Biographical Dictionary
of the Union

BIOGRAPHICAL DICTIONARY OF THE UNION

Northern Leaders of the Civil War

Edited by
John T. Hubbell & James W. Geary

Jon L. Wakelyn, *Advisory Editor*

GREENWOOD PRESS
Westport, Connecticut • London

Library of Congress Cataloging-in-Publication Data

Biographical dictionary of the Union : Northern leaders of the Civil
    War / John T. Hubbell and James W. Geary.
       p. cm.
    Includes bibliographical references (p.).
    ISBN 0–313–20920–0 (alk. paper)
      1. United States—History—Civil War, 1861–1865—Biography.
    I. Hubbell, John T. II. Geary, James W.
    E467.B56   1995
    973.7'092'2—dc20
    [B]   94–46934

British Library Cataloguing in Publication Data is available.

Library of Congress Catalog Card Number: 94–46934
ISBN: 0–313–20920–0

First published in 1995

Greenwood Press, 88 Post Road West, Westport, CT 06881
An imprint of Greenwood Publishing Group, Inc.

Printed in the United States of America

The paper used in this book complies with the
Permanent Paper Standard issued by the National
Information Standards Organization (Z39.48–1984).

10 9 8 7 6 5 4 3 2 1

For

Norma and Linda

Contents

Introduction

The Civil War continues to interest, preoccupy, and bemuse a wide and various population. The public men and women who lived and died during that time have in some instances become part of a national consciousness; others have faded from the collective memory. The *Biographical Dictionary of the Union* brings together 872 of those individuals in a series of entries both factual and interpretive.

The primary editorial tasks were the selection of those who should write the entries and of the subjects themselves. The main criterion used in determining the final choice of biographical entries centered on those men and women who influenced the course of public policy, opinion, and events. The list is comprehensive for political leaders (presidents, congressmen, senators, governors, cabinet officers, Supreme Court justices) and selective for others (e.g., foreign service officials, editors, photographers, abolitionists). Military leaders were selected for specific contributions to the Union cause; included here are most of those who were at least division commanders. We understand that the choices may not be satisfactory to all readers, but they should serve as topics of conversation in Civil War Round Tables across the country.

The authors of the entries include historians of varied backgrounds, each of whom has contributed significantly to the writing on the war. They were asked to include biographical information about the person but to stress the war years and to offer an assessment of the individual's place in the Union. They were also asked to list their principal monographic sources with emphasis upon accessibility. Whenever possible, we have added other (usually more recent) works on a subject and updated editions of certain books for selected entries. There are few references to scholarly journals and collections of primary sources. Nor, as a rule, are there references to standard works such as the *Dictionary of American Biography* or Ezra Warner's *Generals in Blue*, although contributors no doubt consulted these and similar volumes.

Included among the entries are some individuals whose obscurity is breathtaking. But for all that, the assessments are often choice, as the authors have managed to capture the essence of a public life. Taken together, they illumine those "mystic chords of memory" that continue to tie us yet to the Civil War generation.

That generation began a long train of debate and denial—about the origins of the war, its aims and execution, and its implications and effects. Amid the political controversies and conflicts, the war took on a remorseless logic of its own. Union or emancipation were competing goals until 1863, but winning the war was always the necessary first step. Abraham Lincoln spoke of higher purposes, while understanding that achieving those purposes meant the defeat of the Confederate armies. This first goal demanded a unity of political purpose and an effective army. These sometimes conflicting elements of Union success— higher purposes, political unity, and military professionalism—are reflected to some degree in the following biographies. A few generals are included who were derelict in the discharge of their duties and whose actions caused the needless expenditure of Union lives. Nevertheless, we decided to include them with the true leaders whose contributions very often represented the epitome of military professionalism.

In adding this volume to the rich traditions of Civil War historiography, we have tried to present an honest history, which is, after all, the mark of a free people. For the inspirational passages, we thank the men and women who saved the Union and the country. For assistance in helping to bring this work to fruition in various ways, we wish to express our gratitude to Ruth Young, Sandy Clark, Kent State University's Division of Research and Graduate Studies, and the University Libraries' Interlibrary Loan Department.

*Biographical Dictionary
of the Union*

A

ADAMS, Charles Francis, *congressman, diplomat,* was born in Boston on August 18, 1807. In 1809, his father, John Quincy Adams, accepted the appointment as U.S. minister to Russia and moved his family to St. Petersburg. After his father returned to Washington in 1817, Charles Francis attended the Boston Latin School, then graduated from Harvard University in 1825. For two years during his father's presidency he resided in the White House, after which he returned to Boston to devote the next ten years to study, writing, and management of his father's financial affairs. He sat on the Massachusetts General Court (1840–1845) and edited the *Boston Whig* (1846–1848).

During the Mexican War, Adams became a Conscience Whig, then bolted the party in 1848 and presided at the Buffalo convention that founded the Free Soil party. That convention nominated Martin Van Buren for the presidency and Adams for the vice presidency. With other Conscience Whigs he drifted into the Republican party, and as a Republican he entered the House of Representatives in 1859. He represented Massachusetts on the House Committee of Thirty-three, formed to deal with the secession crisis. At the request of the committee chairman, Thomas Corwin (*q.v.*), Adams introduced the committee's resolution to protect slavery, where it existed, by constitutional amendment.

Abraham Lincoln (*q.v.*), acting on the advice of Secretary of State William H. Seward (*q.v.*), appointed Adams minister to Great Britain; he resigned his congressional seat on May 1, 1861. His arrival in London later that month coincided with the Queen's Proclamation of Neutrality toward the American Civil War. Adams conveyed to the London government Seward's forceful admonitions against British recognition of the Confederacy, fortunately without damaging U.S.–British relations. When, in 1862, he could not prevent the departure of the *Florida,* the *Alabama,* and other Confederate raiders built in British shipyards, he warned the London government that it would be held liable for the damages inflicted on Northern shipping by Confederate commerce destroyers. In April 1863 British officials, conscious of the mounting Confederate toll on the high seas, prevented the sailing of the *Alexandra.* Adams's efforts were finally successful when, in September 1863, the British government seized the two ironclad Laird rams being built at Liverpool for the Confederates. Adams did not leave England until May 1868. In 1871–1872, he sat on the tribunal in Geneva that settled the *Alabama* Claims. He died in Boston on November 21, 1886. Duberman, *Charles Francis Adams.*

Norman A. Graebner

ALDRICH, Cyrus, *congressman,* was born on June 18, 1808, in Smithfield, Rhode Island. He attended local common schools, then worked as a sailor, farmer, and public works contractor. After moving to Illinois in 1837, Aldrich became a mail contractor and Whig activist, served from 1845 to 1847 in the Illinois legislature, ran unsuccessfully for Congress in 1848, then served from 1849 to 1853 as receiver in the Federal Land Office at Dixon, Illinois. In 1854, he moved to Minneapolis, entered the lumber business, and helped establish the Republican party in Minnesota. After an unsuccessful bid in 1857, Aldrich won the Second District seat in Congress in 1858 and was reelected in 1860. He was a loyal supporter of his old friend Abraham Lincoln (*q.v.*) on all major issues, including the war effort, but his enormous affinity for brandy somewhat impaired his effectiveness.

Aside from continuous patronage battles with Governor Alexander Ramsey (*q.v.*), Aldrich's favorite cause was the welfare of Minnesota's men in blue. He cofounded the Minnesota Soldiers' Aid Society to help wounded Minnesota soldiers in hospitals near Washington and articulated the complaints of 1st Minnesota Regiment enlistees, whose tours had been extended from three months to three years. Following the 1862 Sioux uprising in Minnesota, he urged unsuccessfully that all 300 Sioux confined at Camp Lincoln be hanged and that $1.5 million be taken from Sioux funds to aid their victims.

Aldrich did not seek reelection in 1862, trying instead to secure the Senate seat being vacated by Henry Rice (*q.v.*), but was passed over in favor of his bitter enemy Ramsey. Following his retirement from Congress in 1863, he served a term in the Minnesota legislature, became chairman of the Minneapolis Board of Supervisors, then served as postmaster of Minneapolis from 1867 until a few weeks before his death in that city on October 5, 1871. Folwell, *History of Minnesota,* vol. 2; Smalley, *Republican Party in Minnesota.*

Roger A. Fischer

ALLEN, James Cameron, *congressman,* was born in Shelby county, Kentucky, on January 29, 1822. His family moved to Parke county, Indiana, in 1830. After graduating from the "seminary" at Rockville, he read law and in 1843 received his license. He served as state's attorney (1845–1847), then moved to Palestine, Illinois. On November 5, 1850, Allen was elected as a Democrat to the state legislature, and in 1852 was elected to the 33rd Congress. He looked upon "slavery, as it exists in the South, as a social evil" but insisted that Congress had no right to interfere. He strongly supported Stephen A. Douglas's (*q.v.*) Kansas–Nebraska Bill. That fall he won reelection by one vote and returned to Congress, only to have his reelection contested. A recount showed his opponent, William B. Archer, to be the winner. The House finally declared Allen's seat vacant on July 18, 1856, and in a special election held on November 4, he beat Archer by nearly 3,000 votes and resumed his place until March 3, 1857. His party then named him clerk of the House of Representatives (1857–1859).

Allen opposed Richard Yates (*q.v.*) in 1860 as the Democratic candidate for governor of Illinois, losing by nearly 13,000 votes. Yates offered him command of the 21st Illinois Volunteers, but Allen refused because he had no military training. Nor would he accept a brigade command from Abraham Lincoln (*q.v.*). He was elected judge of the 25th Judicial Circuit on June 3, 1861, and elected congressman-at-large on November 4, 1862. When he sought at-large reelection in 1864, he lost by 31,442 votes. He practiced law until 1873, when he became judge of the 21st Circuit.

When the appellate court system was inaugurated on July 1, 1877, the Illinois Supreme Court appointed Allen for the Southern District. He thus sat on both circuit and appellate benches at the same time. In 1879, he returned to private practice and retired in 1907. However, he continued to act as U.S. commissioner for southern and eastern Illinois, a position he had held since 1896. Allen died in Olney, Illinois, on January 30, 1912. *Biographical and Reminiscent History of Richland, Clay and Marion Counties, Illinois*; Cole, *Era of the Civil War.*

Wayne C. Temple

ALLEN, Robert, *general,* was born on March 15, 1811, in Morrow county, Ohio. He graduated from West Point in 1836 and was commissioned into the 2nd U.S. Artillery. He performed routine garrison duties at various posts, transferred from the artillery to the Quartermaster's Department in 1846, and was promoted to major (brevet) for gallant and meritorious conduct at Cerro Gordo. After the Mexican War, Allen became the chief quartermaster of the Department of California and Oregon, and achieved the permanent rank of major in 1861.

Allen's successful Civil War career resulted in his promotion from colonel to brevet major general of Volunteers on March 13, 1865. He served as chief quartermaster of the turbulent Department of Missouri, which was later expanded to cover the entire Mississippi Valley and the western territories. Allen's record from 1832 to 1878, when he retired as assistant quartermaster general, shows that he disbursed over $100 million without a penny being disallowed by the Treasury. He died on August 5, 1886, in Geneva, Switzerland. Weigley, *Quartermaster General of the Union Army.*

Alan C. Aimone

ALLEN, William, *congressman,* was born near Hamilton, Butler county, Ohio, on August 13, 1827. He attended public schools, studied law, and was admitted to the bar in 1849. In 1850, he established a law practice in Greenville, Ohio, and began his political career by becoming the prosecuting attorney for Darke county. After being elected as a Democrat to the 36th and 37th Congresses, Allen declined to seek renomination to the 38th Congress. During his tenure in the first Civil War Congress, he chaired the Committee on Expenditures in the Department of the Interior. A fiscal conservative, Allen frequently employed dilatory tactics to force discussion on tax legislation and other controversial measures. To this end, he frequently joined Clement L. Vallandigham (*q.v.*), Chilton A. White (*q.v.*), and other Ohio Democrats in voting to delay quick passage of certain bills in the Republican-dominated House. Unlike most of his fellow Buckeye Democrats, however, Allen leaned more toward the Unionist faction in his party. Indeed, by the end of the Civil War, he had joined the Republicans.

After the war, Allen was appointed judge of the Court of Common Pleas for the 2nd Judicial District and pursued banking interests. In 1878, he declined the Republican nomination to the 46th Congress because of poor health. Allen died in Greenville, Ohio, on July 6, 1881. Curry, *Blueprint for Modern America.*

James W. Geary

ALLEN, William Joshua, *congressman,* was born on June 9, 1829, in Wilson county, Tennessee. His family moved to Williamson county, Illinois, in 1830. After admission to the bar in 1849, he began his legal practice at Metropolis, and served as a clerk of the Illinois House of Representatives (1849–1851). In 1854, he was appointed an Illinois prosecuting attorney and was elected to the legislature (1855–1857). In 1855, Allen was appointed U.S. district attorney, and was elected judge of the Illinois 26th Judicial Circuit in 1859 (succeeding his father, Willis, one of southern Illinois's most powerful politicians), serving until 1861. In May 1862 he was elected as a Peace Democrat to fill a vacancy in the U.S. Congress and was reelected that November, serving from June 2, 1862, to March 3, 1865. He was defeated in his reelection bid in 1864 and was an unsuccessful candidate for Congress in 1866.

While in Congress, Allen was an "ultraconservative." He opposed the war and was involved with the Knights of the Golden Circle, a group seeking the secession of southern Illinois from the state and the Union. His efforts landed him in jail (1862–1863), and he was freed only through Abraham Lincoln's (*q.v.*) intervention. Allen remained active in Illinois Democratic politics, practicing law at Cairo, later at Carbondale, and then at Springfield, where he moved in 1886. In 1887, he was appointed U.S. district judge for the Southern District of Illinois. He served in that capacity until his death, while vacationing in Hot Springs, Arkansas, on January 26, 1901. Bogart, *Industrial State*; Cole, *Era of the Civil War*.

Leslie J. Stegh

ALLEY, John Bassett, *congressman,* was born on January 7, 1817, in Lynn, Massachusetts. After attending the Lynn public schools and serving as a shoemaker's apprentice, he embarked upon what would become a remarkable career. With the money he saved while a merchant trader in the Ohio Valley, he returned home to enter the shoe manufacturing business. By 1860, he was the richest man in Lynn, with assets worth $250,000. Alley, whose father was an antislavery Quaker, was an early foe of the expansion of slavery, having been a Liberty party member in the 1840s, and then a Free Soiler and a Republican. From 1847 to 1851, he was a member of the Governor's Council; in 1852 he represented Lynn in the state Senate; and in the following year he was a member of the state Constitutional Convention. Alley was active on the State Central Committee of the Republican party, and in 1858 he defeated Democratic and Know-Nothing opponents to win election to Congress. He was reelected for three consecutive terms.

The belief in a slave power conspiracy convinced Alley of the need to gird for battle against the South, and during the war years he was an uncompromising Radical Republican. He later took a slightly less Radical position than would have been expected, given his voting record. In 1866, he supported the candidacy of a close business associate, Benjamin F. Butler (*q.v.*), to succeed him in Congress. Alley retired from politics in 1886 and became involved in railroad enterprises and land speculation in the West. He died in West Newton, Massachusetts, on January 19, 1896. Dawley, *Class and Community*; Rand, *One of a Thousand*.

Dale Baum

ALLISON, William Boyd, *congressman,* was born on March 2, 1829, in Perry Township, Ohio. He attended Wooster Academy (Ohio) and Allegheny College Academy (Meadville, Pennsylvania). After a year of teaching school and a year (1850) at Western Reserve College, he returned to Wooster, read law, and was admitted to the bar. Politically, Allison moved from Whig to anti-Nebraska fusion, then to Republican and Know-Nothing, and finally, in late 1856, to straight Republican. He went to Dubuque, Iowa, in 1857, and by 1861 he was established in the Dubuque business community and a friend of Grenville M. Dodge (*q.v.*), with whom he was to be associated in railroad promotion and Iowa Republican politics for the rest of his life. In 1861, Governor Samuel Kirkwood (*q.v.*) appointed him a special aide, with the rank of lieutenant colonel, assigned to help enroll and outfit Iowa volunteers for military service.

In 1862 Allison won the first of four consecutive terms to Congress. His opponent that year was Dennis Mahony (*q.v.*), editor of the *Dubuque Herald,* then on his way to becoming one of the leading Copperheads in the Midwest. During his first term Allison was both a party regular and a developing Radical. He supported all war measures, favored confiscation of lands belonging to rebels, and voted for the Wade–Davis Bill. After the war he moved closer to a center position within the party, but he opposed Andrew Johnson's (*q.v.*) Reconstruction policies and voted for his impeachment. After an unsuccessful try for the Senate in 1870, he won in 1872. Although touched by the Crédit Mobilier scandal, Allison emerged relatively unscathed. He was coauthor of the Bland–Allison Act, chairman of the Appropriations Committee for twenty-five years, and a proponent of Philippines annexation. He died in Dubuque on August 4, 1908. Sage, *William Boyd Allison.*

Hubert H. Wubben

ALVORD, Benjamin, *general,* was born on August 18, 1813, in Rutland, Vermont. After graduation from West Point in 1833, he served with the 4th U.S. Infantry, including duty in the Florida and Mexican Wars, until 1854. He then became a paymaster with the rank of major and continued to serve in the Pacific Northwest, mainly at Fort Vancouver, until 1865.

The Civil War brought a major change in Alvord's career. General George Wright (*q.v.*), commander of the Department of the Pacific, wanted a proven Regular, not a controversial Volunteer, to head the large and remote District of Oregon. Thus, from July 1862 until March 1865, Alvord commanded Oregon, Washington, and Idaho from headquarters at Fort Vancouver. He visited public and private leaders, asking how the military might protect and promote the underdeveloped region, and with Oregon Governor Addison Gibbs (*q.v.*) enthusiastically watched for evidence of secessionist activity. He sought to encourage immigration by the construction of Fort Boise, by patrols along remote trails, and by military action, especially in 1864 against the Snake Indians in eastern Oregon.

Alvord convinced his superiors of the need to fortify the mouth of the Columbia River, but his efforts to improve this defense and to protect Puget Sound failed. Because of pressing military needs and sluggish enlistments in Oregon and Washington, he favored conscription. Failing to win support for that controversial measure, he urged a state bounty for enlistments. Alvord was removed from command because General Ulysses S. Grant (*q.v.*) thought him ill-suited for the task; because Oregon's Republican Congressman, John R. McBride (*q.v.*), accused him of being "a tool and plaything" of anti-Union men; and because he angered some Oregon politicians by advocating a draft and a bounty.

In 1865, Alvord became a paymaster in New York City and eventually paymaster general (1872–1880). Although this intelligent and devoted brigadier general of Volunteers was unfairly removed from command, his solid service is honored by the fact that the Alvord Valley in southeastern Oregon bears his name. He died in Washington, D.C., on October 16, 1884. Edwards, "Department of the Pacific."

G. Thomas Edwards

AMES, Oakes, *congressman,* was born on January 10, 1804, in Easton, Massachusetts. After attending local schools, he entered his father's shovel manufacturing business, which he and his brother Oliver inherited in 1844. By the time of the Civil War, it was valued at $4 million. Ames was an avowed free soiler, and joined the Republican party upon its formation. In 1862, he was elected to the 38th Congress, and was returned to his seat four times. Ames did not play an important role in Congress but generally supported the Radical Republicans in their efforts to promote emancipation and equal rights for blacks, including the right to vote, and in their struggle with President Andrew Johnson (*q.v.*) over Reconstruction. He remains best known for his promotion of the Union Pacific Railroad, a cause that eventually involved him in the Crédit Mobilier scandal. In 1873 the House of Representatives voted overwhelmingly to condemn Ames's conduct but chose not to expel him. His reputation ruined, Ames died on May 8, 1873, in North Easton, Massachusetts. Howard, *Great Iron Trail.*

Richard H. Abbott

ANCONA, Sydenham Elnathan, *congressman,* was born on November 20, 1824, in Warwick, Pennsylvania. He taught school, and in 1846 obtained a position with the Reading Railroad Company, rising to head bookkeeper. He became active in local politics as a member of the school board for Reading and as an organizer of a volunteer rifle club, the Reading Rifles. Having failed to gain the nomination for the state Senate, he announced his candidacy for a congressional seat in 1860 and defeated the Republican candidate. Ancona was reelected in 1862 but served with no particular distinction. He was numbered among the Peace Democrats and spoke against the war. Although challenged in 1864 by a War Democrat, Ancona won a third term, then failed to be nominated in 1866.

In 1867, Ancona organized the Reading Fire Insurance Company and grew wealthly. He retained an interest in politics, however; in 1880, he was a delegate to the Democratic National Convention. As late as 1907 he contended that thousands would have lived, millions of dollars would have been saved, and slavery would have ended in due course if the war had been avoided. In 1912, Ancona was honored by the House of Representatives as the sole surviving member of the 1861 Civil War Congress. He died in Reading on June 20, 1913. Montgomery, *Historical and Biographical Annuals of Berks County, Pennsylvania*, vols. 1, 2.

W. Wayne Smith

ANDERSON, Lucian, *congressman,* was born on June 23, 1824, in Mayfield, Kentucky. He was educated in the local schools, read law, and was admitted to the bar on October 30, 1845. Anderson, a Whig presidential elector in 1852, joined the Democrats and was elected to one term in the Kentucky legislature (1855–1857). On August 3, 1863, Anderson was elected to the 38th Congress as a Union Democrat. In the fall, he was taken prisoner by Confederate forces, but was exchanged shortly afterward and took his seat at the beginning of the next session of Congress. He immediately broke with the Union Democrats and allied himself with the Republicans in Congress. Nevertheless, he attempted to represent the interests of pro-Union slave owners in his district. An advocate of compensated emancipation, Anderson initially opposed the conscription of slaves in 1864. However, his subsequent support of the Enrollment Bill, which provided for limited compensation to slave owners whose "property" was lost through military service, added to his growing unpopularity at home.

By the spring of 1864, Anderson was an active spokesman for Kentucky's newly formed Unconditional Union party, which strongly supported the Lincoln administration. He played a major role at the state Republican convention on May 25, 1864, and subsequently served as a delegate to the Republican National Convention. On September 2, 1864, Governor Thomas Bramlette (*q.v.*) charged Anderson, Brigadier General Eleazer A. Paine (*q.v.*), Union commander of the District of Western Kentucky, and other prominent Unionists with "extorting money and property from citizens for their own private gain." Paine fled the state to avoid arrest, and Anderson became the subject of a congressional investigation. Although he was cleared of the charge, Anderson's defense of Paine's official conduct cost him considerable support.

Declining to run for a second term, Anderson returned to Mayfield, where he resumed the practice of law. Although he never again sought public office, he remained active in politics and is regarded as one of the founders of the Republican party in Kentucky. He died in Mayfield on October 18, 1898. Hood, "For the Union," *Register of the Kentucky Historical Society*; Kleber, *Kentucky Encyclopedia.*

James M. Prichard

ANDERSON, Robert, *general,* was born on June 14, 1805, near Louisville, Kentucky. After graduating from West Point in 1825, he served with distinction in the Seminole and Mexican wars and became one of the leading artillery specialists in the army, attaining the rank of major in 1857. In November 1860 the War Department appointed him commander of the garrison at Charleston, South Carolina, hoping that because he was a Southerner and a slave owner, his presence would soothe the South Carolinians. Although he was loyal to the Union, Anderson opposed using force to keep the South from seceding and desired to avoid a clash that might lead to war. Hence, on learning that the South Carolinians planned to seize Fort Moultrie, where most of his garrison was stationed and that was defenseless against land attack, he transferred the garrison to Fort Sumter in Charleston Harbor on the night of December 26, 1860. In January, President James Buchanan (*q.v.*) sent the *Star of the West* to resupply Anderson's garrison, but the ship turned back when South Carolina batteries opened fire and when Anderson—still seeking to avoid war—refrained from answering their fire.

Early in April, President Abraham Lincoln (*q.v.*) ordered another relief expedition to Fort Sumter. The Confederates called upon Anderson to surrender. He refused but stated that he would have to abandon the fort if it was not supplied soon. The Confederates, wishing to force the issue of Southern independence, began bombarding Sumter on the morning of April 12. Anderson returned their fire, and the civil war he had hoped to prevent was under way. On April 14, further resistance being pointless, Anderson surrendered the fort and the Confederates allowed him and his troops to proceed to the North, where they were greeted as heroes. Lincoln placed Anderson, promoted to brigadier general, in command of Kentucky, which vital state he helped save for the Union. In October 1861 Anderson retired from active service for reasons of health. On April 14, 1865, he returned to Fort Sumter and raised the same flag he had lowered four years before. On October 26, 1871, he died in Nice, France. Crawford, *History of Fort Sumter*; Swanberg, *First Blood*.

Albert Castel

ANDREW, John Albion, *governor*, was born on May 31, 1818, in Windham, Maine. He graduated from Bowdoin College in 1837 and moved to Boston, where he was admitted to the bar in 1840. His attachment to antislavery began early in life and deepened through constant association with Boston abolitionists. He participated in several fugitive slave cases in the 1840s and 1850s, and he helped raise money for John Brown's (*q.v.*) legal defense and for the support of the Brown family following the Harpers Ferry raid.

Andrew entered politics during the Mexican War, gravitating toward the Conscience Whigs and into the orbit of Charles Sumner (*q.v.*); in 1848 he joined the Free Soil party. Active in the formation of the Massachusetts Republican party, he won a seat in the lower house of the state legislature in 1857. On the strength of his oratory, his forceful yet sociable personality, and most of all his skillful resistance to the conservative, Know-Nothing element in the party, Andrew quickly rose to prominence among Bay State Radical Republicans. In 1860, he chaired the Massachusetts delegation to the Republican National Convention, and later that year he was elected governor, the first of five consecutive terms.

In his tireless devotion to total victory, emancipation, and the welfare of black troops, Andrew was without equal among war governors. Even before delivering his first inaugural address, he had taken steps to place Massachusetts upon a war footing, and he was able to dispatch 3,000 troops to the Federal government immediately after Abraham Lincoln (*q.v.*) called out the militia on April 15, 1861. Andrew was effectively the unofficial war minister for New England, directing and assisting governors of neighboring states at the same time that he undertook to raise money, purchase ships, and organize and equip his own state troops. He was equally energetic in urging official Washington to prosecute the war with more vigor and to embrace emancipation as a war aim.

Among the most vocal of the state executives calling for the removal of General George B. McClellan (*q.v.*) following the Peninsula campaign, Andrew was also instrumental in calling the Altoona conference of governors, which assembled in September 1862 to revive Northern war enthusiasm. By January 1863, having finally won official authorization for his long campaign to enlist black soldiers, he was wholeheartedly engaged in raising the 54th Massachusetts Regiment, which he took special pains to turn into a showcase unit. He also fought for the rights of black soldiers to receive equal pay and to serve as officers.

In general agreement that Andrew was the most energetic and radical of Northern war governors, historians have debated whether he was responsible or reckless in his efforts to influence war policy. A fair judge would account him restrained in his conduct, for by his own admission Andrew was radical in principles but conservative in measures. He worked hard for Lincoln's reelection despite having opposed his renomination, and he refrained from openly criticizing Andrew Johnson (*q.v.*) even when Johnson's Reconstruction policy diverged sharply from his own. Indeed, Andrew's famous Valedictory Address, delivered in January 1866 upon his leaving office, was a moderate plea for enfranchising the former Confederates but not all of the former slaves. After he resumed his law practice, Andrew directed much of his energy toward channeling Northern capital into the agricultural South. He died in Boston on October 30, 1867.

Hesseltine, *Lincoln's War Governors*; Pearson, *Life of John A. Andrew.*

Lawrence N. Powell

ANDREWS, George Leonard, *general,* was born on August 31, 1828, in Bridgewater, Massachusetts. He graduated from West Point in 1851, first in his class. Andrews served with the Corps of Engineers on the construction of Fort Warren in Boston Harbor and as an instructor in civil and military engineering. In 1855 he resigned his commission to take a position with a manufacturing company in Manchester, New Hampshire, and in 1857 became a civil engineer with the Federal government. With the outbreak of war, he became lieutenant colonel of the 2nd Massachusetts Volunteers and commanded the regiment during the Federal retreat from Strasburg to Winchester during General Nathaniel P. Banks's (*q.v.*) Shenandoah Valley campaign. Promoted to colonel on June 13, 1862, Andrews became a brigadier general of Volunteers in November 1862 and was commended for his service at Winchester, Cedar Mountain, and Antietam.

Ordered to the Department of the Gulf, Andrews commanded the defenses around New Orleans (2nd Division, XIX Corps) and, as Banks's chief of staff, fought at Fort Bisland and Port Hudson. His assignments also included command of the military district of Baton Rouge and Port Hudson. He later became provost marshal general for the Army of the Gulf, and was present during the Mobile campaign. Andrews concluded his wartime duties as General Edward R.S. Canby's (*q.v.*) chief of staff. As a cap to his service, he was promoted to brevet major general of Volunteers. Andrews's record seems unimpeachable. He fought in eighteen battles and several minor actions, and his steady rise in rank demonstrates that his superiors recognized his abilities.

From 1865 until 1867, Andrews was a planter in Washington County, Mississippi. In 1867, he became the U.S. marshal for Massachusetts. He held that post until February 1871, when President Ulysses S. Grant (*q.v.*) appointed him professor of French at West Point. Andrews retired on August 31, 1892, and spent his last years in Brookline, Massachusetts, where he died on April 4, 1899. Hewitt, *Port Hudson*; Sears, *Landscape Turned Red.*

Frank J. Wetta

ANTHONY, Henry Bowen, *senator,* was born to Quaker parents on April 1, 1815, in Coventry, Rhode Island. He graduated from Brown University in 1833 and became editor and co-owner of the *Providence Journal* in 1840. As a voice of the Whig party, Anthony joined the resistance to the movement for suffrage reform led by Thomas Wilson Dorr in 1842. This opposition was an early expression of the anxiety among nativists and the established political structure in Rhode Island over the influx of Irish Catholics into the state. Anthony was rewarded by the Whigs with election to the governorship in 1849 and 1850. In 1855 he was influential in the organization of the Republican movement in Rhode Island, which in that state was dominated by Whig and nativist elements whose concern over the spread of slavery was matched by their continued hostility to immigrants.

Anthony's political and journalistic labors contributed heavily to the maintenance of a system of property qualifications for voting in Rhode Island until late in the nineteenth century. In 1858 he was elected to the U.S. Senate, where he became a consistent supporter of the administration of Abraham Lincoln (*q.v.*). He was among the majority of Republican senators who voted for conviction in the impeachment of Andrew Johnson (*q.v.*), though his vote was apparently a reluctant one. Anthony continued to exercise a dominant influence in party affairs in Rhode Island, and held his Senate seat until his death in Providence on September 2, 1884. Bicknell, *History of Rhode Island*; Carroll, *Rhode Island*, vol. 3.

Mario R. DiNunzio

ANTHONY, Susan Brownell, *abolitionist, women's rights activist,* was born on February 15, 1820, in Adams, Massachusetts. She was a precocious child and advanced rapidly from home education to graduation in 1838 from a Quaker boarding school near Philadelphia. She then taught school until 1849, when she took up active reforming. By 1850, Rochester, New York, had become her home, and her circle of associates had broadened to include the North's foremost agitators on behalf of temperance, abolition, and women's rights. Anthony crusaded for emancipation and women's rights, enduring taunts for wearing the famous "Bloomer costume" and for consorting with blacks such as Frederick Douglass (*q.v.*). She supported William Lloyd Garrison's (*q.v.*) position that the North must withdraw from the "proslavery" Federal Union, but when the Civil War came, she enthusiastically embraced armed conflict.

Anthony was extremely influential in the drive for emancipation, developing a national reputation as a compelling lecturer and organizer. At war's end, she took the position, contrary to William Lloyd Garrison (*q.v.*), that slavery could never be ended unless African Americans were guaranteed full civil equality by constitutional amendment. She supported Wendell Phillips's (*q.v.*) efforts to continue the American Anti-Slavery Society, but by 1867, Phillips and Anthony had split over her belief that black male suffrage and the vote for women must be united under a demand for "impartial" suffrage.

In 1869, Anthony and other feminists formed the National Woman Suffrage Association, pledged to securing the vote for women through the passage of a constitutional amendment. For the next thirty-five years, she spoke on behalf of women's rights while showing increasing indifference to the political rights of other minorities. She died in Rochester on March 13, 1906. DuBois, *Feminism and Suffrage*; Harper, *Life and Work of Susan B. Anthony*.

James Brewer Stewart

APPLETON, William, *congressman*, was born on November 16, 1786, in Brookfield, Massachusetts. He attended schools in New Ipswich and Francestown, New Hampshire, and in Tyngsboro, Massachusetts. In 1807 he moved to Boston, where he established a successful business in the West Indian trade. Appleton was president of the Boston branch of the Bank of the United States from 1832 to 1836 and was elected as a Whig to the 32nd and 33rd Congresses. He was defeated for reelection to Congress in 1854 and 1856 by Anson Burlingame (*q.v.*), who ran on the American party ticket. His narrow victory over Burlingame in 1860 prevented a Republican sweep of the state's congressional seats. Appleton served in the 37th Congress until September 27, 1861, when he resigned because of failing health.

As long as the Massachusetts Whig party was able to represent economic progress and moral superiority, Appleton, like other members of Boston's Episcopalian and philanthropical business elite, exercised inordinate influence in public affairs. When the intrusion of the slavery issue into state politics made the Whigs appear to place economic self-interest above moral precepts, opponents attacked Appleton and conservatives like him for an indifference to the question of slavery that was in direct proportion to the amount of wealth they had amassed. Appleton died on February 15, 1862, in Brookline, Massachusetts. Crawford, *Famous Families of Massachusetts*, vol. 1; O'Connor, *Lords of the Loom*.

Dale Baum

ARNOLD, Isaac Newton, *congressman,* was born on November 30, 1815, in Hartwick, New York. He attended local schools and the Hartwick Seminary. In 1835, he was admitted to the bar after studying with Judge E. B. Morehouse and Richard Cooper, a nephew of the novelist James Fenimore Cooper. In 1836, Arnold moved to Chicago and, from 1842 to 1846, served in the Illinois state legislature as a Democrat. He joined the Free Soil movement in 1848 and eventually the Republican party. In 1860, Arnold was elected to the 37th Congress and in 1862 was reelected to the 38th Congress. He served on the Committee on Defenses and Fortifications of the Great Lakes and Rivers, the Committee on Manufactures, and the Committee on Roads and Canals. He voted to abolish slavery in the District of Columbia, supported various confiscation measures, and urged that the Constitution be amended to end slavery.

Despite his record, Arnold frequently broke ranks with other Radical Republicans to give unequivocal support to President Abraham Lincoln's (*q.v.*) policies. His support of the President did not waver in the 38th Congress; on one occasion, Thaddeus Stevens (*q.v.*) singled out Arnold as the only Lincoln Republican left in the House of Representatives. Lincoln may have depended on Arnold to initiate certain controversial measures. For example, Arnold suggested in the closing minutes of the 37th Congress that the $300 exemption fee in the national draft bill that had just passed Congress be repealed. He renewed this proposal in the opening minutes of the 38th Congress. Regardless of whether Lincoln had a role in these related actions, Arnold represented the sentiments of Midwestern congressmen generally that their region carried a disproportionate burden in furnishing troops for the Union Army.

Arnold also was instrumental in lifting the ban that had been imposed on the publishing of the *Chicago Times* in June 1863. He returned to his law practice in 1865 and briefly served as auditor of the treasury for the Post Office Department. His greatest accomplishment in later life was the publication of *History of Abraham Lincoln and the Overthrow of Slavery* (1866), which was revised and posthumously published as *The Life of Abraham Lincoln* (1885). Arnold died on April 24, 1884, in Chicago. Bogue, *Congressman's Civil War*; Curry, *Blueprint for Modern America*; Geary, *We Need Men.*

Thomas F. Schwartz

ARNOLD, Richard, *general,* was born on April 12, 1828, in Providence, Rhode Island. Arnold graduated from West Point in 1850 and was commissioned in the artillery. He served at Key West, Florida, at San Francisco, on the Northern Pacific Railroad surveys in Washington Territory, and as aide-de-camp to Brevet Major General John E. Wool (*q.v.*). Arnold was placed in command of Battery D of the 2nd U.S. Artillery at First Bull Run; he lost of all his guns as he was attempting to cover the retreat of the panic-stricken Union Volunteers. In the spring of 1862, Arnold was promoted to chief of artillery of William B. Franklin's (*q.v.*) division of the Army of Potomac and appointed inspector general of the VI Corps during the Peninsula campaign. He earned a brevet as major for his services at the battle of Savage's Station during the withdrawal to Harrison's Landing.

By November 29, 1862, Arnold was promoted to brigadier general of Volunteers and assigned to duty as chief of artillery, XIX Corps and Department of the Gulf. He was in charge of the artillery at the siege and surrender of Port Hudson, and during the Red River campaign was in charge of both the artillery and cavalry when Union forces had to retreat. Arnold was again in charge of artillery at the siege and capture of Fort Morgan in Mobile Bay. He served the remainder of the war as a member of the Retiring Board for disabled Regular officers at Wilmington, Delaware. At the end of the war he received brevets through major general for both Regular and Volunteer service but later reverted to his Regular commission as captain and served as a brevet colonel in command of Battery G, 5th U.S. Artillery at Little Rock, Arkansas. His last service was as acting assistant inspector general, Department of the East. Arnold died at Governors Island, New York, on November 8, 1882. Johnson, *Red River Campaign.*

Alan C. Aimone

ARNOLD, Samuel Greene, *senator,* was born in Providence, Rhode Island, on April 12, 1821. He graduated from Brown University (1841) and Harvard Law School (1845). Arnold was elected lieutenant governor in 1852 as a Democrat and was returned to that office in 1861 and 1862 by a coalition of Democrats and Conservative Republicans who had organized against those Republicans labeled Radical because of their emphasis on the slavery issue. In 1861, he was a delegate to the peace convention held in Washington.

Arnold was representative of a large body of Rhode Island political leaders who feared that emphasis on the slavery question would bring war but who, when the war came, served the Union cause with dedication. Arnold served for extended periods as acting governor while Governor William Sprague (*q.v.*) traveled with Rhode Island troops to the front lines. He also helped to raise a company of light artillery. He was elected to the U.S. Senate in 1862 to fill the unexpired term of James F. Simmons (*q.v.*). After his brief Senate service, Arnold devoted himself to charitable activities and to his historical studies, serving as president of the Rhode Island Historical Society for over a decade. He died in Providence on February 13, 1880. Carroll, *Rhode Island,* vol. 3; Field, *State of Rhode Island,* vol. 3.

Mario R. DiNunzio

ASHLEY, James Mitchell, *congressman,* was born on November 14, 1824, in Allegheny, Pennsylvania. In 1826 his family moved to Portsmouth, Ohio. He left home at the age of fourteen and came under the influence of a Quaker abolitionist family. His major employment was as a printer and editor for various Democratic newspapers in Ohio, although he was admitted to the bar in 1849.

Ashley broke with the Democrats in 1853 because of his disillusionment with President Franklin Pierce's proslavery and pro-Southern views. He played a leading role in the establishment of both the Ohio and the national Republican parties, and was an active supporter of Salmon P. Chase's (*q.v.*) 1856 and 1860 presidential efforts.

In 1858, Ashley was elected to Congress, where he was an early and unceasing advocate of political and civil rights for African Americans. He successfully guided the District of Columbia Emancipation Bill and the 13th Amendment through the House, and was the House's foremost exponent of the territorialization theory of Reconstruction. He was a major proponent of the impeachment of Andrew Johnson (*q.v.*), but his at times erratic role in the process and his support of African American suffrage in Ohio in 1867 contributed to his failure to win reelection in 1868. Ashley served for a time as the territorial governor of Montana, practiced law, and eventually became the president of the Toledo, Ann Arbor, and Northern Michigan Railroad. He died in Ann Arbor, Michigan, on September 16, 1896. Horowitz, *Great Impeacher.*

Robert F. Horowitz

AUGUR, Christopher Columbus, *general,* was born on July 10, 1821, in Kendall, New York, but grew up in Michigan. He graduated from West Point in 1843, and fought in the Mexican War and in several skirmishes with western Indian tribes. In 1861, Major Augur was commandant of cadets at West Point. Promoted to brigadier general of Volunteers (November 1861), he later joined the II Corps of General Nathaniel P. Banks (*q.v.*), which was maneuvering near the old Bull Run battlefield in conjunction with the offensive command by General John Pope (*q.v.*). Banks foolishly engaged Stonewall Jackson's forces near Cedar Mountain (August 9, 1862), where Augur's division took heavy losses and Augur himself was badly wounded. Augur was later promoted to major general for his gallantry at Cedar Mountain.

After recovering from his wound, Augur again commanded a division (in the XIX Corps) under Banks in Louisiana. Banks intended to capture Port Hudson, a strongly fortified position on the Mississippi River, second in importance only to Vicksburg. On May 27, 1863, Augur's troops struck at the center of the Confederate works, but heavy fire stopped the charge. Augur succeeded to command of the Union left wing in early June, and after a siege, Port Hudson surrendered on July 9, 1863. From 1863 to 1866, Augur commanded the XXII Corps and the defenses of Washington, where he was serving when Jubal Early made his exciting "raid" on the capital.

In 1869, Augur was promoted to brigadier general in the Regular Army and subsequently commanded several western military departments. He was senior officer in Louisiana during the crucial Reconstruction election of 1876. Augur retired from the Army in 1885, and died in Georgetown on January 16, 1898.

Harrington, *Fighting Politician*; Hewitt, *Port Hudson*; Krick, *Stonewall Jackson at Cedar Mountain.*

Joseph G. Dawson III

AVERELL, William Woods, *general,* was born in Bath, New York, on November 5, 1832. He graduated from West Point in 1855, was commissioned in the cavalry, and was engaged in operations (in one of which he was severely wounded) against the Indians in the Southwest. Averell's Civil War career began with his appointment on August 23, 1861, as colonel of the 3rd Pennsylvania Cavalry. As the head of an untrained, undisciplined regiment, Averell instituted drills in horsemanship and in such basic cavalry duties as picketing, scouting, and acting as rear guard. In his first five months with the regiment, he forced the resignation of sixteen officers he considered incompetent. His was one of eight regiments of cavalry in the Peninsula campaign, in which it was joined to the III Corps.

Averell was promoted to brigadier general of Volunteers in September 1862, and upon General Joseph Hooker's (*q.v.*) grouping of the cavalry of the Army of the Potomac into brigades and divisions, he was given command of the 2nd Cavalry Division. He led 2,100 of his men in a fight against Confederate cavalry at Kelly's Ford on March 17, 1863, an inconclusive affair that received far more postwar glorification than it deserved. Transferred to West Virginia on May 8, 1863, presumably because in Hooker's opinion he had not measured up to the requirements of high command, Averell was placed at the head of the Fourth Separate Brigade of cavalry and mounted infantry, and later of the 2nd Division. He engaged in numerous skirmishes and in two major efforts to break the Virginia & Tennessee Railroad in order to disrupt General James Longstreet's communications with the eastern seaboard.

In the spring of 1864, Averell defeated the Confederate cavalry that had burned Chambersburg, Pennsylvania, an action for which he was breveted major general in the Regular Army. On August 7, 1864, Philip Sheridan (*q.v.*) was given the Shenandoah Valley command. Included in his forces were four divisions and an extra brigade of cavalry, overall command of which, for reasons not to be found in the records, was given not to Averell but to the modestly competent Alfred T.A. Torbert (*q.v.*), his junior in rank. In the operations preceding the battle of the Opequon, Averell incurred Sheridan's ill will by an apparent misunderstanding of orders, but he played a creditable role in the battle itself. Still, he had given Sheridan reason to think that the elevation of Torbert over him had made Averell a balky, unreliable subordinate.

Following the Union victory at Fisher's Hill, on September 22, and acting without orders, Averell halted his division's pursuit of the beaten and demoralized enemy. He and Sheridan quarreled over Averell's apparent lack of energy in pressing the enemy retreat. Later that day Sheridan learned that Averell, again acting without orders, had gone into camp, and at once relieved him of his command. For the remaining months of the war, Averell remained unemployed, and he resigned from the army in May 1865. He died in Bath on February 3, 1900. Starr, *Union Cavalry*, vols. 1, 2.

Stephen Z. Starr

AYRES, Romeyn Beck, *general*, was born in East Creek, New York, on December 20, 1825. He graduated from West Point in 1847 and was commissioned in the artillery. He performed occupation duty in Mexico and garrison service at numerous eastern and western posts, and saw active service against California and Minnesota Indians. In 1859–1861, Ayres was a 1st lieutenant at the Fort Monroe Artillery School; when the war began, he became captain of the new Battery F, 5th Artillery. He commanded Battery E, 3rd Artillery at First Bull Run, then was William F. Smith's (*q.v.*) divisional and corps chief of artillery in the Peninsula, Maryland, and Fredericksburg campaigns. His ability earned him promotion to brigadier general on November 29, 1862, but, like many artillerists, he had to leave that branch to receive promotion.

Returning from a ten-week sick leave in April 1863, Ayres took over Joseph Hooker's (*q.v.*) Artillery Reserve for a week, then assumed command of the 1st (Regular) Infantry Brigade, 2nd Division, V Corps, which he led at Chancellorsville. Just before Gettysburg, he took charge of the division, which he commanded until March 1864. Then the Army of the Potomac's consolidation reduced him to his old brigade (now in the 1st Division, V Corps), but on June 5, he resumed charge of the 2nd Division, V Corps, which he capably led through Petersburg and Appomattox.

After the war, Ayres commanded the short-lived 3rd Division, Provisional Corps. After leaving the Volunteers in 1866, he served as lieutenant colonel of the 28th and 19th Infantry and 3rd Artillery, and as colonel of the 2nd Artillery. He performed occupation and staff duties in the South (1865–1872); did garrison service in New York, Maryland, and Florida (1872–1887); and saw strike duty in Pennsylvania (1877). He also was a member of the Tactics Board (1866–1867) and William B. Hazen's (*q.v.*) Court of Inquiry (1883–1884)—reprising his service on Ambrose E. Burnside's (*q.v.*) Court of Inquiry (1864). Neither brilliant nor dashing, Ayres was a reliable, competent commander who could wield a division effectively in combat. Such ability won his superiors' respect and his men's loyalty. Ayres died on December 4, 1888, at Fort Hamilton, New York. Rhea, *Battle of the Wilderness*; Sommers, *Richmond Redeemed*.

Richard J. Sommers

B

BABBITT, Elijah, *congressman,* was born in Providence, Rhode Island, on July 2, 1795. He received a common school education, studied law, and was admitted to the bar in Northumberland county, Pennsylvania, in 1824. In 1826, he resettled in Erie, where he began a legal career that lasted for a half century. Babbitt became active in local politics as a Whig and served as the attorney for the city of Erie. From 1834 to 1846, he was state deputy attorney general, member of the lower house, and state senator. In 1858, Babbitt was among the leading organizers of the Republican party in northwestern Pennsylvania and was elected to Congress.

With Abraham Lincoln (*q.v.*) gaining over 75 percent of the vote in Erie county in 1860, Babbitt was among the Republicans who urged immediate emancipation; he also called for the enrollment of African Americans as soldiers in the Union Army. He did not run for reelection in 1862 and retired from public office. He died in Erie on January 9, 1887. *Biographical Encyclopedia of Pennsylvania of the Nineteenth Century*; Whitman, *Nelson's Biographical Dictionary and Historical Reference Book of Erie County, Pennsylvania.*

W. Wayne Smith

BAILEY, Goldsmith Fox, *congressman,* was born on July 17, 1823, in Westmoreland, New Hampshire. He grew up in Fitchburg, Massachusetts, where he worked on a farm and attended the local public schools. At the age of seventeen, he became an apprentice in a printing office in Bellows Falls, Vermont. Before he had completed his apprenticeship, he bought the office in which he worked, and became the editor and publisher of the *Bellows Falls Gazette.* In 1844, he returned to Fitchburg, where he was employed by the *Fitchburg Sentinel* as a compositor. Shortly thereafter he embarked upon the study of law, gaining admittance to the bar in 1848.

As a Whig, Bailey was appointed postmaster of Fitchburg (1853–1858), and as a Republican, he served in the state legislature (1856–1858). Although he played no active role in the early antislavery movement, he received the Republican nomination for Congress in 1860. In a memorable campaign he defeated the incumbent, Eli Thayer, a Republican-turned-conservative who ran as an independent. Bailey entered Congress as a relatively young man; thus his losing battle against tuberculosis and his death in Fitchburg, on May 8, 1862, were viewed as particularly tragic and untimely by his colleagues and constituents. Emerson, *Fitchburg, Massachusetts.*

Dale Baum

BAILEY, Joseph, *congressman,* was born to a Quaker family in Pennsbury Township, Pennsylvania, on March 18, 1810. He was active in local politics and represented Chester county in the legislature. Attracted by the investment possibilities of an iron furnace in Perry county, he moved there in 1845. The village that emerged around the furnace became known as Baileysburg (later Bailey Station) and today is a town on the Pennsylvania Railroad called Bailey. Bailey resumed his interest in politics and was elected to the state Senate in 1851. He also began to study law, and in 1860 was admitted to the bar.

Bailey was elected to the 37th Congress and became one of a small band of War Democrats who voted for the call for a peace convention with the Confederacy and consistently supported the war aims of Abraham Lincoln's (*q.v.*) administration. He also supported the abolition of slavery and called for the enlistment of African Americans in the Union Army. In 1862, the Democratic party refused to renominate Bailey, he accepted the Republican nomination and waged a successful contest against a Peace Democrat. Bailey was one of seven War Democrats reelected that year. He retired from Congress in 1865 and served as a delegate to the Pennsylvania Constitutional Convention in 1872, but held no other public office. He died in Bailey Station on August 26, 1885. Dell, *Lincoln and the War Democrats*; Hain, *History of Perry County, Pennsylvania.*

W. Wayne Smith

BAIRD, Absalom, *general,* was born in Washington, Pennsylvania, on August 20, 1824. He earned a diploma from Washington College in 1841 and read law before graduating from West Point in 1849. Commissioned in the artillery, Baird was posted to Florida and later became a mathematics instructor at West Point (1853–1859). He spent several months on frontier service in Texas (1859–1860) and then was assigned to Fort Monroe, Virginia, during the secession crisis. In April 1861, he became a captain in the Adjutant General's Office in Washington, D.C., and Brigadier General Daniel Tyler (*q.v.*) temporarily appointed him as a division staff officer during the First Bull Run campaign. Baird was promoted to major in the Inspector General's Office in November 1861 and soon thereafter became chief of staff of the IV Corps under Major General Erasmus D. Keyes (*q.v.*). He served with Keyes during the Peninsula campaign until being promoted to brigadier general of Volunteers and transferred to the West in May 1862.

In the West, Baird saw his most significant service to the Union, becoming one of the army's best and most commended division commanders. He led a brigade in the division of Major General George W. Morgan (*q.v.*) in the Army of the Ohio and was made division commander in the Reserve Corps in Major General William S. Rosecrans's (*q.v.*) Army of the Cumberland. He saw action during the Tullahoma campaign in the summer of 1863, transferred to temporary command of Lovell H. Rousseau's (*q.v.*) division in the XIV Corps, and participated in the combat around Chattanooga in August 1863. In the battle of Chickamauga, Baird did well with the division, and Rosecrans recommended him for promotion to major general of Volunteers. He was not given that rank but was promoted to lieutenant colonel in the Regulars. Rousseau returned to his division, and Baird took command of the 3rd Division in the XIV Corps, an assignment he held until July 1865.

Baird led his division in the attack up Missionary Ridge, was promoted to colonel in the Regulars, and was again recommended for major general in the Volunteers. He performed well in the Atlanta campaign, leading an assault against a Confederate position near Jonesboro, Georgia, on September 1, 1864, an action for which he was awarded the Medal of Honor in 1896. Baird commanded his division through the March to the Sea and the Carolinas, and was finally promoted to major general of Volunteers, effective March 13, 1865. As commander of troops near New Orleans at the time of the riot on July 30, 1866, he failed to deploy his forces in a way that might have averted the violence directed against blacks. Baird served again in the Inspector General's Office and was made inspector general of the army in 1885, with the rank of brigadier general. He retired in 1888, and died on June 14, 1905, near Relay, Maryland. Castel, *Decision in the West*; Cozzens, *This Terrible Sound.*

Joseph G. Dawson III

BAKER, Edward Dickinson, *senator, general,* was born in London on February 24, 1811. After living in Philadelphia, the family moved to Carrollton, Illinois. Much of Baker's education came from his schoolteacher father. He honed his oratorical skills by preaching to the Disciples of Christ, and he practiced law. In 1845, Baker moved to Springfield, Illinois, where he made important friendships, the most famous with Abraham Lincoln (*q.v.*). He represented Sangamon county in the state House (1837–1840) and in the state Senate (1840–1844). In 1843 Baker failed to receive the Whig nomination to Congress, but he was successful two years later. He supported expansionism and resigned from office for service in Mexico, where he won praise for leading his Illinois regiment at Cerro Gordo. He was reelected to Congress, and after an economic venture in Panama, moved his family to San Francisco in 1852.

Baker helped found California's Republican party but failed to win public office there because the Democrats were too powerful. Responding to the invitation of Republican leaders in Oregon, he traveled to the state in 1859 and 1860 and campaigned for the party. In October 1860 a fusion of Douglas Democrats and Republicans elected the "Grey Eagle of Republicanism" to the U.S. Senate. Baker was Lincoln's major source of information about secessionist activity on the Pacific Slope, and his Senate speeches, including his opposition to the Crittenden Compromise and his endorsement of the proposals of the Peace Convention, drew considerable attention. He argued that a compromise plan should be submitted to the people because the Republicans, a minority party, had no right to force a policy on the majority. Following Fort Sumter, Baker abandoned compromise and advocated war. To this end he raised a regiment in the East; to protect his distant constituents, he organized a cavalry regiment in Oregon. He was also named major general of Volunteers and led a brigade at Ball's Bluff, where he was killed on October 2, 1861. Blair, *Lincoln's Constant Ally.*

G. Thomas Edwards

BAKER, Lafayette Curry, *general, chief of National Detective Bureau,* was born near Stafford, New York, on October 13, 1826. In 1841, he moved with his family to a farm near Lansing, Michigan, but upon coming of age, he returned to the east coast. In 1852, he sailed to California and engaged in what he described as the "mechanical business" in San Francisco and Sacramento. In 1856, Baker was active in San Francisco's Second Vigilance Committee, an extralegal organization that had widespread public support because of the ineffectiveness of the city government in dealing with crime and violence. His participation no doubt influenced his later employment of similar tactics against disloyalty to the Union.

In January 1861 Baker sailed for New York. He arrived at about the time of Fort Sumter, and promptly volunteered his services as an undercover agent to General Winfield Scott (*q.v.*). Sent on a fact-finding mission to Richmond in July, he was taken prisoner but escaped and returned to Washington. The success of this mission recommended him to Secretary of State William H. Seward (*q.v.*), for whom he conducted investigations and made arrests until February 1862, when responsibility for internal security was transferred to Secretary of War Edwin M. Stanton (*q.v.*). Baker served the War Department as chief of a secret police force known as the Bureau of the National Detective Police. From September 1862 to November 1863 he was also a special provost marshal for the department, reporting directly to Stanton.

In June 1863 Baker was appointed colonel of the 1st Regiment of District of Columbia Cavalry, whose nucleus was a battalion he had recruited within the District. Known as Baker's Mounted Rangers, the regiment was effective in suppressing pro-Confederate activities in the area of the capital. Under the field command of Lieutenant Colonel Everton J. Conger, the regiment saw action with the Army of the Potomac. Early in 1864, Baker was relieved of the command and once again assigned to Stanton as a special provost marshal. In April 1865 he was promoted to brigadier general, and in January 1866, after a bitter quarrel with President Andrew Johnson (*q.v.*), he was honorably discharged from the Army.

Ruthless in his efforts to stamp out treason, espionage, and sabotage, Baker was hated and feared by individuals opposed to the war. He also made enemies among the war's supporters, for he was arrogant and unscrupulous, and, as special provost marshal and an Army officer, functioned outside the normal chains of command. His secret investigations and arbitrary imprisonments could not be condoned in time of peace but were perhaps inevitable during the war because of the prevalence of disloyalty in the North. Baker's exposure of frauds and other crimes committed by contractors, speculators, government employees, counterfeiters, bounty jumpers, bounty brokers, and others was of undoubted value to the government. After Abraham Lincoln's (*q.v.*) assassination, Baker organized the expedition that tracked down John Wilkes Booth.

A reaction against his wartime excesses was natural when peace was restored. Baker magnified it by testifying before a congressional committee in 1867 that the diary carried by Booth at the time of his capture had been mutilated by the executive branch, and that he had seen and could produce evidence proving that Andrew Johnson was a traitor, a Confederate spy posing as a Unionist. Later he all but withdrew the first charge, and he could not substantiate the second. In an apparent attempt to avenge himself against the President, he succeeded only in administering the coup de grâce to his own already dubious reputation. Although Baker's power was virtually unrestrained, he did not use it to enrich himself, as has been sometimes alleged, for he died a poor man in Philadelphia on July 3, 1868. Baker, *History of the United States Secret Service*; Hanchett, *Lincoln Murder Conspiracies*; Murdock, *Patriotism Limited*.

William Hanchett

BAKER, Stephen, *congressman*, was born on August 12, 1819, in New York City. Following an education in the common schools, he found employment as an importer and wool jobber in the New York City area. He moved to Poughkeepsie, New York, in the decade prior to the Civil War. Elected to the 37th Congress as a Republican, Baker is best known for his indictment of Salmon P. Chase's (*q.v.*) administration of the Treasury Department. At the end of his term, he abandoned his business pursuits and lived in retirement in New York state. On June 9, 1875, he died near Ogden, Utah. Curry, *Blueprint for Modern America*; Lanman, *Biographical Annals*.

Frank R. Levstik

BALDWIN, Augustus Carpenter, *congressman*, was born December 24, 1817, in Salina (now Syracuse), New York. In 1837, he moved to Oakland county,

Michigan, where he taught school, studied law, and was admitted to the bar in 1842. His first law practice was at Milford, Michigan; in 1849 he moved to Pontiac, where he spent the rest of his life with one brief exception. Baldwin held numerous public offices: representative in the state legislature (elected 1843 and 1845, speaker in 1846); prosecuting attorney (1852); representative in the 38th Congress; brigadier general of the state militia (1845–1862); member of the Pontiac board of education (1868–1886); mayor of Pontiac (1874); and judge of the 6th Judicial Circuit of Michigan (1875–1879).

Baldwin was a lifelong Democrat. His earliest political memories were of Andrew Jackson, whom he greatly admired. A delegate to the Democratic conventions at Charleston and Baltimore in 1860, and at Chicago in 1864, and the National Peace Congress at Philadelphia in 1866, he actively campaigned for the Democratic ticket in every presidential election from 1840 until his death. In Congress he took a Douglas Democrat position in supporting the war, though he also voted for the 13th Amendment. After his congressional career Baldwin opposed the 14th and 15th Amendments because he believed that servitude had made the freedman unfit for self-government. Besides engaging in politics, holding public office, and practicing law, he farmed, was a trustee of the Eastern Insane Asylum at Ypsilanti, was a member of the Pioneer Society in Oakland county, and maintained an impressive private library. Baldwin died in Pontiac, Michigan, on January 21, 1903. Dunbar, *Michigan: A History of the Wolverine State*; Utley, *Michigan as a Province, Territory, and State*, vol. 3.

George M. Blackburn

BALDWIN, John Denison, *congressman*, was born on September 28, 1809, in North Stonington, Connecticut. He attended public school, and after graduating from Yale Divinity School in 1834, was a licensed minister for the next fifteen years. He was elected as a Free Soiler to the Connecticut legislature, where he helped establish the state's first normal school. While still in the legislature, Baldwin left the ministry in 1849 to become editor of the Free Soil *Charter Oak* in Hartford. In 1852 he moved to Boston, where he became part owner and editor of the *Daily Commonwealth*, the antislavery newspaper that had supported Charles Sumner's (*q.v.*) election to the Senate in 1851. In 1859 he purchased the *Worcester Spy*, an established Massachusetts newspaper with a long history.

At the 1860 Republican National Convention, Baldwin suggested that Hannibal Hamlin (*q.v.*) receive the vice presidential nomination. He was elected to Congress in 1862 and was twice reelected. His identification with the Radical wing of the Massachusetts Republican party was a prerequisite for nomination and election to Congress from the old Free Soil stronghold in Worcester county. In the House, Baldwin consistently supported Radical positions until the second session of the 39th Congress, when he began to vote occasionally with the Conservative opposition. In 1868 his influential editorial column in the *Spy* supported the candidacy of George Frisbie Hoar to succeed him in Congress. He died on July 8, 1883, in Worcester, Massachusetts. *BDUSC.*

Dale Baum

BANKS, Nathaniel Prentice, *general*, was born in Waltham, Massachusetts, on January 30, 1816. After three defeats, he won election to the Massachusetts legislature in 1848. At first an orthodox Democrat, he allied with the Free Soilers in the early 1850s, then joined the Know-Nothings, and ended as a Republican. Elected to the House in 1852, Banks rose to be Speaker and then won the governorship of Massachusetts in 1857, 1858, and 1859. His hopes of securing the Republican nomination for the presidency in 1860 were wrecked by the hostility of Massachusetts Radical Republicans, who found the governor too bland for their taste. Somewhat embittered by his failure, Banks abandoned politics for a well-paid position with the Illinois Central Railroad.

Although Banks had no military experience worth mentioning and had done little to aid Abraham Lincoln (*q.v.*) in the 1860 campaign, the President nevertheless made him a senior major general soon after the Civil War began. After a brief tour of duty in Maryland, Banks took command in the Shenandoah Valley, where he won imperishable fame as the victim of Stonewall Jackson's Valley campaign. Banks lost to Jackson again at Cedar Mountain, where he was disabled when his horse fell on him. Lincoln then gave this political white elephant the task of enlisting an army of soldier-settlers to occupy Texas and raise cotton for New England's mills. At the last moment, however, Lincoln sent Banks to clear the lower Mississippi, and so he sailed for New Orleans to replace another white elephant, Benjamin F. Butler (*q.v.*), in command of the Gulf Department.

Under Lincoln's guidance, Banks tried to make Louisiana a model of presidential Reconstruction. Opinions differ as to his degree of success. In the field, where he spent a good deal of his time hunting for cotton, Banks won a few minor engagements, received the surrender of Port Hudson in the aftermath of Ulysses S. Grant's (*q.v.*) capture of Vicksburg, and led his troops in the disastrous Red River campaign, whereupon he was relieved of all nonpolitical duties.

After the war, Banks returned to Congress. A jingoist in foreign policy, he apparently accepted a bribe as his price for supporting the purchase of Alaska. While posing as a champion of labor, he was on the take from businessmen. In 1872, Banks lost the House seat he had held since 1865 when he switched to the Liberal Republicans. He then recanted, was reelected, and waved the ''Bloody Shirt'' for Rutherford B. Hayes (*q.v.*) in 1876. Finally overtaken by his reputation as a political chameleon, he failed to win renomination in 1878. The rest of his career was spent in comparative obscurity. Banks died in Waltham on September 1, 1894. Harrington, *Fighting Politician*; Johnson, *Red River Campaign.*

Ludwell H. Johnson

BARLOW, Francis Channing, *general*, was born in Brooklyn, New York, on October 19, 1834, and grew up in Brookline, Massachusetts. He graduated from Harvard at the top of his class in 1855, practiced law, and wrote for the *New York Tribune* until the Civil War began. In April 1861 the young lawyer enlisted as a private in the 12th New York Volunteers, and after a brief stint in Washington joined the 61st New York as a lieutenant colonel, thereafter serving in the field with the Army of the Potomac. As a regimental, brigade, and division commander, the "Boy General" participated in some of the bloodiest battles of the war, including Antietam, Chancellorsville, Gettysburg, Spotsylvania, and Cold Harbor. Absent due to sickness during most of the Petersburg campaign, Barlow returned in time for the final encounters at Sayler's Creek and Farmville.

A youthful, unkempt appearance and a lackluster personality camouflaged the hard-bitten, savagely combative leader that Barlow was. Cold, sardonic, and exacting, he earned the respect rather than the affection of his men. The young commander never squandered the lives of his troops and held in contempt those officers who did. Personally impetuous and unflinchingly brave, Barlow invariably stationed himself where the fighting was heaviest; as a result he suffered severe wounds at Sharpsburg and on the first day at Gettysburg. On May 12, 1864, he capped his wartime career by leading a division in the predawn assault at Spotsylvania. This action netted almost 4,000 Confederate prisoners, a loss the Army of Northern Virginia could ill afford.

Because he never exercised high-level, independent command, Barlow has been relegated to the status of intrepid and highly competent but not very significant. Valid as far as it goes, this evaluation disregards the fact that he and his peers probably influenced the outcome of a given battle as much as, if not more than, the senior officers who planned and directed but did not lead. Barlow is also important as a representative of the Volunteer at his best. Biased by the ineptitude of most amateur officers, historians tend to forget that there were some, like Barlow, who outshone the professionals.

At the end of the war, Barlow entered New York Republican politics. A protégé of Ulysses S. Grant (*q.v.*), he was, nevertheless, an active reformer. As a federal marshal and subsequently state attorney general, he eliminated political corruption in southern New York and prosecuted the Tweed Ring. He also served on the commission that investigated Florida voting frauds in the 1876 presidential election. Afterward, Barlow resumed his law practice in New York City, where he died on January 11, 1896. Catton, *Never Call Retreat*; Coddington, *Gettysburg Campaign*; Rhea, *Battle of the Wilderness*.

James L. Morrison, Jr.

BARNARD, George N., *photographer*, was born in Coventry, Connecticut, on December 23, 1819. In 1843, he opened a daguerreotype gallery in Oswego, New York, where in 1853 he made daguerreotypes of burning mills that are believed to be the earliest news photos taken in the United States. At that time he was secretary of the New York State Daguerrian Association. In the 1850s, the daguerreotype was made obsolete when the "wet plate" or collodion process came into general use. Barnard's first known collodion photographs were taken at Manassas in 1862, after the area had been reoccupied by Union troops. He was almost certainly part of Matthew Brady's (*q.v.*) "Photographic Corps."

In 1863, Barnard moved to the West when he was named the official photographer of the Military Division of the Mississippi. He experienced the high point of his professional career when he followed General William T. Sherman's (*q.v.*) campaigns in Georgia and the Carolinas. The cumbersome photographic process Barnard had to use, which required fragile glass plates, chemicals, and a portable dark room, precluded his presence during the fighting and was so slow that the recording of military units in movement was not possible. Barnard assembled a collection of hauntingly stark and quiet images of burned cities and broken forests from which soldiers and inhabitants alike seem to have recently departed. The picturesque Georgia landscapes, classically composed and featuring spectacular, luminous cloud formations (printed from separate negatives), are both eerie and poignant when one imagines the violence that earlier took place in them.

With Sherman's endorsement, Barnard privately published *Photographic Views of Sherman's Campaign*, a portfolio of sixty-one original photographs, in 1866. The size of the edition was small; the price of the book was $100. Today the work is highly regarded for its historical and artistic value. In 1869, Barnard established a gallery in Chicago that was destroyed two years later by the great fire. He recorded the aftermath of destruction in a series of photographs of the ruined city. Barnard died in Cedarville, New York, on February 4, 1902. Barnard, *Photographic Views.*

Ben Bassham

BARNARD, John Gross, *general,* was born on May 15, 1815, in Sheffield, Massachusetts. He graduated from West Point in 1833 and was commissioned in the Corps of Engineers. He worked on coastal fort construction and performed similar duties during the Mexican War, then headed a survey commission investigating a commercial route to California via the Isthmus of Tehuantepec. Despite tropical illness and inherited deafness that gave the appearance of premature aging, Barnard was acclaimed as an authority on American coast defense. He was one of the original incorporators of the National Academy of Sciences, received A.M. and LL.D. degrees from Alabama (1838) and Yale (1864), and wrote studies on the North Sea Canal of Holland (1872) and on interrelationships of the gyroscope, equinoxes, and pendulum (1872). The Federal government relied on Barnard's scientific expertise, and he served as president of the Fortification, River, and Harbor Improvements Board prior to his retirement in 1881.

Barnard is an overlooked figure of the Civil War. He not only served in major eastern campaigns but also counseled military and civilian leaders on military problems, largely on the basis of his reputation as one of the Army's foremost engineers. As Irvin McDowell's (*q.v.*) engineer at Bull Run, it was his flank reconaissance that dictated the course of the Federal battle plan. As George B. McClellan's (*q.v.*) chief engineer on the Peninsula, he advised returning the Army of the Potomac to Washington. Barnard's fixation with defending Washington, and his engineering responsibility in that regard (1861–1864), led to his foremost contribution in the war. The extensive defenses of Washington embraced thirty-five miles of fieldworks (seventy-four enclosed forts and armed batteries mounting over 1,000 guns), served by thirty-two miles of military roads (both still linchpins in the city's park system), earned him the sobriquet "Father of the Defenses of Washington." Barnard also planned the defenses of Pittsburgh and returned to field duty as Ulysses S. Grant's (*q.v.*) chief engineer in the Petersburg campaign. Grant employed him as personal envoy to William T. Sherman (*q.v.*) to ascertain the state of the latter's army following the March to the Sea.

Barnard possessed undisputed engineering skills, but his military reputation remains enigmatic. Neither Henry W. Halleck (*q.v.*) nor Secretary of War Edwin M. Stanton (*q.v.*) had confidence in his judgment. This may have resulted from Barnard's clear identification as part of the McClellan faction in the Army of the Potomac, and his affiliation with the early defeats in the East dimmed his star in the eyes of many contemporaries. He emerged from the war bearing the brevet of major general in both the Volunteer and Regular service. These rested on his contributions as an engineer—principally the fortifications surrounding Washington. Barnard died in Detroit on May 14, 1882. Cooling, *Symbol, Sword, and Shield.*

B. Franklin Cooling

BARNES, James, *general,* was born in Boston on December 28, 1801. He was a graduate of the Boston Latin School and West Point, class of 1829. Barnes saw duty in the Black Hawk Indian campaign and later served as an instructor of infantry tactics at West Point until July 1836, when he resigned to become a civil engineer for railroads in New York, Massachusetts, Virginia, North Carolina, and Illinois. In 1861, he was appointed a colonel of the 18th Massachusetts Volunteers, which served in the defenses of Washington D.C., and in the Peninsula campaign. He was commissioned on November 29, 1862, as a brigadier general of Volunteers and commanded a brigade in George Morell's (*q.v.*) division of the V Corps at Antietam, Fredericksburg, and Chancellorsville. At Gettysburg, Barnes commanded the 1st Division in the absence of Charles Griffin (*q.v.*), who had been wounded at Chancellorsville. On July 2, in the face of the powerful Confederate attack near the Wheat Field, Barnes withdrew portions of his division, perhaps prematurely. He was later criticized, possibly as a means of excusing the poor performance of Daniel Sickles (*q.v.*).

Barnes's personal courage was never questioned, but doubts about his actions that day led to his removal from field command. After his recovery from wounds received at Gettysburg, he commanded the garrisons at Norfolk and Portsmouth,

Virginia, and was president of several general courts martial. On March 13, 1865, he was breveted a major general of Volunteers and mustered out of service. In 1868, Barnes was appointed to a commission investigating the building the Union Pacific Railroad and telegraph line. He died on February 12, 1869, in Springfield, Massachusetts. Coddington, *Gettysburg Campaign*; Pfanz, *Gettysburg: The Second Day.*

Alan C. Aimone

BARNES, Joseph K., *Surgeon General*, was born in Philadelphia on July 21, 1817. He attended Harvard and graduated with a medical degree from the University of Pennsylvania in 1838. In 1840, he became a military surgeon and served in the Seminole Wars, in Mexico, and on the frontier. In 1862 he was posted to Washington, D.C., where he became Secretary of War Edwin Stanton's (*q.v.*) personal physician. When Surgeon General William A. Hammond (*q.v.*) ran afoul of Stanton, Barnes became acting Surgeon General, and in 1864, after Hammond's dismissal, Surgeon General. Barnes was personally more acceptable to his friend Stanton, and carried out most of Hammond's long overdue reforms in the medical service. He was at Abraham Lincoln's (*q.v.*) deathbed and treated James A. Garfield (*q.v.*) after his wounding in 1881. In 1869 he was a pallbearer for Stanton. Barnes died in Washington on April 5, 1883. Adams, *Doctors in Blue.*

John T. Hubbell

BARRY, William Farquhar, *general*, was born on August 18, 1818, in New York City. He graduated from West Point in 1838 and was assigned to the Canadian border as a lieutenant in the 4th U.S. Artillery. He later served in the Mexican War as an adjutant and aide to Major General Francis Patterson and Major General W.J. Worth. His extensive service as a captain in the 2nd U.S. Artillery included pacification of the Florida Seminoles and the warring parties in Kansas. From 1856 to 1859, Barry was a member of the Board of Light Artillery, which revised field artillery tactics.

At the start of the Civil War, Barry was at Fort Pickens, Florida; he then served as acting chief of artillery under Major General Irvin McDowell (*q.v.*) at First Bull Run, and later under Major General George B. McClellan (*q.v.*). He reorganized and refitted the ordnance of the Army of the Potomac. Barry was appointed brigadier general of Volunteers on August 20, 1861. After the Peninsula campaign he was transferred to Washington, D.C., as the chief of artillery of the capital's fortifications. He also served on a number of ordnance boards. In early 1864, Barry was reassigned as chief of artillery on the staff of General William T. Sherman (*q.v.*), and was with Sherman from northern Georgia to Atlanta to Savannah and through the Carolinas, until the Confederate surrender.

Barry received brevet major generalships of both the Volunteers and the Regular Army. He was promoted to colonel of the 2nd U.S. Artillery on December 11, 1865. Barry was commander of the northern frontier during the Fenian uprising and served at various posts as an artillery officer. He died at Fort McHenry, Maryland, on July 18, 1879. Longacre, *Man Behind the Guns.*

Alan C. Aimone

BARTON, Clara, *nurse,* was born on December 25, 1821, in North Oxford, Massachusetts. After receiving her education in local schools, she began teaching in her hometown. She later taught in New Jersey, where she founded that state's first public school. In 1854, Barton was hired as a clerk in the Patent Office in Washington, D.C., the first woman who was regularly appointed as a civil servant. When the Civil War began, Barton aided homesick soldiers from Massachusetts who were stationed in Washington. After viewing the inadequate first aid facilities at the Bull Run battlefield, she began advertising for medical provisions and other necessities, which she distributed to hospitals, battlefields, and camps. She also ministered to the wounded and dying at the front.

Barton kept her nursing operations separate from the Union's Sanitary Commission and thus managed to circumvent regular military channels. Her deeds and initiative won her the respect of military officers and surgeons and the title "Angel of the Battlefield." Once the Sanitary Commission became better organized, Barton's role as a battlefield nurse lessened. After a brief respite in Port Royal, South Carolina, she was named head nurse in General Benjamin F. Butler's (*q.v.*) Army of the James in 1864.

In 1865, Barton opened an office in Annapolis, Maryland, to assist in locating soldiers who were missing in action. Later, she headed the endeavor to mark the graves of the Union dead at Andersonville Prison. Her hard work and accomplishments convinced the Federal government to finance these efforts. Barton is perhaps best known as the founder of the American Red Cross. She devoted most of the rest of her life to its organization and operation, and became one of the most honored women of her generation. She died in North Oxford on April 12, 1912. Oates, *Woman of Valor*; Ross, *Angel of the Battlefield.*

Donna M. DeBlasio

BATES, Edward, *Attorney General,* was born in Belmont, Virginia, on September 4, 1793. He was educated privately and at Charlotte Hall Academy; saw military service in 1813, when Norfolk was threatened by the British; and moved to St. Louis, where he studied law and was admitted to the bar in 1816. Bates was a circuit attorney in 1818, a member of the Constitutional Convention in 1820 when Missouri was admitted to the Union; a member of the state legislature (1822–1824); U.S. district attorney (1824–1826); and a member of Congress (1827–1829). In the 1830s, he emerged as the leader of Missouri's Whig party, but in a state overwhelmingly Democratic this offered little hope of political success beyond the local level. Bates served again in the legislature (1830–1834) and achieved national recognition in 1847 as presiding officer of the River and Harbor Improvement Convention in Chicago, with a stirring address on national unity and western expansion.

Although Bates declined appointment by President Millard Fillmore as Secretary of War in 1850, his views were increasingly sought by Whig politicians around the country. He opposed the repeal of the Missouri Compromise, moved slowly toward the new Republican party, and presided over the last Whig convention at Baltimore in 1856. Bates was a prominent contender for the Republican presidential nomination in 1860, and following the election of Abraham Lincoln (*q.v.*), he accepted the post of Attorney General.

During the early years of the war, Bates was a close adviser to the President because of their mutual western interests and moderate views. He reorganized the Justice Department to make it more responsive to wartime demands but found himself in frequent conflict with Secretary of State William Seward (*q.v.*), and later Secretary of War Edwin Stanton (*q.v.*), over the implications of martial law and the encroachments of the military on constitutional rights. Although Bates was handicapped by lack of background as he grappled with problems of international law involving the blockade, he successfully steered the government's prosecution of the prize cases through the Supreme Court and generally upheld the President's extensive powers as commander in chief in the absence of congressional mandate. In the *Trent* affair he counseled moderation to avert the possibility of war with England. Bates was influential in the decision to use armored gunboats on the Mississippi and other western waters, which greatly aided the campaigns there in 1862 and 1863. He supported compensated emancipation in the border states in 1862 and favored some form of colonization.

As the brother-in-law and confidant of Governor Hamilton R. Gamble (*q.v.*) of Missouri, Bates was a frequent mediator between state officials and the Lincoln government over matters in that war-torn state. After 1863, his influence began to decline, in part because of his opposition to statehood for West Virginia and his continued disagreement with the legal abuses committed by the military. He resigned his cabinet post on November 24, 1864, and returned to St. Louis, where he fought unsuccessfully against the adoption of a new state constitution proposed by the Radicals in 1865. Bates died in St. Louis on March 25, 1869. Parrish, *Turbulent Partnership.*

William E. Parrish

BAXTER, Portus, *congressman,* was born in Brownington, Vermont, on December 12, 1806. He attended Norwich Military Academy and the University of Vermont, which he left after his junior year in 1823. In 1828, Baxter moved to Derby Line, Vermont, where he gained a reputation as a merchant and farmer, and served as an assistant judge of Orleans county in 1846–1847. His marriage to Ellen Janette Harris in 1832 wedded him to a prominent Vermont family with ties to Justin Smith Morrill (*q.v.*). Though he repeatedly declined elective office, Baxter, a Henry Clay Whig, became politically influential in Orleans county. In 1848, he was the only New England Whig at the party's national convention to initially support Zachary Taylor. As presidential elector in 1852, Baxter supported Winfield Scott (*q.v.*). He attended the informal Republican National Convention in 1856, and as a presidential elector supported John C. Frémont (*q.v.*).

After twice declining nominations for Congress, Baxter successfully ran in 1860. Preferring behind-the-scenes maneuvering to speechmaking, he was a close friend of Edwin Stanton (*q.v.*) and was associated with the Radical Republicans. Known as the soldier's friend, his special concern was exemplified in 1864 when he went to Fredericksburg to take personal care of Vermont casualties. Baxter failed to obtain renomination in 1866 and withdrew from the contest. He died in Washington, D.C., on March 4, 1868. Crockett, *Vermont*, vols. 3, 4.

Samuel B. Hand

BAYARD, George Dashiell, *general,* was born in Seneca Falls, New York, on December 1, 1835, and was raised in Iowa. He graduated from West Point in 1856 and served with the 1st U.S. Cavalry in Kansas and Colorado. His killing of Kiowa Chief Big Pawnee in September 1859 apparently ignited a Kiowa–Comanche uprising. Bayard was severely wounded in one of the actions. He was appointed colonel of the 1st Pennsylvania Cavalry and commanded this regiment until April 28, 1862, when he was promoted to brigadier general. His cavalry brigade served with General John C. Frémont (*q.v.*) in the Shenandoah against Jackson, and participated in the battle of Port Republic on June 9, 1862. In August 1862, General John Pope (*q.v.*) named Bayard and Brigadier General John Buford (*q.v.*) to command his first-line cavalry brigades.

Bayard covered the Union retreat from Cedar Mountain with his 1st Pennsylvania Cavalry, losing 103 of 164 officers and men in the severe fighting. Bayard and Buford almost captured Confederate general J.E.B. Stuart when they surprised his headquarters at Verdiersville. At Gainesville, on August 28, he clashed with Stuart in the opening movements of the Second Bull Run campaign, and after Antietam his brigade drove Stuart back at Snicker's Gap. At Fredericksburg, on December 13, 1862, Bayard, at the headquarters of General William Franklin (*q.v.*), was mortally wounded when struck by a solid shot fired by Stuart's Horse Artillery. He died in Fredericksburg the next day. Starr, *Union Cavalry*, vol. 1; Wheeler, *Lee's Terrible Swift Sword.*

Roy P. Stonesifer, Jr.

BAYARD, James Asheton, *senator,* was born in Wilmington, Delaware, on November 15, 1799. He attended Princeton University and was graduated from Union College in 1818. Admitted to the Delaware bar in 1822, he began to practice law in Wilmington. He ran unsuccessfully for Congress as a Jacksonian Democrat in 1828, and he remained a consistent and unwavering Democrat throughout his life. From 1838 to 1843 he was U.S. district attorney for Delaware. The General Assembly elected him to the U.S. Senate in 1850, 1856, and 1862. At the beginning of the Civil War, Bayard was sympathetic to the South, but he opposed secession. He was highly critical of abuses of civil rights by the

Lincoln (*q.v.*) administration, and spoke out strongly against the requirement that senators take a "test" or loyalty oath. Although he took such an oath, he resigned in protest in 1864.

Upon the death of his successor in 1867, Governor Gove Saulsbury (*q.v.*) appointed Bayard to fill the vacancy until the legislature met. On January 19, 1869, Bayard and his son, Thomas F., were both elected to the U.S. Senate, the father to fill out the unexpired senatorial term and the son to serve as his successor. At noon on March 4, 1869, Bayard retired from senatorial life and his son took his place, an unprecedented event in the annals of Congress. He died in Wilmington on June 13, 1880. Hancock, *Delaware During the Civil War.*

Harold B. Hancock

BEAMAN, Fernando Cortez, *congressman,* was born on June 28, 1814, in Chester, Vermont. The family subsequently moved to New York, where he attended district schools and Malone Academy, taught school, and studied law. In 1838 he moved to Michigan, was admitted to the bar, and began practicing law; in 1843, he settled and lived for the rest of his life in Adrian. Beaman held a number of local offices, including prosecuting attorney for Lenawee county, mayor of Adrian, and judge of the Probate Court of Lenawee county (1856–1860, 1871–1880). An inveterate foe of slavery, he participated in the convention that met in Jackson and organized Michigan's Republican party.

Beaman served in the U.S. House of Representatives (1861–1871), where he denounced secession and urged firmness in dealing with the South. He held that Congress alone had constitutional authority to reconstruct the South; he voted to impeach Andrew Johnson (*q.v.*); and he actively supported the 14th and 15th Amendments. For personal reasons he declined appointments as justice of the Michigan Supreme court, U.S. Commissioner of Indian Affairs, and U.S. senator to fill the vacancy created by the death of Zachariah Chandler (*q.v.*). Stress and hard work so impaired Beaman's health that he chose not to stand for reelection to Congress in 1870. He died in Adrian on September 27, 1882. Barnard, *American Biographical History; BDUSC.*

Frederick D. Williams

BEECHER, Henry Ward, *abolitionist, clergyman,* was born in Litchfield, Connecticut, on June 24, 1813. Among his twelve siblings was Harriet Beecher Stowe (*q.v.*). Beecher attended district schools and graduated from Amherst College in 1834. He entered the Lane Theological Seminary in Cincinnati, over which his father presided, and after three years of study became a minister. During the next decade, he was affiliated with various churches in the Midwest; his skill and reputation as a preacher led to his being named minister of Plymouth Congregational Church in Brooklyn in 1847, where he remained until his death. Beecher became one of the most influential preachers in the antebellum era by involving himself in a variety of reform causes, but his sermons often revealed strains of ambivalence. Although he contended that Congress had no legal authority to interfere with slavery in the individual states, he urged disobedience to the Fugitive Slave Law. He allied himself very early with the Republican party, and supported the presidential candidacies of John C. Frémont (*q.v.*) in 1856 and of Abraham Lincoln (*q.v.*) in 1860.

During the Civil War, Beecher supported the Union through numerous speeches and by visiting England in 1863 to urge support for the Northern war effort. After the war, he supported President Andrew Johnson's (*q.v.*) moderate Reconstruction policies. He also was involved in various newspapers, published *Evolution and Religion* (1885) and other works, and supported the franchise for women and African Americans. Beecher is best remembered for an alleged affair with the wife of Theodore Tilton (*q.v.*). Although he was acquitted of charges of adultery, this sensationalized episode eclipsed the other achievements in Beecher's life. He died on March 8, 1887, in Brooklyn, New York. Clark, *Henry Ward Beecher*; Waller, *Reverend Beecher and Mrs. Tilton.*

James W. Geary

BELMONT, August, *diplomat, financier,* was born on December 8, 1816, in Alzie, Rhenish Palatinate, Germany. Of Jewish descent, he went to work at the age of fourteen for the Rothschilds, who in 1833 sent him to their branch office in Naples, where he initiated financial negotiations with the papal court. In 1837, while in Havana on business, Belmont realized that economic opportunity awaited him in the United States. Once in New York City, he established August Belmont and Company and, after becoming a citizen, immersed himself in Democratic party activities. In 1850 he was appointed consul general for Austria in the United States, and in 1853 President Franklin Pierce named him minister to the Netherlands. In 1860, Belmont supported the Stephen A. Douglas (*q.v.*) wing of the Democratic party and served as national chairman.

At the outbreak of the Civil War, Belmont supported the war effort and continued that support throughout the conflict. In April 1861, he assisted in the raising and fitting out of a German-American regiment known as the 1st New York Regiment of Rifles. Through his assistance, an early domestic Treasury bond issue met with success. In 1861, he sailed to Europe to visit his vacationing family. With the approval of Treasury Secretary Salmon P. Chase (*q.v.*) and Secretary of State William Seward (*q.v.*), Belmont gained European diplomatic and financial support for the Union cause. His contacts with the major European banking firms, especially the Rothschilds, did much to discourage investments in the Confederate cause. Belmont also reported to the administration on commercial and diplomatic policies that might further the Union cause. After the war, Belmont remained active in Democratic party politics. He died in New York City on November 24, 1890. Belmont, *Letters and Speeches*; Katz, *August Belmont.*

Frank R. Levstik

BENHAM, Henry Washington, *general,* was born on April 17, 1813, in Meriden, Connecticut. He attended Yale and graduated from West Point in 1837.

He was commissioned a lieutenant in the Corps of Engineers, and participated in the construction of Savannah River improvements and coast defenses at Fort Marion, and of the seawall at St. Augustine, Florida. As a captain of engineers during the Mexican War, Benham was wounded slightly at Buena Vista. He subsequently supervised harbor and fortification repairs and improvements at Annapolis, Philadelphia, Washington, D.C., New York City, and Boston. Brigadier General George B. McClellan (*q.v.*) appointed Benham chief of engineers of the Department of the Ohio in 1861. His leadership of the advance guard that pursued Confederate General Robert S. Garnett from Laurel Hill to Carrick's Ford, Virginia, led to his brevet promotion to colonel in the Regular Army and a commission as brigadier general of Volunteers.

An ineffective field commander, Benham was relieved by Brigadier General David Hunter (*q.v.*) after his unsuccessful attack on Secessionville, South Carolina, in June 1862. His commission was revoked, but President Abraham Lincoln (*q.v.*) canceled the revocation. For the remainder of the war, Benham commanded the engineer brigade of the Army of the Potomac, which laid a 2,200-foot pontoon bridge across the James River on June 15, 1864; for that service he received the brevets of major general in both the Regulars and Volunteers. As a colonel in the Corps of Engineers, Benham was in charge of constructing the defenses of the harbors of Boston and New York (1867–1882). He died in New York City on June 1, 1884. Carse, *Department of the South*; Sommers, *Richmond Redeemed.*

Alan C. Aimone

BENNETT, James Gordon, Sr., *editor*, was born in Keith, Banffshire, Scotland, in 1795. He came to the United States in 1819, and worked as a freelance writer and typesetter until settling in New York City. In 1835, he established the most successful penny newspaper in America, the *New York Herald*. The paper drew heavily on local police and court news and trivial curiosities, and had a strong sensationalistic tone. It was an immediate success among the working class, and by the 1860s its circulation was 135,000. Politically, the *Herald* was Democratic, pro-South, and vehemently antiabolition. Widely read in both the North and South and in England, it was taken seriously by Abraham Lincoln (*q.v.*) and his administration, which it daily criticized and lampooned, especially after the preliminary Emancipation Proclamation.

Bennett could tolerate the Republican President only as long as the war was being fought to save the Union. When slavery became the central issue, he moved to the attack. The *Herald* had the best news coverage of the war, with more than forty reporters in the field. It also published war maps, showing the placement of armies and troop strength. Lincoln viewed the *Herald*'s editorial support as being so vital, especially among pro-McClellan soldiers, that he went to extreme lengths to try to guarantee its backing. He offered Bennett the French ambassadorship; although that was not enough to obtain his endorsement in the 1864 election, it at least kept the paper neutral. As the war neared its end and

Lincoln announced a moderate Reconstruction policy, Bennett supported the President.

Enigmatic, irascible, often mean-spirited and temperamental, Bennett was a powerful force in the development of modern journalism who also played a significant role during the Civil War with his paper's editorials and extensive news coverage. He died in New York City on June 1, 1872. Carlson, *The Man Who Made News*; Seitz, *James Gordon Bennetts*.

Fredric F. Endres

BERRY, Hiram Gregory, *general,* was born on August 27, 1824, in Rockland, Maine. He pursued a business career, eventually becoming a bank president. A Democrat, he served in the state legislature and as mayor of Rockland. Berry was active in the militia during the 1850s and, due largely to this experience, was chosen colonel of the 4th Maine in 1861. He led his regiment to the defense of Washington prior to First Bull Run and distinguished himself from that battle until his death, rising in the process from regimental to division command, with the final rank of major general of Volunteers. Berry's brigade performed admirably in the battles of Williamsburg and Fair Oaks, and during General George B. McClellan's (*q.v.*) retreat to the James, thus earning Berry accolades from III Corps commander Samuel P. Heintzelman (*q.v.*) as well as from McClellan. Injured in a fall from his horse, slightly wounded, and further incapacitated by malaria and overwork, Berry was furloughed to Rockland, thus missing Second Bull Run and Antietam. He returned to command in time to win praise from Confederate General A. P. Hill at Fredericksburg, for having the ''best behaved brigade'' that Hill had ever witnessed under fire. Little wonder that Berry succeeded to Joseph Hooker's (*q.v.*) division command in time for Chancellorsville.

Berry should be remembered as ''a soldier's general'' and leader of men. His gallantry under fire and the admiration of his subordinates are recorded in numerous accounts. He was unmilitary in appearance, much in the manner of Ulysses S. Grant (*q.v.*), but was devoted to the Union and to his soldiers. He would resort to political intercession by Vice President Hannibal Hamlin (*q.v.*) when he felt his military contributions slighted. Berry was mortally wounded on May 3, 1863, while consolidating Federal positions at Chancellorsville, following Jackson's rout of the XI Corps. De Trobriand, *Four Years with the Army of the Potomac*; Furgurson, *Chancellorsville*.

B. Franklin Cooling

BERRY, Nathaniel Springer, *governor,* was born in Bath, Maine, on September 1, 1796, and moved with his family to Lebanon, New Hampshire, in 1802. Apprenticed to a tanner in 1812, Berry owned his own tannery by the age of twenty-four and engaged in that business for the next thirty-seven years. He served five terms in the New Hampshire House of Representatives and two in the state Senate between 1828 and 1854. His strong opposition to slavery led him away from the Democratic party, and in 1845 he ran unsuccessfully for governor as the candidate of the Free Soil and Liberty parties. Four more times the Free Soil party nominated him for governor, but without success. Running for the same office as a Republican in 1861, Berry won by a wide margin, and he was reelected in 1862.

In his second term, Berry attended the Northern governors' conference at Altoona, Pennsylvania, where he was chosen to present their findings to President Abraham Lincoln (*q.v.*). He was responsible for recruiting fifteen of the state's eighteen infantry regiments, as well as its only battery of field artillery and a squadron of cavalry. At times Berry hampered his own efficiency by ill-advised political appointments to military positions, but his state always met its quotas while he served. He remained fiercely loyal to the Union cause but criticized the Lincoln administration for failing to view slavery as the principal target of the war. In 1863, Berry retired from politics and moved to Andover, Massachusetts, where he served five years as a justice of the peace. He died in Bristol, New Hampshire, on April 27, 1894. Musgrove, *History of the Town of Bristol*; Rayback, *Free Soil*.

William Marvel

BIDDLE, Charles John, *congressman, editor,* was born in Philadelphia on April 30, 1819, the son of Nicholas Biddle, president of the Second Bank of the United States. He graduated from Princeton in 1837, read law, and in 1840 began a practice in Philadelphia. At the outset of the Mexican War, Biddle raised a company of Volunteers. He led an assault on Chapultepec for which he was commended by General Winfield Scott (*q.v.*) and promoted to brevet major. Upon the outbreak of the Civil War, Biddle served as a colonel in the training of the 13th Pennsylvania Reserve Regiment and for a short time was assigned to defend the Pennsylvania border as a commander of the 5th Pennsylvania Reserve Regiment.

When Congressmen Edward Joy Morris (*q.v.*) received a diplomatic assignment, Biddle entered the special election in April 1861 for the vacant congressional seat. Biddle was suspected of being tepid about the war, but his brief military service warded off charges that he was a Southern sympathizer. He narrowly won the election, and when the 37th Congress met in December 1861, Biddle became one of the conservatives who resisted Republican demands for emancipation. His conservatism stiffened as the war progressed, and he became an outspoken critic of the military draft, the arrest of Clement Vallandigham (*q.v.*), and the emancipation policies of the Lincoln (*q.v.*) administration. His antiwar position was better known in 1862, and the voters rejected his reelection bid.

Biddle continued to be active in the Democratic party, and in 1863 he became chairman of the Pennsylvania Central Committee. He also became the proprietor and editor of *The Age*, a conservative Democratic newspaper in Philadelphia,

and served as its editor until his death in Philadelphia on September 28, 1873.
Davis, *Pennsylvania Politics*; Fisher, *Philadelphia Perspective.*

W. Wayne Smith

BIGELOW, John, *diplomat*, was born on November 25, 1817, in Bristol (now
Malden), New York. He graduated in 1835 from Union College, studied law,
was admitted to the bar in 1839, and opened a law office in New York City;
he spent most of his time, however, writing for such journals as John O'Sullivan's *Democratic Review.* Bigelow became a close friend and political associate
of O'Sullivan, William Cullen Bryant (*q.v.*), and Samuel Tilden, leaders of the
New York City Democratic party. After participating strenuously in the 1848
Free Soil party presidential campaign, Bigelow became a partner and coeditor
with Bryant of the *Evening Post*, which they led into the Republican party in
1856. As one of the leading advocates of John Charles Frémont (*q.v.*) for President, and as his authorized campaign biographer, Bigelow became nationally
known as a political strategist and propagandist. During an extended trip to
Europe from late 1858 until June 1860, he became acquainted with leading
journalists and politicians in France and Great Britain, establishing contacts that
proved valuable to the North during the Civil War. Having favored William
Seward (*q.v.*) in 1860, Bigelow was distressed when Bryant backed the candidacy of Abraham Lincoln (*q.v.*) in the columns of the *Post.*

Following Lincoln's nomination, however, Bigelow worked for his election.
In August 1861, Seward, now Secretary of State, persuaded Lincoln to appoint
Bigelow U.S. consul at Paris, hoping that he could influence the French press
and thus help to counteract increasingly effective Confederate propaganda efforts in Europe. In this task Bigelow was eminently successful. His personal
magnetism, his fluent idiomatic French, and his judicious expenditure of money
among the journalists of Paris soon helped to alter French public opinion in
favor of the North. During the *Trent* affair, Bigelow wrote for the signature of
General Winfield Scott (*q.v.*) a conciliatory public letter that reduced antagonism
toward the United States in London and aided in obtaining a peaceful settlement.
Later, Bigelow located documents proving that the French government was allowing Confederate agents to construct warships in French shipyards. The rev-
elation forced Emperor Louis Napoleon to order the sale of the offending
vessels. The *Rappahannock*, a formidable Confederate gunboat, was detained at
Calais until the end of the war. Moreover, it was Bigelow who persuaded Seward
to send Robert J. Walker to Europe to undermine confidence there in the heavily
subscribed Confederate cotton loan and to sell U.S. war bonds to foreign investors.

Upon the death of the U.S. minister to France late in 1864, Bigelow became
for several months charge d'affaires at Paris and then minister, a position he
held until resigning early in 1867. Afterward, he briefly edited the *New York
Times* and became a prolific author. He published a ten-volume edition of the
works of Benjamin Franklin, a monograph titled *France and the Confederate*

Navy (1888), and biographies of his friends Bryant and Tilden. His five-volume *Retrospections of an Active Life* is one of the most important autobiographical works of his era. Bigelow's admiration for Tilden finally lured him back into politics and, after twenty years as a Republican, to the Democratic party. As president of the Tilden Trust, Bigelow helped to found the New York Public Library and, as a close friend and adviser to Philippe Bunau-Varilla, he aided in bringing about the treaty of 1903 establishing the Republic of Panama and paving the way for the Panama Canal. Bigelow died on December 19, 1911, in New York City. Bigelow, *Retrospections*; Case, *The United States and France.*

Norman B. Ferris

BINGHAM, John Armor, *congressman*, was born on January 21, 1815, in Mercer, Pennsylvania, and moved with his family to Ohio at an early age. He received a common school education, worked as a printer, and attended Franklin College when it was a center of antislavery activity. Residing in the heart of the Quaker and Associated Reformed communities in Cadiz, Ohio, Bingham practiced law and was active in the Whig party. He was elected to Congress as a Republican in 1854 and, with the exception of one term (1863–1865), served until 1873. After he lost his reelection bid in 1862, President Abraham Lincoln (*q.v.*) appointed him a judge advocate in the Union Army and a solicitor of the Court of Claims.

Bingham was a consistent advocate of emancipation. Following Lincoln's assassination, he served as a prosecutor in the trial of the conspirators. He wrote the privileges and immunities, equal protection of the laws, and due process clauses of section 1 of the 14th Amendment, but consistently fought the Reconstruction policies of Thaddeus Stevens (*q.v.*) and James M. Ashley (*q.v.*). Although he initially opposed the impeachment of Andrew Johnson (*q.v.*), he supported the third impeachment attempt and was chairman of the House managers during Johnson's trial before the Senate. Bingham served as U.S. minister to Japan (1873–1885), then returned to Ohio and the practice of law. He died in Cadiz on March 19, 1900. Graham, *Everyman's Constitution*; Ten Broek, *Equal Under Law.*

Robert F. Horowitz

BINGHAM, Kinsley Scott, *senator*, was born on December 16, 1808, in Camillus, New York. Early in life he was a farmer but also secured an academic education and studied law. In 1833 he moved to Green Oak, Michigan, which was his home for the rest of his life. Elected a local official during Michigan's territorial period, he was also a member of the first state legislature in 1836 and was reelected in 1838, 1839, 1841, and 1842; he was speaker of the Michigan House three times. In 1846 and 1848 Bingham was elected to the U.S. House of Representatives, where he voted for the Wilmot Proviso and opposed the Fugitive Slave Law. From 1850 to 1854 he was a Free Soil Democrat, and in 1854 he secured nomination as governor on the Free Soil ticket. Attending the meeting "under the oaks" in Jackson (June 1854), when the Republican party was formed, Bingham was nominated for governor and elected. Reelected in 1856, he was chosen by the legislature as U.S. senator in 1859.

Bingham's public life involved a transformation from a Democrat to a Republican, with a Free Soil transitional stage. Throughout his legislative career he supported agricultural pursuits. In Congress, he successfully opposed the patenting of the Wood cast-iron plow; and as a former governor he championed the creation of the Michigan Agricultural College (now Michigan State University). His second major concern was the controversy arising from the slavery issue. He supported the Wilmot Proviso and opposed secession. Bingham died in Green Oak on October 5, 1861. Dunbar, *Michigan: A History of the Wolverine State*; Utley, *Michigan as a Province, Territory, and State*, vol. 3.

George M. Blackburn

BIRGE, Henry Warner, *general,* was born in Hartford, Connecticut, on August 25, 1830. In 1861, he resided in Norwich, where he worked as a merchant and served on the staff of Governor William A. Buckingham (*q.v.*). On April 25, 1861, Birge began the organization of the first three-year regiment from his state, the 4th Connecticut Volunteers. He served in Maryland and Virginia until appointed a colonel in the 13th Connecticut in February 1862. Birge joined General Benjamin F. Butler (*q.v.*) in New Orleans and had charge of the city's defenses following its occupation. When General Nathaniel P. Banks (*q.v.*) succeeded Butler, Birge served under him through the first Red River campaign. In 1863, Banks assigned Birge to the 3rd Brigade, 4th Division, of the XIX Corps, and promoted him to brevet brigadier general. Birge commanded a Volunteer battalion at Port Hudson in the summer of 1863, with orders to carry the works by assault. Virtually the entire 13th Connecticut volunteered to follow their former commander. The fall of Vicksburg precipitated the surrender of Port Hudson on July 8, two days before Birge's attack was scheduled to begin. His promotion to full brigadier followed on September 9, 1863.

In 1864, Birge's command participated in the second Red River campaign; the actions at Sabine Cross Roads, Pleasant Hill, and Cane River; and in the occupation of Alexandria and Baton Rouge. In July 1864, Birge moved north with the 2nd Division of the XIX Corps to Virginia, where he joined General Philip Sheridan (*q.v.*) in the Shenanadoah Valley campaign. In February 1865, he moved to Savannah, where his brigade became a division of the X Corps. After Joseph E. Johnston's surrender in April 1865, Birge commanded the occupation forces in the Savannah district until he resigned his comission in November 1865. Birge remained in Savannah as a cotton planter and lumber dealer, and invested in similar businesses in Texas. Later he moved to New York City, where he died on June 1, 1888. Barrett, *Sherman's March Through the Carolinas*; Sprague, *History of the 13th Infantry Regiment*.

Archie P. McDonald

BIRNEY, David Bell, *general,* was born on May 29, 1825, in Huntsville, Alabama, the son of slave owner James G. Birney. In 1838, James Birney freed his slaves and moved his family to Cincinnati, Ohio, where he became an outspoken abolitionist. Educated at Andover School, David Birney subsequently opened a mercantile business and read law, being admitted to the bar in Michigan and Pennsylvania. His Philadelphia practice prospered, and he supported the Republican party. In 1860, Birney read military treatises and gained a commission as lieutenant colonel of militia. His unit, the 23rd Pennsylvania, became a three-year regiment with Birney as its colonel.

After service in West Virginia, Birney fought with the Army of the Potomac from First Bull Run to Petersburg. He was promoted to brigadier general of Volunteers (February 1862) and commanded a brigade in the division of Philip Kearny (*q.v.*). On the Peninsula, Birney's conduct at Fair Oaks necessitated a court martial, which found him not guilty of disobeying orders. He was acting division commander after Kearny's death (September 1862) at Chantilly, and in Kearny's honor, he designed a bronze cross (the Kearny Medal) to be awarded to enlisted men for valor. Promoted to major general of Volunteers (May 1863) for meritorious service at Chancellorsville, Birney took charge of Kearny's old division and led it well at Gettysburg in the III Corps under Daniel Sickles (*q.v.*). He succeeded to acting corps command after Sickles was wounded.

Birney's pivotal day was at Gettysburg, on July 2, 1863, when his thinly stretched division fought against attacks from Longstreet's Corps. A breakdown in the division of General James Barnes (*q.v.*) in the Wheat Field left part of Birney's flank uncovered. His division suffered heavy casualties and had to withdraw, but Birney returned to lead a division in the II Corps under Winfield S. Hancock (*q.v.*). His men fought with inspiration at Spotsylvania (May 12, 1864), and he received command of the X Corps in the Army of the James in June 1864. He contracted malaria and returned to Philadelphia, where he died on October 18, 1864. Furgurson, *Chancellorsville*; Pfanz, *Gettysburg: The Second Day*; Sommers, *Richmond Redeemed.*

Joseph G. Dawson III

BLAINE, James Gillespie, *congressman,* was born on January 31, 1830, in West Brownville, Pennsylvania. At age thirteen, he entered his father's alma mater, Washington College, where he distinguished himself as a debater. A few weeks before his eighteenth birthday, Blaine landed a job teaching mathematics and ancient languages at Western Military Institute in Georgetown, Kentucky. He taught from 1851 to 1854 at Philadelphia's Pennsylvania Institute for the Blind, then moved to his wife's hometown, Augusta, Maine, to edit the *Kennebec Journal,* the state's leading Whig paper. For a time he also edited the *Portland Advertiser.* In 1858, Blaine was elected to the Maine House, where he served three terms, the last two as speaker. In 1859, he became chairman of the Republican State Committee (he was a founder of the Republican party, abandoning the Whigs in 1854), a post he held until 1881.

In 1862, the same year he won a seat in Congress, Blaine purchased a fine house across the street from the State House, and this became the Republican party's nerve center in Maine. (Eventually his heirs would present it to the state of Maine for use as the governor's mansion.) Blaine strongly supported President Abraham Lincoln (*q.v.*) and the Union cause, and contributed significantly to the Union (Republican) party victories of 1863 and 1864. In Reconstruction, Blaine favored votes for blacks but espoused a less retributive policy for the defeated Confederate states than did the Republican Radicals. He also opposed general amnesty for former Confederates, especially Jefferson Davis.

Blaine was Speaker of the House (1869–1876), U.S. senator (1876–1881), an unsuccessful presidential candidate in 1884, and Secretary of State (1889–1892). No statesman aroused such contrasts of adoration and loathing as the man whom worshippers dubbed the "plumed knight of the Republican party" and whom detractors called the "continental liar from the State of Maine." Myriad ailments ended Blaine's life in Washington, D.C., on January 27, 1893. Morgan, *From Hayes to McKinley*; Stanwood, *James Gillespie Blaine.*

H. Draper Hunt

BLAIR, Austin, *governor*, was born on February 8, 1818, in Tompkins county, New York. He graduated Phi Beta Kappa from Union College in 1839, studied law, and was admitted to the New York bar in 1841. Later that year he moved to Michigan, and in 1844 settled permanently in Jackson. Entering politics as an antislavery Whig, Blair served in the state legislature in 1846, joined the Free Soil party in 1848, and was a founder of the Republican party in 1854. As a Republican he was a state senator (1855–1856), governor (1861–1865), and member of the U.S. House of Representatives (1867–1873).

Influenced by his parents, longtime abolitionists, and by the liberalism of western New York, where he was raised, Blair became a zealous advocate of humanitarian reforms. In the antebellum period he supported black voting rights, abolition of capital punishment, statewide prohibition, personal liberty laws, and the nonextension of slavery in the territories. In 1860, Blair was disappointed by the failure of the Republican National Convention to nominate William H. Seward (*q.v.*), but he campaigned vigorously for Abraham Lincoln (*q.v.*). In that same year he was elected governor of Michigan.

As a proud nationalist and principled reformer, Blair identified with the Radical Republicans, denounced secession as treason, advocated confiscation of Southerners' property (including slaves), and supported vigorous prosecution of the war. His leadership in providing prudent, honest government, and his contributions to the Union cause entitle him to be ranked as one of the most able and effective Civil War governors. In Congress he promoted civil and political rights for blacks and backed the impeachment of Andrew Johnson (*q.v.*). However, he was critical of the administration of Ulysses S. Grant (*q.v.*), calling in particular for civil service reform and a return to honest government. In 1872, Blair joined the Liberal Republicans, campaigned for Horace Greeley (*q.v.*), and was himself defeated for the governership. Not until 1880 did he again support the Republican presidential ticket. He died in Jackson on August 6, 1894. Hesseltine, *Lincoln's War Governors*; *Michigan Biographies*, vol. 1.

Frederick D. Williams

BLAIR, Francis Preston, Jr., *congressman, general*, was born on February 19, 1821, in Lexington, Kentucky, the son of Francis Preston Blair, influential editor of the *Globe*. He was expelled from several academies and universities before graduating from Princeton in 1841. After studying law, Blair moved to St. Louis, to practice with his brother, Montgomery Blair (*q.v.*). Though himself a slave owner, Blair was adamantly opposed to the extension of slavery into the territories. He organized Missouri's Free Soil party prior to the 1848 presidential campaign. In 1852, Blair was elected to the Missouri legislature as a Free Soil Democrat, and was elected to the U.S. House in 1856, the only Free Soiler in Congress from a slave state. In 1860, he won reelection while campaigning for Abraham Lincoln (*q.v.*).

During the secession crisis, Blair organized the Union party in St. Louis while secretly drilling and equipping the Unionist elements for the defense of the city. Fearful of the secessionist minority, he used the influence of his brother, now a member of Lincoln's cabinet, to force the removal of the Department of the West commander, replacing him with Nathaniel Lyon (*q.v.*), commander of the Federal arsenal in St. Louis. The two then enlisted into Federal service several thousand Home Guard militia and captured a secessionist state militia encampment located outside the city. Blair led one of Lyon's volunteer brigades to Boonville, then in July 1861 left to take his seat in Congress, where he chaired the House Committee on Military Affairs.

Blair left Congress in 1862 and was appointed brigadier general of Volunteers. He led a brigade in the Vicksburg campaign under his friend William T. Sherman (*q.v.*), then was promoted to major general. Leaving the front once to participate in a stormy session of Congress, Blair successively commanded the XV and XVII Corps in Sherman's campaign through Georgia and the Carolinas. After the war, he reentered politics, was the running mate in 1868 of presidential candidate Horatio Seymour (*q.v.*), and ultimately served as U.S. senator from Missouri. He died in St. Louis on July 8, 1875. Bearss, *Vicksburg Campaign*; Castel, *Decision in the West*; Smith, *Francis Preston Blair.*

Christopher Phillips

BLAIR, Jacob Beeson, *congressman*, was born on April 11, 1821, in Parkersburg, Virginia (now West Virginia). After attending public schools, he studied the law and in 1844 was admitted to the bar. For several years, Blair was prosecuting attorney for Ritchie county, Virginia, then returned to Parkersburg prior to the Civil War. In late 1861, he was elected as a Unionist to the 37th Congress, following the resignation of John S. Carlile (*q.v.*). Reelected as an Unconditional Unionist to the 38th Congress, Blair served on the Committees on Public Buildings and Grounds and Public Expenditures. After the war, he was U.S. minister to Costa Rica (1868–1873). For twelve years, Blair was a Wyoming Supreme Court justice (1876–1888), then a Utah probate judge (1892–1895). In 1897, he became surveyor general of Utah, serving until his death on February 12, 1901, in Salt Lake City. Ambler, *West Virginia*; Lanman, *Biographical Annals*.

                                                                        Frank R. Levstik

BLAIR, Montgomery, *Postmaster General,* was born on May 10, 1813, in Franklin county, Kentucky. He graduated from West Point in 1835, served in the Seminole War, and resigned his commission in 1836 to study law at Transylvania University. In 1837 he moved to St. Louis, where he served a term as mayor (1841–1843) and four years (1845–1849) as judge of the Court of Common Pleas. He left the bench to resume his law practice, and in 1853 moved to Maryland, where he regularly argued before the Supreme Court. Sympathetic with Western viewpoints, Blair was a Free Soiler who believed the issue of slavery could be settled peacefully. He left the American party because it failed to take a stand on slavery, spent an active decade as a Democrat, and finally became a Republican. Blair's reputation among antislavery partisans loomed large because of his famous client, Dred Scott.

   After presiding over the Maryland Republican Convention at Baltimore in 1860, Blair went to Chicago as a delegate to the Republican National Convention. Abraham Lincoln (*q.v.*) repaid Blair for his party service by appointing him Postmaster General. A strong supporter of the President, Blair nonetheless held independent views. He so strongly believed Fort Sumter should be reinforced that he threatened to resign if it were not. He irritated the Radical wing of the party by denouncing the seizure of Mason and Slidell and by befriending George B. McClellan (*q.v.*). The Radicals demanded his dismissal from the cabinet in 1864; Lincoln subsequently requested Blair's resignation and received it. Blair firmly believed in Lincoln's plan of Reconstruction, and opposed the disenfranchisement of Southern whites and the enfranchisement of blacks. He returned to the Democratic party after the war, and unsuccessfully ran for Congress in 1882. He died on July 27, 1883, in Silver Spring, Maryland. Leech, *Reveille in Washington*; Smith, *Francis Preston Blair Family in Politics*.

                                                                        Robert H. Jones

BLAIR, Samuel Steel, *congressman,* was born in Indiana, Pennsylvania, on December 5, 1821. He graduated from Jefferson College in 1838, studied law, and in 1846 established a practice in Hollidaysburg, Pennsylvania. He was active in Whig politics, but in the 1850s, like most Northern Whigs, switched to the newly formed Republican party. Blair attended the first Republican National Convention at Philadelphia in 1856, and ran for Congress in 1859. He won the seat, which he held for two terms. When the Civil War began, Blair took a strong, uncompromising attitude toward the South. He strenuously objected to pleas for conciliatory talks with the Confederacy, demanded a vigorous prosecution of the war, and especially supported proposals to confiscate Rebel property. In 1862, the antiwar Democrats enjoyed a revival in Pennsylvania and ousted several Republicans, Blair among them. He made an unsuccessful bid for Congress in 1874. He died on December 8, 1880, in Hollidaysburg. Davis, *Pennsylvania Politics.*

W. Wayne Smith

BLAKE, Harrison Gray, *congressman,* was born in Newfane, Vermont, on March 17, 1819. His parents froze to death in December 1821, and he was reared by a Mrs. Jesse Rhoades in Salem, New York, and Guilford, Ohio. After first studying medicine, Blake's interests turned to law, and he was admitted to the Ohio bar. In the 1840 presidential election, he supported William Henry Harrison, and entered politics himself. In 1846, he was elected to the Ohio House of Representatives, and in 1848, to the Ohio Senate. As a Republican, he was elected to the 36th Congress, filling a vacancy left when the incumbent died. He was reelected in 1859. As a loyal Republican, Blake chaired a special committee that exonerated fellow Ohio Republican James M. Ashley (*q.v.*) of charges of corruption in arranging for a patronage appointment. His interests in medicine continued, and he argued for expansion of the army's medical service. Not seeking reelection in 1863, Blake became colonel of the 166th Ohio Volunteers in 1864. After the war, he resumed his law practice and his interest in politics, although he declined the governorship of the Idaho Territory. He died in Medina, Ohio, on April 16, 1876. Bogue, *Congressman's Civil War.*

Thomas H. Smith

BLISS, George, *congressman,* was born in Jericho, Vermont, on January 1, 1813. He graduated from Granville College and moved to Akron, Ohio, in 1832. There he studied law and was admitted to the Ohio bar in 1841. In 1850, Bliss was elected mayor of Akron, and March 15, 1851, was appointed the president judge of the Summit County Court of Common Pleas, filling the vacancy left when Benjamin F. Wade (*q.v.*) was elected to the U.S. Senate. As a Democrat, Bliss was elected to the 33rd Congress in 1852. Not seeking another term in 1855, he moved to Wooster, Ohio. He assisted in the famous *ex parte Bushnell* case that resulted from the Wellington Rescue case in 1859, a test of the 1850 Fugitive Slave Act.

Bliss successfully ran for Congress in 1862 and served on the House Judiciary Committee. He criticized Abraham Lincoln's (*q.v.*) administration, believing the President held too much power and was subverting the civil rights of the people. He blamed the Republicans and Northern abolitionists for the war. After being defeated for reelection in 1864, Bliss returned to Wooster, where he died on October 24, 1868. Doyle, *Centennial History of Summit County*; Lane, *Fifty Years and over of Akron and Summit County.*

Thomas H. Smith

BLOW, Henry Taylor, *diplomat, congressman,* was born in Southampton county, Virginia, on July 15, 1817, and moved with his family to St. Louis in 1830. He graduated with distinction from St. Louis University, became an important figure in the development of lead mining in southwest Missouri, and was involved in a variety of business enterprises, including the Iron Mountain Railroad. After serving in the Missouri Senate as a Whig in 1854, he moved to the American party and worked with Francis Blair (*q.v.*) and B. Gratz Brown (*q.v.*) to organize the Republican party in Missouri. Blow was a delegate to the Republican National Convention in 1860 and was active in the Union cause in St. Louis during the critical first half of 1861.

Abraham Lincoln (*q.v.*) appointed Blow minister to Venezuela on June 8, 1861, but he returned in early 1862 to assume an active role within the emerging Radical Republican coalition in Missouri. Favoring the speedy emancipation of the state's slaves, he was elected to Congress as a "Charcoal" (Emancipationist) in the fall of 1862 and was reelected two years later. Blow was a member of the Missouri Radical delegation to the 1864 Republican National Convention that opposed the renomination of Lincoln. He supported Thaddeus Stevens (*q.v.*) in the early stages of Reconstruction, but he realized the need for reconciliation because of the variety of his business contacts in St. Louis. Following his retirement from Congress in 1867, Blow was minister to Brazil (1869–1871) and a member of the Board of Commissioners of the District of Columbia (1874–1875). He devoted most of his time to his mining and other business interests, however. He died in Saratoga Springs, New York, on September 11, 1875.
Parrish, *Missouri Under Radical Rule*; Reavis, *St. Louis.*

William E. Parrish

BLUNT, James Gillpatrick, *general,* was born on July 21, 1826, in Trenton, Maine. He served in the merchant marine, then studied medicine, and in 1849 graduated from Starling Medical College, Columbus, Ohio. In 1856, he moved to Greeley, Kansas Territory, where he became active in politics and in the antislavery movement. After supporting John Brown (*q.v.*) in his Kansas adventures, Blunt was a member of the 1859 convention that framed the constitution of Kansas. In this body he served as chairman of the militia committee, an appointment that likely influenced his future military career.

In July 1861, Blunt became a lieutenant colonel of the 3rd Kansas Volunteers, but soon commanded the cavalry attached to the brigade of James H. Lane (*q.v.*). In April 1862 he was made brigadier general and appointed commander of the Kansas Military Department. In October 1862 he routed Colonel Douglas H. Cooper's Confederate Indian forces, on their way north to invade Kansas, at Old Fort Wayne, near the southwest corner of Missouri. In November 1862 Blunt continued his aggressive operations and overwhelmingly defeated Brigadier General John S. Marmaduke at Cane Hill, Arkansas. For these successful campaigns he was promoted to major general. Blunt attacked the Confederates commanded by Major General Thomas C. Hindman at Prairie Grove, Arkansas, in December 1862 and, with the cooperation of Brigadier General Francis J. Herron (*q.v.*), drove Hindman fifty miles to the Arkansas River, causing him to abandon his plan to occupy Missouri. During the same month Blunt captured Van Buren, Arkansas.

In June 1863 Blunt led his Army of the Frontier into Indian Territory and defeated a concentration of Confederate Indians and Texans under Brigadier General Cooper at Honey Springs. Fort Smith, Arkansas, fell the following September. Blunt's last combat duty was in October 1864 at Newtonia, Missouri, when his forces gave the final blow to Major General Sterling Price's invasion of Missouri.

Even though he had no formal military education, Blunt understood the significance of mobility and offensive operations. His major campaigns were uniformly successful and without exception accomplished their primary objectives. Uniquely, his forces usually contained Indian and African American troops in addition to whites. Because of his strong personality and the isolation of his campaigns in the trans-Mississippi West, Blunt never received the recognition or command advancement he deserved during the war.

After discharge from the Army in July 1865, Blunt settled in Leavenworth, Kansas, and practiced medicine. In 1869 he moved to Washington, D.C., where he served as a claims agent. His health began to fail as a result of viral encephalitis contracted during his military service, and in 1879 he was admitted to the government's hospital for the insane in Washington, D.C., where he died on July 27, 1881. Castel, *Sterling Price*; Josephy, *Civil War in the American West.*

LeRoy H. Fischer

BOREMAN, Arthur Ingraham, *governor*, was born in Waynesburg, Pennsylvania, on July 24, 1823. After completing a common school education, he studied law, was admitted to the bar in 1845, and opened a law practice in Parkersburg, Virginia (now West Virginia). In 1855, he was elected to the Virginia House of Delegates, where he served until 1861. Boreman repudiated the secession ordinance passed by the Virginia Secession Convention of 1861, returned to northwestern Virginia, and joined in the unsuccessful fight against ratification.

Boreman was elected to and presided over the Second Wheeling Convention, which established the Reorganized Government of Virginia on June 20, 1861, recognized by President Abraham Lincoln (*q.v.*) as the de jure state government. Boreman served the Reorganized Government as judge of the 19th Virginia Judicial Circuit until June 1863. Nominated by an "Unconditional Union" (Republican) convention to be the first governor of the state of West Virginia, Boreman was elected without opposition. He served until 1868, and in 1869 was elected to the U.S. Senate. As war governor, Boreman was active and able, but his administration was hampered by the fact that the southern half of West Virginia was plagued by guerrilla warfare and internal strife over which Union troops and state authorities had little control. Nearly half of the counties included in West Virginia were Confederate in sympathy and opposed to the creation of the new state.

In 1870, a coalition of conservative Union and ex-Confederate Democrats gained power and consigned most of the "statemakers" to political oblivion. In 1868, however, the state legislature, still under the control of Republicans, had elected Boreman to the U.S. Senate, where he served one term. He replaced Peter G. Van Winkle (*q.v.*), one of eight Republican senators to vote against President Andrew Johnson's (*q.v.*) conviction in the impeachment trial of 1868. In 1889, Boreman was elected judge of West Virginia's 5th Circuit, a position he held until his death in Parkersburg on April 19, 1896. Ambler, *Makers of West Virginia*; Curry, *House Divided.*

Richard Orr Curry

BOUTWELL, George Sewall, *congressman,* was born on January 28, 1818, in Brookline, Massachusetts. Largely self-educated, he eventually became a practicing lawyer in Groton, Massachusetts, but he devoted most of his time to political pursuits. Boutwell became an active Democrat and served in the state legislature from 1842 to 1850. In 1850, and again in 1851, a coalition of Democrats and Free Soilers elected him governor of Massachusetts. Boutwell's antislavery leanings led him to join the Republican party in 1855. In 1861, he was a representative to the Washington Peace Conference, where he resisted concessions on slavery and warned that secession would lead to civil war and destruction of the South.

After the Civil War began, Boutwell called for emancipation as the quickest way to end the conflict. In July 1862 he became the first Commissioner of Internal Revenue, and worked diligently to organize that new office and to draft its basic rules and regulations. In March 1863 he resigned to take a seat in the House of Representatives, a post he held for the next six years. Boutwell voted consistently with the Radicals and was an early champion of black suffrage. He later was one of the leading advocates of the impeachment of President Andrew Johnson *(q.v.).*

Boutwell, a loyal party man, served as Secretary of the Treasury from 1869 to 1873, and as senator from Massachusetts from 1873 to 1877. He broke with the Republican party, however, over the annexation of the Philippines after the Spanish-American War, and served as president of the Anti-Imperialist League. He died in Groton on February 27, 1905. Benedict, *Compromise of Principle*; Boutwell, *Reminiscences.*

Richard H. Abbott

BOWDEN, Lemuel Jackson, *senator,* was born on January 16, 1815, in Williamsburg, Virginia. After graduation from William and Mary College at the age of seventeen, he studied law and was admitted to the bar in 1838. He served in the Virginia House of Delegates (1841–1846) and as a delegate to the state constitutional convention of 1850–1851. Bowden was a presidential elector for the Constitutional Union ticket in 1860. The outbreak of hostilities found him still loyal to the Union cause, a loyalty that made his property the target of frequent depredations by Confederate troops. However, he was still mayor of Williamsburg when George B. McClellan (*q.v.*) launched the Peninsula campaign in the spring of 1862. The hospitality Bowden extended to the ''invaders'' led former neighbors to denounce him as a traitor. He joined the Republican party and in 1863 was elected to the U.S. Senate. He died in Washington, D.C., on January 2, 1864. *BDUSC.*

James M. Prichard

BOWLES, Samuel, III, *editor,* was born in Springfield, Massachusetts, on February 9, 1826, and began working for his father's weekly, the *Springfield Republican,* when he was seventeen. Largely responsible for the paper by the time he was twenty, he made the daily edition the leading paper in western Massachusetts and took complete control by the time of his father's death in 1851. Aside from Horace Greeley (*q.v.*), no other editor was as well known or as influential, and Bowles made the *Republican* into one of the nation's best newspapers not published in a large city. By 1860, it had a circulation of 12,000 for the weekly edition and around 6,000 for the daily. Bowles supported the Wilmot Proviso and the Compromise of 1850, opposed the Kansas–Nebraska Bill, and called for a constitutional end to slavery. He was a founder of the Republican party in Massachusetts and was a key figure in organizing the national Republican party.

Bowles denounced the hanging of John Brown (*q.v.*), and supported Abraham Lincoln (*q.v.*) for President in 1860 and 1864. He favored a vigorous prosecution of the war and supported Lincoln's moderate views on Reconstruction. He avoided the Radical views of other Republican newspaper editors but favored Andrew Johnson's (*q.v.*) impeachment. A leading critic of President Ulysses S. Grant's (*q.v.*) administration, Bowles joined the Liberal Republican movement that nominated Horace Greeley for President in 1872.

Bowles's most solid achievement was his contribution to news reporting. He insisted on high editorial standards, and by recruiting college graduates for his staff, tried to make journalism a profession. ''My own observation,'' he once said, ''is that the Press rarely does injustice to a thoroughly honest man or cause.'' He died in Springfield, Massachusetts, on January 16, 1878. Merriam, *Life and Times of Samuel Bowles*; Weisner, *Embattled Editor.*

Ronald D. Rietveld

BOYD, Sempronius Hamilton, *congressman,* was born near Nashville, Tennessee, on May 28, 1828, and moved with his parents to a farm near Springfield, Missouri, when he was twelve. He followed the gold rush to California in 1849, returned to Springfield in 1854, was appointed clerk of the Greene County Court, studied law, and was admitted to the bar. In 1856 he was elected mayor of Springfield as a Whig and served two terms. Although three of his brothers joined the Confederate cause, Boyd and his father, Marcus, organized Union regiments.

Boyd was colonel of the 24th Missouri and saw extensive duty in southern Missouri and northern Arkansas. Although his father had been a slaveholder, Boyd early realized the need for Missouri to rid itself of slavery. He was elected to Congress as a "Charcoal" (Emancipationist) in 1862, but continued to serve with his regiment until December 1863. In the House, he helped to draw up the measures establishing the Freedmen's Bureau. Boyd, who did not seek reelection in 1864, was appointed circuit judge the following year and showed strong support for black civil rights. Indeed, he recommended the use of African American troops to help ensure order.

Boyd was a member of the Missouri Radical delegation to the 1864 Republican National Convention that opposed the renomination of Abraham Lincoln (*q.v.*), and served on the Republican National Committee (1864–1868). He was active in the building and operation of the Southwest Pacific Railroad (1867–1874), served another term in Congress, and supported the Liberal Republicans in Missouri in 1870. President Benjamin Harrison appointed Boyd minister resident and consul general to Siam (now Thailand), where he served for two years (1890–1892). He died in Springfield, Missouri, on June 22, 1894. Parrish, *History of Missouri*, vol. 3; Stewart, *Bench and Bar of Missouri*.

William E. Parrish

BOYLE, Jeremiah Tilford, *general,* was born in Mercer (now Boyle) county, Kentucky, on May 22, 1818. Educated at Centre and Princeton colleges and the law school of Transylvania University, he had a successful legal practice at Harrodsburg, Kentucky, and, after 1842, at Danville. Although he was a slaveholding Whig, Boyle favored gradual emancipation at the Kentucky constitutional convention of 1849. In 1860, he supported the Constitutional Union party. He served briefly as a commonwealth attorney in 1861 before becoming involved in military affairs.

A staunch Unionist, Boyle began raising troops when Kentucky's neutrality ended in September 1861. Although his commission as brigadier general was dated November 9, 1861, he did not receive it until early 1862. Boyle was commended for gallantry while leading his brigade at Shiloh. Apparently at the request of the Kentucky congressmen, Boyle was appointed the state's military commander on May 27, 1862. After November, he commanded the District of Western Kentucky, headquartered in Louisville. Boyle had little success in halting John Hunt Morgan and the depredations of guerrillas. Never given the soldiers necessary for his mission, he was blamed for his lack of success.

In his zeal for the Union cause, Boyle violated such civil rights as freedom of speech and the press, interfered in elections, and issued economic decrees that antagonized even Unionists. His plans to imprison or deport female Confederate sympathizers aroused particular opposition, but he also annoyed the national administration by opposing the use of African American soldiers. His efforts to become governor or a member of Congress failed miserably, and demands for his removal increased. In late 1863 he was ordered to collect his scattered troops and join a Union army at Knoxville. Instead, Boyle resigned his commission, effective January 26, 1864.

Although he was respected for his personal integrity and devotion to the Union cause, Boyle's zeal and heavy-handed administration led him to make many unwise decisions. Critics called him militarily inept, but it is doubtful if anyone could have done much better with his inadequate troops. Boyle became president (1864–1866) of the Louisville City Railway Company, which brought streetcars to that city. His presidency of the Evansville, Henderson and Nashville Railroad Company and shrewd investments in western lands and railroads made him wealthy. Boyle died in Louisville, Kentucky, on July 28, 1871. Coulter, *Civil War and Readjustment in Kentucky*; Kleber, *Kentucky Encyclopedia.*

Lowell H. Harrison

BRADFORD, Augustus Williamson, *governor*, was born in Bel Air, Maryland, on January 9, 1806. After attending Bel Air Academy, he graduated from St. Mary's College in Baltimore. He was admitted to the bar in 1826 and in 1831 moved to Baltimore, where he resided for the rest of his life. Bradford became an active Whig and served as a Clay elector in 1844. In 1845 he was appointed clerk of the Baltimore County Court and served until 1851. He then remained politically inactive until the Civil War. Bradford, a delegate to the Washington Peace Conference in 1861, and was nominated for governor in August 1861 by the Union party. Aided by military interference, a light vote, and Unionist support, he was overwhelmingly elected.

Differing over methods but not purpose, Bradford supported the Lincoln (*q.v.*) administration, but he was also vigilant in upholding civil authority in Maryland. He strongly protested Federal intervention in state affairs, but despite occasional sharp clashes, especially in the 1863 elections, he cooperated with the military. He initially opposed the introduction of the slavery issue, but by 1863 he accepted gradual emancipation and took the lead in recommending the calling of a constitutional convention to end slavery. Bradford's refusal to throw out the soldiers' vote in the referendum saved the new constitution from defeat and freed Maryland from its "peculiar institution." Following his governorship, Bradford was surveyor of the Port of Baltimore until his removal by Ulysses S. Grant (*q.v.*) in 1869. He died in Baltimore on March 1, 1881. Baker, *Politics of Continuity*; Clark, *Politics in Maryland During the Civil War.*

Richard R. Duncan

BRADY, Mathew B., *photographer*, was born in Warren county, New York, in 1823. When Brady was a boy, William Page, the "American Titian," gave him lessons in pastel and painting, and in 1841 took him to New York City to study with Samuel F.B. Morse, who had begun to make daguerreotypes in order to supplement his income. Brady studied daguerreotypy with Morse for three years, and when he opened his own gallery in 1844, he was almost immediately a critical and financial success. In the mid-1840s he began recording and collecting the likenesses of major American personalities. The result was his *Gallery of Illustrious Americans*, published in 1850. Brady opened another New York gallery and an establishment in the nation's capital in the late 1850s. The Washington gallery did an enormous business as the city filled with soldiers. Meanwhile, Brady increased his already considerable reputation by photographing Lincoln in New York in 1860, and the young Prince of Wales later that year.

At the outbreak of the Civil War, Brady assembled a team of cameramen to make a historical record of the conflict. The venture was financed by income from his galleries and a line of credit from a photographic supply house. Brady was confident that the American people would purchase views of camp scenes and battlefields in great numbers. Above all, he felt he was destined to be the photographic historian of the Civil War, demonstrating the great usefulness of the photograph as a historical document. Brady trained and equipped some ten cameramen and dispatched them to scenes of battle in the East. Brady himself photographed views at First Bull Run and throughout the Peninsula campaign. He was also at Antietam, Fredericksburg, and many other battlefields. Brady and his men took more than 3,500 photographs during the war. Because of the slowness of the photographic process, the fragility of the glass plates, and the cumbersomeness of the equipment, most of the views show posed groups of men or scenes of destruction in the aftermath of the fighting.

After the brief initial excitement generated by Brady's war photographs, the public lost interest and the venture was a financial failure. Brady realized some return on his work and investment in 1895 when the government purchased 2,000 of the photographs for $25,000. Another set of war views became the property of Brady's supplier of equipment and materials. Brady maintained his Washington gallery until 1895 (he lost his New York gallery in the Panic of 1873), but increased competition and the gradual loss of his eyesight made the last twenty years of his life very difficult. He died in New York City on January 15, 1896. Horan, *Mathew Brady*; Meredith, *Lincoln's Camera Man*; Taft, *Photography and the American Scene.*

Ben Bassham

BRAMLETTE, Thomas Elliott, *governor,* was born on January 3, 1817, in Cumberland (now Clinton) county, Kentucky. After education in local schools, he read law and was admitted to the bar in 1837. A Whig until the death of that party, he was elected a state representative in 1841 and was a commonwealth attorney from 1848 to 1850. In 1852, he moved to Columbia, Kentucky, where in 1856 he was elected judge of the 6th Circuit. An uncompromising Unionist, Bramlette resigned his judgeship to raise the 3rd Kentucky Infantry while Kentucky was still neutral. He resigned his commission in early 1862 over a command dispute and was appointed U.S. district attorney by Abraham Lincoln (*q.v.*). He left that position in 1863 to organize a division, but soon he accepted the Union Democrats' nomination for governor and won easily. Within a year he declined a congressional seat and forbade the Kentucky delegation to nominate him for Vice President.

A strong supporter of the administration in 1863, Bramlette soon became an outspoken critic. He bitterly opposed the use of African American troops, and he quarreled with General Stephen G. Burbridge (*q.v.*) over his arbitrary military measures. Bramlette opposed Lincoln's nomination in 1864 and seemed to be on the verge of rebellion. But a meeting with Lincoln eased relations, and Burbridge's removal in early 1865 helped modify Bramlette's opinion of the President. Bramlette recommended ratification of the 13th Amendment if slave owners were compensated, but the legislature rejected the amendment.

An able spokesman for the majority of Kentuckians, Bramlette blocked some of Burbridge's obnoxious measures. His efforts toward reconciliation eased the return of former Confederates to the state and the removal of disqualifications against them. When he failed to get a senatorial nomination in 1867, Bramlette moved to Louisville, where he practiced law until his death on January 12, 1875. Coulter, *Civil War and Readjustment in Kentucky*; Levin, *Lawyers and Lawmakers of Kentucky*.

Lowell H. Harrison

BRANDEGEE, Augustus, *congressman,* was born on July 15, 1828, in New London, Connecticut. He graduated from Yale University and its law school, and was admitted to the Connecticut bar in 1851. A Whig, then a Republican, Brandegee was elected to the Connecticut House of Representatives in 1854, serving that year and in 1858 and 1861. He was speaker of the Connecticut House in 1861 and eulogized Stephen A. Douglas (*q.v.*), who died in June 1861, thus: "The loss of such a man, at such a crisis, is an unspeakable calamity." Brandegee was elected to the 37th Congress in 1862 and reelected in 1864. When his party did not nominate him in 1867, he returned to New London and again practiced law. During his later years he attended two Republican National Conventions, in 1880 and 1884. He died in New London on November 10, 1904. Lane, *Political History of Connecticut*; Niven, *Connecticut for the Union*.

Joanna D. Cowden

BRANNAN, John Milton, *general,* was born on July 1, 1819, in Washington, D.C. He graduated from West Point in 1841 and was commissioned in the artillery. During the Mexican War he was breveted captain for his service at Contreras and Churubusco as adjutant of the 1st U.S. Artillery. He later saw action against the Seminoles in Florida. With the outbreak of the Civil War, Brannan was appointed brigadier general of Volunteers, and as commander of the Department of Key West, he directed operations on the St. John's River and at Pocotaligo, South Carolina. After temporary command of the Department of the South following General Ormsby M. Mitchel's (*q.v.*) death on October 30,

1862, he served as a infantry division commander with General William S. Rosecrans (*q.v.*) in the Tullahoma campaign and with General George H. Thomas (*q.v.*) at Chickamauga. Brannan lost 38 percent of his command at Horseshoe Ridge, and his bravery led to his brevet colonelcy in the Regular Army.

Brannan was appointed chief of artillery of the Army of the Cumberland when Major General Ulysses S. Grant (*q.v.*) relieved Rosecrans. He oversaw the defenses of Chattanooga and of Atlanta after October 1864. He then served as inspector of the Department of the Cumberland until the end of the war. He was breveted a major general in both the Regular and Volunteer services but reverted to his prewar rank of major, 1st U.S. Artillery. Brannan's postwar assignments included suppressing the Fenian raiders near Ogdensburg, New York. He retired as a colonel of the 4th U.S. Artillery in 1882 and settled in New York City, where he died on December 16, 1892. Cozzens, *This Terrible Sound*; Lamers, *Edge of Glory.*

Alan C. Aimone

BRECKINRIDGE, Robert Jefferson, *abolitionist, clergyman,* a member of Kentucky's premier political family, was born near Lexington on March 8, 1800. He attended local schools, Jefferson College (Pennsylvania), Yale College, and Union College (New York), graduating from the last in 1819. Breckinridge represented Fayette county in the Kentucky legislature (1825–1830). After the deaths of two of his children, and his own serious illness, he turned to the Presbyterian Church and in 1832 was licensed to preach. He studied briefly at Princeton, then replaced his brother John at Baltimore's Second Presbyterian Church. After two years (1845–1847) as president of Jefferson College, he returned to Lexington as pastor of the First Presbyterian Church.

Active in state and national church affairs, Breckinridge was an outstanding superintendent of public instruction (1847–1853). From 1851 until 1869 he was a professor at Danville Theological Seminary. Emancipation and temperance were among his continuing concerns, and he was a prolific editor and author in both theology and politics. An uncompromising Unionist, Breckinridge saw his family divide over secession. Abraham Lincoln (*q.v.*) consulted him frequently, as did civil and military authorities in Kentucky. Unlike many state Unionists, he supported most of the administration's wartime measures. In 1864, he was temporary chairman of the Union Convention that renominated Lincoln. Convinced of the righteousness of his causes, Breckinridge was a harsh foe and a difficult ally. He and George Prentice (*q.v.*) were probably the two most important Kentucky Unionists during the Civil War. Breckinridge died in Danville, Kentucky, on December 27, 1871. Coulter, *Civil War and Readjustment in Kentucky*; Klotter, *The Breckinridges of Kentucky.*

Lowell H. Harrison

BRIDGES, George Washington, *congressman,* was born on October 9, 1825, in Charleston, Tennessee. After attending East Tennessee University at Knoxville, he studied law and was admitted to the bar in 1848. Establishing a practice in Athens, he subsequently served as attorney general of Tennessee (1849–1860). Like many residents of East Tennessee, Bridges remained loyal to the Union. He was a delegate to the East Tennessee Convention in Knoxville (May 30–31, 1861) that passed a resolution denouncing the state's ordinance of secession. As a delegate to the Greenville Convention (June 17–20, 1861), he joined Unionists who petitioned the pro-Confederate government in Nashville for permission to create a new state.

Elected to the 37th Congress on the Union ticket, Bridges immediately fled his home to avoid arrest. He made his way through the mountains to neutral Kentucky, where he halted at Monticello to await the arrival of his family. Learning of his whereabouts, Confederate border forces detained his family and sent word that his wife was gravely ill. Bridges set out to join her, and on August 7, 1861, was seized three miles inside the Kentucky line. He remained a prisoner in his own home for over a year, then escaped to the North.

Bridges took his seat in Congress on February 25, 1863, but left office on March 3 and returned to Tennessee. On August 25, he joined the Union army with the rank of captain and afterward helped organize the 10th Tennessee Volunteer Cavalry. As its lieutenant colonel, Bridges saw active service in operations against Nathan B. Forrest in northern Alabama and middle Tennessee, and in the Nashville campaign. Discharged on December 29, 1864, Bridges resumed his judicial career. He died in Athens, Tennessee, on March 16, 1873. Humes, *Loyal Mountaineers of Tennessee.*

James M. Prichard

BRIGHT, Jesse David, *senator,* was born in Norwich, New York, on December 18, 1812, moved to Kentucky with his family in 1819, and to Madison, Indiana, in 1820. After attending local schools and studying law, he was admitted to the bar in 1833. His election as a Democrat as Jefferson county probate judge (1834–1839), appointment as U.S. marshal for Indiana (1840–1841), and subsequent election to the Indiana House of Representatives (1841–1843) demonstrated his popularity. Bright was elected lieutenant governor (1843–1845), serving with Indiana's first Democratic governor, James Whitcomb. He was in the U.S. Senate (1845–1862) and its president pro tem (1854–1857, 1860–1861) while maintaining near-autocratic control over Indiana's Democratic party.

Bright, who led the Buchanan (*q.v.*) and later the Breckinridge factions, favored admitting Kansas under the proslavery Lecompton Constitution, whereas the majority of Hoosier Democrats supported the popular sovereignty policy espoused by Stephen A. Douglas (*q.v.*). In 1860, Bright denounced Douglas as "venal and corrupt." However, pro-Douglas Democrats seized control of the state convention, and Bright's political career in Indiana quickly deteriorated. In the spring of 1861, after opposing strong action against secession, Bright seemingly severed his connections with Indiana. His move to his farm with twenty-one slaves in Gallatin county, Kentucky, caused many Indiana representatives to seek his ouster.

In August 1861, Federal authorities in Cincinnati arrested a man carrying a letter from Bright to Jefferson Davis, introducing a friend who had improved firearms to sell. The Senate voted 32–14 to expel him on February 5, 1862, thereby allowing Governor Oliver H.P. Morton (*q.v.*) to appoint former Governor Joseph A. Wright (*q.v.*), a War Democrat and Bright's archenemy, to fill the unexpired term. In 1864, Bright officially moved to Carrollton, Kentucky, and in 1866 won election to the Kentucky legislature (1867–1871). An owner of substantial landholdings and interests in West Virginia coal mines, Bright moved to Baltimore in 1874, where he died on May 20, 1875. Stampp, *Indiana Politics During the Civil War.*

David G. Vanderstel

BROOKS, James, *congressman,* was born in Portland, Maine, on November 10, 1810. His father was killed during the War of 1812, and Brooks was bound out to a storekeeper. His master sent him to school, and he graduated at the head of his class from what is now Colby College. While studying the law, he wrote a series of articles for the *Portland Advertiser.* He settled in New York City in 1835, and a year later he started the *New York Express*, with which he was connected for the rest of his life.

As a Whig in the 31st and 32nd Congresses, Brooks voted to support the Compromise of 1850. In 1856, he supported James Buchanan (*q.v.*) for President, and Stephen A. Douglas (*q.v.*) in 1860. He believed that a civil war must be avoided at all costs, and therefore urged in the spring of 1861 that the South be allowed to depart peacefully. An extreme Copperhead Democrat, he advocated overthrowing the Lincoln (*q.v.*) administration and installing General George B. McClellan (*q.v.*). He was elected in 1862 as a Democrat from New York City to the 38th Congress; remained in the 39th Congress until April 7, 1866, when his seat was successfully contested by William E. Dodge. Brooks returned to the 40th and the three following Congresses. He tried to end sectional hostilities so that the North and South could return to their strong commercial relations. He did not favor slavery and believed that the ''peculiar institution'' would eventually die of natural causes. In an attempt to speed the easing of sectional tensions after the war, he advocated a rapid and mild Reconstruction, and opposed Andrew Johnson's (*q.v.*) impeachment and the Radical governments in the South.

In 1873, a House investigating committee found Brooks and others guilty of taking bribes from the Crédit Mobilier. The House did not expel him but passed a resolution of censure against him and Oakes Ames (*q.v.*). The experience embittered Brooks, but his district overwhelmingly reelected him in 1872. He died in Washington, D.C., on April 30, 1873. Fitch, *Encyclopedia of Biography of New York*, vol 1.

Richard W. Brown, Jr.

BROOKS, Noah, *journalist*, was born on October 24, 1830, in Castine, Maine. He moved to Boston in 1847, studied landscape painting, joined the Taylor Club, and campaigned for public office as a Whig. He was a reporter for the *Boston Atlas*, a Whig paper, and also contributed to weeklies—including *The Carpet-Bag*—under the pen name Jacques. Financial difficulties forced Brooks to leave Boston in 1854 and settle in Dixon, Illinois. After a paint and furniture shop failed, he secured employment at the *Dixon Telegraph* and met Abraham Lincoln (*q.v.*) in the 1856 campaign. Brooks helped form the Illinois Republican party on the local level. Having strong antislavery feelings, he moved to Kansas Territory in 1857 to farm and to vote. Being no farmer, he returned less than a year later to edit the *Dixon Telegraph* and cover the 1858 Lincoln–Douglas debates.

To escape certain financial ruin, Brooks joined the Pikes Peak gold rush in 1859. However, he bypassed the diggings and trekked on to Marysville, California, where he established a profitable paint shop and contributed to the *San Francisco Evening Mirror* as John Riverside. For the first time, he saved his money, and bought a coeditorship of the *Marysville Appeal* in October 1860. He organized torchlight parades, served on Republican committees, and composed editorials in favor of Lincoln.

At the end of 1862, Brooks became the Washington correspondent of the *Sacramento Daily Union,* and renewed his social and political acquaintance with Lincoln. His popular column, which he signed Castine, influenced the entire West Coast in support of the Union. Occasionally he performed political chores for Lincoln, such as ''spying'' on the Democratic National Convention at Chicago in 1864. Had Lincoln not been assassinated, Brooks would have replaced John Nicolay as his private secretary.

Brooks served as a clerk in the House of Representatives (1863–1865), and President Andrew Johnson (*q.v.*) appointed him naval officer in charge of the Port of San Francisco in May 1865. However, he ardently supported the Radical Republicans, and Johnson removed him in September 1866. Thereupon Brooks became the managing editor of a new Republican newspaper, the *San Francisco Daily Times*, and with his facile pen he took revenge upon Johnson. In June 1867 he became the managing editor of the *Alta California* and also wrote for the *Overland Monthly* and other publications. In 1871, Brooks accepted the night editorship of the *New York Tribune*; in 1874, he signed on with the *New York Times* as night editorial writer; in 1884 he took the position of editor in chief of the *Newark* (New Jersey) *Daily Advertiser*. He retired on August 1, 1893, but continued to write, including his famous *Washington, D.C., in Lincoln's Time* (1895). He died on August 15, 1903, in Pasadena, California. Brooks, *Washington, D.C., in Lincoln's Time*; Temple, ''Lincoln's 'Castine,' '' *Lincoln Herald*.

Wayne C. Temple

BROOKS, William Thomas Harbaugh, *general*, was born in Lisbon, Ohio, on January 28, 1821. He graduated from West Point in 1841, served in Florida, and won commendations for service in Mexico. After assignments on the frontier, he was named a brigadier general of Volunteers on September 28, 1861. On the Peninsula, he commanded a brigade of Vermont soldiers that took some of the highest casualties in the campaign. Brooks himself was wounded. After leading his brigade at Antietam, where he was again wounded, Brooks was promoted to division command.

In the bitter aftermath of Fredericksburg, Ambrose Burnside (*q.v.*) ordered "Bully" Brooks's arrest for insubordination and then attempted to have him, and other critics, dismissed from the service. Brooks's division was at Chancellorsville, under the army command of Burnside's severest critic, Joseph Hooker (*q.v.*), and directly under the command of John Sedgwick (*q.v.*), whose VI Corps was to press the Confederate rear at Fredericksburg.

Brooks led well enough, but Sedgwick was less than aggressive. During the next year, Brooks commanded the Department of the Monongahela, where he was instrumental in the capture of John Hunt Morgan. He again led a division at Cold Harbor and Petersburg, where he was involved in the fruitless campaign at Bermuda Hundred. In July 1864 he resigned because of poor health and later settled on a farm near Huntsville, Alabama. Brooks seems to have been popular with his Southern neighbors, perhaps because his commanding officers had not been particularly effective in the field. He died in Huntsville on July 19, 1870.

Furgurson, *Chancellorsville*; Marvel, *Burnside*; Robertson, *Back Door to Richmond.*

John T. Hubbell

BROOMALL, John Martin, *congressman,* was born on January 19, 1816, in Upper Chichester Township, Pennsylvania. He was active for nearly three decades in national and state politics. Broomall served in the 38th, 39th, and 40th Congresses, where he was a strong supporter of the Republican party's war effort and an equally strong advocate of the party's Reconstruction policy. Initially, he embraced President Abraham Lincoln's (*q.v.*) plan for a speedy, lenient restoration of the Union, but later introduced a resolution that declared the Confederacy was conquered territory and that the Federal government would decide what power the people of the seceded states possessed and which people within those states possessed that power.

Broomall urged passage of the 13th Amendment and chided his border state colleagues who were reluctant to authorize the conscription of slaves into the Union Army. When white voters of the District of Columbia rejected a measure to grant suffrage to the District's blacks, Broomall recommended that another referendum be held, this time with blacks voting to decide whether whites within the District should vote. Convinced that loyal Southerners, especially the freedmen, required and deserved protection from the former Confederates, Broomall urged passage of the Civil Rights Act, the Reconstruction Acts, and a universal suffrage amendment. He died in Philadelphia on June 3, 1894. McKitrick, *Andrew Johnson.*

Philip J. Avillo, Jr.

BROUGH, John, *governor*, was born on September 17, 1811, in Marietta, Ohio. After briefly attending Ohio University, he began a law practice and, by publishing a series of newspapers that were strongly Democratic, launched a political career. In 1837 he was elected to the state legislature, and from 1839 to 1845 he was state auditor. In 1845, after the Whigs regained control of the state, he served as president of a succession of railroads. After the Civil War began, Brough, who had moved to Indianapolis, refused to join fellow Democrats in attacking the Lincoln (*q.v.*) administration.

In 1863, Republicans opposed to the renomination of incumbent governor David Tod (*q.v.*) brought Brough back to his home state, where he delivered strong speeches in behalf of the Union cause. His absence from Ohio had kept him from alienating potential supporters, and his advocacy of a railroad consolidation scheme opposed by Tod won other adherents. In a close vote he won the nomination, and in the general election overwhelmed Democrat Clement Vallandigham (*q.v.*) by more than 100,000 votes. Brough made perhaps his greatest contribution to the Union cause by administering this crushing defeat to a prominent peace candidate at a critical point in the war. He faced the same problems—raising troops, wrestling with the Federal draft, and providing for Ohio's soldiers in the field—that had confronted his predecessors.

Although by 1864 many state governors were calling either for abandoning conscription or for liberalizing bounties to attract recruits, Brough opposed both proposals. He complained to Washington that the bounty system had led to great corruption and that many of the provost marshals in Ohio should be removed. Although he supported the draft, he insisted that the quota system was faulty, and with the aid of ex-governor Tod managed to get Secretary of War Edwin Stanton (*q.v.*) to reduce the number of men required of the state. He did not hesitate, however, to call upon Ohio to provide needed manpower, and on his own initiative in 1864 he raised over 34,000 militia for 100 days' service to relieve veteran troops from garrison duty around Washington.

To meet the needs of Ohio troops in the field, Brough obtained passage of legislation increasing support for soldiers' families, enlarged the number of welfare agencies watching over Ohio troops, and insisted that his own state agents, rather than officials of the United States Sanitary Commission, handle the state's money and stores. Although this activity proved popular with the soldiers, Brough's decision to base army promotions solely on seniority led to acrimonious disputes with officers that helped erode support for his renomination in 1865. Also, as the war neared its end, Republicans wanted one of their own, preferably a military man, selected as governor. Brough chose not to campaign actively, and the Unionists nominated General Jacob D. Cox (*q.v.*). Brough did not live to complete his term of office; the last of Ohio's wartime governors contracted gangrene in hand and foot, and died in Cleveland on August 29, 1865. Abbott, *Ohio's War Governors*; Hesseltine, *Lincoln's War Governors*.

Richard H. Abbott

BROWN, Benjamin Gratz, *senator,* was born on May 28, 1826, in Lexington, Kentucky. He graduated from Yale in 1845, and after being admitted to the Kentucky bar, he moved to St. Louis to practice law. He served in the Missouri state legislature (1852–1859), where he consistently opposed slavery, advocated emancipation, and supported free-soil expansion. In 1857, Brown was narrowly defeated in the state's gubernatorial election. After taking an active part at the 1860 Chicago convention that nominated Abraham Lincoln (*q.v.*), Brown in 1861 assisted Nathaniel Lyon (*q.v.*) and Francis P. Blair (*q.v.*) in mobilizing St. Louis Unionists for the city's defense, then participated in Lyon's Springfield campaign as colonel of a volunteer Home Guard regiment under Franz Sigel (*q.v.*).

Brown was returned to the Missouri legislature in 1862, and in 1863, he was elected to the U.S. Senate, where he quickly aligned with the Radical Republicans in their support for vigorous prosecution of the war. As senator, he called for full implementation of the Emancipation Proclamation and the immediate abolition of slavery in all states and territories. Brown also supported women's suffrage, abolition of voting tests, an eight-hour workday for government employees, and civil service reform. In 1864, he helped to organize the Cleveland convention that opposed Lincoln's renomination and supported the candidacy of John C. Frémont (*q.v.*). Following the war, Brown was elected governor of Missouri, opposed Radical Reconstruction, and in 1872 was nominated as the running mate of Democratic presidential candidate Horace Greeley (*q.v.*). He died in St. Louis on December 13, 1885. Peterson, *Freedom and Franchise.*

Christopher Phillips

BROWN, James Sproat, *congressman,* was born on February 1, 1824, in Hampden, Maine. At age sixteen, he settled in Cincinnati, then, in 1844, in frontier Milwaukee. He received a public school education and studied law and German in Cincinnati. In 1843, he was admitted to the Ohio bar, but established his legal practice in Milwaukee. In 1845, Brown was elected district attorney for Milwaukee county, and in 1848 became Wisconsin's first attorney general. In 1861, he was elected mayor of Milwaukee, and in 1862 was elected as a War Democrat to the 38th Congress, defeating the popular incumbent, John Fox Potter (*q.v.*). He served one term, failing in his reelection bid in 1864.

Brown seems not to have distinguished himself in his brief congressional career. As Milwaukee's mayor he helped to put down a bank riot, but his regard for law and order failed to extend to the city's small African American community when he seemingly condoned the lynching of a black man by a mostly Irish mob. Brown opposed a proposal to set up a special police force to deal with growing lawlessness, particularly among the state's immigrant population, which figured prominently in the bank riots and in violent demonstrations against the draft. In failing health, Brown went to Europe in 1865, hoping to recuperate. Upon his return in 1873, he resumed his law practice, but his health continued to deteriorate. He died in Chicago on April 15, 1878. Gregory, *History of Milwaukee, Wisconsin*, vol. 2.

Michael J. McManus

BROWN, John, *abolitionist*, was born on May 9, 1800, in Torrington, Connecticut. He grew up in Hudson, Ohio, where he acquired a limited formal education. He married twice and became the deeply religious patriarch of a large family, which he could not adequately support as a tanner or through other generally unsuccessful business ventures. Within the antislavery movement, Brown was especially drawn to direct action. In the 1840s, he helped fugitive slaves in Ohio. At Springfield, Massachusetts, in 1851, he organized a black vigilance committee designed to resist enforcement of the Fugitive Slave Act of 1850. As early as 1847 he had begun to consider going into the South to lead a massive slave revolt. It was the violent struggle between free-state and slave-state forces in Kansas Territory that provided Brown with the experience and reputation that allowed him to initiate this scheme.

Drawn to Kansas in 1855, Brown emerged as a famous free-state guerrilla captain after having massacred five slave-state men at Potawatomi Creek in 1856. In 1858, he crossed the Missouri border, violently liberated eleven slaves, and guided them to freedom. Now able to command the financial support of leading abolitionists, Brown, on October 16, 1859, led a small band in the capture of the Federal arsenal at Harper's Ferry, Virginia. The aim was to acquire weapons for his planned slave rebellion. Instead, Brown was overwhelmed by U.S. Marines, and was convicted of treason against Virginia. His raid contributed to a Southern commitment to secession as a means of protecting slavery. His bravery and eloquence during the weeks prior to his execution convinced many Northerners of the morality of a war to abolish slavery. He was hanged at Charleston, Virginia (now West Virginia), on December 2, 1859. Oates, *To Purge This Land with Blood*; Rossbach, *Ambivalent Conspirators*.

Stanley Harrold

BROWN, William Gay, Sr., *congressman*, was born on September 25, 1800, in Kingwood, Virginia (now West Virginia). After attending public schools, he studied law and in 1823 was admitted to the bar. He served as prosecuting attorney of Preston county, Virginia (1823–1832), and was elected to the Virginia House of Delegates (1832, 1840–1843). Brown subsequently won election as a Democrat to the 29th and 30th Congresses (1845–1849). In 1850, he was a delegate to the Virginia Constitutional Convention and, in 1860, to the Democratic National Conventions in Charleston, South Carolina, and Baltimore, Maryland. At the latter, he was a Stephen Douglas (*q.v.*) elector.

As a delegate to the Virginia Convention in early 1861, Brown opposed secession. In May 1861, he was elected as a Unionist to the 37th Congress and was reelected to the 38th Congress as an Unconditional Unionist. After the war, Brown served in the West Virginia legislature and as president of a bank. He died in Kingwood, West Virginia, on April 19, 1884. Lanman, *Biographical Annals*; Morris, *Who Was Who in American Politics.*

Frank R. Levstik

BROWNE, Charles Farrar, *editor, satirist,* was born in Waterford, Maine, on April 26, 1834. He was a printer until 1851, when he began working for a Boston humor magazine called the *Carpet-Bag.* In it, he published his first article (on Cornwallis) in 1852. Browne was a journeyman printer in the South and West until he joined the *Cleveland Plain Dealer* in 1857, first as a reporter, then as the "local" editor, providing columns of quips and observations. The American and English publics first became aware of him as a writer of comic letters in the *Plain Dealer*, which he signed as Artemus Ward. When a New York comic magazine, *Vanity Fair*, contracted to print his popular humorous material, Browne left the *Plain Dealer*. He eventually became the managing editor of *Vanity Fair.*

Browne gathered his Artemus Ward letters into a book and hit the lecture circuit, beginning at New London, Connecticut, on November 26, 1861. He polished his act in various New England towns and eventually left a declining *Vanity Fair* for even larger audiences. His comic lectures were delivered in the midst of the agonies of the Civil War. The tubercular Browne could not serve as a soldier, but he was a loyal Unionist and freely donated lecture profits to the Union cause. A trip to Washington, D.C., inspired "Artemus Ward in Washington," which developed an imaginary meeting with President Abraham Lincoln (*q.v.*), whom he never really met. Lincoln, however, knew of Browne and admired both his humor and his pro-Union sympaties. He read Browne's "High Handed Outrage in Utica" to his Cabinet on September 22, 1862, just before he read them his draft of the Emancipation Proclamation.

In the winter of 1863–1864, Browne toured California, Nevada, and Utah. He encountered the Mormons in Salt Lake City, a meeting that gave birth to his popular lecture "Artemus Ward Among the Mormons," which delighted Eastern audiences. In 1866, Browne toured England, fell ill, and died in Southampton on March 6, 1867. Blair, *America's Humor*; Seitz, *Artemus Ward.*

Ronald D. Rietveld

BROWNE, George Huntington, *congressman,* was born in Gloucester, Rhode Island, on January 6, 1811. He graduated from Brown University in 1840 and was admitted to the Rhode Island bar in 1843. He entered politics as a Democrat sympathetic to the efforts of Thomas Wilson Dorr for suffrage reform. After serving in the state legislature (1845–1851), Browne was appointed U.S. attorney for Rhode Island (1852–1861). He was a delegate to the Democratic National Convention of 1860 and to the Peace Convention held in Washington in January 1861. He was elected to the 37th Congress as a candidate of the successful coalition of Democrats and Conservative Republicans who had feared that emphasis on the slavery issue would lead to war.

Defeated in his bid for reelection in 1862, Browne was commissioned a colonel and ordered to raise and command the 12th Regiment of Rhode Island Volunteers. After initial assignment to the defense of Washington, Browne led the regiment to Fredericksburg in December 1862 where he was ordered to the center of Union lines. Fierce fighting on December 13 took a toll of 109 killed and wounded and 95 missing. After the battle, Browne and his troops were transferred to Kentucky but saw no more heavy combat. The regiment was mustered out of service in the summer of 1863. Browne resumed the practice of law and again served in the state legislature in 1872 and 1873. He died in Providence on September 26, 1885. Bartlett, *Memoirs of Rhode Island Officers*; Tillinghast, *History of the Twelfth Regiment*.

Mario R. DiNunzio

BROWNING, Orville Hickman, *senator*, was born in Cynthiana, Kentucky, on February 10, 1806. He attended Augusta (Kentucky) College. In 1836 he was elected as a Whig to the Illinois Senate, but he declined to run again in 1840. Browning successfully ran for the legislature in 1842 but lost elections to the U.S. House in 1843 to Stephen A. Douglas (*q.v.*), and in 1850 and 1852 to William A. Richardson (*q.v.*). In 1856, he was a delegate to the anti-Nebraska convention held at Bloomington, Illinois, where he played a key role, as he did at the 1860 Republican National Convention.

When Douglas died, Browning was appointed to fill his Senate seat, serving from July 1861 to January 1863; he was not returned to the Senate because the Illinois legislature chose Democrat William A. Richardson. Browning was a conservative who rejected the idea that Congress had authority to legislate on the slavery issue in the states (although he agreed that Congress had the right to deal with the slavery issue in the District of Columbia). He consistently opposed his more radical colleagues in debates over taxation on slaves, emancipation, and the confiscation of the property of rebelling Southerners. He also objected to any expansion of congressional "war powers" because Southerners were still citizens of the United States. Believing that freed slaves would not be able to adapt to American society, Browning supported the idea of colonization. Although he maintained the close personal relationship that he had developed with Abraham Lincoln (*q.v.*) in Illinois, they often disagreed politically.

Browning's senatorial career was briefer than most, and his positions on issues did not make him famous. His enduring contribution was that he kept one of the few good diaries written by a congressman during the era. He returned to Washington in 1863 to practice law, and as a lobbyist he took full advantage of the connections that he had made. He was appointed Secretary of the Interior (1866–1869) and served briefly as interim U.S. Attorney General. He was a delegate to the Illinois Constitutional Convention in 1869–1870 as a Democrat, but his post-Washington years were mostly devoted to his law practice in Quincy, especially as counsel to the Chicago, Burlington & Quincy Railroad.

He died in Quincy on August 10, 1881. Baxter, *Orville H. Browning*; Browning, *Diary of Orville Hickman Browning.*

Leslie J. Stegh

BROWNLOW, William Gannaway, *clergyman, editor*, was born in Wythe county, Virginia, on August 29, 1805. He entered the Methodist ministry in 1826 and served as an itinerant preacher for ten years in Tennessee and South Carolina. In 1838 he became the editor of the *Knoxville Whig*, and his unsparing treatment of political opponents earned him the sobriquet of the "fighting parson." Brownlow opposed secession and maintained the *Whig* as a champion of the government through the outbreak of the Civil War. He refused to take down the United States flag from his house or take the oath of allegiance to the new Confederacy.

The *Whig* was suppressed, and Brownlow moved to East Tennessee in October 1861. He was charged with burning railroad bridges and was to be shot on sight by Confederate soldiers. He fled to North Carolina, where he remained until he received a promise of a pass into Kentucky if he would return to Knoxville, which he did. He was arrested and jailed. Brownlow's imprisonment created one of the most troublesome problems for the Confederacy, and ended up taking the time of various officials from Richmond to Knoxville. On March 15, 1862, he was released to Union lines.

Encouraged by Abraham Lincoln (*q.v.*) and others, Brownlow made a triumphant lecture tour through the North, from Ohio to New England. Lionized for his deeds and suffering in East Tennessee, he accumulated enough money to return to Knoxville in September 1863 and republish the *Whig*. He became the journalistic lord of East Tennessee and served as a delegate to the National Union (Republican) Convention at Baltimore in June 1864. He took an active part in renominating Lincoln and in the selection of Andrew Johnson (*q.v.*) of Tennessee as the vice presidential nominee on the Union ticket. By a vote of 23,352 to 35 he was elected governor to reconstruct Tennessee; as governor (1865–1869), he disfranchised Confederate veterans and attempted to break the Ku Klux Klan. He served as U.S. senator from 1869 to 1875 and wrote *Sketches of the Rise, Progress, and Decline of Secession in 1862*, which enjoyed wide circulation in the North. Upon leaving the Senate, he returned to Tennessee and resumed editing the *Whig*. He died in Knoxville on April 29, 1877. Brownlow, *Sketches*; Coulter, *William G. Brownlow.*

Ronald D. Rietveld

BRYANT, William Cullen, *editor*, was born on November 3, 1794, in Cummington, Massachusetts. He attended Williams College, studied law, and for ten years practiced law in Great Barrington. He also achieved fame as a poet, and in 1825 went to New York City to edit a literary periodical. In 1826, he joined the *New York Evening Post*, becoming editor in 1829 and later its principal owner. Bryant was a moderate, practical man whose political loyalties tempered his principles. He supported the Jacksonian Democrats, who, he thought, best represented his beliefs in individual freedom, limited government, antimonopoly, and a gold or silver currency. Although he defended the right of the abolitionists to speak their views, he denounced their immoderate zeal and hoped that the natural progress of civilization would end slavery in the United States.

During the 1840s, Bryant followed the Van Buren, or Barnburner, Democrats in opposing the annexation of Texas and supporting the Wilmot Proviso and the Free Soil party. In the early 1850s, he accompanied the Van Burenites back into the Democratic party and supported President Franklin Pierce until the Kansas–Nebraska Act opened those territories to slavery. Then Bryant advocated sending free-state settlers to Kansas and accepted the possibility of bloodshed in the territory. He was one of the earliest supporters of the Republican party in New York, but his Democratic past influenced his Republican loyalties.

In 1860, Bryant favored either Salmon P. Chase (*q.v.*) or Abraham Lincoln (*q.v.*) for the nomination over his long-time Whig opponent William Henry Seward (*q.v.*). He denounced secession and compromise, favored use of military force against the Confederacy, and criticized Lincoln's caution on emancipation. He also opposed the administration's high-tariff, paper money, and national banking policies. After the war, Bryant favored a generous policy toward the South, but his desire to protect the rights of the former slaves caused him to oppose President Andrew Johnson's (*q.v.*) plan of Reconstruction. Still, he believed that African Americans would require considerable time to acquire the education, property, and experience needed for full citizenship. Although he disliked much that he saw in Ulysses S. Grant's (*q.v.*) administration, he found more defects in the Democrats, and thus maintained his loyalty to the Republican party until his death in New York City on June 12, 1878. Brown, *William Cullen Bryant*; Nevins, *The Evening Post.*

George McJimsey

BUCHANAN, James, *President,* was born in Cove Gap, near Mercersburg, Pennsylvania, on April 23, 1791. He graduated from Dickinson College in 1809, read law, and was admitted to the bar in 1812. Elected as a Federalist to the state Assembly in 1812, he was elevated to Congress in 1820. For thirty-seven of the next forty-one years, he was never out of national office, earning the nickname "Old Public Functionary." With the Federalists' demise, Buchanan led his followers into the Democratic party. As a reward, he was appointed ambassador to Russia (1831–1833) and elected to the U.S. Senate (1834–1845). He was Secretary of State during the Mexican War, and later ambassador to England. There Buchanan drafted the Ostend Manifesto (1854), a statement that the United States should buy Cuba or take it from Spain by force. The resulting international furor was overshadowed by the controversy surrounding the Kansas–Nebraska Bill.

At the Democratic National Convention in Cincinnati in April 1856, Buchanan secured the nomination, defeating Illinois's Stephen A. Douglas (*q.v.*). In

November, Buchanan defeated the first Republican presidential candidate, John C. Frémont (*q.v.*), and the only Native American party presidential candidate, former President Millard Fillmore. Buchanan's term was not marked by success, despite his image as a nationalist and a master politician. A military expedition against the Mormons ended in inglorious compromise. A bill to appropriate money to purchase Cuba died in the Senate. The House of Representatives formally censured Buchanan and his Navy Secretary, Isaac Toucey, in 1860 for their handling of naval contracts and the patronage. Most important, Buchanan's 1858 decision to support the pro-slavery Lecompton Constitution for Kansas led to a bitter conflict with Douglas. Buchanan failed to secure the Lecompton Constitution's adoption, and failed in limited attempts to turn Douglas out of the Senate.

By 1860, Buchanan was all but ignored by his party, and played almost no role in the presidential campaign, except to bear responsibility for splitting the Democracy and thereby ensuring Abraham Lincoln's (*q.v.*) election. Buchanan vacillated in dealing with secession, partly because of his lame-duck status. Fort Pickens and Fort Sumter became the symbols of an unbroken Union, but other Federal posts were turned over to the seceding states without protest. Military expeditions to reinforce both forts were ordered, but at Fort Pickens, Buchanan agreed to a truce that forbade landing the troops and supplies. The warship originally scheduled to deliver supplies and reinforcements to Fort Sumter was replaced by the unarmed *Star of the West.* Clear instructions about the *Star*'s purpose were not given to Fort Sumter's commander, Major Robert Anderson (*q.v.*). When the *Star*, unsupported by Sumter's guns, fled under Confederate fire, Buchanan neither responded nor made further efforts to reinforce or resupply the garrison.

Buchanan left his successor a nation at peace on March 4, 1861, but at the price of a weakened government and a nation far from indivisible. When war broke out, he loyally supported a nonpartisan military effort to put down the rebellion. Wartime emotions sometimes brought threats of physical violence against him and quashed his efforts to place his version of prewar events before the public. Not until 1866 was his book on the secession crisis published. Buchanan had a fine legal mind and was an upholder of the Constitution, but as President he placed adherence to the forms of law above justice in the Lecompton crisis, and contributed significantly to the Democratic party's destruction. He might have been a successful national leader in the 1840s, but in the late 1850s he was not the man for the times or the position, and his presidency must be judged a failure. On June 1, 1868, Buchanan died in Lancaster, Pennsylvania. Klein, *President James Buchanan*; Nichols, *Disruption of American Democracy*; Stampp, *America in 1857.*

David E. Meerse

BUCKALEW, Charles Rollin, *senator,* was born on December 28, 1821, in Columbia county, Pennsylvania. He was elected district attorney of Columbia county in 1845, served eight years in the Pennsylvania Senate, and was named ambassador to Ecuador in 1858 by President James Buchanan (*q.v.*). In 1863 Buckalew was elected to the U.S. Senate, defeating his Republican opponent, former Secretary of War Simon Cameron (*q.v.*). The contest was a particularly bitter struggle, and Buckalew's victory was largely dependent upon factionalism in the Republican ranks and attempts by Cameron supporters to bribe state senators.

Buckalew voted against expanding the war powers of the central government, the creation of the Freedmen's Bureau, and high tariff legislation. He also voted to acquit Andrew Johnson (*q.v.*) during the President's impeachment trial. Buckalew was defeated for reelection and returned to Pennsylvania state politics. A brief resurrection came in 1887 when he was elected to the House of Representatives. After two terms in the House, Buckalew retired to his home in Bloomsburg, where he died on May 19, 1899. Dell, *Lincoln and the War Democrats*; McClure, *Old Time Notes of Pennsylvania*, vol. 2.

David Dixon

BUCKINGHAM, William Alfred, *governor*, was born on May 28, 1804, in Lebanon, Connecticut. He attended Bacon Academy in Colchester, and worked for a time as a teacher and as a surveyor's apprentice. After accumulating a fortune in business, Buckingham, until then a Whig, became involved in Republican party politics. In 1857, he tried unsuccessfully to secure the Republican nomination for governor, and a year later was the party's choice. He was elected governor in 1858 and was reelected every succeeding year through 1865. His seven years as governor is one of the longest terms on record. Buckingham was an able administrator and a loyal Lincoln (*q.v.*) supporter.

Through proclamations and demands for special sessions of the Connecticut Assembly, Buckingham increased the state's contribution to the war effort and expanded the exercise of executive power in the state. His activist approach corresponded with his moral opposition to slavery. Before April 1861 he rejected the pleas of conciliationists who wanted him to demand the repeal of Connecticut's Personal Liberty Law. When he chose delegates to the February 1861 peace conference, Buckingham instructed the delegates to make no concessions to Southern demands. Before the war began, Buckingham acted as a bridge between the conservative followers of Senator James Dixon (*q.v.*) within Connecticut's Republican party and James Hawley and Charles Dudley Warner of the *Hartford Press*, who led the party's Radical wing. During the war years, however, Buckingham's aversion to slavery and to the South intensified, and he drew closer to the Radicals.

Buckingham's postwar effort was less impressive than his work as governor. He failed to gain election to the Senate in 1866 but succeeded in 1868. His senatorial record was not distinguished. He died on February 5, 1875, in Norwich, Connecticut. Buckingham, *Life of William A. Buckingham*; Niven, *Connecticut for the Union*.

Joanna D. Cowden

BUELL, Don Carlos, *general,* was born near Marietta, Ohio, on March 23, 1818. He graduated from West Point in 1841 and served in the Seminole and Mexican Wars, advancing to the rank of major and participating in the battles of Monterey, Contreras, and Churubusco. He was severely wounded at the last engagement. Buell was a lieutenant colonel in the Adjutant General's Department at the outbreak of the Civil War. On May 17, 1861, he was commissioned a brigadier general of Volunteers and helped to organize and train the Army of the Potomac. A more important assignment soon followed: command of the Army of the Ohio at Louisville, with orders to advance into East Tennessee and Knoxville. He recommended an alternative plan, appreciated by neither General George B. McClellan (*q.v.*) nor President Abraham Lincoln (*q.v.*), of striking south by the Cumberland and Tennessee Rivers and into Nashville.

When Ulysses S. Grant's (*q.v.*) advance on Forts Henry and Donelson forced a Confederate retreat, Buell was able to march into Bowling Green and Nashville without opposition. Placed under the orders of General Henry W. Halleck (*q.v.*), who headed the new Department of the Mississippi, Buell was instructed to advance on Savannah, Tennessee, and join forces with the troops moving up the Tennessee River. His lead division did not arrive on the Tennessee River until April 6, 1862, the day of the Confederate attack at Shiloh. The division helped to boost Union morale when it crossed the river and began taking a position on the Federal left late in the first day of battle. On the morning of April 7, with two more divisions up, Buell's fresh forces joined in the attack and contributed significantly to the Union victory.

Now a major general of Volunteers, Buell took part in the advance on Corinth, which the Confederates soon abandoned. Buell's subsequent move across north Alabama, with Chattanooga as the objective, was unsuccessful, primarily due to Confederate attacks on his railroad supply line. In late summer, when Generals Braxton Bragg and Edmund Kirby Smith launched a two-pronged invasion of Kentucky, Buell left a small force to cover Nashville and retreated to protect the supply line from Louisville. North of Bowling Green, in mid-September, he found that Bragg was between him and Louisville, but Bragg marched northeast and Buell reached Louisville safely. On October 1, with reinforcements bringing his strength to 60,000, Buell moved southeast; at Perryville, on October 8, he stumbled onto a portion of Bragg's command. A bloody but indecisive battle ensued. Buell failed to use his superior numbers effectively, and when Bragg realized that the Union forces were united while his own command was scattered, he retreated toward East Tennessee. Before the month was over, Buell was relieved of command and succeeded by General William S. Rosecrans (*q.v.*). A military commission investigating his conduct reported the facts without making a recommendation. After awaiting orders for a year, Buell was discharged as a major general of Volunteers, whereupon he resigned his commission in the Regular Army on June 1, 1864.

A man of high principle, personally courageous, and a good organizer and disciplinarian, Buell nevertheless failed to reach the heights that his pre-Civil

War reputation seemed to promise. He was unable to inspire his troops or gain the confidence of the administration. But most important, Buell lacked aggressiveness. Writing to McClellan about Grant's advance up the Cumberland and Tennessee Rivers, Buell dwelt upon the problems involved and said he could not support Grant without placing his own army in a hazardous position. His belief that he saved Grant's army from destruction at Shiloh is a debatable point. In any case, Buell was much too slow in arriving at Savannah. He allowed Bragg to steal a march on him in Kentucky, and after the poorly fought battle of Perryville, he again, as at Shiloh, showed little inclination to pursue the foe. Buell's good qualities thus were largely negated by his excessive caution. After the war Buell settled in Kentucky, engaging in mining and serving for a time as a pension agent. He died near Paradise, Kentucky, on November 19, 1898. Hafendorfer, *Perryville*; McDonough, *Shiloh.*

James Lee McDonough

BUFFIN[G]TON, James, *congressman*, was born on March 16, 1817, in Fall River, Massachusetts. Although sources tend to spell his surname with a ''g,'' the correct version is Buffinton. His parents were Quakers, and he was educated at the Society of Friends' school in Providence, Rhode Island. Before establishing himself as a merchant in Fall River, Massachusetts, Buffinton studied medicine, went to sea as a whaler, and worked in a print shop. As a Whig he served three consecutive terms as a selectman before being elected mayor of Fall River as a Know-Nothing in 1853 and 1854. He resigned in 1855 in order to take a seat in the 34th Congress, to which he was elected with Know-Nothing support in 1854. As a Republican he was easily reelected in 1856, 1858, and 1860. In 1862, redistricting made Fall River part of the 1st Congressional District, which was then, and continued to be, represented by Republican Thomas D. Eliot (*q.v.*) of New Bedford.

In 1863, Buffinton was appointed a Treasury agent and then collector of internal revenue for the 1st District, in which post he served until 1868, when Eliot retired. Buffinton was elected to the 41st Congress and reelected to the three succeeding Congresses. He won the nomination on the basis of his earlier experience in Congress, his expertise in financial matters, and his effectiveness as a party organizer. By 1870, he had secured the support of the Radical Republican press in his district through patronage rather than through his continued support in Congress for a thoroughly Radical position on the issues of Reconstruction. Buffinton died in Fall River on March 7, 1875. Blank, ''The Waning of Radicalism.''

Dale Baum

BUFORD, John, *general*, was born in Woodford county, Kentucky, on March 4, 1826. He graduated from West Point in 1848, served with the 2nd Dragoons on the Plains, in Kansas, and as quartermaster of his regiment in the Utah Expedition. In 1861, he was promoted to major and given a desk job in the

Inspector General's Corps in Washington. John Pope (*q.v.*) arranged for his transfer to the Army of Virginia, to command a brigade of cavalry with the rank (from July 27, 1862) of brigadier general. With George Bayard's (*q.v.*) cavalry brigade, Buford's command participated in the operations that culminated in Pope's disastrous defeat at Second Bull Run. Buford himself was wounded in an action at Lewis's Ford, after he had reported the approach of James Longstreet's corps through Thoroughfare Gap. After recovering from his wound, Buford was given command of a two-brigade division of cavalry in the Army of the Potomac. Joseph Hooker (*q.v.*) claimed that he wanted to give Buford command of his newly organized Cavalry Corps but was obliged to give it to Alfred Pleasonton (*q.v.*) instead, by reason of the latter's eleven-day seniority in rank.

Following his outstanding performance at Gettysburg, Buford led his division in General George Meade's (*q.v.*) halfhearted pursuit of Lee's army. He had a number of fights with Stuart's cavalry around Williamsport; and at one near Boonsborough, Buford himself led the dismounted skirmish line against the enemy. Up to the time of Buford's death, the senior officers of the Union cavalry, and the Union cavalry as a whole, had only begun to rise to the level of mediocrity. Only Buford was thought to have the qualities to reach the highest level of competence in performing the traditional functions of cavalry and in its increasingly important role as mounted infantry. At Brandy Station, for example, after the initial contact with the enemy, Buford took his division into action dismounted.

His fellow officers believed that Buford was the best cavalry general in the Army of the Potomac, a model commander who would not curry favor with newspaper reporters. It is not impossible that if Buford had lived, he, and not Philip Sheridan (*q.v.*), would have had command of the Cavalry Corps of the Army of the Potomac in the final year of the war. He died in Washington, D.C., on December 16, 1863. Coddington, *Gettysburg Campaign*; Starr, *Union Cavalry*, vol. 1.

Stephen Z. Starr

BURBRIDGE, Stephen Gano, *general,* was born in Scott county, Kentucky, on August 19, 1831. After attending Georgetown College and Kentucky Military Institute, he studied law but did not open a practice. When the Civil War began, Burbridge raised the 26th Kentucky Volunteers and became its colonel. His performance at Shiloh brought promotion to brigadier general on June 9, 1862. Burbridge then saw extensive duty in the western theater, usually as commander of a brigade in the XIII Corps of the Army of the Tennessee. In February 1864 he was given command of the District of Kentucky, with extensive civil as well as military authority. Much of his military service consisted of encounters with Confederate raiders. Burbridge was breveted major general on July 4, 1864, after defeating John Hunt Morgan at Mount Sterling and Cynthiana. Later that year Burbridge led large but not totally successful raids against the important salt and lead mines in southwestern Virginia.

Harsh and tactless in exercising his powers within the state, Burbridge earned the undying hatred of many Kentucky Unionists. Although he was unjustly blamed for carrying out such administrative measures as the use of African American troops and suspension of habeas corpus, his own zeal and excesses contributed to his poor reputation. He interfered with the 1864 elections; he was accused of cheating farmers in the "Hog Swindle"; and he employed harsh measures, including executions and banishment, against Confederate sympathizers in his efforts to curb guerrilla activities. Governor Thomas E. Bramlette (*q.v.*) led the demands that secured Burbridge's dismissal from the command in January 1865. He resigned his commission in December. Kentuckians' hatred of Burbridge continued into the postwar era, and forced him and his family to leave the state. He had become a political liability, and his requests for Federal appointments were rejected. The most detested Kentuckian of the Civil War died in Brooklyn, New York, on December 2, 1894. Coulter, *Civil War and Readjustment in Kentucky*; Johnson, *History of Kentucky and Kentuckians*, vol. 1; Kleber, *Kentucky Encyclopedia.*

Lowell H. Harrison

BURLINGAME, Anson, *diplomat*, was born on November 14, 1820, in New Berlin, New York, and moved with his family to Ohio and later to Michigan. He attended the University of Michigan and then Harvard Law School, from which he graduated in 1846. In 1848, he supported the Free Soil presidential ticket, and following the Compromise of 1850, he joined in the fight against the Fugitive Slave Law. In 1852, he was elected to the Michigan Senate. In 1854 he joined the Know-Nothing party in an act of political survival and won election to Congress. Soon after the 1854 election Burlingame entered the new Republican party. He served three consecutive terms in the U.S. House of Representatives, from 1855 to 1861. In 1856, after Preston Brooks's attack upon Charles Sumner (*q.v.*) in the Senate chamber, Burlingame made a rousing speech on the House floor defending Massachusetts, praising his friend Sumner, and comparing Brooks to the biblical Cain. Brooks challenged Burlingame to a duel; and although the confrontation never occurred, Burlingame's acceptance of the challenge established him as a Northern regional hero.

The Brooks affair and Burlingame's own spellbinding oratory made him one of the Republican party's most effective campaigners in 1856 and 1860. His efforts for Abraham Lincoln (*q.v.*) in 1860 contributed to the Republican success in the Great Lakes states, but Burlingame neglected his own reelection campaign and lost his House seat. In 1861, Lincoln rewarded Burlingame by appointing him the first U.S. minister plenipotentiary to reside in Peking (now Beijing), China.

Burlingame played a peripheral role in the Civil War by preventing Confederate ships access to Chinese ports; he became better known for his opposition to the coercive policies of Western nations in China. As both an antislavery politician and an innovative diplomat, he was an eloquent advocate of change.

In 1867, he resigned as U.S. minister and accepted the Chinese government's appointment as its first official envoy to the United States and the European nations. After negotiating a treaty between the United States and China in 1868 that bears his name, Burlingame traveled to Europe. While in St. Petersburg, Russia, still serving as China's emissary, he died on February 23, 1870. Anderson, *Imperialism and Idealism*; Williams, *Anson Burlingame.*

David L. Anderson

BURNETT, Henry Cornelius, *congressman,* was born in Essex county, Virginia, on October 5, 1825. During his childhood his family settled in Kentucky, where he was educated in the common schools. After attending Hopkinsville Academy, he studied law and was admitted to the bar in 1847. He established a practice in Cadiz, Kentucky, and subsequently served as Trigg county Circuit Court clerk (1851–1853). A staunch proslavery Democrat, Burnett served three terms in Congress (1855–1861). During the secession crisis, he emerged as a leading Southern rights advocate who denounced Republican measures to "coerce" the seceded states. After Congress adjourned on March 2, 1861, Burnett returned to Kentucky, where he was nominated by the Southern Rights party as its candidate for the emergency session of Congress scheduled to meet on July 4.

The only Southern Rights candidate elected from Kentucky, Burnett openly denounced Abraham Lincoln's (*q.v.*) war policy. The Confederate seizure of Hickman and Columbus in early September ended Kentucky's neutrality and prompted the pro-Union legislature to call on the Federal government for aid. Burnett served as president of the Kentucky Southern Conference (October 29–31) at Russellville, where the Unionist legislature was denounced. He later served as president of the Russellville Sovereignty Convention, which passed an ordinance of secession and organized a new state government. Burnett was in Richmond, seeking to gain Kentucky's admission to the Confederacy, when he was expelled from Congress on December 3, 1861.

Burnett was commissioned colonel of the 8th Kentucky Infantry (C.S.A.) on November 11, 1861. Although he never took active command, he was with the regiment at Fort Donelson; he escaped capture by fleeing with General John B. Floyd. On February 26, 1862, he took a seat in the Confederate Senate, where he remained for the duration of the war. He reported to the Union authorities at Danville, Virginia, on May 19, 1865, and took the Amnesty Oath. He took the Oath of Allegiance to the United States on June 19, 1865, in Washington.

Burnett was en route to his home when he was arrested in Louisville on an 1863 treason charge. Released on $10,000 bail, he waited quietly at home while prominent Kentucky Unionists petitioned President Andrew Johnson (*q.v.*) for a pardon. Ironically, it was Burnett's willingness to support the 13th Amendment that prompted them to rally to his support. Burnett resumed the practice of law in Cadiz shortly after the war. He died in Hopkinsville, Kentucky, on October

1, 1866. Craig, "Henry Cornelius Burnett," *Register of the Kentucky Historical Society*; Kleber, *Kentucky Encyclopedia.*

James M. Prichard

BURNHAM, Alfred Avery, *congressman*, was born on March 8, 1819, in Windham, Connecticut. He attended preparatory school and one year of college, then studied law and was admitted to the Connecticut bar in 1843. He established a law practice in Windham and, a year later, was elected as a Whig to the Connecticut House of Representatives. There he served three terms (1845, 1850, 1858), and in 1858 was speaker of the House. In 1857 he was lieutenant governor under Governor Alexander Holley, a Republican whose election demonstrated the supremacy of that party over the Know-Nothings.

Burnham was elected to Congress in 1859 and reelected in 1861. He opposed efforts by Republican conservatives as well as Democrats to placate Southern leaders, and in December 1861 he voted against the establishment of the House Committee of Thirty-three (one member from each state), which was to seek ways of averting war. Burnham opposed an amendment to the Constitution emanating from this committee that would prevent Congress from interfering with slavery in any state. This proposed amendment, adopted by the House and Senate in March 1861, was never ratified. When Burnham did not seek reelection in 1863, his congressional career ended. After his return to Windham, he was again elected to the Connecticut House and again chosen speaker. He died in Windham on April 11, 1879. Niven, *Connecticut for the Union.*

Joanna D. Cowden

BURNS, William Wallace, *general*, was born in Coshocton, Ohio, on September 3, 1825. He graduated from West Point in 1847 and was commissioned a 2nd lieutenant in the 3rd U.S. Infantry, but saw no combat in the Mexican War. He was promoted to 1st lieutenant in the 5th U.S. Infantry in 1851 and served at posts in Texas and in Florida during the third Seminole War (1855–1858). While stationed at Fort Myers, Burns was appointed depot commissary and quartermaster for his regiment, the beginning of a series of commissary positions that he held for rest of his life. He was appointed chief commissary of subsistence for the "Utah War" of 1857–1858, and was chief commissary for Arkansas and Texas at Fort Smith when the Civil War began.

Escaping internment in Texas, Burns was appointed chief commissary for the Department of Ohio under Brigadier General George B. McClellan (*q.v.*), and served under McClellan in the West Virginia campaign. On September 28, 1861, Burns was named brigadier general of Volunteers and brought to Washington, where he served on various boards and courts martial. On March 13, 1862, he received his first field command when he was appointed commander of the Philadelphia Brigade (the 69th, 71st, 72nd, and 106th Pennsylvania Volunteers). Burns turned out to be a surprisingly good field officer. Although wounded at Savage Station, he continued to command the Philadelphia Brigade throughout the Peninsula campaign. After a lengthy sick leave, he led the 1st Division, IX Corps at Fredericksburg.

In February 1863 Burns refused to report to General William S. Rosecrans (*q.v.*), and on March 6, 1863, resigned his Volunteer commission and reverted to his Regular Army rank of major. He served as chief commissary of subsistence for the Department of the Northwest from March 20, 1863, until the end of the war; during Reconstruction, he was chief commissary to the Military Departments of Georgia, Florida, and the South. Burns retired in 1889 with the rank of colonel and a brigadier general's brevet for gallantry at Savage Station. He died in Beaufort, South Carolina, on April 19, 1892. Banes, *History of the Philadelphia Brigade*; Bates, *History of Pennsylvania Volunteers*, vol. 2; Marvel, *Burnside*.

Allen C. Guelzo

BURNSIDE, Ambrose Everett, *general,* was born in Liberty, Indiana, on May 23, 1824. He graduated in 1847 from West Point, but saw little active service in the Mexican War. After routine postings in garrison duty and on the frontier, he resigned from the Army in October 1853. When he had difficulty in manufacturing a breech-loading rifle he had invented, and fell on hard times, George B. McClellan (*q.v.*) secured "Burn" a job with the Illinois Central Railroad. When the Civil War began, Burnside was named colonel of the 1st Rhode Island; he was an ineffective brigade commander at First Bull Run. He gained prominence—along with the Union Navy—by successfully leading a force that captured lightly defended New Bern, North Carolina, in early 1862. Some of his troops fought with John Pope (*q.v.*) in the Federal defeat at Second Bull Run in August. In command of the right wing of McClellan's Army of the Potomac, Burnside captured Turner's Gap and Fox's Gap at South Mountain on September 14, 1862, but he failed miserably at Antietam, three days later, delaying his futile attacks beyond the "Burnside Bridge" on the Union left.

Despite his accurate protestations of limited ability, Burnside was named by Abraham Lincoln (*q.v.*) to the command of the Army of the Potomac in early November 1862 and led that 122,000-man force to a disastrous defeat—in sixteen separate, piecemeal assaults—at Fredericksburg in mid-December against Robert E. Lee's army of 78,000. Relieved of his command, Burnside headed the Department of the Ohio and successfully withstood James Longstreet's siege of Knoxville, Tennessee. Burnside performed ineptly as a corps commander under George G. Meade (*q.v.*) and Ulysses S. Grant (*q.v.*) in the Overland campaign of 1864, failing especially lamentably in the battle of the Crater at Petersburg in July, after which he resigned his commission.

Despite the fact that almost everyone liked Burnside personally, he revealed himself at Antietam and in 1864 to be unfit as a corps commander and, at Fredericksburg, to be incompetent as an army commander. He later acknowledged Lincoln's wisdom in removing him from command of the Army of the Potomac, although he should never have been entrusted with such a large and vitally important assignment in the first place. After the war Burnside was president of several large companies, a three-time governor of Rhode Island (1866–1869), a mediator in the Franco–Prussian War in 1871, and a U.S. senator from 1874 until his death, on September 13, 1881, in Bristol, Rhode Island. Hassler, *Commanders of the Army of the Potomac*; Marvel, *Burnside.*

Warren W. Hassler, Jr.

BURTON, William, *governor,* was born on October 16, 1789, in rural Sussex county, Delaware. After attending local schools, he graduated from the medical school of the University of Pennsylvania. He then began to practice medicine in Milford, Delaware. He joined the Whig party and was elected sheriff of Kent county in 1830. Following the Mexican War he became a Democrat. He ran unsuccessfully for governor in 1854, but in 1858 he was elected to a four-year term. At the time of the Civil War, he sympathized with the South, but cautiously and reluctantly cooperated with Federal authorities in war measures. He was concerned about Federal encroachment on states' rights and thought the use of Federal troops at polling places in the state in November 1862 was unconstitutional. Some of his political advisers, such as former Governor William Ross, more openly sympathized with the Confederacy. Burton's term ended on January 4, 1863, when he was succeeded by William Cannon (*q.v.*). He returned to Milford and practiced medicine there until his death on August 5, 1866. Hancock, *Delaware During the Civil War.*

Harold B. Hancock

BUTLER, Benjamin Franklin, *general,* was born in Deerfield, New Hampshire, on November 5, 1818. Educated at Lowell High School and Waterville (now Colby) College, he established a flourishing law practice in Lowell, Massachusetts. In politics a Democrat, he was twice elected to the Massachusetts General Court, where he championed the rights of immigrants and labor. At the 1860 Democratic National Convention in Charleston, he cast his vote for Jefferson Davis and subsequently became the Breckinridge candidate for governor.

At the outbreak of the Civil War, Butler was commissioned a brigadier general in the Massachusetts Volunteers, and promptly led his troops to the relief of isolated Washington and the occupation of Baltimore. Promoted to major general, he was sent to Fortress Monroe, where he coined the term "contrabands" for runaway slaves. In 1862, he was given command of the military forces accompanying David G. Farragut's (*q.v.*) naval expedition against New Orleans; after the city's capture, he assumed authority there. Although Butler succeeded in preventing epidemics by rigorous sanitary measures, his stern rule earned him the bitter hatred of the South. He hanged a gambler for tearing down the American flag, issued the notorious General Orders No. 28 (threatening to treat any "Female" annoying his troops as "a woman of the town plying her avocation"), and engaged in so much controversy with foreign consuls that in December he was recalled.

In the meantime, however, Butler had experienced a complete political conversion. Joining the Radical Republicans, he raised one of the first African American military units in the nation. In 1863, he was put in command of the Department of Virginia and North Carolina, and in 1864 of the Army of the James, but his incompetence in the assault on Richmond and his failure to take Fort Fisher led to his final recall in 1865.

After the war, Butler served in Congress from 1867 to 1875 and again from 1877 to 1879. He was one of the managers in the impeachment trial of Andrew Johnson (*q.v.*) and consistently favored measures for the protection of African Americans, including the Civil Rights Act of 1875, for which he was largely responsible. Despite his enthusiastic advocacy of payment of the principal of the national debt in greenbacks, he strongly supported the administration of President Ulysses S. Grant (*q.v.*). After several attempts to become governor of Massachusetts, Butler finally was successful in 1882, after returning to the Democrats. Defeated for reelection one year later, in 1884 he was nominated for the presidency by the People's party, an inflationist antimonopoly group secretly subsidized by the Republicans.

One of the most controversial politicians in nineteenth-century America, Butler was often considered a shameless demagogue ready to advance himself by unsavory means. Notwithstanding his faults, however, he did yeoman work in uplifting the freedmen; he was innovative and anxious to move with the times; and he sympathized with the aspirations of labor in newly industrialized America. He was an able politician who, despite his ruthless reliance on his machine and his dubious financial transactions, contributed materially to several necessary reforms. He died in Washington, D.C., on January 11, 1893. Robertson, *Back Door to Richmond*; Trefousse, *Ben Butler*; West, *Lincoln's Scapegoat General.*

Hans L. Trefousse

BUTTERFIELD, Daniel, *general,* was born on October 31, 1831, in Utica, New York. He graduated from Union College in 1849. On the eve of the Civil War he was a superintendent of the American Express Company and an officer in the New York militia. After Fort Sumter, he was mustered into the Federal service and rose steadily in rank and responsibility: colonel of the 12th New York (May 2, 1861); lieutenant colonel in the Regular Army (May 14, 1861); brigadier general of U.S. Volunteers (September 7, 1861); major general of Volunteers (November 29, 1862); chief of staff, Army of the Potomac (Chancellorsville and Gettysburg campaigns); and chief of staff of the Army of the Cumberland (Chattanooga and the start of the Atlanta campaign). In recognition of his bravery at Gaines' Mill, Congress awarded him the Medal of Honor in 1892.

Butterfield's main legacy endures in his two contributions to American military tradition. First, in response to an order from General Joseph Hooker (*q.v.*), Butterfield devised a system of badges to identify the corps comprising the Army of the Potomac. The distinctive insignia were sewn to the soldier's hats and became marks of unit pride. Second, Butterfield took a special interest in bugle calls. He composed the haunting ''Taps'' (sounded to summon soldiers to bed in camp or fort, and now also to accompany military burials). Butterfield resigned from the Army on March 14, 1870. For the rest of his life he was a prominent figure in Republican politics, public affairs, national and international business, and philanthropy. He died in New York City on July 17, 1901. Castel, *Decision in the West*; Hennessy, *Return to Bull Run.*

Frank J. Wetta

C

CALDWELL, John Curtis, *general*, was born on April 17, 1833, in Lowell, Vermont. He attended Amherst College, became a teacher, and in 1861 was principal of Washington Academy in East Machias, Maine. Caldwell had strong political connections with the Republican party in Maine, which won him a commission as colonel of the 11th Maine, and subsequent promotion to brigadier general of Volunteers. He was assigned to command a brigade in the II Corps of the Army of the Potomac, and saw action in every major battle from the Seven Days through Chancellorsville, except Second Bull Run. Following Chancellorsville, Caldwell was assigned to command the veteran 1st Division, II Corps, by virtue of seniority. He led the division at Gettysburg, where it was severely engaged in the area of the Wheat Field on July 2 and lost 40 percent of its members. Although initially successful, the division was struck in the flank and routed from the field. Winfield Scott Hancock (*q.v.*) investigated the circumstances and was satisfied with Caldwell's performance.

When the Army of the Potomac was reorganized for the 1864 campaign, however, Hancock recommended that Caldwell be relieved. In Hancock's opinion he was not active enough and lacked self-reliance at critical times. He never again led troops in the field. Caldwell was an agreeable man and well liked by nearly all who knew him. As a soldier, he was a brave and competent infantry brigade commander. Although he did well at Gettysburg, the rigors of permanent division command were beyond his abilities. Following the war, Caldwell received many political appointments, including adjutant general of Maine and U.S. consul to Chile, Uruguay, and Costa Rica. He died in Calais, Maine, on

August 31, 1912. Gallagher, *Second Day at Gettysburg*; Pfanz, *Gettysburg: The Second Day.*

D. Scott Hartwig

CALVERT, Charles Benedict, *congressman*, a descendant of colonial proprietors and the son of a wealthy planter, was born in Riverdale, Prince Georges county, Maryland, on August 23, 1808. He received his preparatory education at Bladensburg Academy and graduated from the University of Virginia in 1827. Calvert became one of Maryland's leading agriculturists and helped to form the Farmers' Club in Baltimore, which became the Maryland State Agricultural Society. For many years he served as its president and became a major leader in the establishment of the Maryland Agricultural College (now University of Maryland). As a member of the U.S. Agricultural Society, he was active in promoting the creation of the U.S. Department of Agriculture.

For Calvert, one of Maryland's largest slave owners, the secession crisis was traumatic. Despite his opposition to abolition, he believed that the interest of the Maryland farmer lay with the Union cause. In 1861, Calvert joined the Unionist coalition and defeated the State Rights Convention nominee in his southern Maryland congressional district, which was one of the most pro-Southern areas on the Western Shore. Calvert became a firm supporter of the government, but strongly opposed emancipation and the enlistment of slaves into the army. Division in the Union party cost him reelection to the 38th Congress. Shortly after leaving politics, he died at his home in Riverdale on May 12, 1864. Baker, *Politics of Continuity*; Clark, *Politics in Maryland During the Civil War.*

Richard R. Duncan

CAMERON, Robert Alexander, *general*, was born on February 22, 1828, in Brooklyn, New York. He moved to Indiana in 1842 and graduated from the Indiana Medical College in 1850. He also attended Rush Medical College in Chicago, and for a time practiced in Valparaiso, Indiana. In 1857, Cameron became the publisher of the *Valparaiso Republican*, and at the beginning of the Civil War was serving in the Indiana legislature. He raised a company on a few days' notice and became its captain in the 9th Indiana Volunteers. Later he was a lieutenant colonel in the 19th Indiana, and colonel of the 34th Indiana. After August 11, 1863, he was brigadier general of Volunteers. Cameron participated in the battles at Philippi, Carrick's Ford, Island No. 10, New Madrid, Port Gibson, Memphis, and Vicksburg. In the Red River campaign of 1864 he commanded the 1st and 3rd Divisions of the III Corps, and ultimately the entire corps when it was detailed to the west bank of the Mississippi River to observe Kirby Smith's command.

Cameron was breveted a major general at war's end in recognition of distinguished service in these actions. In 1864, he became district commander at Thibodaux, Louisiana, in the Department of the Gulf. His administration so pleased Louisianans that the state legislature later changed the name of Sabine Parish, in extreme southwest Louisiana, to Cameron Parish. Following the war, Cameron did not return to medicine or publishing, but instead founded the community of Greeley, Colorado. He was prominent in Colorado politics and the economic development of the state until his death in Canon City, Colorado, on March 15, 1894. Cameron Pass in Larimer county is named in his honor. Josephy, *Civil War in the American West.*

Archie P. McDonald

CAMERON, Simon, *Secretary of War, diplomat,* was born on March 8, 1799, in Maytown, Pennsylvania. From the early 1820s, his business and political ventures—the former very much dependent upon the latter—were almost always successful. Cameron moved into journalism, married the daughter of a director of the Bank of Harrisburg, and by 1827 had a fortune of $20,000. Branching out into construction, he received lucrative canal-building, as well as state printing, contracts and moved into railroading, iron manufacturing, and banking. Cameron also proved to be an astute and imaginative politician. On the national level, he supported Andrew Jackson, and on the state level, James Buchanan (*q.v.*). In 1845, aided by Whig votes, Cameron was elected as an insurgent Democrat to the U.S. Senate, where in 1846 he opposed the Walker Tariff (protection was his one consistent political principle) with the only memorable speech of his career. Failing reelection in 1849, he returned to Pennsylvania, where he cultivated a political following. In 1855, Cameron narrowly missed election to the U.S. Senate by a Whig-Nativist coalition; in 1857, running as a Republican, he won, after bribing three Democrats.

When Pennsylvania Republicans, who had backed Cameron for the presidential nomination in 1860, switched to Abraham Lincoln (*q.v.*), they earned Cameron a Cabinet post. As Secretary of War, and despite his business acumen, he was a badly organized administrator. To raise, equip, and supply an army, Cameron had to utilize a department unprepared to handle large undertakings. These difficulties were further complicated by a division of responsibilities between state and national governments. Cameron was personally free of corruption, but his poorly chosen political appointments, his wasteful administration, and his careless letting of contracts offset his achievements.

Charges of inefficiency and corruption, compounded by Cameron's unsavory reputation and his demand that the North recruit African American soldiers, led to his removal in January 1862 and to his exile as minister to Russia. His eclipse was temporary. He returned from Russia in November 1862 to keep his political machine from deteriorating, and in early 1863 he tried bribing Democratic legislators to get back in the Senate; publicity caused his attempt to fail. Cameron conspicuously supported Lincoln's renomination and successfully managed his campaign in Pennsylvania, where he remained the President's chief consultant on patronage. With his election to the U.S. Senate in 1867, his political organization proved itself more formidable than Andrew G. Curtin's (*q.v.*) popularity or Thaddeus Steven's (*q.v.*) prestige. When reelected in 1873, Cameron was the undisputed chief of the ruling party in Pennsylvania. In 1877, he turned over his Senate seat and his machine to his son Don. He died near Maytown, Pennsylvania, on June 26, 1889. Bradley, *Simon Cameron.*

Ari Hoogenboom

CAMPBELL, James Hepburn, *congressman, diplomat*, was born in Williamsport, Pennsylvania, on February 8, 1820. He attended Dickinson College and graduated from its law department in 1841. In 1840, he was a representative to the Whig Young Men's Ratification Convention, and in 1844 was a delegate to the Whig National Convention. In 1854, he was elected to Congress from a district that was largely Democratic, but failed to gain reelection. In 1858, he ran as a Republican and regained the seat, which he held for two terms. He denounced James Buchanan's (*q.v.*) administration for its support of the Lecompton Constitution, and in 1860–1861, he opposed any compromise that would allow the extension of slavery.

In the 37th Congress, Campbell supported the confiscation of Rebel property and emancipation. He also chaired a select committee to determine the route of the transcontinental railroad. Primarily due to his leadership, the committee recommended, and Congress endorsed, the central route. He also supported the high tariff policy that was so vital to Pennsylvania's industrial interests. He did not run for reelection in 1862.

Campbell served as a major in the 25th Pennsylvania Volunteers in 1861, and when Lee invaded Pennsylvania in 1863, he helped to recruit a new volunteer unit of 1,100 men, the 39th Pennsylvania Volunteers. In 1863, Secretary of State William H. Seward (*q.v.*) offered Campbell an appointment to the Court for the Suppression of the Slave Trade. Campbell declined the offer, but in 1864 he accepted an appointment as minister to Sweden and Norway. He held that post until 1867, when he was offered an appointment as minister to Colombia, which he declined. He died in Delaware county, Pennsylvania, on April 12, 1895. *Biographical Encyclopedia of Pennsylvania of the Nineteenth Century*; Davis, *Pennsylvania Politics.*

W. Wayne Smith

CANBY, Edward Richard Sprigg, *general*, was born on November 9, 1817, at Piatt's Landing, Kentucky, and in 1818 moved with his family to Crawfordsville, Indiana. He graduated from West Point in 1839, and subsequently served in the Second Seminole War and in the removal of the Civilized Tribes to Indian Territory. During the Mexican War, he took part in every major action from the siege of Veracruz to the capture of Mexico City. After the war he served in various military posts, including the Utah expedition against the Mormons. In 1861, Canby, then at Fort Defiance, New Mexico, to campaign against the Navajos, was promoted to colonel and commander of the Department of New Mexico. He was to defend the territory against a Confederate force under Henry Hopkins Sibley.

Although defeated at Valverde on February 21, 1862, Canby retained Fort Craig. Part of his command from Fort Union, augmented by Colorado Volunteers, stopped the Confederates at Glorieta on March 28, and destroyed their supply train. Canby now combined his forces and attacked Peralta on April 15. Though he was criticized for not capturing the half-starved Confederate column, Canby realized that the resources of the territory were inadequate to support such a large number of prisoners. His successful defense of New Mexico, which cost Sibley at least one-third of his command, saved the West from Confederate domination.

Canby was named brigadier general on March 31, 1862, and assigned to special advisory duty at the War Department in Washington, D.C. Later he was detached to help suppress the New York draft riots of 1863. On May 7, 1864, he was promoted to major general in command of the Military Division of West Mississippi. Canby helped plan the expedition that resulted in the capture of Mobile on April 12, and of Montgomery on April 27, 1865. He received the surrenders of the last Confederate field armies: those of Richard Taylor at Citronelle, Alabama, on May 4, and of General Kirby Smith on May 26, 1865, at New Orleans. In 1870, he became commander of the Department of Columbia and later the Division of the Pacific. He was murdered by Modoc Indians on April 11, 1873, while engaged in a peace conference with Captain Jack's band near the Lava Beds, Siskiyou county, California. Heyman, *Prudent Soldier.*

Martin Hardwick Hall

CANNON, William, *governor,* was born in Bridgeville, Delaware, on March 15, 1809. Educated in local schools, he became a prominent merchant and landowner, and promoted the construction of the Delaware Railroad into Sussex county. An active Democrat, he served in the Delaware House of Representatives in 1844 and 1846, and was state treasurer in 1851. He attended the Peace Conference in Washington in 1861, and supported the Crittenden Compromise as a way to solve the difficulties between North and South. Perhaps patriotism led him to become a strong supporter of the Republican party, though another explanation might be that he became disenchanted with the Democratic party, whose members upon three occasions had failed to nominate him as governor.

The Union party nominated Cannon for governor in 1862, and he won in a close election. Democrats charged that the presence of Federal troops at many polling places influenced the returns. Cannon and the Democratic legislature frequently quarreled over the cooperation of the state with the Federal government and the refusal of the legislature to support emancipation within the state. Cannon was succeeded by the Democratic presiding officer of the Senate, Gove Saulsbury (*q.v.*), after his sudden death at his home in Bridgeville on March 1, 1865. Hancock, *Delaware During the Civil War.*

Harold B. Hancock

CARLILE, John Snyder, *senator,* was born in Winchester, Virginia, on December 16, 1817. He studied law, and was admitted to the bar in 1840. After establishing his practice at Beverly, [West] Virginia, Carlile served in the Virginia Senate (1847–1851). At the Constitutional Convention of 1850–1851, he championed the right of western counties to proportional representation in the state legislature on the basis of universal white male suffrage. In 1855, he was elected to the U.S. House of Representatives, serving one term. In the Virginia Convention of 1861, Carlile voted against the ordinance of secession and later wrote the "Clarksburg Resolutions," which not only repudiated secession but called for the creation of the state of New Virginia. In the First and Second Wheeling Conventions (May and June 1861), he led the fight for separate statehood that culminated in the creation of the Reorganized Government of Virginia on June 20, 1861, the first major step toward creating the state of West Virginia in 1863.

Carlile, the most prominent and popular of all northwestern Virginia leaders during the secession crisis and early stages of the war, was elected to the 37th Congress in the spring of 1861. After the Lincoln (*q.v.*) administration recognized the Reorganized Government as the de jure state government, Carlile was elected to the U.S. Senate, serving until 1865. As a conservative Union Democrat, he found himself at odds with some of the policies of the administration, especially the suspension of the writ of habeas corpus, arbitrary arrests, and emancipation. When the Republican majority in Congress demanded the ratification of the Willey Amendment (a gradual emancipation proviso included in the West Virginia state constitution) by the electorate as a condition of statehood, Carlile led an unsuccessful fight against it. He was labeled a "Copperhead" by his opponents, and his opposition to the Willey Amendment destroyed his once promising political career. He moved to Frederick, Maryland, where he unsuccessfully attempted to reenter national politics as a champion of the Maryland Democracy. Returning to West Virginia in 1868, Carlile resumed his law practice in Clarksburg. He was nominated by President Ulysses S. Grant (*q.v.*) for a diplomatic post in Sweden, but the Senate did not confirm his appointment. Carlile died in Clarksburg on October 24, 1878. Curry, *House Divided*; Moore, *Banner in the Hills.*

Richard Orr Curry

CARLIN, William Passmore, *general,* was born in Greene county, Illinois, on November 24, 1829. He graduated from West Point in 1850, and served with the 6th U.S. Infantry through the Sioux War (1855–1856), the Cheyenne War (1857), and the Mormon Rebellion (1858). Named captain on March 2, 1861, he was promoted to colonel, 38th Illinois Volunteers, in August. He defeated Jeff Thompson at Fredericktown, Missouri, in October 1861 and pursued Beauregard in Mississippi. His subsequent commands included a brigade in the Army of the Mississippi (June–September 26, 1862) and a brigade in the Army of the Ohio at Perryville. Described by a fellow Illinois officer as "careful, painstaking," and a man with "two o'clock courage," Carlin led a smashing attack on Hardee's lines at Perryville, causing the ultimate failure of Bragg's assault on Don Carlos Buell (*q.v.*).

As brigiadier general, promoted November 29, 1862, Carlin led the 2nd brigade, 1st Division, of Alexander McDowell McCook's (*q.v.*) right wing during the fighting at Knob Gap, Nolensville, and Stones River. In the latter battle, he was forced to retire, taking new positions on the Murfreesboro Pike. He continued his command through Liberty Gap and Chickamauga until October 19, 1863, when he assumed command of the 1st Brigade, 1st Division, XIV Corps at Lookout Mountain and Ringgold Gap. Carlin participated in the action at Buzzard Roost, Resaca, and Kennesaw Mountain, and in the siege of Atlanta. He was the division commander at Jonesboro and, during the campaign in the Carolinas, he commanded the 1st Division, XIV Corps, Army of Georgia. At Bentonville, Carlin's division was in the van of the attack but was forced to turn back in heavy fighting. Breveted major general in both the U.S. Army and the Volunteers, Carlin continued in the Regular Army, assuming command of the Department of Columbia and retiring as a brigadier general. Carlin died near Whitehall, Montana, on October 4, 1903. Barrett, *Sherman's March Through the Carolinas*; Cozzens, *This Terrible Sound.*

Victor Hicken

CARNEY, Thomas, *governor,* was born on August 20, 1824, in Delaware county, Ohio. After becoming a successful wholesale merchant in Cincinnati, in 1858 he removed to Leavenworth, Kansas Territory, where he established a thriving mercantile business. In 1861, he was elected a member of the Kansas legislature as a Republican, and the following year was elected governor, serving creditably in that office until 1865. During this time he organized for border defense against guerrilla raids from Missouri (even paying some companies from his private resources), and in 1864 he committed the entire state militia to the successful repulsion of a large Confederate cavalry raid, led by Sterling Price, into Missouri and eastern Kansas.

In February 1864, Carney was elected U.S. senator from Kansas, but because the election was held prior to the established date in November (and its legality was thus in question), Carney never claimed the seat. He retired to private life in 1865, ran unsuccessfully for Congress, and was again a successful businessman. Carney died in Leavenworth on July 28, 1888. Castel, *Frontier State at War.*

Christopher Phillips

CARR, Eugene Asa, *general,* was born on March 20, 1830, in Concord, New York. He graduated from West Point in 1850, and began a distinguished career of forty-three years, most of it on the frontier in the cavalry. He was involved in several skirmishes with Indians, in one of which (near Limpia, Texas, October 10, 1854) he was severely injured by an arrow, the first of many wounds. He was promoted to captain in 1858, and at the beginning of the Civil War was stationed at Fort Washita in Indian Territory. Sent to join General Nathaniel Lyon's (*q.v.*) command in Missouri, he distinguished himself at the battle of Wilson's Creek and was appointed colonel of the 3rd Illinois Cavalry a few days later. Carr then commanded a brigade in John C. Frémont's (*q.v.*) Army of Southwest Missouri and participated in the pursuit of Confederate General Sterling Price's troops into northern Arkansas.

A highlight of Carr's military career occurred at Pea Ridge. In one of the most important battles west of the Mississippi, Carr commanded a division in General Samuel R. Curtis's (*q.v.*) army. In the fierce fighting around Elk Horn Tavern, on Curtis's right, Carr was wounded three times but refused to leave the field, having his wounds bandaged as he sat on his horse. He later received the Medal of Honor for his gallantry in this action. Appointed brigadier general of Volunteers on March 7, 1862, Carr served briefly as commander of the Army of Southwestern Missouri in the fall of 1862, and of the District of St. Louis until March 1863. In the Vicksburg campaign he led a division of the XIII Corps and took part in the battles at Port Gibson, Champion's Hill, and Big Black River, as well as the assaults on Vicksburg. Afterward, he served in Arkansas, where, in command of a cavalry division, he took part in General Frederick Steele's (*q.v.*) Camden expedition.

Early in 1865, Carr led the 3rd Division of the XVI Corps in General Edward R.S. Canby's (*q.v.*) attack on Mobile, Alabama. He was mustered out of the Volunteer service on January 15, 1866, with the brevet rank of major general, served for a time in North Carolina and Washington, and then returned to the frontier. From 1868 until 1891, Carr served almost continuously in Indian country with the 5th and 6th Cavalry. He was given the Regular Army rank of brigadier general on July 19, 1892, and retired the following year. He died in Washington, D.C., on December 2, 1910. Bearss, *Vicksburg Campaign*, vols. 2, 3; Monaghan, *Civil War on the Western Border*; Shea, *Pea Ridge*.

James J. Hudson

CARRINGTON, Henry Beebee, *general*, was born on March 2, 1824, in Wallingford, Connecticut. He graduated from Yale in 1845, taught school, and entered Yale Law School. In 1848, he moved to Columbus, Ohio, where he practiced law with William Dennison (*q.v.*). Carrington was active in the organization of the Republican party in Ohio, and in 1857 Governor Salmon P. Chase (*q.v.*) recruited him to reorganize the state militia. Carrington was retained as adjutant general when Dennison became governor in 1861. He recruited nine regiments of the Ohio militia to assist General George B. McClellan (*q.v.*) in his western Virginia campaign. In May 1861 he was commissioned a colonel of the 18th U.S. Infantry while retaining the post of Ohio adjutant general.

In mid-1862, Indiana Governor Oliver H.P. Morton (*q.v.*) appointed Carrington to organize and recruit Indiana troops. He retained his Regular Army assignment and avoided field service through the assistance of Governor Morton, who had Federal authorities create a special District of Indiana as Carrington's jurisdiction. Carrington focused on secret political societies in Indiana, especially the Knights of the Golden Circle. He composed an exaggerated report on the subversive work and strength of the society, and in July 1863, at the time of John Hunt Morgan's raid into Ohio and Indiana, charged the Knights with aiding Morgan. In reality, Carrington was drunk at the time of the raid and had to be temporarily removed from duty.

Less than a year later, Carrington charged the Sons of Liberty, another secret society, with a conspiracy to establish a Northwest Confederacy. The "Carrington Report" contended that the group was organized in twelve states; in Indiana alone it had over 30,000 members, and as such posed a threat to civil government. In reality, the report dealt a deathblow to an organization without a following. In both reports, Carrington took liberties with the truth, creating biased and exaggerated accounts of secret society activity. In 1865, he was mustered out of service as a brigadier general of Volunteers and in 1866 returned to the Regular Army for service in the West. He died on October 26, 1912, in Hyde Park, Massachusetts. Klement, *Dark Lanterns*; Reid, *Ohio in the War*, vol. 1.

Frank R. Levstik

CARROLL, Anna Ella, *pamphleteer,* was born near Pocomoke City, Maryland, on August 29, 1815. Her lifelong interest in politics manifested itself in her writings. She was a propagandist of the Know-Nothing party, gave a series of anti-Catholic lectures, and wrote political tracts and a book on the party itself. At the outbreak of the Civil War, Carroll moved to Washington, D.C., where she wrote letters supporting Maryland Governor Thomas Hicks's (*q.v.*) efforts to keep his state in the Union. Her defense of Abraham Lincoln's (*q.v.*) suspension of the writ of habeas corpus was distributed among government officials. Carroll was an effective propagandist, writing pamphlets on such topics as the illegality of secession and the colonization of freed slaves. Although her significance as a political writer is acknowledged, her role as a military strategist is questionable. She claimed that she had planned the Tennessee River strategy used by General Ulysses S. Grant (*q.v.*) to divide the Confederacy in 1862. The details of the story are unclear, but she probably heard the idea from the wife of a river pilot on the Tennessee.

Carroll periodically petitioned Congress to recognize her contribution to the war effort and provide her with adequate financial remuneration. She had some powerful supporters of her claim, including former Assistant Secretary of War Thomas Scott and Senator Benjamin F. Wade (*q.v.*). Feminists like Matilda Joselyn Gage and Mary Livermore (*q.v.*) also bolstered Carroll's cause, seeing her as a woman who was cheated out of her just rewards because of her sex. But there is no real evidence for Carroll's assertions, and Congress never acknowledged her requests. Carroll died on February 19, 1893, in Washington, D.C. Coryell, *Neither Heroine nor Fool*; Greenbie, *My Dear Lady*.

Donna M. DeBlasio

CARROLL, Samuel Sprigg, *general,* was born on September 21, 1832, in Takoma Park, Maryland. He graduated from West Point in 1856, was commissioned in the infantry, and spent most of the antebellum era on the western frontier. Just before the Civil War, he returned to West Point as quartermaster. In December 1861 he took command of the 8th Ohio Volunteers and soon afterward, a brigade in James Shields's division. In contrast with his lackluster division commander, Carroll demonstrated outstanding skill and aggressiveness during the Shenandoah Valley campaign. After recovering from wounds, he served for a short while in the Washington defenses, then joined the Army of the Potomac as a brigade commander, a position he held until again incapacitated by wounds at Spotsylvania. On returning to duty in December 1864, Carroll was assigned to the Department of West Virginia, and later to the Army of the Shenandoah.

Throughout the war, "Sprigg" Carroll consistently vindicated the reputation for valor and skill he had first earned in the Shenandoah Valley. At Gettysburg, for instance, he conducted a successful night attack in a murky situation where a single mistake on his part would have spelled disaster. Not surprisingly, Carroll emerged from the conflict with six brevets. He was a soldier's soldier. After the war, he remained in the Army until forced to retire for disability in 1869. He died in Washington, D.C., on January 28, 1893. Rhea, *Battle of the Wilderness;* Tucker, *Hancock the Superb.*

James L. Morrison, Jr.

CASEY, Samuel Lewis, *congressman,* was born in Union county, Kentucky, on February 12, 1821. Though he had little formal education, he early demonstrated an interest in business. As a youth he began working as a surveyor but soon developed an interest in geology that enabled him to become an early entrepreneur in Kentucky's developing coal industry. Casey's political career was short. He entered the Kentucky legislature in 1860 and served for two years. In March 1862 he was elected to the U.S. House of Representatives as a Unionist, to complete the unexpired term of Henry C. Burnett (*q.v.*), who had been expelled from Congress.

In 1863, Casey declined the position of U.S. attorney for Kentucky in order to reenter the business world. In 1864, however, he became Abraham Lincoln's (*q.v.*) personal emissary to Mississippi, and later served as military governor of that state. Although a strong Unionist, Casey did not consider himself a politician. He retired from politics at the first opportunity, to resume his business interests in Kentucky. He died in St. Joseph, Missouri, on August 25, 1902. Collins, *History of Kentucky,* vol. 2; *History of Union County, Kentucky.*

Marion B. Lucas

CASEY, Silas, *general,* was born on July 12, 1807, in East Greenwich, Rhode Island. He graduated from West Point in 1826, and served with the 2nd Infantry along the Great Lakes. From 1837 to 1842, he fought in the Second Seminole

War, during which he contracted the swamp fevers that weakened his health for the rest of his life. He earned a distinguished combat record in the Mexican War. During Winfield Scott's (*q.v.*) advance on Mexico City, Casey received two brevets for gallantry and a severe wound during the assault on Chapultepec. After recovering from the wound, he met with boards of officers in the early 1850s to evaluate weapons and tactics. The tactics board endorsed a two-volume work written by Captain William J. Hardee to replace the manual by Winfield Scott.

Casey was promoted to lieutenant colonel in 1855 and posted to the new 9th Infantry on the West Coast; in 1861 he became its colonel. He was promoted to brigadier general of Volunteers on August 31, 1861, and journeyed east to command a division. Meanwhile, Hardee had resigned to join the Confederate Army, and the War Department did not want to rely upon a tactical manual written by a Confederate. Therefore, Casey revised Hardee's work and issued the three-volume *Infantry Tactics* (1862), which became the official manual of the Union forces.

At the battle of Fair Oaks (Seven Pines) on May 31, 1862, a Confederate division led by A.P. Hill smashed Casey's 3rd Division of the IV Corps, under Erasmus D. Keyes (*q.v.*). Although Casey was promoted to major general of Volunteers and brevet brigadier general in the Regular Army (May 31, 1862), he never held another field command. Instead, he commanded a brigade, and then a division, in the defenses of Washington, D.C. In addition to supervising the training of recruits, he sat as president of a board that examined applicants for commissions in the new regiments of black soldiers. Casey issued a revised edition of his manual, *Infantry Tactics for Colored Troops* (1863). He also served on the controversial court martial of Major General Fitz John Porter (*q.v.*). Casey left the Volunteers on August 24, 1865, and retired from the Army on July 8, 1868. He died in Brooklyn, New York, on January 22, 1882. Cornish, *Sable Arm*; Glatthaar, *Forged in Battle*.

Joseph G. Dawson III

CATRON, John, *Supreme Court justice*, was born in Pennsylvania around 1786, and was a resident of Tennessee when he served in the War of 1812 with Andrew Jackson. Despite a lack of formal education, he was admitted to the bar shortly after the war and became a successful lawyer in Nashville. He served on the Tennessee Supreme Court (1824–1835) and was appointed by President Jackson to the U.S. Supreme Court on March 3, 1837. Catron was part of the orthodox states' rights contingent on the Court, but in decisions involving fugitive slaves, he was equally adamant in sustaining national authority. As the Court listened to the arguments in the *Dred Scott* case, he kept his friend and political ally President James Buchanan (*q.v.*) informed about the deliberations. Catron broke with his Southern brethren in asserting that Congress had the power to govern the national territories, but rather lamely argued that the terms of the Louisiana Purchase prevented Congress from abolishing slavery there.

In March 1861, Catron courageously attempted to hold circuit court in Tennessee, but a vigilante group persuaded him to transfer his activities to Kentucky. Although he issued writs of habeas corpus for prisoners arrested by military authorities in Kentucky, he did not protest when the prisoners were transferred to New York. His uncompromising Unionism did not translate into complete support for the policies of the Lincoln (*q.v.*) administration; for example, in the Prize Cases, he joined the dissenters in declaring Lincoln's blockade proclamation unconstitutional. He died in Washington, D.C., on May 30, 1865. Silver, *Lincoln's Supreme Court*; Swisher, *The Taney Period.*

George C. Rable

CHAMBERLAIN, Jacob Payson, *congressman,* was born on August 1, 1802, in Dudley, Massachusetts. In 1807, he moved with his parents to New York, where he attended public schools, and then farmed and taught school in Varick. He later settled in Seneca Falls, where he continued farming and operated flour mills, malt houses, the Phoenix Woolen Mills, and the first savings bank in Seneca Falls. Chamberlain's position as a successful businessman led him into politics, and he served locally as a village supervisor and member of the board of education before being elected to the New York State Assembly in 1859. A moderate Republican, Chamberlain had not yet completed his first term in the Assembly when he won a seat in the House of Representatives in November 1860. He served on the Agriculture Committee and was not a candidate for renomination. Chamberlain died October 5, 1878, in Seneca Falls. Lanman, *Biographical Annals; Portrait and Biographical Record of Seneca and Schuyler Counties.*

Lori A. Lisowski

CHAMBERLAIN, Joshua Lawrence, *general,* was born in Brewer, Maine, on September 8, 1828. He was educated at a military academy in Ellsworth, Maine, graduated from Bowdoin College in 1852, and completed a course of study at Bangor Theological Seminary in 1855. Abandoning the idea of the ministry, he joined the Bowdoin faculty in 1855, and taught a variety of subjects. Chamberlain became lieutenant colonel of the 20th Maine in August 1862. He fought in twenty-four engagements, large and small. At Gettysburg, on July 2, 1863, as colonel of the 20th Maine, he led his regiment in a bayonet charge down the side of Little Round Top, captured twice his regimental strength, helped save that crucial position, and subsequently won the Congressional Medal of Honor ''for daring heroism and great tenacity.''

A supposedly mortal wound at Petersburg in 1864 brought Chamberlain a battlefield promotion to brigadier general from General Ulysses S. Grant (*q.v.*); he recovered to preside over the surrender ceremony at Appomattox. Chamberlain ended the Civil War as a brevet major general, declined the offer of a Regular Army colonelcy, and returned to Maine, where the Republican party elected him governor for four terms (1867–1871). From 1871 to 1883, Chamberlain was president of Bowdoin, also teaching there from 1874 to 1879 and from 1883 to 1885. As militia major general, he helped avert a virtual civil war that threatened Maine because of a disputed gubernatorial election during the winter of 1878–1879. During the postwar years, he wrote widely on Civil War and Maine history, and held important offices in a variety of veterans' organizations. He also served as surveyor of the port of Portland, Maine, from 1900 until 1914.

Chamberlain is one of the finest examples of the talented citizen–soldier of the Civil War. Completely inexperienced in military affairs before the war, he managed, by dint of hard work, courageous example, and selfless devotion to the Union cause, to become an outstanding leader. Chamberlain died in Portland on February 24, 1914, as a result of the most serious of the six wounds he had received during the war. Trulock, *In the Hands of Providence*; Wallace, *Soul of the Lion*.

H. Draper Hunt

CHANDLER, Zachariah, *senator*, was born in Bedford, New Hampshire, on December 10, 1813. After attending the Bedford common schools and the academies at Pembroke and Derry, he spent a short time as a teacher and business clerk. In 1833, he moved to Detroit, where he built the most profitable wholesale establishment in Michigan. In 1848, Chandler supported Whig presidental candidate Zachary Taylor, who was running against Michigan Democrat Lewis Cass. He was elected mayor of Detroit for 1851, and ran unsuccessfully for governor the following year. In 1854, he joined a group of anti-Nebraska Whigs to form the Republican party at Jackson, Michigan, and in 1856 defeated the popular Cass for the U.S. Senate; he retained his seat until 1875. Chandler early won a reputation as an uncompromising foe of the Democrats through his bitter attacks against the Lecompton constitution. He was also an ardent expansionist, supporting the annexation of Cuba, Santo Domingo, and Canada. He controlled Michigan through the patronage system and satisfied the state's need for internal improvements as the chairman of the Committee on Commerce.

The Civil War catapulted Chandler into national prominence as a leading Radical. He monitored President Abraham Lincoln's (*q.v.*) handling of the war through the Committee on the Conduct of the War. He opposed Andrew Johnson (*q.v.*) over the pardoning of former Confederates and stood firm for the President's impeachment. Chandler's close association with President Ulysses S. Grant (*q.v.*) brought the loss of his Senate seat in 1875 to a Democrat, Isaac Christiancy. Grant immediately appointed his friend Secretary of the Interior. During the two years Chandler held this office, he surprised the reform elements of his party by his firm stand against corruption in the fraud-ridden bureaus relating to Indian, pension, and land affairs. Chandler was Republican national chairman in 1868 and 1876. The election of Rutherford B. Hayes (*q.v.*) was a disappointment to him, however, and he retired to Michigan until his return to the Senate in 1879. Chandler died in Chicago on November 1, 1879. Bogue, *Earnest Men*; George, *Zachariah Chandler.*

Emily George, R.S.M.

CHANLER, John Winthrop, *congressman,* was born in New York City on September 14, 1826. Following graduation from Columbia College in 1847, he traveled extensively in Europe, studied the law, and was admitted to the bar. He served in the New York State Assembly in 1858–1859 and was elected as a Democrat to the 38th, 39th, and 40th Congresses. In 1864, he voted against a resolution supporting the use of blacks as soldiers. He believed that the Freedmen's Bureau was a Republican attempt to force the South into the Republican party. He voted against the 14th Amendment (1866) and the 1867 Reconstruction Act, which imposed military rule on the South.

Chanler's major importance was at the local level. Deeply involved in the struggle for domination of New York City politics between Tammany Hall and Fernando Wood's (*q.v.*) rival Mozart Hall, he worked hard for Tammany's eventual victory. Chanler opposed William Marcy Tweed, and "the Boss" exacted revenge when the Tammany machinery destroyed Chanler's chances for reelection in 1868. With Tweed's imprisonment and fall from power after the election of 1871, Chanler returned to influence inside Tammany Hall. He was a Sachem and chairman of its General Committee until 1875, when he retired for health reasons. He died in Rhinebeck, New York, on October 19, 1877. *BDUSC.*

Richard W. Brown, Jr.

CHASE, Salmon Portland, *senator, Secretary of the Treasury, Chief Justice,* was born in Cornish, New Hampshire, on January 13, 1808. He lived for several years with his uncle, Philander Chase, Episcopal bishop of Ohio. While in Ohio, Chase was confirmed in the church, and throughout his life retained a strong religious faith. He graduated from Dartmouth College in 1826, moved to Washington, read law with William Wirt, and was admitted to the bar in 1829. For the next twenty years he combined the practice of law in Cincinnati with a commitment to the antislavery movement and gained much publicity for his controversial defense of fugitive slaves. Rather than immediate abolition, he advocated the divorce of the Federal government from any responsibility for sanctioning or protecting slavery. Chase left the Whigs for the Liberty party and was among its most active leaders in the 1840s. He helped lead the Liberty men into the more moderate Free Soil party, and at the Buffalo convention of 1848, he was instrumental in drafting the party's platform and selecting Martin Van Buren as its candidate.

In 1849, Chase won a seat in the U.S. Senate in an election that brought Free Soilers and Democrats together in a coalition of convenience. Chase never viewed political parties as ends in themselves, but rather as a means to his personal and antislavery goals. Thus he attempted to lead the Free Soilers into a coalition with Northern Democrats. With the introduction of the Kansas–

Nebraska Bill in 1854, he wrote the "Appeal of the Independent Democrats," which stressed his hopes for a Democratic party free from proslavery control.

When the Republican party emerged, Chase was among its early supporters, and in 1855 was elected the first Republican governor of Ohio. He served two terms while observing the deepening sectional conflict and carefully preparing himself for the White House. A candidate for the presidency in 1856 and 1860, he failed to receive the united support of Ohio Republicans, many of whom still remembered his controversial role in the Senate election of 1849. Chase actively supported Abraham Lincoln (*q.v.*) in 1860 and was rewarded by being named Secretary of the Treasury. Inheriting a difficult set of financial conditions, he dealt with the problems in a competent way. Reluctantly he accepted greenbacks as legal tender to help finance the war, and with the help of Senator John Sherman (*q.v.*) of Ohio, proposed reform measures that were embodied in the National Bank Act of 1863.

Throughout the war, Chase urged a policy of emancipation and was an important influence in moving the President toward the Emancipation Proclamation. He also took a special interest in the plight of the freedmen, urging that they be accepted as soldiers and be granted the right to vote. Chase sought a role in military policy decisions, and was constantly in conflict with congressmen, generals, and the President. Despite his close working relationship with Lincoln, he permitted his supporters to seek his nomination for President in 1864. This challenge, plus differences over appointments and military policies, led Lincoln to accept his resignation in June 1864. Nevertheless, at the end of that year, the President appointed Chase Chief Justice.

In his remaining years, Chase was not always at his best. At odds with Republican leaders over Reconstruction policies, he fought their efforts to deny him a major role in the impeachment trial of Andrew Johnson. His desire for the presidency remained constant, and while on the bench he broke with his party and actively sought the Democratic nomination in 1868. His devotion to principle remained strong, however; his advocacy of black suffrage cost him his new party's nomination. Chase never attained his primary goal of the presidency. A self-righteous and opinionated man, he was puritanical and lacked a sense of humor. Ambition for personal political power was so obvious that his enemies were many and his constant friends few. Nevertheless, he maintained a moral courage that helped push the country toward eventual emancipation and greater equality. He died in New York City on May 7, 1873. Blue, *Salmon P. Chase*; Chase, *Inside Lincoln's Cabinet*.

Frederick J. Blue

CHEEVER, George Barrell, *clergyman, abolitionist,* was born on April 17, 1807, in Hallowell, Maine. In 1833, after attending Bowdoin College and Andover Seminary, he was ordained a Congregational preacher. Although he endorsed abolition, he chose to champion more conservative causes, such as capital punishment and compulsory Bible reading in public schools, and to assail Unitarianism and intemperance. The Compromise of 1850 brought Cheever back into the antislavery movement. From the pulpit of the Church of the Puritans in New York City, he directed his considerable oratorical skills against Southern policies, and after 1854 he became a leading proponent of the Higher Law doctrine. He delivered antislavery sermons throughout New England and Pennsylvania and as far west as Milwaukee. Cheever preached and wrote in defense of John Brown (q.v.). With his brother Henry, he helped found the Church Anti-Slavery Society, which during the Civil War pressed politicians to take abolitionist positions.

In 1860–1861, Cheever spoke in England and Scotland to further support for the Union cause, and upon his return he strongly urged emancipation as a war aim. He addressed a joint session of the wartime Pennsylvania legislature on the subject, and at the invitation of Owen Lovejoy (q.v.), George W. Julian (q.v.), Thaddeus Stevens (q.v.), and others, preached antislavery sermons in the House of Representatives and the Smithsonian Institution. He regarded Abraham Lincoln's (q.v.) policies toward slavery and Reconstruction as inadequate, and supported John C. Frémont's (q.v.) presidential candidacy in 1864. He finally abandoned both Lincoln and Frémont, and endorsed the movement to hold a new Republican nominating convention at Cincinnati. After Frémont withdrew, Cheever still refused to support Lincoln. He opposed the 14th Amendment as a "robbery of the colored race." In 1867, he retired from his New York pastorate and move to Englewood, New Jersey, where he died on October 1, 1890. Smith, *Revivalism*; York, *Cheever.*

Merton L. Dillon

CLARK, Ambrose Williams, *congressman*, was born on February 19, 1810, near Cooperstown, New York. While receiving a common school education, he worked in a Cooperstown printing office. When he became of age, Clark began publishing the *Otsego Republican.* In 1836, he established and published the *Northern Journal* in Lewis county, and in 1844 the *Northern New York Journal* at Watertown. He was elected to the 37th Congress in 1860 and reelected in 1862. Clark was a Radical on Southern issues and used his position on the Committee on Printing to expedite the dissemination of Republican tracts. In 1865, President Abraham Lincoln (q.v.) appointed Clark consul at Valparaiso, Chile. He also served as chargé d'affaires at Santiago, Chile, during the absence of Minister Judson Kilpatrick in 1869. Clark died in Watertown, New York, on October 13, 1887. Bogue, "William Parker Cutler's Congressional Diary," *Civil War History*; Lanman, *Biographical Annals.*

Lori A. Lisowski

CLARK, Daniel, *senator*, was born on October 24, 1809, in Stratham, New Hampshire. He graduated from Dartmouth in 1834, studied for the bar, and opened a practice in Manchester, New Hampshire, in 1839. He served five terms as a Whig in the state legislature, and in 1855 he sought election to the U.S.

Senate. He lost to James Bell, who died in office two years later. Clark—now a Republican with a strong statewide party behind him—was elected to fill the unexpired term, and reelected in 1860. Clark answered the Crittenden Compromise with substitute resolutions obnoxious to Southern senators. Republicans embraced his resolutions, effectively derailing the peace process and bringing upon Clark the wrath of congressional moderates. He resisted Andrew Johnson's (*q.v.*) administration, opposing all of Johnson's constitutional amendments. That provoked some resentment in his home state, which was sliding back into the conservative camp.

In 1866, Clark sought reelection to the senate, contrary to the system of rotation in office that held a firm grip on the New Hampshire legislature. That same legislature had recently refused to reelect John P. Hale (*q.v.*), and although Clark was second only to Hale as the Granite State's most prominent politician he, too, went down to defeat. Perhaps wishing to be rid of a perennial obstructionist, President Johnson offered Clark a position as judge of the Federal District Court in Concord before his term in the Senate expired. Clark resigned to accept the appointment and held that office until his death. Clark is remembered in New Hampshire for his refusal to accept the tradition of rotation in office. At the national level he is largely forgotten, except for his scuttling of the Crittenden Compromise. He died in Manchester, New Hampshire, on January 2, 1891. McClintock, *History of New Hampshire*; Welles, *Diary*, vols. 1, 2.

William Marvel

CLARKE, Freeman, *congressman,* was born in Troy, New York, on March 22, 1809. In 1837, he began his banking career as cashier at the Bank of Orleans in Albion, New York; in 1845, he moved to Rochester, where he helped to found several banks and a telegraph company. He was also involved with railroads in the area, and was a director of several banks in New York City. Clarke's statewide business reputation was reflected in his political prominence. In 1850, he was vice president of the state Whig convention, but made an early shift from the dying Whig party to the new Republican party. He was chosen vice president of the state's first Republican convention in 1854. As a former Whig who was interested in business matters, Clarke represented the more conservative wing of the Republican party. His career at the national level began with his election to the 38th Congress. Abraham Lincoln (*q.v.*) appointed him Comptroller of the Currency in 1865, in which capacity he served until 1867. He reappeared on the national scene as a representative in the 42nd and 43rd Congresses. He died in Rochester, New York, on June 24, 1887. Peck, *History of Rochester.*

Richard W. Brown, Jr.

CLAY, Brutus Junius, *congressman,* was born on July 1, 1808, in Richmond, Kentucky. His father, Green Clay (a second cousin of Henry Clay), was one of the wealthiest men in the state. After attending the common schools, young Clay was taught by tutors before completing his education at Centre College. He was active in agricultural pursuits for most of his public life. After being elected to the Kentucky legislature on the Union ticket in 1860, in August 1861 Clay saw one of his sons leave home to serve as an officer in the Confederate Army. The death of John J. Crittenden (*q.v.*) in 1863 forced the Union Democrats of Kentucky's 7th District to select his replacement. Clay was nominated, and was elected to the 38th Congress in August. Composed of former Whigs and War Democrats, the Union Democrats of Kentucky fought for the "Union As It Was." In this respect, Clay, unlike his famous younger brother, the fiery abolitionist Cassius M. Clay (*q.v.*), represented the views of the majority of Kentuckians.

Convinced that the Democrats were reluctant to crush the rebellion, Clay initially allied himself with congressional Republicans on most issues related to the war effort. However, as a large slave owner, he denounced the Emancipation Proclamation, which he felt wrongfully deprived loyal Southerners of their property. He was particularly vocal in his opposition to the creation of the Freedmen's Bureau and the enrollment of African Americans in the Union Army. Clay returned to the Democratic fold in 1864, campaigned for George B. McClellan (*q.v.*), and opposed the passage of the 13th Amendment. He sought a second term in 1865 but failed to win the nomination. Returning to Auvergne, his estate in Bourbon county, Clay resumed the life of a gentleman farmer. He died near Paris, Kentucky, on October 11, 1878. Hood, "The Union and Slavery," *Register of the Kentucky Historical Society*; Kleber, *Kentucky Encyclopedia.*

James M. Prichard

CLAY, Cassius Marcellus, *abolitionist, general, diplomat*, was born on October 19, 1810, in White Hall, near Lexington, Kentucky. A son of a prominent slaveholder, Clay graduated from Yale College in 1832. First elected to the Kentucky legislature as a Whig in 1835, his outspoken opposition to slavery led to his defeat for reelection in 1841. Thereafter, Clay increased his contacts with Northern abolitionists, and in 1845 established in Lexington an antislavery newspaper named the *True American.* His writings, speeches, and near martyrdom when a proslavery mob attacked his newspaper in August 1845 made him a hero of the antislavery movement. Clay's service in 1846, in what many regarded as a proslavery war against Mexico, briefly estranged him from other antislavery activists. By 1849, however, he had regained his standing by leading an unsuccessful effort to place a gradual abolition clause in the Kentucky constitution.

Clay promoted the establishment of the Republican party in 1856, identified with that party's Radical antislavery wing, and faced violent opposition to his efforts to organize the party in Kentucky. For most of the Civil War years he served as President Abraham Lincoln's (*q.v.*) ambassador to Russia. During a brief return to the United States in 1862, Clay pressured Lincoln to make emancipation a war aim. On April 11, 1862, he was commissioned major general of

Volunteers, but saw only limited service. He is more significant for the encouragement he gave to the antislavery movement, and the fear he engendered among slavery's defenders before the war, than for his role in the war itself. Following the end of his ambassadorial service in 1869, Clay became disillusioned with Republican Reconstruction policies. He died in White Hall on July 22, 1903. Smiley, *Lion of White Hall.*

Stanley Harrold

CLEMENTS, Andrew Jackson, *congressman,* was born on December 23, 1832, in Clementsville, Tennessee. He received a common school education, attended Burritt College, and upon completion of his medical studies, began a practice in Lafayette, Tennessee. Clements opposed secession and ran for the 37th Congress on the Union ticket. Both he and his Confederate opponent claimed victory in the 4th District on August 1, 1861, and set out to take their seats in Washington and Richmond, respectively. The validity of Clement's election was challenged by members of the Republican party, and his case was referred to the Committee on Elections. Clements took his seat on January 13, 1862, and served until the expiration of his term on March 3, 1863.

Clements joined the Union Army as a surgeon with the 1st Tennessee Mounted Infantry, which was organized during the winter of 1863–1864. The regiment served in middle Tennessee, guarding the Nashville and Chattanooga Railroad. Clements reentered politics after the war and served in the Tennessee legislature (1866–1867). He subsequently returned to his medical practice and eventually established a school to provide greater educational opportunities for the people of the Cumberland highlands. He died on November 7, 1913, in Glasgow, Kentucky. Fertig, *Secession and Reconstruction of Tennessee*; Patton, *Unionism and Reconstruction in Tennessee.*

James M. Prichard

CLIFFORD, Nathan, *Supreme Court justice,* was born on August 18, 1803, in Rumney, New Hampshire. After admission to the New Hampshire bar in 1827, he settled in Newfield, Maine. In the Maine legislature and the U.S. House (1839–1843), he was a fervent Jacksonian, in favor of state banking and opposed to a protective tariff, federal financing of internal improvements, and abolition. He was Attorney General in President James K. Polk's Cabinet, a peace commissioner, and American minister to Mexico. After he returned to Portland, Maine, and private practice in 1849, his political career foundered even as his party loyalty held firm. In 1857, President James Buchanan (*q.v.*) rewarded Clifford for supporting his Kansas policies with an appointment to the Supreme Court, but his lackluster legal background and his doughface politics made confirmation a very close call.

The Civil War had little impact on Clifford's strict constructionism. He labeled secession a ''wicked heresy'' but was unwilling to accept an expanded interpretation of the war powers in the Prize Cases. As a circuit judge, Clifford issued a writ of habeas corpus for a prisoner arrested by the military for treasonable correspondence with the Confederacy. However, when the writ could not be delivered, he refused to press the issue beyond lamenting the Lincoln (*q.v.*) administration's defiance of the Federal courts. His votes on Reconstruction questions were equally conservative, and he defended state regulation of railroads against Federal encroachment. Clifford died in Washington, D.C., on July 25, 1881. William Gillette, "Nathan Clifford," in Friedman, *Justices of the U.S. Supreme Court*, vol. 2, pp. 963–988; Silver, *Lincoln's Supreme Court*.

George C. Rable

COBB, Amasa, *congressman, general,* was born on September 27, 1823, in Crawford county, Illinois. He moved to Wisconsin in 1842 and began preparing for a career in law. After serving in the Mexican War as a private in the Illinois Volunteers, he returned to Wisconsin and set up a law practice in Mineral Point. Cobb was elected Iowa county district attorney in 1850 as a Whig; in 1855 he entered the state Senate as a Republican. He was also Wisconsin's adjutant general (1855–1860), and was speaker of the state Assembly when the Civil War began. Cobb was instrumental in raising troops for the 5th Wisconsin Volunteers and was commissioned its first colonel. He saw action at Williamsburg and Antietam, and, while still in the field, was elected in 1862 to the House of Representatives, a seat he held until 1871.

Cobb was appointed chairman of the Committee on Enrolled Bills, a job that required him to deliver to the President every successful measure that originated in the House. On Reconstruction issues, Cobb usually voted with the Radicals and supported the impeachment of President Andrew Johnson (*q.v.*). While Congress was adjourned in the autumn of 1864, Cobb helped to raise another regiment, the 43rd Wisconsin. For the remainder of the war he held two government positions, congressman and colonel. He was mustered out of the service in June 1865 as brigadier general. In 1871, Cobb moved to Lincoln, Nebraska, and in 1873 was appointed its mayor. He was elected an associate justice of Nebraska's Supreme Court (1878–1892) and for four years was chief justice. He died in Los Angeles on July 5, 1905. *History of Iowa County, Wisconsin.*

Michael J. McManus

COBB, George Thomas, *congressman,* was born in Morristown, New Jersey, on October 13, 1813. Although orphaned in childhood and having little opportunity for schooling, he amassed a fortune in the iron business. A "free trade Whig" with antislavery proclivities, Cobb became a Democrat during the 1850s. Democratic factionalism led party managers in 1860 to turn to Cobb, who supported efforts to create a statewide fusion electoral ticket of Breckinridge, Bell, and Douglas supporters. He was elected to the House by a majority of about 1,000 votes. Cobb was recognized as the most forthright supporter of the war effort among New Jersey Democrats in Congress in 1861 and 1862, and thereby outraged the increasingly powerful Peace faction of his party.

When he refused in October 1862 to run on a platform challenging the constitutionality of the Emancipation Proclamation, Cobb was denied renomination. There were rumors that he could have had the Union–Republican nomination, but he gave grudging support to the strongly antiadministration Democratic nominee, Andrew J. Rogers (*q.v.*). Cobb became a Republican in 1863 and was twice elected to the state Senate, in 1865 and 1868. He was a leader of the movement to enact black suffrage in New Jersey, but severe Republican losses on this issue in the 1867 state elections delayed equal suffrage until implementation of the 15th Amendment. After 1865, Cobb served as mayor of Morristown and as state senator from Morris county. He died in a railroad accident near Allegheny, Virginia, on August 6, 1870. Knapp, *New Jersey Politics.*

Daniel W. Crofts

COBURN, Abner, *governor*, was born on March 22, 1803, in Skowhegan, Maine. He worked on his father's farm and snatched what education he could at the district school and from a few terms at Bloomfield Academy. From 1825 to 1830, he was a surveyor, then joined his father and a younger brother in founding E. Coburn & Sons, a land-buying and lumbering firm on the banks of the Kennebec River. Ultimately, the firm became Maine's biggest landowner. Coburn also bought extensive timber acreage in Wisconsin and received 50,000 acres through his connection with the Northern Pacific Railroad.

Throughout the Kennebec Valley, the Coburn brothers' name became synonymous with fair dealing and help in hard times. Coburn was active in Maine railroads and banking. He cast his first vote for John Quincy Adams for President in 1824. Later he became a Whig and won three terms in the Maine House. He helped Anson P. Morrill (*q.v.*) found Maine's Republican party, and held a seat on the party's executive council under governors Morrill, Hannibal Hamlin (*q.v.*), and Joseph H. Williams. Israel Washburn, Jr. (*q.v.*), defeated Coburn for the Republican gubernatorial nomination in 1860 but made way for him in 1863.

As governor, Coburn ran an honest, businesslike administration, refusing to play politics with appointments and contracts. He loyally supported President Abraham Lincoln (*q.v.*) and the war effort. But his unpopularity with hungry politicos, coupled with the decision of Maine's jittery Republican leadership to nominate a War Democrat for governor, cost Coburn the renomination customary for Maine governors. He never held important elective office again. When he died in Skowhegan on January 4, 1885, he capped a lifetime of generosity by donating over $1 million to a variety of religious, educational, and charitable institutions. Hesseltine, *Lincoln's War Governors*; Williams, *Life of Abner Coburn.*

H. Draper Hunt

COCHRANE, John, *general*, was born on August 27, 1813, in Palatine, New York. He graduated in 1831 from Hamilton College, was admitted to the bar in 1834, and established a law practice in upstate New York. In 1846, Cochrane moved to New York City, where he became an important figure in legal and political circles. A "soft" Tammany Democrat, he was appointed in 1853 by President Franklin Pierce to the politically sensitive position of surveyor of the port in the New York City Customhouse. Four years later, Cochrane became a Tammany Representative to the 35th Congress, and was reelected to the 36th. In 1860, he served as a Stephen A. Douglas (*q.v.*) delegate to the Charleston and Baltimore conventions, and played a key role in forging a fusion state Democratic presidential ticket. Despite these efforts at party harmony, Cochrane became a victim of Tammany's conflict with Mozart Hall and lost his congressional seat.

When the Civil War began, Cochrane reassessed his political loyalties. At first a War Democrat, he shifted to Unionism before joining the Republican party. His military career began when he raised the 65th New York Volunteers and was commissioned a colonel on June 11, 1861. The regiment fought in the Peninsula campaign, where Cochrane was cited for bravery. On July 17, 1862, he was promoted to brigadier general and led his command until Antietam. Forced to resign because of physical disabilities on February 25, 1863, he returned to New York, and in the fall of 1863 was elected state attorney general. Cochrane had advocated the enlistment and arming of African American troops, a position that won the approval of many Radical Republicans and in 1864 brought him nomination for the vice presidency on the Independent Republican national ticket.

At war's end, Cochrane reestablished his law practice and supported President Andrew Johnson (*q.v.*). Now considered a maverick by both Democrats and Republicans, he backed Ulysses S. Grant (*q.v.*) in 1868, then became a leader of the Liberal Republican movement and was instrumental in Horace Greeley's (*q.v.*) nomination for President in 1872. He held a number of minor patronage and political offices until he died in New York City on February 7, 1898. Alexander, *Political History of the State of New York*, vol. 2; Mushkat, *Reconstruction of the New York Democracy.*

Jerome Mushkat

COFFROTH, Alexander Hamilton, *congressman,* was born on May 18, 1828, in Somerset county, Pennsylvania. After studying law, he was admitted to the bar in February 1851. He was a delegate to several Democratic state conventions, and in 1860 and 1872 was a delegate to the Democratic National Convention. In 1862, he ran as a Democrat for the 38th Congress, narrowly defeating the Union party candidate, Edward McPherson (*q.v.*), by 550 votes. Coffroth was active for a first-term representative, channeling most of his energies into the debates surrounding conscription and the abolition of slavery. His primary concern focused on the question of substitutes, but regardless of the final form the legislation took, Coffroth voted consistently against conscription. Initially, Coffroth opposed emancipation, charging that Republican partisanship had precipitated the Civil War and that the proposed 13th Amendment would cause a mass migration of free blacks to the North.

When the Wade–Davis Bill, which contained an abolition clause, came before the House, Coffroth voted against it. Less than a year later, however, he and several other House Democrats voted in favor of the 13th Amendment and helped provide the two-thirds' vote necessary for its passage. According to the initial election returns, Coffroth had been reelected to the 39th Congress by seventy-three votes. He took his seat February 19, 1866, but on July 18, 1866, lost it to Republican William H. Koontz, who had successfully contested the election. He was elected to the 46th Congress and resumed his law practice in Somerset at the completion of his term. He died in Markleton, Pennsylvania, on September 2, 1906. Cox, *Politics, Principles, and Prejudice.*

Philip J. Avillo, Jr.

COLE, Cornelius, *congressman, senator,* was born on September 17, 1822, in Lodi, New York. Following his graduation from Wesleyan University in 1847, he studied law in the office of former New York Governor William H. Seward (*q.v.*), with whom he established a long and influential friendship. In 1849, he became a miner in El Dorado county, California, but sold his claim and returned to the practice of law in San Francisco and Sacramento. Cole began as a Jacksonian, antibanking Democrat, then became one of the founders of the Republican party in the state and served on the Republican National Committee from 1856 to 1864. The results of the 1863 state election sent Cole to Congress as the only Republican in the California delegation; the other two Union party congressmen were Free Soil Democrats. Cole had been one of the incorporators of the Central Pacific Railroad company in June 1861, and though he had disposed of his interest, he aided his friend Collis P. Huntington in modifying the railroad bill in 1864. He supported the administration's war measures, particularly emancipation and arming the freedmen.

In spite of his good record, patronage disputes with Senator John Conness (*q.v.*) and widespread Free Soil Democratic influence within the wartime Union party prevented Cole's renomination in 1864. Elected to the Senate in December 1865, he served from March 1867 to March 1873, and became chairman of the Senate Committee on Appropriations. He was a staunch supporter of Reconstruction and influenced the purchase of Alaska. Cole kept an interest in public affairs, and lived to become the sole surviving Civil War congressman. He died in Hollywood, California, on November 3, 1924. Cole, *Memoirs*; Phillips, *Cornelius Cole.*

Robert J. Chandler

COLE, George Edward, *territorial delegate,* was born in Trenton (now Trenton Falls), New York, on December 23, 1826. In 1850, he joined the California gold rush. When his ship landed at Umpqua city, Oregon, he remained to become a merchant and to promote steamboat transportation on the Willamette River. He served in the Oregon territorial legislature (1852–1853) and was clerk of the U.S. District Court (1859–1860). In 1860 Cole moved to the Walla Walla

Valley of Washington Territory, where in May 1863, he was nominated as the Democratic Union candidate for territorial delegate. Cole had opposed secession and supported the war effort, but he opposed the administration's abolition policies and suspensions of the writ of habeas corpus.

According to the *Washington Statesman*, the Democratic newspaper in Walla Walla, Republicans put abolition before the Union and the Democrats made preservation of the Union the primary war aim. The territory had been strongly Democratic until the Civil War gave control to the Republicans. However, Cole was able to take advantage of internal bickering within Republican ranks and was elected, the last Democratic delegate to serve the territory until 1885. He supported the Union cause, and after Abraham Lincoln's (*q.v.*) death, backed Andrew Johnson (*q.v.*), who appointed him governor of Washington Territory in November 1866. Cole was not confirmed by the Radicals, who controlled Congress, although he served as governor until March 1867. He shifted his allegiance to the Republican party, and in 1873 President Ulysses S. Grant (*q.v.*) appointed him postmaster of Portland, an office he held until 1881. He died in Portland on December 3, 1906. Meany, ''George E. Cole,'' *Washington Historical Quarterly.*

Kent D. Richards

COLFAX, Schuyler, *congressman, Speaker of the House*, was born on March 23, 1823, in New York City, and in 1836 moved with his family to New Carlisle, Indiana. He campaigned for Henry Clay in 1844, was a delegate to the Whig National Conventions of 1848 and 1852, served in the state constitutional convention in 1850, and was narrowly defeated as a Whig candidate for Congress from a Democratic district in 1851. With the disintegration of the Whig party, Colfax, a temperance advocate, experimented with the Know-Nothing party, then became active in the People's party, the forerunner of the Republican organization in Indiana. In 1854, he was elected to the U.S. House of Representatives on the People's party ticket. As a Republican, he served in Congress continuously until 1869 and was Speaker of the House from 1863 until 1869.

As outspoken antislavery advocate, Colfax opposed the admission of Kansas as a slave state, and after the outbreak of the Civil War strongly supported a vigorous prosecution of the conflict. His speeches on these and similar topics were widely circulated. Colfax's prominence and possibly his Radical Republican sentiments brought him the vice presidential nomination in 1868. Elected with President Ulysses S. Grant (*q.v.*), Colfax served one term, his consideration by the Liberal Republicans as a possible presidential candidate possibly costing him the vice presidential nomination in 1872. Also in 1872, Colfax declined the editorship of the *New York Tribune.*

Colfax was implicated in the Crédit Mobilier scandal of 1872–1873. Although he escaped formal censure on the grounds that any misconduct had occurred before he became Vice President, his denial of any wrongdoing was not convincing, and his political career was ruined. After his retirement, Colfax continued to be in demand as a public speaker. He died in Mankato, Minnesota, on January 13, 1885. Hollister, *Life of Schuyler Colfax*; Smith, *Schuyler Colfax.*

Lorna Lutes Sylvester

COLLAMER, Jacob, *senator,* was born in Troy, New York, on January 8, 1791. His family moved to Burlington, Vermont, in 1795, and he graduated from the University of Vermont in 1810. Although a call to militia service in 1812 interrupted his law studies, he was admitted to the Vermont bar in 1813. During the 1820s he served in the legislature and as Windsor county's prosecuting attorney. From 1834 until 1842, Collamer was an associate justice of the Vermont Supreme Court and led a successful movement for a bicameral legislature. In 1842, he was elected as a Whig to the U.S. House of Representatives, where he served three terms. In 1849, he was appointed Postmaster General by Zachary Taylor, but upon Taylor's death in 1850, he returned to Vermont and served as a judge until 1854, when he was elected to the Senate as an antislavery Whig.

As a member of the Committee on Territories, Collamer came into conflict with Stephen A. Douglas (*q.v.*), particularly during the Kansas controversy. His early conversion to the Republican party and his efforts on behalf of the protective tariff in 1857 gained attention, and at the Republican nominating convention of 1860, he received ten votes on the first ballot. An adherent to the concept of congressional authority, Collamer nonetheless is credited with drafting the act of July 13, 1861, that provided congressional authorization for the President's exercise of extraordinary powers. Following Ambrose Burnside's (*q.v.*) defeat at Fredericksburg, Collamer became spokesman for a caucus of Republican senators who sought to wrest conduct of the war from Abraham Lincoln (*q.v.*), and to force important Cabinet changes. He died on November 9, 1865, in Woodstock, Vermont. Bogue, *Earnest Men*; Crockett, *Vermont*, vols. 2, 3, 4; Curry, *Blueprint for Modern America.*

Samuel B. Hand

CONKLING, Frederick Augustus, *congressman,* was on born August 22, 1816, in Canajoharie, New York. His father served in the 17th Congress and his brother, Roscoe (*q.v.*), served in the U.S. House and Senate. Conkling followed classical studies and later attended the Albany Academy. Prior to the Civil War, he was involved in the mercantile trade and served three terms in the New York State Assembly. In June 1861, Conkling organized the 84th New York Volunteers and became its colonel. Elected as a Republican to the 37th Congress, he was one of two party members to oppose the Pacific Railroad Bill. Later, while on the Naval Affairs Committee, he opposed a resolution introduced by his brother that pertained to Erie Canal construction.

Conkling ran unsuccessfully for the 38th Congress, and rejoined the 84th New York during the summer of 1864 until the regiment was mustered out that October. In 1868, Conkling ran unsuccessfully for mayor of New York City.

He helped organize the West Side Savings Bank and became president of the Aetna Fire Insurance Company. A prolific writer, Conkling produced numerous pamphlets on a variety of political, commercial, and scientific subjects. He died in New York City on September 18, 1891. Curry, *Blueprint for Modern America*; Phisterer, *New York in the War of the Rebellion*, vol. 1.

Frank R. Levstik

CONKLING, Roscoe, *congressman, senator*, was born on October 3, 1829, in Albany, New York. An indifferent student, he read for the law in Auburn, New York, and in 1850 was admitted to the bar. He moved to Utica, where he was appointed to fill the vacant Oneida county district attorneyship. Defeated in the 1850 election, Conkling spent the next few years building his legal and political career. He was elected mayor of Utica in 1858, and then to the 36th and 37th Congresses. Conkling's record in his first two terms is difficult to categorize. As an orthodox Republican, he opposed the extension of slavery and criticized President James Buchanan's (*q.v.*) leadership, yet he supported parts of the Crittenden Compromise and rejected the Legal Tender Act as inflationary. Even his friendship with Radical Republicans was conditional. He helped his mentor, Thaddeus Stevens (*q.v.*), form the Committee on the Conduct of the War, but backed President Abraham Lincoln's (*q.v.*) gradualist, compensated emancipation proposals. In 1862, Conkling was defeated for reelection, but won the first of two additional terms in 1864 and built sufficient backing to become a U.S. senator.

The second phase of Conkling's Washington career began with opposition to President Andrew Johnson (*q.v.*), service on the Joint Committee on Reconstruction, support for the 14th Amendment, and eventual alignment with Ulysses S. Grant (*q.v.*). When Grant won the presidency, Conkling became his chief patronage agent and the leader of the Republican Stalwarts. Two presidents offered him Supreme Court appointments (one as Chief Justice), both of which he rejected. He was reelected to the Senate in 1873 and 1879, but in 1881, he resigned his seat to protest Federal appointments in New York. When Republican legislators refused to renominate him, he established a law practice in New York and became a leader of the bar. He died in New York City on April 18, 1888. Chidsey, *Gentleman from New York*; Jordan, *Roscoe Conkling*.

Jerome Mushkat

CONNESS, John, *senator*, was born on September 22, 1821, in County Galaway, Ireland. He immigrated to the United States in 1836, and settled in New York City, where William A. Walker, one of his teachers in the public schools and later a Democratic congressman (1853–1855), made a lasting impression. Conness arrived in California in July 1849 and settled in El Dorado county. He was a Free Soil Democrat, and in 1853 and 1854 represented El Dorado county in the Assembly. He was a candidate for lieutenant governor on the Free Soil Democratic ticket in 1859 and lost the race for governor in 1861. To counter

Republican domination of the state, Conness advocated a fusion of those who supported the war, and became a leading figure in the Union party after its formation in the summer of 1862. A bribery scandal during the 1863 legislative session discredited Timothy Phelps (*q.v.*), the leading Republican senatorial candidate. The Senate seat went to Conness, the second choice of most. His methods were rough, and he once bragged that he bullied President Abraham Lincoln (*q.v.*) into making a patronage removal. He prevailed upon Lincoln to appoint Stephen J. Field (*q.v.*), a Free Soil Democrat, to the U.S. Supreme Court.

During the 1864 presidential campaign, Conness inclined toward Salmon P. Chase (*q.v.*) and only reluctantly campaigned for Lincoln. He supported Lincoln's war measures and Radical Reconstruction. He also advocated the national bank system and the use of legal tender in gold-producing California, and supported the Central Pacific Railroad. His 1864 bill turned the Yosemite Valley and the Mariposa big trees over to the state for protection. In 1866, they formed the first state park in the nation. Mount Conness, near Tioga Pass in the park, commemorates him. Conness left the Senate in 1869, and Democratic control of the state made his reelection impossible. He settled in Boston after his remarriage in 1869 and died in Jamaica Plain, Massachusetts, on January 10, 1909.
Rice, *Reminiscences of Abraham Lincoln.*

Robert J. Chandler

CONNOR, Patrick Edward, *general,* was born in County Kerry, Ireland, on March 17, 1820, and came to New York City as a child. He enlisted in the Regular Army and served in Florida, in the Texas Volunteers, and in the Mexican War. He resigned from the Army in 1847 and went to California, where he engaged in mining and other ventures. At the start of the Civil War, Connor, a leading citizen of Stockton, California, was named colonel of the 3rd California Volunteers. He was anxious to see fighting duty in the East, but instead was given command of the District of Utah and ordered to Utah Territory to protect the trails from western Wyoming to Nevada.

Connor's 700 troops entered Salt Lake City in October 1862 and established Camp Douglas east of the city on a high bench. From the start there was confrontation between Connor and Brigham Young (*q.v.*). Although Connor's official task was to protect the trails against Indian raids, which he did quite effectively, he also believed it was a portion of his duty to keep a watch on the Mormons, which he did untiringly. Well aware of the geographical importance of Utah Territory, Connor developed a dislike and even hatred of the Mormons, as is shown in his official correspondence. He pacified the Indians and obtained some treaties that had more effect than such agreements usually had. In violent and bitter weather, Connor led a portion of his force to Bear River (near present Franklin, Idaho), where on January 29, 1863, they defeated a force of Bannock and Shoshone Indians. His skillful campaign against the Indians won him promotion to brigadier general of Volunteers on March 30, 1863.

Connor continued his struggle with the Mormons throughout the remainder of the war and even tried to entice "gentile" miners to Utah Territory in order to "water down" Mormon control. He also set up an army-run newspaper, the *Union Vidette*, in opposition to the Mormon-controlled *Deseret News*. In March 1865, Connor was given command of the District of the Plains and was victorious on the Tongue River against the Arapaho. However, the campaign as a whole was a failure, and he was relieved of his command. He left the army on April 30, 1866, a brevet major general of Volunteers. Connor was in business in Stockton, California, and Salt Lake City, where he died on December 17, 1891. Long, *Saints and the Union.*

E. B. Long

CONWAY, Martin Franklin, *congressman,* was born on November 19, 1827, near Fallston, Maryland. In 1854, he moved from Baltimore to Kansas, and as correspondent for the *Baltimore Sun* attracted some attention as a leader of the Free State movement. When Conway arrived in Kansas Territory, he offered his services to territorial Governor Andrew W. Reeder. Although the legislative council election of March 1855 was carried by the proslavery party—many feel fraudulently—Conway won a seat—the only Free State man to do so. He resigned the position, but did not resign from politics. At the Free State Convention on September 5, 1855, he was appointed a member of the Free State Executive Committee. A few weeks later, he was elected a delegate to the Topeka Constitutional Convention and wrote the resolutions of that body. He was elected a Kansas Supreme Court justice. On February 28, 1859, in response to what he considered a slanderous newspaper letter, Conway caned Governor Charles Robinson (*q.v.*).

In 1858, Conway was a delegate to the Leavenworth Constitutional Convention and became its president. In October 1859, as the Republican nominee for Congress, he was elected by a majority of 2,107 votes. Since Kansas did not become a state until January 21, 1861, his first term was a short one, but he was reelected in June 1861. As a member of the 37th Congress, his fight to withhold money from the war effort until all slaves were freed earned him the distrust of the administration and condemnation resolutions from the Kansas House and Senate. He often broke party ranks to vote with the opposition and was one of two Republicans to vote against the final passage of the national conscription bill.

After failing to be nominated for a third term, Conway retired to private life in Washington. A strong congressional supporter of President Andrew Johnson (*q.v.*), he was rewarded with the position of U.S. consul at Marseilles, France, in June 1866. He was removed after Ulysses S. Grant (*q.v.*) became President. It was never determined whether his insanity was a result of "disappointed ambition" or medical disability. Conway's mental deterioration progressed rapidly after he left public service. He died at Saint Elizabeth's Insane Asylum, near Washington, D.C., on February 15, 1882. Castel, *Frontier State at War*; Geary, *We Need Men.*

Larry Jochims

CONY, Samuel, *governor*, was born on February 27, 1811, in Augusta, Maine. His parents provided private tutors, then sent him to China Academy and Wakefield College. He graduated from Brown University in 1829, read law, and gained admission to the bar in 1832. In common with many lawyers then and now, Cony early felt the tug of politics. He entered the Maine House of Representatives in 1835, serving two terms. He was a member of Governor John Fairfield's Executive Council in 1839. From 1840 to 1846, he was judge of the Probate Court of Penobscot county, then was land agent for Maine from 1847 to 1850. Five years as state treasurer (1850–1855) followed, necessitating the Cony family's move to Augusta. During the late 1850s, Cony, a strong antislavery Democrat, joined Illinois Senator Stephen A. Douglas (*q.v.*) in opposing the Lecompton Constitution for Kansas Territory. In 1860, he supported Douglas for President.

When the war came, Cony strongly backed the Lincoln (*q.v.*) administration's war policies. He became a Republican in 1862, winning election to the Maine House that year. There he steadfastly voted for men, supplies, and other war measures. In 1863, he won the governorship with 57.4 percent of the vote, and was reelected in 1864 and 1865. A vigorous and patriotic war governor, he furthered Maine's massive war contribution of men and matériel. During Reconstruction, Cony was a strong opponent of President Andrew Johnson's (*q.v.*) restoration policies, which he believed represented a betrayal of the Northern people and a surrender of the "fruits of victory" to the former Confederacy. Highly popular, Cony could have easily won another term in 1866, but ill health caused him to step down. He died in Augusta on October 5, 1870. *BDGUS*, vol. 2; North, *History of Augusta.*

H. Draper Hunt

COOPER, Thomas Buchecker, *congressman*, was born in Coopersburg, Pennsylvania, on December 29, 1823. He attended the public schools, the Pennsylvania College in Gettysburg, and the medical school of the University of Pennsylvania, from which he graduated in 1843. He devoted no attention to political officeholding until he won election to the House of Representatives in 1860 as a Democrat. Cooper held little sympathy for the Southern cause. Though he made no rhetorical record in Congress, his vote could be counted consistently among the War Democrats. He died in Coopersburg on April 4, 1862. Dell, *Lincoln and the War Democrats.*

W. Wayne Smith

CORNING, Erastus, *congressman, industrialist*, was born on December 14, 1794, in Norwich, Connecticut. In spite of his limited education and poor health,

Corning rose to prominence as a successful businessman and politician. By 1833, he headed the Utica and Schenectady Railroad, and when it merged with the New York Central in 1853, he became its president. His business activities coincided with his increasing influence in the social and political circles of Albany, New York. In 1833, he was named a regent of the University of New York, then was selected as one of its vice chancellors. Through his affiliation with the Albany regents, Corning was elected in 1834 to the first of four successive terms as Albany's mayor. He was a state senator (1842–1846) and was elected as a Democrat to the 35th, 37th, and 38th Congresses.

Although Corning opposed the North's increasingly militant position toward the South, his iron manufacturing company, in which he was a silent partner, would later produce cannon and other weaponry for the Union Army. His firm also received the contract for the construction of the U.S.S. *Monitor.* Despite these vested interests and a preference for behind-the-scenes activity, Corning assumed an important leadership role among wartime Democrats. As a member of the powerful Ways and Means Committee in the 37th Congress, he opposed the legal tender bill and similar legislation that was designed to support the war effort. He also participated in the 1861 Peace Conference held in Washington, and headed a delegation of New York Democrats in the spring of 1863 in denouncing the arrest of Clement L. Vallandigham (*q.v.*). Although reelected to the 38th Congress, Corning resigned his seat before it convened, citing poor health as the reason. Thereafter, he concentrated on his many and varied business interests until his death in Albany on April 9, 1872. Curry, *Blueprint for Modern America*; Neu, *Erastus Corning.*

James W. Geary
{: style="text-align: right"}

CORSE, John Murray, *general,* was born in Pittsburgh, Pennsylvania, on April 27, 1835; his family moved to Iowa in 1842. Corse attended West Point from 1853 to 1855, when he withdrew and returned home to study law. He was an attorney in Burlington, Iowa, and an active figure in state Democratic politics when the Civil War began. In July 1861, Corse was made major of the 6th Iowa Volunteers and with that regiment served in the early campaigns in Missouri before being detailed as judge advocate and inspector general on the staff of Major General John Pope (*q.v.*). He returned to his regiment as lieutenant colonel and was promoted to colonel in March 1863. Corse served at Corinth and Vicksburg, and in August 1863 was made brigadier general of Volunteers. He led a brigade of the XV Corps until he received a severe leg wound at Missionary Ridge in November 1863. When Corse returned to duty, he was assigned to Major General William T. Sherman's (*q.v.*) staff. In July 1864 he was made a division commander in the XVI Corps.

Corse's conduct at the battle of Allatoona won wide acclaim. He rushed to the aid of a small Federal force defending the supply depot at Allatoona. From fifteen miles away Sherman, by signal flags, ordered the garrison to "hold fast. We are coming." In response, he received a message that could only be read in part: "CRSEHER." This was taken to mean "Corse is here." The incident became the inspiration for a popular nineteenth-century hymn, "Hold the Fort; I Am Coming." When the battle was over and the Confederates had been repulsed, Corse sent another message: "I am short a cheek bone and ear, but am able to whip all h __ l yet." For this service, he was later made a brevet major general of Volunteers. He participated in the March to the Sea and the Carolinas campaign.

After the war, Corse declined a lieutenant colonelcy in the Regular Army and was mustered out in 1866. Unlike some prewar Democrats, he remained true to his party, and President Grover Cleveland named him to several government offices. He served as collector of internal revenue in Chicago and as postmaster of Boston. He was also chairman of the Massachusetts State Democratic Committee. When not holding political office, he was involved in railroad, harbor, and bridge construction. He died in Winchester, Massachusetts, on April 27, 1893. Castel, *Decision in the West.*

Richard M. McMurry

CORWIN, Thomas, *congressman, diplomat,* was born on July 29, 1794, in Bourbon county, Kentucky. In 1798, the family moved to Lebanon, Ohio, which was Corwin's lifelong home. In 1817 he was admitted to the Ohio bar and turned to politics, spending several terms in the Ohio legislature. Corwin represented Ohio in the U.S. House (1831–1840), was governor of Ohio (1840–1842), served in the U.S. Senate (1845–1850), and from 1850 until 1853 was Secretary of the Treasury. As an ardent Whig he adopted the creed of Henry Clay, and throughout his political career defended high tariffs, internal improvements, and a conservative foreign policy. In 1859, Corwin entered the House of Representatives as a reluctant Republican, at odds especially with the party's role in agitating the slavery issue. During the secession crisis, Corwin, as chairman of the House Committee of Thirty-three, battled the forces of disunion.

Corwin, a Unionist, was willing to compromise even the territorial issue to prevent a civil war, and condemned Northern and Southern extremists alike for preventing agreement in the committee. He sought to assure the South that the moderate Whig tradition lived on in the Republican party. During the closing days of the session, in January and February 1861, both houses of Congress adopted the Committee of Thirty-three's proposed amendment to bar congressional interference with slavery in the states. Corwin left Congress for the last time in March 1861. Several days later Abraham Lincoln (*q.v.*) appointed him minister to Mexico, where he attempted unsuccessfully to forestall the French intervention by negotiating an American loan that would enable Mexico to satisfy its European creditors. He returned to Washington, D.C., in 1864 and died there on December 18, 1865. Corwin, *Life and Speeches of Thomas Corwin*; Russell, *Thomas Corwin.*

Norman A. Graebner

COUCH, Darius Nash, *general,* was born on July 23, 1822, in Putnam county, New York. He graduated from West Point in 1846, was commissioned in the artillery, and was breveted for gallant and meritorious service in the Mexican War. In 1853–1854, he participated in a scientific expedition to northern Mexico and gathered zoological specimens for the Smithsonian Institution. He resigned from the Army in 1855 to join his wife's family's copper manufacturing business in Taunton, Massachusetts, but in 1861 he became colonel of the 7th Massachusetts. With the accession of his old friend George McClellan (*q.v.*) to command of the Army of the Potomac, Couch rose rapidly to divisional command in the Peninsula and Antietam campaigns, and leadership of the II Corps as major general of Volunteers at Fredericksburg and Chancellorsville. As second in command under Joseph Hooker (*q.v.*) at the latter battle, he functioned as temporary army commander after Hooker's incapacitation. Nonetheless, Couch held a profound dislike and distrust of Hooker's generalship. His desire to serve elsewhere led to command of the Pennsylvania militia during the Gettysburg campaign, and divisional command in the XXIII Corps at the battle of Nashville and during William T. Sherman's (*q.v.*) campaign in the Carolinas.

An enthusiastic member of McClellan's entourage, Couch nevertheless enjoyed sufficient favor with the Lincoln (*q.v.*) administration to be given the important task of organizing the militia to oppose Lee's campaign in Pennsylvania. Insufficiently supported by the administration and the people of Pennsylvania, Couch and Governor Andrew G. Curtin (*q.v.*) labored indefatigably to shape citizens into soldiers on the eve of Gettysburg. If nothing more, this effort provided George Meade (*q.v.*) with flank coverage and intelligence information in support of the main battle. Couch also helped preserve law and order in the coal mining districts, but his close association with McClellan and his unstinting disgust with Hooker, coupled with poor health, surely contributed to his lusterless service in the latter stages of the war.

Couch served briefly as collector of the Port of Boston after the war, and failed in his Democratic bid for the Massachusetts governorship. He headed a Virginia mining and manufacturing company prior to his retirement to Norwalk, Connecticut, in 1870. From then until his death in Norwalk on February 12, 1897, Couch occasionally served the state as quartermaster and adjutant general. Coddington, *Gettysburg Campaign*; Furgurson, *Chancellorsville*; Sears, *To the Gates of Richmond.*

B. Franklin Cooling

COVODE, John, *congressman,* was born on March 18, 1808, in Westmoreland county, Pennsylvania. His first political office was justice of the peace. Labeled "Honest John" for his judicial services, Covode parlayed his reputation into a seat in the state legislature, a position he held for two terms. He won election to the 34th Congress as a Whig and was reelected, this time as a Republican, to the 35th Congress, a seat he retained through the 37th Congress. In 1863, he declined his party's nomination, but reentered congressional politics in 1866,

winning seats in the 40th and 41st Congresses. Covode gained national prominence in March 1860 when he introduced a resolution calling for the formation
of a congressional committee to investigate possible corruption in President
James Buchanan's (*q.v.*) administration. He chaired the committee, but the results of its investigation proved inconclusive. Since it did bring to the public's
attention the possibility of widespread corruption within the Democratic party,
many of Covode's contemporaries, as well as students of the period, have described the committee's work as a partisan effort designed to enhance the Republican party's election prospects that autumn.

Covode solidified his place in history when on February 28, 1868, he introduced a resolution initiating impeachment proceedings against President Andrew
Johnson (*q.v.*). Throughout his political life, Covode generally remained loyal
to the Republican party, a fact noticed by President Lincoln (*q.v.*), who honored
many of his patronage requests, and by the House leadership, which appointed
him to such important committees as the Committee on the Conduct of the War.
Pennsylvania Republicans treated him less well. Twice Covode sought the gubernatorial nomination, only to have the state's Republican party machine abandon him for another candidate. He died in Harrisburg, Pennsylvania, on January
11, 1871. Bradley, *Triumph of Militant Republicanism.*

Philip J. Avillo, Jr.

COWAN, Edgar, *senator,* was born on September 19, 1815, in Greensburg,
Pennsylvania. He graduated from Franklin College in 1839, and in 1842 began
practicing law in Westmoreland county. Initially, he was a Jacksonian Democrat,
but subsequently joined the Whigs. In 1856, he declared himself a Republican,
but by the end of the Civil War he ran as a Democrat for the U.S. Senate.
Liberal Republicanism beckoned him in the early 1870s. Cowan's political career began in 1861, as a Republican candidate for the Senate. Relatively unknown in state politics, he confronted a strong challenge for the nomination
from the nationally known former congressman David Wilmot (*q.v.*). The state
Republican party endorsed Cowan, however, and Wilmot's challenge dissipated.
Cowan defeated the Democratic candidate, Henry D. Foster, and served one
term in the Senate.

Once in the Senate, he quickly drifted away from the Republican party's
position. He spoke against the Confiscation Act and the Conscription Act—not,
he insisted, because he opposed the war but because measures such as these
jeopardized more than aided the war effort. Confiscation of slaves, he reasoned,
threatened the support of loyal Union men in the border states, and conscription
challenged the very tenets of the American ideal. Cowan in fact voted for both
of these measures, but the breach with his party widened considerably by the
end of the war. He voted against the creation of the Joint Committee on Reconstruction, the Civil Rights Bill of 1866, the Reconstruction Act of 1867, and
the 14th Amendment. He encouraged President Andrew Johnson (*q.v.*) to veto
the Civil Rights Bill, and later in 1866 drafted for Johnson a veto message

against the bill establishing the Freedmen's Bureau. In that same year Cowan joined several other senators to organize the National Union party, which endorsed Johnson's plan for Reconstruction. Republicans throughout Pennsylvania denounced him, and when he ran for the Senate again in 1867, as a Democrat, he was unsuccessful. When Johnson nominated him to serve as ambassador to Austria, Senate Republicans refused to confirm him. His political career over, Cowan resumed the practice of law until his death in Greensburg, Pennsylvania, on August 31, 1885. Bradley, *Triumph of Militant Republicanism.*

Philip J. Avillo, Jr.

COX, Jacob Dolson, *general,* was born of American parents on October 27, 1828, in Montreal, Canada. He graduated from Oberlin College in 1851, practiced law in Warren, Ohio, and was a member of the Ohio Senate when the Civil War began. Thanks to his personal and political connections, he became a brigadier general and participated in the 1861 campaign that secured western Virginia for the Union. In September 1862, having been assigned to the Army of the Potomac, he commanded a division and was acting commander of the IX Corps at the battles of South Mountain and Antietam. From April to December 1863, Cox commanded the District of Ohio, then joined the XXIII Corps in Tennessee as a division commander. In that capacity he participated in the Atlanta campaign (May–September 1864), and then in the Tennessee campaign (November–December 1864), during which he also commanded the XXIII Corps at Spring Hill and Franklin. His performance in both campaigns was excellent, gaining him a much overdue promotion to major general. Early in 1865, Cox was transferred with the XXIII Corps to North Carolina, where he soon took charge of "Cox's Provisional Corps," with which he defeated a Confederate force under Braxton Bragg at the battle of Kinston (March 8–10), following which he joined William T. Sherman's (*q.v.*) army and witnessed Joseph E. Johnston's surrender at Durham Station.

Tall, handsome, and highly intelligent, Cox was among the best of the North's "political generals," one who exemplified the contention he made in his *Military Reminiscences* that once they acquired the needed experience, nonprofessionals possessing the requisite personal qualities were as capable of commanding troops as the typical West Pointer. In particular, he displayed outstanding ability at Kennesaw Mountain in late June 1864, conducting a flanking operation that forced the Confederates to relinquish a position that was invulnerable to direct assault. His historical works, although afflicted with strong biases, remain valuable sources on the Civil War. Cox served as governor of Ohio (1866–1867), as Secretary of the Interior (1869–1870), in the House of Representatives (1877–1879), as dean of the Cincinnati Law School (1881–1897), and as president of the University of Cincinnati (1885–1889). He also published numerous articles and books pertaining to the Civil War. On August

4, 1900, Cox died in Gloucester, Massachusetts. Castel, *Decision in the West*; Cox, *Military Reminiscences*, vols. 1, 2; Losson, "Jacob Dolson Cox."

Albert Castel

COX, Samuel Sullivan, *congressman*, was born on September 30, 1824, in Zanesville, Ohio. He graduated from Brown University in 1846, practiced law briefly in Cincinnati as George Pugh's partner, then moved to Columbus. In 1853, he became editor and part owner of the *Daily Ohio Statesman*, the foremost Democratic newspaper in the state capital. A lifelong Democrat, he was first elected to Congress in 1856. He actively supported Stephen A. Douglas's (*q.v.*) position on slavery in the western territories and on Kansas. Denouncing extremism and agitation as a sure way to war, Cox urged conciliation and accommodation between North and South. As a delegate to the 1860 convention in Charleston, he lamented the breakup of the party but remained loyal to Douglas. In the dark winter of 1860–1861, he advocated compromise to save the Union.

When war came, Cox became leader of the Democratic opposition in the House, where he urged limited support for a limited war to restore the Union but not to subjugate the South. He regularly denounced the Lincoln (*q.v.*) administration for its limitation of free speech, suppression of political critics, suspension of habeas corpus, and arbitrary arrests and military trials of civilians. At Clement L. Vallandigham's (*q.v.*) trial in 1863, Cox testified that he had written the words for which Vallandigham was being tried. He criticized the trend toward centralized power in Washington and in the hands of the executive, and he dragged his feet on emancipation. Gerrymandered out of office at war's end by Ohio's Republican legislature, Cox moved to New York City and a safe Democratic district. He opposed Radical Reconstruction and urged amnesty, a speedy restoration of the South to the Union, and full political rights for Southerners. He opposed protective tariffs but advocated civil service reform, hard money, and the ending of government subsidies to railroads.

Cox's tireless efforts won approval of laws establishing the Life Saving Service, providing better working conditions and pay for letter carriers, and authorizing a broader information base in the U.S. census. For many years he served as a regent of the Smithsonian Institution, and in 1885 was named minister to Turkey. Beyond politics, Cox made a name as a man of letters, a popular lecturer, a wit, and a writer. His political works provide the perceptive analysis of a shrewd insider. Following his death in New York City, on September 10, 1889, appreciative letter carriers erected a monument to him in Greenwood Cemetery, Brooklyn. Lindsey, *"Sunset" Cox*.

David Lindsey

CRAPO, Henry Howland, *governor*, was born in Dartmouth, Massachusetts, on May 22, 1804. He received little formal schooling, but self-education prepared him to teach school in Dartmouth during the 1820s. After moving to New Bedford, Massachusetts, in 1832, Crapo held numerous local governmental and military positions there during the 1830s and 1840s. An aspiring entrepreneur in many fields, particularly shipping and insurance, he moved in 1856 to Flint, Michigan, to supervise development of the land he had recently purchased. Crapo built the first of his three sawmills in the Flint area and started logging a vast area of land. By the beginning of the Civil War, he operated one of the state's largest individually owned lumber firms.

Formerly a Whig, Crapo became a Republican during the mid-1850s. He was elected mayor of Flint in 1860 and state senator in 1862. In 1864 and 1866 he was elected governor. As governor he backed the 13th Amendment and all other measures of Radical Reconstruction. In response to President Andrew Johnson's (*q.v.*) vetoes of the Freedmen's Bureau Act and the 1866 Civil Rights Act, Crapo declared April 19, 1866, a "day of fasting, humiliation and prayer," and issued a proclamation emphasizing the need to reconstruct the South. He also supported Johnson's impeachment. Crapo achieved his greatest recognition by his encouragement of the influx of new capital and labor into Michigan. He died in Flint on July 23, 1869. Crapo, *The Story of Henry Howland Crapo*; Lewis, *Lumberman from Flint.*

Roger L. Rosentreter

CRAVENS, James Addison, *congressman*, was born on November 4, 1818, in Rockingham county, Virginia. His family subsequently moved to Hardinsburg, Indiana, where he attended common schools. During the war with Mexico, he was major of the 2nd Indiana Volunteers. Cravens represented Washington county in Indiana's House of Representatives (1848–1850) and Senate (1850–1853), and was among four Indiana Democrats to win in the critical 1860 election, which returned a Republican majority. Cravens served in the 37th and 38th Congresses.

After the election of Abraham Lincoln (*q.v.*), several southern Indiana leaders advocated a reconstructed Union or a Northern confederacy with ties to the South. A supporter of this option, Cravens proposed creating the "state of Jackson" from the southern portions of Illinois and Indiana, which would align with the South. Later, despite his public indecision, he became a zealous supporter of an energetic war policy to preserve the Union. Indiana Governor Oliver H.P. Morton (*q.v.*) acknowledged that southern Indiana remained highly loyal to the Union, and that the devotion of Cravens and fellow Democrat William Steele Holman (*q.v.*) remained unsurpassed. Following the war, Cravens was a delegate to the Union National Convention of Conservatives at Philadelphia (1866) and several Democratic National Conventions. He died in Hardinsburg on June 20, 1893. Shepherd, *Biographical Directory of the Indiana General Assembly*, vol. 1; Stampp, *Indiana Politics During the Civil War.*

David G. Vanderstel

CRAWFORD, Samuel Johnson, *governor*, was born on April 10, 1835, near Bedford, Indiana. He graduated from the law school of Cincinnati College in 1858, and moved to Kansas Territory, where he was elected to the legislature. In 1861, he resigned from the newly formed legislature and was made captain in the ninety-day 2nd Kansas Volunteers, which was bloodied in the battle of Wilson's Creek (August 10, 1861). Crawford was subsequently commissioned a captain in the 2nd Kansas Cavalry, which campaigned in northwest Arkansas in 1862: at Maysville (or Old Fort Wayne, October 22), Cane Hill (November 28), and Prairie Grove (December 7). He was frequently cited for bravery, and he served as brigade and regimental commander. He was commissioned colonel in the 2nd Kansas Colored Infantry, which distinguished itself at Jenkins' Ferry, Arkansas (April 30, 1864).

Selected as Republican candidate for governor of Kansas, Crawford had his campaign interrupted by Sterling Price's expedition into Missouri in 1864. He was at the battles of Westport and Mine Creek. As a war hero, he was elected governor in 1864 and again in 1866. Crawford resigned as governor in 1868 and led a Kansas militia regiment in an abortive campaign against the Indians. Although he ran for Congress in the 1870s as both a Liberal Republican and a Greenbacker, he was not elected. He subsequently became a successful claims agent for the Federal government on behalf of the state of Kansas and certain Indian tribes. He died in Topeka on October 21, 1913, one of the last surviving Civil War governors. Plummer, *Frontier Governor*.

Mark A. Plummer

CRAWFORD, Samuel Wylie, *general*, was born near Chambersburg, Pennsylvania, on November 8, 1829. After graduating from the University of Pennsylvania (1846) and its medical school (1850), he was appointed army assistant surgeon (1851). During the 1850s, he served on the frontier and engaged in scientific research and writing on the Southwest and Mexico. War's eve found Crawford at Charleston, where during the Fort Sumter crisis he was both a medical and an artillery officer. Commissioned a major in the 13th Infantry on May 14, 1861, and brigadier general on April 25, 1862, he initially served as a staff officer with William S. Rosecrans (*q.v.*) and Nathaniel P. Banks (*q.v.*). He commanded the 1st brigade of Alpheus S. Williams's (*q.v.*) division at Cedar Mountain and Second Bull Run. At Antietam, he briefly led the division until wounded.

In June 1863, Crawford took command of the Pennsylvania Reserve Division, which soon rejoined the V Corps. He fought gallantly at Gettysburg but ineptly at the Wilderness and Spotsylvania. After the Reserves left service in June 1864, he led the 3rd Division, V Corps, but with no greater success. At Petersburg, Crawford temporarily commanded the corps, but when a permanent V Corps commander was needed, Ulysses S. Grant (*q.v.*), who had previously considered relieving Crawford, let him be passed over in favor of the junior but abler Charles Griffin (*q.v.*).

Crawford was an inquisitive scientist and a brave fighter, but a clumsy, rash general. His vanity was hardly justified by his sorry record of blunders. Elevated beyond his ability through his chance presence at Fort Sumter, he repeatedly demonstrated the folly of such promotion. By war's end, he was the worst division commander remaining in the Army of the Potomac. During Reconstruction, he served briefly in Louisville, Kentucky, and Huntsville, Alabama, but was mostly on leave. He retired as a colonel on February 19, 1873; in 1875, however, a controversial law elevated him to brigadier general (retired). He died in Philadelphia on November 3, 1892. Matter, *If It Takes All Summer*; Rhea, *Battle of the Wilderness*.

Richard J. Sommers

CRESWELL, John Angel James, *congressman*, was born in Port Deposit, Maryland, on November 18, 1828. After attending a local academy, he entered Dickinson College and graduated with honors in 1848. For two years he studied law, and was admitted to the Maryland bar in 1850. Creswell entered politics as a Whig, but upon that party's collapse he became a Democrat. In 1856, he was a delegate to the Democratic National Convention, but with the outbreak of the Civil War he joined the Union party. As a Unionist he was elected to the Maryland House of Delegates in 1861, and in the following year he was appointed assistant adjutant general for the state. With the support of the Unconditional Unionist faction, he was nominated for Congress over John Crisfield (*q.v.*), the incumbent Unionist. The nomination bitterly divided the party, but with the aid of the military, Creswell won the seat. In Congress, he worked closely with Henry Winter Davis (*q.v.*), and became an advocate of emancipation.

In 1864, Creswell was defeated for reelection by a resurgence of the Democratic party in his nominally Democratic district. On the death of Senator Thomas Hicks (*q.v.*) in 1865, he was elected to serve out the remainder of his term. He advocated manhood suffrage, demanded strict enforcement of the Civil Rights Act, and defended congressional Reconstruction. His Radical views prevented his reelection to the Senate. By 1868, Creswell had become a Republican, and after an internal struggle he gained control over the party in Maryland. In 1869, he was appointed Postmaster General, and his reforms and improvements in the department won him high praise. Following his resignation in 1874, he became U.S. counsel in the *Alabama* claims proceedings before returning to his law practice. Creswell died in Elkton, Maryland, on December 23, 1891. Baker, *Politics of Continuity*; Clark, *Politics in Maryland During the Civil War*.

Richard R. Duncan

CRISFIELD, John Woodland, *congressman*, was born in Kent county, Maryland, on November 8, 1808. After attending Washington College, he studied law, and was admitted to the Maryland bar in 1830. He served as a Whig in the Maryland House of Delegates in 1836, and as editor of the *Somerset Herald*, he supported William Henry Harrison in 1840. Seven years later, Crisfield was elected to Congress but served only one term, during which he opposed the Mexican War. He was briefly a member of the 1850 Maryland Constitutional Convention. With the collapse of the Whigs, he refused to identify with any party, but in the worsening sectional crisis he joined the emerging Unionist coalition. He was a delegate to the Washington Peace Conference, and was elected to Congress as a Unionist.

Crisfield supported the prosecution of the war but opposed emancipation. He denied that slavery was the cause of the war and maintained that the two issues should be kept separate. His bid for reelection in 1862 failed when Unconditional Unionists seized control of the party and nominated John A.J. Creswell (*q.v.*) instead. Crisfield's supporters ran him as an independent Unionist, but party division and the support of the military for Creswell spelled defeat. Crisfield briefly served as a delegate to the National Union Convention in 1866, but he devoted most of his time to business affairs. He became the leading promoter of the Eastern Shore Railroad and served as its president. Crisfield died in Princess Anne, Maryland, on January 12, 1897. Baker, *Politics of Continuity*; Clark, *Politics in Maryland During the Civil War*.

Richard R. Duncan

CRITTENDEN, John Jordan, *congressman*, was born near Versailles, Kentucky, on September 10, 1787. He attended the local Pisgah Academy, then studied at Washington College in Virginia before graduating from William and Mary in 1807. In 1809–1810, he was attorney general for the Illinois Territory, and in the War of 1812, he saw extensive service as an aide-de-camp. Elected to the state House of Representatives for seven consecutive terms (1811–1817), Crittenden was speaker in 1815 and 1817. In the latter year he was picked to fill a vacancy in the U.S. Senate. He returned to Illinois in 1819, then served in the state House in 1825 and 1829–1832, being speaker for the last four years. John Quincy Adams nominated Crittenden to the Supreme Court, but Jacksonian senators blocked the appointment. He became Kentucky's secretary of state in 1834, then was elected to the U.S. Senate as a Whig in 1835. Reelected in 1840, he resigned in 1841 to become U.S. Attorney General. Disagreements with President John Tyler led to his resignation in September of that year.

Crittenden returned to the Senate in 1842 to fill out Henry Clay's term, and he was elected to a full term in 1843. He opposed the admission of Texas and favored an amicable solution to the Oregon dispute. He also opposed the Mexican War. His support of Zachary Taylor for the 1848 Whig nomination caused a break with Clay, but Crittenden refused Taylor's offer of a Cabinet post. Elected governor of Kentucky in 1848, he resigned in 1850 to become U.S. Attorney General. He returned to the Senate in 1854. Crittenden owned a few household slaves but hoped that slavery would gradually disappear. However, he opposed the abolitionists, and he deplored the reopening of the slavery issue with the Kansas–Nebraska Bill. When the Whig party broke up, Crittenden became a Know-Nothing, and in 1860 he was a Constitutional Unionist.

Crittenden viewed secession as a calamity, and in December 1860 he introduced compromise proposals that would have restored the Missouri Compromise line by constitutional amendment. He fought to keep Kentucky in the Union, and he advocated the neutrality that the state followed until September 1861. After election to the House of Representatives in June 1861, he introduced a resolution declaring that the purpose of the war was to preserve the Constitution and the Union with the rights of the states unimpaired. Crittenden opposed the Confiscation Acts, the use of African American soldiers, the Emancipation Proclamation, and military interference in Kentucky. During most of his pre-1850 career he was overshadowed by Clay. During the last years of his life he was a moderate who could not cope with the radical forces that dominated events. As much as any man, he represented the failure of moderation in the sectional crisis. Crittenden was a candidate for reelection to the House when he died in Frankfort, Kentucky, on July 26, 1863. Collins, *History of Kentucky*, vol. 2; Kirwan, *John J. Crittenden.*

Lowell H. Harrison

CRITTENDEN, Thomas Leonidas, *general,* was born on May 15, 1819, in Russellville, Kentucky, the son of John J. Crittenden (*q.v.*). After business endeavors failed, he studied law, and was admitted to the Kentucky bar in 1840. A Mexican War volunteer, he was an aide to General Zachary Taylor and then lieutenant colonel of the 3rd Kentucky Infantry in 1847–1848. After his father helped get Taylor elected president, Crittenden was appointed consul in Liverpool (1849–1853). Then he resumed his law practice but was colonel of a Volunteer regiment in 1858 when a "Mormon war" seemed imminent. By the late summer of 1861, Crittenden, an old-line Whig who had supported the Constitutional Union ticket in 1860, commanded the state militia after many Kentuckians, including his brother George, had joined the Confederacy. Commissioned a brigadier general of Volunteers on September 27, 1861, he commanded the 5th Division in the Army of the Ohio at Shiloh. His performance won him promotion to major general on July 17. Crittenden pursued Braxton Bragg's 2nd Corps during the invasion of Kentucky in the late summer of 1862, but he saw little fighting at Perryville.

Crittenden helped prevent a possible Union disaster at Stones River (Murfreesboro), where he led the three-division left wing of William S. Rosecrans's (*q.v.*) Army of the Cumberland. His firm stand there resulted in a belated brevet to brigadier general in the Regular Army on March 2, 1867. Crittenden commanded the XXI Corps in the campaign leading to the battle of Chickamauga. Rosecrans blamed Crittenden and two other generals for the defeat there, and Crittenden was relieved of command on September 29. However, in February 1864 a court of inquiry called his performance "most creditable." Shifted to the Army of the Potomac but given only a division, Crittenden was relieved at his request on June 7, 1864. Denied another appointment, he resigned from the Army on December 13.

Aware of his lack of military training, Crittenden depended for advice upon more experienced subordinates. His performance was usually satisfactory, but he was one of those unfortunates to whom luck never seemed to come. He may have strained his competence as a corps commander. Appointed Kentucky state treasurer in January 1866, Crittenden resigned to accept President Andrew Johnson's (*q.v.*) offer of a colonelcy in the Regular Army. He retired on May 19, 1881, and lived on Staten Island. He died in Annandale, New York, on October 23, 1893. Kirwan, *John J. Crittenden*; Lamers, *Edge of Glory.*

Lowell H. Harrison

CROCKER, Marcellus Monroe, *general,* was born in Franklin, Indiana, on February 6, 1830; his family moved in 1840 to Illinois and in 1844 to Jefferson county, Iowa. He was appointed to West Point in 1847, but poor health compelled his resignation in mid-February 1849. Upon returning to Iowa, Crocker read law and began a practice in Keokuk county in 1851. He was mustered into Federal service as captain of Company D, 2nd Iowa Infantry, on May 27, 1861; at the regiment's Keokuk rendezvous four days later, he was elected its major. On September 6, he was promoted lieutenant colonel of the 2nd Iowa, then stationed at Bird Point, Missouri. In October, Crocker returned to Iowa to become colonel of the 13th Iowa, then being organized at Davenport. After duty in Missouri, Crocker's regiment was ordered to Tennessee and assigned to a brigade in John A. McClernand's (*q.v.*) division. At Shiloh, Crocker assumed command of the brigade when Colonel A. M. Hare was wounded. On April 8, the famed Iowa Brigade was constituted and placed under Crocker's command. He led the brigade in the siege of Corinth and was promoted brigadier general to rank from November 29, 1862.

On May 2, 1863, Crocker became a division commander in James B. McPherson's (*q.v.*) XVII Corps. The division spearheaded the May 14 attack on Jackson and, at Champion Hill on May 16, smashed a Confederate charge and participated in the counterattack that won a key victory for the Union. His body wracked by tuberculosis, Crocker returned to Iowa on sick leave in late May 1863. In early August, he rejoined the Army of the Tennessee and assumed command of the XVII Corps's 4th Division, which he led on the Harrisonburg raid and the Meridian expedition. In May, his physical condition became critical, and he submitted his resignation. It was rejected, and he was ordered to the Southwest, where he reported for duty at Fort Sumner, New Mexico, as commandant of the Bosque Redondo. His health seemingly improved, and he was ordered to Washington in March 1865. He died there on August 26, 1865. Bearss, *Vicksburg Campaign*, vols. 1, 2; Miers, *Web of Victory*; Williams, *Lincoln Finds a General*, vol 4.

Edwin C. Bearss

CROOK, George, *general,* was born near Dayton, Ohio, on September 8, 1828. He graduated from West Point in 1852, and was wounded in action against Indians in the Northwest. In September 1861 he was appointed colonel of the 36th Ohio and served in the West Virginia campaign. Crook was promoted to brigadier general, and his brigade, attached to the IX Corps, served at South Mountain and Antietam. Transferred to the West, he commanded a cavalry division at Chickamauga and defeated Joseph Wheeler's cavalry at Farmington, Tennessee, in October 1863. He returned to West Virginia in February 1864 and led a successful raid into southwestern Virginia that routed Albert G. Jenkins's force at Cloyd's Mountain and destroyed the New River Bridge. In August 1864, he held dual command of the Department of West Virginia, and of a cavalry division in General Philip Sheridan's (*q.v.*) army in the victories at Winchester, Fisher's Hill, and Cedar Creek.

Crook was promoted to major general in October 1864. On February 21, 1865, he and General Benjamin F. Kelley were captured by a daring raid led by Captain Jesse O'Neill's Partisan Rangers. Exchanged in March 1865, he rejoined Sheridan for the final actions of the war at Dinwiddie, Sailor's Creek and Appomattox. Although promoted to brevet major general of Regulars, Crook accepted the lieutenant colonelcy of the 23rd Infantry after the war.

An eccentric in dress and beard, Crook was one of the most effective and intelligent Indian fighters. His defeat of the Apaches in 1871 brought promotion to brigadier general in the Regular Army. His column was repulsed by massed Sioux at the Rosebud River in the Great Sioux Uprising of 1876. In 1883, he again defeated the Apaches, including Geronimo's band. In 1885, when Geronimo began to raid again, Crook was not able to capture him, and was relieved. He died in Chicago on March 21, 1890. Sheridan, *Memoirs,* vols. 1, 2; Starr, *Union Cavalry,* vol. 2.

Roy P. Stonesifer, Jr.

CRUFT, Charles, *general,* was born in Terre Haute, Indiana, on January 12, 1826. He graduated from Wabash College in 1842, worked as a bank clerk, studied law, and was admitted to the bar in 1848. He served as president of the St. Louis, Alton and Terre Haute Railroad from 1855 until 1858. After witnessing the battle of First Bull Run, Cruft enlisted on September 20, 1861, as a colonel in the 31st Indiana Volunteers. He commanded a brigade in Lew Wallace's (*q.v.*) division at Fort Donelson, where he vigorously pressed his men forward and showed courage under fire. Under heavy attack at Shiloh, Cruft's brigade repulsed the charging Confederates four times. Cruft was seriously wounded in the leg and shoulder, and had to retire from the field. As a result of these actions, he received promotion to the rank of brigadier general. Commanding raw troops and greatly outnumbered, he again performed well during the Union debacle at the battle of Richmond, Kentucky.

Assigned a brigade in John M. Palmer's (*q.v.*) division, Cruft rallied his soldiers against several Confederate attacks at Chickamauga and later complained that no one had informed him of a general order to withdraw. He commanded a division at Chattanooga and in the relief of Ambrose Burnside (*q.v.*) at Knoxville. At the battle of Nashville, Cruft commanded several detachments of black troops near Fort Negley, along the Granny White Pike. At the end of the war, he was breveted a major general and stationed at Huntsville, Alabama. Cruft was mustered out of the Army on August 24, 1865, returned to Terre Haute, and resumed his legal career. He died in that city on March 23, 1883. Cozzens, *This Terrible Sound*; Horn, *Decisive Battle of Nashville*.

George C. Rable

CURTIN, Andrew Gregg, *governor,* was born on April 22, 1817, in Bellefonte, Pennsylvania. In 1839, he was admitted to the Pennsylvania bar and became active in Whig politics. Beginning in 1840, he stumped effectively for all Whig presidential candidates, and in 1855 narrowly missed election to the U.S. Senate by a Whig–Nativist combination. Throughout most of that year Curtin and his rival Simon Cameron (*q.v.*) remained deadlocked for the nomination while charges and countercharges (focusing on Cameron's attempt to bribe potential supporters) made them enemies. Their bitter rivalry continued in the newly established Republican party, which in 1860 nominated and elected Curtin governor of Pennsylvania. Following President-elect Abraham Lincoln's (*q.v.*) advice, he was the first Northern governor to advocate force to keep the South in the Union. The Republican legislature responded by passing a resolution that the South did not have the right to secede, pledged Pennsylvania to support the Union, and doomed the February 1861 Washington Peace Convention by sending an unsympathetic delegation.

Curtin was the first governor Lincoln consulted in Washington (April 8, 1861), and he enthusiastically implemented Lincoln's call for troops. War added fuel to the Curtin–Cameron feud because Cameron, as Secretary of War, constantly dealt with Curtin and frequently clashed with him. When Baltimore rioters cut communications with Washington, Curtin called for 25,000 additional troops, whom Cameron refused to accept until after the disaster at Bull Run. The Cameron faction attacked Curtin for providing troops with inferior supplies and temporarily undermined confidence in his administration, but the troops were aware of Curtin's concern for them and called him the ''Soldier's Friend.'' Besides improving care of the sick and wounded and bringing Pennsylvania dead home for burial, Curtin induced the legislature to establish a fund to educate war orphans.

Under Curtin's leadership, Pennsylvania raised and equipped 270 regiments in addition to many detached companies. At the Altoona Governors' Conference in September 1862, Curtin helped contain the wrath of the Radical Republicans. Since George B. McClellan (*q.v.*) had just turned back Robert E. Lee at the battle of Antietam and Lincoln had just issued the preliminary Emancipation Proclamation, Curtin persuaded the conference to approve Lincoln's policies rather than to demand McClellan's replacement with John C. Frémont (*q.v.*).

Curtin further annoyed the Radicals in 1863 by arguing that only Congress—not the President—could suspend the writ of habeas corpus. He did not plan to run for reelection, but the Republicans needed his popularity because his margin of victory in 1863 was only 15,000 out of 500,000 votes cast. After his second inauguration, his health failed, and Lincoln ordered a naval vessel to carry him to Havana to recuperate. In mid-March 1864, Curtin returned to Harrisburg to continue his support of the war effort.

When he retired as governor in 1867, Curtin was the most popular Republican in Pennsylvania, yet Cameron, with his superb political organization, easily defeated him for the U.S. Senate. After Pennsylvania Republicans unsuccessfully urged Curtin for Ulysses S. Grant's (*q.v.*) running mate in 1868, Cameron in 1869 got Grant to appoint Curtin minister to Russia, thus exiling him to St. Petersburg. When Curtin returned to Pennsylvania in 1872, he joined the anti-Grant Liberal Republican movement and later was elected a delegate to the 1873 Constitutional Convention. The new Pennsylvania constitution was meant to curtail Cameron's power, but when reform was not forthcoming, Curtin moved into the Democratic party and ran for Congress. He lost in 1878 but succeeded in the three following elections. In 1887, he retired to his home in Bellefonte, where he died on October 7, 1894. Egle, *Andrew Gregg Curtin.*

Ari Hoogenboom

CURTIS, Samuel Ryan, *congressman, general,* was born on February 3, 1805, near Champlain, New York, and moved in 1809 to Licking county, Ohio. He graduated from West Point in 1831 but resigned from the Army a year later. He was a civil engineer on the National Road, and chief engineer of the Muskingum River improvement project. After studying law, Curtis was admitted to the Ohio bar. During the Mexican War, he served as Ohio adjutant general, as commander of the 3rd Ohio Infantry, and finally as a member of General John E. Wool's (*q.v.*) staff. In 1847, he moved to Keokuk, Iowa, where he was chief engineer of the Des Moines River improvement project. Curtis also became involved in railroads, law, and Republican politics, and was elected mayor of Keokuk in 1856. In that same year, he won the first of three consecutive terms to Congress, where he devoted himself to the promotion of the Pacific railroad.

In June 1861, Curtis took the 2nd Iowa Volunteers into Missouri to guard the railroad between Hannibal and St. Joseph. After sitting in the special session of Congress, he resigned his seat and was appointed brigadier general. As commander of the Southwest District of Missouri, he defeated the Confederates at the battle of Pea Ridge. After his appointment as major general in March, and as military governor of Arkansas in May, his troops were resupplied, then completed a sweep to Helena, Arkansas, on July 14. Curtis took leave to preside over the organizational meeting of the incorporators of the Pacific Railroad. Made commander of the Department of the Missouri in September 1862, he clashed with Governor Hamilton R. Gamble (*q.v.*), who objected to his stern treatment of Rebel sympathizers.

Removed in May 1863 in an unsuccessful effort to calm factional strife in Missouri, Curtis was assigned to command the Department of Kansas in January 1864. He took the field again in the summer of 1864 and drove Sterling Price's forces from Kansas. He took over the Department of the Northwest in January 1865, and when it was dissolved in July, he was appointed a commissioner to treat vith Indian tribes on the Upper Missouri. Curtis left the Army on April 30, 1866, and soon afterward was appointed to a commission to inspect work on the Pacific Railroad. After an inspection trip, he died in Council Bluffs, Iowa, on December 26, 1866. Shea, *Pea Ridge*.

Hubert H. Wubben

CUSTER, George Armstrong, *general,* was born on December 5, 1839, in New Rumley, Ohio. He graduated from West Point, last in the class of 1861. He fought at Bull Run and joined General George B. McClellan's (*q.v.*) staff as a captain. Under Alfred Pleasonton (*q.v.*), his aggressive spirit and daring at Aldie brought him a direct promotion to brigadier general and command of the Michigan Brigade. He fought with distinction at Hanover, Pennsylvania, and at Rummel's Farm in the Gettsyburg campaign. He found that in seemingly impossible situations, such as at Trevilian Station (June 11, 1864), he could fight his way out. He became a division commander in Philip Sheridan's (*q.v.*) Army of the Shenandoah and fought with skill and success in the actions from Winchester to Waynesboro. In the final battle of the war at Appomattox Station, it was Custer who blocked Lee's retreat. He ended the war as a major general, but received appointment as lieutenant colonel of the 7th Cavalry in 1866.

Often insubordinate to his superiors, Custer insisted on obedience from his commands. In Kansas in 1867, he ordered his troopers to fire on a group of deserters (one died), but then left his unit without orders. He was court martialed, found guilty, and suspended for one year. Sheridan, unable to catch the Cheyenne in summer campaigns, used Custer in November 1868 to destroy their camp on the Washita. Custer led the Black Hills expedition in 1874 that confirmed gold in the area. At the outbreak of the Great Sioux Uprising of 1876, he attempted to defeat, with only his 7th Cavalry, an Indian force that outnumbered them as much as ten to one. After the reckless division of his regiment, the 266 officers and men who rode with his segment at the Little Big Horn on June 25, 1876, were all killed. Longacre, *Cavalry at Gettysburg*; Starr, *Union Cavalry*, vols. 1, 2.

Roy P. Stonesifer, Jr.

CUTLER, Lysander, *general,* was born on February 16, 1807, in Worcester county, Massachusetts. After obtaining a common school education, he taught in Dexter, Maine, where he became a successful entrepreneur and civic leader. He commanded a local regiment in the Aroostook War, and was a selectman, railroad director, state senator, and trustee for Tufts College. Ruined by the depression of 1857, Cutler established a grain brokerage firm in Milwaukee, remaining there until the Civil War began. Appointed colonel of the 6th Wisconsin Volunteers, he accompanied the regiment to Washington in July 1861. There he trained his raw Midwestern troops and eliminated unfit officers. The combat record of this unit, an element of the Iron Brigade, eloquently attests to the competence of the man who molded it.

At Gainesville, the first battle in which his regiment fought, Cutler suffered a leg wound that left him permanently crippled. Notwithstanding this disability and the chronic rheumatism that also afflicted him, he had proven to be such an effective leader that John Gibbon (*q.v.*), upon relinquishing command of the Iron Brigade, recommended that Cutler replace him. Politics thwarted the appointment, but Cutler did lead a brigade at Fredericksburg and Chancellorsville. He saw little action in either engagement; at Gettysburg, on the other hand, his was one of the first Federal infantry units on the scene, where it saw hard combat on July 1. Although severely punished in its initial actions, the brigade maintained cohesion under Cutler's inspired leadership and participated on the second and third days.

Cutler went on to lead troops in the Wilderness, where he assumed command of a division, and in the early stages of the Petersburg campaign. At that point his health failed and, at age fifty-seven, he was detailed to recruiting duty for the remainder of the war. When Civil War scholars mention Lysander Cutler at all, they dismiss him with a footnote or at most a few cursory remarks. Admittedly, if significant accomplishment is the most important criterion, he warrants no more than that. But he deserves recognition for what he was, if not for what he did.

An exacting disciplinarian and a self-taught soldier, Cutler trained and commanded with a skill seldom equaled by Civil War Volunteer officers. In this regard, the fact that the men who grumbled about the elderly officer's seemingly unreasonable demands in 1861 had come to appreciate his worth by 1864 speaks for itself, as does the recommendation of John Gibbon, who knew a soldier when he saw one. Devoid of flamboyance and dash, Cutler possessed a character and determination that neither illness, anguish, nor advancing age could diminish. He was, indeed, the beau ideal of the Union Volunteer. In June 1865 he resigned from the Army and returned to Milwaukee, where he died on July 30, 1866. Catton, *Glory Road*; Love, *Wisconsin in the War of the Rebellion*; Rhea, *Battle of the Wilderness*.

James L. Morrison, Jr.

CUTLER, William Parker, *congressman,* was born in Marietta, Ohio, on July 12, 1812. His grandfather, Mannasseh Cutler, was instrumental in the passage of the Ordinance of 1787. Cutler attended public school and spent several years at Ohio University. Primarily a farmer, he helped to organize the Belpre and Cincinnati Railroad (of which he was president), the Marietta and Pittsburgh Railroad, and the Hocking Valley Railroad. He also had interests in developing the coal mining business in the Hocking Valley region. As a Whig, Cutler was elected to the Ohio House (1844–1847) and selected speaker for his last term. He was also a member of the 1850 Constitutional Convention, was an outspoken abolitionist, and was elected as a Republican to Congress in 1860.

Although he seldom spoke in the House, Cutler performed a significant service when he decided to keep a private diary from December 16, 1862, to February 9, 1863. Among the subjects he discussed were the widespread disenchantment in party ranks with the President and his Cabinet, and the secret caucuses of the House Republicans that met in the waning months of the 37th Congress. Cutler also helped to raise troops from southeastern Ohio, and organized railroad employees to intercept Major John Hunt Morgan during his famous raid through Ohio in 1863. Cutler returned to Marietta, engaged in the development of railroads in Ohio and the Midwest, and for a number of years was on the board of trustees of Marietta College. He died in Marietta on April 11, 1889. Bogue, *Congressman's Civil War*; Bogue, "William Parker Cutler's Congressional Diary," *Civil War History*.

Thomas H. Smith

D

DANA, Charles Anderson, *editor, assistant secretary of war*, was born on August 8, 1819, in Hinsdale, New Hampshire. He attended Harvard College and later visited Brook Farm, the early socialist experiment. There he met Horace Greeley (*q.v.*), who hired him and named him managing editor of the *New York Tribune*. Dana remained with the *Tribune* until 1862, when he split with Greeley over war-related issues. During his work on the *Tribune*, he met Secretary of War Edwin Stanton (*q.v.*). Shortly after his separation from the *Tribune*, Dana was appointed by Stanton to a War Department commission that audited unsettled claims against the quartermaster's department at Cairo, Illinois. His work impressed Stanton and Lincoln, and in 1863 Stanton named him a special commissioner of the War Department, purportedly to investigate the pay service in the western armies.

Dana's real task, however, was to report on the activities of the western armies and, especially, on Ulysses S. Grant's (*q.v.*) character and ability as a commanding officer. Rumors circulated that Grant was an alcoholic, and Stanton and Lincoln wanted to know the truth. Dana traveled with Grant during the Vicksburg campaign and came to admire him greatly. His glowing reports to Stanton, filed in code, supposedly played a part in Lincoln's decision to promote Grant. Upon Dana's return to Washington, Stanton named him assistant secretary of war, a position he held until the war ended.

After the war, Dana returned to his real love, newspapering. In 1868, he purchased the *New York Sun*, the original penny newspaper, and established a reputation as an excellent editor of the inexpensive, mass-circulation daily. Dana moved his paper into a more modern appearance and more extensive local, and sensational, coverage. He was known as a reporter's editor, allowing his staff great leeway in reporting and in writing styles. Dana died in Glen Cove, New York, on October 17, 1897. Dana, *Recollections*; Rosebault, *When Dana Was the Sun*; Steele, *The Sun*.

Fredric F. Endres

DANA, Richard Henry, Jr., *author, lawyer*, was born on August 1, 1815, in Cambridge, Massachusetts. The son of a noted literary figure, he graduated from Harvard College in 1837, and briefly taught elocution there before gaining admission to the Massachusetts bar in 1840. It was a two-year therapeutic voyage as a common sailor, following Dana's junior year at Harvard, that shaped his literary reputation and legal career. In 1840, he published *Two Years Before the Mast*, a major contribution to the reform of the American merchant marine and a literary classic. Dana's experience at sea also led him to concentrate his law practice in admiralty cases.

In politics, Dana described himself as "a highly conservative Whig," and opposed action against slavery in the South. He did, however, enthusiastically support efforts to bar slavery from the western territories. He attended the Free Soil Convention of 1848 and helped establish the Republican party in Massachusetts in 1855. He successfully defended the individuals charged with rescuing the fugitive slave "Shadrack" from a Boston courtroom in 1851, but failed to prevent the surrender of Anthony Burns, another fugitive slave, in 1854.

During the Civil War, Dana's greatest achievement was to convince the U.S. Supreme Court to uphold the Union blockade of the Confederacy. Immediately after the war, Dana was a government counsel in the truncated effort to convict Jefferson Davis of treason. An aristocrat who fared poorly in elective politics, Dana devoted the rest of his life to literary pursuits and legal theory. He died in Rome on January 7, 1882. Dana, *Journal*; Shapiro, *Richard Henry Dana, Jr.*

Stanley Harrold

DAVIDSON, John Wynn, *general*, was born on August 18, 1823, in Fairfax county, Virginia. He graduated from West Point in 1845, was commissioned in the cavalry, and served on the frontier in Kansas and Wisconsin. During the Mexican War he was mainly in California. Davidson subsequently was assigned to frontier service again, and fought Indians at Clear Lake, the Russian River, and the Sacramento River. In 1854, he defeated the Jicarilla Apaches at Cieneguillo, New Mexico, where he was badly wounded. He was promoted to captain of the 1st Dragoons in 1855 and was stationed at Fort Tejon, near Los Angeles, at the time of Fort Sumter.

Davidson was offered a commission in the Confederate Army, but although a Virginian by birth, education, and family ties, he remained loyal to the Union. He was assigned to the 1st U.S. Cavalry in August 1861 and become a major in the 2nd U.S. Cavalry on November 14. In February 1862, Davidson was appointed brigadier general and commanded a brigade in the Peninsula campaign. He participated in the battles of Gaines' Mill and Golding's Farm, and won the brevets of lieutenant colonel and colonel for gallant conduct. In addition, he took part in the actions at Lee's Mill, Mechanicsville, Savage Station, and Glendale. After the Peninsula, Davidson was transferred to the West, where he commanded the St. Louis District and, for a brief time, the Army of Southeast Missouri. In 1863–1864, he commanded the Army of Arkansas and served in the Little Rock expedition. He was breveted through all the grades to major general in both the Regular Army and the Volunteers.

On January 15, 1866, Davidson was mustered out of the Volunteers and assigned to the 2nd U.S. Cavalry. He served briefly in the Inspector General's Department, was a professor of military science at Kansas Agricultural College (1868–1871), and held various commands in Indian Territory and Texas. In March 1879 he was promoted to colonel of the 2nd Cavalry and served in the District of the Yellowstone and at Fort Custer, Montana, where he was severely injured when his horse fell on him. He died four months later, on June 26, 1881, in St. Paul, Minnesota. Castel, *Sterling Price*; Monaghan, *Civil War on the Western Border.*

James J. Hudson

DAVIES, Henry Eugene, *general,* was born in New York City on July 2, 1836. After attending Harvard and Williams College, he graduated from Columbia in 1857. Davies was practicing law in New York City when the Civil War began. He obtained a captaincy in the 5th New York and fought at Bethel, Virginia (June 1861). Subsequently he accepted a major's commission in the Harris Light Cavalry (2nd New York), and served thereafter with mounted units. Davies fought at Second Bull Run and Beverly Ford, Virginia. Promoted successively to lieutenant colonel, colonel, brigadier (September 1863), and major general of Volunteers (May 1865), Davies led brigades, and sometimes divisions, in the Cavalry Corps of the Army of the Potomac. He rode in the Richmond raids (1864) and showed well in the Appomattox campaign.

Davies's most important battles were in the last twelve months of the war, under General Philip Sheridan (*q.v.*). He pursued a Confederate force after the battle at Todd's Tavern, dismounted and led a charge at Beech Grove Church, fought off Fitzhugh Lee's attack against Sheridan's rear guard on the way to Yellow Tavern, and ripped up six miles of railroad track and destroyed a locomotive near Ashland Station. In the Appomattox campaign, Davies's brigade was driven back by a Confederate assault at Dinwiddie Courthouse, but at Paineville they attacked and burned a wagon train carrying Robert E. Lee's headquarters files, capturing several prisoners and five cannon.

A reliable and valiant brigade commander, Davies was one of many talented Volunteer officers who served creditably in the war. He resigned his commission in January 1866 and, as a Republican, held the offices of public administrator of New York City (1866–1869) and assistant district attorney for the Southern District of New York (1870–1872). After 1872, he resumed his law practice and wrote several books—including an admiring biography of Sheridan. Davies died on September 7, 1894, in Middleboro, Massachusetts. Sheridan, *Memoirs*; Starr, *Union Cavalry*, vol. 2.

Joseph G. Dawson III

DAVIES, Thomas Alfred, *general,* was born on December 3, 1809, in St. Lawrence county, New York. He graduated from West Point in 1829, and served in the 1st Infantry on the Wisconsin frontier and as quartermaster at the Military Academy before resigning his commission in 1831 to practice civil engineering in New York City. He eventually became a successful New York City merchant.

Davies, elected colonel of the 16th New York in May 1861, led the regiment at First Bull Run and in the defenses of Washington, D.C., until his promotion to brigadier general of Volunteers on March 7, 1862. He had a good reputation as a field commander, especially for his performance at the battle of Corinth, where his division bore the brunt of the Confederate attack. Davies was less fortunate in his first independent command; he was roundly criticized for destroying and abandoning the defenses of Island No. 10 and New Madrid, and unnecessarily concentrating Union forces at Columbus, Kentucky, during Forrest's 1862 raid. Distrusted thereafter by Ulysses S. Grant (*q.v.*), he was relegated to a succession of commands remote from the active theaters of the war.

Davies was mustered out of the service on August 24, 1865, as brevet major general of Volunteers. After the war, he made a substantial fortune in New York real estate and wrote a number of books supporting the divine inspiration of the Bible. He also wrote a practical guide titled *How to Make Money, and How to Keep It*, which was later revised and reissued by Henry Ford. Davies died on August 19, 1899, in Odgensburg, New York. Bearss, *Vicksburg Campaign*, vol. 1; Grant, *Papers*, vols. 5, 6, 7; Williams, *Lincoln Finds a General*, vol. 4.

Bruce J. Dinges

DAVIS, David, *Supreme Court justice,* was born on March 9, 1815, in Cecil county, Maryland. He attended Kenyon College in Ohio, read law in Lenox, Massachusetts, and graduated from the New Haven Law School in 1835. Moving to Illinois, Davis worked as an attorney and railroad lobbyist. Although he became a circuit judge in 1847, his passion, like that of his confidant Abraham Lincoln (*q.v.*), was Whig politics. Davis saw his friend as a coming man in the party and joined the Lincoln inner circle. He was a masterful campaign manager for Lincoln at the 1860 Republican Convention in Chicago and was instrumental in wooing those two reluctant prima donnas, Salmon P. Chase (*q.v.*) and William H. Seward (*q.v.*), into the Cabinet. Davis would have been satisfied with a district judgeship, but the candidacy of his political enemy Orville H. Browning (*q.v.*) for a vacant seat on the U.S. Supreme Court roused him to action.

After several delays, Lincoln nominated Davis as an associate justice in August 1862. From the beginning, Davis was uncomfortable on the Court. He disliked writing and could not stay out of patronage wrangles. Although he joined the majority in the Prize Cases in upholding Lincoln's authority to proclaim a blockade of the Confederate states, he broke with the administration over the question of military trials for civilians. He further irritated Lincoln by warning that the Emancipation Proclamation would be politically costly in Illinois and suggesting that it be withdrawn. He opposed the elevation of Salmon P. Chase to the Chief Justiceship but accepted the appointment with good grace.

As a result of his opposition to military tribunals in the North, Davis wrote his only important opinion. Speaking for a unanimous Court in *Ex Parte Milligan*, he ruled that the military trial of Lambdin P. Milligan (*q.v.*) had been illegal because the President could not authorize the trials of civilians by military commissions. He made an eloquent defense of constitutional liberties in wartime, but he was not inclined to interfere with military Reconstruction in the South. Davis remained unhappy on the Court and began nursing presidential ambitions, which undoubtedly hampered his effectiveness as a justice. Forced to resign his seat after his election in 1877 to the U.S. Senate, Davis played the role of a nonpartisan political broker. He retired from the Senate in 1883 and died on June 26, 1886, in Bloomington, Illinois. King, *Lincoln's Manager*; Swisher, *The Taney Period.*

George C. Rable

DAVIS, Garrett, *senator*, was born in Montgomery county, Kentucky, on September 10, 1801. After a common school education, he worked in the county clerk's office while preparing for the bar. He served in the Kentucky legislature as a Whig in 1833 and in 1839 entered the U.S. Congress, where he served for eight years. In 1849 Davis was a member of the Kentucky Constitutional Convention and actively supported the end of slavery. His virulent anti-Catholicism led him to the American party after the collapse of the Whig party.

A strong Unionist, Davis entered the U.S. Senate in 1861. His reputation rests upon his Civil War career. In a period when much of Kentucky's leadership faltered, Davis stood uncompromisingly for the Union. He tirelessly supported Abraham Lincoln's (*q.v.*) efforts to keep Kentucky in the Union, and when elected to the Senate advocated the confiscation of Rebel property. The adoption of increasingly Radical legislation during the last years of the war, however, led Davis to a scathing attack on Lincoln and Republican party policies. By the end of hostilities Davis had returned to the Democratic party, which reelected him to the Senate in 1867. He died in Paris, Kentucky, on September 22, 1872. Collins, *History of Kentucky*, vol. 2; Levin, *Lawyers and Lawmakers of Kentucky.*

Marion B. Lucas

DAVIS, Henry Winter, *congressman*, was born in Annapolis, Maryland, on August 16, 1817. He graduated from Kenyon College in 1833, studied law at the University of Virginia, and in 1840 moved to the District of Columbia, where he set up a flourishing law practice. At the age of twenty-seven he was admitted to the bar of the U.S. Supreme Court, became involved in Whig politics, and soon attracted considerable notice. Following the death of his wife, Davis moved to Baltimore, where he entered Maryland politics and served as a Whig elector in 1852. With the collapse of that party, he joined the Know-Nothings in 1855, and as an American ran for, and won, the U.S. House seat from Baltimore. He was overwhelmingly reelected, but in 1859, in the wake of John Brown's (*q.v.*) raid and charges of being anti-Southern, he was seriously challenged for reelection. Victorious after the most lawless election in Baltimore history, Davis returned to the House of Representatives. He provoked censure by the Maryland House of Delegates when he voted for William Pennington (*q.v.*) in the deadlocked speaker's contest.

Davis was willing to cooperate with other factions in creating an opposition party united against the Democrats. In 1860, he preferred the Republicans but reluctantly supported the Constitutional Union ticket. He endorsed the compromise proposals of the Committee of Thirty-three, and in Maryland became one of the most influential leaders in rallying support for the Union cause. In his bid for reelection to the special session of Congress, Davis ran on a platform calling for the "unconditional maintenance of the Union." He lost the election but became the leader of the Unconditional Unionists in Maryland.

By 1863, Davis, never proslavery, led the demand for immediate emancipation and was overwhelmingly elected to Congress. He became increasingly disenchanted with Abraham Lincoln (*q.v.*). He was passed over for a Cabinet post, questioned the legality of the Emancipation Proclamation—not its effect—and opposed Lincoln's Proclamation of Amnesty and Reconstruction. In opposing Lincoln's approach to Reconstruction, Davis championed the role of Congress in dealing with the problem in the Wade–Davis Bill. Lincoln's pocket veto angered Davis, and in conjunction with Benjamin Wade (*q.v.*) in the Senate, he struck back at the President in the Wade–Davis Manifesto. Meanwhile, in Maryland, conservative Unionists gained control of the party, and Davis was denied renomination. He remained an important Radical spokesman until his death in Baltimore on December 30, 1865. Belz, *Reconstructing the Union*; Henig, *Henry Winter Davis*.

Richard R. Duncan

DAVIS, Jefferson Columbus, *general*, was born in Clark county, Indiana, on March 2, 1828. In 1846, he enlisted in Colonel James Lane's 3rd Indiana Regiment and was made a 2nd lieutenant in the Regular Army's 1st Artillery for his gallant conduct at the battle of Buena Vista. He was promoted to 1st lieutenant (1852) and stationed at Fort Sumter when the Civil War began. In May 1861, Davis was made captain in the Regular Army. He organized the 22nd Indiana, with the help of his good friend Governor Oliver H.P. Morton (*q.v.*), and was made its colonel.

In December 1861, after he had captured a numerically superior Confederate force at Milford, Mississippi, Davis was promoted to brigadier general of Volunteers and given command of a brigade. At the battle of Pea Ridge in March

1862, he commanded a division and was instrumental in the defeat of the Confederate forces. Following Shiloh, his command participated in the capture of Corinth. In August, Davis returned to Indiana on sick leave. On August 30, however, General William Nelson was badly defeated by Confederate General Edmund Kirby Smith at Richmond, Kentucky, and was in danger of losing the city of Louisville. Davis reported to Nelson in Louisville and offered his services. Unfortunately, Nelson insulted Davis over a minor matter, Davis overreacted, and the result was a confrontation in the Galt House. Nelson slapped Davis, after which Davis borrowed a pistol and killed Nelson. Davis was arrested but never brought to trial.

Governor Morton interceded, and there was a command shake-up. Davis would receive increased responsibility but would not be promoted. He commanded a division at Murfreesboro (Stones River), Chickamauga, and Atlanta, during which he distinguished himself. He was made commander of the XIV Corps during William T. Sherman's (*q.v.*) March to the Sea and retained that position until the end of the war. Both William S. Rosecrans (*q.v.*) and Ulysses S. Grant (*q.v.*) recommended his promotion, but to no avail. Although he was breveted a major general, Davis never rose above the rank he had obtained nearly four years earlier. He never regretted killing Nelson, but he was always bitter about not being promoted.

Davis remained on active duty following the war and became commander of the 23rd Infantry. He was stationed on the Pacific Coast and served two years in Alaska. In 1873, he was sent to Oregon to campaign against the Modoc Indians, following the death of General Edward R.S. Canby (*q.v.*), and forced their surrender. Davis died in Chicago on November 30, 1879. Jones, "General Jefferson C. Davis," *Georgia Historical Quarterly.*

Raymond L. Shoemaker

DAVIS, Theodore Russell, *artist, journalist,* was born in Boston in 1840. He attended the Rittenhouse Academy in Washington, D.C., before moving to Brooklyn in 1845. Davis received some training in drawing and wood engraving from James Walker or Henry W. Herrick, or possibly both. In 1861, he joined *Harper's Weekly* and became one of the most productive artist–correspondents of the Civil War. He covered the battle between the *Monitor* and the *Merrimac,* the battles at Shiloh and Antietam, the siege of Atlanta, and Sherman's campaign through Georgia and the Carolinas. His drawings in the field, like those of Alfred Waud (*q.v.*) and Winslow Homer (*q.v.*), were the basis for many of the wood engravings that form a rich visual record of the war. He was wounded twice and is said to have held off at gunpoint surgeons who wanted to amputate his leg.

After the war, Davis traveled extensively throughout the South and the boom-towns and mining districts of the West, especially in Colorado. During the spring and summer of 1867 he spent four months in the saddle and covered an estimated 3,000 miles to observe and record the Indian Wars. For a brief time, he accompanied George A. Custer (*q.v.*) in Nebraska and Colorado. Drawing on his firsthand knowledge, Davis became one of America's premier illustrators of life on the frontier. He retired to Asbury Park, New Jersey, in 1884 and died there on November 10, 1894. Samuels, *Illustrated Biographical Encyclopedia of Artists of the American West*; Taft, *Artists and Illustrators of the Old West.*

Ben Bassham

DAVIS, Thomas Treadwell, *congressman,* was born in Middlebury, Vermont, on August 22, 1810, and moved to Clinton, New York, in 1817. He graduated from Hamilton College in 1831, settled in Syracuse, studied law, and was admitted to the bar in 1833. Davis practiced law and was involved in various business ventures, including the organization of the Oswego and Syracuse Railroad Company, the incorporation of the Syracuse Savings Bank, and the mining of coal.

Although Davis refused to run for office under a party label, the ardent Unionist was elected to the 38th Congress. To demonstrate his commitment to the war effort, he spoke in favor of conscription, higher taxes, and other revenue-raising plans. Davis was also active in legislation relating to railroads, fire engine companies, and gas lighting companies. After serving two terms in Congress, he declined to run again, and returned to his law practice in Syracuse. He died May 2, 1872, in Washington, D.C. Clayton, *History of Onondaga County.*

Lori A. Lisowski

DAVIS, William Morris, *congressman,* was born in Keene Valley, New York, on August 16, 1815. He moved to Philadelphia early in his adulthood and entered the sugar refining business. He made only a short venture into politics by successfully running for Congress in 1860. As a novice congressman, he supported a high tariff policy and abolitionist demands for emancipation. He was among the Pennsylvania Republicans who lost their political offices in a Democratic landslide in the 1862 elections. Davis died in Keene Valley on August 5, 1891. Davis, *Pennsylvania Politics.*

W. Wayne Smith

DAWES, Henry Laurens, *congressman,* was born on October 30, 1816, in Cummington, Massachusetts. After graduating from Yale College in 1839, he opened a law office in Pittsfield, Massachusetts, and entered state politics as a Whig. In 1856, after serving several terms in the state legislature, Dawes was elected as a Republican to the U.S. House of Representatives, where he served until 1875. In that year he was elected to the U.S. Senate, where he remained until retiring in 1892.

During the Civil War, Dawes was the leading member of the House War Contracts Committee, which uncovered a number of questionable contracts granted by the War and Navy departments and considerably embarrassed President Abraham Lincoln (*q.v.*). As chairman of the House Committee on Elections, which made recommendations to the House concerning the seating of representatives from conquered areas of the South, Dawes influenced congressional policy on Reconstruction. He was a moderate on most issues relating to slavery and Reconstruction, opposed confiscation of Confederate property, and favored weakening the emancipation provisions of the 1862 Confiscation Act. He steered so closely to Lincoln's position on Reconstruction that he asked the House to relieve his Elections Committee of Reconstruction matters, lest he lose the chairmanship of the committee.

After the Civil War, Dawes's influence continued to grow in Congress when he became chairman of the important House Ways and Means and Appropriations committees. In the Senate, he was chairman of the Committee on Indian Affairs, and drafted the Dawes Act of 1887. He died in Pittsfield on February 5, 1903. Belz, *Reconstructing the Union*; Nicklason, "Civil War Contracts Committee," *Civil War History.*

Richard H. Abbott

DAWSON, John Littleton, *congressman,* was born in Uniontown, Pennsylvania, on February 7, 1813. In 1833, he graduated from Washington College, and two years later was admitted to the bar. In 1838, he was elected deputy attorney general for Fayette county, and in 1845 was appointed U.S. district attorney for western Pennsylvania, a post he held until 1848. He was active in Democratic politics, and in 1844, 1848, 1860, and 1868 served as a delegate to the Democratic National Convention. He ran unsuccessfully for the 31st Congress but was elected to the 32nd and 33rd Congresses. Although Dawson declined renomination in 1854, he accepted the nomination in 1862 and 1864, and was elected.

Dawson established himself as a consistent critic of the war and a staunch advocate of a Democratic peace. He tried, for example, to amend conscription bills in a manner that would reduce Pennsylvania's future quota requirements. When conscription bills came before the House, he joined most of his Democratic colleagues in voting against them. Dawson also objected to what he considered unconstitutional expansion of the war's aims: specifically, emancipation. Concealing his hostility to black freedom in constitutional rhetoric, he argued that the war was to defend the Union, and nothing else. He opposed the 13th Amendment, the Freedmen's Bureau, black suffrage in the District of Columbia, the Civil Rights Act of 1866, the 14th Amendment, and the 1867 Reconstruction Act. Dawson introduced a resolution that sought to limit President Lincoln's (*q.v.*) power to negotiate a peace settlement with the seceded states. His political career concluded at the end of the 39th Congress, and he died in Springfield Township, Pennsylvania, on September 18, 1870. Bradley, *Triumph of Militant Republicanism.*

Philip J. Avillo, Jr.

DAYTON, William Lewis, *diplomat,* was born in Somerset county, New Jersey, on February 17, 1807. After attending Trenton Academy and graduating from Princeton College, he studied law, and was admitted to the New Jersey bar in 1830. While practicing law in Freehold, New Jersey, he became an associate justice of the state Supreme Court. In 1842, Dayton was appointed by Governor William Pennington (*q.v.*) to fill a vacant U.S. Senate seat; in 1844, as a Whig, the legislature elected him for a full term. Having opposed both American entry into the Mexican War and the Compromise of 1850, Dayton was defeated for reelection in 1850. In 1856, he was nominated by the new Republican party as its first vice presidential candidate. After John C. Frémont (*q.v.*) lost the election, Dayton served as attorney general of New Jersey from 1857 until 1861.

At the 1860 Republican National Convention in Chicago, Dayton received New Jersey's votes for the presidential nomination on the first ballot. By the third and final ballot, all fourteen votes had been switched to Abraham Lincoln (*q.v.*). Following his election, Lincoln desired to appoint Dayton as U.S. minister to England but finally, yielding to Secretary of State William Seward's (*q.v.*) insistence that Charles Francis Adams (*q.v.*) be sent to London, he instead selected Dayton to be U.S. minister to France. Handicapped by ignorance of the language and lack of diplomatic experience, Dayton endeavored to keep France from aiding the Confederates. He neglected to utilize social channels for this purpose, however, and had to be constantly prodded by Seward, John Bigelow (*q.v.*), and Henry S. Sanford (*q.v.*), the U.S. minister at Brussels, to show more energy and initiative. He tended to react rather than to act.

Dayton failed to prevent Napoleon III from sponsoring a European invasion of Mexico that led in time to the establishment of a French client state there. Moreover, Napoleon's desire for European intervention in the American Civil War was little diminished by Dayton's remonstrances. Suffering during much of his mission at Paris from depression and various physical ailments, Dayton died in Paris on December 1, 1864. Bigelow, *Retrospections*, vols. 1, 2; Case, *The United States and France*.

Norman B. Ferris

DE TROBRIAND, Philippe Régis Dénis de Keredern, *general*, was born on June 4, 1816, near Tours, France. Educated to be a soldier, he was graduated in 1834 from the University of Orléans. Three years later he completed legal studies at Poitiers. He moved to New York City, married well, wrote articles for French reviews, and hobnobbed with New York's literati.

In 1861, de Trobriand supported the Union, and his militia unit—the Gardes Lafayette—was mustered in as the 55th New York Volunteers, a three-year regiment. He served throughout the war as a brigade or division commander, notably on the Peninsula and at Fredericksburg, Chancellorsville, Gettysburg, Petersburg, and Five Forks. He became a brigadier general of Volunteers (January 5, 1864), and major general of Volunteers (April 9, 1865).

The high point of de Trobriand's active service was at Gettysburg, where he led a brigade in the III Corps, commanded by General Daniel E. Sickles (*q.v.*).

In the Peach Orchard on July 2, his flank and rear became vulnerable when troops under General James Barnes (*q.v.*) failed to keep their place in line. De Trobriand bravely exposed himself to Confederate fire to steady and rally his men, but they suffered heavily. By the evening, his regiments had been badly mauled and were withdrawn. After the war, de Trobriand was chosen as colonel of the 31st Infantry Regiment, which was subsequently merged into the 13th Infantry.

Between trips to France, de Trobriand served with his regiment at various frontier posts, mainly in the Dakotas and Montana. A special contribution to the Union record of the war came from his talented pen, the opinionated but valuable *Four Years with the Army of the Potomac*. His most important postwar duty was during Reconstruction in Louisiana, where he ousted improperly elected Democrats from the state legislature in 1875. De Trobriand retired from the Army in 1879 and died at Bayport, New York, on July 15, 1897. Pfanz, *Gettysburg: The Second Day*; Sommers, *Richmond Redeemed.*

Joseph G. Dawson III

DELANO, Charles, *congressman*, was born in New Braintree, Massachusetts, on June 24, 1820. He attended public schools in Amherst, graduated from Amherst College in 1840, studied law, and was admitted to the bar in 1842. In 1850, he was appointed treasurer of Hampshire county, an office he held until his election to Congress in 1858. In spite of his election as a Republican to the 36th and 37th Congresses, Delano never had a wide reputation or excerised much influence beyond his own district. After declining to be a candidate for renomination in 1862, he resumed the practice of law in Northampton. In 1877 he became a trustee of the Clarke School for the Education of the Deaf. The following year he served as counsel for the state in matters relating to the Troy and Greenfield Railroad and the Hoosac Tunnel. He died in Northampton, Massachusetts, on January 23, 1883. *BDUSC.*

Dale Baum

DELAPLAINE, Isaac Clason, *congressman*, was born on October 27, 1817, in New York City. He graduated from Columbia College in 1834 and established a law practice in New York City, where he became active in the complicated factional politics of the Democratic party. In 1860, after the national Democratic party failed to agree upon a single presidential candidate and both Stephen A. Douglas (*q.v.*) and John Breckinridge entered the race, the Democratic factions of New York City struck an uneasy truce at the local level. Although they continued to disagree on national policy, they did not want to risk a self-defeating division of their supporters in the city against a united Republican opposition.

Those Democratic candidates who agreed to the truce, including Delaplaine, were known as Fusionists. The strategy worked in Delaplaine's district, and he won election to the House of Representatives. Following Fort Sumter, Delaplaine publicly defended the integrity of the national government, although not the specific policies of the Republican administration. In the 37th Congress, he was regarded as a regular, centrist Democrat and served a single term before returning to the practice of law in 1863. Delaplaine died in New York City on July 17, 1866. *BDUSC.*

James C. Mohr

DEMING, Henry Champion, *congressman,* was born on May 23, 1815, in Colchester, Connecticut. A graduate of Yale University (1836) and Harvard Law School (1839), he began his law practice in New York City, where he also edited a literary monthly, *New World.* He returned to Connecticut in 1847 and in 1849 was elected to the Connecticut House of Representatives. He served in 1849, 1850, and 1859–1861. Deming, a Democrat, was mayor of Hartford from 1854 to 1858 and developed a reputation as one of the most eloquent speakers in New England. In 1860, he opposed coercive measures against the seceding states, but after the war began in 1861, declared his willingness to set aside partisan feelings and concentrate on the war crisis.

Deming supported Governor William Buckingham's (*q.v.*) war policies. As a result, his Republican colleagues, by acclamation, chose him speaker pro tem to replace Assemblyman Augustus Brandegee (*q.v.*). That same year, he left the Democrats and joined the Republicans. In September 1861, Deming accepted a commission as colonel of the 12th Connecticut Volunteers, which participated in the capture of New Orleans. Shortly thereafter, he was appointed mayor of New Orleans and remained there until 1863. He was elected to the 37th Congress, was reelected to the 38th, and was defeated in 1866.

From 1869 to 1872, Deming was collector of internal revenue for his Connecticut district. He was remembered for his able administration as mayor of New Orleans and for his ability to obtain war contracts for Connecticut manufacturers. He was also remembered for his eloquence, notably a eulogy for Abraham Lincoln (*q.v.*) presented to the Connecticut General Assembly in 1865. He died in Hartford on October 8, 1872. Lane, *A Political History of Connecticut;* Niven, *Connecticut for the Union.*

Joanna D. Cowden

DENISON, Charles, *congressman,* was born in Wyoming Valley, Pennsylvania, on January 23, 1818. He graduated from Dickinson College in 1838, was admitted to the bar in 1840, and practiced law in Wilkes-Barre for the next twenty years. Elected to the 38th, 39th, and 40th Congresses, Denison remained a staunch Peace Democrat, opposing most legislation designed to assist the Union war effort. He voted against the 13th Amendment, opposed conscription measures brought before the House, and rejected legislation that called for confiscation of Confederate property. At the conclusion of the war, he opposed the Freedmen's Bureau bill, the Civil Rights Act, and the Reconstruction Act. On the few occasions he addressed the House, he objected to congressional legislation that, he argued, usurped the constitutional prerogatives of the states. He believed that emancipation and the Reconstruction measures which sought to elevate blacks through suffrage, land distribution, and the protection of civil rights challenged the natural order. Denison died in Wilkes-Barre on June 27, 1867. Shankman, *Pennsylvania Antiwar Movement.*

Philip J. Avillo, Jr.

DENNIS, Elias Smith, *general,* was born in Newburgh, New York, on December 4, 1812. In 1836, he settled in Carlyle, Illinois, where he taught school and served as clerk of the Circuit Court. Dennis served a term in the Illinois General Assembly (1842–1844) and one in the state Senate (1846–1848). In 1857, he was appointed a U.S. marshal in "bleeding Kansas." On August 18, 1861, Dennis was mustered into service as lieutenant colonel of the 30th Illinois. He fought at Belmont and commanded the regiment at Forts Henry and Donelson, earning the commendation of his superiors. Dennis became colonel of the regiment on May 1, 1862, and participated in the siege of Corinth. On September 1, he commanded at Britton's Lane, Tennessee, where his regiment mauled a Confederate column.

Dennis's comrades thereupon petitioned President Abraham Lincoln (*q.v.*) to promote him to brigadier general. Among those pressuring the administration was Lyman Trumbull (*q.v.*), a powerful Illinois senator. The bureaucracy moved slowly, and it was not until April 13, 1863, that Dennis was made a brigadier general to rank from the previous November 29. He assumed command of the 2nd Brigade, 3rd Division, XVII Corps, then stationed at Lake Providence, Louisiana, leading it at the battles of Port Gibson, Raymond, and Jackson. On May 15, he was ordered to take command of the District of Northeast Louisiana, where he was responsible for guarding vital magazines and warding off attempts to relieve Vicksburg. After the surrender of Vicksburg, Dennis rejoined the XVII Corps and commanded the garrison there. In August 1864 he was ordered to the Department of the Gulf and headed a brigade in the campaign leading to the capture of Mobile, for which he was breveted major general.

Mustered out on August 24, 1865, Dennis established himself as a planter in Madison Parish, Louisiana, across the Mississippi from Vicksburg. In 1887, he returned to Carlyle, where he died on December 16, 1894. Bearss, *Vicksburg Campaign,* vols. 2, 3; Williams, *Lincoln Finds a General,* vol. 4.

Edwin C. Bearss

DENNISON, William, *governor, Postmaster General,* was born on November 23, 1815, in Cincinnati, Ohio. After graduating from Miami University in 1835, he moved to Columbus, established a law practice, and eventually achieved prominence as a wealthy businessman. In 1848, Dennison was elected as a Whig to the state legislature, where he fought to repeal laws discriminating against blacks. An opponent of slavery expansion, he joined the Republican party as soon as it was organized in Ohio, and in 1859 won election to a two-year term as governor of the state. The Civil War found the government of Ohio poorly prepared to raise and supply the troops called for by Washington. Many of the early misfortunes of Dennison's administration stemmed from incompetence in the War Department, but Dennison was also slow to improve the organization of his own administration. By the end of 1861, however, he had ended loose spending and mismanagement, and had raised over 100,000 men, exceeding by 20,000 the quotas set for the state.

Although he lacked legal authority, Dennison used money refunded to the state from Washington to supply Ohio's soldiers, and accounted for every penny spent. Concerned for the defense of his southern border, he used Ohio troops to help secure western Virginia for the Union, and also assumed control of his state's transportation and communication systems to prevent movement of war supplies into Kentucky. Although Dennison had acted capably in meeting the exigencies of war, the inevitable problems and mistakes of his early wartime administration cost him the limited popularity he enjoyed. Ohio Republicans, eager to find a Democrat to run on a Union ticket, refused to renominate him in 1861. His successor, David Tod (*q.v.*), used Dennison's services frequently in his administration, and in 1864 Lincoln made Dennison Postmaster General, a position he held until resigning from Andrew Johnson's (*q.v.*) Cabinet in 1866. Dennison died in Columbus on June 15, 1882. Abbott, *Ohio's War Governors*; Hesseltine, *Lincoln's War Governors*.

Richard H. Abbott

DEVENS, Charles, Jr., *general,* was born on April 4, 1820, in Charlestown, Massachusetts. He graduated from Harvard (1838) and Harvard Law School (1840), and began a successful public career. Devens was a brigadier general in the militia and commanded the 15th Massachusetts Volunteers at Ball's Bluff. After promotion to brigadier general of Volunteers, he led a brigade on the Peninsula and at Fredericksburg, and a division in the XI Corps at Chancellorsville. At the latter, Devens, in command only twelve days, disregarded and ridiculed several reports of Confederate movements in his sector, as did the staff officers at corps headquarters. This almost criminal neglect of security was compounded by Devens's inability to control his division as it broke before the Confederate assault. Only the resolute action of scattered regiments and companies tempered the disaster.

Notwithstanding his part in the debacle at Chancellorsville, Devens returned to division command in the Army of the James, and after the war headed the District of Charleston, South Carolina. He became a judge in Massachusetts and in 1877 was appointed Attorney General of the United States. His honors in civilian life were more than commensurate with his performance as a field commander. He died in Boston on January 7, 1891. Furgurson, *Chancellorsville*.

John T. Hubbell

DICKINSON, Anna E., *abolitionist,* was born on October 28, 1842, in Philadelphia. A birthright Quaker, she later was converted to Methodism. She worked as a copyist, as a schoolteacher, and at the U.S. Mint in Philadelphia, which position she lost in 1861 after having delivered a speech denouncing General George B. McClellan (*q.v.*). Dickinson contributed to William Lloyd Garrison's (*q.v.*) *Liberator*, and in 1860 she spoke before the Pennsylvania Anti-Slavery Society. When her effectiveness as a public speaker came to Garrison's attention, he arranged in 1862 for her to lecture in New England under auspices of the Massachusetts Anti-Slavery Society. In 1863, Dickinson turned to electoral politics and campaigned with great success for Republican candidates in the New Hampshire state elections. She also was credited with contributing through her oratory to Republican victories in Connecticut. Large and enthusiastic crowds turned out to hear "the Joan of Arc" of the antislavery movement and the Republican cause. She was second only to Wendell Phillips (*q.v.*) in demand as a lecturer.

On January 16, 1864, in the U.S. House of Representatives, Dickinson addressed an audience that included President Lincoln (*q.v.*) and Mrs. Lincoln (*q.v.*). Only with reluctance, however, did she support Lincoln in the election of 1864. She had denounced what she regarded as the President's dilatory policy toward slavery; she was also outspokenly critical of his Reconstruction policies, as well as those later pursued by Andrew Johnson (*q.v.*) and Ulysses S. Grant (*q.v.*). For a few years after the war Dickinson lectured on the lyceum circuit, advocating rights for the freedmen and for women, though she did not join the women's suffrage movement.

In the 1870s, interest in Dickinson's message and personality declined, and her subsequent efforts to become a playright and actress had little success. An attempt at a comeback as a Republican political orator in 1888 proved a failure. The last forty years of her life were lived in obscurity. Dickinson died in Goshen, New York, on October 22, 1932. Chester, *Embattled Maiden*; Dickinson, *Ragged Register*.

Merton L. Dillon

DIVEN, Alexander Samuel, *congressman, general,* was born in Catharine, New York, on February 10, 1809. In 1856, he left his law practice in Elmira to help organize the state Republican party. He later served a term in the legislature, was the Free Soil candidate for governor in 1859, and waged a successful congressional campaign in 1860. As a member of the House Judiciary Committee in the 37th Congress, Diven supported Abraham Lincoln's (*q.v.*) 1862 plan of compensated emancipation, as well as later, more sweeping measures to abolish slavery; he was also one of the first congressmen to propose the recruitment of African American troops. Fiscally conservative, Diven opposed confiscation of slaveholders' property and the issuance of paper money, and he fought to recapture funds paid to unscrupulous contractors.

On August 13, 1862, Diven left Congress to be mustered in as lieutenant colonel of a regiment he had helped to organize, the 107th New York Volunteers. He served competently at Antietam and as colonel led the regiment at

Chancellorsville. Discharged on May 11, 1863, he reentered the army as assistant provost marshal-general for the Western District of New York and served well enough to be breveted brigadier general on August 30, 1864.

After the war, Diven served as mayor of Elmira and as vice president of the Erie Railroad, and helped build the southwestern branch of the Missouri Pacific. He also owned a street railway and a waterworks in Elmira, where he died on June 11, 1896. Bogue, *Congressman's Civil War*; Curry, *Blueprint for Modern America*.

Edward G. Longacre

DIX, Dorothea Lynde, *superintendent of army nurses*, was born on April 4, 1802, in Hampden, Maine. She began teaching at the age of fourteen and in 1821 opened a "dame school" for girls in Boston. In 1841, she began her career as a crusader for the mentally ill, after seeing how these unfortunates were imprisoned and treated as criminals. Dix traveled throughout the country to promote state legislation to improve conditions for the mentally ill and fund hospitals for their care. Her work was widely publicized and she became one of the most famous women in America, which led to her appointment as superintendent of army nurses on June 10, 1861, and the responsibility for the recruitment of all female nurses. She had strict requirements: nurses had to be over thirty, plain, and with no romantic notions about the job. She barred Roman Catholic nuns and members of other religious sisterhoods.

Elizabeth Blackwell's assertion that Dix lacked organizational skills was not unfounded. She was overly concerned with details, unable to delegate tasks to subordinates. She helped set up and staff infirmaries, issued detailed instructions to volunteer sewing societies, and stockpiled medical supplies. Dix constantly quarreled with hospital administrators over their nurses' duties and publicly criticized those she felt were not up to her standards. She was censured for dismissing volunteer nurses not appointed by her. In order to keep Dix in line, the Surgeon General was given the authority to appoint nurses who were under medical officers in Union hospitals.

In 1866, Dix resigned from her post in order to work on various causes, including aid for orphans as well as the mentally ill. She died on July 17, 1887, at the Trenton (New Jersey) State Hospital, which she had helped to found. Marshall, *Dorothea Dix*; Wilson, *Stranger and Traveler*.

Donna M. DeBlasio

DIX, John Adams, *general*, was born on July 24, 1798, in Boscawen, New Hampshire. He received a commission as ensign at the age of fourteen, and served in the War of 1812, most notably at Lundy's Lane. Remaining in the Regular Army until 1826, Dix managed to study law and obtain admission to the District of Columbia bar. After moving to Cooperstown, New York, in 1828 to manage his father-in-law's properties, Dix soon gained acceptance as the county's leading Jacksonian Democrat. His power in the party earned him positions as the state adjutant general and state school superintendent.

Dix was elected to fill an unexpired term in the U.S. Senate (1845–1850), where he became a strong supporter of free-soil policies. His ties in the Democratic party brought him an appointment as postmaster of New York City in 1859; two years later he was named Secretary of the Treasury for the last few days of James Buchanan's (*q.v.*) administration. Shortly after taking office, Dix issued his famous "American Flag Dispatch" to a harried Treasury official in New Orleans: "If anyone attempts to haul down the American flag, shoot him on the spot."

When the war began, Dix received the first commission as major general of Volunteers on May 16, 1861, thereby outranking all other Volunteer officers until the end of the war. By this time Dix was considered too old for field service. He performed department and garrison duties in the Department of Annapolis, the Department of Pennsylvania, the Middle Department, the Department of Virginia, and the Department of the East. His most distinguished contribution to the Union war effort was the forceful suppression of the New York draft riots in 1863. After the war Dix continued a successful political career. He died in New York City on April 21, 1879. Dix, *Memoirs of John Adams Dix*; Randall, *Lincoln the President*, vol. 3.

Mitchell A. Yockelson

DIXON, James, *senator*, was born in Enfield, Connecticut, on August 5, 1814. He graduated with distinction from Williams College, and practiced law in Enfield and Hartford. Dixon was elected to the Connecticut House of Representatives in 1837, 1844, and 1854, and to the U.S. House of Representatives from 1845 to 1849. He remained a Whig until 1854, and was editor of the *Hartford Courant*, an organ of Connecticut's Whig party. Dixon shifted to the Know-Nothing party in 1855, and in 1858 to Connecticut's Republican party. He was elected to the U.S. Senate in 1856 and reelected in 1862. Upon the secession of South Carolina, Dixon demanded that concessions be offered to Southern leaders. He proposed a Senate committee to seek sectional compromise and declared that if Republican leaders rejected Southern demands, he would abandon the party. When it became clear that negotiations had failed, he predicted war and national ruin.

Dixon's wartime views were compatible with those of War Democrats who supported the war solely as a means of preserving the Union. He rejected war measures, including emancipation. He further declared that the states were indestructible entities and that rebellion did not alter that status. He denounced the Emancipation Proclamation but supported Lincoln's (*q.v.*) 10 percent plan in 1864. When President Andrew Johnson (*q.v.*) challenged congressional Republicans over control of the Reconstruction process, Dixon was one of the few who supported him. His persistent conservatism ultimately weakened his position in the Senate and in his state party, and in 1868 he defected to the Democrats. Although his bid for the Senate nomination that year failed, he received the Democratic nomination for Congress. His defeat in the 1868 election marked the end of his political career. Dixon died in Hartford on March 27, 1873. Niven, *Connecticut for the Union*; Silbey, *Respectable Minority.*

Joanna D. Cowden

DIXON, Nathan Fellows, Jr., *congressman,* was born in Westerly, Rhode Island, on May 1, 1812. A graduate of Brown University (1833), he studied law in Cambridge and New Haven, and developed an extensive law practice in southern Rhode Island and eastern Connecticut. Dixon's long political service was divided between the Rhode Island legislature and the Congress. He was a member of the state legislature from 1840 to 1849 and was elected to Congress as a Whig in 1849 for one term. He returned to the state legislature in 1852 and from 1855 to 1863. Republicans returned him to Congress from 1863 to 1872, and he concluded his political career in the state legislature from 1872 to 1877. Dixon's role in Congress was a quiet one with little evidence of any important influence on major legislation. He died in Westerly on April 11, 1881. Bicknell, *History of Rhode Island.*

Mario R. DiNunzio

DODGE, Grenville Mellen, *general,* was born on April 12, 1831, in Danvers, Massachusetts. He graduated as an engineer from Norwich Academy (1851), and began a career in railroad building after moving to Council Bluffs, Iowa. He served in the Iowa militia and on July 6, 1861, was appointed colonel of the 4th Iowa Volunteers. As a brigade commander Dodge was wounded at Pea Ridge. He was promoted to brigadier (March 21, 1862) and major general (June 7, 1864). Because of his engineering background, he was given responsibility for maintaining the border between Tennessee and Alabama. Dodge's significant field service was as commander of the XVI Corps (Army of the Tennessee) in the Atlanta campaign. He performed effectively at Resaca, Dallas, and Nickajack Creek, but missed the bloodletting at Kennesaw.

At the battle of Atlanta, Dodge's corps was deployed on General James B. McPherson's (*q.v.*) left, in anticipation of a general assault, which indeed happened. General William T. Sherman (*q.v.*) had earlier ordered the XVI Corps to destroy the railroad to Decatur, but McPherson asked that execution of the order be delayed. This circumstance may have saved the Army of the Tennessee from casualties even more severe than it suffered that day. Dodge credited McPherson for his leadership, but the steadiness of the corps commanders—Dodge, Francis Blair (*q.v.*), and John A. Logan (*q.v.*)—must be noted.

On August 19, 1864, Dodge suffered a head wound that kept him out of action until December, when he became commander of the Department of Missouri. In February 1865 he also became commander of the Department of Kansas. He left the Army in January 1866 and embarked upon a distinguished career as chief engineer of the Union Pacific Railroad, and as a railroad builder in the

United States and Cuba after the Spanish–American War. He served a term in Congress (1867–1869) and was active in veterans' affairs. He died in Council Bluffs on January 3, 1916. Bearss, *Vicksburg Campaign*; Castel, *Decision in the West*; Dodge, *Personal Recollections*.

John T. Hubbell

DONNELLY, Ignatius Loyola, *congressman*, was born on November 3, 1831, in Philadelphia. He attended public schools, read law, became an attorney, then in 1857 moved to Minnesota to develop Nininger (Dakota county) as a speculative venture. When Nininger languished, Donnelly turned to Republican politics, winning the lieutenant governorship in 1859 and again in 1861. Although he wielded considerable authority during Governor Alexander Ramsey's (*q.v.*) frequent absences, the lieutenant governorship satisfied neither Donnelly's need for funds nor his personal ambition. In 1862, he was elected to represent Minnesota's 2nd District in Congress and was reelected in 1864 and 1866. He supported Abraham Lincoln's (*q.v.*) war measures and liked the President personally, but believed that his Reconstruction proposals were too generous to the South. An early proponent of the "state suicide" theory, Donnelly was the only Minnesotan in either chamber to support the Wade–Davis Manifesto. He voted with the Radical bloc on all major Reconstruction issues, including the impeachment of Andrew Johnson (*q.v.*). On other issues, Donnelly urged reform of the Indian Office, argued for approval of the purchase of Alaska, and wrote the resolution creating the National Bureau of Education.

After leaving the Republican party after 1869, Donnelly carved his major niche in American history as a leader of lost causes, perpetual candidate, and author. He was involved in the Granger, Greenbacker, and Anti-Monopolist movements, then became a founding father of Populism. He sought public office fifteen times after 1869, winning five of seven legislative races but losing five bids for Congress and one each for the Senate, governorship, and vice presidency. His writings included the futuristic novel *Caesar's Column* and treatises offering elaborate "proof" that Atlantis had existed and that the works of Shakespeare, Marlowe, and Cervantes had really been written by Sir Francis Bacon. Donnelly died in Nininger on January 1, 1901. Folwell, *History of Minnesota*, vols. 2, 3; Ridge, *Ignatius Donnelly*.

Roger A. Fischer

DOOLITTLE, James Rood, *senator*, was born in Hampton, New York, on January 3, 1815. He graduated from Geneva (later Hobart) College in 1834, studied law, and was admitted to the bar in 1837. Doolittle was active in the Van Buren campaigns of 1840 and 1844, and was elected district attorney for Wyoming county in 1845 and in 1847. In September 1847 he attended the New York State Democratic Convention and aligned himself with the Barnburner faction of the party. In 1848, he was a Free Soiler, once again supporting Van Buren.

In 1851, Doolittle settled in Racine, Wisconsin, and in 1853 he was elected circuit judge of the 1st District, a position he held until his appointment in 1854 to chair a three-man committee to revise and codify the laws of Wisconsin. He threw his support to John C. Frémont's (*q.v.*) candidacy in 1856, and Wisconsin Republicans, now the majority in both houses of the state legislature, sent Doolittle to the U.S. Senate in 1857. He took an active role in the Kansas and Oregon debates and attempted to disassociate his party from John Brown (*q.v.*) in 1859. Although he endorsed William H. Seward (*q.v.*) in 1860, Doolittle was not disappointed in the nomination of Abraham Lincoln (*q.v.*), and worked throughout the North on his behalf. He was confident that the South would accept the election outcome, but when events proved otherwise, he worked for compromise, serving as a member of the Committee of Thirteen.

Doolittle, unswerving in his support of Lincoln's policies, was reelected to the Senate in 1863. As chairman of the Committee on Indian Affairs, he attempted to maintain a fair and judicious attitude, although he believed—with the majority—that the Indian race would soon cease to be and that it was not within his province to delay the hand of destiny. Nonetheless, he called for an investigation of the Sand Creek Massacre of November 29, 1864, and the actions of Colonel John M. Chivington, commanding officer of the 3rd Colorado Volunteers. Doolittle also introduced the bill for the establishment of Indian Territory, a measure that provided for the beginning of representative government.

Doolittle's singular strength was his effectiveness as a speaker. At no time did he use this strength to greater purpose than before a mass meeting of some 20,000 at Springfield, Illinois, in May 1864, when Lincoln's renomination was not yet assured. Illinois Governor Richard Yates (*q.v.*) had expressed doubts as to the desirability of a second Lincoln administration, but Doolittle brought the crowd to a wild, thirty-minute ovation with his support of the President. However, his loyalty to Lincoln, subsequently transferred to Andrew Johnson (*q.v.*), would prove politically fatal. At the 1865 Illinois State Convention, where Doolittle served as chairman of the Platform Committee, he presented a set of resolutions in support of Johnson's Reconstruction policies. These were adopted, but the party schism became evident to all in the winter of 1865–1866.

Doolittle's refusal to vote to override several Johnson vetoes resulted in the Wisconsin legislature's demand that he resign. This he refused to do. He was not renominated, and his subsequent political involvements—all unsuccessful—were as a Democrat. The price he paid for his principled loyalty was large indeed. Doolittle died in Providence, Rhode Island, on July 27, 1897. Current, *Civil War Era; Dictionary of Wisconsin Biography.*

Charles E. Twining

DOUBLEDAY, Abner, *general,* was born in Ballston Spa, New York, on June 26, 1819. While attending school in nearby Cooperstown, he may have invented baseball. Doubleday graduated from West Point in 1842, was commissioned in the artillery, served in coastal garrisons, fought in Mexico, and campaigned against the Seminoles before reporting to Fort Moultrie in 1858. At Fort Sumter in April 1861, he reputedly aimed the first gun to respond to the secessionists' bombardment. The following May, Doubleday took command of a regiment in the Shenandoah Valley, then led a brigade at Groveton and a division at Second Bull Run. Commanding another division at Antietam, he won a brevet for his actions. Although it was present at Fredericksburg and Chancellorsville, Doubleday's division played minor roles in both engagements.

At Gettysburg, Doubleday's brigades were the first Federal infantry units to enter the battle on July 1. When John Reynolds (*q.v.*) was killed, Doubleday took over the I Corps and, under the circumstances, performed satisfactorily. Nevertheless, George G. Meade (*q.v.*), the army commander, believing that Doubleday had bungled, ordered John Newton (*q.v.*), Doubleday's junior, to assume command of the corps. Indignant at this injustice, Doubleday left the Army of the Potomac on July 5, 1863, and spent the rest of the war on administrative duty in Washington. While there, he impugned the competence and loyalty of Meade in testimony before the Joint Committee on the Conduct of the War.

Cautious, petulant, and prudish, Doubleday obviously lacked both the ability and the élan of such soldiers as Francis Barlow (*q.v.*), John Buford (*q.v.*), John Gibbon (*q.v.*), and John Reynolds, his near contemporaries or juniors. Indeed, Meade, although unjust in the specific instance, was correct in assuming Newton would make the better corps commander. Doubleday's self-serving attempt to slander Meade speaks for itself. All told, it is appropriate that Doubleday's ostensible association with baseball, rather than his generalship, should fix his place in American history. After Appomattox, he served as a lieutenant colonel with the 35th Infantry in Texas and as superintendent of the Recruiting Service in San Francisco, where he obtained a patent for a cable railway. His final assignment took him again to Texas, where he commanded the 24th Infantry, an African American regiment. After retiring in 1873, Doubleday made his home in Mendham, New Jersey, where he died on January 26, 1893. Coddington, *Gettysburg Campaign*; Hassler, *Commanders of the Army of the Potomac*; Hennessy, *Return to Bull Run*.

James L. Morrison, Jr.

DOUGLAS, Stephen Arnold, *senator*, was born in Brandon, Vermont, on April 23, 1812. He studied at academies in New York, read law, taught school in Winchester, Illinois, and was admitted to the Illinois bar in 1834. Douglas was a primary builder of the Illinois Democratic party and held several state offices before being elected to the U.S. House of Representatives in 1842, and in 1846 to the U.S. Senate. His role as spokesman for the West was recognized by his selection as chairman of both the House and the Senate Committee on the Territories. An outspoken expansionist and Mexican War supporter, Douglas was notably identified with "popular sovereignty" and was instrumental in writing this concept into bills organizing the New Mexico and Utah territories in 1850, and the Kansas–Nebraska Bill of 1854. The latter bill, however, repealed the

Missouri Compromise of 1820, which had barred slavery from the region, and thereby caused a political revolution in the North that produced the Republican party, headed in Illinois by Douglas's longtime political rival, Abraham Lincoln (*q.v.*).

Despite Southern support in 1856, Douglas was passed over, as he had been in 1852, for his party's presidential nomination, the prize going to a less controversial candidate, James Buchanan (*q.v.*). When proslavery voters in Kansas petitioned for statehood in 1857, with a constitution recognizing slavery, Douglas denounced this document as fraudulent and unrepresentative of the popular will. His opposition caused a break with a majority of Democratic senators and President Buchanan, and forced a resubmission of the Lecompton Constitution to the Kansas electorate. Kansans overwhelmingly rejected the document in August 1858, while Douglas was campaigning for reelection. He was victorious in the contest, which included the seven famous debates with Lincoln. His success made him the spokesman for the Northern Democratic party, but it cost him the little Southern support he had after his opposition to Lecompton.

At the Democratic National Convention in Charleston and Baltimore in 1860, Southern delegations walked out rather than accept Douglas as the nominee. He received the nomination of the Northern majority, and Southerners nominated Vice President John C. Breckinridge. He actively campaigned for popular votes in New England, the Northwest, and the South, turning his Southern speeches into denials that Lincoln's election justified secession. In the postelection Congress, he vainly sought a compromise that would preserve the Union.

Douglas aroused more popular emotion, favorable and unfavorable, than any other public man of his day. His "great principle," popular sovereignty, sought to deal dispassionately with a highly emotional moral issue, and was thus a failure. After Fort Sumter, Douglas advocated strong measures against the South, urging Lincoln to call 200,000 instead of 75,000 volunteers to suppress the rebellion. He returned to Illinois to rally support for the war effort but, exhausted by his presidential campaign, died in Chicago on June 3, 1861. His death at the outset of the war deprived the Northern Democracy of its foremost spokesman, with a consequent loss of effectiveness and responsibility as the wartime opposition. Johannsen, *Stephen A. Douglas.*

David E. Meerse

DOUGLASS, Frederick, *abolitionist, editor,* was born in 1817 or 1818 in Tuckahoe, Maryland. His mother was a slave; his father's identity is unknown. Sent to Baltimore in 1825, he remained there for thirteen years, then escaped in 1838 and settled at New Bedford, Massachusetts, where he became an odd-job laborer. In 1841, after making a spontaneous speech at the convention held by the Massachusetts Anti-Slavery Society, he was hired as an agent of that organization. Douglass became an eloquent speaker and for twenty years traveled widely, denouncing slavery and championing reformist movements in general. By the time of the Civil War, he was firmly established as the best-known and most influential African American leader. The outbreak of the war had a bracing effect on Douglass. He viewed the conflict as a crusade to wipe out slavery, once and for all. Thus he was doubly anxious that blacks themselves become participants. In the columns of his periodical, *Douglass' Monthly*, he urged them to form militia companies, and he called upon Abraham Lincoln (*q.v.*) to enlist blacks, slave and free, into a "a liberating army."

During the first eighteen months of the war, Douglass acted as whip and spur to the Lincoln administration, strongly criticizing it for its slowness in striking directly at slavery. Hence he was overjoyed when, on January 1, 1863, Lincoln signed the Emancipation Proclamation, a measure doubly important, in the Douglass viewpoint, because it gave the presidential stamp of approval to the raising of African American soldiers. Too old to shoulder a gun, Douglass served as a recruiting agent, enlisting two of his sons and traveling throughout the North, urging young African Americans to sign up. He protested against the discriminations encountered by the black soldiers, including a differential in monthly pay, and took the matter to the White House.

In August 1864, Douglass had a second audience with Lincoln, who broached a plan for assisting slaves to escape if it appeared that the war might end in a stalemate. No such preemptive operation was necessary, however, and as a Union victory became more and more evident, Douglass began to concentrate on such issues as equal voting rights for blacks. From the end of the Civil War until his death thirty years later, Douglass was regarded by the majority of African Americans as somewhat of an elder statesman, guiding them by precept and example. He was a staunch supporter of the Republican party, crediting it with having abolished slavery and making blacks both soldiers and citizens. Under Republican administrations, he was appointed marshal of the District of Columbia, recorder of deeds for the District, and U.S. minister to Haiti. He died on February 25, 1895, in Washington, D.C. Blight, *Frederick Douglass' Civil War*; McFeely, *Frederick Douglass*; Quarles, *Frederick Douglass*.

Benjamin Quarles

DOW, Neal, *reformer, general,* was born on March 20, 1804, in Portland, Maine. He broke with his Quaker heritage over his refusal to eschew the use of force. His business successes gave him the means to engage in lifelong agitation against alcohol, and he won statewide prohibition through the nationally famous Maine Law of 1851. Serving twice as mayor of Portland and once in the state legislature, he was a pioneer Maine Republican. In a classic example of a political military appointment, Dow was commissioned colonel of the 13th Maine in November 1861 and recruited a number of temperance men for his regiment. To his frustration, he was assigned to Benjamin F. Butler's (*q.v.*) mainly Democratic expedition against New Orleans in 1862.

Although Dow's friends obtained his commission as brigadier general as of April 28, 1862, Butler kept him in isolated commands. But under Nathaniel Banks (*q.v.*), Dow commanded a brigade in the unsuccessful charge at Port

Hudson on May 27, 1863. He was wounded and was captured while convalescing. His experiences in prisons at Richmond and at Mobile, to which he was sent for investigation of charges that he had encouraged slaves to revolt, confirmed his hatred of the Confederates, which he expressed in subsequent propagandistic attacks. Exchanged in March 1864, Dow worked for Abraham Lincoln's (q.v.) reelection. He resigned his commission in November 1864. Dow advocated a thorough postwar Reconstruction. In 1880, he was the Prohibition party's candidate for President. He died in Portland on October 2, 1897. Byrne, *Prophet of Prohibition*; Dow, *Reminiscences*.

Frank L. Byrne

DOWNEY, John Gately, *governor*, was born on June 24, 1827, at Castle Sampson, County Roscommon, Ireland. In 1842, he joined relatives in Maryland, completed his education at a private school, and became an apprentice druggist in Washington, D.C. He lived in Vicksburg in 1845 and in Cincinnati from 1846 until 1849, when he caught gold fever. In December 1850, Downey moved to Los Angeles, where he opened the town's first drugstore, engaged in banking, and purchased land. He held local offices and in 1859 was elected lieutenant governor. On January 14, 1860, Downey succeeded to the governorship when Governor Milton S. Latham (q.v.) became a U.S. senator. He was efficient and progressive, but the growing sectional crisis ended his political career.

On May 11, 1861, when San Franciscans held a monster mass meeting, Downey sent a letter calling for an "honorable compromise." At the Northern Democratic convention that began on July 4, he lost renomination on the fourteenth ballot. In the summer of 1861, he raised five regiments of infantry and one and one-half of cavalry, although he disputed the war's purpose. Downey left office on January 10, 1862, still claiming that "compromise" could have averted conflict, and fearing the "subjugation and impoverishment of the white race" through emancipation. In 1863, a united Democracy chose Downey for governor. He denounced the "tyranny, usurpation, and corruption" of the administration and singled out the Emancipation Proclamation not only for raising "an almost impassable barrier to the reconstruction of the Union" but also for encouraging freed slaves to migrate to California.

In 1864, the Democratic party asked Downey to represent it at the national convention, and then to become a congressional candidate. Downey declined the latter honor, but participated in party affairs for the next twenty years. In 1865, he began subdividing 75,000 acres around the town of Downey to encourage settlement, and in February 1868 opened the first Los Angeles bank. He was a founder of the University of Southern California in 1879 and of the Historical Society of Southern California in 1883. Downey died on March 1, 1894, in Los Angeles. Hittell, *History of California*, vol. 4; Melendy, *Governors of California*.

Robert J. Chandler

DRAKE, Charles Daniel, *Republican party leader,* was born in Cincinnati, Ohio, on April 11, 1811. He was appointed to the U.S. Naval Academy in 1827, but resigned in 1830 to study law. He was admitted to the bar at Cincinnati in 1833, and moved in 1834 to St. Louis. Originally a Whig, he turned to the American party in the mid-1850s and then to the Democrats. In 1860, Drake supported Stephen A. Douglas (*q.v.*), but did not take an active role in the political events of 1861 that kept Missouri in the Union. In 1862, he moved rapidly to the forefront of those calling for prompt action on emancipation. After the failure of the legislature to act on the issue during the winter of 1862–1863, Drake joined those calling for the state convention to meet again to handle the matter. He was elected as a "Charcoal" to fill a vacancy in the convention, and when it met in June 1863, he assumed the leadership of those who wanted slavery ended quickly.

After the convention chose 1870 as the termination date for slavery, Drake took the lead in organizing the Radical Union party. He led a delegation to Washington to urge Abraham Lincoln (*q.v.*) to oust the provisional government of Missouri and appoint a more radically minded military commander in St. Louis, a move the President rejected. Drake worked to keep the Radicals in the Republican party, but the Radical delegation he led to the Republican National Convention at Baltimore in 1864 was the only group to vote against Lincoln's renomination. The Radicals swept the 1864 elections in Missouri, including passage of a referendum for a new convention to reconsider emancipation and other constitutional changes. Drake dominated the convention of 1865 that voted for immediate emancipation and produced a new state constitution.

During the next four years Drake was the major figure in Missouri's Radical party. He was elected to the U.S. Senate in 1867, but resigned after the Liberal Republican split brought Radical defeat in 1870. Appointed chief justice of the U.S. Court of Claims, he served until 1885. Drake died in Washington, D.C., on April 1, 1892. Parrish, *Missouri Under Radical Rule*; Parrish, *Turbulent Partnership.*

William E. Parrish

DRIGGS, John Fletcher, *congressman,* was born on March 8, 1813, in Kinderhook, New York. With limited education, he was apprenticed to learn the trade of sash, door, and blind manufacturing, became a master mechanic, and built a prosperous business. He stayed in New York until 1856, when he moved to East Saginaw, Michigan, where he resided for the rest of his life. An intense antislavery advocate since boyhood and a vice president of an antislavery society as a young man, Driggs was one of the original members of the Liberty or Free Soil party. He first actively engaged in a political campaign in 1844, as a supporter of James Harper in his successful campaign for mayor of New York City. Soon thereafter, Driggs was appointed superintendent of the penitentiary on Blackwell's Island for two years.

When Driggs moved to East Saginaw, he became an active member of the

Republican party. He belonged to the Austin Blair (*q.v.*) or Outstate faction, which was locked in unsuccessful and bitter conflict with the Zachariah Chandler (*q.v.*) or Detroit faction. He was elected president of the village of East Saginaw in 1858 and a member of the Michigan legislature in 1859; after Abraham Lincoln's (*q.v.*) election as President, Driggs was appointed registrar of the U.S. Land Office for the Saginaw district. He was elected to Congress in 1862, 1864, and 1866. He did not obtain his party's nomination in 1868, and in 1870 was nominated but defeated in a bitter election characterized by intense factional infighting.

Driggs represented a huge district stretching north from the middle of Michigan's Lower Peninsula to include the Upper Peninsula. He labored diligently to promote the economic development of this vast, largely unpopulated area. He actively sought and received land grants from the Federal government for railroad and canal construction, and helped secure upward revision of the tariffs on iron, copper, salt, and lumber, the four major economic interests of his district. Toward the end of the war he helped raise a regiment of infantry. Driggs strongly supported the 13th Amendment. His last effort in public life ended when he withdrew from the mayoral contest as a candidate for the Democratic party. Upon his return to private life, Driggs engaged in salt manufacture and managing real estate interests. He died in East Saginaw on December 17, 1877. *BDUSC; Michigan Biographies*, vol. 1.

George M. Blackburn

DU PONT, Samuel Francis, *admiral,* was born on September 27, 1803, in Bergen Point (now Bayonne), New Jersey. In 1815 he was appointed a midshipman in the U.S. Navy. His career was typical of the early nineteenth century: service abroad at various naval stations and on a number of ships. After the Mexican War, in which he distinguished himself while commanding the sloop-of-war *Cyane*, Du Pont was assigned to shore duty. In 1855, he was promoted to captain and shortly afterward took command of the Philadelphia Navy Yard. He was still in this command when the Civil War broke out.

During the early months of the war, Du Pont was senior officer of a board of strategy to plan naval operations, including the blockade of the Southern coastline. On September 18, 1861, he was appointed to command the South Atlantic Blockading Squadron, considered at that time the most important tactical command in the Navy. He was to have control of all naval operations along the Atlantic coast south of the boundary between the Carolinas. Ordered to cooperate in an amphibious expedition to seize Port Royal, South Carolina, Du Pont assembled a squadron of some seventy-five vessels and on November 7, 1861, attacked Confederate forts in the vicinity of Port Royal. After an action that lasted nearly five hours, the Confederates evacuated their positions and Union troops moved in to assume control.

Du Pont's victory was important because the North badly needed one at that time, but more important, it provided the Navy with a base to support its blockade. The blockade off Charleston, Savannah, and other ports along the Atlantic coast could not have been maintained without it. Du Pont's ships continued to cooperate with army units in the occupation of islands and coastal areas along South Carolina, Georgia, and Florida. The effectiveness of the blockade gradually improved as more vessels were added to his squadron.

By early 1863, the only serious weakness in the blockade was Charleston. Under pressure from Washington, Du Pont agreed to attack and reduce the forts guarding Charleston harbor, using primarily ironclad warships. On April 15, seven monitors, along with the *New Ironsides* and *Keokuk*, attacked Forts Sumter and Moultrie. After an engagement that lasted slightly less than two hours, his battered vessels were withdrawn. This repulse resulted in public criticism, and in July 1863 Du Pont asked to be relieved of the command. For the remainder of the war he remained inactive, serving only as a member of a promotion board.

Du Pont was oversensitive and far too concerned about his reputation. His aristocratic demeanor, which led one officer to refer to him as "that stately and courtly potentate, elegant as one's ideal French marquis," caused him to look down upon army officers, who lacked "the slightest idea of civility," and civilians, including Secretary of the Navy Gideon Welles (*q.v.*). Du Pont was not brilliant or very aggressive, but he was an able naval officer. His work on the blockade board and his implementation of the blockade in his area of command were well done. The only blot on his career was the failure to take Charleston. Yet, historians generally agree that his warnings to the Navy Department about utilizing monitor-type vessels in attacks against land fortifications were well founded, and also most would agree with Admiral John D. Hayes, the editor of the Du Pont papers, that "no commander could have succeeded in the Navy Department's plan to run the forts and to force Charleston to surrender." Du Pont died in Philadelphia on June 23, 1865. Du Pont, *Samuel Francis Du Pont*; Merrill, *Du Pont*; Reed, *Combined Operations in the Civil War*.

                                                            William N. Still, Jr.

DUDLEY, Thomas Haines, *diplomat,* was born on October 9, 1819, in Burlington county, New Jersey. He was admitted to the New Jersey bar in 1845. As a Whig, Dudley held a number of Camden city offices, and in 1852 became a member of the state Executive Committee. When the Whig party disintegrated, Dudley's antislavery and protariff beliefs led him naturally into the Republican ranks, where he rose to chairman of the state Executive Committee in 1856. In 1860, he was a delegate to the Republican National Convention in Chicago and played a crucial role in Abraham Lincoln's (*q.v.*) nomination.

Lincoln rewarded Dudley with the U.S. consulship in Liverpool, the center of Confederate financial and purchasing operations in the British Isles. Dudley worked tirelessly and effectively to counter Southern agents. He forwarded precise descriptions of over 300 Confederate blockade runners and often included detailed listings of their cargoes; he helped compile pamphlets and disseminated Union propaganda; and he made his office into the clearinghouse for intelligence secured by other Union consuls. Even more important, he gathered and cast into proper legal form the information that helped convince the British government to detain the *Alexandria* and the Laird Rams, and to halt Confederate shipbuilding operations at Liverpool and Glasgow.

Following the war, Dudley supervised the disposal of Confederate property in Britain, and assisted the American delegation during the arbitration of the *Alabama* claims in 1871. He resigned in 1872 and returned to New Jersey, where he resumed his law practice, became a director of several businesses, helped found the American Protective League in the 1880s, and played an active role in Republican politics until his death in Camden on April 15, 1893. Dyer, "Thomas H. Dudley," *Civil War History.*

Joseph A. Fry

DUELL, Rodolphus Holland, *congressman,* was born on December 20, 1824, in Warren, New York. He attended public school and the Syracuse Academy, studied law, and was admitted to the bar in 1845. Duell began practicing law in Fabius, and in 1848 moved his practice to Cortland, where he gained a reputation as one of the top lawyers in central New York. He was elected district attorney of Cortland county as a Whig in 1850 and county judge in 1855. He soon joined the fledgling Republican party, however, and in 1856 was a delegate to the party's first national convention. He remained county judge until 1859, when he was elected to the 36th Congress.

Duell was an outspoken supporter of the war and fought for the proper equipping of troops in the field. He was an early advocate of the confiscation of Southern slaves, and he scoffed at those who hoped to restore the Union "as it was." Duell served two terms in Congress before returning to Cortland to practice law and chair the county committee. He was a delegate to the Republican National Convention that nominated Ulysses S. Grant (*q.v.*) for President, and afterward was appointed assessor of internal revenue for the 23rd District of New York. He left that post in 1871 to return to Congress for two terms. On October 1, 1875, Grant appointed Duell U.S. commissioner of patents, and he served until January 30, 1877. He died in Cortland, New York, on February 11, 1891. Smith, *History of Cortland County.*

Lori A. Lisowski

DUMONT, Ebenezer, *general, congressman,* was born in Vevay, Indiana, on November 23, 1814. After attending Indiana University, he taught school, studied law, was admitted to the bar, and served in the state legislature and as town treasurer in Vevay. During the Mexican War, he achieved the rank of lieutenant colonel. On his return to Indiana, Dumont became active in Democratic politics and was again elected to the Indiana House. In 1852, he was a presidential elector for Franklin Pierce. By 1860, he had moved to Indianapolis and become an outspoken antisecession Democrat.

On April 27, 1861, Dumont was mustered into the Army as colonel of the

7th Indiana Volunteers. His regiment fought well in George B. McClellan's (*q.v.*) West Virginia campaign, and Dumont was promoted to brigadier general of Volunteers. His most notable military accomplishments came against Confederate raider John Hunt Morgan. After nearly capturing Morgan in Nashville, Dumont's 17th Brigade, Army of the Ohio, threw back Morgan's cavalry at Lebanon, Kentucky. In September 1862 Dumont took command of the 12th Division of Don Carlos Buell's (*q.v.*) Army of the Cumberland but did not play an active role in repulsing Braxton Bragg's invasion of Kentucky.

Deteriorating health forced Dumont to go on leave in December 1862, and he resigned his commission on February 28, 1863. Elected to Congress as a Unionist in 1863, he served two terms, declining to run for reelection in 1866. President Ulysses S. Grant (*q.v.*) appointed Dumont governor of the Idaho Territory, but before he could take office, he became ill and died in Indianapolis on April 16, 1871. Brown, *Bold Cavaliers.*

George C. Rable

DUNLAP, George Washington, *congressman,* was born in Walnut Hills, Kentucky, on February 22, 1813. After demonstrating superior intellect in the county schools, he entered Transylvania University, from which he graduated in 1834. He then studied law, and in 1838 began to practice in Lancaster, Kentucky. Dunlap had a long and distinguished legal and political career at the state level, and in March 1861 entered the U.S. House of Representatives as a Unionist. A vigorous supporter of the Union, he worked diligently for a compromise solution. In May 1861 he was a delegate to the Border State Convention, where he labored to avert conflict. When compromise failed, Dunlap regularly voted for Abraham Lincoln's (*q.v.*) war program until he left Congress in 1863. In 1864, however, Dunlap, disenchanted with Lincoln, served as an elector for the Democratic ticket of George B. McClellan (*q.v.*). After the Civil War, Dunlap resumed his law practice in Kentucky. He died in Lancaster on June 6, 1880. Collins, *History of Kentucky,* vol. 2; Levin, *Lawyers and Lawmakers of Kentucky.*

Marion B. Lucas

DUNN, William McKee, *congressman,* was born December 12, 1814, in Hanover, Indiana Territory. A graduate of Indiana University (1832) and Yale College (1835), he studied law and was admitted to the bar in 1837. He was a member of the Indiana House of Representatives (1848–1849) and served as a delegate to the Indiana Constitutional Convention (1850–1851). During the convention's debate over an article that would effectively exclude blacks from Indiana, Dunn voiced his opposition and was the only delegate from southern Indiana to vote against the clause. He was elected as a Republican to the 36th and 37th Congresses. He opposed Radical Republican efforts to abolish slavery, warning that abolition would destroy the Union and pledging to combat ''these Northern fanatics at every step.''

Dunn served briefly in the Union Army as volunteer aide-de-camp to General

George McClellan (*q.v.*) during the 1861 campaign in western Virginia. After an unsuccessful bid for reelection, he became major and judge advocate of Volunteers, Department of the Missouri (March 1863–July 1864), and was appointed lieutenant colonel and assistant judge advocate general of the U.S. Army (June 22, 1864). He was named brigadier general and judge advocate general in December 1875. Dunn retired in January 1881 and died on July 24, 1887, in Fairfax county, Virginia. Shepherd, *Biographical Directory of the Indiana General Assembly*, vol. 1; Walsh, *Centennial History of the Indiana General Assembly*.

David G. Vanderstel

DWIGHT, William, Jr., *general*, was born on July 14, 1831, in Springfield, Massachusetts. He entered West Point in 1849, but was discharged prior to graduation in 1853. He enlisted in the 13th U.S. Infantry in New York City on May 14, 1861. Later that month, Dwight was commissioned a captain, and in June became lieutenant colonel of the 70th New York Volunteers, whose colonel was Daniel E. Sickles (*q.v.*). At the battle of Williamsburg on the Peninsula, the regiment suffered 50 percent casualties. Dwight received three wounds and was left for dead. He survived, however, was taken prisoner, and later was exchanged and promoted for gallantry in this action to brigadier general of Volunteers on November 29, 1862.

In command of the 1st Brigade in Cuvier Grover's (*q.v.*) division of Nathaniel P. Banks's (*q.v.*) army in Louisiana, Dwight led in the attack on Port Hudson and served on the commission to settle the terms of Port Hudson's surrender. In 1864, he was Banks's chief of staff in the Red River campaign, and later commanded the 1st Division of the XIX Corps. Ugly rumors indicate that Dwight's staff job really involved trafficking in contraband cotton. Later, when the XIX Corps moved to Virginia to serve under General Philip Sheridan (*q.v.*), Dwight led his command in battles at Winchester, Fisher's Hill, and Cedar Creek. Again he came under a cloud for absence from his command during an action—reportedly to eat his lunch. He was placed under arrest but later released from charges.

Possibly for this reason, Dwight was excluded from brevet promotion prior to being discharged on January 15, 1866. After the war, he moved to Cincinnati and entered the railroad business with members of his family. He died in Boston on April 21, 1888. Hewitt, *Port Hudson*; Phisterer, *New York in the War of the Rebellion*, vols. 4, 5.

Archie P. McDonald

DYER, Alexander Brydie, *general*, was born on January 10, 1815, in Richmond, Virginia. He graduated from West Point in 1837, was posted to Fortress Monroe, and then served in the Second Seminole War in Florida. In 1838, he transferred to the Ordnance Corps, and during the Mexican War served as chief of ordnance for the army invading New Mexico. He saw considerable combat and was wounded in February 1847. Until the Civil War, Dyer performed routine duty at a number of government facilities. His brilliance and organizational ability were recognized but opportunities were limited, although he was promoted to captain in 1853.

When the Civil War came, Dyer remained loyal to the Union. In August 1861 he was named superintendent of the Springfield Armory in Massachusetts, the only government small arms manufactory in the United States. Dyer's Southern birth led many, including members of Congress, to challenge his fitness for such an important post, but in the following three years he proved his worth. The armory was expanded from a facility producing about 10,000 arms annually to one producing more than 300,000. In addition, Dyer supervised the distribution of patterns and gauges to private arms manufacturers in order to assure weapons of quality and interchangeability with government issue.

Although he was considered for the post of chief of ordnance as early as 1863, Dyer requested that he be passed over in order to prevent the jealousy of officers senior to him. On September 12, 1864, however, he received the appointment and proved to be the most able and progressive of all who served in that post. He increased efficiency, reduced administrative costs, and was able to lower the price the government was required to pay for contract arms. His actions were often unpopular with contractors, who in time were able to force Dyer to defend himself against charges of unfairness and favoritism. This he successfully did. Dyer moved to expand the use of breech-loading arms and metallic self-contained ammunition, called for improved rifled artillery, and provided a banded artillery projectile of his own design. Further, he wished to produce all of these items at government facilities. Great advancements were made in the acquisition of better weapons, but the full fruit of Dyer's aims were not realized because the war ended.

Following the war, Dyer was able to oversee the conversion to breech-loading, metallic cartridge small arms, but the lack of appropriations did not permit arms as advanced as he would have liked. Artillery improved little after the war because Dyer's requests went largely unheeded. He supervised the disposal of surplus arms, many of which went to Europe, and got the best prices possible. He died while still in office, on May 20, 1874, in Washington, D.C. Davis, *Arming the Union*; Edwards, *Civil War Guns*.

Carl L. Davis

E

EADS, James Buchanan, *inventor, manufacturer,* was born in Lawrenceburg, Indiana, on May 23, 1820. His family moved to Cincinnati and Louisville before settling in St. Louis when Eads was thirteen. He received only a primary education and by 1838 was working as a purser on a Mississippi River steamboat. He invented a diving bell, and in 1842 established a partnership to salvage sunken steamboats. When President Abraham Lincoln (*q.v.*) called upon Eads for advice on how best to use the western waterways to Union advantage, he urged the construction of an armor-plated, steam-propelled fleet of gunboats.

Eads received the contract to build seven of these gunboats, established a shipyard at Carondolet (near St. Louis) in September 1861, and had the first of the gunboats ready by October 12. Employing 4,000 men at Carondolet and a second shipyard near Mound City, Illinois, he delivered the remainder within 100 days of his start, a remarkable feat. These ships played a key role in the war on the Mississippi, Tennessee, and Cumberland rivers. Before war's end, Eads had completed seven more, equipping them with several ordnance inventions that he had patented. He also produced seven converted transports, which came to be known as tinclads, and constructed four heavy mortar boats. After the war, Eads bridged the Mississippi at St. Louis and designed a system of jetties that greatly improved navigation at the mouth of the Mississippi. He died in Nassau, the Bahamas, on March 8, 1887. Dorsey, *Road to the Sea*; Gosnell, *Guns on the Western Waters.*

William E. Parrish

EATON, John, *general,* was born on December 5, 1829, in Sutton, New Hampshire. He worked his way through Thetford Academy (Vermont) and Dartmouth

College, from which he graduated Phi Beta Kappa in 1854. After two years as a school principal in Cleveland, Ohio, he was appointed superintendent of education in Toledo. Although a staunch Unionist who probably voted Republican in 1856 and 1860, Eaton was no abolitionist. In August 1861 he returned to Toledo, where he enlisted as chaplain in the 27th Ohio Volunteers and was ordained by the Maumee Presbytery. When his regiment fought at Shiloh, Iuka, and Corinth, Eaton ministered to physical as well as spiritual wounds and served as brigade sanitary inspector. In November 1862 General Ulysses S. Grant (*q.v.*) ordered him to take charge of the hundreds of runaway slaves pouring into Union lines, and a month later named him general superintendent of contrabands for the Department of the Tennessee. Eventually, he and his staff supervised more than 100,000 freedmen throughout the Mississippi Valley.

Eaton resigned his chaplaincy in October 1863 to become colonel of the 9th Louisiana Volunteers of African Descent (later 63rd USCT). At the close of the war he served briefly as assistant commissioner of the Freedmen's Bureau for the District of Columbia, Maryland, and northern Virginia. Breveted brigadier general in October 1865, he was mustered out in December. Eaton's later career included three years in Reconstruction Tennessee, where he edited the Radical *Memphis Post* and was elected state superintendent of public instruction (1867–1869), and sixteen years as U.S. commissioner of education (1870–1886). He was president of Marietta College (1886–1891) and of Sheldon Jackson (now Westminster) College in Salt Lake City (1895–1899). He was also the first American superintendent of schools in Puerto Rico. Eaton died in Washington, D.C., on February 9, 1906. Eaton, *Grant, Lincoln, and the Freedmen*; Gerteis, *From Contraband to Freedman.*

Cam Walker

ECKLEY, Ephraim Ralph, *congressman*, was born on December 3, 1811, near Mount Pleasant, Ohio. In 1814, he moved with his family to Ashland, and in 1816 settled in Hayesville, Ohio. He graduated from Vermillion Institute, taught school, surveyed, and studied law. In 1835, Eckley laid out the first lots in Crestline, Ohio, which became an important rail center. He moved to Carrollton in 1836 and entered the Ohio bar that year. Eckley served two terms in the Ohio Senate, ran unsuccessfully for lieutenant governor in 1851, was elected to the Ohio House in 1853, and lost an election for the U.S. Senate in 1853. In 1856, he attended the Republican National Convention in Philadelphia and as a Republican was elected to the 38th, 39th, and 40th Congresses. He supported Abraham Lincoln's (*q.v.*) administration and its war policies, and was an outspoken critic of the Democratic party. Eckley did not seek reelection in 1868 but returned to his law practice. He died in Carrollton on March 27, 1908. *BDUSC.*

Thomas H. Smith

EDEN, John Rice, *congressman*, was born in Bath county, Kentucky, on February 1, 1826. In 1831, his family moved to a farm in Rush county, Indiana.

At eighteen, he began to teach at the local school, but left in 1850 to read law in Rushville. Eden migrated to Shelbyville, Illinois, passed the bar there on July 1, 1852, and opened a law office. In 1856, he ran as a Democrat for prosecuting attorney of the 17th Judicial Circuit and easily won. Four years later he lost a race for the legislature. Elected to the 38th Congress in 1862, Eden voted for those bills necessary to prosecute the war. He failed to win reelection in 1864, and in 1868, the Illinois Democrats selected him to run for governor against John M. Palmer (*q.v.*), who defeated him by more than 50,000 votes. He was elected to Congress in 1872, 1874, and 1876. Eden served as chairman of the Committee on War Claims, and in 1876 sat on the committee that investigated the presidential voting in South Carolina. He failed to be renominated in 1878, but when his congressional district was reorganized in 1884, he was elected and served one term. He died in Sullivan, Illinois, on June 9, 1909. *Combined History of Shelby and Moultrie Counties, Illinois.*

Wayne C. Temple

EDGERTON, Joseph Ketchum, *congressman*, was born in Vergennes, Vermont, on February 16, 1818. He attended the common schools and an academy at Plattsburgh, New York. In 1835, he studied law with Dudley Selden in New York City and was admitted to the bar in 1839. Edgerton moved to Fort Wayne, Indiana, in 1844. In 1855, he was made president of the Fort Wayne and Chicago Railroad, and became a director of the Pittsburgh, Fort Wayne, & Chicago Railroad when his company was consolidated with others to form that line. He was a Whig until the party's dissolution and then joined the Democratic party. Edgerton supported Stephen A. Douglas (*q.v.*) for President in 1860, and in 1862 was elected to the U.S. House of Representatives, where he served on the Committee on Naval Affairs. He was defeated for reelection in 1864 and took no active part in politics after the war. He died in Boston on August 25, 1893. *Biographical History of Eminent and Self-Made Men of the State of Indiana; Memorial Record of Northeastern Indiana.*

Raymond L. Shoemaker

EDGERTON, Sidney, *congressman*, was born in Cazenovia, New York, on August 17, 1818. He attended and taught in local schools, including Wesley Seminary in Lima, New York, before he traveled to Akron, Ohio, and began to study law with Rufus P. Spalding (*q.v.*). In 1846, he graduated from the Cincinnati Law School, was admitted to the Ohio bar, and began a practice in Akron. Fervently antislavery, Edgerton was a delegate to the Buffalo, New York, convention that formed the Free Soil party. He was prosecuting attorney for Summit county (1852–1856), attended the Philadelphia convention at which the Republican party was organized in 1856, and, as a Republican, was elected to the 36th and 37th Congresses. He did not seek reelection in 1862. He supported Abraham Lincoln's (*q.v.*) war policies and was an outspoken critic of the Democratic party. In 1863, Lincoln appointed Edgerton U.S. judge for the Idaho

Territory. He paved the way for the organization of the Montana Territory and served as its governor in 1865 and 1866. He returned to his law practice in Akron, where he died on July 19, 1900. Doyle, *Centennial History of Summit County*; Lane, *Fifty Years and over of Akron and Summit County.*

Thomas H. Smith

EDWARDS, Oliver, *general,* was born on January 30, 1835, in Springfield, Massachusetts. In 1856, he moved to Warsaw, Illinois, and became a partner in a foundry. At the outbreak of the Civil War, Edwards returned home and recruited an infantry company. When this unit was incorporated into the 10th Massachusetts Volunteers, he became the regimental adjutant. He assumed command of the 37th Massachusetts Volunteers in September 1862, leading that regiment at Fredericksburg, Chancellorsville, and Gettysburg. After commanding a special brigade in New York during the draft riots, Edwards returned to Virginia, where he directed a regiment, and later a brigade, in the Wilderness. At Spotsylvania, units under his command held the "Bloody Angle" throughout twenty-four hours of continuous combat.

Edwards accompanied General Philip Sheridan (*q.v.*) in the Shenandoah Valley but rejoined the Army of the Potomac in time to lead a brigade in the final assault on Petersburg and accept the mayor's surrender. A few days later, his troops participated in capturing a Confederate brigade. Edwards personified the ideal Civil War citizen-soldier. Although he lacked prior military experience, his intelligence, devotion, and courage enabled him to succeed as a leader in some of the bloodiest fighting of the conflict. After the war, Edwards became postmaster of Warsaw, Illinois, but soon returned to manufacturing. He served three terms as mayor of Warsaw before his death there on April 28, 1905. Matter, *If It Takes All Summer.*

James L. Morrison, Jr.

EDWARDS, Thomas McKay, *congressman,* was born on December 16, 1795, in Keene, New Hampshire. He graduated from Dartmouth, and was admitted to the bar in 1816. In 1845, he gave up the law to become a railroad president and an executive of banking and insurance companies. Edwards served several terms in the New Hampshire legislature, gravitating toward the Know-Nothing party in the 1850s. After becoming prominent in the new Republican party, he was a frequent runner-up for higher office, losing a bid for speaker of the state House of Representatives in 1855, and a campaign for the legislature's approval as U.S. senator in 1857, when the incumbent died. In 1856 he was a Republican presidential elector, and in 1858 his district sent him to Congress. Reelected in 1860, Edwards took a moderate course through the early stages of the war, opposing some arbitrary arrests but resisting the use of Federal troops for enforcement of the Fugitive Slave Laws. He lost his party's nomination to James W. Patterson (*q.v.*) in 1862, and in 1864 he failed in another attempt at the U.S.

Senate. After the war Edwards returned to his business interests in Keene, and died there on May 1, 1875. Lyford, *Life of Edward H. Rollins.*

William Marvel

ELDREDGE, Charles Augustus, *congressman,* was born on February 27, 1820, in Bridport, Vermont. He studied law, taught school to support himself, and in 1846 was admitted to the New York bar. In 1848, Eldredge settled in Fond du Lac, Wisconsin. A conservative Democrat, he served in the state Senate in the mid-1850s, and in 1862 was elected to the first of his six terms in the U.S. House of Representatives. He supported a vigorous prosecution of the war, although he resisted proposals that threatened to impede the restoration of the Union and the integrity of the Constitution. These included the draft, the Emancipation Proclamation, and the 13th Amendment. Later, Eldredge became a Johnson Democrat, advocated a policy of leniency toward the South, and opposed the Civil Rights Laws and the 14th and 15th Amendments. As a member of the House Judiciary Committee in 1868, he helped to draft the minority report against President Andrew Johnson's (*q.v.*) impeachment. After leaving Congress, Eldredge resumed his law practice in Fond du Lac, where he died on October 26, 1896. Benedict, *Compromise of Principle; History of Fond du Lac County, Wisconsin.*

Michael J. McManus

ELIOT, Thomas Dawes, *congressman,* was born on March 20, 1803, in Boston. After graduating from Columbia College in Washington, D.C., he was admitted to the Massachusetts bar in 1829, and began practice in New Bedford, Massachusetts. He served in both houses of the state legislature, and in 1854 was elected as a Whig to fill a vacancy in the 33rd Congress, where he attracted attention for his speeches against the Kansas–Nebraska Bill. In 1855, he helped found the Republican party in Massachusetts, and was elected as a Republican to five successive terms in Congress (1859–1869).

During the Civil War, Eliot was appointed to the Commerce Committee and the Select Committee on Confiscation and Emancipation; in the 39th Congress he was chairman of the Select Committee on Freedmen. He was an outspoken advocate of emancipation and of congressional protection for the equal rights of the former slaves. He played an important role in the drafting and passage of the Second Confiscation Act, and in the winter of 1864–1865 he was instrumental in the enactment of the Freedmen's Bureau Bill. Eliot was critical of Abraham Lincoln's (*q.v.*) hesitancy to emancipate slaves, and at first opposed him on Reconstruction issues. Originally he supported the Wade–Davis Reconstruction Bill, but by December 1864 he was attempting to negotiate a compromise with Lincoln over the admittance of Louisiana to the Union. He continued to be influential in debates over Reconstruction during the postwar years. Eliot died in New Bedford on June 14, 1870. Belz, *New Birth of Freedom*; Benedict, *Compromise of Principle.*

Richard H. Abbott

ELLIOTT, Washington Lafayette, *general,* was born on March 31, 1825, in Carlisle, Pennsylvania. He studied at Dickinson College before entering West Point in 1841. Elliott left the Academy in 1844 to study medicine, but at the outset of the Mexican War he received a commission as 2nd lieutenant of Mounted Rifles. He saw action at Veracruz, but after becoming ill, he was assigned to recruiting duty. Following the war, Elliott saw action on the frontier and in 1854 was promoted to captain. Shortly before the outbreak of the Civil War, he was transferred to St. Louis. He served under Nathaniel Lyon (*q.v.*) during the 1861 Missouri campaign and saw action at Wilson's Creek. On September 14, 1861, Elliott was commissioned in the Volunteers as colonel of the 2nd Iowa Cavalry, and under John Pope (*q.v.*) he took part in operations against New Madrid and Island No. 10.

Transferred to northern Mississippi, Elliott was given command of a cavalry brigade during the siege of Corinth and commanded the war's first cavalry raid, against the Mobile & Ohio Railroad. Promoted to brigadier general of Volunteers, he was transferred to Virginia, where he was wounded at Second Bull Run. He served briefly as chief of cavalry of the Army of Virginia, commanded the Department of the Northwest, led the 3rd Division of the III Corps at Chancellorsville and Gettysburg, then commanded the 1st Cavalry Division of the Army of the Cumberland, reinforcing Ambrose Burnside (*q.v.*) in East Tennessee. During the Atlanta campaign, he was chief of cavalry under George H. Thomas (*q.v.*), and took part at the battles near Nashville as a division commander in the IV Corps. After serving in the District of Kansas, having been breveted major general in both the Regular Army and the Volunteers, Elliott was promoted to lieutenant colonel and colonel. He retired from the Army in 1879, and engaged in banking in San Francisco until his death there on June 29, 1888. Starr, *Union Cavalry,* vol. 3.

Christopher Phillips

ELY, Alfred, *congressman,* was born on February 15, 1815, in Lyme, Connecticut. He moved in 1835 to Rochester, New York, where he became a lawyer for a number of large milling firms. Long active in city politics, Ely was elected in 1858 to the House of Representatives as a Republican, and was reelected in 1860. As spokesman for a district that Southerners regarded as a hotbed of abolitionism, Ely took a hard line against slaveholders. On July 21, 1861, he was one of several congressmen who rented carriages in Washington and drove to Manassas, Virginia, hoping to observe the death of the Confederacy at the battle of Bull Run. Cut off from colleagues in the subsequent melee, Ely was captured by Confederates and imprisoned in Richmond. Although treated reasonably well, he was all but put on display as a Radical Republican trophy. He was released Christmas Day 1861, in exchange for a Confederate political prisoner.

A diary Ely kept during his incarceration was published at New York in 1862 as *Journal of Alfred Ely: Prisoner of War at Richmond.* In 1862, with the Union war effort sputtering and the Republican party in Rochester splintering, Ely reluctantly stepped aside to allow the nomination of a more centrist candidate. In 1864, though tacitly promised renomination, he lost out to a more powerful Radical rival. Ely resumed his lucrative law practice after the war and remained active in civic and cultural affairs. He died in Rochester on May 18, 1892. McKelvey, *Rochester: The Flower City.*

James C. Mohr

EMERSON, Ralph Waldo, *essayist, poet,* was born in Boston on May 25, 1803. A son of a Unitarian minister, he became one of the leading literary figures of nineteenth-century America. He graduated from Harvard College in 1821 and preached until 1832, when his extreme individualism led to his break with the Unitarian Church. Thereafter, Emerson was a popular Transcendentalist lecturer, traveling throughout the North. In his lectures and essays he conceptualized the values of the modernizing culture of New England. Quite conventional in his racism and disinclination to interfere with slavery in the South, Emerson was initially critical of abolitionists. It was the Fugitive Slave Act of 1850, which he interpreted as a Southern assault on Northern states' rights, that got him actively involved in the sectional conflict. In the 1850s, he frequently spoke against what he regarded as proslavery aggression. Nevertheless, his public praise of John Brown (*q.v.*) as a ''new saint,'' following Brown's Harper's Ferry raid, was balanced by private misgivings.

When the Civil War began, Emerson enthusiastically backed the Union war effort with lectures, poems, service on the Board of Visitors for West Point, and visits to Washington, D.C. Meanwhile, he despaired that President Abraham Lincoln (*q.v.*) was not a gentleman, and joined abolitionists and Radical Republicans in pressing Lincoln to make emancipation a war aim. Emerson also criticized Lincoln's mild Reconstruction policy. In all, he played an important role in convincing Northerners that the war and emancipation were patriotic and moral necessities. After the war, Emerson became increasingly senile, and although he remained active, he achieved no new insights in his literary work. He died in Concord, Massachusetts, on April 27, 1882. Porte, *Representative Man.*

Stanley Harrold

EMORY, William Hemsley, *general,* was born on September 7, 1811, in Poplar Grove, Maryland. He graduated from West Point in 1831, and became one of the best topographical engineers in America. He consistently avoided involvement in party politics and remained ardently loyal to the Union. In 1861, Lieutenant Colonel Emory commanded four forts in Indian Territory. Pressured by Texas troops, he took his soldiers to Kansas, and then sent them to Missouri, where they reinforced an army forming under Nathaniel Lyon (*q.v.*). In 1862, Emory was promoted to brigadier general of Volunteers and assigned to command a cavalry brigade in the Army of the Potomac. In the Peninsula campaign he distinguished himself leading a charge at Hanover Court House, which was perhaps the personal high point of his military career.

From 1862 to 1864, Emory commanded a division of the XIX Corps in Louisiana under Nathaniel P. Banks (*q.v.*). His troops showed well in a defensive role against Richard Taylor's Confederates at the battle of Mansfield. Emory also participated in the Port Hudson campaign and temporarily commanded the defenses of New Orleans. After taking command of the XIX Corps in May 1864, he transferred to the East, serving in the Shenandoah Valley under Philip H. Sheridan (*q.v.*). At Winchester and Cedar Creek, Confederates broke the line of the XIX Corps, but Emory partially redeemed his reputation by supporting Sheridan's successful counterattack at Cedar Creek. Sheridan personally recommended that he be promoted to brevet major general of Volunteers for his actions.

Emory remained in the Army at his Regular rank of colonel, but his postwar career turned so sour that he might have been better off retiring. He became involved in the machinations of the Radicals, out to impeach President Andrew Johnson (*q.v.*), who told him that the Command of the Army Act was unconstitutional. In 1871, Emory took charge of troops in the Department of the Gulf and became entangled in Louisiana's Reconstruction politics. In 1875, he and Sheridan disagreed over when and how to use troops to support Louisiana's Republican government, leading Sheridan to demand that Emory be forcibly retired. Emory's promotion to brigadier general on the retired list in 1876 helped to ease the pain of being abruptly separated from the Army after forty-three years of faithful service. He died in Washington, D.C., on December 1, 1887.

Catton, *Stillness at Appomattox*; Dawson, *Army Generals and Reconstruction.*

Joseph G. Dawson III

ENGLISH, James Edward, *congressman,* was born on March 13, 1812, in New Haven, Connecticut. He attended public schools briefly, then was apprenticed to a farmer and later to a carpenter. Not content to be a skilled laborer, English became a successful entrepreneur, purchasing the Jerome Clock Company and, in 1855, the New Haven Clock Company. He expanded the latter firm into one of the largest clock manufacturing businesses in the country; by 1861, it employed 300 people and produced 250,000 clocks per year. English became a member of the New Haven Common Council and served in the Connecticut legislature. In 1860, he was the Democratic nominee for lieutenant governor but was defeated. He was offered the gubernatorial nomination in 1861 but refused it, instead accepting nomination to Congress from the New Haven district. He won that election and was reelected in 1862.

English, a self-proclaimed War Democrat, supported most of Abraham Lincoln's (*q.v.*) war measures, including appropriations bills and recruitment measures. He challenged the Peace Democrats, who supported former Governor Thomas H. Seymour's (*q.v.*) demand for an immediate end to the war. English opposed the Emancipation Proclamation but, in 1865, voted for the 13th Amendment. During the postwar years, he helped reestablish Connecticut's Democratic party. He received the nomination for governor in 1866 and, though defeated, was renominated each succeeding year until 1871. He defeated his Republican opponents in 1867, 1868, and 1870. In 1875, when Senator Orris Ferry died, English assumed his seat. These political successes may be attributed to his support for war measures and, despite his entrepreneurial prowess, to his continuing rapport with Connecticut's working people. He died in New Haven on March 2, 1890. Lane, *Political History of Connecticut*; Niven, *Connecticut for the Union.*

Joanna D. Cowden

EVERETT, Edward, *Unionist vice presidential candidate, orator*, was born in Dorchester, Massachusetts, on April 11, 1794. He epitomized a nationalism located in the parochial environment of Boston that manifested itself in the Civil War. After graduating from Harvard in 1811, he went directly to the prestigious Brattle Street Church as a Unitarian minister. In 1814, Everett was appointed professor of Greek at Harvard, and in 1819, after studying at Göttingen, he became the first American to receive a German Ph.D. He was the editor of the *North American Review*, and pursued a career in Whig politics that brought him election to Congress (1825–1835) and to the governorship of Massachusetts (1836–1840). Aside from an unhappy three years (1846–1849) as president of Harvard, Everett never returned to academic life. After serving in Congress and the statehouse, he was as minister plenipotentiary to England from 1841 to 1845, and Secretary of State at the end of Millard Fillmore's administration, succeeding Daniel Webster.

Throughout his public career, Everett was identified as a moderate and a Southern sympathizer, the latter charge provoking his resignation from the Senate in 1854. His political sensibilities and the quality of his judgment were probably best expressed by his candidacy in 1860 for Vice President on the Constitutional Union party ticket with John Bell of Tennessee. The party was the heir to the Whig party that would preserve the Union by reviving the Missouri Compromise.

However, it was not as a diplomat or as a politician that Everett won his fame; it was as a lecturer. He was a brilliant speaker, imposing in the rhetorical tradition of the nineteenth century, and during the Civil War used his talents to support the North and the reelection of Abraham Lincoln (*q.v.*). It is more fitting than ironic that Everett was the main speaker at Gettysburg, speaking for two hours while the President spoke for two minutes. He died in Boston on January 15, 1865. Frothingham, *Edward Everett*; Kaplan, "The Brahmin as Diplomat," *Civil War History.*

Lawrence S. Kaplan

EWING, Thomas, Jr., *general*, was born on August 7, 1829, in Lancaster, Ohio. His father was a U.S. senator whose powerful presence gained his son, at age nineteen, a position as one of President Zachary Taylor's private secretaries. Ewing attended Brown University, and studied and practiced law in Cincinnati. In 1856, he and his brother, Hugh, moved to Leavenworth, Kansas, where they opened a law practice and sold real estate with their foster brother, William T. Sherman (*q.v.*). Ardently antislavery, Ewing opposed the Lecompton Constitution, which sought statehood for Kansas as a slave state. When Kansas entered the Union as a free state in 1861, Ewing was its first chief justice. He resigned that office in the fall of 1862 to organize and recruit the 11th Kansas Volunteer Cavalry, of which he was named colonel. Assigned to the Army of the Frontier under James G. Blunt (*q.v.*), he saw action at Cane Hill and Prairie Grove, Arkansas.

In March 1863, Ewing was promoted to brigadier general and was assigned to command the District of the Border (Kansas and western Missouri). In an effort to suppress local proslavery guerrillas, he issued his notorious Order No. 11, which depopulated four Missouri counties of both proslavery and antislavery residents. In the fall of 1864, during Sterling Price's Missouri raid, Ewing was ordered to delay the Confederate approach to St. Louis. He commanded Federal troops at Pilot Knob, and his stubborn resistance and subsequent withdrawal allowed Federal forces in the West to concentrate against Price's invasion. For his conduct, he was breveted major general in February 1865, but in March he resigned from the Army. After the war, Ewing practiced law in Washington, D.C., then returned to Ohio, where he entered politics. He served in the U.S. House, and ran for the state's governorship as a Greenback Democrat. Ewing died on January 21, 1896, in New York City. Goodrich, *Bloody Dawn.*

Christopher Phillips

F

FAIRBANKS, Erastus, *governor*, was born in Brimfield, Massachusetts, on October 28, 1792. In 1815 his family moved to St. Johnsbury, Vermont. In 1830, his brother Thaddeus conceived the platform scale that made the Fairbanks' fortune. Thaddeus's invention was patented, and in 1834 he and his brothers founded E. & T. Fairbanks and Company to manufacture the scales. Erastus became head of the firm and remained so until his death. In 1836, he was elected from St. Johnsbury to the Vermont House of Representatives, and for the next twenty years was among the most influential Vermont Whigs.

In 1848, Fairbanks declined nomination to the U.S. Congress. In 1852 he was elected governor. The most important act of his administration was a prohibitory liquor law that he strongly supported. Although this act remained substantially in force for fifty years, the disaffection of wets and antislavery elements with the Whig party combined to deny Fairbanks a bid for reelection. This threw the election into the legislature, where, despite his plurality in the general election, he was defeated.

After joining the Republican party, Fairbanks regained the governorship in September 1860 and pursued a militantly pro-Union policy. Vermont stood ready, he informed President James Buchanan (*q.v.*), to respond to any requisition for troops. When President Abraham Lincoln (*q.v.*) did issue a requisition, Fairbanks secured appropriations for seven regiments rather than the one requested by the President, and pledged the credit of E. & T. Fairbanks and Company to facilitate the purchase of military equipment. Six regiments were raised and equipped before Fairbanks left office. He died on November 20, 1864, in St. Johnsbury. Crockett, *Vermont*, vol. 3; Newell, "Erastus Fairbanks," *Vermont History*; Williams, *Biographical Encyclopedia of Vermont of the Nineteenth Century.*

Samuel B. Hand

FARNSWORTH, Elon John, *general,* was born in Green Oak, Michigan, on July 30, 1837. He left the University of Michigan to join General A.S. Johnston's Mormon expedition as a forage master in 1857–1858. With the outbreak of the Civil War, he was commissioned 1st lieutenant and adjutant of the 8th Illinois Cavalry, rising to captain on December 25, 1861. The 8th Illinois saw duty on the Peninsula, at Antietam, and at Fredericksburg. In the spring of 1863, Farnsworth served as an acting chief quartermaster with General Erasmus Keyes's (*q.v.*) IV Corps. When General Alfred Pleasonton (*q.v.*) consolidated the Union cavalry into a single corps, he appointed Farnsworth to his staff. On June 29, 1863, Farnsworth and George Custer (*q.v.*) were promoted directly from captain to brigadier general.

As commander of the 1st Brigade of General H. Judson Kilpatrick's (*q.v.*) 3rd Division, Farnsworth immediately saw action at the battle of Hanover, Pennsylvania, June 30, 1863. Confederate General J.E.B. Stuart struck Kilpatrick's division, which was passing through the town. Farnsworth's brigade halted the Southern charge and counterattacked—driving the Confederates out of the town and almost capturing Stuart. The Union victory at Hanover deflected Stuart's cavalry northeast, away from Gettysburg and out of most of that campaign at a critical moment. On the afternoon of July 3, at Gettysburg, Kilpatrick rashly ordered Farnsworth's brigade to make a charge in the area south of Devil's Den. The charge would have to be made over rough ground, through timber, against an infantry brigade supported by artillery. Farnsworth objected, and Kilpatrick insinuated that Farnsworth was "afraid." Farnsworth hotly denied this, led the desperate and ill-fated charge, and fell dead with five wounds. The charge was needless and cost the life of a promising officer. Longacre, *Cavalry at Gettysburg*; Starr, *Union Cavalry*, vol. 1.

Roy P. Stonesifer, Jr.

FARNSWORTH, John Franklin, *congressman, general,* was born in Eaton, Canada, on March 27, 1820. His family moved to Livingston county, Michigan, in 1834; there he surveyed with his father and read law with Judge Josiah Turner. After moving to St. Charles, Illinois, he was admitted to the bar on April 18, 1844. Although raised a Democrat, Farnsworth became "a full blown [Owen] Lovejoy [*q.v.*] abolitionist" and won election to Congress on November 4, 1856, as a Republican. He was reelected easily in 1858, but two years later was not renominated. When the Civil War came, he raised the 8th Illinois Cavalry and was mustered in as its colonel on August 18, 1861. The regiment took part in the Peninsula campaign, and Farnsworth soon commanded the 2nd Brigade. He was elected to the 38th Congress on November 4, 1862, which perhaps hastened his promotion to brigadier general on December 5, 1862, to rank from

November 29. Although Farnsworth had to resign his commission before Congress convened, the War Department gave him special authority to raise the new 17th Illinois Cavalry at St. Charles. According to plan, his old law partner, John L. Beveridge of Evanston, became the colonel (he had served as major in the 8th under Farnsworth).

President Abraham Lincoln (*q.v.*) sometimes consulted Farnsworth and always addressed him as "General," yet in the House, he became allied with the Radical Republicans. He was reelected in 1864, 1866, 1868, and 1870. In 1872, Kane county, Illinois, became part of 4th District, and he failed to be nominated, largely because he favored Horace Greeley (*q.v.*). In his place, the local Republicans picked Stephen A. Hurlbut (*q.v.*). Two years later, Farnsworth changed parties and ran as a Democrat against Hurlbut but lost by over 1,000 votes. He practiced law in St. Charles until 1879, when he moved to Washington, D.C. He invested his money in real estate and became one of the wealthiest men in the capital city. Farnsworth died in Washington, D.C., on July 14, 1897. Dunne, *Illinois: The Heart of the Nation*, vols. 2, 3.

Wayne C. Temple

FARRAGUT, David Glasgow, *admiral,* was born on July 5, 1801, at Campbell's Station, near Knoxville, Tennessee. His family moved to New Orleans in 1807. After the death of his mother and the enlistment of his father in the Navy, he was adopted by Commander David Porter, in charge of the New Orleans naval station. At the age of nine Farragut was appointed a midshipman. In 1811, Porter was given command of the frigate *Essex,* and Farragut sailed with him. In the War of 1812, the *Essex* captured a number of prizes in the Pacific, and Farragut, as prize master, took one of them into Valparaiso, Chile. He was twelve at the time. After the war, Farragut served primarily in the Mediterranean and the West Indies, in a career that was varied but not spectacular. He received his first command, the sloop *Decatur,* in 1842, and his last, the *Brooklyn,* in 1860. He commanded the *Saratoga* during the Mexican war, and had several shore assignments.

When the Civil War broke out, the Navy Department was apparently suspicious of Farragut because of his Southern birth and upbringing; he remained unemployed until September 1861, when he was appointed to a retirement board. However, in January 1862, he was given command of the West Gulf Blockading Squadron. Opening the Mississippi River and seizing New Orleans were the major objectives of his command. On April 24, 1862, seventeen ships, led by Farragut on the *Hartford,* passed Forts Jackson and St. Philip, and after defeating a small Confederate river flotilla, reached New Orleans. The city surrendered without bloodshed. For this feat, he was promoted to rear admiral—the first officer in that grade in the U.S. Navy.

For the next sixteen months, Farragut concentrated on securing control of the lower Mississippi. In June–July 1862, he attempted to take Vicksburg; and from August through February 1863, he was at Pensacola and then New Orleans, chiefly strengthening the blockade along the Gulf coast. In March 1863 he attacked the batteries at Port Hudson. With the reduction of Port Hudson and the surrender of Vicksburg in July, Farragut considered the Mississippi River campaign complete. In August, he sailed for New York and remined there until January 1864, when he returned to his station in the Gulf. His major objective was Mobile, the most important Gulf port remaining in Confederate hands. On August 4, Farragut led four monitors and fourteen wooden vessels into Mobile Bay. The fleet successfully passed the forts defending the bay and defeated the small Confederate squadron, after which the forts surrendered. Mobile Bay marked the high point of his career, and for this victory he was promoted to vice admiral.

Because his long service in the Gulf had undermined his health, Farragut declined the command of the Fort Fisher expedition, and spent the remainder of the war on inactive service. He was the most competent naval officer on either side during the Civil War. His operational plans were carefully prepared and thorough. His tactics, based on an analysis of his weaknesses and those of his opponent, were superb. The lashing of weak vessels to the sides of more powerful warships was a brilliant innovation. He grasped the limitations of land fortifications in naval actions, and on the Mississippi River and in Mobile Bay utilized this tactical understanding successfully. Finally, he was extremely energetic and aggressive, traits that are absolutely necessary for a successful military commander.

In July 1866, Farragut was commissioned admiral, a grade specially created for him; the following year, he took command of the European Squadron, his last active command. He suffered a heart attack in 1869, and died on August 14, 1870, in Portsmouth, New Hampshire. Dufour, *Night the War Was Lost*; Lewis, *David Glasgow Farragut*; William N. Still, Jr., "David Glasgow Farragut: The Union's Nelson," in Bradford, *Captains of the Old Steam Navy*, pp. 166–193.

William N. Still, Jr.

FARWELL, Nathan Allen, *senator,* was born in Unity, Maine, on February 24, 1812. He attended local schools sufficiently to be able to teach in 1832–1833, then moved to the coastal town of East Thomaston, where he manufactured lime and constructed ships. The sea must have gotten into his blood, for he became a master mariner and trader. He also studied law. Farwell moved to Rockland, founded the Rockland Marine Insurance Company, and served as its president. He was a member of the Maine Senate in 1853, 1854, 1861, and 1862, presiding over that body during his final term. In addition, he won a seat in the Maine House in 1860, 1863, and 1864, and went to Baltimore in 1864 as a delegate to the Union (Republican) National Convention.

In October 1864, Farwell was selected to fill the U.S. Senate vacancy created by the departure of William Pitt Fessenden (*q.v.*) to become Secretary of the Treasury. A partisan of Hannibal Hamlin (*q.v.*), Farwell hoped to see the outgoing Vice President win his seat in 1865. However, Fessenden defeated Hamlin handily, and Farwell returned to Maine and his insurance business. He served as a delegate to the anti-Andrew Johnson (*q.v.*) "loyalist" convention held at Philadelphia in 1866. Farwell died on December 9, 1893, in Rockland, Maine. *BDUSC*.

H. Draper Hunt

FENTON, Reuben Eaton, *congressman, governor,* was born on July 4, 1819, in Chautauqua county, New York, where he amassed a substantial fortune in lumber and real estate. An outspoken opponent of slavery, Fenton was elected in 1852 to the House of Representatives, where he helped lead the revolt of the Free Soil Democrats against the Kansas–Nebraska Bill. After failing to be re-elected as a Democrat in 1854, Fenton helped organize the Republican party in 1855, presided over the first Republican Convention in New York State, and regained his House seat, running as a Republican, in 1856. Uninterrupted re-elections kept him in the House through December 1864.

During the secession crisis, Fenton opposed any compromises that might extend slavery. Once the war began, he earned a strong reputation as a friend of the Union soldier by consistently supporting bills designed to expedite or increase military benefits and by investigating alleged frauds in the letting of army contracts. In 1864, Republicans nominated Fenton for governor of New York. With a strong boost from absentee ballots cast by soldiers voting at the front for the first time, Fenton replaced Horatio Seymour (*q.v.*) in the statehouse at Albany. His victory represented an important political shift in the Union's most powerful state, and his strong showing helped Abraham Lincoln (*q.v.*) secure New York's electoral votes.

As governor, Fenton presided over a Radical Republican coalition that passed reform legislation in the areas of education, fire protection, public health, tenement housing, and labor. Running against President Andrew Johnson's (*q.v.*) Reconstruction policies, he was reelected in 1866. New York's Radical coalition came unglued in 1867 over the issue of racially equal suffrage in the state. Fenton found his version of Republicanism in disarray by 1868, but retained sufficient personal strength to secure election to the U.S. Senate in 1869, where he served until March 1875. At odds throughout his term with New York's other Republican senator, Roscoe Conkling (*q.v.*), and with Ulysses S. Grant's (*q.v.*) administration, Fenton joined the short-lived Liberal Republican movement in 1872. He died in Jamestown, New York, on August 25, 1885. Mohr, *Radical Republicans and Reform in New York.*

James C. Mohr

FERRERO, Edward, *general,* was born in Grenada, Spain, on January 18, 1831; and his family came to New York City shortly thereafter. Ferrero was a dance master (at West Point for a time) and something of a dandy. He entered the service as colonel of the 51st New York Volunteers, which he led in Ambrose Burnside's (*q.v.*) North Carolina expedition. As a brigade commander, he led an attempt to seize Burnside's Bridge at Antietam, and at Fredericksburg his brigade was almost destroyed in the assault on the Confederate center. At the siege of Knoxville, Ferrero commanded a division of the IX Corps. The Union victory at Fort Sanders (November 28–29, 1863) may have obscured a subordinate's charge that he had remained safely under cover. Ferrero should have been removed as a field officer, but instead was given command of a division of black soldiers.

At the infamous battle of the Crater, Burnside chose Ferrero's division to lead the assault through the break in the Confederate lines, and the division trained for the task. George G. Meade (*q.v.*), with Ulysses S. Grant's (*q.v.*) approval, overruled Burnside, who then, after the other division commanders drew straws, gave the assignment to James H. Ledlie's (*q.v.*) division. Ferrero was to follow. By the time Ferrero's division was ordered forward, the advantage of surprise had been lost. Confederate defenders had recovered from the effects of Ledlie's attack, and Ferrero's men plunged into the Crater, where they were slaughtered. Ferrero himself had joined the drunken Ledlie in a bombproof shelter, there to share a bottle while their divisions were destroyed. A court of inquiry found Ferrero negligent but recommended censure rather than criminal charges. In December 1864 he was breveted a major general. After the war he managed dance halls. Ferrero died in New York City on December 11, 1899. Catton, *Stillness at Appomattox*; Marvel, *Burnside*.

John T. Hubbell

FESSENDEN, Samuel Clement, *congressman,* son of the noted abolitionist Samuel Fessenden and half brother of Senator William Pitt Fessenden (*q.v.*) and full brother to Congressman Thomas A. D. Fessenden (*q.v.*), was born in New Gloucester, Maine, on March 7, 1815. He graduated from Bowdoin College in 1834 and from the Bangor Theological Seminary in 1837, and became an ordained Congregational minister. He turned to the study of law and was admitted to the bar in 1858. Subsequently he was appointed judge of the Rockland Municipal Court and, as a Republican, won a seat in the 37th Congress, where he served a single term. In that same Congress, his brother Thomas sat with him in the House and his half brother William Pitt sat in the Senate. Samuel Fessenden received the post of examiner in the U.S. Patent Office in 1865, serving until 1879, when he became U.S. consul at St. John, New Brunswick, Canada. He stepped down from that office in 1881 and died in Stamford, Connecticut, on April 18, 1882. *BDUSC.*

H. Draper Hunt

FESSENDEN, Thomas Amory DeBlois, *congressman,* was born in Portland, Maine, on January 23, 1826. He studied at North Yarmouth Academy and Dartmouth College before graduating from Bowdoin College in 1845. He became a lawyer in 1848, setting up his office in the village of Mechanic Falls, before moving his practice to Auburn. A zealous Republican, he served as delegate to the 1856 Republican National Convention and sat in the Maine House of Representatives in 1860. In 1861, he was prosecuting attorney of Androscoggin county, and in December 1862 he entered Congress as the replacement for Charles W. Walton (*q.v.*), who had resigned. There he joined his brother Samuel Fessenden (*q.v.*) in the House and his half brother William Pitt Fessenden (*q.v.*) in the Senate. He did not seek a second term but returned to Maine and his law practice. He served a second Maine House term in 1868, and that same year went to Chicago as a delegate to the Republican National Convention that nominated Ulysses S. Grant (*q.v.*) for the presidency. He also served as a Republican elector before his death in Auburn on September 28, 1868. *BDUSC*.

H. Draper Hunt

FESSENDEN, William Pitt, *senator, Secretary of the Treasury*, was born on October 16, 1806, in Boscawen, New Hampshire, and spent his formative years in New Glouster, Maine, where his father practiced law. Fessenden attended Bowdoin College, and entered politics at the age of twenty-five, when he was elected to the Maine legislature as a Whig. In 1840, he was elected to Congress, where he worked diligently to implement Henry Clay's American System. Disillusioned with Washington politics, he returned home after one term and was again elected to the Maine legislature. In 1854, Fessenden was elected U.S. senator and took his seat in time to oppose the Kansas–Nebraska Bill. He began his second term in the Senate as chairman of the powerful Finance Committee. Fessenden gradually began to distance himself from his Radical colleagues.

When Secretary of the Treasury Salmon P. Chase (*q.v.*) resigned to accept an appointment to the U.S. Supreme Court in June 1864, President Abraham Lincoln (*q.v.*) nominated Fessenden to the position. He reluctantly agreed to accept the post and went to work to secure new loans for the financially troubled government. After revitalizing the Union's fiscal state, Fessenden resigned and returned to the Senate for a third term, beginning in March 1865. He was named chairman of the Joint Committee on Reconstruction, which put him squarely at odds with Lincoln's successor, Andrew Johnson (*q.v.*). Despite his objections to Johnson's policies, Fessenden courageously voted to acquit the President during his impeachment trial. Fessenden's influence perhaps did more to spare Johnson from conviction than did the more dramatic votes of Senators Joseph Fowler and Edmund Ross. He died in Portland, Maine, on September 8, 1869. Fessenden, *Life and Public Services*; Jellison, *Fessenden of Maine*.

David Dixon

FIELD, Richard Stockton, *senator*, was born in Whitehills, New Jersey, on December 31, 1803. A member of the most politically powerful family in New Jersey, graduated from Princeton in 1821, became a lawyer, practiced for a time in Salem, and in 1832 settled in Princeton, which thereafter was his home. Field, a Whig, served in the Assembly (1838), for three years was attorney general (1838–1841), and played a prominent role in the 1844 state Constitutional Convention. He taught at the Princeton Law School (1847–1862) and was a founder of the New Jersey Historical Society. He led the movement in 1855 and 1856 to establish the State Normal School, later Trenton State College.

New Jersey's Union–Republican party, in which Field played a leading role, had suffered a crushing defeat in the November 1862 elections, but Governor Charles S. Olden (*q.v.*) appointed him to fill the Senate vacancy caused by the death (September 12, 1862) of John R. Thomson (*q.v.*). Field held office just long enough to denounce New Jersey Democrats for obstructing the war effort, and to defend President Abraham Lincoln's (*q.v.*) suspension of habeas corpus. The legislature retaliated by replacing him with the most prominent Peace Democrat in the state, James W. Wall (*q.v.*). Lincoln then appointed Field to a vacancy on the Federal District Court, even though the state congressional delegation had united behind the candidacy of Representative John T. Nixon (*q.v.*). Field served as a Federal judge until a few weeks before his death in Princeton on May 25, 1870. Keasbey, "Richard S. Field," *Proceedings of the New Jersey Historical Society.*

Daniel W. Crofts

FIELD, Stephen Johnson, *Supreme Court justice,* was born on November 4, 1816, in Haddam, Connecticut. He graduated valedictorian of his class at Williams College in 1837, and became a lawyer. He practiced for several years in New York, but was lured to California by the gold rush. The intricacies of local politics and the complexities of California land disputes provided a perfect stage for a man of Field's substantial ability and blustery temperament. Elected to the Supreme Court of California in 1857, he spent most of his time straightening out land titles. Strong lobbying from powerful Californians induced President Abraham Lincoln (*q.v.*) to appoint Field to a tenth and recently created seat on the U.S. Supreme Court on May 20, 1863.

Although he was a longtime Democrat, Field joined the Union party during the Civil War. Before his arrival in Washington, he issued an opinion in the Circuit Court of the Northern District of California in a case involving Confederate privateers. Field maintained that privateering constituted levying war against the United States, and was punishable by both imprisonment and fine. He continued to work on California land cases. When Roger Taney (*q.v.*) died, Field pressed for the nomination of Salmon P. Chase (*q.v.*) as Chief Justice.

Field was a consistent and unyielding proponent of untrammeled capitalism and suspicious of most government regulation. He developed the idea of substantive due process to protect corporate property and converted a majority of colleagues to his views. Although Field apparently had presidential ambitions, he was obviously unsuited for popular politics. He resigned from the Court because of ill health and died on April 9, 1899, in Washington, D.C. Robert J. McCloskey, "Stephen J. Field," in Friedman, *Justices of the U.S. Supreme Court,* vol. 2, pp. 1069–1112; Swisher, *Stephen J. Field.*

George C. Rable

FINCK, William Edward, *congressman,* was born in Somerset, Ohio, on September 1, 1822. He graduated from St. Joseph's College, clerked in a store in Somerset, and studied law. In 1843, he was admitted to the Ohio bar and later served as prosecuting attorney for Perry county. Finck attended the Whig National Conventions of 1844, 1848, and 1852, made an unsuccessful bid for Congress in 1850, and in 1851, was elected to the Ohio Senate. Because of the slavery issue and the Know-Nothings, Finck became a Democrat. In 1862, he won a seat in the 38th Congress, and in 1864 was reelected to the 39th Congress. He opposed the abolition of slavery, believing it an issue to be settled by the states and not by the Federal government. Finck returned to Ohio in 1867, and in 1874 filled the unexpired term of Hugh J. Jewett, who had resigned from Congress. He died in Somerset on January 25, 1901. *BDUSC.*

Thomas H. Smith

FISHER, George Purnell, *congressman,* was born on October 13, 1817, in Milford, Delaware. After attending local schools, he entered St. Mary's College in Baltimore, transferring after one year to Dickinson College, from which he graduated in 1838. He read law in the office of John M. Clayton in Dover, and was admitted to the bar in 1841. Active in Whig politics, Fisher served as clerk of the Delaware Senate in 1843, and was elected to the Delaware House of Representatives in 1844. In 1846, he was appointed secretary of state by Governor Joseph Maull and continued in this office under Maull's successor, William Temple (*q.v.*).

When Clayton became U.S. Secretary of State in 1849, Fisher accompanied him to Washington, serving as his secretary and also working with the State Department to press the claims of American citizens against the Brazilian government. Fisher returned to Dover in 1852 and resumed his practice of law. In 1855, Peter Causey, a former Whig, was elected governor by the American party and named Fisher attorney general of the state. In 1858, Fisher joined the local People's party, composed mostly of former Whigs. A combination of members of the People's party, the Constitutional Union party, and the Republican party elected him to Congress in 1860.

In 1861, President Abraham Lincoln (*q.v.*) consulted with Fisher about a compensated emancipation plan to free the slaves in Delaware, but the measure was not introduced into the legislature after Fisher found that it would be defeated by one vote. The Union party nominated him for the U.S. House of Representatives in 1862, but he was defeated. Lincoln appointed Fisher associate justice of the Supreme Court of the District of Columbia in March 1863, and he participated in the trial of John Surratt. He resigned this post in 1870 in order to become U.S. district attorney in the District of Columbia. He resigned in 1875 and returned to the practice of law. Fisher continued to be prominent in politics, but was not again elected to office. In 1889, President Benjamin Harrison appointed him first auditor of the Treasury Department, a post he held for four years. He died on February 10, 1899, in Washington, D.C. Conrad, *History of the State of Delaware*, vols. 1, 3.

Harold B. Hancock

FLANDERS, Benjamin Franklin, *congressman*, was born on January 26, 1816, in Bristol, New Hampshire. After attending New Hampton Academy, he graduated from Dartmouth College in 1843 and began the study of law. Throughout the antebellum era, Flanders was active in New Orleans journalism, local politics, and business ventures. After editing the *New Orleans Tropic* (1845), he was elected to two terms as alderman (1847, 1852) and served as superintendent of public schools (1850). He helped organize the New Orleans, Opelousas and Great Western Railroad, and was its secretary and treasurer when the war broke out.

After New Orleans fell to Union forces, Flanders was appointed city treasurer by General Benjamin Butler (*q.v.*) on July 20, 1862, and elected as a Unionist to the 37th Congress on December 3, 1862. The admission of Flanders and fellow Louisiana Representative G. Michael Hahn (*q.v.*) was a victory for Abraham Lincoln (*q.v.*), whose Reconstruction policy met fierce opposition in Congress. Although permitted to take his seat, Flanders never had the opportunity to serve because his term expired on March 3, 1863. After brief military service as a captain in the 5th Louisiana Volunteer Infantry, he was appointed special agent of the Treasury Department for the Southern District (1863). Flanders remained active in politics, making an unsuccessful bid for governor on the Republican ticket in 1864. The first president of the First National Bank of New Orleans (1864), he was reappointed special Treasury agent after the end of the war.

During Reconstruction, Flanders was appointed by General Philip Sheridan (*q.v.*) as military governor of Louisiana on June 3, 1867. Taking his seat without a formal inauguration, he resigned on January 8, 1868. After serving as mayor of New Orleans (1870–1872) and assistant U.S. treasurer in that city (1873–1882), he died near Youngsville, Louisiana, on March 13, 1896. *BDGUS*, vol 2.

James M. Prichard

FLETCHER, Thomas Clement, *governor*, was born in Herculaneum, Missouri, on January 22, 1827. At age seventeen he secured employment in the circuit clerk's office, and was elected clerk in 1849. He was admitted to the bar in 1856, and shortly thereafter was appointed land agent for the southwest branch of the Pacific Railroad. Although Fletcher came from a slaveholding family, he embraced the antislavery cause in the mid-1850s and helped to organize the Republican party in Missouri. In 1860, he was a delegate to the Republican National Convention, where he supported the nomination of Abraham Lincoln (*q.v.*).

At the outbreak of war, Fletcher was appointed assistant provost marshal at St. Louis by General Nathaniel Lyon (*q.v.*). Early in 1862, he helped raise the

31st Missouri Volunteers and served as their colonel. He saw action at Chickasaw Bayou, where he was wounded and captured. Exchanged in May 1863, he served in the Vicksburg campaign and at Chattanooga. He commanded a brigade during the Atlanta campaign but was forced to return to Missouri in the summer of 1864 because of illness. He recovered in time to participate in the defense of Missouri against Sterling Price's raid that fall.

In the meantime, Fletcher had been nominated by the Radical Union party as its candidate for governor, and he was elected by a wide margin. The Radicals now controlled the state, and the voters approved a convention to consider constitutional revisions. This convention provided for immediate emancipation, which Fletcher proclaimed on January 11, 1865. It later adopted a new constitution toward which Fletcher was lukewarm because he considered it too proscriptive. He also was disappointed that it did not provide for black suffrage. Nevertheless, his administration saw considerable progress in economic development, the attraction of immigrants, and education for both races. Fletcher retired in 1869 to practice law in St. Louis. He died in Washington, D.C., on March 25, 1899. Parrish, *Missouri Under Radical Rule.*

William E. Parrish

FOOT, Solomon, *senator,* was born in Cornwall, Vermont, on November 19, 1802. He graduated from Middlebury College in 1826, taught at Castleton Seminary and the University of Vermont while reading law, and in 1831 was admitted to the Vermont bar. He served in the Vermont legislature during the 1830s, and from 1836 until 1842 also was prosecuting attorney for Rutland county. In 1842, Foot was elected to Congress as a Whig, serving two terms before declining renomination. His service in the House was most notable for his opposition to the Mexican War. He returned to the Vermont legislature in 1847, and in 1850 he was elected to the U.S. Senate. Ardently antislavery, Foot was twice reelected as a Republican.

A popular platform speaker, though relatively ineffective as a debater, Foot preferred to serve as presiding officer, a function he exercised frequently and well. He received praise from his peers for his ability as president pro tempore during the 36th and 37th Congresses. As chairman of the Committee on Public Buildings and Grounds, he pushed through the completion of the Capitol despite the onset of the Civil War. Foot never achieved national distinction, although he was the senior senator, with sixteen continuous years in office, at the time of his death in Washington, D.C., on March 28, 1866. Bogue, *Earnest Men*; Crockett, *Vermont,* vols. 3, 4; Curry, *Blueprint for Modern America.*

Samuel B. Hand

FORBES, Edwin, *artist,* was born in New York City in 1839. In 1859, he became a pupil of Arthur Fitzwilliam Tait, and his skill in drawing animals, especially horses, was probably acquired in Tait's studio. In 1861, he was hired as a staff artist by Frank Leslie's (*q.v.*) *Illustrated Newspaper* and assigned to the Army of the Potomac, which he accompanied from the occupation of Manassas in 1862 to the siege of Petersburg in 1864. Like Winslow Homer (*q.v.*), Forbes concentrated on the day-to-day camp life of the Union soldiers and only occasionally drew a battlefield scene. His drawings of long marches, the boring lulls between the fighting, and the ingenious ad hoc architecture of winter quarters reveal a detached reporter's attempt to assemble a documentary record of the soldier's life. His frankness and aversion to sentimentality lend credibility to his art.

Forbes kept his wartime sketches and used them as inspiration and models for paintings, etchings, and illustrations. His oil painting of 1865, *The Lull in the Fight*, from a drawing made during the battle of the Wilderness, was exhibited at the National Academy of Design in New York and at the Boston Atheneum. In 1876, forty etchings he based on earlier sketches, published without text as *Life Studies of the Great Army*, received a gold medal at the Philadelphia Centennial Exposition. William T. Sherman (*q.v.*) purchased the original prints for his office in the War Department. From 1878, Forbes painted landscapes, but was largely dependent for his living on illustrating children's books, such as *General William T. Sherman, His life and Battles, Mostly in One Syllable Words* (1886), by his wife, Ida B. Forbes.

Forbes wrote his own reminiscences, *Thirty Years After: The Artist's Story of the Great War*, in 1891, to accompany the publication of some 300 of his sketches and reproductions of his paintings. In his last years, he was paralyzed on his right side and taught himself to work with his left hand. He died in Brooklyn, New York, on March 6, 1895. Forbes's collection of about 300 drawings, etched plates, and the original impressions of the etchings published in *Life Studies of the Great Army* was acquired by John Pierpont Morgan, who gave it to the Library of Congress in 1919. Forbes, *A Civil War Artist*; Forbes, *Thirty Years After*.

Ben Bassham

FORCE, Manning Ferguson, *general*, was born in Washington, D.C., on December 17, 1824. He graduated from Harvard in 1845 and from Harvard Law School in 1848. Force then moved to Cincinnati, where, in 1850, he was admitted to the bar and practiced law until 1861. When the Civil War began, Force became major of the 20th Ohio Volunteers, then its lieutenant colonel, and in May 1862 its colonel. He was with Major General Ulysses S. Grant (*q.v.*) at Fort Donelson, at Shiloh, and in the 1862–1863 campaigns in western Tennessee and northern Mississippi. In the Vicksburg campaign he was in the XVII Corps with Major General James B. McPherson (*q.v.*), and on August 11, 1863, he was promoted to brigadier general of Volunteers. Force commanded a brigade in the XVII Corps during the Meridian expedition and the Atlanta campaign. On July 22, 1864, his command played a significant role in repulsing a Confederate assault during the battle of Atlanta. In this fighting, Force received a severe facial wound and was disabled for about three months. For his performance at Atlanta he was later made a brevet major general of Volunteers and (in 1892) awarded a Medal of Honor.

Force returned to duty in October 1864 and led his brigade in the March to the Sea. In January 1865 he took command of the 3rd Division, XVII Corps, and led that unit and the 1st Division, XVII Corps, in the Carolinas campaign. Force was a competent officer who won high praise from his superiors and respect from his men. In 1866, he was mustered out of the Army and returned to Cincinnati to resume his law practice. On several occasions he was elected to judicial offices. He wrote several books on law, archaeology, and military campaigns, and a biography of General William T. Sherman (*q.v.*). Force was commandant of the Ohio Soldiers' and Sailors' Home at Sandusky, where he died on May 8, 1899. Bearss, *Vicksburg Campaign*, vols. 2, 3; Cox, *Atlanta*; Lewis, *Sherman*.

Richard M. McMurry

FORNEY, John Weiss, *editor*, was born on September 30, 1817, in Lancaster, Pennsylvania. Like many early journalists, his formal education was scant. In 1833, he went to work for the *Lancaster Journal* as a printer. By the time he was twenty, he had purchased a competing newspaper, *The Intelligencer*, and had become its editor and publisher. Forney worked on other papers and, while in Philadelphia, began covering Washington, D.C., politics. A former Democrat, he switched to the Whig and then to the Republican party. In 1857, he founded the *Philadelphia Press* and turned it into a enthusiastic Lincoln paper. He also met Abraham Lincoln (*q.v.*), and the two struck up an immediate friendship. Forney was as close to Lincoln as any journalist or politician, visiting the White House almost every day. He also edited the weekly *Washington Chronicle*.

In 1862, Lincoln convinced Forney to convert the paper to a daily. The President attended the dedication of the new building and saw to it that the paper received government advertising and patronage. That patronage included the purchase of several thousand copies daily of the *Chronicle* and/or *Press* for distribution to Union soldiers in Virginia. Forney's unquestioning allegiance to the President and his attempts to lift Northern morale also earned him Lincoln's political support. Lincoln was an important behind-the-scenes force when Forney was named secretary of the U.S. Senate during the war. However, Forney's devout support also gained him the title of ''Lincoln's dog'' from the Democratic press. The *Press* and *Chronicle* were known nationally for their strong editorials, and the *Press* even had a California edition. Although Lincoln broke tradition and had no single newspaper to serve him and the Republican party as an ''official'' voice, the *Press* and *Chronicle* were watched closely for indications of the President's thinking. Forney continued his journalistic career until his death in Philadelphia on December 9, 1881. Harper, *Lincoln and the Press*.

Fredric F. Endres

FOSTER, John Gray, *general*, was born in Whitefield, New Hampshire, on May 23, 1823. He graduated from West Point in 1846. Foster was commissioned in the Corps of Engineers and immediately attached to the company of sappers, miners, and pontoniers recently organized to accompany General Winfield Scott (*q.v.*) to Mexico. During the Mexican War, Foster won two brevets and was severely wounded at Molino del Rey. After the war, he performed routine engineering duties, and taught for two years at the Military Academy.

At the outbreak of the Civil War, Foster was the engineer in charge of fortifications at Charleston harbor. Forced to surrender with the garrison at Fort Sumter, he went to Washington, where he was promoted to brigadier general of Volunteers. He was assigned the command of a New England brigade and led them to victory during the battles of Roanoke Island and New Berne on the coast of North Carolina.

Receiving high praise from his superior, Major General Ambrose E. Burnside (*q.v.*), Foster was named military governor of New Bern and vicinity on March 15, 1862. Thereafter, he held administrative posts in various commands, seeing little field action. In late 1863, Foster was transferred to Tennessee and assisted in the relief of the siege of Knoxville. His next assignment was to command the Department of Ohio in December 1863, but he was forced to relinquish the position two months later due to a fall from his horse. Fully recovered from his injury, Foster was assigned to command the Department of the South, where he cooperated with General William T. Sherman (*q.v.*) in the sieges of Savannah and Charleston. For the remainder of the war, Foster was in command of a Regular unit in Florida, as a brevet major general. When the war ended, he went back to engineering along the New England coast until his death on September 2, 1874, in Nashua, New Hampshire. Burton, *Siege of Charleston*; Marvel, *Burnside*.

Mitchell A. Yockelson

FOSTER, LaFayette Sabine, *senator*, was born November 22, 1806, in Franklin, Connecticut. He graduated from Brown University in 1828, and was admitted to the Connecticut bar in 1831. In 1835, he was editor of the *Norwich Republican*, an organ of Connecticut's Whig party. Foster served in the Connecticut House of Representatives in 1839 and 1840, and was speaker of the House from 1846 to 1849. He was the Whig nominee for governor in 1850 and in 1851, but lost to Thomas H. Seymour (*q.v.*) both times. He returned to the Connecticut House in 1854 and was again elected speaker. In that year, Foster filled the U.S. Senate seat that Truman Smith, a Whig, had vacated. He was on friendly terms with key members of Connecticut's Know-Nothing organization, but when the state's Republican party was organized in 1856, Foster immediately joined. He opposed slavery on principle and voted against the Kansas–Nebraska Act and the Lecompton Constitution.

During the secession crisis, Foster (reelected as a Republican in 1860) supported sectional compromise, but once the war began, associated himself closely with Abraham Lincoln (*q.v.*) and upheld his views in the Senate. Yet, when confronted with the struggle between Republican conservatives like James Dixon (*q.v.*) and the Radical element in Connecticut's state party organization,

Foster vacillated. His refusal to align himself with either faction persuaded Connecticut's Republicans to reject his 1866 bid for reelection. After leaving the Senate, Foster served briefly in the Connecticut House, and in 1870 was appointed associate justice of the Connecticut Supreme Court. In 1872, he supported Horace Greeley (*q.v.*), the Liberal Republican candidate for the presidency. Foster lost a final attempt at election to the House of Representatives in 1874, this time as a Democrat. He died in Norwich, Connecticut, on September 19, 1880. Croffut, *Military and Civil History of Connecticut During the War*; Lane, *Political History of Connecticut*; Niven, *Connecticut for the Union.*

Joanna D. Cowden

FOSTER, Robert Sanford, *general,* was born in Vernon, Indiana, on January 27, 1834. In April 1861 he became a captain in the 11th Indiana Volunteers, and in June, major of the 13th Indiana. Throughout 1861, he fought in western Virginia, winning notice at Romney and Rich Mountain. In 1862, he served in the Shenandoah Valley, on the Virginia Peninsula, and (until mid-1863) at Suffolk, Virginia. As a brigadier general of Volunteers, he led a brigade in the early stages of the Charleston siege and, for a brief period, in Florida. In April 1864, with most of the X Corps, Foster was transferred to the Army of the James. After a stint as chief of staff of the X Corps, he returned to brigade command. In August 1864 he received a division, eventually a part of the XXIV Corps, which overwhelmed Fort Gregg, key to the Petersburg defenses, on April 2, 1865.

Foster was among the ablest Volunteer officers to attain a division command. His proficiency in both administration and command seems not to have been seriously affected by his occasional intemperance. After the war, one of his regiments' historians noted that "he attracted universal attention by his faultless military bearing; and he was as brave in battle as he was imposing in appearance on review." Shortly after war's end—having helped try Abraham Lincoln's (*q.v.*) assassins—Foster resigned his brevet major generalship in the Volunteers, refusing a lieutenant colonelcy in the Regulars. He held various administrative and commercial positions in Indianapolis, where he died on March 3, 1903. Smith, *Life and Military Services of Brevet Major-General Robert S. Foster*; Sommers, *Richmond Redeemed.*

Edward G. Longacre

FOUKE, Philip Bond, *congressman,* was born on January 23, 1818, in Kaskaskia, Illinois. After studying in the public schools, he became a civil engineer. He published the *Belleville Advocate* (1841), but left it for the practice of law. He served one term in the Illinois House (1851) and lost to Lyman Trumbull (*q.v.*) in a bid for Congress in 1854. Fouke was elected as a Democrat to the 36th and 37th Congresses. In December 1861 he assumed the lead in the House of Representatives among those demanding that government employees have the opportunity to defend themselves against allegations of disloyalty. Although he failed to infuse due process into the deliberations of John Fox Potter's (*q.v.*) Select Committee on the Loyalty of Clerks and Other Persons Employed by the Government, his motion encouraged members of both parties to begin scrutinizing the power that had been invested in the creation of "Bowie Knife" Potter's committee in July 1861.

Fouke declined a reelection bid to the 38th Congress, preferring to serve in the military. He joined the 30th Illinois Volunteers, obtained the rank of colonel, and saw action at the battle of Belmont, where he was wounded. After the war, Foulk returned to the practice of law in Washington, D.C., where he died on October 3, 1876. Bogue, *Congressman's Civil War.*

Thomas F. Schwartz

FOX, Gustavus Vasa, *assistant secretary of the navy,* was born on June 13, 1821, in Saugus, Massachusetts. He was appointed a midshipman on January 12, 1838, and for thirteen years served on sailing vessels, including action in Mexico. In 1851, Fox—who had resolved to learn steam navigation—received a leave of absence to serve initially as second in command, and ultimately as captain, of mail steamers. In 1855, he married, gave up the sea at his wife's request, began managing a textile factory in Lawrence, Massachusetts, and in 1856 resigned his commission as a lieutenant in the U.S. Navy. He left the textile mill in 1860, and was unemployed when the secession crisis came.

Fox conceived a plan to reinforce Fort Sumter that the Buchanan (*q.v.*) administration rejected. The Lincoln (*q.v.*) administration—in which his wife's brother-in-law, Montgomery Blair (*q.v.*), was Postmaster General—adopted it, precipitating the Confederacy's attack on Sumter, and the Civil War. Though Fox's relief expedition failed, it "heightened" him in the estimation of Lincoln, who insisted that Secretary of the Navy Gideon Welles (*q.v.*) accept Fox as his assistant. In the specially created position of assistant secretary of the Navy, Fox was responsible both for naval operations and for the acquisition of new vessels. Sturdy ships—with the requisite size, speed, draft, and seaworthiness—and proper bases were needed for the blockade. Fox was well equipped to accomplish these tasks. His experience and his connections enabled him to mediate between the politicians and the sailors.

Fox had boundless energy, and an enthusiasm for the Union, for the Navy, and for ships, guns, and the men with whom he worked. Although he was self-confident and unafraid to make decisions, he often consulted experts. His enthusiasms were usually for the plans and designs of others in whose genius he trusted. Following the suggestion of Alexander Dallas Bache of the Coast Survey, Fox constituted a Blockade Board, which met in June and July 1861 and whose reports guided the Navy in making the blockade effective. Fox scrapped the seniority system (under which he had suffered) and awarded commands to able officers regardless of rank. His enthusiasm for turreted monitors, armed with fifteen-inch guns, accounts for their extensive use. Since Fox was primarily responsible for naval strategy, the expeditions against the Hatteras forts, Port

Royal, New Orleans, Mobile Bay, and Fort Fisher, as well as operations on the Tennessee, Cumberland, and Mississippi Rivers, were his triumphs. But the Navy's failure to capture Charleston was largely his failure because his wish to humble that city clouded his judgment. In these efforts Fox and Welles made a good team, with Welles deciding in consultation with Fox, whose judgment he trusted.

In 1866, Fox publicized the monitor by using one to carry the congressional resolution congratulating Czar Alexander II on his escape from an assassination attempt. After retiring from government service, Fox made an abortive effort to take over the Southwest Pacific Railroad (later called the St. Louis–San Francisco). In January 1869 he returned to the textile business, managing the Middlesex Mills in Lowell; he moved in 1874 to Boston, where he became a partner in Mudge, Sawyer & Company. After Fox retired in 1878, he traveled, researched geographical problems including Columbus's landfall, contemplated writing a naval history of the Civil War, and maintained close friendships with many veterans of that conflict. He died in Boston on October 29, 1883. Fox, *Confidential Correspondence*; Hoogenboom, ''Gustavus Vasa Fox and the Relief of Fort Sumter,'' *Civil War History*.

Ari Hoogenboom

FRANCHOT, Richard, *congressman*, was born on June 2, 1816, in Morris, New York. After graduation from the Hartwick and Cherry Valley academies, he studied civil engineering at the Polytechnic Institute in Troy, New York, and for several years headed the Albany and Susquehanna Railroad. In early 1861, he was elected as a Republican to the 37th Congress. Soon after taking office, Franchot was appointed to a select committee reviewing a proposal for a railroad to the Pacific, which he actively supported.

Deciding not to be a candidate for renomination, Franchot obtained authority in July 1862 to recruit the 121st New York Infantry. A month later, the regiment was mustered into Federal service with Franchot as colonel. Its first engagement came in September at Crampton Gap, Maryland. Later that month, Franchot was discharged from the service. After the war, he returned to the railroad business and became associated with the Central Pacific Railroad Company. He died in Schenectady, New York, on November 23, 1875. Curry, *Blueprint for Modern America*; Phisterer, *New York in the War of the Rebellion*, vols. 1, 4.

Frank R. Levstik

FRANK, Augustus, *congressman*, was born July 17, 1826, in Warsaw, New York. He attended public school, and helped his father manage his mercantile businesses until he went into business for himself in 1847. He soon became a director and vice president of the Buffalo and New York City Railway Company. A Whig, Frank cast his first vote for Zachary Taylor in 1848 and gave his first political speeches during that campaign. In 1855, he became a Republican and helped to organize the party in New York. He was a delegate to the party's national convention and actively campaigned for John C. Frémont (*q.v.*). In 1858, he was elected to the 36th Congress and was reelected in 1860 by a majority of nearly 8,000 votes. During his three terms, Frank was a strong antislavery voice in the House. He chose not to run for a fourth term and returned to the banking business. Frank participated in the New York Constitutional Convention in 1867 and 1868 and again in 1894. From 1870 until 1882 he was a manager of the Buffalo State Hospital for the Insane. He died in New York City on April 29, 1895. *History of Wyoming County.*

Lori A. Lisowski

FRANKLIN, William Buel, *general*, was born in York, Pennsylvania, on February 27, 1823. In 1843, he graduated from West Point first in his class and joined the engineers. After service on the Great Lakes, in the Southwest, and in Mexico, Franklin supervised several large government construction projects in Washington, D.C. He reached the rank of captain in 1857, but once the Civil War began, his rise was rapid. He became major general of Volunteers as of July 4, 1862, commanded a brigade at First Bull Run, and a division and then a corps on the Peninsula. His corps arrived too late to play a significant part at Second Bull Run, and during the Maryland campaign its principal accomplishment was to drive the Confederates from Crampton's Gap, although it failed in its mission to rescue the Federal garrison at Harper's Ferry. At Fredericksburg, he commanded the left wing of the Army of the Potomac. Franklin came from a Democratic background and was known as a favorite of the leading Democratic general, George B. McClellan (*q.v.*).

Republican efforts to discredit McClellan and his associates, especially Democratic generals, undoubtedly hurt Franklin's military career. Both Ambrose Burnside (*q.v.*) and the Joint Committee on the Conduct of the War tried to make him the scapegoat for the Fredericksburg fiasco. Although Franklin defended himself with spirit, he was assigned to that graveyard of military reputations, the Gulf Department. There he took charge of the XIX Corps and performed creditably, although he was unable to compensate for the ineptitude of his commanding officer, Nathaniel P. Banks (*q.v.*). During the ill-starred Red River expedition, Franklin suffered a troublesome wound at the battle of Mansfield. He returned to the East on sick leave and recovered his health, but never held another command.

Franklin resigned his commission in November 1865, and the next year the Colt Firearms Company made him its general manager, a position he held for twenty-two years. Throughout his Civil War career, Franklin proved to be a capable general, and was certainly to some extent the victim of political and military circumstances beyond his control. Nevertheless, when all allowances are made, it must be said that he seems to have lacked drive, aggressiveness, and initiative. He made no blunders, but he won precious few victories. No wonder he and McClellan saw eye to eye. He died in Hartford, Connecticut, on March 8, 1903. Marvel, *Burnside*; Sears, *To the Gates of Richmond*.

Ludwell H. Johnson

FRÉMONT, John Charles, *general*, was born on January 21, 1813, in Savannah, Georgia. He briefly attended Charleston College before being expelled in 1831. After being assigned to the topographical engineers in 1838, he accompanied the distinguished scientist J.N. Nicollet on an expedition to the upper Iowa territory. Through this acquaintance, Frémont met and married Jessie Benton, daughter of the influential Missouri senator Thomas Hart Benton. From 1842 to 1846, Frémont led several surveying expeditions to the American West, including much of the Mexican territory. His published reports of his journeys had wide public appeal, sharpening the nation's appetite for aggressive expansion and securing his national reputation as the "Pathfinder." At the outbreak of the Mexican War, Frémont played a prominent role in California's Bear Flag Revolution, but after a controversial court martial for mutiny, he resigned from the service. He served briefly as U.S. senator from California and ran unsuccessfully for the presidency in 1856, the first candidate of the Republican party.

In July 1861, Frémont was appointed major general in the Regular Army and assumed command of the Department of the West, with headquarters at St. Louis. Proving unequal to the large task, he drew the enmity of Abraham Lincoln (*q.v.*) by rashly issuing an emancipation proclamation for Missouri's slaves. Applauded by Radical Republicans, he then refused to rescind the edict, forcing the embarrassed President to order modification of the proclamation. In an attempt to regain Lincoln's favor, Frémont led his army from St. Louis in futile pursuit of a retreating force of Missouri Confederates under Sterling Price. In November 1861, in the midst of this aborted campaign, Frémont was removed from command.

Pressured by harsh criticism from Radicals, Lincoln reinstated Frémont in March 1862, assigning him to a command in western Virginia. Despite his superior force, Frémont showed poor generalship in his sound defeat by Stonewall Jackson at Cross Keys, during Jackson's brilliant Valley campaign. When Lincoln placed him under the command of John Pope (*q.v.*), whom Frémont detested, he requested to be relieved of command. In 1864, Frémont was nominated for President by a coalition of Radicals, Missouri Germans, and War Democrats, but withdrew his name in return for the ousting from the Cabinet of conservative Montgomery Blair (*q.v.*). Frémont died in New York City on July 13, 1890. Rolle, *John C. Frémont*.

Christopher Phillips

FRENCH, William Henry, *general*, was born in Baltimore on January 13, 1815. He graduated from West Point in 1837, and served as an artillery officer in the 1837–1838 Seminole War and in Mexico. He was promoted to brigadier general of Volunteers in September 1861 and assigned to command an infantry brigade in the II Corps. Following service on the Peninsula, French was assigned to command a newly formed division in the II Corps. He led his division at the Sunken Lane at Antietam, where it suffered 1,750 casualties. Following Antietam, French was promoted to major general of Volunteers and performed competently at Fredricksburg and Chancellorsville, where his division was heavily engaged. During the Gettysburg campaign, he was assigned to command the Union garrison at Harper's Ferry, with which French provided important support to the rear of the Army of the Potomac.

Following Gettysburg, French was posted to command of the III Corps. He did well enough until the last days of the Mine Run operations, when the tardy movement of his corps delayed the entire army. Army commander George G. Meade (*q.v.*) was unhappy with French's performance, and was further angered by the "lying report" of a *New York Herald* correspondent traveling with French's headquarters. Despite Meade's displeasure with French's performance at Mine Run, he attempted unsuccessfully to retain him as a division commander when the army was reorganized in the spring of 1864. French served the remainder of the war in unimportant posts. After the war, he remained in the Regular Army and eventually obtained the rank of colonel of the 4th Artillery. He died on May 20, 1881, in Washington, D.C. Meade, *Life and Letters of George G. Meade*, vol. 2.

D. Scott Hartwig

FRY, James Barnet, *general,* was born on February 22, 1827, in Carrollton, Illinois. He graduated from West Point in 1847, and served in Mexico City and at various posts in the southern and western United States before returning to the Academy in 1853. He remained there until 1859, and gained valuable administrative experience as its adjutant before being ordered to Fort Monroe. He returned to West Point for a brief period in 1860 to assist in revising the curriculum. Prior to his appointment as Provost Marshal General on March 17, 1863, he participated in the battles of First Bull Run, Shiloh, and Perryville. Although his defense of Don Carlos Buell's (*q.v.*) actions at Shiloh troubled Ulysses S. Grant (*q.v.*) and William T. Sherman (*q.v.*), Grant nevertheless recommended Fry as "the officer best fitted" to head the newly created National Conscription Bureau. In April 1864 he was promoted to brigadier general and remained at that rank until his agency was dissolved on August 28, 1866.

Although Fry wrote a number of books after the war, he is best remembered for his administration of the Federal draft. As the individual directly responsible for implementation, he bore the brunt of the virulent criticism of his agency. With varying degrees of success, he addressed numerous complaints from Northern citizens who accused him and his subordinates of inefficiency, corruption, and abuses of power. Despite the negative views of his contemporaries, the preponderance of historical opinion finds that Fry was a capable leader who did his best to administer the draft as judiciously and as fairly as possible. After the war, he was an adjutant general in various military departments, and in February 1868 received a belated promotion to major general by brevet for his wartime service. He retired from the Army in 1881, and died in Newport, Rhode Island, on July 11, 1894. Geary, *We Need Men*; Murdock, *One Million Men.*

James W. Geary

FULLER, John Wallace, *general,* was born in Harston, Cambridgeshire, England, on July 28, 1827, and came with his family to Oneida county, New York, in 1833. He operated his own book publishing business in New York City, then moved to Toledo, Ohio, in 1858 to establish a similar business. When the Civil War began, Fuller was selected to drill troops at Grafton, Virginia (now West Virginia), and was appointed colonel of the 27th Ohio Volunteers in August 1861. He led his regiment at New Madrid and Island No. 10 under the command of John Pope (*q.v.*), and in the autumn of 1862 was a brigade commander at Iuka and Corinth.

Most of 1863 was taken up by garrison duty, as Fuller's brigade went through a series of transfers and reorganizations as a unit of the Army of the Tennessee. In 1864, they played a major role in the battle of Atlanta and were with William T. Sherman (*q.v.*) during his March to the Sea. After the Confederates surrendered, Fuller received a brevet as major general for meritorious service during the war. He resigned from the military on August 15, 1865, and returned to Ohio for a life as a businessman and public servant. Fuller died on March 12, 1891, in Toledo. Bearss, *Vicksburg Campaign*, vols. 1, 2; Castel, *Decision in the West.*

Mitchell A. Yockelson

G

GAMBLE, Hamilton Rowan, *governor*, was born in Winchester, Virginia, on November 29, 1798. Educated at Hampden-Sydney College, he studied law, and was admitted to the Virginia bar. In 1818, he moved to St. Louis and in 1821 was appointed prosecuting attorney of Howard county, which then covered much of mid-Missouri. In 1825, he was appointed secretary of state by Governor Frederick Bates but relinquished that post when Bates died later in the year. He then returned to St. Louis and entered into law practice with his brother-in-law, Edward Bates (*q.v.*). Gamble served one term in the legislature (1846–1848), and as chief justice of the Missouri Supreme Court. When the *Dred Scott* case came before the court, he alone decided in favor of Scott.

Ill health forced Gamble's retirement in 1854, and he moved to Norristown, Pennsylvania. He returned to St. Louis early in 1861 to become a delegate to the convention to decide secession. He chaired the committee that reported against secession and dominated the convention. When the convention met again in July 1861, in the wake of the flight of Governor Claiborne F. Jackson to join the Confederacy, Gamble was the unanimous choice to serve as provisional governor. He immediately secured the endorsement of President Abraham Lincoln (*q.v.*) and worked closely with the administration as heavy fighting raged in western Missouri and guerrilla warfare threatened the rest of the state. From the outset, Gamble maintained that the state should do as much as it could to protect itself with Federal aid. He persuaded Lincoln, against the advice of General John C. Frémont (*q.v.*) at St. Louis, that a new state militia could help maintain order. That fall the Provisional Government offered amnesty to those who wanted to return to their Union allegiance and would take an oath of loyalty. Many took advantage of the offer, but the state was plagued by guerrilla activity throughout the war.

Initially unsympathetic to emancipation, Gamble came to realize its inevitability following the Emancipation Proclamation. He thereupon worked out a program of gradual emancipation through the state convention of July 1863. His unwillingness to move more rapidly spawned the Radical Union party, which challenged the Provisional Government both at home and in Washington. Gamble kept a firm hand on the state, however, and managed to retain the support of Lincoln through frequent trips to Washington and the intercession of Attorney General Bates. Although criticized for his conservatism and moderation, Gamble undoubtedly played a major role in keeping most Missourians loyal to the Union. He died in St. Louis on January 31, 1864. Parrish, *Turbulent Partnership.*

William E. Parrish

GANSON, John, *congressman,* was born on January 1, 1818, in Le Roy, New York. His grandfather, a pioneer in western New York, was an officer in the Revolutionary War and had been wounded at Bunker Hill. Ganson graduated from Harvard University in 1838, studied law, and practiced in Le Roy, Canandaigua, and Buffalo, forming partnerships with some of the area's foremost lawyers. A Democrat, he was politically active during the Civil War, winning election to the state Senate in 1862, and to a term in the 38th Congress at the end of the year. He was a delegate to the Democratic National Convention at Chicago in 1864, and refused a nomination for a second congressional term. In 1865, Ganson returned to Buffalo to practice law, and was elected to the state Senate in 1873. He died on September 28, 1874, in Buffalo. *BDUSC.*

Lori A. Lisowski

GARDNER, Alexander, *photographer,* was born in Paisley, Scotland, on October 27, 1821. He had served an apprenticeship to a jeweler, worked as a reporter, and risen to the position of newspaper editor when an interest in "cooperative communities" led him in 1856 to join a workers' community in Iowa; but an epidemic there led him to settle in New York City. Gardner's interests in physics and chemistry, and his good business sense, led to his involvement with photography. He was hired in 1858 by Mathew Brady (*q.v.*), who appreciated his knowledge of the collodion ("wet plate") process, and his ability to keep impeccable business records. Brady sent Gardner to Washington, D.C., to manage the National Photographic Art Gallery, which prospered under his innovative guidance.

At the beginning of the Civil War, Brady dispatched Gardner to accompany the Army of the Potomac as part of his ambitious plan to record a photographic history of the war. From 1861 to 1863, Gardner took many of the pictures that were at one time routinely attributed to Brady. His views of the mangled and contorted bodies of the dead at Antietam and at Gettysburg brought the terrible reality of the war to the people at home. Although he did not do all the work himself, Gardner must nevertheless be given much of the credit for having made some of the most moving photographs of the nineteenth century.

In 1863, Gardner left Brady when the two disagreed over copyright ownership of the plates Gardner had exposed in the field. He established his own gallery in Washington, and sent photographers to the front to record the major battlefields and events of the war while he gave the major portion of his time (except for the work at Gettysburg) to the photocopying of maps and documents for the War Department. He also did a brisk business in individual and group portraits of statesmen, dignitaries, and Indian visitors to the capital. In 1866, he published *Gardner's Photographic Sketchbook of the War* in two volumes, with original prints made from plates taken by himself and his assistants. This collection of pictures is a milestone in documentary war photography.

Gardner photographed Lincoln's funeral procession, the conspirators against Lincoln, and the trial and execution of Jacob Wirz. In 1867, he became field photographer for the Union Pacific Railroad, following covered wagons in his own photographic darkroom wagon along the Chisholm Trail through Kansas and Texas. His photography business continued in Washington in the 1870s, but there is evidence that social pursuits and other business interests claimed increasing amounts of his time. He died in Washington in 1882. Frassanito, *Antietam*; Frassanito, *Gettysburg*; Horan, *Mathew Brady.*

Ben Bassham

GARFIELD, James Abram, *general, congressman*, was born in Orange Township (now Moreland Hills), near Cleveland, Ohio, on November 19, 1831. His studies at a Disciples of Christ Academy and the Western Reserve Eclectic Institute (now Hiram College), bent his inclinations toward scholarship and the ministry. After completing his education at Williams College, he returned to Hiram to become president of the Eclectic Institute. He won election as a Republican to the Ohio Senate in 1859, and was serving in that body when the Civil War began. Garfield raised the 42nd Ohio Volunteers, largely from his students at Hiram, and was commissioned its colonel.

Assigned to the Department of the Ohio, Garfield was ordered by Don Carlos Buell (*q.v.*) to take the 18th Brigade into eastern Kentucky to meet a threatened invasion by Confederate General Humphrey Marshall. Despite his lack of experience, Garfield turned back Marshall at Middle Creek and drove the Confederates into Virginia. This minor campaign was to be Garfield's only independent command. Promoted to brigadier general (as of the battle of Middle Creek), he was given command of the 20th Brigade, 6th Division, of the Army of the Ohio, which arrived at Shiloh just after the battle was over, and then participated in the siege of Corinth. Garfield returned to Ohio on sick leave in the summer of 1862, and while there was nominated for Congress.

After an interlude at Washington, where he was a member of the Fitz John Porter (*q.v.*) court martial, Garfield was assigned to the Army of the Cumberland in January 1863. His executive ability so impressed the commanding general,

William S. Rosecrans (*q.v.*), that he appointed Garfield his chief of staff. Garfield served in that capacity for the remainder of his military career, handling all the administrative business of the Army of the Cumberland and planning the brilliant Tullahoma campaign (as well as the considerably less successful cavalry raid by Colonel Abel D. Streight). The battle of Chickamauga (September 19–20, 1863) was Garfield's farewell to arms. When the Union line crumbled, he was unable to persuade Rosecrans to halt his panicky flight to Chattanooga. Garfield salvaged his own reputation by joining General George H. Thomas (*q.v.*) in his famous stand.

Although he was a self-trained soldier, Garfield combined a broad grasp of strategic principles with a tireless capacity for detailed staff work. Resigning his major general's commission (which dated from Chickamauga), he took his seat in Congress in December 1863. By virtue of his military record, he was appointed to the House Committee on Military Affairs. He served in Congress for seventeen years, until elected President of the United States in 1880. On July 2, 1881, he was shot by a religious fanatic, Charles J. Guiteau, and died on September 19, 1881, in Elberon, New Jersey. Peskin, *Garfield*; Williams, *The Wild Life of the Army.*

Allan Peskin

GARRARD, Kenner, *general,* was born on or about September 1, 1828, in Fairfield, Kentucky. He spent his childhood in Cincinnati, attended Harvard in 1844–1845, and then entered West Point, from which he graduated in 1851. For most of the next ten years he served along the frontier, rising to the rank of captain in the 2nd Cavalry. On April 23, 1861, Texas state troops took Garrard prisoner, but he was allowed to return to the North on parole. In September 1862 he became colonel of the 146th New York, which he commanded at Fredericksburg, Chancellorsville, and Gettysburg, where he took charge of his brigade upon the death of Brigadier General Stephen H. Weed.

Promoted to brigadier general, Garrard participated in the Bristoe and Mine Run operations in Virginia, served briefly as chief of the Cavalry Bureau (January 2–29, 1864), and then was given command of the 2nd Cavalry Division of the Army of the Cumberland. During the Atlanta campaign, Garrard's division, like the other Federal mounted forces, spent most of its time covering the flanks of William T. Sherman's (*q.v.*) army. Otherwise, it made, or attempted to make, several raids on enemy communication lines and on July 9 secured a crossing over the Chattahoochee River at Roswell, Georgia. Dissatisfied with what he deemed to be Garrard's lack of aggressiveness and enterprise, Sherman relieved him of command following the fall of Atlanta and sent him to Tennessee. There, in December 1864, he became commander of an infantry division in the XVI Corps, which he led ably at the battle of Nashville and, in the spring of 1865, in siege operations that led to the capture of Mobile.

Unfortunately for Garrard, his historical reputation derives largely from Sherman's criticisms, many of which were unfair. While leading cavalry during the

Atlanta campaign, he was more unfortunate than inept; he demonstrated at Nashville and Mobile that he was a competent infantry commander. Late in 1866, having reverted to the Regular Army rank of major, Garrard resigned his commission and returned to Cincinnati, where he engaged in the real estate business and various civic and cultural activities until his death there on May 15, 1879. Castel, *Decision in the West*; Starr, *Union Cavalry*, vol. 3.

Albert Castel

GARRISON, William Lloyd, *abolitonist, editor*, was born on December 12, 1805, in Newburyport, Massachusetts. His career as editor of *The Liberator*, the newspaper that carried his controversial views for thirty-five years, began on January 1, 1831. His demand for immediate emancipation was adopted by the American Anti-Slavery Society and its state-level affiliates. The great Yankee crusade against chattel servitude, intimately associated with Garrison's name, caused mob violence in the North and a furious reaction in the South. After 1838, Garrison added nonresistance, anticlerical "come-outerism," and women's rights to his list of radical causes. Garrisonians declared that abolitionists must boycott all elections, and that the North must secede from the proslavery Union, a position they generally maintained until the outbreak of the Civil War. Their direct influence on sectional parties was small, but their role in fostering sectional consciousness in Northern popular culture was substantial.

Garrison's name increasingly connoted to angry Southern planters all that was inherently evil, misguided, and dangerous about Yankee ways. Yet, once the Civil War began, he became increasingly favorable to the Republican party, and ever less critical of Abraham Lincoln's (*q.v.*) leadership. In 1864, he endorsed Lincoln for reelection and insisted in 1865 that the American Anti-Slavery Society disband because the 13th Amendment had abolished slavery. His lifelong friend Wendell Phillips (*q.v.*) and many others dissented from this view, and insisted that emancipated blacks must be guaranteed full citizenship before slavery would be abolished in fact. Garrison resigned from the American Anti-Slavery Society in 1865 and ended his editorship of *The Liberator.* The American Anti-Slavery Society remained active until 1870, when the 15th Amendment was passed. Garrison became an occasional contributor to the temperance, women's rights and antiprostitution movements. He died in Roxbury, Massachusetts, on May 24, 1879. Stewart, *William Lloyd Garrison*; Thomas, *The Liberator.*

James Brewer Stewart

GAY, Sidney Howard, *abolitonist, editor*, was born on May 22, 1814, in Hingham, Massachusetts. He attended Harvard, and then spent three years traveling, suffering business reversals, and reading law. Abolitionism furnished him with a cause, and by 1842 he had moved to New York City as editor of the *National Anti-Slavery Standard.* His duties assured a close association with New England's most extreme abolitionist figures. In 1845, he married Elizabeth

Neale, a Quaker from one of Philadelphia's most prominent families, and became active in efforts to harbor fugitive slaves. In 1857, Gay joined the *New York Tribune*, and became its managing editor in 1862. Throughout the Civil War, he took a strong emancipationist position in the *Tribune*.

After the passage of the 13th Amendment, Gay retired from organized abolitionism and in 1867 became managing editor of the *Chicago Tribune*. His commitment to Radical Reconstruction began to waver, and in 1872, when he joined the editorial staff of the *New York Evening Post*, his career as a reformer was in decline and his interest in writing popular history was rising. Gay was the principal (though unacknowledged) author of a four-volume history of the United States publicly attributed to William Cullen Bryant (*q.v.*). He also published a critical biography of James Madison, and was at work on a biography of his old abolitionist friend Edmund Quincy when he died on June 25, 1886, in New Brighton, New York. Friedman, *Gregarious Saints.*

James Brewer Stewart

GEARY, John White, *general,* was born on December 30, 1819, in Westmoreland county, Pennsylvania. He graduated from Jefferson College in 1839, studied law and civil engineering, was admitted to the bar, and worked as a surveyor. Geary was active in the Pennsylvania militia. During the Mexican War, he was lieutenant colonel of a Pennsylvania regiment and was wounded at Chapultepec. President James K. Polk sent Geary to organize the post office in San Francisco, and he became mayor of the city. He prospered in real estate until his wife's health forced the family to return to Pennsylvania. In 1856, President Franklin Pierce appointed Geary governor of Kansas—a position in which his antislavery-inspired attempt at fairness angered the proslavery faction. In 1857, disgusted at the lack of support he received from Washington, he resigned and retired to his Pennsylvania farm.

When the Civil War began, Geary was active in raising troops, and in June 1861 was made colonel of the 28th Pennsylvania Volunteers. He was promoted to brigadier general of Volunteers on April 25, 1862, and on January 15, 1863, brevet major general of Volunteers. Until late 1863, Geary served with the Army of the Potomac, commanding his regiment, a brigade, and then a division in the II and XII corps. He was wounded at Cedar Mountain. In the fall of 1863, his division was with the force sent to the relief of Chattanooga, and was assigned to the Army of the Cumberland as part of the XII (later XX) Corps. Geary participated in the fighting around Chattanooga, the Atlanta campaign, the March to the Sea, and the Carolinas campaign. He was briefly military governor of Savannah.

Geary was an imposing figure, a competent but not a spectacular officer. After his son was killed in late 1863, he sometimes expressed a desire to punish the South. His tenure as military governor, however, was characterized by moderation and restraint. Geary left military service in 1866, became a Republican, and associated himself with the Simon Cameron (*q.v.*) wing of the party in

Pennsylvania. In 1866, he was elected governor of Pennsylvania, and served two terms. He often feuded with the legislature, but he proved to be a competent executive whose administration was marked by a reduction in the state debt and the passage of laws intended to aid African Americans, public schools, and laborers. He left office amid allegations of financial irregularities, but investigation of the charges was dropped after his death in Harrisburg, Pennsylvania, on February 18, 1873. Castel, *Decision in the West*; Krick, *Stonewall Jackson at Cedar Mountain*; Tinkcom, *John White Geary*.

Richard M. McMurry

GETTY, George Washington, *general,* was born in Georgetown, D.C., on October 2, 1819. He graduated from West Point in 1840, was commissioned in the artillery, and was breveted for gallantry in Mexico. After service against the Seminoles, he was at Fort Randall, Dakota Territory, when the Civil War began. Made senior captain of the new 5th Artillery and soon promoted to lieutenant colonel of Volunteers, Getty initially directed artillery at Cincinnati and at Budd's Ferry, Maryland. In 1862, he commanded an artillery brigade on the Peninsula, and was chief of artillery for Ambrose Burnside (*q.v.*) in the Maryland campaign. Promoted to brigadier general on September 25, 1862, he, like many artillerists, transferred to another branch to exercise higher rank.

Getty led the 3rd Division, IX Corps at Fredericksburg but did not accompany the corps to Kentucky. His division (redesignated the 2nd Division, VII Corps) remained at Suffolk, which he ably helped to defend in the spring of 1863. He led the VII Corps briefly that summer, and for the balance of 1863 commanded the Norfolk–Portsmouth garrison. Getty rejoined the Army of the Potomac as acting assistant inspector general, then as commander, 2nd Division, VI Corps until June 1865 (except when he was absent due to wounds, May 6–June 21, 1864). He fought with great distinction at the Wilderness, in Philip Sheridan's (*q.v.*) Shenandoah battles, at Petersburg (where he spearheaded the decisive charge, April 2, 1865), and at Sailor's Creek.

Getty was one of many artillerists who gained prominence in the Civil War by commanding infantry divisions. A capable, dependable subordinate who excelled in combat tactics, he could be counted on to deliver powerful attacks on the battlefield. After the war he commanded the Districts of Baltimore, the Rio Grande, Texas, and New Mexico. Getty returned to the ''long arm'' as colonel, 3rd Artillery (1871–1882), and colonel, 4th Artillery (1882–1883). He then served at Atlantic coastal posts, except during labor disturbances in 1877. He had charge of the Fort Monroe Artillery School (1877–1883), and he was on the Fitz John Porter (*q.v.*) court of inquiry (1878–1879). He retired in 1883, and died in Forest Glen, Maryland, on October 1, 1901. Catton, *Stillness at Appomattox*; Rhea, *Battle of the Wilderness*.

Richard J. Sommers

GIBBON, John, *general,* was born on May 20, 1827, in Holmesburg, Pennsylvania, and grew up in Charlotte, North Carolina. Commissioned an artilleryman on graduation from West Point in 1847, he served in Mexico, Florida, and Texas before returning to the Academy as an instructor. While teaching there, he wrote *The Artillerist's Manual*, which was adopted throughout the Army in 1859. After participating in the Mormon pacification expedition, Gibbon commanded a battery at Fort Leavenworth until the war began.

Despite close ties with the Confederacy, Gibbon remained loyal to the Union, and in October 1861 became chief of artillery under Irvin McDowell (*q.v.*). In May 1862 he took over an infantry brigade and led it with distinction at Second Bull Run. The following fall this unit, under Gibbon's command, won the nickname "Iron Brigade" for its conduct at Boonesboro in the Maryland campaign. Gibbon then led divisions at Fredericksburg, where he was severely wounded, and in the assault on Marye's Heights during the battle of Fredericksburg. At Gettysburg, Gibbon not only directed his own unit but also took over the II Corps on two occasions. Wounded on the third day of the battle, he resumed command of his division in December 1863 and led it throughout the Wilderness, Spotsylvania, and Cold Harbor engagements. At Reams's Station in August 1864, Gibbon's command, depleted by casualties, performed poorly. The mortified general prohibited the guilty regiments from carrying colors until they had redeemed their honor at Hatcher's Run. In January 1865 he took command of the XXIV Corps and led it for the rest of the war.

His contemporaries, Ulysses S. Grant (*q.v.*) included, consistently ranked Gibbon as one of the finest commanders in the Army of the Potomac. Independent, outspoken, stubborn, and at times contentious, he may well have reached his limit at the corps level, but this is irrelevant. He deserves to be remembered for what he was: a soldier's soldier, the epitome of professional competence. Notwithstanding six brevets, Gibbon began his postwar career as a colonel. He led troops in the ill-fated Sioux campaign of 1876 and against the Nez Percé in 1877. Gibbon was wounded, and his command almost annihilated, at Big Hole, Montana, but this did not prevent him from later befriending Chief Joseph, the brilliant Nez Percé leader. Promoted to brigadier general in 1885, he commanded departments in Oregon and California before retiring to Baltimore in 1891. He devoted his time to writing on military matters and working with the Loyal Legion, which he was commanding at the time of his death in Baltimore on February 6, 1896. Coddington, *Gettysburg Campaign*; Gibbon, *Personal Recollections of the Civil War*; Rhea, *Battle of the Wilderness*.

James L. Morrison, Jr.

GIBBS, Addison C., *governor*, was born on July 9, 1825, in East Otto, New York. He was admitted to the New York bar in 1849, then joined the California gold rush. In 1850, he moved to the southern Oregon coast, where he promoted Gardiner, his town site. In 1852, Gibbs was elected to the Oregon territorial legislature; the following year he soldiered in the Rogue River Indian war and received appointment as collector of customs. He moved to Portland in 1858. As a Douglas Democrat and antislavery politician, Gibbs was elected to the state legislature in 1860. He helped form the Union party in 1862, and received its gubernatorial nomination. Gibbs easily defeated his Democratic opponent and served as governor until September 1866. In his inaugural address, he urged his fellow citizens to show loyalty by accepting paper money and higher taxes. He quoted the pro-Southern sentiments of Senator Joseph Lane (*q.v.*) and accused General Albert Sidney Johnston and other Federal officials of treason.

To counteract the Knights of the Golden Circle, Gibbs helped form, and became the head of, Oregon's Union League in 1863. In 1864, he successfully urged the legislature to pay a bounty to Volunteer soldiers, and he called the legislature into special session so that Oregon could ratify the 13th Amendment. In 1866, he was the choice of the Union–Republican caucus for U.S. senator but was defeated. In 1868 and 1870 Gibbs was elected prosecuting attorney; in 1872, President Ulysses S. Grant (*q.v.*) appointed him a U.S. district attorney for the District of Oregon. He suffered another political disappointment when George H. Williams, his former law partner and now President Grant's (*q.v.*) Attorney General, summarily removed him from office while he was probing charges of Federal election fraud. He died in London on December 29, 1886.

Edwards, "Department of the Pacific"; Johannsen, *Frontier Politics.*

G. Thomas Edwards

GIBSON, James F., *photographer,* was born in Scotland in 1828 or 1829. He served under Alexander Gardner (*q.v.*) on the staff of Mathew Brady's (*q.v.*) National Photographic Art Gallery from 1860 to about 1862; in March 1862 he joined Brady's cameramen in the field. Some 150 photographs of the Civil War can be attributed to him, including many of the well-known photographs from the Peninsula campaign traditionally associated with Brady. Gibson, working alongside John Woods, the official photographer of the Quartermaster's Department, accompanied the Army of the Potomac up the York River peninsula in the spring of 1862 and saw action at Fair Oaks, Gaines' Mills, Savage Station, and Malvern Hill. Working with both large-plate and stereo cameras, he made photographs under the most challenging conditions. His group portraits of officers and their staffs, and of the Union ironclad warships (including the *Monitor*), are especially notable.

In May 1862, Gibson worked with George N. Barnard (*q.v.*) while photographing the battleground of First Bull Run, some eight months after the combat there. He accompanied Gardner to the battlefield at Antietam later that year to take some of the war's most haunting photographs of the human cost of the conflict; their pictures of the unburied dead caused a sensation when they were exhibited in New York City shortly afterward. After Gardner left Brady in 1862, he and Gibson were partners for a short time. They photographed General Joseph Hooker's (*q.v.*) campaign in Virginia and the aftermath of the battle at Gettysburg.

In 1863–1864, Gibson was active at Brandy Station and other scenes of battle in Virginia. He then parted company with Gardner to manage Brady's financially troubled gallery in Washington, D.C. Brady persuaded Gibson to join him as a partner, but as the firm slid into bankruptcy, the two ended their professional relationship with a bitter exchange of lawsuits. Gibson left Washington in 1868 and is believed to have moved to Kansas. His activity in the West and the place and date of his death are unknown. Waldsmith, "James F. Gibson," *Stereo World.*

Ben Bassham

GIDDINGS, Joshua Reed, *abolitionist, diplomat,* was born in Bradford county, Pennsylvania on October 6, 1795. He grew up in the "Burned-over" district of western New York and in Ohio's Western Reserve. The prevalent religious revivalism and antislavery sentiment in these regions shaped Giddings's life. A child of farmers, he made the most of limited educational opportunities to become a successful lawyer, and from 1838 to 1858 was the Reserve's representative in Congress. Although technically Giddings was not an abolitionist, his career linked the abolitionists' moral antagonism to slavery with conventional politics.

As a Whig congressman in the late 1830s and early 1840s, Giddings cooperated in John Quincy Adams's successful assault upon the gag rule against antislavery petitions. Censured by the House of Representatives in 1842 for his advocacy of slave escape, Giddings resigned his seat, then was overwhelmingly reelected by his constituents. Giddings was a fierce opponent of the Mexican War and of the expansion of slavery which that war entailed. In 1848, he carried his constituency into the Free Soil party's campaign against slavery extension, and in 1856 he helped establish the Republican party.

An advocate of equal rights for African Americans, Giddings labored to make Republicans conform to the equal rights principles of the Declaration of Independence. Poor health and his persistent radicalism forced his retirement from Congress in 1858. He supported Abraham Lincoln (*q.v.*) in 1860, and Lincoln appointed him consul general to Canada, where he died on May 27, 1864, in Montreal. Giddings's significance for the Civil War lay not in this post, however, but in his earlier interjection of antislavery principles into national politics. Stewart, *Joshua R. Giddings.*

Stanley Harrold

GILBERT, James Isham, *general,* was born in Louisville, Kentucky, on July 16, 1823, and moved with his parents to Illinois and then to Prairie du Chien, Wisconsin. In the 1840s, as a commission merchant and Indian trader, he engaged in rafting timber on the Mississippi and Wisconsin rivers. In 1851, he helped plat the town of Lansing, Iowa, and resided there until entering the military. On October 3, 1862, Gilbert turned over management of his livery stable and real estate business to others, and became colonel of the 27th Iowa Volunteers. The regiment saw its first field service in Minnesota, and in late November 1862 was sent to Memphis. It served in northern Mississippi and

West Tennessee until the late summer of 1863, when it participated in the Meridian expedition and the Red River campaign.

Gilbert led the attack on Fort De Russy, distinguished himself at Pleasant Hill, and was placed in command of a brigade in June 1864. He led his brigade in the Tupelo campaign, the Oxford expedition, the pursuit of Sterling Price, and the battle of Nashville. His distinguished service as a brigade commander earned him promotion to brigadier general, to rank from February 9, 1865. At Fort Blakely, he led one of the onrushing columns that smashed the foe's defenses, resulting in a hurried Confederate evacuation of Mobile. Gilbert was breveted major general for his service during the Mobile campaign and returned to civilian life on August 4, 1865. He reentered the lumber business in Burlington, Iowa. He moved to Topeka, Kansas, in 1882, and died there on February 9, 1884. Stuart, *Iowa Colonels and Regiments.*

Edwin C. Bearss

GILLMORE, Quincy Adams, *general,* was born on February 28, 1825, in Black River, Ohio. He graduated first in the West Point class of 1849, and received a commission in the prestigious Corps of Engineers. Prewar service included construction duty at Forts Monroe and Calhoun, teaching and administrative posts at his alma mater, and command of the Engineer Agency in New York. Late in 1861, Captain Gillmore became chief engineer of the expedition that seized Confederate works at Port Royal, South Carolina. In early 1862, he supervised operations against Fort Pulaski, which guarded the mouth of the Savannah River. After building a vast array of batteries southeast of the fort, he directed a two-day barrage that forced the surrender of the 400-man garrison on April 11. His success in Georgia brought Gillmore a brigadier generalship in the Volunteer service and command of various military districts in Kentucky and western Virginia.

In April 1863, Gillmore returned to South Carolina to head the Department of the South and the X Corps. For ten months he oversaw the siege of Charleston. At first, his efforts—including the descent on Morris Island and the capture of Fort Wagner—bore fruit. By April 1864, however, his long-range bombardment of Charleston appeared to be an exercise in futility. Most of his corps was assimilated into General Benjamin Butler's (*q.v.*) Army of the James, and Gillmore's tactical incapacity cost that army more than one opportunity to seize Richmond or Petersburg during the 1864 campaign. Following a wretched performance at Petersburg on June 9, he was relieved of command and sent to Washington. He led two XIX Corps divisions in helping repulse General Jubal Early's raid on the capital, then a riding injury relegated him to minor duties until February 1865, when he regained command of the Department of the South.

Like many engineer officers elevated to high field command, Gillmore proved expert at constructing works and managing siege operations. His foresight in massing rifled cannon and heavy mortars against Fort Pulaski demonstrated the vulnerability of masonry fortifications. In open combat, however, he displayed glaring shortcomings. Unnerved by heavy losses suffered while attacking the Charleston defenses, he was unable to commit himself to the offensive warfare demanded by the 1864 campaign. After the war he served in the Engineer Bureau and as president of the Mississippi River Commission; he also published treatises on military engineering. He died in Brooklyn, New York, on April 7, 1888. Gillmore, *Engineer and Artillery Operations Against the Defenses of Charleston Harbor in 1863*; Robertson, *Back Door to Richmond*; Wightman, *From Antietam to Fort Fisher*.

Edward G. Longacre

GILMORE, Joseph Albree, *governor*, was born in Weston, Vermont, on June 10, 1811. In 1842, he opened a wholesale grocery in Concord, New Hampshire, and in 1848 was appointed superintendent of construction for the Concord & Claremont Railroad. By 1856, he had become superintendent of the Concord Railroad, one of the bigger independent lines of that period. Originally a Whig, Gilmore was elected to the state Senate in 1858 as a Republican, reelected to another one-year term in 1859, and chosen Senate president. He held no political office when the Civil War began. In 1862, he was tentatively offered command of a new regiment and began dispensing commissions to political cronies, but Governor Nathaniel Berry (*q.v.*) appointed someone else.

''Colonel'' Gilmore succeeded Berry in 1863, after a three-way race in which the Democratic contender outpolled Gilmore. None of the three secured a majority, however, so the election was thrown into the Republican-controlled legislature. Within a few days of taking office, the excitable Gilmore had to deal with scattered violence in reaction to the first draft lottery. He responded by mounting cannon in the statehouse yard, ordering a shipment of hand grenades, and demanding the return of the 5th New Hampshire from the Army of the Potomac. While Gilmore spent most of his term trying to meet Federal enlistment quotas, he was criticized for keeping his four sons out of the Army. Near the end of the war, he appointed one of them as a lieutenant in an artillery battery. His second term expired in the summer of 1865, and shortly afterward he retired from business, because of ill health. Gilmore died in Concord, New Hampshire, on April 17, 1867. Waite, *New Hampshire in the Great Rebellion*.

William Marvel

GOOCH, Daniel Wheelwright, *congressman*, was born on January 8, 1820, in Wells, Maine. He attended Phillips Academy and Dartmouth College, from which he graduated in 1843. In 1846, he began practicing law in Boston, served in the Massachusetts House of Representatives in 1852, and was present at the Massachusetts Constitutional Convention of 1853. In 1858 he was elected to Congress as a Republican, in a special election held to fill the vacancy caused by the resignation of Nathaniel P. Banks (*q.v.*), who had been elected governor. Gooch was reelected to the four succeeding Congresses, but resigned September

1, 1865, to accept a more lucrative position as naval officer of the Port of Boston. In less than a year he was removed from this position by President Andrew Johnson (*q.v.*).

In 1872, the Republicans chose Gooch to run for Congress after Banks bolted to the Liberal Republicans. Gooch defeated Banks, but lost his seat in an 1874 rematch. In 1875, Gooch was appointed pension agent in Boston and served in that capacity until 1886. During the Civil War, Gooch served on the Joint Congressional Committee on the Conduct of the War, maintaining a relatively Radical position. Gooch died in Melrose, Massachusetts, on November 11, 1891. Baum, *The Civil War Party System.*

Dale Baum

GOODELL, William, *abolitionist, editor,* was born in Chenango county, New York, on October 25, 1792. He helped found the American Anti-Slavery Society; edited its official newspaper, *The Emancipator,* and became one of its most important lecturers. In 1836, he became the editor of an abolitionist paper in Utica, the *Friend of Man.* By 1840, Goodell was a strong proponent of the Liberty party and a leading opponent of William Lloyd Garrison's (*q.v.*) anticlerical, antigovernment, and profeminist views. Whereas Garrison condemned voting by abolitionists, Goodell supported the Liberty party presidential candidate, James G. Birney, in 1840 and 1844. He argued his view that the Constitution permitted legislated emancipation of the slaves in two impressive legal treatises: *Views upon American Constitutional Law, in Its Bearing Upon American Slavery* (1844) and *American Slave Code, in Theory and Practice* (1853).

Goodell, an opponent of the Liberty party's merger with the Free Soil party, helped to found the Liberty League, which opposed slavery, land monopoly, the liquor traffic, tariffs, and war, and ran Gerrit Smith (*q.v.*) for President in 1844, 1852, 1856, and 1860. In 1854, Goodell moved to New York City to edit the *Radical Abolitionist* (later the weekly *Principia*), which upheld Liberty League principles. During the secession crisis, he became a supporter of Abraham Lincoln (*q.v.*), and thereafter made *Principia* an influential voice for emancipation. After the war, he moved to Janesville, Wisconsin, where he was active in the National Prohibition party until his death there on February 14, 1878. Perry, *Radical Abolitionism.*

James Brewer Stewart

GOODWIN, Ichabod, *governor,* was born in North Berwick, Maine, on October 8, 1794. He was a merchant ship captain, and in 1832 he opened a business in Portsmouth, New Hampshire. He invested in numerous ventures, including the first local railroad, serving as president of two lines for a quarter of a century. As a Whig, Goodwin won election to the state legislature six times, beginning in 1838. He stayed with the party until it dissolved, running for Congress several times without success; in 1856 he was the last Whig candidate for governor. As a Republican, he was elected governor in 1859 and 1860. Goodwin devoted his first term, and most of his second, to expansion of the state's railroad network, but in his last days as governor he answered Abraham Lincoln's (*q.v.*) first calls for troops.

Despite an empty treasury, Goodwin raised a ninety-day militia regiment and recruited a three-year infantry regiment that acquitted itself creditably at First Bull Run. To do this, he borrowed more than $750,000 on his own responsibility, fearing it would take too long to call a special session of the General Court. He may also have suspected that conservative legislators would reject requests for money to support coercion. Over just such a protest by a sizable minority, the legislature approved Goodwin's illegal expenditures a few days after he left office. After his political retirement, Goodwin began reducing his business activities to the presidency of the two railroads and two banks. He died in Portsmouth on July 4, 1882. McClintock, *History of New Hampshire*; Waite, *New Hampshire in the Great Rebellion.*

William Marvel

GOODWIN, John Noble, *congressman, territorial delegate*, was born in South Berwick, Maine, on October 18, 1824. He attended Berwick Academy, graduated from Dartmouth College in 1844, read law, and was admitted to the bar in 1848. Goodwin served in the Maine Senate in 1854, and in 1860, as a Republican, won election to Congress. After a lackluster term, he lost his reelection bid by 127 votes. When Congress organized the Arizona Territory, President Abraham Lincoln (*q.v.*) appointed Goodwin territorial chief justice on March 6, 1863. Before he could leave for Arizona, however, Governor John Gurley (*q.v.*) died, and Lincoln replaced him with Goodwin, who reached Arizona in December 1863. Goodwin toured Arizona, then settled in a log house near Fort Whipple. The town of Prescott (named for historian William Hickling Prescott) grew up around this "executive Mansion."

Arizona, its tiny population largely pro-Confederate, needed careful handling, and received it from the canny Goodwin. He appointed a number of Southern sympathizers to office, and skillfully turned attention away from the war and toward internal development. Goodwin worked effectively with the squabbling factions and the first legislature, pushed for railroad development, and made many friends and few enemies. His election as territorial delegate to Congress in 1865 attests to his popularity. At the end of one term, Goodwin settled in New York City to practice law. His significance in the Civil War period lies in the skill with which he defused the pro-Confederate spirit in Arizona and gave that territory honest, strong, and stable government. Like many another Mainer of his era, he made his greatest mark outside his native state. Goodwin died on April 19, 1887, in Paraiso Springs, California. *BDUSC*; Farish, *History of Arizona*, vols. 2, 3, 4.

H. Draper Hunt

GORDON, George Henry, *general,* was born on July 19, 1823, in Charlestown, Massachusetts. After completing his education at Framingham Academy, he graduated from West Point in 1846. With Winfield Scott's (*q.v.*) army in Mexico, he participated in the siege of Veracruz, and the battles of Cerro Gordo (where he was wounded), Contreras, and Chapultepec. He took part in the capture of Mexico City, after which he was wounded again. Gordon was breveted 1st lieutenant in the Regular Army for bravery at Cerro Gordo. From 1850 until 1854, when he resigned his commission, he served on the frontier in the Oregon, Washington, and Kansas territories. In 1855 and 1856, he attended Harvard Law School, then practiced law until the bombardment of Fort Sumter.

In May 1861, Gordon was commissioned colonel of the 2nd Massachusetts Volunteers, and a year later was promoted to brigadier general of Volunteers for his service in the Shenandoah Valley. He fought in the battles of Winchester, Cedar Mountain, Chantilly, South Mountain, and Antietam. In poor health for most of 1863, he engaged in operations around Charleston Harbor, South Carolina. In July 1864, Gordon campaigned on the White River in Arkansas. In March 1865 he commanded the Eastern District of Virginia. Gordon was breveted major general of Volunteers in April 1865, but four months later poor health forced him to resign. He devoted considerable energy to the military history of the campaigns with which he had been involved. Gordon died August 30, 1886, in Framingham, Massachusetts. Krick, *Stonewall Jackson at Cedar Mountain*; Sears, *Landscape Turned Red.*

Robert H. Jones

GRAHAM, Charles Kinnaird, *general,* was born in New York City on June 3, 1824. He served as a midshipman in the Gulf Squadron during the Mexican War, then pursued a civil engineering career. In the 1850s he surveyed Central Park, and constructed docks and landings at the Brooklyn Naval Yard. In 1861, he was an officer in the 70th New York Volunteers, then became colonel of the 74th New York in February 1862. He participated in the Peninsula campaign, during which he contracted an illness that incapacitated him for several months. In 1863, he was given a brigade and, briefly, a division in the III Corps, Army of the Potomac, and served conspicuously at Chancellorsville and Gettysburg. On July 2, 1863, he suffered a head wound and was captured. Exchanged late that year, Graham, now a brigadier general of Volunteers, went to General Benjamin Butler's (*q.v.*) Army of the James. Under Butler, he commanded a fleet of gunboats, manned by heavy artillerists, on the James and Appomattox Rivers, then a division garrisoning the army's main base at Bermuda Hundred.

Breveted major general of Volunteers in 1865, Graham was mustered out in August. With his naval and engineering background, he was a multitalented soldier. He considered himself a field commander above all else, but after 1863 his superiors deemed him too valuable a gunboat and garrison leader to be spared for combat assignments. Certainly his "Naval Brigade" rendered valuable service to Butler's army. Graham was best known in the South for torching

the Virginia home of the brother of the Confederate secretary of war—on Butler's orders. After the war, he was chief engineer of the New York Department
of Docks and surveyor and naval officer of the Municipal Port until his death
in Lakewood, New Jersey, on April 15, 1889. Phisterer, *New York in the War of
the Rebellion*, vol. 4; Robertson, *Back Door to Richmond.*

                                                                                          Edward G. Longacre

GRANGER, Bradley Francis, *congressman*, was born on March 12, 1825, in
Lowville, New York. He attended public schools, studied law, and was admitted
to the bar in 1847. He began practicing in Tecumseh, Michigan, and a short
time later moved to Ann Arbor. He held a number of local offices, including
clerk of Washtenaw county (1852) and judge of probate (1856). In his profession, he was regarded as "a strong and forceful advocate" who was "thoroughly
informed on the principles of jurisprudence in many departments." He was a
Republican member of the U.S. House of Representatives from 1861 to 1863.
Following his term in the 37th Congress, where he remained in the background,
he returned to Ann Arbor and practiced law until his death there on November
4, 1882. Beakes, *Past and Present of Washtenaw County, Michigan.*

                                                                                          Frederick D. Williams

GRANGER, Gordon, *general*, was born on November 6, 1822, in Joy, New
York. He graduated from West Point in 1845, and was assigned first to the
infantry and then the cavalry. In the Mexican War he was with Winfield Scott's
(*q.v.*) campaign from Veracruz to the capture of Mexico City, and earned two
brevets. Granger later served on the western frontier in various Indian campaigns. His first action in the Civil War was at Wilson's Creek, and his able
performance in that battle won him appointment as colonel of the 2nd Michigan
Cavalry in September 1861. He performed capably in the New Madrid and
Island No. 10 operations in the spring of 1862, and was named brigadier general
of Volunteers, dating from March 26, 1862. When John Pope's (*q.v.*) force was
moved eastward to serve under Henry W. Halleck (*q.v.*) in the advance on
Corinth, Mississippi, Granger commanded a brigade. Dating from September
17, 1862, he was given the rank of major general of Volunteers, and until the
summer of 1863 was a division commander in garrison duty and in secondary
operations in Kentucky and Tennessee.

   Granger joined the Army of the Cumberland under William S. Rosecrans
(*q.v.*) in the advance on Chattanooga, and in September 1863 took part in the
momentous battle of Chickamauga, his most illustrious and best-known action
of the Civil War. Guarding a pass in reserve behind of the Union lines on
September 20, Granger "marched to the sound of the guns," and arrived on
the field in time to buttress George H. Thomas's (*q.v.*) gallant defense of Snodgrass Hill. Thomas and Granger held their positions until dark and prevented
the possible destruction of the army. During the siege of Chattanooga and the
battle of Missionary Ridge, Granger commanded the IV Corps. He led a division

and sometimes a corps in the relief of Knoxville, Tennessee; in operations against the forts outside Mobile in 1864; and in the capture of Mobile in 1865.

Granger, brusque and tough with an irascible, outspoken manner, often acted independently. He frequently clashed with his men, his subordinates, and his superiors. But when action was required, Granger was at his best. He left the Volunteer service in January 1866 to become a colonel of infantry in the Regular Army. He commanded the District of Memphis in 1867–1869, and intermittently commanded the District of New Mexico between 1871 and 1876. He died on January 10, 1876, in Santa Fe, New Mexico Territory. Cozzens, *This Terrible Sound*; Starr, *Union Cavalry*, vol. 3.

E. B. Long

GRANT, Ulysses S., *general*, was born on April 27, 1822, in Point Pleasant, Ohio. He attended school in Ohio and had two years of academy instruction before appointment to West Point in 1839. Originally named Hiram Ulysses Grant, he decided to reverse the first and middle name, but through confusion in his appointment was registered as Ulysses S. Grant, a name he finally accepted, persistently asserting that the "S." stood for nothing. Grant graduated in 1843, and was assigned as brevet 2nd lieutenant to the 4th U.S. Infantry at Jefferson Barracks, near St. Louis. After service in Louisiana and at Corpus Christi, Grant participated in the opening battles of the Mexican War at Palo Alto, Resaca de la Palma, and Monterrey. Transferred to the expedition of Winfield Scott (*q.v.*), and assigned quartermaster duty, he did not rejoin the fighting until the final battles for Mexico City.

In 1848, Grant married and settled into garrison duty at Sackets Harbor, New York, and Detroit. Assignment to the Pacific coast in 1852 disrupted family life when Grant refused to take his pregnant wife on the hazardous journey across the Isthmus of Panama. Lonely, underpaid, ill, and without prospect of promotion, Grant spent two years at Fort Vancouver, Washington Territory, and Fort Humboldt, California, before resigning on April 11, 1854, to rejoin his wife and two sons. He hoped to start a new life as a farmer in St. Louis county, but the farm failed in the Panic of 1857, as did subsequent business ventures in St. Louis.

On the eve of the Civil War, Grant worked in his father's leather goods store in Galena, Illinois. Leaving Galena with a company of Volunteers, Grant's military experience soon brought him a position as aide to Governor Richard Yates (*q.v.*) of Illinois. Two frustrating months elapsed before he took command of a regiment, later mustered as the 21st Illinois Volunteers. Through the influence of U.S. Representative Elihu B. Washburne (*q.v.*), Grant was appointed brigadier general before he had engaged an enemy. Placed in command at Cairo, Grant promptly occupied Paducah when Confederates violated the neutrality of Kentucky. An expedition to Belmont, Missouri, opposite the Confederate bastion of Columbus, Kentucky, led to an indecisive battle on November 7, 1861. In February 1862, Grant cooperated with naval forces on the Tennessee River in an expedition against Fort Henry, which fell before the army arrived. Grant then marched overland against Fort Donelson on the Cumberland River, surrounded it, demanded "unconditional and immediate surrender," and won the first major Union victory of the Civil War.

Promoted to major general, Grant was in command at Shiloh when Union forces were driven to the Tennessee River in the first day; aided by reinforcements brought by Don Carlos Buell (*q.v.*), he swept the enemy from the field on the second day. Grant received considerable criticism for the success of the surprise Confederate attack and for resulting heavy casualties. His superior, General Henry W. Halleck (*q.v.*), took personal command of Grant's forces, so humiliating him that he considered resigning. In late 1862, Grant began an overland campaign along the line of the Mississippi Central Railroad that aimed at the Confederate bastion of Vicksburg. When Confederate cavalry raids cut his supply lines in December, he withdrew to Memphis, then moved downriver to Vicksburg, where he failed in several attempts to gain a dry foothold. In April 1863, his fleet ran the batteries and landed troops below Vicksburg. Grant veered to the east, captured Jackson, Mississippi, then won a series of battles that pushed the enemy back to Vicksburg. After two unsuccessful assaults, he began a siege that culminated in the surrender of Vicksburg on July 4.

Sent to relieve the siege of Chattanooga, Grant led a three-day battle that swept the enemy from Lookout Mountain and Missionary Ridge. Appointed lieutenant general and given command of all the U.S. armies, he accompanied the Army of the Potomac through the bloody Wilderness campaign, which included the battles of Spotsylvania and Cold Harbor, and finally forced the Army of Northern Virginia into fortifications at Petersburg. When the line cracked in early April 1865, Grant quickly pushed Robert E. Lee to surrender at Appomattox.

Grant's aggressiveness, resilience, and determination led to military success. In the campaigns of 1864–1865, he had numerical superiority, but so had his predecessors in command; Grant made the numbers count. At Fort Donelson, Vicksburg, and Appomattox he captured entire Confederate armies; at Chattanooga he destroyed another. Victories at Vicksburg and Chattanooga were notable for low Union casualties; the Wilderness campaign was a bloodbath. As a commander, Grant operated unpredictably, perhaps a key to his success. His career also reflects administrative ability, versatility, openness to innovation, and capacity to learn.

Grant commanded the Army until his inauguration as President on March 4, 1869. In two terms, he upheld fiscal conservatism, negotiated a settlement of difficulties with England, and enforced Reconstruction legislation, albeit with waning ardor. Nonetheless, financial scandals remain the best-remembered feature of the Grant administration. After a celebrated tour around the world and failure to win nomination for a third term, Grant settled in New York City, where he lost all he possessed in a Wall Street swindle. Penniless and dying of cancer, Grant wrote his classic *Memoirs*. He died on July 25, 1885, in Mount

McGregor, New York. Catton, *Grant Moves South*; Catton, *Grant Takes Command*; McFeely, *Grant*.

John Y. Simon

GRAY, Joseph William, *editor*, was born on August 5, 1813, in Bridport, Vermont. His family moved to New York in the 1830s, and he graduated in 1836 from St. Lawrence Academy in Potsdam. That year he moved to Cleveland, Ohio, where he was admitted to the bar, taught school, and practiced law before embarking on a newspaper career. Gray and his brother purchased the *Cleveland Advertiser* in 1842, renamed it the *Plain Dealer*, and started weekly and eventually daily publication. Gray soon was sole proprietor. He editorially supported the Mexican War and became a close friend of Stephen A. Douglas (*q.v.*). Gray was a delegate to the 1852 Democratic National Convention, and served as postmaster of Cleveland (from 1853 to 1858). He relinquished editorial control of the paper during his term, fearing a potential conflict of interest. He also served as school examiner and as secretary of the Cleveland Lyceum.

Although untrained in journalism, Gray was a good writer and editor. He supported Douglas in 1860, and when Douglas lost, he followed his lead in giving fairly strong support to the war effort, although he criticized Abraham Lincoln (*q.v.*) and the war on occasion. Although rarely as vituperative as other Democratic editors, Gray nonetheless felt the wrath of the prowar community. He followed personal principle and Douglas Democratic philosophy until his death. Most Americans and historians, however, have looked at the *Plain Dealer*'s course during the entire war and labeled Gray a Copperhead. It was actually after Gray's death that the newspaper, embroiled in a complicated battle for ownership, began a bitter attack on Lincoln and the war. Gray's initial War Democrat stance was largely ignored. He died in Cleveland on May 26, 1862. Hooper, *History of Ohio Journalism*; Shaw, *The Plain Dealer*.

Fredric F. Endres

GREELEY, Horace, *editor*, was born on February 3, 1811, in Amherst, New Hampshire. His formal education was sparse, but he read widely and became an expert, at least by his own reckoning, on almost any subject. Greeley founded *The New-Yorker* magazine in 1834. Its excellent content and commentary earned him a regional reputation, and his Whiggish stand on major issues brought him to the attention of New York political boss Thurlow Weed (*q.v.*), who hired him to edit Whig papers (*The Jeffersonian* and the *Log Cabin*). In 1841, while still editing *The New-Yorker*, Greeley launched the *New York Tribune*, a mass-circulation penny paper with a popular orientation. The paper proved successful, quickly reaching an 11,000 circulation. More important, however, was the *Weekly Tribune*, a compendium of news, farming advice, and strong editorials begun in the fall of 1841. Its circulation reached 200,000, much of it in the politically volatile Midwest.

Greeley now had a national reputation and following. The *Tribune* reflected his broad interests, discussing socialism, agrarian reform, and workers' rights. Its staffers and contributors included Henry Raymond (*q.v.*), Charles A. Dana (*q.v.*), and such literary figures as Margaret Fuller and William Dean Howells. It was one of the most socially conscious, inexpensive, mass-circulation urban dailies of the period. Greeley was a staunch Whig until the 1850s, when he shifted to the new Republican party and its 1860 candidate, Abraham Lincoln (*q.v.*). Strongly antislavery and eager to get the war over quickly after the surrender of Fort Sumter, Greeley—and much of the nation—tired of the lack of military movement. His 1861 editorial campaign "Forward to Richmond" probably reflected the attitude of most people in the North. However, the Union rout at Bull Run brought severe public criticism of the editor from a public that blamed him for the premature action.

Greeley and Lincoln corresponded often, especially when the editor chastised the President or told him what to do. In August 1862, for example, Greeley published his famous "Prayer of Twenty Millions" editorial, urging a stronger emancipation policy. Though occasionally inconsistent in his support of Lincoln, he backed his reelection in 1864, and supported the President's call for a draft in 1863, a move that brought a public assault on the *Tribune* building.

After Ulysses S. Grant's (*q.v.*) election in 1868, Greeley became impatient with the policies and corruption in the administration. Liberal Republicans, or mugwumps, led by such editors as Greeley, Samuel Bowles (*q.v.*), and Murat Halstead (*q.v.*), split form the regular party, held a nominating convention, and emerged with Greeley as their candidate. The splintered and weak Democratic party also nominated Greeley, who won only six of the thirty-seven states. Disenchanted and tired, and despondent over the recent death of his wife, Greeley fell ill and moved to Pleasantville, New York, where he died on November 29, 1872. Horner, *Lincoln and Greeley.*

Fredric F. Endres

GREENE, George Sears, *general,* was born on May 6, 1801, in Apponang, Rhode Island. He graduated from West Point in 1823, and remained to teach mathematics until 1827. He served at various posts in New England and was promoted to 1st lieutenant in 1829. In 1836 he resigned from the Army to enter engineering, primarily railroad construction. In January 1862 he became colonel of the 60th New York Volunteers and was stationed near Washington, D.C., until he was appointed brigadier general of Volunteers in April. He commanded a brigade under General Nathaniel P. Banks (*q.v.*) in the Shenandoah Valley, fought at Cedar Mountain, and commanded a division at Antietam. Returned to command of his brigade, a part of the XII Corps of the Army of the Potomac, Greene fought at Chancellorsville and again with distinction at Culp's Hill.

Severely wounded in October 1863, Greene saw no further action until 1865. He commanded a brigade in the North Carolina campaign in March and April 1865. Breveted major general, he was mustered out in April 1866. Greene resumed work as an engineer in New York, involved in water supply and elevated railroads. He worked on other engineering projects in Washington, D.C., Detroit, and Troy and Yonkers, New York. He served as president of the American Society of Civil Engineers, 1875–1877. Greene died January 28, 1899, in Morristown, New Jersey. Pfanz, *Gettysburg—Culp's Hill and Cemetery Hill*; Sears, *Landscape Turned Red.*

Robert H. Jones

GREGG, David McMurtrie, *general,* was born in Huntingdon, Pennsylvania, on April 10, 1833. He graduated from West Point in 1855, then served in New Mexico and on the West Coast. Upon the establishment of the 6th U.S. Cavalry in the summer of 1861, he was transferred to the new regiment with the rank of captain, and served in the defenses of Washington until he was appointed colonel of the 8th Pennsylvania Cavalry in January 1862. After service on the Peninsula and at Antietam, Gregg was promoted to brigadier general of Volunteers on November 29, 1862, and given command of a cavalry division. From June 1863 he alternately commanded the 2nd Division and the entire Cavalry Corps of the Army of the Potomac. In the fall and winter of 1864–1865, in the absence of Philip Sheridan (*q.v.*) and the 1st and 3rd Divisions of the Cavalry Corps in the Shenandoah Valley, Gregg's division represented the total cavalry force of the army, and under his leadership it participated in all of Ulysses S. Grant's (*q.v.*) repeated probes of the Confederate defenses of Petersburg.

In his long tour with the Army of the Potomac, Gregg participated in four major combats. At Brandy Station his division formed the left side of a two-pronged attack on J.E.B. Stuart's cavalry. At the crossing of the Rappahannock at Kelly's Ford, he was delayed by General Alfred N. Duffie's unaccountable slowness, but he came up to Fleetwood Heights, the practically undefended key to Stuart's position, from the south. Bewildered by the fire of a single howitzer, Gregg hesitated to order an attack on the Heights, and when at last he did so, it was too late.

On July 3, 1863, at Gettysburg, Gregg was posted to the southeast of Culp's Hill with two of the three brigades of his division, plus George Custer's (*q.v.*) brigade of Hugh Judson Kilpatrick's (*q.v.*) division; in a fierce combat, he checked the attack of four brigades of Stuart's cavalry. Had he failed to do so, Stuart would have been able to attack the rear of the Union infantry on Cemetery Ridge at the same time that it was attacked frontally by Pickett's infantry. This was Gregg's most significant victory, and it is fittingly commemorated by his statue at Gettysburg, erected by his native state.

The third of Gregg's major combats occurred on May 28, 1864, at Haw's Shop (Salem Church), when, fighting dismounted and aided by Custer's brigade, he drove off two divisions of Confederate cavalry in the severest cavalry fighting of the war. The fourth combat took place a month later, at Saint Mary's (or ''Samaria'') Church. On his return from his Trevilian Station raid, Sheridan was ordered to escort a train of 900 army wagons from the Pamunkey River across the Peninsula. Gregg and his division were sent to reinforce Sheridan. Marching to the right of the road to Charles City Courthouse, on which the wagons were traveling, Gregg's division had to bear the brunt of the attacks led by Wade Hampton. Gregg held the enemy long enough to allow the wagons to make their way to safety.

On February 3, 1865, after a winter of nearly constant activity, Gregg resigned his commission. Why he did so and why, so far as is known, no effort was made to keep so able and dependable an officer in the Army, are a mystery. In the postwar years he served as U.S. consul at Prague and as auditor general of Pennsylvania. He was active in the commandery of the Loyal Legion and served as its national commander from 1903 to 1905. He died on August 7, 1916, in Reading, Pennsylvania. Sommers, *Richmond Redeemed*; Starr, *Union Cavalry*, vols. 1, 2.

Stephen Z. Starr

GRESHAM, Walter Quintin, *general*, was born on March 17, 1832, near Lanesville, Indiana. He was caught up in the political chaos of the mid-1850s, first as a leader in the anti-Nebraska movement and later in the Republican party. After his election to the Indiana legislature in 1860, Gresham made several speeches in Kentucky, appealing to citizens there to remain in the Union. After the war broke out, Gresham clashed with Governor Oliver H.P. Morton (*q.v.*) over military appointments, and enlisted in the Army as a private. However, Morton appointed him a colonel on March 10, 1862, and he raised the 53rd Indiana Regiment. Though Gresham was anxious to take his men into action at Shiloh, General Ulysses S. Grant (*q.v.*) ordered him to remain at Savannah, Tennessee. After his regiment fought well at Vicksburg, Gresham was promoted to brigadier general on August 11, 1863. Assigned a command in Natchez, he had to contend with the usual problems of occupation duty and also with the effects of the Emancipation Proclamation.

In 1864, Gresham became a division commander in General William T. Sherman's (*q.v.*) army, then on its advance toward Atlanta. A serious leg wound ended Gresham's military service and kept him either in bed or on crutches for five years. He resumed his law practice in Indiana and entered several unsuccessful political races. After serving as a U.S. district judge, he was appointed Postmaster General by President Chester A. Arthur in 1883 and later became Arthur's Secretary of the Treasury. After being appointed a circuit judge, Gresham drifted away from the Republican fold, and President Grover Cleveland named him Secretary of State in 1893. He died in Washington, D.C., on May 28, 1895. Calhoun, *Gilded Age Cato*; Gresham, *Life of Walter Q. Gresham*.

George C. Rable

GRIDER, Henry, *congressman*, was born on July 16, 1796, in Garrard county, Kentucky. He was educated at schools in Greensburg and Bowling Green; his legal studies were supervised by two Bowling Green attorneys. With his father and a brother, he served as a private in Governor Isaac Shelby's command in the invasion of Canada during the war of 1812. Grider never achieved the first rank among Kentucky politicians, but he had an active career. He was elected to the state House of Representatives in 1827 and 1831; he served in the state Senate from 1833 to 1837; and he won election as a Whig to the U.S. House of Representatives in 1843 and 1845. As a Union Democrat he won House elections in 1861, 1863, and 1865.

Although Grider supported many war measures, he was jealous of states' rights, especially in regard to slavery, and he voted consistently against such measures as the 13th Amendment. Grider merited his reputation as an attorney, and his numerous elections testified to his popularity, but he was never a real leader in state politics, and he had little impact in the House of Representatives. He died in Bowling Green, Kentucky, on September 9, 1866. *Biographical Encyclopedia of Kentucky*; Levin, *Lawyers and Lawmakers of Kentucky.*

Lowell H. Harrison

GRIER, Robert Cooper, *Supreme Court justice,* was born on March 5, 1794, in Cumberland county, Pennsylvania. He graduated from Dickinson College in 1812, and when his father died in 1815, replaced him as president of Northumberland Academy. Admitted to the bar in 1817, Grier became a successful attorney and won appointment in 1833 to a district judgeship in Allegheny county. In 1845, President James K. Polk named him to the Supreme Court seat left vacant by the death of Henry Baldwin. In opinions on the commerce clause, corporate contracts, vested rights, and banking, Grier established himself as a consistent defender of states' rights.

When the *Dred Scott* case reached the Court, Grier wisely suggested handing down a decision with no reference to the constitutionality of the Missouri Compromise. Under prodding from President James Buchanan (*q.v.*), he drafted a brief opinion agreeing with Chief Justice Roger Taney's (*q.v.*) position on that explosive question. He thereby came in for a full share of partisan abuse from angry Republicans. At the beginning of the Civil War, Grier called for the suppression of the rebellion, no matter what the cost. As a circuit judge, he ruled that the government could attack the rebels and treat their shippers as pirates without recognizing the Confederacy as a nation. He likewise endorsed, albeit indirectly, the constitutionality of conscription.

Grier's most notable contribution to wartime jurisprudence was his ringing vindication of President Abraham Lincoln's (*q.v.*) policies in the famous decision of the Prize Cases. Counsel for shipowners whose vessels had been seized contended that Lincoln could not proclaim a blockade because Congress had not declared war. Grier countered that civil wars are seldom declared and that the President had ample powers to use a blockade to suppress an insurrection. He also agreed that people residing in the Confederacy were ''enemies'' whose property was subject to seizure. Grier thus upheld the legality of the blockade without forcing the United States to recognize the Confederacy as a belligerent power.

During Reconstruction, Grier reverted to his habitual conservatism and looked askance at congressional policies and attempts to modify the Court's appellate jurisdiction. He resigned in December 1869 and died in Philadelphia on September 25, 1870. Frank Otto Gatell, "Robert C. Grier," in Friedman, *Justices of the U.S. Supreme Court*, vol. 2, pp. 873–894; Silver, *Lincoln's Supreme Court*; Swisher, *The Taney Period.*

George C. Rable

GRIERSON, Benjamin Henry, *general*, was born in Pittsburgh, Pennsylvania, on July 8, 1826. He attended a Youngstown, Ohio, academy, and taught music there and at Jacksonville, Illinois. In 1861, Grierson entered service as a Volunteer aide to General Benjamin M. Prentiss (*q.v.*), but received no pay because his rank of captain was never confirmed. He was commissioned major of the 6th Illinois Cavalry on October 1, 1861, but he continued to serve on Prentiss's staff until December 1. In March 1862, the regiment was ordered to Pittsburg Landing but was detained at Paducah, where Grierson became its colonel. In early summer he was ordered to Memphis, and during the next five months led his regiment in sweeps through West Tennessee and northwestern Mississippi. On November 26, the regiment left Memphis in advance of William T. Sherman's (*q.v.*) wing and then participated in the pursuit of Earl Van Dorn's force on its return from the Holly Springs raid.

During the winter of 1862–1863, Grierson commanded a brigade posted at La Grange, Tennessee, and on April 17, launched one of the war's great cavalry raids. Striking southward into Mississippi, his command disrupted communications and scattered General John C. Pemberton's strategic reserve. On May 2, after a 450-mile ride through the Confederate heartland, the raiders reached Baton Rouge. In recognition of this exploit, Grierson was promoted to brigadier general. After the surrender of Port Hudson, the brigade returned to West Tennessee and Grierson was given a division. He accompanied General William S. Smith's (*q.v.*) column, which Nathan Bedford Forrest turned back at Okolona in February 1864.

During the late spring and summer, Grierson fought at Brice's Cross Roads and participated in the Tupelo campaign and the Oxford expedition. At the Cross Roads, he was outbattled and outgeneraled by Forrest, and his division was routed. In December, Grierson's command wrecked the Mobile & Ohio Railroad, then being used to supply John Bell Hood's army on its retreat from Middle Tennessee, and defeated a Confederate force at Egypt Station. Grierson then led his columns on a swath of destruction through the Mississippi hill counties, and reached Vicksburg on January 4, 1865. In March, he reported to General E.R.S. Canby (*q.v.*), as commander of Canby's Cavalry Corps, then operating on the approaches to Mobile. In the closing weeks of the war, he led a sweep from Mobile Bay to Columbus, Georgia, by way of Eufaula, Alabama.

Grierson was promoted major general of Volunteers to rank from May 27, 1865, and was mustered out of the service on April 30, 1866. In July 1866 he was commissioned colonel of the 10th U.S. Cavalry, one of the Army's two postwar black mounted units. They served with distinction at a number of southwestern frontier posts. On April 5, 1890, while commanding the District of Arizona, Grierson was promoted to brigadier general. Three months later, on reaching his sixty-fourth birthday, he retired from the Army. Grierson died in Omena, Michigan, on August 31, 1911. Brown, *Grierson's Raid*; Utley, *Frontier Regulars.*

Edwin C. Bearss

GRIFFIN, Charles, *general,* was born in Granville, Ohio, on December 18, 1825. He graduated from West Point in 1847, and was commissioned in the artillery. After service in Mexico and various eastern, southern, and western posts, he returned to West Point in September 1860 as an instructor of artillery. Griffin led the new West Point Battery (later Battery D, 5th Artillery) to Washington, D.C., in January 1861 and commanded it at First Bull Run, where it was overrun. Promoted to captain in the Regular Army (April 1861) and brigadier general of Volunteers (June 1862), he was chief of artillery of Porter's (later Morell's) division on the Peninsula, then took over the 2nd Brigade, 1st Division, V Corps, on June 26, 1862.

Like many artillerists, Griffin had to enter the infantry to exercise his higher rank. His new service began promisingly in the Seven Days' battles but appeared doomed at Second Bull Run, where he was accused of undercutting General John Pope (*q.v.*). Unlike Fitz John Porter (*q.v.*), Griffin survived such accusations. He led his brigade at Antietam and the 1st Division, V Corps in the Fredericksburg, Chancellorsville, and Second Bristoe campaigns. Illness and court duty often kept him from the field, but he resumed command for the war's final year. He fought splendidly in Ulysses S. Grant's (*q.v.*) Overland campaign and at Petersburg. When command of the V Corps fell vacant after Five Forks, Griffin was chosen over more senior officers to fill it. His corps intercepted Robert E. Lee at Appomattox Court House, after which he became one of three Federal commissioners to implement Lee's surrender.

Proud, abrasive, and bellicose, but a fighting soldier, Griffin could inspire and agressively and effectively lead his troops in combat. He was the V Corps's best general. After the war, Griffin commanded the District of Maine, then served on a small-arms board. As colonel, 35th Infantry, he had charge of the District of Texas and briefly of the Fifth (Reconstruction) Military District. His abbreviated Southern tour (November 1866–September 1867) proved him to be a vigorous executor of congressional Reconstruction. He died in Galveston, Texas, on September 15, 1867. Powell, *Fifth Army Corps*; Sommers, *Richmond Redeemed.*

Richard J. Sommers

GRIFFING, Josephine Sophia, *abolitionist, relief worker,* was born on December 18, 1814, in Hebron, Connecticut. In 1842, with her husband, Charles

S.S. Griffing, she moved to Litchfield, Ohio. She became an antislavery activist, sheltering fugitive slaves, serving as an officer of the Western Anti-Slavery Society, and contributing to the Salem (Ohio) *Anti-Slavery Bugle*. Griffing also participated in the women's rights and temperance movements. She criticized the orthodox churches for their conservative stands on slavery and women's rights, and for a time supported the Ohio Friends of Human Progress, a radical offshoot of the Quakers. In the early 1850s, she toured Ohio and other western states as an abolitionist agent. Upon resuming this activity in the winter of 1860–1861, Griffing encountered a wave of pro-Union, antiblack sentiment and was mobbed. Like most Garrisonians she doubted the antislavery character of the Republican party in 1860.

During the war Griffing lectured as an agent of the National Woman's Loyal League, which promoted emancipation as a war aim. But her war service was practical aid to the freedmen rather than propaganda. In 1863, she went to Washington, D.C., as an agent of the Western Freedmen's Aid Committee, and remained there. For a short time Griffing served as subassistant commissioner of the Freedman's Bureau for Washington, and she continued relief work through the National Freedman's Relief Association of the District of Columbia. She appealed for support from private philanthropy and regularly appeared before congressional committees to urge appropriations for freedmen's relief. She helped form the National Woman Suffrage Association and became its corresponding secretary. Griffing died in Washington, D.C., on February 18, 1872.

McPherson, *Struggle for Equality*; Stanton, *History of Women's Suffrage*, vol. 2.

Merton L. Dillon

GRIMES, James Wilson, *senator*, was born on October 20, 1816, in Deering, New Hampshire. He attended Dartmouth but left to read law. Grimes moved to Wisconsin Territory in 1836, and then settled at what was to become Burlington, Iowa. After work as a secretary to a commission that concluded treaties with the Sac and Fox Indians, and as city solicitor, he was elected in 1838 on the Whig ticket to the first Iowa territorial legislature, and in 1843 to the sixth. By 1852, when he was elected to the state legislature, Grimes was a railroad advocate, real estate speculator, banker, and proponent of scientific agriculture. He won the governorship in 1854 as a Whig with strong abolitionist leanings. Strongly opposed to the Kansas–Nebraska Act, Grimes was a major figure in the founding of the Iowa Republican party.

After a second term as governor, Grimes was elected to the U.S. Senate, taking office March 4, 1859. He favored a Pacific railroad, but was distrustful of business monopoly and cool toward protective tariffs. He also favored a more progressive wartime income tax than was eventually enacted. A supporter of emancipation and war measures, including confiscation and the building of iron-clad ships, Grimes did not, however, favor the Wade–Davis Reconstruction Bill. A member of the Joint Committee on Reconstruction, he voted against President Andrew Johnson's (*q.v.*) impeachment, arguing that although his acts were lamentable, they were not criminal. This brought him great abuse. His health broken, he died in Burlington on February 7, 1872. Dykstra, *Bright Radical Star*; Sage, *History of Iowa*.

Hubert H. Wubben

GRINNELL, Josiah Bushnell, *abolitionist, congressman*, was born on December 22, 1821, in New Haven, Vermont. He graduated from Oneida Institute in 1843 and from Auburn Theological Seminary in 1846, and served as pastor at the racially integrated Congregational church of Union Village, New York. In 1851, he left to found the first Congregational church in Washington, D.C., but following a series of abolitionist sermons he was forced to leave the city. Grinnell and two associates purchased over 5,000 acres in Poweshiek county, Iowa, in 1854 and founded the town of Grinnell, which quickly assumed a New England character. Iowa College (renamed Grinnell College in 1909) moved there from Davenport in 1856, and Grinnell became president of the trustees and a lifelong supporter.

Present at the founding of the Iowa Republican party in 1856, Grinnell served in the state Senate, 1856–1860. He became known as a proponent of prohibition and free schools, and as Iowa's foremost abolitionist. In 1859, he sheltered John Brown (*q.v.*), who was transporting a group of fugitive slaves to Canada. A delegate to the Chicago Republican National Convention of 1860, Grinnell won two terms in Congress (1863–1867). He supported greater efforts to enlist black troops and approved of Abraham Lincoln's (*q.v.*) broad use of war powers, including "political arrests" and detention without trial of opponents of the war.

Grinnell's outspoken manner and his continuing concern for black rights won him the hatred of many Iowa Democrats. He was on good terms with Lincoln, which led him to vote "under protest" for the Wade–Davis Bill. He opposed Andrew Johnson's (*q.v.*) Reconstruction policies and readmission of the Southern states until they gave African Americans the vote. He was defeated for renomination to a third term by the Radical William Loughridge. He supported Horace Greeley (*q.v.*) for President in 1872, contributing further to his waning influence in the party. Grinnell espoused some Greenback principles and advocated a policy of reconciliation with the South. Because of his interest in scientific agriculture, he was elected president of the American Agricultural Association in 1885. He died in Grinnell on March 31, 1891. Grinnell, *Men and Events of Forty Years*; Payne, *Josiah B. Grinnell*.

Hubert H. Wubben

GRISWOLD, John Augustus, *manufacturer, congressman*, was born on November 11, 1818, in Nassau, New York. He attended the common schools, and in the mid-1830s, moved to Troy to live with his uncle, General John E. Wool (*q.v.*). Griswold worked for hardware and manufacturing firms, married the daughter of ironmaster Richard P. Hart, and became a partner in the Rensselaer

Iron Works. He was elected mayor of Troy in 1855, and two years later was president of the Troy City Bank and three railroads.

In the spring of 1861, Griswold helped raise and equip five regiments for Union service; one, the 21st New York, became known as Griswold's Light Cavalry. His major contribution was building monitors for the Union Navy. With C.S. Bushnell and John F. Winslow, Griswold convinced the Navy to consider a novel ironclad designed by John Ericsson, and put up $275,000 to begin construction. Their *Monitor* (while still privately owned) successfully engaged the Confederate *Merrimack* in an epic battle at Hampton Roads, Virginia. Griswold and his partners subsequently constructed six additional monitors, including the famous *Dictator*. In 1862, Griswold won election to the U.S. House of Representatives as a War Democrat and was reelected as a Republican in 1864 and 1866. He also helped introduce the Bessemer process into the United States and in 1865 built a plant in Troy that rolled the first steel railroad rails in the nation.

An energetic, highly successful businessman, John Griswold made a major contribution to the Union war effort by raising troops, risking money on an untried ironclad vessel, and promoting the rise of the steel industry in the nation. He also was active in politics. Unlike many businessmen, who seized on the war to satisfy short-term greed, Griswold offered time and money to support the Union during its lengthy ordeal. He ran unsuccessfully for governor of New York in 1868, and died on October 31, 1872, in Troy, New York. Rezneck, *Profiles out of the Past of Troy, New York.*

Harwood P. Hinton

GROVER, Cuvier, *general,* was born on July 29, 1828, in Bethel, Maine. He graduated from West Point in 1850, was breveted into the artillery, and was assigned to an exploratory expedition for the Northern Pacific Railroad route. It was in the winter of 1854 that Grover first evidenced those qualities of leadership and perseverance that later marked his Civil War career. Defying inclement weather and hostile Indians, he took a four-member team over the Rocky Mountains, thus dispelling many doubts about the feasibility of this route. He became a 1st lieutenant in the 10th Infantry in 1855, and his distinguished service as provost marshal with the Mormon expedition brought him notice throughout Army circles.

The outbreak of the Civil War found Grover on duty at Fort Union, New Mexico. Following a leave of absence, from November 1861 until April 1862, he was appointed a brigadier general of Volunteers and assumed command of the 1st Brigade, 2nd Division, in Samuel Heintzelman's (*q.v.*) III Corps, Army of the Potomac. Grover won brevets for gallant service at Williamsburg and Fair Oaks, but his greatest fame probably derived from the heavy fighting at Second Bull Run. Here, his brigade displayed élan and valor by penetrating Stonewall Jackson's position behind the railroad embankment at Groveton. Grover had thoroughly scouted the position, and he personally led his command forward. The brigade incurred 25 percent casualties in twenty minutes, but gained itself a reputation for hard fighting.

Grover subsequently transferred to the Department of the Gulf, where he commanded the 4th Division of Nathaniel P. Banks's (*q.v.*) XIX Corps during operations in Louisiana. Again his command took heavy casualties, due mostly to Grover's ability to be at the forefront of the battle. He commanded Bank's right wing at Port Hudson, where he displayed customary tenacity (if not much originality) in conduct of siege operations. Returning once more to the East with the XIX Corps, now commanded by William H. Emory (*q.v.*), his conduct at Winchester, Fisher's Hill, and Cedar Creek (where he was wounded) earned him brevet ranks of major general of Volunteers and brigadier general, U.S. Army.

At the end of the war, Grover was in command of the District of Savannah, having earned the brevet of major general in the Regular Army. His postwar career found him commanding the 38th (Black) Infantry and 3rd Cavalry as a lieutenant colonel, superintendent of the General Mounted Recruiting Service, and colonel of the 1st Cavalry. Grover's health, impaired by facial neuralgia contracted at Port Hudson, led him to move to Atlantic City, New Jersey, where he died on June 6, 1885. Hennessy, *Return to Bull Run*; Hewitt, *Port Hudson*.

B. Franklin Cooling

GROW, Galusha Aaron, *congressman, Speaker of the House*, was born on August 31, 1822, in Windham county, Connecticut. He graduated from Amherst College in 1844, studied law, and in 1847 was admitted to the bar in Pennsylvania. Significantly, his first law partner was Congressman David Wilmot (*q.v.*), who just a year earlier had introduced his controversial proviso. When Wilmot's prospects for reelection in 1850 dimmed, Grow became a compromise candidate, personally endorsed by Wilmot and satisfactory to the more conservative Democrats. Grow's election to the 32nd Congress began a career that spanned eleven Congresses between 1851 and 1903. Ironically, he entered the House as the youngest member of the 32nd Congress; he left in 1903 as the oldest member of the 57th.

Initially a Democrat, Grow embraced the Free Soil ideology, and in 1854 participated actively in the formation of the Republican party. He concentrated his early effort on the passage of homestead legislation. Free distribution of public lands, he reasoned, would contribute not only to the settlement of the American frontier but also to the development of the native industries necessary to support such rapid settlement. A homestead bill similar to the one he envisioned finally became law in 1862. Its passage and his election as Speaker of the House in the 37th Congress appeared to place Grow at the zenith of his profession.

Pennsylvania politics offered a different reality, however. The state legislature's realignment of congressional districts presented Grow with a predominantly Democratic constituency, and he lost his bid for reelection to the 38th Congress. During the next thirty years, he maintained his interest in politics, serving as a delegate to the Republican National Convention in 1864, 1884, and 1892. He also engaged in a number of business pursuits, including four years in Texas (1871–1875) as the president of the Houston and Great Northern Railroad. Grow returned to Congress in 1893, when he was elected to fill the unexpired term of Pennsylvania's congressman at large, who had died in office. He was elected to the following four Congresses. Grow retired from politics in 1903, and died on March 31, 1907, in Glenwood, Pennsylvania. Ilisevich, *Galusha Grow.*

Philip J. Avillo, Jr.

GURLEY, John Addison, *congressman,* was born in East Hartford, Connecticut, on December 9, 1813. He was pastor of the Universalist church in Methuen, Massachusetts (1835–1838), then moved to Cincinnati, where he owned and edited the *Star and Sentinel,* later renamed the *Star of the West.* In 1854, he sold the newspaper, retired from preaching, and lived on a farm in Hamilton county, Ohio. Gurley was an unsuccessful Republican candidate for Congress in 1856, but won election in 1858. He favored keeping black labor in the South through the organization of freedmen colonies and openly criticized the Federal government's telegraphic censorship of the press.

In December 1861, Gurley introduced a resolution that called on the House Judiciary Committee to investigate the censorship. His action served as a catalyst that ultimately led to the committee's interviewing various officials, including Assistant Secretary of State Frederick W. Seward (*q.v.*). Gurley lost his bid for reelection in the 1862 Democratic sweep. For a brief period in 1861, he had served as a colonel, and was an aide-de-camp to General John C. Frémont (*q.v.*) in St. Louis. He accepted President Abraham Lincoln's (*q.v.*) appointment as governor of the Arizona Territory, but died in Green Township, near Cincinnati, on August 19, 1863, before he took office. Bogue, *Congressman's Civil War.*

Thomas H. Smith

GUROWSKI, Adam, *publicist,* was born near Kalisz, Poland, on September 10, 1805. Russian authorities, then in control of Poland, expelled him from schools because of his expressions of Polish nationalism. For the next several years he studied in Germany, plotted against Russian authority, and was sentenced to death in absentia. In 1834, Gurowski turned to Pan-Slavism, and advocated Russia as the unifying nation for all Slavic peoples. Czar Nicholas pardoned him, but Gurowski fled Russia in 1844 and in 1849 came to the United States. He wanted to teach at Harvard University but failed to impress its faculty. In New York City, he found employment on the editorial staff of Horace Greeley's (*q.v.*) *New York Tribune.* His articles and pamphlets supported Russia in the Crimean War. He also denounced slavery and in 1860 published *Slavery in History.*

The sectional crisis brought Gurowski to Washington, D.C., in early 1861, and he at once became a leading Radical Republican propagandist. His efforts took the form of his published *Diary*, counsel with government officials through interviews and letters, and frequent conversations with Radical Republican friends. After working in the State Department for nearly two years as a translator and adviser to Secretary of State William H. Seward (*q.v.*), Gurowski published the first volume of his *Diary*. He expressed disgust at Seward's policies, caustically criticized President Abraham Lincoln's (*q.v.*) actions, and praised Secretary of War Edwin M. Stanton (*q.v.*). Seward then dismissed Gurowski, and through an employee sued him for libel; a Radical Republican judge dismissed the case for lack of evidence that Gurowski had written the *Diary*.

Gurowski's admitted purpose in publishing the *Diary* was to warn the American people of the flaws and schemes of government officials. The second and third volumes treated Seward severely and urged Lincoln to lead the nation vigorously instead of prolonging the war by slow and wavering policies. Gurowski promoted the raising of African American troops, petitioned the Secretary of War for the colonelcy of a black regiment, and recommended a special book of tactics for their use. He praised Stanton as the savior of the Union and heavy-handedly criticized Lincoln's leading generals, although Ulysses S. Grant (*q.v.*) won his enthusiastic commendation.

Gurowski was the only man Lincoln feared as a possible assassin. Many contemporaries considered him a crank, a splenetic eccentric to be ignored with a smile if not with disgust. But to many Radical Republicans his beliefs were those of a sage, for in their hopes he found a sacred calling, and by the end of the war his severe judgments undoubtedly assisted the Radical Republicans in prevailing in the South and nationwide. Gurowski died on May 4, 1866, in Washington, D.C. Fischer, *Lincoln's Gadfly*.

LeRoy H. Fischer

H

HACKLEMAN, Pleasant Adam, *general*, was born on November 15, 1814, in Franklin county, Indiana. As a prominent attorney in Rush county, he was active in local politics and held several county offices. He served a single term in the Indiana House of Representatives (1841–1842), and twice ran unsuccessfully for a seat in the U.S. Congress, as a Whig in 1847 and as a Republican in 1857. He was a delegate to the 1860 Republican National Convention and a commissioner to the Washington Peace Convention in February 1861.

On May 20, 1861, Hackleman was appointed colonel of the 16th Indiana, and in July was assigned to Colonel John J. Abercrombie's brigade in the Department of the Shenandoah. The regiment earned a commendation for "steadiness and coolness" at Edward's Ferry, Virginia, following the Union debacle at Ball's Bluff. Hackleman was promoted to brigadier general on April 28, 1862, and in June was assigned to command the 1st Brigade of General Thomas A. Davies's (*q.v.*) 2nd Division, Army of West Tennessee. He was mortally wounded on October 3, 1862, while rallying Union troops during the Confederate assault on Corinth, Mississippi, and died that evening in Corinth. Hackleman died before he had a chance to prove himself as a field commander, but his performance at Corinth showed promise. Generals Davies, William S. Rosecrans (*q.v.*), and Ulysses S. Grant (*q.v.*) praised his bravery, and President Abraham Lincoln (*q.v.*) telegraphed regret at the news of Hackleman's death. Grant, *Papers*, vol. 6; Williams, *Lincoln Finds a General*, vol. 4.

Bruce J. Dinges

HAHN, Georg Michael Decker, *congressman, editor, governor*, was born in Klingenmunster, Bavaria, on November 24, 1830. After emigrating to New

York, Hahn's widowed mother settled in New Orleans about 1840. Hahn graduated from the New Orleans city high school, and received a law degree from the University of Louisiana (now Tulane) in 1851. In addition to serving as president of the New Orleans school board, he joined the Democratic party and became active in Louisiana politics. An outspoken critic of slavery, he opposed the Slidell wing of the party in the state and supported Stephen A. Douglas's (*q.v.*) bid for the presidency in 1860. Hahn actively opposed secession and openly refused to support the Confederacy.

After New Orleans fell to the Federals in 1862, Hahn expressed his loyalty to the U.S. government. The Louisiana congressional elections of December 1862, in which he was chosen 1st District representative, provided the first significant test of Abraham Lincoln's (*q.v.*) Reconstruction policy. The admission of Hahn and fellow Representative Benjamin F. Flanders (*q.v.*) in the face of strong opposition in the House was a major victory for the President. Hahn was prevented from actually serving by the expiration of the congressional term on March 3, 1863. Appointed prize commissioner at New Orleans in 1863, he purchased the *New Orleans Daily True Delta* in 1864. He was elected governor on February 22, 1864, and actively supported Lincoln's Reconstruction policy in the state.

Following his election to the U.S. Senate, Hahn resigned as governor on March 4, 1865. His opposition to President Andrew Johnson's (*q.v.*) Reconstruction policy prompted him to decline his senatorial seat and return to Louisiana. Hahn was seriously wounded during a New Orleans riot in 1866. In 1867, he started the *New Orleans Republican*, which he operated until 1871. After a brief retirement, he became publisher of the *St. Charles* (Louisiana) *Herald.* He was elected to a term in the state legislature (1872–1876), then served as judge of the 26th District (1879–1885). Hahn was a member of the 49th Congress from March 4, 1885, until his death in Washington, D.C., on March 5, 1886. *BDGUS*, vol. 2.

                                                                    James M. Prichard

HAIGHT, Edward, *congressman,* was born on March 26, 1817, in New York City. Though he had only a limited common school education, Haight achieved financial success first in wholesale dry goods and later in banking and investment. In 1850, he moved to Westchester county and continued to prosper as a director of the National Bank of New York. In 1856, he founded the Bank of the Commonwealth of New York City and remained its president through 1870.

In 1860, Haight was elected to the House of Representatives as a Democrat. Consistent with his financial knowledge, he was appointed to the Committee on Manufactures, where he favored the higher tariffs advocated by the Republicans. Indeed, though elected as a Democrat, Haight supported most of Abraham Lincoln's (*q.v.*) policies, becoming one of only two Democrats in the 37th Congress to endorse the Emancipation Proclamation. In 1862, he ran for reelection on the Republican–Union ticket, which attempted to combine War Democrats and moderate Republicans in a united front. However, the regular New York Democratic party closed its factional ranks to defeat him. Haight returned to investment banking and expanded into insurance while continuing to serve as director of several corporations. He died in Westchester county on September 15, 1885. Curry, *Blueprint for Modern America.*

James C. Mohr

HALE, James Tracy, *congressman,* was born on October 14, 1810, in Towanda, Pennsylvania. He attended the public schools, was admitted to the bar, and began his practice in Bellefonte, Pennsylvania. In 1851, he was appointed president judge of the 20th Judicial District. In 1858, as a Republican, he was elected to the House of Representatives. He was reelected in 1860, and as an Independent Unionist in 1862. During the secession crisis, Hale consistently voted for the various compromise measures and served on a committee that attempted to resolve the controversy. As a strict-constructionist during the war, he opposed confiscation, conscription, and the Wade–Davis Bill. He was absent from the House during the last months of the war, and died in Bellefonte on April 6, 1865. *BDUSC.*

J. K. Folmar

HALE, John Parker, *senator,* was born in Rochester, New Hampshire, on March 31, 1806. After graduation from Bowdoin (1827), Hale moved to Dover, New Hampshire, where in 1830 he was admitted to the bar. In 1832, he won election to the state legislature as a Democrat. Defeated for reelection, he accepted an appointment in 1834 as U.S. district attorney for New Hampshire. He steadily enlarged his influence among New Hampshire Democrats, who in 1843 secured his election to the U.S. House of Representatives.

On most issues, Hale took an orthodox Democratic position, but his growing antislavery convictions prompted him to vote against both the ''gag'' rule on abolitionist petitions and the admission of Texas as a slave state. When, in 1845, New Hampshire Democrats, led by Franklin Pierce, responded to Hale's ''insubordination'' by dropping him from the ticket, a group of self-styled Independent Democrats took up his candidacy. In 1846, with open support from the Liberty party and covert aid from New Hampshire Whigs, the Independent Democrats elected Hale to the state legislature (where he became speaker) and then to the U.S. Senate. His prominence in antislavery circles reached a peak in 1847, when Hale received the Liberty party's nomination for President. In 1848, he relinquished that nomination and backed Martin Van Buren.

In the Senate, Hale condemned the Mexican War, championed the Wilmot Proviso, proposed abolition of slavery in the District of Columbia, and attacked Henry Clay's compromise in 1850. He led the fight to outlaw flogging in the Navy. In 1852, he ran for President as a Free Democrat; his bid for reelection to the Senate having failed, he returned to private life. The political realignment of parties that followed the Kansas–Nebraska Act restored his political fortunes, however, and in 1855 New Hampshire Republicans returned Hale to the U.S. Senate. After filling a four-year vacancy, he was reelected to a full term in 1858. Now overshadowed by such Radicals as Charles Sumner (*q.v.*), Benjamin Wade (*q.v.*), and Zachariah Chandler (*q.v.*), Hale continued to attack the "Slave Power," condemning the "plot" to make Kansas a slave state, opposing Southern designs on Cuba, and denouncing proposals for compromise during the secession crisis.

Throughout most of the Civil War, Hale served as chairman of the Senate Naval Affairs Committee, engaging in a running feud with Secretary of the Navy Gideon Welles (*q.v.*), whom Hale accused of nepotism, extravagance, and general mismanagement of the Navy Department. This bootless vendetta served not only to diminish Hale's influence within the Senate and within his own committee but also to prevent him from giving more than fitful attention to the completion of the antislavery crusade. He did, however, support various measures that led to the 13th Amendment and endorsed Reconstruction policies proposed by his Radical colleagues. His letters and speeches during these years reveal a genuine concern for the welfare of African Americans and a skepticism about the supposedly innate inferiority of that race, which placed him well in advance of most contemporaries, including fellow Republicans.

Rebuffed in his quest for reelection (partly because of an unproven charge that he had peddled his influence as a senator), Hale gratefully accepted from President Abraham Lincoln (*q.v.*) an appointment as U.S. minister to Spain. His years in Madrid were largely uneventful, save for a quarrel with his secretary of legation, who accused Hale of having abused his privilege of importing goods free of duty. Replaced by Daniel Sickles (*q.v.*) in 1869, Hale returned to his home in Dover, New Hampshire.

The high point of Hale's career came during political abolitionism's formative years. Yet, as the antislavery movement grew stronger, his role in it weakened. The very qualities that made him so admirable a minority spokesman—especially his partisanship and distrust of compromise—ultimately kept him from offering constructive leadership once the Republicans came to power. Well before the war against slavery had been won, therefore, Hale found himself shouldered aside by more malleable, politically ambitious men. He died in Dover on November 19, 1873. Sewell, *John P. Hale.*

Richard H. Sewell

HALL, Willard Preble, *governor*, was born in Harper's Ferry, Virginia, on May 9, 1820, the brother of William Augustus Hall (*q.v.*). He graduated from Yale College in 1839, and in 1840 accompanied his family to Randolph county, Missouri, where he studied law and was admitted to the bar. He was appointed circuit attorney, became active in the Democratic party, and served as a presidential elector in 1844. Although a candidate for Congress, Hall enlisted as a private in the Missouri Volunteers in 1846 and accompanied them to Santa Fe. There he worked with Colonel Alexander W. Doniphan to draft the basic legal code that would serve New Mexico for the next decade. Hall served three terms in Congress (1846–1852), then retired to his law practice in St. Joseph. He played a prominent role in the deliberations of the state convention that decided against secession in March 1861.

When the convention established the Provisional Government in July to replace the Claiborne Jackson regime, which had gone over to the Confederacy, Hall was chosen lieutenant governor. He worked closely with Governor Hamilton R. Gamble (*q.v.*) and exercised the full powers of the office when Gamble was absent. He also had a major voice in both militia and administrative appointments. When Gamble died in January 1864, Hall succeeded to the governorship and served until a regularly elected government took office the following year. He closely coordinated state militia with Federal troops to resist the Sterling Price raid in the fall of 1864. He led a conservative delegation to the Republican National Convention that year, but they were turned aside for rival Radical claimants. Following his retirement from office, Hall resumed his law practice in St. Joseph. He died there on November 2, 1882. Parrish, *Turbulent Partnership*.

William E. Parrish

HALL, William Augustus, *congressman*, was born in Portland, Maine, on October 15, 1815. He was the brother of Willard Preble Hall (*q.v.*). He attended Yale College and accompanied his family to Randolph county, Missouri, in 1840. After studying law, he was admitted to the bar in 1841, and established a practice at Fayette. Hall became active in the Democratic party, served as a presidential elector in 1844, and was a captain with the Missouri Volunteers during the Mexican War. He was a circuit judge (1847–1861), and was elected as a Union delegate to the state convention that decided against secession in March 1861.

At the July 1861 session of the convention, Hall served on the committee that recommended the establishment of the Provisional Government. He declined appointment to the U.S. Senate in January 1862, having already been elected to the House of Representatives to fill the vacancy caused by the expulsion of John B. Clark. He was reelected to a full term that fall. Hall took a strong conservative position, especially with regard to President Abraham Lincoln's (*q.v.*) plan for compensated emancipation in the border states, which he saw as unwarranted Federal interference and an unnecessary burden on the taxpayer. By July 1863, however, he had changed his mind and was a member of the state convention committee that reported the gradual emancipation proposal adopted at that time. Hall did not stand for reelection in 1864, but was a delegate to the Democratic National Convention that year. After the war he was active in party affairs while practicing law and farming. He died at his farm near Darkville, Missouri, on December 15, 1888. Parrish, *Turbulent Partnership*.

William E. Parrish

HALLECK, Henry Wager, *general,* was born on January 16, 1815, in Westernville, New York. He attended Union College and the U.S. Military Academy, from which he graduated in 1839, third in his class, and where he remained as an assistant professor. In 1846, he published *Elements of Military Art and Science,* an influential treatise based on French scholarship. Sent to California during the Mexican War, Halleck arrived after its conquest and in time to participate in its fortification and administration, two areas in which he excelled. On August 1, 1854, he resigned as captain to practice law full-time and to complete a treatise titled *International Law* (1861).

Halleck's substantial reputation in the Old Army led to his appointment as major general, August 19, 1861, and early assignment to command the Department of the Missouri, left in disorder by his predecessor, John C. Frémont (*q.v.*). From headquarters in St. Louis, he eliminated fraud and disorder, then rested contentedly. Reluctantly, he permitted Ulysses S. Grant (*q.v.*) to attack Fort Henry, and never gave formal permission for the expedition to Fort Donelson, although he later claimed credit for it, as he did for Samuel R. Curtis's (*q.v.*) victory at Pea Ridge and that of John Pope (*q.v.*) at Island No. 10. Halleck's command was enlarged to the Department of the Mississippi, encompassing all the territory between the Allegheny and Rocky Mountains. After the battle of Shiloh, he took command in the field for the first and last time. Reorganizing and drilling his troops, while insisting on entrenchments and fortifications at every point, he slowly moved against the railroad center of Corinth, Mississippi, which fell without a battle on May 30.

One month later, Halleck went to Washington as general in chief, a post effectively occupied for months by President Abraham Lincoln (*q.v.*) after the demotion of George B. McClellan (*q.v.*). Halleck operated as an administrator, not a strategist; Lincoln and Secretary of War Edwin M. Stanton (*q.v.*) continued as war managers until Grant's appointment as lieutenant general in March 1864. As superior officer, Grant automatically superseded Halleck, whom he left in his Washington office as chief of staff to continue his administrative work. At the close of the war, Grant sent Halleck to Richmond to supervise the restoration of Virginia, but after he quarreled with William T. Sherman (*q.v.*), he was transferred to the Division of the Pacific, where he sat out the tumult of Reconstruction.

How could a man regarded as expert on matters military, a man who declined an appointment as professor of engineering at the Lawrence Scientific School of Harvard University (1848), have come to be a figure ridiculed by most Civil War scholars? As military administrator, Halleck sought to claim credit for victories won by his subordinates while evading responsibility for their failures. He feared field service, avoided it, and bungled his one Civil War campaign. When Confederate Jubal A. Early approached the defenses of Washington in July 1864, Halleck's panic burdened the defense. Above all, this consummate bureaucrat lacked all trace of moral courage. By war's end, officials in Washington joined commanding generals in viewing Halleck with contempt. In July

1869 he took command of the Division of the South in Louisville, Kentucky, where he remained until his death on January 9, 1872. Ambrose, *Halleck*; Catton, *Grant Takes Command*; Williams, *Lincoln and his Generals;* Williams, *Lincoln Finds a General*, vols. 2, 3.

John Y. Simon

HALLOCK, Gerard, *editor*, was born on March 18, 1800, in Plainfield, Massachusetts. He graduated from Williams College in 1819, and attended Andover Seminary. Hallock operated a private school in Salem, Massachusetts, then edited religious newspapers in Boston and New York City. In 1828, he became editor and part owner of the *New York Journal of Commerce*; with the death of his partner in 1849, he assumed full control. Vigorous and innovative in news-gathering techniques, he made his paper a financial success and served as head of cooperative news-gathering organizations.

Hallock consistently sought to conciliate the South by attacking Northern opponents of slavery. Although his views reflected New York business opinion, they also derived from his religious attitudes. A strict observer of religious forms and conventions, Hallock denounced abolitionists as a disruptive minority in Congregational churches, and at one time threatened to withhold his sizable contributions if their doctrines were allowed to hold sway. He defended the Fugitive Slave Act and the repeal of the Missouri Compromise, and urged New York Democrats to declare their willingness to admit new slave states. In 1856, he called upon all Democrats to unite to crush Republican sectionalism.

During the winter of 1860–1861, Hallock declared that secession was unconstitutional, but feared that reunion could be achieved only by drenching the nation in blood and extinguishing constitutional liberty. Unwilling to pay such a price, he charged the war to Republican intransigence and advocated a treaty between North and South to accomplish peaceable secession. In August 1861, a Federal grand jury denounced his paper for sympathizing with the Confederacy, and the Postmaster General excluded it from the mails. Declaring he did not want others associated with the paper to suffer for his opinions, Hallock retired from journalism.

If Hallock had remained with the *Journal of Commerce*, he would probably have become one of the Civil War's outstanding Peace Democrats. As it was, his decision to retire left it to others to pursue the causes of negotiation with the Confederacy and the rights of a free press. His acceptance of peaceable secession, however, revealed at an early stage the logical consequences of the Peace Democrats' policies. Hallock died in New Haven, Connecticut, on January 4, 1866. Hallock, *Life of Gerard Hallock.*

George McJimsey

HALPINE, Charles Graham, *satirist*, was born on November 20, 1829, near Oldcastle, County Meath, Ireland. Christened Charles Boyton Halpin by his father, a parish priest in the Church of Ireland (Episcopal), he added the "e" to his name (radically changing its pronunciation) and took the middle name Graham at the time of his emigration to America in 1850. Although a Protestant throughout his life, Halpine was an ardent Irish nationalist. Through his writings and the solid support of the New York Irish, he acquired influence and political power.

Among the first to respond to Abraham Lincoln's (*q.v.*) April 15, 1861, call to arms, Halpine served for three months with New York's famous 69th Regiment of Irish Volunteers. Late in the summer of 1861, he became an officer on the staff of General David Hunter (*q.v.*) and participated in some of the notable events of the war. He helped compile the bill of particulars against John C. Frémont (*q.v.*), which resulted in that officer's removal from command in Missouri in 1861; he accepted the surrender of Fort Pulaski, Georgia, in 1862; he witnessed and later publicly defended the attack of the monitors on Fort Sumter in 1863; he was involved in Hunter's pioneering experiment with African American soldiers at Port Royal, South Carolina; and he was at the general's side during the 1864 expedition up the Shenandoah Valley and during the disastrous retreat through the mountains of West Virginia.

Following the July 1863 riots in New York, Halpine served temporarily on the staff of John A. Dix (*q.v.*), commander of the Department of the East, and made an important contribution to the Union victory. His assignment was to cultivate support for the war among the Irish, so many of whom had just demonstrated their opposition to it. He accomplished his objective through a series of humorous stories about a mythical Private Miles O'Reilly, who got into scrapes with the military brass, and even with the Secretary of War and the President, by artlessly practicing the democratic egalitarianism he heard so much talk about. A lovable and popular character in the North, O'Reilly helped to improve the image of the Irish among the native born. At the time of his sudden death on August 1, 1868, in New York City, Halpine's political future seemed bright; he was serving as the registrar of New York county, the most remunerative elective office in the United States. Hanchett, *Irish.*

William Hanchett

HALSTEAD, Murat, *editor*, was born on September 2, 1829, in Butler county, Ohio, near Cincinnati. Although he had planned to enter law practice, he wrote articles for several Cincinnati newspapers while attending Farmers' College, and decided to make journalism his career. In the early 1850s, he became a reporter for the *Cincinnati Daily Commercial*. Within a few years he was news editor, and by 1865 was its editor and publisher. Halstead covered the 1856 Republican National Convention and the John Brown hanging. By 1860, his reporting had brought him a regional reputation, and after his coverage of the nominating conventions that year, he became well known nationally.

Initially independent in politics, Halstead moved into the liberal wing of the Republican party. During the Civil War, he was a staunch supporter of Abraham Lincoln (*q.v.*), a position that put him in direct opposition to the Democratic

Cincinnati Enquirer. Halstead's paper achieved a national reputation for both its excellent editorial page and its strong war reporting. The *Commercial* was so supportive of the war that it became known as the "soldiers' paper," because of its popularity among Northern troops. Its support of Lincoln and the war was important not only in Cincinnati but also in nearby northern Kentucky and southern Indiana.

Halstead probably is best known for his part in the 1872 presidential campaign, when he and other liberal Republicans bolted the regular party, held their own convention, and nominated Horace Greeley (*q.v.*). Halstead continued as editor of the *Commercial* until 1890, when he took over the *Brooklyn Standard-Union.* That association lasted only a short time, however, and he completed his career writing dozens of books about the Spanish–American War, famous politicians, and America's foreign policy. Halstead died in Cincinnati on July 2, 1908. Curl, *Murat Halstead*; Halstead, *Three Against Lincoln.*

Fredric F. Endres

HAMILTON, Charles Smith, *general,* was born on November 16, 1822, in Westernville, New York. He graduated from West Point in 1843, a classmate of Ulysses S. Grant (*q.v.*). As a 2nd lieutenant, 5th Infantry, in the Mexican War, Hamilton served under both Zachary Taylor and Winfield Scott (*q.v.*), was severely wounded at Molino del Rey, and received promotion to brevet captain. He resigned from the Army in 1853, and entered business in Fond du Lac, Wisconsin. Hamilton organized the 3rd Wisconsin Volunteers and soon received appointment as brigadier general, backdated to May 17, 1861.

Serving in the Army of the Potomac as division commander, Hamilton was labeled unfit by George B. McClellan (*q.v.*), and transferred to the command of William S. Rosecrans (*q.v.*). He performed creditably in the battles of Iuka and Corinth, and won Grant's recommendation for promotion to major general. Yet, Grant was lukewarm; he called Hamilton competent and pointed out that Wisconsin had no major general. By the time the Senate confirmed Hamilton, he had plotted to displace James B. McPherson (*q.v.*) and had quarreled bitterly and unnecessarily with Stephen A. Hurlbut (*q.v.*), both of whom held corps command.

Thwarted in seeking advancement, Hamilton resigned as of April 13, 1863, in the midst of the Vicksburg campaign. His marginal capacity as soldier was overmatched by his quarrelsome spirit, fever for higher command, and nasty temper. In a private letter to a Wisconsin senator, Hamilton denounced Grant as a drunkard. Unaware of this duplicity, Grant nonetheless accepted Hamilton's resignation with relief, and the Army of the Tennessee suffered no great loss. In 1869, President Grant appointed Hamilton U.S. marshal. He also served on the board of regents of the University of Wisconsin and was active in veterans' groups. Hamilton died in Milwaukee on April 17, 1891. Catton, *Grant Moves South*; Lamers, *Edge of Glory.*

John Y. Simon

HAMILTON, Schuyler, *general,* was born on July 25, 1822, in New York City, a grandson of Alexander Hamilton and great-grandson of Philip Schuyler. He graduated from West Point in 1841, served in the infantry in the Midwest, and was an instructor at West Point before the Mexican War. Hamilton was breveted 1st lieutenant and captain for gallantry in Mexico, and was severely wounded twice. From 1847 to 1854, he served as an aide-de-camp to General Winfield Scott (*q.v.*), and resigned from the Army in 1855. He resided in California and Connecticut, and at the start of the Civil War enlisted as a private in the 7th New York Infantry. Shortly thereafter, he was made acting aide to General Benjamin F. Butler (*q.v.*), and then became military secretary to General in Chief Winfield Scott, with the rank of lieutenant colonel.

After Scott's retirement, Hamilton was assistant chief of staff to General Henry Wager Halleck (*q.v.*), his brother-in-law. He was made a brigadier general, dating from November 12, 1861, and skillfully commanded a division in the New Madrid and Island No. 10 campaign of 1862. He led the left wing of the Army of the Mississippi in the advance on Corinth, but became ill from malaria and went on sick leave. Hamilton had been appointed a major general to date from September 17, 1862, but was not confirmed. He resigned from the Army early in 1863, because no officer unfit for service could be named to the Senate for confirmation. For years he tried, without success, to have his name placed on the retired list.

Hamilton was an officer who showed promise. His service as a staff officer seemed to give him experience for field operations. He was said to have suggested the successful canal-digging operation at Island No. 10. After the war, ill health prevented his steady employment, but he was at one time hydrographic engineer for the docks in New York City, where he died on March 8, 1903. Williams, *Lincoln Finds a General,* vol. 3.

E. B. Long

HAMLIN, Hannibal, *Vice President,* was born in Paris Hill, Maine, on August 27, 1809. He attended local schools and spent a year at Hebron Academy. He ran the family farm, briefly edited the Jacksonian Democratic *Oxford Jeffersonian,* read law on his own, and studied for a time in the prestigious Portland law firm of Samuel Fessenden. In 1835, Hamlin won a seat in the Maine House of Representatives, serving a total of six terms (the last one in 1847), with three terms as speaker. He moved on to the U.S. House of Representatives for two terms (1843–1847). In Augusta and Washington, Hamlin spoke out against the expansion of slavery, and he coauthored the Wilmot Proviso. As a congressman and U.S. senator (1848–1861), Hamlin played an important role in alerting Maine citizens to the danger of slavery expansion and made bitter enemies of the proslavery faction of the Maine Democracy.

In 1850, Hamlin championed California's admission, but resisted the notion that a comprehensive compromise of North–South differences was needed. The Fugitive Slave Act appalled him, and popular sovereignty seemed to him an unacceptable alternative to congressional exclusion of slavery from the territories. Hamlin fought the passage of the Kansas–Nebraska Act, although in other areas he loyally supported President Franklin Pierce. In June 1856 he left the Democratic party, and joyful Maine Republicans drafted him for governor. He won a thunderous victory, burying his Democratic opponent by more than 25,000 votes. By prearrangement, the legislature made Hamlin a senator a month after he assumed the governorship.

In 1860, the Republican National Convention nominated Hamlin for Vice President. During the Civil War, he chafed at the restrictions and powerlessness of the purely ceremonial "second office" of the land. Previously a skilled dispenser of patronage, he lamented that as Vice President he could do "little for my friends." At Abraham Lincoln's (*q.v.*) request, he did choose the New England member of the Cabinet, but Hamlin and that choice, Navy Secretary Gideon Welles (*q.v.*), became bitter enemies during the war. A Radical Republican, he longed for greater influence with Lincoln in such areas as emancipation and military policy. Hamlin wanted a second term, if only as recognition of his fidelity to nation and party, but Lincoln had other plans. He engineered the vice presidential nomination of Andrew Johnson (*q.v.*) of Tennessee, believing that this Southern War Democrat would have far greater voter appeal than Hamlin.

The Vice President hid his disappointment well, and spent the summer of 1864 serving as a cook in the Maine Coast Guard. In 1865, Hamlin failed to defeat William Pitt Fessenden (*q.v.*) for the U.S. Senate, but received the Boston collectorship from President Johnson as a consolation prize. He broke with Johnson over Reconstruction policy the following year and resigned. In 1869, he won a narrow victory over Lot M. Morrill (*q.v.*), and served twelve more years in the Senate, loyally supporting President Ulysses S. Grant (*q.v.*) and feuding bitterly with President Rutherford B. Hayes (*q.v.*). In 1877, Hamlin became chairman of the Foreign Relations Committee, and in 1881, his old Maine comrade-in-arms, Secretary of State James G. Blaine (*q.v.*), obtained his appointment as U.S. minister to Spain. He died on July 4, 1891, in Bangor, Maine, where he had lived since 1862. Hunt, *Hannibal Hamlin.*

H. Draper Hunt

HAMMOND, William Alexander, *Surgeon General,* was born in Annapolis, Maryland, on August 28, 1828. He graduated from the University of the City of New York in 1848, and took further medical training at the Pennsylvania Hospital in Philadelphia. He joined the Army Medical Corps as an assistant surgeon in 1850, and for the next ten years served in various frontier posts in the West and South and at West Point. He resigned in 1859 to become a professor of anatomy and physiology at the University of Maryland in Baltimore. As a staff physician at the medical school, he treated wounded soldiers of the 6th Massachusetts following the attack by a secessionist mob as the regiment passed through the city.

In May 1861, Hammond rejoined the Regular Army as an assistant surgeon.

He was placed in the lowest rank because his resignation had cost him his seniority, but through influential friends he became Surgeon General with the rank of brigadier general. The irregularities of Hammond's advancement, however, angered Secretary of War Edwin M. Stanton (*q.v.*). Hammond immediately began to revolutionize medical treatment in the Union Army. Although the Civil War took place in a primordial medical age, Hammond represented the best that the medical arts and sciences had to offer. Despite the obvious failures to prevent death from diseases and infections, by 1865 Northern soldiers were the best cared for in the history of warfare. Improvements in the selection of medical officers, the design of hospitals, the distribution of medical supplies, and the elimination of bureaucratic "bloody red tape," among other achievements, marked Hammond's intelligent, humane, and progressive administration. It is estimated that improved treatment of the wounded alone saved approximately 25,000 lives.

Despite these remarkable successes, Hammond was court martialed and dismissed from the Army on August 18, 1864. It was a disgraceful affair, based apparently on minor, trumped-up charges having more to do with personalities than with performance, and brought on by the abrasive natures of Hammond and Stanton. But Hammond's reputation did not really suffer. Soon he was practicing medicine, lecturing, teaching, publishing, and conducting research in the field of nervous and mental diseases. His legacy includes the multivolume *Medical and Surgical History of the War of the Rebellion*, which he began during his tenure as Surgeon General. In 1888, Congress authorized his restoration to the Army's retired list, and he officially ended his career as a brigadier general. Hammond died on January 5, 1900, in Washington, D.C. Freemon, "Lincoln Finds a Surgeon General," *Civil War History*; Key, *William Alexander Hammond*.

Frank J. Wetta

HANCHETT, Luther, *congressman,* was born on October 25, 1825, in Middlebury, Ohio. He attended common schools, studied law, and was admitted to the bar in 1846. He commenced his legal career in Fremont, Ohio, and in 1849 moved to Portage county, Wisconsin, settling in the little town of Plover. Hanchett became involved in lumbering and mining activities, and interested in local politics. He was elected district attorney of Portage county in 1852, became an early member of the Republican party, and was elected to the state Senate in 1856 and 1858. In 1860, he was elected to Congress and reelected in 1862. He died in Plover on November 24, 1862. *Columbian Biographical Dictionary . . . Wisconsin Volume; Dictionary of Wisconsin Biography.*

Charles E. Twining

HANCOCK, Winfield Scott, *general,* was born on February 14, 1824, in Montgomery Square, Pennsylvania. He attended Morristown Academy, and graduated from West Point in 1844. Hancock won two brevets in the Mexican War, then served in Florida, Kansas, Utah, and on the Pacific Coast. Dashing and handsome, he was imposing in appearance and possessed a commanding presence. Shortly after the Civil War began, Hancock was named brigadier general of Volunteers. At the battle of Williamsburg, May 5, 1862, his brigade captured several Confederate redoubts, and he led it ably in the Seven Days' battles, at South Mountain, and at Antietam.

Promoted to major general, Hancock commanded a division with skill at Fredericksburg and Chancellorsville. His greatest achievements came in 1863 as a corps and wing commander at Gettysburg, where he selected the battlefield, supported the Union left wing on the second day of the engagement, and repulsed George Pickett's charge on the third day, when he was wounded severely in the groin. After capable service under George G. Meade (*q.v.*) and Ulysses S. Grant (*q.v.*) in the 1864 Overland campaign, Hancock was obliged, by his Gettysburg wound, to return to Washington, D.C., on less active duty. According to George B. McClellan (*q.v.*), who dubbed him "The Superb," Grant, and others, Hancock was one of the very ablest corps commanders on either side in the Civil War, and his masterful performance at Gettysburg was pivotal in helping to win that crucial victory for the Federals.

After Appomattox, Hancock took the field again, this time in the West against the Indians, and was a department commander. He ran unsuccessfully as the Democratic candidate for President in 1880, against James A. Garfield (*q.v.*). He died on February 7, 1886, at Governor's Island, New York. Jordon, *Winfield Scott Hancock*; Rhea, *Battle of the Wilderness*; Tucker, *Hancock the Superb*.

Warren W. Hassler, Jr.

HARDING, Aaron, *congressman,* was born in Taylor (later Green) county, Kentucky, on February 23, 1805. Although his formal education was limited to local schools, he embarked upon a rigorous course of self-education and learned shorthand to assist his note taking. He taught school while reading law, and established a successful practice at Greensburg in 1833. Harding called himself "an Old Whig" who remained loyal to the party's principles after it dissolved. After serving as Green county attorney in 1837–1839, he was elected to the state House of Representatives in 1840. For the next twenty years he devoted himself to the law, until the secession crisis brought him back into politics.

A determined opponent of secession, Harding condemned extremists in both sections, and it was as a moderate Union Democrat that he won election to the U.S. House of Representatives in 1861, 1863, and 1865. Although he supported the war measures he considered necessary, he opposed the 13th Amendment as an invasion of states' rights, and he was critical of Abraham Lincoln's (*q.v.*) administration for what he saw as an unwarranted interference in Kentucky affairs. While Harding earned an enviable reputation as a lawyer and a man, he did not achieve much success as a congressman. When he failed to secure election as U.S. senator in 1867, Harding moved to Danville, Kentucky, and resumed his legal practice. Never in robust health, he died in Georgetown, Kentucky, on December 24, 1875. Coulter, *Civil War and Readjustment in Kentucky*; Perrin, *Kentucky. A History of the State.*

Lowell H. Harrison

HARDING, Benjamin Franklin, *senator*, was born on January 4, 1823, in Wyoming county, Pennsylvania. He attended public schools and became a lawyer in Illinois. In 1849 he joined the gold rush in California, and in 1850 he moved to Oregon. He abandoned his Whig affiliations because he realized that his political ambitions could more easily be attained in the powerful Democratic party. He was a territorial legislator, U.S. district attorney, secretary of the territory, and speaker of the state House of Representatives. In September 1861 the War Department, upon the recommendation of Senator Edward Baker (*q.v.*), chose Harding to help raise a Volunteer cavalry regiment. Harding resigned a few months later because he wanted a political, not a military, career.

In 1860, as a Douglas Democrat, Harding had helped to form a fusion of his political faction and Republicans that led to the election of Douglas Democrat James Nesmith (*q.v.*) and Republican Baker to the U.S. Senate. His efforts helped secure his election in 1862 to fill the remaining portion of Baker's Senate term; thus he served from September 1862 until March 1865. He was not a candidate for reelection, and he did not win another important state office.

Harding's political success was in large part the result of his participation in a political faction, the "Salem Clique." He played a limited role in the U.S. Senate, but he supported Lincoln and his war measures. When he sought to improve relations with his Democratic opponents, some of whom were Copperheads, Unionists denounced him for his political shift and for his opposition to enlisting soldiers by means of a state bounty. Harding was unable to attract Democratic party support, and his political star burned out. He died in Cottage Grove, Oregon, on June 16, 1899. Hendrickson, *Joe Lane*; Johannsen, *Frontier Politics.*

G. Thomas Edwards

HARKER, Charles Garrison, *general*, was born December 2, 1835, in Swedesboro, New Jersey. He graduated from West Point in 1858, was commissioned in the infantry, and was sent to duty on the frontier. At the beginning of the Civil War, Harker was assigned to drill Ohio troops, and in November 1861 he was named colonel of the 65th Ohio Volunteers. He served with the Army of the Ohio and the Army of the Cumberland, often commanding a brigade. Harker fought at Shiloh, the siege of Corinth, Perryville, Murfreesboro (where he won praise and a recommendation for promotion), and Chickamauga. In April 1864 Harker was made a brigadier general of Volunteers with his date of rank set at September 20, 1863—the second day at Chickamauga, when he and his brigade had played a crucial role in holding the Union position when it appeared that the Confederates would sweep all before them.

In November 1863, Harker's brigade, then a part of the IV Corps, was in the fighting around Chattanooga. He also led the brigade in the Atlanta campaign. He bore a conspicuous part in the fighting along Rocky Face Ridge, and was wounded at Resaca but he refused to absent himself from duty. On June 27, 1864, Harker's brigade was in the assaulting column sent against Cheatham's Hill, a part of the strongly fortified Confederate position at Kennesaw Mountain. It was a desperate assault, and when Harker's brigade fell back, he galloped forward to rally the men to the attack. Within a few yards of the Southern line, his horse was killed, and he fell with what proved to be a mortal wound. In the renewed attack inspired by Harker's gallant example, the battle flag of the 27th Illinois floated briefly over the Confederate breastworks. Harker died a few hours after the attack ended. Castel, *Decision in the West*; Cozzens, *This Terrible Sound.*

Richard M. McMurry

HARLAN, James, *senator, Secretary of the Interior*, was born on August 26, 1820, in Clark county, Illinois. The family moved to Park county, Indiana, in 1824. He graduated from Asbury University (later DePauw) in 1845, and moved to Iowa in 1846 to head Iowa City College. Soon active in Whig politics, he was elected state superintendent of public instruction, only to be deprived of his victory by apparently fraudulent means.

Admitted to the bar in 1850, Harlan practiced law until he became president of the Mount Pleasant Collegiate Institute (later Iowa Wesleyan). During his presidency he arranged for the school to receive support from the Iowa Conference of the Methodist Episcopal Church. The Methodist constituency, a numerous and assertive body, became a major factor in his political life and complemented his activities in the Free Soil and temperance movements. In 1855, running as an anti-Nebraska candidate, Harlan was elected by a rump legislative body to the U.S. Senate. The election was invalidated, but he won reelection from the full legislature in 1857 for the remainder of the term, and again in 1860 to a full term.

During the Civil War, Harlan became identified with the Radical wing of his party. Certain that African Americans were inferior, he nevertheless was an early supporter of emancipation and of their service in the Army. He also favored the draft, but advocated a sliding scale of exemption payments based on ability to pay. Harlan predictably backed measures of particular benefit to the West and had a major role in pushing through the Pacific Railroad Bill. During Robert Todd Lincoln's courtship of his daughter Mary, Harlan became closer to President Abraham Lincoln (*q.v.*). Appointed Secretary of the Interior just before Lincoln's assassination, he stayed on under Andrew Johnson (*q.v.*). Increasingly angered by Johnson's Reconstruction policies, he resigned in July 1866.

Harlan sought and regained his Senate seat for a six-year term, but at the cost of party harmony and his own political future. He favored black votes as a means to ensure Southern loyalty, and took an active part in the effort to impeach Johnson. Having failed in his attempt to gain renomination in 1872, in a bitter intraparty fight, Harlan never regained political office. He did, however, serve on the court that settled the *Alabama* claims dispute. He died in Mount Pleasant, Iowa, on October 5, 1899. Brigham, *James Harlan*; Sage, *William Boyd Allison.*

Hubert H. Wubben

HARRINGTON, Henry William, *congressman,* was born near Cooperstown, New York, on September 12, 1825. He attended school in Fredonia, New York, in 1842, and Temple Hill Academy in 1845. He was admitted to the bar in 1848, and commenced his law practice in Nunda, New York. In 1856, he set out for Kansas, but became ill and stopped to recuperate in Madison, Indiana. He eventually settled in Madison, opened a law office, and remained there until 1872. Harrington was active in politics from the time he reached Madison. In 1860, he was a delegate to the Democratic National Convention in Charleston, South Carolina, and was elected to represent Indiana on the Democratic National Committee, a position he also held in 1868 and 1872.

Harrington was also elected to Congress in 1862, but was defeated for re-election in 1864. As a Democrat in an overwhelmingly Republican House, he accomplished little. In 1866, he was appointed collector of internal revenue in Indiana's 3rd District, a position he held for less than a year before returning to his law practice. Harrington became affiliated with the Greenback movement, and in 1876, after the withdrawal of Anson Wolcott, the Greenback nominee for governor, was chosen to succeed him. He polled nearly 13,000 votes, more than the Greenback presidential nominee received in the state. Despite this modest success, Harrington did not again enter politics. He died in Indianapolis on March 21, 1882. Thornbrough, *Indiana in the Civil War Era.*

Raymond L. Shoemaker

HARRIS, Benjamin Gwinn, *congressman,* a member of an old-line Maryland family, was born in St. Mary's county, Maryland, on December 13, 1805. He attended Yale College, studied law at the Cambridge Law School in Massachusetts, and in 1840 was admitted to the Maryland bar. Harris became a wealthy planter, owning slaves and 1,600 acres of land. As a Democrat he was elected to the Maryland House of Delegates in 1833 and 1836, and by 1861 he had become the party's leader in southern Maryland. In that year he ran for Congress as the candidate of the State Rights Convention, only to suffer defeat by a Unionist, Charles B. Calvert (*q.v.*). A second try in 1863 was successful, owing to the bitter division in the Union party, although Harris polled less than the combined votes for the two Union candidates.

Harris's speeches in Congress against the ''illegal'' methods of the government caused considerable embarrassment to many Democrats. Harris strongly opposed emancipation and the enlistment of slaves, which he regarded as being unconstitutional. In one debate he expressed gratification over the secession of the South, which provoked a move to expel him from Congress. His critics lacked the necessary two-thirds' majority and censured him instead. Harris won reelection in 1864, but in his second term he ran afoul of the military authorities. In May 1865, charged with harboring two paroled Confederate soldiers, he was tried by court martial. He was sentenced to three years' imprisonment and disqualified from future officeholding. Shortly thereafter, President Andrew Johnson (*q.v.*) remitted the sentence. By 1866, opposition within his own party denied Harris renomination, and he retired to private life. He died near Leonardtown, Maryland, on April 4, 1895. Baker, *Politics of Continuity*; Clark, *Politics in Maryland During the Civil War.*

Richard R. Duncan

HARRIS, Charles Murray, *congressman*, was born on April 10, 1821, in Munfordsville, Kentucky. After attending the common schools, he studied law and was admitted to the bar. He moved to Oquawka, Illinois, where he established a law practice and became affiliated with the Democratic party. Successful in his bid for office as a result of the Democratic sweep in the 1862 congressional elections, Harris was undoubtedly the least effective member of the Illinois delegation in the 38th Congress. Failing to be reelected, he returned to Illinois. He died in Chicago on September 20, 1896. *BDUSC.*

Thomas F. Schwartz

HARRIS, Ira, *senator*, was born on May 31, 1802, in Charleston, New York. He graduated from Union College in 1824 and settled in Albany, where he came to be regarded as one of the most able lawyers in the state. Harris helped establish Albany Medical College in 1838 and Albany Law School in 1850, and held a professorship at the latter until his death. With the support of Anti-Rent forces, whose opposition to old Dutch landholding laws provided a rallying point for progressive politics in New York, Harris was elected as a Whig to the state Assembly in 1845 and 1846, to the state constitutional convention of 1846, and to the state Senate in 1847. Named to the New York Supreme Court in 1847, he served with distinction until stepping down in 1859.

In 1861, Harris was elected to the U.S. Senate when more powerful Republican chieftains blocked one another. He quickly became a close counselor to President Abraham Lincoln (*q.v.*) and, despite friction over appointments, a generally staunch supporter of the administration's policies. He also organized a regiment of cavalry. As a member of the Judiciary and Foreign Relations committees, Harris exercised considerable power in the Senate. When the war drew to a close, he was named as well to the influential Joint Committee on Reconstruction.

On most issues, Harris was regarded as a cautious, even conservative, Republican, and in the New York party caucus of 1867, he lost the nomination to Roscoe Conkling (*q.v.*). He returned to Albany and served in the state constitutional convention of 1867. Continuing lifelong commitments to higher education and religion, he also served as trustee of Union College and of Vassar College, as chancellor of the University of Rochester, and as chairman of the

American Baptist Missionary Union. Harris died in Albany on December 2, 1875. Benedict, *Compromise of Principle*; Brummer, *Political History of New York State*.

James C. Mohr

HARRISON, Richard Almgill, *congressman*, was born in Thirsk, Yorkshire, England, on April 8, 1824, and in 1832 came with his parents to Springfield, Ohio. He attended local schools and in 1846 graduated from the Cincinnati Law School, was admitted to the bar, and set up his office in London, Ohio. As a Democrat, he served in the Ohio House in 1858, and in the Ohio Senate in 1860–1861. Following Thomas Corwin's (*q.v.*) resignation from Congress, Harrison was elected as a Unionist to fill the unexpired term. He introduced several resolutions that called for investigations into charges of fraud in government contracting and in the pension system. He kept his party affiliation as a Union Democrat, but did not wander too far from his support of Abraham Lincoln's (*q.v.*) administration, as is evidenced by his votes in favor of confiscation, prohibiting slavery in the territories, and conscription. Harrison moved in 1873 to Columbus, Ohio, where he practiced law until his death on July 30, 1904. Curry, *Blueprint for Modern America*.

Thomas H. Smith

HARROW, William, *general*, was born on November 14, 1822, in Winchester, Kentucky. He moved with his family to Lawrenceville, Illinois, where he practiced law and came to know Abraham Lincoln (*q.v.*). In 1859, he moved to Mount Vernon, Indiana, to open a law practice. Harrow was a staunch Republican, and aligned himself with the Radical Republicans during the war. When war broke out, he immediately offered his services and was commissioned a captain in the 14th Indiana Volunteers. In less than one year, he was promoted successively from major to colonel of the regiment. At Antietam, where the 14th lost over half its men, Harrow handled his regiment well enough to earn praise from his brigade commander. The following spring he was promoted to brigadier general and given a brigade in John Gibbon's (*q.v.*) division of the II Corps.

Following the wounding of Gibbon at Gettysburg, Harrow temporarily commanded the division, but Alexander Webb (*q.v.*) observed that he was universally disliked and enjoyed little respect. In the fall of 1863, he was transferred to the West and led a division in the XV Corps during the Atlanta campaign. He won praise from his corps commander for the fighting around Atlanta, but he was not included in General William T. Sherman's (*q.v.*) army that marched through Georgia and the Carolinas. He resigned on April 20, 1865, and returned to Vincennes, Indiana, to resume his law practice.

Although Harrow was a brave soldier who possessed some ability, he was coarse and profane, traits that some of his subordinates found offensive, and he lacked the ability to inspire confidence. The war perhaps softened his harsh political views toward the South, for he aligned himself with Horace Greeley (*q.v.*) in the presidential election of 1872. Harrow was killed in a train accident at New Albany, Indiana, on September 27, 1872. Brown, *Cushing of Gettysburg*; Castel, *Decision in the West*.

D. Scott Hartwig

HARTSUFF, George Lucas, *general*, was born in Seneca county, New York, on May 28, 1830. His family moved to Michigan in 1842, and he was appointed to West Point from that state in 1848. After graduation, he served in the artillery in Texas and Florida, where in 1855 he was badly wounded in a fight with Seminoles. At the time Fort Sumter was attacked, he had just been promoted to captain and assigned to the Adjutant General's Department. Hartsuff accompanied the expedition to reinforce Fort Pickens, and in the summer of 1861 he went to western Virginia as chief of staff to William S. Rosecrans (*q.v.*).

In April 1862, Hartsuff was named brigadier general of Volunteers, and led a brigade in the Army of Virginia through Cedar Mountain and Second Bull Run. After being transferred to the Army of the Potomac in September, he commanded a brigade at South Mountain and Antietam, where he was severely injured by a shell fragment. While recovering from his wounds, Hartsuff was promoted to major general of Volunteers, and in the spring of 1863 was sent to Kentucky to assume command of the XXIII Corps. With Ambrose Burnside (*q.v.*) he led his corps into East Tennessee, serving in and around Knoxville. His health remained poor, however, and he yielded his command in November. He remained inactive until three weeks before Lee's surrender, when he returned to the field as commander of the defenses of Bermuda Hundred, between Richmond and Petersburg.

Hartsuff was a solid, courageous, competent officer on whom superiors could always depend. Because of his wounds he never realized an opportunity to display battlefield brilliance. Indeed, he may have possessed none, but neither did he have any of the overweening ambition that infected many of his contemporaries. When mustered out, he resumed his duties with the Adjutant General's Office, retiring because of his wounds in 1871. He died in New York City on May 16, 1874. Krick, *Stonewall Jackson at Cedar Mountain*; Marvel, *Burnside*.

William Marvel

HARVEY, Louis Powell, *governor*, was born in East Haddam, Connecticut, on July 22, 1820; shortly thereafter his family moved to Strongsville, Ohio. He attended Western Reserve College, taught school, and in 1841 moved to Southport (now Kenosha), Wisconsin Territory, where he founded his own academy. He was the editor of the *Southport American*, a Whig paper. In 1850, he moved to Shopiere, a small community that thereafter was his home. Harvey had been a delegate to the Wisconsin Constitutional Convention in 1847–1848, and was one of the organizers of the Republican party in 1854. He served in the state Senate (1854–1857) and as secretary of state (1860–1862).

In 1861, Harvey participated in the formation of the Republican–Union party, on whose ticket he replaced the incumbent governor, Alexander Randall (*q.v.*), running successfully with a Democratic nominee for lieutenant governor, Edward Salomon (*q.v.*). As governor, Harvey quickly learned the limits of patriotism. Although the legislature enthusiastically voted its support for the war, fiscal appropriations were another matter. Harvey struggled to match rhetoric and funding, and his troubles were not limited to political colleagues. As a result of financial confusion, the 17th Wisconsin refused his plea that they depart to Camp Randall without the promised payment. The governor sadly watched them riot, and even more sadly witnessed intercession of a regiment called from Chicago to quell the disturbance. In his less than three months as governor, Harvey established a reputation for genuine concern with the welfare of Wisconsin soldiers, particularly the sick and wounded. He was also successful in working out the state's claims against the Federal government, arranging for the retention of the direct Federal tax to compensate the state.

In April 1862, having returned from a trip to the St. Louis area, where he had visited soldiers, Harvey received word of the battle of Shiloh. He set forth again, with a party of surgeons and fellow governors. On the way to the battlefield they visited hospitals, and at Pittsburg Landing, he paid tribute to Shiloh survivors. But that would be his final contribution. On April 19, Harvey lost his footing while transferring between boats and drowned in the Tennessee River. On May 3, 1862, his body was recovered and returned to Madison for burial. Current, *Civil War Era*; Hesseltine, *Lincoln's War Governors*.

Charles E. Twining

HATCH, Edward, *general*, was born in Bangor, Maine, on December 22, 1832. He spent two years at Norwich University in Vermont, went to sea briefly, moved to Muscatine, Iowa, and entered the lumber business. On September 5, 1861, Hatch was commissioned a captain in the 2nd Iowa Cavalry, which he had helped to organize. The regiment took the field in February 1862, and Hatch led a battalion in the campaign that resulted in the capture of New Madrid and Island No. 10. The 2nd Iowa accompanied General John Pope's (*q.v.*) Army of the Mississippi up the Tennessee River in April and participated in the siege of Corinth. In June 1862, Hatch became colonel of the regiment. The regiment was at Iuka in mid-September, and Hatch participated in the battle of Corinth as a brigade commander.

The 2nd Iowa left La Grange, Tennessee, on April 17, 1863, with Colonel Benjamin H. Grierson (*q.v.*), but four days later, Grierson detached Hatch. Grierson rode to the southwest; Hatch and his Iowans, after threatening the Mobile & Ohio Railroad, returned to La Grange, followed by the Confederate cavalry. In December, Hatch was severely wounded in a skirmish at Moscow, Tennessee. While recuperating from his injury, he commanded the St. Louis Cavalry Depot. He was commissioned a brigadier general of Volunteers to rank from April 27, 1864, and soon after was ordered to Memphis. Hatch led a cavalry division in the Oxford expedition and during John Bell Hood's invasion of Middle Tennessee. In the latter campaign, he screened the Union retreat and led his division in the battles of Franklin and Nashville. He was breveted major general for gallantry at Nashville.

After he left the Volunteer service on January 1, 1866, Hatch was commissioned colonel of the 9th U.S. Cavalry, one of the Army's two black mounted regiments. He died at Fort Robinson, Nebraska, on April 11, 1889. Bearss, *Vicksburg Campaign*; Stuart, *Iowa Colonels and Regiments*; Sword, *Embrace an Angry Wind.*

Edwin C. Bearss

HAUPT, Herman, *general,* was born in Philadelphia on March 26, 1817. He graduated from West Point in 1835, and in 1836 was appointed the principal assistant engineer of the state of Pennsylvania. Later, he entered the field of railroad engineering and was instrumental in the construction of several of the more important railroad segments in New York, New England, and Pennsylvania. He also taught civil engineering, mathematics, and architecture at Penn College in Gettysburg.

Haupt did not serve during the first year of the Civil War, but in April 1862 he was placed in charge of U.S. military railroading and appointed aide-de-camp to General Irvin McDowell (*q.v.*), with the rank of colonel. Haupt immediately made an impression through the construction of blockhouses and stockades to protect the railroad from Confederate raiding parties, as well as arming and drilling his railroad personnel. More spectacular was his success rate in repairing damaged bridges and rail lines. On September 5, 1862, Haupt was promoted to brigadier general of Volunteers. However, fearing a limitation on his freedom to conduct private business, he refused the appointment and returned to civilian life.

After resigning from the military, Haupt continued to display his skill in engineering through the publication of technical books, and positions as the chief engineer and general manager of many railroads. In addition to his skill in railroad engineering, Haupt was a pioneer in oil pipeline development and the use of compressed air for motors and mine machinery. The railroad was always his first love, and appropriately he died aboard a train in Jersey City, New Jersey, on December 14, 1905. Catton, *Mr. Lincoln's Army*; Lord, *Lincoln's Railroad Man.*

Mitchell A. Yockelson

HAVEN, Gilbert, *clergyman, abolitionist,* was born on September 19, 1821, in Malden, Massachusetts. He attended Wesleyan Academy and Wesleyan University, taught at Amenia (New York) Seminary, and was ordained in 1851 as a Methodist Episcopal minister in the New England Conference. Although the temperance cause attracted him, antislavery became his chief concern. Haven was especially noted for sermons expounding the Higher Law doctrine. He enthusiastically supported Abraham Lincoln (*q.v.*) in the election of 1860, writing a pamphlet, *Te Deum Laudamus: The Cause and Consequence of the Election of Abraham Lincoln* (1860).

When the war began, Haven was commissioned chaplain of the 8th Massachusetts Volunteers for a three-month term. Upon discharge, he visited Europe, where he spoke in defense of the Union cause, and then resumed his ministry in Boston. Haven was one of the few abolitionists to advocate complete civil and social equality of the races and to urge interracial marriage. He was critical of racial discrimination in the North and succeeded in desegregating many Methodist churches in New England. He also opposed segregation in the army.

From 1867 to 1872, Haven edited *Zion's Herald*, which he used as a forum for the advocacy of Radical Reconstruction, as well as for women's suffrage and temperance reform. He also lobbied for the impeachment of Andrew Johnson (*q.v.*). In 1872, he was elected bishop of the Methodist Episcopal Church and stationed in Atlanta. Haven advocated freedmen's rights and exposed Southern resistance to Reconstruction. He helped establish Methodism in Mexico City in 1873 and visited Methodist missions in Liberia in 1876. Haven died in Malden, Massachusetts, on January 3, 1880. Gravely, *Gilbert Haven*; McPherson, *Struggle for Equality*; Prentice, *Life of Gilbert Haven*.

Merton L. Dillon

HAWKINS, John Parker, *general,* was born in Indianapolis on September 29, 1830. He graduated from West Point in 1852, and was breveted 2nd lieutenant in the 6th U.S. Infantry. In 1854, he became a full 2nd lieutenant and served as a regimental quartermaster on the northwestern frontier. After Fort Sumter, Hawkins transferred to the Commissary Department, served in various assignments, and rose to the rank of brigadier general of Volunteers in 1863. After his return from sick leave in 1863, he led a brigade of African American soldiers in the District of Northeastern Louisiana. In February 1864 he received command of the 1st Division, U.S. Colored Troops, and later participated in the capture of Mobile.

Although considered a strict disciplinarian, Hawkins was an enlightened leader. He was one of the few individuals who insisted on additional junior officers to assist in training and drilling black troops in order to prepare them for combat service. He combined his appreciation for the efficacy of small unit leadership with prohibition of any practices that threatened to demean his troops. Indeed, he was the only general of African American soldiers to abolish bonding because his men found such humiliating forms of punishment too reminiscent of slavery. Hawkins's compassion extended to all former slaves. In the fall of 1863, he objected strenuously to the paternalism inherent in the contract labor system, and argued that blacks were entitled to be paid real wages.

In 1865, Hawkins was breveted major general of Volunteers and Regulars, but in February 1866 he reverted to his Regular rank of captain in the Subsistence Department. He remained in the Army and served at various locations until he retired as a brigadier general in September 1894. He returned to Indianapolis, where he died on February 7, 1914. Gerteis, *From Contraband to Freedman*; Glatthaar, *Forged in Battle*.

                                                                    James W. Geary

HAWLEY, Joseph Roswell, *general*, was born on October 31, 1826, in Stewartville, North Carolina; in 1837 his family moved to Connecticut. He graduated in 1847 from Hamilton College, and during the next fourteen years he was a teacher, law student, editor, antislavery advocate, and a founder of the Republican party in Connecticut. As a captain in the 1st Connecticut Volunteers he served at First Bull Run, then helped Alfred H. Terry (*q.v.*) recruit the 7th Connecticut. By mid-1862, he had risen to command the regiment.

Through early 1864, Hawley participated in the Port Royal expedition, in operations against Fort Pulaski and Charleston, and in the battle of Olustee; he also served as a military governor in eastern Florida. Commanding a X Corps brigade, in April 1864 he joined General Benjamin Butler's (*q.v.*) Army of the James for the Richmond–Petersburg campaign, during portions of which he led a division. That September, Hawley became a brigadier of Volunteers, and two months later commanded troops sent to New York City to prevent anticipated election riots. Following the January 1865 capture of Fort Fisher, he headed a military district in North Carolina, and in September 1865 he received the brevet of major general of Volunteers.

Hawley was a brigade leader of above-average ability and courage, and great zeal (he considered the Union's struggle a "holy war"). He served long and faithfully, though often crippled by rheumatism and derogated by his men, who considered him a martinet. His greatest weaknesses were a quick temper and a tendency to feud with other political generals, such as Butler, which limited his military usefulness. After the war, Hawley was governor of Connecticut, a congressman, and, from 1881 until his death in Washington, D.C., on March 18, 1905, a senator from Connecticut. Hawley, *Major General Joseph R. Hawley*; Robertson, *Back Door to Richmond*.

                                                                Edward G. Longacre

HAYES, Rutherford Birchard, *general*, was born in Delaware, Ohio, on October 4, 1822. After graduating from Kenyon College and attending Harvard Law School, he settled into respectable life as a rising Cincinnati lawyer, Methodist by religion and Whiggish (and later moderate Republican) in his political convictions. Enlisting shortly after Fort Sumter, he was commissioned a major in the 23rd Ohio Volunteer Infantry and, after the promotion and resignation of earlier colonels, became the regiment's commander for the remainder of the war. The 23rd proved to be an unusually talented group. Within its ranks were a future major general, William S. Rosecrans (*q.v.*); two diplomats, Eliakim P. Scammon and James M. Comly; a Supreme Court justice, Stanley Matthews; and two future Presidents of the United States, Hayes and William McKinley.

That Hayes was able to stand out in such distinguished company was a tribute to his often underrated capacity for leadership. His rise through the command structure was steady, as was his active service. Put in charge of a brigade and then, temporarily, a division, he was promoted to brigadier general late in 1864 and brevet major general by war's end.

Hayes's service was confined to the Eastern theater: the Kanawha and Shenandoah valleys and the Antietam campaign. He was wounded four times, most seriously at South Mountain, where his gallantry and skill won special commendation. As a military commander, Hayes was dutiful rather than imaginative, steady rather than brilliant—qualities that could also characterize his political career. Elected to Congress during the war, he took his seat in 1865 but resigned after less than two terms to serve the first of his three terms as governor of Ohio. He was elected President of the United States in 1876. Declining to run for reelection, he devoted himself to business and charitable causes. He died in Fremont, Ohio, on January 17, 1893. Barnard, *Rutherford B. Hayes*; Williams, *Hayes of the Twenty-Third.*

Allan Peskin

HAYS, Alexander, *general,* was born in Franklin, Pennsylvania, on July 8, 1819. He graduated from West Point in 1844, was assigned to the 4th Infantry, and served in the Mexican War, during which he was wounded at Resaca de la Palma. Cited for gallantry in that action, he was promoted to 1st lieutenant and transferred to the 8th Infantry. At war's end Hays resigned his commission to take up iron manufacturing near Franklin; he left two years later to join the California gold rush. He returned to Pennsylvania in 1851, and went into civil engineering.

In April 1861, Hays left his position with the Allegheny Valley Railroad to enlist in a militia company, called the City Guard, in Pittsburgh, and was elected captain. His company became part of the 12th Pennsylvania, a ninety-day regiment, and Hays was promoted to major. When the regiment's term expired, he returned to Pittsburgh to raise a new unit, which became the 63rd Pennsylvania Volunteers. As colonel of the 63rd, he was popular with his men, and served with distinction during the Peninsula campaign, during which he gained two brevet promotions for gallantry at Fair Oaks and Malvern Hill.

Hays was seriously wounded at Second Bull Run, and was assigned to the defenses of Washington for the next nine months, obtaining a promotion to brigadier general of Volunteers on September 29, 1862. He resumed active duty in the Army of the Potomac as commander of the 3rd Division of Winfield S. Hancock's (*q.v.*) II Corps on June 28, 1863, and at Gettysburg he inspired confidence by his open display of courage, particularly during Pickett's charge. Hays continued to serve brilliantly until May 5, 1864, when he was killed while riding forward to rally his men at the Wilderness. Coddington, *Gettysburg Campaign*; Rhea, *Battle of the Wilderness.*

Walter L. Powell

HAYS, William, *general*, was born in Richmond, Virginia, on May 9, 1819. He was commissioned in the artillery on graduating from West Point in 1840. During the Mexican War, Hays won two brevets. Later he campaigned against the Seminoles and served on the western frontier. At the beginning of the Civil War, he served in the Washington defenses; later he commanded a brigade of horse batteries during the Peninsula campaign. After leading artillery units at Sharpsburg and Fredericksburg, Hays assumed command of an infantry brigade in the Army of the Potomac. Wounded and captured at Chancellorsville, he was released in time to command the II Corps at Gettysburg, after Winfield S. Hancock (*q.v.*) and John Gibbon (*q.v.*) were wounded. In August 1863 Hays was named provost marshal of New York, and the following February he returned to Virginia and led a division in the II Corps until just before Appomattox, when General Andrew A. Humphreys (*q.v.*) relieved him of his command for sleeping on duty.

Considering his background, Hays should have been a better general. His failure seems to have stemmed more from carelessness and lack of zeal than from ignorance of tactics. At best, he was a mediocre leader. After the war he resumed his place in the 5th Artillery but never rose above the rank of major. Hays died in Boston on February 7, 1875. Longacre, *Man Behind the Guns*; Naisawald, *Grape and Canister*.

James L. Morrison, Jr.

HAZEN, William Babcock, *general*, was born on September 27, 1830, in West Hartford, Vermont; his family moved to Ohio in 1833. He graduated from West Point in 1855, and served with the 8th U.S. Infantry on the frontier. He was severely wounded in 1859 in an Indian fight and was on medical leave until early 1861. From February to September 1861, Hazen taught at the Military Academy. In October 1861 he was made colonel of the 41st Ohio Volunteers. He commanded a brigade in both the Army of the Ohio and the Army of the Cumberland, serving in the early Kentucky campaigns and at Shiloh, Corinth, Perryville, Murfreesboro, Chickamauga, and in the battles around Chattanooga. Meanwhile, he was promoted to brigadier general of Volunteers with date of rank November 29, 1862.

Hazen led his brigade in the Atlanta campaign until August 1864, when he was transferred to the Army of the Tennessee to command the 2nd Division, XV Corps. He held that position until May 1865, participating in the closing battles around Atlanta and in William T. Sherman's (*q.v.*) March to the Sea. On December 13, 1864, Hazen captured Fort McAllister, and thereby opened the Ogeechee River, secured a base on the coast (ensuring the success of the march), and made certain the capture of Savannah. The date of the fort's capture later became his date of rank as a major general of Volunteers. Hazen led his division through the Carolinas campaign and in May 1865 took command of the XV Corps.

Hazen was a brave and competent officer who possessed what one contemporary called an "aggressive and disputatious" temperament. This trait was especially apparent in the postwar years, when he became involved in bitter quarrels with political and military figures. Hazen remained in the Army after the war, serving in the West with the 38th and 6th Infantry regiments. Twice (1870–1871, 1876–1877) he was sent to Europe to study military matters. He wrote extensively on military history, and in 1880 President Rutherford B. Hayes (*q.v.*) named him chief signal officer, a post in which he served well until his death in Washington, D.C., on January 16, 1887. Castel, *Decision in the West*; Cozzens, *This Terrible Sound.*

Richard M. McMurry

HEINTZELMAN, Samuel Peter, *general*, was born in Manheim, Pennsylvania, on September 30, 1805. He graduated from West Point in 1826, was commissioned into the infantry, and spent the next six years on frontier duty in the West. Heintzelman served on a Tennessee River surveying team and in the Seminole campaigns in Florida. A participant in Winfield Scott's (*q.v.*) campaign against Mexico City, he was breveted for gallantry at Huamantla. Major Heintzelman was called to Washington in 1861 as inspector for the Volunteer Army assembling there. In May 1861 he led the Federal advance across the Potomac to occupy the Arlington heights, and as brigadier general of Volunteers, commanded the 3rd Division at First Bull Run, where he was wounded.

The most controversial incident of Heintzelman's career occurred on the Peninsula in 1862. As one of the senior generals in the Army, he was initially hostile to the younger George B. McClellan (*q.v.*), particularly the latter's Urbanna plan. Heintzelman and three other senior generals—Erasmus Keyes (*q.v.*), Irvin McDowell (*q.v.*), and Edwin Vose Sumner (*q.v.*)—functioned in conflict with the clique of younger officers surrounding McClellan. Many of the command problems; dilatory action before Yorktown, Williamsburg, and during the Seven Days; and the lackluster performance of the III Corps can be attributed to the aging Heintzelman. Basically unable to perform above brigade-level command, he never lacked for gallantry; he ascended in Professor T.S.C. Lowe's balloon at night to discover the Confederates evacuating Yorktown. He repeatedly appeared on the battlefield to inspire his subordinates, and on July 4, he was promoted to major general of Volunteers.

Heintzelman's corps was sent to aid John Pope (*q.v.*) at Second Bull Run, after which Heintzelman received command of the defenses of Washington, a post he held until October 1863. Finally sent to Columbus, Ohio, he served out the Civil War on courts martial duty, although during Early's raid in 1864 he rushed "100-days men" from Ohio to Washington, D.C.

Heintzelman may be seen as the epitome of the Regular soldier of the period. Jealous of his prerogatives as corps commander, uncharitable toward junior and senior officers alike, he was not quite an effective corps commander. He lacked initiative and magnified difficulties, due possibly to his inability to cope with the mass, pace, and significance of modern warfare. Heintzelman assumed command of the 17th Infantry in the Southwest in August 1865 and retired from the army in February 1869. He resided in Washington, D.C., until his death on May 1, 1880. Hennessy, *Return to Bull Run*; Sears, *To the Gates of Richmond.*

B. Franklin Cooling

HENDERSON, John Brooks, *senator,* was born in Danville, Virginia, on November 16, 1826, and moved with his parents to Lincoln county, Missouri, when he was five. He taught school, read law, and was admitted to the bar in 1848. Henderson was active in Democratic politics, served in the legislature (1849–1850, 1857–1858), and made three unsuccessful attempts to gain a seat in Congress (1850, 1858, 1860). A presidential elector in 1856 and 1860, he attended the Charleston and Baltimore Democratic National Conventions in 1860, as a Stephen A. Douglas (*q.v.*) delegate. As a delegate to the state convention that decided against secession in March 1861, Henderson opposed secession and coercion equally. After Fort Sumter he changed his position, supported the establishment of the Missouri Provisional Government, and became a brigadier general in the state militia.

Henderson was active in efforts to control guerrilla activity in northeast Missouri in the fall of 1861. Following the expulsion of Trusten Polk from the U.S. Senate, he was appointed to the vacancy by acting Governor Willard P. Hall (*q.v.*) on January 17, 1862, and was elected to a full term in 1863. He served on the Finance and District of Columbia committees, and played an important role in securing passage of much of the wartime financial legislation. Henderson supported President Abraham Lincoln's (*q.v.*) 1862 efforts at compensated emancipation in the border states and played a prominent role in the 1863 state convention that provided for gradual emancipation in Missouri. He moved into the emerging Radical coalition in Missouri in 1864, and in that same year introduced the measure that became the 13th Amendment.

Henderson generally acted with the Radicals in the postwar era, but opposed the impeachment of President Andrew Johnson (*q.v.*), which cost him reelection. Nevertheless, he remained active in Republican politics. He was the party's gubernatorial candidate in 1872 and served as president of the Republican National Convention in 1884. He died in Washington, D.C., on April 12, 1913. Parrish, *Missouri Under Radical Rule*; Parrish, *Turbulent Partnership.*

William E. Parrish

HENDRICKS, Thomas Andrews, *senator, governor,* was born on September 7, 1819, near Zanesville, Ohio; his family moved to Madison, Indiana, in 1820 and to Shelby county in 1822. He graduated from Hanover College (1841), studied law in Pennsylvania, and was admitted to the Indiana bar (1843). A Democrat, Hendricks served in Indiana's House of Representatives (1848–1849); was a delegate to the state constitutional convention (1850–1851), where he favored an amendment excluding blacks from Indiana; and won election to Congress (1851–1855). Appointed commissioner of the General Land Office

(1855–1859), he advocated a homestead law and improved departmental efficiency. In January 1860, Indiana Governor Ashbel Willard broke from the Jesse Bright (*q.v.*)-dominated state Democratic party and nominated Hendricks for governor. After waging a campaign to unite party factions, the Hendricks–David Turpie (*q.v.*) ticket lost to Republicans Henry S. Lane (*q.v.*) and Oliver H.P. Morton (*q.v.*) by 10,000 votes. This Republican win may have swayed Hoosier voters to Abraham Lincoln (*q.v.*) in the November presidential election.

Afterward, Hendricks moved to Indianapolis and established a law practice that became one of the state's leading firms. He supported a vigorous policy to preserve the Union, but Republicans accused him of treason and associating with secret societies, which he denied. Following Bright's 1862 expulsion from the Senate and a renewal of Democratic strength in Indiana, Hendricks won election to the U.S. Senate (1863–1869), where he supported the war effort but criticized what he considered to be dictatorial and sometimes unconstitutional administration policies. He opposed emancipation, Radical Reconstruction, and the 13th, 14th, and 15th Amendments, calling the times unpropitious for such changes. Although he opposed national conscription, he advocated compliance with the law until it was repealed or nullified by the courts.

Hendricks campaigned three times for the governorship (1860, 1868, 1872), winning on his third try. As Indiana's sixteenth governor (1873–1877), he was the the first Democrat elected to that position in the North since the war. A contender for the presidency in 1868, 1872, and 1876, Hendricks accepted the Democratic vice presidential nomination (1876) on the ticket headed by Samuel J. Tilden. He again accepted the second spot in 1884, winning alongside Grover Cleveland. Hendricks died in Indianapolis on November 25, 1885. Gray, *Gentlemen from Indiana*; Holcombe, *Life and Public Services of Thomas A. Hendricks*; Shepherd, *Biographical Directory of the Indiana General Assembly*, vol. 1.

David G. Vanderstel

HERRICK, Anson, *congressman,* was born on January 21, 1812, in Lewiston, Maine. At Wiscasset, Maine, in 1833, he established the *Citizen,* then moved to New York City in 1836 and established the weekly *New York Atlas.* Rising through the ranks of the New York City Democratic party, Herrick was elected alderman from 1854 to 1856 and was appointed naval storekeeper for the Port of New York from 1857 to 1861. While an alderman, he attacked the Democratic mayor, Fernando Wood (*q.v.*), as a corrupt autocrat, only to be counterattacked with accusations of bribery.

In 1862, Herrick was elected to the 38th Congress. An extreme Peace Democrat in the first session of that Congress, he broke with fellow Democrats in the second session to vote for an end to slavery, apparently in exchange for patronage favors from the Lincoln (*q.v.*) administration. Herrick stood for reelection in 1864, in a redrawn district, against Fernando Wood. They split the Democratic majority, allowing a Republican to capture the seat. Herrick returned to publishing and used the *Atlas* to support President Andrew Johnson's (*q.v.*)

unsuccessful efforts to fashion a new conservative party after the war. Herrick died in New York City on February 6, 1868. Benedict, *Compromise of Principle.*

James C. Mohr

HERRON, Francis Jay, *general,* was born on February 17, 1837, in Pittsburgh, Pennsylvania. He briefly attended what is now the University of Pittsburgh, and in 1855 moved to Dubuque, Iowa, where he and three brothers established a bank. In 1859, he organized and commanded an independent company known as the Governor's Grays. In January 1861, Herron offered his fully equipped and uniformed unit to the War Department, but was turned down. Following Fort Sumter, he commanded a company of the 1st Iowa, a three-month organization, in combat at Boonville, Dug Springs, and Ozark, and at the Federal defeat at Wilson's Creek. In September 1861 he became lieutenant colonel of the 9th Iowa Volunteers and distinguished himself at Pea Ridge, until disabled and taken prisoner. After being exchanged, he was promoted to brigadier general of Volunteers and received the Medal of Honor (thirty-one years later).

In December 1862, Herron marched two divisions 125 miles in three days, from Wilson's Creek to Prairie Grove, Arkansas, to reinforce the small Union force under James G. Blunt (*q.v.*), before Thomas C. Hindman could march half that distance to overwhelm Blunt. Although Hindman's timidity aided in the Confederate defeat, Herron's spectacular feat made Union victory possible. For this achievement, he was appointed major general of Volunteers in March 1863. In the siege of Vicksburg, Herron commanded a division on the Union left wing, and later the XIIIth Corps in the Department of the Gulf, with headquarters at Brownsville, Texas.

Herron's extraordinary ability to command forces in crisis periods won deserved commendation. Both in combat and in tactical situations he demonstrated unique judgment and troop control. Unfortunately, he did not serve in the pivotal campaigns and battles of the East. At the close of the war he was appointed a commissioner to negotiate with the Five Civilized Tribes of Indian Territory, and in August 1865 he resigned from the Army. As a lawyer in Louisiana, Herron engaged in mercantile business, and served as U.S. marshal (1867–1869) and secretary of state for Louisiana (1871–1872). In 1877, he moved to New York City and worked for a manufacturing establishment until his death there on January 8, 1902. Bearss, *Vicksburg Campaign,* vol. 3; Josephy, *Civil War in the American West*; Shea, *Pea Ridge.*

LeRoy H. Fischer

HICKMAN, John, *congressman,* was born in West Bradford Township, Pennsylvania, on September 11, 1810. Educated in classical studies by private tutors, he studied law, and was admitted to the bar in West Chester. In 1844, he was a delegate to the Democratic National Convention but was defeated in a bid for Congress. After having served one term as county district attorney, and with the emergence of the Kansas crisis, he was elected to the 34th Congress as a Democrat–Know-Nothing candidate. Hickman supported President James Buchanan's (*q.v.*) sectional policies, but following his reelection to the House in 1856, he gradually adopted free-soil principles. Reelected in 1858 as a Douglas Democrat, he soon broke with that party completely and began to vote with the Radical faction of the Republican party.

In 1860 Hickman won reelection, as a Republican, to the 37th Congress. There he used his oratorical skills, intellectual energy, and political experience to great effect in support of Radical economic, military, and political measures. He did not seek renomination in 1862, but served one term in the state legislature in the late 1860s. Hickman died in West Chester on March 23, 1875. *Biographical Encyclopedia of Pennsylvania of the Nineteenth Century*; Futhey, *History of Chester County, Pennsylvania.*

J. K. Folmar

HICKS, Thomas Holliday, *governor, senator,* was born in Dorchester county, Maryland, on September 2, 1798. At the age of twenty-one he was elected town constable, and a series of public offices followed: county sheriff; member of the House of Delegates, the Maryland Electoral College, and the Governor's Council; member of the 1850 state constitutional convention; and registrar of wills. Originally a Democrat, he became a Whig in the 1830s; with the collapse of that party, he joined the newly formed American party. As its candidate in 1857, Hicks was elected governor of Maryland. In the sectional crisis, his role in preventing precipitate action in Maryland was crucial. He refused to call the legislature into special session until after the rioting in Baltimore on April 19, 1861.

Despite his waverings, Hicks was determined to hold Maryland in the Union, and in this he was successful. His subsequent actions strengthened his Unionist stance and materially aided the extension of Federal control over Maryland. Following his retirement from office in January 1862, he was appointed a brigadier general. Poor health prevented his serving, but with the death of Senator James Pearce (*q.v.*) in 1862, Governor Augustus Bradford (*q.v.*) appointed him to serve out the term. In 1864, Hicks was elected to a full term. Owing to failing health, he made few speeches in the Senate but continued his support of the administration. Originally strongly proslavery, he cautiously and pragmatically moved to acceptance of emancipation. Hicks's great achievement was his handling of the crisis in Maryland while governor. He died in Washington, D.C., on February 18, 1865. Clark, *Politics in Maryland During the Civil War*; Radcliffe, *Governor Thomas Hicks.*

Richard R. Duncan

HIGBY, William, *congressman,* was born August 18, 1813, in Willsboro, New York. He graduated from the University of Vermont in 1840, taught school, studied law, and gained admission to the bar in 1844. He practiced at Elizabethtown, New York, until stricken with gold fever in 1850. Arriving on August

15, Higby worked at his profession in San Francisco, and in September 1851 turned to mining in Plumas county. The next year he settled in Calaveras county. County district attorney from 1853 to 1859, Higby also served on the Free Soil Democratic State Central Committee in 1858 and 1861. During his term as state senator in 1863, he supported the right of blacks to testify in court and various war measures. That summer he became one of the three Union party candidates for Congress. Successful in 1863, Higby was reelected in 1864 and 1867, but failed to receive the nomination in 1868.

Higby was a staunch supporter of the Lincoln (*q.v.*) administration and ably advocated the 13th Amendment and Reconstruction measures. He returned to San Francisco and practiced law until his appointment as collector of internal revenue in January 1877. After his retirement in 1881, he devoted himself to horticulture. He died in Santa Rosa, California, on November 27, 1887. Phelps, *Contemporary Biography*, vol. 2.

Robert J. Chandler

HINCKS, Edward Winslow, *general,* was born on May 30, 1803, in Bucksport, Maine. In 1849, he moved to Boston and later served in the Massachusetts legislature. He was appointed a 2nd lieutenant in the Regular Army (April–June 1861), and in August 1861 was named colonel of the 19th Massachusetts Volunteers. The regiment was at Ball's Bluff and on the Peninsula, where Hincks was wounded. He was severely wounded again at Antietam, and while on sick leave he was promoted to brigadier general of Volunteers. After recruiting duty and a brief stint as commander of a prisoner of war camp at Camp Lookout, Maryland, he was given command of an all-black division of the XVIII Corps in the Petersburg campaign.

Hincks showed admirable initiative in the capture of City Point in early May 1864. William Farrar Smith (*q.v.*), the corps commander, hesitated unduly and lost the opportunity to move on a weekly defended Petersburg. Benjamin F. Butler (*q.v.*) launched a poorly coordinated attack on June 8, during which Hincks seemed to be the one division commander who wanted to carry the objective. Had Butler allowed Hincks, rather than Quincy A. Gillmore (*q.v.*), to command the expedition, the Union forces could have achieved a valuable, if not decisive, advantage. As it was, Hincks left his field command for recruiting duty. Following the war he was given the rank of lieutenant colonel in the Regular Army, and in 1870 retired with the rank of colonel. Hincks died in Cambridge, Massachusetts, on February 14, 1894. Robertson, *Back Door to Richmond.*

John T. Hubbell

HITCHCOCK, Ethan Allen, *general,* was born on May 18, 1798, in Vergennes, Vermont. He graduated in 1817 from West Point, where he was later commandant of cadets. He served in the wars with the Indians and with Mexico, in the latter as inspector general for Winfield Scott (*q.v.*). In 1856, Hitchcock resigned his colonel's commission after a dispute with Secretary of War Jefferson Davis, and devoted himself to the philosophical and literary studies that would occupy much of his remaining life.

Scott's influence obtained Hitchcock's appointment as major general of Volunteers in February 1862. He wisely rebuffed, on grounds of age and frail health, the desperate suggestion of the new Secretary of War, Edwin M. Stanton (*q.v.*), that he should become commander of the Army of the Potomac. Instead, Hitchcock became one of Stanton's advisers (one of the few authorized to sign for him) and applied his considerable administrative experience to the reorganization of the War Department, often tempering his chief's angry impatience.

On November 15, 1862, Hitchcock became commissioner for the exchange of prisoners, and in that position rendered his most significant service. He was intellectually well qualified to uphold his government's stand in the interminable bickering with his Confederate counterpart. Convinced of Union rectitude, he set forth in published correspondence legalistic arguments, concerning the handling of paroles and black prisoners, that attempted to justify the developing Federal policy of refusing to exchange prisoners. On November 3, 1865, Hitchcock became commissary general of prisoners and supervised the settling of a large number of postwar claims. With the closing of the office on August 19, 1867, he was mustered out. He moved South for his health and died on August 5, 1870, in Sparta, Georgia. Hitchcock, *Fifty Years.*

Frank L. Byrne

HOBSON, Edward Henry, *general,* was born on July 11, 1825, in Greensburg, Kentucky. He attended local schools in Greensburg and Danville, then entered business with his father. In May 1846 he enlisted in the 2nd Kentucky Infantry, was elected 2nd lieutenant, and won promotion to 1st lieutenant for gallantry at Buena Vista. Mustered out in 1847, he resumed his successful business career. When Kentucky entered the Civil War, Hobson recruited the 13th Kentucky Infantry, mustered into service on December 30, 1861, and became its colonel. Assigned to Thomas L. Crittenden's (*q.v.*) division, Hobson earned praise for his leadership at Shiloh.

After the summer campaign in Tennessee and northern Alabama, Hobson returned to Kentucky when General Don Carlos Buell (*q.v.*) hurried northward to check the Braxton Bragg–Edmund Kirby Smith invasion. He did not participate in the Perryville battle that led to Confederate withdrawal. He was left in southern Kentucky to help guard against guerrillas and Confederate raiders, particularly John Hunt Morgan. Hobson was promoted to brigadier general in April 1863 with rank from November 29, 1862. He chased Morgan across Kentucky, Indiana, and Ohio in July 1863, and helped capture several hundred Confederates at Buffington Island. Hobson then resumed his guard duties in south-central Kentucky. He was embarrassed at Cynthiana on June 11, 1864, when he was captured by Morgan. Ill health prevented him from accepting a more active command, and he headed the 1st Division, Department of Kentucky, until mustered out of service on August 24, 1865.

Hobson performed well for most of his military career, although success in his Kentucky assignment was impossible. The major blot on his record was his surrender and questionable parole at Cynthiana, but he was exonerated of all charges. Hobson became interested in postwar Republican politics, but he was defeated for clerk of the Court of Appeals. In 1869, President Ulysses S. Grant (*q.v.*) appointed him a district collector of internal revenue. His business interests prospered, and he was active in the Grand Army of the Republic. Hobson was attending a GAR encampment in Cleveland, Ohio, when he died on September 15, 1901. Keller, *Morgan's Raid*; Ramage, *Rebel Raider*; Speed, *Union Regiments of Kentucky.*

Lowell H. Harrison

HOFFMAN, William, *general,* was born in 1808 at the military post of his Army lieutenant father, who obtained his appointment to West Point. After graduating in 1829, he fought in the Indian and Mexican Wars, and at the start of the Civil War was among the troops whom David E. Twiggs surrendered in Texas. As a paroled prisoner, Hoffman was appointed on October 7, 1861, as commissary general of prisoners. He was formally exchanged on August 27, 1862, and promoted to colonel of the 3rd U.S. Infantry. As warden for the Union's prisoners, he supervised construction of the depot on Johnson's Island, Ohio, in Lake Erie. He also directed the expansion of the Federal prison system and kept records of the unprecedented numbers of captives, infinitely more men than he had ever commanded in peacetime.

Hoffman was an efficient administrator, but his insistence on rigid economy in furnishing food and housing contributed to suffering and death among the prisoners. Except from November 11, 1864, to February 1, 1865, when his duties were limited to prisoners west of the Mississippi, Hoffman supervised, from his headquarters in Washington, all Confederates in Union captivity until November 3, 1865. He was breveted brigadier general in the Regular Army on October 7, 1864, and major general on March 13, 1865. Hoffman continued in the Regular Army until he retired in 1870. He died at Rock Island, Illinois, in August, 1884. Hesseltine, *Civil War Prisons.*

Frank L. Byrne

HOLBROOK, Frederick, *governor,* was born at Warehouse Point, Connecticut, on February 15, 1813. He attended the Brattleboro common schools and Berkshire Academy, and after graduation worked in a Boston bookstore. Holbrook's influence in promoting more efficient agriculture through adaptation of European methods was widely acknowledged, and crossed state borders through his numerous articles. Harnessing his agricultural concerns to politics, he was elected to the Vermont Senate in 1849 and again in 1850. For the remainder of the decade, he declined to participate in electoral politics while his public and professional reputation continued to grow.

In 1861, Holbrook was courted by both the Republicans and the Democrats as a gubernatorial candidate, and received the Republican nomination. He was elected with 77 percent of the popular vote in September 1861 and was reelected in 1862 with over 88 percent. Holbrook's principal achievements as governor were to negotiate a bond sale at rates that facilitated the state's ability to adhere to his plan to pay half of the war expenses "as we go," and in 1862, in association with Abraham Lincoln (*q.v.*), to call for the raising of additional troops in the face of Vermont's declining reserves.

Under Holbrook, Vermont became the first state to have hospitals for its soldiers. After completing his second term in 1863, he returned to Brattleboro, where he maintained his interest in scientific farming, engaged in banking, and wrote his *Reminiscences*. He died in Brattleboro on April 28, 1909. Crockett, *Vermont*, vol. 3; Moore, "Frederick Holbrook," *Vermont History*.

D. Gregory Sanford

HOLMAN, William Steele, *congressman*, was born on September 6, 1822, in Aurora, Indiana. After attending common schools and Franklin College, he taught school, studied law, and was admitted to the bar (1843). A Democrat, he held the offices of judge of Probate Court (1843–1847), prosecuting attorney (1847–1849), member of the state's constitutional convention (1850–1851), and judge of the Court of Common Pleas (1852–1856). He also served in the U.S. House of Representatives (1859–1865, 1867–1877, 1881–1895).

On December 16, 1860, Holman, a War Democrat from southern Indiana, introduced a resolution condemning secession and declaring it the duty of the government to maintain the Union. He opposed abandonment of Federal property in the South. Although antislavery, he refused to endorse emancipation and the 13th Amendment, arguing that slavery was dead and the amendment unnecessary. In 1864, Holman declined to run on his party's platform, which declared the war a failure. During his thirty years in Congress, he earned the title of "watchdog of the Treasury" for his tight fiscal policies. He died on April 22, 1897, in Washington, D.C. Shepherd, *Biographical Directory of the Indiana General Assembly*, vol. 1; Stampp, *Indiana Politics During the Civil War*; Thornbrough, *Indiana in the Civil War Era*.

David G. Vanderstel

HOLT, Joseph, *Postmaster General, Secretary of War, Judge Advocate General*, was born in Breckinridge county, Kentucky, on January 6, 1807. Educated at St. Joseph's and Centre colleges, he became a lawyer. He supported the election of President James Buchanan (*q.v.*) and received successive appointments as commissioner of patents, Postmaster General, and Secretary of War. Although previously opposed to Federal coercion of a state, Holt urged firmness when Buchanan faced the secession crisis. After the inauguration of Abraham

Lincoln (*q.v.*), he played an important part in winning his native Kentucky for the Union. The grateful President appointed Holt Judge Advocate General, ranking as colonel from September 3, 1862, and as brigadier general from June 22, 1864. Also holding the title of head of the Bureau of Military Justice, Holt reviewed the proceedings of courts martial and military commissions. In this function, he was careful to insist that correct procedure be followed.

More controversial was Holt's involvement in the arrests of civilians and their trials by military commissions. Of these the most notorious were the cases of Clement L. Vallandigham (*q.v.*) and Lambdin P. Milligan (*q.v.*). The assassination of President Lincoln and the decision to try the alleged assassins by military commission thrust Holt into the limelight. He personally headed the prosecutions of the accused and supervised that of the keeper of Andersonville Prison, Henry Wirz. His strong belief that the Confederacy's former leaders had conspired in the crimes of all of the accused made him easy prey for perjured witnesses, whose testimony did much to discredit him. Especially damaging to his reputation was a public confrontation with former President Andrew Johnson (*q.v.*) over whether Holt had shown him the petition for clemency for Mary E. Surratt, signed by some members of the military commission that sentenced her to be hanged. Even after his retirement in 1875, Holt wrote in defense of his side of this disputed matter. Of more enduring effect was the frequent citation of his precedents on points of military law. Holt died in Washington, D.C., on August 1, 1894. Hanchett, *Lincoln Murder Conspiracies.*

Frank L. Byrne

HOMER, Winslow, *artist,* was born on February 24, 1836, in Boston; in 1842 his family moved to nearby Cambridge. His father encouraged his early indication of artistic talent, and in 1855 apprenticed him to John H. Bufford, a publisher of lithographs. By 1859, Homer was a freelance illustrator, contributing mainly to *Harper's Weekly.* He attended the National Academy of Design, presumably to receive instruction in drawing. His only formal training in oil painting, from Frederick Rondel, a French artist, was acquired at this time.

In 1861, Homer became a freelance artist–correspondent for *Harper's.* He was in Washington that year to sketch Lincoln's inauguration, then in Virginia for his first assignment with the Army of the Potomac. In the spring of 1862, he covered the Peninsula campaign with the staff of Colonel Francis C. Barlow (*q.v.*), whose portrait Homer later painted as the Union officer in *Prisoners from the Front* (1866). In early 1862, *Harper's* published a Homer drawing almost every week. With few exceptions, his illustrations are colorful, realistic, and frequently humorous impressions of camp scenes and the dull life of the Union soldier. For the Boston publisher Louis Prang, Homer executed two sets of lithographs, *Campaign Sketches* and *Life in Camp,* in an even more broadly humorous style.

The paintings Homer began to do at this time, and for which he received his first critical attention, are quite a different matter: they are sober and matter-of-fact depictions of everyday events (*Home, Sweet Home* in 1863 and *Pitching Horseshoes* in 1865, for example) that have a timeless human appeal. The paintings, produced in his New York studio from drawings made during three visits to the Virginia front, reveal Homer's dislike of military pomp and the conventional rhetoric of nineteenth-century battle art; of some twenty Civil War paintings, only five show action. *Prisoners from the Front*, acclaimed in 1866 as a picture that summed up the meaning of the war, made his reputation and is still thought to be the greatest painting inspired by the conflict.

After an extended visit to Paris in 1867, Homer settled into a pattern of drawing and painting scenes of everyday life in rural Massachusetts, New Jersey, and New York. He began painting in watercolor around 1873; some of his most memorable work in this medium was painted in 1881–1882 near Tynemouth, on the east coast of England, where he depicted the fishermen and their wives in a heroic and elemental struggle with the North Sea. In his later years, Homer made his permanent home at Prout's Neck in Scarboro, Maine, where he built a studio cottage near the ocean and continued to paint the epic theme of men's effort's to win a living from the sea. During the summers, he traveled north into the Maine woods, Canada, and the Adirondacks; in the winters he often went south to Florida, Nassau, Bermuda, or Cuba. From these travels Homer created perhaps the century's greatest works on the theme of outdoor life. He died at Prout's Neck on September 29, 1910. Gardner, *Winslow Homer*; Goodrich, *Winslow Homer's America*; Wilmerding, *Winslow Homer.*

Ben Bassham

HOOKER, Joseph, *general,* was born on November 13, 1814, in Hadley, Massachusetts. He graduated from West Point in 1837, served in Florida (1837–1838), and in the Mexican War won three brevets for gallantry and meritorious conduct. He then served on the Pacific Coast, and resigned from the Army as a captain in 1853. When the Civil War came, Hooker journeyed to the East, seeking a command. Although named a brigadier general of Volunteers on May 17, 1861, he was only a private observer at Bull Run. George B. McClellan (*q.v.*) named him a brigade, and then a division, commander later in 1861, and it was in this capacity that he ably participated in the Peninsula and Second Bull Run campaigns.

A major general of Volunteers since May 1862, Hooker capably commanded the Army of the Potomac's I Corps in the Maryland campaign. At Fredericksburg, in December 1862, he again demonstrated his ability as a commander of a grand division. In each of these operations Hooker always seemed to know what to do and when to do it, and he was highly regarded as a general. A fine figure of a soldier, with graying light hair, a ruddy complexion, and dominant blue eyes, he had been known by some, however, for his fondness of women and the bottle, and he had been a sharp-tongued, carping critic of a number of his superiors and subordinates.

Although most of the Union's ablest generals questioned his ability to command an army, and in spite of his denunciation of Abraham Lincoln (*q.v.*) and his call for a military dictatorship, headed by himself, Hooker was named commander of the Army of the Potomac. He thoroughly reorganized the army during the winter of 1862–1863, and drew up an imaginative plan of operations to attack Robert E. Lee's army in front and rear at Fredericksburg. In early May, outgeneraling Lee at first, Hooker swung his army through the Wilderness toward the Confederate rear. But then, losing his nerve and uncharacteristically refusing to fight offensively, he withdrew into the Wilderness, to an area around Chancellorsville. He thus surrendered the initiative to Lee, who promptly attacked and defeated him. Hooker was injured in the battle.

In most of his military campaigns, Hooker performed most creditably. The exception was at Chancellorsville, where he exercised command of the largest army (some 132,000) raised by either side during the Civil War. Against some 62,000 Confederates, and also against the advice of nearly all of his subordinate generals, Hooker, after a most promising, even brilliant, opening of the campaign, suddenly and astonishingly lost confidence (as he later admitted) and withdrew his army from open ground, where his superior artillery could be used to good effect, into a cramped, wooded position around the crossroads at Chancellorsville.

Some historians think that Hooker's abrupt end to heavy drinking, in which he apparently had engaged in for years, caused a severe physical, emotional, and psychological letdown. After a sharp battle of several days, in which he lost over 17,000 men, "Fighting Joe" refused to throw many reserve troops into combat, and retreated against the advice of a majority of his top generals. As *New York Times* war correspondent William Swinton averred, "Not the Army of the Potomac was beaten at Chancellorsville, but its commander."

Although he maneuvered his army dexterously in the early stages of the Gettysburg campaign, Hooker was relieved of command at his own request three days before the opening of the great battle. Returning again as a corps commander—his true level of ability—he performed well at the battle of Chattanooga in November 1863, and was with William T. Sherman's (*q.v.*) army in the advance on Atlanta. But when Oliver O. Howard (*q.v.*) was promoted ahead of him, Hooker resigned. Until his retirement in 1868, he served as the commander of several military departments. He died in Garden City, New York, on October 31, 1879. Furgurson, *Chancellorsville*; Hassler, *Commanders of the Army of the Potomac*; Herbert, *Fighting Joe Hooker*.

Warren W. Hassler, Jr.

HOOPER, Samuel, *congressman,* was born on February 3, 1808, in Marblehead, Massachusetts. After obtaining a common school education, he moved to Boston and began a business career. He inherited considerable wealth from his father, married well, and proceeded to make wise investments in shipping, banking, industrial, and railroad properties. During the 1850s, Hooper served for four years in the Massachusetts legislature, and by 1858 was influential in the Republican party in Boston. When the Civil War began, he devoted himself wholly to public affairs.

In 1861, Hooper was elected to Congress, and was returned to his seat six consecutive times. He had already gained a reputation for his knowledge about currency and financial affairs, and was given committee assignments on Ways and Means, Banking and Currency, and Coinage, Weights, and Measures committees. By the end of the war, he was acknowledged as the foremost Republican financial expert in the House. Along with most of the Massachusetts delegation, he voted for Radical measures regarding emancipation, freedmen's rights, and treatment of Southern rebels.

Hooper's chief legislative efforts were devoted to supporting the administration's financial program, on which he worked closely with Secretary of the Treasury Salmon P. Chase (*q.v.*). He helped draft tax measures, was a strong supporter of issuing legal-tender notes, and sponsored the National Bank Bill in the House. After the war he advocated a policy of greenback contraction and played an important role in framing the Currency Act of 1873. On February 14, 1875, Hooper died in Washington, D.C. Curry, *Blueprint for Modern America*; Nugent, *Money and American Society.*

Richard H. Abbott

HORTON, Valentine Baxter, *congressman*, was born in Windsor, Vermont, on January 29, 1802. He graduated from and taught at Partridge Military Academy; moved to Middletown, Connecticut, to study law with Samuel Dana; and was admitted to the bar in 1830. In 1831, he moved to Pittsburgh, and in 1833 to Cincinnati. In Pomeroy, Ohio, Horton engaged in the economic development of the region's rich coal and salt resources. He helped to organize the Pomeroy Coal Company and used tow barges to transport coal to market on the Ohio River. Horton was a Whig member of the 1850 Ohio Constitutional Convention, and was elected to the 34th and 35th Congresses. He did not seek reelection in 1858, but he was elected in 1860, as a Republican. Horton was one of Ohio's representatives to the 1861 Peace Conference in Washington, D.C.

His knowledge of government financing caused Horton to support the issuance of government notes, but as one of the most conservative House Republicans, he usually joined a handful of others in voting against measures such as the Negro Troop Bill and confiscation legislation. He returned to Pomeroy, continued his study of natural resources in Ohio, and was the first chairman of the board of trustees of the Ohio Agricultural and Mechanical College (now Ohio State University). He died in Pomeroy on January 14, 1888. Curry, *Blueprint for Modern America.*

Thomas H. Smith

HOTCHKISS, Giles Waldo, *congressman*, was born in Windsor, New York, on October 25, 1815. He attended Windsor and Oxford academies, studied law, and was admitted to the bar in 1837. Hotchkiss was one of the founders of the

Republican party in New York, and a delegate to its 1860 national convention in Chicago. He was part of the Radical wing of the party while maintaining a close and supportive friendship with President Abraham Lincoln (*q.v.*). At one point, Hotchkiss intended to resign from the 38th Congress and enlist in the Army despite his frail constitution, but Lincoln persuaded him to remain in Washington.

Reelected in 1864, Hotchkiss lost his battle for a third nomination in 1866, although he did return to Congress in 1869. After serving in the 41st Congress, Hotchkiss retired to his law practice in Binghamton, New York. He refused offers of judicial and legal posts from his friends Roscoe Conkling (*q.v.*) and Ulysses S. Grant (*q.v.*). Hotchkiss died in Binghamton on July 5, 1878. *Biographical Review . . . of Broome County.*

Lori A. Lisowski

HOVEY, Alvin Peterson, *general,* was born on September 26, 1821, near Mount Vernon, Indiana. He served as an officer of Volunteers in the Mexican War but saw no combat. Hovey was active in Indiana Democratic politics, and in 1856 President Franklin Pierce named him U.S. district attorney for Indiana, a position he held until 1858, when his support of the Stephen A. Douglas (*q.v.*) wing of the Democratic party led to his removal from office by President James Buchanan (*q.v.*). He became a Republican and was that party's unsuccessful candidate for Congress in 1858.

When the Civil War began, Hovey devoted himself to raising troops, and in July 1861 was made colonel of the 24th Indiana Volunteers. Promoted to brigadier general of Volunteers for his conduct at Shiloh, he served in Arkansas and in the Vicksburg campaign as a division commander in the XIII Corps. He won high praise for his conduct at Champion Hill, Mississippi. In the winter of 1863–1864, Hovey was sent to raise a new division, and with this command he was assigned to the XXIII Corps, Army of the Ohio. He participated in the first movements of Major General William T. Sherman's (*q.v.*) Atlanta campaign, but saw little action and soon expressed great unhappiness with the organization of his command. Sherman allowed him a leave of absence pending a decision on his resignation. Shortly afterward, Hovey was made a brevet major general of Volunteers. This promotion was a recognition of his earlier services, but the timing was unfortunate. It became the subject of some sharp comments from Sherman, who believed that Hovey had in effect left his comrades at a time of crisis. Not even President Abraham Lincoln (*q.v.*) could completely mollify Sherman.

Hovey held an administrative command in the North until the end of the war. He was U.S. minister to Peru (1865–1870), then returned to Indiana and resumed his law practice. In 1872, he declined the Republican gubernatorial nomination, but four years later he was elected to Congress, where he busied himself introducing and supporting veterans' pension bills. In 1888, he was elected governor of Indiana. Hovey died in Indianapolis on November 23, 1891. Bearss, *Vicksburg*

Campaign; Castel, *Decision in the West*; Tredway, *Democratic Opposition to the Lincoln Administration in Indiana.*

Richard M. McMurry

HOWARD, Jacob Merritt, *senator*, was born on July 10, 1805, in Shaftsbury, Vermont. He attended academies in Bennington and Brattleboro, graduated from Williams College in 1830, and studied law in Ware, Massachusetts. In 1832, he moved to Detroit, where in the following year he was admitted to the bar. Howard was city attorney of Detroit (1834), a member of the state legislature (1838), and a Whig member of the U.S. House of Representatives (1841–1843). He reentered politics in 1854 when he drew up the platform of the convention that met "under the oaks" in Jackson, Michigan, and organized the Republican party. Two years later, he attended the convention in Pittsburgh that worked to establish the Republican party as a national organization.

Howard was attorney general of Michigan (1856–1861) and a U.S. senator (1862–1871). On important political issues he consistently demonstrated the courage of his convictions. An outspoken foe of slavery, he denounced the Fugitive Slave Act of 1850, defended the personal liberty laws, and opposed the extension of slavery in the territories. In the Senate he served on the Judiciary and the Military Affairs committees. As a supporter of vigorous prosecution of the war, Howard favored confiscation of Rebel property, conscription, and firmness toward disloyal persons.

After Appomattox, Howard lost patience with Andrew Johnson (*q.v.*), sided with the Radical Republicans, and served on the Joint Committee on Reconstruction. He argued that the Southern states had forfeited their rights and were conquered provinces, and that Congress alone had constitutional authority to reconstruct them. He voted to impeach President Johnson and supported the 14th and 15th Amendments. Howard was widely respected as an honest, principled man of unusual intellectual strength. He died in Detroit on April 2, 1871. Barnard, *American Biographical History*; Bogue, *Earnest Men.*

Frederick D. Williams

HOWARD, Oliver Otis, *general*, was born in Leeds, Maine, on November 8, 1830. He graduated from Bowdoin College in 1850, and from West Point in 1854. Following service in ordnance, he taught mathematics at West Point until the outbreak of the war. Howard was elected colonel of the 3d Maine Infantry, and after Bull Run he was promoted to brigadier general and assigned to the II Corps. He lost his right arm at Fair Oaks, but within two months he had returned to the army and was learning to write with his left hand. In March 1863 he was promoted to major general and given command of the XI Corps.

At Chancellorsville, Howard's neglect led to the rout of his corps by Stonewall Jackson's flank attack. After the death of General John Reynolds (*q.v.*) on the first day at Gettysburg, Howard commanded the Union forces on the field until relieved by General Winfield S. Hancock (*q.v.*). He selected the Union position on Cemetery Hill, but his generalship on that day was sharply criticized by both peers and subordinates. In September 1863, Howard was reassigned, participating in the battles around Chattanooga, the Atlanta campaign, and General William T. Sherman's (*q.v.*) campaign through Georgia and the Carolinas. He was named commander of the Army of the Tennessee after the death of General James B. McPherson (*q.v.*).

After the war, Howard was appointed commissioner of the Freedmen's Bureau, where he proved to be an inefficient administrator. He was instrumental in founding Howard University and was director of the Freedmen's Bank. During the 1870s and 1880s, he served on the frontier, including the arduous campaign against the Nez Perce in 1877. In 1893, he was awarded the Medal of Honor for his accomplishments at Fair Oaks. Howard was a deeply religious, sincere man. In battle he was personally brave, but as a commander never rose above mediocrity. His promotion after McPherson's death owed much to Sherman's bias against "political generals," such as the estimable John A. Logan (*q.v.*), whom Howard replaced. Howard retired in 1894 and died in Burlington, Vermont, on October 26, 1909. Carpenter, *Sword and Olive Branch*; Castel, *Decision in the West*; Furgurson, *Chancellorsville*.

D. Scott Hartwig

HOWE, Timothy Otis, *senator*, was born on February 24, 1816, in Livermore, Maine. He attended Maine Wesleyan Seminary, studied law, and was admitted to the bar in 1839. Howe was active in local politics and was elected as a Whig to the Maine House of Representatives in 1844. In 1845, he opened a law office in Green Bay, Wisconsin, and in 1848 was nominated by the Whigs for Congress. Whigs selected him again the next year, but this time for lieutenant governor. The Barnburner Democrats, however, captured the free-soil issues, the voters, and the election. In 1850, Howe was elected to a six-year term as judge of the 4th District Circuit Court. Although he took no direct part in the organizational meeting of the Republican party following passage of the Kansas–Nebraska Act, many delegates to the first Republican convention expressed enthusiasm for Howe's nomination to the Senate. He resigned from the bench, largely because of his reluctance to support personal liberty laws, and lost the nomination for senator to James R. Doolittle (*q.v.*) in 1857.

After the election of 1860, Howe gained favor with many of the state's conservative Republicans. He faced strong opposition from Governor Alexander Randall (*q.v.*) and Cadwallader C. Washburn (*q.v.*), until Randall accepted a promise of an equal share in the patronage; the opposition then weakened, and Howe was nominated. He was elected by the legislature, and on March 4, 1861, became a member of the U.S. Senate. He supported Abraham Lincoln's (*q.v.*) war policies, from issuance of greenbacks to the suspension of the writ of habeas corpus. During one of his visits to Green Bay, in November 1862, it appeared so likely that a group of draft resisters was preparing to mob his home that he was forced to escape by a side door. As the war dragged on, Howe became increasingly tired of the administration's "limping policy" and seriously considered backing the presidential candidacy of Salmon P. Chase (*q.v.*). When that failed, Howe returned to the Lincoln camp, although without much enthusiasm.

As the war ended, Howe assumed a Radical Republican position, arguing in a January 10, 1866, speech that territorial governments should be established to replace the former states of the Confederacy. In January 1867, he was unopposed in his reelection to the Senate. Although his alliance with the Radicals caused some problems with patronage, he was successful in obtaining an impressive program of internal improvements for Wisconsin. Howe opposed Andrew Johnson's (*q.v.*) postwar program, but those within the President's circle did not regard him as among their principal antagonists. He was briefly considered for a Cabinet position in James Garfield's (*q.v.*) administration, but it was Chester Arthur who finally brought him back as Postmaster General. Howe died on March 25, 1883, in Kenosha, Wisconsin. Current, *Civil War Era*; Nesbit, *Wisconsin: A History.*

Charles E. Twining

HUBBARD, Asahel Wheeler, *congressman*, was born on January 19, 1819, in Haddam, Connecticut. He attended the common schools, worked on the family farm, and learned the stonecutter's trade. After further schooling at an academy in Middletown, he moved in 1838 to Rushville, Indiana. There Hubbard taught school, worked as a book agent, and studied law. Following admission to the bar, he practiced in Rushville for sixteen years and served as a Whig representative (1847–1849) in the Indiana legislature. Hubbard moved to Sioux City, Iowa, in 1857, and became involved in real estate speculation, railroad promotion, the law, and the Republican party. Elected as judge of Iowa's 4th Judicial District, he served in that post from 1859 to 1862. In 1862, Hubbard won the first of three successive terms to the U.S. Congress. He was a consistent supporter of war measures, but only reluctantly voted for the Wade–Davis Bill.

After the war, Hubbard opposed Andrew Johnson's (*q.v.*) Reconstruction policies and voted for the President's impeachment. He did not vote on either the Reconstruction Act of 1867 or the 15th Amendment. At the end of his congressional career, he was considered to be, along with John Kasson (*q.v.*), more of a moderate among the generally Radical Iowa congressional delegation than was agreeable to the dominant wing of the party. When he left office, Hubbard returned to the law, railroad promotion, the organization of the First National Bank of Sioux City, and mining interests in Colorado. Hubbard died in Sioux City on September 22, 1879. Clark, *History of the Counties of Woodbury and Plymouth, Iowa*; Sage, *William Boyd Allison.*

Hubert H. Wubben

HUBBARD, John Henry, *congressman*, was born on March 24, 1804, in Salisbury, Connecticut. He attended public schools, then studied law, and was admitted to the Connecticut bar in 1828. Hubbard, a Whig, served two years in the Connecticut Senate (1847–1849). He was appointed Connecticut's prosecuting attorney in 1849 and held that office for three years. During his service in the 37th and 38th Congresses, Hubbard was a loyal Republican, fully in sympathy with Lincoln's (*q.v.*) war policies. He was instrumental in organizing recruitment drives in Litchfield and regularly gave speeches on the Litchfield green, exhorting those who sought exemptions from service to heed the call to arms. When he was not nominated for a third term in 1867, he returned to his law practice. Hubbard died in Litchfield on July 30, 1872. Croffut, *Military and Civil History of Connecticut During the War.*

Joanna D. Cowden

HUGHES, John Joseph, *archbishop*, was born in County Tyrone, Ireland, on June 24, 1797. Fleeing religious persecution by Protestants in Northern Ireland, he emigrated to the United States in 1817. In 1823, he enrolled at Mount St. Mary's College in Maryland to study for the priesthood, and in 1826 he completed his studies. After serving as a priest in Philadelphia, Hughes was appointed in 1838 as coadjutor to the bishop of New York. In 1839, he sailed to Europe to raise money for the American Catholic Church, some of which he used to found the College of St. John (later Fordham University). In 1841, he sought municipal funding for Catholic schools in New York City but was rebuffed by the Public School Society and later by the state legislature, despite the backing of Governor William H. Seward (*q.v.*). In 1842, Hughes was able to persuade the legislature to remove the schools of New York City from the control of the private (and Protestant) Public School Society, and place them under public jurisdiction.

On December 20, 1842, Hughes became bishop of New York, and in 1847, he was invited to address a joint session of Congress. In 1850 he became the first Roman Catholic archbishop of New York, with jurisdiction over New England as well. In 1858, he laid the cornerstone of St. Patrick's Cathedral, the location and design of which he personally determined. In 1861 and 1862, Hughes traveled in Europe, speaking in favor of the Union cause to Catholics, including Pope Pius IX and Emperor Napoleon III, in France, Italy, and Ireland. A year later, although in declining health, he worked to help quell the draft riots in New York City. He died there on January 3, 1864. Hassard, *Life of the Most Reverend John Hughes*; Lannie, *Public Money and Parochial Education.*

Norman B. Ferris

HULBURD, Calvin Tilden, *congressman*, was born on June 5, 1809, in Stockholm, New York. He graduated from Middlebury College in 1829, and attended Yale Law School. Although admitted to the bar in 1833, he chose to farm instead. In 1839, he and his brother bought 600 acres of land around Brasher Falls, where they constructed a gristmill and dry goods store. Hulburd became the town's first postmaster, a member of the New York State Assembly (1842–1844), and a town supervisor (1859, 1860).

When the Civil War began, Hulburd was a member of a town committee that directed local efforts to meet volunteer quotas. In 1862, he was elected as a Republican to the 38th Congress, where he served on the Agriculture, Public Expenditures, Library, Customhouse Frauds, and Reconstruction committees. He was an ardent supporter of the Emancipation Proclamation. He died in Brasher Falls on October 25, 1897. Durant, *History of St. Lawrence County.*

Lori A. Lisowski

HUMPHREYS, Andrew Atkinson, *general,* was born in Philadelphia on November 2, 1810. He graduated from West Point in 1831, was commissioned in the artillery, and served in the South before resigning in 1836. After two years as civilian engineer with the Army, he reentered the service as lieutenant (later captain) in the Corps of Topographical Engineers. The U.S. Coast Survey, routes for the Pacific railroad, and—most enduring—a hydrographical study of the Mississippi River brought him international recognition. Still suspect as an Old Army protégé of Jefferson Davis, Humphreys was passed over until December 1861, when he joined George B. McClellan's (*q.v.*) staff. The following spring, he became chief topographical engineer, Army of the Potomac, for the Peninsula campaign.

Ever anxious for command, Humphreys took charge of a new Pennsylvania division in September 1862. He almost lost this post to a War Department favorite, but he managed to get his troops to the V Corps just after Antietam. At Fredericksburg, he inspired his inexperienced soldiers to one of the most famous (albeit unsuccessful) charges of the war, but his division saw less action at Chancellorsville. Transferred to command the 2nd Division, III Corps, Humphreys again fought gallantly in a losing effort at Gettysburg, but at least managed to extricate his troops from the perilous position where Daniel Sickles (*q.v.*) had placed them.

On July 8, 1863, George G. Meade (*q.v.*) named Humphreys chief of staff, Army of the Potomac, with promotion to major general. The two generals worked well together, both professionally and personally. Humphreys's nobility of person and aggressiveness complemented Meade's personal abrasiveness and military prudence. Such differences produced balance at headquarters. Both Meade and Ulysses S. Grant (*q.v.*) understood Humphreys's contributions; they also understood his yearning to resume command. Finally, in November 1864 they entrusted him with the II Corps, as a worthy successor to Winfield Scott Hancock (*q.v.*). The corps, badly shredded that spring and summer, regained its strength over the winter, and Humphreys knew how to use its fighting qualities: defensively at Second Hatcher's Run, offensively at Watkins' Farm, White Oak Road, Sailor's Creek, High Bridge, and Cumberland Church. His relentless pursuit helped pin Robert E. Lee at Appomattox.

Many officers did one thing well; Humphreys did everything well. He was an acclaimed scientific engineer, an original member of the National Academy of Sciences, a pioneering historian of Meade's campaign, a mapmaker, a military administrator, a translator of his superiors' intentions into plans and orders, an inspiring, aggressive, and effective combat commander. Had he not been suspect in 1861, and had he been allowed more field than staff duty, he would likely have received still higher office and fame. Although not the most renowned, Humphreys nevertheless ranks among the best Northern generals. After the war, he briefly commanded the District of Pennsylvania and inspected levees on the Mississippi River. In 1866, he became brigadier general and chief of engineers, a post he filled with distinction until retiring in 1879. He died in Washington, D.C., on December 27, 1883. Humphreys, *Andrew Atkinson Humphreys*; Rhea, *Battle of the Wilderness*; Sommers, *Richmond Redeemed.*

Richard J. Sommers

HUNT, Henry Jackson, *general,* was born on September 14, 1819, in Detroit. He graduated from West Point in 1839, and for the next two decades he served on garrison duty in various parts of the country. During the Mexican War, as a light artillery lieutenant, he was twice wounded and won two brevets for gallantry in action. By 1856, Hunt's reputation as a military theorist gained him a place on a three-officer panel revising artillery tactics. A few years later, the board's work was used extensively by Federals and Confederates alike. During the 1860 election, while serving in Washington, D.C., he voted for John Breckinridge.

When war came, however, Hunt refused to follow friends into Confederate service. As a major in the 5th U.S. Artillery, he protected the Union left flank from attack at First Bull Run. After the withdrawal to Washington, he won a colonelcy and command of the Army of the Potomac's Artillery Reserve. During the Peninsula campaign he led the Reserve with conspicuous ability, especially at Gaines' Mill and Malvern Hill. In the latter battle, 100 of his cannon shattered the Southern assault and ensured the safety of the retreating army under General George B. McClellan (*q.v.*).

Shortly before Antietam, McClellan named Hunt a brigadier general of Volunteers and the army's artillery commander. He served ably at Antietam, and at Fredericksburg he planned the army's crossing of the Rappahannock River, then opened the battle with his 147 guns. At Chancellorsville, General Joseph Hooker (*q.v.*) temporarily stripped him of authority—thus ensuring Union defeat.

On July 3, 1863, at Gettysburg, Hunt duplicated his performance at Malvern Hill, destroying Pickett's charge and helping gain the pivotal victory of the war. From June 1864 to April 1865, he headed siege operations at Petersburg. By war's close he was a brevet major general in both the Regular and Volunteer services. Early in 1866, however, he reverted to field grade in the 3rd Artillery and in 1869 became colonel of the 5th Artillery, a position he held for the rest of his career.

Hunt singlehandedly revamped the Union artillery, streamlining its administration, promoting massed firepower, and discouraging excessive expenditure of ammunition. Partially because of his outspoken political views, the government failed to reward him fully for his services. In 1885, President Chester Arthur killed a bill to restore him to brigadier and grant him an adequate pension. As a result, he died deep in debt and virtually forgotten by the War Department. After his retirement in 1883, he became governor of the Washington, D.C., Soldier's Home, where he died on February 11, 1889. Coddington, *Gettysburg Campaign*; Longacre, *Man Behind the Guns*; Naisawald, *Grape and Canister.*

Edward G. Longacre

HUNTER, David, *general,* was born on January 21, 1802, in Washington, D.C. After graduating from West Point in 1822, he served in the Old Northwest, but resigned in 1836 to go into business in Chicago. He reentered the army as a paymaster in 1842, and served in the Mexican War. In 1860, Hunter began a correspondence with Abraham Lincoln (*q.v.*), was invited to accompany him on his postelection trip to Washington, and later was made head of the Volunteer force guarding the White House. Thus closely associated with the President, he was commissioned a colonel of cavalry and a brigadier general of Volunteers in May 1861, the latter promotion probably raising him above his level of ability. Hunter was seriously wounded at Bull Run. In November 1861 he replaced John C. Frémont (*q.v.*) as head of the Western Department at St. Louis, and then was transferred to command in Kansas.

In March 1862, Hunter took charge of the Department of the South. He captured Fort Pulaski near Savannah, but a defeat at Secessionville on June 16 ended the possibility of the early capture of Charleston. His most conspicuous act occurred on May 9, 1862, when he declared the freedom of all slaves in his department, an order revoked by Lincoln as exceeding his authority. Hunter then repeatedly was on court and inspection duty. He served Judge Advocate General Joseph Holt (*q.v.*) in such roles as president of the court that convicted Fitz John Porter (*q.v.*). In May 1864 he replaced the defeated Franz Sigel (*q.v.*) in command of the Shenandoah Valley campaign. After winning at Piedmont, he retreated from the reinforced Confederates at Lynchburg and, by retiring into West Virginia, left the valley open for the raid on Washington by Jubal Early and for the burning of Chambersburg, in retaliation for Hunter's destruction of property in Virginia.

After Lincoln's assassination, Hunter accompanied his body to Springfield and later was president of the military commission that tried those accused of the assassination conspiracy. He was especially hated by Confederates for organizing one of the first black regiments (the 1st South Carolina) and for burning the buildings of the Virginia Military Institute. Hunter retired in 1866, and died in Washington, D.C., on February 2, 1886. Cornish, *Sable Arm*; Taylor, *With Sheridan up the Shenandoah Valley.*

Frank L. Byrne

HURLBUT, Stephen Augustus, *general,* was born on November 29, 1815, in Charleston, South Carolina. A regimental adjutant in the Seminole War in Florida in 1840, he thereafter served as a law clerk for the eminent South Carolina Unionist and jurist James Louis Petigru. Denounced as a swindler, he left Charleston in disgrace in 1845, established a law firm at Belvidere, Illinois, and served as a Whig delegate to the Illinois Constitutional Convention of 1847. Although an unsuccessful Republican congressional candidate throughout the 1850s, Hurlbut served twice in the Illinois legislature before the Civil War. He entered the U.S. Volunteers as a brigadier general in June 1861, but his lack of strategic ability and drunkenness on duty in northeast Missouri resulted in his removal from command in the fall of that year. Subsequently elevated to a division command under Ulysses S. Grant (*q.v.*) in West Tennessee, he bravely held the Union left at the battle of Shiloh.

Two months after Hurlbut's promotion to major general in September 1862, Grant made him commander of the XVI Corps at Memphis, Tennessee. Hurlbut resumed his heavy drinking and came under official scrutiny for allegedly accepting bribes from cotton speculators and for extorting ransoms from pro-Confederate political prisoners and contraband smugglers. Ordered home to Belvidere in April 1864, Hurlbut maintained a loyalty to President Abraham Lincoln (*q.v.*) that won him command of the Department of the Gulf in September of that year. Through his corrupt financial scheming in New Orleans, Hurlbut helped Southern conservatives to subvert Lincoln's liberal "ten percent" government in Louisiana. In April 1865 a military investigation panel charged Hurlbut with bribery and perjury, but the War Department seems to have suppressed incriminating evidence against him.

After the war, Hurlbut practiced law in Belvidere, served as the Grand Army of the Republic's first national commander, and sat in the Illinois legislature in 1867. As a reward for his political and military service, he was U.S. minister to Colombia (1869–1872). Elected as a Grant Republican to Congress in 1872 and 1874, he lost his bid for a third term in 1876. An attorney in Washington, D.C., until May 1881, Hurlbut served as U.S. minister to Peru during the War of the Pacific between Chile and Peru. His exercise of blatantly partisan diplomacy, his self-serving support of exploitative American investment interests in Peru, and his bitter opposition to the equally partisan U.S. minister to Chile, Hugh Judson Kilpatrick (*q.v.*), frustrated and discredited the State Department's peacemaking efforts during the war. Hurlbut died in Lima, Peru, on March 27, 1882. Bearss, *Vicksburg Campaign*; Sword, *Shiloh*; Williams, *Lincoln Finds a General*, vols. 3, 4, 5.

Jeffrey Lash

HUTCHINS, John, *congressman*, was born in Vienna, Ohio, on July 25, 1812. He graduated from Western Reserve College, studied law with David Tod (*q.v.*), who later was governor of Ohio, and was admitted to the bar in 1837. Hutchins was a clerk in the Common Pleas Court for Trumbull county, was mayor of Warren, Ohio, and for six years served on the Warren board of education. In 1846, he made an unsuccessful bid for Congress as an abolitionist. He served in the Ohio House (1848–1850), and in 1858 was elected to Congress as a Republican.

Hutchins introduced two bills that would prohibit slavery in the District of Columbia. Although a Radical Republican, he usually supported Abraham Lincoln's (*q.v.*) administration in all its policies, and especially defended the Emancipation Proclamation. Along with Benjamin F. Wade (*q.v.*), he help recruit men for the 2nd Ohio Volunteer Cavalry. Hutchins was not reelected in 1862. In 1868, he moved to Cleveland to continue his practice of law, and died there on November 20, 1891. Curry, *Blueprint for Modern America; Historical Collections of the Mahoning Valley.*

Thomas H. Smith

HUTCHINS, Wells Andrews, *congressman,* was born in Hartford, Ohio, on October 8, 1818. He read law in Warren, Ohio, with his cousin John Hutchins (*q.v.*), and in 1842 began practicing law in Portsmouth, Ohio. In 1851, Hutchins was elected as a Whig to the Ohio House of Representatives, and in 1855 attended the convention that organized the Ohio Republican party. However, in 1856 he became a Democrat and won election as city solicitor, an office he held until 1861. He was elected in 1862 to the 38th Congress, where he mildly supported Abraham Lincoln's (*q.v.*) administration and called for the use of African American troops in combat. Hutchins was defeated for reelection in 1864 and again in 1880. Returning to Portsmouth after his years in Congress, he practiced law until his death there on January 25, 1895. Evans, *History of Scioto County.*

Thomas H. Smith

I

INGALLS, Rufus, *general*, was born in Denmark, Maine, on August 23, 1818. He graduated from West Point in 1843, saw service with the 1st Dragoons in the Mexican War, and served principally as a quartermaster until the outbreak of the Civil War. In July 1861 General George B. McClellan (*q.v.*) named him chief quartermaster of the Union forces south of the Potomac River. Ingalls superintended the movement of Union forces by water to the Virginia Peninsula during the spring of 1862. He solved numerous problems and exhibited extraordinary skill in carrying out the transfer of over 100,000 troops and their equipment. His reputation as a quartermaster of unsurpassed ability was firmly established during the Peninsula campaign, and he held the position of chief quartermaster of the Army of the Potomac through its succession of commanders.

In every campaign, Ingalls assured that the Army of the Potomac was well supplied. When Ulysses S. Grant (*q.v.*) assumed command of Union forces in 1864, he made Ingalls chief quartermaster of all the armies operating against Richmond, a position he held until the end of the war. McClellan probably echoed a universal sentiment when he declared that Ingalls was without equal as a quartermaster in the field.

Following the war, Ingalls received the post of assistant quartermaster general, and in 1882 was promoted to brigadier general and named chief quartermaster of the army. He retired in 1883 after forty years of service, and died in New York City on January 15, 1893. Hagerman, *American Civil War and the Origins of Modern Warfare.*

D. Scott Hartwig

INGERSOLL, Ebon Clark, *congressman,* was born on December 12, 1831, in Dresden, New York. He followed his itinerant preacher father to Wisconsin Territory and Paducah, Kentucky, where he read law with Illinois Democratic Congressman Willis Allen in Marion, Illinois, and was admitted to the bar in 1854. In 1856 he was elected to the Illinois House of Representatives as a Douglas Democrat, but was defeated by a Republican in 1858. His "metamorphosis" into a Republican came after his brother, Robert G. Ingersoll (*q.v.*), organized and led a cavalry unit into the Civil War, and Ebon was selected by the Illinois Union Republican party to run for congressman at large in 1862.

Although he lost, after conducting an anti-Copperhead campaign, Ingersoll was elected to the seat left vacant by the death of abolitionist Owen Lovejoy (*q.v.*) in 1864, as a supporter of Abraham Lincoln's (*q.v.*) administration. He was reelected to Congress in the regular elections of 1864, 1866, and 1868, as a Radical Republican, but was defeated in 1870. After his retirement from politics, he established a law practice in Washington, D.C. He died there on May 31, 1879, and was memorialized by his brother Robert in an oration often cited as a classic. Cramer, "Political Metamorphosis of Robert Green Ingersoll," *Journal of the Illinois State Historical Society*; Plummer, *Robert G. Ingersoll.*

Mark A. Plummer

INGERSOLL, Robert Green, *orator,* was born on August 11, 1833, in Dresden, New York. In 1854, he was admitted to the Illinois bar, and between 1858 and 1877 practiced law and politics in Peoria. His political metamorphosis was from Douglas Democrat, to Lincoln Republican, to Radical Republican. In late 1861, he recruited the 11th Illinois Cavalry. He and a small detachment of his men were captured by General Nathan Bedford Forrest, near Lexington, Tennessee, on December 18, 1862. He was paroled and resigned his commission. In 1864, when his brother, Ebon Clark Ingersoll (*q.v.*), was elected to Congress as a Republican, Robert began to exercise his political oratory in favor of Abraham Lincoln (*q.v.*) and Illinois gubernatorial candidate Richard J. Oglesby (*q.v.*). He continued to manage his brother's campaigns as a Radical Republican until Ebon's defeat in 1870.

In 1867, Governor Oglesby appointed Ingersoll attorney general, the only political office he ever held, although he was a candidate for Congress in 1860 and 1864, and for governor in 1868. After Ebon's defeat, Ingersoll continued to practice criminal and probate law. His Republican patriotic speeches were in great demand, most notably his "bloody shirt" speech to veterans. In 1877, Ingersoll moved to Washington, D.C., and later to New York City, where he continued to practice law and launched his speaking tours. He died in Dobbs Ferry, New York, on July 21, 1899. Anderson, *Robert Ingersoll*; Plummer, *Robert G. Ingersoll.*

Mark A. Plummer

J

JACKSON, James Streshly, *congressman, general,* was born in Fayette county, Kentucky, on September 27, 1823. He studied at Centre College, Kentucky, and graduated from Jefferson College, Pennsylvania, then took a law degree at Transylvania University in 1845. His legal practice at Greenupsburg was interrupted by the Mexican War. Jackson enlisted as a private in the 1st Kentucky Cavalry, which he helped recruit, but he was soon made 3rd lieutenant. After fighting a duel with Colonel Thomas F. Marshall, he resigned his commission to escape a court martial.

Originally a Whig, Jackson became a Know-Nothing in the 1850s. Elected as a Unionist to the 37th Congress, he recruited and organized the 3rd Kentucky Cavalry during the autumn of 1861. He resigned his seat to take active command as colonel on December 13, 1861. As a part of Thomas L. Crittenden's (*q.v.*) division, the regiment reached Shiloh but was not actively engaged. Jackson showed sufficient promise to be promoted to brigadier general of Volunteers on July 19, 1862; soon afterward he was given command of the cavalry in General William Nelson's Army of Kentucky.

Fortunately for his reputation, Jackson was not involved in the Richmond debacle. On September 29, 1862, he was given command of the newly organized 10th Division in Alexander McDowell McCook's (*q.v.*) corps of the Army of the Ohio. At the battle of Perryville, on October 8, 1862, Jackson was killed while directing his defense against a strong Confederate assault. Both of his brigade commanders, Brigadier General William R. Terrill and Colonel George Webster, also were killed at Perryville. Jackson's handsome appearance and engaging personality led admirers to say, ''He was the highest type of Kentucky gentleman.'' He performed well in a number of minor engagements and showed considerable promise before his untimely death. Hafendorfer, *Perryville*; Speed, *Union Regiments of Kentucky*; Tenney, *Military and Naval History of the Rebellion.*

Lowell H. Harrison

JENCKES, Thomas Allen, *congressman,* was born in Cumberland, Rhode Island, on November 2, 1818. After graduation from Brown University in 1838, he read for the law, and was admitted to the bar in 1840. Jenckes was secretary of the Rhode Island Constitutional Convention of 1842, and was elected to the state legislature in 1854 as a Whig. He followed the path of many Rhode Island Whigs into the nativist American–Republican fusion, which dominated the state until the outbreak of the war. He was elected to Congress in 1862 as a Republican, and held that office until 1870.

Jenckes was the principal author of the National Bankruptcy Act of 1867, and was one of the earliest supporters in Congress of civil service reform. He was defeated for reelection in 1870, in a bitter campaign during which he accused Senator and former Governor of Rhode Island William Sprague (*q.v.*) of having traded with Confederate agents during the Civil War. Despite the public uproar over the sensational accusation, the issue faded after the election and Jenckes retired from politics. He died in Cumberland on November 4, 1875. Belden, *So Fell the Angels*; Field, *State of Rhode Island*, vol. 3.

Mario R. DiNunzio

JOHNSON, Andrew, *senator, military governor, Vice President, President,* was born in Raleigh, North Carolina, on December 29, 1808. He moved as a teenager to Greeneville, Tennessee, which he considered his home for the rest of his life. He had no formal education but acquired elementary skills while apprenticed to a Raleigh tailor, and his wife helped him further his self-education. After several years in Greeneville politics, Johnson won a seat in the General Assembly of Tennessee in 1835. His defeat in 1837 was the first of only two popular elections he ever lost. After gaining another term in 1839, he served in the Tennessee Senate from 1841 to 1843, by which time his identity as a Democrat was unmistakable.

Johnson served in the U.S. House of Representatives from 1843 to 1853. Now distinctly middle class, a prosperous small businessman and property owner, and the master of several slaves, he adopted strong positions on national issues. He favored reduction of government spending, free homesteads for poor families, and a vigorously nationalist stance toward Mexico and on the Oregon question. Although he supported slavery as a matter of states' rights, the cotton aristocracy of the deep South distrusted him. He voted for four of the five compromise measures of 1850.

As governor of Tennessee from 1853 to 1857, Johnson faced a hostile legislature, and his office lacked powers of veto and appointment. His proposals thus languished, and he could do little but try to remain in the public eye until his election to the Senate in 1857. Johnson saw himself as a possible presidential candidate in 1860, but the Democratic polarization was too strong. During the South Carolina crisis, he made a two-day speech in favor of the Union, against the right of secession, and in support of the individual's right to own slaves. After Tennessee seceded, he continued in his seat until 1862, when Abraham Lincoln (*q.v.*) appointed him military governor of Tennessee, with the charge to organize a loyal state government. The course of military operations, however, made this a slow and frustrating task.

As a border-state Unionist and War Democrat, Johnson was an obvious nominee as Lincoln's Vice President on the Union ticket in 1864. Lincoln's death, however, left leadership of a wartime coalition made up primarily of Republicans in the hands of a lifelong Democrat. For the remainder of 1865, during the absence of Congress, Johnson conducted Reconstruction on his own, appointing provisional governors, issuing pardons, and establishing lenient terms for the South. Disagreements with Congress over policy marked the period from December 1865 until March 1867, when the Reconstruction Acts established more rigorous terms of readmission. Rancorous veto battles, which had begun in the spring of 1866 over civil rights legislation, continued as Johnson encouraged native white Southern leaders, showed no interest in using Federal authority in behalf of blacks, and supported Democratic positions and candidates.

An increasingly alienated Republican majority impeached Johnson for high crimes and misdemeanors on February 24, 1868, alleging violation of the Tenure of Office Act in his removal of Secretary of War Edwin M. Stanton (*q.v.*), as well as general unfitness for office. The Senate trial ended in May with a vote of 35–19 for conviction, one vote less than necessary. Johnson left office on March 4, 1869, and returned immediately to Tennessee. He ran for congressman at large and senator before winning a Senate seat in 1875. He served briefly that spring before returning home for the summer. He died in Greeneville on July 31, 1875. Castel, *Presidency of Andrew Johnson*; Sefton, *Andrew Johnson*.

James E. Sefton

JOHNSON, Philip, *congressman,* was born in Polkville, New Jersey, on January 17, 1818. He moved in 1839 to Mount Bethel, Pennsylvania, where he attended the public schools. He also attended Lafayette College and Union Law School in Easton, Pennsylvania, was admitted to the bar in 1848, and immediately became active in local Democratic politics. Johnson was county court clerk (1848–1853), served one term in the legislature (1853–1854), and was revenue commissioner of the 3rd Judicial District (1859–1860). In 1860, he was elected to the 37th Congress. Johnson was an extreme Peace Democrat during the war and, in the early phases of Reconstruction, voted with the congressional faction that supported the policies of President Andrew Johnson (*q.v.*). Reelected twice, he served in Congress from July 1861 until his death in Washington, D.C., on January 29, 1867. *BDUSC*; Benedict, *Compromise of Principle.*

J. K. Folmar

JOHNSON, Reverdy, *senator,* was born in Annapolis, Maryland, on May 21, 1796. After graduating from St. John's College in 1811, he read law until he was admitted to the bar in 1815. In 1821, after serving as a state's attorney and deputy attorney general, Johnson was elected to the Maryland Senate. In the political realignment of the 1830s he became a Whig, but held no further public office until his election to the U.S. Senate in 1845. Resigning his Senate seat in 1849, he accepted an appointment to Zachary Taylor's Cabinet as Attorney General, but following Taylor's death in 1850, he resigned and returned to his legal practice. With the collapse of the Whig party, Johnson became a Democrat.

In the sectional crisis, Johnson strongly supported the Union and denounced secession in Maryland. As a member of the emerging Union coalition, he was elected in 1861 to the Maryland House of Delegates, and in the following year to the U.S. Senate. Johnson's Unionist approach to the Civil War, reflecting his legal background, was often a conservative one. He initially supported the Lincoln (*q.v.*) administration, but after differing over specific policies and believing Lincoln to be incompetent, Johnson broke with the President and supported George B. McClellan (*q.v.*) in 1864. Personally antagonistic to slavery, Johnson approached the issue as a constitutionalist. He opposed the Emancipation Proclamation but later voted for the 13th Amendment.

His position on Reconstruction varied, but having returned to the Democratic party, Johnson generally supported Presidential Reconstruction and became an important figure in preventing Andrew Johnson's (*q.v.*) conviction at his impeachment trial in the Senate. In 1868, he was appointed minister to Great Britain, but after Ulysses S. Grant's (*q.v.*) election in 1872, he returned to his law practice. Johnson died in Annapolis on February 10, 1876. Clark, *Politics in Maryland During the Civil War*; Steiner, *Life of Reverdy Johnson.*

Richard R. Duncan

JOHNSTON, William, *congressman,* was born in Ireland in 1819 and emigrated to the United States. Little is known of his early years except that he attended public schools in Ohio, studied law, and was admitted to the Ohio bar. In 1844 he published the *Richland Bugle*, a campaign newspaper, and was thereafter called "Bugle Bill." Johnston practiced law in Mansfield, Ohio, and in the 1862 Democratic landslide in Ohio, was elected to the 38th Congress. He was antiadministration during the war and was very critical of the Republican party. Defeated for reelection in 1864, Johnston returned to Mansfield, where he died on May 1, 1866. Baughman, *Centennial Biographical History of Richland County.*

Thomas H. Smith

JULIAN, George Washington, *congressman,* was born on May 5, 1817, in Centreville, Indiana. His father died when George was seven years old, and he was reared by his mother in a strict Quaker faith, a religious setting that accounts in part for Julian's antislavery proclivities. He entered politics in the early 1840s as a Whig, but a combination of reforming zeal and political ambition led him into the Free Soil party in 1848, under whose banner he was elected to Congress in 1848, and thus was initiated into national politics during the debate over the Compromise of 1850. His exemplars were John P. Hale (*q.v.*), Charles Sumner (*q.v.*), and Joshua R. Giddings (*q.v.*), whose daughter Julian married after the death of his first wife.

Unsuccessful in his pursuit of office until 1860, Julian became the leader of the Radical Free Soil faction of the emerging Republican party in Indiana in the 1850s, in opposition to the powerful Oliver H.P. Morton (*q.v.*). The enmity between the two men lasted until Morton's death. Elected to Congress again in 1860 by Indiana's most thoroughly antislavery district, Julian served in the House of Representatives for ten years. As a member of the famous Joint Committee on the Conduct of the War, with Senators Benjamin Wade (*q.v.*) and Zachariah Chandler (*q.v.*), he made his reputation as a doctrinaire Radical. He championed the Homestead Act and became chairman of the House Committee on Public Lands, a position he kept throughout the war and into the Reconstruction era. In the Southern Homestead Act of 1866, one can see how Julian combined his crusade for free land for actual settlers with his antislavery activities.

Julian broke with the regular Republican party under Ulysses S. Grant (*q.v.*), and became a leader in the Liberal Republican party in 1872. During the 1870s and early 1880s, he practiced law and wrote his memoirs, a biography of Joshua R. Giddings, and a number of articles. By 1876, he had become a Democrat, and in 1885 President Grover Cleveland appointed him surveyor general of New Mexico Territory, where he served until 1889. In his later years, Julian abandoned the cause of African Americans and devoted himself to tariff and monetary reform. In 1896, he bitterly opposed William Jennings Bryan and joined the Gold Democrats, the sixth political party with which he was affiliated during a long and restless career. Julian died in Irvington, near Indianapolis, on July 7, 1899. Riddleberger, *George Washington Julian.*

Patrick W. Riddleberger

K

KALBFLEISCH, Martin, *mayor, congressman*, was born in Vlissingen (Flushing), Holland, on February 8, 1804. After emigrating to New York in 1826, he sold paint on Long Island, then opened a chemical works. In 1852–1854, he served as supervisor of Bushwick, New York, and upon the village's incorporation into Brooklyn, became an alderman. His rising popularity led to Kalbfleisch's election as mayor of Brooklyn on the eve of the Civil War. Ostensibly a War Democrat, he alienated his Unionist and moderate constituents by his stringent conservatism and disdain for compromise. Ignoring public opinion, he refused to appropriate large sums to raise regiments and provide relief to soldiers' families.

In 1862–1863 Kalbfleisch criticized Abraham Lincoln's (*q.v.*) policies, including emancipation and conscription. Yet, although labeled a Copperhead, he never embraced the extreme views of the Peace Democrats. In 1863, the quarrelsome mayor was denied renomination. Flouting the Democratic leadership, he suffered defeat on a third-party ticket. Months earlier, however, Kalbfleisch had won a House seat in the 38th Congress. In Washington, he continued to oppose legislation to abolish slavery, enlist African Americans, and establish the Freedmen's Bureau.

Upon returning to Brooklyn in March 1865, Kalbfleisch mended local political fences and waged an unsuccessful mayoral campaign; he was returned to the mayoralty three years later. Refused renomination in 1871, he bolted his party to run yet again, thus ensuring his own and the Democracy's defeat. Shouldered out of public life, the "Old Dutchman" managed his expanded business holdings until his death in Brooklyn on February 12, 1873. Brummer, *Political History of New York State.*

Edward G. Longacre

KASSON, John Adam, *congressman,* was born in Charlotte, Vermont, on January 11, 1822. After graduation from the University of Vermont in 1842, he studied law, was admitted to the bar, and practiced in Massachusetts, and in Missouri after moving to St. Louis in 1850. A Free Soiler who for four years owned at least one slave, Kasson moved to Des Moines, Iowa, in 1857. By 1858, he was Republican state chairman and, in 1860, a delegate to the party's national convention. He and Horace Greeley (*q.v.*) were credited with being the primary authors of the Chicago platform. Appointed by Abraham Lincoln (*q.v.*) as first assistant postmaster general, he served until 1863.

Elected to Congress in 1862, Kasson served two terms, failing to gain renomination for a third. He won a reputation as perhaps the least Radical of a generally Radical Iowa delegation, a reputation that, after the war, left him vulnerable to the attacks of Iowa party leaders who favored sterner measures against the South, black suffrage, and qualified support of business enterprise (including high tariffs). During the war years, Kasson was an administration supporter, backing the Emancipation Proclamation and opposing peace negotiations. He favored a stiff confiscation bill and the drafting of African Americans into the Army. However, he abstained from voting on the Wade–Davis Bill, a mark against him among many Iowans.

After the war, Kasson tried to walk a narrow line on Reconstruction issues. He supported efforts to restore the South to the Union and opposed unlimited black suffrage, but he voted for establishment of the Joint Committee on Reconstruction, for a strengthened Freedmen's Bureau, and for the Civil Rights Bill. He usually fought to limit the scope and force of Reconstruction measures, and against efforts designed to limit President Andrew Johnson's (*q.v.*) power. After two terms in the Iowa legislature, Kasson returned to Congress for two terms (1873–1877), served as minister to Austria-Hungary (1877–1881), returned to Congress for two more terms (1881–1884), and was minister to Germany (1885) and delegate to various international conferences relating to the status of colonial territories, to postal services, and to tariff reciprocity. Kasson defended American acquisitions in the Far East and supported arbitration of international disputes. He died on May 19, 1910, in Washington, D.C. Cook, *Baptism of Fire*; Stiles, *Recollections and Sketches*; Younger, *John A. Kasson.*

Hubert H. Wubben

KAUTZ, August Valentine, *general,* was born on January 5, 1828, in the German province of Baden. His family later emigrated to Georgetown, Ohio. During the Mexican War, he served in the Ohio Volunteers and received a West Point appointment. He graduated from West Point in 1852, served in the 4th U.S. Infantry, then in the 6th Cavalry, and was twice wounded while fighting

Indians. After early Civil War service in the Washington defenses and on the Peninsula, Kautz was sent west to command the 2nd Ohio Cavalry.

In 1863, Kautz commanded Camp Chase, helped capture John Hunt Morgan's raiders, and was chief of cavalry in the XXIII Corps. From January to April 1864, he was executive officer of the Cavalry Bureau in Washington. Until March 1865 he commanded the cavalry division of the Army of the James, receiving promotions to brigadier and brevet major general of Volunteers. His lack of conspicuous tactical success and poor relations with his superiors finally led to his transfer to a black infantry division in the XXV Corps, which he led into evacuated Richmond on April 3, 1865.

Although a gifted administrator and regimental leader, Kautz proved unequal to the demands of division command. A bookish sort (during the war he published works on military duties and customs), he was too methodical and overly reliant on textbook tactics. He was especially unsuited to lead black troops, whose abilities he mistrusted. His field performance was sometimes affected by seizures of malaria and by his apparent addiction to quinine. Following the war, Kautz helped try Abraham Lincoln's (*q.v.*) assassins, then served in the 34th, 15th, and 8th Infantry in the West and Southwest. Almost four years before his death in Seattle, Washington, on September 4, 1895, he retired from the service as a brigadier general. Robertson, *Back Door to Richmond*; Starr, *Union Cavalry*, vol. 2; Wallace, "General August V. Kautz."

Edward G. Longacre

KEARNY, Philip, *general,* was born in New York City on June 1, 1814. He graduated from Columbia College in 1833. Although left a fortune of approximately $1 million, he obtained a commission in the 1st Dragoons, commanded by Stephen Watts Kearny, his uncle. In 1839, he was sent to France to study cavalry tactics, and he saw combat at Algiers in 1840. Upon returning to the United States, Kearny became aide-de-camp to generals in chief Alexander Macomb and Winfield Scott (*q.v.*). In Scott's campaign for Mexico City, Kearny won promotion for gallant conduct at Churubusco, where he lost an arm while leading a charge. In 1851, he resigned from the Army, later serving on the staff of Napoleon III's army in 1859, and participating in the battles of Magenta and Solferino.

Upon the outbreak of the Civil War, Kearny returned to America and was named brigadier general of Volunteers. He fought courageously in 1862 under George B. McClellan (*q.v.*) on the Peninsula and under John Pope (*q.v.*) at Second Bull Run. In Pope's retreat on September 1, 1862, while covering the rear guard at Chantilly (Ox Hill), Kearny mistakenly rode into the Confederate lines and was shot dead when he refused to dismount and surrender.

Throughout his colorful career, Phil Kearny gained the devotion, respect, and admiration of his soldiers by his zeal and alacrity in performing his duties. He was, said Winfield Scott, "the bravest man I ever knew, and a perfect soldier." Initially buried in Trinity Churchyard, New York City, Kearny's body was reinterred in Arlington National Cemetery in 1912. Hennessy, *Return to Bull Run*; Sears, *To the Gates of Richmond.*

Warren W. Hassler, Jr.

KELLEY, William Darrah, *congressman,* was born in Philadelphia on April 12, 1814. He became active in local Democratic politics as a debater and writer, particularly as a defender of the rights of workingmen. He was named prosecuter of pleas in 1845, and judge of common pleas in 1847, an office to which he was reelected for a ten-year term in 1851, on the Independent ticket. With the emergence of the sectional crisis, Kelley joined the Republican party, and was an unsuccessful candidate for Congress in 1856. In 1860, he was elected to the House of Representatives, for the first of fifteen terms. Kelley was a Radical Republican and an ardent Unionist who vigorously supported the prosecution of the war. Although he represented an urban district, he voted for controversial civil rights measures regarding the use of black troops, the abolition of slavery, and black suffrage.

Arguably the most effective Republican debater in Congress, Kelley gave one speech in particular that prompted such applause from the galleries that the Democrats demanded the removal of all specatators from the House before resuming discussion on the national conscription bill. He opposed the strategies for Reconstruction that Abraham Lincoln (*q.v.*) and Andrew Johnson (*q.v.*) put forward, and instead emphasized that the seceded states should be treated as "alien enemies." A free-trader prior to the Panic of 1857, Kelley became a leading spokesman for a protective tariff. Somewhat ironically, he was also a significant inflationist during the postwar years.

Kelley established himself for his humanitarianism, independence, and honesty. As chairman of the Centennial Committee, he played a major role in the success of the Centennial Celebration of 1876. Kelley died in Washington, D.C., on January 9, 1890. Brown, "William D. Kelley," *Pennsylvania Magazine of History and Biography*; Geary, *We Need Men.*

J. K. Folmar

KELLOGG, Francis William, *congressman,* was born on May 30, 1810, in Worthington, Massachusetts. In 1833, he moved to Columbus, Ohio, and in 1855 to Grand Rapids, Michigan, where he entered the lumber business. A Republican, he served in the state legislature in 1857 and 1858, and was a member of the U.S. House of Representatives from Michigan (1859–1865) and from Alabama (1868–1869). During the Civil War, Kellogg raised the 2nd, 3rd, and 6th Michigan Cavalry. He was for a short time colonel of the 3rd, being replaced by Robert H. G. Minty before the regiment left for the field. An active worker for the Union war effort, he gave loyal but not uncritical support to the Lincoln (*q.v.*) administration. In addition to his congressional service after the war, he was collector of internal revenue for the Southern District of Alabama (1866–

1868). From Alabama, Kellogg moved to New York City and later to Alliance, Ohio, where he died on January 13, 1879. Goss, *History of Grand Rapids.*

Frederick D. Williams

KELLOGG, Orlando, *congressman,* was born on June 18, 1809, in Elizabethtown, New York. In 1833, he began studying law, and in 1838 was admitted to the bar and opened a practice in Elizabethtown. He was appointed county surrogate in 1840 and served for four years. Kellogg was known as a great stump speaker, and in 1846 his talents helped him win election, as a Whig, to the 30th Congress. There he became friends with another freshman Whig, Abraham Lincoln (*q.v.*). In 1860, as a delegate to the Republican National Convention in Chicago, he was able to help nominate his friend for President. When not busy with politics, Kellogg continued his law practice in Elizabethtown. After the war broke out, he was instrumental in organizing and equipping the 118th New York Volunteers. In 1862, he was elected to the 38th Congress and served on the Committee on the Militia. Kellogg, an early supporter of the 13th Amendment, was reelected in 1864. He died on August 24, 1865, in Elizabethtown. Smith, *History of Essex County.*

Lori A. Lisowski

KELLOGG, William, *congressman,* was born on July 8, 1814, in Kelloggsville, Ohio. Educated in the local schools, he studied law, then moved to Canton, Illinois, where he opened a law practice in 1837. Elected as a Whig to the Illinois legislature for one term (1849–1850), he served as a state circuit court judge from 1850 to 1855. He was elected as a Republican to the 35th, 36th, and 37th Congresses. Kellogg opposed the extension of slavery in the territories, and offered his own set of resolutions as a substitute for the Crittenden Compromise in 1861. He supported measures that benefited his district, especially the protective tariff and sound monetary policies. He also supported the Homestead Act and a transcontinental railroad.

The close friendship that had existed between Kellogg and Abraham Lincoln (*q.v.*) may have become strained even before the Civil War began. Evidently Kellogg badgered the President about patronage and urged him to intercede in the reinstatement of the congressman's son to West Point. Such requests for personal favors not only troubled Lincoln but also incurred the displeasure of Secretary of War Edwin M. Stanton (*q.v.*) and Secretary of the Treasury Salmon P. Chase (*q.v.*). In February 1863 Kellogg announced that he, as a member of the Judiciary Committee, was investigating the allegation that Postmaster General Montgomery Blair (*q.v.*) had excluded certain newspapers from the U.S. mail.

Even though Kellogg failed to be reelected, such allegations would continue to embarrass the President after the 38th Congress convened. Kellogg was dismayed when Lincoln offered to appoint him minister to Chile because he considered the position beneath him. Lincoln remained unmoved, and Kellogg returned to Illinois. Ever the office seeker, he was appointed chief justice of the Nebraska Territory by President Andrew Johnson (*q.v.*) on December 20, 1865. He served until 1867, when he became the collector of internal revenue for Peoria, Illinois. In 1869, Kellogg was appointed to a judgeship under Mississippi's Provisional Government. After his failure to be elected to Congress in 1869, following Mississippi's readmission to the Union, Kellogg returned to Peoria, where he died on December 20, 1872. Bogue, *Congressman's Civil War.*

Thomas F. Schwartz

KENNEDY, Anthony, *senator,* was born in Baltimore on December 21, 1810. In 1820, his family moved to Charlestown, (West) Virginia, where he attended Jefferson Academy. As a country gentleman, Kennedy became involved in Virginia politics, and as a Whig he represented his county in the Virginia House of Delegates from 1838 to 1842. He also was magistrate of the Jefferson County Court for over ten years. A bid in 1847 to represent his district in Congress failed, and in 1851 Kennedy returned to Baltimore. He was elected as an American party candidate to the state House of Delegates in 1856, and in the following year, with strong ties to the Know-Nothing clubs, was elected to the U.S. Senate, where he supported the Buchanan (*q.v.*) administration. In 1859, with the mounting sectional crisis, Kennedy, along with other American party leaders, saw the need for a new party to preserve the Union on the basis of the Constitution and the exclusion of the slavery question.

As a border state conservative, Kennedy supported the Union, but was often at odds with the Federal government. He attacked as unconstitutional the suppression of the writ of habeas corpus and the arrests stemming from it. His conservatism extended to opposing any moves supporting emancipation. Opposed by the more Radical elements in the Unionist coalition, Kennedy was not a candidate for reelection to the Senate in 1862. He retired to private life, and except for serving as a delegate to the Maryland Constitutional Convention in 1867, he remained politically inactive until his death in Annapolis on July 31, 1892. Baker, *Politics of Continuity;* Clark, *Politics in Maryland During the Civil War.*

Richard R. Duncan

KERNAN, Francis, *congressman,* was born on January 14, 1816, in Wayne, New York. He graduated from Georgetown College in 1836, and eventually established a law practice in Utica, New York. From 1854 to 1857, he was reporter for the New York Court of Appeals. Kernan was elected as a Democrat to the state legislature in 1861 and quickly became one of the most influential Democrats in New York. He opposed the use of force against the Confederacy during the secession crisis, but pledged loyalty to the national government once war broke out. In 1862, he defeated Roscoe Conkling (*q.v.*) for a seat in the House of Representatives. During the 38th Congress, Kernan helped lead the loyal opposition, especially against the Wade–Davis Bill. He lost to Conkling in 1864, but his power increased after the war.

Kernan played an active role in the New York Constitutional Convention of 1867 and Constitutional Commission of 1874. He was instrumental in the presidential nominations of Horatio Seymour (*q.v.*) in 1868 and Samuel Tilden in 1876, having worked with both of them to rid the New York Democracy of the Tweed machine. In 1872, Kernan was defeated for governor of New York, in part because of his Roman Catholicism. From 1875 to 1881 he represented New York in the U.S. Senate, the first Democrat to do so in almost a quarter of a century. He died in Utica on September 7, 1892. Brummer, *Political History of New York State*; Mushkat, *Reconstruction of the New York Democracy.*

James C. Mohr

KERRIGAN, James, *congressman*, was born in New York City on December 25, 1828. After attending what is now Fordham University, he served in the Mexican War, and in 1855 accompanied William Walker's filibustering expedition to Nicaragua. After returning to New York City, he entered Democratic politics, became an alderman, and served as clerk of the Tombs Police Court. As the Civil War approached, Kerrigan professed Southern sympathies, but after the shooting started, he supported the Union. Elected to the House of Representatives in 1860, he promptly secured leave to recruit the 25th New York Volunteers, of which he was elected colonel. The regiment acquired a reputation for poor discipline and rowdiness; on several occasions its men brawled with Republicans in other outfits. In December 1861 Kerrigan was arrested for drunkenness on duty, court martialed for conduct unbecoming an officer, and discharged on February 21, 1862.

Belatedly taking his seat in the House, Kerrigan spent the next year fighting every major piece of legislation advanced by the Lincoln (*q.v.*) administration, especially the raising of war taxes and the freeing of slaves. When Lincoln issued his preliminary Emancipation Proclamation, Kerrigan harangued the President in public; on one occasion police had to save him from an angry mob. After completing his term in March 1863, Kerrigan worked ardently for a free Ireland. In 1866, he led a band of Fenians in an unsuccessful attempt to capture Canada from the British, and the following year he ran arms to the Irish coast. He died in Brooklyn, New York, on November 1, 1899. Curry, *Blueprint for Modern America*; Dell, *Lincoln and the War Democrats.*

Edward G. Longacre

KEYES, Erasmus Darwin, *general*, was born in Brimfield, Massachusetts, on May 29, 1810. He graduated from West Point in 1832. Dispatched to Charleston, South Carolina during the Nullification Crisis (1832–1833), Keyes came to the attention of General Winfield Scott (*q.v.*), and served as his aide-de-camp (1837–1841). He was an instructor at West Point (1844–1848) and skirmished against Indians in Washington Territory. In January 1861, when Robert E. Lee declined the position of Scott's military secretary, the general picked Lieutenant Colonel Keyes for the office. When the Civil War began, Keyes gained command of the

11th U.S. Infantry and a few days later was promoted to brigadier general of
Volunteers. His brigade fought ineffectually but not disgracefully at First Bull
Run.

In May 1862 Keyes was promoted to major general of Volunteers and made
commander of the IV Corps in the Army of the Potomac. He was the only one
of four new corps commanders to approve of the controversial Urbanna Plan of
General George B. McClellan (*q.v.*). Keyes was heavily engaged at Fair Oaks,
and after Malvern Hill, where part of his corps, under General Darius N. Couch
(*q.v.*), held the center of the Union line, he organized the rear guard to protect
McClellan's retreat. In 1863, the IV Corps remained in the Department of Virginia under General John A. Dix (*q.v.*). Keyes and Dix argued over Keyes's
alleged failure to carry out a diversionary attack on Richmond (July 1863). A
tremendous row ensued, prompting Keyes to resign his commission (May 6,
1864).

Years later, Keyes wrote *Fifty Years of Observations of Men and Events*
(1884), which reveals little about its author but much about a host of high
officers on both sides in the Civil War. Keyes prospered at San Francisco in a
variety of businesses—banking, gold mining, and grape growing. He died in
Nice, France, on October 14, 1895. Davis, *Bull Run*; Dowdey, *Seven Days*; Sears,
To the Gates of Richmond.

Joseph G. Dawson III

KILLINGER, John Weinland, *congressman*, was born in Annville, Pennsylvania, on September 18, 1824. He attended the public schools and Lebanon
Academy, and graduated from Mercersburg Preparatory School and Franklin
and Marshall College. Admitted to the bar in 1846, he began his practice in
Lebanon. Killinger was elected to the state House of Representatives (1848–
1849) and the state Senate (1854–1859). A delegate to the Republican National
Convention in 1856, he was elected to the 36th and 37th Congresses, where he
tended to follow the party's leadership on the sectional issues and supported the
prosecution of the war effort. His voting behavior was moderate in regard to
confiscation and emancipation. From 1864 to 1866, Killinger was an assessor
of internal revenue. During the postwar years, he was elected to the U.S. House
of Representatives in the 42nd, 43rd, 45th, and 46th Congresses. He was also
a solicitor for the Philadelphia & Reading Railroad Company. Killinger died in
Lebanon, Pennsylvania, on June 30, 1896. *BDUSC.*

J. K. Folmar

KILPATRICK, Hugh Judson, *general*, was born on January 14, 1836, near
Deckertown, New Jersey. He graduated from West Point in 1861. As a captain
in the 5th New York (Duryee's Zouaves), he was severely wounded at Big
Bethel, then became the lieutenant colonel of the 2nd New York Cavalry. As a
colonel, he commanded a brigade at Brandy Station (June 9, 1863), and led
several charges at the end of this action that covered the Union withdrawal. At

Aldie, his counterattack won the day. At Hanover, Pennsylvania (June 30, 1863), in an important preliminary to the Gettysburg campaign, J. E. B. Stuart struck the rear of Kilpatrick's division. Counterattacked by Elon Farnsworth (*q.v.*) and George Custer (*q.v.*), Stuart turned northeast and did not return to Lee's army until July 2.

On July 3, Kilpatrick rashly ordered Farnsworth's brigade to make a charge over the rough ground south of Devil's Den. This reckless attack cost the life of Farnsworth. Kilpatrick acquired the nickname "Kil-cavalry" for the aggressive way he used up men and horses. In February 1864 his division attempted a raid on Richmond, hoping to free Union prisoners. The raid failed, and cost the life of Colonel Ulric Dahlgren. Kilpatrick was transferred to command a cavalry division in William T. Sherman's (*q.v.*) army and was badly wounded at Resaca, Georgia. Although he could not ride, he accompanied his unit on the March to the Sea and on the last campaign through the Carolinas. He was promoted to brevet major general, but resigned to serve as minister to Chile (1865–1868). While a director of the Union Pacific Railroad, Kilpatrick ran unsuccessfully for Congress in 1880. He returned to the Chile ministry, and died in Santiago on December 2, 1881. Longacre, *Cavalry at Gettysburg*; Starr, *Union Cavalry.*

Roy P. Stonesifer, Jr.

KIMBALL, Nathan, *general,* was born on November 22, 1822, in Fredericksburg, Indiana. He attended Asbury College, then taught school in Independence, Missouri, farmed, studied medicine, and was practicing medicine when the Mexican War began. Kimball helped recruit, and was commissioned captain of, Company C, 2nd Indiana Volunteers, a one-year regiment. The unit panicked at Buena Vista, but Kimball rallied his company and continued fighting. He was mustered out on June 23, 1847, and returned to Indiana.

On April 23, 1861, Kimball reentered the military as captain of Company C, 14th Indiana Volunteers, and on June 7 became its colonel. He led the regiment at Cheat Mountain and Greenbrier in western Virginia, and in January 1862 commanded a brigade guarding the upper Potomac. His division commander having been wounded the previous evening, Kimball fought and defeated General Thomas J. Jackson at Kernstown on March 23, 1862. For this service he was promoted to brigadier general, to rank from April 16. On July 4, Kimball and his brigade were reassigned to the Army of the Potomac's XI Corps. He led the brigade in savage attacks at Antietam and Fredericksburg. In the latter battle, he was seriously wounded and was carried from the field.

In mid-March 1863, Kimball reported to the XVI Corps, Army of the Tennessee. Placed in command of a provisional division, he joined General Ulysses S. Grant (*q.v.*) near Vicksburg in early June, and led several expeditions up the Mechanicsburg Corridor. On May 22, 1864, Kimball was assigned a brigade in the Army of the Cumberland's IV Corps. His distinguished service at the battle of Peachtree Creek earned him command of a division. Some three weeks after the capture of Atlanta, he returned to southern Indiana to assist in suppressing the Copperheads, but rejoined his division in time to lead it at Franklin and Nashville. He was breveted major general on February 1, 1865, and was mustered out on October 7, 1865.

Kimball had an active role in organizing the Grand Army of the Republic in Indiana, and became its first state commander. He also served two terms as state treasurer and one in the state legislature. President Grant appointed Kimball surveyor general of the Utah Territory in 1873, and President Rutherford B. Hayes (*q.v.*) named him the Ogden postmaster. He held the latter position until his death in Odgen on January 21, 1898. Bearss, *Vicksburg Campaign*, vol. 3; Castel, *Decision in the West*; Murfin, *Gleam of Bayonets*.

Edwin C. Bearss

KING, Austin Augustus, *congressman*, was born in Sullivan county, Tennessee, on September 21, 1802. He moved to Columbia, Missouri, in 1830, served as a colonel of Missouri troops in the Black Hawk War of 1832, and became acquainted with Abraham Lincoln (*q.v.*). A strong Jacksonian Democrat, King was elected to the Missouri House (1834, 1836), and served eleven years as circuit judge for Northwest Missouri (1837–1848). During his tenure on the bench, he presided over the trials of Joseph Smith and other church leaders, following the Mormon War of 1838.

Elected in 1848, King was governor during a period that witnessed the dissolution of the Jacksonian coalition put together by Thomas Hart Benton and paved the way for the party factionalism of the 1850s. He ran unsuccessfully as a Benton Democrat for Congress in 1852 and for the legislature in 1854. As a delegate to both the Charleston and Baltimore Democratic National Conventions in 1860, he supported Stephen A. Douglas (*q.v.*). He again served as circuit judge in 1862–1863, resigning when he was elected to the 38th Congress as a War Democrat.

King followed a staunch conservative course during his one term in the House. A lifelong slaveholder, he was one of eleven Democrats to vote against submission of the 13th Amendment, even though Missouri had abolished slavery two weeks earlier. He was defeated for reelection in 1864 because of the Radical sweep in Missouri, but was active in the postwar reorganization of the Democratic party. He died in St. Louis on April 22, 1870. *BDUSC*.

William E. Parrish

KING, John Haskell, *general*, was born either at Sackett's Harbor, New York, or in Michigan on February 19, 1820. He obtained a 2nd lieutenant's commission two months prior to his eighteenth birthday and became a career soldier, serving in the Seminole Wars, the Mexican War, and along the frontier, rising to the rank of captain. Following the outbreak of the Civil War, he escaped to New York from Texas with nine companies of Regulars. He commanded detachments of Regular troops at Shiloh, Corinth, and Stones River, where he was wounded. Promoted to brigadier general of Volunteers in April 1863, King headed an all-Regular brigade, the only one in the Army of the Cumberland, at Chickamauga, where his troops suffered the highest casualties of any Federal unit engaged. It would seem, however, that this poor showing was more the consequence of circumstances than of any failure on King's part.

During the Atlanta campaign, King commanded the 2nd Brigade of the 1st Division of the XIV Corps, an outfit consisting of two Volunteer regiments and portions of five Regular regiments. His troops saw little action until early August, when they were heavily engaged and suffered severe losses during a futile attempt to turn the Confederate flank southeast of Atlanta, and on September 1, in the second battle of Jonesboro. On both occasions King, as senior brigadier, served as acting commander of his division, and hence did not personally lead his brigade.

After the fall of Atlanta, King and his Regulars were assigned to the District of the Etowah under Major General James B. Steedman (*q.v.*), but did not participate with the rest of Steedman's forces in the battle of Nashville. When the war ended, King was promoted to colonel in the Regular Army and assigned command of the 9th Infantry, in which capacity he served at various frontier outposts until his retirement in 1882. He moved to Washington, D.C., where he died on April 7, 1888. Castel, *Decision in the West*; Cozzens, *This Terrible Sound.*

Albert Castel

KING, Preston, *senator,* was born on October 14, 1806, in Ogdensburg, New York. He graduated from Union College with honors in 1827, and attracted the attention of Silas Wright, a leader of Martin Van Buren's Albany Regency. In 1829, King was admitted to the bar and established his practice in rural St. Lawrence county. He established the *St. Lawrence Republican* in 1830 to support the administration, and through Van Buren's influence became postmaster of Ogdensburg. In 1834, he was elected to the first of his four terms in the state Assembly, where he established a reputation as a fiscal conservative and an opponent of Whig economic policies.

King was elected to four congressional terms (1843–1847, 1849–1853). During the late 1840s, his political loyalties shifted. In Congress, he worked closely with David Wilmot, and in 1848 deserted the Democracy for the Free Soil party. His opposition to the extension of slavery convinced King to join the Republicans, and in 1857 his new party selected him to run for the U.S. Senate. King rejected secession, opposed any sectional compromise, and urged Republicans to stand by their principles. He guided important naval appropriations bills through the Senate, supported President Abraham Lincoln's (*q.v.*) war policies, and joined the Radical Republicans.

An intraparty split cost King reelection in 1863. He established his law practice in New York City and remained active in the Republican party. At the 1864 Baltimore convention, King was instrumental in securing Andrew Johnson's (*q.v.*) nomination for Vice President, and when Johnson became President, King was one of his closest associates. On August 15, 1865, Johnson named him to the politically important position of collector of customs in New York City. King was extremely reluctant to assume the office, particularly because the President expected him to harmonize Republican factionalism and conciliate Democrats. King snapped under the strain. Long haunted by mental breakdowns, he committed suicide by leaping from a ferryboat in New York Harbor on November 2, 1865. Alexander, *Political History of the State of New York*, vol. 2; Bogue, *Earnest Men.*

Jerome Mushkat

KING, Rufus, *general, diplomat,* was born on January 26, 1814, in New York City, the grandson of Federalist statesman Rufus King. After attending Columbia College, he was appointed to West Point, from which he graduated in 1833. In 1836, he resigned his commission to work as a surveyor for the New York & Erie Railroad. Subsequently, he edited the *Albany Daily Advertiser* and then the *Albany Evening Journal*, in association with Thurlow Weed (*q.v.*). King also served as adjutant general of New York State during the governorship of William H. Seward (*q.v.*). In 1845, he moved to Milwaukee, and edited the *Milwaukee Sentinel* until 1861. He was superintendent of schools in Milwaukee, and a regent of the University of Wisconsin.

With the bombardment of Fort Sumter, King received a commission as brigadier general of Volunteers, and took command of the ''Iron Brigade'' in the defenses of Washington. In August 1862 his division, as part of John Pope's (*q.v.*) Army of Virginia, fought General Thomas J. ''Stonewall'' Jackson near Gainesville. After holding his ground until dark, King retreated. On the following day Jackson and Robert E. Lee defeated Pope's army at Second Bull Run. King's retreat left him under suspicion, but he remained in active service until 1863, when poor health forced his resignation.

Appointed minister to the Papal States when he left the army, King assisted in the apprehension of John Surratt, a conspirator in Abraham Lincoln's (*q.v.*) assassination, who had fled to Italy. He resigned his mission in 1868, and was deputy collector of the Port of New York until 1869, when his health failed again. He died in New York City on October 13, 1876. Current, *Civil War Era*; Hennessy, *Return to Bull Run.*

Robert H. Jones

KIRKWOOD, Samuel Jordan, *governor,* was born on December 20, 1813, in Harford county, Maryland. After schooling at an academy in Washington, D.C., he clerked in a drugstore and taught school for two terms. In 1835, his family moved to Richland county, Ohio, where he farmed, taught school, served as deputy county assessor, ran a store and tavern, and studied law. In 1845, Kirkwood, running as a Democrat, became county prosecuting attorney. He served from 1850 to 1851 in the Ohio Constitutional Convention. In 1855, he moved to Coralville, Iowa, to engage in milling and farming.

An early opponent of the Kansas–Nebraska Act and a worker in the Underground Railroad, Kirkwood became an early leader in the Iowa Republican party. After service in the state Senate (1856–1859), he won two terms as governor, serving from 1860 to 1863. In his first inaugural address, he angered Democrats by declaring that he approved the spirit animating John Brown's (*q.v.*) raid on Harper's Ferry, even though he deplored the act. When Virginia demanded extradition of Barclay Coppoc, one of Brown's group who had escaped capture, Kirkwood's insistence that all legal forms be satisfied enabled Coppoc's friends to spirit him out of the state.

With the outbreak of war, Kirkwood used his own funds and those borrowed from friends to help equip Iowa's Volunteer units until the state legislature could act. He appointed War Democrats as well as Republicans to important civil and military positions, but he had limited tolerance for Peace Democrats and generally approved arrests of the most vocal ones. Under his leadership, Iowa successfully met its manpower and financial obligations. Following the Altoona conference of loyal governors in September 1862, Kirkwood personally urged President Abraham Lincoln (*q.v.*) to remove George B. McClellan (*q.v.*) from command as a means of strengthening the Union cause.

In 1866–1867, Kirkwood filled James Harlan's (*q.v.*) unexpired Senate term. Elected governor again in 1875, he relinquished the office upon being elected to the Senate; he served from 1877 to 1881, then was appointed Secretary of the Interior by James A. Garfield (*q.v.*). He resigned on April 17, 1882, following Garfield's assassination. In 1886, Kirkwood lost a race for Congress because of a split in the Republican party. In the years he was not in public office, he engaged in law, banking, and railroad promotion. He died in Iowa City on September 1, 1894. Clark, *Samuel Jordan Kirkwood*; Sage, *William Boyd Allison*.

Hubert H. Wubben

KNAPP, Anthony Lausett, *congressman,* was born in Middletown, New York, on June 14, 1828, and moved to Jerseyville, Illinois, in 1839. He studied law, and began practicing there in 1849. He served in the Illinois Senate (1859–1861) as a Democrat, and was reelected to a second term. He did not finish that term, however, because he was elected to the U.S. House in 1861 to fill a vacancy in the 37th Congress. Knapp was elected to a full term to the 38th Congress in 1862, but did not seek reelection in 1864. While in Congress he was a Peace Democrat. In 1865 he moved to Chicago, remaining there until 1867, when he moved to Springfield, Illinois. There he practiced law with James C. Robinson (*q.v.*), one of his former colleagues in Congress. He died in Springfield on May 24, 1881. Cole, *Era of the Civil War.*

Leslie J. Stegh

KNIPE, Joseph Farmer, *general,* was born on March 30, 1823, in Mount Joy, Pennsylvania. In 1842, he enlisted in the 2nd U.S. Artillery, with which he served in the Mexican War; he was honorably discharged at Veracruz as a sergeant when his enlistment expired. Until 1861, he worked in the Pennsylvania Railroad's Harrisburg mail office. When war came, Knipe served ninety days as a militia brigade inspector, then raised a three-year infantry regiment, the 46th Pennsylvania. He fought through the Shenandoah Valley, at Cedar Mountain, and (after missing Second Bull Run due to wounds) at Antietam, where he succeeded to command of his brigade.

After Chancellorsville, Knipe went home on sick leave and was still in Harrisburg when Lee invaded Pennsylvania. Knipe volunteered to command a New York militia brigade sent to observe and deter the Confederate advance. Between June 20 and 28, he withdrew slowly to the Susquehanna, probably causing some delay in Confederate movements. Rejoining his own brigade after Gettysburg, in September he moved to Tennessee, guarding a section of the Nashville–Chattanooga rail link until April 1864, then fought through the Atlanta campaign, during the last month as acting division commander.

In poor health, Knipe took a staff appointment, but soon became commander of the 7th Cavalry Division of James H. Wilson's (*q.v.*) cavalry corps, playing a commendable part in the battle of Nashville. Early in 1865, his division was transferred to E. R. S. Canby's (*q.v.*) command for the Mobile campaign. Canby next planned an offensive into Alabama, but lack of horses dictated consolidation of cavalry units, relegating Knipe to brigade command. This precipitated an insubordinate protest from Knipe that brought his immediate relief, although he was not mustered out until August 24, 1865.

Despite his excellent combat record, including months as a division commander, Knipe was denied the brevet promotion to major general granted to most brigadiers of comparable or even less impressive performance. He was postmaster of the House of Representatives, and from 1880 to 1889 was a civilian functionary with the Quartermaster's Department at Fort Leavenworth, Kansas. He died in Harrisburg, Pennsylvania, on August 18, 1901. Nye, *Here Come the Rebels!*; Sword, *Embrace an Angry Wind.*

John B. B. Trussell, Jr.

KNOX, Samuel, *congressman,* was born in Blandford, Massachusetts, on March 21, 1815. He graduated from Williams College in 1836, and after reading law for a term, he entered Harvard's law department, from which he graduated in 1838. He moved to St. Louis that same year and established a successful practice. An ardent Whig, Knox was elected to the St. Louis House of Delegates in 1843 and 1844, and served as its chairman in his second year. He was appointed city counsellor (1845–1846), but declined the office to devote himself to his law practice.

Knox was strongly antislavery, and was persuaded to stand for Congress as a "Charcoal" (Emancipationist) against Francis Blair (*q.v.*) in 1862. Although Blair was declared the winner, Knox successfully contested the election and was seated on June 10, 1864. During his brief tenure he served on the Military Affairs Committee and was active in efforts to secure the same pension and bounty benefits for members of the Missouri State Militia as those enjoyed by the Volunteer troops. He was defeated for reelection in 1864, but continued to be active in the Radical party in Missouri. He died in Blandford on March 7, 1905. Stewart, *Bench and Bar of Missouri.*

William E. Parrish

L

LANE, Henry Smith, *senator*, was born on February 24, 1811, near Sharpsburg, Kentucky. Around 1834, he moved to Crawfordsville, Indiana, where he practiced law until 1854, then entered the banking business with his father-in-law, Isaac C. Elston. Like many Whigs, Lane broke with President John Tyler over banking issues, and he campaigned for Henry Clay in 1844. Unlike a number of Northern Whigs, he strongly supported the Mexican War and served as lieutenant colonel of the 1st Indiana Volunteer Infantry. At least nominally antislavery, Lane opposed the methods of the radical abolitionists and favored compromise. With the disintegration of the Whig party in the 1850s, he aided in the formation of the Republican party in Indiana. He served as president of the Republican National Convention in 1856, was defeated in a bid for the U.S. Senate in 1858, and in 1860 supported Abraham Lincoln's (*q.v.*) nomination for the presidency.

Lane was elected governor of Indiana in 1860. Two days after his inauguration, in accordance with a previous understanding, he was selected by the legislature as U.S. senator and resigned the governorship in favor of Lieutenant Governor Oliver H.P. Morton (*q.v.*). Lane was a member of the Committee on Pensions and the Committee on Military Affairs, zealously supported the Union cause during the Civil War, and to a somewhat lesser degree backed Congressional Reconstruction. At the expiration of his term in 1867, he was appointed Indian peace commissioner. He was a delegate to the Republican National Conventions of 1868 and 1872, and served for many years as a trustee of Asbury College (now DePauw University). Tremendously popular, Lane took few openly controversial stands, and thus made few political or personal enemies.

He died in Crawfordsville on June 18, 1881. Peat, *Portraits and Painters of the Governors of Indiana*; Shepherd, *Biographical Directory of the Indiana General Assembly*, vol. 1; Thornbrough, *Indiana in the Civil War Era*.

Lorna Lutes Sylvester

LANE, James Henry, *senator, general,* was born on June 22, 1814, in Lawrenceburg, Indiana. He served admirably as a colonel of an Indiana Volunteer regiment during the Mexican War, then won election in 1849 as Indiana's lieutenant governor, and in 1853 was elected to Congress. His vote in favor of the Kansas–Nebraska Bill ruined his political reputation in the state, and in 1855 he moved to Kansas, where he joined the Free State movement. An electrifying orator, Lane presided over the 1855 Topeka Convention that framed an extralegal state constitution, and directed the fortification of Lawrence against invading Missourians during the "Wakarusa War."

His reputation thus established, in 1856 Lane went to Washington to gain statehood for Kansas; when unsuccessful, the self-styled "crusader for freedom" promoted migration to Kansas. Upon returning to the territory, he waged a private war against proslavery "border ruffians." In 1859, he was elected as Kansas's first U.S. senator and took his seat in 1861, when the territory became a state. Lane organized a "Frontier Guard" to protect President Abraham Lincoln (*q.v.*), thus beginning an intimate friendship that gave him great influence in the management of Kansas affairs.

In June 1861, Lincoln appointed Lane a brigadier general of Volunteers with authority to raise two regiments. This Kansas Brigade participated in actions in western Missouri and Kansas, raiding and confiscating the property of Missouri slaveholders—including slaves—while assisting fugitive slaves to escape. Acting as recruiting commissioner for Kansas, in 1863 Lane raised one of the first black regiments mustered into the Union Army. He maintained unflagging support for Lincoln's reelection in 1864, and in Congress was a strong advocate of western expansion, supporting the Homestead Act and Pacific Railroad Bill, and helping to secure land grants in Kansas for the construction of railroads.

Lane broke with the Radicals over Reconstruction, and publicly supported President Andrew Johnson (*q.v.*) in his veto of the Civil Rights Bill. This brought almost universal condemnation in Kansas, and in a state of depression brought on in large part by overwork, Lane took his life near Leavenworth on July 11, 1866. Bailes, *Rider on the Wind*; Castel, *Frontier State at War*.

Christopher Phillips

LANE, Joseph, *senator,* was born in Buncombe county, North Carolina, on December 14, 1801, and in 1804 moved with his parents to Kentucky. He later moved to Indiana and won election to the state legislature, where he served as a Democrat from 1822 to 1846. The Mexican War, in which he became a brigadier general of Indiana Volunteers, with significant service under Zachary Taylor and Winfield Scott (*q.v.*), gave him a national reputation. In 1848, President Polk appointed Lane governor of the recently created Oregon Territory. After leaving office in 1850, he won good majorities in four successive elections as Oregon's delegate to Congress. In 1853, he successfully led a force in the Rogue River Indian War and negotiated an important treaty. In 1858, Lane was elected as a Democrat to the U.S. Senate. Southern Democrats nominated him as Vice President in 1860, but the Breckinridge–Lane ticket failed to carry Oregon.

Lane returned to semiretirement on his farm in the Umpqua Valley in 1861. Many Oregonians could accept his proslavery sentiments, but they rejected his defense of secession and his opposition to a war for the Union. Some accused him of plotting western secession. In time, political animosity subsided, and Lane received considerable public support, even affection. The old politician also changed, for he accepted the results of the Civil War—this was symbolized when Lane rode in a stagecoach with Republican President Rutherford B. Hayes (*q.v.*) while General William T. Sherman (*q.v.*) was perched on top. Lane died in Roseburg, Oregon, on April 19, 1881. Edwards, "Holding the Far West for the Union," *Civil War History*; Hendrickson, *Joe Lane*; Johannsen, *Frontier Politics.*

G. *Thomas Edwards*

LANGSTON, John Mercer, *lawyer, chief recruiting agent for African American troops in the West,* was born on December 14, 1829, at Louisa Courthouse, Virginia, the son of a white planter father and a mother of Indian and African American blood. Following his parents' death, Langston and his brothers moved as a family to Chillicothe, Ohio. He attended the public schools there and in Cincinnati. In 1844, he entered Oberlin College's preparatory department, receiving a B.A. degree in 1849 and an M.A. degree in 1852. Admitted to the Ohio bar in September 1854, Langston settled into community life near Oberlin. In 1855, he was elected Brownhelm Township clerk, running on the Liberty party ticket. The victory at the polls probably made him the first African American elected to public office in the United States.

In 1859, John Brown (*q.v.*) approached Langston for assistance in a large-scale slave liberation expedition in the Virginia mountains, a project in which he declined to participate. Following the Altoona Conference in early 1863, Governor John Andrew (*q.v.*) of Massachusetts persuaded George L. Stearns (*q.v.*) to begin organizing African American regiments for Union service. Stearns subsequently appointed Langston chief recruiting agent for the western part of the country. Traveling throughout Ohio, Indiana, and Illinois, he was able to recruit major portions of the 54th and 55th Massachusetts and 5th (Ohio) U.S. Colored Troops.

Following the Civil War, Langston served as general inspector of schools for the Freedmen's Bureau. Active in the Republican party and higher education, he occupied a number of posts, including minister resident to Haiti, president of Howard University, and president of the Virginia Normal and Collegiate Institute. In 1888, he was the Republican nominee for the U.S. House of Representatives from Virginia. Although his election was contested, the House voted to seat him in September 1890, making Langston the first African American congressman from Virginia. Defeated for reelection, he returned to a law practice in Washington, D.C., and died there on November 15, 1897. Cheek, *John Mercer Langston*; Langston, *From Virginia Plantation to the National Capitol.*

Frank R. Levstik

LANPHIER, Charles Henry, *editor,* was born in Alexandria, Virginia, on April 14, 1820. In 1824, his family moved to Washington, D.C., where Lanphier received a good primary school education. In 1836, he went to work as an apprentice printer for his brother-in-law, William Walters, who had been persuaded to start a Democratic paper in Vandalia, Illinois. On February 12, 1836, the first issue of the *Illinois State Register and Vandalia Republican* appeared. When the state capital was moved from Vandalia to Springfield, the paper followed, and on August 10, 1839, the *Illinois State Register and People's Advocate* was published in Springfield.

For more than ten years, Lanphier was a member of the Democratic State Committee and directed the policies of the Democratic party in Illinois. He was an intimate friend and personal adviser to Stephen A. Douglas (*q.v.*), who relied upon his judgment and considered him to be his spokesman. It was Lanphier's task to defend Douglas's authorship of the Kansas–Nebraska Act, laud his supporters, and castigate his critics.

When the Civil War broke out, Lanphier subordinated his party loyalty and editorial position on the *Register* to champion the preservation of the Union and uphold the authority of the national government. The Illinois legislature was summoned to meet in special session on April 23, 1861, and Lanphier urged Douglas to be in Springfield when it met. It was later revealed that Douglas called on President Abraham Lincoln (*q.v.*) and apprised him of Lanphier's appeal, but offered to remain in Washington if the President needed him. Lincoln, however, agreed with Lanphier that Douglas would probably do more good in Illinois.

During the war, Illinois Governor Richard Yates (*q.v.*) appointed Lanphier to the Board of Army Auditors. He later began a political career as clerk of the circuit court, and was defeated for Illinois state treasurer in 1872. Lanphier took an interest in Springfield municipal affairs and, as a member of the city council, shaped legislation and organized the Springfield public school system. He was largely instrumental in laying out and opening Oak Ridge Cemetery, in which Lincoln and other prominent Illinois figures, including himself, are buried. Lanphier died in Springfield on March 19, 1903. Johannsen, *Stephen A. Douglas.*

Ronald D. Rietveld

LANSING, William Esselstyne, *congressman,* was born in Sullivan, New York, on December 29, 1822. He graduated from Cazenovia Seminary in 1841, studied law in Utica, was admitted to the bar in 1845, and began practicing in Chittenango. Lansing was elected district attorney of Madison county in 1850, president of the trustees of Chittenango in 1853, and county clerk in 1855. He made the leap from local to national politics when he was elected to the 37th Congress in 1860. A Radical Republican, he supported the various confiscation acts proposed during his term. "I am in favor of emancipating the slaves of all rebels," he said in May 1862. "None but the blindest devotees of slavery itself now doubt or deny that it was the cause of this war." Lansing did not stand for renomination to a second term, but in 1870 he was elected to the 42nd Congress and served two terms. He died in Syracuse, New York, on July 29, 1883. Smith, *Our Country and Its People.*

Lori A. Lisowski

LATHAM, Milton Slocum, *senator,* was born in Columbus, Ohio, on May 23, 1827. He attended the University of Ohio, and graduated in 1845 from Jefferson College in Pennsylvania. He moved to Russell county, Alabama, taught school, and studied law in the office of Solomon Heydenfeldt, who later was a justice of the California Supreme Court. Latham also imbibed the principles of state sovereignty and white supremacy, which had a lasting influence on his political career. He left Alabama in 1849 with Heydenfeldt and arrived in San Francisco in April 1850. He served one term in Congress (1853–1855) and as collector of the Port of San Francisco (1855–1857). Latham's nomination for governor on the successful Southern Democratic ticket in 1859 interrupted his Sacramento law practice.

Latham sought the governorship as a stepping-stone to the U.S. Senate, and the death of David Broderick in a duel gave him his opportunity. At age thirty-two he was the youngest California governor, and the one who served the shortest term: January 9–14, 1860. In the Senate, Latham actively promoted the transcontinental railroad and other California interests, but his war record put his career in doubt. Although a good friend of Stephen A. Douglas (*q.v.*), he misread California sentiment in 1860 and supported John C. Breckinridge in the presidential election; he did not remain in the state for the conclusion of the campaign. Again misinterpreting public opinion, in November 1860 he advocated that California form an independent Pacific Republic.

In Congress, Latham voted regularly for war measures, but attacked the administration for its alleged violations of the Constitution and for abolitionism. Influential friends warned that he was out of touch with California's Unionism, and when he returned in August 1862 to campaign for reelection, he discovered his political errors. The voters returned a strong Union legislature, and Latham retired from politics. During a tour of Europe, he helped organize the London and San Francisco Bank, which opened in San Francisco on July 1, 1865, with Latham as president. He also promoted local California and Oregon railroads, steamers on the inland waters, and other financial ventures. Latham died in New

York City on March 4, 1882. Melendy, *Governors of California*; Phelps, *Contemporary Biography*, vol. 1.

Robert J. Chandler

LAUMAN, Jacob Gartner, *general*, was born in Taneytown, Maryland, on January 20, 1813, and moved shortly thereafter with his family to nearby York county, Pennsylvania. In 1844, he settled in Burlington, Iowa, where he engaged in mercantile pursuits until the Civil War came. He was active in recruiting and organizing a three-year infantry regiment, the 7th Iowa, and was mustered in on July 11, 1861, as its colonel. After training around Cairo, Illinois, the regiment fought at Belmont, Missouri, and Lauman was seriously wounded. He returned to duty to lead a brigade in Charles F. Smith's (*q.v.*) division at Fort Donelson, and in recognition of his service there, was promoted to brigadier general.

At Shiloh, Lauman commanded a brigade in General Stephen A. Hurlbut's (*q.v.*) division and was engaged in the savage fighting in the Peach Orchard. He led a brigade during the Corinth siege and at the battle of the Hatchie. On December 9, 1862, Lauman assumed command of a division and led it in General Ulysses S. Grant's (*q.v.*) thrust down the Mississippi Central Railroad from Grand Junction to the Yacona River. The division spent the winter and early spring in West Tennessee, and rejoined Grant's army near Vicksburg, where it was attached to the XIII Corps. The day after the surrender of Vicksburg, Lauman's division marched east to attack Jackson. On July 12, 1863, he botched a forced reconnaissance, losing more than half the force committed.

Lauman was relieved by his corps commander and ordered to report to Grant at Vicksburg; Grant directed him to return home and await instructions. Broken in spirit and health, he did not again take the field, although he was breveted major general to rank from March 13, 1865. Lauman died in Burlington on February 9, 1867. Bearss, *Battle of Jackson*; Bearss, *Vicksburg Campaign*, vols. 1, 3; Cooling, *Forts Henry and Donelson*.

Edwin C. Bearss

LAW, John, *congressman*, was born October 28, 1796, in New London, Connecticut. A graduate of Yale College (1814), he studied law before moving to Vincennes, Indiana, in 1817, where he established a practice and won election as prosecuting attorney. Law was a member of the Indiana General Assembly (1823–1824), served as judge of the 7th Judicial Circuit (1830–1831, 1844–1850), held the position of receiver of land sales money at Vincennes (1838–1842), and lost five races for the U.S. Congress. After he moved to Evansville, Indiana, in 1851, President Franklin Pierce appointed Law judge of the Court of Land Claims for Indiana and Illinois (1855–1857). In the 1860 elections, Indiana voters elected Republicans by a substantial majority. Only four of eleven congressmen elected, including Law, were Democrats, and all were from the southern part of the state.

During his terms in the 37th and 38th Congresses, Law supported the Union but opposed confiscation bills and national emancipation legislation. After the war he served as president of the Indiana Historical Society (1859–1873) and as historian of Vincennes. Law retired to Evansville and resumed his law practice until his death there on October 7, 1873. Shepherd, *Biographical Directory of the Indiana General Assembly*, vol. 1; Woollen, *Biographical and Historical Sketches of Early Indiana.*

David G. Vanderstel

LAZEAR, Jesse, *congressman,* was born near Waynesburg, Pennsylvania, on December 12, 1804. Although he received little formal education, he taught school and was county recorder for one term, and cashier of the Waynesburg Farmers' and Drovers' Bank (1835–1867). He was active in public affairs and was elected as a Democrat to the 37th and 38th Congresses. Lazear opposed confiscation, emancipation, conscription, efforts to expand the national currency, and all Radical Reconstruction measures. Defeated for reelection in 1864, he was a delegate to the Union National Convention in 1866. After a brief retirement, he was president of the Baltimore & Powhatan Railroad Company from 1871 to 1874. Lazear died in Baltimore county, Maryland, on September 2, 1877. *BDUSC.*

J. K. Folmar

LE BLOND, Francis Celeste, *congressman,* was born in Bellville, Ohio, on February 14, 1821. He was educated in the local schools and studied law in Norwalk, Ohio. In 1844, he was admitted to the Ohio bar and began to practice law in St. Marys. In 1848, he moved to Celina, Ohio, and continued his law career. Le Blond became interested in politics and was elected as a Democrat to the Ohio House from 1851 to 1855, serving as speaker in 1854 and 1855. In 1862, he was elected to the 38th Congress, and won reelection in 1864 to the 39th Congress. Le Blond did not agree with Abraham Lincoln's (*q.v.*) war policies and opposed emancipation. He did not seek reelection in 1866, but returned to Celina, where he practiced law and successfully promoted railroad construction. He died in Celina on November 9, 1902. *BDUSC.*

Thomas H. Smith

LEARY, Cornelius Lawrence Lublow, *congressman,* was born in Baltimore on October 22, 1813. After attending public schools, he graduated from St. Mary's College in 1833. He entered politics as a Whig, and served in the Maryland House of Delegates in 1838 and 1839. Meanwhile, he studied law and was admitted to the Maryland bar in 1840. With the collapse of the Whig party, Leary joined the Know-Nothings and served as an American party presidential elector in 1856.

With the coming of the Civil War, Leary joined the Union coalition and in 1861 defeated his State Rights opponent for his district's congressional seat. From a position of dubious loyalty, Leary became a stronger Conditional

Unionist by 1863. He opposed any interference with slavery, but by early 1863, during the political maneuvering over an ill-fated measure that would provide for compensated emancipation in Maryland, he had begun to change his position. As a result of the 1860 census, Maryland lost a congressional seat in 1863, and in the newly constructed district the Union nomination went to Edwin Webster (*q.v.*), also an incumbent. Leary returned to his law practice, and died in Baltimore on March 21, 1893. Clark, *Politics in Maryland During the Civil War.*

Richard R. Duncan

LEDLIE, James Hewett, *general,* was born in Utica, New York, on April 14, 1832. He attended Union College, and was an engineer when the Civil War began. After service as a major with the 19th New York Volunteers (later the 3rd New York Artillery) and promotion to lieutenant colonel, Ledlie was appointed a brigadier general of Volunteers on December 24, 1862. He commanded an artillery brigade on the Carolina coast, then became an infantry brigade commander in Ambrose Burnside's (*q.v.*) IX Corps. Although his service in the Petersburg campaign was ineffective, through a series of ill-advised command decisions his division was chosen to spearhead the assault on the Confederate lines in the aftermath of the mine explosion of July 30, 1864. Burnside had intended to use Edward Ferrero's (*q.v.*) all-black division for the first assault, and that division was trained for the task.

George G. Meade (*q.v.*), with Ulysses S. Grant's (*q.v.*) approval, overruled Burnside, who then allowed his division commanders to draw straws to see who would lead the attack. Ledlie won the draw, and the Union soldiers lost. When the time came to attack, a drunken Ledlie skulked in a bombproof shelter. He was joined by Ferrero when that general's division went forward. Ledlie and Ferrero deserved a firing squad, but Burnside, Meade, and Grant must be blamed for their command blunders. Ledlie left the service on January 23, 1865, to resume his career as a civil engineer. He died on Staten Island, New York, on August 15, 1882. Catton, *Stillness at Appomattox*; Marvel, *Burnside.*

John T. Hubbell

LEE, Albert Lindley, *general,* was born in Fulton, New York, on January 16, 1834. He graduated from Union College at Schenectady, which also claimed Henry W. Halleck (*q.v.*) as an alumnus, in 1853, then studied law. He practiced law in New York until 1858, then moved to Kansas Territory. He was elected a district judge and, in early 1861, a justice on the new state's Supreme Court. Lee resigned this post on October 29 to accept a commission as major of the 7th Kansas Cavalry, of which he became colonel in 1862. Following service in Kansas and western Missouri, the regiment served under Ulysses S. Grant (*q.v.*) in the Vicksburg campaign.

Lee was promoted to brigadier general and acted as John A. McClernand's (*q.v.*) chief of staff in the actions at Champion's Hill and Big Black River. He suffered a wound during the siege of Vicksburg, and when he returned to active duty, was ordered to join Nathaniel P. Banks's (*q.v.*) command. As Banks's chief of cavalry, Lee commanded the cavalry in the action at Sabine Cross Roads and, like others responsible for Union arms at that ill-fated battle, came under severe criticism.

Thereafter, Lee's career was blighted. He commanded a cavalry division in the Department of the Gulf, but quarreled with Banks's successor, General Edward R.S. Canby (*q.v.*). Lee continued at his post for a time, but exercised little authority. In early 1865, he received orders to report to the adjutant general in Washington, who ordered him to return to Louisiana. In April, Canby ordered him to remain in New Orleans until further notice. Lee resigned from the service on May 4, 1865, and remained in New Orleans. He entered several businesses, traveled, then moved to New York to join a banking and brokerage firm. Lee became an active member of the Union League Club and the Loyal Legion. He died in New York City on December 31, 1907. Bearss, *Vicksburg Campaign*; Starr, *Jennison's Jayhawkers.*

Archie P. McDonald

LEE, S[amuel] Phillips, *admiral*, was born on February 13, 1812, in Fairfax county, Virginia, the eldest son of Francis Lightfoot Lee and a grandson of Richard Henry Lee. President John Quincy Adams gave Lee an acting midshipman's warrant in 1825, shortly after his third cousin, Robert Edward Lee, entered the Military Academy at West Point. Phillips Lee's forty-six-year naval career began in 1827, with orders to Norfolk. His first training followed the Old Navy pattern: at sea on the *Hornet* (West India Squadron), and the *Delaware* and the *Java* (Mediterranean Squadron). After passing the examination for midshipman in 1831, Lee won his first distinction aboard the *Brandywine* when its rudder was carried away off Cape Horn in 1834; his prompt actions as sailing master saved the ship.

Lee transferred to the *Vincennes* in early 1835 for a world cruise, during which he was made acting lieutenant; promotion to lieutenant came in early 1837. Briefly in the exploring expedition (1838–1842) under Charles Wilkes, he returned home in 1839 and met Elizabeth Blair, daughter of the Jacksonian editor Francis Preston Blair. Overcoming family opposition, Lee married her in April 1843, thus allying himself with a politically powerful family who were strong supporters of Abraham Lincoln (*q.v.*) before and throughout the Civil War.

For most of the 1840s, Lee served on the Coast Survey, charting, inter alia, Chesapeake and Delaware bays. Commanding the *Washington* in 1847, he participated in the second Tabasco expedition. Exemplary performance on the survey led in 1851 to command of the *Dolphin* in making deep-sea soundings. Publication of his *Cruise of the Dolphin* (1854) helped gain Lee his 1855 promotion to commander. After various duties in Washington, Lee sailed the *Vandalia* out of New York in late 1860, with orders to the East Indies.

Learning at Capetown of the outbreak of war, Lee returned home to join the

Union blockade and to perform distinguished service throughout the war, winning promotion to captain in 1862, to commodore in 1866, and to rear admiral in 1870. His Civil War service can be divided into four parts: aboard the *Vandalia* off Charleston until October 1861, when he took command of the *Oneida*, a new steam sloop; up the Mississippi with David Farragut (*q.v.*) to capture New Orleans and threaten Vicksburg; then command of the North Atlantic Blockading Squadron as acting rear admiral from September 1862 to October 1864; and command of the Mississippi Squadron from November 1864 to midsummer 1865.

Lee's greatest contribution to the Union victory came in the two years on blockade. He developed an effective triple girdle of cruisers that became the model for other blockaders. A long list of prizes taken and ships destroyed proved the utility of his organization and brought him substantial prize money. His last sea duty was in command of the North Atlantic Squadron. Lee retired in 1873 and turned to farming in Silver Spring, Maryland, where he died on July 5, 1897. Cornish, *Lincoln's Lee*.

Dudley T. Cornish

LEGGETT, Mortimer Dormer, *general,* was born near Ithaca, New York, on April 19, 1821. In 1836, his family moved to Ohio, where Leggett studied law and medicine, and was admitted to the bar in 1844. He practiced as a partner of Jacob D. Cox (*q.v.*), became interested in public education, and served as superintendent of schools for several towns. In the early months of the Civil War, Leggett was a volunteer aide-de-camp on the staff of his friend George B. McClellan (*q.v.*), and in December 1861 became a lieutenant colonel of the 78th Ohio Volunteers. In January 1862, he was promoted to colonel, and in November of the same year to brigadier general of Volunteers. Meanwhile, he had fought at Fort Donelson, Shiloh, and Corinth. Leggett commanded a brigade in the XIII and XVII Corps in the Vicksburg campaign, and led the 3rd Division, XVII Corps in the Atlanta campaign, the March to the Sea, and the Carolinas campaign. For a part of this time, however, he was absent from his division because of sickness, and for another part he briefly commanded the XVII Corps.

Leggett's most distinguished service was on July 21 and 22, 1864, as his division, part of the Army of the Tennessee, approached Atlanta from the east, marching along the Georgia Railroad. On July 21, Leggett's command assaulted Bald Hill, an important Confederate position. After a desperate battle, the hill was taken and held against counterattacks. On July 22, the Confederates lapped around the hill and attacked Leggett from the rear. Leggett's men jumped to the outside of their breastworks and repulsed the attack. When other Confederates attacked from the original front side of the works, Leggett's men quickly resumed their first position and repulsed that attack. On September 1, 1864, Leggett was made a brevet major general of Volunteers, and on August 21, 1865, a full major general of Volunteers. In September 1865 he resigned, ending a distinguished military career. He died in Cleveland, Ohio, on January 6, 1896.

Bearss, *Vicksburg Campaign*; Castel, *Decision in the West*; Jones, *"Black Jack:" John A. Logan.*

Richard M. McMurry

LEHMAN, William Eckart, *congressman*, was born in Philadelphia on August 21, 1821. He graduated from the University of Pennsylvania, studied law, and was admitted to the bar in 1844. Lehman was appointed post office examiner for Pennsylvania and New York during the Polk administration, and in 1860 was elected to Congress. Although the results were contested, he was seated. A War Democrat, he supported most of the Republican leadership's policies. In April 1862, being proemancipation, Lehman was appointed to a committee that would consider and recommend gradual emancipation in the border states. He was one of only four Democrats to support a national conscription bill, and in March 1863 was the only one to vote for a measure granting the President the power to suspend the writ of habeas corpus.

Excessive absences and abstentions marred Lehman's brief congressional career. He did not receive his party's nomination in 1862, and his Democratic successor, Samuel J. Randall (*q.v.*), won handily. As a reward for supporting controversial administration policies, Abraham Lincoln (*q.v.*) appointed Lehman provost marshal in Pennsylvania's 1st District. During his two-year tenure, draft officials under his direction were accused of corruption, but subsequent investigations revealed that the charges were without foundation and Lehman was exonerated of any wrongdoing. He died in Atlantic City, New Jersey, on July 19, 1895. *BDUSC*; Geary, *We Need Men.*

J. K. Folmar

LESLIE, Frank, *publisher*, was born Henry Carter in Ipswich, England, on March 29, 1821. He began an artistic career under the pseudonym Frank Leslie, which he later adopted legally as his name. In 1842, Leslie joined the *Illustrated London News* as an engraver, and in 1848 emigrated with his family to Boston, where he did engraving for *Gleason's Pictorial Drawing Room Companion*, illustrated programs for Jenny Lind's American tour, and became managing foreman for P. T. Barnum's *Illustrated News*. In 1854, he started *Frank Leslie's Ladies Gazette of Fashion*; his most important publication was his *Illustrated Newspaper*, established in 1855. The New York weekly, known more for its spectacular, sensational illustrations than for its editorial content, was an immediate success and reached a circulation of 100,000 by 1858. Ever the innovator, Leslie developed a new engraving technique for large pictures. A double-page illustration, which would ordinarily require two weeks for an engraver to complete, could be produced within a day with the new process, which was eventually adopted by every large engraving house in the country.

Leslie opposed abolitionism, denounced John Brown (*q.v.*) as a maniac, and criticized Wendell Phillips (*q.v.*) for his Toussaint oration at Cooper Union. At the outbreak of the war, the *Illustrated Newspaper* tried nonpartisanship, and as a result was criticized in both the North and the South. The bombardment of Fort Sumter was illustrated in a dramatic folding picture, and the paper offered to pay any soldier, North or South, for sketches. Leslie sent artists and correspondents to all Union armies; Alfred Waud (*q.v.*) and Edwin Forbes (*q.v.*), among others, provided on-the-spot views of battles and camps. Sketches of battles in progress were sent to New York, where they were embellished and engraved. Thus readers saw the war in vivid, if romanticized, illustrations. The newspaper issued extras, many full and double-page battle pictures, and occasionally four-page folding scenes.

The 1860s was the most prosperous decade for Leslie's publishing empire. Between 1854 and 1869, he founded fifteen publications. In 1867, Leslie received a gold medal from Napoleon for his services as a U.S. commissioner at the Paris Exposition. In 1876, he was named president of the New York State Centennial Commission. The 1870s brought personal scandal and near financial ruin to Leslie, however, and by 1877 his business was conducted by an assignee. Leslie died in New York City on January 10, 1880. Gambee, *Frank Leslie*; Mott, *History of American Magazines*, vols. 2, 3.

Kathleen L. Endres

LEWIS, James Taylor, *governor*, was born in Clarendon, New York, on October 30, 1819. His father had invested considerably in Wisconsin lands, and in 1845 young Lewis settled in Columbus, Wisconsin, where he began his law practice and dabbled in politics. As a Democrat, Lewis was a delegate to the 1847–1848 Wisconsin Constitutional Convention, after which he served as county judge. He was elected to the Assembly in 1852 and the state Senate the following year. He ran successfully for lieutenant governor in 1854, then retired from politics in 1856. When he reentered politics, in the 1861 contest for attorney general, Lewis won as a Republican.

In 1863, his new party nominated Lewis for governor. At the time it seemed impossible for Republicans to lose statewide elections, and so it was with Lewis. His already substantial margin of 16,000 swelled by half again when the soldier vote was tallied, giving him a record majority. Lewis was stronger in supporting Abraham Lincoln's (*q.v.*) policies than were most Midwestern governors, although he worked diligently to postpone the draft and argued about the fairness of quotas. His most important contribution may have been his attention to Wisconsin's war casualties, in the tradition of his predecessors in office. Lewis tirelessly toured hospitals and camps, traveling as far as New Orleans and Norfolk to visit the sick and wounded from Wisconsin. He was also committed to the care of the families of fallen soldiers, and his administration oversaw the founding of orphans' homes as well as hospitals.

In 1864, Lewis was an enthusiastic backer of the Lincoln–Johnson ticket, but he did not stand for reelection, having promised to be a one-term governor. With the exception of the 1876 Republican National Convention, to which he was a Rutherford B. Hayes (*q.v.*) delegate, Lewis contented himself with the practice of law and an active involvement in civic affairs. He died in Columbus on August 4, 1904. Current, *Civil War Era*; Hesseltine, *Lincoln's War Governors.*

Charles E. Twining

LIEBER, Francis, *educator, political theorist,* was born on March 18, 1798, in Berlin, Germany. His youthful experience in Europe included military service, academics, and political dissent. He fought against Napoleon in 1815, and for Greek independence in 1822. He earned a Ph.D. from the University of Jena in 1820. His espousal of nationalistic and liberal politics led to imprisonments, which in turn motivated his migration to the United States in 1827. Following his arrival, Lieber pursued a variety of educational, scholarly, and reform activities in the North.

In 1835, Lieber became professor of history and political economy at South Carolina College, where he remained until 1857. During his tenure at the college, he published a series of political studies that stressed institutional limits on individual rights. Lieber owned slaves while simultaneously criticizing the institution of slavery. His ambiguous position contributed to his return to the North in 1857 to accept a professorship at Columbia University. During the Civil War, he served as an adviser on constitutional questions to the U.S. Attorney General and denounced Northern critics of the war.

Lieber's *Code for the Government of Armies,* published in 1863 and adopted by the U.S. Army, constituted the first practical effort to establish a code for the conduct of armies at war and helped define international law on the subject. His Loyal Publication Society of New York printed 900,000 tracts to counter calls for an early peace. Following the war, Lieber became the official keeper of the captured Confederate archives and promoted the codification of international law. He died on October 2, 1872, in New York City. Fredrickson, *Inner Civil War*; Freidel, *Francis Lieber.*

Stanley Harrold

LINCOLN, Abraham, *President,* was born on February 12, 1809, in Hardin county, Kentucky. His family moved to Indiana in 1816, and to Illinois in 1830. Despite his typical frontier background, Lincoln never entirely conformed to the image of the pioneer. He had very little formal education but was an avid reader; he held no readily definable set of religious beliefs but had a strong religious sense. In 1831, Lincoln settled at New Salem, near Springfield, and from the mid-1830s, the law and politics were his chief preoccupations. A staunch Whig, he served in the state legislature (1834–1841) and became his party's floor leader.

After an anguished and intermittent courtship, Lincoln married Mary Todd (*q.v.*) on November 4, 1842. They had four sons, of whom only the eldest, Robert Todd, survived to manhood. Elected to the House of Representatives in 1846, Lincoln served only one term (1847–1849). The lone Illinois Whig in the House, he made no great impression in Washington, but he expressed mounting opposition to the Mexican War and supported the Wilmot Proviso. After several years devoted to law, the Kansas–Nebraska controversy brought him back into public life in 1854. Emerging as the most prominent Republican in Illinois, Lincoln was a candidate for the party's vice presidential nomination in 1856, and the challenger for Stephen A. Douglas's (*q.v.*) Senate seat in 1858. Through his "House Divided" speech, and his much-publicized debates with Douglas, he won a new and wider reputation, but not the Senate seat.

At the 1860 Republican National Convention in Chicago, Lincoln, with the advantage of a high reputation too newly acquired to be tarnished, offered an attractive alternative to more prominent but more controversial candidates like William H. Seward (*q.v.*) and Salmon P. Chase (*q.v.*), and won the nomination on the third ballot. He went on to win a clear majority in the electoral college, with under 40 percent of the popular vote. He took no public part in the campaign, and remained generally silent during the four months until his inauguration on March 4, 1861, while seven Southern states seceded from the Union. Lincoln remained firm on two fundamental points: the preservation of the Union and the prevention of any further extension of slavery in the territories. His refusal to surrender Fort Sumter in Charleston Harbor left the Confederate leaders with the choice between challenge and acquiescence. They chose to fire the first shots, and Fort Sumter fell on April 12–13, 1861.

Lincoln now found himself the untutored leader of an improvised war effort. Political and personal, as well as strategic, disagreements soured his relations with his commanders in the East and the West. He tolerated George B. McClellan's (*q.v.*) delays, reluctantly sanctioned his strategy on the Virginia Peninsula in 1862, and persevered with him until his failure to follow up his half-success at Antietam led to his removal. Other generals—Ambrose E. Burnside (*q.v.*) and Joseph Hooker (*q.v.*)—came, failed, and departed. George G. Meade (*q.v.*) won the vital defensive victory at Gettysburg, but incurred Lincoln's displeasure for failing to exploit it. In the West, the feats of Ulysses S. Grant (*q.v.*), culminating in the capture of Vicksburg, convinced the President that he had found one general, at least, who shared his strategic conceptions and acted upon them.

Meanwhile, on the home front, Lincoln faced political storms, and his party suffered a sharp setback in the midterm elections of 1862. Beset by critics in his own party, who demanded immediate emancipation, and by others in both parties, who insisted that the war was simply to save the Union and not to free the slaves, Lincoln steered a difficult middle course. He failed to win support for a policy of gradual, compensated emancipation associated with projects for colonizing freedmen overseas, but he prepared the way for the Emancipation Proclamations of September 22, 1862, and January 1, 1863, which declared free only those slaves in areas still in rebellion. However, the demise of slavery was now assured if the North won the war. In 1864–1865, Lincoln supported the passage of the 13th Amendment, which abolished slavery once and for all.

Lincoln was accused of executive tyranny for his attempts to deal with the problem of internal security by arbitrary arrests, aimed at preventing rather than punishing subversion. But he consistently argued that the Constitution gave special powers to the President in time of war or rebellion. By 1864, massive Northern superiority had laid the basis for an ultimate victory, which was still difficult to achieve. Throughout the arduous campaigns of that year, the President solidly supported Grant and William T. Sherman (*q.v.*), in the face of mounting frustration and war weariness. Lincoln's apparently lenient and flexible approach to the reconstruction of the Southern states brought him into sharp conflict with members of his own party, culminating in his pocket veto of the Wade–Davis Bill (July 4, 1864) and the fierce denunciation of the President in the Wade–Davis Manifesto.

The election of 1864 was the crucial test for Lincoln as war leader and as party leader. His mastery of the party organization assured his renomination in June, but a midsummer slump in the fortunes of war, and in his own political standing, inspired moves to replace him. Lincoln briefly succumbed to deep pessimism about his prospects, but new military successes, notably the capture of Atlanta, came to his rescue. By November, the issue was not in doubt, and Lincoln won an impressive, if scarcely overwhelming, victory over McClellan. In the closing months of the war, he toyed with various peace proposals and met Confederate leaders at Hampton Roads (February 3, 1865), but maintained his insistence on reunion and abolition as basic conditions for peace. When Richmond finally fell, Lincoln walked unharmed through the streets of the Confederate capital on April 3, 1865.

Few presidents have come to the White House with less experience in the Federal government or in executive office of any kind. Lincoln's presidential style proved to be a blend of the unpretentious, the unpredictable, and the unprecedented—quite unlike that of the major twentieth-century presidents. His public appearances were limited, and his speeches astonishingly rare. As an administrator, he was unsystematic, and he dealt with a Cabinet of strong and often dissonant personalities as separate individuals rather than as a group. He made little attempt to lead Congress, and pressed no great program of legislation upon it. Lincoln was frequently derided as a fumbling incompetent or patronized as a decent and well-meaning man struggling out of his depth.

Not all of the criticism was ill-founded; there were chapters of confusion, indecision, and mismanagement in the history of his administration. But Lincoln drew upon unsuspected skill and strength. He was a master politician, never too busy directing the war to give attention to appointments to office, party maneuvers, or vote-getting tactics. Though never short of critics within his own party, he managed its affairs with subtlety and perseverance. In using party politics as a device for containing internal conflict, Lincoln made it one of the vital tools of war. On military matters, he made serious mistakes but learned quickly from them. In defiance of the conventional military wisdom of the day, he insisted that the North must exploit its superiority in numbers and resources through relentless pressure, and that destruction of the opposing army, not occupation of territory, must be the highest priority. Lincoln took a broad view of the wartime powers of the President; in tackling the slavery question, for example, he was determined to keep control in his own, rather than in congressional, hands.

Lincoln's sensitive political antennae, his sense of timing, his unwillingness to commit himself prematurely, and his predilection for achieving great ends by small and unspectacular stages were nowhere better illustrated than in the tortuous route that led to the Emancipation Proclamations and the 13th Amendment. His racial attitudes had been shaped by the social, political, and scientific conventions of his day. Although they changed during the war, at the time of his death he was still struggling toward a new conception of the role and status of free black citizens in American society. The war revealed in Lincoln a determination and a resilience, even a ruthlessness, that enabled him to prosecute to final victory a struggle that proved infinitely more bloody, costly, and destructive than he or anyone had imagined in 1861.

The sharp contrast between the hesitant, clumsy, even incompetent Lincoln depicted by his contemporary critics, and the shrewd politician, iron-willed war leader, and inspired statesman of later fame, may be explained partly by his capacity for growth, partly by his deceptive low-key style, partly by his somewhat enigmatic personality, and partly by the distinction between history and myth. Remarkably free from pomp and self-importance, he had an almost unlimited capacity to accept burdens and absorb punishment, to operate simultaneously at several different levels, and, under fierce and constant pressure, to reconcile the desirable with the possible. Lincoln seldom erred in his judgment of what really mattered and what did not. His impact upon the popular mind was not sudden and dramatic, but gradual and profound. Although he made few speeches as President, he talked individually to thousands of people, and he made incomparable use of the written word.

From the outset, Lincoln perceived the underlying purpose of the struggle to be not simply preservation of the Union, nor indeed freedom for the slaves, but the survival of the great American experiment in liberal democracy, with the promise of opportunity for all, "the last, best hope of earth." His articulation of the fundamental issues reflected his personal identification with them. Lincoln's final achievement was to be both the successful day-to-day manager and the enduring symbol of his cause. Five days after Robert E. Lee's surrender at Appomattox, Abraham Lincoln was shot by John Wilkes Booth at Ford's Theatre in Washington, D.C. He died the next morning (April 15, 1865) without regaining consciousness. Fehrenbacher, *Lincoln in Text and Context*; McPherson, *Abraham Lincoln and the Second American Revolution*; Oates, *With Malice Toward None*; Randall, *Lincoln the President*; Thomas, *Abraham Lincoln*.

Peter J. Parish

LINCOLN, Mary Todd, *first lady*, was born on December 13, 1818, in Lexington, Kentucky. The Todd family was prosperous, and Mary received the best of everything, including a good education. In 1839, she was sent to Springfield, Illinois, to live with her sister, Elizabeth Edwards. It was there that she met Abraham Lincoln (*q.v.*), and in 1842 married him. Mary Todd Lincoln was destined to become one of the most controversial first ladies in history. Her Southern background made her a natural target for accusations of being a traitor. Despite her education and social skills, she was scorned by Washington society as being from the frontier. The press continually censured her for her lavish entertainments and expenditures, especially when she began a sorely needed remodeling of the White House.

At a time when women were supposed to be mere ornaments to their husbands, Mary Lincoln stepped out of this role. She had a lively interest in politics, enjoyed being the center of attention, and was the first President's spouse to be so constantly in the public eye. She was also emotionally unstable, which manifested itself in hysterical outbursts and a flirtation with spiritualism. Her jealousy of other women, especially Kate Chase, daughter of Salmon P. Chase (*q.v.*), and her emotional problems were aggravated by the deaths of loved ones. Her mother died when Mary was a girl. She lost two young sons: Edward, when he was three, and Willie, who died in 1862, at the age of eleven. The death of her husband was the worst blow, and the rest of Mary Lincoln's life was marked by great sorrow. Her son Tad died in 1871. Four years later, her son Robert called for a sanity trial, at which she was adjudged insane and committed to a sanatorium for four months. She died on July 16, 1882, in Springfield, Illinois. Baker, *Mary Todd Lincoln*; Neely, *The Insanity File*; Randall, *Mary Lincoln.*

Donna M. DeBlasio

LITTLEJOHN, DeWitt Clinton, *congressman,* was born on February 17, 1818, in Bridgeport, New York. Although well educated, he did not attend college. In 1839, he moved to Oswego, where he formed a business partnership with Henry Fitzhugh that concentrated on lake commerce and flour milling. Littlejohn was elected mayor of Oswego in 1849 and 1850, then served three terms in the New York State Assembly, one as speaker, prior to the Civil War. In late 1860, President-elect Abraham Lincoln (*q.v.*) offered him the U.S. consulship in Liverpool, but he declined the office. On July 29, 1862, he was appointed colonel of the 110th New York Infantry, a post he retained until his discharge on February 3, 1863, at New Orleans. Littlejohn was elected as a Republican to the 38th Congress, but declined to run for renomination. After the war, he served several terms as speaker of the New York State Assembly. He died in Oswego on October 27, 1892. Phisterer, *New York in the War of the Rebellion*, vols. 1, 4.

Frank R. Levstik

LIVERMORE, Mary Ashton Rice, *abolitionist, journalist, relief worker*, was born on December 19, 1820, in Boston. She attended Miss Martha Whiting's Female Seminary, where she was retained as an instructor of Latin, Italian, and French. In 1839, she became a tutor on a plantation in Virginia. When Mary returned to Boston in 1842, she subscribed to *The Liberator* and attended every accessible antislavery meeting. She also became involved in the temperance movement, and in 1845 married Daniel Parker Livermore, a Universalist minister. She augmented the family income by contributing essays, stories, and poems to various magazines and local papers.

In 1857, Daniel Livermore resigned his ministry and planned to move his family to a Kansas antislavery colony to which he had given financial support. The illness of a daughter forced the family to settle in Chicago, where Daniel became editor of the Universalist weekly newspaper of the Northwest—the *New Covenant*. Mary became associate editor and ran the newspaper when her husband traveled. In 1860, she was the only woman reporter at the Chicago Republican National Convention. The Livermores backed the Union cause, although it meant losing many readers.

Mary had a dual career as a journalist and as an associate member of the Sanitary Commission, headquartered in Chicago. She appealed for supplies and donations; wrote circulars, bulletins, and monthly reports of the commission; toured hospitals; and helped plan, organize, and conduct a number of Sanitary Fairs. She and a friend, Jane Hoge, proposed the first Sanitary Fair but received little encouragement from the men on the commission. The extremely successful fair became the model of the others that followed. As a journalist, Livermore wrote extensively for the *New Covenant* and other periodicals in the Northwest. In addition, she contributed war sketches to magazines. She appealed to women to provide hospital supplies, and wrote scornfully of what she regarded as treasonable opinion or sympathy with secession held by army officers and civil authorities.

After the Civil War, Livermore became a leader in the women's rights movement. She arranged a suffrage convention in Chicago, and was elected president of the Illinois Woman Suffrage Association, and later president of the American Woman Suffrage Association. In 1869, she established *The Agitator*, which advocated suffrage and temperance. In 1870, it was merged into Lucy Stone's (*q.v.*) *Woman's Journal*, and Livermore was editor in chief until 1872, when she resigned to pursue a career in lecturing. She was also involved in Republican party politics; twice she was sent as a delegate to the Massachusetts Republican Convention, with the responsibility of presenting temperance and woman's suffrage resolutions. She died on May 23, 1905, in Melrose, Massachuetts. Brockett, *Woman's Work in the Civil War*; Livermore, *Story of My Life*.

Kathleen L. Endres

LOAN, Benjamin Franklin, *congressman*, was born in Hardinsburg, Kentucky, on October 4, 1819. He moved to St. Joseph, Missouri, in 1838. He continued his study of law there and was admitted to the bar in 1840. A prewar Democrat, Loan moved quickly to the support of the Union cause in northwest Missouri in 1861. He helped sustain the pro-Union *St. Joseph Journal* in 1861, and organized troops and procured arms from Fort Leavenworth. He supported the establishment of the Provisional Government in July 1861 and received a commission as brigadier general in the Missouri State Militia in November. He played a prominent role in the defense of the state against guerrillas during the next two years.

Staunchly antislavery, Loan was elected to Congress in 1862 as a "Charcoal" (Emancipationist). He played a leading role in the establishment of the Radical Union party in Missouri in 1863, and became increasingly critical of the conservative posture of the Provisional Government. His military experience and Radical tendencies were recognized in the 38th Congress by his appointment to the Joint Committee on the Conduct of the War. Loan was a member of the Missouri Radical delegation to the 1864 Republican National Convention and, with the rest of the group, opposed the renomination of Abraham Lincoln (*q.v.*).

Reelected to Congress in 1864 and 1866, Loan became a key link between Missouri Radicals and their congressional counterparts during the early days of Reconstruction. An unsuccessful candidate for reelection in 1868, he resumed his law practice in St. Joseph. A delegate to the Republican National Convention in 1876, he declined several diplomatic and territorial appointments. Loan was again an unsuccessful candidate for Congress in 1876. He died in St. Joseph on March 30, 1881. Parrish, *Turbulent Partnership; Portrait and Biographical Record of Buchanan and Clinton Counties, Missouri.*

William E. Parrish

LOCKE, David Ross, *editor, satirist,* better known as Petroleum V. Nasby, was born on September 20, 1833, in Vestal, New York. He was largely self-educated, and in 1845 he was apprenticed as a printer. After four years he became an itinerant printer, his travels in 1853 taking him to Ohio, where he entered editorial journalism. From 1853 to 1865, Locke edited at least three weekly papers in Plymouth, Bucyrus, and Findlay, Ohio. In March 1861 he began writing the Nasby columns, the Copperheadish outpourings of a patently and purposefully stereotyped poor white from the town of "Confedrit X Roads, Kentucky." It was not long before Nasby's ludicrous, earthy philosophy and satirical antiwar articles became quite popular in the North, thanks in large part to their popularity with Abraham Lincoln (*q.v.*).

The letters from Nasby continued until about 1870. From 1865 to 1871, Locke owned and edited the *Toledo Blade,* for which he continued to write strong, Liberal Republican editorials, and to serve as a buffer between the moderate and Radical Republicans. He also continued his lifelong battle for African American rights. In 1871, Locke moved to New York City and became an editor of the *Evening Mail,* but returned to Toledo in 1880 to serve as publisher of the *Blade* and as a civic and political activist.

Of several Civil War humorists, Locke was the most prominent and influential. The Nasby letters remain fairly alive and vibrant, though much has been lost for the modern reader. Yet Locke has largely been forgotten, his identity lost to, or stolen by, the implacable, irascible Nasby. Locke died in Toledo on February 15, 1888. Austin, *Petroleum V. Nasby*; Harrison, *The Man Who Made Nasby*.

Fredric F. Endres

LOGAN, John Alexander, *general,* was born on February 9, 1826, in Jackson county, Illinois. After service as a lieutenant of Illinois Volunteers in Mexico, he became active in Democratic politics. He was a state legislator and congress-man (1858–1861), and managed to become an informal member of a Michigan regiment at Bull Run. In the late summer of 1861, he formed the 31st Illinois Volunteers and was named its colonel in September. Logan acquired an early and deserved reputation as an effective field commander. He fought at Belmont and Fort Donelson, and was promoted to brigadier general in March 1862. After service as a brigade commander, he led a division during the Corinth campaign and, with distinction, at Vicksburg. His division, part of James B. McPherson's (*q.v.*) XVII Corps, led the triumphant march into that city after the surrender.

During the Atlanta campaign, Logan commanded the XV Corps, in which position he continued to excel. He was conspicuously present at Resaca, Dallas, and Kennesaw. On July 22, 1864, at the battle of Atlanta, after McPherson was killed, Logan took command of the Army of the Tennessee. One account has it that Logan shouted, "McPherson is dead, boys! Will you follow me?" The Union soldiers responded with chants of "Black Jack! Black Jack!," his popular nickname. Notwithstanding Logan's admirable record of command, from regi-ment to army, William T. Sherman (*q.v.*) chose Oliver O. Howard (*q.v.*) as McPherson's successor, ostensibly because George H. Thomas (*q.v.*) said that he would resign if Logan were elevated to army command. Sherman was also skeptical of "political" generals (as if West Pointers were not masters of the political arts!), and in fact Logan returned that fall to Illinois to help elect candidates friendly to Abraham Lincoln's (*q.v.*) administration.

Logan joined the XV Corps at Savannah and led it through the Carolinas. Before that, in mid-December, Ulysses S. Grant (*q.v.*) had decided to send him to Nashville, where Thomas seemed to be unduly slow in attacking Hood. Logan was in Louisville when he learned of Thomas's smashing victory, which ren-dered his mission unnecessary. He was at Joseph E. Johnston's surrender, and in a fine touch of irony was named commander of the Army of the Tennessee in time to lead that redoubtable fighting machine in the Grand Review at Wash-ington.

Logan left the service for politics, veterans' affairs, and a failed bid (1884) for the vice presidency. He wrote *The Volunteer Soldier of America* (1887), at times a thinly disguised attack upon the professional officer corps. Its petulant tone was unbecoming and unnecessary. John A. Logan was a soldier's soldier. He died in Washington, D.C., on December 26, 1886. Castel, *Decision in the West*; Jones, *"Black Jack": John A. Logan.*

John T. Hubbell

LONG, Alexander, *congressman,* was born in Greenville, Pennsylvania, on December 24, 1816. He was educated in the public schools, studied law, was admitted to the Ohio bar, and began his practice in Cincinnati. As a Democrat, Long was elected to the Ohio House (1848–1849). When the Civil War began, he was an outspoken critic of Abraham Lincoln's (*q.v.*) administration. Dubbed a Copperhead by his political opponents, he was elected to the 38th Congress in the 1862 Democratic landslide. At the 1864 Democratic National Convention in Chicago, he supported the peace plank of his party's platform. In October 1864 a small group of Midwestern Democrats met in Cincinnati, repudiated Democratic nominee George B. McClellan (*q.v.*), called for peace, upheld slavery, and urged Long to run for President. He refused, and the bolt ended.

On April 12, 1864, Long delivered a speech in Congress calling for immediate peace and the recognition of Southern independence. A resolution for his expulsion from Congress was defeated, but he was censured. He was unsuccessful in his 1865 reelection attempt, but was nominated for governor on the Ohio Democratic ticket. He was soundly defeated by Unionist Jacob D. Cox (*q.v.*). Long continued his law practice in Cincinnati, remained active in Democratic politics, and attended the Democratic National Conventions in 1868, 1872, and 1876. He died in Cincinnati on November 28, 1886. Porter, *Ohio Politics During the Civil War.*

Thomas H. Smith

LONG, Eli, *general,* was born on June 16, 1837, in Woodford county, Kentucky. He graduated from a military school in Frankfort in 1855, and the following year received a 2nd lieutenant's commission in the 1st U.S. Cavalry, with which he served until 1861. Following the outbreak of the Civil War and promotion to captain, he commanded a company in the 4th U.S. Cavalry until wounded at Stones River. Upon recovering, and having been promoted to colonel, Long headed the 4th Ohio Cavalry during the Chickamauga campaign, then commanded the 2nd Brigade of the 2nd Cavalry Division, Army of the Cumberland, during operations around Chattanooga and in an expedition to Knoxville.

Because of a lack of horses, Long's brigade did not join William T. Sherman's (*q.v.*) army in the Atlanta campaign until June 1864. It then served in the division of Brigadier General Kenner Garrard (*q.v.*), its most notable achievement being the capture of McAfee's Bridge across the Chattahoochee on July 9. Temporarily assigned to the command of Brigadier General Hugh Judson Kilpatrick (*q.v.*), it took part in his unsuccessful Jonesboro raid, during which Long was wounded twice while conducting a rearguard action. In October 1864, now a brigadier general and again fit for duty, Long was placed in command of Garrard's division and assigned to the cavalry corps of Brigadier General James H. Wilson (*q.v.*) in Tennessee. He then proceeded to take an important part in the battle of Nashville (December 15–16, 1864) and in Wilson's expedition into Alabama in the spring of 1865. On April 2, while leading his division in a successful dismounted assault on the Confederate fortifications at Selma, he suffered yet another wound that put him out of action for the rest of the war.

Cool, courageous, and intelligent, Long was praised by all of the generals under whom he served and undoubtedly was one of the finest, most professional Union cavalry leaders to emerge during the Civil War. In 1867, he retired with the rank of major general (reduced in 1875 to brigadier general). He then practiced law in Plainfield, New Jersey, until his death in New York City on January 5, 1912. Starr, *Union Cavalry*, vols. 1, 3; Wilson, *Under the Old Flag*, vol. 2.

Albert Castel

LONGYEAR, John Wesley, *congressman,* was born in Shandaken, New York, on October 22, 1820. He moved in the early 1840s to Ingham county, Michigan, where he taught school, read law, and was admitted to the bar in 1846. In 1847, he moved to Lansing, where in partnership with his brother Ephriam, he became one of the first lawyers to establish a practice in Michigan's newly designated capital. At first a Whig, Longyear had become a Republican by the outbreak of the Civil War. In 1862, he was elected to the 38th Congress, and was reelected in 1864.

Longyear firmly believed that slavery was the main cause of the war, which he declared would continue as long as even "a vestige of this accursed institution" remained. A staunch Radical Republican, he actively supported the 13th Amendment and Congressional Reconstruction. By early 1866, Longyear openly criticized President Andrew Johnson (*q.v.*), especially his pardoning of former Rebels. He was a delegate to the Union National Convention in Philadelphia in 1866, and in 1867 was a delegate to the Michigan Constitutional Convention. In 1870, Longyear reached the pinnacle of his public career by being appointed a Federal judge for the Eastern District of Michigan. He died in Detroit on March 11, 1875. Leake, *History of Detroit; Michigan Biographies*, vol. 2.

Roger L. Rosentreter

LOOMIS, Dwight, *congressman,* was born on July 27, 1821, in Columbia, Connecticut. He attended public school there, and academies in Monson, Connecticut, and in Amherst, Massachusetts. In 1847, he was admitted to the Connecticut bar and established a law practice in Rockville. He was elected as a Whig to the Connecticut House of Representatives in 1851, and to the Connecticut Senate in 1857. Loomis was a delegate to the Republican National Convention in 1858, was elected to Congress in 1860, and was reelected in 1862. During the months preceding the war, he and a fellow Republican, Alfred Burnham (*q.v.*), challenged the conservatives in their party, notably Connecticut Senators James Dixon (*q.v.*) and LaFayette Foster (*q.v.*), who wished to conciliate the South. Loomis opposed the establishment of the House Committee of Thirty-three, which sought compromise. He also chastised President James Buchanan (*q.v.*) for his vacillation during the secession crisis, and in December

1860 demanded that Congress ignore Buchanan's efforts to influence its decisions.

Loomis's four years in Congress ended in 1863, and he returned to Connecticut. In 1864, he began a distinguished career on Connecticut's Superior Court. He was reelected to this post in 1872, and in 1875 became justice of the state's Supreme Court of Errors. Loomis retired from the court in 1891, and for the next two years served as an instructor at the Yale University School of Law. He also was a member of the state Board of Mediation and Arbitration, from 1891 until his death in a train accident in Waterbury, Connecticut, on September 17, 1903. Niven, *Connecticut for the Union.*

Joanna D. Cowden

LOVEJOY, Owen, *abolitionist, clergyman, congressman,* was born on January 6, 1811, in Albion, Maine. Educated in the common schools, he attended Bowdoin College until 1833, when his father died. He taught school and studied law, but abandoned both professions in favor of the church. In 1836, he moved to Alton, Illinois, to study for the ministry under his brother, Elijah Lovejoy, and to assist him in the publishing of the antislavery *Alton Observer.* On November 7, 1837, a mob attacked the newspaper office and murdered Elijah. Undeterred by the death of his older brother, Lovejoy resolved to devote his life to slavery's abolition. By 1839, he was ordained pastor of the Congregational church in Princeton, Illinois, served as a conductor for the Underground Railroad, and in 1854 was elected to the Illinois legislature on the "Abolition" ticket, although he became an active proponent of Republican party principles.

Lovejoy was elected to the 35th through 38th Congresses. He remained steadfast in his opposition to slavery but broke ranks with other Radical Republicans such as Thaddeus Stevens (*q.v.*) when it came to opposing Abraham Lincoln's (*q.v.*) general war policies and Reconstruction program. Indeed, Lovejoy came to Lincoln's defense in 1862 when William Lloyd Garrison (*q.v.*) criticized the President. He introduced the bill abolishing slavery in the territories and was heartened by the Emancipation Proclamation. Lovejoy died in Brooklyn, New York, on March 25, 1864, during his last congressional term. Magdol, *Owen Lovejoy.*

Thomas F. Schwartz

LOW, Frederick Ferdinand, *congressman, governor,* was born near Frankfort (now Winterport), Maine, on June 30, 1828. He attended the common schools and Hampden Academy. In 1843, an apprenticeship to Russell, Sturgis & Company of Boston, which traded extensively with the East Indies, followed. Here Low acquired an interest in California and the Far East. He arrived in San Francisco in June 1849 and went to the gold mines. With his earnings, he returned to San Francisco in late 1849 and engaged in mercantile pursuits, moving to Marysville, the supply center for the northern mines, in 1850. There, with two older brothers, he formed Low & Brothers Company to engage in merchandising and shipping.

Low became a Republican upon the formation of the party in 1856, and was elected to Congress in 1861 on the theory that the results of the census of 1860 entitled California to a third representative. A special act of Congress admitted Low, and he served from June 3, 1862, to March 3, 1863. His record in Congress and his ability to solve complicated revenue problems earned the backing of San Francisco's business community. An alliance with Senator John Conness (*q.v.*) gave Low control of the Sacramento and San Francisco delegations to the 1863 Union party conventions, and he easily won nomination for governor over the incumbent Leland Stanford (*q.v.*).

Low was the first governor to serve a four-year term, occupying the office from December 1863 until December 1867. He supported the war measures of the Federal government, and called for black suffrage and ratification of the 14th Amendment. Low, who took special interest in financial and revenue measures, agriculture, and education, laid the foundation for the University of California. He died in San Francisco on July 21, 1894. Anderson, ''Frederick F. Low in China,'' *California History*; Low, *Reflections*; Melendy, *Governors of California*.

Robert J. Chandler

LOWELL, James Russell, *editor, educator, poet,* was born on February 22, 1819, in Cambridge, Massachusetts. A son of an aristocratic New England family, he was among the foremost literary figures of nineteenth-century America. He graduated from Harvard College in 1838, and from Harvard Law School in 1840. He did not practice law, but devoted his life to literature, teaching, and social criticism. Between 1844 and his death forty-seven years later, Lowell published numerous volumes of poetry and prose. In 1848, he was corresponding editor of the *National Anti-Slavery Standard*, and from 1857 to 1861 edited the *Atlantic Monthly*. Between 1864 and 1866, he was a major contributor to the *North American Review*, and from 1855 to 1886 he was professor of literature at Harvard.

In politics, Lowell was a conservative nationalist. Although he associated with the circle of abolitionists led by William Lloyd Garrison (*q.v.*), he dissented from such Garrisonian precepts as disunionism and nonresistance. Nevertheless, the first series of Lowell's *Biglow Papers*, published serially in 1846 and 1847, helped raise Northern opposition to slavery and the political power of slaveholders. Writing in Yankee dialect, Lowell portrayed the war against Mexico as a proslavery plot and warned Northern whites, ''Chaps thet make black slaves o' niggers/Want to make wite slaves o' you.''

When the Civil War began, Lowell's nationalism overcame his abolitionism. An early advocate of coercing the South, he argued that slavery was peripheral to national unity and defended President Abraham Lincoln's (*q.v.*) cautious approach to emancipation. Consequently, Lowell's primary role during the war lay in his articulation of the views of many Northerners who regarded the war as a means of nation-building rather than of securing racial justice. Lowell died in Cambridge on August 12, 1891. Duberman, *James Russell Lowell*; Fredrickson, *Inner Civil War*.

Stanley Harrold

LYON, Nathaniel, *general,* was born on July 14, 1818, in rural Eastford, Connecticut. He graduated from West Point in 1841, and served with the 2nd U.S. Infantry in Florida, California, and Kansas, and in the Mexican War. Throughout his career Lyon exhibited a violent, hair-trigger temper, and proved a contentious and nearly unpromotable subordinate. His experience in "Bleeding Kansas" caused him to condemn the slave states for inciting internecine warfare there and for attempting to usurp democratic government. By 1860, Lyon had aligned with the Republican party, publicly supporting Abraham Lincoln (*q.v.*) and condemning the Democrats for pandering to the "Slavocracy."

In February 1861, Lyon and two companies of infantry were transferred to St. Louis to protect the government arsenal there. Although Missouri would vote to maintain neutrality, the state boasted an active secessionist minority, including the governor and several legislators. Fearing an attack upon the arsenal, Lyon allied himself with Congressman Francis P. Blair (*q.v.*), leader of St. Louis's Unionists and highly connected in Washington. The two forced the removal of the department commander, then enlisted several thousand (mostly German) Home Guard militia into Federal service. On May 10, Lyon used these men to capture a small encampment of secessionist state militia located on the city's outskirts. While returning to the arsenal, Lyon's troops fired upon a civilian mob, precipitating two days of rioting in St. Louis and driving thousands of hitherto neutral Missourians into the Confederate camp.

In June, when Missouri's governor traveled to St. Louis to effect peace, Lyon (now a brigadier general of Volunteers) ended the meeting by audaciously declaring war on the state. After conducting a successful campaign up the Missouri River, capturing the state capital, and easily scattering a concentration of state militia forces at Boonville, he pressed southward after them to Springfield. On August 10, 1861, he rashly attacked the combined force at Wilson's Creek. During the pitched battle, Lyon was killed. In defeat and death, he became the North's first battlefield hero, although his temerity brought war to a neutral border state. Phillips, *Damned Yankee*.

Christopher Phillips

M

McALLISTER, Archibald, *congressman,* was born in Dauphin county, Pennsylvania, on October 13, 1813. In 1842, he moved to Blair county, where he became involved in the iron industry. Riding the antiwar sentiment that swept through Pennsylvania in 1862, McAllister ran successfully as a Democrat for a seat in the 38th Congress. In a pattern unusual even for new congressmen, he remained virtually silent throughout his term. His voting record on Civil War issues, however, reflected a shift in his initial position from a Peace Democrat to a more compromising Democrat who recognized the necessity of employing strong measures in order to reunite the nation.

Nothing reveals this more clearly than his vote in favor of the 13th Amendment, after he had helped defeat an earlier effort. In prepared remarks that he had the clerk of the House read, McAllister argued that Southern determination to perpetuate slavery had prolonged the war. His vote, combined with that of his Pennsylvania Democratic colleague Alexander H. Coffroth (*q.v.*), contributed significantly to the two-thirds' vote necessary to pass the amendment. He also opposed the Freedmen's Bureau Bill, the Wade–Davis Bill, confiscation measures, and conscription legislation. At the conclusion of the 38th Congress, McAllister withdrew from public life and returned to iron manufacturing. He died in Royer, Pennsylvania, on July 18, 1883. Cox, *Politics, Principles, and Prejudice*; Shankman, *Pennsylvania Antiwar Movement.*

Philip J. Avillo, Jr.

McARTHUR, John, *general,* was born in Erskine, Scotland, on November 17, 1826. He emigrated to the United States, and by 1861 was the owner of the

Excelsior Iron Works in Chicago. Following the outbreak of war, he became the colonel of the 12th Illinois Volunteers (First Scotch Regiment) in August 1861. He was promoted to brigadier general on March 21, 1862, and on April 6, after General William H. L. Wallace (*q.v.*) was killed at Shiloh, McArthur took command of the 2nd Division. Later, during the heavy fighting at Corinth and Iuka, he commanded the 6th Division, Army of the Tennessee. Although his division was in the XVII Corps under James B. McPherson (*q.v.*) at Vicksburg, his command was often detached for service with John A. McClernand's (*q.v.*) or William T. Sherman's (*q.v.*) corps.

From the autumn of 1863 to August 1864, McArthur was post commander at Vicksburg. Later service included rear-guard duties in Georgia, and action against Sterling Price in Missouri. In November 1864, his 1st Division was part of the XVI Corps, Andrew J. Smith (*q.v.*) commanding, which was rushed to the support of George H. Thomas (*q.v.*), who was under siege by John Hood at Nashville. On December 15, McArthur led the strike at enemy positions on the Hillsboro Pike, and on the following day, his troops played a major role in the final rout of Hood at Nashville. Breveted major general, he served under Edward R.S. Canby (*q.v.*) in the Alabama campaign until the end of the war.

McArthur was known as a soldier's general; Ulysses S. Grant (*q.v.*) saw him as "zealous and efficient"; Thomas thought so highly of him that he recommended his last promotion. McArthur died in Chicago on May 15, 1906. Bearss, *Vicksburg Campaign*; Sword, *Embrace an Angry Wind.*

Victor Hicken

McBRIDE, John Rogers, *congressman,* was born near St. Louis on August 22, 1832, and in 1846 went with his parents to Oregon. He was a county superintendent of schools, studied for the law, and in 1855 opened a practice in Lafayette, Oregon. Aided by his father—who had been a Whig leader in Oregon and a founder of its Republican party—McBride rose at an early age to political importance. At the state constitutional convention in 1857, he shared the popular aversion to blacks' coming to Oregon; he was especially critical of the *Dred Scott* decision. In 1860 he was elected to the state Senate, where he played a role in the political deal that sent Douglas Democrat James Nesmith (*q.v.*) and Republican Edward D. Baker (*q.v.*) to the U.S. Senate.

McBride's role in these events and his hostility to secession and abolition led Oregon's new Union party to nominate him for Congress in 1862. In an emotional election, he easily defeated his Democratic foe. McBride enthusiastically supported the war and Abraham Lincoln (*q.v.*), including his Reconstruction plan, and worked for his constituents, especially through securing passage of a bill that provided for a branch mint at The Dalles. Because Oregon politicians believed that the congressional seat should be shared, not dominated, by an individual, and because of the rivalry over the location of the mint, McBride was not renominated. Lincoln rewarded him for his service by appointing him chief justice of Idaho Territory. McBride later practiced law, and from 1880 to

1892 was a member of the Republican National Committee. He died in Spokane, Washington, on July 20, 1904. Johannsen, *Frontier Politics*.

G. Thomas Edwards

McCLELLAN, George Brinton, *general, Democratic presidential candidate*, was born in Philadelphia on December 3, 1826. He graduated second in the West Point class of 1846, and was commissioned in the engineers. While serving in the Mexican War he won two brevets (and declined a third as unearned) for meritorious conduct. This service was followed by routine duty in exploration and railroad survey work. More important was Captain McClellan's 1855 tour with the American mission to observe the siege of Sevastopol in the Crimean War, after which he ably studied and reported on military institutions throughout Europe, and developed the famous "McClellan saddle." He resigned from the Army in 1857, and by 1860 was a railroad president.

Upon the outbreak of the Civil War, McClellan was named a major general and quickly won a series of small but significant victories over the Confederates in western Virginia. Following Irvin McDowell's (*q.v.*) defeat at Bull Run in July 1861, McClellan was named to command the Army of the Potomac, which sturdy force he built into a magnificent fighting host. Four months later, on November 1, 1861, he was named general in chief. Circumspect and too much the perfectionist, McClellan delayed advancing against Richmond and the Confederates until the spring of 1862, when he embarked on his Peninsula campaign. After a one-month siege of Yorktown, he inched toward Richmond; at Seven Pines (Fair Oaks) he won a defensive victory over Joseph E. Johnston at the end of May. But in the great Seven Days' battles in late June, Robert E. Lee, now in command of the Southerners, successfully defended Richmond, though he was unable to drive McClellan's army away. The Federals lost 15,849 men, compared with 20,614 Confederate casualties.

The Army of the Potomac was ordered back to Washington over McClellan's vehement protests, and assigned in large part to John Pope's (*q.v.*) Army of Virginia. Reorganizing his army on the march, McClellan repulsed Lee's first invasion of the North with a crucial victory at South Mountain on September 14, and a strategic success at Antietam (Sharpsburg) three days later. Owing to his delay in pursuing the retreating enemy, and for political reasons, he was relieved of his command on November 7. He never held another one. In 1864, having resigned his commission, McClellan failed in his bid for the presidency on the Democratic ticket against Abraham Lincoln (*q.v.*).

McClellan's just claim to fame rests largely on his building of the truly superb Army of the Potomac, on his grasp of the realities of grand strategy in his brief tenure as general in chief of all the Union armies, on his able tactical defensive handling of his force on the Peninsula in the Seven Days' battles, on his turning back of Lee's invasion in the Maryland campaign, and on the trust, admiration, and inspiration he instilled in his soldiers. In his pressing for an amphibious movement to the Peninsula—taking advantage of Federal naval superiority—he was on sounder ground than Lincoln and others who advocated the overland route. That he fell just short of conspicuous success was due largely to his tendency to magnify difficulties, and to his inability to trust to the military inspiration of the moment, instead of extreme caution and minute planning.

Nevertheless, it was most fortunate, and possibly vital for the Union cause, that a lesser man was not in command early in the Civil War. McClellan's contributions were substantial—some masterful. After the war, he directed several large engineering enterprises, and was an able governor of New Jersey from 1878 to 1881. A man of culture and a connoisseur of the arts, he often traveled abroad and enjoyed mountain climbing. Late in life he wrote his memoirs, *McClellan's Own Story*, which were published after his death. He died in Orange, New Jersey, on October 29, 1885. Hassler, *Commanders of the Army of the Potomac*; Hassler, *General George B. McClellan*; Sears, *George B. McClellan*.

Warren W. Hassler, Jr.

McCLERNAND, John Alexander, *congressman, general,* was born in 1812 near Hardinsburg, Kentucky. He moved to Shawneetown, Illinois, where he read law and was admitted to the bar. McClernand served in the state Assembly (1836–1843), where he supported the vast Illinois internal improvement scheme. As a congressman, he achieved national recognition during the speakership struggles of the 31st and 36th Congresses. Although he broke with Stephen A. Douglas (*q.v.*) over the Kansas–Nebraska Bill in 1854, the two eventually reconciled during the momentous congressional struggles from 1856 to 1861. McClernand became a War Democrat in 1861, leaving Congress to accept a commission as brigadier general. Being Abraham Lincoln's (*q.v.*) Springfield neighbor probably helped him obtain this recognition, but the real reason was McClernand's strong influence in southern Illinois, where there was much sympathy to the Confederate cause.

McClernand proved extremely valuable, not only in securing the loyalty of ''Egypt'' but also in raising numerous regiments out of that area. He quickly learned the art of war, but he never failed to keep his political lines to Washington open. He commanded a division at Belmont, Fort Donelson, and Shiloh, and though some historians have tended to disparage McClernand's performance in all three places, he and his troops fought bravely. At Shiloh, where both Ulysses S. Grant (*q.v.*) and William T. Sherman (*q.v.*) were surprised, McClernand was not. He had warned Grant of the possibilities of a Confederate attack several days before April 6, and his division was on semialert at the time.

While Grant was in temporary eclipse after Shiloh, McClernand obtained leave to visit Washington, where he persuaded Lincoln to allow him to raise an Army of the Mississippi, to capture Vicksburg and to cut Southern railroads eastward to the sea. General in Chief Henry W. Halleck (*q.v.*), who disliked McClernand, placed a subtle addendum on McClernand's orders allowing Grant to take command if necessary. McClernand managed to capture Arkansas Post before Grant exercised the privilege in Halleck's addendum. Thereafter, he commanded the XIII Corps, arguably the hardest-fighting corps in the Army of the Tennessee; both the troops and their commander performed well at Champion's Hill and Grand Gulf. The XIII Corps was the first to cross the Big Black River, and it participated in the May 22 assault against Vicksburg.

After the failure of this attack, McClernand issued a congratulatory order, which Grant interpreted as denigrating the efforts of other corps. Grant therefore relieved his most contentious subordinate and sent him back to Springfield. Not wanting a court of inquiry—McClernand had made substantial charges concerning Grant's drinking problem—Lincoln eventually returned him to the XIII Corps. But McClernand, now suffering from ill health and a general disgust with General Nathaniel Banks's (*q.v.*) failures in the Red River campaign, resigned his commission and returned to politics.

McClernand had used all of his political skills in his efforts against his superior, but Grant was not without weapons of his own. He had become a Republican after 1862, and he had not only Halleck on his side but also Charles A. Dana (*q.v.*), an influential secret interrogator sent by the War Department to investigate the situation at Vicksburg. McClernand never had a chance against them. He died in Springfield on September 10, 1900. Catton, *Grant Moves South*; Hicken, *Illinois in the Civil War.*

Victor Hicken

McCLURG, Joseph Washington, *congressman,* was born in St. Louis county, Missouri, on February 22, 1818. After attending Xenia (Ohio) Academy and Miami University, and teaching school in Louisiana and Mississippi, he moved to Columbus, Texas, in 1839. There he studied law and was admitted to the bar. He returned to St. Louis in 1841, and followed the gold rush to California in 1849. Upon returning to Missouri in 1852, he established a prosperous mercantile business with two partners at Linn Creek, on the edge of the Ozark frontier. McClurg was elected as a Union delegate to the convention that decided against secession in March 1861, and with the outbreak of war he organized the Osage Regiment of Missouri Volunteers and equipped it at his own expense. He supported the establishment of the Provisional Government at the July 1861 session of the convention, and that fall was appointed a colonel in the Missouri State Militia.

McClurg became increasingly antislavery, and in 1862 freed the slaves his wife had inherited. They continued to work for him, by their own preference, at regular wages. That fall, McClurg was elected as a "Charcoal" (Emancipationist) to Congress, and in 1863 helped organize the Radical Union party in Missouri. He became an increasingly outspoken opponent of the conservative Provisional Government, and at the 1864 Republican National Convention was a member of the Missouri Radical delegation, which opposed the renomination of Abraham Lincoln (*q.v.*).

Reelected to Congress in 1864 and 1866, McClurg followed the lead of Thaddeus Stevens (*q.v.*) on Reconstruction. In 1868, he was elected governor of

Missouri on the Radical ticket, but was defeated for reelection two years later because of the Liberal Republican split over reenfranchisement of Southern sympathizers, which McClurg opposed. He resumed his mercantile business at Linn Creek, engaged in steamboating and lead mining, and was registrar of the Federal land office in Springfield (1889–1893). He died in London, Missouri, on December 2, 1900. Morrow, "Joseph Washington McClurg," *Missouri Historical Review*; Parrish, *Missouri Under Radical Rule*.

William E. Parrish

McCOOK, Alexander McDowell, *general*, was born on April 22, 1831, in Columbiana county, Ohio, the fifth son of a Scotch–Irish family known as "the Fighting McCooks"; the immediate family provided eight sons to the Union cause. He graduated from West Point in 1852, became a brevet 2nd lieutenant in the 3rd Infantry, and until December 1857 served in a number of military campaigns against the Utes and Apaches. In early 1858, McCook became an instructor in military tactics at the Military Academy; he remained there until April 1861, when he was appointed colonel of the 1st Ohio Volunteers. At Vienna, Virginia, and First Bull Run he served with distinction. In August, he was reappointed colonel of the 1st Ohio, and soon thereafter was a commissioned brigadier general of Volunteers.

While stationed in Kentucky, McCook organized, equipped, and trained the 2nd Division, Army of the Ohio. During early 1862, he and his command distinguished themselves at Shiloh, Corinth, and Nashville. Promotion to the rank of major general of Volunteers came in July 1862, and at the battle of Perryville he commanded the I Corps, Army of the Ohio. Later that year, General William S. Rosecrans (*q.v.*) reorganized his forces, and McCook led the XX Corps, Army of the Cumberland, at Stones River and in the Tullahoma campaign. During the battle of Chickamauga, on September 20, 1863, troops under McCook's command retreated to Chattanooga, fearing that the entire Union army was subject to destruction. On October 6, 1863, he was relieved of command and became subject to a court of inquiry. The court exonerated him of responsibility for the Union reverse, but subsequent military assignments were decidedly undistinguished.

For the remainder of the war, McCook's duty included the defense of Washington and command of the District of East Arkansas. Following the war, he became lieutenant colonel of the 26th U.S. Infantry. From 1875 to 1881, he was aide-de-camp on the staff of General William T. Sherman (*q.v.*). Subsequent service was in the West, including command at Fort Leavenworth, Kansas. In 1890, he was promoted to brigadier general, followed four years later by appointment to major general. McCook retired from military service in April 1895 and died on June 12, 1903, in Dayton, Ohio. Cozzens, *This Terrible Sound*; Hafendorfer, *Perryville*; McDonough, *Stones River*.

Frank R. Levstik

McCOOK, Daniel, Jr., *general*, was born on July 22, 1834, in Carrollton, Ohio. He was the sixth son of a Scotch-Irish family known as "the Fighting McCooks"; the immediate family furnished eight sons to the Union cause. Daniel graduated from a Florence, Alabama, college in 1857, took up the study of law, and in 1858 was admitted to practice. After moving to Leavenworth, Kansas, he became a law partner of William Tecumseh Sherman (*q.v.*) and Thomas Ewing, Jr. (*q.v.*). Following the attack on Fort Sumter, McCook organized a militia company called the Shield Grays, and entered them into Federal service with the 1st Kansas. Later that year, through the efforts of his brother Alexander (*q.v.*), the colonel of the 1st Ohio, he obtained a transfer as adjutant of the unit. He joined his brother in the advance on Nashville and in the battle of Shiloh.

In May 1862, Governor David Tod (*q.v.*) called on McCook to recruit the 52nd Ohio, and that July he was appointed colonel of the regiment. Two months later, he was promoted to command the 36th Brigade, 11th Division, of the Army of the Ohio, headed by General Philip Sheridan (*q.v.*). On October 8, 1862, at the battle of Perryville, McCook's brigade relieved the imperiled command of his brother Alexander.

In early 1863, at the battle of Stones River, troops under McCook's command saved an ammunition train from capture. Later that year, in the Chickamauga campaign, his brigade held the extreme left wing of Union General George H. Thomas's (*q.v.*) position against tremendous odds. McCook's brigade was in Sherman's command at Missionary Ridge, was with Ambrose E. Burnside (*q.v.*) in the Knoxville campaign, and was chosen to lead the assault on Kennesaw Mountain by General Sherman. The main assault of June 27 at Kennesaw Mountain was led by McCook's brigade in General Jefferson Columbus Davis's (*q.v.*) division. McCook was severely wounded in the assault, and on July 17, 1864, he died in Steubenville, Ohio. A day earlier, he had been promoted to brigadier general. Castel, *Decision in the West*; Reid, *Ohio in the War*, vol. 1.

Frank R. Levstik

McCOOK, Edward Moody, *general*, was born on June 15, 1833, in Steubenville, Ohio. The eldest son of Dr. John McCook, he and his three brothers served in the Civil War. In 1849, he left Steubenville for Minnesota, then moved to Arapahoe county, Colorado, where he eventually opened a law practice. In 1859, he served as district delegate in the territorial legislature of Kansas. At the outbreak of the Civil War, McCook joined the Kansas Legion, and in May 1861 obtained a lieutenancy in the 1st U.S. Cavalry, soon followed by one in the 4th U.S. Cavalry. After transferring to the Volunteers in September 1861, he rose rapidly from major to colonel of the 2nd Indiana Cavalry.

McCook's conspicuous service at Shiloh, Perryville, and Chickamauga led to brevet promotions and commands in the Army of the Ohio and the Army of the Cumberland. In April 1864 he was promoted to brigadier general of Volunteers, and at the close of the war to brevet brigadier general in the Regular Army and major general of Volunteers. During the Atlanta campaign, his cavalry command prevented the reinforcement of Confederate General John Bell Hood. In March and April 1865, his cavalry division participated in General James H. Wilson's (*q.v.*) raid on Selma, Alabama.

Following the war, McCook served as military governor of Florida for a short time. In 1866, he resigned his military commission to become U.S. minister to Hawaii. Three years later, President Ulysses S. Grant (*q.v.*) appointed him territorial governor of Colorado, a post he held (with a brief interruption) until 1875. For the remainder of his life, he engaged in a number of successful business enterprises. He died in Chicago on September 9, 1909. Castel, *Decision in the West*; Coons, *Indiana at Shiloh.*

Frank R. Levstik

McCOOK, Robert Latimer, *general,* was born on December 28, 1827, in New Lisbon, Ohio. He was the fourth son of a Scotch-Irish family known as "the Fighting McCooks"; the immediate family provided eight sons to the Union cause. McCook began the study of law under Ephraim R. Eckley (*q.v.*), and completed it at the Steubenville law firm of Edwin M. Stanton (*q.v.*) and his brother George Wythe McCook. During the late 1850s, he joined a Cincinnati law firm, and in April 1861 was commissioned a colonel in the 9th Ohio Volunteers, an ethnic German unit. Although his knowledge of military matters was limited, the Germans saw in McCook a man of standing and character who could protect them from anti-German prejudice.

McCook was brigade commander at Carnifex Ferry, [West] Virginia, September 10, 1861, during George B. McClellan's (*q.v.*) campaign. He later commanded the 2nd Brigade, Division of the Kanawha, Army of Western Virginia, then the 3rd Brigade, 1st Division, in General Don Carlos Buell's (*q.v.*) Army of the Ohio. At the battle of Mill Springs, his brigade figured prominently in the defeat of the Confederates during hand-to-hand combat. McCook received a leg wound and had his horse shot out from under him. Two months later, he was commissioned a brigadier general of Volunteers. From Mill Springs, McCook's brigade came to serve in Buell's Army of the Ohio, participating in the Forts Henry and Donelson campaign, and later at the battle of Shiloh.

During the summer of 1862, McCook contracted a case of camp dysentery so severe that surgeons urged his return to Nashville for rest and recovery. He refused, however, and remained with his command, directing them from a cot fitted into a field ambulance. Responding to a threat by Confederate John Hunt Morgan's forces in East Tennessee, the brigade was ordered to a position near Decherd, Tennessee. On August 5, 1862, McCook and his escort were attacked by a party of Confederate guerrillas. While the escort attempted to flee, the ambulance was surrounded by guerrillas who fired several shots, one of which struck McCook. Taken to Winchester, Virginia, he died there on August 6, 1862. Grebner, *"We Were the Ninth"*; Reid, *Ohio in the War*, vol. 1.

Frank R. Levstik

McCULLOCH, Hugh, *Secretary of the Treasury*, was born in Kennebunk, Maine, on December 7, 1808. After attending Bowdoin College, he taught school and studied law in Boston. In 1833, he moved to Indiana, was admitted to the bar, and settled into a practice in Fort Wayne. In 1835, he went to work for the State Bank of Indiana and eventually became its president. In 1862, McCulloch traveled to Washington to lobby against the establishment of a new national bank, which he feared would impair state financial institutions. He dropped his opposition to the new bank when he realized it was necessary to help promote the war. In March 1863 he accepted the position of comptroller of the currency.

Two years later, President Abraham Lincoln (*q.v.*) appointed McCulloch to serve as Secretary of the Treasury. During his tenure, he worked for the retirement of Federal notes and a resumption of the gold standard, all the while striving to reduce the public debt following the war. He left the Treasury Department at the end of Andrew Johnson's (*q.v.*) term, and moved to London to form a partnership with Philadelphia financier Jay Cooke. In 1884, he was again Secretary of the Treasury under President Chester Arthur. He died in Prince Georges county, Maryland, on May 24, 1895. Hendrick, *Lincoln's War Cabinet*; McCulloch, *Men and Measures of Half a Century.*

David Dixon

McDOUGALL, James Alexander, *senator*, was born in Bethlehem, New York, on November 19, 1817. He attended the public schools, assisted in the survey of the railroad between Albany and Schenectady, and studied law. In 1837, McDougall migrated to Cook county, Illinois, became attorney general of Illinois for two terms (1842–1846), and in 1843 was an unsuccessful candidate for Congress. He settled in San Francisco in 1850, and was elected attorney general of California in the fall of that year. He resigned December 20, 1851, and in 1852 was elected to Congress as a Democrat. The Free Soil wing of the party renominated McDougall in 1854; failing to be elected, he returned to his practice of law in San Francisco.

The repudiation of the Southern Democracy in the election of 1860 gave a majority in the 1861 California legislature to the Free Soil Democrats and Republicans. McDougall, the compromise senatorial candidate, served from March 1861 until March 1867. He showed his loyalty through the support of various war measures and, as chairman of the Senate Committee on the Pacific Railroad, guided the transcontinental railroad bill to passage in June 1862. However, McDougall's partisanship and excessive drinking discredited him. He opposed the administration on several measures, including emancipation in the District of Columbia. He was the only member of the California delegation to take a strong interest in foreign policy, and advocated that Congress demand France remove its troops from Mexico and that the United States actively aid the Republic of Mexico.

The California legislature, by resolution, repudiated McDougall on February

7, 1864, for his political and personal conduct. He did not, however, mend his ways. In 1864, he served as a delegate to the Democratic National Convention, and two years later was a delegate to the Union National Convention. In his sober moments, he was a strong supporter of President Andrew Johnson's (*q.v.*) plan of Reconstruction. McDougall chose not to run for reelection, and died on September 3, 1867, in Albany, New York. Shuck, *Representative and Leading Men of the Pacific.*

Robert J. Chandler

McDOWELL, Irvin, *general*, was born in Columbus, Ohio, on October 15, 1818. He attended the College de Troyes in France, and graduated from West Point in 1839. He served on the Mexican border before returning to the Military Academy to teach tactics (1841–1845). During the Mexican War, he served on the staff of General John E. Wool (*q.v.*) and was breveted captain for gallant conduct at the battle of Buena Vista. Thereafter, McDowell served in the office of the adjutant general of the army.

While in Washington, McDowell made the acquaintance of Salmon P. Chase (*q.v.*), which would prove beneficial when the Civil War started. Through Chase's intervention, he was appointed a brigadier general in the Regular Army on May 14, 1861. This was a disastrous decision, for McDowell had no command experience and was put in charge of a half-trained army. Political pressure forced him to advance his army against an equally untrained Confederate force at Bull Run, Virginia, where he was soundly defeated. McDowell was relieved in March 1862 and placed in command of a corps in the Army of the Potomac. Controversy surrounded most of his remaining Civil War career. General George B. McClellan (*q.v.*) publicly vented his dislike for McDowell and the fact that he was protecting Washington while McClellan was trying to take Richmond.

During McClellan's failure in the Peninsula campaign, McDowell and the III Corps of John Pope's (*q.v.*) Army of Virginia faced the Confederacy once again at Bull Run, with similar results. McDowell's conduct, along with Pope's, was severely criticized. McDowell was brought before a court of inquiry and exonerated, but for two years he was exiled. He was assigned to command the Department of the Pacific on July 1, 1864, and remained in that post for a year, then was reassigned to the Department of the East and South. McDowell received a promotion to major general in 1872 through the army's seniority system. In 1876, he returned to California and took command of the Division of the Pacific. Retiring in 1882, McDowell remained in California and became the parks commissioner of San Francisco. He died in that city on May 4, 1885. Davis, *Bull Run*; Hennessy, *Return to Bull Run*; Sears, *George B. McClellan.*

Mitchell A. Yockelson

McDOWELL, James Foster, *congressman*, was born on December 3, 1825, in Mifflin county, Pennsylvania. In 1835 his family moved to Ohio, where he attended public schools, worked in a printing office, studied law, and was admitted to the bar in 1846. McDowell established the *Greenville* (Ohio) *Herald* in 1847, and became the prosecuting attorney of Darke county, Ohio, in 1848. Moving to Marion, Indiana, in 1851, he established a law practice and founded the *Marion Journal.* McDowell served as a Democratic presidential elector in 1852 and 1860, and was elected to the 38th Congress in 1862. After an unsuccessful reelection bid, he returned to practice law in Marion and to serve as president of the Marion & Kokomo Narrow Gauge Railroad. McDowell died in Marion on April 18, 1887. *Biographical History of Eminent and Self-Made Men of Indiana.*

David G. Vanderstel

McINDOE, Walter Duncan, *congressman*, was born on August 22, 1819, in Dunbartonshire, Scotland. After coming to the United States in 1834, he worked as a bookkeeper in New York City, Charleston, South Carolina, and St. Louis. In 1845, he settled in Wausau, Wisconsin, after becoming a partner in a saw-milling operation. McIndoe was elected as a Whig to the state Assembly in 1850, became an early member of the Republican party, and was reelected to the Assembly in 1854 and 1855. In 1857, he sought the Republican nomination for governor but was defeated, the nomination and election going to Alexander Randall (*q.v.*). In December 1862 he won election to Congress, replacing Luther Hanchett (*q.v.*), whose death had created the vacancy.

McIndoe was reelected to the 38th and 39th Congresses, then declined renomination in 1866. During the Indian scares in the summer of 1863, he was appointed an investigator by the commissioner of Indian affairs. He arrived on the scene after the Winnebagos had broken up into small hunting bands, thereby no longer posing any real threat. McIndoe was reassured and reassuring, although he did recommend early removal of the tribe. In 1867, he returned to his lumber business on a full-time basis, continuing until his death in Wausau on August 22, 1872. Current, *Civil War Era; Dictionary of Wisconsin Biography.*

Charles E. Twining

McKEAN, James Bedell, *congressman*, was born on August 5, 1821, in New York State, near the border with Vermont. He taught school in Rensselaer county, served on the faculty of Jonesville Academy, and in 1842 became school superintendent in Half Moon, New York. In 1849, he began a law practice in Ballston Spa, then moved to nearby Saratoga Springs in 1851. From 1854 to 1858, McKean sat as Saratoga county judge. Running as a Republican, he won a seat in the House of Representatives in 1858, and was reelected in 1860.

When war broke out, McKean, who had been elected colonel in the New York militia in 1844, drew upon his military experience to organize the 77th New York Volunteers. He served as colonel of that regiment until July 1863, when he resigned his commission. He had not run for reelection in 1862. McKean, who had chaired the House Committee on State Department Expenditures, served as treaty commissioner to Honduras in 1865, but declined a consulship in Santo Domingo. In 1867, as the Republican candidate for New York secretary of state, he lost decisively. President Ulysses S. Grant (*q.v.*) appointed him chief justice of the Supreme Court of Utah Territory in 1870. He died in Salt Lake City on January 5, 1879. *BDUSC.*

James C. Mohr

McKEAN, Thomas Jefferson, *general,* was born on August 21, 1810, in Burlington, Pennsylvania. He graduated from West Point in 1831, then served as a 2nd lieutenant in the 4th Infantry in Louisiana and Mississippi, and at Jefferson Barracks, Missouri. He left the Army in 1834 to practice civil engineering, but reentered the service briefly during the Seminole Wars. In 1840, McKean migrated to Marion, Iowa. Despite his West Point training, he was unable to secure a commission during the Mexican War; he served as a noncommissioned officer and was seriously wounded at the battle of Churubusco. In recognition of his service, he was offered a brevet commission in the 1st Dragoons, but he chose to return to engineering and farming in Iowa.

On November 21, 1861, McKean was commissioned brigadier general of Volunteers, commanding the Central District of Missouri at Jefferson City. From April through December 1862, he led a division during Union operations in northern Mississippi, including the battle of Corinth, where he commanded the Federal garrison. At his own request, McKean was removed from field duty and served out the remainder of the war in command of a succession of military districts in Missouri, Nebraska, Kansas, Florida, and Louisiana. Although perhaps a bit old for military service, he nonetheless acquired a creditable reputation as a dependable, if unspectacular, field commander, and as an efficient military administrator. He received the brevet of major general of Volunteers on March 13, 1865, and at the close of the war returned to his Iowa farm. McKean died in Marion on April 19, 1870. Lamers, *Edge of Glory*; Welcher, *Union Army*, vol. 2.

Bruce J. Dinges

McKENZIE, Lewis, *congressman,* was born on October 7, 1810, in Alexandria, Virginia. He was involved in shipping and mercantile interests there and was active in local politics. McKenzie served three terms in the Virginia House of Delegates, followed by terms on the Alexandria city council (1855–1859). In 1861, he became mayor of Alexandria, serving until his election as a Unionist to a seat in the 37th Congress that had been left vacant by the expulsion of Charles H. Upton. His term lasted from February 16 to March 3, 1863, after which he remained on the Alexandria city council until 1866. After Virginia's readmission to the Union, McKenzie was elected as a Union Conservative to the 41st Congress. In subsequent years, he became Alexandria's postmaster and served additional years on the city council. He died in Alexandria on June 28, 1895. Lanman, *Biographical Annals.*

Frank R. Levstik

McKIM, James Miller, *abolitonist, relief worker,* was born in Carlisle, Pennsylvania, on November 14, 1810. He graduated from Dickinson College (1828), then studied theology at Andover and Princeton (1831–1833) before taking a pastorate as a Presbyterian minister. William Lloyd Garrison's (*q.v.*) attacks on the American Colonization Society focused McKim's attention on the problem of slavery, and he resigned his pulpit for full-time antislavery agitation. In 1834, he joined Theodore D. Weld's (*q.v.*) famous band of "seventy agents," who assisted in the formation of local antislavery societies throughout Ohio, Pennsylvania, and New York. McKim resided in Philadelphia and became a principal leader of the abolitionist community there, and was a fervent supporter of Garrison's anticlerical and disunionist views. He was an active opponent of the Fugitive Slave Law and a notable supporter of John Brown (*q.v.*).

When the Civil War began, however, McKim took a major role in efforts to recruit black soldiers. In 1862, when over 10,000 South Carolina slaves were liberated by Union armies, he organized the Philadelphia Post Royal Relief Committee and the Pennsylvania Freedman's Relief Association. By 1869, he had ended this work, and moved to journalism by furnishing some of the capital to found the *Nation,* with which his son-in-law, Wendell Phillips Garrison, was closely associated. He died on June 13, 1874, in Orange, New Jersey. McPherson, *Struggle for Equality.*

James Brewer Stewart

McKINNEY, John Franklin, *congressman,* was born near Piqua in Miami county, Ohio, on April 12, 1827. He attended the Piqua Academy and spent one year at Ohio Wesleyan College. He studied law with his brother, was admitted to the bar in 1850, and began to practice law. McKinney became a strict Democrat and attended all the Democratic National Conventions between 1850 and 1888. He was elected to the 38th Congress in 1862, but was defeated in 1864. In 1870, McKinney was elected to the 42nd Congress, and was chairman of the Democratic State Executive Committee in 1879 and 1880. He died in Piqua on June 13, 1903. Robson, *Biographical Encyclopaedia of Ohio.*

Thomas H. Smith

McKNIGHT, Robert, *congressman,* was born in Pittsburgh, Pennsylvania, on January 20, 1820. A graduate of Princeton, he studied law and, after being admitted to the bar, began a long and prestigious career. He was a Whig city councilman for five years, including two as president of the council, and was a founder of the Republican party in Pittsburgh. He was elected to the 36th and 37th Congresses, where he was a party regular on the sectional issues and most war-related measures. He voted for confiscation, emancipation, and funding bills, but opposed the National Currency Act and abstained from voting on habeas corpus bills. After the war, he resumed his law practice until his death in Pittsburgh on October 25, 1885. *BDUSC.*

J. K. Folmar

McLEAN, Samuel, *territorial delegate*, was born on August 7, 1826, in Summit Hill, Pennsylvania. After attending Lafayette College, he studied law, and was admitted to the bar in 1849. He was prosecuting attorney of Carbon county (1855–1860), then joined in the rush to the Pike's Peak mines. When the government failed to organize the mining region into a separate state or territory, McLean was one of those in 1860 who created the provisional Territory of Jefferson, which he served as attorney general. He moved to Bannack in early 1862, and later settled in Virginia City. This area became part of Idaho Territory in 1863, and in 1864 it was split off as part of the new Montana Territory.

Both territories (like Colorado and Nevada earlier) were created to provide legal institutions for newly discovered mining areas and to bind the citizens more closely to the Union. The number of Confederate loyalists in those territories is a matter of dispute. Republican estimates that from one-half to four-fifths of the territory's population were secessionists were reflected in the 1864 campaign to elect a territorial legislature and delegate to Congress, for which McLean ran as a Democrat. Although opponents charged that McLean was a Peace Democrat, he was elected, and in 1865 was reelected to a regular two-year term. Like many territorial delegates before him, he castigated the Federal government for its tightfisted control over the territory.

McLean achieved the most notoriety by threatening, in 1866, that oppressive legislation would drive Montanans into the arms of Canada. His constituents rejected this as an absurdity, and it was partly for this reason that he was not nominated for another term. He returned to Montana to become president of a silver mining company, but rumors of rich new deposits failed to materialize. In 1870, McLean moved to a plantation near Burkeville, Virginia, where he died on July 16, 1877. Spence, *Territorial Politics and Government in Montana.*

Kent D. Richards

McLEAN, Washington, *publisher*, was born on May 14, 1817, in Cincinnati, Ohio. After an elementary education he was apprenticed to a machinist and acquired a knowledge of boilermaking. In time, he set up his own boiler factory, which served the growing steamboat industry on the Ohio and Mississippi rivers. During the race riots in Cincinnati in the 1830s, McLean became captain of the Cincinnati Rover Guards, whose purpose was to keep order. He next organized the Miami Tribe, a secret social/political group that controlled Hamilton county politics for a generation. McLean became Democratic boss of Cincinnati, and in time of Ohio. He bought into the *Cincinnati Enquirer* in 1853, and on August 23, 1857, the same day as the financial panic, he became its principal stockholder and publisher.

McLean believed that the sectional crisis had been encouraged by Northern and Southern extremists at the expense of the West, and in 1860 saw Stephen A. Douglas (*q.v.*) as the only candidate who could save the Union. With Douglas's defeat, he turned to the Crittenden Compromise as the only solution to North–South differences. In a special citywide meeting, he maneuvered

Cincinnati into officially endorsing the compromise, much to the embarrassment of Republicans. After Fort Sumter, McLean decided to support the Federal government regardless of party, a policy that lasted only two months because he feared a military dictatorship. He headed the opposition party through his control of the *Enquirer*, and maintained a separate Democratic party organization that favored peace by negotiation. He held to this position until the announcement of the Emancipation Proclamation.

The purpose of the war now changed, McLean changed the policy of the Democratic party and the paper to opposition to the war itself. He supported Clement L. Vallandigham (*q.v.*) in his campaign for governor in 1863, befriended him after his arrest, and supplied him with money during his exile. After the defeat of Vallandigham in the fall of 1863, McLean steered the *Enquirer* from a call for negotiations to a "peace-at-any-price" position that he maintained until the Democratic National Convention met at Chicago in late August 1864. There he made a deal whereby Ultra Peace Democrats, such as Vallandigham, supported General George B. McClellan (*q.v.*) as Democratic presidential candidate, in return for which George H. Pendleton (*q.v.*), a Peace Democrat and McLean favorite, was nominated for Vice President.

Although it was primarily McLean who kept the Democratic party in Ohio alive during the war, he succumbed to current passions and played upon race prejudice in his columns. After the war, he supported Andrew Johnson (*q.v.*), and ran one of the most astute campaigns in journalism history in his fight against suffrage for blacks. Large increases in subscriptions, sometimes amounting to 200 a day, convinced him of the rightness of his course. At the 1868 Democratic National Convention, McLean tried to make poverty and wealth, rather than Reconstruction, the issue of national politics, and he nearly succeeded. Conservatives were able to defeat McLean's plan, however, thus removing from national politics the most meaningful issue the Democratic party had. McLean promoted Horace Greeley (*q.v.*) for the presidency in 1872. In 1875, he left the management of the *Enquirer* to his son, and moved to Washington, D.C., where he died on December 8, 1890. Klement, *Copperheads in the Middle West*; Merrill, *Bourbon Democracy of the Middle West*.

James G. Smart

McMILLAN, James Winning, *general,* was born on April 28, 1825, in Clark county, Kentucky. During the Mexican War, he served with Volunteer regiments from Illinois and Louisiana, reaching the rank of sergeant. After being mustered out, he resided in Indiana, occupying himself with several business pursuits. In 1861, McMillan helped to organize the 21st Indiana Volunteers and led the regiment in campaigns in the Department of the Gulf. He acquitted himself well during the defense of Baton Rouge (August 5, 1862) and in a skirmish at St. Charles Courthouse the next month.

Following his promotion to brigadier general of Volunteers, McMillan commanded the 2nd Brigade, 1st Division, XIX Corps, in Nathaniel Banks's (*q.v.*)

Red River campaign. He fought at Monett's Ferry and Mansfield, and led his brigade in a counterattack at Pleasant Hill that helped to win a Union victory (April 9, 1864). Subsequently, the XIX Corps was transferred to the Shenandoah Valley. At Winchester and Cedar Creek, McMillan displayed outstanding leadership in crucial situations, and General Philip H. Sheridan (*q.v.*) complimented him on his troop-handling abilities. McMillan had his worst and best day as a soldier at Cedar Creek. In the morning Confederates routed his division, along with the rest of the XIX Corps, and the battle appeared to be lost. However, McMillan re-formed his brigade and beat back an attack. Spurred on by Sheridan, the whole Union line counterattacked at midafternoon, with the 2nd Brigade in the thick of the fighting.

McMillan repeatedly demonstrated his reliability, often set a personal example of bravery, and merited his promotion to major general of Volunteers in March 1865. For a decade after the war, he had various business enterprises in Kansas; in 1875 he obtained an appointment to the board of review in the Pension Office. McMillan died in Washington, D.C., on March 9, 1903. Irwin, *History of the Nineteenth Army Corps*; Pond, *Shenandoah Valley in 1864*; Winters, *Civil War in Louisiana*.

Joseph G. Dawson III

McPHERSON, Edward, *congressman*, was born in Gettysburg, Pennsylvania, on July 31, 1830. He graduated from Gettysburg College, known then as Pennsylvania College, in 1848, and after a brief period spent studying the law, he turned to journalism. He was associated with a number of newspapers in Pennsylvania, including the *Harrisburg American*, the *Independent Whig* (Lancaster), the *Pittsburgh Daily Times*, and the *Philadelphia Press*. In 1880, he purchased the Gettysburg *Star and Sentinel*, and served as its editor until his death.

In 1858 and 1860, McPherson ran successfully for Congress as a Republican. In both elections, his winning margin was slim: less than 300 votes in 1858 and just over 500 in 1860. The Democratic sweep of Pennsylvania in 1862 brought McPherson's career as an elected official to an end. While in Congress, he no doubt understood the political ramifications of his narrow victories. During the secession winter, for instance, McPherson reassured his Southern colleagues that neither the Republican party nor the President-elect would interfere with slavery in the states. He reaffirmed that position several weeks later, voting with the majority to pass a constitutional amendment prohibiting such interference. In an effort further to demonstrate his sentiment that the war was being fought for the Union and not for the abolition of slavery, in the opening session of the 37th Congress McPherson opposed a confiscation bill that threatened slave property in the seceded states. He qualified these conciliatory gestures, however, by frequently reminding the House that if preserving the Union necessitated war, then "let it come, and upon the aggressors rest the responsibility."

McPherson gained national notice as the clerk of the House of Representatives (1863–1875). Many of the Southern states elected to the Congress individuals who had held prominent positions in the Confederacy, and Republicans decided in caucus to block their admission by refusing to acknowledge their presence. Consequently, when McPherson called the roll to assemble the 39th Congress, he omitted the names of the former Confederates.

McPherson wrote major books on politics: *Political History of the Great Rebellion* (1864) and *The Political History of the United States of America During the Period of Reconstruction* (1871). He published the *Political Manual* annually from 1866 to 1869, and beginning in 1868 compiled (1868–1894) the *Handbook of Politics* biennially. McPherson was twice reappointed clerk of the House (1881–1883, 1889–1891). He died in Gettysburg on December 14, 1895. McKitrick, *Andrew Johnson.*

Philip J. Avillo, Jr.

McPHERSON, James Birdseye, *general,* was born on November 14, 1828, in Sandusky county, Ohio. Following his father's death in 1841, James left home to work for a merchant in a neighboring community. With his employer's encouragement, he attended Norwalk (Ohio) Academy and then the U.S. Military Academy, from which he graduated in 1853, at the head of his class. McPherson then taught for one year at West Point, followed by service as a military engineer in New York City and San Francisco. Saddened by the worsening sectional conflict, he held the abolitionists and Southern "fire-eaters" largely responsible. His political conservatism was noticeable in 1856, when he supported Millard Fillmore, the American party candidate, and in 1860, when he favored John Bell and the Constitutional Union ticket.

After the attack on Fort Sumter, McPherson returned to the East as a captain of engineers. Eager for duty in the field, and for an opportunity for promotion, he appealed to Henry W. Halleck (*q.v.*), commanding the Department of the West, who appointed him lieutenant colonel of engineers on Ulysses S. Grant's (*q.v.*) staff. A collateral duty may have been to report on Grant's "bad habits." His service at Forts Henry and Donelson and at Shiloh won McPherson command of the XVII Corps during the Vicksburg campaign. In the Atlanta campaign, he commanded the Army of the Tennessee.

That McPherson possessed outstanding personal qualities is not disputed; opinions vary as to his military ability. He was an excellent staff officer and subordinate commander, as is evidenced by his record at the division and corps levels. William T. Sherman (*q.v.*) chided him for being overly cautious at Resaca (May 1864) but continued to give him great responsibility throughout the advance on Atlanta. His intelligent deployment of his army at Atlanta very likely averted a disaster for Union arms. On July 22, 1864, McPherson died of wounds received in the early stages of John Bell Hood's attack on the Union left. His death at age thirty-five, near Atlanta, left unanswered the question of his potential. Castel, *Decision in the West*; Liddell Hart, *Sherman.*

John T. Hubbell

MAGOFFIN, Beriah, *governor*, was born in Harrodsburg, Kentucky, on April 18, 1815. After attending local schools, he graduated from Centre College in 1835, and the Transylvania College of Law in 1838. After practicing law in Jackson, Mississippi, Magoffin returned to Kentucky in 1839 and established a lucrative practice in Harrodsburg. As a Democrat, he was a candidate for presidential elector in every election from 1844 to 1856. He was elected to the state Senate in 1850 and was a delegate to the Democratic National Conventions of 1848, 1856, 1860, and 1872. Magoffin lost the race for lieutenant governor in 1855 but was successful in the 1859 gubernatorial election.

Magoffin, a Southern sympathizer, supported states' rights and slavery. He favored compromise instead of war, and as a result Kentucky generally followed a course of neutrality. Magoffin resigned in August 1862 after Unionists in the state legislature consistently overrode his vetoes. After selecting his successor, he returned to his law practice in Harrodsburg. He proposed a plan to the slave state governors to preserve the Union, but it failed.

When hostilities began, Magoffin refused Abraham Lincoln's (*q.v.*) call for troops. A week later he refused a similar request from Confederate President Jefferson Davis, although both sides recruited in the state. Magoffin unsuccessfully attempted to form a union of border states for mediation of the war. Ultimately he supported civil rights for African Americans and served in the state legislature from 1867 to 1869. He died in Harrodsburg on February 28, 1885.

Coulter, *Civil War and Readjustment in Kentucky*; Harrison, *Kentucky's Governors*.

Boyd Childress

MAHONY, Dennis Aloysius, *editor*, was born in County Cork, Ireland, on January 20, 1821. His family emigrated to Philadelphia when he was nine, and he moved in 1843 to Iowa, where he was active in law, business, and politics. Mahony became known as a defender of the public interest against corporate wealth, particularly Easter-financed railroads. He also promoted Irish and German immigration and vigorously defended immigrants against nativist attacks. Although sometimes identified as a Douglas Democrat after 1858, Mahony was never far removed from the Buchanan regulars, intent mainly on sustaining Democratic unity in face of the Republican challenge.

After Abraham Lincoln's (*q.v.*) election, Mahony's *Dubuque Herald* called for Republican capitulation to Southern demands, including separation if the South would settle for nothing less. With the outbreak of war, he was increasingly antiwar and challenged the Republicans on all fronts. He also challenged Iowa Republicans to back up their sentiments by enlisting. In August 1862 Mahony was arrested, allegedly for discouraging enlistments, and imprisoned in Old Capitol Prison. Nominated to run for Congress against William B. Allison (*q.v.*), he campaigned from prison as best he could, but lost.

Released without trial or hearing any official charges against him, Mahony returned to the *Herald* and continued his attack against the Lincoln administration. In 1863, he wrote two antiadministration polemics, the autobiographical

Prisoner of State, and *Four Acts of Despotism.* In the summer of 1863, he returned to Dubuque, sold his interest in the *Herald,* and ran for and was elected Dubuque county sheriff. Near the end of a second term, Mahony moved to St. Louis and established the *St. Louis Times.* He returned to Dubuque in 1871. He took over the *Dubuque Telegraph* and made it into one of the leading Greenback papers in the country before he died on November 5, 1879. Wubben, *Civil War Iowa.*

Hubert H. Wubben

MALLORY, Robert, *congressman,* was born on November 15, 1815, in Madison county, Virginia. Educated at the University of Virginia, he established himself in 1839 as a lawyer and farmer in Oldham county, Kentucky. Mallory was elected to Congress in August 1859 on the Opposition ticket, although the Democrats carried most of the state. He won reelection in 1861 as a Unionist, and in 1863 as a Union Democrat. In the crisis of 1860–1861, Mallory, like other conservative Kentuckians, deplored the disruptive influence of antislavery Republicans and proslavery Southern Democrats. Until the death of John J. Crittenden (*q.v.*) in 1863, Mallory was a friend and supporter of the Kentucky elder statesman.

As early as December 1860, Mallory introduced in the House a resolution that would have instructed the Committee of Thirty-three to report back compromise proposals essentially identical to the Crittenden Compromise, which was laid before the Senate a few days later. He consistently supported the war for the Union, but resisted what he considered to be its pernicious effects upon the rights of the states and property owners. Mallory invariably opposed antislavery measures in Congress, and as late as 1865 spoke out in the House against the 13th Amendment. In February 1863 he denounced military conscription as a violation of states' rights and of the Constitution's militia provisions. He was especially annoyed by efforts to exclude Kentucky's elected state officials from the supervision of the draft.

Mallory was a competent representative, with a good grasp of the techniques of congressional logrolling and parliamentary procedure. Although his attachment to slavery was out of step with the times, he usually refrained from taxing the patience of his House colleagues with lengthy, impassioned speeches in its defense. As chairman of the Roads and Canals Committee, his main concern was to block projects that would have lessened the advantage of Louisville's strategic location on the Ohio River. Defeated for reelection in 1865, Mallory returned to farming. In 1866, he was a delegate to the National Union Convention in Philadelphia, and ten years later was a commissioner and vice president of the Centennial celebration held in the Quaker City. Mallory died near La Grange, Kentucky, on August 11, 1885. Curry, *Blueprint for Modern America.*

Richard G. Stone

MANSFIELD, Joseph King Fenno, *general,* was born on December 22, 1803, in New Haven, Connecticut. He graduated from West Point in 1822, five months before his nineteenth birthday. As an engineer officer he spent several years working on coastal fortifications in the Southeast. During the Mexican War, Mansfield won three brevets as General Zachary Taylor's chief engineer. In 1853, Secretary of War Jefferson Davis appointed him to the Inspector General's Department, where he attempted unsuccessfully to establish savings banks for enlisted men and to abolish the practice of having soldiers farm at frontier posts.

When the Civil War began, Mansfield took command of the Washington defenses. Under his direction, Union forces seized and fortified positions on the south bank of the Potomac. Subsequently, he was posted to Fortress Monroe. Mansfield was directing Union shore batteries there on March 8, 1862, when the U.S.S. *Congress* struck its colors to the C.S.S. *Virginia.* Disregarding the capitulation, he ordered the Union guns to continue the bombardment. When a subordinate protested this breach of protocol, Mansfield responded that although the ship had surrendered, he had not. Two days before the battle of Sharpsburg, he assumed command of the XII Corps, Army of the Potomac. Taking over an organization demoralized by poor leadership and filled with raw recruits, he quickly whipped it into shape.

Had he lived, Mansfield undoubtedly would have proved a splendid corps commander. But this was not to be. After making a difficult night march, he was wounded on September 17, 1862, while deploying troops in the East Wood during the battle of Antietam. He died from his wound the next day. Mansfield, who had graduated from West Point before his commanding general at Antietam was born, led troops with the endurance, vigor and competence of a far younger man. His natural soldierly instincts were enhanced by character, education, and experience. Catton, *Mr. Lincoln's Army*; Hassler, *Commanders of the Army of the Potomac*; Sears, *Landscape Turned Red.*

James L. Morrison, Jr.

MARBLE, Manton Malone, *editor,* was born in Worcester, Massachusetts, on November 16, 1834. He grew up in Albany, New York, and graduated from the University of Rochester in 1855. He gained his early experience in journalism in Boston and with the *New York Evening Post.* In June 1860 he was hired as night editor of the newly established *New York World,* became editor two years later, and was sole owner in 1869. Before 1862, when he became editor of the *World,* Marble exerted little influence on national affairs. A conservative Republican with nativist sympathies, he joined the Democratic party to obtain financial backing for his paper.

During the Civil War, Marble attacked Abraham Lincoln's (*q.v.*) policies on emancipation, paper money, and military arrests of civilians. He also opposed the Peace Democrats and called for a military victory over the Confederacy, but only to restore the Union and not to interfere with the rights of the states or with slavery. He strongly supported his personal friend, General George B. McClellan (*q.v.*), for the Democratic presidential nomination in 1864.

After the war, Marble tried to broaden the Democratic party's popular appeal.

He urged white Southerners to accept Congressional Reconstruction and black suffrage, and wanted the Democrats to nominate Salmon P. Chase (*q.v.*) in 1868 and Charles Francis Adams (*q.v.*) in 1872. Frustrated in these efforts, he turned to support his friend and longtime Democratic regular, Samuel J. Tilden, whom he supported for governor of New York in 1874 and for President in 1876.

Under Marble's editorship, the *New York World* became the most important organ of the Democratic party. His efforts to mold the party into a loyal opposition to the Lincoln administration contributed to Northern unity against the Confederacy. By calling upon Democrats to accept the results of the war, he paved the way for his party's "new departure" and alliance with the Liberal Republicans in 1871–1872. In the end, however, party loyalty among grassroots Democrats and Republicans undermined his postwar efforts, so that the Democrats' resurgence in the 1870s owed less to his efforts than to economic discontent, the corruption of Ulysses S. Grant's (*q.v.*) administration, and the campaign of Southern Democrats for home rule and white supremacy. In 1876, Marble sold the *World* and retired from journalism, although he remained active in politics. In 1897, he took up permanent residence in England and died at Allington Castle, Kent, on July 24, 1917. McJimsey, *Genteel Partisan.*

George McJimsey

MARCY, Daniel, *congressman,* was born in Portsmouth, New Hampshire, on November 7, 1810 (one source says 1809). He left school at fourteen to go to sea, and at twenty-one he was master of a vessel. In 1842, he joined two New Orleans businessmen in a shipbuilding venture at Portsmouth, and with his brother continued to build ships until the outbreak of the Civil War. Marcy served in the New Hampshire legislature as a Democrat (1854–1860), and in 1860 attended the Democratic National Convention in Charleston. He was nominated for Congress, but lost to Gilman Marston (*q.v.*). Marston entered the Army and was not renominated, and in 1863 Marcy won the seat. He opposed government underwriting of the Union Pacific Railroad, among other internal improvements, and he spent much of his time in Washington attending to the needs of his state's sick and wounded soldiers.

Marcy was the only Democrat in New Hampshire's five-man delegation, and Republican resurgence assured his defeat in 1865. In 1871, he returned to the state Senate for a year, and later he was elected to several terms in the legislature. In 1876 and 1877, he lost races for governor. Thereafter Marcy withdrew from politics, applying his attention to banks and other corporate interests. He died in Portsmouth on November 3, 1893. McClintock, *History of New Hampshire.*

William Marvel

MARSTON, Gilman, *congressman, general,* was born in Orford, New Hampshire, on August 20, 1811. He graduated from Dartmouth in 1837, studied law at Harvard, and in 1841 began a practice in Exeter, New Hampshire. From 1845 until the end of his life, he was active in politics, serving five consecutive terms in the legislature before being elected to Congress as a Republican in 1858. Marston won reelection in 1860 and finished out his term, although he went to war as colonel of the 2nd New Hampshire Volunteers in June 1861. Wounded in the shoulder at First Bull Run, he returned to duty and was promoted to brigadier general, to rank from November 29, 1862. He divided his time between the field and the forum, but his party failed to renominate him at the end of his second term.

Later Marston commanded the Maryland district that included Point Lookout military prison. In the summer of 1864 he narrowly missed being chosen by the New Hampshire legislature for the U.S. Senate, but the next winter he was elected to another term in Congress. He resigned from the Army on April 20, 1865. Marston served five more terms in the New Hampshire House of Representatives, lost another bid for Congress in 1876, and was appointed to fill a vacancy in the U.S. Senate on March 4, 1889. A successor was elected in June, and Marston stepped down after 106 days as a senator. He died in Exeter on July 3, 1890. Haynes, *History of the Second Regiment*; Lyford, *Life of Edward H. Rollins.*

William Marvel

MARTINDALE, John Henry, *general,* was born in what is now Hudson Falls, New York, on March 20, 1815. He graduated third in the West Point class of 1835, but resigned from the Army a year later. Admitted to the New York bar in 1838, he was practicing in Rochester at the outbreak of the Civil War. He advised Abraham Lincoln's (*q.v.*) administration to graduate the first and second classes at West Point immediately, and to distribute those officers among the Volunteers to train them. The Secretary of War pretended to dismiss the letter, but within weeks he had followed Martindale's recommendations.

Commissioned a brigadier general of Volunteers in August 1861, Martindale led a brigade under Fitz John Porter (*q.v.*) during the Peninsula campaign. His troops fled the battle of Gaines' Mill, and a month after the battle of Malvern Hill, Porter charged that on the morning after that fight, Martindale advised his men to lay down their arms and surrender as soon as they could obtain terms. A court was appointed to investigate, but it found the charge to be untrue. By then Martindale had fallen ill with typhoid, and he did not resume the command of his brigade. In February 1863, Martindale became military governor of the District of Columbia, holding the post until the beginning of the 1864 campaign. Given a division in the XVIII Corps, he took part in early operations around Bermuda Hundred and in the fighting at Cold Harbor. Although he commanded the corps briefly that summer, his name does not appear prominently in accounts of the campaign, and he resigned on September 13 because of poor health.

Despite apparent early influence with the administration, and an appointment as brigadier that placed him ahead of most of his contemporaries, Martindale never won promotion until the massive distribution of brevets at the close of the war. That left him with one of the oldest brigadier's commissions in the

Army when he resigned. That relative lack of success may have resulted equally from his political disagreements with superiors, his luck in drawing unspectacular assignments, and his limited military ability. After the war Martindale served a term as attorney general of New York and practiced law. He died in Nice, France, on December 13, 1881. Robertson, *Back Door to Richmond.*

William Marvel

MARVIN, James Madison, *congressman,* was born on February 27, 1809, in Ballston Spa, New York. He established himself in the hotel business, first in Albany and then in Saratoga Springs. He served in the state Assembly as a Whig, but switched to the Democratic party in 1856. With the outbreak of war in 1861, Marvin found himself more in sympathy with the Lincoln (*q.v.*) administration than with the President's Democratic opponents. Accordingly, he abandoned the Democrats and in 1862 accepted the nomination of the Republican–Union coalition in Saratoga Springs, whose voters sent him to the House of Representatives. Voting as a cautious Republican during the war, he was reelected as a member of that party in 1864 and again in 1866. Although consistently conservative by Republican standards, especially on economic issues, Marvin supported the 14th and 15th Amendments. He did not run for reelection in 1868, returning to his hotel business in Saratoga Springs, which after the war was a favorite vacation spot for the rich. He died in Saratoga Springs on April 25, 1901. Benedict, *Compromise of Principle.*

James C. Mohr

MASON, Charles, *journalist,* was born on October 24, 1804, in Pompey, New York. Following education at a district school and Pompey Academy, he graduated from West Point at the top of the class of 1829, just ahead of his friend Robert E. Lee. After two years as assistant professor of engineering at the Academy he resigned from the Army, read law, and was admitted to the bar in 1832. In 1838, he was appointed chief justice of Iowa Territory, a post he held until Iowa became a state in 1846. Mason became a leader in law, business, railroad promotion, and the Democratic party, eventually winning appointment as U.S. patent commissioner in 1853. He resigned in 1857, but worked in Washington for many years as a patent lawyer.

Although a supporter of James Buchanan (*q.v.*) against Stephen A. Douglas (*q.v.*), Mason had great prestige among all Iowa Democrats, partly because of his many contacts with important national Democrats and partly because most of them never learned the depth of his pro-Southern feelings. He privately hoped for Southern military success throughout the war. Doubts about his commitment to the war caused War Democrats to pressure him into declining the party nomination for governor in 1861. Writing under the pseudonym X for the *Dubuque Herald,* Mason excoriated the Lincoln (*q.v.*) administration, scoffed at Union victory claims, magnified Confederate victories, and defended conservative interpretations of the Constitution. His wartime pamphlet ''The Election in Iowa''

(1863), published under his own name, was mainly a diatribe against emancipation and its imagined consequences.

Mason labored for George B. McClellan's (*q.v.*) election in 1864, assuming that a Democratic victory would bring peace and satisfaction of Southern demands. He saw Lincoln's assassination as both "retributive justice" and a golden Democratic opportunity. He became a strong supporter of Andrew Johnson (*q.v.*), assuming that a speedy reunion of Northern and Southern Democrats in Congress would permanently oust the Republicans from power. Mason ran for the Iowa Supreme Court in 1863, and for governor in 1867, losing decisively both times. In the 1870s, he wrote frequently on financial matters, accepting part of the Greenback program. Mason died in Burlington, Iowa, on February 25, 1882. Wubben, *Civil War Iowa.*

Hubert H. Wubben

MAY, Henry, *congressman,* was born in Washington, D.C., on February 13, 1816. He attended Columbia College (now George Washington University), finished his studies by reading law, and was admitted to the bar in 1840. May became a prominent Washington lawyer, and in 1850 he moved to Baltimore. In 1852, he won election as a Democrat to the 33rd Congress, but suffered defeat in his bid for a second term. In 1861, May, now an independent Unionist, challenged and defeated Henry Winter Davis (*q.v.*) for his congressional seat. Professing loyalty to the Union and defending the rights of Marylanders, he denounced all measures that he regarded as oppressive.

For May, constitutional rights were paramount, even at the expense of the Union. He attacked the suppression of the writ of habeas corpus, the arrest of the Baltimore police commissioners, and Federal funding of a new police force there. The House refused his resolutions calling for an armistice to end the war, with the possibility of peaceful separation. The prospect of emancipation was an anathema to May. Even before he took his congressional seat, Unionists in the House challenged his loyalty, and during the session they tried unsuccessfully to expel him. In September 1861 he was arrested and imprisoned by the military, but after an appeal to President Abraham Lincoln (*q.v.*) by his brother, he was released in December and completed his term. Despite his arrest, May remained outspoken. He died in Baltimore on September 25, 1866. Clark, *Politics in Maryland During the Civil War.*

Richard R. Duncan

MAY, Samuel Joseph, *abolitionist,* was born in Boston on September 12, 1797. He graduated from Harvard College in 1817 and from its Divinity School in 1822, adopted Unitarianism, and embarked on a lifetime of radical reform. In the early 1830s, he became an abolitionist and was a founding member of the American Anti-Slavery Society. He was a general agent for the Massachusetts Anti-Slavery Society, an active abettor of fugitive slaves, and an uncompromising proponent of female equality both within the antislavery movement and in society. During the early 1850s, May found himself especially disturbed by the conflict he experienced between his commitment to nonviolence and his desire to defy the Fugitive Slave Law. Despite this ambivalence, he assisted in the rescue of the fugitive Jerry McHenry from Federal marshals in 1851.

In 1861, May reluctantly supported recourse to arms, and became one of Abraham Lincoln's (*q.v.*) staunchest abolitionist supporters. After the passage of the 13th Amendment, he declared his crusade against slavery to be a success and resigned from the American Anti-Slavery Society. He remained interested in race and reform issues, and a critic of Andrew Johnson's (*q.v.*) Reconstruction policies. May provided in his will that his personal papers be placed in the Cornell University Archives, where they remain as one of the richest collections of documents bearing on antebellum reform. He died in Syracuse, New York, on July 1, 1871. Yacovone, *Samuel Joseph May.*

James Brewer Stewart

MAYNARD, Horace, *congressman*, was born on August 30, 1814, in Westboro, Massachusetts. After attending the local common schools and Millbury Academy, he graduated from Amherst College as class valedictorian in 1838. Maynard was a tutor and professor of mathematics at East Tennessee College (now the University of Tennessee) before establishing a successful law practice in Knoxville. A presidential elector on the Whig ticket in 1852, he failed to win election to Congress in 1853. He was elected on the American ticket to the 35th Congress in 1857, to the 36th Congress as a member of the Opposition party in 1859, and actively supported the Constitutional–Union ticket during the presidential election of 1860.

Although an outspoken critic of both Abraham Lincoln (*q.v.*) and the Republican party, Maynard was strongly opposed to secession. He attended the East Tennessee Convention in Greeneville (June 17–20, 1861), at which Unionists petitioned the pro-Confederate legislature in Nashville for permission to create a new state. On August 8, 1861, he was elected to the 37th Congress on the Union ticket, then was forced to flee the state to avoid arrest. Despite his devotion to the Union, Maynard was challenged by Republicans who questioned his admission as a representative of a ''disloyal state.'' He strongly opposed Radical efforts to reduce Tennessee and other seceded states to territorial status. Although highly critical of the ''Loyalty Oath'' amendment of Lincoln's plan, he continued to support Presidential Reconstruction throughout the remainder of his term.

After Andrew Johnson (*q.v.*) was elected military governor of Tennessee, Maynard was appointed state attorney general (1863–1865). Bitter political foes before the war, they became the leading advocates of sending Federal forces to ''liberate'' East Tennessee. Maynard strongly supported Johnson for the vice presidency in 1864, and effectively thwarted his old rival Thaddeus Stevens (*q.v.*) when he sought to deny Southern Unionists a place in the electoral college.

Maynard was elected to the 39th Congress as an Unconditional Unionist in

1866, but broke with Johnson and allied himself with the President's opponents—an act that made him a pariah to his former conservative allies. He subsequently was elected to three additional terms in Congress as a Republican. In 1874, Maynard returned to state politics and made an unsuccessful bid for the governorship. Appointed minister to Turkey on March 9, 1875, he left that position in May 1880 to serve as Postmaster General (June 2, 1880–March 5, 1881). He died in Knoxville on May 3, 1882. Park, *Life and Services of Horace Maynard.*

James M. Prichard

MEADE, George Gordon, *general,* was born in Cadiz, Spain, on December 15, 1815, the son of a wealthy businessman who was also an American naval agent in Spain. He graduated from West Point in 1835, and served in Florida, in the Seminole War, for one year before resigning from the Army to pursue surveying and engineering work. In 1840, he married Margaretta Sergeant; they had six children. Meade returned to the Army in 1842, and until 1861 was engaged in routine engineering duties, interrupted only by participation in Zachary Taylor's northern campaigns during the Mexican War, winning a brevet at Monterey.

A captain when Civil War began, Meade was named a brigadier general and given command of one of the three brigades in the famous Pennsylvania Reserves. In this capacity, he served with George B. McClellan's (*q.v.*) Army of the Potomac on the Peninsula, where he was severely wounded at Glendale. He returned to duty in time to fight with John Pope (*q.v.*) at Second Bull Run and, as a division and temporary corps commander, with McClellan at South Mountain and Antietam. In November 1862 Meade was named a major general, and was a division commander at Fredericksburg and a corps commander at Chancellorsville. In all of these operations he performed with distinction.

Although slightly stooped and balding, Meade was graceful and soldierly in appearance and bearing, and he had a commanding presence. At times, however, he was irritable. He possessed an excellent eye for terrain and showed ability in combined operations with infantry, artillery, and cavalry. When John Reynolds (*q.v.*) refused command of the Army of the Potomac, Meade was named to that onerous position on June 28, 1863, just three days before the opening of the battle of Gettysburg. Meade showed that although not a brilliant general, he was, withal, a sound, steady, and competent commander. He outgeneraled Robert E. Lee at Gettysburg and won a crucial but not crushing victory that forced the Confederates to retreat into Virginia. No further serious battles were fought in the East until the following spring, when, under General in Chief Ulysses S. Grant's (*q.v.*) overall direction, Meade continued to lead the Army of the Potomac ably in the Wilderness, Spotsylvania, Cold Harbor, Petersburg, and Appomattox campaigns, which led to Lee's eventual surrender on April 9, 1865.

A man and soldier of the highest character, integrity, and dedication to duty, Meade was bluntly honest and aware of his own limitations, and possessed a fine and wide-ranging combination of personal and military talents. His permanent claim to fame rests largely on his magnificent defensive triumph over Lee at Gettysburg, with the outcome of the Civil War possibly hanging in the balance. Although perhaps too circumspect in his pursuit of Lee's defeated army after Gettysburg, Meade did not merit the sharp criticism Abraham Lincoln (*q.v.*) leveled at him. Although unable to win from his soldiers the spontaneous enthusiasm and trust that McClellan could, Meade nonetheless commanded support, obedience, and respect.

The permanence of the American Republic depended to a large extent upon Meade's qualities, and he more than met this stern test at Gettysburg. Yet few commanders of a great army in such a decisive battle are so little spoken of by posterity as Meade. After the war, he held several important department commands in the South and East. His last was in Philadelphia in 1869, where he had enough time to indulge his tastes in literature and the arts. He died on November 6, 1872, in Philadelphia. Cleaves, *Meade of Gettysburg*; Coddington, *Gettysburg Campaign*; Hassler, *Commanders of the Army of the Potomac.*

Warren W. Hassler, Jr.

MEAGHER, Thomas Francis, *general,* was born on August 3, 1823, in Waterford, Ireland. His involvement with Free Ireland groups resulted in his banishment to a penal colony on Tasmania, from which he escaped to America in 1852. He settled in New York, where his imposing appearance, Democratic credentials, and spellbinding oratory soon made him one of the most prominent Irish nationalists in the New World. Viewing Unionism as a means of promoting ethnic pride and his political ambitions, Meagher (pronounced ''Marr'') helped organize a company of Zouaves that joined the 69th New York Militia, in which he rose to major.

After winning fame out of proportion to his service at First Bull Run, Meagher raised a New York brigade of infantry composed largely of native- and American-born Irishmen. To command the organization, Abraham Lincoln (*q.v.*) appointed ''Meagher of the Sword'' a brigadier general of Volunteers in February 1862. Although the Irish Brigade fought gallantly and suffered heavily from the Peninsula through Gettysburg, its commander fell from his horse, drunk, at Antietam, and reportedly abandoned his command and fled to the rear at Fredericksburg. He tried to resign in May 1863, but the War Department blocked his action. Meagher returned to the field to lead a division of rear-echelon personnel during William T. Sherman's (*q.v.*) March to the Sea.

Before the war's end Meagher defected to the Republican party, and in 1865 he accepted a patronage post as territorial secretary (and later served as acting governor) of Montana. He died on July 1, 1867, after falling, while drunk, from a steamboat near Fort Benton, Montana. Athearn, *Thomas Francis Meagher*; Jones, *Irish Brigade.*

Edward G. Longacre

MEDARY, Samuel, *editor,* was born on a farm in Montgomery county, Pennsylvania, on February 25, 1801. After attending Norristown Academy, teaching school, and working in a print shop, he moved in 1825 to Bethel, Ohio, to establish the *Ohio Sun.* In 1837, in Columbus, he founded the *Ohio Statesman,* destined to become the leading Democratic journal in the Northwest and earn its editor-owner the sobriquet "the Old Wheelhorse of Ohio Democracy." Medary supported the Kansas–Nebraska Act of 1854, and successively served as the governor of Minnesota Territory, postmaster of Columbus, and governor of Kansas Territory.

After Abraham Lincoln's (*q.v.*) election, Medary resigned his Kansas assignment and returned to Columbus. On January 1, 1861, he established *The Crisis* to promote peace and compromise, as well as the sectional interests of the upper Midwest. His eight-page weekly aired partisan views with a vigor that ruffled Republican feathers. He cursed abolitionists, opposed a tariff as detrimental to Western interests, damned "the monstrous Bank Bill," called Lincoln "the Prince of Rails," wrote learned treatises opposing suspension of the writ of habeas corpus, condemned arbitrary arrests, and even suggested the impeachment of the President. Medary deplored Lincoln's emancipation policy, opposed Federal conscription, and carried on a passionate crusade for peace and compromise—on almost any terms.

On March 5, 1863, soldiers from nearby Camp Chase visited the building that housed *The Crisis,* and wrecked Medary's office. He worked for a "peace plank" and a peace candidate at the Chicago Democratic National Convention, rejecting George B. McClellan's (*q.v.*) nomination. With states' rights as the alpha and omega of his political philosophy, he opposed the centralization of the government during the Civil War, the ascendancy of industrialism, and emancipation. His partisanship veiled a keen intellect, astute political judgment, and "a courageous heart." Medary died in Columbus on November 7, 1864, the day before Lincoln's reelection. Dorn, "Samuel Medary," *Ohio State Archaeological and Historical Quarterly*; Roseboom, "The Mobbing of the *Crisis*," *Ohio State Archaeological and Historical Quarterly.*

Frank L. Klement

MEDILL, Joseph, *editor,* was born on April 6, 1823, in St. John, New Brunswick, Canada, and moved with his family to Ohio in 1832. He graduated from a local academy, studied law, and was admitted to the bar in 1846. He practiced law near Canton, Ohio, and also set type and wrote editorials for local papers. In 1850, Medill purchased the Coshocton, Ohio, paper, and in 1852 the *Daily Forest City* in Cleveland. His law and newspaper background brought him into contact with a number of political leaders, including Salmon P. Chase (*q.v.*) and Edwin M. Stanton (*q.v.*). In 1855, he moved to Chicago and began editing *The Tribune,* building the paper into the leading Whig/Republican voice in the Midwest.

Medill became friends with Abraham Lincoln (*q.v.*), who often visited *The*

Chicago Tribune office. *The Chicago Tribune* gave Lincoln extensive coverage and pushed his candidacy for the presidency. Indeed, Medill, active in the Republican party, was in charge of seating arrangements for the 1860 Republican National Convention and packed the auditorium with Lincoln supporters. He was an ardent abolitionist, and pushed the President to free the slaves outright, and to pursue the war more vigorously. Lincoln showed a good deal of patience with Medill, but on one occasion bluntly told his friend to stop trying to run the war. Lincoln had issued a draft call, which included a heavy quota of men from Illinois. Medill complained that Chicago and the state were being asked to do more than their share. Lincoln supposedly told Medill that he had done as much as anyone to bring about the war, and that he should go back to Chicago and help raise the troops. Medill did.

After the war, Medill dabbled in local and state politics, serving as mayor of Chicago in 1872. He returned to full-time editing of *The Chicago Tribune* after that, and remained editor until his death on March 16, 1899, near San Antonio, Texas. Kinsley, *Chicago Tribune.*

Fredric F. Endres

MEIGS, Montgomery Cunningham, *general,* was born May 3, 1816, in Augusta, Georgia. He graduated from West Point in 1836, entered the artillery, and became a lieutenant of engineers in 1837. He served in various border fortification and river improvement projects, and on the Board of Engineers for Atlantic Coast Defenses in Washington. Both able and socially well connected, Meigs was appointed on March 29, 1853, just after his promotion to captain, as supervising engineer of the extension of the Capitol as well as of the Washington Aqueduct. How much he contributed to the Capitol dome and the legislative chambers is obscured by a conflict between him and the architect, a dispute significant in the separation of the architectural and engineering professions.

Meigs also became embroiled in a dispute with Secretary of War John B. Floyd, over his resistance to what he saw as Floyd's efforts to misuse contracts for political purposes. When Floyd tried to remove Meigs, the latter turned to his friends Senator Jefferson Davis and others in Congress; through their efforts the Civil Works Appropriation Act of June 25, 1860, required his superintendency. Regarding this proviso as an unwarranted intrusion on executive power, on November 1, 1860, President James Buchanan (*q.v.*) ordered Meigs to Fort Jefferson in the Dry Tortugas, Florida. On January 30, 1861, Meigs was ordered back to the Capitol and aqueduct, but his acquaintance with the Florida situation soon involved him in the expedition for the relief of Fort Pickens.

His conflict with Floyd had earned Meigs a reputation for assertive integrity, which was instrumental in his promotion to brigadier general and appointment as quartermaster general on June 13, 1861 (both retroactive to May 15). He promptly helped bring order out of the chaos of Union army contracting. He emerged from the war a brevet major general as of July 5, 1864, and continued as quartermaster general until his retirement, February 6, 1882. He believed the death of his eldest son, Major John R. Meigs, in the Shenandoah Valley on October 3, 1864, was a murder by bushwhackers; his consequent embitterment sealed his political transformation from prewar Democrat to a Republican of Radical inclinations, favoring land redistribution for the freedmen. It also inspired him in his efforts to make Robert E. Lee's estate at Arlington into a national cemetery. In retirement, Meigs designed the Pension Office in Washington, completed in 1866 and known to generations as "Meig's barn." Formally an Episcopalian, Meigs retained an ethical code reminiscent of his Puritan forebears in its combination of stern, inner-directed demands on himself with a humorless self-righteousness.

The assertive integrity that won him the chief logistical post in the Army assured that no financial scandal approached Meigs or anything he could control, despite the wartime expansion of military supply. While insisting on the strictest accounting and contracting standards, however, he also judiciously decentralized quartermaster operations to assure flexibility. He encouraged considerable discretion, first among quartermasters with the field armies, then, after 1864, among the divisions into which the Quartermaster's Department was reorganized, each concerned with a major area of supply. Meigs died in Washington, D.C., on January 2, 1892. Huston, *Sinews of War*; Risch, *Quartermaster Support of the Army*; Weigley, *Quartermaster General of the Union Army*.

Russell F. Weigley

MENZIES, John William, *congressman*, was born in Bryant's Station, Kentucky, on April 12, 1819. He graduated in 1840 from the University of Virginia, read law, and in 1841 opened a law practice in Covington, Kentucky. In 1848, and again in 1855, Menzies won election as a Whig to the Kentucky legislature. After the breakup of the party, Menzies supported Millard Fillmore and the Know-Nothings in 1856, and the Constitutional Union candidacy of John Bell in 1860. In 1861, Menzies worked with a conservative Unionist coalition to block the secession of the Bluegrass State. In June of that year, he was elected as a Unionist to Congress.

Never previously sympathetic to the Democratic party, Menzies endorsed the platform of the 1862 Union Democratic Convention in Louisville. Decrying what he perceived to be a Radical Republican program to subvert property rights and the Constitution, he became an increasingly vocal critic of the administration. Menzies vehemently denounced proposals to liberate or purchase slaves belonging to loyal border-state Unionists. He also attempted to weaken the measure that in April 1862 abolished slavery in the District of Columbia. In May 1862, Menzies bitterly attacked the Second Confiscation Act, which became law in July. He asserted that he was prepared to hang rebels, but not thereafter to sequester the slaves of their wives or minor children.

Among the most outspoken of the Kentucky Unionists, Menzies consistently adhered to the principles enunciated by the July 1861 Crittenden Resolution, in which Congress declared its determination to preserve the Constitution and the

Union, but not to subjugate the South or interfere with slavery. His dilemma was that of many conservative border-state loyalists, who found it difficult to adapt to revolutionary changes in the American social and political environment. Defeated for reelection, Menzies resumed his Covington law practice. He was a delegate to the 1864 Democratic National Convention in Chicago. From 1873 to 1893 he served as a chancery judge. Menzies died in Falmouth, Kentucky, on October 3, 1897. *Biographical Encyclopedia of Kentucky.*

Richard G. Stone

MEREDITH, Solomon, *general*, was born on May 29, 1810, in Guilford county, North Carolina, and at age nineteen moved to Wayne county, Indiana. He was elected sheriff in 1834, and to four terms in the state legislature. In 1849, he was appointed U.S. marshal. In July 1861 Meredith's staunch support of the Republican party, and his close friendship with Governor Oliver H.P. Morton (*q.v.*), helped him gain the colonelcy of the newly formed 19th Indiana Volunteers, whose men had unanimously chosen him for that position.

Meredith saw his first major action at Brawner Farm (or Groveton), Virginia, on August 28, 1862; his Hoosiers, part of General John Gibbon's (*q.v.*) Iron Brigade, performed well in a costly standoff battle with Stonewall Jackson. Meredith was injured in a fall from his horse, and following the action at South Mountain on September 14, took a brief leave to recuperate. Returning to Indiana, he lobbied for a brigade command, and upon learning of Gibbon's promotion, used his political connections to secure the leadership of the Iron Brigade, much to Gibbon's chagrin. Although relieved of his command at Fredericksburg under unclear circumstances, he was quickly restored, and performed creditably at Chancellorsville.

At Gettysburg, Meredith had his finest hour, as his brigade played a key role in defending McPherson's Ridge on July 1. Early in the action, while leading his men in an attack, he was severely wounded and, like his unit, rendered largely unfit for further service. In the spring of 1864 he accepted a post at Cairo, Illinois, and that September was transferred to Paducah, Kentucky, where he remained until war's end. From 1867 to 1869 Meredith served as surveyor general of Montana Territory, then returned to his farm near Cambridge City, Indiana, where he died on October 2, 1875. Nolan, *Iron Brigade.*

Walter L. Powell

MEREDITH, Sullivan Amory, *general*, was born on July 4, 1816, in Philadelphia. In business in Philadelphia at the war's start, he was made colonel of the 10th Pennsylvania, a militia unit, and supervised the training and equipping of over 30,000 men. He then participated in the unsuccessful campaign of Robert Patterson. In 1862, Meredith organized and became colonel of the 56th Pennsylvania Infantry. It served as part of Irvin McDowell's (*q.v.*) III Corps in the battle of Second Bull Run, in which he was seriously wounded. On November 29, 1862, he was promoted to brigadier general of Volunteers. When partially recovered from his wounds, Meredith was appointed agent for prisoner exchange on July 25, 1863. He continued and sharpened ongoing controversies with the Confederate exchange commissioner over the counting of paroled and ex-changed prisoners, and over the status of black soldiers and their white officers. The outcome was a deadlock and the continued breakdown of exchange.

In January 1864, Benjamin F. Butler (*q.v.*), the department commander at Fort Monroe, replaced Meredith as exchange agent. After acting briefly under Butler's instructions, Meredith was ordered to St. Louis to report to William S. Rosecrans (*q.v.*). Mustered out there on August 25, 1865, he remained in St. Louis and acted as commissioner of exchanged prisoners. He moved in 1866 to Buffalo, New York, where he went into the wholesale drug business. He died there on December 26, 1874. Hesseltine, *Civil War Prisons.*

Frank L. Byrne

MERRITT, Wesley, *general*, was born in New York City on June 16, 1834, and graduated from West Point in 1860. After serving as aide-de-camp to cav-alry leaders Philip Cooke and George Stoneman (*q.v.*), he was given command of the Reserve Cavalry Brigade, served at Chancellorsville and Gettysburg, and was promoted to brigadier general. He became an aggressive division com-mander under Alfred Torbert (*q.v.*) in Philip Sheridan's (*q.v.*) army, and played a major role in the victories at Winchester, Tom's Brook, and Cedar Creek— where he led a counterattack that reversed the battle. Merritt's troopers took part in the destruction of the Shenandoah Valley, after which he replaced Torbert as commander of Sheridan's cavalry corps and participated in the victory at Five Forks. He was promoted to major general but accepted the lieutenant colonelcy of the 9th Cavalry after the war.

In 1876, Merritt was promoted to colonel of the 5th Cavalry. He served as superintendent of West Point (1882–1887); commanded the Departments of Mis-souri, Dakota, and the East (1887–1897); and was promoted to major general in the Regular Army. In May 1898, with the outbreak of the Spanish–American War, Merritt organized and sailed with an expedition to consolidate the Amer-ican position in the Philippines. Although he found the Spanish garrison of Manila surrounded by the guerrillas of Emilio Aguinaldo, he captured the city on August 13, and on August 14 established military government in the islands. Merritt was ordered to Paris to participate in negotiating the treaty that ended the war, resumed command of the Department of the East, and retired in June 1900. He died at Natural Bridge, Virginia, on December 3, 1910. Sheridan, *Mem-oirs*; Starr, *Union Cavalry*, vols. 1, 2.

Roy P. Stonesifer, Jr.

MIDDLETON, George, *congressman*, was born in Philadelphia on October 14, 1800. He developed a tanning business in Burlington, New Jersey, and later moved it to Allentown, not far from Trenton. Middleton was elected as a Dem-ocrat to two terms in the state legislature and unsuccessfully sought nomination for a congressional seat in 1860. In 1862, he secured the nomination after four ballots at the Democratic district convention. The Republicans, instead of renominating the incumbent, John L.N. Stratton (*q.v.*), honored the "rotation principle" by selecting William F. Brown. Republicans also suffered a disproportionate erosion of strength because New Jersey soldiers had no way to cast absentee ballots.

Middleton, a member of the Society of Friends who quite likely was able to gain some support from other members of this usually anti-Democratic religious group, won by a margin of over 1,300 votes. He was among a small minority of House Democrats in the 38th Congress who gave unequivocal support to the war; in January 1865 his conspicuous absence during a crucial House vote on the 13th Amendment helped its supporters gather a narrow two-thirds' majority. Middleton was renominated in 1864, though his candidacy drew some opposition from Peace Democrats. Republicans nominated the popular former governor, William A. Newell, who gained the seat by about 200 votes. The defeat marked the end of Middleton's modest political career. He died in Allentown on December 31, 1888. *BDUSC.*

Daniel W. Crofts

MILES, Nelson Appleton, *general,* was born on August 8, 1839, near Westminster, Massachusetts. He was commissioned a 1st lieutenant in the 22nd Massachusetts Volunteers on September 9, 1861, and was later promoted to lieutenant colonel of the 61st New York. On May 12, 1864, he became a brigadier general, then was breveted major general of U.S. Volunteers (August 1864). Miles's service during the Civil War included the Peninsula campaign, where he served on General Oliver O. Howard's (*q.v.*) staff, Antietam, Fredericksburg, Chancellorsville, the Wilderness, Spotsylvania, Petersburg, and the Appomattox campaign. He was wounded four times during the war: at Fair Oaks during the Peninsula campaign, at Fredericksburg (where he was shot in the throat), at Chancellorsville, and at Petersburg. In 1892, Congress awarded him the Medal of Honor for his bravery at Chancellorsville.

When the war ended, Miles received a commission in the Regular Army as the colonel of the 40th U.S. Infantry, an African American regiment. He also served at Fortress Monroe, where he supervised the imprisonment of Jefferson Davis. By 1895, he had become the general in chief of the U.S. Army. Miles retired from the army on August 8, 1903. His career was one of the most remarkable in American military history, lasting through four wars: the Civil War, the Indian campaigns, the Spanish–American War and the Philippine insurrection. He died on May 15, 1925, in Washington, D.C. Sommers, *Richmond Redeemed*; Wooster, *Nelson A. Miles.*

Frank J. Wetta

MILLER, Samuel Franklin, *congressman,* was born on May 27, 1827, in Franklin, New York. He graduated from Hamilton College in 1852, studied law, and was admitted to the bar in 1853. He devoted little time to his law practice, however, remaining actively involved in farming and lumbering, and serving as a colonel in the state militia. Miller's political career began in 1850, with his election as a town supervisor in Franklin, a post he held for most of the 1850s. In 1854, he was elected to the legislature, and served one term. A worsening case of rheumatism kept Miller from joining the Union Army, but he was elected as a Republican to the 38th Congress in 1862.

After one term, Miller returned to Franklin and continued farming and lumbering. By 1867, when he participated in the New York Constitutional Convention, he was forced to use crutches to reach the speaker's platform. In 1869, Miller was appointed district collector of internal revenue and a member of the state Board of Charities. He resigned his position as collector in 1873, and was elected to the 44th Congress in 1874. Miller died in Franklin on March 16, 1892. *Biographical Review . . . of Delaware County.*

Lori A. Lisowski

MILLER, Samuel Freeman, *Supreme Court justice,* was born on April 5, 1816, in Richmond, Kentucky. He received his M.D. degree in 1838 from Transylvania University. Bored by routine medical practice, Miller began reading law, and in 1847 was admitted to the county bar. His belief in the gradual emancipation of the slaves made a successful political career in his native state impossible, so in 1850 he moved to Keokuk, Iowa. Like many other successful frontier lawyers, Miller prospered by litigating disputed land titles. A loyal Whig who worshiped Henry Clay, he exemplified the moderate reformism of his day. Outraged by the Kansas–Nebraska Act, he joined the new Republican party and became a diligent organizer.

By the eve of the Civil War, Miller was a leading figure in Iowa Republican circles and an enthusiastic supporter of Abraham Lincoln (*q.v.*). Nevertheless, it took the complex rearrangement of judicial circuits by Congress, and a strong lobbying effort by influential Iowans, to secure him a seat on the U.S. Supreme Court. When Lincoln submitted the nomination on July 16, 1862, Miller was unknown in most of the country. Although seemingly a plain, jovial country lawyer, he possessed a splendid legal mind and a talent for drafting precise, clear, and forceful opinions. Miller's vote was critical in a 5–4 decision upholding the constitutionality of Lincoln's blockade proclamation in the Prize Cases. He defended the Federal loyalty oath in two postwar cases, but he generally followed his fellow justices in avoiding judicial entanglement in sectional questions and in narrowly construing the rights secured to black Americans by the postwar constitutional amendments.

Miller was often suspicious of the new industrial capitalists and their motives. He believed the states should not use their taxing power to subsidize private corporations, and in the Slaughterhouse Cases adopted a limited interpretation of the 14th Amendment that precluded using substantive due process to protect business interests. Twice passed over for Chief Justice, Miller may have had presidential ambitions. He died in Washington, D.C., on October 13, 1890. Fairman, *Mr. Justice Miller.*

George C. Rable

MILLER, Stephen, *governor,* was born on January 17, 1816, in Perry, Pennsylvania. He attended local common schools; worked in Harrisburg as a clerk, forwarding agent, temperance lecturer, and editor of a Whig weekly; then served from 1855 to 1858 as flour inspector of Philadelphia. He moved to St. Cloud, Minnesota, in 1858 and opened a general store. Brought into Minnesota Republican politics by his old friend Alexander Ramsey (*q.v.*), Miller served as a national convention delegate and Lincoln elector in 1860.

When war came, Miller joined the 1st Minnesota as a private, but was quickly promoted by Ramsey to the rank of lieutenant colonel. He commanded the regiment's right flank at Bull Run, earning respect for mounting a charge against Beauregard's forces during the Union retreat. Miller also saw action at Yorktown, West Point, Fair Oaks, the Peach Orchard, Savage Station, Nelson's Farm, and Malvern Hill, where he sustained serious injuries in a fall from his horse. He was then promoted to colonel and given command of the 7th Minnesota, stationed at Camp Lincoln, near Mankato, where 300 Sioux warriors condemned for the 1862 uprising were imprisoned. After preventing a mass lynching by a vigilante mob, Miller presided over the hanging of thirty-eight of the Sioux on December 26, 1862, then supervised the establishment of a network of forts along the Minnesota frontier to prevent further Indian attacks.

Miller received the Republican gubernatorial nomination in August 1863, was given a patently political promotion to brigadier general by Abraham Lincoln (*q.v.*), then easily defeated his Democratic rival in November. As Minnesota's governor during the last sixteen months of the war, he worked to fill enlistment quotas and, with little success, to enforce conscription quotas. He did not seek reelection in 1865, partly because two sons had been implicated in a California postal scandal. Miller's last years were marked by prolonged periods of unemployment, heavy drinking, poverty, and poor health. He served as a state legislator in 1873, and as an elector for Rutherford B. Hayes (*q.v.*) in 1876. He died in Worthington, Minnesota, on August 18, 1881. Folwell, *History of Minnesota,* vol. 2; Imholte, *First Volunteers.*

Roger A. Fischer

MILLER, William Henry, *congressman,* was born in Landisburg, Pennsylvania, on February 28, 1829. He graduated from Franklin and Marshall College in 1846, studied law, and began his practice in Harrisburg. In 1854, he became clerk of the Pennsylvania Supreme Court and served in that capacity until 1863. From 1858 to 1859, Miller also held the post of clerk of the state Senate. In 1862 he was elected as a Democrat to the 38th Congress, defeating the Union candidate by a slim majority. Miller opposed legislation supporting the Northern war effort, voted consistently against conscription bills, opposed the Wade–

Davis Bill, and protested the 13th Amendment. When Congress passed the Freedmen's Bureau Bill, Miller voted against it.

Miller directed his strongest criticism toward his fellow Pennsylvania Democrats, Alexander H. Coffroth (*q.v.*) and Archibald McAllister (*q.v.*), who had earlier declared their support for the 13th Amendment, and whose votes contributed to its passage. He had won his seat in 1862 on a wave of antiwar sentiment that swept though Pennsylvania, and lost it by a similar margin in 1864, when the Democratic share of the vote dropped significantly throughout the state. At the conclusion of his term, Miller resumed his law practice. He died in Harrisburg, Pennsylvania, on September 12, 1870. Shankman, *Pennsylvania Antiwar Movement.*

Philip J. Avillo, Jr.

MILLIGAN, Lambdin P., *lawyer,* was born in Belmont county, Ohio, on March 24, 1812. After ten years as a lawyer in Belmont county, he moved to Huntington, Indiana, in 1845. He was active in county politics as a confirmed Democrat and a strict constitutionalist. Milligan opposed the Civil War from the beginning, calling himself "a free trader" who detested New England's *isms* (abolitionism, prohibitionism, Know-Nothingism, and protectionism). He dominated the Democratic county convention that adopted antiwar resolutions in August 1861, but at the Democratic state convention in January 1862 his bid to become a congressional nominee failed. When Alexander J. Douglas, a state senator, was arrested in May 1863 for antiwar utterances, and was tried before a military commission in Cincinnati, Milligan served as his lawyer, arguing unsuccessfully that a military court had no right to try a civilian when the civil courts were open.

Friends promoted Milligan as a gubernatorial nominee at the Democratic state convention in July 1864 but failed. General Alvin P. Hovey (*q.v.*), at the urging of Indiana Governor Oliver H. P. Morton (*q.v.*), arrested Milligan and others on October 5, 1864, and charged them with "disloyal practices," engaging in a conspiracy, and belonging to the Sons of Liberty. As far as Milligan was concerned, the charges were false and the conspiracy a Republican fantasy. In the second Indianapolis "treason trial," begun in January 1865, a military commission found four of the prisoners guilty, and three (including Milligan) were sentenced to be hanged. Milligan's lawyer sought a writ of habeas corpus in the U.S. Circuit Court, and the execution of the three was postponed.

In early 1866, Associate Justice David Davis (*q.v.*) wrote the majority decision in *Ex Parte Milligan,* declaring the military trial invalid. After an imprisonment of eighteen months, Milligan returned to Huntington, Indiana, and, seeking revenge against those responsible for his arrest, sued twenty-four persons for $500,000. The case went through several name changes, eventually evolving into *Milligan* v. *Hovey.* The jury ruled in Milligan's favor, but Indiana law limited damages to $5.00 in such cases. He died on December 21, 1899. Kelley,

Milligan's Fight Against Lincoln; Frank L. Klement, "The Indianapolis Treason Trials and *Ex Parte Milligan*," in Belknap, *American Political Trials*, pp. 101–128.

Frank L. Klement

MILROY, Robert Huston, *general,* was born on June 11, 1816, near Salem, Indiana; his family moved to Delphi, Indiana, in 1826. He graduated from Norwich University in Vermont in 1843. Thwarted in his efforts to gain either appointment to West Point or a military commission, he turned to the law, graduating from Indiana University with a law degree in 1850. His earlier Volunteer service (1846–1847) in the Mexican War had earned Milroy no distinction, and his legal career was equally routine. He was a member of the second Indiana Constitutional Convention, and became a circuit judge in 1852.

With the outbreak of the Civil War, Milroy was made colonel of the 9th Indiana Volunteer Infantry. Dubbed the "Gray Eagle," he saw early field service in West Virginia and rapidly rose to the rank of major general. As a political general and an abolitionist, Milroy subscribed to a style of warfare wherein spirit counted for more than discipline. He was impatient with system, authority, and "scientific" warfare; rushed into frequent disputes with fellow officers; and exhibited an impulsive, excited courage that West Pointers looked upon as walleyed frenzy. He had an abiding hatred for West Point generally, which focused on the person of Henry W. Halleck (*q.v.*), whose own contempt for Milroy was nearly perfect. In West Virginia, his stern measures against secessionists resulted in a "dead or alive" reward being placed on his head.

Nevertheless, overwhelming testimony exists in praise of Milroy's courage, devotion, and truthfulness. He loved combat and was respected by his soldiers. In 1863, his command was surprised and surrounded at Winchester, Virginia, during Robert E. Lee's invasion of the North. This disaster led to a board of inquiry that, although it exonerated Milroy, marked the effective end of his military hopes. Shortly after the war, Milroy became a trustee of the Wabash & Erie Canal. In 1872, he accepted a position as superintendent of Indian affairs in the state of Washington, and subsequently became Indian agent at Olympia, Washington, where he died on March 29, 1890. Hennessy, *Return to Bull Run.*

Jack Nortrup

MITCHEL, Ormsby MacKnight, *general,* was born July 28, 1809, in Union county, Kentucky; in 1816 his family moved to Lebanon, Ohio. Although his schooling was sporadic, he had unusual facility in mathematics, which apparently was his motivation for entering West Point, from which he graduated in 1829. For two years Mitchel taught mathematics at the Academy, read law, and worked on surveys of two railroads in Pennsylvania. After service at St. Augustine, Florida, he resigned his commission on July 30, 1832, moved to Cincinnati, and opened a law office. His major interest was science, and from 1836 to 1844, he taught mathematics and astronomy at Cincinnati College. In the winter of 1842–1843, Mitchel's public lectures on astronomy aroused such enthusiasm that he raised enough money to buy a refracting lens in Munich and build the first major observatory in America. His lectures on astronomy were very popular in Boston and New York, and in 1860 he became director of Dudley Observatory in Albany, New York, which he had helped design.

On August 9, 1861, Abraham Lincoln (*q.v.*) appointed Mitchel brigadier general and commander of the Department of the Ohio. During the autumn, he supervised the defense of Cincinnati. After William T. Sherman (*q.v.*) rejected his proposal to invade East Tennessee and seize the East Tennessee & Virginia Railroad, he resigned his commission. His resignation was refused, and he was assigned to command the 3rd Division in the army being organized under Don Carlos Buell (*q.v.*). After occupying Shelbyville, Tennessee, on March 28, 1862, Mitchel led his troops to Huntsville, Alabama, which he entered on April 11, covering fifty-seven miles in forty-eight hours and capturing the Memphis & Charleston Railroad. (Twenty-four men from his command came to be known as the Andrews Raiders, or occasionally as the Mitchel Raiders.) In late June, Buell inspected Mitchel's command at Huntsville, where he found discipline lax and was also incensed by the fact that Mitchel communicated directly with the Secretary of War.

Mitchel again submitted his resignation, and he was assigned a shadow command with the rather grandiose designation of Department of the South, at Hilton Head, South Carolina. His one military exploit, the capture of Huntsville, which earned him promotion to major general, was conducted with enterprise and daring. He recognized the importance of rail transport sooner than most Northern leaders, and his technical knowledge might have proved valuable in the Shenandoah Valley or in Georgia, but his vanity and impetuosity make it doubtful that he could have served effectively for long under Sherman, Philip Sheridan (*q.v.*), or anyone else. Mitchel died of yellow fever on October 30, 1862, in Beaufort, South Carolina. Mitchel, *Ormsby MacKnight Mitchel*; Reid, *Ohio in the War*, vol. 1.

William Coyle

MITCHELL, William, *congressman*, was born on January 19, 1807, in Root, New York. He attended common schools, studied law, and was admitted to the bar in 1836. That same year, he moved to Kendallville, Indiana, and established his law practice. On December 7, 1836, Mitchell was appointed the first postmaster of Kendallville, a position he held until March 1846 and again from 1849 to 1851. He represented Lagrange and Noble counties in Indiana's House of Representatives (1841), and also served as a justice of the peace. Mitchell won election as a Republican to the 37th Congress, but was an unsuccessful candidate for reelection. Afterward, he became involved in the cotton business. He died in Macon, Georgia, on September 11, 1865. Shepherd, *Biographical Directory of the Indiana General Assembly*, vol. 1.

David G. Vanderstel

MONTGOMERY, James, *colonel,* was born in Ashtabula county, Ohio, on December 22, 1814. As a youth he moved to Kentucky, where he taught school for twelve years, thence to Missouri, and in 1854 to the Kansas Territory. By then, he had become a true Jayhawker—a rabid abolitionist who believed that "the South should be devastated with fire & sword." In 1855, Montgomery joined other militants, such as John Brown (*q.v.*) and Charles R. Jennison, in raiding proslavery settlements. In 1859, he led an unsuccessful mission to rescue Brown from the gallows.

In 1861, Governor Charles Robinson (*q.v.*) of Kansas commissioned Montgomery colonel of the 3rd Kansas Volunteers, part of a brigade led by Senator James H. Lane (*q.v.*). At intervals Montgomery commanded the brigade as well as the garrison at Fort Scott. He spent several months fending off Confederate raids into Kansas and leading retaliatory strikes across the Missouri border. Late in 1862, Montgomery secured authority to organize and command one of five African American regiments being raised in the Department of the South. Soon he was leading the 2nd South Carolina Volunteers against Confederate enclaves in Florida and Georgia. In June 1863 he created controversy by shelling and burning Darien, Georgia. Later he commanded a brigade of blacks outside Charleston and in the February 1864 battle of Olustee, Florida. Montgomery returned to Missouri to lead a Kansas militia regiment in curtailing Sterling Price's raid of September–October 1864. He spent his postwar years in uncharacteristic quietude, dying in Linn county, Kansas, on December 6, 1871. Castel, *Frontier State at War*; Shaw, *Blue-eyed Child of Fortune.*

Edward G. Longacre

MOORHEAD, James Kennedy, *congressman,* was born in Halifax, Pennsylvania, on September 7, 1806. He attended public schools, was a tanner's apprentice, and with borrowed capital, became a canal contractor on the Susquehanna division of the Pennsylvania Canal. In 1838, he founded a packet company that offered passenger service between Philadelphia and Pittsburgh. Moorhead moved to Pittsburgh, where he became a wealthy and influential businessman, particularly in the development of river navigation and in the telegraphic industry. A leader within the Democratic party, he was, briefly, named adjutant general of the state and deputy postmaster of Pittsburgh.

In the mid-1850s, Moorhead joined the Know-Nothing party and participated in the fusion that led to the Republican domination of the city. In 1858, he was elected to the 36th Congress, and reelected to four additional terms. During the secession crisis, Moorhead was a party regular. However, during the Civil War and Reconstruction era, he voted with the Radical faction on every major issue. A strong protectionist, he was a persistent protariff force in Congress on the Manufactures Committee, which he chaired for three terms. A delegate to the Republican National Convention in 1868, Moorhead was also a candidate for the U.S. Senate in 1869 and 1880. From 1877 until his death in Pittsburgh on

March 6, 1884, he was president of the Pittsburgh Chamber of Commerce. Benedict, *Compromise of Principle*; Holt, *Forging a Majority*.

J. K. Folmar

MORAN, Benjamin, *diplomat,* was born in Chester county, Pennsylvania, on August 1, 1820. He became a printer in Philadelphia, and began to write articles and essays for magazines. In 1851 and 1852, he journeyed throughout Great Britain, supporting himself by publishing travel sketches in American journals. When James Buchanan (*q.v.*), with whom his father had transacted business, became U.S. minister in London, Moran became first a legation clerk and then, in 1854, Buchanan's private secretary. When the Civil War began, he was second secretary of the London legation under Minister George Dallas, and he remained in that office under Charles Francis Adams (*q.v.*).

During the war years, Moran proved an industrious worker, heavily relied upon by Adams for his detailed knowledge of British customs, diplomatic lore, and legation archives. His voluminous *Journal*, covering the years 1857 to 1874 (published only through 1865), is one of the most important source documents for Civil War diplomatic history. In 1864, he was promoted to first secretary of the legation, an office he continued to occupy for the next decade. The *London Times* described him, at the time of his departure, in December 1874, to become U.S. minister in Portugal, as the "ablest and most honest" representative the United States had ever sent to England. Moran remained in Lisbon (as chargé d'affaires after 1876) until 1882. He died in Braintree, Essex, England, on June 21, 1886. Moran, *Journal.*

Norman B. Ferris

MORELL, George Webb, *general,* was born in Cooperstown, New York, on January 8, 1815. He graduated first in his class at West Point in 1835, and after two years in the engineers, resigned to work in railroad construction. In 1842, he became a lawyer and practiced in New York City until the Civil War began. He was a staff officer in the New York militia and in the defenses of Washington until August 9, 1861, when he was named a brigadier general of Volunteers. During the Peninsula campaign he was a brigade and division commander. Although his division was overwhelmed at Gaines' Mill, Morell proved himself a competent and inspirational leader. At Malvern Hill, his division held its position, again at a high cost. He had lost 3,136 men in two battles, the most of any of the divisions in Fitz John Porter's (*q.v.*) V Corps.

In the Second Bull Run campaign, Morell's division, with the rest of the army, was victimized by John Pope's (*q.v.*) vagaries and Porter's petulance. At Antietam, Morell's division was in the tactical reserve, and at one point he was to relieve Ambrose Burnside (*q.v.*) if that general did not move with greater enthusiasm. After Antietam, Morell was caught up in the Fitz John Porter controversy and saw no further service in the field. He commanded the defenses of the capital and a draft rendezvous until he left the service on December 15,

1864. Morell lived in Scarborough, New York, until his death there on February 11, 1883. Hennessy, *Return to Bull Run*; Sears, *Landscape Turned Red*; Sears, *To the Gates of Richmond.*

John T. Hubbell

MORGAN, Edwin Denison, *governor, senator*, was born on February 8, 1811, in Washington, Massachusetts. In 1822, his family moved to Windsor, Connecticut, and in 1829 Morgan went to Hartford to clerk in his uncle's grocery. Shortly afterward, he became a partner in the grocery and a member of the city council. In 1836 he left for New York City, where he amassed a fortune in wholesale groceries, banking, and brokerage. In 1849, Morgan became active in Whig politics, and was a two-term state senator and a commissioner of immigration. He was an early Republican and served as the party's chairman from 1856 to 1864. Morgan was elected governor by a slight plurality in 1858, and two years later won by the largest majority of any candidate to that point. He favored a policy of moderation, conciliation, and compromise to save the Union, but when those failed, he proved an effective war governor. He helped the state raise its early quota of seventeen regiments, and President Abraham Lincoln (*q.v.*) appointed him, on September 28, 1861, a major general of Volunteers and commander of the New York Military District.

By the time Morgan retired from office in 1862, because of the state's no-third-term tradition, he had assisted in enrolling and equipping 223,000 soldiers in 120 regiments. In 1863, he won a U.S. Senate seat over fierce Radical opposition. Although he sponsored little legislation, Morgan was a member of several influential committees, including the Congressional Campaign Committee, of which he was cochairman. During the early stages of Reconstruction, he backed President Andrew Johnson (*q.v.*), but soon broke with him and eventually supported impeachment.

In 1869, Morgan lost his reelection bid, under questionable circumstances, to the Radical Reuben Fenton (*q.v.*). The remainder of his political career was anticlimactic. Although he served as Republican national chairman from 1872 to 1876, he failed to secure another senatorial nomination in 1875, and was defeated for governor in 1876. After these setbacks, Morgan spent his remaining years in philanthrophic activities. He died in New York City on February 14, 1883. Benedict, *Compromise of Principle*; Rawley, *Edwin D. Morgan.*

Jerome Mushkat

MORGAN, George Washington, *general*, was born in Washington county, Pennsylvania, on September 20, 1820. He attended West Point but resigned in 1843 because of academic problems. After studying law, he became prosecutor of Knox county, Ohio, and in 1846 was named colonel of the 2nd Ohio Volunteers in the Mexican War. He served with Zachary Taylor until March 3, 1847, when he was appointed colonel of the 15th U.S. Infantry. During Winfield Scott's (*q.v.*) advance on Mexico City, Morgan was breveted brigadier general for gallantry at Contreras and Churubusco. After leaving the Army in 1848, he was an attorney in Mt. Vernon, Ohio, U.S. consul at Marseilles, and minister to Portugal.

In November 1861, Morgan was commissioned a brigadier general of Volunteers. He commanded a division in the Army of the Ohio at Cumberland Gap, a division under William T. Sherman (*q.v.*) at Chickasaw Bayou, and the XIII Corps at the capture of Arkansas Post. In the aftermath of the bitter Union defeat at Chickasaw Bayou, Sherman criticized Morgan for his handling of his division, suggesting that if Morgan had been more aggressive, he could have carried the day. The hard feelings remained, although Sherman insisted that he was confident of Morgan's abilities and devotion to the Union cause. Morgan held that his division had paid the price for an ill-advised assault.

Morgan's considerable military career ended with his resignation on June 8, 1863. The ostensible reason was his objection to the plan to recruit black soldiers, but his resentment toward Sherman emerged in his account of Chickasaw Bayou in *Battles and Leaders*. Morgan became an open and ardent Democrat, supported George B. McClellan (*q.v.*) in the election of 1864, and served three terms in Congress, where he strongly opposed Radical Reconstruction. He died at Fort Monroe, Virginia, on July 26, 1893. Bearss, *Vicksburg Campaign*, vol. 1; Williams, *Lincoln Finds a General*, vols. 3, 4.

John T. Hubbell

MORRILL, Anson Peaslee, *congressman,* was born in Belgrade, Maine, on June 10, 1803. Educated in local schools, he became postmaster of Dearborn, Maine, and kept a general store. In 1844, he settled in Readfield, where he purchased a nearly bankrupt woolen mill. He made the mill profitable, and was financially comfortable for life. Morrill entered politics in 1834, winning a Maine House seat as a Democrat. He was sheriff of Somerset county (1839–1840) and state land agent (1850–1853). After breaking with the Democracy on the temperance issue in 1853, Morrill ran unsuccessfully for governor as an Independent, supported by ''Morrill Democrats.'' In 1854, he was Maine's Anti-Nebraska candidate and won 44,000 votes to 28,000 for his nearest opponent. Four candidates in the field prevented his winning a majority, but the legislature made Morrill the first Republican governor of Maine in January 1855.

Morrill won a seat in Congress in 1860 but declined to stand for reelection, making way for his close friend James G. Blaine (*q.v.*), who had swallowed his own ambitions in deference to Morrill two years earlier. Except for a single legislative term (1881–1882), Morrill's political career was over. From 1871 until his retirement from business, he headed the Maine Central Railroad. An honest, rugged, independent-minded, salt-of-the-earth Mainer, Morrill helped popularize temperance and antislavery in Maine, and played a key role in laying the foundations of the Maine Republican party, which effectively dominated the state for a century. He died on July 4, 1887, in Augusta. Hatch, *Maine: A History*, vols. 2, 3; Moulton, *Memorials of Maine.*

H. Draper Hunt

MORRILL, Justin Smith, *congressman,* was born in Strafford, Vermont, on April 14, 1810. He amassed a fortune large enough for him to retire by 1848. Subsequently, he expanded his efforts for the Whig party and rose rapidly within the state organization. In 1854, Morrill entered his first election and won a seat in the U.S. House as an antislavery Whig and temperance advocate. Converting to Republicanism even before taking his seat, Morrill remained in the House until he was elected to the Senate in 1866, and served there until his death in 1898. His forty-three years in Congress established a record for longevity.

Morrill made his most significant contributions in the House, where his adeptness at parliamentary maneuvering assured him a leadership position. Appointed to the Ways and Means Committee in 1858, he relinquished an opportunity to become chairman in favor of Thaddeus Stevens (*q.v.*). He did become chairman in 1865, however, and served on the Joint Committee on Reconstruction. An ardent protectionist, Morrill opposed the low tariff bill of 1857 and gained the animosity of the South for the high ''Morrill Tariff'' of 1861. His most celebrated legislative achievement was the 1862 Land Grant College Act. He had introduced similar legislation in 1858, but Southern opposition, and eventually President James Buchanan's (*q.v.*) veto, kept it from becoming law.

As a senator, Morrill voted Andrew Johnson (*q.v.*) ''guilty'' in the impeachment trial, and became the embodiment of the Republican domestic legislative program. As chairman of the Banking and Finance Committee, he opposed inflationary policies, and as a member of the Buildings and Grounds Committee, placed his imprint on the Washington Monument, the Library of Congress, and Statary Hall. Always a stern moralist, in his later career he was closely associated with the Mugwump faction. Morrill died in Washington, D.C., on December 28, 1898. Parker, *Life and Public Service of Justin Smith Morrill.*

D. Gregory Sanford

MORRILL, Lot Myrick, *senator,* was born on May 3, 1813, in Belgrade, Maine. His older brother, Anson P. Morrill (*q.v.*), became Maine's first Republican governor in 1855. Lot attended local schools and Belgrade Academy, and enrolled in Waterville College (now Colby). He soon left college to spend a year as a private school principal in New York, then returned to Maine to read for the law. Admitted to the bar in 1839, Morrill moved in 1841 to Augusta, where he specialized in work before legislative committees and built one of Maine's most distinguished law practices. He chaired the Democratic State Committee from 1849 to 1856 and served in the Maine House in 1854 and the Senate in 1856 (he was elected president of the latter). However, he opposed further concessions to the South on slavery and broke with the Democrats over the Cincinnati platform (1856), which endorsed popular sovereignty. As a Republican, Morrill became governor of Maine in 1858, winning two additional terms. As legislator and governor, he strongly resisted repeal of Maine's prohibition law.

In January 1861 the legislature chose Morrill to succeed U.S. Senator Hannibal Hamlin (*q.v.*), who had become Vice President. Morrill served as a Maine delegate to the February 1861 Peace Convention in Washington and ably opposed its compromise resolutions. During the Civil War, he supported a bill to confiscate slaves of rebels, strongly endorsed the Emancipation Proclamation, and, as chairman of the Senate District of Columbia Committee, championed a bill to emancipate slaves in the District. After the war, he fought for black suffrage, strongly supported Congressional Reconstruction, and, unlike his colleague William Pitt Fessenden (*q.v.*), voted to convict President Andrew Johnson (*q.v.*). As chairman of the Senate Committee on Indian Affairs, he became well known as a loyal supporter of Indian rights.

Morrill won a full Senate term in 1863, but found himself pitted against the redoubtable Hannibal Hamlin (*q.v.*) in 1869 and lost his seat by a single vote. Fessenden's death that same year restored Morrill to his former place, however, and he was reelected in 1871. President Ulysses S. Grant (*q.v.*) made Morrill Secretary of the Treasury in July 1876 (earlier he had declined the War portfolio), and he proved a most able Treasury head, aided by his experience as chairman of the Senate Appropriations Committee. President Rutherford B. Hayes (*q.v.*) offered the British ministership to Morrill in March 1877, but he declined for health reasons. Morrill accepted the collectorship of Portland, Maine, which he held until his death there on January 10, 1883. Hatch, *Maine: A History*, vols. 2, 3; Hunt, *Hannibal Hamlin*; Moulton, *Memorials of Maine*.

H. Draper Hunt

MORRIS, Daniel, *congressman,* was born in Fayette, New York, on January 4, 1812. He attended public school and the Canandaigua Academy, worked as a farmer and schoolteacher, studied law, and was admitted to the bar in 1845. He began practicing in Rushville and then moved to Penn Yan in Yates county, where he was elected district attorney in 1847. Morris joined the Republican party, and in 1859 was elected to the legislature for one term. In 1862, he won a seat in the 38th Congress, where his legal reputation gained him a place on the Judiciary Committee. He also took a special interest in the sick and wounded soldiers of his district, and was outspoken in favor of emancipation. After serving two terms in Congress, Morris declined another nomination and returned to his law practice in Penn Yan, where he died on April 22, 1889. Aldrich, *History of Yates County.*

Lori A. Lisowski

MORRIS, Edward Joy, *congressman, diplomat,* was born in Philadelphia on July 16, 1815. He attended the University of Pennsylvania, and graduated from

Harvard in 1836. He became a lawyer in Philadelphia, then served in the Pennsylvania lower house (1841–1843) and in the U.S. House of Representatives (1843–1845). Morris's erudition and politics obviously helped him to gain an appointment as chargé d'affaires in Naples (1850–1853). He was one of the principal organizers of the Republican party in Philadelphia, and was elected to Congress in 1856, where he became an outspoken advocate of a high tariff. He was reelected in 1858 and 1860.

As a member of the Simon Cameron (*q.v.*) faction of the Pennsylvania Republican party, Morris benefited from the patronage that Cameron had at his disposal. At Cameron's insistence, he received an appointment as minister to Turkey in 1861. His previous travels in the Middle East, and his foreign service experience and education, made him highly qualified for the post.

During his diplomatic tour in that faraway corner of the world, Morris protected the freedom of American trading vessels to sail through the Bosporus and the Dardanelles. In March 1862 the Ottoman government issued an order prohibiting the entrance of privateers or any other class of vessels into the waters of the Ottoman Empire to prey upon American commerce. In addition, in February 1862 Morris was instrumental in the adoption of a new commercial treaty that enhanced trade between the two nations. The treaty lowered export duties from Turkey that American traders had to pay, appointed a new tariff commission to revise rates, and gave the United States a "favored nation" position in Turkish trade. That American exports to Turkey tripled during Morris's tenure suggests he served American commercial interests well.

Morris resigned his post in 1870 and returned to Philadelphia, where he continued to dabble in politics as a Liberal Republican, but held no other public office. He died in Philadelphia on December 31, 1881. Bradley, *Triumph of Militant Republicanism*; Howard, *Turkey, the Straits and U.S. Policy.*

W. Wayne Smith

MORRIS, James Remley, *congressman*, was born in Rodgersville, Pennsylvania, on October 10, 1820; his family moved to Waynesburg, Ohio, in 1829. He studied law, was admitted to the Ohio bar in 1840, and practiced law in Woodsfield. He acquired his interest in politics from his father, Joseph Morris, who was Monroe county treasurer and was elected to the 28th Congress. Young Morris was elected to fill his father's unexpired term as county treasurer. He edited the *Spirit of Democracy*, a local Democratic newspaper, and in 1848 was elected as a Democrat to the Ohio House. Morris was elected to the 37th Congress in 1860, and was reelected to the 38th Congress. He mildly supported Abraham Lincoln's (*q.v.*) war policies and recognized the President's constitutional means to suppress the rebellion. But he also joined forces with Clement L. Vallandigham (*q.v.*) in opposing such measures as the Illinois Ship Canal Bill. Morris was defeated in 1864, returned to Woodsfield, and continued his practice of law. He died in Woodsfield on December 24, 1899. Curry, *Blueprint for Modern America.*

Thomas H. Smith

MORRISON, William Ralls, *congressman,* was born on September 14, 1824, in Prairie du Long, Illinois. Educated at McKendree College, he served in several minor elected offices before enlisting for service in the Mexican War. After panning for gold in California, Morrison returned to Illinois in 1851. He then studied law, was admitted to the bar in 1855, and established a law practice in Waterloo. As a Douglas Democrat, he was a member of the Illinois legislature from 1854 to 1860, serving as its speaker in 1859 and 1860. After the war began, Governor Richard Yates (*q.v.*) asked Morrison to raise a regiment, resulting in the creation of the 49th Illinois Volunteers.

Morrison was elected colonel, and led the regiment at Fort Donelson, where he was severely wounded. He recovered enough to witness the siege at Corinth. In 1862, voters elected Morrison to Congress, where he joined the War Democrats but produced an undistinguished record. He lost his bid for reelection in 1864 by only seventy-five votes; in 1873 he was returned to the 43rd Congress, and remained for six terms. He led the attack against high tariffs and supported bimetallism. From 1887 until 1897, Morrison was a member of the Interstate Commerce Commission and chaired it from March 1892 to December 1897. He returned to his law practice in Waterloo, where he died on September 29, 1909. Robbins, ''Congressional Career of William Ralls Morrison''; Scott, ''Political Career of William R. Morrison,'' *Transactions of the Illinois State Historical Society.*

Thomas F. Schwartz

MORTON, Oliver Hazard Perry Throck, *governor, senator,* was born on August 4, 1823, in Wayne county, Indiana. After attending a local seminary and apprenticing as a hatter, he studied at Miami University (Ohio), read law, and was admitted to the bar in 1846. He established a practice at Centerville before serving out an eight-month term in 1852 as judge of Indiana's 6th Judicial Circuit. Originally an antislavery Democrat, Morton left the party in 1854 over the Kansas–Nebraska issue, and became a leader in the new People's party (forerunner of the Republican party), serving as its first gubernatorial nominee in 1856. Elected lieutenant governor in 1860, Morton became Indiana's fourteenth governor when, under a prearranged agreement, the Republican-dominated state legislature sent newly elected Republican governor Henry S. Lane (*q.v.*) to the U.S. Senate.

Morton, the first native Hoosier to hold the governorship, was an effective spokesman for the Union and Abraham Lincoln's (*q.v.*) conduct of the war. Among his first acts as governor was the appointment of five staunch Republicans to represent Indiana at the Washington, D.C., Peace Conference, directing them to reject any guarantees of slavery. He opposed compromise with the rebellious South, united War Democrats and Republicans in his Union party, and often used unconstitutional means to consolidate his power. In April 1861, determined to demonstrate Indiana's loyalty to the Union, Morton offered Lincoln 10,000 troops "for the defense of the Nation" and called a special legislative session to pass nearly $2 million in military appropriations. He subsequently worked to fill Indiana's quotas, earning the state second place among the Northern states in both absolute numbers and percentage of troops provided to the war effort. The rendezvous point at Indianapolis, for soldiers headed for Federal service, was appropriately called Camp Morton.

Earning the sobriquet "the soldier's friend," Morton was deeply interested in the welfare of Hoosier troops and devised ways of supplying them when regular channels failed. On his own authority, he established a state arsenal at Indianapolis that not only supplied Indiana soldiers but also sold ammunition to the Union government. After Democrats secured a majority in the 1862 legislative elections, the General Assembly sought to strip Morton of his powers and to transfer military authority to Democratic state officials. Republicans, determined to block passage of "obnoxious" Democratic legislation, prevented a quorum in 1863 by abandoning Indianapolis for Madison. When the Republican minority refused to return, and the legislature adjourned without making budgetary appropriations, Morton conducted state affairs on his own until January 1865, using funds generated by the state arsenal, appropriated by county governments, and borrowed from private and public sources.

Morton considered Democratic challenges to his authority to be treasonous, charged secret societies with planning to seize the state and secede from the Union, and advocated the suppression of opposition newspapers and the arrest of individuals critical of his and Lincoln's administrations. He justified his unprecedented use of executive power as a necessary wartime measure. Initially opposed to emancipation, Morton defended the policy not as a humanitarian program but as a "stratagem of war." Leading a Republican resurgence in the state legislature, Morton won a second term as governor in 1864. Upon Lincoln's death, he supported President Andrew Johnson (*q.v.*), but after realizing the power of the Radical Republicans, quickly joined them.

Upon resigning as governor in January 1867 to enter the U.S. Senate, Morton became a leader of the Radicals, a converted advocate of the 15th Amendment, and a trusted adviser in Ulysses S. Grant's (*q.v.*) administration while maintaining control of Indiana Republicans. He won reelection in 1873, and with strong support from Southern Republicans, sought the 1876 presidential nomination, which he lost to Rutherford B. Hayes (*q.v.*). Morton died in Indianapolis on November 1, 1877. Foulke, *Life of Oliver P. Morton*; Thornbrough, *Indiana in the Civil War Era.*

David G. Vanderstel

MOTLEY, John Lothrop, *diplomat, propagandist, historian*, was born in Dorchester, Massachusetts, on April 15, 1814. He personified the Boston Brahmin in public life. He graduated from Harvard in 1831, and went on to Göttingen and Berlin for two years. Motley entered foreign service in 1841, a career he pursued with mixed results over the next generation. His entry into diplomacy as secretary of legation in St. Petersburg lasted only a few months. Later he served as minister to Austria (1861–1867) and minister to England (1869–1870). The larger part of his career centered on his work as a historian, notably his distinguished history of the Netherlands. Motley's strong sense of nationalism was reflected in the way he contrasted Latin, Catholic Spain and Nordic, Protestant Holland—to the advantage of the latter. America had all the virtues of Holland, he wrote, in addition to the special grace that came with its location in a new world.

To Motley, the Civil War appeared to threaten the integrity of the nation, and he employed his talents to win Europeans to the Union cause. Two articles for the *Times of London* explained to Englishmen the inseparability of the Union. As minister to Austria, he was an eloquent spokesman for the war and a devoted follower of Abraham Lincoln (*q.v.*), despite their disparate backgrounds. Motley's emotional attachments to the Union and republicanism made his role as propagandist more successful than his role as diplomat. He died in England on May 29, 1877. Kaplan, ''The Brahmin as Diplomat,'' *Civil War History*; Levin, *History as Romantic Art.*

Lawrence S. Kaplan

MOTT, Gershom, *general,* was born in Lamberton, New Jersey, on April 7, 1822. He spent most of the prewar years as a dry-goods clerk, Lamberton port collector, and official of Bordentown canal and bank companies. Mott was a 2nd lieutenant in the 10th Infantry but did not serve in Mexico. He was the lieutenant colonel of the 5th New Jersey in 1861, and served at Budd's Ferry, Yorktown, and Williamsburg. On May 7, 1862, he became colonel of the 6th New Jersey, which he led until severely wounded at Second Bull Run. Promoted to brigadier general in September 1862, he assumed command of the 2nd Jersey Brigade (3rd Brigade, 2nd Division, III Corps) on December 24, 1862. He was again badly wounded at Chancellorsville, and remained inactive until August 29, 1863.

When the III Corps was discontinued on March 24, 1864, Mott led the 1st Brigade, 4th Division, II Corps; he succeeded to division command on May 2. His inept handling of the 4th Division at the Wilderness and Spotsylvania resulted in its absorption into the 3rd Division, II Corps. Mott accepted demotion to that division's 3rd Brigade rather than be mustered out. Slightly wounded on May 19, he remained on duty and eventually commanded the division. Although his debut in higher command at Petersburg and Weldon Railroad was no better than his service that spring, Mott subsequently directed his troops more skillfully at Second Deep Bottom and at First and Second Hatcher's Run. At Sailor's Creek, he received his fourth wound.

Neither a Regular nor a political general, Mott characterized the citizen-soldier who served during crises. His loyalty and bravery made him a good regimental officer, but hardly qualified him for a star. Through June 1864 his conduct as a general was mediocre, even inept. Yet he matured with experience until, by war's end, he had become at least a competent division commander. Made major general of Volunteers on December 1, 1865, Mott left the service on February 20, 1866. He served on commissions that convicted Henry Wirz and that investigated overseas recruiting by Massachusetts. Mott was active in New Jersey business and politics, and as a militia major general, commanded the state's National Guard. He died in New York City on November 29, 1884. McAllister, *Civil War Letters of General Robert McAllister*; Rhea, *Battle of the Wilderness*; Sommers, *Richmond Redeemed.*

Richard J. Sommers

MOWER, Joseph Anthony, *general,* was born in Woodstock, Vermont, on August 22, 1827; in 1833 his family moved to Lowell, Massachusetts. He attended Norwich Academy in Vermont, and was employed as a carpenter when he enlisted on March 29, 1847, as a private in Company A, U.S. Engineers. He was mustered out on July 25, 1848, but on June 18, 1855, was commissioned a 2nd lieutenant in the 1st U.S. Infantry, and served with the regiment for several years at Fort McKavett, Texas. Upon the surrender of the Texas garrisons to Confederate forces in February 1861, Mower was ordered to Key West, Florida. In February 1862 he reported to Missouri and General John Pope (*q.v.*), whose army was closing in on New Madrid and Island No. 10. On May 3, Mower was commissioned colonel of the 11th Missouri, and placed in command of a brigade at Iuka and Corinth. At the latter battle, he was severely wounded and captured, but was left on the field when the Confederates retired.

After returning from convalescence leave, Mower was promoted to brigadier general on November 29, 1862, and placed in command of the Eagle Brigade. He led that famed brigade, assigned to William T. Sherman's (*q.v.*) XV Corps, at Jackson on May 14, 1863; in the May 22 assault on Vicksburg; and in the Vicksburg siege. In March 1864 Mower was assigned to command a XVI Corps division, and headed it during the Red River campaign, at the battle of Tupelo, and in the Oxford expedition. His conduct during the Tupelo campaign earned him a major generalcy. In late October, he was ordered to Georgia and took command of a XVII Corps division, leading it on the March to the Sea and through the Carolinas. On April 3, 1865, Sherman gave him command of the XX Corps.

Mower was mustered out of the Volunteer service on February 1, 1866, and six months later reentered the Regulars as colonel of the 39th U.S. Infantry, one of the Army's black regiments stationed in the deep South. While serving as commander of the Department of Louisiana, he died in New Orleans on January 6, 1870. Barrett, *Sherman's March Through the Carolinas*; Bearss, *Forrest at Brice's Cross Roads.*

Edwin C. Bearss

MYERS, Amos, *congressman,* was born in Clarion Furnace, Pennsylvania, on April 23, 1824. This region of western Pennsylvania was a stronghold for Jacksonian Democrats, and he grew up in an atmosphere steeped in politics. Educated at Allegheny College, Myers later studied law, and was admitted to the bar in 1846. Abandoning the Democrats, he first joined the Free Soil party and then, with his influential father, became a leading Republican in Clarion county. In 1862 he was elected to Congress, where he served as chairman of the Committee on Expenditures. After one term, Myers was defeated, and returned to Clarion to resume his law practice. Although he was regarded as a talented lawyer, he left the bar and was ordained a Baptist minister. Myers died in Kent, New York, on October 18, 1893. Davis, *History of Clarion County.*

David Dixon

MYERS, Leonard, *congressman,* was born on November 13, 1827, in Attleboro, Pennsylvania. Educated at the University of Pennsylvania, he studied law, and was admitted to the bar in 1848. After opening a practice in Philadelphia, he drifted into politics and held a number of municipal offices. When Robert E. Lee's Maryland campaign threatened the Keystone State in the fall of 1862, Myers was offered a commission as major in the 9th Pennsylvania Militia. Under the political patronage of Governor Andrew Curtin (*q.v.*), he was elected to serve in the 38th Congress, where he avoided controversy and gradually built a solid constituency that returned him to the House for four more terms.

During his tenure as a congressman, Myers served inconspicuously on the Committee of Patents, the Foreign Affairs Committee, and the Special Committee on Civil Service. In the wake of the Panic of 1873, he bolted from the party ranks to declare himself an Independent Republican candidate for reelection in 1874. After his defeat, he retired from public life to resume his law practice. He died in Philadelphia on February 11, 1905. Evans, *Pennsylvania Politics.*

David Dixon

N

NAST, Thomas, *cartoonist,* was born in Landau, Germany, on September 27, 1840. His mother brought him to New York City in 1846; his father, a Bavarian army bandsman, joined the family four years later. Nast studied art briefly before landing his first job in 1855 with Frank Leslie's (*q.v.*) *Illustrated Newspaper.* In 1859, he began contributing to *Harper's Weekly*; later that year, he joined the staff of the *New York Illustrated News,* for which he covered the funeral of John Brown. In 1860, the *News* sent Nast to England to cover a world heavyweight championship fight, after which he was off to Italy to follow Garibaldi's campaign.

Following the outbreak of the Civil War, Nast went to Baltimore and Washington as a freelancer for the *News,* Leslie's *Illustrated,* and *Harper's.* He sent back to New York drawings of Abraham Lincoln's (*q.v.*) inauguration and the early departure of Northern troops. In the summer of 1862, Nast joined *Harper's* as a staff artist, beginning an association that was to last for twenty-four years. He drew a number of battle pieces, but he quickly began to specialize in large, sentimental allegories such as "Christmas Eve," "The War in the Border States," and "Compromise with the South." Clearly intended to marshal support on the home front for the Union cause, these pictures made Nast nationally famous. Abraham Lincoln called him "our best recruiting sergeant." After the war Nast devoted his efforts to political cartoons in which the enemies of the steadfastly Republican *Harper's Weekly* were ruthlessly caricatured. His most famous artistic campaign was waged against New York City's corrupt Tweed Ring in 1870–1871.

The secret of Nast's great success was his ability to invent symbols for political personalities, parties, or nations. He popularized the Tammany tiger and conceived the Democratic donkey and the Republican elephant. He also developed the popular allegorical figures of Uncle Sam, John Bull, and Columbia. Santa Claus, who made his first appearance in *Harper's* during the Civil War, was another of Nast's definitive pictorial creations. Nast, a fixture at *Harper's* until 1886, published his own unsuccessful paper, *Nast's Weekly*, in 1892–1893. He spent most of his time during the 1890s painting in oils at his New Jersey home. In 1902, President Theodore Roosevelt appointed him consul at Guayaquil, Ecuador, where he died of yellow fever on December 7, 1902. Keller, *The Art and Politics of Thomas Nast*; Paine, *Thomas Nast*; St. Hill, *Thomas Nast*.

Ben Bassham

NEGLEY, James Scott, *general,* was born into a prominent family near Pittsburgh, Pennsylvania, on December 22, 1826. He attended the public schools and the Western University of Pennsylvania. Negley enlisted and served in the Mexican War with Company K of the Duquesne Greys, 1st Pennsylvania Volunteers. After the war, he engaged in business, including horticulture, for which he became nationally known. His service continued with the state militia and, by 1859, he was a brigadier general. After Fort Sumter, he was placed in charge of raising and arming "three months" recruits in the district, and participated in the ill-fated campaign against Joseph E. Johnston. With the expiration of his troops' enlistments, Negley returned to Pittsburgh, where he quickly raised another brigade. Ordered to Kentucky as colonel, he was assigned to the Army of the Ohio and promoted to brigadier general.

In early 1862, Negley was active in the Union advance into central Tennessee and northern Alabama. When Braxton Bragg invaded Kentucky in the late summer, Negley commanded the exposed Nashville defenses. Promoted to major general in the Army of the Cumberland, he led his division in the battle of Stones River. He also played a key role in the strategic advance that led to the evacuation of Chattanooga in the autumn of 1863. At Chickamauga, his command was swept back with the right wing, and Negley was relieved of duty for alleged cowardice. He was exonerated by a court martial but was not restored to command, and bitterly resigned in January 1865.

An aggressive recruiter and organizer early in the war, Negley was a capable brigade and division commander. After Chickmauga, however, military politics and the reorganization of the western armies prevented his continued service to the Union cause. After the war, Negley resumed his business career in Pittsburgh and was elected, as a Republican, to the U.S. House for four terms (1869–1875, 1885–1887). A railroad executive, he moved to New York City in 1886, where he lived until his death in Plainfield, New Jersey, on August 7, 1901. Cozzens, *This Terrible Sound*; James, "General James Scott Negley," *Western Pennsylvania Historical Magazine*.

J. K. Folmar

NELSON, Homer Augustus, *congressman,* was born on August 31, 1829, in Poughkeepsie, New York. He studied law, and after admittance to the bar, practiced in the Poughkeepsie area. In 1855, he was elected a judge of Dutchess county, a post he held until 1862. In September 1862 Nelson received authority to recruit the 167th New York Volunteers, but recruitment moved slowly and the regiment was consolidated with the 159th New York in early November 1862. Mustered in as a colonel of the 167th, Nelson resigned later in the month to run for the 38th Congress. He failed to win reelection in 1864, but was a delegate to the New York State Constitutional Convention (1867), secretary of state of New York (1867–1870), and, in the early 1880s, a state senator. He died in Poughkeepsie on April 25, 1891. Lanman, *Biographical Annals*; Phisterer, *New York in the War of the Rebellion,* vol. 5.

Frank R. Levstik

NELSON, Samuel, *Supreme Court justice,* was born on November 10, 1792, in Washington county, New York. He graduated from Middlebury College in 1813, read law, and set up practice in Cortland, New York. As chief justice of the New York Supreme Court, Nelson handed down a number of significant decisions on state incorporation and banking laws, but usually showed restraint in reviewing the acts of the state legislature. President John Tyler named him to the U.S. Supreme Court, where he generally followed the lead of Chief Justice Roger Taney (*q.v.*). But in the *Dred Scott* case, Nelson urged his brethren to send the case back to Missouri for lack of jurisdiction, thereby avoiding the explosive questions of black citizenship and the constitutionality of the Missouri Compromise. When the other justices insisted on handing down a broad decision, he stubbornly issued his original opinion, which had been first drafted as the opinion of the Court.

Like many other Old Whigs, Nelson desperately believed that only sectional compromise could save the country, and served as an intermediary between Secretary of State William H. Seward (*q.v.*) and the Confederate commissioners. Although apparently taken in by Seward's pledge that the Lincoln (*q.v.*) administration would evacuate Fort Sumter, Nelson soon withdrew from the negotiations. He doubted the nation could be reunited by force and lamented the "plunge of Emancipation" and the approach of "military despotism." As the spokesman for the dissenters in the Prize Cases, Nelson condemned Lincoln for illegally conducting a "personal war" against the insurrectionary states. Only Congress could impose a blockade, he said, because only Congress could declare war.

As a circuit judge, Nelson carefully examined blockade seizures and ruled against the government more often than the other justices. His service on the *Alabama* Claims Commission helped resolve a complex dispute between the United States and Great Britain but also ruined his health. Nelson resigned from the Court in November 1872 and died on December 13, 1873, in Cooperstown, New York. Silver, *Lincoln's Supreme Court*; Swisher, *The Taney Period.*

George C. Rable

NESMITH, James Willis, *senator,* was born on July 23, 1820, in New Brunswick, Canada. After several family moves, Nesmith traveled to Oregon in 1843. He became a lawyer, but concentrated on farming and politics. In 1845, he began his public career as a judge and then legislator in the provisional government of Oregon. He served as a Volunteer officer, attaining the rank of colonel, in three Indian wars. In the 1850s, he became a U.S. marshal and superintendent of Indian affairs in Oregon and Washington. Although Joe Lane (*q.v.*), the ranking Democratic politician in Oregon, had assisted him politically, Nesmith broke with Lane late in the 1850s. To defeat Lane and his Breckinridge Democrats, the ambitious Nesmith helped unite Douglas Democrats and Republicans in 1860; his reward was election to the U.S. Senate. He incorrectly reported that Lane favored western secession and a Pacific Republic.

An ardent Unionist, a white supremacist, a critic of Radical Republicans, and skeptical of Abraham Lincoln's (*q.v.*) abilities, Nesmith was very active on the Senate Committee on Military Affairs. He attempted to improve and enlarge the Army, favoring conscription without dubious exemptions. Army officers appreciated his efforts and his earthy comments. Nesmith, who championed measures that he considered to be in the best interests of Westerners, was not reelected for a variety of reasons, including his support of McClellan (*q.v.*) in 1864 and Johnson (*q.v.*) in 1866, his independent spirit, and the fluidity of Oregon politics. He never lost favor among the people, however, and was elected as a Democrat to the U.S. House in 1872. He died in Rickreall, Oregon, on June 17, 1885. Hendrickson, *Joe Lane*; Johannsen, *Frontier Politics; Portrait and Biographical Record of the Willamette Valley.*

G. Thomas Edwards

NEWTON, John, *general,* was born in Norfolk, Virginia, on August 24, 1823. He graduated from West Point in 1842, was commissioned a lieutenant of engineers, taught at the Academy, worked on waterway improvement, and built forts along the Eastern Seaboard, the Gulf Coast, and the Great Lakes. He subsequently participated in the Mormon pacification expedition, then spent the remainder of his prewar career supervising fortification construction on Delaware Bay. Between April and September 1861, Newton served as chief engineer in the departments of Pennsylvania and the Shenandoah, then erected forts around Washington. Afterward, he took over a brigade in the capital defenses and commanded another in the Peninsula campaign with the Army of the Potomac.

At Crampton's Gap, Newton, on his own initiative, assumed command of the field and led a bayonet charge that dislodged the Confederates. He headed a division at Fredericksburg but saw little action; during the battle of Chancellorsville, however, he won commendation for storming Marye's Heights. At Gettysburg, he took command of the I Corps and led it until its deactivation in March 1864. Subsequently, Newton joined the Army of the Cumberland as a division commander in the IV Corps. He saw heavy combat in the Atlanta campaign, winning a brevet for his conduct at Peach Tree Creek. After the fall of Atlanta, he commanded a military district in Florida until the end of the war.

Newton's accomplishments as an engineer cannot be challenged, but the same does not hold true for his performance as a field commander. Brave, intelligent, and decisive though he was on occasion, two contemporaries, Charles Wainwright and Marsena Patrick (q.v.), thought him unreliable and second-rate. Moreover, by complaining directly to President Abraham Lincoln (q.v.) about General Ambrose Burnside (q.v.) and subsequently testifying to his incompetence before the Committee on the Conduct of the War, Newton displayed questionable judgment as well as a gross disregard for propriety. Although an effective division commander, he lacked the prerequisites for higher command.

In 1865, reduced to a lieutenant colonel, Newton resumed his career as a military engineer. His most notable achievement in the postwar era was the removal of obstructions from New York Harbor, a series of operations that entailed exploding 125 tons of dynamite in underwater chambers. In 1884, Newton became chief of engineers, retiring two years later at his own request. He died in New York City on May 1, 1895. Castel, *Decision in the West*; Catton, *Never Call Retreat*.

James L. Morrison, Jr.

NIXON, John Thompson, *congressman,* was born in Fairton, New Jersey, on August 31, 1820. He graduated from Princeton in 1841, was admitted to the bar in 1845, and settled in Bridgeton, the Cumberland county seat. He was elected as a Whig to the state leqislature in 1849, and served in 1850 as speaker. In 1858, he won election to Congress as a member of the Opposition party, a Whiggish coalition of Americans and Republicans, and was reelected in 1860. Nixon played a significant role at the beginning of his first term in winning the bitterly contested speakership of the 36th Congress for his New Jersey Opposition colleague, William Pennington (q.v.), and collaborated with the minority of Republicans who attempted to devise a conciliatory formula to hold the Union together. He at first opposed confiscation of slaves, but in a speech on April 11, 1862, he indicated his willingness to support extreme measures, if they were necessary to win the war.

Nixon declined renomination in 1862, but he remained active in New Jersey Republican politics and was associated with the faction that seized control of the party after 1865. Nixon hoped for appointment as a Federal judge in 1863, but interim Senator Richard S. Field (q.v.) was selected instead. After Field's death in 1870, Nixon was finally appointed, and held the position until his death in Stockbridge, Massachusetts, on September 28, 1889. Keasbey, "John T. Nixon," *Proceedings of the New Jersey Historical Society*; Smith, *Charles Perrin Smith.*

Daniel W. Crofts

NOBLE, Warren Perry, *congressman*, was born in Luzerne county, Pennsylvania, on June 14, 1820, moved to Wayne county, Ohio, in the early 1830s, and in 1836 settled in Seneca county, Ohio. He graduated from Wadsworth Academy in 1840, was admitted to the Ohio bar in 1844, and began his law career in Tiffin. Noble, a Democrat, served in the Ohio House of Representatives (1846–1850), and was twice elected Seneca county prosecuting attorney. He was elected to the 37th and 38th Congresses, where he was known as a War Democrat. Defeated for reelection in 1864, he returned to his law practice in Tiffin. Governor Rutherford B. Hayes (*q.v.*) appointed him to the board of trustees of the Ohio Agricultural and Mechanical College (now Ohio State University), a position he held for a decade. He was active in banking and promoted railroad construction in Ohio. Noble died in Tiffin on July 9, 1903. Lang, *History of Seneca County.*

Thomas H. Smith

NOELL, John William, *congressman*, was born in Bedford county, Virginia, on February 22, 1816. In 1833, he moved to Perryville, Missouri, where he established a successful mercantile and milling business. While clerk of the circuit court for Perry county (1841–1850), he studied law and was admitted to the bar. Noell was active in the Democratic party, and was elected to the state Senate in 1851, where he served one term, and to Congress in 1858, where he served until his death. When President Abraham Lincoln (*q.v.*) proposed compensated emancipation for the border states in July 1862, Noell, alone of Missouri's House delegation, supported him. He joined seven other border-state congressmen who wrote to the President, pledging their support.

Following the 1862 election, which showed increased support for some form of emancipation in Missouri, Noell introduced legislation providing the state $10 million in compensation if it endorsed emancipation by January 1, 1864. This passed the House, but the issue was lost when the Senate passed a different version that Noell and his allies would not accept. Noell died in Washington, D.C., on March 14, 1863. Parrish, *Turbulent Partnership*; Stewart, *Bench and Bar of Missouri.*

William E. Parrish

NORTON, Elijah Hise, *congressman*, was born near Russellville, Kentucky, on November 21, 1821. He was educated at Centre College and took his legal training at Transylvania University, from which he graduated in 1842. He moved in 1845 to Platte City, Missouri, where he was elected county attorney in 1850 and was a circuit judge from 1852 until his election to Congress as a Democrat in 1860. Norton was a delegate to the state convention that decided against secession in March 1861 and strongly supported its stand, although he also opposed coercion. He believed that a peaceful separation could lead eventually to the South's realization of the need for reunion. This could be followed by some plan for the gradual extinction of slavery, with colonization.

A staunch conservative, Norton opposed President Abraham Lincoln's (*q.v.*) efforts at compensated emancipation in the border states in 1862, and voted against the congressional attempt to accomplish it. He was defeated for reelection in 1862, and retired to his law practice in Platte City. Norton remained active in Democratic politics following the war, and was a prominent member of the state constitutional convention of 1875. He was appointed to the state supreme court in 1876 and served until his retirement in 1888. He died in Platte City on August 5, 1914. Parrish, *Turbulent Partnership*.

William E. Parrish

NORTON, Jesse Olds, *congressman*, was born on December 25, 1812, in Bennington, Vermont. Educated at Williams College, he taught in Wheeling, Virginia (now West Virginia), and Potosi, Missouri. In 1838, he moved to Illinois and settled in Joliet. After serving as city attorney, county judge, delegate to the 1848 state constitutional convention, and state legislator, he was elected as a Whig to the 33rd Congress, and reelected as a Republican to the 34th Congress. Norton declined renomination to the 35th Congress, and returned to Illinois to serve as judge of the 11th Judicial Circuit until he was returned to the 38th Congress. He supported Abraham Lincoln's (*q.v.*) policies on the war and Reconstruction, and steadfastly refused to recognize that states had the power to secede or that Congress had the power to expel states from the Union.

Norton declined renomination to the 39th Congress, but was a delegate to the 1866 Union National Convention in Philadelphia. After he left Congress, he served as the U.S. district attorney for the Northern District of Illinois, practiced law, and was Chicago's corporation counsel until his death there on August 3, 1875. *Biographical Encyclopedia of Illinois of the Nineteenth Century*; Cole, *Era of the Civil War*.

Thomas F. Schwartz

NUGEN, Robert Hunter, *congressman*, was born near Hallidays Cove, Pennsylvania, on July 16, 1809. He moved to Ohio with his parents in 1811 and settled in Columbiana county. Before the Civil War, he engaged in farming in Tuscarawas county and did some contracting. In 1860, Nugen was a delegate to the Democratic National Convention in Charleston, South Carolina. He was elected to the 37th Congress and served until 1863. Opposing many of the Republican war measures, Nugen argued against the confiscation of Confederate property, believing that could be accomplished only after treason was proven and the Constitution provided specifically for that charge. Upon returning to Ohio in 1863, he became superintendent of the Ohio Canal. Nugen died in Newcomerstown, Ohio, on February 28, 1872. *BDUSC*.

Thomas H. Smith

NYE, James Warren, *governor, senator,* was born in De Ruyter, New York, on June 10, 1814 or 1815. He attended the common schools and Courtland Academy, and was admitted to the bar in 1838. In 1839, he was elected district attorney of Madison county, became a probate judge in 1845, and county judge in 1847. In 1848, Nye ran for Congress unsuccessfully on the Free Soil ticket, and in 1852 campaigned for Democrat Franklin Pierce. He joined the Republican party, and in 1856 worked for John C. Frémont (*q.v.*). In 1860, Nye fought mightily to nominate William Henry Seward (*q.v.*), and then to have the party choose Hannibal Hamlin (*q.v.*) as Vice President.

Congress organized Nevada Territory on March 2, 1861, and Nye was appointed governor. In 1861 and 1862, he opposed sections in the Crimes and Punishments Act that banned black testimony in cases involving whites. Nye raised troops to guard the Overland Mail route, and he organized the militia. He drew on troops at Fort Churchill to control secessionist speakers, and in September 1864 used the soldiers to overawe the Miners' League and keep down wages during an economic depression. Nye lobbied extensively for an enabling act to grant Nevada statehood, which came on October 31, 1864, when Nevada had only 16,400 active voters. On December 16, Nye became Nevada's second senator. He supported black rights and Radical Reconstruction, and served until March 3, 1873. He died in White Plains, New York, on December 25, 1876.
Gray, *Source and the Vision*; Myles, *Nevada's Governors.*

Robert J. Chandler

O

ODELL, Moses Fowler, *congressman,* was born in Tarrytown, New York, on February 24, 1818. He rose from Customhouse clerk in New York City to become a mover in state Democratic circles. In 1860, he was elected to the House of Representatives from Brooklyn. His early support of the Union cause found favor with the House leadership, and brought Odell the chairmanship of the Committee on Expenditures. In December 1861 he was one of two Democrats to win seats on the powerful Joint Committee on the Conduct of the War. An "advanced moderate" Democrat, Odell voted to raise the tariff to finance the war effort; endorsed the Conspiracy Bill, which imposed fines or jail sentences on plotters against the government; backed a resolution that Congress raise funds and troops to suppress the rebellion as quickly as possible; and voted to table several peace resolutions. He called for the removal of slow, conservative commanders such as George B. McClellan (*q.v.*).

The only House Democrat to reject the use of troops in returning fugitive slaves, Odell was an early supporter of black regiments. Twice he voted in support of the 13th Amendment. One of only seven War Democrats to retain their House seats in 1862, he was appointed to the Military Affairs Committee in the 38th Congress. Two years later, however, he failed to win renomination. Shortly before vacating his seat, he criticized his party's sympathy with slavery in a well-publicized floor speech. In 1865, Odell was appointed naval agent in New York City and served until his death in Brooklyn on June 13, 1866. Curry, *Blueprint for Modern America*; Dell, *Lincoln and the War Democrats.*

Edward G. Longacre

OGLESBY, Richard James, *general, governor,* was born in Oldham county, Kentucky, on July 25, 1824. His parents died of cholera when he was eight years old, and he moved to Decatur, Illinois, with an uncle. He read law, and was admitted to the bar in 1845. In 1846, Oglesby was commissioned in the 4th Illinois Volunteers, and participated in the battles of Cerdo Gordo and Veracruz. In 1849, he joined the California gold rush, then returned to Decatur, where he was a successful land developer, attorney, and Whig politician. An unsuccessful Republican candidate for Congress in 1858, in the Republican state convention of 1860, Oglesby devised the ''Lincoln the rail-splitter'' slogan. He was elected to the Illinois state Senate in 1860.

After the firing on Fort Sumter, Oglesby organized the 8th Illinois Volunteer Infantry. He was promoted to brigadier general after leading a brigade at Fort Donelson, and to major general after being ''shot through'' at Corinth in October. While on sick leave in Illinois, Oglesby made telling speeches in support of Abraham Lincoln (*q.v.*) and the war effort. He was returned to duty as commander of the left wing of the XVI Corps in Tennessee. Reassigned to court martial duty in Washington, D.C., he presided over the trial of Surgeon General William Hammond (*q.v.*). Before the trial was completed, he resigned to run successfully for governor of Illinois. As governor, he was a strong supporter of the President, although he argued for an adjustment of Illinois's draft quota.

Oglesby arrived in Washington on April 14, 1865, and was among the last persons to call on the President. He was at Lincoln's deathbed, helped organize the removal of the body to Oak Ridge Cemetery in Springfield, and headed the organization that successfully solicited contributions to build the Lincoln tomb. A founding father of the Grand Army of the Republic, Oglesby opposed the lenient Reconstruction policy of President Andrew Johnson (*q.v.*). In 1872, he was again elected governor, but served only a few days before being elected to the U.S. Senate. In 1884, Oglesby was again elected governor as a ''last hurrah'' of the Illinois veterans. He died in Elkhart, Illinois, on April 24, 1899. Bearss, *Vicksburg Campaign,* vols. 2, 3; Johns, *Personal Recollections of Early Decatur;* Plummer, ''Richard J. Oglesby,'' *Journal of the Illinois State Historical Society.*

Mark A. Plummer

OLDEN, Charles Smith, *governor,* was born near Princeton, New Jersey, on February 19, 1799. He became a prosperous merchant and banker and built Drumthwacket, the Princeton home now used as the official residence of the New Jersey governor. Olden was twice elected as a Whig to the state Senate (1845–1851). He later affiliated with the American party, and supported Millard Fillmore for President in 1856. In 1859, a more unified Opposition party— Americans, Republicans, former Whigs, and Anti-Lecompton Democrats—selected Olden as its candidate for governor. He narrowly defeated the Democratic nominee, Edwin R.V. Wright.

Olden and the New Jersey Opposition party supported Abraham Lincoln (*q.v.*) in 1860, and the victorious Republican nominee gained four of the state's seven electoral votes because of divisions among Democrats. The only governor to attend the Washington Peace Conference in February 1861, Olden supported a compromise on the divisive territorial issue. The patriotic groundswell following the attack on Fort Sumter placed New Jersey firmly on the Union side and imposed heavy responsibilities on the governor. Olden called a special session of the legislature, which readily supported military mobilization. He worked tirelessly during 1861 and 1862 to sustain the war effort, and his party, which adopted a "Union" designation, gained precarious control of the legislature with support from several War Democrats.

Olden's position became more difficult in 1862, as Union losses mounted. Aware that the Emancipation Proclamation divided the Union coalition in New Jersey, he refused to join other Republican governors in supporting it. State elections held in November 1862 produced a sweeping Democratic victory. Forbidden by the state constitution to run for a second consecutive term, Olden suffered the disappointment of seeing the Union–Republican nominee, Marcus L. Ward, soundly defeated by Democrat Joel Parker (*q.v.*). Democrats also gained solid control over the legislature. In his last annual message to the legislature (January 1863), Olden urged continued support of the war effort. He was elected president of the New Jersey Loyal League in 1863, and was one of the state's presidential electors for Ulysses S. Grant (*q.v.*) in 1872. He died in Princeton on April 7, 1876. Knapp, *New Jersey Politics*; Stellhorn, *Governors of New Jersey*.

Daniel W. Crofts

OLIN, Abram Baldwin, *congressman,* was born in Shaftsbury, Vermont, on September 21, 1808. After graduating from Williams College in 1835, he studied law, and was admitted to the bar in 1838. He established a practice in Troy, New York, and served as that city's recorder from 1844 to 1852. This was his only known local office before being elected as a Republican to the 35th, 36th, and 37th Congresses. Olin served without particular notice until the war came. When the 37th Congress convened, he was appointed to the House Committee on Military Affairs and the Militia. This body, which was relatively unimportant before the war, assumed great significance with the outbreak of hostilities.

By July 1862 Olin was the committee's chair due to the resignation of Francis Blair (*q.v.*) from his congressional seat. After this appointment, Olin's demeanor toward his colleagues became obstreperous. In his effort to amass power, he proposed that his committee consider a variety of measures. These included Thaddeus Stevens's (*q.v.*) Negro Troop Bill in January 1863 and the Illinois Ship Canal Bill, which William Holman (*q.v.*) and other Midwestern Democrats found objectionable for reasons that included Olin's decision to report a bill that he favored over the sentiments of other members of his committee.

Olin's penchant for enraging Republicans and Democrats alike reached its greatest intensity in late February 1863, when he reported out the National Conscription Act. As in the past, he relied on deception and other underhanded tactics to steer the controversial measure through the House. Once it became evident that he had no intention of honoring his earlier promise to consider amendments to the legislation, the Democratic minority filibustered, and with the assistance of Stevens and other Republicans, forced major modifications to the bill.

Despite Olin's influential position, he was an ineffectual leader because of his disregard for his colleagues. Having failed to secure reelection to the 38th Congress, and with his legislative career at an end, he received an appointment as an associate justice of the Supreme Court in the District of Columbia on March 11, 1863. He served in this position until his retirement on January 13, 1879. He died near Sligo, Maryland, on July 7, 1879. Curry, *Blueprint for Modern America*; Geary, *We Need Men*.

James W. Geary

OLMSTED, Frederick Law, *author, landscape architect, general secretary, U.S. Sanitary Commission*, was born on April 26, 1822, in Hartford, Connecticut. He is best remembered as the originator of landscape architecture in the United States, but he was also a significant figure in the sectional conflict that preceded the Civil War. From his boyhood, the land attracted Olmsted. He responded through travel, studying engineering, farming, and finally the creation of artificial landscapes. In the 1850s, he made three excursions into the South, which he recorded in *A Journey in the Seaboard Slave States* (1856), *A Journey Through Texas* (1857), and *A Journey in the Back Country* (1860). Although Olmsted was no abolitionist, his portrayal of Southern economic stagnation, the negative impact of slavery on the Southern work ethic, and the sad condition of many nonslaveholding Southern whites contributed to Northern antipathy toward the South.

Beginning in 1857, with his appointment as superintendent of New York City's new Central Park, Olmsted concentrated on landscape design. Shortly after the start of the Civil War, however, he took a leave of absence to serve as general secretary of the U.S. Sanitary Commission, a semiofficial civilian agency designed to promote the health of Union soldiers and to provide care for the sick and wounded. Olmsted also helped establish the Union League Club, which aimed at suppressing criticism in the North of the Union war effort. Such war-related endeavors ended in August 1863 when Olmsted accepted the superintendency of what became Yosemite National Park in California. He devoted the rest of his life to landscape architecture. Olmsted died on August 28, 1903, in Waverly, Massachusetts. Fredrickson, *Inner Civil War*; Mitchell, *Frederick Law Olmstead*.

Stanley Harrold

O'NEILL, Charles, *congressman*, was born in Philadelphia on March 21, 1821. After graduating from Dickinson College, he studied law, and was admitted to the bar in 1843. O'Neill served one term in the state legislature, and in 1861 campaigned for Congress against Democrat Charles Biddle (*q.v.*), son of financial magnate Nicholas Biddle. Enthusiasm for the Union cause was already beginning to subside in Philadelphia, a city known for its Southern sympathies, and O'Neill was defeated by 200 votes in what was described as a "listless campaign." One observer believed that any reasonable candidate could have beaten Biddle, who was suspected of being a Southern sympathizer.

By 1862, the political atmosphere in Philadelphia had changed dramatically, as the city's banking institutions began to prosper through war loans. O'Neill ran for Congress again, this time defeating Biddle. He won three more terms before losing in 1870. O'Neill was returned to the House of Representatives in 1873, and served without interruption until his death in Philadelphia on November 25, 1893. Weigley, *Philadelphia.*

David Dixon

O'NEILL, John, *congressman,* was born in Philadelphia on December 17, 1822. He was probably one of the best-educated representatives from Ohio to serve in Congress during the war years. Following a secondary education in the public schools in Frederick, Maryland, he attended Georgetown College and graduated from Mount St. Mary's College. In 1841, he received a law degree from Georgetown College, was admitted to the bar in 1842, and moved to Zanesville, Ohio. In 1845, he was Muskingum county's prosecuting attorney.

Elected as a Democrat to the 38th Congress, O'Neill participated little in debates but did call for an exchange of prisoners on a "white man for white man" basis. Following his years in Congress, he returned to his law practice. In 1883, he was elected to the Ohio Senate, where he was instrumental in the passage of the bill that granted state assistance to Wilberforce University, a school for African Americans founded in 1856. He also served on the board of trustees of Wilberforce. O'Neill died in Zanesville on May 25, 1905. *BDUSC.*

Thomas H. Smith

ORD, Edward Otho Cresap, *general,* was born in Cumberland, Maryland, on October 18, 1818. He graduated from West Point in 1839, was commissioned a 2nd lieutenant, 3rd Artillery, and fought the Seminole Indians (1839–1842). He spent the Mexican War mostly in California. Ord married into a slave-owning family in 1854, and was involved in John Brown's (*q.v.*) hanging in 1859. Despite his early proslavery views, Ord was appointed a brigadier general of Volunteers as of September 14, 1861. He commanded a brigade in the Army of the Potomac and won the battle of Dranesville, Virginia, on December 20, resulting in his promotion to major general. He caught Ulysses S. Grant's (*q.v.*) eye as a division commander during the battles of Iuka and Corinth, Mississippi.

Severely wounded at the battle of the Hatchie, Ord spent several months recuperating, then returned to replace John A. McClernand (*q.v.*) as commander of the XIII Corps during the siege of Vicksburg. Grant further demonstrated his confidence in Ord by making him commander of the XVIII Corps in July 1864, during operations near Petersburg. Wounded again during the assault and capture of Fort Harrison, Virginia, he did not return to action until December. In January 1865, Grant gave Ord command of the Army of the James and the Department of Virginia and North Carolina. He played an important role in the final battles around Petersburg and witnessed Robert E. Lee's surrender.

Ord proved himself an aggressive commander once engaged in battle, but exhibited little independent initiative. He found the perfect niche for his considerable abilities under Grant's immediate direction, and deserves to be remembered as one of the better corps commanders in the Union Army. After the Civil War, he became a brigadier general in the Regular Army, briefly commanded the 4th Military District during Reconstruction, and then commanded various departments in the West and on the frontier. He quarreled with Philip H. Sheridan (*q.v.*) and retired in 1880. Ord contracted yellow fever on a business trip and died in Havana, Cuba, on July 22, 1883. Cresap, *Appomattox Commander*; Sommers, *Richmond Redeemed.*

David L. Wilson

ORTH, Godlove Stein, *congressman*, was born April 22, 1817, in Lebanon, Pennsylvania. He attended Pennsylvania (now Gettysburg) College, studied law, and was admitted to the bar in 1839. Later that year, he moved to Indiana, settling in Lafayette and becoming involved in local Whig politics. Orth served for six terms in the state Senate (1843–1849; president pro tem, 1845–1846), and unsuccessfully sought the Whig gubernatorial nomination in 1846. During the 1850s, he was active in Indiana's Know-Nothing movement and was its president (1854–1855). A fusionist, he later became involved in the Republican party.

In 1861, Indiana Governor Oliver H.P. Morton (*q.v.*) selected Orth as one of five delegates to the Washington Peace Conference. At the conference he pledged to oppose constitutional amendments or any propositions that recognized slavery in the territories. Orth later served in the U.S. House of Representatives (1863–1871, 1873–1875, 1879–1882). He also was U.S. envoy to Austria-Hungary (March 1875–May 1876), resigning to accept his party's gubernatorial nomination. Because of criticism for his earlier Know-Nothing affiliation, Orth withdrew at the party convention and was replaced by Benjamin Harrison. Orth died in Lafayette, Indiana, on December 16, 1882. Shepherd, *Biographical Directory of the Indiana General Assembly*, vol. 1; Walsh, *Centennial History of the Indiana General Assembly.*

David G. Vanderstel

OSTERHAUS, Peter Joseph, *general*, was born in Koblenz, Germany, on January 4, 1823. He received a military education, and in the wake of the failed revolution of 1848, he settled in Belleville, Illinois in 1849. Osterhaus worked for a while as a dry-goods clerk, then moved to Lebanon, Illinois, where he operated a general merchandising business. In 1851, he moved to St. Louis and took a position as a bookkeeper for a wholesale hardware firm. In 1861, Osterhaus volunteered as a private in the 12th Missouri Volunteers, but because of his prior training and military experience, he was commissioned captain in the 2nd Missouri, and a few days later promoted to major.

Osterhaus fought at the battle of Wilson's Creek and in December 1861 was made colonel of the 12th Missouri Volunteers. At the battle of Pea Ridge he commanded a division in General Samuel Curtis's (*q.v.*) army. His heroic stand in the Leetown area on the first day of that fierce combat probably had much to do with saving the Union forces from disaster. In June 1862, Osterhaus was appointed brigadier general in the U.S. Volunteers. He led a division in the Vicksburg campaign and was wounded by a shell fragment at the battle of Big Black River. His next command was the 1st Division of the XV Corps at Chattanooga. In the brutal fighting along Missionary Ridge, Osterhaus's troops drove the Confederates' southern wing from the crest of the ridge.

On July 23, 1864, during the Atlanta campaign, Osterhaus was promoted to major general of Volunteers over General William T. Sherman's (*q.v.*) objections. Nonetheless, he remained with Sherman's command and performed ably in Georgia and the Carolinas. During the drive northward through the Carolinas, Osterhaus temporarily commanded the XV Corps. After the war, he held various commands in Mississippi until he was mustered out of the service on January 17, 1866.

Osterhaus was one of the most effective of the foreign-born officers who served in the Union Army. He was consul to France (1866–1877), and after some twenty years in private business, served as vice and deputy consul in Mannheim, Germany (1898–1900). He died on January 2, 1917, in Duisburg, Germany. Bearss, *Vicksburg Campaign*; Monaghan, *Civil War on the Western Border*; Shea, *Pea Ridge*.

James J. Hudson

O'SULLIVAN, Timothy H., *photographer*, was born in New York City in 1840. In his midteens, he learned photography while working at the New York and Washington galleries of Mathew Brady (*q.v.*), and during the first years of the Civil War, he became one of the leading cameramen in ''Brady's Photographic Corps.'' O'Sullivan is said to have been present at the first battle of Bull Run in July 1861, and would have photographed the fighting but for the fact that a shell from one of the Confederate field pieces destroyed his camera. During the winter and spring of 1861–1862, he accompanied Union forces to South Carolina, where he photographed ruined Confederate forts, graves of Union soldiers, plantation scenes, and regiments on parade. By the midsummer of 1862, he was traveling with Union forces in Virginia. His photographs taken on or near the Cedar Mountain battlefield are the most outstanding of this phase of his wartime activity. O'Sullivan returned to Washington following the rout of the Army of the Potomac at Bull Run, on August 30.

In 1863, O'Sullivan left Brady to work for Alexander Gardner (*q.v.*), who had established his own gallery in Washington. On July 5, Gardner and O'Sullivan, along with James F. Gibson (*q.v.*), arrived at Gettysburg to photograph the torn and bloated corpses awaiting burial, some of which the cameramen moved in order to create more interesting compositions. O'Sullivan's unforgettable photograph of the Union dead, "A Harvest of Death," was one of his forty-four prints that appeared in Gardner's *Photographic Sketch Book of the War* (1866).

When Gardner closed his gallery in 1867, O'Sullivan joined the government-sponsored exploring party in the West led by Clarence King. He was photographer on an expedition to Panama that investigated possible routes for a canal. From 1871 to 1875, O'Sullivan was active again in the West, both independently and with the Corps of Engineers. In 1880, he was named photographer of the Treasury Department, but served only five months. He died at Staten Island, New York, on January 14, 1882. Frassanito, *Gettysburg*; Naef, *Era of Exploration*; Newhall, *T.H. O'Sullivan*.

Ben Bassham

OWEN, Joshua Thomas, *general*, was born on March 29, 1821, in Caermarthen, Wales, and came to the United States with his parents in 1830. He graduated from Jefferson College in 1845, and after several unsuccessful business ventures, founded the Chestnut Hill Academy for Boys, outside Philadelphia. He also turned to the law, sat in the Pennsylvania legislature, and rose high enough in Philadelphia society to be admitted to the exclusive First City Troop.

At the outbreak of the Civil War, Owen became colonel of the 24th Pennsylvania, a three-month regiment. In August 1861 he recruited a new regiment in Philadelphia for General Edward D. Baker (*q.v.*), which would bear the designation 2nd California, as a surrogate for troops from Baker's Pacific Coast constituency. The California regiment, however, was composed mainly of Irish Americans, and it marched under a green flag bearing traditional Irish insignia, along with the national colors. Owen was appointed its colonel on August 18, 1861, and when Baker was killed at Ball's Bluff, the regiment was reclaimed by Pennsylvania as one of its own units and renumbered the 69th Pennsylvania. It was brigaded together with three other Philadelphia-based regiments (the 71st, 72nd, and 106th Pennsylvania) under General William Wallace Burns (*q.v.*), and became known as the Philadelphia Brigade.

The brigade served with distinction on the Peninsula, and Owen was particularly commended by division commander Joseph Hooker (*q.v.*) for leading the 69th Pennsylvania in a successful bayonet charge at White Oak Swamp. Owen succeeded Burns in command of the Philadelphia Brigade, and was appointed brigadier general of Volunteers on November 29, 1862. He commanded the brigade in late 1862 and early 1863 as part of the 2nd Division, II Corps. However, three days before Gettysburg, Owen was abruptly removed from command by General John Gibbon (*q.v.*), an action that seems to have been connected with a disagreement over Owen's orders to his officers to remove rank markings from their uniforms before going into battle, so as not to present obvious targets to enemy sharpshooters.

Owen was posted to brigade command in the 3rd Division, II Corps, but he returned to command the Philadelphia Brigade on April 25, 1864. Gibbon, who had returned to division command after recuperating from wounds received at Gettysburg, revived his quarrel with Owen. After another round of confrontations at Cold Harbor, Owen demanded either a transfer or a court martial. Gibbon prepared a court martial for Owen on grounds of disobedience of orders under fire at Spotsylvania. The case lacked evidence, however, and Owen was quietly mustered out of service on July 18, 1864. He returned to an active political life in Philadelphia, and was a charter member of Philadelphia's Post 2 of the Grand Army of the Republic. Owen remained a favorite at Philadelphia Brigade reunions until his death in Chestnut Hill on November 7, 1887. Banes, *History of the Philadelphia Brigade*; Bates, *History of Pennsylvania Volunteers*, vol. 2; Rhea, *Battle of the Wilderness*.

Allen C. Guelzo

P

PAINE, Eleazer Arthur, *general,* was born in Parkman, Ohio, on September 10, 1815. He graduated from West Point in 1839. After brief service on the staff of General Zachary Taylor during the Seminole War, he resigned from the Army in 1840. He studied law and practiced in Painesville, Ohio, was U.S. deputy marshal for Ohio, and was brigadier general of the Ohio Militia. Moving to Illinois, Paine practiced law at Monmouth and became a personal friend of Abraham Lincoln (*q.v.*). He was named colonel of the 9th Illinois on July 26, 1861, and made brigadier general of Volunteers on September 3.

During the fall of 1861, Paine was brigade commander at Paducah, Kentucky. He was at Cairo, Illinois, early in 1862, and commanded the 4th Division of General John Pope's (*q.v.*) army in the New Madrid and Island No. 10 campaign in the spring. He was a division commander in the advance on Corinth, and participated in the fighting around Farmington, Mississippi. Then Paine was in areas away from the front. He guarded the Louisville & Nashville Railroad from November 1862 to May 1864, and commanded the District of Western Kentucky from July to September 1864. After this, he awaited orders and resigned his commission, which was accepted to date from April 5, 1865. He died on December 16, 1882, in Jersey City, New Jersey. Hughes, *Battle of Belmont*; Williams, *Lincoln Finds a General,* vol. 3.

E. B. Long

PAINE, Halbert Eleazar, *general,* was born on February 4, 1826, in Chardon, Ohio. He graduated from Western Reserve University in 1845, taught school in Mississippi for a brief time, and then moved to Cleveland, where he read law.

Admitted to the bar in 1848, he moved in 1857 to Milwaukee, Wisconsin, where he formed a partnership with Carl Schurz (*q.v.*). Like Schurz, Paine was an abolitionist and a Republican. When the Civil War began, Paine, who handled most of the law firm's business because of Schurz's frequent absences due to politics, closed the office, and became colonel of the 4th Wisconsin Cavalry on July 2, 1861.

Promoted to brigadier general of Volunteers, Paine commanded two divisions of the XIX Corps of the Army of the Gulf (January–June 1863). While under General Benjamin F. Butler's (*q.v.*) command, he defied orders to burn Baton Rouge; as an abolitionist he refused to return fugitive slaves to their masters. During the attack on Port Hudson, Paine was wounded and lost a leg, but remained in the Army as a member of military boards and commissions, commander of forts in the Washington, D.C., area, and commander of the Military District of Illinois. Paine is a good example of the "political" general, the citizen-soldier Abraham Lincoln (*q.v.*) relied upon to ensure support for the war effort and to fill the new commands. A man of steady competence, he could be relied upon to hold the line.

In November 1864 Paine entered Congress, and served consecutive terms in the 39th, 40th, and 41st Congresses. He supported Thaddeus Stevens's (*q.v.*) "state suicide" theory regarding the status of the Southern states. In 1870, Paine left Congress to practice law in Washington, and later served as U.S. commissioner of patents. In this position, he introduced important reforms and innovations, including the substitution of scale drawings for working models, and the use of typewriters by the department's staff. He died in Washington, D.C., on April 14, 1905. Hewitt, *Port Hudson.*

Frank J. Wetta

PALMER, Innis Newton, *general,* was born in Buffalo, New York, on March 30, 1824. He graduated from West Point in 1846, served in Winfield Scott's (*q.v.*) Mexico City campaign, and remained on frontier duty until the outbreak of the Civil War. Palmer commanded the Regular Army cavalry during the campaign of First Bull Run, for which he won a brevet promotion to lieutenant colonel, and in September 1861 was commissioned a brigadier general of Volunteers. During the Peninsula campaign, he commanded a brigade of Silas Casey's (*q.v.*) division, taking part in the battles of Williamsburg and Fair Oaks.

After the brigade was lost in an administrative consolidation, he took temporary charge of a brigade under Darius Couch (*q.v.*), which he led at Glendale and Malvern Hill. Palmer was left without a command when the Army of the Potomac departed the Peninsula, and he spent the autumn organizing and drilling recruits. At the end of 1862, he was assigned to the Department of North Carolina, where he remained for the rest of the war. He successively commanded the XVIII Corps, the defenses of New Bern, the District of North Carolina, and the combined Department of Virginia and North Carolina.

Notwithstanding his long prewar service and early prominence, Palmer's assignment to unfortunate commands and less active locations slowed his professional advancement. Breveted colonel in the Regular Army and major general of Volunteers at the end of the war, he was mustered out of the Volunteers in 1866 and took command of his old unit, the 2nd Cavalry, retiring in 1879 as full colonel. He died in Chevy Chase, Maryland, on September 9, 1900. Barrett, *Civil War in North Carolina.*

William Marvel

PALMER, John McCauley, *general,* was born in Scott county, Kentucky, on September 13, 1817, and moved with his family to Illinois in 1831. He attended Shurtleff College for two years, moved to Carlinville in 1839, studied law, and began his practice. Palmer supported Martin Van Buren for President in 1840. As an Independent Democrat, he was delegate to the Illinois Constitutional Convention in 1847, county judge, and Illinois senator in 1851, and opposed Senator Stephen A. Douglas's (*q.v.*) Kansas–Nebraska Bill of 1854. In 1856, Palmer had an important role in forming the Republican party in Illinois, and was a delegate to the national convention. He was defeated for the U.S. House of Representatives in 1859, and in 1860 he was a delegate at the Chicago convention, which nominated Abraham Lincoln (*q.v.*). He also was a delegate to the Washington Peace Convention in 1861.

In May 1861, Palmer began his military career as colonel of the 14th Illinois Volunteers, served under John C. Frémont (*q.v.*) in Missouri, and was named brigadier general of Volunteers in December. His first major action was as a division commander under John Pope (*q.v.*) in the New Madrid and Island No. 10 campaign in the spring of 1862. He led a brigade during the advance on Corinth, Mississippi, and at Stones River performed effectively as a division commander. On March 13, 1863, he was promoted to major general, to rank from November 29, 1862. Palmer again fought commendably at Chickamauga, and was also in the battles around Chattanooga. He commanded the XIV Corps in the Atlanta campaign, but refused to take orders from John M. Schofield (*q.v.*), who, he claimed, was his junior in rank. After an altercation with William T. Sherman (*q.v.*), he asked to be relieved and was next given command of the Department of Kentucky.

Although Palmer was a "political" general, his performance in brigade, division, and corps command, while not brilliant, was certainly able. After leaving the Army in 1866, he resumed his law practice in Springfield, Illinois, and was elected governor of Illinois as a Republican in 1868. Upset with the corruption in Ulysses S. Grant's (*q.v.*) administration, he supported the Liberal Republicans and Horace Greeley (*q.v.*) in 1872. Palmer then returned to the Democrats, and in 1888 was defeated as the Democratic candidate for governor. In 1891, he was elected to the U.S. Senate, and in 1896 was the presidential candidate of the National or Gold Democrats, polling only 130,000 votes. Palmer died in

Springfield on September 25, 1900. Castel, *Decision in the West*; Hicken, *Illinois in the Civil War.*

E. B. Long

PARKE, John Grubb, *general,* was born near Coatesville, Pennsylvania, on September 22, 1827. He attended the University of Pennsylvania and received an appointment to West Point, graduating in 1849. Parke joined the engineers, performed surveys in the West, and in 1861 was stationed in Washington Territory as a 1st lieutenant of topographical engineers. In October, Parke went east as a captain and soon was made brigadier general of Volunteers (November 23, 1861). Ambrose Burnside (*q.v.*) specifically asked for Parke to serve as a brigade commander in his Roanoke Island expedition, one of the earliest Union offensives. Parke handled his brigade well, especially in the siege of Fort Macon, near Beaufort, North Carolina. Burnside tapped him for command of the 3rd Division, IX Corps, and he was promoted to major general of Volunteers.

Parke was chief of staff of the IX Corps for the Antietam campaign and chief of staff of the Army of the Potomac when Burnside succeeded George B. McClellan (*q.v.*). After Fredericksburg, he moved west with his mentor to the Army of the Ohio, taking command of the IX Corps. Parke reinforced Ulysses S. Grant (*q.v.*) at Vicksburg, and William T. Sherman (*q.v.*) at Jackson, Mississippi. After a leave due to malaria, Parke was transferred to Burnside's command in engagements against James Longstreet near Knoxville (fall and winter of 1863). With Burnside, he again shifted to the eastern theater, and was chief of staff of the IX Corps in fighting through the Wilderness and along the James River.

Parke again suffered from malaria, and was on leave at the time of the battle of the Crater. He replaced Burnside as commander of the IX Corps, which fought well at Petersburg and in the Appomattox campaign. He was promoted to brevet major general in the Regular Army for his accomplishments at Fort Stedman. He held temporary command of the Army of the Potomac (December 30–January 11, 1865) while George G. Meade (*q.v.*) was on leave.

After the war, Parke commanded the District of Alexandria outside Washington, and was mustered out of Volunteer service on January 15, 1866. He received promotions to major (1864), lieutenant colonel (1879), and colonel (1884) in the Regulars, and closed out his career as superintendent of West Point (1887–1889). After retirement in 1889, he became a businessman in Washington, D.C., where he died on December 16, 1900. Marvel, *Burnside*; Sommers, *Richmond Redeemed.*

Joseph G. Dawson III

PARKER, Ely Samuel, *general,* was born sometime in 1828 near Indian Falls, New York. A Seneca of pure lineage, he was the last grand sachem of the Iroquois League of the Five Nations. He attended a school operated by Baptist missionaries near his home, and at ten, was taken into the Canadian wilds, where he became skilled in archery and gunnery. The experience was followed by attendance at the Cayuga Academy, in western New York. Parker studied law, but was refused admittance to the bar because only white males could enter practice in New York. He studied civil engineering at Rensselaer Polytechnic Institute, and upon graduation superintended improvements on the western terminal of the Erie Canal. In 1855, Parker was appointed chief engineer of the Chesapeake & Albemarle Ship Canal in Virginia. Two years later, he became superintendent of construction for a customhouse and marine hospital in Galena, Illinois, where he met Ulysses S. Grant (*q.v.*).

The firing on Fort Sumter sparked Parker's interest in the Unionist cause, and he returned to New York to seek a military commission. Rebuffed by the governor, he left for Washington, D.C., only to have his request refused by the War Department. In May 1863 President Abraham Lincoln (*q.v.*) commissioned him a captain and assistant adjutant general of Volunteers. Parker reported to Brigadier General John E. Smith (*q.v.*) near Vicksburg, where he served as the division engineer of the 7th Division, XVII Corps. He was at the battles of Lookout Mountain and Missionary Ridge, and in the Wilderness campaign laid out breastworks and entrenchments.

In late August 1864 Parker became military secretary to Grant. He transcribed much of Grant's correspondence, in addition to preparing letters, orders, and reports for the general's signature. At Appomattox, he joined Grant and his staff inside the McLean House. Grant called for his order book to transcribe the letter of surrender and passed it to Parker for review. The book was then passed to Robert E. Lee for his review, after which Lee suggested certain additions. Due to the nervousness of Union Colonel Theodore S. Bowers, the document was turned over to Parker, who transcribed the official copies of the document that ended the Civil War.

Parker served as colonel and as aide-de-camp to Grant until March 4, 1869, rising to the rank of brevet brigadier general. In April 1869 President Grant appointed Parker commissioner of Indian affairs. He resigned the post in August 1871 to enter private business, where he made and lost several fortunes. Parker died on August 30, 1895, in Fairfield, Connecticut. Armstrong, *Warrior in Two Camps*.

Frank R. Levstik

PARKER, Joel, *governor*, was born near Freehold, New Jersey, on November 24, 1816. He was graduated from Princeton University in 1839, and began a law practice in Freehold. Parker was elected as a Democrat to the state legislature (1848–1851) and in 1860 was chosen a presidential elector, one of the three New Jersey Democrats on both the "fusion" slate and the separate slate supporting Stephen A. Douglas (*q.v.*).

A brigadier general in the New Jersey militia, Parker was appointed a major general by Governor Charles S. Olden (*q.v.*) once the Civil War began. As a War Democrat, he won his party's nomination to succeed Olden, and in November 1862 defeated Union–Republican Marcus L. Ward. Democrats also gained a majority in both houses of the legislature, making New Jersey the only Northern state under solid Democratic control. Parker, who took office in January 1863, criticized Abraham Lincoln's (*q.v.*) administration for the Emancipation Proclamation, the military arrest of civilians, and the suspension of the writ of habeas corpus. To placate the substantial antiwar element in his party, he signed "Peace Resolutions" passed by the legislature in March 1863 that urged Lincoln to appoint commissioners to meet with Confederate counterparts in order to find a way to end the war.

In other ways, however, Parker assisted the Union war effort. He arranged quietly with the War Department to allow New Jersey to continue to meet its manpower quotas with volunteers, rather than risk implementing Federal conscription in 1863 (a draft did go into effect in 1864). He also worked energetically to supply the state's men in the field, and to care for those who were wounded or hospitalized. Parker nevertheless remained an outspoken critic of the Lincoln administration, which he accused in August 1864 of preventing a peaceful settlement of the war. When the administration threatened to open a rail line across New Jersey to compete with the Camden & Amboy Railroad monopoly, he denounced the threat to states' rights. He also opposed allowing soldiers to vote in the field, a policy that helped George B. McClellan (*q.v.*) carry his home state in 1864. Parker opposed passage of the 13th Amendment, and when the war ended, called for the rapid readmission of Southern states.

Parker was forbidden by the state constitution to run for a second consecutive term. He returned to his law practice, and in 1871 he won a second three-year term as governor (1872–1875). He was a justice of the New Jersey Supreme Court until his death in Philadelphia on January 2, 1888. Knapp, *New Jersey Politics*; Stellhorn, *Governors of New Jersey*.

Daniel W. Crofts

PARSONS, Lewis Baldwin, *general,* was born on April 5, 1818, in New York. He graduated from Yale College in 1840, and after two years spent teaching in Mississippi, he entered Harvard Law School, receiving a Bachelor of Laws degree in 1844. Parsons practiced law in Alton, Illinois, until 1854, when he moved to St. Louis to take charge of the Ohio and Mississippi Railroad's legal affairs. He rose in the company until he became president, a position from which he retired in 1860. A strong Union man, Parsons joined the staff of Francis P. Blair (*q.v.*), and participated in the capture of Camp Jackson. He then went to Washington, where he was commissioned a captain but did not receive the combat assignment he sought. Instead, he was assigned to St. Louis, where he was placed in charge of all transport in the Department of the Mississippi.

River transport was a serious problem because of shortages of vessels and tonnage, and of schedules entirely too casual for the expanded needs of the war. But railroads offered even greater problems. Lack of sufficient rolling stock and locomotives, unstandardized track gauge and equipment, and lines that did not connect proved a nightmare. Parsons created the first organized modern transport system. Schedules were set, procedure was organized, and wagons, men, and animals were made available where water and rail transit were impossible or needed augmenting. With his promotion to colonel in February 1862, backed by General Henry W. Halleck (*q.v.*), and with the passage of a railroad act in 1862, Parsons was able to impose this effective system. In August 1864 he was ordered to Washington and placed in charge of all U.S. Army transport, a post he held until after the war.

Parsons was one of a number of able men whose skill and organization allowed the Union Army to move and fight. Tens of thousands of men could be transported from one front to another in a matter of days. Hundreds of thousands of tons of munitions and supplies moved on tight schedules. Still needed after the end of the war, Parsons, now a brigadier general, did not leave the service until April 30, 1866. The effort and exhaustion had broken his health, and it was two years before he could lead an active life. Returning to St. Louis in 1869, he later moved to Flora, Illinois, where he served on boards of directors of several railroads and as a bank president, and was an unsuccessful Democratic candidate for lieutenant governor of Illinois. He died in Flora on March 16, 1907. Turner, *Victory Rode the Rails.*

Carl L. Davis

PATRICK, Marsena Rudolph, *general,* was born near Watertown, New York, on March 11, 1811. He graduated from West Point in 1835, and was commissioned in the infantry. Following troop assignments in Michigan, Wisconsin, and Florida, he became chief of commissariat for John Wool's (*q.v.*) column in the Mexican War. Resigning from the Army in 1850, Patrick farmed at Geneva, New York, headed a local railroad, and promoted a state agricultural society. Named president of the New York State Agricultural College when it opened at Ovid in 1859, he held that office until the Civil War began.

Between May 1861 and February 1862, Patrick served as inspector general of New York Volunteers. In the spring of 1862, he took command of a force manning the Washington defenses, then led a brigade of the 1st Division, III Corps, Army of Virginia, at Second Bull Run. After this unit was transferred to the Army of the Potomac, Patrick led it at Boonesboro and Sharpsburg, seeing heavy fighting at the West Woods and the Cornfield in the latter battle. Appointed provost marshal general, Army of the Potomac, on October 6, 1862, he retained that assignment for the rest of the war, and in July 1864 assumed similar responsibilities for the other armies operating against Richmond. Patrick made strenuous efforts to enforce regulations, particularly those prohibiting trade with Confederates, but with mixed results. After Appomattox, he commanded the military district surrounding Richmond until relieved for showing excessive leniency to white Virginians.

A competent but unpopular brigade commander and provost marshal, Patrick is important to Civil War historiography mainly because of his wartime diary, a gossipy but fairly reliable account of field headquarters. Upon resigning his commission and returning to New York in June 1865, Patrick, displeased with the Republicans, ran on the Democratic ticket for state treasurer. Defeated, he then became a farmer near Manlius. In 1867, he became president of the New York State Agricultural Society, and for twelve years pursued his interest in scientific agriculture and pioneered in conservation and reforestation. Appointed governor of the Central Branch, National Home for Disabled Soldiers, at Dayton, Ohio, in 1880, Patrick remained in that post until his death there on July 27, 1888. Catton, *Grant Takes Command*; Patrick, *Inside Lincoln's Army*.

James L. Morrison, Jr.

PATTERSON, James Willis, *congressman,* was born in Henniker, New Hampshire, on July 2, 1823. He graduated from Dartmouth in 1848, studied for both the bar and the ministry, then returned to Dartmouth in 1852 as a tutor. Two years later he accepted a professorship there, holding it for the next thirteen years. In 1863, after a single term in the New Hampshire legislature, Patterson was elected to Congress. He served four years in the House, working for the establishment of freedmen's schools, and in 1866 he was elected to the U.S. Senate. Patterson lost a bid for reelection in 1872, his defeat coming largely as a result of his alleged involvement in the Crédit Mobilier scandal.

Patterson's political strengths included the force of his rhetoric and adherence to a moderate doctrine. His political demise was self-inflicted, however, for if he was not actively corrupt, he was at least sufficiently negligent to give the appearance that he was. Returning to his home in Hanover, New Hampshire, Patterson reentered politics briefly as a state legislator. In 1881, he was named state superintendent of public instruction, a post he held for a dozen years. He died in Hanover on May 4, 1893. Lyford, *Life of Edward H. Rollins.*

William Marvel

PATTON, John, *congressman,* was born in Covington, Pennsylvania, on January 6, 1823. He lacked a formal education, but after working in the mercantile and lumbering business, he was able to establish a successful career in banking. In the late 1840s, he was appointed an aide to Governor William F. Johnston and commissioned a brigadier general in the state militia. A Henry Clay Whig, Patton was elected delegate to the 1852 convention. He was a delegate to the 1860 Republican National Convention, and was elected to the U.S. House of Representatives. Patton consistently voted for measures that furthered the Union war effort, particularly confiscation, the suspension of habeas corpus, and emancipation. He was not a candidate in 1862, but he was a Republican elector in 1864.

After the war, Patton resumed his career in banking and became well known for his philanthrophy and leadership within the Methodist Episcopal Church. In 1884, he reentered the political arena and was defeated for Congress. Two years later he was elected to the 50th Congress. He died in Philadelphia on December 23, 1897. *BDUSC; Biographical Album of Prominent Pennsylvanians,* vol. 3.

J. K. Folmar

PEARCE, James Alfred, *senator,* was born in Alexandria, Virginia, on December 14, 1805. He attended a private academy in Alexandria, graduated from the College of New Jersey (now Princeton), studied law in Baltimore, and was admitted to the bar in 1824. He began his practice in Cambridge, Maryland, but within a year he accompanied his father to Louisiana to manage a sugar plantation. After three years he returned to Maryland, where he resumed his law practice in Chestertown. Pearce's long public career began in 1831, with his election to the Maryland House of Delegates. He served as a Whig in Congress from 1835 to 1843, with the exception of one term (1839–1841), when he was defeated for reelection. In 1843, he was elected to the U.S. Senate, and remained in that body until his death. With the collapse of the Whigs, Pearce became a Democrat, and in 1861 he was returned to the Senate for a fourth term by that party.

In the sectional crisis, Pearce pleaded for conciliation. He denied that a state had the right to secede, but he was opposed to coercion. His support for the Union was tempered by conservative instincts, which subordinated the preservation of the Union to the protection of constitutional rights. He strongly protested the suspension of the writ of habeas corpus and the use of military arrests. Pearce's opposition to a joint congressional resolution approving Abraham Lincoln's (*q.v.*) actions taken during the crisis brought demands from some Marylanders for his resignation. Reluctant to speak on the slavery issue, he opposed any interference with the institution by the Federal government. In March 1862, in ill health, he made his final Senate appearance. He died on December 20, 1862, in Chestertown, Maryland. Baker, *Politics of Continuity;* Clark, *Politics in Maryland During the Civil War.*

Richard R. Duncan

PECK, John James, *general,* was born in Manlius, New York, on January 24, 1821. He graduated from West Point in 1843, then served with distinction in the Mexican War and on the frontier until he resigned on March 31, 1853, to pursue banking and railroad interests in his native state. Twice nominated for Congress as a Democrat, he was a delegate to the national conventions that nominated James Buchanan (*q.v.*) and Stephen A. Douglas (*q.v.*).

A brigadier general of Volunteers (August 9, 1861), Peck commanded a brigade in the defenses of Washington and in the Peninsula campaign, taking over Silas Casey's (*q.v.*) division just before the Seven Days' battles. His service proved so satisfactory that he was promoted to major general, to date from the end of that campaign. Peck remained on the James when the rest of the army moved north. He stymied James Longstreet's siege of Suffolk early in 1863, wisely opting for a defensive maneuver with a force that consisted largely of untried Volunteers and short-term militia. Injured in an accident that spring, he went on leave until August, when he took command of the District of North Carolina and later the Department of Virginia and North Carolina. His health forced him to leave the latter post in April 1864. In November 1864 Peck assumed command of the Canadian frontier in the wake of international incidents caused by Confederate activities along the border. He remained in that capacity until August 24, 1864, when he returned to civilian life.

Peck's civil and military careers were marked with success, and his performance at Suffolk prevented a major Union setback at a crucial juncture. Had he remained with a major army, he would likely have achieved a significant reputation. After the war he established a life insurance company. Peck died in Syracuse, New York, on April 21, 1878. Sears, *To the Gates of Richmond.*

William Marvel

PENDLETON, George Hunt, *congressman, vice presidential candidate,* was born in Cincinnati, Ohio, on July 29, 1825. He attended Cincinnati College, studied with private tutors, and interspersed study at Heidelberg University with travel through most of Europe and an extensive journey to the Holy Land and Egypt. In 1846, he married Alice Key, daughter of Francis Scott Key and niece of U.S. Supreme Court Chief Justice Roger B. Taney (*q.v.*). Pendleton was admitted to the Ohio bar, and began practicing law as a partner of George E. Pugh. In 1853, he won election to the Ohio legislature as a Democrat, and his talents and vigor proved impressive enough to win him nomination to Congress. Although defeated in 1854, he was elected to four successive terms, running from 1857 to 1865. With other Northern Democrats, he backed Stephen A. Douglas (*q.v.*) in blocking Kansas's admission as a slave state, and supported Douglas again in the 1860 presidential race.

In the winter of 1860–1861, Pendleton gave vigorous support to the Crittenden Compromise proposals, and when the war did come, he viewed it as an advoidable tragedy. He strongly opposed the Lincoln (*q.v.*) administration's suspension of habeas corpus, arbitrary arrests of civilians, and military trials of dissidents. He also criticized the centralizing tendencies that the war engendered. As the vice presidential running mate of George B. McClellan (*q.v.*) in 1864, Pendleton suffered a resounding defeat.

Out of Congress, Pendleton became an ardent Greenbacker. Although he did not originate the "Ohio Idea" to pay off the war debt with issues of greenbacks, he became closely associated with it. That position, which angered Eastern Democrats, likely cost him the presidential nomination in 1868. In 1869, he lost the Ohio gubernatorial race to Rutherford B. Hayes (*q.v.*), and left politics to serve as president of the Kentucky Central Railroad. Chosen in 1879 as one of Ohio's senators, Pendleton won in his single term a degree of fame as a reformer. As chairman of the Committee on Civil Service, he pushed through a bill that created the Civil Service Commission and authorized the President to classify Federal positions that could be filled only through competitive examinations. It was the basis for the modern civil service system, but the alienation of party spoilsmen cost him renomination. In 1885, President Grover Cleveland appointed Pendleton minister to Germany, a post he held until his death in Brussels, Belgium, on November 24, 1889. Bloss, *Life and Speeches of George H. Pendleton*; Fish, *Civil Service and Patronage.*

David Lindsey

PENNINGTON, William, Jr., *congressman, Speaker of the House,* was born in Newark, New Jersey, on May 4, 1796. He graduated from the College of New Jersey (now Princeton) in 1813. After clerking in the U.S. District Court and studying law, he was admitted to the bar and began a law practice in 1820. In 1828, Pennington was elected as a Whig to the state General Assembly, and in 1837 the legislature appointed him governor and chancellor of New Jersey. He was reelected in each of the next six years. After he left the governor's office in October 1843, he returned to his law practice and declined various appointments, including the governorship of Minnesota Territory.

In the late 1850s, Pennington resumed his interest in politics and was elected as a Republican to the 36th Congress. Although this was his first and only national office, he would have a pivotal role in the secession crisis. Within hours after the 36th Congress convened in December 1859, a bitter contest erupted over the selection of the Speaker of the House. After two months of acrimonious debate, forty-four ballots, and the elimination of various contenders, including skilled politicians such as John Sherman (*q.v.*) and John A. McClernand (*q.v.*), Pennington was selected as the most viable compromise candidate. Henry Winter Davis (*q.v.*) cast the deciding vote. The divisiveness over the speakership portended the difficulties that were to emerge at this critical hour, which were compounded by Pennington's inexperience at the national level.

When the second session of the 36th Congress convened in December 1860, Pennington appointed the members of the Committee of Thirty-three, a representative from each state. In an attempt to achieve balance, he selected fourteen Democrats, sixteen Republicans, and three Opposition members, more on the basis of their political affiliation than the leadership that they could bring to this cumbersome and factious group. However well-intentioned, the effort failed to develop compromise proposals that might have averted the Civil War.

After Pennington failed to win reelection to the 37th Congress, he returned to Newark, New Jersey, where he died on February 16, 1862. Henig, *Henry Winter Davis*; Nichols, *Disruption of American Democracy*; Potter, *Impending Crisis.*

James W. Geary

PERHAM, Sidney, *congressman,* was born on March 27, 1819, in Woodstock, Maine. Educated in local schools and at Bethel Academy, he made farming his lifetime occupation. He specialized in sheep raising, keeping 250–500 animals at a time. Perham addressed numerous agricultural fairs and served in 1853–1854 as a member of the Maine Board of Agriculture. From 1854 to 1858, he spoke for prohibition all over Maine, as an agent of the Maine Temperance Society, having already organized Woodstock's first temperance society. His speeches at national temperance conventions won him many invitations to speak on a variety of patriotic occasions. Perham was also a state and national leader of the Universalist Church. He served on the board of trustees of the Universalist General Convention for twenty-seven years, and was board president part of the time.

Initially a Democrat, Perham held local offices in Woodstock, but broke with his party to support fellow temperance advocate Anson P. Morrill's (*q.v.*) unsuccessful gubernatorial bid in 1853. He helped found the Republican party in Maine, and served as a Republican state representative in 1854, being elected speaker on his first day in the House. He was a Republican presidential elector in 1856, and clerk of courts of Oxford county (1859–1863). In 1862, Perham won a seat in Congress, and served there until 1869. He immersed himself in pension law revision and allied matters as chairman of the House Committee on Pensions, and still found time to speak frequently on Reconstruction issues. He urged that the South be treated mercifully but that rebellion be made impossible, and that civil and political rights, including suffrage, be guaranteed to all loyal citizens regardless of race or color. He also strongly favored the impeachment of Andrew Johnson (*q.v.*).

From 1871 to 1874, Perham was governor of Maine. In 1875, he ran unsuccessfully for the U.S. Senate against the incumbent, Hannibal Hamlin (*q.v.*), and filled a vacancy as Maine secretary of state. From 1877 to 1885, Perham served as appraiser in the Portland, Maine, customhouse, apparently a reward for faithful party service and his concern for Union soldiers and veterans. Perham died in Washington, D.C., on April 10, 1907. *BDUSC*; Hatch, *Maine: A History*, vols. 2, 3.

H. Draper Hunt

PERRY, Nehemiah, *congressman,* was born in Ridgefield, Connecticut, on March 30, 1816. Arriving in Newark, New Jersey, in 1836, he developed a cloth manufacturing and retail business through which he amassed an ample fortune. He was elected to the state Assembly in 1855 as a Whig, with Know-Nothing support. Not long afterward he became a Democrat. By 1860, Perry was chairman of the New Jersey Democratic Executive Committee, in which capacity he worked to arrange a fusion ticket of Douglas, Bell, and Breckrinridge supporters.

Perry won a bitterly contested election to Congress in 1860 from the populous and fast-growing 5th District, centered in Newark. His opponent, Speaker of the House William Pennington (*q.v.*), was a conservative Republican, but some of Pennington's previous National American supporters among the Newark elite could not accept his endorsement of the "sectional" presidential candidate, Abraham Lincoln (*q.v.*). Aided by such Bell–Everett voters, who regarded both Pennington and Perry as renegades, but Perry as the lesser evil, Perry won by about 400 votes in a heavy turnout.

In Congress, Perry became an increasingly outspoken opponent of administration policies and contended that emancipation doomed the Union war effort. As a member of the Commerce Committee, he firmly defended the Camden &

Amboy Railroad monopoly against threatened Federal interference. Perry easily won reelection in 1862. Redistricting had made the seat more Democratic; he maintained his hold on well-to-do former Whigs; and Republican fortunes were at a low ebb in any case. But in 1864, the nomination went to E.V.R. Wright when New Jersey Democrats observed the rotation principle. Perry was elected mayor of Newark as a Democrat in 1873, but became a Republican after being denied renomination. He died in Newark on November 1, 1881. Knapp, *New Jersey Politics.*

Daniel W. Crofts

PHELPS, John Smith, *congressman, general, military governor,* was born in Simsbury, Connecticut, on December 22, 1814. Educated at Washington College (now Trinity University), he studied law with his father, and was admitted to the bar in 1835. In 1837, he moved to Springfield, Missouri, where he began the practice of law. A Jacksonian Democrat, Phelps served Greene county in the legislature (1840–1842), and in 1844 he was elected to Congress, where he served for the next eighteen years. He was particularly active in promoting western expansion and protection for the settlers of California and Oregon. During the sessions of the 37th Congress he was principally involved in noncongressional activities, although he retained his seat until 1863.

In 1861, Phelps organized a regiment of six-month volunteers known as Phelps's Regiment, and led it at Pea Ridge, where he was wounded. His wife turned their Springfield home into a hospital for those wounded at Wilson's Creek and Pea Ridge, and was later awarded $20,000 by Congress for her services. This she used to establish an orphans' home at Springfield for the children of veterans from both sides. In July 1862, President Abraham Lincoln (*q.v.*) appointed Phelps military governor of Arkansas, and on November 29 commissioned him major general of Volunteers, to rank from July 19. Phelps established his headquarters at Helena, but by January 1863 he was ill in St. Louis, and did not return to his post. His appointment expired on March 4, 1863, for lack of senatorial confirmation.

Phelps was a delegate to the Democratic National Convention in 1864, and after the war was active in reorganizing the Missouri Democratic party. He ran unsuccessfully for governor in 1868, but was elected in 1876 and served until 1881. He died in St. Louis on November 20, 1886. Staples, *Reconstruction in Arkansas.*

William E. Parrish

PHELPS, Timothy Guy, *congressman,* was born in Chenago county, New York, on December 20, 1824. Lacking a formal education, he engaged in mercantile pursuits with an older brother in New York City (1846–1848), then entered the study of law. He arrived in San Francisco in December 1849 and mined in Tuolumne county until 1851, when failing health forced him back to San Francisco. Phelps entered politics as a Whig and became a Republican in

1856. Election as an assemblyman followed that year, then two terms (1858–1862) in the California Senate. A Unionist, he was the main opponent of Leland Stanford (*q.v.*) for the governorship.

Phelps served in Congress from December 1861 until March 1863, supporting the administration's war measures. With both of California's senators Democratic, he dominated the other two Republican congressmen to build a strong following through use of the Federal patronage. The remainder of Phelps's forty-year political career, except for two appointments as collector of the Port of San Francisco, consisted of unfilled promise and near election to office. In 1863, he outmaneuvered Governor Stanford to become the leading Republican contender for the U.S. Senate. However, a friend and Federal official attempted to bribe members of the legislature. The resulting scandal sent John Conness (*q.v.*) to the Senate, and Phelps to his real estate business and farm in San Mateo county. He lost races for Congress in 1867, for governor in 1875, and for Congress in 1889. He was a regent of the University of California and chairman of the board of regents of Lick Observatory. Phelps died in San Mateo county on June 11, 1899. Phelps, *Contemporary Biography*, vol. 2; Shuck, *Representative and Leading Men of the Pacific*.

Robert J. Chandler

PHILLIPS, Wendell, *abolitionist*, was born on November 29, 1811, in Boston. He joined the American Anti-Slavery Society in 1837, and became the close collaborator of William Lloyd Garrison (*q.v.*). Phillips was an exceptional orator, and his greatest contributions to the crusade against slavery undoubtedly came from the speaker's platform. He attracted national attention for his espousals of immediate emancipation, women's rights, and the need for the North to withdraw from the ''proslavery'' Federal Union. When the Civil War began, however, Phillips embraced the Union, demanded the military annihilation of the Confederacy, and called for all slaves to be granted full citizenship. He made several highly publicized speaking tours that did much to shape public opinion in favor of emancipation. In 1864, disillusioned with Abraham Lincoln's (*q.v.*) leadership, Phillips joined the abortive attempt to elevate John C. Frémont (*q.v.*) as the Republican presidential candidate. His attacks on Lincoln and his demands for African American political equality soon put him at odds with Garrison and many others within the abolitionist movement, which split over such issues in 1865.

At war's end, when Garrison retired, Phillips assumed the presidency of the American Anti-Slavery Society. From then until 1870, when the 15th Amendment was finally ratified, he used his position to further his comprehensive version of Radical Reconstruction. While insisting on universal male suffrage, he demanded that confiscated Confederate estates be distributed to the freed slaves, that Confederate leaders be permanently disenfranchised, and that the rebel states be placed under long-term military occupation. At the same time, Phillips became increasingly involved in the Northern labor movement, supporting its demands for an eight-hour day. In 1872, he ran unsuccessfully at the Temperance and Labor party's candidate for the Massachusetts governorship. He died in Boston on February 3, 1884. Stewart, *Wendell Phillips.*

James Brewer Stewart

PIERPONT, Francis Harrison, *governor,* was born in Monongalia county, Virginia (now West Virginia), on June 25, 1814. He graduated from Allegheny College in 1840, then migrated to Mississippi, where he taught school and studied law. Returning to northwestern Virginia in 1842, Pierpont opened his law practice at Fairmont and gained a reputation as an outspoken critic of the "slavocracy" and the Democratic party. Bitterly opposed to secession, he was elected to the First Wheeling Convention (May 1861) and was also a member of the Second Wheeling Convention, which, on June 20, 1861, formed the Reorganized Government of Virginia and elected Pierpont governor.

Recognized by President Abraham Lincoln (*q.v.*) as the de jure governor of Virginia, Pierpont actively engaged in recruiting and equipping ten regiments for Federal service. Guerrilla warfare, internecine strife, and insufficient manpower made life difficult for him, for the Union Army, and for Unionists who lived in areas outside the extreme northwestern section of the state. After West Virginia's admission into the Union in 1863, Pierpont remained head of the Reorganized Government, moving his headquarters from Wheeling to Alexandria. His jurisdiction was confined to a few counties in the vicinity of Washington, D.C., the Eastern Shore, and the region in and about Norfolk.

When the war ended, the legitimacy of the Reorganized Government was recognized by President Andrew Johnson (*q.v.*). Thus, Pierpont served as Reconstruction governor of Virginia in Richmond. He urged the Virginia Assembly to ratify the 14th Amendment, but without success. He also supported and enforced the Military Reconstruction Acts. Despite this, Virginia Radical Republicans, led by Judge John C. Underwood, succeeded in having Pierpont removed from office (April 4, 1868) by General John M. Schofield (*q.v.*).

Pierpont campaigned for Ulysses S. Grant (*q.v.*), and was elected to a two-year term in the West Virginia House of Delegates. In 1872, he was a delegate to the Republican National Convention, but his opposition to Grant's renomination and his support of Horace Greeley (*q.v.*) cost him his influence. In 1897, he moved to Pittsburgh, where he died on March 24, 1899. Ambler, *Francis H. Pierpont*; Curry, *House Divided.*

Richard Orr Curry

PIKE, Frederick Augustus, *congressman,* was born in Calais, Maine, on December 9, 1816. He attended local schools and Washington Academy in East Machias, Maine, then went on to Bowdoin College, from which he graduated in 1837. He read law, and began his practice in Calais in 1840. Pike served as mayor of Calais in 1852–1853, and as a member of the Maine House for three terms (1858–1860), holding the speakership in 1860. A Republican, he won a seat in Congress in 1860, and remained there until 1869. He strongly advocated emancipation, made naval affairs a specialty, and eventually rose to the chairmanship of the House Naval Affairs Committee.

In April 1865 Pike was a member of a national committee that escorted Abraham Lincoln's (*q.v.*) body home to Illinois. Although a Radical Republican, he resisted President Andrew Johnson's (*q.v.*) impeachment until the latter's February 21, 1868, removal of Secretary of War Edwin M. Stanton (*q.v.*). Defeated for renomination in 1868, he began practicing law again, and won a Maine House seat in 1870 and 1871. An unsuccessful independent candidacy for Congress in 1872 ended Pike's political career, although he supported Liberal Republican candidate Horace Greeley (*q.v.*) for the presidency that year. Pike died in Calais on December 2, 1886. *BDUSC*; Blaine, *Twenty Years of Congress*.

H. Draper Hunt

PIKE, James Shepherd, *diplomat*, was born in Calais, Maine, on September 8, 1811. He accumulated a modest fortune before turning to politics and journalism in the late 1840s. An ardent Whig who failed to win in several tries for political office in Maine, he began spending winters in Washington, D.C., in 1844 and writing political letters for the *Boston Courier*. His forceful style and strong antislavery sympathies led Horace Greeley (*q.v.*) to invite Pike to write for the *Tribune*, which was well on the way to becoming the most important antislavery newspaper in the nation. When the Republican party was born in 1854, both Pike and the *Tribune* became its strong partisans.

Even more radical than Greeley, Pike was also remarkably candid in his racial views. His vigorous articles and editorials made it clear that his staunch support for "free soil" before the Civil War sprang partly from his belief that the West should belong to white people; that he advocated a Garrisonian-like disunionism in the late 1850s because he despaired of living alongside what he regarded as arrogant slaveholders and their repulsive human property; that he urged peaceful secession in 1860–1861 partly because he saw a chance to rid the country of a "mass of barbarism"; and that during some of the Civil War's gloomier moments for the North, he would have settled for a compromise peace if it meant only that a deep South "negro pen" would be lost to the Union.

Identified with the Radical wing of his party, Pike realized an old dream of a diplomatic appointment when President Abraham Lincoln (*q.v.*) named him as minister to the Netherlands in 1861, a post that he occupied until his return to the United States in 1866. He resumed his journalistic career on the *Tribune* and supported Congressional Reconstruction, but in 1872 he, like Greeley, bolted the party to become a Liberal Republican. Following that party's defeat, Pike visited South Carolina and wrote a series of articles on the alleged Republican and black misrule there. These were soon published in *The Prostrate State: South Carolina Under Negro Rule*, which not only had a large impact at the time but was long cited by historians who took a negative view of Reconstruction. In 1879, Pike published *First Blows of the Civil War*, a valuable collection of his articles and of letters from many important Republicans in the 1850s. Pike died in Calais on November 24, 1882. Durden, *James Shepherd Pike.*

Robert F. Durden

PILE, William Anderson, *general*, was born near Indianapolis, Indiana, on February 11, 1829, but grew up in St. Louis, Missouri, where he was ordained in the Methodist Episcopal Church. He became active in abolitionist circles, and on June 12, 1861, was appointed chaplain of the 1st Missouri Light Artillery. On March 1, 1862, Pile moved into a combat role as a battery commander, fighting at Shiloh. After the occupation of Corinth, Mississippi, on September 5, 1862, he was appointed lieutenant colonel of the 33rd Missouri Volunteers, and became its colonel on December 23. As colonel he took part in the January 1863 White River expedition against Devall's Bluff, Arkansas, and in the February–March 1863 Yazoo Pass expedition.

In May, Pile became superintendent of colored troops in Missouri. His near fanatic zeal brought protests from pro-Union slave owners, but he was successfully defended by his friend, General John M. Schofield (*q.v.*), and on December 26, 1863, was promoted to brigadier general. After recruiting seven colored regiments, he was assigned in November 1864 to command the garrison of Brazos Santiago, Texas. Repeatedly demanding more active service, Pile finally obtained assignment on February 25, 1865, to command the 1st Brigade of General John P. Hawkins's (*q.v.*) 1st Division, U.S. Colored Troops, for the impending Mobile campaign. He distinguished himself in the siege and the April 9, 1865, assault on Fort Blakely, Alabama. On August 24, 1865, he was mustered out as a brevet major general of Volunteers.

Pile was forceful and courageous, self-righteous and domineering, traits that made him a strong commander but a difficult subordinate. A capable brigadier at the tactical level, he is chiefly noteworthy for attaining the highest rank among the clergymen who served in the Union Army as combat officers. In 1866, Pile was elected to Congress as a Republican, but his radicalism contributed to his defeat in 1868. In 1869, President Ulysses S. Grant (*q.v.*) appointed Pile territorial governor of New Mexico, an office he held until May 23, 1871, when he became the U.S. minister resident in Venezuela. In 1874, Antonio Guzman Blanco named him the Venezuelan government's agent in the United States. He continued in that post until Guzman Blanco's fall in 1888. Pile then moved to Monrovia, California, where he died on July 7, 1889. Andrews, *History of the Campaign of Mobile*; Honeywell, *Chaplains of the United States Army.*

John B.B. Trussell, Jr.

PINKERTON, Allan, *detective*, was born in Glasgow, Scotland, on August 25, 1819, the son of a policeman. In 1842, he came to America, and in 1843 opened a cooperage at Dundee, Illinois. Becoming deputy sheriff first of Kane county and then of Cook county, he sold his business and in 1850 moved to Chicago, where he formed an organization to capture thieves stealing the property of the railroads. By 1852, it had become Pinkerton's National Detective Agency. Pinkerton's success brought him national publicity and enabled him to expand his operations.

Hired early in 1861 to investigate rumors of impending sabotage of the Philadelphia, Wilmington, & Baltimore Railroad, Pinkerton and his operatives, posing as secessionists, discovered a plot to assassinate President-elect Abraham Lincoln (q.v.) as he passed through Baltimore en route to Washington, D.C. On the night of February 21, he met Lincoln in Philadelphia and warned him of the danger. As a result, Lincoln, who had also learned of the plot through detectives working for General Winfield Scott (q.v.), altered his plans.

In May 1861, at the request of George B. McClellan (q.v.), whom he had previously met, Pinkerton toured from Kentucky and Tennessee to Mississippi to assess public opinion. When he returned, he organized a secret service bureau for the Department of the Ohio, commanded by McClellan, and assumed the name E.J. Allen, by which he was known throughout the war. He and a large number of male and female operatives continued to provide military intelligence when McClellan became commander of the Army of the Potomac. Upon McClellan's removal from command in November 1862, Pinkerton severed his connections with the army, but continued to work for the government in the investigation of claims against it.

In 1865, Pinkerton returned to Chicago and the practice of his profession, which increasingly involved industrial espionage and union busting. With branch offices in New York and Philadelphia, the Pinkerton Agency's services were much in demand, and the organization accumulated the largest storehouse of data concerning crime and criminals in the United States. One of its many successful actions was the frustration in 1876 of an attempt by two counterfeiters to steal Lincoln's body from its tomb in Springfield, Illinois, and hold it for ransom.

Pinkerton's books read like fiction, and are no doubt liberally laced with it, but there is no question about the daring and enterprise he and those who worked for him exhibited during the war. What is questionable is the value of the intelligence he gathered. In addition to reporting their personal observations about the size and deployment of Confederate units, he and his spies interrogated Southern refugees, deserters, and slaves, the latter being considered "my best source of information." To the end of his life, Pinkerton continued to insist that his reports to McClellan were accurate. Charges that he had overestimated the size of the opposing army originated, he believed, with McClellan's political enemies in Washington and with "irresponsible historians."

The consensus of responsible military historians today is that Pinkerton grossly overestimated the strength of the enemy, and thus contributed to McClellan's failure. In at least one other matter he misled McClellan. He accompanied Lincoln to Washington after the President's visit to the Army of the Potomac at Antietam, and reported that he had had a long talk with him aboard the train. "All is at present bright and beautiful as regards your future prospects," he told McClellan one month before the general was dismissed from command. Pinkerton died in Chicago on July 1, 1884. Fishel, "Pinkerton and McClellan," *Civil War History*; Horan, *The Pinkertons*; Pinkerton, *Spy of the Rebellion.*

William Hanchett

PLEASONTON, Alfred, *general,* was born on June 7, 1824, in Washington, D.C. He graduated from West Point in 1844, was promoted to brevet 1st lieutenant for service at Palo Alto and Resaca de la Palma in the Mexican War, and saw duty against the Indians in Florida, Kansas, Oregon, and Washington. With the outbreak of the Civil War, he served as a major in the 2nd U.S. Cavalry, and was promoted to brigadier general in July 1862. He commanded a cavalry division from South Mountain through Chancellorsville. In the latter action, he gathered twenty-two artillery pieces that helped to stop Thomas Jackson's initial attack. Promoted to major general, he reorganized the scattered cavalry units of the Army of the Potomac that could finally challenge J.E.B. Stuart.

Pleasonton's new corps surprised and almost defeated Stuart at Brandy Station on June 9, 1863, in the largest cavalry battle of the war. He defeated Stuart at Aldie, Middleburg, and Upperville, Virginia, and Hanover, Pennsylvania, in preliminary actions of the Gettysburg campaign. His cavalry under John Buford (*q.v.*) opened the battle, and his repulse of Stuart at Rummel's Farm ended it. Pleasonton harassed Lee's retreat with victories at Williamsport and Boonsboro, Maryland. His last operation in the East was ordering the ill-fated Kilpatrick–Dahlgren raid against Richmond in February 1864.

Pleasonton was transferred to Missouri in March 1864 to make way for Philip Sheridan (*q.v.*). He defended Jefferson City against Sterling Price's last raid through Missouri; defeated Price at Westport, in one of the largest battles in the trans-Mississippi West; and thoroughly routed the Confederates at Mine Creek, Kansas. He resigned in 1868 and served with the Treasury Department until 1872. Pleasonton spent his last years on a military pension and died in Washington, D.C., on February 17, 1897. Longacre, *Cavalry at Gettysburg*; Starr, *Union Cavalry.*

Roy P. Stonesifer, Jr.

PLUMMER, Joseph Bennett, *general,* was born in Barre, Massachusetts, on August 10, 1815. He graduated from West Point in 1841, served at various posts in the Midwest and in Florida, was in the Mexican War, and had quartermaster duty in Texas (1848–1861). Plummer assisted General Nathaniel Lyon (*q.v.*) in the capture of Camp Jackson at the outbreak of the Civil War, and was severely wounded while commanding Regulars at the battle of Wilson's Creek. As colonel of the 11th Missouri (September 1861), he defeated the Confederates at Fredericktown, and then commanded the post at Cape Girardeau. On March 11,

1862, he was named brigadier general of Volunteers, and on April 25, 1862, was promoted to major of Regulars.

Plummer commanded the 5th Division of John Pope's (*q.v.*) army in the New Madrid campaign, and led a brigade in the advance on Corinth and the pursuit of the Confederates. He died on August 9, 1862, in camp near Corinth, from the effects of his old wound and exposure in the field. Although Plummer's career was short, it would seem that, had he lived, he could have achieved at least modest distinction as an able and popular officer. Hughes, *Battle of Belmont*; Monaghan, *Civil War on the Western Border*.

E. B. Long

POMEROY, Samuel Clarke, *senator*, was born on January 3, 1816, in Southampton, Massachusetts. He attended Amherst College, became active in the Liberty party, and held several local political offices in Onondaga county, New York, before being appointed financial agent of the New England Emigrant Aid Company in 1854. That fall he accompanied a party of settlers to Kansas, and was present at Lawrence when ''border ruffians'' threatened the town in 1855 and 1856. In 1856, Pomeroy served as a delegate to the first Republican National Convention, where he delivered a sensational speech demanding Southern reparations to Kansas for the depredations of proslavery Missourians.

In 1861, when Kansas was admitted to the Union, Pomeroy used his personal wealth and influence to gain election to the U.S. Senate, where he aligned himself with the Radical Republicans in his support of the immediate abolition of slavery as a war measure. He never achieved the personal influence with Lincoln (*q.v.*) enjoyed by James H. Lane (*q.v.*), and forever resented his colleague's near monopoly of Federal patronage in Kansas. In part, this jealousy caused Pomeroy to oppose Lincoln's 1864 renomination, supporting Salmon P. Chase (*q.v.*) in a widely circulated campaign circular.

Pomeroy's reelection to the Senate in 1867 engendered charges of fraud, which caused a congressional committee to investigate the election and conclude unanimously that Pomeroy had bribed members of the Kansas General Assembly. Similar charges in 1873 cost him a third term and ended his political career, though he was nominated for President in 1884 by the American Prohibition party. Pomeroy died in Whitinsville, Massachusetts, on August 27, 1891. Castel, *Frontier State at War*.

Christopher Phillips

POMEROY, Theodore Medad, *congressman*, was born on December 31, 1824, in Cayuga, New York. Following his graduation from Hamilton College in 1842, he studied law in William H. Seward's (*q.v.*) firm, and in 1846 became an attorney. Establishing a prosperous practice in Auburn, Pomeroy was elected district attorney of Cayuga county (1851–1856) and to the state Assembly (1856). He was instrumental in the passage of the Metropolitan Police Act of 1857, which set a pattern of state control over New York City's local autonomy.

A protégé of Seward's, Pomeroy was a Whig-turned-Republican. In 1860, he was a delegate to the Republican National Convention and followed his mentor to Washington as a representative in the 37th and three following Congresses.

Pomeroy served on a variety of House committees, notably Foreign Affairs, where as a conservative Republican he championed Seward's interests. He consistently backed Republican policies, ranging from the Conspiracies Act, to higher tariffs, to the 13th Amendment. During Reconstruction, he briefly broke with Seward's support of President Andrew Johnson (*q.v.*) and backed the Radical wing of the Republican party. Pomeroy capped his congressional career in 1869 when he was elected Speaker of the House on the last day of the 40th Congress. In 1868, he declined renomination but remained politically active as mayor of Auburn (1875–1876), temporary chairman of the Republican National Convention (1876), and state senator (1877–1879). Pomeroy died in Auburn on March 23, 1905. Bogue, *Congressman's Civil War*; Storke, *History of Cayuga County, New York*.

Jerome Mushkat

POORE, Benjamin Perley, *journalist*, was born on November 2, 1820, near Newburyport, Massachusetts. In 1836, his father introduced him to Andrew Jackson at the Hermitage, where he obtained the President's autograph, a part of his collection of the signatures of 15,000 famous people, including Washington and Lafayette. His father desired a military career for his son, but young Ben ran away from home to learn the printer's trade. In 1839, he became editor of the *Southern Whig* and, in 1841, attaché of the American legation in Belgium. During 1844–1848, Poore was in Paris as the historical agent for Massachusetts, to copy important papers relating to American history. As Perley, he contributed letters to the *Boston Atlas* that were read by thousands.

At the request of Thurlow Weed (*q.v.*), Poore wrote the campaign biography of General Zachary Taylor in 1848. He went to Washington, D.C., in 1854 as correspondent for the *Boston Journal*, which he served for the next twenty years. Among his political friends were Abraham Lincoln (*q.v.*), Ulysses S. Grant (*q.v.*), Charles Sumner (*q.v.*), Ambrose Burnside (*q.v.*), Samuel Hooper (*q.v.*), and Henry Wilson (*q.v.*). Poore was the first compiler and editor of the *Congressional Directory*, which was published for the first time in 1865.

In the spring of 1852, Poore had organized the 1st Battalion of Rifles in Newburyport, which became known as Ben Poore's Savages and in 1861 formed companies A, B, and C of the 19th Massachusetts. Poore was commissioned a major in the 8th Massachusetts under the command of General Benjamin F. Butler (*q.v.*) within weeks of the fall of Fort Sumter. After three months of drilling recruits at Annapolis, he returned to Washington as a civilian, and reported the political and military aspects of the war as correspondent for the *Journal.* Poore opposed censorship, and led a delegation of journalists to Secretary of State William Seward's (*q.v.*) home to protest the closing of telegraph offices in the early days of war. Like other Washington correspondents, he believed his essential work was to build both civilian and military morale.

Massachusetts Governor John A. Andrew (*q.v.*) praised Poore's Washington services as being as important as a regiment in the field. His career began to wane with the end of Reconstruction, however, although he still commanded the respect of his fellow journalists, who elected him the first president of Washington's Gridiron Club. He was one of the city's most popular after-dinner speakers because of his humor and contact with many of the leading statesmen of his day. Poore died in Washington, D.C., on May 29, 1887. Poore, *Perley's Reminiscences*; Rice, *Reminiscences of Abraham Lincoln.*

Ronald D. Rietveld

POPE, John, *general*, was born on March 16, 1822, in Louisville, Kentucky. He graduated from West Point in 1842, and performed survey work in the topographical engineers in Florida and along the northeastern boundary of the United States and Canada. Pope won two brevets with Zachary Taylor's army in the Mexican War, then performed army survey work in Minnesota, route surveys for a transcontinental railroad, and lighthouse construction. After serving as a mustering officer in Chicago from mid-April through most of July 1861, he was named major general of Volunteers. In command of the Federal Army of the Mississippi, Pope, skillfully employing artillery and engineering tactics, captured New Madrid and Island No. 10, thereby opening the Mississippi to a point near Memphis. These capable operations were marred when he asserted that he had captured ten times as many prisoners as he had actually taken.

The imposing and overconfident Pope came a cropper when brought east in the summer of 1862 to command the Union Army of Virginia. Handicapped by his own prevarications and bluster, and by deprecations he heaped upon his own soldiers, he incautiously advanced against the Confederates, only to be outgeneraled by Robert E. Lee, James Longstreet, and Stonewall Jackson and decisively defeated at Bull Run in August 1862. Throughout the campaign, Pope seldom could locate the Southern forces, and often he did not know where his own troops were. Although outnumbering the enemy 70,000 to 55,000, his forces suffered some 17,000 casualties. Blaming others—such as George B. McClellan (*q.v.*), Henry W. Halleck (*q.v.*), and Abraham Lincoln (*q.v.*)—for his own blunders, Pope was relieved of his command on September 5, 1862, and sent to Minnesota to ride herd on the Indians. Later, based at Fort Leavenworth, Kansas, he ably campaigned against the Indians and aided in opening the West for settlement.

Although Pope's operations in the Mississippi Valley early in the Civil War were ably conducted, his venomous public relations, lackluster intelligence system, and bungling command at Second Bull Run overshadowed these earlier accomplishments, as did his carping criticisms of others. But in the post–Appomattox years, his grasp of realities of Indian problems, and his almost intuitive appreciation of the relationship of the Regular Army to the people and nation as a whole, are worthy of commendation. Pope was commander of several military departments before he was retired from the Army on March 16, 1886. He died on September 23, 1892, in Sandusky, Ohio. Hassler, *Commanders of the Army of the Potomac*; Hennessy, *Return to Bull Run.*

Warren W. Hassler, Jr.

PORTER, Albert Gallatin, *congressman,* was born on April 20, 1824, in Lawrenceburg, Indiana. He attended Hanover College, and in 1843 graduated from Asbury College (now DePauw University). Porter read law briefly in Lawrenceburg, then moved in 1845 to Indianapolis, where he established his law practice and began his political career. Because of the Kansas–Nebraska Act, Porter severed his connection with the Democrats and joined the newly formed Republican party. He was twice elected to the U.S. House of Representatives on the Republican ticket, serving from 1859 to 1863. He was a member of the Judiciary Committee and favored a vigorous prosecution of the war. Declining a third term because of the small salary, Porter returned to Indianapolis in 1863 and established one of the most successful law firms in Indiana.

In 1876, President Rutherford B. Hayes (*q.v.*) appointed Porter first comptroller of the currency, in which capacity he settled numerous claims against the government, many of which grew out of the Civil War. He resigned in 1880 to run for governor of Indiana. His administration (1881–1885) was distinguished for its public health measures, including the establishment of a state board of health, the building of hospitals for the insane, and the drainage of swamplands in northern Indiana. In 1889, President Benjamin Harrison, Porter's former law partner, appointed him minister to Italy. He served ably in this position until 1892, when he returned home to concentrate on the collection of material about and the writing of Indiana history. Porter died in Indianapolis on May 3, 1897. Peat, *Portraits and Painters of the Governors of Indiana*; Taylor, *Biographical Sketches and Review of the Bench and Bar of Indiana.*

Lorna Lutes Sylvester

PORTER, David Dixon, *admiral,* was born on June 8, 1813, in Chester, Pennsylvania, the son of Commodore David Porter. His father served in the Mexican Navy in 1826, after resigning his U.S. commission because of a controversy that had culminated in a court martial. Dixon was appointed a midshipman in the Mexican Navy, and three years later received an appointment as a midshipman in the U.S. Navy. Tours of sea duty were followed by service in the Coast Survey and on board merchant vessels. During the Mexican War, he commanded the steamer *Spitfire* and gained recognition as a "brave and zealous officer."

With the outbreak of the Civil War, Porter was given command of the *Powhatan* and ordered to relieve Fort Pickens. He later received orders to join the blockade off the mouth of the Mississippi, and from there attempted without success to run down the Confederate raider *Sumter.* He next was given command of a flotilla of mortar boats that took part in the attack on the forts below New

Orleans and the bombardment of Vicksburg. On October 9, 1862, Porter was chosen to relieve Charles Henry Davis as commander of the Mississippi River Squadron, with the rank of acting rear admiral. He was chosen over some eighty officers for this command. For nearly twenty-one months he commanded this squadron, which had as its primary responsibility the support of amphibious operations along the Mississippi and its tributaries.

In January 1863 Porter, with units of the squadron, cooperated in the capture of Arkansas Post; in May and July he took part in the battle of Grand Gulf and the siege of Vicksburg. In the spring of 1864 he led a naval force that ascended the Red River; when General Nathaniel Banks's (*q.v.*) army was defeated, he had to withdraw his vessels under difficult circumstances. In the summer of 1864, Porter was selected to command the North Atlantic Blockading Squadron, with orders to reduce Fort Fisher, the chief defense for Wilmington, North Carolina. In the fall of 1864, he assembled a powerful force of over 120 vessels for the Fort Fisher attack. His initial effort in December failed, but a second attempt in January succeeded. For the remainder of the war, Porter's activities were confined primarily to the James and York rivers. After the war, he spent four years as superintendent of the Naval Academy and in 1869 was "advisor" to Secretary of the Navy Adolph Borie. In 1866, he was promoted to vice admiral, and upon the death of Admiral David Farragut (*q.v.*) in 1870, he received the fourth star.

Porter's career, particularly during the Civil War, was spectacular and controversial. He was ambitious and self-confident to the point that he irritated his seniors and others. He was politically minded and the most publicity-conscious naval officer of the war. He had no compunction about undercutting his fellow naval officers, including Farragut. Nevertheless, Porter was intelligent, enterprising, and extremely competent. He was by far the most successful officer in the Union Navy in joint operations with the Army. In the years before his death in Harrisburg, Pennsylvania, on February 13, 1891, he spent much of his time writing parables, poems, novels, and historical works. Tamara Moser Melia, "David Dixon Porter: Fighting Sailor," in Bradford, *Captains of the Old Steam Navy*, pp. 227–247; Reed, *Combined Operations in the Civil War*; West, *Second Admiral*.

William N. Still, Jr.

PORTER, Fitz John, *general,* was born in Portsmouth, New Hampshire, on August 31, 1822. He graduated from West Point in 1845, and won two brevets for gallantry and meritorious conduct in the Mexican War. He was an instructor at West Point (1849–1855), then held routine Army assignments. Promoted to brigadier general of Volunteers shortly after the Civil War began, Porter served first in the Shenandoah Valley. In 1862, as a division and corps commander under George B. McClellan (*q.v.*) on the Peninsula, he performed outstandingly at Mechanicsville, Gaines' Mill, and Malvern Hill. His corps was heavily engaged under Pope (*q.v.*) at Second Bull Run in August 1862. Porter disliked Pope and criticized him severely—especially when the latter, not believing Porter's correct intelligence that Longstreet's corps had arrived on the battlefield to bolster Stonewall Jackson, issued inoperative orders to Porter. Pope brought unfair charges against Porter, who was court martialed, convicted, and cashiered from the Army on January 21, 1863.

Porter was one of the Civil War's ablest corps commanders, but he is best remembered for the contretemps at Second Bull Run. That he knew much more about the battlefield situation than did Pope is apparent; that he was partly a political victim of the Radical Republicans is now acknowledged by most scholars. In 1879, Porter was exonerated, and in 1886 was reinstated in the Army. In the meantime, he engaged in business and was the fire commissioner, commissioner of public works, and police commissioner of New York City. He died in Morristown, New Jersey, on May 21, 1901. Hassler, *Commanders of the Army of the Potomac*; Hennessy, *Return to Bull Run*; Sears, *To the Gates of Richmond*.

Warren W. Hassler, Jr.

POTTER, John Fox, *congressman,* was born on May 11, 1817, in Augusta, Maine. He attended Phillips Exeter Academy, studied law, and was admitted to the bar in 1837. In 1838, he moved to Wisconsin Territory, settling in East Troy, where he began his law practice and became involved in politics as a Whig–Free Soiler. He served as Walworth county judge (1842–1856), and was a delegate to the Whig National Conventions at Baltimore in 1852 and 1856, despite having joined the Republican party in 1854. He served as a delegate to the 1860 and 1864 Republican National Conventions. In 1856, Potter was elected on the Republican ticket to the 35th Congress. He was reelected in 1858 and 1860, but not even the Republican soldier vote could save him in 1862, and his political career ended with that defeat.

While he was in Congress, Potter's most important post was chairmanship of the Committee on Public Lands. He is best remembered, however, for his role in a tragicomic affair that took place on the House floor in April 1860. When Roger A. Pryor of Virginia squared off against Owen Lovejoy (*q.v.*) of Illinois, Potter took Lovejoy's side. Although order was quickly restored, Pryor was so angered that he challenged Potter to a duel. After some hesitation and with an appreciation of Pryor's reputation with a pistol, Potter suggested that they duel with bowie knives at close quarters. Pryor declined the offer, and "Bowie Knife" Potter thus became something of a Northern folk hero. After his 1862 defeat, Potter was appointed consul general to the British Provinces in North America, a position he held until 1866. He died in East Troy on May 18, 1899. Current, *Civil War Era; Dictionary of Wisconsin Biography.*

Charles E. Twining

POTTER, Robert Brown, *general,* was born on July 16, 1829, in Schenectady, New York. He attended Union College, was admitted to the New York bar, and practiced in New York City until the outbreak of the Civil War. He entered the service as major of the 51st New York, and was quickly promoted to lieutenant colonel. Potter participated in Ambrose Burnside's (*q.v.*) North Carolina campaign in early 1862. He commanded part of his regiment in the fight at Roanoke Island, and in March he was wounded in the successful assault on New Bern. At Antietam, Potter led his regiment as it made the perilous crossing of Burnside's Bridge, and he commanded it at Fredericksburg as a full colonel.

Transferred to Kentucky with the IX Corps in 1863, Potter was commissioned a brigadier general of Volunteers, leading the 2nd Division of that corps through the campaign to Jackson, Mississippi, that summer and into East Tennessee later that year. During the siege of Knoxville, he commanded the corps. In 1864, Potter resumed command of his division in Virginia and led it capably from the Wilderness to Petersburg. It was Potter's troops who dug and armed the mine at Elliott's Salient, and they were among the first into the Crater after the charge was exploded. Potter was the only IX Corps division commander whose reputation did not suffer because of that debacle. His division was decimated at the Crater, and it disintegrated at Poplar Springs Church two months later. Potter himself was badly wounded again in the final assault on Petersburg, April 2, 1865.

Potter was one of the brighter lights among the civilian soldiers who served the Union Army. Known for his personal courage and competence, he was offered the rare honor of a field commission in the Regular Army when his Volunteer commission expired. Potter's name might be as familiar as that of Joshua Chamberlain (*q.v.*) but for his own modesty and his longtime association with the ill-fated IX Corps. He left the Army as a major general of Volunteers, and worked as a receiver for a railroad after the war. His wounds troubled him for the rest of his life, and after a long sojourn in England, he died in Newport, Rhode Island, on February 19, 1887. Cox, *Military Reminiscences*; Lyman, *Meade's Headquarters*; Marvel, *Burnside*.

William Marvel

POWELL, Lazarus Whitehead, *senator*, was born near Henderson, Kentucky, on October 6, 1812. After a common school education, he attended St. Joseph College in Bardstown, from which he graduated in 1833. He read law before entering the law school at Transylvania University. Shortly after beginning his law practice in 1835, Powell was elected to the state legislature as a Democrat. After several unsuccessful campaigns for governor, in 1851 he became the first Democrat to win that office since the days of Andrew Jackson. On March 4, 1859, he entered the U.S. Senate, where he served until 1865.

In many ways Powell represented the dilemma of Kentuckians during the secession crisis. He did not believe in secession, yet he adamantly opposed a policy of coercion. He believed that compromise was a viable option, even after secession. When Kentucky's neutrality failed, Powell became such an outspoken opponent of Abraham Lincoln's (*q.v.*) policies that the Kentucky legislature requested his resignation in October 1861. An attempt by the Senate to expel him failed.

Although a Unionist, Powell viewed the Republican party as despotic and an enemy of individual rights. In 1862, he opposed the suspension of the writ of habeas corpus; in 1863 he decried Ulysses S. Grant's (*q.v.*) expulsion of Jews from his military department. Throughout the war, Powell opposed a constitutional amendment to free the slaves as a violation of the right of private property. Saddened by his inability to shape events, he retired from the Senate in March 1865. He died in Henderson on July 3, 1867. Levin, *Lawyers and Lawmakers of Kentucky*; Starling, *History of Henderson County, Kentucky.*

Marion B. Lucas

PRENTICE, George Dennison, *editor*, was born in New London county, Connecticut, on December 18, 1802. He attended local schools, taught school, and graduated from Brown University in 1823. He studied law, but became more interested in journalism and politics. Sent to Kentucky in 1830 to write a campaign biography of Henry Clay, Prentice remained to edit the *Louisville Journal*, an anti-Jackson paper. Blessed with ability, wit, and courage, he made the *Journal* the most important Whig paper in the South, and earned a national reputation. In an era of personal journalism, he was often involved in duels and physical encounters.

Southern sympathizers sought his support in 1860–1861, but Prentice never wavered in his support of the Union. Both of his sons enlisted in the Confederate Army, and after one was killed, Prentice joined the Episcopal Church. He was critical of the Emancipation Proclamation and some other war measures, but he came to see the end of slavery as inevitable, and urged ratification of the 13th Amendment. His favorite enemy was John Hunt Morgan, with whom he exchanged barbs until Morgan's death. Prentice was a Union Democrat leader throughout the war, and a supporter of George B. McClellan (*q.v.*) in the 1864 presidential campaign. After the war he opposed Radical policies and urged Kentuckians to accept reconciliation.

One of the nation's outstanding editors for several decades, Prentice exerted great influence on Kentucky's social and cultural life. No one was more influential in holding Kentucky in the Union in 1861. Worn out by his intense labors, Prentice retired and allowed Walter N. Haldeman to form the *Louisville Courier–Journal* in late 1868. He died in Louisville on January 22, 1870. Coulter, *Civil War and Readjustment in Kentucky*; Evans, *The Newspaper Press in Kentucky.*

Lowell H. Harrison

PRENTISS, Benjamin Mayberry, *general*, was born on November 23, 1819, in Belleville, Virginia, and moved with his family to Marion county, Missouri, in 1835, where he began manufacturing cordage. He moved to Quincy, Illinois, in 1841, joined a militia company, and served against the Mormons at Nauvoo. A captain in the 1st Illinois Volunteers during the Mexican War, he returned home to study law. Prentiss joined the Republican party, and ran unsuccessfully for Congress in 1860. Appointed colonel of the 10th Illinois Volunteers in April

1861, he took control of Cairo, Illinois. Promoted to brigadier general of Volunteers as of May 17, Prentiss engaged in an acrimonious dispute with Ulysses S. Grant (*q.v.*) over seniority; Grant won the dispute.

During the fall of 1861, Prentiss campaigned in Missouri, then took command of the 6th Division, Army of the Tennessee, at Pittsburg Landing, late in March 1862. On April 6, at Shiloh, he stubbornly defended the Hornets' Nest, a sunken roadbed, against repeated Confederate attacks, surrendering the remnants of his division late that afternoon. He returned to duty after his exchange in October, serving on the court martial of Major General Fitz John Porter (*q.v.*). Grant assigned Prentiss to command the District of Eastern Arkansas in February 1863, and he was promoted to major general in March, to date from November 29, 1862. On the day that Vicksburg surrendered, Prentiss repulsed a determined Confederate assault on Helena, Arkansas. He resigned on August 3, having "been without an adequate command" since that battle.

Prentiss's political connections secured his appointment as brigadier general, but his dispute with Grant and his surrender at Shiloh did not further his military career. His tenacious defense at Shiloh, however, allowed Grant to stabilize the Union lines, possibly preventing a Union defeat. Prentiss again proved his abilities as a defensive fighter at Helena, but received little credit for his accomplishments and quietly returned to civil life. Grant appointed him U.S. pension agent in Quincy, Illinois. In 1878, Prentiss returned to Missouri, and served as postmaster of Bethany from 1889 until his death there on February 8, 1901. McDonough, *Shiloh*; Sword, *Shiloh*.

David L. Wilson

PRICE, Hiram, *congressman*, was born January 10, 1814, in Washington county, Pennsylvania. He moved to Davenport, Iowa, in 1844 and became a successful merchant. He was active in local government, and advocated building the Iowa portion of what eventually became the Rock Island Railroad. Price was secretary of the Mississippi & Missouri Railroad, and after a year as head of the Davenport branch of the Iowa State Bank, he became president of the state bank system. Elected as a Democrat to his first public offices, Price, who was a strong prohibitionist and an opponent of slavery extension, played an active role in the organization of the Iowa Republican party in 1856.

When the Civil War began, Price took the lead in contributing and raising private funds to pay and outfit the soldiers of Iowa's first three Volunteer regiments until the state could assume the responsibility. He served three terms in Congress (1863–1869), becoming identified with the Radicals on war measures and racial issues, and with Western business and railroad interests. Price was an early supporter of the Freedmen's Bureau, voted consistently in opposition to Andrew Johnson's (*q.v.*) Reconstruction policies, and cast an affirmative vote for the President's impeachment.

In Iowa, Price was a leader in the successful fight to open the suffrage to African Americans. He also chaired the House Committee on the Pacific Railroad. He declined renomination for a fourth term, but in 1877 returned for two more terms in Congress, where he spoke for the remonetization of silver. In 1881, President James A. Garfield (*q.v.*) appointed him commissioner of Indian affairs, a post he held until 1885. He died on May 30, 1901, in Washington, D.C. Cook, *Baptism of Fire*; Stiles, *Recollections and Sketches.*

Hubert H. Wubben

PRICE, Thomas Lawson, *congressman,* was born near Danville, Virginia, on January 19, 1809. Having inherited a considerable fortune from his planter father, he emigrated to the Missouri frontier in 1829. Settling in the new capital of Jefferson City, he was active in land speculation and in the mercantile business. He established the first stage line between St. Louis and the capital in 1838, and then an expanding network of stage lines around Missouri. In the 1850s, he was a major figure in the development of the state's railroads. A strong Jacksonian Democrat, Price served as Jefferson City's first mayor (1839–1842) and as lieutenant governor of Missouri (1849–1853). The choice of the Benton Democrats for governor in 1852, he lost the nomination because of party factionalism. A bid for Congress in 1854 was also unsuccessful, but Price was elected to the state legislature in 1860 and strongly supported the movement to keep Missouri in the Union.

With the establishment of the Provisional Government in July 1861, Price accepted a commission as brigadier general in the militia but was not involved in any major fighting. He was elected to Congress to fill the unexpired term of John W. Reid, who had been expelled, and took his seat on January 21, 1862. He opposed compensated emancipation in the border states, and worked to thwart congressional moves in this direction. Price was defeated for reelection in 1862 and contested the results unsuccessfully. In 1864, the Democrats nominated him for governor, but he was badly defeated in the Radical landslide. He also was a delegate to the Democratic National Conventions in 1864 and 1868. Price died in Jefferson City on July 15, 1870. Parrish, *Turbulent Partnership.*

William E. Parrish

PRINCE, Henry, *general,* was born on June 19, 1811, in Eastport, Maine. He graduated from West Point in 1835, fought Indians in Florida, and participated in the Mexican War, winning two brevets and suffering a severe wound. After recovering, he served as a paymaster on the Western frontier and in Washington, D.C. At the beginning of the Civil War, Prince commanded a brigade and then a division in the Army of Virginia. Captured at Cedar Mountain, he took over a division on the North Carolina coast upon being released from prison. In July 1863 he assumed command of the 2nd Division, III Corps, and later the 3rd Division, VI Corps, Army of the Potomac.

In January 1864, Prince took command of a military district in Tennessee and spent the remainder of the war in that and other administrative positions. Except for the Mine Run fiasco, in which he played a part, he seems to have been an

adequate brigade and division commander, but nothing more. Although courageous, Prince failed to perform at a level commensurate with his military education and experience. With the return of peace, he resumed his duties as a
paymaster, retiring in 1879. Wracked by pain from his wounds, Prince committed suicide on August 19, 1892, in London, England. Krick, *Stonewall Jackson
at Cedar Mountain.*

James L. Morrison, Jr.

PRINGLE, Cyrus Guernsey, *conscientious objector*, was born on May 6,
1838, in East Charlotte, Vermont. Although he gained public notice after 1865
when he headed expeditions into the western United States, eastern Canada, and
Mexico in search of new plant species, his role during the Civil War has gone
largely unnoticed. Drafted in July 1863, Pringle refused to pay a $300 com-
mutation fee to gain exemption from service because it ran counter to his Quaker
principles. He also declined the entreaties of other Friends who offered to pay
the fee for him. Instead, he entered the Army and endured severe treatment from
other soldiers. Much of this discomfort he brought on himself when he refused
to shoulder a rifle or to sign for his uniform, because he believed such actions
would be tantamount to endorsing war as a way of life.

Pringle continued his uncompromising behavior until November 1863, when
his case gained the notice of Abraham Lincoln (*q.v.*). Upon hearing of Pringle's
deep convictions, the President ordered his release, along with other devout
Quakers, from further military service. Shortly thereafter, on December 15,
1863, the War Department directed provost marshals to parole all conscripted
Quakers, who would not need to report until "called for."

Despite the concerted wartime efforts of influential Quaker elders and influential government officials to have the Federal government grant a special exemption from the draft to all Friends, it required the courage and fortitude of a
quiet and unassuming Vermont plant breeder to transform those efforts into
reality. Pringle died in Vermont on May 25, 1911. Brock, *Pacifism in the United
States*; Geary, *We Need Men.*

James W. Geary

PRUYN, John Van Schaick Lansing, *congressman*, was born in Albany, New
York, on June 22, 1811. After attending private schools in Albany and studying
the law, he was admitted to the bar in 1832. He was involved in corporate
affairs, especially banking and railroads, and drew up the agreement that created
the New York Central Railroad in 1853. Joining Erastus Corning (*q.v.*) and
Chauncey Vibbard (*q.v.*) as its executives, he became secretary and treasurer,
and remained with the New York Central until 1866. Pruyn was involved in a
landmark case in corporate law when he made the final arguments before the
U.S. Supreme Court for the Hudson River Bridge Company. The Court ruled

in favor of the company and ended a long series of controversies throughout the country concerning the right to bridge navigable rivers.

A lifelong Democrat and close friend of Horatio Seymour (*q.v.*), Pruyn viewed politics as just one facet of his public career. Nominated for the state Assembly in 1861, he accepted, with the proviso that not a single dollar be spent on his campaign. On December 7, 1863, he filled a vacancy in the 38th Congress created by the resignation of Erastus Corning, and served until March 3, 1865. While supporting a vigorous prosecution of the war, Pruyn opposed some Republican measures, such as the Confiscation Acts and the Currency Bill. He doubted that Abraham Lincoln (*q.v.*) had the power to emancipate the slaves because of the possible violation of property rights.

Pruyn was elected to the 40th Congress, and during the turmoil surrounding Andrew Johnson (*q.v.*) spoke out against impeachment. After his congressional term, he returned to his law practice, philanthropic causes, and educational interests. He died in Clifton Springs, New York, on November 21, 1877. Hungerford, *Men and Iron*.

Richard W. Brown, Jr.

PURVIS, Robert, Sr., *abolitionist*, was born on August 4, 1810, in Charleston, South Carolina. In 1819, he was sent to Philadelphia for schooling; soon thereafter his father, a wealthy cotton broker, left him a bequest of $120,000. Purvis then turned his attention to the concerns that would dominate his public life: the abolition of slavery and the improvement of the African American community. He developed close associations with Benjamin Lundy and with William Lloyd Garrison (*q.v.*), who was beginning his controversial reform career. Purvis participated prominently in the founding of the American Anti-Slavery Society before traveling to England in 1834 to secure international support for the cause.

Purvis was one of the most prominent African American participants in the Society and its affiliate, the Pennsylvania Anti-Slavery Society, of which he was president (1845–1850). He also assumed the presidency of the Vigilance Committee of Pennsylvania and the General Vigilance Committee, which assisted numerous fugitive slaves. Harriet Purvis, daughter of the wealthy black abolitionist and sailmaker James Forten, joined her husband in helping fugitives, turning their home into a haven for runaways.

Purvis fought unsuccessfully against measures to disenfranchise African Americans in Pennsylvania and to prevent out-of-state free blacks from settling in the state. He opposed public school segregation by refusing to pay local taxes, and used his wealth and standing to promote the establishment of manual labor schools, libraries, and other self-improvement groups. During the Civil War, he was a vocal critic of Abraham Lincoln's (*q.v.*) reluctance to declare emancipation, and he sided with Wendell Phillips (*q.v.*), Frederick Douglass (*q.v.*), and others who refused to disband the American Anti-Slavery Society until the 14th and 15th Amendments had secured the promise of black political freedom. The last surviving founder of the American Anti-Slavery Society, Purvis died in Philadelphia on April 15, 1898. Quarles, *Black Abolitionists.*

James Brewer Stewart

Q

QUINBY, Isaac Ferdinand, *general*, was born on a farm near Morristown, New Jersey, on January 29, 1821. He graduated from West Point in 1843, was commissioned a brevet 2nd lieutenant, and was assigned to the 2nd Artillery. He joined his regiment at Fort Mifflin, Pennsylvania. In August 1844 he returned to West Point as an assistant professor of mathematics, and then as an assistant professor of natural and experimental philosophy. After duty with the 3rd Artillery at Forts Monroe and Adams, Quinby resigned his 1st lieutenant's commission (March 1852) to teach science and mathematics at the University of Rochester.

In May 1861 Quinby was mustered into service as colonel of the 13th New York Volunteers, a ninety-day regiment, which he led at First Bull Run. On August 4, he resigned and returned to the University of Rochester, but on March 17, 1862, he was appointed brigadier general of Volunteers and assigned command of the post at Columbus, Kentucky. He held a succession of post and district commands in the Department of the Tennessee before being assigned on November 1, 1862, to lead the Army of the Tennessee's newly constituted 7th Division. The division participated in the unsuccessful Yazoo Pass expedition, marched with General James B. McPherson's (*q.v.*) XVII Corps from Milliken's Bend to Hard Times, and crossed the Mississippi at Bruinsburg on May 2.

Quinby was under a surgeon's care before resuming command of the division immediately after the battle of Champion Hill. He was in the May 22 assault on Vicksburg, and on June 3, was invalided home on sick leave. On July 28, he was placed in charge of the draft rendezvous at Elmira, New York, a position he held until December 31, 1863, when he resigned from the Army because of ill health.

Quinby resumed his teaching career at the University of Rochester until 1884, when he become city surveyor. He served as provost marshal of New York's 28th Congressional District (January 21–October 15, 1865) and as U.S. marshal for the Northern District of New York during Ulysses S. Grant's (*q.v.*) administration. Quinby died in Rochester on September 18, 1891. Bearss, *Vicksburg Campaign*; Williams, *Lincoln Finds a General*, vol. 4.

Edwin C. Bearss

R

RADFORD, William, *congressman*, was born on June 24, 1814, in Pough-keepsie, New York. In 1829, he moved to New York City, where he entered business and Democratic politics. In 1862, he was elected to the House of Representatives from a district that included his residence in Yonkers, New York. In the first session of the 38th Congress he voted as a moderate Peace Democrat, but shifted to favor abolition during the second session. He was reelected in 1864, and voted as a steady Democratic centrist through the 39th Congress. In the 38th Congress, he sat on the Committee on Public Buildings and Grounds; in the 39th, on the Elections Committee and on a committee to look into a postal road to New York.

Along with many other Democrats around the nation, Radford lost his House seat in the elections of 1866, which resulted in a Republican landslide. Following expiration of the 39th Congress in 1867, Radford returned to the life of a New York City merchant. He died in Yonkers on January 18, 1870. Benedict, *Compromise of Principle.*

James C. Mohr

RAMSAY, George Douglas, *general*, was born on February 21, 1802, in Alexandria, Virginia. He graduated from West Point in 1820, served as an artillery officer, and was promoted in 1835 to captain in the Ordnance Corps. He served at various arsenals until 1845, when he was assigned to General Zachary Taylor's command in Texas. Ramsay's record in the Mexican War led to his nomination as Taylor's chief of ordnance in June 1847. After the war, he returned to arsenal duties, where his able and dedicated work, though recognized, did not result in promotion.

Ramsay was in command of the Washington Arsenal, the post he loved best, when the Civil War began. He was promoted to major in April 1861 and lieutenant colonel in August. The Washington Arsenal became the largest one serving the Union Army, and Ramsay did his work well. In addition to supplying arms and munitions, the arsenal handled all kinds of military supplies. A good deal of testing of new arms and equipment took place there, and because of this testing, Ramsay gained something of a reputation as a progressive ordnance officer. This reputation proved to be largely undeserved when he was promoted to brigadier general and named chief of ordnance, succeeding General James W. Ripley (*q.v.*) on September 15, 1863.

Although more modern weapons were acquired in larger numbers than before, Ramsay still showed a marked conservatism in all areas of ordnance, which restrained purchases and contracts for these arms. His efforts as head of the Ordnance Department were hampered by a constant interference from Secretary of War Edwin M. Stanton (*q.v.*), either directly or through officers in the department loyal to Stanton. Ramsay retired as chief of ordnance on September 12, 1864, but continued as inspector of arsenals until June 8, 1866, when he was named commandant of his beloved Washington Arsenal. He retired from active duty in 1870, and lived in Washington, D.C., until his death on May 23, 1882. Bruce, *Lincoln and the Tools of War*; Davis, *Arming the Union*.

Carl L. Davis

RAMSEY, Alexander, *governor, senator,* was born in Hummelstown, Pennsylvania, on January 8, 1815. He attended common schools in Hummelstown and Harrisburg, studied at Lafayette College and Reed Law School, and was admitted to the bar in 1839. He became a Whig activist in 1840, was chief clerk of the Pennsylvania House in 1841, and served two terms in Congress from 1843 to 1847. Ramsey then became Whig state chairman, engineered Zachary Taylor's victory in Pennsylvania in 1848, and was rewarded by being appointed territorial governor of Minnesota in 1849. He served until 1853, then was a land speculator and railroad lobbyist, revealing flexible ethics in both pursuits. He became a Republican, narrowly lost an 1857 gubernatorial race, then won the Minnesota governorship two years later.

In 1860, Ramsey led a delegation to the Republican National Convention that favored William H. Seward (*q.v.*), but quickly made his peace with Abraham Lincoln (*q.v.*), and stumped Minnesota on his behalf. In Washington pressing patronage claims when Lincoln issued his call for troops in April 1861, Ramsey immediately pledged a thousand Minnesota volunteers to the Union cause, then returned to Minnesota to help raise and staff seven Volunteer regiments. An ardent Unionist, he untypically put merit above politics in selecting senior officers, including his appointment of former Governor Willis A. Gorman, a Democrat, to command the 1st Minnesota Regiment. Ramsey was reelected overwhelmingly in 1861, then in 1862 had to deal with the Sioux uprising that claimed more than 500 lives.

In 1863, Ramsey resigned the governorship to replace Henry Rice (*q.v.*) in the U.S. Senate. As a Civil War senator, he played a rather insignificant role. He loyally supported Lincoln on all war-related measures, but spent most of his time on such parochial concerns as patronage, Minnesota–Canada border issues, and home state railroad land grants. As a result, "Bluff Aleck" developed little influence in the Senate, but perpetuated his dominance of Republican politics in Minnesota for a generation. During the struggle to define Reconstruction, Ramsey followed a straight Radical Republican line, including a vote to remove Andrew Johnson (*q.v.*) from office, but again abstained from major involvement.

Reelected to a second term in 1869, Ramsey became a loyal supporter of President Ulysses S. Grant (*q.v.*), with whom he often played poker, and generally lined up with the "Stalwart" faction, led by Roscoe Conkling (*q.v.*). An unabashed reactionary, he continued to champion subsidies for railroads, opposed appropriations for the Civil Service Commission, and voted for the 1873 "Salary Grab." He was retired involuntarily in 1875, after which he devoted most of his time to the land investments that had made him a millionaire, and to civic affairs in St. Paul. He served as Secretary of War under Rutherford B. Hayes (*q.v.*) from 1879 to 1881, then from 1882 to 1886 headed the Utah Commission investigating Mormon polygamy. He died in St. Paul on April 22, 1903. Folwell, *History of Minnesota*, vols. 1, 2, 3; Ryland, *Alexander Ramsey*.

Roger A. Fischer

RANDALL, Alexander Williams, *governor, diplomat, assistant postmaster general*, was born on October 31, 1819, in Ames, New York. In 1840, he moved to Prairieville (soon to be Waukesha), in Wisconsin Territory. Although he had been a Whig, he became identified with the Democratic party, so much so that President James K. Polk appointed him postmaster of Waukesha. In 1848, Randall supported the Van Buren Free-Soil Democrats, subsequently becoming active in the Barnburner faction. In 1855, he served one term in the state Assembly as an Independent Democrat, but he also supported the election of Wisconsin's first Republican senator, Charles Durkee. Randall was defeated in a Republican bid for attorney general in 1855, but was appointed to fill an unexpired term as judge of the Milwaukee Circuit Court. He secured the Republican nomination for governor in 1857, evidencing the opportunities afforded in a new party in a new state, and was reelected in 1859.

Randall had previously worried over the erosion of states' rights, but when he delivered his annual message on January 10, 1861, he seemed a nationalist to the core. Still, his less-than-enthusiastic support of Abraham Lincoln (*q.v.*) altered little in the days following. Lincoln seemed too hesitant, too uncertain, too willing to compromise. The President's call to arms on April 15, 1861, was, in Randall's view, typically insufficient. The governor was eager to offer several more regiments than the one requested, but the War Department declined. A month later, Randall was in Cleveland to meet with other Western governors, all of them troubled by economic and military problems that demanded immediate resolution. Some proposed taking matters into their own hands, even to the point of marching their troops to the front. Randall was delegated to communicate their concerns to the President, a responsibility he willingly accepted.

Randall stressed the importance of keeping the Ohio and Mississippi open to the trade of the Northwest. Specifically, he advised the calling up of 300,000 troops, warning that should the Federal government fail to lead, the individual states would have no choice but to act on their own. In fact, the governors already were busy responding to the May 3 call-up of forty regiments for a three-year duration. Randall remained enthusiastic in the task, and would raise 25,000 men during his term of office. Sending Wisconsin boys off to a distant war was a large and difficult administrative task, and inevitably there were complaints about provisioning, patronage, and corruption. Eventually tiring of the responsibility, Randall decided not to seek a third term.

Although Randall likely would have preferred a military position, he accepted Lincoln's assignment as minister to the Papal States. But apparently he grew homesick, and upon returning to Washington, accepted appointment as first assistant postmaster general, an office that had limited duties but significant patronage opportunities. He was heavily involved in Lincoln's reelection campaign in 1864. In July 1866 President Andrew Johnson (*q.v.*) promoted Randall to Postmaster General. He was one of few Republicans who supported Johnson throughout, although his loyalty would cost him heavily. He chose not to return to Wisconsin at the conclusion of the Johnson administration, settling instead in Elmira, New York, where he practiced law until his death on July 26, 1872.
Current, *Civil War Era*; Hesseltine, *Lincoln's War Governors*.

Charles E. Twining

RANDALL, Samuel Jackson, *congressman,* was born in Philadelphia on October 10, 1828, and educated at the city's University Academy. He operated a successful iron firm, but devoted a great deal of time to politics. He began his political career as a city councilman, and in 1858 was elected to the state Senate as a Democrat. When the Civil War began, he enlisted in a company of the Philadelphia Home Guard and rose to the rank of captain. Elected to Congress in 1862, Randall presented himself as a member of the loyal opposition and served throughout the war in an inconspicuous fashion. He gained national prominence in 1875 when he led the fight in the House to defeat the Force Bill, designed to give extreme powers to President Ulysses S. Grant (*q.v.*) in dealing with the remaining unreconstructed Southern states.

Randall's abilities as a parliamentarian and party leader led to his election as Speaker of the House in 1876 and immediately embroilment in the contested election of 1876. His challenge to the legitimacy of the special electoral commission that decided in favor of Rutherford B. Hayes (*q.v.*) was unsuccessful, but his efforts helped ensure the Compromise of 1877. Randall continued to serve in the House until his death in Washington, D.C., on April 12, 1890. Evans, *Pennsylvania Politics*; McClure, *Old Time Notes of Pennsylvania*, vol. 2.

David Dixon

RANDALL, William Harrison, *congressman*, was born on July 15, 1812, near Richmond, Kentucky. He studied law, and was admitted to the bar in 1835. In 1836, he was appointed clerk of the Circuit and County Court of Laurel county and served in that capacity until 1850, when a constitutional change necessitated his election. Randall remained on the bench until 1855. In 1863, he was elected as a Republican to the 38th Congress, representing the 8th Congressional District of Kentucky, and was reelected to the 39th Congress in 1865. Randall voted for the 13th and 14th Amendments, against overriding the presidential veto on several occasions, and usually failed to vote on bills affecting the Army. He served on few committees, and his only significant action in Congress was to present petitions from Kentuckians whose property was damaged during the war. Although he was ineffective in the House for four years, he became a well-respected judge in Kentucky's 15th District (1870–1880). Randall died in London, Kentucky, on August 1, 1881. Hood, ''For the Union,'' *Register of the Kentucky Historical Society*; Tapp, *Kentucky: Decades of Discord.*

Boyd Childress

RANSOM, Thomas Edward Greenfield, *general*, was born on November 29, 1834, in Norwich, Vermont. He was graduated from Norwich College, and soon afterward moved to Fayette county, Illinois, where he engaged in engineering and real estate. In 1861, he joined the 11th Illinois Volunteers, then commanded by William H.L. Wallace (*q.v.*). Almost rashly brave, Ransom was wounded in personal combat with a Confederate officer at Charleston, Missouri, on August 19, 1861; he killed his opponent. He was wounded again at Fort Donelson, on February 15, 1862.

As colonel of the 11th Illinois at Shiloh, Ransom was wounded yet again, but refused to leave his command during the remainder of the day (April 6, 1862). In the Corinth campaign, as a brigadier general, he commanded the 2nd Brigade, 6th Division, XVI Corps. His brigade was eventually attached to the XVII Corps during the Vicksburg campaign, and following this, he was given command of the 4th Division, XIII Corps in the Texas expedition to Matagorda Bay. Due to the inadequate handling of Union troops at Sabine Cross Roads by General Nathaniel Banks (*q.v.*), Ransom was forced to fight an uneven battle against strong Confederate forces. Here he was wounded again. Still recovering from his injury, Ransom was assigned to command of the 4th Division, XVI Corps, taking part in the siege of Atlanta. He commanded the corps in the magnificent turning movement that cut Confederate communications at Jonesboro.

Presbyterian by religion, and described as ''Cromwellian'' by those who knew him, Ransom might well have become a dominant force in postwar American history. But his rashness was such that he did not survive the war. The added burdens of command, plus the numerous injuries inflicted in battle, made him increasingly ill. Although Ransom attempted to retain command, he died on October 29, 1864, while traveling to Rome, Georgia, on a litter. Bearss, *Vicksburg Campaign*, vols. 2, 3; Hirshson, *Grenville M. Dodge*.

Victor Hicken

RAUM, Green Berry, *general*, was born on December 3, 1829, in Golconda, Illinois. He practiced law in Harrisburg, Illinois, and nearby towns. A southern Illinois Democrat, he was an alternate delegate in 1860 to the Democratic National Convention that nominated Stephen A. Douglas (*q.v.*). With the fall of Fort Sumter, Raum became a vigorous exponent of the war and was commissioned as major of the 56th Illinois Volunteers. He was promoted to lieutenant colonel on June 26, 1862, colonel on August 31, 1862, and brigadier general on February 24, 1865. His combat record included the leadership of a bayonet charge at Corinth and the command of a brigade at Champion's Hill and Missionary Ridge. Wounded in this last battle, upon recovery he was given command of the 2nd Brigade, 3rd Division, XV Corps, which was placed in rearguard positions during William T. Sherman's (*q.v.*) siege of Atlanta and the subsequent March to the Sea.

Raum resigned his commission on May 6, 1865, and returned to Illinois. Elected as a Republican to the 40th Congress, he opposed Andrew Johnson's (*q.v.*) Reconstruction policies and voted for the articles of impeachment. Although defeated in the next election, he remained politically active, becoming the commissioner of internal revenue (1876–1883). In 1889, he was named the commissioner of pensions, but was found guilty of malfeasance in office by a congressional committee. As for his 56th Illinois Volunteers, most of the remaining men died at sea while being moved to another post at the end of the war. Raum died in Chicago on December 18, 1909. Bearss, *Vicksburg Campaign*, vol. 3; Jones, *"Black Jack": John A. Logan*.

Victor Hicken

RAWLINS, John Aaron, *general*, was born on February 13, 1831, in Galena, Illinois. He acquired an indifferent education, but was admitted to the bar in 1854. Rawlins caught the attention of fellow townsman Ulysses S. Grant (*q.v.*) through patriotic speeches when the Civil War began, and in August 1861 Grant gave him a staff appointment that lasted throughout the war. As Grant rose, Rawlins followed, attaining the rank of brigadier general after the fall of Vicksburg, and promotion to major general and chief of staff of the Army at war's end. As adjutant, he issued orders for Grant and presided over his military household. Far the better writer, Grant frequently drafted orders and always wrote his own reports.

Rawlins's role was normally that of friend, adviser, and guardian. A fanatical foe of liquor, he privately dramatized his role in preventing Grant from drinking, and issued stern but probably unnecessary warnings to his commander. After Vicksburg, Grant sent Rawlins to Washington as an advocate to justify the removal of John A. McClernand (*q.v.*). As Grant's right-hand man throughout the Civil War, he implemented Grant's decisions. When he vehemently protested William T. Sherman's (*q.v.*) plan to march from Atlanta to the sea, Grant brushed away these objections.

Friends tried to claim that Rawlins had been the brains behind Grant's meteoric rise, arguing that his death explained the contrast between Grant's brilliant military record and unsuccessful presidency. Military records will not sustain this theory. Instead, Rawlins had hitched his wagon to Grant's star. After the war, he continued as chief of staff until Grant took office as President in 1869. Aware that Rawlins's health was declining due to tuberculosis, Grant intended to send him to Arizona to recover, but acquiesced in his ambition to serve as Secretary of War. Within six months, on September 6, 1869, Rawlins died in Washington, D.C. Wilson, *Life of John A. Rawlins*.

John Y. Simon

RAYMOND, Henry Jarvis, *editor*, was born on January 24, 1820, near Lima, New York. He graduated from the University of Vermont, and while in college, contributed articles and poems to several publications, including Horace Greeley's (*q.v.*) *The New-Yorker*. Raymond demonstrated traits that would affect his journalistic and political careers. He disliked personal disputes, seeking compromise whenever possible, and he usually saw both sides of a political argument.

Raymond's political and journalistic careers were mixed early in his life. He worked with Greeley on Thurlow Weed's (*q.v.*) *Albany, Evening Journal* and *The New-Yorker*. When Greeley started the *New York Tribune*, Raymond was hired as assistant editor. He later worked on the *New York Courier and Enquirer* and *Harper's Magazine*. In 1850, he was elected to the New York State Assembly, where he was a consistent proponent of a strong central government, the national bank, and internal improvements at government expense. On the issue of slavery and emancipation, he was cautious and conservative, in contrast to his journalistic mentor, the liberal Greeley.

In 1851, Raymond founded the *New York Times*, an inexpensive, mass-circulation newspaper with an emphasis on news objectivity and a moderate Whig editorial policy. The *Times* supported the Republican party and consistently and staunchly backed Abraham Lincoln (*q.v.*). It warmly endorsed Lincoln's call for a gradual, compensated emancipation program in areas where the people wanted it, but it easily switched to strongly supporting the Emancipation Proclamation. Indeed, of all Republican editors in the country, Raymond was one of the few who consistently and enthusiastically supported Lincoln and the war.

Raymond was a major journalistic force, but fared less well as a politician. During his tenure in the New York State Assembly and one term in the 39th

Congress, the traits that made him a good journalist (fairness, compromise, and the ability to see both sides of issues) made him a poor politician. His journalistic legacy is the *New York Times* and its commitment to accuracy, balance, and objectivity. His political legacy is limited to his often lonely, if consistent and sympathetic, support of Lincoln. And that, in the context of the partisanship of the time, is of no small consequence. Raymond died June 18, 1869, in New York City. Brown, *Raymond of the Times.*

Fredric F. Endres

REID, Hugh Thompson, *general,* was born in Union county, Indiana, on October 18, 1811. He attended Miami University, graduated from Indiana College, read law, and was admitted to the bar. In 1839, he went to Fort Madison, Iowa, and moved to nearby Keokuk in 1849. Reid was prosecuting attorney for five southeast Iowa counties (1840–1842), and for four years was president of the Des Moines Valley Railroad.

In October 1861 Reid began recruiting a three-year regiment, the 15th Iowa Volunteers, which on February 22, 1862, was mustered in at Keokuk, with Reid as its colonel. The regiment reached Pittsburg Landing on Sunday, April 6, and he led his troops off the boat and into battle. Reid was shot through the neck, but refused to leave the field. He led the regiment at Corinth, and commanded the famed Hawkeye Brigade in the fall of 1862 while Marcellus M. Crocker (*q.v.*) was on leave. During the early spring of 1863, when Adjutant General Lorenzo Thomas (*q.v.*) visited the XVII Corps to seek support for the administration's program for enlisting and organizing black units, Reid championed this policy in a compelling speech to the assembled brigade. As chairman of a brigade conference, he forwarded to Governor Samuel Kirkwood (*q.v.*) of Iowa a resolution endorsing the Emancipation Proclamation.

On April 9, Reid was promoted to brigadier general, and on April 22, assumed command of the 1st Brigade, 6th Division, XVII Corps, then stationed at Lake Providence, Louisiana. His brigade guarded local plantations growing cotton until late summer. On October 3, 1863, Reid was named to command the District of Cairo, a position he held until resigning his commission on April 4, 1864. He was active in affairs of the Des Moines Valley Railroad Company and played a key role in expediting construction of Keokuk's bridge spanning the Mississippi. He died in Des Moines on August 21, 1874. Bearss, *Vicksburg Campaign,* vol. 3; Belknap, *History of the Fifteenth Regiment*; Stuart, *Iowa Colonels and Regiments.*

Edwin C. Bearss

REID, Whitelaw, *journalist,* was born on October 27, 1837, near Xenia, Ohio. Born to comfortable circumstances, he excelled at the Cedarville Academy and at Miami University, from which he graduated in 1856. With financial aid from his family, Reid purchased the *Xenia News* in 1858 and became its editor. He was an early supporter of Abraham Lincoln (*q.v.*), and worked for the Republican party in the fall of 1860. He was Columbus correspondent for several newspapers and, because of his friendship with William Henry Smith, who wrote for the *Cincinnati Gazette*, became a full-time employee of that paper.

Reid's talent was for rapid, accurate, descriptive writing—and he always wrote in a legible hand. Readers respected the column signed Agate. His account of the battle of Shiloh vaulted him to fame. His thrilling report had no rival, although he exaggerated Union unpreparedness on the first day of the battle. The country then, and historians since, have relied heavily on his account. He produced a similar tour de force the next year at Gettysburg. Reid found much to criticize in the government's prosecution of the war: its early failure to accept African Americans into the Union Army; George B. McClellan's (*q.v.*) tardiness in western Virginia; and Ulysses S. Grant's (*q.v.*) tactics in Tennessee. His report "In the Midst of Revolution," written after the battle of Fredericksburg, held Lincoln personally responsible for the Union disaster, and hinted that the Cabinet would somehow discipline or replace him. He brilliantly, if not convincingly, defended William S. Rosecrans's (*q.v.*) performance at Chickamauga.

The *Gazette*, in the meantime, had become recognized as one of the country's outstanding Radical newspapers, and Reid as its most distinguished reporter. Never enthusiastic for Lincoln, Reid occasionally praised him for his unique politics, and his column "April, 1865" was a moving tribute to the fallen leader. After the war, Reid took several trips through the South, and reported on the conditions and attitudes of the freedmen, investment opportunities, and the absence of strong Federal policy on Reconstruction. In 1868, he accepted Horace Greeley's (*q.v.*) offer to be managing editor of the *New York Tribune.*

The passage of the 15th Amendment in 1870 marked the end of Reid's interest in Civil War issues. He worked for the Liberal Republican movement, and after Greeley's death in 1872, he bought a majority interest in the *Tribune*, which he controlled and dominated for the rest of his life. He returned to the Republican party in 1875 and became one of its most reliable and steadfast members, contributing to it both money and publicity. As a reward for his service, Reid was named minister to France (1889–1892) and ambassador to England (1905–1912). He died in London on December 15, 1912. Duncan, *Whitelaw Reid*; Reid, *A Radical View.*

James G. Smart

REILLY, James William, *general,* was born on May 20, 1828, in Akron, Ohio. A graduate of Mount St. Mary's College in Emmitsburg, Maryland, he practiced law in Wellsville, Ohio. In 1861, he was elected as a Republican to the state legislature. Appointed colonel of the 104th Ohio on August 30, 1862, he commanded a brigade in the XXIII Corps at the siege of Knoxville and during the Atlanta campaign. Promoted to brigadier general of Volunteers on July 30, 1864, he distinguished himself as a division commander at the battle of Franklin, where his entrenched troops broke under an overwhelming Confederate assault, then rallied to capture 1,000 prisoners and twenty-two battle flags. As part of

General John Schofield's (*q.v.*) forces, Reilly participated in William T. Sherman's (*q.v.*) campaign in the Carolinas.

A competent organizer and dependable field commander, Reilly frequently exercised higher command than his rank indicated. He also cared deeply for his soldiers. He broke down in tears after his 1,500-man brigade suffered 306 casualties in an August 6, 1864, attack on Confederate works near Atlanta. He resigned his commission on April 20, 1865, just six days before General Joseph Johnston's final surrender. Reilly practiced law and was active in political and community affairs until his death in Wellsville, Ohio, on November 6, 1905. Castel, *Decision in the West*; Sword, *Embrace an Angry Wind.*

Bruce J. Dinges

RENO, Jesse Lee, *general*, was born on June 20, 1823, in what is now Wheeling, West Virginia. He graduated from West Point in 1846, was assigned to the ordnance department, and earned two brevet promotions in Winfield Scott's (*q.v.*) campaign to Mexico City. After a stint as professor of mathematics at West Point, he spent most of the next dozen years on duty at various arsenals. He commanded the Mount Vernon arsenal in Alabama until it was seized by Confederates in January 1861. Assigned next to the arsenal at Leavenworth, Kansas, Reno remained there until the fall of that year, when Ambrose Burnside (*q.v.*) requested his services for his amphibious division.

Commissioned brigadier general of Volunteers on November 12, 1861, Reno led one of Burnside's brigades into the North Carolina sounds in January 1862. After the capture of Roanoke Island and New Bern, he was promoted to major general and given a division. In that capacity, he engaged in a spirited dispute with Colonel Rush Hawkins over the latter's conduct at the battle of South Mills. Burnside took the IX Corps to Virginia that summer, and Reno led his own division and another to the assistance of John Pope (*q.v.*) at Second Bull Run.

Reno took over the IX Corps during the Maryland campaign, when Burnside rose to wing command. His troops assaulted Fox's Gap at South Mountain on September 14, 1862, carrying the crest at dusk, and Reno rode to the front line to inspect the situation. A sudden Confederate volley brought him out of the saddle with a bullet in the chest; he died within hours. A short, muscular man, Reno was known for his aggressive demeanor on the battlefield. His death robbed Burnside of his most experienced, capable, and dependable subordinate, as well as one of his best friends. Had Reno lived, the history of the IX Corps might have been different. Hennessy, *Return to Bull Run*; Marvel, *Burnside.*

William Marvel

REYNOLDS, John Fulton, *general*, was born in Lancaster, Pennsylvania, on October 20, 1820. He graduated from West Point in 1841, and was commissioned in the artillery. Reynolds served four years in East Coast garrisons, then was posted to Texas. Subsequently, he fought in the Mexican War under Zachary Taylor's command and earned two brevets. Afterward, he held command

and staff positions on both coasts and on the frontier. In September 1860 he became commandant of cadets at West Point, remaining in that office until the Civil War began.

Appointed lieutenant colonel, 14th Infantry, in May 1861, Reynolds commanded a unit in the Washington defenses until April 1862, when he was named military governor of Fredericksburg. Two months later, he assumed command of a brigade in the 3rd Division, V Corps, Army of the Potomac, and led it in the Peninsula campaign. Captured at Frayser's Farm, he was repatriated in August 1862 and took over the 3rd Division, Pennsylvania Reserves. After commanding this organization at Second Bull Run, Reynolds returned to Pennsylvania at the governor's request, and prepared the militia for repelling an anticipated Confederate invasion. He then took command of the I Corps, Army of the Potomac; soon afterward, at Fredericksburg, George G. Meade's (*q.v.*) division of this corps achieved the only penetration of the Confederate lines. At Chancellorsville, on the other hand, the I Corps saw little action.

In June 1863, Reynolds commanded a wing of Joseph Hooker's (*q.v.*) Army of the Potomac on the march north. When Meade replaced Hooker during this operation, Reynolds gracefully acquiesced to serving under his former subordinate. On July 1, 1863, in response to reports of Confederate concentrations near Gettysburg, Reynolds rushed forward to find General John Buford's (*q.v.*) cavalry hotly engaged northwest of the town. A little later, while deploying his forces to support Buford, Reynolds was killed by an enemy sniper. His death affected soldiers of all ranks. Meade called him the noblest and bravest of his subordinates. Another officer equated the loss of Reynolds at Gettysburg to that of Nelson at Trafalgar.

Military historians have consistently sustained these evaluations. Reynolds brought to the Civil War the best of the natural soldierly attributes honed by years of active service. But he was more than an inspiring combat leader; he was a better operational strategist than most of his titular seniors. Indeed, had John Pope (*q.v.*), Burnside, and Hooker accepted his counsels, they might have avoided the defeats that stained their reputations. It is idle to speculate about what Reynolds might have accomplished had he lived, but certainly he would have emerged from the war equal, if not superior, in stature to John Sedgwick (*q.v.*), Winfield Scott Hancock (*q.v.*), and Meade. Catton, *Terrible Swift Sword*; Coddington, *Gettysburg Campaign*; Hennessy, *Return to Bull Run*.

James L. Morrison, Jr.

REYNOLDS, Joseph Jones, *general*, was born in Flemingsburg, Kentucky, on January 4, 1822. He graduated from West Point in 1843 and, as a brevet 2nd lieutenant in the 4th Artillery, served in Texas at the outbreak of the Mexican War. Promoted to 2nd lieutenant in the 3rd Artillery on May 11, 1846, he spent most of the following decade as an instructor of geography, history, and philosophy at the Military Academy. He resigned at Fort Washita, Indian Territory, on February 28, 1857, to accept a teaching post at Washington University in St. Louis.

Reynolds was engaged in the family mercantile business in Lafayette, Indiana, when he was appointed colonel of the 10th Indiana Volunteers on April 27, 1861. Promoted to brigadier general of Volunteers on May 10, he commanded the Cheat Mountain District, West Virginia, until his resignation on January 23, 1862, to attend to business following the death of his brother. Reynolds was reappointed to the Army in the late summer of 1862, and was promoted to major general of Volunteers on November 29. He distinguished himself as a division commander at Chickamauga and as General George H. Thomas's (*q.v.*) chief of staff at Chattanooga. Reynolds supervised the defenses of New Orleans during the first six months of 1864, then assumed command of the XIX Corps and organized forces for the capture of Mobile. He commanded the Department of Arkansas from November 29, 1864, until April 25, 1866.

Mustered out of the Volunteer service on September 1, 1866, Reynolds was commissioned colonel of the 26th Infantry, to date from July 28. Appointed to a military command in Texas during Reconstruction, he supported the state's moderate Republican faction, served as provisional governor, and lost a contested election for U.S. senator in 1871. Assigned to the 25th Infantry in 1869, he transferred to the 3rd Cavalry on December 15, 1870, and commanded the regiment in Nebraska and Wyoming. His military career disintegrated after a court martial criticized his conduct during the 1876 Powder River campaign, and suspended him from rank and pay for a year. Although President Ulysses S. Grant (*q.v.*) remitted the sentence, Reynolds was unable to bear the stigma, and resigned on June 25, 1877. He died in Washington, D.C., on February 25, 1899. Cozzens, *This Terrible Sound*; Richter, *The Army in Texas During Reconstruction*.

Bruce J. Dinges

RICE, Alexander Hamilton, *congressman,* was born on August 30, 1818, in Newton Lower Falls, Massachusetts. He worked in his father's paper mill, attended local schools, and in 1844 graduated from Union College. Rice had a successful career in politics as well as business. He served as a Whig member of Boston's Common Council in 1853 and 1854, and then joined the Republican party, which elected him mayor of the city in 1856 and 1857. In 1858, he was sent to Congress, and served there for four terms. He won a reputation as a fiscal conservative, voted with moderate Republicans on issues relating to slavery and Reconstruction, served on the Committees on the District of Columbia and on Expenditures in the Treasury Department, and was an influential member of the Committee on Naval Affairs throughout the war. Rice chose not to seek reelection in 1866, and devoted himself to his business interests in Boston. Ten years later, he returned to politics and served as governor from 1876 to 1878. Rice died in Melrose, Massachusetts, on July 22, 1895. Benedict, *Compromise of Principle*.

Richard H. Abbott

RICE, Henry Mower, *senator,* was born on November 29, 1817, in Waitsfield, Vermont. He studied at a local academy, read law, worked as a surveyor in Michigan, then in 1839 entered the fur trade in what would become Minnesota. Rice was instrumental in several Indian negotiations, including the Sioux cession of 1851 that opened the "Su-land" (nearly all of southern and southwestern Minnesota) to white settlement. In 1849, he teamed with Henry Sibley (*q.v.*) to lobby for legislation establishing the Minnesota Territory, settled in St. Paul, and helped create the Minnesota Democratic party. He served as territorial delegate to Congress from 1853 to 1857, then in 1858 engineered Minnesota's statehood.

In December 1857, Rice was elected to the U.S. Senate, where he began as a Buchanan (*q.v.*) loyalist, often siding with the southern Democratic bloc against the Douglasites. In 1860, he opposed the nomination of Stephen A. Douglas (*q.v.*), then campaigned in Minnesota for John C. Breckinridge. During the secession crisis, Rice served on the Senate Committee of Thirteen, which sought a compromise on slavery to avert disunion. He supported John J. Crittenden's (*q.v.*) proposal to extend the Missouri Compromise line to the Pacific, but twice tried to end the issue of territorial slavery altogether by proposing immediate statehood for all western territories. When secession became inevitable, he urged that it be accepted peacefully.

In July 1861, Rice reversed his position to unyielding support of the war effort, a move prompted by fear for the Union after Bull Run, as well as by enormous political pressure from Minnesota. He became a key member of the Senate Committee on Military Affairs, and was instrumental in making military mobilization successful. Rice opposed Abraham Lincoln (*q.v.*) on conscription but supported him on virtually every other war measure, including the Emancipation Proclamation. His support was so pronounced that when his Senate term ended in 1863, and the choice of a successor was in the hands of the Republican-dominated Minnesota legislature, such Senate Republicans as Benjamin Wade (*q.v.*) of Ohio wrote letters urging Rice's reelection. The advice was not heeded, however, and Alexander Ramsey (*q.v.*) was given the seat.

In 1864, Rice supported the Lincoln–Johnson ticket, stumping Minnesota on its behalf. In 1865, he was privately offered Morton S. Wilkinson's (*q.v.*) Senate seat if he would switch parties, but he chose instead to run, unsuccessfully, for the governorship as a Democrat. After 1865, Rice devoted most of his time to land investments and civic affairs, serving on the University of Minnesota board of regents and as president of the Minnesota Historical Society. He was Ramsey county treasurer from 1878 to 1884, and served on the commission that negotiated the 1888 Red Lake Treaty with the Chippewa. He died in San Antonio, Texas, on January 15, 1894. Folwell, *History of Minnesota,* vols. 1, 2; Nichols, *Disruption of American Democracy.*

Roger A. Fischer

RICE, John Hovey, *congressman,* was born in Mt. Vernon, Maine, on February 5, 1816. He secured a clerkship in the office of the registrar of deeds for Kennebec county, holding that post and living in Augusta until 1841. Rice then moved to Monson, Maine, where he worked in a general store, read law, and was admitted to the bar in 1848. From 1852 to 1860, he served as county attorney of Piscataquis county, where he helped build the Republican party. Rice won a seat in Congress in 1860, and made a name for himself as a friend of the common soldier, particularly the sick and wounded. He frequently consulted with President Abraham Lincoln (*q.v.*) on soldiers' problems.

Lincoln offered Rice the collectorship of the Port of Bangor (Rice had moved his family there during the war) when he learned that Rice planned to retire from Congress in 1865. Rice, who served in the House until 1867, accepted the Bangor collectorship from President Andrew Johnson (*q.v.*). He hoped to make money from his new post and assorted business enterprises. In the early 1870s, he moved his family to Washington, where he opened a law office with the former Treasury solicitor Edward Jordan. Rice practiced before Federal and state courts and legislative committees for twelve years, then went to New York City in 1884 for fifteen more years of practice. A charming man with a great sense of humor, he was a practicing Universalist in later life. He died on March 14, 1911, in Chicago. *BDUSC.*

H. Draper Hunt

RICHARDSON, Israel Bush, *general,* was born on December 26, 1815, in Fairfax, Vermont. He graduated from West Point in 1841, and fought against the Seminoles in Florida in 1841–1842. He campaigned from Veracruz to Mexico City in the Mexican War, during which he acquired the sobriquet "Fighting Dick," and was breveted twice for gallant and meritorious service. Following the war, Richardson served on the frontier until 1855, when he resigned from the Army to settle and farm in Pontiac, Michigan.

In 1861, Richardson organized and became the colonel of the 2nd Michigan. Three days before Bull Run he commanded a brigade in a reconnaissance that revealed such Confederate strength at Blackburn's Ford that General Irvin McDowell (*q.v.*) changed his plan of attack. Richardson's brigade saw little actiom during the battle, but it did serve as a rear guard covering the Union retreat to Washington, D.C. For his performance Richardson was promoted to brigadier general of Volunteers. As commander of a division in the Peninsula campaign, he earned a reputation as a hard fighter and brilliant leader. In battle he was calm, resolute, and personally fearless. Esteem for his generalship is revealed in the reports of his superiors and of officers in other commands, who praised him as a courageous and skillful military leader.

On July 4, 1862, Richardson was promoted to major general of Volunteers. During the Confederate invasion of Maryland, he fought at South Mountain and in the battle of Antietam, where he led his division to a position immediately in front of enemy troops holding the sunken road soon to be known as Bloody Lane. There, while directing his men, he was mortally wounded by Confederate artillery fire. He was carried to Pry House, George B. McClellan's (*q.v.*) headquarters, where he died on November 3, 1862. Davis, *Bull Run*; Sears, *Landscape Turned Red*; Sears, *To the Gates of Richmond*.

Frederick D. Williams

RICHARDSON, William Alexander, *senator*, was born near Lexington, Kentucky, on January 16, 1811. He was educated at an academy at Walnut Hill, Centre College, and Transylvania University. In 1831, he moved to Illinois, was admitted to the bar, and began practicing law at Shelbyville. He was a state's attorney (1834–1836) and a member of the Illinois House of Representatives (1837–1839), the Illinois Senate (1839–1843), and the House again (1845–1847). He was speaker in 1845.

After service during the Mexican War, Richardson was elected in 1847 as a Democrat to the 30th Congress, filling the vacancy created by Stephen A. Douglas's (*q.v.*) resignation. He was reelected several times, serving in the House until 1856. He supported the Compromise of 1850, and was Douglas's key ally in backing the Kansas–Nebraska Act. He resigned in 1856 to run for governor of Illinois, but was unsuccessful. With Douglas' backing, in 1858, Richardson was appointed territorial governor of Nebraska, serving for less than a year. He was elected to the House again in 1860, but resigned in January 1863 to take the Senate seat formerly held by Douglas and temporarily filled by Orville H. Browning (*q.v.*).

Richardson served in the Senate from January 30, 1863, to March 3, 1865, being replaced by Republican Richard Yates (*q.v.*). During his political career he was a partner, supporter, and key assistant to Stephen A. Douglas, especially at the Democratic National Conventions in 1856 and 1860. He was a partisan Democrat, opposed abolition, and was a bitter opponent of Abraham Lincoln's (*q.v.*) administration. He became the Illinois leader of the Peace Democrats, and opposed the the Conscription Bill in 1863. After his service in Congress, he moved to Quincy, Illinois, where he resumed his law practice and, for a time, managed the *Quincy Herald*. He was elected in 1874 to the board of supervisors of Adams county. Richardson died in Quincy on December 27, 1875. Cole, *Era of the Civil War*; Johannsen, *Stephen A. Douglas*.

Leslie J. Stegh

RICKETTS, James Brewerton, *general*, was born in New York City on June 21, 1817. A graduate of West Point in 1839, he served as an artillery lieutenant at the battles of Monterey and Buena Vista during the Mexican War. He subsequently campaigned against the Seminoles in Florida and bandits in Texas, and was promoted to captain in 1852. He still held that rank at the outset of the Civil War.

Ricketts's service began with the capture of his battery on Henry House Hill at First Bull Run on July 21, 1861, an event that effectively turned the tide of battle against Federal arms. Ricketts was wounded, and spent the next six months in a Confederate prison. Exchanged in January 1862, he received the rank of brigadier general of Volunteers on April 30, 1862. He commanded a division of General Irvin McDowell's (q.v.) III Corps, covered Nathaniel P. Banks's (q.v.) retreat from Cedar Mountain, and participated in the campaigns of Second Bull Run and Antietam. Two horses were shot from beneath him at Antietam, one falling and severely incapacitating him.

At this point Ricketts's career became checkered, flawed by controversial conduct at Thoroughfare Gap before Second Bull Run; a court of inquiry accused him of retiring without orders when he might have contained Longstreet's drive to reinforce Jackson at Groveton. In addition, he was appointed to the court of inquiry for Fitz John Porter (q.v.); his lack of enthusiasm for the vendetta against Porter may have cost him higher rank. Unable to return to combat service, due to his wounds, until March 1864, Ricketts received a division in John Sedgwick's (q.v.) VI Corps, and held this command from the Wilderness to Petersburg.

In the summer of 1864, Ricketts's star rose when his division of less than 5,000 men was sent to aid Lew Wallace (q.v.) in containing Early's thrust against Washington and Baltimore. His men bore the brunt of the battle of Monocacy and, although swept from the field by overwhelming numbers, delayed the Confederates for an important twenty-four hour period. Ricketts subsequently fought with Philip H. Sheridan (q.v.) in the Shenandoah Valley, and was again wounded while temporarily commanding a corps at Cedar Creek. Nonetheless, he returned to his division in time to witness Lee's surrender at Appomattox. He was breveted major general of Volunteers on August 1, 1864, and in the Regulars as of March 13, 1865.

Ricketts remains an enigmatic figure of the Civil War. He epitomized the brave and dedicated, quick and bluff-mannered, professional soldier who inspired his subordinates. His early problems were a result of the "politicization" of George B. McClellan's (q.v.) army, and were offset by later, even pivotal, service when opportunities for dedicated action, such an Monocacy and Cedar Creek, presented themselves. Retired in 1867 due to his war wounds, Ricketts continued on courts martial duty until 1869. He lived in Washington, D.C., until his death there on September 22, 1887. Hennessy, *Return to Bull Run*; Rhea, *Battle of the Wilderness*; Sears, *Landscape Turned Red.*

                                                                                          B. Franklin Cooling

RIDDLE, Albert Gallatin, *congressman,* was born in Monson, Massachusetts, on May 28, 1816. In 1817, his family migrated to Geauga county, in Ohio's Western Reserve. Riddle received a common school education, worked as a carpenter, and was admitted to the Geauga county bar in 1840. He was county prosecuting attorney (1840–1846), and in 1848 was elected as a Whig to the Ohio House of Representatives, where he served until 1850. Passionately opposed to slavery, Riddle issued the call (1848) for a mass meeting that culminated in the formation of the Ohio Free Soil party. In 1859, he was one of the attorneys for the Oberlin Rescuers, and in his summation he invoked the "higher law" doctrine.

Riddle was elected as a Republican to Congress in 1860, but served only one term. Unwilling to compromise once the South had seceded, he was one of only two congressmen to vote against the Crittenden Resolutions. He believed that the Civil War should be fought to destroy slavery, and spoke publicly in favor of arming the slaves. He also supported the District of Columbia Emancipation Bill.

In 1863 and 1864, Riddle served as U.S. consul in Matanzas, Cuba. Upon returning to Washington, D.C., he began a law practice, and was later one of the prosecutors in the trial of John H. Surratt. Riddle maintained his Republican party connections, practiced law in the capital, and was active in the affairs of Howard University while writing novels, political biographies, and reminiscences. He died in Washington, D.C., on May 16, 1902. Riddle, *Recollections of War Times.*

Robert F. Horowitz

RIDDLE, George Read, *senator,* was born in New Castle, Delaware, in 1817. Educated at Delaware College, he studied engineering, and was active in the construction of railroads and canals in several states. In 1848, he was admitted to the bar in New Castle county, and began to practice law in Wilmington. In 1849, he was one of the commissioners to retrace the Maryland and Delaware boundary. In 1850, Riddle was appointed deputy attorney general of New Castle county. Active in Democratic politics, he served two terms in the U.S. House of Representatives (1851–1855). He attended Democratic National Conventions in 1844, 1848, and 1856. Upon the resignation of Senator James A. Bayard (*q.v.*) in protest against the "iron-clad" oath, Riddle was appointed to fill his unexpired term on February 2, 1864, and served until his death in Washington, D.C., on March 29, 1867. Conrad, *History of the State of Delaware.*

Harold B. Hancock

RIPLEY, James Wolfe, *general,* was born on December 10, 1794, in Windham county, Connecticut. He was appointed to West Point in 1813, but because of a heavy demand for officers during the War of 1812, his class was graduated in 1814. After serving as an artillery officer in New York, Ripley was posted to Florida. After admirable service in Florida and eight years of garrison and recruiting duty, Ripley, now a captain, was assigned to the sensitive command of General Winfield Scott (*q.v.*) in Charleston, South Carolina, where the nullification controversy threatened the Union. Again he won praise, this time from Scott. In 1833, after the ordnance corps was separated from the artillery, Ripley was assigned to command the arsenal at Kennebec, Maine, where he improved efficiency and won promotion to major.

In 1841, Ripley became superintendent of the Springfield Armory, where he increased production, lowered costs, and helped develop the means for manufacturing the new rifled musket, which would go into production the year after his departure. In 1854, he was promoted to lieutenant colonel and transferred to the Watertown Arsenal, but within a year was appointed chief of ordnance for the Pacific Department and, in 1857, inspector of arsenals. On the eve of the Civil War, Ripley had begun a special mission to observe munitions, particularly powder manufacturing, in Japan and the Far East. On hearing of the outbreak of war, he immediately returned and went directly to Washington, where he was promoted to colonel and chief of ordnance on April 23, 1861. His experience and ability made him the logical choice, and his promotion to brigadier general in August was deserved.

Short of arms and with inadequate manufacturing facilities, the Union forces accepted a wide variety of weapons. The national and state governments and private businessmen flooded the United States and Europe with purchasing agents, many of whom were inexperienced or dishonest. The Ordnance Department had little control over these acquisitions except through the inspection process, which suffered greatly from a shortage of personnel. Political favoritism and graft became rampant in the arms business, and Ripley fought them with all his considerable will, eventually reducing the level of corruption. The number of substandard arms issued to troops was high during the early months of the war, but the situation was largely corrected by early 1862. Although Ripley was a champion of the new rifled musket, he was less progressive in other areas. Although accepting the concept of breech-loading arms for the cavalry, he disdained similar weapons for the infantry. Valid reasons existed for caution in purchasing some of these arms, but Ripley exaggerated their weaknesses and almost ignored their virtues.

Political pressures as well as demands by a significant minority of field commanders forced Ripley to yield on many occasions and purchase large numbers of advanced arms. Despite his shortcomings, he and the Ordnance Department supplied the basic small arms and artillery needs of the Union Army very well. Ripley retired as chief of ordnance on September 15, 1863, but continued in service as inspector of armaments until 1869. He died on March 15, 1870, in Hartford, Connecticut. Davis, *Arming the Union*; Shannon, *Organization and Administration of the Union Army*.

Carl L. Davis

ROBINSON, Charles, *governor,* was born on July 21, 1818, in Hardwick, Massachusetts. He attended Amherst College, studied medicine, and became a doctor. Robinson lived briefly in California, serving as a state assemblyman, before being appointed Kansas resident agent of the New England Emigrant Aid Company. In 1854, he led the first two groups to the present site of Lawrence and assisted in the construction of the town. The fraudulent first territorial election caused Robinson to advocate armed resistance by Free State settlers, and when proslavery Missourians gathered on the Wakarusa River in 1855, threatening to destroy Lawrence, Robinson acted as commander of the town's defenders.

In 1856, Robinson assisted in the organization of the Free State party at Big Springs, led the party's radical wing at the constitutional conventions at Topeka, and was chosen Free State governor of the territory. While traveling east to gain aid for the Kansas Free Staters, he was arrested for treason and imprisoned at Lecompton for four months. In 1859, after the Free State party had captured control of the territorial government, it nominated Robinson for governor, and in 1861, when Kansas became a state, he served one term as its first chief executive. Later, he served two terms in the state Senate and ran unsuccessfully for U.S. congressman and for governor before his death in Lawrence on August 17, 1894. Blackmar, *Charles Robinson*; Castel, *Frontier State at War*.

Christopher Phillips

ROBINSON, James Carroll, *congressman*, was born on August 19, 1823, near Paris, Illinois; his family moved to Clark county in 1825. He served as a corporal in the Mexican War (1846–1847), studied law, and was admitted to the bar in 1850. Elected as a Democrat to the 36th through 38th Congresses, he did not seek reelection in 1864 in order to run, unsuccessfully, for governor. While in Congress, Robinson was a Peace Democrat, seeking compromise with the South. He opposed Abraham Lincoln's (*q.v.*) administration, supported states' rights, and opposed the Emancipation Proclamation. He returned to Marshall, Illinois, after the war and was the unsuccessful Democratic nominee for the U.S. Senate in 1865. In 1868, he moved to Springfield, where he practiced law in partnership with Anthony Lausett Knapp (*q.v.*). Robinson was elected to the 42nd and 43rd Congresses as a Democrat. He died in Springfield on November 3, 1886. Cole, *Era of the Civil War*.

Leslie J. Stegh

ROBINSON, James Fisher, *governor*, was born in Scott county, Kentucky, on October 4, 1800. He was educated by private tutors, at Forest Hill Academy, and at Transylvania University, from which he graduated in 1818. After reading law, he established a successful practice in Georgetown while living at Cardome, his Kentucky farm. A Whig until that party disintegrated, Robinson then became a Democrat. Although he agreed that the South had grievances, he rejected secession and remained loyal to the Union. Robinson was not politically ambitious, and his only office before 1860 was a term (1851) in the state Senate. He was elected again to that body in 1861.

In August 1862 pro-Southern Governor Beriah Magoffin (*q.v.*) agreed to resign if an acceptable conservative replaced him, the office of lieutenant governor being vacant. The Senate speaker resigned, Robinson was elected speaker, then resigned to become governor after Magoffin resigned. He served until the term ended in September 1863. Although supportive of the war effort, he denounced

Abraham Lincoln's (*q.v.*) Emancipation Proclamation and military interference with civilian affairs.

Upon leaving office, Robinson returned to his farm and law practice. In 1864, he was a delegate to the Union Democratic Convention, and in 1867 he received some support for the U.S. Senate, but he sought no political office. For years, he was chairman of the board of trustees of Georgetown College and president of Georgetown's Farmers' Bank. Robinson died at his home near Georgetown, Kentucky, on October 31, 1882. Coulter, *Civil War and Readjustment in Kentucky*; Harrison, *Kentucky's Governors*.

Lowell H. Harrison

ROBINSON, John Cleveland, *general,* was born on April 10, 1817, in Bing-hamton, New York. He was dismissed from West Point in his second year (1832), but was commissioned in 1839. After service in Mexico and on the frontier, he was at Fort McHenry when the Civil War began. He commanded a brigade on the Peninsula, at Second Bull Run, and at Fredericksburg, after which he was named a division commander in John F. Reynolds's (*q.v.*) I Corps. His division missed the worst of Chancellorsville, but on the first day at Gettysburg it took part in brutal fighting that effectively blunted the Confederate advance. Robinson's division lost almost two-thirds of its members in casualties and prisoners, but he was praised for his fighting spirit and for effectively with-drawing his command under great pressure.

In the reorganization of the army after Gettysburg, Robinson commanded a division in the V Corps. In leading an assault at Spotsylvania, he lost his left leg and served no more in the field. He headed the Freedmen's Bureau in North Carolina before retirement in 1869. He was active in New York politics and veterans' affairs, and headed the Grand Army of the Republic and the Society for the Army of the Potomac. In 1894, Robinson received the Congressional Medal of Honor for his actions at Spotsylvania. He died in Binghamton on February 18, 1897. Coddington, *Gettysburg Campaign*; Rhea, *Battle of the Wilderness.*

John T. Hubbell

RODMAN, Isaac Peace, *general,* was born on August 18, 1822, in South King-ston, Rhode Island. He was a successful businessman and served in the Rhode Island legislature. Although he was a Quaker, he accepted a commission as a captain in the 2nd Rhode Island Volunteers, but resigned to become colonel of the 4th Rhode Island Volunteers in October 1861. The regiment was in Ambrose Burnside's (*q.v.*) Carolinas expedition, after which Rodman was promoted to brigadier general. He commanded a division in the IX Corps at Antietam, and after the standstill on the Union left, was dispatched to ford the creek below Burnside's Bridge. The ford was unusable, and Rodman had to search for a crossing further downstream. He did get across, but because of the mishandling of the army by George B. McClellan (*q.v.*) and of the IX Corps by Burnside, the wasted time allowed Confederate forces under A.P. Hill to halt the Union advance. While attempting to deploy his troops, Rodman was shot from his horse by a sharpshooter. He died in a field hospital on September 30, 1862. Sears, *Landscape Turned Red.*

John T. Hubbell

ROGERS, Andrew Jackson, *congressman,* was born in Hamburg, New Jersey, on July 21, 1828. He had little formal education, but studied law, and was admitted to the bar in 1852. Rogers's reputation as a Peace Democrat originated in September 1861, when he refused to support prowar resolutions adopted by a bipartisan meeting in Newton, New Jersey. He won the Democratic nomination for Congress in October 1862 when the district convention dumped incumbent Democrat George T. Cobb (*q.v.*), who had supported the war effort and refused to condemn emancipation. Rogers was an effective stump speaker who warned that emancipated slaves would swarm into New Jersey, undercut free labor, and soon be "crawling into bed with your wives and daughters."

Once in Congress, "Jack" continued to voice the resentments of the New Jersey Peace Democracy. He found the Conscription Law "despotic" and "degrading to the white race of America." He called the 13th Amendment a violation of states' rights, yet incredibly, for a crucial vote on January 31, 1865, was one of the eight Democratic absentees who allowed the amendment to achieve a precarious two-thirds' House majority. His claim of sickness did not stop rumors that he had been bribed.

Rogers showed no signs of deviating from Democratic orthodoxy in the Reconstruction Congress, to which he was reelected in 1864. He was one of the fifteen members appointed to the Joint Committee on Reconstruction, no doubt as a token gesture to extreme Democrats. He opposed Congressional Reconstruction, which cost him his 1866 bid for reelection. Rogers lived for many years in New York City, where he was a city counsel. He was also police commissioner of Denver (1892–1896). He died in New York City on May 22, 1900. Knapp, *New Jersey Politics.*

Daniel W. Crofts

ROLLINS, Edward Henry, *congressman,* was born in Rollinsford, New Hampshire, on October 3, 1824. He became a drugstore clerk in 1845, and in 1847 bought a pharmacy in Concord, New Hampshire. In 1855, he won a seat in the New Hampshire House of Representatives, and in 1856 was elected speaker. A Republican by way of the Whig and Know-Nothing parties, Rollins served as a Whig committeeman and as chairman of the New Hampshire Republican Committee for five years. In 1861, he closed his drugstore after winning election to Congress. Rollins preached strong antislavery doctrine from his earliest days as a Whig, and in his first days in Congress, he voted in favor of a resolution against the use of Federal troops to capture and return fugitive slaves. Late in 1861, he supported a resolution disavowing Abraham Lincoln's (*q.v.*) right to suspend habeas corpus, but otherwise was a loyal supporter of the President throughout the war.

In 1866 and 1872, Rollins failed in bids for the Senate. He served as treasurer of the Union Pacific Railroad until 1876, when he finally won election to the Senate. Failing to be reelected in 1882, he established a bond company and banking firm, and in 1886 became president of the Boston, Concord, & Montreal Railroad. Unlike many antislavery politicians, Rollins was wily, practical, and predatory. Such qualities helped make him the only Granite State congressman to keep his seat through the entire Civil War. Rollins died on the Isle of Shoals, New Hampshire, on July 31, 1889. Lyford, *Life of Edward H. Rollins*.

William Marvel

ROLLINS, James Sidney, *congressman*, was born in Richmond, Kentucky, on April 19, 1812. Educated at Washington College and Indiana University, he took his legal training at Transylvania University, from which he graduated in 1834. He established a practice at Columbia, Missouri, and became involved in local politics. Rollins was elected as a Whig to the state House of Representatives in 1838, and to the state Senate in 1846. He was a delegate to the Whig National Convention in 1844, and by the end of the decade was the acknowledged leader of the party in Missouri. A bid for governor was unsuccessful in 1848, but he secured the largest vote for a Whig candidate to that date. Again elected to the legislature in 1854, Rollins was nominated for governor in 1857 by a coalition of Whigs, Know-Nothings, and Benton Democrats. This time he lost by only 329 votes.

Rollins was elected to Congress in 1860 on the Constitutional Union ticket, and easily secured a second term in 1862 as a Conservative–Unionist. Although he had good personal relations with Abraham Lincoln (*q.v.*), he opposed the President's plan for compensated emancipation in the border states. Unlike many of his conservative colleagues, he supported the 13th Amendment. Rollins did not seek reelection in 1864, but was elected to the Missouri House in 1866, and the Senate in 1868.

Rollins did yeoman's work in securing the Morrill land grants for the University of Missouri at Columbia, thereby thwarting its removal to another place by the Radicals. He moved into the Democratic party, following the lead of Francis Blair (*q.v.*), with whom he had been allied in the 1850s, but he was never completely comfortable there. He died in Columbia, Missouri, on January 9, 1888. Parrish, *Turbulent Partnership*; Smith, *James Sidney Rollins*.

William E. Parrish

ROSECRANS, William Starke, *general*, was born in Delaware county, Ohio, on September 6, 1819. He graduated from West Point in 1842, pursued engineering work on the fortifications at Hampton Roads, and returned to West Point in 1843 to serve four years on the faculty. After serving at various posts in New England, Rosecrans resigned his commission in 1854 to become a civil engineer, architect, and coal and oil refiner. He lived most of the time in Cincinnati, where he resided in 1861.

Soon after the start of the war, Rosecrans was made a brigadier general in the Regular Army and served with General George B. McClellan (*q.v.*) in West Virginia. He commanded a brigade at Rich Mountain, one of the first battles of the war. On March 21, 1862, he was named major general of Volunteers. In the fall of that year he won a victory at Iuka, Mississippi, then drove the Confederates out of Corinth. These successes largely explain why Rosecrans was selected to succeed General Don Carlos Buell (*q.v.*) when the latter was relieved after his overly cautious campaigning in Kentucky.

Reorganizing his command as the Army of the Cumberland, Rosecrans moved southeast toward Murfreesboro and General Braxton Bragg's Army of Tennessee. The two armies met on the west fork of Stones River, just west of the town, on the last day of 1862, and fought one of the bloodiest battles of the war. Bragg launched his attack first and rolled up the Union right wing, but Rosecrans with great vigor established a new line covering the railroad and pike to Nashville. Fighting continued for the next two days, then Bragg retreated to a line near Tullahoma.

In the summer of 1863, Rosecrans conducted an excellent campaign, skillfully forcing Bragg to retreat to Chattanooga. Next he maneuvered Bragg out of the city but, hastening to follow, overextended his lines. Bragg received reinforcements, turned, and defeated him at Chickamauga on September 19 and 20. Through mistaken orders, Thomas J. Wood's (*q.v.*) division was pulled out of the Union line at the very time a major Confederate attack struck the wide gap thus created. A large portion of the Union forces fled in disorder, and Rosecrans himself was caught up in the rapid retreat to Chattanooga. The error at Chickamauga, together with his unfortunate tendency to irritate his superiors, cost him his command. Relieved on October 19, he was assigned to command the Department of Missouri. He saw very little action thereafter, and resigned from the Army in March 1867.

Rosecrans was active in business and politics, serving as minister to Mexico, engaging in mining operations, and becoming a Democratic congressman from California (1881–1885). Independent, outspoken, occasionally short of temper, and with an uncompromising moral sense, he sometimes made enemies, needlessly and unwisely, in high places. Always in his military career he was energetic, displayed a vast theoretical knowledge of war, was popular with the soldiers he led, and seemed to be a capable military commander except for the crisis at Chickamauga. Rosecrans died on March 11, 1898, on his ranch in Redondo, California. Cozzens, *This Terrible Sound*; Lamers, *Edge of Glory*; McDonough, *Stones River*.

James Lee McDonough

ROSS, Lewis Winans, *congressman*, was born near Seneca Falls, New York, on December 8, 1812. In 1821, he accompanied his father to Illinois, where the new town of Lewistown was named after him. He attended Illinois College, where he was a friend of Richard Yates (*q.v.*), who was to be the Civil War governor of Illinois. Ross studied law with a Jacksonville attorney, was admitted to the bar, and began practice in Lewistown in 1839. He was an early friend of Stephen A. Douglas (*q.v.*) and active in Democratic politics. In 1840–1841, and again in 1844–1845, he was a member of the state legislature. After service in the Mexican War, he returned to law and Democratic politics. Ross was an elector on the Cass–Butler ticket of 1848, and a delegate to the Charleston and Baltimore Democratic National Conventions of 1860.

Ross's most notable political service was in the 38th through 40th Congresses. He steadfastly followed the route of states' rights, strict construction, limited Federal government, implacable opposition to the military, hostility to Radical Reconstruction, and the impeachment of Andrew Johnson (*q.v.*). He supported the war because he favored the Union, but thought that by refusing to compromise, Republicans were as guilty of causing the war as the secessionists. Ross favored free trade in theory, but accepted a tariff as practical necessity. He could always be found on the anti-''Robber Baron'' slope of any economic question, and against New England. He championed the cause of the ''common man'' against the powerful, and of the Indians against the bureaucracy, but had little sympathy for the slave or former slave.

In 1868, Ross was not a candidate for Congress; he remained in Illinois, where he resumed the practice of law. In 1870, he served in the state constitutional convention, and in 1876, he supported Samuel J. Tilden's nomination. He died in Lewistown, Illinois, on October 20, 1895. *BDUSC.*

Jack Nortrup

ROUSSEAU, Lovell Harrison, *general,* was born on August 4, 1818, near Stanford, Kentucky. In the 1830s, he read law in Louisville, and in 1840 moved to Bloomfield, Indiana, where he was admitted to the bar. Rousseau served in the Indiana legislature (1844–1845), fought in Mexico as a captain in the 2nd Indiana Volunteers, and in 1847 won the first of two terms in the Indiana Senate. Returning to Louisville in 1849, he practiced law and, in 1860, was elected to the Kentucky Senate.

Rousseau opposed secession, and in September 1861 enlisted pro-Union Kentuckians in the 3rd Kentucky Infantry and became its colonel. He gallantly led the 4th Brigade in the 2nd Division under General Alexander McCook (*q.v.*) at the battle of Shiloh. His brigade twice turned back attacks launched by General Braxton Bragg, resulting in Rousseau's promotion to brigadier general of Volunteers (October 1862). The brigade also fought well at Perryville, leading to his promotion to major general of Volunteers. Rousseau then took command of the 5th Division in the Army of the Cumberland, under General George H. Thomas (*q.v.*). He fought at Stones River, performed valuable service in leading cavalry on a raid to destroy railroad tracks and equipment from Montgomery to Opelika, Alabama (July 1864), and defended Nashville against John Bell Hood.

In addition, he was military commander of Nashville and the District of Tennessee (November 1863–November 1865).

Rousseau's postwar career was distinguished. Elected to Congress as a Republican in 1865, he quickly sided with President Andrew Johnson (*q.v.*) against the Radicals over Reconstruction policy. After an argument, he caned Iowa Republican Josiah B. Grinnell (*q.v.*). The House censured Rousseau, who resigned; he was reelected, however, and served until 1867. In 1867, President Johnson appointed Rousseau to the rank of brigadier in the Regular Army, and assigned him to head the U.S. delegation that received the Alaska Territory from the Russians. In September 1868 Johnson sent Rousseau to command the 5th Military District. He neglected to enforce Federal civil rights and state election laws in Louisiana, giving the state's electoral votes to Democratic presidential aspirant Horatio Seymour (*q.v.*). He died in New Orleans on January 7, 1869. Dawson, *Army Generals and Reconstruction*; Sword, *Embrace an Angry Wind*; Sword, *Shiloh*.

Joseph G. Dawson III

ROWLEY, Thomas Algeo, *general,* was born on October 5, 1808, in Pittsburgh, Pennsylvania. He was active in local politics, and at the beginning of the Civil War was commissioned a colonel of the 13th Pennsylvania, a ninety-day regiment, by virtue of his service with a local militia regiment, the Jackson Blues, during the Mexican War. The 13th was redesignated the 102nd Pennsylvania at the expiration of its enlistment, and as commander of this unit, Rowley served competently but without distinction in the Peninsula and Second Bull Run campaigns. On November 29, 1862, he was promoted to brigadier general and commanded a brigade at Chancellorsville. At Gettysburg, he briefly took command of General Abner Doubleday's (*q.v.*) division when the latter assumed the leadership of John Reynolds's (*q.v.*) I Corps, but he did not manage it effectively, a fact the I Corps artillery chief, Charles Wainwright, attributed to his apparent intoxication.

Although Rowley was cited by Doubleday for gallantry, serious questions about his competence prompted a decision to relieve him of active duty in the Army of the Potomac. Court martialed at Culpepper, Virginia, on April 23, 1864, he was convicted of charges ranging from drunkenness to incompetence. Judge Advocate General Joseph Holt (*q.v.*) recommended a dismissal of the conviction, however, because of conflicting testimony. After an unsuccessful attempt to get General Ulysses S. Grant (*q.v.*) to reassign him to the Army of the Potomac, Secretary of War Edwin Stanton (*q.v.*) gave Rowley charge of the District of the Monongahela. He resigned this post on December 29, 1864, and devoted the rest of his life to a law practice. He died in Pittsburgh on May 14, 1892. Coddington, *Gettysburg Campaign*; Wainwright, *Diary of Battle*.

Walter L. Powell

RUGER, Thomas Howard, *general,* was born in Lima, New York, on April 2, 1833. In 1846, he moved with his family to Janesville, Wisconsin, and at age seventeen entered West Point, from which he graduated in 1854. After less than one year, he resigned from the Army and established a law practice in Janesville. Upon the outbreak of the Civil War, he became lieutenant colonel, then colonel, of the 3rd Wisconsin, which he led at Cedar Mountain and Antietam. Promoted to brigadier general on November 23, 1862, he commanded a brigade in Alpheus S. Williams's (*q.v.*) division of the XII Corps at Chancellorsville and Gettysburg. In the latter battle, after Williams took charge of the corps, Ruger headed the division and showed initiative and foresight by occupying an abandoned line of entrenchments, thus preventing the Confederates from outflanking the Union right.

In October 1863, Ruger went with the XII Corps to Tennessee, where his brigade spent the rest of the year guarding supply lines. He took part in the Atlanta campaign, during which he continued to command a brigade in Williams's division, now part of Joseph Hooker's (*q.v.*) XX Corps. At Resaca, Kolb's Farm, and Peachtree Creek the brigade helped repulse strong Confederate attacks, and at New Hope Church it was repulsed. Following the fall of Atlanta, Ruger became a commander of a division in the XXIII Corps that played a key role in defeating the Confederate assault at Franklin, Tennessee and, after having been transferred to North Carolina, did the same at the battle of Kinston.

Ruger was an excellent brigade and division commander who fully deserved by 1865 what he did not obtain until thirty years later—the rank of major general. He remained in the Army after the war, receiving first the rank of colonel in 1866, then being promoted to brigadier general in 1886 and to major general in 1895. After retiring in 1897, he moved to Stamford, Connecticut, where he died on June 3, 1907. Castel, *Decision in the West*; Coddington, *Gettysburg Campaign.*

Albert Castel

RUSSELL, David Allen, *general,* was born in Salem, New York, on December 10, 1820. He graduated from West Point in 1845, served in the Mexican War, and campaigned against the Yakima Indians in the Pacific Northwest. He was a captain when the Civil War began, and in early 1862 took a Volunteer commission as colonel of the 7th Massachusetts. Russell led his regiment through the Peninsula campaign without particular distinction, and he arrived at the battle of Antietam after the fighting was over. Nevertheless, he was commissioned a brigadier general of Volunteers in November 1862. His brigade took a passive part in the battle of Fredericksburg, and did not lose a man at Gettysburg. Russell had temporary command of a division of the VI Corps at the battle of Rappahannock Station on November 7, 1863, where one of his brigades captured 1,300 Confederates and eight stands of colors.

Russell continued at the head of a division from the Wilderness to Petersburg. He followed the VI Corps to the Shenandoah Valley that summer, commanding his division at the battle of Winchester, Virginia, on September 19. He was wounded early in that action, but declined to leave the field; he was struck and killed by a piece of shell several hours later. Known principally for his hour of glory at Rappahannock Station and his death at Winchester, Russell is an example of a mediocre military figure whose reputation was salvaged from oblivion largely by circumstances. Matter, *If It Takes All Summer.*

William Marvel

S

SALOMON, Edward, *governor,* was born in Stroebeck, Prussia, on or about August 11, 1828. While attending the University of Berlin, he became involved in the revolutionary activities of 1848, and he left his homeland. He initially settled in Manitowoc, Wisconsin, and worked as a teacher, county surveyor, and deputy court clerk. In 1852, he moved to Milwaukee, where he studied law and was admitted to the bar. Like most Milwaukee Germans, Salomon considered himself a Democrat, but his support of Abraham Lincoln (*q.v.*), combined with his ethnic appeal, resulted in his nomination in 1861 for lieutenant governor on the Republican–Union ticket. The tragic death of Governor Louis P. Harvey (*q.v.*) in April 1862 thrust Salomon into that office.

Although relatively inexperienced in American politics, Salomon learned quickly. One of his more contentious opponents was Secretary of War Edwin M. Stanton (*q.v.*). In May 1862, Salomon received a request from Stanton to raise additional troops. He expressed a willingness to continue to meet his quotas, but only if certain changes were made in the procedures, most importantly that the War Department pay its expenses promptly. Since the problems enumerated were common throughout the North, Salomon's determination served to rally the support of his fellow governors. The War Department finally agreed to meet the demands, and recruiting once again proceeded.

There were problems following passage of the Militia Act of 1862, with its implied power of conscription, problems particularly troublesome in Wisconsin's Lake Michigan counties, where large numbers of German Catholics opposed the Lincoln administration. Efforts to attract volunteers had not been successful, and it was presumed that the draft would make up the shortfalls. The law was scheduled to go into effect on November 10, 1862, but there were violent reactions in several communities. Senator Timothy Howe (*q.v.*) was personally threatened, draft commissioners were driven off, and angry mobs roamed the streets. Governor Salomon was forced to call out some of the newly raised regiments, a decision that would have serious political consequences. Although many of those "drafted" disappeared, more than 1,700 were mustered in. One regiment, the 34th, was composed of nine-month conscripts, the majority of whom were Germans. There were still legal problems involving the rioters who had been arrested, but administrative and judicial delays served to diminish the urgency, and the affair was more or less forgotten.

Despite these disturbances, Salomon attended the governors' meeting at Altoona, Pennsylvania, on September 23, 1862, the results of which proved to be more satisfying to the President than to the state participants. When Lincoln imposed the Conscription Act of March 1863, there was little violence in Wisconsin, which is not to say that the draft worked well. Salomon did what he could to encourage volunteering, but was distressed with many of his fellow German immigrants, who now claimed to be aliens solely for the purpose of avoiding service. It was apparent that Salomon had become a liability to the Republican cause, no longer appealing to those German voters who had supported him previously. Thus, James T. Lewis (*q.v.*) became the party's nominee and the next governor. Salomon returned to his law practice, moved to New York City in 1867, and in 1894 returned to his native Germany. He died in Frankfurt-am-Main, on April 21, 1909. Current, *Civil War Era*; Hesseltine, *Lincoln's War Governors*.

Charles E. Twining

SALOMON, Frederick, *general,* was born on April 7, 1826, in the village of Stroebeck, Prussia. He received a good education and became a government surveyor, then a lieutenant of artillery. He was studying architecture in Berlin when the revolutionary movement of 1848 swept Europe. To escape the turmoil, he emigrated to the United States in 1849 with three brothers; two were breveted brigadier generals during the Civil War, and another, Edward Salomon (*q.v.*), served as governor of Wisconsin (1862–1863). Salomon settled in Manitowoc, Wisconsin, engaged in surveying, served as county registrar of deeds, and worked as a civil engineer during construction of the Manitowoc & Wisconsin Railroad.

With the outbreak of the Civil War, Salomon became a captain in the 5th Missouri, a Volunteer three-month regiment commanded by one of his brothers. They saw combat at Carthage, Dug Springs, and Wilson's Creek. On November 26, 1861, Salomon reentered the Volunteer service as colonel of the 9th Wisconsin, which he commanded in Missouri, Arkansas, and the Indian Territory. On July 16, 1862, he was commissioned a brigadier general and assigned to command a brigade of the Army of the Frontier in Kansas. At the battle of Helena, Arkansas, on July 4, 1863, while commanding a division of the XIII

Corps, he demonstrated superior ability in fighting off a sustained and determined attack by Confederate forces under Lieutenant General Theophilus H. Holmes. This won high commendation from his district commander, Major General Benjamin M. Prentiss (*q.v.*). During the Red River expedition, in command of the 3rd Division of the VII Corps at the battle of Jenkins' Ferry, Arkansas (April 30, 1864), Salomon again distinguished himself. His able and energetic defense against a much larger Confederate force enabled Major General Frederick Steele's (*q.v.*) exhausted troops to escape across the Saline River.

On March 13, 1865, Salomon was breveted major general for meritorious service, and then mustered out of the Army on August 25. After the war, he became the surveyor general of Missouri. When Rutherford B. Hayes (*q.v.*) became President in 1877, Salomon was made U.S. surveyor general of Utah Territory, an office he held until 1885. On March 8, 1897, he died in Salt Lake City. Bearss, *Vicksburg Campaign*, vols. 1, 3; Josephy, *Civil War in the American West*; Love, *Wisconsin in the War.*

LeRoy H. Fischer

SANFORD, Henry Shelton, *diplomat,* was born on June 15, 1823, in Woodbury, Connecticut. He graduated from the Episcopal Academy at Cheshire in 1839. Health problems forced him to withdraw from Washington College in 1840, and he spent eight years traveling in Europe, where he learned several languages and earned a Doctor of Laws degree from the University of Heidelberg. Sanford was an inactive member of the Whig and Republican parties, but the political influence of his uncle, Philo S. Shelton, with William H. Seward (*q.v.*), secured him appointments as secretary of the American legation in Paris (1849–1854) and as minister resident to Belgium in 1861.

Sanford's service in Europe was diverse and significant. Soon after his arrival in April 1861, he initiated a broad-ranging secret service system for the surveillance of Confederate agents. This system, which drew upon Union consuls, ministers, and private detectives, provided the prototype for subsequent Union efforts. He also coordinated a major portion of the North's purchases of European war matériel during 1861, contracting for 400 tons of saltpeter and 125,000 arms. He completed his 1861 assignments by carrying the offer of a Union command to Giuseppe Garibaldi.

During the remainder of the war, Sanford continued his surveillance activities, participated actively in Northern propaganda work, and ably represented U.S. interests in Belgium. His tenure in Brussels ended with the inauguration of President Ulysses S. Grant (*q.v.*) in 1869. He subsequently exercised considerable influence over American policy toward the Congo by engineering recognition of Leopold II's African International Association in 1884, and by serving as a delegate to the Berlin West African Conference of 1884–1885 and the Brussels Antislavery Conference of 1889–1890. Sanford died in Healing Springs, Virginia, on May 21, 1891. Fry, *Henry S. Sanford.*

Joseph A. Fry

SARGENT, Aaron Augustus, *congressman,* was born in Newburyport, Massachusetts, on September 28, 1828. His political ambition surfaced early when he became secretary to a member of Congress. In 1849, he left Washington for California and settled in Nevada City. Sargent was active in Whig politics and was proprietor of the *Nevada City Journal,* which became a Whig organ. He gained admission to the bar in 1854, served as Nevada county district attorney from 1855 to 1857, and sat on the state central committee of a settlers' and miners' party. As a Republican, he tried for the state Senate in 1856; ran for state attorney general in 1857; served on the Republican Central Committee in 1858 and 1859; and was a delegate to the Republican National Convention in 1860.

Sargent's service to the party was rewarded with a term in Congress. He formed a close association with Theodore D. Judah, engineer for the Central Pacific Railroad, and his bill for its construction was passed in 1862. He strongly supported the administration's war measures, and voted for emancipation in the District of Columbia. Sargent was unsuccessful in his attempt to become senator in 1863, governor in 1863, and senator in 1865 and 1867. His only consolation was to serve on the California Republican Central Committee in 1864. Sargent was elected to Congress in 1868 and in 1871, and in 1872, to the U.S. Senate.

At the expiration of his term (March 1879), Sargent resumed the practice of law in San Francisco. He had mastered the German language through private study, and President Chester Arthur appointed him minister to Germany. He returned to his law practice in San Francisco, and remained active in Republican politics and anti-Chinese agitation. He died in San Francisco on August 14, 1887. *BDUSC.*

Robert J. Chandler

SAULSBURY, Gove, *governor,* was born on May 29, 1815, in Mispillion Hundred, Delaware, the eldest of three brothers active in Delaware Democratic party politics. He attended local schools and Delaware College in Newark. In 1842, he graduated from the Medical College of the University of Pennsylvania, opened a practice, and involved himself with the Democratic party. In 1856, Saulsbury was a delegate to the Democratic National Convention, as was his brother Willard (*q.v.*). In 1862, he was elected to the Delaware Senate, and was a major figure in the Delaware Democratic party. During the 1863–1864 sessions of the state legislature, he supported resolutions inquiring into the enlistment of African American troops into the Federal service.

In early 1865, Saulsbury was elected state Senate president. In March, Governor William Cannon (*q.v.*) died. Under the state constitution in effect at that time, there was no office of lieutenant governor, so Saulsbury became acting governor. After taking office, he reprimanded the U.S. Congress for interfering with the institution of slavery, and actively opposed Delaware's ratification of the 13th Amendment. In November 1866, Saulsbury was elected governor in his own right, and retained that office until 1871.

In 1871, Saulsbury and his brothers Eli and Willard were candidates for U.S. senator from Delaware. After several ballots, Eli emerged the winner, with support from Willard. After that election, Gove never again held public office, although he was a delegate to the 1876 and 1880 National Democratic Conventions. He died in Dover, Delaware, on July 31, 1881. Hancock, *Delaware During the Civil War*; McCarter, *Historical and Biographical Encyclopaedia of Delaware.*

Frank R. Levstik

SAULSBURY, Willard, Sr., *senator,* was born in Kent county, Delaware, on June 2, 1820. Educated in local schools, he then attended an academy in Denton, Maryland, and spent one year at Delaware College and another at Dickinson College. After reading law, he was admitted to the bar in Dover in 1845. He began to practice law in Georgetown, Delaware, the county seat of Sussex county. Because of his intellect and brilliance as an orator, Saulsbury advanced rapidly in politics. An active member of the Democratic party, he served as Delaware's attorney general (1850–1855). He attended the Democratic National Conventions of 1856 and 1864. In 1859 the General Assembly elected him to serve in the U.S. Senate, and he was reelected in 1865.

During the Civil War, Saulsbury sympathized with the South, and was critical of violations of civil rights by the Lincoln (*q.v.*) administration. Unfortunately, he attained notoriety for his drinking habits. In 1871, the Democratic caucus and the Democratic General Assembly chose his brother Eli as a candidate for the U.S. Senate, rather than Willard or another brother, Gove (*q.v.*). In 1873, his brother-in-law, Governor James Ponder, chose Saulsbury to be chancellor of the state's judicial system. He filled this office with great ability and distinction until his death in Dover, Delaware, on April 6, 1892. Hancock, *Delaware During the Civil War.*

Harold B. Hancock

SAXTON, Rufus, *general,* was born in Greenfield, Massachusetts, on October 19, 1824. He graduated from West Point in 1849, served in the Seminole Wars, surveyed railroad routes, and observed European campaigns. Stationed at St. Louis in 1861, Saxton helped Brigadier General Nathaniel Lyon (*q.v.*) disperse disloyal militia before transferring to western Virginia as chief quartermaster to Major General George B. McClellan (*q.v.*). In October, he accompanied the Port Royal expedition, and the following spring joined the headquarters of the Department of the South. Promoted to brigadier general of Volunteers in April 1862, a month later, he was moved to Virginia, where he won a Medal of Honor for repulsing a Confederate assault on Harper's Ferry. Returning to South Carolina with responsibility over all blacks in the Department of the South, Saxton, a moderate abolitionist, won authority to recruit up to 5,000 African Americans as ''military laborers.'' Later his troops were authorized to conduct defensive operations and raid enemy territory.

In 1863–1864, as military governor of the Sea Islands off South Carolina and

Georgia, Saxton placed black civilians on abandoned plantations and provided them with tools and seed. In May 1865 he became assistant commissioner of the Freedmen's Bureau in South Carolina, Georgia, and Florida. His tenure was ineffective due to a lack of resources and military support. Early in 1866, he was mustered out of the Volunteers as a brevet major general. Saxton remained in the Regular service for another twenty-two years, rising to assistant quartermaster of the Army. He died in Washington, D.C., on February 23, 1908. Quarles, *Negro in the Civil War*; Rose, *Rehearsal for Reconstruction*.

Edward G. Longacre

SCHENCK, Robert Cumming, *general, congressman,* was born October 4, 1809, in Franklin, Ohio. He graduated from Miami University in 1827 and moved to Dayton to practice law. In 1840, he won a seat in the state legislature, and two years later went to Congress as a Whig. He served for eight years before Millard Fillmore appointed him minister to Brazil. After returning to Ohio in 1853, Schenck identified with the new Republican party, and worked energetically for the nomination and election of Abraham Lincoln (*q.v.*). His support brought him in a commission as brigadier general on June 5, 1861.

Although inexperienced in things military, Schenck was popular in Ohio and as a general could help raise troops. He led a brigade in Daniel Tyler's (*q.v.*) division at First Bull Run, but it was the only one that did not cross Bull Run and enter the battle. In 1862, Schenck commanded a brigade in the campaign against Jackson, finally turning up at Second Bull Run with a division in Franz Sigel's (*q.v.*) I Corps. Here he received a bad wound that rendered him unfit for further service in the field.

Promoted to major general on August 30, 1862, Schenck held administrative command of the Middle Department, with headquarters at Baltimore. His administration was very unpopular with the largely pro-Southern population of Maryland, and his harsh attitude toward secessionists did not help the situation. He resigned his commission on December 5, 1863, in order to take his seat in the 38th Congress, to which he had been elected as a Republican. On the basis of his military expertise, he was appointed chair of the House Committee on Military Affairs and the Militia. Despite some difficulties from the chair of the Senate Military Committee, Henry Wilson (*q.v.*), and from some powerful House Republicans, Schenck proved relatively successful in securing needed changes in the national Conscription Bill.

Schenck remained in Congress until 1871, when President Ulysses S. Grant (*q.v.*) rewarded him with an appointment as minister to Great Britain, where his chief service came in amicably settling the *Alabama* claims. In 1876, he resigned his post in some disgrace following a business difficulty, and returned to Washington, D.C., to practice law until his death there on March 23, 1890. Davis, *Bull Run*; Geary, *We Need Men*; Hennessey, *Return to Bull Run*.

William C. Davis

SCHOFIELD, John McAllister, *general,* was born in Gerry, New York, on September 29, 1831. He graduated from West Point in 1853, was posted to the 1st Artillery in Florida, and returned to West Point for four and a half years as an instructor in philosophy. When the Civil War began, Schofield was in St. Louis, a professor at Washington University. He became an aide-de-camp to General Nathaniel Lyon (*q.v.*), and thus was at the head of the Union column that forced the surrender of the secessionists at Camp Jackson. Lyon thought highly of Schofield, but unfortunately did not heed his advice to retreat before the battle at Wilson's Creek. Schofield opposed the division of the command that sent Franz Sigel (*q.v.*) marching on an ill-fated flanking attempt. Lyon lost his life in the ensuing chaotic engagement.

In November 1861 Schofield became a brigadier general of Volunteers and held various territorial commands until the autumn of 1862. He commanded the Army of the Frontier in Missouri, but grew impatient when advancement did not keep pace with his expectations. His most strenuous efforts seemed to accomplish little. A discouraged Schofield at last wrote General in Chief Henry W. Halleck (*q.v.*), pleading for a transfer to some other command. President Abraham Lincoln (*q.v.*) placed him in charge of the vast Department of Missouri, which included Kansas, Indian Territory, and part of Arkansas, as well as the state of Missouri. Schofield was unable, however, to resolve the tense political situation, and in late 1863 Lincoln gave him command of the Department of the Ohio, with headquarters in Knoxville.

In the spring of 1864, Schofield received the kind of appointment that he had long awaited: as an army commander in William T. Sherman's (*q.v.*) Atlanta campaign. But this assignment did not bring him the opportunity to distinguish himself. He always kept up with his paperwork, and handled his command well on occasional flanking movements, but any hope of glory eluded him. Schofield finally gained a measure of fame in the Spring Hill–Franklin–Nashville campaign in late 1864. When General George H. Thomas (*q.v.*) began a concentration of troops at Nashville, Schofield, with his XXIII Corps and part of the IV Corps, covered the concentration of John Bell Hood's Army of the Tennessee. Gradually retiring toward Nashville, he escaped Hood's attempt to trap him at Spring Hill and then fought the bloody battle at Franklin, which badly shattered the Confederate army. Schofield then joined Thomas, taking part in the battle of Nashville, which almost destroyed Hood's command. Breveted a major general in March 1865, he rejoined Sherman in North Carolina for the conclusion of the war.

Schofield proved himself one of the better army administrators as military director of Reconstruction in Virginia. Only thirty-six when he was appointed Secretary of War in 1868, he held thereafter several prominent positions: commander of the Divisions of the Pacific, the Missouri, and the Atlantic; superintendent of the U.S. Military Academy; and commanding general of the Army from 1888 to 1895, the year of his retirement. Schofield's record in Georgia and Tennessee shows that he was a good second-echelon battle leader. As an administrator, he demonstrated realistic good sense, attention to avoiding mistakes, and an ability, in most cases, to remain above personal prejudices. Schofield died in St. Augustine, Florida, on March 4, 1906. Castel, *Decision in the West*; McDonough, *Schofield*; Sword, *Embrace an Angry Wind*.

James Lee McDonough

SCHURZ, Carl, *diplomat, general,* was born on March 2, 1829, in Liblar, Germany. As a student at the University of Bonn, he took an active part in the Revolution of 1848–1849. He was almost captured at Rastatt, but succeeded in reaching France. He returned secretly to Germany to free Professor Gottfried Kinkel from Spandau prison and take him to Great Britain, a feat that made him famous. Finding refugee life in Paris and London uncongenial, in 1852 Schurz came to the United States, and settled in Watertown, Wisconsin, where there was a large German population. Because of his antislavery convictions, he was naturally attracted to the Republican party, for which he performed valuable services as a journalist and orator by winning over many of his normally Democratic compatriots.

Abraham Lincoln (*q.v.*) rated Schurz's aid in 1860 so highly that he rewarded him with the legation in Madrid. In 1862, Schurz returned to the United States to join the Army. He established a creditable record at Second Bull Run, but suffered a serious reverse at Chancellorsville when his division, together with the rest of the XI Corps, was overrun by Stonewall Jackson. Temporarily in command of the XI Corps on the first day at Gettysburg, he was forced to withdraw to Cemetery Hill. Subsequently, Schurz participated in the engagements around Chattanooga, where General Joseph Hooker (*q.v.*) unjustly accused him of tardiness at Wauhatchie. Although fully vindicated by a court of inquiry, he was transferred to the command of a replacement depot near Nashville and did not see active service again until the last days of the war, when he became General Henry W. Slocum's (*q.v.*) chief of staff.

During Reconstruction, Schurz was at first an active Radical; his devastating report on conditions in the South (1865) was an effective indictment of President Andrew Johnson's (*q.v.*) policy. After two brief newspaper ventures in Washington and Detroit, he became an editor of the St. Louis *Westliche Post*. He was elected U.S. senator from Missouri in 1869. Schurz advocated the repeal of disabilities of former Confederates and opposed the annexation of Santo Domingo, which led to a complete break with President Ulysses S. Grant (*q.v.*). In 1872, he was a leader of the national Liberal Republican revolt, but in 1876 supported Rutherford B. Hayes (*q.v.*), who appointed him Secretary of the Interior. He utilized this position to further civil service reform, better treatment of the Indians, and the conservation of natural resources. From 1881 to 1883, Schurz edited the *New York Evening Post*, and in 1884 again broke with his party to urge the election of Grover Cleveland over James G. Blaine (*q.v.*). A foe of inflation, in 1896 he backed William McKinley, only to break with him because of his strong anti-imperialist convictions.

Schurz's distinguished career was made possible by his success as an ethnic politician. Serving as a model for German-Americans everywhere, he was able to appeal to their national pride and to imbue them with confidence in their future; he also showed them how to combine loyalty to their traditions with full participation in the life of their adopted country. His literary skills were remarkable, his oratorical talents unusual, and his goodwill convincing. If he lacked greatness as a military commander, and a certain sense of humility, he nevertheless performed important services. He rallied the Germans to the cause of the Union and helped them adjust to their new surroundings. His pleas for tolerance and clean government make him a good example of a leading nineteenth-century liberal. He died in New York City on May 14, 1906. Fuess, *Carl Schurz*; Schafer, *Carl Schurz*; Trefousse, *Carl Schurz*.

Hans L. Trefousse

SCOFIELD, Glenni William, *congressman*, was born in Dewittville, New York, on March 11, 1817. He graduated from Hamilton College in 1840, taught school, read law, and was admitted to the Pennsylvania bar in 1842. He entered practice in Warren, which became his home and political base. Scofield entered politics in 1849 as a Democratic state legislator, and served in the Pennsylvania General Assembly for two years. His strong opposition to slavery was well known, and as the sectional crisis deepened, he advocated its restriction. In 1856, as the Republican candidate for the state Senate, he won in an area that had been a traditional Democratic stronghold, and served for three terms.

In 1862, Scofield was elected to Congress, where he served until his retirement in 1875. During Ulysses S. Grant's (*q.v.*) administration, he became implicated in the Crédit Mobilier scandal but escaped prosecution. He withdrew from elective office, but Rutherford B. Hayes (*q.v.*) appointed Scofield a registrar of the U.S. Treasury in 1878, and in 1881 he accepted a seat on the U.S. Court of Claims. He died in Warren on August 30, 1891. *Biographical Encyclopedia of Pennsylvania of the Nineteenth Century*; Evans, *Pennsylvania Politics 1872–1877*.

W. Wayne Smith

SCOTT, John Guier, *congressman*, was born in Philadelphia on December 26, 1819. He graduated from Bethlehem Academy in civil engineering, and in 1842 moved to Iron Mountain, Missouri, to become general manager of the Iron Mountain Company. He established the Irondale Iron Company at Irondale in 1858. Following the death of Congressman John W. Noell (*q.v.*) in March 1863, Scott was elected as a Democrat to fill the vacancy, and served for the rest of the 38th Congress. Little is known of his congressional career; there is no record of his having participated in a single debate during his two years in Congress. He did not stand for reelection, but entered the drug business in St. Louis. He established iron furnaces at Scotia, Missouri, in 1868 and at Nova Scotia, Missouri, a year later. He lived in St. Louis during the 1870s, and moved to eastern

Tennessee around 1880. He died in Oliver Springs, Tennessee, on May 16, 1892.
BDUSC.

William E. Parrish

SCOTT, Winfield, *general,* was born near Petersburg, Virginia, on June 13, 1786. His distinguished service at Lundy's Lane during the War of 1812 led to a brevet as major general. He was instrumental in building the Regular Army, and in 1847 led the brilliant campaign from Veracruz to Mexico City that ended the Mexican War. He quarreled with other officers and with President James K. Polk, revealing an unfortunate side of his nature. In 1852, he was the Whig candidate for President, but lost to Franklin Pierce. He was general in chief at the beginning of the Civil War but was physically unable to take the field. Nor could he convince his fellow Virginian, Robert E. Lee, to serve his country rather than his state.

Scott would have pursued a conservative strategy against the South: a combination of economic pressures and blockade, and a massive offensive by a large, well trained army. The political pressure for an early advance led to Bull Run, a humiliation of Union arms, and retirement (October 31, 1861) for General Scott. Had his health permitted, he would have been a splendid general in chief. As it was, he was replaced by George B. McClellan (*q.v.*). Variations of his "anaconda" plan were tried, but McClellan, Don Carlos Buell (*q.v.*), and Henry W. Halleck (*q.v.*) were unable to make it succeed, as it should have, in 1862. Scott died at West Point on May 29, 1866. Elliott, *Winfield Scott.*

John T. Hubbell

SCRANTON, George Whitfield, *congressman,* was born in Madison, Connecticut, on May 1, 1811. In 1839, he and his brother Selden formed a partnership in an iron furnace business. In 1840, they organized the Lackawanna Iron & Coal Company and purchased a large parcel of land in Lackawanna, Pennsylvania, that contained rich deposits of coal. In that same year Scranton founded the city of Scranton. Within a few years, both the business and the city were thriving. In addition to the coal industry, Scranton introduced railroad transportation into the Lackawanna Valley, and he served for several years as president of two railroads. In 1858, he won election to Congress on the Union ticket, and two years later was reelected as a Republican.

During the two-month struggle to elect a Speaker, Scranton emphasized his desire to organize the House rapidly. Initially he supported John A. Gilmer of North Carolina, but later declared that because he was elected by the "People's Party," he remained independent of party politics and could support any candidate whom a majority in the House found acceptable. Scranton shifted his vote to William Pennington, (*q.v.*), who became the Speaker. Throughout the remainder of the 36th Congress, he generally supported Republican legislation, particularly that dealing with the secession crisis. He voted in favor of a proposed 13th Amendment protecting slavery where it already existed, and he rejected, again with most other House Republicans, Senator John J. Crittenden's (*q.v.*) compromise proposals. Scranton remained conscious, too, of his own district, supporting, whenever possible, tariff policies that promised protection for American industries. He died in Scranton on March 24, 1861. Bogue, *Congressman's Civil War*.

Philip J. Avillo, Jr.

SEATON, William Winston, *editor*, was born on January 11, 1785, in King William county, Virginia. From 1803 to 1812, he edited newspapers in Virginia and North Carolina. In October 1812, Seaton became a partner with his brother-in-law, Joseph Gales, Jr., in publishing the *National Intelligencer*, the first recognized political organ in the United States. It championed James Madison's administration, and the British destroyed its office when they captured Washington, D.C., in 1814. The paper reported the debates of Congress exclusively from 1812 to 1829; all other papers in the nation reprinted these proceedings from the *Intelligencer*. Seaton and Gales published forty-two volumes of *The Debates and Proceedings in the Congress of the United States* (covering 1789–1824) between 1834 and 1856. As the first official reporters of Congress, they provided the nation with notes on the Missouri Compromise debates and other major oratorical clashes. Daniel Webster reportedly said that he believed Gales and Seaton were the two wisest heads in the nation.

Seaton was active in local politics, led the movement for the Washington Monument, and was a founder and organizer of the Smithsonian Institution. As an official of the American Colonization Society for many years, he favored gradual emancipation and freed his own slaves. However, he objected to the Garrisonian abolitionists and took the firm position that the national government should not interfere with the institution of slavery. Although he favored compromise on the slavery issue, Seaton was a firm Unionist. He retired from the *National Intelligencer* in January 1865. The paper had lost two-thirds of its circulation through the secession of the Southern states, and Seaton found it impossible to continue to function when two governments were at war. He died in Washington, D.C., on June 16, 1866. Hudson, *Journalism in the United States*; Seaton, *William Winston Seaton*.

Ronald D. Rietveld

SEDGWICK, Charles Baldwin, *congressman*, was born on March 15, 1815, in Pompey, New York. After attending Hamilton College, he studied law, and became an attorney in Syracuse. Attracted to the Free Soil party in 1848, he opposed the Compromise of 1850, defended fugitive slaves in court, and eventually joined the Republican party. His constituents elected him to the 36th and 37th Congresses. Prior to secession, Sedgwick, a member of his party's Radical wing, labored for a constitutional amendment to emancipate slaves and pressed for black colonization. After secession, he argued that Republicans must support both the Union and liberty by avoiding concessions to the South.

The outbreak of the war found Sedgwick in the sensitive position of chairman of the House Naval Committee. He at once ran into procedural and personal differences with Secretary of the Navy Gideon Welles (*q.v.*). Although they often shared similar goals, they clashed over Welles's impatience with congressional rules and Sedgwick's insistence that they must be honored. Even so, Sedgwick did sponsor several measures Welles wanted: expansion of the department's bureaucracy; increased appropriations; manufacture of ironclads; and the enlargement of shipyards. At the same time, he backed a drastic program of confiscation, and lobbied for enlistment of fugitive slaves into military service.

Meanwhile, Welles had uncovered purported frauds in the purchase of supplies at navy yards. According to his allegations, several prominent Republicans, including Sedgwick, were involved. Although President Abraham Lincoln (*q.v.*) helped quash the investigation, Sedgwick's reputation was ruined. In 1862, his constituents denied him renomination, and the following year, he failed in a bid for the U.S. Senate. For the remainder of the war, Sedgwick gained Welles's grudging approval to codify naval laws for the department. In 1865, he returned to Syracuse and continued his law practice until his death there on February 3, 1883. Curry, *Blueprint for Modern America*; Foner, *Free Soil, Free Labor, Free Men*; Welles, *Diary*, vol. 1.

Jerome Mushkat

SEDGWICK, John, *general*, was born in Cornwall Hollow, Connecticut, on September 13, 1813. He graduated from West Point in 1837, and was commissioned in the artillery. Sedgwick battled Seminoles, participated in the Cherokee removal, served on the frontier, and then fought in the Mexican War. Subsequently, he spent eight years in eastern garrisons. Following his transfer to the cavalry in 1855, he campaigned on the Great Plains and participated in the Mormon pacification expedition.

When the Civil War began, Sedgwick was stationed at Fort Wise, Colorado. Returning east in June 1861, he served in the capital defenses for a month before becoming inspector general of the Department of Washington. Between August 1861 and February 1862, he commanded units near the capital, then led a division in the II Corps, Army of the Potomac, in the Peninsula campaign until he was wounded at Frayser's Farm. After recuperating, Sedgwick resumed command of his division, seeing heavy action at Antietam, where he was wounded again. Upon returning to duty on December 26, 1862, he temporarily commanded the II and III Corps.

On February 5, 1863, Sedgwick took over the VI Corps, the organization associated with his name thereafter. In the battle of Chancellorsville, he directed the effort to outflank Robert E. Lee by crossing the Rappahannock at Fredericksburg. This maneuver failed largely because of the ineptitude of Joseph Hooker (*q.v.*), the army commander, but Sedgwick's slowness was also a factor. In contrast, during the Gettysburg campaign, Sedgwick's troops marched thirty-five miles in twenty hours, reaching the battlefield only to remain idle for most of the engagement. In its next major encounters, Rappahannock Station and Mine Run, the VI Corps fought well, capturing a Confederate division in the first action. In the Wilderness, however, the men broke when outflanked, and only Sedgwick's timely action averted disaster.

A few days later, on May 9, 1864, a sniper killed Sedgwick as he was inspecting the lines at Spotsylvania. The death of "Uncle John," probably the most loved general in the Army of the Potomac, severely dampened troop morale. Ulysses S. Grant (*q.v.*) said that his loss hurt as much as losing a division. Yet Grant also maintained that Sedgwick, though brave and conscientious, lacked the attributes of military greatness. Most of his contemporaries and military historians have shared that view. Furgurson, *Chancellorsville*; Rhea, *Battle of the Wilderness*.

James L. Morrison, Jr.

SEGAR, Joseph Eggleston, *congressman,* was born on June 1, 1804, in King William county, Virginia. After attending public schools, he studied law, and was admitted to the bar. He was elected to the Virginia House of Delegates (1836–1838, 1848–1852, 1855–1861) and, in October 1861, as a Unionist, to the 37th Congress. However, the House decided he was not entitled to the seat. Soon thereafter, Segar was elected to the same Congress, serving from March 15, 1862, to March 3, 1863. Although he was reelected to the 38th Congress, an 1864 House resolution declared him ineligible. In February 1865 he presented credentials as U.S. senator-elect and again was not permitted to take his seat. In the years after the war, Segar was elected to the 41st Congress, and again declared not eligible. From 1877 to 1880, he served on the Spanish Claims Commission. He died on April 30, 1880, aboard a steamer en route from Norfolk, Virginia, to Washington, D.C. Lanman, *Biographical Annals*; Morris, *Who Was Who in American Politics*.

Frank R. Levstik

SEWARD, Frederick William, *assistant secretary of state,* was born on July 8, 1830, in Auburn, New York, where his father, William Henry Seward (*q.v.*), was a rising politician and lawyer. On graduating from Union College in 1849, the younger Seward served as private secretary to his father, who had just been elected to the U.S. Senate. Although he was admitted to the bar in 1851, Seward chose journalism as his career. Until March 1861 he served as assistant editor for his father's friend, Thurlow Weed (*q.v.*), the proprietor of the *Albany Evening Journal*, and played an important role in the politics of New York.

President Abraham Lincoln (*q.v.*) appointed Seward assistant secretary of state at the outset of the Civil War. In that office he served as his father's closest subordinate throughout the Lincoln and Andrew Johnson (*q.v.*) administrations. He had special authority over the consular service, but also wrote many diplomatic instructions and, when his father was ill or out of Washington, acted in his place. On the night of April 14, 1865, Seward was attacked by the same assassin who tried to murder his father; both narrowly survived.

Seward left the State Department with his father in March 1869, and they traveled together extensively for the next two years, until the elder Seward became too weak to continue. Following his father's death in 1872, Seward served one term in the New York legislature and was narrowly defeated by John Bigelow (*q.v.*) in 1875 for the office of New York secretary of state. From March 1877 until October 1879, he resumed the post of assistant secretary of state in Washington, where he negotiated a treaty for an American protectorate in Samoa. His last years were spent in business near his home at Montrose, New York, where he died on April 25, 1915. Seward, *Reminiscences.*

Norman B. Ferris

SEWARD, William Henry, *Secretary of State,* was born on May 16, 1801, in Florida, New York. He graduated from Union College in 1820, and in 1822 was admitted to the New York bar. He entered the practice of law at Auburn, New York, and maintained his home there for the rest of his life. Seward served in the New York Senate (1830–1834) as a member of the Anti-Masonic party. With the demise of that party he, like other anti-Jacksonians, became a Whig. He was governor of New York from 1839 to 1843, and entered the U.S. Senate in 1849 as an antislavery Whig. He opposed Henry Clay's compromise proposals in 1850, as well as the Kansas–Nebraska Bill four years later. As the Whig party disintegrated after 1854, Seward led its New York remnants into the Republican party. Thereafter, he became a serious candidate for the Republican presidential nomination, but he lacked the appeal of John C. Frémont (*q.v.*) in 1856 or Abraham Lincoln (*q.v.*) in 1860.

Lincoln chose Seward as his Secretary of State. To prevent civil war, Seward assured commissioners of the seceded states that the Federal government would evacuate Fort Sumter. When Lincoln overruled him, Seward, on April 1, 1861, suggested that a war against the major powers of Europe would destroy the divisive forces within the country and thereby save the Union. Again Lincoln overruled him. With the fall of Fort Sumter, Seward undertook the task of keeping Europe neutral. He reminded London and Paris that the United States remained one country; any recognition of the Confederacy could lead to war. Seward deflated the *Trent* crisis of December 1861 by admitting the superiority of the British case and permitting the Confederate agents to proceed to their European destinations.

During the critical year of 1862, Seward withstood British and French pressure to end the war by insisting that the North would win and that he and Lincoln, under no circumstance, would give up the Union. Seward failed to prevent the French involvement in Mexico but, convinced that the Mexican people would never accept a French-supported European monarch, he refused to commit the United States to an active anti-French policy. When he could not stop British shipyards from launching commerce raiders for the Confederacy,

Seward perfected the case against Britain that later permitted a satisfactory financial settlement.

On April 5, 1865, Seward suffered an injury in a fall from his carriage. Nine days later, while recuperating in his Washington home, he was wounded by a member of the conspiracy that took Lincoln's life. Seward regained his health and remained in Andrew Johnson's (*q.v.*) Cabinet. Throughout the struggle over Reconstruction, he supported Johnson. In 1867, he negotiated the purchase of Alaska from Russia, and in March 1869 returned to private life. He died in Auburn on October 10, 1872. Van Deusen, *William Henry Seward.*

Norman A. Graebner

SEYMOUR, Horatio, *governor*, was born on May 31, 1810, in Pompey Hill, New York. After graduation from a Connecticut military academy in 1824, he returned to his family home in Utica and became an attorney. In 1833, he became Governor William L. Marcy's military secretary, an appointment that began an alliance of twenty-four years. A conservative Democrat, or Hunker, Seymour was the state's chief expert on canal expansion, an issue that contributed to the Democratic party's fragmentation.

As the split between the Hunkers and Barnburners escalated into the Free Soil movement, Seymour labored for reconciliation. His reward came in 1850 when the temporarily united Democracy gave him the first of his six nominations for governor. Narrowly defeated, he won two years later. His term was highlighted by new Democratic schisms because of the Kansas–Nebraska Bill and ethnoculturalism symbolized by conflicts over temperance and anti-Catholicism. These issues led to his defeat in 1854. The campaign of 1860 marked his political revitalization; Seymour supported Stephen A. Douglas (*q.v.*) and was instrumental in forming a state fusion slate of electors. He opposed coercion of the seceded states, pleaded for moderation, and urged compromise through the Crittenden Resolutions.

When the war began, Seymour loyally encouraged Volunteer enlistments, even though he doubted that force could restore the Union. He rejected the administration's growing centralism, particularly its denials of civil liberties. Moreover, Seymour's political philosophy was at odds with other wartime developments, including protective tariffs, legal tender, centralized banking, and internal revenue taxation. Such conservatism, plus his antagonism to emancipation, contributed to his second gubernatorial victory in 1862. As governor of the Union's largest and richest state, he automatically became a national figure and, somewhat reluctantly, the focal point of the Democratic opposition. As a result, Seymour supported some wartime measures, such as Volunteer enlistments, as long as they were under state control. This position reached critical dimensions during his controversial involvement in the 1863 New York City draft riots, which clouded not only his remaining term but also his historical reputation.

In 1864, Seymour seemed committed to the Peace Democrats, yet worked with their opponents on behalf of George B. McClellan (*q.v.*). This uncertainty, plus Republican charges of disloyalty, led to his defeat. After turning again to farming, he became the unexpected, if not unwilling, candidate for President in 1868, when the Democrats deadlocked. After his loss, he retired from politics, and in the following years refused another gubernatorial nomination and a chance to become a U.S. senator. His only involvement lay in helping Samuel J. Tilden's crusade against the Tweed Ring. Seymour died in Utica on February 12, 1886. Brummer, *Political History of New York*; McCabe, *Life and Public Services of Horatio Seymour*; Mitchell, *Horatio Seymour*.

Jerome Mushkat

SEYMOUR, Thomas Hart, *governor*, was born on September 29, 1807, in Hartford, Connecticut. He attended public schools in Hartford, and graduated in 1829 from Captain Alden Partridge's Institute in Middletown. He then studied law, and in 1833 was admitted to the Connecticut bar. From 1837 to 1838, Seymour edited *The Jeffersonian*, an organ of the Democratic party in Hartford. He was elected judge of the Probate Court, and in the 1840s became an influential figure in Hartford's Democratic party.

In 1843, Seymour served his first and only term in Congress. He was a major in the Mexican War, and participated in the capture of Chapultepec. He was defeated for election as governor in 1849, but was elected in each of the three succeeding years. President Franklin Pierce appointed him minister to Russia in 1853, so he served as governor only a portion of that year and for the next four years was in St. Petersburg. In the spring of 1860, Seymour was Democratic candidate for governor, but lost to William Buckingham (*q.v.*); he ran again in 1863.

The outbreak of war horrified Seymour. He had long considered the South to be an ideal society, one that should be protected, not attacked, by Northern leaders. An elitist, he disapproved of the expanding managerial class in his own state, and was appalled by the concomitant growth of manufacturing and urban centers. He denied the necessity of war, and throughout the conflict demanded that hostilities be ended and the South appeased. Thus, in his campaign for governor in 1863, the war was the issue. Republican opponents denounced him as a defeatist, a Southern sympathizer, and a Copperhead. After Union victories at Vicksburg and Gettysburg, Seymour's influence waned, and when delegates who favored the war were chosen for the 1864 Democratic National Convention, he assumed that his own party had rejected him.

Although he was absent, Peace Democrats who did attend the national convention named Seymour as their candidate, even though they recognized that George B. McClellan (*q.v.*) was the favorite of the majority. Despite this vindication, Seymour remained despondent. In an 1863 letter to Franklin Pierce, he declared, ''I have no longer a country, nothing left but the 'graves of knaves' and friends. And so I will go and weep for what is no more forever.'' Seymour died in Hartford on September 3, 1868. Niven, *Connecticut for the Union*; Norton, *The Governors of Connecticut.*

Joanna D. Cowden

SEYMOUR, Truman, *general,* was born in Burlington, Vermont, on September 24, 1824. He graduated from West Point in 1846, and with the 1st Artillery, distinguished himself in the Mexico City campaign. Talented as an artist as well as an artillerist, he subsequently taught drawing at West Point, fought the Seminoles, and served at several Atlantic forts. Commissioned captain in November 1860, Seymour commanded half the Charleston garrison when war came. After Fort Sumter, he joined the new 5th Artillery, still as captain but frequently as commander of the regiment. He thereafter served as chief of artillery and commander of the 3rd (later 1st) Brigade, Pennsylvania Reserve Division, and was promoted to brigadier general on April 28, 1862. His brigades fought well at the Seven Days, Second Bull Run, South Mountain, and Antietam; at Malvern Hill he directed the division.

Upset at being passed over and concerned about his health, Seymour transferred to the Department of the South (November 1862), where he served as chief of staff, chief of artillery, and commander of the Beaufort and Hilton Head garrisons, and of the 2nd Division, X Corps. In July 1863 he fell severely wounded at Battery Wagner. Worse defeat came in February 1864, when his expedition to conquer Florida was crushed at Olustee. Recalled north that spring, he commanded the 2nd Brigade, 3rd Division, VI Corps in the Wilderness, but was captured on May 6, 1864. Exchanged in August, he led the 3rd Division, VI Corps from late October through Appomattox.

Seymour blended marked contrasts. He was sensitive with friends, artistic, diffident, yet militarily quick to offend, was ambitious, and aggressive, even reckless. As a subordinate, he proved a capable hard-hitting combat leader. But as a senior subordinate or a quasi-independent commander, Seymour repeatedly came to grief through his rashness and ambition. Such weaknesses made him unfit for higher command, and caused his demotion to levels better suited to his fighting ability. Seymour left Volunteer service after the war, commanded various artillery posts, and served on the Artillery Board. He retired in 1876, and in 1885 settled in Florence, Italy, where he died on October 30, 1891. Rhea, *Battle of the Wilderness.*

Richard J. Sommers

SHANKS, John Peter Cleaver, *congressman, general,* was born in Martinsburg, Virginia, on June 17, 1826. His family moved to Jay county, Indiana, in 1839. The self-educated Shanks read law, and was admitted to the bar in 1850. In 1851, as a Whig, he was elected prosecuting attorney of the Circuit Court, and in 1855 was elected to the Indiana General Assembly as a Fusionist. In 1856, Shanks became a Republican, and his support of free blacks and prohibition contributed to his defeat for reelection that year. He campaigned for John

C. Frémont in 1856, and they became friends. Elected to the U.S. House of Representatives in 1860, he became a vigorous supporter of the war effort, both in Congress and on the battlefield.

Shanks was at Bull Run—like many others, he went out to see the opening battle. He found himself caught in the retreat of a leaderless New York regiment and successfully rallied the unit. He refused a brigadier general's commission, but did accept a position on Frémont's staff. He may have drafted Frémont's manumission proclamation, issued on August 30, 1861, freeing the slaves of owners in active rebellion. The proclamation was revoked by the administration. Shanks returned to Congress in December 1861, in time to support passage of a bill preventing the army from returning former slaves to their masters. He served on Frémont's staff in the spring of 1862, during Frémont's losing contest with Stonewall Jackson in the Shenandoah Valley.

Because of his abolitionist views and his advocacy of conscription, Shanks was defeated in the 1862 elections. Under the authority of Indiana Governor Oliver H.P. Morton (q.v.), he raised a regiment of cavalry and was appointed its colonel in October 1863. He served in the West and Southwest, successively commanding a regiment, a brigade, and a division of cavalry. He was breveted brigadier general in December 1864 and, upon the recommendation of Secretary of War Edwin Stanton (q.v.), was breveted a major general in March 1865.

Shanks was reelected to Congress in 1866, and served on the Committee on Militia and the Committee on Indian Affairs. He was chairman of a committee to investigate the treatment of Union prisoners of war; in March 1869 it issued a 1,200-page report. Shanks favored the impeachment of Andrew Johnson (q.v.) and generally all measures of Congressional Reconstruction. He also supported the 13th, 14th, and 15th Amendments, the Freedmen's Bureau, a preamble to the 1875 Civil Rights bill calling for equality of all before the law, a bill providing that the lands contained in lapsed railroad land grants be distributed among the freed slaves, and measures to protect the Indians from exploitation. Shanks also advocated support for Civil War veterans on matters from pension and pay to artificial limbs. He was reelected to his seat three more times, finally losing in 1874. He died on January 23, 1901, in Portland, Indiana. Curry, *Blueprint for Modern America*; Shepherd, *Biographical Directory of the Indiana General Assembly*, vol. 1.

Raymond L. Shoemaker

SHANNON, Thomas Bowles, *congressman*, was born in Westmoreland county, Pennsylvania, on September 21, 1827, and attended the common schools. In 1844 he moved to Illinois, and in 1849 to Plumas county, California, where he engaged in mining and mercantile pursuits. Originally a Whig, Shannon acted with the Free Soil wing of the Democratic party. He was a member of the California Central Committee in 1860; represented Plumas county in the assembly in 1859, 1860, and 1862; and was elected to the state Senate in 1863. Shannon actively supported black testimony in 1862 and 1863, a campaign issue that Democrats unsuccessfully used against him during two elections. As a supporter of Senator John Conness (*q.v.*), Shannon went to Congress in 1863, and served until March 1865. He participated little in debate, but consistently voted for administration measures. He was not a candidate for reelection.

Conness saw to Shannon's appointment as surveyor of the Port of San Francisco on August 11, 1865, a post he held for five years. He represented San Francisco in the Assembly during the 1871–1872 legislative session and became speaker. He succeeded Timothy Guy Phelps (*q.v.*) as collector of the port on July 1, 1872, and, appointed to an unprecedented second term, held the position until August 10, 1880, when he returned to mining and mercantile activities. Shannon died in San Francisco on February 21, 1897. Phelps, *Contemporary Biography*, vol. 2; Shuck, *Representative and Leading Men of the Pacific*.

Robert J. Chandler

SHAW, Robert Gould, *colonel*, was born in Boston on October 10, 1837. When the Civil War approached, he dropped out of Harvard, moved to New York, and joined an elite militia unit. Transferring to the 2nd Massachusetts Volunteers, he fought ably at Cedar Mountain and Antietam. Early in 1863, family connections brought Shaw the opportunity to command the 54th Massachusetts Infantry, the first unit of black soldiers raised in the North. He initially declined the offer, but by early June he had recruited the regiment to fighting strength and led it to South Carolina. Although occasionally guilty of racial insensitivity, Shaw came to decry the way the Army discriminated against black troops. Aware that his men must prove themselves in battle, he fought superiors who relegated them to rearguard duty outside Charleston. When they finally were assigned to active service, Shaw protested being forced to accompany an expedition that wantonly burned Darien, Georgia.

Thanks to Shaw's efforts, the 54th experienced a successful baptism of fire in a skirmish on James Island, South Carolina, on July 16, 1863. Two days later, Shaw accepted an offer to lead an attack on Battery Wagner, which guarded the main approach to Charleston. In the doomed assault the regiment lost almost half its men, including its commander, killed as he topped the parapet of the fort. Glatthaar, *Forged in Battle*; Shaw, *Blue-eyed Child of Fortune*.

Edward G. Longacre

SHEAHAN, James Washington, *editor*, was born in Baltimore on February 22, 1824. He was admitted to the practice of law in the Federal courts of the District of Columbia in 1845, and reported congressional proceedings for the District's press and the New York Associated Press for many years. He moved to Chicago and founded the *Chicago Times* in August 1854. The *Times* was established by friends of the Franklin Pierce administration, with Stephen A. Douglas (*q.v.*) the most prominent among them. With the political separation of President James Buchanan (*q.v.*) and Douglas, the *Times* remained loyal to Douglas and supported him in the 1858 contest with Abraham Lincoln (*q.v.*).

Although loyal to Douglas, Sheahan failed to make the *Times* "a campaign paper," and thus provoked concern and dissatisfaction in Democratic ranks. As early as 1858, the paper was having financial problems that, together with political difficulties, forced the owners to sell it in December 1860 to Cyrus McCormick, who consolidated it with his *Herald* as the *Times and Herald*.

Sheahan then went to Springfield, Illinois, and contributed to the *Springfield Register* during the 1860 campaign. That same year, the *Chicago Post* was launched under the general editorship of Sheahan, with a declaration of devotion to commercial, literary, and local happenings rather than to politics. However, the public's eagerness for war news forced the *Post*'s sale in April 1865. Sheahan remained, and accepted an editorial position on the *Tribune* (as it was now called). He still held that position in 1875.

The *Times* under Sheahan had been an honest Democratic journal, as Lincoln once described it, but after he left, the paper became a sensation-mongering sheet without conscience or principle. After McCormick bought it, E.W. McComas, a bitter proslavery Virginian, became its editor. It remained Democratic, but supported the war and, for a time, the Lincoln administration until it began a series of attacks on the President and Northern generals after the Emancipation Proclamation was issued. Its virulent attacks caused General Ambrose Burnside (*q.v.*) to suspend the paper in June 1864, but three days later Lincoln rescinded the order.

From 1854 to 1860, Sheahan had been active in Democratic politics as well as the press, but he managed to continue his literary interests, addressing literary societies and preparing a comprehensive biography of Douglas, which was published in 1860. Sheahan died in Chicago on June 17, 1883. Johannsen, *Stephen A. Douglas*; Sheahan, *Life of Stephen A. Douglas*.

Ronald D. Rietveld

SHEFFIELD, William Paine, *congressman,* was born in New Shoreham, Rhode Island, on August 30, 1820. He was educated at Kingston Academy and studied law at Harvard. Sheffield was a delegate to the Rhode Island Constitutional Convention of 1842, and a member of the Law and Order party that successfully frustrated efforts to achieve universal manhood suffrage and constitutional reform in Rhode Island. He served in the state legislature for eleven of the years between 1843 and 1861, first as a Whig and by 1857 as an American–Republican. He was elected to the 37th Congress by the coalition of Democrats and Conservative Republicans who had organized in 1860 because they feared that the slavery issue would bring war. Sheffield returned to the state legislature in 1863 and served there until 1884, when he was appointed to fill the unexpired term of Senator Henry B. Anthony (*q.v.*). No important Federal legislation bears the mark of his name or influence. He died in Newport, Rhode Island, on June 2, 1907. *BDUSC*.

Mario R. DiNunzio

SHELLABARGER, Samuel, *congressman,* was born in Clark county, Ohio, on December 19, 1817. He graduated from Miami University in 1841, studied law, was admitted to the Ohio bar in 1844, and began his law career in Springfield. He was elected as a Whig to the Ohio House in 1852 and 1853, became a Republican, and was elected to the 37th Congress, where he supported Abraham Lincoln's (*q.v.*) administration in its war efforts. So strong was Shellabarger's support for the President that near the end of the 37th Congress, he and Isaac Arnold (*q.v.*) of Illinois were reputed to be the only two Republicans who refrained from criticizing Lincoln in private conversations. Shellabarger urged the use of African American troops, and favored ending slavery in the territories and the District of Columbia, but did not support Federal emancipation. In 1862, he ran against Samuel S. Cox (*q.v.*) and was defeated for reelection.

Shellabarger was elected to the 40th Congress, and declined a reelection bid in 1868. President Ulysses S. Grant (*q.v.*) appointed him minister to Portugal, a post he held for nine months in 1869. He was again elected to Congress in 1870. During 1874 and 1875, he served on the Civil Service Commission. In 1875, Shellabarger moved his law practice to Washington, D.C., where he died on August 7, 1896. Bogue, *Congressman's Civil War;* Robson, *Biographical Encyclopaedia of Ohio.*

Thomas H. Smith

SHERIDAN, Philip Henry, *general,* was born on March 6, 1831, in Albany, New York, and attended the local school in Somerset, Ohio, where his family moved soon after his birth. Sheridan spent five years at the U.S. Military Academy, accumulated many demerits, and graduated in 1853, a year behind his class; he had been suspended for striking a cadet sergeant. He took a commission in the infantry, serving well, if obscurely, as a 2nd lieutenant for almost eight years. While on duty in Oregon in March 1861, he was promoted to 1st lieutenant, and to captain two months later.

After the Confederates shelled Fort Sumter, Sheridan was anxious for combat, but acted as a quartermaster, notably on the staff of General Henry W. Halleck (*q.v.*) in the Corinth campaign. In May 1862 he obtained the colonelcy of the 2nd Michigan Cavalry, and effectively commanded a brigade on a raid on Booneville, Mississippi, in July 1862. Promoted to brigadier of Volunteers, Sheridan led a division at Perryville, and won high praise from General William S. Rosecrans (*q.v.*) for defending the Union center at Stones River, actions that earned him promotion to major general of Volunteers.

Sheridan's next battles were studies in contrast. At Chickamauga, the Confederates struck the poorly deployed Union lines, disrupting Rosecrans's defense and sending Sheridan's division into retreat. Two months later, at Chattanooga, Sheridan's troops took their initial objectives and then, acting on their own, charged headlong up Missionary Ridge. Sheridan joined the charge, routing the Confederate defenders. In April 1864, General Ulysses S. Grant (*q.v.*) appointed Sheridan to reorganize and command the cavalry corps of the Army of the

Potomac, allowing him to use the Union horse soldiers directly against J.E.B. Stuart's cavalry. Following a battle at Todd's Tavern, Sheridan took advantage of his numerical superiority and good equipment, besting Stuart's poorly supplied cavalrymen at Yellow Tavern, where Stuart was killed. Although not decisive, this "raid on Richmond," coupled with the publicity from other cavalry engagements, such as Trevilian Station, made Sheridan a hero to the Northern public.

In July 1864, General Jubal Early and his army threatened Washington, D.C., and Grant ordered Sheridan to devastate Early's base of supply, the Shenandoah Valley of Virginia. Grant gave him a combined force of more than 40,000 infantry, cavalry, and artillery, and Sheridan aggressively set to his task. Again outnumbering his opponents, this time two to one, he found and defeated Early at Winchester (Opequon) and Fisher's Hill, and laid waste the rich valley where several Union generals had been defeated. Sheridan was promoted to brigadier general in the Regular Army, but despite appearances, Early was not whipped. On the morning of October 19, 1864, while Sheridan was absent, Early attacked the unprepared Army of the Shenandoah at Cedar Creek, pushed the Federals out of their camps, and seemed on the verge of victory. Hearing the guns, Sheridan left Winchester and rode to Cedar Creek. Gathering stragglers along the road, exhorting wayward companies, castigating wavering officers, he personally galvanized his army and launched a counterattack that swept Early from the field.

Cedar Creek was a sterling victory that aided Abraham Lincoln's (q.v.) reelection. Congress gave Sheridan a vote of thanks, and he was promoted to major general in the Regulars. Subsequently, he fought at Dinwiddie Courthouse, Five Forks, and Sayler's Creek. Following Appomattox, he commanded troops along the Rio Grande and became a strong supporter of the Radical Republicans, sternly administering the 5th Military District and later backing Grant's presidency. Sheridan supervised the Military Division of the Missouri during some of the most intense Indian wars. He was promoted to lieutenant general in 1869 and to full general in 1888. He held the post of commanding general of the Army from 1884 until his death on August 5, 1888, in Nonquitt, Massachusetts. O'Connor, *Sheridan*; Pond, *Shenandoah Valley in 1864*; Sheridan, *Memoirs*.

Joseph G. Dawson III

SHERMAN, John, *senator*, was born on May 10, 1823, in Lancaster, Ohio. He left school at fourteen after only a rudimentary education, and went to work on canal construction. In 1840, he began the study of law and, after being admitted to the bar in 1844, practiced in Mansfield, Ohio. Sherman became active in local politics and attended the Whig National Conventions of 1848 and 1852. Capitalizing on the anti-Nebraska sentiment, he sought and won a seat in the House of Representatives, where he served as a Republican from 1855 to 1861. A moderate on slave-related issues, he was also a partisan who skillfully exploited the Kansas situation by writing a House report that blamed the Democratic party for the crisis. The report became an important Republican campaign document in the 1856 election.

In Congress, Sherman became increasingly interested in financial questions, and in 1859 was made chairman of the House Ways and Means Committee. He was an economic conservative, although at times he was willing to compromise his principles to satisfy the more radical demands of Ohio voters. He was in line to be elected Speaker of the House when a vacancy occurred in the Senate, following Lincoln's appointment of Salmon P. Chase (*q.v.*) as Secretary of the Treasury. The Ohio legislature balloted seventy-nine times before choosing Sherman. Thus began his thirty-two years in the Senate, interrupted only by a four-year period as Treasury Secretary under President Rutherford B. Hayes (*q.v.*).

As a highly influential member of the Senate Finance Committee, Sherman frequently worked with Secretary Chase, although at times they disagreed over policy. He persuaded Chase to accept the bill to give greenbacks the status of legal tender, but he usually advocated more traditional means of financing the war: increased taxes, loans, and tariffs. Perhaps Sherman's most important service during the war years was in helping Chase to reform the nation's banking system. The National Bank Act of February 1863 (revised in June 1864) created a system of federally supervised national banking associations empowered to issue banknotes guaranteed by the Federal government and based upon U.S. bonds. This highly controversial system created a more secure currency and helped to bring order to the previously unstable Civil War economy.

More controversial than his financial role was Sherman's often stormy relationship with President Abraham Lincoln (*q.v.*). As a moderate on the emancipation question, he supported Lincoln's war objective of saving the Union and agreed with his initial efforts to resist abolition. His eventual support of emancipation was inspired by pressure from Ohio Radicals and the apparent reversal of public opinion in that state. Yet Sherman was at odds with Lincoln on other matters, for in his view, the President failed to provide the strong leadership of Congress necessary in a time of crisis. He questioned the President's treatment of his brother, William Tecumseh Sherman (*q.v.*), and privately referred to Lincoln as a fool and a baboon. He foolishly cooperated with those seeking to defeat Lincoln in 1864, and his support of Chase for the nomination accomplished little except to make him less popular with Ohio Republicans, who rallied behind the President.

Sherman later regretted this purely political act, and preferred to remember only his economic contributions to the war effort. He opposed what he believed to be the overly harsh Reconstruction plans of Thaddeus Stevens (*q.v.*) and Charles Sumner (*q.v.*). Although sympathizing with President Andrew Johnson (*q.v.*) in his struggle with Radical Republicans, he nevertheless voted for conviction in the impeachment trial; apparently he feared the political repercussions if he voted for acquittal. As chairman of the Senate Committee on Finance,

Sherman played a dominant role in the complicated economic issues of the postwar years. After serving in the Hayes Cabinet, he unsuccessfully sought the Republican presidential nomination in 1880. He returned to the Senate (1881–1897) and sponsored the Sherman Antitrust Act. Sherman ended his political career with a brief stint as Secretary of State under William McKinley. He died in Washington, D.C., on October 22, 1900. Burton, *John Sherman*; Jeannette P. Nichols, "John Sherman," in Wheeler, *For the Union*, pp. 377–438; Sherman, *Recollections*.

Frederick J. Blue

SHERMAN, Socrates Norton, *congressman*, was born on June 22, 1801, in Barre, Vermont. After graduation from Mount Castleton Medical College in 1824, he established a practice in Ogdensburg, New York. Sherman took an active interest in politics and eventually supported the Republican party's attempt to limit the extension of slavery. These efforts led to his election in 1860 to the 37th Congress, but shortly after taking his seat, Sherman joined the 34th New York Volunteers as a surgeon, with the rank of major. He managed to fill both offices simultaneously, largely because his regiment was stationed near Washington. In fact, he used his congressional contacts to advance certain critical medical needs, such as improved facilities, higher pay to attract more surgeons, and professional nursing staffs. Because of his experience in the field, many of Sherman's suggestions won approval. Moreover, his voting record strengthened administration preparedness for war.

These essentially political activities ended in June 1862 when his regiment went into action. Sherman served in campaigns ranging from the Seven Days through Antietam to Chancellorsville, during which his regiment suffered heavy casualties. Although he enjoyed influence in the 37th Congress, he refused renomination and continued to serve as a surgeon until he was mustered out on October 7, 1865, a brevet lieutenant colonel. He returned to Odgensburg and continued his practice until his death there on February 1, 1873. Bogue, *Congressman's Civil War*.

Jerome Mushkat

SHERMAN, Thomas West, *general*, was born on March 26, 1813, in Newport, Rhode Island. He graduated from West Point in 1836, was commissioned in the artillery, and was promoted to 1st lieutenant two years later. He served in the Second Seminole War and in the removal of the Cherokees to the Indian Territory. After 1842, Sherman was engaged in routine duty in coastal fortification. During the Mexican War, he served with Zachary Taylor, commanded an artillery battery, and was praised for his work at Buena Vista. Following the war, Sherman returned to garrison and fortification duties, and commanded two expeditions against the Sioux.

Shortly after the outbreak of the war, Sherman was promoted to brigadier general of Volunteers and placed in command of Regular artillery and Pennsylvania Volunteers who guarded transportation and communication lines above Washington and Baltimore. In May 1861, he was named chief of light artillery guarding the capital, and in late June he began the planning and organizing of expeditions to seize key locations on the southern coast, which would be needed by the Union blockade fleet. Bull's Bay, South Carolina, and Fernandina, Florida, were taken, and Sherman commanded the land forces that captured Port Royal, South Carolina, in October 1861.

By this time Sherman's Old Army discipline was a source of friction with his Volunteer command. It was a problem that he never overcame or, perhaps, understood. In April 1862 he was given command of a division of the Army of the Tennessee in operations against Corinth, Mississippi, and of a larger force pursuing the Confederates after their withdrawal. Following a leave of absence, he was placed in command of a division in defense of New Orleans in August 1862. Sherman was in a minority of generals who argued against the attack on Port Hudson in May 1863. Nevertheless, he commanded the Union left, was wounded while leading an assault, and lost his right leg. He returned to duty in February 1864 and was placed in command of reserve artillery and the forts guarding New Orleans. In addition, he was given administrative duties in Louisiana. In March, he was promoted to brevet major general in both the Volunteers and Regulars.

Following the war, Sherman commanded at various coastal fortifications and, for a time, the Department of the East. Retiring as a major general on December 31, 1870, he died in Newport on March 16, 1879. Hewitt, *Port Hudson.*

Carl L. Davis

SHERMAN, William Tecumseh, *general,* was born on February 8, 1820, in Lancaster, Ohio. After his father's death in 1829, he was raised as a foster son by Thomas Ewing, U.S. senator, Cabinet officer, and a power in Whig politics. After graduation from West Point in 1840, Sherman served in South Carolina, Florida, and California, but not in Mexico, where many of his contemporaries gained reputations and rank. In 1853, he left the Army and turned successively and unsuccessfully to banking and law. In 1859, he was named superintendant of a military school near Pineville, Louisiana (now Louisiana State University at Baton Rouge). He accepted this post over an offer to become a bank official in England, and over the urgings of his wife, Ellen Ewing, and her family.

Sherman left Louisiana when that state seceded, and with the support of his brother, John Sherman (*q.v.*), recently elected U.S. senator from Ohio, obtained a commission as a Regular Army colonel. He commanded a brigade in Daniel Tyler's (*q.v.*) division at Bull Run (July 21, 1861), and was discouraged and frightened by the disintegration of the Union forces. In August 1861 he was named a brigadier general of Volunteers, and in September was posted to Kentucky as a deputy to Robert Anderson (*q.v.*), commander of the Department of the Cumberland. Kentucky was of great importance, politically and militarily, and both sides were determined to control the state. Sherman believed that to defend Kentucky, he would need 60,000 men; to take the offensive, he would need 200,000. His pessimism and generally high-strung manner led to criticism, stress, and a near nervous collapse.

On November 13, 1861, Sherman was relieved by Don Carlos Buell (*q.v.*) and sent to Henry W. Halleck's (*q.v.*) staff in St. Louis. He was assigned to a training command while friends and family defended him against charges of insanity. In February 1862, Halleck named Sherman to a command headquartered in Paducah, Kentucky. More important, he would serve with Ulysses S. Grant (*q.v.*), commander of the Department of West Tennessee. Grant's aura of organization, purpose, and professionalism greatly encouraged Sherman. April 1862 brought Shiloh and a division command. Tactically surprised by the Confederate attack on April 6, Sherman managed to steady his forces and lead in the Union counterattack on the following day. Shiloh was a Union victory, but much too costly. Grant and Sherman were guilty of overconfidence, but both showed great presence as field commanders.

Sherman was named major general of Volunteers, to date from May 1, 1862, and for a time was military governor of Memphis. He commanded a disastrous operation at Chickasaw Bayou, Mississippi, on December 27, 1862, ordering a frontal assault that would have done justice to Burnside (*q.v.*) or Lee. He did penance by serving under John A. McClernand (*q.v.*) in an expedition against Arkansas Post (January 12, 1863). It was a victory, if not a great one, and Sherman was notable for placing himself near the front, where he was often in some danger. Perhaps this was further penance for Chickasaw Bayou. Sherman's depression over his failures and having to serve under McClernand was eased by words of praise from Grant, Buell, and David Dixon Porter (*q.v.*). He had been named commander of the XV Corps before Arkansas Post, and in that rank took part in the Vicksburg campaign. After a series of false starts and missteps (and Sherman's misgivings), Grant launched his grand maneuver in late April, and from late May to July 4, conducted a siege of the city. Sherman credited Grant for his superb and steady leadership, and for removing McClernand from command of the XIII corps. Vicksburg brought Sherman fame second only to Grant.

After a time in Mississippi, Sherman led a corps in the relief of Union forces at Chattanooga and at Knoxville. When Grant was named general in chief, Sherman took command in the West, with the task of taking Atlanta and destroying Joseph E. Johnston's Army of Tennessee. The great campaign began in May 1864 with a flanking movement against Resaca by the Army of the Tennessee, now commanded by James B. McPherson (*q.v.*). Sherman hoped that the threat to his rear would force Johnston out of his strong position at Dalton. Johnston did retreat, but McPherson was unable to seize Resaca or seriously threaten the Confederates. Sherman was vastly disappointed in McPherson's "timidity," but he himself has been criticized for not leading with his strongest force, the Army of the Cumberland, commanded by George H. Thomas (*q.v.*). Sherman now fought, maneuvered, and pursued Johnston, with major engagements at Cassville, Allatoona, and especially at Kennesaw Mountain (June 27, 1864). The bloody frontal assault at Kennesaw was a major error in judgment by Sherman, a decision based upon impatience, for which thousands of Union soldiers paid the price.

Ironically, Johnston abandoned Kennesaw for fear of being flanked, and withdrew across the Chattahoochee and into Atlanta. Jefferson Davis aided Sherman's cause on July 17 when he replaced Johnston with John Bell Hood. Hood attacked Thomas on July 20 and, after failing, attempted an envelopment of McPherson on July 22. He failed again, but McPherson was killed. Sherman, grieving for his friend and protégé, drew Hood into a third failed attack, at Ezra Church on July 28. An exultant yet frustrated Sherman settled in for a siege before deciding in mid-August to circle Atlanta with some 60,000 men. He would cut the roads, isolate the city, and force Hood into another attack or a retreat. Hood chose to save his army, and Sherman could wire Washington "Atlanta is ours and fairly won." It was a victory rich in military and political meaning, and for Sherman an immeasurable personal triumph. Sherman sent Thomas back to Tennessee to deal with Hood, and led a picked army of light infantry to Savannah (captured December 25, 1864), and thence northward through the Carolinas until his war ended with the surrender of Joseph Johnston at Durham, North Carolina. With the surrender of the Confederate field armies, Sherman could remark, "War's over—occupation's gone."

Sherman remained in government service until 1884, including a tour as general in chief. He shunned politics even while he advocated an early return to peace between North and South, and early occupation of the West, and a sometimes benign neglect of the former slaves. He accepted the idea of a small Army, but urged a more professional officer corps. Withal, he ended the Civil War with reputation enhanced, the premier soldier of his generation. Perhaps his most admirable quality was his refusal to exalt military glory or to capitalize unduly upon his fame. In 1865, he mused on his victory: "Even success the most brilliant is over dead and mangled bodies, with the anguish and lamentations of distant families, appealing to me for sons, husbands and fathers." It was Sherman's sense of the true price of glory that led his soldiers to admire him and follow him in war and peace. Sherman died in New York City on February 14, 1891. Castel, *Decision in the West*; Liddell Hart, *Sherman*; Marszalek, *Sherman*.

John T. Hubbell

SHIEL, George Knox, *congressman*, was born in Ireland in 1825. He emigrated to the United States, settled in New Orleans, and then moved to Ohio, where he became a lawyer. In 1854, he moved to Salem, Oregon, practiced law, and was elected to minor public offices. Joe Lane Democrats nominated him in April 1860 as their candidate for the House of Representatives; he narrowly won election in June. Douglas Democrats declared his election unconstitutional and elected Andrew J. Thayer (*q.v.*) in November 1860. Disagreement in the House of Representatives in July 1861 between the two claimants, including exchanges between Thayer and Shiel, resulted in Shiel's victory. He voted with Representative Clement Vallandigham (*q.v.*), embraced the views of New York City Mayor Fernando Wood (*q.v.*), and apparently invested heavily in Benjamin Wood's (*q.v.*) antiwar newspaper. Shiel also worked for the passage of the Pacific Railroad Act, which he unsuccessfully attempted to amend so that Portland, not San Francisco, would be the western terminus.

Following his voluntary return to Oregon in 1863, Shiel vehemently denounced the war and Abraham Lincoln (*q.v.*), whom he compared to Benedict Arnold. He refused to take an oath of allegiance to the United States, and thus could not practice law. His resulting economic decline and bitter comments about the consequences of the war attracted considerable local comment. Few politicians were more angry about defeat or paid a higher personal price because of their stubbornness. Shiel died in Salem, Oregon, on December 12, 1893. Johannsen, *Frontier Politics.*

G. *Thomas Edwards*

SIBLEY, Henry Hastings, *general,* was born on February 20, 1811, in Detroit, Michigan Territory. He joined the American Fur Company at Mackinac in 1829, then served in 1831–1832 as purchasing agent for the company in Cleveland, Ohio. By 1834, he managed trade with the Sioux Indians along the border of British America, from Minnesota to the Rocky Mountains. In 1835, he built a stone house at Mendota where he entertained explorers, missionaries, traders, and Indians. After serving as a territorial delegate to Congress from both the Wisconsin and Minnesota territories, Sibley, a Democrat, became the first governor of Minnesota in 1858. He chose not to stand for reelection the next year.

In 1862, when the Sioux devastated the Minnesota Valley, Sibley was appointed brigadier general in command of Minnesota troops then being enlisted at Fort Snelling, and led them against the Sioux. After raising the siege at New Ulm, he won a decisive victory at Wood Lake. In 1863 and 1864, serving under the command of John Pope (*q.v.*), Sibley led punitive expeditions against the Sioux in the Dakotas. In 1865–1866, he was a commissioner and assisted in making new peace treaties that relocated the Minnesota Sioux on reservations in the Dakotas. In later years, he moved to St. Paul, Minnesota; became president of a gas company, an insurance company, and a bank; served a term in the Minnesota legislature in 1871; and for many years presided over the board of regents of the University of Minnesota and the Minnesota Historical Society. He died in St. Paul on February 18, 1891. Jones, *Civil War in the Northwest.*

Robert H. Jones

SICKLES, Daniel Edgar, *general,* was born in New York City on October 20, 1818. After attending New York University and passing the bar, he entered politics as a Tammany Democrat. Following terms in state and local office, and diplomatic service in London, Sickles became a U.S. senator in 1855, and a representative two years later, remaining in the latter office until the Civil War began. In 1859, while a member of Congress, he killed his wife's lover. Defended by Edwin M. Stanton (*q.v.*), Sickles established a legal precedent by winning the first acquittal on grounds of temporary insanity in an American court.

Having recruited the Excelsior Brigade in New York City during the spring of 1861, Sickles led it in the Peninsula campaign, seeing action at Seven Pines and Malvern Hill. Subsequently, while commanding the 2nd Division, III Corps at Fredericksburg, he won a brevet for gallantry and meritorious service. When commanding the III Corps at Chancellorsville, he launched an uncoordinated attack that contributed to the Federal defeat, but the primary responsibility for this fiasco rested with Joseph Hooker (*q.v.*), the army commander.

At Gettysburg, where he won a second brevet and the Medal of Honor, Sickles became involved in another imbroglio when, without permission, he deployed his corps in a salient beyond the main line. James Longstreet's attack on this point decimated Sickles's command and jeopardized the entire Union position. Later, Sickles and his defenders defamed General George G. Meade (*q.v.*), the commander of the Army of the Potomac, and attempted to argue the tactical benefits of Sickles's actions; however, their case was unconvincing. Having lost a leg at Gettysburg, Sickles never returned to field duty.

Except for a few apologists, scholars have accepted the nearly universal view of Sickles's military contemporaries: that he was a fearless but mediocre commander, perhaps not the worst of the political generals but far below the best. Appointed military governor of the Carolinas at the end of the war, Sickles was dismissed by President Andrew Johnson (*q.v.*) for displaying excessive zeal on behalf of African Americans. In 1869, President Ulysses S. Grant (*q.v.*) named him minister to Spain, but Sickles resigned in 1873, following several diplomatic blunders and a lurid affair with the deposed queen. Returning to New York politics, he held state offices; sat in the House of Representatives, where he acted to preserve the Gettysburg battlefield; and became involved in yet another scandal. Sickles died in New York City on May 3, 1914. Coddington, *Gettysburg Campaign*; Pfanz, *Gettysburg: The Second Day*; Swanberg, *Sickles the Incredible.*

James L. Morrison, Jr.

SIGEL, Franz, *general,* was born on November 18, 1824, in Sinsheim, Baden, Germany. In 1842, he graduated from the military academy at Karlsruhe and received a commission in the army of Grand Duke Leopold. In the revolutions of 1848, Sigel was war minister for the unsuccessful revolutionaries and a very inept field commander. He fled to the United States in 1852, finally moving to St. Louis, where he became prominent in German-American activities. Like several other German expatriates, he was fervidly pro-Union and had excellent political connections. Sigel received a brigadier's commission on August 7, 1861, more in recognition of the impact it would have on recruiting Germans for the Union Army than for his military prowess.

Sigel took part in Nathaniel Lyon's (*q.v.*) capture of Camp Jackson at St. Louis, and later in the little fight at Carthage. At Wilson's Creek, as second in command, he failed Lyon in the battle and then abandoned his command, retreating to Springfield. At Pea Ridge, he performed well—his only good showing of the war—then went to Virginia, where he commanded a relatively inactive corps under John Pope (*q.v.*) and Ambrose Burnside (*q.v.*), and then a grand division. Relieved of command due to ill health and pique at having his grand division taken from him, Sigel spent much of 1863 politicking shamelessly for command of the Department of West Virginia. In February 1864 he got it, organized its forces rather efficiently, and then completely mismanaged his only offensive campaign of the war.

In the campaign leading to the battle at New Market, Sigel started with double the Confederates' numbers, yet on the field of battle managed to be outnumbered and overwhelmed. Two months later, when he showed equal incompetence during Early's raid on Washington, he was finally removed from active command, and in May 1865 resigned his commission. Following the war, Sigel published German-language newspapers, first in Baltimore and then in New York City, where he lived out his life. He became prominent in city politics, held several patronage positions, and changed from a Republican to a Democrat when the city's political winds shifted. On August 21, 1902, he died in New York City. Davis, *New Market*; Engle, *Yankee Dutchman*.

William C. Davis

SIMMONS, James Fowler, *senator,* was born in Little Compton, Rhode Island, on September 10, 1795. He began his political career in the state legislature, serving for eleven of the thirteen years between 1827 and 1840, and was elected to the U.S. Senate in 1841 as a Whig. Though no friend of Dorrism, he supported the release from prison of Rhode Island political rebel Thomas Wilson Dorr, a stand that probably accounts for the defeat of his effort for a second term in the Senate. By 1857, Simmons had joined the American–Republican nativist movement in Rhode Island and was again elected to the U.S. Senate. He resigned from the Senate in 1862, and died in Johnston, Rhode Island, on July 10, 1864. Field, *State of Rhode Island*, vol. 3.

Mario R. DiNunzio

SLOAN, Andrew Scott, *congressman,* was born on June 12, 1820, in Morrisville, New York. He attended Morrisville Academy, was admitted to the bar in 1842, and began his practice in Morrisville. In 1854, Sloan moved to Beaver Dam, Wisconsin, where he opened a law office and was involved in local politics. A Whig of the Henry Clay tradition, he became an enthusiastic Republican and was elected to the state Assembly in 1857. The next year, Governor Alexander Randall (*q.v.*) appointed him to fill an unexpired term on the Circuit Court, but he lost the subsequent election.

In the spring of 1860, Sloan was a candidate for chief justice of the Wisconsin

Supreme Court, but lost a close race to the incumbent. In the fall of that year, however, he was swept along with the Republican landslide and elected to the 37th Congress. He served a single term, declining renomination in 1862. Sloan again ran for Congress in 1864, this time on the Union party ticket along with most regular Republicans. Unsuccessful, he was appointed clerk of the Federal District Court for Wisconsin.

Beginning in 1868, Sloan served as judge of the Dodge County Court until he became the Reform party candidate for attorney general. In 1881, Sloan was elected judge of the 13th Judicial Circuit, and was reelected in 1887 and 1893. In 1886, he presided over the trials of the leaders of labor riots that broke out in Milwaukee the day after the Haymarket Riot in Chicago. Sloan died in Beaver Dam on April 8, 1895. Berryman, *Bench and Bar of Wisconsin; Dictionary of Wisconsin Biography.*

Charles E. Twining

SLOAN, Ithamar Conkey, *congressman,* was born on May 9, 1822, in Morrisville, New York. He studied law, was admitted to the bar in 1848, and in 1854 moved to Janesville, Wisconsin. In 1858, Sloan was elected as a Republican to the office of district attorney of Rock county, a position he held until 1862, when he was elected to the U.S. House of Representatives. He retired from Congress in 1867, deferring to the "iron-clad rule" in his district that a representative should voluntarily step down after serving two terms. In 1875, he moved to Madison to assist his brother, Andrew Scott Sloan (*q.v.*), then the state's attorney general, as a special counsel in prosecuting railroads deemed to be in violation of the state's Granger Law.

In 1876, Sloan joined the faculty of the University of Wisconsin School of Law, a post he held until 1894. He was reputed to be honest and diligent, his casework noteworthy for its thorough research and clear, concise presentation. In the Civil War Congress, he generally voted with the Radical wing of his party. Sloan died in Janesville on December 24, 1898. Benedict, *Compromise of Principle; Biographical Review of Dane County, Wisconsin.*

Michael J. McManus

SLOCUM, Henry Warner, *general,* was born on September 24, 1827, in Delphi Falls, New York. He attended Cazenovia Seminary and taught school before his appointment to West Point, from which he graduated in 1852. As a lieutenant in the 1st Artillery, he served in the Florida Seminole War and at Fort Moultrie, South Carolina, until his resignation on October 31, 1856, to practice law in Syracuse. He was elected Onondaga county treasurer, served in the New York legislature, and was artillery instructor for the state militia.

Appointed colonel of the 27th New York Volunteers on May 21, 1861, Slocum was wounded in the thigh at First Bull Run. Promoted to brigadier general of Volunteers on August 9, 1861, and to major general on July 4, 1862, he commanded a division of William B. Franklin's (*q.v.*) VI Corps in fighting at

Gaines' Mill and Malvern Hill during the Peninsula campaign. Slocum covered the Union retreat after Second Bull Run, and during the Antietam campaign routed Confederate forces at Crampton's Gap. As commander of the newly created XII Corps and the right wing of the Army of the Potomac, he pressed the initial attack at Chancellorsville. The XII Corps sustained 2,824 casualties, and Slocum immediately became a vociferous critic of Joseph Hooker's (*q.v.*) faltering conduct of the battle.

On July 1–3, 1863, Slocum commanded the Union right wing at Gettysburg. When the XI and XII corps were ordered west following the Union defeat at Chickamauga, he angrily submitted his resignation rather than serve again under Hooker. To avoid a clash, Slocum was shunted off to guard the Nashville & Chattanooga Railroad, and later commanded the District of Vicksburg. In August 1864, William T. Sherman (*q.v.*) designated him to succeed Hooker as commander of the XX Corps, after Hooker protested Oliver O. Howard's (*q.v.*) elevation to command the Army of the Tennessee and asked to be relieved. On September 2, Slocum led the vanguard of the Union Army into Atlanta. He and Howard commanded the left (Army of Georgia) and right (Army of the Tennessee) wings, respectively, of the Federal advance through Georgia and the Carolinas.

An intelligent, disciplined, and aggressive officer, Slocum distinguished himself at successive levels of command and in some of the severest fighting of the Eastern and Western theaters. His contributions no doubt would have been greater if his volatile temper and acerbic tongue had not relegated him to backwater commands during the advance on Atlanta. Slocum resigned from the Army on September 28, 1865, and ran unsuccessfully on the Democratic ticket for New York secretary of state. Declining a Regular Army appointment as colonel of the 31st Infantry, he practiced law in Brooklyn and served three terms in the U.S. Congress. As a member of the House Committee on Military Affairs, he staunchly supported Fitz John Porter's (*q.v.*) efforts to overturn his court martial. Slocum died in Brooklyn, New York, on April 14, 1894. Castel, *Decision in the West*; Furgurson, *Chancellorsville*; Pfanz, *Gettysburg—Culp's Hill and Cemetery Hill.*

Bruce J. Dinges

SMALLS, Robert, *naval pilot,* was born at Ashdale Plantation on Ladies Island, off the coast of South Carolina, on April 5, 1839. His mother was Lydia, a slave; his father may have been her owner, John McKee. Smalls grew up as a slave in the McKee home in Charleston. The McKees hired him out, and he learned to be a master seaman, working the boats in Charleston's waters for many years.

When the Civil War began, Smalls was the wheelman on *The Planter*, a Confederate dispatch boat. He was determined to escape, and at 3 A.M. on May 13, 1862, after the white officers went home, Smalls and the black crewmen guided the ship out of the harbor, stopping briefly to pick up their families. Smalls steered the ship past the Confederate forts, passing Fort Sumter in broad daylight. Once outside of Sumter's range, he surrendered to a Federal blockade ship. *The Planter* was quite a prize for the Union. Smalls, who was commissioned a 2nd lieutenant, was himself a valuable asset, bringing information and piloting vessels along the Carolina coast. He fought in seventeen battles and was prominent in several engagements.

Despite his accomplishments, Smalls faced discrimination. In an attempt to discredit him, in May 1864 the navy sent him with *The Planter* to Philadelphia, where he knew little of the coastline. He successfully piloted the ship north and stayed in Philadelphia during *The Planter*'s overhaul. While there, he was thrown off a streetcar because of his race, which outraged many Philadelphians. This led to the passage of a Pennsylvania law in 1867 prohibiting discrimination on public transportation. Smalls later was active in politics, becoming a staunch Republican. From 1868 to 1870, he served as a representative in the South Carolina General Assembly. In 1870, he was elected a state senator, and in 1874, to the U.S. Congress, where he served until 1886. Smalls died in Beaufort, South Carolina, on February 22, 1915. Quarles, *Negro in the Civil War*; Uya, *From Slavery to Public Service.*

Donna M. DeBlasio

SMITH, Andrew Jackson, *general,* was born in Bucks county, Pennsylvania, on April 28, 1815. He graduated from West Point in 1838, and was commissioned a 2nd lieutenant in the 1st Dragoons. After short tours of duty at Carlisle Barracks, Pennsylvania, and in the recruiting service, he was ordered to frontier duty at Fort Leavenworth and Fort Gibson. He was promoted to 1st lieutenant in May 1845, and saw service during the Mexican War in New Mexico and southern California. He spent the years 1849–1861 at various Pacific Coast posts, and participated in the Rogue River War (1855–1856). He was a captain at Fort Walla Walla, Washington, when the Civil War began.

Smith was commissioned colonel of the 2nd California Cavalry, but resigned on November 3, 1861, to become Henry W. Halleck's (*q.v.*) chief of cavalry. He held this position until the following July. Earlier, on March 20, he had been named a brigadier general of Volunteers. He led one of William T. Sherman's (*q.v.*) four divisions at Chickasaw Bayou, and commanded a division under John A. McClernand (*q.v.*) at Arkansas Post. During the Vicksburg campaign, Smith's XIII Corps division was heavily engaged at Port Gibson on May 1, and in the May 22 assault on Vicksburg. At Champion Hill, on May 16, his failure to vigorously attack a Confederate brigade on the Raymond road allowed General John C. Pemberton's battered army to withdraw across Baker's Creek.

"Whiskey" Smith and his division were a part of Sherman's army that advanced on Jackson and drove General Joseph E. Johnston's command east of the Pearl River in July. In March 1864, after participating in the Meridian expedition, Smith, commanding units of the XVI and XVII Corps that were detached from the Army of the Tennessee, participated in Nathaniel P. Banks's (*q.v.*) ill-starred Red River campaign. On May 14, Smith was promoted to major general. He led his command, soon referred to as the "lost tribes of Israel," against the formidable Nathan Bedford Forrest at the battle of Tupelo and on the Oxford expedition, and in the autumn of 1864 across Missouri in pursuit of Sterling Price. Smith and his men returned to Tennessee to battle the Confederates before Nashville. Advancing out of the Mobile Point enclave, he and his XVI Corps played a vital role in the campaign leading to the April 12, 1865, capture of Mobile.

Upon the demobilization and reorganization of the Army, Smith, in 1866, became colonel of the 7th U.S. Cavalry. In 1869, he resigned his commission to accept appointment as postmaster of St. Louis, and from 1877 to 1889, served as city auditor. Smith died in St. Louis on January 30, 1897. Bearss, *Vicksburg Campaign*; Johnson, *Red River Campaign*; Sword, *Embrace an Angry Wind.*

Edwin C. Bearss

SMITH, Caleb Blood, *Secretary of the Interior,* was born in Boston on April 16, 1808. In 1814, the family moved to Cincinnati; he attended Cincinnati College and, later, Miami University. Moving across the border to Connersville, Indiana, Smith opened a law practice and became editor of a Whig newspaper, the *Indiana Sentinel.* After serving several terms in the state legislature, he was elected to Congress and served until 1849.

During the presidential campaign of 1860, Smith worked hard to secure the nomination of Abraham Lincoln (*q.v.*), and was rewarded when the President named him Secretary of the Interior, a position for which he seemed wholly unsuited. Incapable of overseeing a technical bureaucracy, he left the daily functioning of the department to assistants. In the fall of 1862, he participated in a Cabinet cabal, led by Secretary of War Edwin M. Stanton (*q.v.*), to undermine Lincoln's authority over military affairs. Smith also vigorously opposed the Emancipation Proclamation. Discontented, ineffective, and ill, he resigned in December 1862 to accept an appointment as a Federal judge in Indiana. Smith collapsed while serving on the bench and died in Indianapolis on January 7, 1864. Hendrick, *Lincoln's War Cabinet*; Richardson, *John Palmer Usher.*

David Dixon

SMITH, Charles Ferguson, *general,* was born in Philadelphia on April 24, 1807. He graduated from West Point in 1825, and began a distinguished military career. Thirteen years at West Point as instructor and commandant (1829–1842) brought him respect and admiration from cadets later prominent as Civil War generals. In the Mexican War, Smith commanded infantry under both Zachary Taylor and Winfield Scott (*q.v.*), winning brevet appointment to colonel. He later led expeditions to the Red River of the North and to Utah, where he held command at the outbreak of the Civil War.

Appointed colonel of Regulars and brigadier general of Volunteers, Smith took command at Paducah under Ulysses S. Grant (*q.v.*), fifteen years his junior, who winced before giving orders to his former commandant. Smith, however, performed admirably as a subordinate, advancing overland to threaten Colum-bus, Kentucky, while Grant fought at Belmont, directly across the Mississippi River. Commanding the right wing at Fort Donelson, Smith moved forward vigorously when Confederates attacked the left wing. His advance led to the unconditional surrender of the garrison on the following day, a great victory for which Grant won public acclaim. Department commander Henry W. Halleck (*q.v.*), however, distrusted Grant and placed Smith in command of the Tennessee River expedition, ordering Grant to remain behind. During that expedition, Smith injured his leg and infection developed. Grant resumed command and fought at Shiloh as Smith lay dying.

Universally admired in the Old Army for his gallantry, tactical skill, and bearing, Smith attracted the suspicion of politicians, some in uniform, while commanding at Paducah. Charges of disloyalty delayed Senate confirmation of his appointment as brigadier general, but his conduct at Fort Donelson silenced such criticism; his promotion to major general occurred little more than a month before his death. William T. Sherman (*q.v.*) believed that had Smith lived, he would have superseded Grant. A model officer, Smith appeared destined for military renown before his untimely demise. After his death in Savannah, Ten-nessee, on April 25, 1862, his body was transported to Philadelphia for burial. Catton, *Grant Moves South*; Grant, *Papers*, vols. 3, 4, 5.

John Y. Simon

SMITH, Edward Henry, *congressman,* was born on May 5, 1809, in Smith-town, New York. He became a prosperous farmer and was elected to a series of local offices: justice of the peace (1833–1843), assessor (1840–1843), and supervisor of Smithtown (1856–1861). He capped his political career by being elected to the 37th Congress. Smith generally identified with the War Democrats and usually supported administration wartime policies, such as the Conspiracies Act of July 31, 1861, and the House resolution to spend all necessary funds and employ sufficient men to crush the rebellion. At the same time, he sponsored several resolutions, especially concerning navigation on Long Island Sound, for his constituents. Beyond that, Smith took little part in House debates and often missed roll calls. In 1862, he declined renomination and resumed farming. Smith died in Smithtown on August 7, 1885. *BDUSC.*

Jerome Mushkat

SMITH, Gerrit, *abolitionist,* was born on March 6, 1797, in Utica, New York. He inherited great wealth and used it to promote a variety of philanthropies, most notably abolitionism. An 1818 graduate of Hamilton College, Smith in the 1820s was deeply influenced by the Second Great Awakening, which inspired his career in reform. Initially a member of the American Colonization Society, he joined the abolitionists in 1835 and quickly became, with William Lloyd Garrison (*q.v.*) and Lewis Tappan (*q.v.*), one of the movement's three most influential leaders. In the 1840s, Smith led the radical wing of the abolitionist

Liberty party in its contention that natural law implicitly sanctioned forceful resistance to slavery, and that the national government had authority to abolish slavery in the Southern states.

Because neither the Free Soil party nor the Republican party endorsed such radicalism, Smith refused to go along with other former Liberty abolitionists in joining them. Instead, from the late 1840s through the 1850s, he headed a tiny abolitionist party. Elected to Congress in 1852, Smith joined in the opposition to the Kansas–Nebraska Bill before resigning his seat in August 1854. Thereafter he grew increasingly convinced that slavery could not be peacefully abolished. This disposition led him to provide moral and financial support to John Brown's (*q.v.*) plan to promote slave revolt.

Deeply depressed following Brown's capture, Smith briefly entered an insane asylum. But this did not end his commitment to the cause. Like other abolitionists during the Civil War, he pressed President Abraham Lincoln (*q.v.*) to make emancipation a war aim. After the war, Smith advocated black suffrage as well as reconciliation with the South. He died on December 28, 1874, in New York City. Friedman, *Gregarious Saints*; Harlow, *Gerrit Smith*.

Stanley Harrold

SMITH, Giles Alexander, *general*, was born in Jefferson county, New York, on September 29, 1829. He was the younger brother of Morgan Lewis Smith (*q.v.*), who also became a Federal general. In 1847, he moved to Ohio, where he lived first in London and then in Cincinnati. He later moved to Bloomington, Illinois, where he was in the dry goods business and operated a hotel.

In June 1861, Smith was made a captain in the 8th Missouri Volunteers, a regiment commanded by his brother. Having served at Forts Henry and Donelson, at Shiloh, and at Corinth, he was promoted to colonel in June 1862 and succeeded his brother as regimental commander. He commanded a brigade in the XIII and XV Corps in Arkansas and along the Mississippi in 1862 and 1863. Promoted to brigadier general of Volunteers as of August 4, 1863, Smith was in the fighting around Chattanooga, where his brigade was part of Major General William T. Sherman's (*q.v.*) force that assaulted the northern end of Missionary Ridge. In this attack Smith was badly wounded. Meanwhile, he had acquired an enviable reputation.

Smith led his brigade in the XV Corps in the first part of Sherman's 1864 campaign against Atlanta. On July 20, he was made commander of a division in the XVII Corps and played a prominent part in repulsing the Confederate attack in the battle of Atlanta on July 22. Smith led his division in the March to the Sea and the Carolina campaign. On September 1, 1864, he was made brevet major general of Volunteers, and in November 1865 he was promoted to full major general of Volunteers.

Smith remained in the Army until 1866, after which he returned to Bloomington. In 1868, he sought election to Congress as a Republican, and in the following year President Ulysses S. Grant (*q.v.*) appointed him second assistant postmaster general, a position he held until ill health forced his resignation in 1872. He died in Bloomington on November 5, 1876. Bearss, *Vicksburg Campaign*; Castel, *Decision in the West.*

Richard M. McMurry

SMITH, Green Clay, *general, congressman,* was born on July 4, 1826, in Richmond, Kentucky, the nephew of Cassius M. Clay (*q.v.*). His education in the common schools of Richmond was interrupted by a year of service in the Mexican War. In 1849, he graduated from Transylvania University, after which he studied at Lexington Law School, graduating in 1852. A strong Unionist, Smith was elected to the state legislature in 1860. He enlisted in the Union Army as a private in 1861, was made colonel of the 4th Kentucky Cavalry in March 1862, and in June was promoted to brigadier general. In May, his regiment had participated in the rout of John Hunt Morgan at Lebanon, Tennessee. Smith's success in his contact with Morgan doubtless led to his promotion a month later. When the Confederate raider entered Kentucky in 1863, Smith was not so fortunate, and his inability to cope with Morgan damaged his military reputation.

Elected to Congress as a Unionist in 1862, Smith resigned his commission in December 1863. He was reelected in 1865, but resigned in 1866 after being appointed governor of the Montana Territory by President Andrew Johnson (*q.v.*). In Congress, he voted for the 13th and 14th Amendments, and generally supported the administration. After he resigned as territorial governor in April 1869, Smith returned to Frankfort, Kentucky, where he was ordained a Baptist minister. In 1876, he received less than 10,000 votes as the presidential candidate of the National Prohibition party. In 1890, Smith became pastor of the Metropolitan Baptist Church in Washington, D.C. He remained in that post until his death on June 29, 1895. McMullin, *Biographical Directory of American Territorial Governors*; Spence, *Territorial Politics and Government in Montana.*

Boyd Childress

SMITH, James Young, *governor,* was born in Groton, Connecticut, on September 15, 1809. He settled in Rhode Island in 1826 and began a successful career in the lumber and cotton textile industries. Smith joined the opposition to the Dorr rebellion in Rhode Island in 1842, and won election to the state legislature as a Whig in 1848. He was chosen mayor of Providence in 1855 as the candidate of the nativist American party, and in 1863 he was elected Republican governor of Rhode Island, holding that office until 1866.

Smith was determined to avoid the use of the draft in raising troops to meet the state's quotas during the war. Large appropriations of money for bounties and the employment of recruiting agents helped him succeed in meeting all demands for troops with volunteers. These included 1,800 black soldiers, called the Corps d'Afrique. Although he was charged with financial irregularities in connection with the raising of troops, an investigation exonerated Smith, and his reelections were by large majorities. After the war, he resumed his business career, which now included extensive banking, insurance, and railroad interests. He died in Providence on March 26, 1876. Bartlett, *Memoirs of Rhode Island Officers*; Field, *State of Rhode Island*, vol. 3; Hesseltine, *Lincoln's War Governors*.

Mario R. DiNunzio

SMITH, John Eugene, *general*, was born in Bern, Switzerland, on August 3, 1816. In 1817, his parents migrated to Philadelphia, where he was educated and learned the jeweler's trade. In 1836, Smith moved from St. Louis to Galena, Illinois, and was elected treasurer of Jo Daviess county in 1860. In mid-April 1861 he reported to Governor Richard Yates (*q.v.*) of Illinois as an aide-de-camp to organize the three-month troops. While on this duty, he recommended a fellow townsman, Ulysses S. Grant (*q.v.*), to Yates as a man who ought to know how to lead a regiment. On July 23, Smith was commissioned a colonel and directed to recruit and organize the 45th Illinois Volunteers, the Lead Miners Regiment.

Soon after being mustered in at Camp Douglas, Illinois, on November 24, 1861, Smith reported to Grant at Cairo, Illinois. He led his regiment at Forts Henry and Donelson, at Shiloh, and during the siege of Corinth. The Lead Miners were posted at Jackson, Tennessee, until November 1, 1862, when they marched to La Grange and participated in Grant's abortive drive to Oxford, Mississippi. On November 24, 1862, Smith became a brigadier general, and in December assumed command of a XVI Corps division stationed in West Tennessee. In April 1863, he reported to Milliken's Bend, Louisiana, to command a brigade in General John A. Logan's (*q.v.*) XVII Corps division. The brigade fought at Port Gibson, Raymond, and Champion Hill, and on June 3, 1863, after Vicksburg was invested, Smith took command of the XVII Corps's 7th Division because General Isaac F. Quinby (*q.v.*) was on sick leave.

Reassigned to the XV Corps in October, Smith accompanied General William T. Sherman (*q.v.*) to Chattanooga, then participated in the battle of Missionary Ridge and the pursuit of the defeated Confederate army to Graysville, Georgia. During the Atlanta campaign, he was charged with guarding railroads over which Sherman supplied his armies. On the March to the Sea and through the Carolinas, Smith led a XV Corps division. He was breveted major general in March, and from June 1865 commanded the District of West Tennessee until he was mustered out on April 30, 1866. Smith reentered the Army in July 1866, as colonel of the 27th U.S. Infantry. He was on the Bozeman Trail in 1866–1867, and at other Western posts until his retirement on May 19, 1881. He settled in Chicago, and died there on January 29, 1897. Bearss, *Vicksburg Campaign*; Jones, *"Black Jack": John A. Logan*.

Edwin C. Bearss

SMITH, John Gregory, *governor*, was born on July 22, 1818, in St. Albans, Vermont. He graduated from the University of Vermont in 1838, read law, entered Yale Law School, and in 1841 joined his father's St. Albans practice. In 1858, he relinquished his law practice, entered fully into his father's extensive railroad enterprises, and gained election to the Vermont Senate. Reelected the following year, Smith next represented St. Albans in the lower house in 1860, 1861, and 1862, serving as speaker the two latter years. Elected governor in 1863, and reelected in 1864, his most noted efforts as the last of Vermont's three war governors were recruiting troops and providing care for the wounded. These concerns brought him to the front on several occasions, and his staunch and effective support of President Abraham Lincoln (*q.v.*) gained him ready access to the White House.

Even before completing his second gubernatorial term, Smith expanded his business interests considerably. In 1864, after consolidating Vermont's railroads, he became involved in the construction and management of the Northern Pacific Railroad, serving as its first president until 1872. Although never holding elective office after 1865, he remained a dominant force in state politics and was active in national Republican party affairs until his death in St. Albans on November 6, 1891. Crockett, *Vermont*, vols. 3, 4; Dowden, "John Gregory Smith," *Vermont History.*

D. Gregory Sanford

SMITH, Morgan Lewis, *general*, was born on March 8, 1821, in Mexico, New York. After teaching school for two years in Indiana, he served in the Army from 1845 to 1850, under the name of Mortimer L. Sanford, becoming a sergeant and drillmaster. Until 1861, he engaged in steamboat operations along the Ohio and Mississippi rivers. Upon the outbreak of the Civil War, he organized and became colonel of the 8th Missouri, a regiment recruited largely from river men and St. Louis roustabouts.

At Fort Donelson, on February 15, 1862, Smith led his and another regiment in a successful assault on a key point in the Confederate line, thereby winning the praise of General Lew Wallace (*q.v.*) for his "courage and coolness." He next commanded a brigade in the Union counterattack at Shiloh on April 7, 1862, and was commended by William T. Sherman (*q.v.*) for his conduct during the siege of Corinth. Promoted to brigadier general on July 26, 1862, he participated in various operations in northern Mississippi until seriously wounded while commanding a division at Chickasaw Bluffs on December 28, 1862. Smith returned to duty as commander of the 2nd Division, XV Corps, Army of the Tennessee in time to take part in a subsequent expedition to Knoxville.

During the Atlanta campaign, Smith continued to lead the 2nd Division until the July 22 battle of Atlanta, during which, as a consequence of John A. Logan's (*q.v.*) assuming command of the Army of the Tennessee upon the death of James B. McPherson (*q.v.*), he took charge of the XV Corps. Soon afterward, when Logan resumed command of the corps, Smith returned to his division and led it at the battle of Ezra Church on July 28. He then obtained sick leave, following which he commanded the District of Vicksburg until he resigned his commission on July 12, 1865.

Without doubt Smith was a superior brigade commander and a competent division head, but these were the limits of his military talent, as he demonstrated during the battle of Atlanta, where his refusal to heed warnings that there was a vulnerable gap in the XV Corps front made possible a potentially disastrous Confederate breakthrough. During the postwar years, Smith served as U.S. consul general in Honolulu, then engaged in various enterprises in Washington, D.C., until his death in Jersey City, New Jersey, on December 28, 1874. Castel, *Decision in the West*; Cooling, *Forts Henry and Donelson*.

Albert Castel

SMITH, Thomas Kilby, *general*, was born in Boston on September 23, 1820; shortly thereafter his family moved to Cincinnati. He studied civil engineering under Ormsby M. Mitchel (*q.v.*), then law under Salmon P. Chase (*q.v.*). He practiced law in Ohio, then moved to Washington and employment as a special agent in the Postal Department. President Franklin Pierce appointed Smith U.S. marshal for the Southern District of Ohio, but he lost his appointment under President James Buchanan (*q.v.*), and for the four years preceding the war he served as deputy clerk of Hamilton county.

On September 9, 1861, Smith was appointed lieutenant colonel of the 54th Ohio Volunteers, and on October 31 became its colonel. In February 1862, the regiment joined William T. Sherman (*q.v.*), and first saw battle at Shiloh. His brigadier was wounded in the action, and Smith commanded the brigade for a time. At Vicksburg, after the wounding of General Morgan L. Smith (*q.v.*) at Chickasaw Bluffs, Thomas K. Smith again commanded his brigade, but was once again relieved. Sherman wrote an impassioned plea for Smith's promotion, but it was delayed. Still under Sherman, Smith participated in the capture of Arkansas Post, and in an expedition to Rolling Ford to relieve Admiral David D. Porter (*q.v.*).

Smith drew staff assignments until August 26, 1863, when he was appointed brigadier general of Volunteers. In September, he received command of the 2nd Brigade, 6th Division, of the Army of the Tennessee, and later commanded the 1st Brigade, 4th Division in active field service at Natchez and on the Black and Yazoo rivers. In 1864, Smith joined Nathaniel P. Banks (*q.v.*) in the ill-fated Red River campaign, and was one of the few officers who escaped with career intact. Smith's command took part in the capture of Fort De Russy, then occupied Alexandria. When the advance was repulsed at Sabine Cross Roads, Smith protected Admiral Porter's descent of the river with land actions on both banks that won the praise of the army. But the exertion left him seriously ill, and he was forced to go on medical leave until January 1865.

Smith was assigned to a division in the Army of the Tennessee, later commanded the South Alabama District at Mobile, and was honorably mustered out of the service on January 15, 1866, with the rank of brevet major general of

Volunteers. He was U.S. consul to Panama (1867–1869), and lived thereafter at Torresdale, Pennsylvania. He died in New York City on December 15, 1887. Smith, *Life and Letters of Thomas Kilby Smith.*

Archie P. McDonald

SMITH, William Farrar, *general,* was born in St. Albans, Vermont, on February 17, 1824. He graduated from West Point in 1845. Smith's academic standing enabled him to become a lieutenant in the Corps of Engineers, member of several survey commissions, and a mathematics professor for two terms at his alma mater. During an 1853 canal survey in Florida, he contracted malaria, recurrent symptoms of which afflicted him at crucial times in his career.

When the Civil War came, Smith, a War Democrat, forged close ties with General George B. McClellan (*q.v.*). Through McClellan's patronage he became a brigadier general of Volunteers in command of a brigade, and later of a division, in the Army of the Potomac. At the start of the 1862 Peninsula campaign, Smith fared poorly, but redeemed himself at White Oak Swamp and Malvern Hill, where his troops safeguarded the Union withdrawal to the James River. Held largely in reserve at Antietam, he commanded the II Corps at Fredericksburg. Following that bloody debacle, he joined others in intriguing against McClellan's successor, General Ambrose Burnside (*q.v.*). When Burnside learned of this, he helped block Smith's pending promotion to major general and relegated him to lesser commands.

After a lackluster performance in command of a militia division during the Gettysburg campaign, Smith went to Tennessee, ultimately as chief engineer in General Ulysses S. Grant's (*q.v.*) Military Division of the Mississippi. He won Grant's admiration for helping construct the ''Cracker Line,'' which in October restored supply routes to the besieged garrison at Chattanooga. As a reward, Grant made him a major general of Volunteers and returned him to Virginia as leader of the XVIII Corps in General Benjamin F. Butler's (*q.v.*) Army of the James. In May and June 1864, through illness and indecisiveness, Smith cost Grant and Butler opportunities to capture Richmond or Petersburg. At Cold Harbor, his corps suffered staggering losses in a series of assaults against impregnable works. Sick, weary, and depressed, Smith made himself obnoxious to his superiors, criticizing Butler for the failures outside Richmond and Petersburg, and Grant and George Gordon Meade (*q.v.*) for Cold Harbor. In mid-July he was relieved, and Grant prevented him from returning to active service thereafter.

Disgusted, Smith left the Volunteers in 1865 and the Regulars in 1867, to serve as New York City police commissioner, a telegraph company president, and a civil engineer. A brilliant engineer, he was a weak field commander. His tactical ability was negated by egotism, a contentious disposition, and a proclivity to undermine any superior whose strategy he questioned. For these reasons he was a ''perfect Ishmaelite'' among his associates, although a humane superior to his men, whose welfare was always uppermost in his mind. Smith died in Philadelphia on February 28, 1903. Robertson, *Back Door to Richmond*; Wightman, *From Antietam to Fort Fisher.*

Edward G. Longacre

SMITH, William Sooy, *general,* was born on July 22, 1830, in Tarlton, Ohio. He graduated from Ohio University in 1849, and from West Point in 1853. Smith resigned from the Army a year later, and applied his skills to the building of the Illinois Central Railroad. Illness forced him to leave that position, and for the next two years he was a high school principal in Buffalo, New York. In 1857, he formed an engineering firm that concentrated on surveying and building railroad bridges and tunnels from New York to Georgia. He improved the pneumatic method of sinking cylinders for bridge piers, and was also an officer in the Trenton Locomotive & Machine Manufacturing Company.

Smith was commissioned colonel of an Ohio infantry regiment on June 26, 1861, and participated in the West Virginia campaign of 1861–1862. Beginning in February 1862, he was involved in campaigns in Tennessee, Kentucky, and Mississippi; much of his time was spent repairing and protecting vital railroads. He was at Shiloh in April and the siege of Corinth in May. Promoted to brigadier general on April 15, and in command of a division in the Army of the Ohio, Smith continued guarding rails in the region. In October, he commanded a division at the battle of Perryville and in the pursuit of Braxton Bragg's defeated army. In the Vicksburg campaign, Smith, now in command of the 1st Division, XVI Corps, was again guarding against Confederate forces attempting to relieve the siege.

In July 1863, Smith was made chief of cavalry of the Department of the Tennessee, and in October, of the Military Division of the Mississippi, until his resignation due to illness on July 15, 1864. In command of 7,000 cavalry during the Meridian campaign, he advanced from Memphis to join General William T. Sherman (*q.v.*), who captured the town, but bad weather delayed preparations and slowed his advance. Sherman withdrew, and Smith's force was threatened by Nathan Bedford Forrest's cavalry. Overestimating the Confederate force, Smith withdrew after a holding action; a later engagement saw one of his regiments panic and nearly turn the retreat into a rout. Smith's force made it safely back to Memphis, but that cold, rainy campaign undoubtedly contributed to his chronic rheumatism and led to his resignation. Sufficiently recovered by 1866, he returned to his engineering practice and became known internationally for his bridge building. Smith died in Medford, Oregon, on March 4, 1916. Bearss, *Vicksburg Campaign*, vol. 3; Starr, *Union Cavalry*, vol. 3.

Carl L. Davis

SMITHERS, Nathaniel Barratt, *congressman,* was born in Dover, Delaware, on October 8, 1818. Educated at local schools, he prepared for college at an academy at West Nottingham, Maryland. He was graduated from Lafayette College in 1836, and then read law under Judge Reed in Carlisle, Pennsylvania. In 1841, Smithers was admitted to the bar in Dover. He served as clerk of the House of Representatives in 1845 and 1847, and in 1848 attended the Whig National Convention. Always opposed to the Democratic party, he helped organize the Independent Temperance party in 1850, and later the American party and the local People's party. He also helped establish the Republican party in Delaware and served as a delegate to the Chicago Convention in 1860.

Governor William Cannon (*q.v.*), the successful Union party gubernatorial candidate, appointed Smithers secretary of state in 1863. In November 1863 he was elected by supporters of the Union party to fill the unexpired term of Representative William Temple (*q.v.*). To show their opposition to the use of Federal troops at polling places, however, the Democrats boycotted the election. Smithers was nominated by the Union party for representative in 1864, but was defeated.

In spite of Smithers's relatively brief congressional service, he made his mark when he introduced the nucleus of the compromise legislation on amendments to the national conscription bill, after earlier proposals had come to naught in both chambers of Congress. At the end of his term, Smithers continued to practice law in Dover and to support the Republican party, attending national conventions in 1868 and 1880. He also served as president of the First National Bank of Dover. In 1895, Governor Joshua H. Marvil appointed him secretary of state, but he resigned the office three months later because of the governor's death. Smithers died in Dover on January 16, 1896. Geary, *We Need Men*; Hancock, *Delaware During the Civil War.*

Harold B. Hancock

SPALDING, Rufus Paine, *congressman,* was born in West Tisbury, Massachusetts, on May 3, 1798. He graduated from Yale in 1817, studied law, and was admitted to the bar. In 1820, he moved to Little Rock, Arkansas, but in 1821, moved east to Ohio and settled in Warren. There he practiced law until 1835, when he moved to Ravenna, Ohio. Spalding was elected to the Ohio House of Representatives in 1839 and served two terms, during one of which he was speaker. From 1849 to 1852, he was associate judge of the Ohio Supreme Court. Fervently antislavery, in 1859 he defended Simeon Bushnell during the famous Wellington rescue case. Spalding attended the anti-Nebraska conventions in 1854 and 1855, and wrote the antiextension of slavery platform that was adopted by the Ohio Republicans in July 1855. He attended the Republican National Conventions in 1856 and 1860, and as a Republican was elected to the 38th through 40th Congresses.

Spalding supported the war efforts of Abraham Lincoln's (*q.v.*) administration. In 1863, he was considered a candidate for Benjamin F. Wade's (*q.v.*) senatorial seat, but was not a candidate for reelection to the House in 1868. He returned to his law practice in Cleveland, where he died on August 29, 1886.

Doyle, *Centennial History of Summit County*; Robson, *Biographical Encyclopaedia of Ohio.*

Thomas H. Smith

SPAULDING, Eldridge Gerry, *congressman,* was born on February 24, 1809, in Summer Hill, New York. He established a lucrative law practice in Buffalo and was active in banking. A Whig, he held minor offices in Buffalo prior to his election as mayor in 1847. During the next eleven years, Spaulding served in the state Assembly and in the 31st Congress, and became New York state treasurer. In 1858, he was elected to the 36th Congress and in 1860 was re-elected to the 37th. When the war began, Spaulding served on the critical Committee on Ways and Means, where he became the chief sponsor of two vital measures involving wartime money and banking. Without consulting Secretary of the Treasury Salmon P. Chase (*q.v.*), he introduced and guided through the House a bill making government notes legal tender. Although Spaulding and many other fiscal conservatives were ideologically opposed to fiat money, his contention that this temporary device, created by necessity, was more reasonable than relying on fluctuating state banknotes, won administration backing.

In 1863, Spaulding sponsored the National Bank Act, probably the most important financial legislation passed during the Civil War. Refusing renomination, and now known as the ''father of the greenbacks,'' he worked for their retirement when war ended and advocated bank currency redeemable in gold. In 1869, he explained his position in a major historical document: ''History of the Legal Tender Paper Money Issued During the Great Rebellion.'' Spaulding was a banker until his death in Buffalo on May 5, 1897. Curry, *Blueprint for Modern America*; Knox, *History of Banking.*

Jerome Mushkat

SPEED, James, *Attorney General,* was born on March 11, 1812, near Louisville, Kentucky. He attended St. Joseph's College in Bardstown, and studied law at Transylvania University in Lexington. Successful as a lawyer in Louisville, he fared less well in politics, for he was an antislavery Whig before the war and a supporter of Radical Republican policies after it. Speed served one term in the lower house of the legislature in the 1840s, another in the upper house in the early 1860s, was backed for the vice presidential nomination in 1868, and was a delegate to the Republican National Conventions of 1872 and 1876. Like his younger brother, Joshua Fry Speed, Abraham Lincoln's (*q.v.*) close friend from early days in Springfield, he was an outspoken Unionist. He corresponded with Lincoln about the perilous situation in Kentucky, and he acted as one of the agents through whom the United States smuggled arms to its friends.

In July 1862, Lincoln read to Speed the text of the preliminary Emancipation Proclamation, apparently the only individual outside the Cabinet whom the President took into his confidence in this matter. When Attorney General Edward

Bates (*q.v.*) resigned in November 1864, Lincoln appointed Speed to the office. He served until July 1866, when he resigned in protest against Andrew Johnson's (*q.v.*) Reconstruction policies. The most important controversy in which Speed was involved as Attorney General was the trial of the eight civilians accused of complicity in Abraham Lincoln's assassination before a military rather than a civil tribunal. Adding to the impression of impropriety was the fact that his justification of the military trial, published in Benn Pitman's officially approved record of the trial, was dated "July—, 1865," a date by which the trial had already ended with verdicts of guilty for all the accused. His opinion thus appeared to be ex post facto.

However, the administration had decided as early as April 20 that the murder of the Commander in Chief in time of war, in a city in which martial law had been declared, was a military crime. Speed's written opinion to this effect had been solicited and published as a rebuttal to the arguments against the jurisdiction of the military commission presented by defense counsel. To the end of his life, Speed defended the military trial and insisted that the defendants had received a fairer trial than they would have had in a civil court. After resigning from the Cabinet, Speed returned to his law practice in Louisville, became a professor at the Louisville Law School in 1872, and remained active in his profession until his death near Louisville on June 25, 1887. Neely, *Abraham Lincoln Encyclopedia*; Randall, *Lincoln the President*, vol. 4.

William Hanchett

SPRAGUE, William, *governor, senator,* was born in Cranston, Rhode Island, on September 12, 1830. By age twenty-six he managed the family enterprises, which included the largest calico printing mill in the world and vast, diversified investments. In 1860, the Republicans of Rhode Island nominated for governor a Radical on the slavery issue. Conservative Republicans joined a fusion movement with the Democrats, lest this extremism bring war and disrupt Rhode Island's cotton commerce with the South. Sprague returned from a trip to Europe to find that he had been nominated for governor by the fusion movement. He won the election after a bitter campaign marred by mutual charges of corruption.

As war governor, Sprague indulged his lifelong fascination with military organizations by insisting that he join Rhode Island troops at the battle front. He fought at the battle of Bull Run, where his horse was shot from under him while he exhorted the troops to hold their ground. He divided his efforts between Providence and the army in Virginia, though he held no military commission, having first requested and then declined appointment to the rank of brigadier general. After Bull Run, Sprague participated in patrol skirmishes in western Virginia and led several scouting missions. He abandoned his unorthodox military role in 1862, when he was elected to the U.S. Senate, where he served two terms with little distinction.

Sprague was a controversial figure throughout his public and private life. In 1863, he married Kate Chase, daughter of the Secretary of the Treasury, and was divorced in 1882 after four children and stormy years of argument, hostility, and scandal. His years in the Senate earned him a reputation for intemperate speeches that insulted fellow senators and vilified Rhode Island leaders who had gradually eased him out of the state's circle of influence. Sprague was most seriously embarrassed by charges that he had traded with agents of the Confederacy in order to obtain cotton for his mills. Despite damaging documentary evidence, a perfunctory Senate investigation in 1871 produced no formal charges against him. After failing in a bid for the governorship in 1883, Sprague retired from politics, spending much of his time abroad with his second wife. He died in Paris on September 11, 1915. Belden, *So Fell the Angels*; Hesseltine, *Lincoln's War Governors*; Sokoloff, *Kate Chase*.

Mario R. DiNunzio

STAHEL-SZAMVALD, Julius, *general*, was born November 5, 1825, in Szeged, Hungary. As a youth he worked in a bookshop in Pest, but when the revolts of the 1850s broke out, he became a lieutenant in the Hungarian rebel army. His valor won him the War Cross of Bravery, but in 1856 he was forced to flee to the United States, where he worked as a journalist for the *New York Illustrated News*. In 1861, he joined with Louis Blenker in raising the 8th New York Volunteers, becoming its lieutenant colonel and fighting with it at First Bull Run. In August 1861 Stahel (who dropped the latter half of his surname) became colonel, and on November 12 was promoted to brigadier general. He formed a close association with Franz Sigel (*q.v.*), who constantly urged his promotion. He fought in the Shenandoah Valley in 1862, and led a division at Second Bull Run.

In November 1863, a major general, Stahel commanded the guard of honor at the Gettysburg Address ceremonies. His final war service came in the Shenandoah Valley in 1864. Commanding Sigel's cavalry in the ill-fated New Market campaign, he was slow to think and act, and did not perform well. Later that summer, heading a cavalry division in David Hunter's (*q.v.*) Lynchburg campaign, he performed bravely at Piedmont on June 5—winning the Medal of Honor—but simply was not equal to the responsibilities of his command. Consigned to court martial duty, he resigned on February 8, 1865. After 1865, Stahel took a consulship at Yokohama, opening additional Japanese ports to American trade, tried mining in the West, then became consul general at Shanghai until 1885. He died in New York City on December 4, 1912. Davis, *New Market*; Hennessey, *Return to Bull Run*.

William C. Davis

STANFORD, Leland, *governor*, was born in Watervliet, New York, on March 9, 1824. In 1845, he moved to Albany, studied law, and was admitted to the bar in 1848. After two years in Port Washington, Wisconsin, he joined his five brothers in their wholesale mercantile firm in Sacramento, California. He began his political life as a Whig and Free Soiler, and became one of the founders of the Republican party in California. Though not an abolitionist, Stanford always claimed that he never held blacks in contempt. In 1857, he ran unsuccessfully for state treasurer, and in 1859 accepted the Republican nomination for governor, in part to prepare the party for the 1860 campaign. He stumped California for Abraham Lincoln (*q.v.*) and traveled to Washington, D.C., in the spring of 1861, to talk with the new president about patronage and Pacific Coast matters.

In 1861, Stanford defeated two Democrats for governor, which signaled public recognition of the triumph of Unionism in California. As governor, he complied with the requisitions from the national government for men and money, and fought for harbor defenses, an improved militia, efficient government, strengthened state finances, and forest conservation. In 1863, he signed measures granting black men and women the right to testify in the courts, requiring loyalty oaths for attorneys and teachers, and prohibiting certain treasonable activities. He encouraged the Sanitary Commission and Union Leagues, and was one of the few major politicians to advocate the use of legal tender notes in gold-producing California.

Stanford's failure in patronage appointments weakened his hold on the party organization, and Timothy G. Phelps (*q.v.*) defeated him as a candidate for the U.S. Senate. In April 1862, Stanford called for Republicans to keep their party organization, but the party fused with Northern Democrats to form the Union party. In 1863, supporters of Frederick Low (*q.v.*) and John Conness (*q.v.*) denied him a second term as governor.

Stanford's major dream in life was to span the continent with a railroad. The Central Pacific Railroad came into being June 28, 1861, with Stanford as president. Aid from the Federal government through the act of July 1, 1862, allowed him to break ground on January 8, 1863. As governor, Stanford signed seven bills in 1863 to aid the enterprise, and the completion of the Central Pacific became the foundation of his fortune and prestige. Stanford was elected to the U.S. Senate in 1865 and in 1891. The early death of his only son was memorialized in the Leland Stanford Junior University, founded in 1885 and opened in 1891. Stanford's health began to decline in 1888, and he died in Palo Alto, California, on June 21, 1893. Melendy, *Governors of California*; Tutorow, *Leland Stanford.*

                                                              Robert J. Chandler

STANLEY, David Sloane, *general,* was born in Cedar Valley, Ohio, on June 1, 1828. He graduated from West Point in 1852, served with the cavalry in California and Texas, was active in the Kansas troubles of 1856, and operated against the Cheyenne. At the outbreak of the Civil War, Captain Stanley was at Fort Washita, Indian Territory. He refused the offer of a colonelcy in Confederate service and led his men in a desperate march to Fort Leavenworth, Kansas. Stanley participated in the Missouri campaign of 1861, and guarded wagon trains at Wilson's Creek. He was named gadier general of Volunteers on September 28, 1861, but was out of action a while because of a broken leg.

Stanley commanded a division in the New Madrid and Island No. 10 campaigns, and in the advance on Corinth, as well as at Iuka and Corinth in the fall. He was recognized for his ability in the New Madrid campaign and for his counterattack at Corinth (October 3–4, 1862). From late 1862 to September 1863, Stanley was cavalry chief for the Army of the Cumberland under William S. Rosecrans (*q.v.*). He was at Stones River and in the important Tullahoma campaign. On sick leave at the time of Chickamauga, he was in the 1864 Atlanta campaign.

Commended for his action at Resaca, Stanley became commander of the IV Corps under William T. Sherman (*q.v.*). He was critized by Sherman for allegedly allowing the Confederates to escape at Jonesboro, near Atlanta, where he was wounded. Sent back to Tennessee by Sherman, he reached Pulaski in time to help George Thomas's (*q.v.*) army escape from Spring Hill. At Franklin, Stanley's counterattack helped to secure the Federal victory over John Bell Hood. However, he received a severe wound that virtually ended his wartime career.

After occupation duty in Texas, Stanley was mustered out of Volunteer service in February 1866 and commissioned colonel of the 22nd Infantry in the Regular Army. He saw extensive service in the Indian campaigns in the West, and led the Yellowstone expedition of 1873. On March 24, 1884, he was promoted to brigadier general of Regulars, and commanded the Department of Texas from 1884 until his retirement in 1892. Known particularly for his long career in the American West and his successful handling of Indian affairs, Stanley is a somewhat neglected Civil War figure. He was generally an able division and corps commander, and well regarded by most of his colleagues. Stanley died in Washington, D.C., on March 13, 1902. Castel, *Decision in the West*; Sword, *Embrace an Angry Wind.*

E. B. Long

STANNARD, George Jerrison, *general,* was born in Georgia, Vermont, on October 20, 1820. In 1845, he began to work for a foundry in St. Albans, and became a partner in 1860. He was also a colonel in the militia. Stannard is credited with being the first Vermonter to volunteer, on April 15, 1861, and was mustered into service as lieutenant colonel of the 2nd Vermont Volunteers on June 21, 1861. After serving at Bull Run and during the Peninsula campaign, he organized the 9th Vermont Volunteers, and was commissioned its colonel on May 21, 1862. He commanded the 9th at Winchester and Harper's Ferry, where the regiment was surrendered. Stannard was paroled, and promoted to brigadier general on March 11, 1863, for bravery at Harper's Ferry.

Stannard was assigned to the 2nd Vermont Brigade, and during the Gettysburg campaign commanded the 3rd Brigade, 3rd Division, I Corps. He was wounded on July 3, 1863, as his brigade's flank attack helped break up Pickett's charge. He commanded the New York Harbor defenses until assigned to brigade command in the X Corps in the spring of 1864. Stannard was transferred to command of the 1st Brigade, 2nd Division, XVIII Corps and was wounded twice at Cold Harbor on June 3, 1864. He led the advance on Petersburg on June 14, subsequently commanded the 1st Division, XVIII Corps, and was wounded at Petersburg. On September 29, 1864, he took Fort Harrison and held it against counterattacks although he was again wounded, losing an arm.

Stannard returned to Vermont to recover, and was commissioned as brevet major general, U.S. Volunteers, dating from October 28, 1864. He commanded the northern frontier following the St. Albans, Vermont, raid. Stannard was assigned to service in the Freedmen's Bureau at Baltimore on June 27, 1866, resigned from the Army in 1867, and served as collector of customs, District of Vermont, until 1872. He was doorkeeper of the U.S. House of Representatives from 1881 until his death on June 1, 1886, in Washington, D.C. Coffin, *Vermonters in the Civil War*; Sommers, *Richmond Redeemed.*

D. Gregory Sanford

STANTON, Edwin McMasters, *Secretary of War,* was born on December 19, 1814, in Steubenville, Ohio. He attended Kenyon College, studied law, and was admitted to the bar in 1836. Practicing law in Ohio and Pennsylvania, he became involved in widely reported cases, which began to win him a national reputation. His most important legal work was in 1858, as special counsel for the United States, fighting fraudulent land claims in California that were based on titles allegedly acquired during Mexican rule. Hardworking and bright, he collected evidence by reassembling the Mexican archives, and then discredited his opponents, among whom was Henry W. Halleck (*q.v.*). More sensationally, in 1859 he won the acquittal of Democratic Congressman Daniel E. Sickles (*q.v.*) for killing his wife's lover.

A Democrat, Stanton was appointed Attorney General on December 20, 1860, when President James Buchanan (*q.v.*) reorganized his Cabinet early in the secession crisis. A staunch Unionist, Stanton joined those urging the President not to abandon Fort Sumter. In the early days of the Abraham Lincoln (*q.v.*) administration, Stanton was a frequent critic who, however, gave legal advice to his fellow Pennsylvanian, Secretary of War Simon Cameron (*q.v.*). Stanton later helped discredit Cameron when, in circumstances still unclear, he wrote language for a report by Cameron that contradicted presidential policy. Cleverly rallying widespread political support, he secured from a President anxious for the backing of War Democrats the appointment as Secretary of War on January 14, 1862.

Stanton was at first a supporter of General George B. McClellan (*q.v.*), but turned against him because of his lack of decisive results. In this Stanton agreed with the Congressional Committee on the Conduct of the War, with which his relationship became close. He reorganized the War Department in the interest of efficiency, and cleaned up many of the contract scandals that had helped to blight Cameron's reputation. Brusque to the point of rudeness, he often irritated associates, especially army officers. He took the responsibility for such unpopular policies as arrests of civilians, enforcement of conscription, and refusing to exchange prisoners of war in 1864. The "Union's Organizer of Victory" thus deflected much criticism from the President. His conspicuous leadership of the hunt for Lincoln's assassins ironically made him the target of false charges of complicity in the conspiracy.

With other Cabinet members, Stanton continued under President Andrew Johnson (*q.v.*), but his views on Reconstruction soon proved to be closer to those of Johnson's opponents. When the President attempted to replace the Secretary of War without the Senate's prior approval, Stanton physically retained possession of his office and became the central figure in the presidential impeachment of 1868.

After the failure to convict Johnson, Stanton returned to private law practice. He received from President Ulysses S. Grant (*q.v.*) an appointment as associate justice of the Supreme Court and died in Washington, D.C., on December 24, 1869, days after senatorial confirmation. Thomas, *Stanton.*

Frank L. Byrne

STANTON, Elizabeth Cady, *abolitionist, women's rights activist,* was born in Johnstown, New York, on November 12, 1815. She received a superior education at Emma Willard's famous seminary for women in Troy, New York, encouraged by a supportive father and her abolitionist cousin, Gerrit Smith (*q.v.*). By 1840, she had married abolitionist attorney Henry B. Stanton, and had befriended leading abolitionist-feminists like Lucretia Mott. After attending the 1840 World's Anti-Slavery Convention in London, Stanton resolved with Mott to promote women's rights, and to this end they organized the famous Seneca Falls convention of 1848. Soon thereafter, Stanton met Susan B. Anthony (*q.v.*), inaugurating fifty-one years of friendship and close association in the cause of women's rights. Temperance also became one of Stanton's major interests, especially after she began demanding that women be granted the right to divorce on the grounds of a husband's drunkenness and physical abuse.

Although by doctrine a "nonresistant" pacifist, Stanton regarded the Civil War as a struggle for women's freedom as well as for black emancipation. Hence, she organized the National Woman's Loyal League, which petitioned and agitated for slave emancipation as essential for Union victory. When William Lloyd Garrison (*q.v.*) proposed dissolving the American Anti-Slavery Society once chattel slavery had been abolished, Stanton argued that the society must remain active until the freedmen had secured full citizenship. She also demanded that women as well as black males be guaranteed the franchise by constitutional amendment, a position that put her at odds with Wendell Phillips (*q.v.*), Frederick Douglass (*q.v.*), and other powerful male abolitionists. By 1869, she had broken completely with them over the female suffrage question and had formed the National Woman Suffrage Association, whose presidency she held until 1890. Stanton remained in the forefront of the feminist cause as a lecturer, author, and organizer until her death in New York City on October 2, 1902. Banner, *Elizabeth Cady Stanton.*

James Brewer Stewart

STARK, Benjamin, *senator,* was born in New Orleans on June 26, 1820. He pursued a business career in New York City and then turned to seafaring, his father's occupation. In 1845, he sailed to Oregon, where he recognized tiny Portland's potential and acquired a section of the town. In the 1850s, Stark was a lawyer and merchant, but the basis for his wealth was a steady income from sales and rentals of his choice land. He served a term as a Whig in the territorial legislature, became a Democrat in 1856, and in 1860 was elected to the state legislature. In 1861, Governor John Whiteaker (*q.v.*) appointed Stark, a fellow Breckinridge Democrat, to replace Republican Senator Edward Baker (*q.v.*), who had died in the battle of Ball's Bluff.

Stark had come to Oregon seeking money and power, and he achieved both. He defended slavery and secession, and opposed the Civil War, which to many Oregonians made him a traitor. They bitterly opposed his replacing Baker, a war hero. Documents from Portlanders, depicting Stark as the "most prominent" Oregon secessionist, were rushed to Washington in an attempt to prevent him from holding office. Radical Republicans, led by Charles Summer (*q.v.*) and Lyman Trumbull (*q.v.*), fought to prevent Stark from taking his seat, but following a bitter debate he was permitted to take the oath of office on February 27, 1862. Political opponents unsuccessfully tried to expel him after a Senate select committee found him to be disloyal. In the fall, the Oregon legislature replaced him.

Stark supported the Union, but his earlier statements for the South and against the war were so unpopular in Oregon that his desperate attempts to gain a second term failed. Income from Portland investments meant that he lived comfortably until his death on October 10, 1898, in New London, Connecticut. Edwards, "Benjamin Stark [Part I and Part II]," *Oregon Historical Quarterly*; MacColl, *Merchants, Money and Power.*

G. Thomas Edwards

STARR, John Farson, *congressman,* was born in Philadelphia on March 25, 1818. He moved in 1844 to Camden, New Jersey, where he established a small iron foundry. The Starr Iron Works became the largest manufacturing enterprise in western New Jersey, and one of the largest smelting foundries in the world. Starr played no political role before the Civil War, though his allegiances were Whiggish.

In 1862, the incumbent from New Jersey's 1st District, John T. Nixon (*q.v.*), decided to retire. Camden county had the right to select the nominee for his safely Republican seat; the honor went to Starr, who had contributed liberally to the equipping of local troops. He ran against Isaac V. Dickerson, an "ultra" Peace Democrat, and was elected by a margin of 1,000 votes in a year that saw

Democrats sweep the other four New Jersey seats. He was reelected by 2,000 votes in 1864, but did not seek renomination in 1866.

Starr's political course in Congress became similar to that of his Pennsylvania ironmaking colleagues, William D. Kelley (*q.v.*) and Thaddeus Stevens (*q.v.*). Although not prominent in debate, Starr regularly voted for Radical Reconstruction measures. He also tried to protect the Camden & Amboy Railroad monopoly against Federal intervention. In later life, Starr continued his business interests, but did not reenter politics. He died in Atlantic City, New Jersey, on August 9, 1904. Knapp, *New Jersey Politics.*

Daniel W. Crofts

STEARNS, George Luther, *abolitionist, editor,* was born in Medford, Massachusetts, on January 8, 1809. He became a wealthy manufacturer and a prominent figure in Massachusetts antislavery circles. Stearns supported the Liberty party in 1840, and then became a Conscience Whig. In 1851, he helped arrange Charles Sumner's (*q.v.*) election to the U.S. Senate, and took the lead in opposing the Fugitive Slave Law. Stearns also ranked high in the Republican "Bird Club," the powerful organization dominated by Massachusetts Governor John A. Andrew (*q.v.*). In 1856, he led efforts to furnish rifles to Free Soilers in Kansas, and began giving money to John Brown (*q.v.*). Ignorant of Brown's exact plans, Stearns fled briefly to Canada after the raid on Harper's Ferry, but returned to testify before the U.S. Senate committee investigating the conspiracy.

During the Civil War, Stearns built significantly on his antebellum political associations in order to further the cause of black freedom. Governor Andrew, for example, authorized him to recruit for the all-black 54th and 55th Massachusetts regiments. His notable successes brought him to the attention of Secretary of War Edwin M. Stanton (*q.v.*), who commissioned him to recruit black soldiers in the Union-occupied South. He continued in this capacity until mid-1864, when he resigned to establish *The Right Way*, a paper dedicated to Radical racial policies (especially land confiscation and black suffrage), and to the views of Charles Sumner and other Massachusetts Republican leaders. *The Right Way* achieved a circulation of 60,000 before Stearns died in New York City on April 9, 1867. McPherson, *Struggle for Equality.*

James Brewer Stewart

STEBBINS, Henry George, *congressman,* was born on September 15, 1811, in Ridgefield, Connecticut. He attended private schools and worked in the banking business. He served as the colonel of the 12th Regiment of the New York Militia until the outbreak of the Civil War, when the unit was reorganized and mustered into Federal service as the 12th New York Volunteers. Elected as a Democrat to the 38th Congress, Stebbins served on the Committee on Ways and Means. He resigned in October 1864 because he supported the war effort, a position he felt was contrary to the peace principles of his constituents. Following the war, he was active in the stock brokerage business and served as president of the New York Stock Exchange. Other civic pursuits included the presidency of the Central Park Commission and the management of the New York Academy of Music. He died in New York City on December 9, 1881. Lanman, *Biographical Annals*; Phisterer, *New York in the War of the Rebellion*, vol. 2.

Frank R. Levstik

STEEDMAN, James Blair, *general,* was born in Northumberland county, Pennsylvania, on July 29, 1817. He learned the printer's trade, and eventually became owner of the *Toledo* (Ohio) *Times.* In the meantime, he volunteered in the Mexican War, followed the gold rush to California, and served in the Ohio legislature. A Douglas Democrat, he was a delegate to the 1860 Charleston Convention, and ran unsuccessfully for Congress.

Appointed colonel of the 14th Ohio Volunteers, Steedman participated in the battle of Philippi, [West] Virginia. He was promoted to brigadier general of Volunteers on July 17, 1862, and commanded a brigade at Perryville and Murfreesboro. During the Tullahoma campaign, he led the sole division of General Gordon Granger's (*q.v.*) reserve corps. At Chickamauga, Steedman rushed to the relief of beleaguered General George H. Thomas (*q.v.*) and staved off Union disaster. Promoted to major general of Volunteers on April 20, 1864, he commanded the garrison at Chattanooga during the Atlanta campaign. His makeshift detachment of 5,200 white and black troops launched the December 15 attack on the Confederate right at Nashville.

Steedman resigned on August 18, 1866, and became collector of customs at New Orleans. Nicknamed "Old Steady," he was an aggressive fighter whose personal habits often generated gossip. His reckless display of bravery inspired his faltering troops to heroic action at Chickamauga, but many of his men detested his high-handed and sometimes brutal treatment. His reputation as a womanizer and his leadership of black troops scandalized his fellow officers. Steedman himself generated controversy when the *New York Times* of June 22, 1881, published his allegations that General John M. Schofield (*q.v.*) had been a "Judas" working behind the scenes to undermine Thomas's command at Nashville. Regardless, Steedman remained popular among Ohio voters. He died in Toledo on October 18, 1883. Cozzens, *This Terrible Sound*; Sword, *Embrace an Angry Wind.*

Bruce J. Dinges

STEELE, Frederick, *general,* was born on January 14, 1819, in Delhi, New York. After graduation from West Point in 1843, he was commissioned as a 2nd lieutenant in the 2nd Infantry, and served briefly in New York and Michigan before seeing action in the Mexican War. He received brevets for gallantry at Contreras and Churubusco, and saw action at Molino del Rey and Chapultepec. Following the war, he served in California and on the Great Plains, and in 1855 received promotion to captain.

In 1861, Steele was transferred from Kansas to St. Louis, and commanded a battalion of Regulars under Nathaniel Lyon (*q.v.*) in his Missouri campaign and at Wilson's Creek. In September 1861 he was appointed colonel of the 8th Iowa Volunteers, and on January 29, 1862, received promotion to brigadier general of Volunteers and briefly commanded the District of Southeastern Missouri. In the summer of 1862, Steele commanded a division of Samuel Curtis's (*q.v.*) Army of the Southwest at Helena, Arkansas, and was transferred to the Army of the Tennessee, where he served as division commander under William T. Sherman (*q.v.*) at Chickasaw Bluffs and Arkansas Post.

On March 17, 1863, Steele received promotion to major general of Volunteers, and commanded a division of the XV Corps during the Vicksburg campaign. After the surrender of Vicksburg, he was named commander of Union forces in Arkansas, and was ordered to clear the state of Confederate troops who might threaten Union operations east of the Mississippi River. In the fall of 1863, he led the Arkansas campaign, capturing Little Rock in September, and successfully gained and maintained control of the strategically vital eastern portion of the state. In the spring of 1864, Steele cooperated with Nathaniel Banks (*q.v.*) in the Red River campaign, and although providing solid leadership, suffered heavy casualties at Jenkins's Ferry and other hard-fought engagements.

Steele retained overall command of Arkansas troops through 1864. In the spring of 1865, he led a division in the campaign against Mobile, then commanded the District of West Florida until war's end. Following the war, Steele remained in the Army and commanded the Department of Columbia. On January 12, 1868, he died in San Mateo, California. Bearss, *Vicksburg Campaign*; Castel, *Sterling Price*; Josephy, *Civil War in the American West*.

Christopher Phillips

STEELE, John Benedict, *congressman*, was born on March 28, 1814, in Delhi, New York. He graduated in law from Williams College in 1838, and was admitted to the bar in 1839. Steele was active in local Democratic party affairs, and was elected to the 37th and 38th Congresses. He proved to be a hardworking, conscientious congressman who missed few roll calls. He introduced a variety of bills that involved the operation of the District of Columbia. Moreover, Steele was a strong War Democrat who often supported the administration. He backed the Conspiracies Act, opposed Alexander Long's (*q.v.*) proposal for a peace commission, and voted to censure Congressman Benjamin Harris (*q.v.*) of Maryland for disloyalty. However, he did insist that the House Republican majority follow proper procedures, as was evident by his participation in a Democratic filibuster on the national conscription bill. Furthermore, he consistently approved higher military appropriations and increased taxes, including internal revenue.

In 1864, Steele lost his bid for reelection. Even so, as a lame duck in 1865, he became one of the few New York Democrats to vote for the 13th Amendment. When Andrew Johnson (*q.v.*) became President, Steele immediately pledged support, and in 1866 campaigned for his former House seat on the

National Union party ticket. During the primary, however, he was accidentally killed on September 24, 1866, in Rondout, near Kingston, New York, when his horses bolted and he was thrown from the carriage. Curry, *Blueprint for Modern America*; Dell, *Lincoln and the War Democrats*; Geary, *We Need Men.*

Jerome Mushkat

STEELE, William Gaston, *congressman,* was born on December 17, 1820, in Somerville, New Jersey, where he spent almost all of his life. The 3rd District, which extended across central New Jersey, was considered the Gibraltar of New Jersey's Democracy. In 1858, the party had denied renomination to the incumbent, Garnet B. Adrian, who opposed President James Buchanan's (*q.v.*) Kansas policies. Adrian, however, won reelection as an anti-Lecomptonite, supported by a fusion of dissident Democrats, Republicans, and National Americans. In 1860, Democrats united behind Steele, a political newcomer supportive of Stephen A. Douglas (*q.v.*) He attempted to rebuild his splintered party base through a fusion electoral ticket of Breckinridge, Douglas, and Bell supporters, which helped him carry the district by a decisive 2,400 votes.

Steele's voting pattern was firmly antiadministration and antiemancipation, though he was not an extreme Peace Democrat by New Jersey standards. He defended the powerful Camden & Amboy Railroad monopoly against threatened Federal interference. Steele was reelected in 1862 by a majority of over 6,600 votes. Republicans nominated Orestes A. Brownson, who had slim ties to the district and far more imposing intellectual than political credentials, and was a radical emancipationist closely allied to Horace Greeley (*q.v.*). In 1864, however, the seat "rotated" to Charles Sitgreaves, and Steele thereafter played a diminishing role in politics. He died in Somerville on April 22, 1892. Knapp, *New Jersey Politics.*

Daniel W. Crofts

STEVENS, Isaac Ingalls, *general,* was born on March 25, 1818, in North Andover, Massachusetts. He graduated first in his class (1839) from West Point, after which he worked on eastern coastal defenses. In the Mexican War, he served as an engineer on General Winfield Scott's (*q.v.*) staff, and emerged from the war as a brevet major. In 1849, he accepted a position as second in command in the U.S. Coast Survey. Stevens sought and received appointment in 1853 as governor and superintendent of Indian affairs for the newly created Washington Territory, and at the same time was named to head the Northern Railroad Survey. As governor (1853–1857) and territorial delegate (1857–1861), he was involved in a number of controversies.

Stevens was an extremely intelligent and energetic leader, but his detractors accused him of harboring Napoleonic ambitions. In 1860, as a delegate to the Democratic National Conventions, he supported the Southern position and then became national campaign manager for the Breckinridge–Lane ticket. He was a strong Union man who repudiated secession, and when President Abraham Lincoln (*q.v.*) called for troops after Fort Sumter, he immediately offered his services. Stevens's connections with the Southern Democrats made him suspect in Republican circles, and despite his military record, he was able to secure only a colonelcy with the 79th New York Highlanders.

Promoted to brigadier general in September 1861, Stevens was attached to the Port Royal expedition that in November seized and occupied the Sea Islands. For the next several months he remained on the islands, wrestling with problems of freedmen, cotton agents, and abolitionists. He had strongly urged his superior, General Henry W. Benham (*q.v.*), not to attempt the move against Charleston in June 1862 that resulted in a defeat at the battle of Secessionville. Transferred to the 1st Division, IX Corps, under General Ambrose Burnside (*q.v.*), Stevens was prominent in the fighting at Second Bull Run. He commanded the rear guard during John Pope's (*q.v.*) retreat and was sent to intercept Stonewall Jackson, who was attempting to move troops between the Union army and Washington, D.C. Stevens met Jackson at Chantilly, Virginia, where he was able to frustrate the Confederate plan. Heroically, but rashly, he led a charge and was fatally wounded on September 1, 1862. He was posthumously promoted to major general.

Contemporaries suggested that Stevens at the time of his death was about to be promoted to command of the Army of the Potomac. Even his detractors admitted that he was the type of fearless, aggressive, perceptive leader needed by the Union. Hennessy, *Return to Bull Run*; Richards, *Isaac I. Stevens*.

Kent D. Richards

STEVENS, Thaddeus, *congressman,* was born in Danville, Vermont, on April 4, 1792. He was educated at Peacham Academy and Dartmouth College, taught school, studied law, and was admitted to the bar in 1816. Entering political life as an anti-Mason, Stevens served, with some interruption, in the state legislature between 1833 and 1842. A bitter opponent of the Jacksonians, he supported the recharter of the National Bank, but cooperated with the Democratic governor in establishing a public school system. He was one of the main protagonists in the Buckshot War to settle a disputed election. Above all, he was a staunch enemy of slavery and consistently defended fugitive slaves.

Active in the Log Cabin campaign of 1840, Stevens had hopes of a Cabinet seat, but was disappointed. He was elected to Congress as an antislavery Whig in 1848 and 1852, and in 1856 became one of the founders of the Republican party in Pennsylvania. In 1858, he was again elected to the U.S. House of Representatives, where he acquired the reputation of an adept parliamentarian, forceful speaker, and uncompromising opponent of slavery. As chairman of the Ways and Means Committee after 1861, he was responsible for procuring funds to carry on the Civil War. He favored high tariffs and greenbacks, and advanced the theory that the seceded states were conquered provinces.

''The Commoner,'' as he was now called, achieved his greatest triumph after the war, when he became the undoubted leader of the Radicals in the House.

An unwavering opponent of Andrew Johnson's (*q.v.*) Reconstruction policies, Stevens was instrumental in blocking the admission in 1865 of Southern members-elect and in the establishment of the Joint Committee on Reconstruction, to which all questions concerning the South had to be referred. Although dissatisfied with its limitations, he piloted the 14th Amendment through the House, and later was the chief sponsor of the Reconstruction Acts. Stevens was one of the principal advocates of the ouster of Johnson, and when the House voted to impeach him, Stevens framed the most important article of impeachment and became one of the managers of the trial.

Stevens was one of the most controversial political leaders of his time. Sardonic, unforgiving, and ever ready to take advantage of parliamentary technicalities, he was an unrelenting foe of the Southern aristocracy. His enemies might accuse him of misanthropic hatreds because of his club foot, and of vindictiveness because of the destruction of his Gettysburg ironworks. They might call him a greedy capitalist seeking to benefit great corporations and a base hypocrite utilizing the race question for partisan purposes, and charge that he was influenced by his mulatto housekeeper, whom they called his mistress. But he always scoffed at these insults.

Stevens proved his devotion to human equality by arranging for his burial in a black cemetery; his hatred of slaveholders long antedated the destruction of his property; and his economic views included soft money and opposition to draft exemptions for the rich, as well as aid to industry. As for his partisanship, he openly avowed it by explaining that the social revolution started in the Civil War could be carried to fruition only by the Republican party. He advocated the distribution of confiscated land to the freedmen, and it was his indomitable will and relentless effort that made possible many of the gains of Reconstruction. Stevens died in Washington, D.C., on August 11, 1868. Brodie, *Thaddeus Stevens*; Current, *Old Thad Stevens*.

Hans L. Trefousse

STEWART, William Morris, *senator*, was born on August 9, 1825 (or 1827), on a farm near Lyons, New York. He attended Lyons Union School and Yale University. He settled in Nevada county, California, in 1850, and in 1852 became a lawyer and an authority on mining law. In March 1860, Stewart settled in the Comstock Lode of Nevada, where the unending litigation over mining titles brought him $200,000 a year in fees. He represented the California corporations and their monopolistic control, and became the dominant political figure in Nevada. He served briefly in the first territorial legislature (1861), where he established basic law, legal procedures, and court districts; settled county boundaries; and placed the capital at Carson City. In 1863, he played a strong role in writing the constitution, and supported statehood in 1863 and again in 1864.

Stewart spoke for the Southern Democrats in the 1860 election, but with war he became a Unionist. However, he remained opposed to black civil rights. On

December 15, 1864, the first state legislature elected him to the U.S. Senate on the first ballot. In the Senate he looked after his corporate supporters, which included the large mines, the Bank of California, and the Central Pacific Railroad. In July 1866, Stewart's bill legalizing local mining rules became the first national act dealing with mining titles, and, as modified in 1872, is the current law.

Stewart supported President Andrew Johnson's (*q.v.*) plan for Reconstruction, but Johnson's veto of the Civil Rights Bill put Stewart in the camp of the Radicals. His lasting national influence came in 1869, when he phrased the wording of the 15th Amendment and, as floor manager, pushed it through the Senate. Reelected on January 12, 1875, Stewart served until March 3, 1881, and again from March 4, 1887, to March 4, 1905. He died in Washington, D.C., on April 23, 1909. Elliott, *Servant of Power*; Gray, *Source and the Vision*.

Robert J. Chandler

STILES, John Dodson, *congressman,* was born in Town Hill, Pennsylvania, on January 15, 1822. He was admitted to the bar in Allentown in 1844, joined the Democratic party, and was elected district attorney for Lehigh county in 1853. He also served as a delegate to the Democratic National Conventions in 1856, 1864, and 1868. Upon the death of Congressman Thomas B. Cooper (*q.v.*) in April 1862, Stiles made a bid for the vacant seat in a special election. He won, and joined the ranks of the antiwar Democrats in Congress. Reapportionment caused him to face a stiff challenge from a War Democrat in the 1862 autumn election, but Stiles was swept into office by that year's Democratic revival in Pennsylvania.

As a Peace Democrat, Stiles strenuously opposed the military and emancipation policies of Abraham Lincoln's (*q.v.*) administration. He did not run for reelection in 1864, but spent considerable time campaigning for the election of George B. McClellan (*q.v.*). Stiles returned to Congress in 1869 for one term, and then retired from public life in 1871. He died in Allentown, Pennsylvania, on October 29, 1896. Jordan, *Historic Homes and Institutions*, vol 2.

W. Wayne Smith

STONE, Lucy, *abolitionist, women's rights activist,* was born on August 3, 1818, near West Brookfield, Massachusetts. In 1843, she enrolled in Oberlin College, where her studies in Greek and Hebrew convinced Stone that crucial passages in the Bible regarding women's role were misinterpreted to justify their unequal treatment. This knowledge helped her later in the many speeches she gave supporting women's rights. Stone began her public career by giving lectures for the American Anti-Slavery Society. She caused some controversy when she introduced feminist rhetoric into her speeches on abolition. In 1850, she led the call for the first National Women's Rights Convention, which was held in Worcester, Massachusetts. In 1855, she married Henry Blackwell but kept her own name, preferring to be known as Mrs. Lucy Stone. Because of this, married women who retained their names were known as "Lucy Stoners."

With the outbreak of war in April 1861, Stone and other feminist leaders agreed to cancel their May convention. Stone herself became one of the founders of the National Woman's Loyal League in 1863, an organization formed to urge the immediate emancipation of all slaves and to support the government in its war for freedom. The league's members collected over 300,000 signatures on a petition presented to the Senate demanding passage of the 13th Amendment.

The war's end brought renewed agitation by Stone on behalf of African Americans and women. Her old friends Susan B. Anthony (*q.v.*) and Elizabeth Cady Stanton (*q.v.*) formed the National Woman Suffrage Association, while Stone and her allies formed the American Woman Suffrage Association. Three years prior to Stone's death on October 18, 1893, in Dorchester, Massachusetts, the two wings of the movement she helped found merged into the National American Woman Suffrage Association. Blackwell, *Lucy Stone*; Hays, *Morning Star*; Kerr, *Lucy Stone.*

Donna M. DeBlasio

STONE, William Milo, *governor*, was born in Jefferson county, New York, on October 14, 1827. His family moved to Coshocton county, Ohio, where he had limited public schooling, was an apprentice chairmaker, and read law. Stone moved to Knoxville, Iowa, in 1854, resumed his legal career for another year, then became owner and editor of the *Knoxville Journal*. A member of the organizing convention of the Iowa Republican party in 1856, he quickly won fame as a public speaker. Twice elected district judge, he resigned in 1861 and organized a company of the 3rd Iowa Infantry. Soon appointed major, Stone fought at the battle of Blue Mills, and was captured at Shiloh. Paroled from Richmond after serving on an officer team that arranged a prisoner exchange, he returned to Knoxville. He took command of the 22nd Iowa and led the unit in the Vicksburg campaign.

Wounded May 22, 1863, Stone returned to Iowa and attended the state Republican convention. His eloquence while giving a patriotic address unexpectedly swung the delegates his way, and he won the party's gubernatorial nomination. Stone won easily in 1863, and again in 1864, although he was somewhat outside of the party's inner circle of lawyers, businessmen, and railroad promoters. Ever concerned about Copperhead influence, he sought to ensure that all public officials in Iowa were "unimpeachably loyal." He supported the controversial movement among Republicans that made Iowa the first of the free states to adopt black suffrage by popular vote.

After his second term, Stone sought nominations to the U.S. House and Senate, but failed to win either, partly because he had aroused the enmity and envy of other important Republicans. He practiced law and entered into mining enterprises in Colorado, then returned to Iowa, where he was appointed assistant commissioner of the General Land Office, then commissioner during President

Benjamin Harrison's administration. Afterward, he moved to Oklahoma Territory, where he died on July 8, 1893. Stuart, *Iowa Colonels and Regiments*; Wubben, *Civil War Iowa.*

Hubert H. Wubben

STONEMAN, George, *general,* was born on August 8, 1822, in Busti, New York. He graduated from West Point in 1846, and as a brevet 2nd lieutenant in the 1st Dragoons, served as quartermaster of the Mormon Battalion in the Mexican War. As a captain in the 2nd Cavalry in 1861, he refused to be included in David E. Twiggs's surrender in Texas, and was given command of the cavalry school at Carlisle, Pennsylvania. On May 9, 1861, Stoneman was promoted to major, and took part in the occupation of Alexandria, Virginia. He served on General George B. McClellan's (*q.v.*) staff in West Virginia, and was made chief of cavalry of the Army of the Potomac when McClellan became general in chief.

When McClellan was relieved, Stoneman took command of the 1st Division, III Corps, and at Fredericksburg, of the entire corps. General Joseph Hooker (*q.v.*) named him chief of cavalry again, but in the Chancellorsville campaign he took most of his corps off on a wide sweep into Lee's rear that was ineffective and left Hooker with practially no cavalry for reconnaissance. He was replaced by Alfred Pleasonton (*q.v.*), served as chief of the Cavalry Bureau, and finally was transferred to the West, where he commanded the XXII Corps and the cavalry corps of the Army of the Ohio. In an attempt to release prisoners of war at Macon and Andersonville, he was captured, but was exchanged in October 1864.

In December 1864, Stoneman began a successful raid into Virginia, Tennessee, and the Carolinas, cooperating with William T. Sherman (*q.v.*). Troubled by hemorrhoids and possessing only modest ability, he achieved limited success as an aggressive cavalry commander. After the war, he served as colonel of the 21st Infantry. Upon retirement in 1871, Stoneman settled in California, becoming governor from 1884 to 1887. He died in Buffalo, New York, on September 5, 1894. Castel, *Decision in the West*; Starr, *Union Cavalry.*

Roy P. Stonesifer, Jr.

STOREY, Wilbur Fisk, *editor,* was born on December 18, 1819, near Salisbury, Vermont. He was self-taught, read voraciously, and became an excellent writer, with a penchant for barbed satire and ridicule. He was apprenticed to the *Middlebury* (Vermont) *Free Press* in 1831, and in 1836 joined the *New York Journal of Commerce*, where he observed the popular and sensationalistic urban journalism of James Gordon Bennett (*q.v.*). In 1838, Storey moved to South Bend, Indiana, where he edited a Democratic weekly, the *LaPorte Herald*; later he edited the *Jackson* (Michigan) *Patriot.*

Storey's ability as a vituperative political editor led to his appointment in 1853 as editor of the Michigan state Democratic organ, the *Detroit Free Press*, which reflected his radical Democratic views. Storey was stridently antiblack (as well as anti-Chinese and anti-Indian), proslavery and proexpansionism, and an ardent supporter of states' rights. His paper became the leading Democratic organ in Michigan and the Midwest.

In 1861, Storey became editor of the *Chicago Times*, a vitriolic paper spewing anti-Lincoln and antiwar sentiment. He soon earned the label of Copperhead, and was linked with such radical Democratic editors as Manton Marble (*q.v.*) of the *New York World* and Samuel Medary (*q.v.*) of the (Columbus, Ohio) *Crisis*, and politicians such as Clement L. Vallandigham (*q.v.*). His paper was hated and feared to the point that citizens, postmasters, politicians, and military officials implored Abraham Lincoln (*q.v.*) to suppress it. However, it was left to General Ambrose Burnside (*q.v.*), commanding the Department of the Ohio, to issue General Orders No. 84, on June 1, 1863, suppressing the *Times*. Reaction from both Democratic and Republican editors and politicians was so immediate and negative, however, that Lincoln rescinded the order two days later.

Storey was so hated that he normally was heavily armed, and the newspaper staff kept weapons handy in case of an attack. The assaults on the paper and its suppression by Burnside focused a substantive and controversial question during the Civil War and later conflicts: What was loyal opposition and what was treason? The *Times* never quite crossed the editorial border of ''legal'' disloyalty, but its antiwar, anti-Lincoln, antiemancipation views brought it to the brink. After the war, the *Times* continued as a major paper.

Storey helped develop urban daily journalism: the initiation of one of the first successful Sunday editions, modernization of newspaper typography, and emphasis on local news. He was a newspaperman for more than forty-five years, yet most historians have focused primarily—and perhaps unfortunately—only on the war years. He died in Chicago on October 27, 1884. Walsh, *To Print the News and Raise Hell.*

Fredric F. Endres

STOWE, Harriet Beecher, *author,* was born on June 14, 1811, in Litchfield, Connecticut. She attended the Hartford Female Seminary, which was established by her sister, Catherine. In 1832, the family moved to Cincinnati, where in 1833 Harriet embarked on her writing career with the publication of an essay in the *Western Monthly Magazine.* She married Calvin Stowe in 1836, and eventually had seven children. She continued writing professionally, making frequent contributions in the genre of domestic literature to magazines like the *Atlantic Monthly.*

In 1850, Stowe moved to Brunswick, Maine, where she wrote her most celebrated work, *Uncle Tom's Cabin.* The impetus for the book was the passage of the Fugitive Slave Act in 1850. The first installment appeared on June 5, 1851, in the *National Era*, and the work was published in book form a year later. It was a sensation, selling over 300,000 copies in its first year. Its graphic portrayal of the evils of slavery, and of unforgettable characters like Simon Legree and Little Eva, had numerous sources, including stories Stowe heard from runaway slaves. The novel also owed much to published slave narratives, other antislavery novels, and Theodore Dwight Weld's (*q.v.*) *American Slavery as It Is*.

It is difficult to measure the impact of *Uncle Tom's Cabin*, but there is no denying its great power to sway those who had tried to ignore the issue of slavery. Southerners were excessively disturbed by the negative depiction of their part of the nation and its "peculiar institution." Abraham Lincoln (*q.v.*), who read the novel and Stowe's defense, *A Key to Uncle Tom's Cabin* (1853), said to her upon their meeting in 1862, "So you're the little woman who wrote the book that made this great war." *Uncle Tom's Cabin* gave Harriet Beecher Stowe her claim to immortality. Although she published for many more years, nothing rivaled its fame or impact. Stowe died in Hartford, Connecticut, on July 1, 1896. Adams, *Harriet Beecher Stowe*; Kimball, *Religious Ideas of Harriet Beecher Stowe*; Wilson, *Crusader in Crinoline*.

Donna M. DeBlasio

STRATTON, John Leake Newbold, *congressman,* was born in Mt. Holly, New Jersey, on November 27, 1817. He graduated from Princeton in 1836, studied law, and was admitted to the bar in 1839. Stratton had been a Whig, but in 1858 was nominated by the Opposition party, a Whiggish coalition of National Americans and Republicans, to run for Congress. He won by over 2,300 votes in a traditional Whig stronghold, and was reelected in 1860. Stratton did not play a prominent role in Congress, but was appointed by House Speaker William Pennington (*q.v.*) to represent New Jersey on the Committee of Thirty-three, which attempted to find some peaceful resolution to the secession crisis. Although Stratton, as a member of the Republican Congressional Executive Committee, had strongly supported Abraham Lincoln's (*q.v.*) election, he was among the minority of Congressional Republicans who favored conciliatory Union-saving overtures to the South in early 1861, and once the war began, became thoroughly estranged from the Radical wing of the party.

Stratton did not run for reelection, apparently because his was a rotating seat. He tried without success in 1864 to win nomination for his old seat, which a Democrat, George Middleton (*q.v.*), had won in 1862. In August 1866 he attended the Union National Convention of Conservatives at Philadelphia, which placed him among the fast dwindling number of conservative Republicans who still supported Andrew Johnson's (*q.v.*) Reconstruction policies. He died in Mt. Holly on May 17, 1899. Knapp, *New Jersey Politics*; Smith, *Charles Perrin Smith*.

Daniel W. Crofts

STRONG, George Templeton, *diarist; treasurer, U.S. Sanitary Commission,* was born on January 26, 1820, in New York City. The son of a prosperous lawyer, he graduated from Columbia College in 1838. He studied law in his father's office, and practiced in New York City from the 1840s until 1873, when he became comptroller of the city's Trinity Episcopal Church. Strong is best known for the diary he kept from 1835 until his death forty years later. It chiefly provides a vivid account of life in New York. But the passages Strong recorded during the Civil War are also significant for the nation, for his service as treasurer of the U.S. Sanitary Commission brought him into contact with Northern war leaders.

An extreme conservative, Strong was uninterested in national politics until 1860, when he supported the candidacy of Abraham Lincoln (*q.v.*). As the deep South seceded in response to Lincoln's victory, Strong demanded that the Union be maintained by force. A Northern victory in the Civil War, he hoped, not only would preserve the Union but also would produce a strong central government that would discourage "democracy and equality." It was a corresponding commitment to order and efficiency that underlay Strong's service with the Sanitary Commission. Like most of the other directors of this semiofficial civilian agency, which aimed to promote the health of Union soldiers and to provide for the sick and wounded, Strong hoped to produce through it a more efficient Union war effort. Nevertheless, his efforts to supplement the ill-prepared Army Medical Bureau certainly eased the suffering of countless Union soldiers. Strong died in New York City on July 21, 1875. Fredrickson, *Inner Civil War*; Strong, *Diary*.

Stanley Harrold

STROUSE, Myer, *congressman,* was born in Bavaria, Germany, on December 16, 1825. He emigrated at age seven with his father to Pottsville, Pennsylvania, was educated in private schools, studied law, and gained admission to the bar in 1855. Strouse was elected to Congress in 1862, a year in which conservative Democrats were particularly strong in Pennsylvania. He opposed Abraham Lincoln's (*q.v.*) war policies, and was especially vocal against conscription. Strouse did not stand for reelection in 1866, and returned to private practice in his hometown. In the 1870s, he represented the Molly Maguires, a secret miners' organization, when it was indicted for violent activities. Strouse died in Pottsville on February 11, 1878. Shankman, *Pennsylvania Antiwar Movement.*

W. Wayne Smith

STUART, John Todd, *congressman,* was born near Lexington, Kentucky, on November 10, 1807. His father, a Presbyterian minister, sent him to Centre College and then to a legal apprenticeship. In 1828, Stuart arrived on horseback in primitive Springfield, Illinois, where he was to become a successful lawyer–politician, serving two terms in the state legislature in the 1830s, and winning election to Congress in 1838 and 1840. From 1849 to 1853, he served in the Illinois Senate. A steady Whig, Stuart disdained the new Republican party, supporting Millard Fillmore in 1856 and the Bell–Everett ticket in 1860.

In 1862, Stuart was endorsed by the Democrats and won election to Congress over Leonard Swett, a favorite of Abraham Lincoln (*q.v.*). Nicknamed "Jerry

Sly,'' Stuart was always a quiet worker and power broker. His influence on Lincoln was immense. Stuart, a major over Lincoln's company in the Black Hawk War, had adopted Lincoln as a protégé and encouraged him to study law. He took him into partnership, became his closest friend, and came to be related through Lincoln's marriage to his cousin Mary Todd (*q.v.*). Although affirming continued personal respect, Stuart broke with Lincoln over wartime policies. He could not abide what he considered to be a revolutionary dismantling of the old Constitution. He opposed secession and favored a vigorous suppression of rebellion, but thought the war could have been avoided, and pleaded for a peace that would not be degrading to the South. He had long favored gradual emancipation and colonization, but regarded the Emancipation Proclamation as unwise.

In 1864, Stuart ran unwillingly for Congress and was defeated. His later years were distinguished by his numerous business and civic activities. He continued to practice law, an ''Old Settler,'' still vigorous, still conservative, but still a horseman from a vanished age. He died in Springfield, Illinois, on November 23, 1885. Angle, *One Hundred Years of Law*; Palmer, *The Bench and Bar of Illinois*; Pratt, ''The Repudiation of Lincoln's War Policy,'' *Journal of the Illinois State Historical Society*.

Jack Nortrup

STURGIS, Samuel Davis, *general*, was born in Shippensburg, Pennsylvania, on June 11, 1822. He graduated from West Point in 1846, was commissioned a brevet 2nd lieutenant in the 2nd Dragoons, and joined his regiment in northern Mexico. Captured while making a reconnaissance near Buena Vista, he was held prisoner for eight days. After the Mexican War, he served at a number of posts in the West. A captain in April 1861, Sturgis commanded two companies of the 1st Cavalry, posted at Fort Smith, Arkansas. Alerted that state troops, sent from Little Rock to capture the post, were approaching, he evacuated the fort on the evening of April 23 and withdrew to Fort Leavenworth by a roundabout route through Indian Territory. He was promoted to major, and at Wilson's Creek succeeded to command of one wing of the army upon the death of Nathaniel Lyon (*q.v.*).

In March 1862, Sturgis was promoted to brigadier general, holding the rank from the day of the Wilson's Creek battle. He led a IX Corps division at Antietam and Fredericksburg, and went west with the corps in the winter of 1863. He was commended for his cavalry leadership in East Tennessee, and in mid-April 1864 was sent to West Tennessee to destroy Nathan Bedford Forrest's corps of mounted infantry. Venturing forth from the Memphis enclave in early May, Sturgis clashed with Forrest but withdrew. In response to orders from William T. Sherman (*q.v.*) to seek out Forrest, he again took the field, and on June 10, his well-appointed 8,000-man column collided with Forrest at Brice's Cross Roads. Sturgis mismanaged his brigades, committing them piecemeal, and compounded Union difficulties when he panicked, and let the retreat become a rout. Sherman, stung by the disaster, called for an investigation. A board questioned Sturgis and most of the ranking Union officers, but adjourned without making any recommendations. Although Sturgis had suffered a crushing defeat, his march had compelled Forrest to abandon a raid on the Nashville & Chattanooga Railroad, the route over which Sherman supplied his army, then closing in on Marietta, Georgia.

Like most Union officers, Sturgis was not forgotten when the brevets were handed out on March 13, 1865. He was mustered out of the Volunteers on August 24, 1865, reverting to his Regular rank of lieutenant colonel of the 6th U.S. Cavalry. On May 6, 1869, he was promoted to colonel of the 7th U.S. Cavalry, with George A. Custer (*q.v.*) as his lieutenant colonel. After service at a number of Western posts, in July 1881 Sturgis was named governor of the Soldiers Home, leading to protests by Brice's Cross Roads survivors. He weathered the uproar to retire in 1886. He died in St. Paul, Minnesota, on September 28, 1889. Bearss, *Forrest at Brice's Cross Roads*; Sears, *Landscape Turned Red*; Sturgis, *The Other Side.*

Edwin C. Bearss

SULLIVAN, Jeremiah Cutler, *general,* was born in Madison, Indiana, on October 1, 1830. He went to sea as a navy midshipman (1848–1854), then resigned his commission to study law. With the outbreak of war, Sullivan answered the call for Volunteers, and in 1861–1862 saw action as a captain in the 6th Indiana and later as colonel of the 13th Indiana. He commanded a brigade in western Virginia, and during the 1862 campaign in the Shenandoah Valley. Following the battle of Kernstown, he was promoted to brigadier general on April 28, 1862, and shortly thereafter commanded a brigade in General William S. Rosecrans's (*q.v.*) Army of the Mississippi. Sullivan participated in the battles of Iuka and Corinth, and in November 1862 was placed in charge of the District of Jackson, Tennessee.

Although criticized by one of his subordinates as possessing a "genius for tardiness," Sullivan was complimented by Ulysses S. Grant (*q.v.*) for dealing with General Nathan Bedford Forrest's December 1862 raid into West Tennessee. He served briefly as Grant's acting inspector general, and during the investment of Vicksburg directed Union forces guarding the supply line between Milliken's Bend and New Carthage, Louisiana. On May 28, 1863, Sullivan was assigned to command the District of Northeastern Louisiana, but the order was revoked when he complained of ill health. After the fall of Vicksburg, he was temporarily General James B. McPherson's (*q.v.*) chief of staff. Grant relieved him of duty in September and ordered him back east.

In the spring of 1864, Sullivan led a division during General Franz Sigel's (*q.v.*) operations in the Shenandoah Valley, but when Philip Sheridan (*q.v.*) reorganized the Middle Military Division in the summer of 1864, he relegated Sullivan to the command of a brigade in West Virginia. Sheridan's successor, Winfield Scott Hancock (*q.v.*), refused to assign him a command and Sullivan resigned on May 11, 1865. After the war, he lived for a time in Maryland and then moved to California. He held a succession of minor clerical jobs, but was frequently unemployed. He died in Oakland, California, on October 21, 1890. Grant, *Papers*, vols. 6, 7, 8, 9; Williams, *Lincoln Finds a General*, vol. 4.

Bruce J. Dinges

SUMNER, Charles, *senator*, was born in Boston on January 6, 1811. He was educated at the Boston Latin School and at Harvard College and Harvard Law School, where he became a protégé of the eminent jurist Joseph Story. Raised as a Unitarian, Sumner became an early champion of pacifism, prison reform, abolitionism, and black equality. He rose to public prominence in 1845 after delivering an antiwar speech at Boston's annual Independence Day celebration and becoming an outspoken critic of Texas annexation. In 1848, he played an active role in the formation of the Free Soil party, and unsuccessfully ran for Congress on its ticket in 1848 and 1850.

In 1851, following a three-month deadlock in the Massachusetts state Senate, a coalition of Democrats and Free Soilers sent Sumner to the U.S. Senate, where he served until his death in 1874. He specialized in lengthy, set-piece speeches punctuated by classical allusions and learned digressions. But for all of his stuffiness, Sunmer had a gift for getting to the moral nub of an issue. His first major address, "Freedom National," a four-hour argument for repealing the 1850 Fugitive Slave Act, sealed his reputation as a champion of political anti-slavery. Southerners scorned him, however. South Carolina Congressman Preston S. Brooks caned him into unconsciousness in May 1856 after Sumner, in the course of his famous "Crime Against Kansas" speech, made insulting remarks about Andrew P. Butler, the Palmetto State's senior U.S. senator and Brooks's kinsman. Besides electrifying the North and hastening the emergence of the Republicans as the nation's second major party, the assault caused Sumner to travel abroad for his health. He resumed his seat three years later, on the eve of the secession crisis, in time to oppose various compromise efforts at averting war and disunion.

During the Civil War, Sumner came to exercise great influence upon American foreign policy. Named chair of the Foreign Relations Committee in 1861, a position he received in recognition of his contacts in Europe and his grasp of international law, he was instrumental in keeping the peace between the United States and England, often moderating the bellicosity of Secretary of State William H. Seward (*q.v.*). During the *Trent* affair, Sumner helped prepare Northern opinion to accept the decision to release Confederate commissioners James Mason and John Slidell. Later, he hardened his attitude toward Great Britain, arguing in his 1869 *Alabama* Claims speech that England should be held accountable for even the indirect costs of the Civil War.

On domestic policy, Sumner was consistently in the vanguard of the black freedom movement. He was one of the first Northern politicians to call for wartime emancipation and equal citizenship for former slaves, and he kept the pressure on President Abraham Lincoln (*q.v.*) throughout the conflict. He advocated awarding the freedmen homesteads in the South, and argued on behalf of Federal enforcement of school integration. The Federal government had unlimited power to reconstruct the South, he argued, because the seceded states had committed "suicide."

During the impeachment trial of Andrew Johnson (*q.v.*), Sumner held that the President should be convicted on the broadest charges possible. His influence on Reconstruction policy, however, was moral rather than substantive. He never served on the influential Joint Committee on Reconstruction, and he opposed the 13th, 14th, and 15th Amendments for falling short of Radical expectations. In fact, the sole piece of legislation for which he is chiefly remembered, the Civil Rights Act of 1875, was not enacted until after his death.

Sumner's power waned during the administration of Ulysses S. Grant (*q.v.*), as he found himself estranged from the pragmatic Stalwarts who had inherited control of the Republican party. By 1872, Sumner bolted the party he had helped build, and threw his support behind the Democrat-dominated Liberal Republican movement. He died in Washington, D.C., on March 11, 1874. Donald, *Charles Sumner and the Coming of the Civil War*; Donald, *Charles Sumner and the Rights of Man*.

Lawrence N. Powell

SUMNER, Edwin Vose, *general,* was born on January 30, 1797, in Boston. Commissioned directly into the Regular Army on March 3, 1819, he successively commanded infantry, dragoon, mounted rifle, and cavalry units prior to becoming colonel of the 1st Cavalry in 1855. He served with particular distinction under Winfield Scott (*q.v.*) in Mexico, suffering a wound at Cerro Gordo and winning brevets for gallantry both at that battle and at Molino del Rey. Sumner functioned as acting governor while serving as military commandant of the New Mexico region in 1852. He attempted to pacify "Bloody Kansas" while commanding Fort Leavenworth in 1856, and the next year fought the Cheyennes. He commanded the Department of the West just prior to the Civil War.

The outbreak of secession found Sumner, a dedicated Unionist, protesting his loyalty to the War Department, undoubtedly because of the rising number of resignations in the officer corps. Scott's belief in Sumner led to his assignment as escort for President-elect Abraham Lincoln (*q.v.*) on his trip to Washington in 1861. He was named brigadier general in March 1861 and replaced Albert Sidney Johnston in command of the Department of the Pacific. Returning east in the fall, he became a division commander in the Army of the Potomac, and the next spring took command of the II Corps. Like Samuel Heintzelman (*q.v.*), with whom his relations were often prickly, Irvin McDowell (*q.v.*), and Erasmus Keyes (*q.v.*), he voted against George B. McClellan's (*q.v.*) Urbanna plan, thus contributing to the politicization of the field force.

Despite age and weakening health, Sumner saved the day at Seven Pines, and won the brevet of major general of Volunteers. This moment of glory only partly offset a decidedly marginal performance earlier at Williamsburg, subsequent indecisiveness at Antietam, and gallant, if blind or unimaginative, adherence to orders for his right grand division to assault Marye's Heights at Fredericksburg. Sumner asked to be relieved upon the appointment of Joseph Hooker (*q.v.*) to command of the Army of the Potomac, and he was reassigned to the Department of the Missouri.

Sumner was unquestionably one of the colorful senior generals of the Union. His troops never forgot the white mane and beard, and loved to apply his Old Army sobriquet of "Old Bull" when his stentorian voice boomed out commands. But warfare and command were changing, and Sumner represented the old guard. He remained the very incarnation of the crusty, Indian-fighting cavalry colonel, rugged and erect in the saddle, strict and duty bound, ill suited to command problems beyond the range of his own voice and sight. Younger officers were commenting about lost opportunities at Williamsburg, half-won actions near the Dunker Church at Antietam, and the inane frontal attacks against Fredericksburg's stone wall. Like so many other early generals in the Eastern armies, Sumner was not capable of high command. He died in Syracuse, New York, on March 21, 1863. Marvel, *Burnside*; Sears, *Landscape Turned Red*; Sears, *To the Gates of Richmond*.

                                                                      B. Franklin Cooling

SWAYNE, Noah Haynes, *Supreme Court justice*, was born on December 7, 1804, in Frederick county, Virginia. After being admitted to the Virginia bar in 1823, Swayne moved to Ohio because of his aversion to slavery. He practiced law there, and was elected to the state legislature in 1829. Appointed a U.S. district attorney by President Andrew Jackson, he served in Columbus until 1841. Swayne was involved in several fugitive slave cases, became an active Republican, and acquired influence with important Ohio politicians. When Supreme Court Justice John McLean died in April 1861, Swayne's political allies urged his nomination.

Confirmed by the Senate in January 1862, Swayne entered upon his duties with little judicial experience but with what Abraham Lincoln (*q.v.*) considered sound political principles. Swayne was quite busy on a Court filled with old men in poor health but, like David Davis (*q.v.*), still found time for politics. As a circuit judge, Swayne criticized arbitrary arrests of civilians by the military, but usually refused to issue writs of habeas corpus. He was a dependable, but not an influential, supporter of the government's war policies; his major problem was that his ego was larger than his judicial ability.

When Roger Taney (*q.v.*) died, Swayne eagerly maneuvered for the chief justiceship. Although a consistent upholder of national authority in various Reconstruction cases, he contributed little to the Court's struggle to interpret the 14th Amendment, except for his dissent in the Slaughterhouse Cases, which anticipated a broader definition of due process. He also became a champion of the railroads in their battles against state regulation. When Salmon P. Chase (*q.v.*) died in 1873, the sixty-nine-year-old Swayne still longed to be Chief Justice. He resigned on January 25, 1881, and died on June 8, 1884, in New York City. Silver, *Lincoln's Supreme Court*; Swisher, *The Taney Period.*

George C. Rable

SWEAT, Lorenzo De Medici, *congressman,* was born on May 26, 1818, in Parsonsfield, Maine. Schooled at local academies and in Effingham, New Hampshire, he graduated with high honors from Bowdoin College in 1837. Law studies in Parsonsfield and Portland, and at Harvard Law School followed. Admitted to the Cumberland county bar in 1840, Sweat traveled to New Orleans, where he spent a few months in the office of the flamboyant Pierre Soulé, future U.S. senator and minister to Spain, then practiced on his own. He returned to Maine in 1841, and for the rest of his long life made Portland his home. Sweat emerged as a prominent Democratic leader in the 1850s. He served as Portland city solicitor from 1856 to 1860, and state senator in 1862; in the latter year he won a seat in Congress. There Sweat strongly advocated a northern Pacific railroad. He failed to be reelected in 1864 and 1866. From 1872 to 1876, Sweat served as a Democratic national committeeman from Maine, and helped Samuel J. Tilden win the 1876 Presidential nomination. He died in Portland on July 26, 1898. *BDUSC.*

H. Draper Hunt

SWEENY, Thomas William, *general,* was born on December 25, 1820, in County Cork, Ireland, and emigrated with his widowed mother to the United States in 1832. Eventually settling in New York City, he found employment with a law publishing firm and took an interest in the local militia. Sweeny enlisted in the Independent Tompkins Blues later known as the Baxter Blues, which served with the 1st New York Volunteers in the Mexican War. During the battle of Churubusco, he received a severe wound that led to the amputation of his right arm. After a period of recuperation, Sweeny accepted a lieutenant's commission in the 2nd U.S. Infantry on March 3, 1848. His unit served in the Southwest and fought Indians on the Great Plains until the commencement of the Civil War.

In May 1861, while stationed in St. Louis, Sweeny resigned his position in the Regular Army and accepted a brigadier generalship in the short-term Missouri Volunteers. Serving under Brigadier General Nathaniel Lyon (*q.v.*), he was severely wounded at Wilson's Creek and carried from the field. Sweeny returned to duty in January 1862 as a colonel of the 52nd Illinois Volunteers, which he led at Fort Donelson and Shiloh. He was once again wounded at Shiloh, while commanding a brigade of William H.L. Wallace's (*q.v.*) division. In October 1862 Sweeny was named brigade commander at Corinth after the death of General Pleasant A. Hackleman (*q.v.*), and promoted to brigadier general on March 16, 1863.

At the outset of the Atlanta campaign, Sweeny commanded a division in

Major General Grenville M. Dodge's (*q.v.*) XVI Corps, Army of the Tennessee. He distinguished himself early in the campaign, but gained notoriety for events that occurred off the battlefield. While entertaining Dodge and Brigadier General John W. Fuller (*q.v.*) at his headquarters on July 25, 1864, he cursed Dodge and struck both Dodge and Fuller. Sweeny was immediately arrested by Dodge and charged with conduct unbecoming an officer, as well as other offenses. He was acquitted in January 1865 by a military court, but not restored to command.

Dismissed from the Regular Army in December 1865, Sweeny used political connections to return to the service in 1866. The rest of his military career was uneventful, except for his involvement with the Fenian movement. Sweeny was placed on the retired list on May 11, 1870, with the rank of brigadier general. He died in Astoria, New York, on April 10, 1892. Castel, *Decision in the West*; Hirshson, *Grenville M. Dodge*.

Mitchell A. Yockelson

SWEET, Benjamin Jeffrey, *general*, was born in northern New York in 1832. His family moved in 1841 to Wisconsin, where Sweet later read law and was admitted to the bar. In 1859, as a Republican and abolitionist, he was elected to the Wisconsin Senate. Beginning the war as a major, he helped to raise several regiments, and was colonel of the 21st Wisconsin when he was badly wounded at Perryville. Having lost full use of his right arm, Sweet was transferred to the Veteran Reserve Corps with the rank of colonel.

On May 2, 1864, Sweet was put in command of the post at Chicago, with headquarters at Camp Douglas. This put him in charge of one of the North's larger war prisons. He learned through spies and other sources of a conspiracy by Confederates from Canada and alleged Copperheads to attack the camp, free the prisoners, and set off a revolt in the Old Northwest. Whatever the reality of these charges, Sweet took precautions during the Democratic National Convention in Chicago, and made arrests just prior to the national election. The Republican press published a lurid exposé of the so-called Chicago or Camp Douglas Conspiracy. Sweet testified at the Cincinnati trial by a military commission of eight of those arrested. He was rewarded by promotion to brevet brigadier general on December 20, 1864. After the war, he engaged in a law practice in Chicago and died there in 1877. Klement, *Dark Lanterns*; Starr, *Grenfell's Wars*.

Frank L. Byrne

SWIFT, Henry Adoniram, *governor*, was born on March 23, 1823, in Ravenna, Ohio. After graduating in 1842 from Western Reserve College, he worked in Mississippi as a tutor before returning to Ohio to study law. Admitted to the bar in 1845, he served as the chief clerk of the Ohio legislature until he moved to St. Paul, Minnesota. In the decade before the Civil War, Swift was involved in various insurance and real estate ventures. Elected to the Minnesota Senate in 1861 as a Republican, he became Senate president in 1862, following the election of Lieutenant Governor Ignatius Donnelly (*q.v.*) to the U.S. Senate. When Governor Alexander Ramsey (*q.v.*) was elected to the U.S. Senate in 1863, Swift automatically ascended to the governorship by virtue of his position in the legislature. He served as Minnesota's third governor from July 10, 1863, until January 11, 1864, and declined to be nominated for another term.

Although one critic finds that Swift "served without disturbance or distinction" compared with other state executives, he discharged his duties reasonably well during his six-month tenure. As is true of so many Civil War governors, he ensured that his constituents did not suffer unfairly from overly burdensome draft quotas and other national demands. In addition to concluding a treaty with the Chippewa Indians that opened another 10,000 square miles of his state to settlers, he and Pennsylvania Governor Andrew Curtin (*q.v.*) proved instrumental in securing the rapid purchase of the Gettysburg battlefield for posterity. After Swift relinquished the governor's seat to his successor, Stephen Miller (*q.v.*), he became the registrar of the St. Peter Land Office in Minnesota. He held this position until he died there on February 25, 1869. Baker, *Governors of Minnesota*; Hesseltine, *Lincoln's War Governors*.

James W. Geary

SWISSHELM, Jane Grey Cannon, *abolitionist, editor, nurse*, was born in Pittsburgh, Pennsylvania, on December 6, 1815. Despite her lack of formal education, she taught school as a young woman. In 1836, she married James Swisshelm, and in 1838 they moved to Louisville, where her firsthand view of slavery strengthened her antislavery sentiment. Her early writings appeared in the *Dollar Newspaper* and *Neal's Saturday Gazette*, under the name Jennie Deans. Concurrently, she contributed articles on slavery and women's rights to the Pittsburgh antislavery paper, the *Spirit of Liberty*.

In 1847, Swisshelm founded the *Pittsburgh Saturday Visitor*, an antislavery, women's rights weekly. At first an organ of the Liberty party, and later a Free Soil paper, it attained modest success nationwide, in England, and in Canada. In 1850, Swisshelm moved to Washington, D.C., where she contributed to the *Visitor* and the *New York Tribune*, and became the first woman admitted to the congressional press gallery. She returned to Pittsburgh later in the year. In 1857, she severed her ties with the *Visitor*, left her husband, and moved with her daughter to St. Cloud, Minnesota, where she founded the *St. Cloud Visitor*, another antislavery paper. Vigilantes destroyed her printing press, but with the financial support of sympathizers, the paper was revived, and its name was changed to the *Democrat.*

Although she shied away from political affiliation, Swisshelm was closely identified with the Republican party. In 1860, she supported the candidacy of William H. Seward (*q.v.*) and Cassius M. Clay (*q.v.*) for the Republican presidential and vice presidential nominations. She was not enthusiastic about Abraham Lincoln (*q.v.*), but advocated support for the war effort and organized her own volunteer aid society. She impatiently branded Lincoln an obstructionist rather than abolitionist, especially when he countermanded the emancipation schemes of John C. Frémont (*q.v.*) and David Hunter (*q.v.*). In 1863, she tried to convince the President of the Indian peril on the frontier. Although she never succeeded in this endeavor, she did become a close friend of Mary Todd Lincoln (*q.v.*) and one of her ardent defenders. Swisshelm was a nurse in the military hospitals, and often appealed for needed hospital supplies. In addition, she was a clerk in the quartermaster's office, a position her old friend Edwin Stanton (*q.v.*) obtained for her.

In 1865, in her newly founded *Reconstructionist*, Swisshelm attacked Andrew Johnson's (*q.v.*) policies and loyalty. Johnson fired her from her clerkship, and the printer's union forbade its members to work where the *Reconstructionist* was printed. Twice her office–residence was set ablaze. After a few months, the publication was suspended and she retired to Swissvale, Pennsylvania, where she died on July 22, 1884. Klement, "Jane Grey Swisshelm," *Abraham Lincoln Quarterly*; Shippee, "Jane Grey Swisshelm," *Mississippi Valley Historical Review*; Swisshelm, *Crusader and Feminist*.

Kathleen L. Endres

SYKES, George, *general*, was born in Dover, Delaware, on October 9, 1822. He graduated from West Point in 1842, a classmate of James Longstreet, whose Confederate troops he would face at Gettysburg. He served in Florida against the Seminoles before taking part in the Mexican War campaign from Veracruz to Mexico City. He spent the next fourteen years in Texas and New Mexico.

Promoted to major on May 14, 1861, Sykes led a battalion of Regulars at First Bull Run. He was appointed a brigadier general of Volunteers in September 1861, and for the next two years he commanded a division composed chiefly of Regulars. These troops served valiantly at Gaines' Mill and at Second Bull Run. In the Maryland campaign, Sykes's division took only a peripheral part, and it never reached the front line in the assaults at Fredericksburg. As a major general, Sykes conducted himself well enough at Chancellorsville, and when George Meade (*q.v.*) was named to lead the army, Sykes took command of the V Corps. At Gettysburg, his troops saved the day by occupying Little Round Top just in time to stop Longstreet's assault on the Union left.

Gettysburg was the peak of Sykes's career. After the Rappahannock and Mine Run campaigns, his superiors accused him of responding lethargically when success depended upon energetic action; he supposedly bore the nickname "Tardy George." Their dissatisfaction may have arisen as much from his politics as from his performance, for in the autumn of 1863 he participated in an effort to compose a testimonial to George McClellan (*q.v.*) that seemed to imply criticism of the army's commanders. The Secretary of War was said to have considered dismissing Sykes and his collaborators, and when the army was reorganized in the spring of 1864, Sykes was relieved of his command and relegated to southern Kansas. Thereafter he returned to the Regular Army and commanded troops west of the Mississippi. He died at Fort Brown, Texas, on February 8, 1880. Davis, *Bull Run*; Hennessy, *Return to Bull Run*; Wainwright, *Diary of Battle*.

William Marvel

T

TANEY, Roger Brooke, *Chief Justice*, was born on March 17, 1777, in Calvert county, Maryland. He attended Dickinson College, where he was graduated class valedictorian at age fifteen. Taney became a staunch Jacksonian in the 1820s, and moved to Washington to become Attorney General in 1831. Taney later became Secretary of the Treasury, and executed Andrew Jackson's order to remove the Federal deposits from the Bank of the United States. Senate Whigs blocked his nomination to other offices, but Jackson chose him to be Chief Justice when John Marshall died in 1835.

Throughout his life Taney held to the doctrine of dual sovereignty, and attempted to maintain a balance between national and state authority over banks, contracts, and commerce. Yet it was the slavery question in general, and the *Dred Scott* decision in particular, that established his historical reputation. By declaring congressional regulation of slavery in the territories unconstitutional, Taney led a divided Court into political quicksand. It did not matter that he had long ago freed his own slaves; Republicans branded him an infamous tool of the slave power.

Taney's poor health and the Court's low prestige relegated both to the sidelines during the Civil War. When President Abraham Lincoln (*q.v.*) authorized the suspension of the writ of habeas corpus in the Baltimore area, military officers arrested one John Merryman, and the case came before Taney in circuit court. The Chief Justice denied the right of the President to suspend the writ, but Lincoln deftly avoided a confrontation by transferring the *Merryman* case to civil jurisdiction. The *Merryman* opinion reflected Taney's deeply held belief that the Federal suppression of civil liberties was more dangerous than the breakup of the Union. Yet Taney refused to hold circuit court in areas under martial law, and preferred to snipe away at government policies. He clashed with Secretary of the Treasury Salmon P. Chase (*q.v.*) over trade regulations and a tax on judges' salaries.

Bedridden for much of the war, Taney carefully prepared in advance of litigation opinions denying the power of Congress to make greenbacks legal tender, and declaring that conscription violated the rights of the states. These cases never came before the Court while Taney was Chief Justice, but there is no doubt that he stood ready to deliver these judicial rebukes to both Lincoln and the Congress. Taney died in Washington, D.C., on October 12, 1864. Frank Otto Gatell, "Roger B. Taney," in Friedman, *Justices of the U.S. Supreme Court*, vol. 1, pp. 635–716; Swisher, *The Taney Period*.

George C. Rable

TAPPAN, Lewis, *abolitionist*, was born on May 23, 1788, in Northampton, Massachusetts. He combined an evangelical faith with great financial resources to become one of the more influential abolitionists. Tappan's formal education was limited to primary schooling and an apprenticeship as a clerk. In 1828, he joined with his brother, Arthur, in the silk business, but it was his establishment in New York City of the nation's first commercial credit-rating agency that produced his wealth. Even before then, the evangelical principle of disinterested benevolence had encouraged Tappan to contribute large portions of his time and finances to organized charitable work, which by the 1830s involved him in the antislavery movement.

Tappan helped establish the American Anti-Slavery Society in 1833. When that society fragmented in 1840, he formed the American and Foreign Anti-Slavery Society to promote church-oriented abolitionism. In 1846, he was the leading spirit in creating the American Missionary Association, designed as an abolitionist alternative to existing missionary organizations and as a means of carrying abolitionist Christianity into the South. Tappan was also instrumental in the initiation of the *National Era* in 1847 as an abolitionist newspaper in slaveholding Washington, D.C.

Although politics was not Tappan's main concern, he was a supporter of the abolitionist Liberty party by 1843. In the early 1850s, he joined Gerrit Smith (*q.v.*) in arguing that the national government could abolish slavery in the Southern states. Thus, Tappan shared in an increasingly confrontational stance toward the South. By the mid-1850s, however, advanced age had begun to limit his influence. He died on June 21, 1873, in Brooklyn, New York. Friedman, *Gregarious Saints*; Wyatt-Brown, *Lewis Tappan*.

Stanley Harrold

TEMPLE, William, *congressman*, was born in Queen Annes county, Maryland, on February 28, 1815. Educated in local schools, he moved to Smyrna, Delaware, as a young man and became a merchant. Active in Whig politics, he was elected to the state House of Representatives and became its speaker. Following the death of Governor Thomas Stockton and of his successor, the presiding officer of the Senate, Joseph Maull, in 1846, Temple became acting governor, serving from May 1846 to January 1847. After his brief term as governor, he served continuously in the state Senate until 1854.

In 1860, Temple was active in forming the Constitutional Union party in Delaware, and attended its national convention in Baltimore. The Democrats nominated him as U.S. representative in 1862, and he won the election. His death in Smyrna, on May 28, 1863, led to the election of Nathaniel B. Smithers (*q.v.*) to fill his unexpired term in November of that year. Conrad, *History of the State of Delaware.*

Harold B. Hancock

TEN EYCK, John Conover, *senator,* was born in Freehold, New Jersey, on March 12, 1814. He was a Whig, even though his original law partner was former U.S. Senator Garret D. Wall, a Democrat. Ten Eyck was prosecuting attorney for Burlington county (1839–1849), and a delegate to the 1844 state constitutional convention. In 1859, he was elected to the U.S. Senate by the Opposition party, a Whiggish coalition of National Americans and Republicans that briefly controlled the state legislature. Ten Eyck was considered an "available" candidate by both factions because his current political allegiance was no more than vaguely Republican. In exchange for electing Ten Eyck, Republicans agreed to support a National American Charles S. Olden (*q.v.*), who ran successfully for governor in 1859.

Ten Eyck positioned himself as a consensus Republican, which frustrated the Radical faction of the state party. He expressed uneasiness about confiscation, the abolition of slavery in the District of Columbia, the arming of blacks, and the possibility of former slaves' leaving the South. He was one of the few Senate Republicans who supported Abraham Lincoln's (*q.v.*) Louisiana Reconstruction policy, and he opposed passage of the Wade–Davis Bill. Unfortunately for Ten Eyck, New Jersey Democrats recovered during the war, blighting his hopes for reelection. He was supported by the Republican legislative caucus in March 1865 but the honor was empty. New Jersey thereby lost its most visible and articulate member of Congress. Ten Eyck retired from politics in 1865 and resumed his law career. He died in Mt. Holly, New Jersey, on August 23, 1879. Knapp, *New Jersey Politics.*

Daniel W. Crofts

TERRY, Alfred Howe, *general,* was born in Hartford, Connecticut, on November 10, 1827. After attending Yale Law School, he was an attorney and clerk of the New Haven Superior Court. As colonel of the 2nd Connecticut Militia he fought at First Bull Run, and afterward he helped form the 7th Connecticut Volunteers. He led his regiment at Port Royal and Fort Pulaski, and in the early operations at Charleston. By the autumn of 1862 he was a brigadier general of Volunteers, commanding at Hilton Head, South Carolina.

Early in 1864, at the head of a X Corps division, Terry went to Virginia to join General Benjamin Butler's (*q.v.*) Army of the James. He served creditably, sometimes exceptionally, in the Richmond–Petersburg campaign. That December, Butler failed to capture Fort Fisher, which guarded the water approach to Wilmington, North Carolina, the last Confederate seaport. Sent to Wilmington with a comparable force, Terry outdid his superior, capturing the formidable earthwork on January 15, 1865, via a series of well-mounted assaults. For this feat, he was named a major general of Volunteers and a brigadier of Regulars, at which rank he led a provisional corps in cooperation with General William T. Sherman's (*q.v.*) North Carolina campaign.

Terry was the most distinguished nonprofessional soldier in the Union ranks, one of very few to attain the highest grade in the postwar Regulars. An able administrator and an innovative tactician, he saw his talents underemployed until the last year of the conflict. After the war, he commanded the Department of Dakota, where he was George Custer's (*q.v.*) superior during the Little Bighorn campaign. He also commanded the Division of the Missouri and served on several military commissions. Terry died in New Haven, Connecticut, on December 16, 1890. Barrett, *Sherman's March Through the Carolinas*; Sommers, *Richmond Redeemed*; Wightman, *From Antietam to Fort Fisher.*

Edward G. Longacre

THAYER, Andrew Jackson, *congressman,* was born on November 27, 1818, in Lima, New York. He attended public schools and then studied law, practicing in Buffalo. In 1853, he moved to Oregon, where he practiced law and farmed near Corvallis. In 1859, President James Buchanan (*q.v.*) appointed him U.S. attorney for Oregon. Thayer was better trained than most frontier lawyers but shared their political ambitions. A strong supporter of popular sovereignty, he came to oppose President Buchanan and Senator Joe Lane (*q.v.*). As a reward for his break with the administration, Douglas Democrats nominated him in October 1860 for the House of Representatives. Breckinridge Democrat George Shiel (*q.v.*) had been elected in June 1860 and successfully challenged the election, replacing Thayer in July 1861.

Oregon Unionists expressed disgust that the House had awarded the contested seat to Shiel, but in 1864 and 1865 some of them complained that Thayer had fundamentally changed his politics by praising the opinions of Copperhead Clement Vallandigham (*q.v.*), and by calling the Union party ''a band of abolitionists.'' His affable disposition and continuing ability to shift his political sentiments contributed to his election as a judge in 1870. Thayer died in Corvallis on April 28, 1873. Evans, *History of the Pacific Northwest*, vol 2.

G. Thomas Edwards

THAYER, John Milton, *general,* was born in Bellingham, Massachusetts, on January 24, 1820. He graduated from Brown University in 1841, read law, and was admitted to the bar. In 1854, he moved to Omaha, Nebraska, where he farmed and resumed the practice of law. During the Pawnee Indian troubles in 1855 and 1859, he was commissioned the first brigadier general of the Nebraska territorial militia. In the Pawnee War of 1859, Thayer's forces were successful in capturing the entire Indian tribe and placing it on a reservation. Perhaps because of his success in handling the Indians, he was elected to the territorial legislature, and was a member of the constitutional conventions of 1860 and 1866.

With the outbreak of the Civil War, Thayer was made colonel of the 1st Nebraska, a regiment originally recruited as infantry but changed to cavalry in 1863. As a part of General Lew Wallace's (q.v.) division, he displayed great bravery at Fort Donelson and at Shiloh. On October 4, 1862, he was appointed brigadier general of Volunteers and was placed in command of five Iowa regiments and a part of the 3rd Illinois Cavalry. Thayer was a part of William T. Sherman's (q.v.) corps at Vicksburg, where once again he performed well. He then accompanied General Frederick Steele (q.v.) to Arkansas, assuming command of the District of the Frontier, with headquarters at Fort Smith, on February 22, 1864. Thayer's troops, known as the Frontier Division, took part in Steele's Camden campaign, which was designed to support General Nathaniel P. Banks's (q.v.) advance up the Red River. The Steele–Banks effort failed in April 1864, and Thayer resumed his Frontier District command until February 27, 1865, when he was given an assignment at St. Charles, in eastern Arkansas.

Thayer was breveted major general of Volunteers on March 13, 1865, and resigned from the service on July 19 of that year. After his return to Nebraska, he assumed a prominent role in organizing the territory into a state, and was elected one of its first U.S. senators, on the Republican ticket. He backed Radical Reconstruction, and was a strong supporter of President Ulysses S. Grant's (q.v.) administration. Thayer was governor of Wyoming Territory (1875–1879) and of Nebraska (1886–1890). He died in Lincoln on November 26, 1901. Bearss, *Vicksburg Campaign*; Sword, *Shiloh*; Williams, *Lincoln Finds a General*, vol. 3.

James J. Hudson

THAYER, Martin Russell, *congressman*, was born in Petersburg, Virginia, on January 27, 1819. He attended Amherst College, graduated as valedictorian from the University of Pennsylvania in 1840, studied law, and was admitted to the bar in 1842. Though not active in politics, Thayer aligned with the Democratic party. When the Civil War began, however, like many other Democrats, he supported Abraham Lincoln's (q.v.) administration rather than acknowledge the independence of the South. Other Philadelphians continued to support the South and formed a vocal Copperhead organization in the state. Thayer responded with a searing public condemnation of their propaganda, and in 1862 won election to Congress as a Union Republican. He was reelected in 1864, and continued to support the war effort. He accepted an appointment as a judge of the Court of Common Pleas in Philadelphia, where he served until 1896. He died in that city on October 14, 1906. *Biographical Encyclopedia of Pennsylvania of the Nine-teenth Century*; Shankman, *Pennsylvania Antiwar Movement.*

W. Wayne Smith

THOMAS, Benjamin Franklin, *congressman*, was born on February 12, 1813, in Boston. After his graduation in 1830 from Brown University, he studied law in Cambridge, and was admitted to the bar in 1834. In 1842, he represented Worcester in the state legislature. From 1844 to 1848, he served as judge of probate for Worcester county, and in 1848 was a presidential elector on the Whig party ticket. Thomas received a LL.D. degree from Brown University in 1853, and a similar degree from Harvard College the following year. In 1853, he was appointed associate justice of the state Supreme Judicial Court, a position he held until 1859. In 1861, he was almost unanimously elected as a Conservative Unionist to the 37th Congress, to fill the vacancy created by the resignation of Charles Francis Adams (*q.v.*), who had been appointed minister to England.

Thomas's course in Congress was more in harmony with the Democratic than with the Republican party, which initially supported him. In 1862, he accepted a nomination for Congress from the anti-Republican "united front" People's party, but was defeated by Republican George S. Boutwell (*q.v.*). If Thomas had been reelected to Congress, he would have been brought forward by conservatives as a challenger to Charles Sumner (*q.v.*) in the 1863 senatorial contest.

After the Civil War, Thomas began to affiliate openly with the Democratic party. When Governor Alexander Bullock nominated him chief justice of the Massachusetts Supreme Court in 1868, Boutwell and Sumner used their influence to defeat the nomination. Thomas died in Beverly Farms, Massachusetts, on September 27, 1878. Reno, *Memoirs of the Judiciary and Bar of New England*, vol. 2.

Dale Baum

THOMAS, Francis, *congressman*, was born on February 3, 1799, in Frederick county, Maryland. After attending St. John's College in Annapolis, he studied law, and was admitted to the bar in 1820. He was elected to the Maryland House of Delegates in 1822, and again in 1827 and 1829, when he became speaker. Instrumental in organizing the Jacksonian party in western Maryland, Thomas represented his district in Congress from 1831 to 1841. He was elected governor in 1841, but his bid for reelection failed. A scandalous divorce hurt him politically.

Thomas generally remained politically inactive until 1860, when he reentered politics in support of Stephen A. Douglas (*q.v.*). With the outbreak of war, he raised regiments for the Union Army, but left their command to younger men. In 1861 he was elected to Congress as a Unionist, serving until 1869. Despite his initial opposition to some Federal policies, Thomas preferred them to the Union's destruction. As a slaveholder, he had been opposed to any interference with slavery, but by 1863, after manumitting his slaves, Thomas accepted emancipation and joined the Unconditional Unionists.

With the loss of power by the Radicals in Maryland, Thomas unsuccessfully attempted to secure Federal intervention under the military Reconstruction Acts and to utilize black suffrage to help the Republican party regain control. At the end of his term, he was appointed an internal revenue collector in 1870, and then minister to Peru (1872–1875). He died in Frankville, Maryland, on January 22, 1876. Baker, *Politics of Continuity*; Clark, *Politics in Maryland During the Civil War*.

Richard R. Duncan

THOMAS, George Henry, *general*, was born in Southampton county, Virginia, on July 31, 1816. He graduated from West Point in 1840, then served in the Second Seminole War and the Mexican War, and as an artillery and cavalry instructor at West Point. In spite of his Virginia birth, Thomas remained with the Union Army, becoming a colonel in May 1861 and commanding a brigade in the opening operations in the Shenandoah Valley. On August 17, 1861, he was made a brigadier general of Volunteers and assigned to duty in Kentucky, where he won the small but important action at Mill Springs, or Logan's Cross Roads, on January 19, 1862. Thomas commanded the 1st Division, Army of the Ohio, in the advance to Pittsburg Landing and at Corinth. Later in the year, Don Carlos Buell's (*q.v.*) retreat to Louisville caused dissatisfaction in Washington, and on September 29 Thomas received orders to supersede him in command. Saying that Buell had already issued orders for an offensive campaign, Thomas declined the command, and served as Buell's second in command during the operations resulting in the battle of Perryville.

Thomas was disappointed when Buell's command was finally given to William S. Rosecrans (*q.v.*), a former junior, but served under him loyally, commanding the XIV Corps, Army of the Cumberland, at Stones River. After the first day of that bloody battle, when Rosecrans was considering the wisdom of retreat, Thomas counseled otherwise. In the Tullahoma campaign and at the battle of Chickamauga, he commanded the XIV Corps. Thomas's greatest moment as a military commander came on the second day at Chickamauga, when, about noon, a gap opened on his right flank, caused by an erroneous movement of a division. The Confederates penetrated the Federal line, driving the troops south of Thomas in disorder, along with two corps commanders and the army commander. Thomas, however, was still in position to protect the line of retreat to Chattanooga that ran through McFarland's Gap. Although his line was bent back severely, Thomas and about half of the army continued to hold Snodgrass Hill throughout the day. Finally, after dark, he retired to Chattanooga.

At West Point, he had been known as "Old Tom" while a cadet, and as "Slow Trot" as an instructor; but now, and ever after, Thomas was best known as "the Rock of Chickamauga." He replaced Rosecrans as commander of the Army of the Cumberland, and his army carried Missionary Ridge in the decisive action of the fighting at Chattanooga. In May 1864 Thomas and his army, constituting over half of William T. Sherman's (*q.v.*) command, moved on Atlanta. They bore the brunt of the Union attack at Kennesaw Mountain and broke the Confederate attack at Peachtree Creek. When Sherman decided to march to the sea, Thomas was dispatched to defend Nashville against John Bell Hood. After the battle of Franklin, where Hood's army was severely bloodied, Ulysses S. Grant (*q.v.*) insisted that Thomas conduct an immediate offensive.

Maintaining that he needed additional strength to gain a decisive victory, Thomas delayed. Both his capacity for independent command and his loyalty were questioned by some. Then, on December 15–16, 1864, just as he was about to be relieved of command, Thomas attacked and completely routed Hood's army in the battle of Nashville. As a defensive fighter Thomas was probably unsurpassed in either army; his conduct of the battle of Nashville indicated an equal capacity for offensive warfare. Continuing in the Regular Army after the war, he died on March 28, 1870, in San Francisco, the commander of the Military Division of the Pacific. Castel, *Decision in the West*; O'Connor, *Thomas: Rock of Chickamauga*; Sword, *Embrace an Angry Wind.*

James Lee McDonough

THOMAS, Henry Goddard, *general*, was born on April 4, 1837, in Portland, Maine. After graduating from Amherst College in 1858, he practiced law in his native state. In April 1861 he enlisted as a private (and soon became an officer) in the 5th Maine Volunteers. After serving at First Bull Run, he attained a captaincy in the newly formed 11th U.S. Infantry. Following several months on recruiting duty, Thomas left his regiment to organize and train black units in Maryland.

In March 1863 Thomas was appointed colonel of the 79th U.S. Colored Troops and, ten months later, of the 19th U.S.C.T. In May 1864 he won command of an African American brigade in the IX Corps, Army of the Potomac, which he led with conspicuous ability in the Petersburg campaign, especially in the Crater assault. That November, Thomas was elevated to brigadier general of Volunteers and, along with the IX Corps U.S.C.T. units, was transferred to the Army of the James. He led a brigade in the XXV Corps until the close of the war, and at its head he entered evacuated Richmond on April 3, 1865. For his war services, he received the brevets of major general of Volunteers and brigadier general of Regulars.

For a young soldier lacking a formal military education, Thomas rose more quickly and saw more varied service than most Union officers. Although capable and courageous in battle, he was chiefly notable as the first Regular Army officer to accept command of a black regiment. Adept at making U.S.C.T. recruits into efficient soldiers, he maintained his interest in African American affairs during Reconstruction, serving in the Freedmen's Bureau in Virginia and Kentucky. After this service, he returned to the 11th U.S. Infantry, became major of the 4th Infantry in 1876, then transferred to the Paymaster's Department. Retiring in July 1891, he resided in Oklahoma City until his death there on January 23, 1897. Cornish, *Sable Arm.*

Edward G. Longacre

THOMAS, Lorenzo, *general,* was born on October 26, 1804, in New Castle, Delaware. He graduated from West Point in 1823, served in the Seminole Wars, was breveted for gallantry in the Mexican War, and from 1853 to the outbreak of the Civil War was chief of staff to Winfield Scott (*q.v.*). In May 1861 he was appointed brigadier general and adjutant general of the Army. Early in 1863, the garrulous, hard-drinking Thomas ran afoul of Secretary of War Edwin M. Stanton (*q.v.*), who virtually banished him from Washington. Sent west to supervise the forming of black units, Thomas traveled to several garrisons and outposts in the West where freedmen and escaped slaves had gathered. In December 1863 he reported to Stanton that he had recruited 25,000 African Americans as combat troops, garrison forces, and military laborers. He had also overseen the hiring of black civilians and had settled other fugitives on abandoned cotton plantations.

Despite Thomas's achievements, in 1864–1865 Stanton relegated him to inspecting provost offices and national cemeteries. After the war, now a brevet major general, Thomas allied himself with Andrew Johnson (*q.v.*), who appointed him interim Secretary of War in place of Stanton. On February 22, 1869, ten days before the embattled President left office, Thomas retired from the Army. He died in Washington, D.C., on March 2, 1875. Cornish, *Sable Arm*; Glatthaar, *Forged in Battle.*

Edward G. Longacre

THOMSON, John Renshaw, *senator,* was born in Philadelphia on September 25, 1800. He attended Princeton, grew wealthy in the China tea trade, and served as U.S. consul at Canton (1823–1825). Upon his return to the United States, Thomson married the sister of Commodore Robert F. Stockton, who was soon to organize the Joint Companies, the Delaware & Raritan Canal and the Camden & Amboy Railroad. This alliance with the most politically powerful family in New Jersey paved the way for a career in business and politics. A Jacksonian Democrat, Thomson stumped the state to promote the constitutional convention of 1844, in which he played a prominent role. Although nominated for governor in 1844, he lost the election.

Thomson wanted a U.S. Senate seat in 1851, but deferred to his brother-in-law. When Robert Stockton resigned from the Senate in 1853, the legislature selected Thomson to finish his term. He was reelected in 1857, and supported President James Buchanan (*q.v.*) during the Lecompton controversy. During the secession crisis, Thomson was a member of a special committee of five senators, and one of the three who vainly supported the Crittenden and Peace Conference compromises. A friend of many Southern senators, he believed forcible reunion impossible. But after Fort Sumter, he became an avowed Unionist and war supporter. Thomson played little role in Congress after the war began, though he spoke in favor of constructing oceangoing ironclads. He died in Princeton, New Jersey, on September 12, 1862. *BDUSC.*

Daniel W. Crofts

TILLSON, Davis, *general,* was born on April 14, 1830, in Rockland, Maine. He entered West Point in July 1849 but left in September 1851 because of an injury that required the amputation of one of his legs. He turned to a career in civil engineering and then to politics. In 1857, Tillson was elected to the Maine legislature as a Republican. He became Maine's adjutant general a year later, and in 1861 received an appointment from Abraham Lincoln (*q.v.*) as a collector of customs. After Fort Sumter, Tillson renewed his interest in a military career, and on November 30, 1861, was appointed a captain in the 2nd Maine Battery. He rose to lieutenant colonel following his unit's participation in the battles of Cedar Mountain and Second Bull Run.

After having served as the chief of artillery on various staffs, Tillson was promoted to brigadier general of Volunteers on March 27, 1863. For the remainder of the war, he served as chief of artillery in General Ambrose Burnside's (*q.v.*) Department of the Ohio, as a infantry brigade commander in the XXIII Corps, and as a divisional commander in the Army of the Cumberland. In this latter assignment, he recruited and organized the all-black 1st U.S. Heavy Artillery and the 3rd North Carolina Mounted Infantry. His experience in raising African American troops led to an offer to serve with the Freedmen's Bureau, and in September 1865 Major General Oliver O. Howard (*q.v.*) assigned Tillson to organize the bureau in Georgia.

Tillson replaced General Rufus Saxton (*q.v.*), who had experienced difficulties in persuading Southern whites to accept the tenets of a free labor system by employing former slaves. In an attempt to make the system work, he tried numerous approaches, which included imposing a uniform wage system, hiring local Georgians as agents, and trying to educate free blacks on the advantages of the system. Nevertheless, Tillson's attempts also foundered as white Georgians increasingly ignored the policies of the Freedmen's Bureau. He was replaced on January 14, 1867, and remained in Georgia as a planter for a year before returning to Maine, where he was successful in the granite business. He died in Rockland on April 30, 1895. Cimbala, "The 'Talisman Power,' " *Civil War History.*

James W. Geary

TILTON, Theodore, *abolitonist, editor,* was born in New York City on October 2, 1835. He wrote for the *New York Tribune,* the *New York Observer,* and the *Independent,* all publications deeply involved in evangelical religion, abolitionism, and other reform movements. He also developed close associations with George B. Cheever (*q.v.*), Lewis Tappan (*q.v.*), and other powerful leaders in New England's crusade against slavery.

The *Independent*, which Tilton helped to found in 1848, became a major voice for emancipation during the Civil War, demanding uncompensated, unqualified freedom for the slaves and an aggressive military strategy against the South. Under his editorship, the *Independent* attracted an impressive list of contributors and supporters, and served as a nationally circulating vehicle for the opinions of such abolitionist luminaries as Wendell Phillips (*q.v.*), William Lloyd Garrison (*q.v.*), Elizabeth Cady Stanton (*q.v.*), and Gerrit Smith (*q.v.*). Tilton remained a consistent yet critical supporter of Abraham Lincoln's (*q.v.*) administration, and allied the *Independent* politically with the Republican party's Radical wing.

As the readership and influence of Tilton's newspaper grew, so did his ability to exercise informal political power. His residence in Brooklyn became well known during the Civil War as a gathering place for prominent antislavery politicians such as Henry Wilson (*q.v.*) and Charles Sumner (*q.v.*). At war's end, he began a new career as a popular lyceum lecturer, espousing Radical Reconstruction, and was widely considered one of the most powerful leaders of the Republican party. The famous scandal that began in 1872—Tilton's wife Elizabeth's sexual liaison with Henry Ward Beecher (*q.v.*)—effectively ended his promising career. Elizabeth's confession of her relationship with Beecher (the exact nature of which still remains in doubt), and the contention, litigation, and divorce growing out of it, destroyed Tilton's reputation. He died in Paris on May 25, 1907. Waller, *Reverend Beecher and Mrs. Tilton.*

James Brewer Stewart

TOD, David, *governor,* was born on February 21, 1805, near Youngstown, Ohio. After attending public schools and Burton Academy, he read law, and was admitted to the bar in 1827. He became active in the Democratic party, and served for one term in the state Senate. In 1844 and 1846, Tod ran unsuccessfully for governor, and from 1847 to 1851 was minister to Brazil. In the 1850s, he turned to business affairs in Youngstown and became one of the founders of that city's iron industry; he also actively promoted railroad development in the state.

In 1861, Tod's staunch support of the Union cause led Ohio Republicans to nominate and elect him governor on a Union ticket; this tactic of merging with prowar Democrats was later emulated by Republicans elsewhere. Tod proved to be an energetic and decisive administrator. One of his foremost responsibilities was raising ever-increasing numbers of troops to meet the repeated calls from Washington, and he constantly badgered Secretary of War Edwin M. Stanton (*q.v.*), a fellow Ohioan, with appeals for assistance and suggestions on recruiting methods. As volunteering slowed in 1862, Tod had to resort to a militia draft, and by 1863 he was asking Stanton to institute a national draft. He blamed antiwar Democrats for discouraging enlistments, and in the summer of 1862 he sanctioned the military arrests of eleven Ohio civilians.

In June 1863, when resistance to the national draft broke out in Holmes county, Tod supported Federal authorities in the use of force to quell the disturbance. During the next month, he faced a more serious threat to the security of his state when Confederate raider John Hunt Morgan, in command of 3,000 cavalry, crossed the Ohio River into Indiana and then entered Ohio. By the time Morgan was apprehended, Tod had sent over 50,000 militia into the field, a number that many Ohioans deemed excessive. As the state elections of 1863 approached, he found his political support slipping away. He had alienated Democrats with his defense of political arrests, and many Republicans were displeased with his failure to support emancipation and his reluctance to recruit blacks to fill Ohio's quotas; they also criticized him for appointing too many Democrats to state offices. In addition, by opposing a railroad consolidation scheme, Tod turned advocates of the plan against him.

The state Democratic party planned to run Clement Vallandigham (q.v.), an outspoken peace proponent, for governor, and Republicans wanted a man who could unite all prowar factions in the state. Hence they rejected Tod and presented the nomination to John Brough (q.v.), another War Democrat. Tod served his state well during his two years in office. He raised over 100,000 men, more than enough to fill the state's quotas. He labored diligently to tend to the needs of Ohio's wounded soldiers, repelled border raids, reorganized the state militia, and upheld the Lincoln (q.v.) administration's prosecution of the war. He continued to support the Union party in Ohio, and in 1866 endorsed Congress's Reconstruction measures. He died in Youngstown on November 13, 1868. Abbott, *Ohio's War Governors*; Hesseltine, *Lincoln's War Governors*.

Richard H. Abbott

TORBERT, Alfred Thomas Archimedes, *general,* was born on July 1, 1833, in Georgetown, Delaware. He graduated from West Point in 1851, then served against the Indians in New Mexico and Florida, and against the Mormons in Utah (1857–1858). With the outbreak of the Civil War, he became colonel of the 1st New Jersey Volunteers, and saw action at Yorktown and the Seven Days. Torbert commanded the 1st Brigade, 1st Division, VI Corps from Second Bull Run through Gettysburg. He was wounded at Crampton's Gap. In April 1864 he was assigned to command the 1st Cavalry Division under Philip Sheridan (q.v.).

Torbert defeated Wade Hampton at Trevilian Station (June 21, 1864), and was named Sheridan's chief of cavalry. In that post he was noted for solid steadiness, leaving aggressive execution of his orders to his flamboyant subordinates, George Custer (q.v.) and Wesley Merritt (q.v.). This team enveloped and routed the Confederate left at the battle of Winchester. Torbert, however, failed to block the Southern retreat from Fisher's Hill. He avenged this with the victory at Tom's Brook. At Cedar Creek, Torbert's cavalry and George Getty's (q.v.) infantry were the only units that did not break, allowing Sheridan to arrive, rally his forces, and go on to win a decisive victory. Torbert's December 1864 raid into central Virginia to break up the railroads failed mainly due to bad weather.

Torbert ended his military career with promotion to brevet major general and entered the diplomatic service. He served as U.S. minister to El Salvador (1869), and consul general to Havana (1871) and Paris (1873). After resigning, he entered into a business venture in Mexico, but en route there, he drowned on August 29, 1880, when his ship was wrecked off the Florida coast. Sheridan, *Memoirs*; Starr, *Union Cavalry*, vol. 2.

Roy P. Stonesifer, Jr.

TOWER, Zealous Bates, *general,* was born on January 12, 1819, in Cohasset, Massachusetts. He graduated from West Point in 1841, first in his class. An engineer with General Winfield Scott's (*q.v.*) army in the Mexican War, he participated in all operations from Veracruz to Mexico City, and was wounded at Chapultepec. Tower was breveted a major in the Regular Army for gallant and meritorious service. Following the Mexican War, he worked as a coastal defense engineer in New England and later San Francisco. Early in 1861, he helped organize the defenses of Fort Pickens. Breveted lieutenant colonel in the Regular Army and commissioned brigadier general of Volunteers, he fought with John Pope's (*q.v.*) Army of Virginia at Cedar Mountain, Thoroughfare Gap, and Second Bull Run, where he was badly wounded.

Breveted colonel and then brigadier general in the Regular Army, Tower returned to duty as superintendent of West Point in 1864. His tour there lasted only two months; then he was sent to Nashville, Tennessee, to take charge of the defenses. His masterful job permitted General George H. Thomas (*q.v.*) to organize safely prior to his attack on General John B. Hood. Tower was breveted major general in both the Volunteers and Regular Army. From 1866 to his retirement in 1883, he was the Army's senior engineering officer. He retired to Cohasset, where he died on March 20, 1900. Hennessy, *Return to Bull Run*; Sword, *Embrace an Angry Wind.*

Robert H. Jones

TOWNSEND, Dwight, *congressman,* was born on September 26, 1826, in New York City. After education in the grammar school of Columbia College, he became active in the sugarcane business. He also joined the board of the Equitable Life Assurance Society, a post he retained throughout the war years. Townsend was elected as a Democrat to the 38th Congress, to fill the vacancy left by the resignation of Henry G. Stebbins (*q.v.*). After the war, he returned to his business activities. Townsend was elected to another term in the 42nd Congress, where he served on the Committee on Commerce. He died in New York City on October 29, 1899. Lanman, *Biographical Annals.*

Frank R. Levstik

TRACY, Henry Wells, *congressman,* was born in Ulster Township, Pennsylvania, on September 24, 1807. He entered Angelica Seminary in Allegany county New York, studied law in the office of Aaron Burr, and then returned to Bradford county in 1830, to join his brother in a prosperous merchandise firm. In the 1850s, he became active in the Republican party, and was a delegate to the Republican National Convention in 1860. He ran for the Pennsylvania lower house in 1861, and served for two terms. In 1862, Tracy was elected to Congress, where he served until his appointment as collector of the Port of Philadelphia in 1866. He retired from that position after a year and returned to private life. He died in Standing Stone, Pennsylvania, on April 11, 1886. Bradsby, *History of Bradford County.*

W. Wayne Smith

TRAIN, Charles Russell, *congressman,* was born on October 18, 1817, in Framingham, Massachusetts. He graduated from Brown University in 1837, studied law at Harvard College, and gained admission to the bar in 1841. He launched his political career in 1840 by making campaign speeches for the Whig party, subsequently held various local political offices in Framingham, and represented his hometown in the state legislature in 1847 and 1848. Train served twice as U.S. district attorney for northern Massachusetts, and was a delegate to the 1860 Republican National Convention. In 1857 and 1858, he was a member of the Governor's Council.

Train captured the 1858 Republican congressional nomination by defeating George S. Boutwell (*q.v.*), and was subsequently elected to the 36th Congress. During the Civil War, he served briefly as a volunteer aide on the staff of Brigadier General George H. Gordon (*q.v.*), and took part in the battle of Antietam. He resigned this position to resume the seat in Congress to which he had been reelected in 1860, but was not a candidate in 1862. In 1863, Train established a law practice in Boston, where he remained politically active. He died in Conway, New Hampshire, on July 28, 1885. *BDUSC*; Herndon, *Men of Progress.*

Dale Baum

TRIMBLE, Carey Allen, *congressman,* was born in Hillsboro, Ohio, on September 13, 1813. He graduated from the Pestalozzian School in Philadelphia, Stubbs's Classical School in Newport, Kentucky, Ohio University (1833), and the Cincinnati Medical College (1836). Trimble began to practice medicine in Chillicothe in 1840. He was elected as a Republican to the 36th Congress, and was reelected to the 37th Congress. He served on the Committee for Public Lands, where he opposed the Land Grant College Act. Trimble supported Abraham Lincoln's (*q.v.*) administration on most war policies, but joined a handful of other Republicans in voting against amendments to the Confiscation Bill. He was defeated in 1862, and returned to Chillicothe to resume his medical practice. Trimble died in Columbus on May 4, 1887. Curry, *Blueprint for Modern America.*

Thomas H. Smith

TROWBRIDGE, Rowland Ebenezer, *congressman,* was born on June 18, 1821, in Horseheads, Chemung county, New York. He moved with his parents in that year to Michigan Territory. Shortly before he graduated from Kenyon College in 1841, his eyes failed suddenly and he returned home, unable to pursue his plan to enter a profession. Upon learning that his affliction was permanent, Trowbridge decided to become a farmer, and in 1848 bought an eighty-acre farm in Barry county. He succeeded in his occupation, and within four years regained his eyesight. In 1851, he exchanged his farm for milling property in Oakland county, in the area in which he was reared.

In politics, Trowbridge was a Whig until 1854, when he became a Republican. He was a state senator from 1856 to 1860, and a member of the U.S. House of Representatives from 1861 to 1863 and from 1865 to 1869. In Congress, he supported vigorous prosecution of the war, Congressional Reconstruction, and the impeachment of Andrew Johnson (*q.v.*). Highly respected for his honesty and reliability, he devoted much time and effort to agricultural experimentation and improvement. In 1873, he took charge of the Zachariah Chandler (*q.v.*) farm near Lansing, Michigan, served for a time as president of the Central Michigan Agricultural Society, and was commissioner of the Bureau of Indian Affairs. Trowbridge died in Birmingham, Michigan, on April 20, 1881. Barnard, *American Biographical History; BDUSC.*

Frederick D. Williams

TRUMBULL, Lyman, *senator,* was born on October 12, 1813, in Colchester, Connecticut. He attended Bacon Academy, taught school, and was admitted to the bar in Georgia. In 1837, he moved to Belleville, Illinois, and became the law partner of John Reynolds. Trumbull, a Jacksonian Democrat, was elected to the Illinois House of Representatives in 1840, and as secretary of state in 1841. He was a justice of the Illinois Supreme Court from 1848 to 1853. Trumbull was elected to Congress as an Anti-Nebraska Democrat in 1854, but the legislature selected him for the U.S. Senate when Abraham Lincoln (*q.v.*) stepped aside to prevent the election of a Douglas Democrat.

Trumbull supported Lincoln for the Senate in 1858 and for the presidency in 1860. He was reelected to the Senate in the legislative session of 1861. Trumbull opposed making concessions to the South during the secession crisis, and favored strong measures to repress the rebellion. His relationship with Lincoln ebbed and flowed as he interpreted his constitutional scruples as chairman of the Judiciary Committee. Trumbull was a leader in the drive to end slavery through the 13th Amendment, and was a major force in enacting a Civil Rights Bill and in extending the Freedmen's Bureau Bill in 1866, which brought him into conflict with President Andrew Johnson (*q.v.*). Trumbull's opposition to Johnson was well received in Illinois, and contributed to his third election to the Senate on 1867, with opposition from John A. Logan (*q.v.*), John M. Palmer (*q.v.*), and Richard J. Oglesby (*q.v.*).

Trumbull's decision to move from Alton to Chicago, where he was supported by the powerful *Tribune* and balanced the two Senate seats between Chicago and downstate, also contributed to his reelection. When Trumbull chose to vote "not guilty" in the 1868 impeachment trial of President Johnson, he lost the support of much of the Republican party. He left the Republicans in 1872, and became an unsuccessful candidate for the presidential nomination of the Liberal Republican party. The Illinois Liberal Republican and Democratic parties supported his reelection to the Senate in 1873, but the Republican majority in the legislature chose Oglesby to take his place. Trumbull rejoined the Democratic party in 1876, and was its unsuccessful candidate for governor in 1880. He died in Chicago on June 24, 1896. Krug, *Lyman Trumbull*, Roske, *His Own Counsel.*

Mark A. Plummer

TRUTH, Sojourner, *abolitionist, women's rights activist,* was born about 1799 in Ulster County, New York. She was the daughter of slaves named James and Elizabeth, who belonged to Charles Hardenbergh. The details of her early life are sketchy, although it is known that her name was Isabella and that her first language was Dutch. She escaped to freedom in 1827, one year prior to the end of slavery in New York state. In 1829, she moved to New York City, where she experienced a religious conversion and became a mystic.

In 1843, "voices" told her to take the name of Sojourner Truth and preach the cause of abolition. She was a magnetic speaker, and quickly became a popular attraction at abolitionist gatherings throughout the East. Her fame spread, and in 1850 she traveled to the West, eventually going as far as Kansas. Her speaking engagements were often interrupted by Southern sympathizers, which sometimes resulted in mob violence.

Besides being an abolitionist, Truth was an ardent feminist. She often shared the dais at women's rights conventions. Her most famous speech, "Ain't I a Woman?," was made at the 1851 Women's Rights Convention in Akron, Ohio. During the Civil War, Truth solicited food and clothing for African American Volunteer regiments and frequently visited army camps in the North, dispensing gifts and comfort. She raised money to help the soldiers by lecturing, singing, and selling copies of her autobiography. In 1864, Abraham Lincoln (*q.v.*) received her at the White House.

The Freedmen's Relief Association appointed Truth "counselor to the freed people" at Freedmen's Village in Arlington Heights, Virginia. After the war, she was one of the few reformers who opposed the passage of the 15th Amendment, because the suffrage was extended to African American men only. She continued lecturing, pressing for the rights of women and African Americans. In 1875, Truth retired to Battle Creek, Michigan, where she died on November 26, 1883. Pauli, *Her Name Was Sojourner Truth*; Quarles, *Negro in the Civil War.*

Donna M. DeBlasio

TUBMAN, Harriet, *slave rescuer, Union spy,* was born in 1821, in Dorchester county, Maryland. She was the child of slaves named Benjamin Ross and Harriet

Greene; her birth name was Araminta. She later called herself Harriet, after her mother. In 1848, she married a free black, John Tubman. When her master died in 1849, Tubman feared she would be sold, so she escaped and made her way to Philadelphia. Not long after fleeing, she made plans to rescue other slaves. In 1850, she freed her sister and two children, the first of an estimated sixty to 300 slaves she rescued. On her more than nineteen trips into Maryland, she was never caught, nor did she ever lose one of her charges. She was so notorious that slaveholders offered a $40,000 reward for her capture.

When the Civil War broke out, Tubman went to Beaufort, South Carolina, where the Federals had recaptured several Sea Islands. There, she served as a spy and scout, making forays into Confederate territory and returning with valuable information and escaped slaves. Tubman led numerous raids that destroyed railroads and bridges, in preparation for the Union invasion of the South. She was able to move freely behind Southern lines and often received her information from slaves who overheard their masters talking strategy. Tubman also served as a nurse, using folk remedies to help injured soldiers. She believed in the Union's cause and convinced many slaves to desert their masters and join the Federal Army.

Tubman, who was not paid for her work, supported herself by selling baked goods, chickens, and eggs. After the war, she fought to secure compensation for her services to the Union. Although her application was supported by such prominent persons as William H. Seward (*q.v.*), it was rejected. It was not until 1897 that Tubman received a government pension of $20 per month. She had settled near Auburn, New York, in 1858, and died there on March 10, 1913.

Bradford, *Harriet Tubman*; Conrad, *Harriet Tubman*; Sterling, *Freedom Train*.

Donna M. DeBlasio

TURNER, John Wesley, *general*, was born on July 19, 1833, near Saratoga, New York. He graduated from West Point in 1855, served in the South and on the frontier as an artillery officer, then transferred to staff duty. By December 1861 he was chief commissary in General David Hunter's (*q.v.*) Department of Kansas. The following year Turner held the same position in the Departments of the South and of the Gulf, the latter under General Benjamin Butler (*q.v.*), whose patronage he thereafter enjoyed. Later he was artillery chief during the early phases of the siege of Charleston. Sent to Butler's Army of the James early in 1864, Turner, now a brigadier of Volunteers, commanded an XVIII Corps division during the Richmond–Petersburg operations. During the Crater offensive of July 30, he was diligent in support of the Army of the Potomac.

That fall, after recovering from a nearly fatal illness, Turner was Butler's chief of staff, then led the Independent Division, XXIV Corps. As a brevet major general of Volunteers, he served ably in the Appomattox campaign, winning the same rank in the Regulars. Turner was one of many energetic, capable commanders who received little publicity during the war. Equally proficient in artillery, infantry, and staff positions, he won praise from virtually every superior—many of whom reaped credit for successes he engineered. His soldiers recognized his worth and especially appreciated his coolness under fire. After the war Turner commanded at Richmond, and was depot commissary at St. Louis. After leaving the Army in 1871, he was a bank director, president of gas and mining companies, and street commissioner of St. Louis, where he died on April 8, 1899. Robertson, *Back Door to Richmond*; Wightman, *From Antietam to Fort Fisher*.

Edward G. Longacre

TURPIE, David, *congressman, senator*, was born on July 8, 1828, in Hamilton county, Ohio. After graduating from Kenyon College in 1848, and studying law, he moved to White county, Indiana. He won election as a Democrat to the state House of Representatives (1852–1853, 1858–1859). Governor Joseph Wright (*q.v.*) appointed Turpie judge of the Court of Commons Pleas (1854–1856); he later served as judge of the 12th Circuit Court (1856). In 1860, he was nominated for lieutenant governor on the Democratic ticket with Thomas A. Hendricks (*q.v.*).

After his defeat, Turpie, a moderate prowar Democrat, won election to the U.S. Senate to fill the vacancy caused by Jesse D. Bright's (*q.v.*) expulsion. He held this position from January 14 to March 3, 1863. The Democrats chose him as their candidate for lieutenant governor in July 1863, but he declined the nomination. Turpie was again in the legislature in 1875, and later served as a commissioner to revise the laws of Indiana (1878–1881). Appointed U.S. district attorney for Indiana in August 1886, he held the position until March 1887, when he returned to the U.S. Senate for two terms (March 1887–March 1899). Turpie died in Indianapolis on April 21, 1909. Shepherd, *Biographical Directory of the Indiana General Assembly*, vol. 1; Turpie, *Sketches of My Own Times*.

David G. Vanderstel

TUTTLE, James Madison, *general*, was born on September 24, 1832, in Summerfield, Ohio. While he was still a boy, the family moved to Iowa and began farming. Tuttle was educated locally and began a career in business and politics, holding several county offices. At the start of the Civil War, he raised and became captain of a company of the 2nd Iowa Volunteers, and on September 6, 1861, he was promoted to colonel. His regiment participated in the siege and capture of Fort Donelson, with Tuttle leading the assault. He suffered a serious wound during the attack, but was only briefly out of action. At Shiloh, he commanded a brigade in General William H.L. Wallace's (*q.v.*) 2nd Division. Because of the collapse of units on its flank, the division found itself surrounded. Wallace chose to fight his way out, but in the attack was mortally wounded. Tuttle assumed division command and, despite heavy casualties, led the unit to safety.

Tuttle was promoted to brigadier general on June 9, 1862, and during the Vicksburg campaign commanded the 3rd Division of General William T. Sherman's (*q.v.*) XV Corps. His division participated in the capture of Jackson, Mississippi, in May 1863. In the fall of 1863, Tuttle was the Democratic candidate for governor of Iowa. Following his defeat, he returned to active duty in Cairo, Illinois, but on June 14, 1864, he resigned to make a second bid for the governorship, also unsuccessful. He served in the state legislature and continued his interest in business, particularly Western mining. Tuttle died in Casa Grande, Arizona, on September 24, 1892. Bearss, *Vicksburg Campaign*, vols. 2, 3; Sword, *Shiloh*.

Carl L. Davis

TYLER, Daniel, *general*, was born January 7, 1799, in Brooklyn, Connecticut. He graduated from West Point in 1819, and became an authority on ordnance. In 1834, he left the service for private business, and during the next twenty-six years scaled the business ladder as a canal and railroad builder, iron manufacturer, and financial entrepreneur. In 1861, Tyler's prominence assured that he would receive a commission. He became colonel of the 1st Connecticut, and very soon thereafter accepted an appointment as brigadier general of Connecticut Volunteers. His rank in June 1861 dictated that he command one of Irvin McDowell's (*q.v.*) divisions, which he led in the First Bull Run campaign.

At Blackburn's Ford, on July 18, Tyler exceeded his orders, bringing on an engagement McDowell did not want and impressing the enemy with Federal strength and intentions. In the major battle three days later, Tyler was slow to go into action but fought well, though perhaps more with an eye to winning personal glory than fulfilling McDowell's battle plans. He joined in the general retreat, and mustered out of state service in August. In March 1862, however, he reentered the Army as a brigadier, fought in the West at Corinth, and, being too old for active service, held post commands and administrative assignments until he resigned on April 6, 1864.

Tyler moved to Alabama after the war, founding the town of Anniston, where he built a significant industrial and manufacturing center based on the rich local iron ore deposits. He entered railroading again, and died a wealthy man on November 30, 1882, in New York City. Davis, *Bull Run*; Mitchell, *Daniel Tyler*.

William C. Davis

TYLER, Erastus Barnard, *general*, was born on April 24, 1822, in Beaconsfield or West Bloomfield, New York. He moved with his parents to New Castle, and later to Ravenna, Ohio. Educated at Granville College (now Dennison University), he joined the American Fur Company, traveling extensively on hunting and buying trips in western Pennsylvania and Virginia, North Carolina, Tennessee, and Kentucky. A prewar brigadier general in the Ohio militia, Tyler recruited and organized Volunteer contingents soon after Fort Sumter. He was elected colonel of the 7th Ohio, and his knowledge of the mountainous regions of Virginia led to assignment as adviser to George B. McClellan (*q.v.*). He proved invaluable as an adviser on topography, but his combat record was spotty—his regiment was surprised and routed at Cross Lanes. William S. Rosecrans (*q.v.*), Tyler's immediate superior, blamed him for the disaster, and subsequent investigations mitigated the onus only slightly.

The next spring, Tyler was in command of a brigade in the Shenandoah Valley. He acquitted himself well enough at Kernstown and Port Republic, where he effectively contained Stonewall Jackson's overwhelming numbers for some six hours before retiring. Commissioned a brigadier general of Volunteers on May 14, 1862, he commanded a brigade of the V Corps, that was comprised largely of nine-month troops from Pennsylvania. The brigade was in a reserve role at Antietam, but saw heavy action at Fredericksburg and Chancellorsville before being mustered out at the expiration of service.

Tyler was reassigned to command Baltimore's northwestern defenses on the eve of Gettysburg. He was praised for his energy and efficiency, and he continued to occupy assignments involving protection of the Baltimore region throughout 1863 and 1864. In this capacity, he performed notable service as part of Lew Wallace's (*q.v.*) holding force against Jubal Early at the battle of Monocacy on July 19, 1864. Later, Tyler had a command in the Kanawha Valley, and in March 1865 was breveted major general.

Tyler, another of the prewar militia generals who fought the war at essentially brigade rank, proves difficult to assess. Something of a rough-hewn woodsman type at the outset, he was popular with the rank-and-file Buckeyes he recruited and commanded in the field. His early disgrace at Cross Lanes may have eclipsed a promising career. His subsequent combat performance proved adequate, though hardly brilliant, for he always projected the image of a "fighting general" at the head of his command in battle. More noteworthy, perhaps, Tyler was an ardent supporter of temperance, and succeeded by his example in suppressing the use of liquor among the men of his command. He died in Baltimore on January 9, 1891. Reid, *Ohio in the War*, vol. 1; Wallace, *Autobiography*, vol. 2.

                                                                                  B. Franklin Cooling

TYLER, Robert Ogden, *general,* was born in Hunter, New York, on December 22, 1831. He graduated from West Point in 1853, and drew an assignment to the 3rd Artillery. He campaigned against Indians in both Washington Territory and Minnesota; the opening of the Civil War found him at Fort Columbus, New York. He was in the expedition that tried to relieve Fort Sumter, helped secure the city of Baltimore, and served as a quartermaster until September 1861, when he became colonel of the 1st Connecticut Heavy Artillery. Tyler's artillery was effective at Gaines' Mill and in the repulse of the Confederate assaults on Malvern Hill. He lost only one gun in the retreat from the Chickahominy to the James, and in November he was appointed a brigadier general of Volunteers.

Tyler commanded the batteries that shelled Fredericksburg, and as commander of the Artillery Reserve for the Army of the Potomac, earned a large measure of the credit for repelling Pickett's charge at Gettysburg. In early 1864, Tyler's heavy artillery was converted to infantry, but he continued to command the brigade. At Harris's Farm, during the fighting around Spotsylvania, his troops threw back Richard Ewell's flanking force, and they took part in the bloody assault at Cold Harbor, where Tyler was badly wounded in the ankle. That ended his field service during the war, at the end of which he was breveted major general in both the Volunteer and Regular services.

Like many who spent most of the war in the artillery, Tyler never achieved recognition commensurate with his talents, which warranted more than the command of a combat brigade. His equal capacity in both artillery and infantry suggests that he would have shone amid the greater opportunities of the latter arm. In 1866, Tyler returned to the Quartermaster's Department as a lieutenant colonel. He died in Boston on December 1, 1874. Coddington, *Gettysburg Campaign*; Wainwright, *Diary of Battle*.

William Marvel

U

ULLMAN, Daniel, *general,* was born in Wilmington, Delaware, on April 18, 1810. After graduating from Yale in 1829, he studied law and opened a practice in New York City. The Whig candidate for state attorney general in 1851, he entered New York's gubernatorial race in 1854 as the candidate of the Know-Nothing party. After Fort Sumter, he was instrumental in raising the 78th New York Infantry, and became its colonel on April 28, 1862. Following garrison duty, his unit participated in the Second Bull Run campaign as part of General Christopher C. Augur's (*q.v.*) division. In the retreat from Cedar Mountain, Ullmann was captured and held in Libby Prison. Released on parole in October 1862, he visited Abraham Lincoln (*q.v.*), and allegedly persuaded the President to begin raising African American troops on a large scale.

Whether Ullmann was a crucial factor in Lincoln's decision to authorize the recruitment of African Americans remains open to conjecture, but he received the first commission to pursue this activity on January 13, 1863. He was also promoted to brigadier general of Volunteers on the same date. Until April 1863 Ullmann remained in New York City, where he enlisted support from such notable officials as Vice President Hannibal Hamlin (*q.v.*) and Secretary of War Edwin M. Stanton (*q.v.*). After he left New York City, Ullmann served in Louisiana under the command of General Nathaniel P. Banks (*q.v.*) until he was ordered to Cairo, Illinois, in February 1865. Throughout his service in raising African American regiments, Ullmann placed great emphasis on selecting the most qualified individuals to serve as officers in these units. His policy combined elements of altruism and pragmatism. He believed that only properly led units performed well in combat, thus enhancing the likelihood that the noble experiment of using black troops would prove successful. He simultaneously created opportunities for white soldiers to advance in rank, thus decreasing criticism of the use of African American soldiers in the Union Army.

Ullmann's insistence on such a high standard was vindicated at Port Hudson and in other battles. In March 1865 he was breveted a major general. After he left the Army in August 1865, he pursued various scientific and literary interests until his death in Nyack, New York, on September 20, 1892. Basso, "Nationalism, Nativism, and the Black Soldier"; Cornish, *Sable Arm.*

James W. Geary

UPSON, Charles, *congressman,* was born in Southington, Connecticut, on April 19, 1821. In 1844 he enrolled in the Yale Law School in New Haven, and in 1845 moved to Constantine, Michigan, where he taught school, read law, and was admitted to the bar in 1847. He was appointed assistant St. Joseph county clerk in 1847, and was elected county clerk in 1849, and county prosecuting attorney in 1852. In 1854, Upson was elected as a Whig to the state Senate and served one term. He moved to Coldwater, Michigan, in 1856 and formed a law partnership with Lieutenant Governor George A. Coe. In 1860, he was elected Michigan attorney general on the Republican ticket. Two years later, he was elected to the 38th Congress, and reelected in 1864 and 1866.

Upson served on the Committee of Elections and reviewed contested congressional elections, especially those in the border states. He fought unsuccessfully for a literal interpretation regarding the distribution of the $100,000 reward offered in the capture of Jefferson Davis. According to Upson, Colonel Benjamin D. Pritchard and the 4th Michigan Cavalry—Davis's captors and Upson's constituents—were entitled to the entire reward.

Upson was a circuit judge and served as a member of the Michigan Constitutional Convention. In 1876, he declined a position as commissioner of the Office of Indian Affairs. He served as Coldwater's mayor in 1877, and in 1880 was again elected to the state Senate. His unsuccessful bid for the Republican nomination to the Michigan Supreme Court in 1883 ended his political career. Upson died in Coldwater on September 5, 1885. Collin, *Twentieth Century History and Biographical Record of Branch County, Michigan; Michigan Biographies,* vol. 2.

Roger L. Rosentreter

UPTON, Emory, *general,* was born near Batavia, New York, on August 27, 1839. He graduated from West Point in 1861, joined the 4th Artillery, and was detailed to drill volunteers for the defense of Washington. Upton became General Daniel Tyler's (*q.v.*) aide in time for Bull Run, where he discovered substantiation for the disdain of amateur soldiers and politically appointed officers that West Point had taught him. Even so, Upton was to serve in only one more campaign—at Antietam—as a Regular. In late 1862, he petitioned for a Volunteer commission and was given command of the 121st New York Volunteers. He was twenty-three.

Despite his youth and the circumstances of his appointment, Upton proved himself a gallant and demanding combat commander, leading the 121st through the Chancellorsville, Gettysburg, and Wilderness campaigns. Increasingly critical of his superiors, he was convinced he could do as well as anyone else in command. He was ever vigilant for an opportunity to advance, and turned more than once to his political friends for preferment. As a brigadier with the VI Corps at Spotsylvania, Upton was tempted by the promise of promotion to assault the Bloody Angle. He led twelve regiments against the enemy fieldworks and momentarily succeeded in gaining the position, only to be forced back when flank supports failed. Despite this setback, Ulysses S. Grant (*q.v.*) persuaded President Abraham Lincoln (*q.v.*) to allow Upton's promotion. Upton finished the campaign at Cold Harbor.

Although he had been wounded on several occasions, Upton was not dangerously hurt until June 1864, when during the battle of Opequan, his leg was nearly shattered by a shell burst. Ordered by General Philip Sheridan (*q.v.*) to quit the field, Upton refused, and directed his men from a stretcher. For this action, he was given his second star at the age of twenty-six. After a long recuperation, he commanded a division of cavalry in James H. Wilson's (*q.v.*) corps for a final sweep through Alabama and Georgia. In his last action, Upton led a frontal assault against palisaded enemy works during the battle of Selma.

Following the war, Upton reverted to captain, married, and took up a new career, writing on military affairs. In his much-cited *Military Policy of the United States*, he poured out his accumulated scorn for citizen soldiers, not realizing the irony that through their efforts he had made good his ambition. In 1876, following the death of his young wife, Upton developed severe headaches. These continued to plague him until, while commanding the 4th Artillery at the Presidio in San Francisco, he killed himself on March 15, 1881. Ambrose, *Upton and the Army*; Michie, *Emory Upton*.

Roger J. Spiller

USHER, John Palmer, *Secretary of the Interior*, was born on January 9, 1816, in Brookfield, New York. He was admitted to the bar in 1839, and a year later moved to Terre Haute, Indiana, where he rode the circuit and argued cases with an Illinois attorney, Abraham Lincoln (*q.v.*). In 1850, he was elected to the Indiana legislature, and in 1856 made an unsuccessful bid for Congress. In 1861, Usher was named assistant Secretary of the Interior under a fellow Indiana Republican, Caleb Blood Smith (*q.v.*). Due to Smith's inability and indifference toward the position, Usher handled the daily affairs of the department.

In December 1862, Smith resigned and Usher was appointed as his successor. He devoted a great deal of time to overseeing the transcontinental railroad project, using his influence in an attempt to advance the fortunes of friends and associates. Usher received stock in the Union Pacific Railroad in return for his support of various financiers and investors. In the presidential election campaign of 1864, political confidants urged President Lincoln to reorganize his Cabinet, and Usher was forced to offer his resignation, which became effective on May 15, 1865.

Usher moved to Lawrence, Kansas, where he became chief counsel for the Union Pacific Railroad, a position he retained for the remainder of his life. He died in Philadelphia on April 13, 1889. Hendrick, *Lincoln's War Cabinet*; Richardson, *John Palmer Usher.*

David Dixon

V

VALLANDIGHAM, Clement Laird, *congressman,* was born on July 20, 1820, in New Lisbon, Ohio. He attended Jefferson College, taught school in Maryland, and studied law in a brother's office. He served his apprenticeship in township, county, and state politics, being elected to the state legislature in 1845 and 1847. In August 1847 he moved to Dayton, where he purchased and edited the *Western Empire*, revived the Democracy of Montgomery county, and built a law practice. Elected to Congress in 1856, he was reelected in 1858 and 1860. Vallandigham supported the Crittenden Compromise proposals, and after Fort Sumter continued to support compromise rather than coercion as the means to reunion. He was a gadfly during the three sessions of the 37th Congress, opposing arbitrary arrests, emancipation measures, the use of black troops, and military conscription.

Defeated for reelection in 1862 because the Republican-controlled state legislature redrew the boundary lines of his district, Vallandigham sought the Democratic gubernatorial nomination in 1863 against the wishes of the party hierarchy. By order of General Ambrose E. Burnside (*q.v.*), he was arrested at his home in Dayton on May 5, 1863, for violating General Orders No. 38, and was tried by a military commission convened in Cincinnati. The commission found him guilty and sentenced him to imprisonment, but President Abraham Lincoln (*q.v.*) changed the sentence to exile in the Confederacy.

In Wilmington, North Carolina, waiting to run the blockade, Vallandigham learned of his nomination as the Democratic gubernatorial candidate. On June 17, he boarded a blockade runner bound for Bermuda, then a mail steamer for Halifax and Montreal. His trek ended at Windsor, Canada West, where he campaigned in absentia. Defeated in the October 13 election by John Brough (*q.v.*), he remained in exile in Canada until June 15, 1864, when he made his way back to Dayton. Meanwhile, in *Ex Parte Vallandigham* (1864), the U.S. Supreme Court ruled that it could not "originate a writ of certiorari to review . . . the proceedings of a military commission." At the 1864 Democratic National Convention in Chicago, Vallandigham helped to write the "peace plank" into the party platform, and reluctantly accepted George B. McClellan (*q.v.*) as the nominee.

Throughout the Civil War, Vallandigham was the best-known advocate of peace and compromise. Although castigated as a "traitor" and "Copperhead," he was essentially a conservative (and a disciple of Edmund Burke) who opposed the changes the war brought to the country: emancipation, ascendancy of industrialism and New England, and the centralization of the national government. He regarded himself as a Western sectionalist. His role as a critic of the Lincoln administration provides a case study of dissent in wartime. After the war Vallandigham developed a successful law practice, but never gained the U.S. Senate seat he wanted as a vindication of his views and a reward for the summary treatment accorded him during the war. He died in Lebanon, Ohio, on June 17, 1871, the result of a self-inflicted, accidental revolver wound. Klement, *Limits of Dissent*; Vallandigham, *Life of Clement L. Vallandigham.*

Frank L. Klement

VAN CLEVE, Horatio Phillips, *general,* was born in Princeton, New Jersey, on November 23, 1809. He attended the College of New Jersey (now Princeton University), and graduated from West Point in 1831. As a 2nd lieutenant in the 5th Infantry, he served on the Wisconsin frontier until his resignation on September 11, 1836. Van Cleve subsequently farmed near Monroe and Ann Arbor, Michigan, taught school in Cincinnati, Ohio, and was a civil engineer. Appointed surveyor of public lands in Minnesota in 1856, he was farming there at the outbreak of the Civil War.

As colonel of the 2nd Minnesota Volunteers, Van Cleve campaigned in Kentucky in 1861–1862, including the fight at Mill Springs on January 19, 1862. Promoted to brigadier general of Volunteers on March 21, he commanded a brigade in the Army of the Ohio during the siege of Corinth, Mississippi. While commanding a division at Stones River, he was wounded in the foot during the Confederate attack on the Union left wing. His division disintegrated in the assault that breached the Federal line at Chickamauga on September 20, 1863. Van Cleve spent the remainder of the war in command of the garrison at Murfreesboro, Tennessee, until he was mustered out on August 24, 1865.

Van Cleve was typical of older West Point graduates who reentered the service at the beginning of the war. By dint of education and some practical experience, he forged new recruits into soldiers and effectively led them into battle. Still, at age fifty-four, he was the oldest division commander in the Army of the Cumberland, and his wound and an uncommonly brutal thrashing at Chickamauga compelled him to step aside in favor of younger, more aggressive officers. After the war, Van Cleve twice served as adjutant general of Minnesota (1866–1870, 1876–1882) and was postmaster at St. Anthony (1871–1873). He died in Minneapolis on April 24, 1891. Cozzens, *This Terrible Sound*; McDonough, *Stones River.*

Bruce J. Dinges

VAN HORN, Burt, *congressman,* was born on October 28, 1823, in Newfane, New York. He attended Hamilton Institution (now Colgate University) until ill health forced his withdrawal shortly before graduation. He became a successful farmer and was attracted to the Republican party's defense of free labor and subsidies for internal improvements. In 1857, he was elected to the state Assembly and served two terms. Van Horn was active in the presidential campaign of 1860, and, as a reward, local Republicans selected him to the 37th Congress. Two years later, he lost his seat when the state reapportioned his district. In 1864, however, he regained the seat for the 39th Congress, and was reelected to the 40th.

Van Horn, moderate to conservative, generally supported administration war measures and Republican legislation. At the same time, he pressed issues vital to his constituents. For example, as a member of the Committee on Roads and Canals, he prepared a bill authorizing a ship canal around Niagara Falls. During Reconstruction, Van Horn opposed President Andrew Johnson (*q.v.*) and shifted toward the Republican party's Radical wing before returning to the center. In 1868, he declined renomination, and retired to farming and a loan business. His last public office was his appointment by President Rutherford B. Hayes (*q.v.*) as an internal revenue collector in Rochester. He died in Lockport, New York, on April 1, 1896. Wiley, *Biographical and Portrait Cyclopaedia of Niagara County, New York.*

Jerome Mushkat

VAN VALKENBURGH, Robert Bruce, *congressman,* was born in Plattsburgh, New York, on September 4, 1821. After attending a local academy, he studied law, was admitted to the bar, and opened an office in Bath, New York. A state assemblyman in 1852, 1857, and 1858, he was elected as a Republican to the 37th and 38th Congresses. In addition, he commanded the recruiting depot at Elmira, New York, and raised the 107th New York Volunteer Infantry. While in command of the regiment at the battle of Antietam, Van Valkenburgh was wounded, and soon afterward relinquished his command. He spent the rest of the war in Congress, where he supported his party's measures. He was acting commissioner of Indian affairs in 1865, and for the next three years served as minister resident to Japan. In November 1869, Van Valkenburgh settled in Florida, where he was especially active in opposing Ulysses S. Grant's (*q.v.*) reelection efforts. In 1874, he was appointed an associate justice of the Florida

Supreme Court, and remained on the bench until his death at Suwanee Springs, Florida, on August 1, 1888. *BDUSC.*

Richard W. Brown, Jr.

VAN WINKLE, Peter Godwin, *senator,* was born in New York City on September 7, 1808. He studied law and began practice at Parkersburg, Virginia (now West Virginia) in the mid-1830s. During the 1840s and 1850s, Van Winkle served as mayor, recorder, and councilman of Parkersburg. Elected to the Virginia Constitutional Convention of 1850–1851, he vigorously advocated a more equitable distribution of representation between eastern and western counties on the basis of universal white male suffrage. An ardent Unionist, Van Winkle was a member of the Second Wheeling Convention, which created the Reorganized Government of Virginia on June 20, 1861. He served as a member of Governor Francis H. Pierpont's (*q.v.*) council until 1863, when he was elected to the Reorganized Government's House of Delegates. He also served in 1862 as a member of the convention that framed a constitution for the proposed state of West Virginia.

After the admission of West Virginia into the Union, Van Winkle, along with Waitman T. Willey (*q.v.*) was elected U.S. senator from West Virginia; he served one term, ending March 4, 1869. Van Winkle was one of only eight Republican senators who voted against President Andrew Johnson's (*q.v.*) conviction after the impeachment trial of 1868. As a result, he became a prime target for Archibald W. Campbell, editor of the influential *Wheeling Intelligencer,* and other leading West Virginia Radicals. In declining health, Van Winkle had no intention of running for reelection, although, in all probability, he would have been passed over had he chosen to do so. He died in Parkersburg on April 15, 1872. Ambler, *Makers of West Virginia*; Curry, *House Divided*; Moore, *Banner in the Hills.*

Richard Orr Curry

VAN WYCK, Charles Henry, *congressman, general,* was born in Poughkeepsie, New York, on May 10, 1824. After early schooling in Bloomingsburg, he graduated at the head of his class from Rutgers in 1843. He was admitted to the bar in 1847, and became district attorney of Sullivan county in 1850. As a member of the Barnburner wing of the Democratic party, he was attracted to the new Republican party because of its stand on the slavery question. Elected as a Republican to the 36th and 37th Congresses, Van Wyck recruited the 56th New York Volunteer Infantry in response to the firing on Fort Sumter, and commanded the unit throughout the war. He was in the Peninsula and South Carolina campaigns, and was promoted to brigadier general in September 1865.

After the war, Van Wyck was elected to the 40th and 41st Congresses. He contested his apparent defeat in the 1868 election, and was seated only in the last year of the term. He helped to investigate the New York Customhouse and contracts made by the War Department. The Liberal Republicans appealed to his reform tendencies, and he joined the revolt against President Ulysses S. Grant (*q.v.*) in 1872. In 1874, Van Wyck moved to Nebraska, where he continued his reform efforts as a member of the Nebraska Senate. Vigorous advocacy of tax relief and railroad regulation led to his election to the U.S. Senate in 1880. The conservatism of the Republican party drove him to the Populists, and in 1892 he was their candidate for governor. He died in Washington, D.C., on October 24, 1895. Parsons, *Populist Context*; Phisterer, *New York in the War of the Rebellion*, vols. 3, 5.

Richard W. Brown, Jr.

VANDEVER, William, *congressman, general,* was born on March 31, 1817, in Baltimore. Educated in the common schools, he moved to Rock Island, Illinois, in 1839 and worked as a surveyor in Illinois, Iowa, and Wisconsin. In 1846, he became editor of the *Rock Island Advertiser*, and campaigned for a railroad connection to Rock Island. Vandever moved to Dubuque, Iowa, in 1851, studied law, went into partnership with Ben M. Samuels, then became clerk of the Iowa Supreme Court in 1855. Active in Republican politics, he won election to Congress in 1858 and 1860.

On September 24, 1861, without resigning his seat, Vandever accepted appointment as colonel of the 9th Iowa Infantry. He fought at Pea Ridge, and won promotion to brigadier general on November 29, 1862. In 1863, Vandever saw action at Arkansas Post and at the siege of Vicksburg. He was a brigade commander throughout most of this period, during the Atlanta campaign of 1864, and in the Carolinas campaign in 1865.

Breveted major general of Volunteers on June 7, 1865, Vandever was mustered out on August 24. He practiced law in Dubuque for several years and hoped to win high political office once again. But he failed, possibly because in both military and civilian life he was less inclined to engage in self-promotion than were his competitors. In 1873 President Ulysses S. Grant (*q.v.*) appointed him U.S. Indian inspector. He served until 1877. Vandever moved to California in 1884, and served two more terms in Congress as a Republican (1887–1891). He died in Ventura, California, on July 23, 1893. Stiles, *Recollections and Sketches*; Stuart, *Iowa Colonels and Regiments.*

Hubert H. Wubben

VEATCH, James Clifford, *general,* was born on December 19, 1819, in the village of Elizabethtown, Indiana. He served as a lawyer and public official from 1840 until August 19, 1861, when he entered the Army as a colonel of the 25th Indiana Volunteers. After service in Missouri, Veatch was at Fort Donelson and commanded a brigade under Brigadier Stephen A. Hurlbut (*q.v.*) at Shiloh. Although the four regiments under his command sustained 630 casualties, Veatch fought well and was appointed brigadier general on April 28, 1862. He next saw action in the siege of Corinth and the occupation of Memphis. Afterward, he participated in the pursuit of Confederate Major General Earl Van Dorn's army after the October 1862 battle of Corinth.

Veatch was placed in charge of the 4th Division on January 24, 1863, despite the objections of Major General Oliver O. Howard (*q.v.*), who had little faith in him as a commander. He led the division during the Atlanta campaign, but went on sick leave on July 17, 1864, and did not return until September. Veatch fulfilled administrative duties in Memphis before taking command of the 1st Division of the Army of the Gulf on February 18, 1865. The division served in the Mobile campaign from March 26 to April 12, 1865; Veatch's duty later earned him a brevet to major general.

Veatch completed his service as the commander of the District of West Louisiana, mustered out in August 1865, and returned to a law practice in Rockport, Indiana. He won appointments as adjutant general of Indiana in 1869, and collector of internal revenue from 1870 to 1883. He died in Rockport on December 22, 1893. Castel, *Decision in the West*; Sword, *Shiloh*; Veatch, *James Clifford Veatch.*

Mitchell A. Yockelson

VERREE, John Paul, *congressman,* was born near Fox Chase Station, Pennsylvania, on March 9, 1817. As a young man he became involved in the manufacture of iron, but soon expanded this interest into the merchandising of edged tools, iron, and steel. He became active in Philadelphia politics in 1851, was elected in 1858 as a Republican to the 36th Congress, and was reelected to the 37th Congress in 1860. Verree's first and only major speech occurred during the first session of the 36th Congress, when he supported a proposed tariff bill, arguing that lack of protection had severely damaged the economic health not only of his district but also of the entire state of Pennsylvania.

On most issues, Verree voted with his party. In the 36th Congress, for example, he voted for William Pennington (*q.v.*) for Speaker; opposed Senator John J. Crittenden's (*q.v.*) compromise measures; and voted for a proposed 13th Amendment, which provided for the protection of slavery where it already existed. Verree also approved Crittenden's resolution that would restrict the purpose of the war to a reunification of the United States. Like most other congressional Republicans, Verree abandoned this posture, refusing to reaffirm Crittenden's resolution later in the Congress. Instead, he endorsed confiscation and conscription, which promoted the war effort and at the same time expanded the scope of the war.

At the conclusion of his second term, Verree withdrew from congressional politics and resumed his business career. He maintained some interest in local politics, however, and from 1875 to 1876 served as president of the Philadelphia Union League. Verree died in Philadelphia on June 27, 1889. *BDUSC.*

Philip J. Avillo, Jr.

VIBBARD, Chauncey, *congressman,* was born in Galway, New York, on November 11, 1811. After working as a clerk in New York City and Montgomery,

Alabama, he became the chief clerk of the recently formed Utica & Schenectady Railroad in 1836. By 1849, he was general superintendent of the railroad and a stockholder. In 1853, he helped Erastus Corning (*q.v.*) form the New York Central Railroad, with which he was associated until 1865.

Vibbard's political career was quite limited. A Democratic member of the 37th Congress, he voted against the use of black soldiers, but did not vote on the Pacific Railroad Act, the Homestead Act, or the abolition of slavery in Washington, D.C. He refused to run again in 1862, evidently deciding to support the Union by utilizing his talents as a director and superintendent of military railroads. He actively supported George B. McClellan's (*q.v.*) bid for the presidency in 1864.

Vibbard's importance to the period lies not in his political activities but in his railroad work. He was a pioneer in devising managerial techniques for controlling complex organizations and worked hard to increase the efficiency of railroad operations and the comfort of passengers. The consolidation of several small railroads into the New York Central presaged the wave of consolidation at the end of the century. Vibbard's efforts on the New York Central later helped to provide the country with a reliable transportation network that was the basis of the national economy which emerged in the Gilded Age. He died on June 5, 1891, in Macon, Georgia. Hungerford, *Men and Iron.*

Richard W. Brown, Jr.

VON STEINWEHR, Adolph Wilhelm August Freidrich, *general,* was born on September 25, 1822, in Blankenburg, Germany. Educated at the military academy in Brunswick, Germany, he served briefly as a lieutenant in the German Army. He resigned in 1847, and came to the United States to offer his services in the Mexican War. Although the United States refused to offer him a commission, he served with Alabama Volunteers. He met and married a woman from Alabama, then returned to Germany. In 1854, they migrated to the United States, and bought a farm near Wallingford, Connecticut.

When the Civil War began, Steinwehr raised and commanded the 29th New York Volunteers, a part of the reserve at the first battle of Bull Run. Appointed brigadier general of Volunteers in October 1861, he served under General John C. Frémont (*q.v.*). He next commanded the 2nd Division of the Army of Virginia under General John Pope (*q.v.*), and participated in the campaigns on the Rapidan and Rappahannock rivers in August 1862. He later fought at Chancellorsville, Gettysburg, and Chattanooga. Steinwehr resigned in July 1865. He published school geographies and maps, and taught for a time at Yale University. Steinwehr died in Buffalo, New York, on February 25, 1877. Furgurson, *Chancellorsville*; Hennessy, *Return to Bull Run.*

Robert H. Jones

VOORHEES, Daniel Wolsey, *congressman,* was born on September 26, 1827, in Butler county, Ohio, and moved with his family to Fountain county, Indiana, that same year. After graduating from Asbury College (later DePauw University) in 1849, he read law with Henry S. Lane (*q.v.*), and entered the law office of former Indiana Senator Edward A. Hannagan. Governor Joseph Wright (*q.v.*) appointed him prosecuting attorney for the Circuit Court (1853–1857). During his first congressional campaign, in 1856, Voorhees, a Jacksonian Democrat, faced Republican James Wilson in a series of debates over slavery, and supported Stephen A. Douglas's (*q.v.*) popular sovereignty position. After losing the election and moving to Terre Haute, he won appointment as U.S. district attorney for Indiana and unsuccessfully pleaded the case of John E. Cook, an accused follower of John Brown (*q.v.*) and brother-in-law of Governor Ashbel Willard.

A renowned orator, Voorhees was one of four Democratic congressmen elected from Indiana in 1860. Facing South Carolina's secession, he vowed never to "vote one dollar, one man, or one gun . . . to make war upon the South," although after the firing on Fort Sumter, he acknowledged the need to preserve the Union. Voorhees opposed emancipation and assailed Abraham Lincoln's (*q.v.*) administration for "despotism," causing Indiana's Union party to characterize him and fellow Hoosier Thomas A. Hendricks (*q.v.*) as traitors more dangerous than armed rebels. The Democrats regained control of Indiana in the fall 1862 elections, winning seven of eleven congressional races and both houses of the General Assembly.

Upon winning a second term, Voorhees became a symbol of Indiana Copperheadism, criticizing the Republicans for enacting economic policies beneficial to Northern industrial interests, resorting to military government, and promoting the 13th Amendment. An opponent of conscription, he ultimately urged compliance with the law until it had been repealed or nullified by the courts. Given his pro-Southern leanings, Voorhees was linked to Clement Vallandigham (*q.v.*) of Ohio and the Sons of Liberty (or Knights of the Golden Circle), who promoted a "Northwest Conspiracy." In retaliation, Voorhees's political enemies raided his Terre Haute office in August 1864, reportedly discovering incriminating Copperhead materials that they printed in the Union press. Voorhees denied participating in any Southern conspiracy that advocated the withdrawal of Midwestern states from the Union, and no evidence exists to prove his involvement.

To defeat Lincoln and to protect American civil liberties, Voorhees urged Democrats in 1864 to unite behind George B. McClellan (*q.v.*). During his successful congressional campaign that year, he stated that Lincoln's administration was a failure, and that peace would come only through a Democratic victory. After Lincoln's death, Voorhees endorsed President Andrew Johnson's (*q.v.*) Reconstruction policy, but lost his seat in the House to Henry D. Washburn. Voorhees later returned to serve in the House (March 1869–March 1873) as an opponent of stringent Reconstruction policies.

In 1876, Voorhees campaigned for James "Blue Jeans" Williams, the Democratic gubernatorial candidate, who defeated Republican Benjamin Harrison in the election. At the death of U.S. Senator and former Indiana Governor Oliver H.P. Morton (*q.v.*) in 1877, Governor Williams appointed Voorhees to fill the vacant seat. Voorhees held the position for twenty years, during which time he opposed Republican economic policies and directed the construction and development of the Library of Congress building. In 1897, he lost his party's nomination and returned to private life. Voorhees, a tall man who had won the sobriquet "Tall Sycamore of the Wabash," died in Washington, D.C., on April 10, 1897. Kenworthy, *Tall Sycamore of the Wabash*; Thornbrough, *Indiana in the Civil War Era;* Tredway, *Democratic Opposition to the Lincoln Administration in Indiana.*

David G. Vanderstel

W

WADE, Benjamin Franklin, *senator,* was born in Feeding Hills, Massachusetts, on October 27, 1800. In 1821, he moved to the Western Reserve of Ohio, worked for a time on the Erie Canal, and in 1825 entered the law office of Elisha Whittlesey, in Canfield. Admitted to the bar in 1828, he settled in Jefferson, where for several years he was in partnership with Joshua R. Giddings (*q.v.*). Wade, an active antislavery Whig, was a prosecuting attorney, state senator, and presiding judge of the 3rd Judicial Circuit. In 1850, he strongly denounced the Fugitive Slave Law, an act of defiance that secured his election to the U.S. Senate by a coalition of Whigs and Free Soilers. After the passage of the Kansas–Nebraska Act, he became a Republican and in 1856 was reelected.

Wade's declared willingness to meet Southerners in combat, and his advocacy of a homestead law and the rights of labor, contributed to his rising fame in the North, and in 1860 he was briefly considered for the presidential nomination. During the secession crisis, he was one of the most outspoken foes of compromise. Disappointed by the rout at Bull Run, which he had personally tried to halt, he concluded that inspired Republican leadership in the Army was necessary for victory. As chairman of the Joint Committee on the Conduct of the War, Wade repeatedly urged Abraham Lincoln (*q.v.*) to dismiss Democratic generals like George B. McClellan (*q.v.*) and advocated the transformation of the war into an antislavery crusade. He was one of the authors of the Wade–Davis Bill for the reconstruction of the South; when Lincoln vetoed it, he joined with Henry Winter Davis (*q.v.*) to publish a manifesto bitterly criticizing the President, but in the end supported the Republican ticket.

After the war, Wade's disappointment with Andrew Johnson (*q.v.*) caused him to become one of the President's most determined antagonists. He favored the President's ouster, and as president pro tem of the Senate, was next in the line of succession. But his colleagues' distrust of him, and his identification with women's suffrage, inflation, and other unconventional causes, contributed to the failure of the impeachment trial. Already defeated for reelection after the Democrats' capture of the Ohio legislature in 1867, Wade failed to win the coveted vice presidential nomination in 1868, and the following year returned to Jefferson, Ohio, to resume his law practice.

Bluff, fearless, and unyielding, Wade unrelentingly advocated emancipation, equal rights, and free land, greatly contributing to their success. It was due to Radicals like him that the Republican party for many years continued to maintain advanced positions and eventually enacted the Reconstruction Amendments. Although by no means free of personal bigotry, he nevertheless believed that reason rather than prejudice should determine voting habits, and pursued his goal of black suffrage even when it resulted in personal defeat. Although his careless language and impulsive actions sometimes lessened his effectiveness, Wade was nevertheless a formidable fighter for freedom. He died in Jefferson on March 2, 1878. Trefousse, *Benjamin Franklin Wade.*

Hans L. Trefousse

WADSWORTH, James Samuel, *general,* was born near Geneseo, New York, on October 30, 1807. He studied at Harvard, read law with Daniel Webster, then returned home to manage the family estate and become a leader in scientific farming. Originally a Democrat, antislavery sentiments led him to join the Free Soil and Republican parties. In early 1861, Wadsworth was a delegate to the Peace Convention in Washington. After declining a commission at the outbreak of the war, he served Irvin McDowell (*q.v.*) as a volunteer aide at First Bull Run. In August 1861 he was appointed a brigadier general and given a command in the Washington defenses. Convinced that the opposing forces were smaller than generally supposed, Wadsworth repeatedly urged General George B. McClellan (*q.v.*) to take the offensive during this period. Then, frustrated by the continued inactivity, he apparently presented his views to President Abraham Lincoln (*q.v.*), thereby increasing the pressure for a decisive campaign.

Ironically, it was Wadsworth who, while subsequently serving as military governor of Washington, protested to Secretary of War Edwin Stanton (*q.v.*) about draining the capital defenses to support the Peninsula campaign, thus initiating the recall of McDowell's corps. Losing hope of obtaining an active command, he ran on the Republican ticket for governor of New York in the fall of 1862, but was defeated. He immediately returned to the army and took over a division in the I Corps, Army of the Potomac. Although remaining in reserve at Chancellorsville, Wadsworth's command saw heavy action at Gettysburg, where both of his brigades—Solomon Meredith's (*q.v.*) and Lysander Cutler's (*q.v.*)—rushed forward to support John Buford's (*q.v.*) cavalry on July 1. Badly punished in the initial fighting, the division nonetheless participated in the subsequent phases of the battle, losing a total of 975 men.

In the reorganization of 1864, Wadsworth commanded a division in the V Corps. On May 6 of that year, he was shot while rallying his troops in the Wilderness, and died in Confederate hands two days later. Entering the Civil War at an advanced age and without military experience, Wadsworth reached the limits of his competence at the division level. Yet his contemporaries mourned him publicly and named a fort in his honor. Wadsworth was an authentic hero who deliberately risked his life for principle. Catton, *Stillness at Appomattox*; Pearson, *James S. Wadsworth*; Rhea, *Battle of the Wilderness*.

James L. Morrison, Jr.

WADSWORTH, William Henry, *congressman*, was born on July 4, 1821, in Maysville, Kentucky. In 1842, he graduated from Augusta College in Bracken county. He then read law, and was admitted to the bar in 1844. In 1853, he won a four-year term as a Whig member of the Kentucky Senate, and in 1860 canvassed the state on behalf of John Bell, the Constitutional Union candidate. In June 1861, Wadsworth was elected to Congress as a Unionist, winning reelection two years later. Also in the summer of 1861, he was active in violating Kentucky's official policy of neutrality by procuring and placing Federal weapons in the hands of the state's pro-Union citizens. He staunchly supported the unconditional restoration of the Union, but took a more conservative stand on issues connected with slavery and Reconstruction.

Although he eventually joined the Republicans, Wadsworth tried to moderate the policies espoused by the Radical wing of that party. After serving in his first term on the Committee on Naval Affairs, Wadsworth was assigned to the Public Lands and Library committees during his second. While Congress was adjourned, he visited the fighting fronts, serving as an aide to General William Nelson in the November 1861 skirmish at Ivy Mountain, Kentucky.

In an era of bitter partisanship, Wadsworth was greatly esteemed in his home state. His conservative Unionism was appropriate to the Kentucky Whig tradition of Henry Clay and John J. Crittenden (*q.v.*), and to Wadsworth's own political base in northern Kentucky. Declining renomination for a third term, Wadsworth returned to his law practice in Maysville, but in 1868 campaigned actively for Ulysses S. Grant (*q.v.*). He refused the new President's offer of the American ministry in Vienna, but accepted appointment as a commissioner to adjust certain claims in dispute with Mexico. From 1885 to 1887, Wadsworth again served in Congress. He died in Maysville on April 2, 1898. *Biographical Encyclopedia of Kentucky*; Levin, *Lawyers and Lawmakers of Kentucky*.

Richard G. Stone

WALKER, Amasa, *congressman*, was born on May 4, 1799, in Woodstock, Connecticut. He grew up in Brookfield, Massachusetts, where he attended the local schools and worked as a farm laborer, clerk, and teacher. In 1825, he established a boot and shoe company in Boston, which he ran until he retired in 1840 in order to pursue his interest in economic issues. Over the next thirty years, Walker published a number of articles and pamphlets, culminating in a widely read treatise on political economy, *The Science of Wealth*, and taught at Oberlin, Amherst, and Harvard. He was involved in social and political movements, promoting temperance, world peace, and the abolition of slavery. He left the Whig party to become a Democrat, then a Free Soiler, and finally a Republican.

Prior to the Civil War, Walker served four terms in the Massachusetts legislature. In 1862, he was elected as a Republican to fill a vacancy in the U.S. House of Representatives, serving in the third session of the 37th Congress. A believer in bank currency based on a 100 percent specie reserve, he gave reluctant support to the wartime issuance of greenbacks, and argued against proposals to increase the number in circulation. Walker was clearly not enamored of the bill to establish national banks, introduced by his friend and colleague Samuel Hooper (*q.v.*), but he agreed that these new banks were preferable to the old state banking systems, and urged enactment of a Federal tax that would drive state banknotes out of existence. Walker advocated a gradual contraction of the currency, championed the income tax, and opposed protective tariffs and eight-hour workday legislation. He died in North Brookfield, Massachusetts, on October 29, 1875. Dorfman, *Economic Mind in American Civilization*, vols. 2, 3; Munroe, *Amasa Walker.*

Richard H. Abbott

WALL, James Walter, *senator,* was born in Trenton, New Jersey, on May 26, 1820. He graduated from Princeton in 1838, qualified for the bar in 1841, moved to Burlington in 1847, and was elected mayor of that city in 1850. He refused the Democratic nomination for a seat in Congress in 1850; in 1856 and 1858 he was the party nominee, but lost both times. In 1860, Wall supported the Breckinridge ticket and took an extreme anticoercion stance during the secession crisis. His outspoken criticism of the Lincoln (*q.v.*) administration brought him his greatest fame and notoriety.

Wall's stinging denunciation of U.S. Postmaster General Montgomery Blair (*q.v.*), who had forced several antiwar newspapers to stop publishing, prompted Secretary of War Simon Cameron (*q.v.*) to have Wall arrested and confined to Fort Lafayette in New York Harbor. For two weeks, until his release on September 24, 1861, after taking an oath of allegiance to the United States, he was held without charges. Peace Democrats in New Jersey immediately made his arrest a major issue in state politics. Popular sympathy for the "martyred" Wall contributed to Democratic gains in the 1861 state elections, despite efforts by Republicans and War Democrats to organize a Union party.

When the Union military offensives of 1862 stalled, and Lincoln began to move toward emancipation, the New Jersey Democracy became incessant in its criticism. The more extreme wing of the party—of which Wall was a prominent leader—advocated an armistice, in the hope of securing Southern agreement to restore "the old Union as it was." The large Democratic majority in the New Jersey legislature, elected in 1862, had the power to fill a two-month interim Senate term resulting from the death of John R. Thomson (*q.v.*), and also to make a full six-year appointment for the term that began in March 1863. Wall eagerly sought the long term, but he was forced to accept the two-month term. He later said that the winner of the six-year term, wealthy manufacturer and former U.S. Senator William Wright (*q.v.*), secured the support of Democratic legislators by the blatant use of money.

Wall used his short Senate term, from January 21 to March 3, 1863, to condemn emancipation as a Union war aim, and to warn that Lincoln was becoming as arbitrary a dictator as Charles I. His direct political involvement thereafter diminished, though he remained active as a newspaper writer. He died in Elizabeth, New Jersey, on June 9, 1872. Knapp, *New Jersey Politics.*

Daniel W. Crofts

WALL, William, *congressman,* was born in Philadelphia on March 20, 1800. He became a rope manufacturer after working as a journeyman, and after moving to Kings county, Long Island, in 1822, he became involved in the political affairs of Williamsburg, serving as trustee, commissioner of highways, supervisor, member of the board of finance, and commissioner of waterworks. As a Whig, he was elected mayor of Williamsburg in 1853, and was a leader in the movement to consolidate Williamsburg with Brooklyn. Another interest was the Williamsburg Savings Bank (later the First National Bank), which he helped to found. Wall's major participation in national affairs came with his election as a Republican to the 37th Congress, where he supported Abraham Lincoln's (*q.v.*) administration. Declining to run for reelection in 1862, he returned to his private interests, especially the Williamsburg Savings Bank, and remained connected with the bank until his death in Brooklyn on April 20, 1872. Ostrander, *History of the City of Brooklyn.*

Richard W. Brown, Jr.

WALLACE, John Winfield, *congressman,* was born near Beaver Falls, Pennsylvania, on December 20, 1818. He graduated from Jefferson Medical College in 1846, and began the practice of medicine. In 1850, he moved to New Castle, where he entered politics. Wallace campaigned successfully as a Republican for the 37th Congress. In this first Civil War Congress, he played only a minor role, but on several occasions he spoke strongly in favor of the Union cause and of his personal area of expertise, medicine. Early in the first session, for example, Wallace submitted a resolution warning all foreign governments that their recognition of the Confederacy would be construed as a hostile act by the United States. When a tax bill under consideration incorporated a tax on medicine, he objected, arguing that medicine is far from a luxury. Shortly afterward, he argued convincingly that the reorganization of the Army's Medical Department should include a provision for appointing physicians as Volunteer officers as well as Regular officers.

Wallace placed himself in the vanguard of Radical Republican policy when he assured the House that in time of war, Congress had the right to confiscate the property of public enemies. Simultaneously, he encouraged Congress to consider Beaver Falls for the location of new armories and foundries necessary for the war effort. On other war-related issues, Wallace adhered to party policy. He supported legislation authorizing the Army to recruit blacks, voted in favor of confiscation, and opposed reaffirming John J. Crittenden's (*q.v.*) resolutions, which limited the objectives of the war to the restoration of the Union.

In addition to his congressional term, Wallace served during the Civil War as a military paymaster. He also was a delegate to several state and national party conventions, and on two occasions (1872, 1888) he was a presidential elector on the Republican ticket. In 1874, he was elected to the 44th Congress, which played a major role in the Compromise of 1877. Wallace died in New Castle on June 24, 1889. Curry, *Blueprint for Modern America*.

Philip J. Avillo, Jr.

WALLACE, Lewis, *general,* was born in Brookville, Indiana, on April 10, 1827. After working as a newspaper reporter, fighting in the Mexican War, and practicing law in Crawfordsville, Indiana, he was elected in 1856 to the state legislature as a Democrat. He was active in the militia, and continued to practice law until the start of the Civil War. Governor Oliver H.P. Morton (*q.v.*) made Wallace adjutant general of the state following the firing on Fort Sumter, and within a week he had 130 companies in camp, seventy more than the state quota.

An excellent disciplinarian and popular with his men, Wallace was promoted rapidly. After Fort Donelson, he rose to the rank of major general. At Shiloh, he lost his way, for reasons that will probably never be entirely clear, and was not engaged on the first day of that desperate battle. This left an enduring cloud over his name. He also incurred the wrath of General Henry W. Halleck (*q.v.*), who twice removed him from command. Abraham Lincoln (*q.v.*) restored him the first time, and Ulysses S. Grant (*q.v.*) the second. In the fall of 1862, Wallace was president of the commission that investigated General Don Carlos Buell's (*q.v.*) military operations. The following year, he strongly defended Cincinnati against the Confederates. Awarded a corps command at Baltimore, he held off a superior force under General Jubal A. Early at Monocacy (July 9, 1864), perhaps his greatest service as a Union general.

After the war, Wallace served on the court martial of Lincoln's assassins, and was president of the court martial that convicted Henry Wirz, commandant of Andersonville Prison. Returning to the practice of law at Crawfordsville, he was an unsuccessful Republican candidate for Congress in 1870. Later, he served as governor of New Mexico and minister to Turkey. Wallace's strong interests were art, music, and literature. He is best remembered for *Ben Hur: A Tale of the Christ*, written while he was living in the governor's palace in Santa Fe. He died in Crawfordsville on February 15, 1905. McDonough, *Shiloh*; McKee, *"Ben Hur" Wallace.*

James Lee McDonough

WALLACE, William Harvey Lamb, *general*, was born on July 8, 1821, in Urbana, Ohio. In 1833, his father moved the family to Illinois, first to La Salle, and then to Mt. Morris, so that his children might attend the Rock River Seminary there. Following graduation from this institution, Wallace studied law and was an apprentice with the Springfield, Illinois, firm of Logan and Lincoln. On his way to the state capital to begin his job, he become acquainted with a prominent Ottawa, Illinois, lawyer, T. Lyle Dickey, with whom he eventually opened a law partnership. At the beginning of the Mexican War, Dickey and Wallace entered military service with the 1st Illinois Volunteers, in which Wallace became a lieutenant.

When the Civil War began, Wallace was named colonel of the 11th Illinois Volunteers. He was recommissioned when the regiment was mustered in permanently, and for a time, commanded the 2nd and 3rd divisions at Cairo. In the Army of the Tennessee, he commanded a division and later a brigade at Forts Henry and Donelson. By the time Wallace was promoted to brigadier general in March 1862, the division was camped at Pittsburg Landing. Like Ulysses S. Grant (*q.v.*) and William T. Sherman (*q.v.*), he foresaw no immediate Confederate attack, and asked his wife to visit him in early April. She arrived an hour after the Confederate attack had begun on April 6. Wallace had already moved his division from its rear position in support of Sherman's faltering division. In desperate fighting quite near the Hornets' Nest, his force was isolated, and Wallace was seriously wounded while attempting an escape. Recovered in the counterattack on the following day, he was brought to Pittsburg Landing, where he died on April 10, 1862, in the arms of his wife. Catton, *Grant Moves South*; Force, *From Fort Henry to Corinth.*

Victor Hicken

WALLACE, William Henson, *territorial delegate, territorial governor*, was born in Troy, Ohio, on July 19, 1811. He attended public schools, and became a lawyer in Indiana. In 1837, Wallace moved to Fairfield, Iowa, where he became a colonel of the state militia. He moved in 1853 to Washington Territory, where he immediately launched an unsuccessful campaign as a Whig candidate for territorial delegate. He was a captain of militia during the Indian war on Puget Sound in 1855–1856, but broke with Governor Isaac Stevens (*q.v.*) over his declaration of martial law. Wallace became one of the governor's leading opponents, served in the territorial legislature, and embraced the new Republican party, which was organized less in response to national issues than as a vehicle to oppose Stevens.

Wallace returned to Washington, D.C., before Abraham Lincoln's (*q.v.*) inauguration to advise him on appointments for Washington Territory, and in the process secured the governorship for himself. Upon his return, he found that the party had nominated him for delegate to Congress. He won easily against the badly divided Democrats, and as territorial delegate (1861–1863), continued as a strong supporter of the President. The discovery of gold east of Lewiston in 1861–1862 created pressure to divide the huge Washington Territory. Wallace supported a proposal to run the eastern boundary of Washington north from Lewiston, and in 1863 Congress created Idaho Territory with that western boundary. Lincoln immediately named Wallace as its first governor, a position he held until elected territorial delegate, a post he filled from February 1864 until March 1865. Wallace was not renominated, and returned to Steilacoom, Washington, where he practiced law until his death there on February 7, 1879. Limbaugh, *Rocky Mountain Carpetbaggers*; Peterson, *Idaho.*

Kent D. Richards

WALTON, Charles Wesley, *congressman,* was born on December 9, 1819, in Mexico, Maine. After reading law, he was admitted to the bar in 1841, and soon had a thriving practice in Mexico and later in Dixfield. From 1847 to 1851, he served as Oxford county attorney. Moving to Auburn in 1855, he held the Androscoggin county attorneyship from 1857 to 1860 and built up a large private practice. In 1860 Walton, a Republican, won a seat in Congress, where he supported its constitutional power to make paper currency legal tender. He resigned his House seat on May 26, 1862, to become an associate justice of the Maine Supreme Judicial Court. There he remained for thirty-five years, playing a key role in the judicial life of the state. A brilliant lawyer with a keen, penetrating mind and a plainspoken manner, Walton was mentor to countless young attorneys. His significance lies not so much in the Civil War period as in a lifetime in the law. He died on January 24, 1900, in Deering, Maine. *BDUSC.*

H. Draper Hunt

WALTON, Eliakim Persons, *congressman,* was born in Montpelier, Vermont, on February 17, 1812. His father was a major general in the Vermont militia, prominent in Whig and Republican politics, and editor and proprietor of the *Vermont Watchman.* Walton took up the study of law, but never practiced. In 1833, he became a partner in his father's paper, became sole owner in 1853, and served as its editor/owner until 1868. Walton also edited Vermont's first legislative newspaper and, at the beginning of the Civil War, published a daily based on his extensive correspondence with the Vermont troops. He was active in Vermont Whig politics, and served in the state House of Representatives in 1853. He actively opposed the Kansas–Nebraska Act, and was a major architect of the Vermont Republican party.

In 1856, at the urging of Senator Solomon Foot (*q.v.*), Walton was elected to the U.S. House of Representatives; he served until 1863, when he declined renomination. During 1858, he urged the admission of Kansas as a free state, and in 1864 was a delegate to the Republican National Convention. In 1860 and 1870, he successfully marshaled opposition to the dropping of one of the state's U.S. representatives, a feat that is frequently cited as his greatest service to Vermont. Walton was a member of the Vermont Senate (1875–1879), and was active in the Vermont Historical Society, for which he edited and published several volumes. He died in Montpelier on December 9, 1890. Crockett, *Vermont*, vol. 3; Williams, *Biographical Encyclopedia of Vermont of the Nineteenth Century*.

D. Gregory Sanford

WARD, Elijah, *congressman*, was born in Sing Sing (now Ossining), New York, on September 16, 1816. He moved to New York City to pursue a business career, attended the law school at New York University, and was admitted to the bar in 1843. He practiced law until 1853, when he was appointed judge advocate general of New York, serving in that capacity until 1855. A lifelong Democrat and close associate of Horatio Seymour (*q.v.*), Ward represented New York City in the 35th Congress. Defeated for reelection, he won election to the 37th and 38th Congresses.

Ward voted against the 13th Amendment because he though it would prolong the war. Climate and soils, he argued, effectively controlled the spread of slavery, and the 13th Amendment would turn the North away from the true goal of the war: preserving the Union. He was, however, not willing to reinstitute slavery where it had been eliminated during the war. He opposed the Reconstruction Amendments because they violated states' rights, but voted in favor of the Pacific Railroad Act and the Homestead Act. Defeated for reelection in 1864, he was returned to the 44th Congress, again from New York City. He did not win reelection in 1876. Ward died in Roslyn, New York, on February 7, 1882. *BDUSC.*

Richard W. Brown, Jr.

WARREN, Gouverneur Kemble, *general*, was born on January 8, 1830, in Cold Spring, New York. He graduated from West Point in 1850, then ran river surveys, fought against the Sioux, mapped the Nebraska and Dakota territories, and was a mathematics instructor at West Point. As a brigade commander in 1862 with George B. McClellan's (*q.v.*) army on the Peninsula, he was wounded at Gaines' Mill, recuperating in time to see action at Second Bull Run, Antietam, Fredericksburg, and Chancellorsville. Promoted to major general of Volunteers on June 3, 1863, Warren was named chief engineer of the Army of the Potomac. In this capacity, on the second day of battle at Gettysburg, seeing the key Federal position of Little Round Top unoccupied, he rushed two brigades—on his own responsibility—to that crucial knob to repulse James Longstreet's attacks and thereby save the Union left wing, and perhaps the army itself.

In command of the V Corps under George G. Meade (*q.v.*) and Ulysses S. Grant (*q.v.*), Warren was heavily engaged in the 1864 Overland campaign. At Five Forks, on April 1, 1865, although arriving promptly to help save the Federal cavalry, Warren was unfairly relieved of his command by Philip Sheridan (*q.v.*), and was unable to gain full exoneration until 1879. He served out the war at Petersburg, Virginia, and was commander of the Department of the Mississippi.

Warren's chief claim to fame—and it is considerable—rests on his military sagacity and brilliance on July 2, 1863, when he saved the critical Little Round Top position for the Federals. His post-Appomattox military career was highlighted chiefly by survey mapping and engineering duties. He died in Newport, Rhode Island, on August 8, 1882. Coddington, *Gettysburg Campaign*; Sommers, *Richmond Redeemed*.

Warren W. Hassler, Jr.

WASHBURN, Cadwallader Colden, *general,* was born in Livermore, Maine, on April 22, 1818. After a brief education in local schools, he taught school in Iowa and Illinois, clerked in a store, surveyed, and read law. He began his law practice in Mineral Point, Wisconsin, in 1842. Soon he branched out into land agency, land speculation, and banking. An early Republican, Washburn won a seat in Congress in 1854, joining his brothers Elihu (*q.v.*), from Illinois (who chose to affix an "e" to his surname), and Israel (*q.v.*), from Maine. The brothers worked closely together, but whereas Elihu became a congressional powerhouse, Cadwallader served a relatively lackluster four terms. He vigorously opposed an amendment to the Constitution that would guarantee slavery permanently, but he strove to prevent war as a member of the 1861 Washington Peace Conference.

When the war came, Washburn rose rapidly in military rank, doubtless aided by his brother Elihu, a close friend of President Abraham Lincoln (*q.v.*) and General Ulysses S. Grant (*q.v.*). Commissioned colonel of the 2nd Wisconsin Cavalry on February 2, 1862, he became a brigadier general of Volunteers in July, and a major general in March 1863. Washburn served competently, if unspectacularly, in Missouri's Army of the Southwest, and finally commanded the Department of West Tennessee, with headquarters in Memphis. He commanded the abortive Yazoo Pass expedition, and later a three-division detachment of the XVI Corps in the siege and capture of Vicksburg.

Returning to Wisconsin in 1865, Washburn won a seat in Congress (1867–1871) and was governor of Wisconsin (1871–1873). But he was first and foremost a businessman. He helped pioneer new milling methods that revolutionized the American flour industry, and in 1877, cofounded Washburn, Crosby & Company (later General Mills) in Minneapolis. Pine lands, lumbering, and railroading were grist for Washburn's financial mill. He also won fame as a philanthropist. Washburn played a modest role in the Civil War itself, but the fact that he, a successful entrepreneur, served in the war sets him apart from such renowned noncombatants as J.P. Morgan, Andrew Carnegie, and John D. Rockefeller. Washburn died in Eureka Springs, Arkansas, on May 14, 1882. Hunt, *Israel, Elihu and Cadwallader Washburn.*

H. Draper Hunt

WASHBURN, Israel, Jr., *governor*, was born on June 6, 1813, in Livermore, Maine. He read law in the office of an uncle, Reuel Washburn, and passed the bar in 1834. Until he moved to Portland in 1863, Orono was his home, and there he held an assortment of local offices. He served as a Whig in the Maine Legislature in 1842–1843, lost a congressional bid in 1848, but won two years later and served in the U.S. House of Representatives until 1861. During part of that decade, brothers Elihu (*q.v.*), who chose to affix an ''e'' to his surname, and Cadwallader (*q.v.*) sat with him, representing Illinois and Wisconsin, respectively.

Few in the United States played a more important part in founding the Republican party than Israel Washburn. The day after the Kansas–Nebraska Act passed, he called together a group of antislavery congressmen who helped create the new antiextension party. Indeed, Washburn probably first coined the name ''Republican'' in a Bangor speech. Throughout his career, he fought the expansion of slavery, and also won a place in the House establishment, serving for a time as Ways and Means Committee chairman.

In 1860, Washburn ran for governor of Maine and won a thumping victory. Tireless, quietly efficient, deeply committed to the Union, he performed prodigious feats of troop raising and equipping. At the outset of the war, he hurried three Maine regiments to the front, rather than the one requested by President Lincoln (*q.v.*). He complained about General McClellan's (*q.v.*) dilatoriness, bemoaned the problems of raising three-year men as the war ground on, worried about an invasion from Canada, and urged speedy emancipation of the slaves and the enlistment of black troops. Reelected governor in 1861, he declined a third term and settled down in Portland in 1863 as collector of the port.

Washburn ran afoul of James G. Blaine (*q.v.*), and consequently failed in several U.S. Senate bids. Blaine was also responsible for Washburn's losing the collectorship in 1878. From March 1878 until his death, he served as president of the Rumford Falls & Buckfield Railroad. A man of parts, Washburn served as a trustee of Tufts from the college's founding in 1852 until his death in 1883, wrote historical works, and frequently had articles published in the *Universalist Quarterly*. The small, mild mannered Washburn deserves to rank with John Andrew (*q.v.*) of Massachusetts, Andrew Curtin (*q.v.*) of Pennsylvania, and Oliver H.P. Morton (*q.v.*) of Indiana as one of the great war governors. Maine's unexcelled war record owes much to his leadership. He died in Philadelphia on May 23, 1883. Hesseltine, *Lincoln's War Governors*; Hunt, *Hannibal Hamlin*; Hunt, *Israel, Elihu and Cadwallader Washburn*.

H. Draper Hunt

WASHBURN, William Barrett, *congressman*, was born in Winchendon, Massachusetts, on January 31, 1820. He attended Westminster, Hancock, and Lawrence academies, and graduated from Yale College in 1844. He became a businessman in Franklin county, Massachusetts, which he represented as a Whig in the state legislature (1850–1855). Washburn, who joined the Republican party in 1856, was elected to the 38th Congress in 1862 and to the four succeeding Congresses. In January 1872 he resigned his seat to be inaugurated governor. He resigned this office during his third term, having been chosen to fill the vacancy in the U.S. Senate created by the death of Charles Sumner (*q.v.*).

Washburn served in the Senate from April 17, 1874, to March 3, 1875, when he withdrew from public affairs. Much of his political success may be attributed to fortuitous circumstances stemming from intraparty factionalism. As a moderate Republican, he demonstrated considerable political acumen by skillfully navigating among the various postwar factions. His rise to the governorship marked the end of the domination of Massachusetts politics by the Sumner wing of the Republican party. He died in Springfield, Massachusetts, on October 5, 1887. BDUSC.

Dale Baum

WASHBURNE, Elihu Benjamin, *congressman*, was born on September 23, 1816, in Livermore, Maine. He attended Kent Hill Seminary, studied at Cambridge Law School, and was admitted to the Massachusetts bar in 1840. He moved to Galena, Illinois, in 1840 and began a successful practice. In 1844 and 1852, he was a delegate to the Whig National Convention. In 1848, Washburne ran unsuccessfully for Congress but was victorious in 1852. He served for nine consecutive terms as a Whig and (after 1856) as a Republican. He had two brothers, who also served in Congress in the prewar era: Israel (*q.v.*), who represented Maine, and Cadwallader Washburn (*q.v.*), who represented Wisconsin. (Of the three brothers, only Elihu affixed the final ''e'' to his surname.)

Much of Washburne's influence in Congress stemmed from his friendship with Abraham Lincoln (*q.v.*) and his seniority. When President-elect Lincoln secretly slipped into Washington, it was Washburne who was chosen to meet him. He chaired the House Committee on Commerce and the Appropriations Committee. After the war, he was a member of the powerful Joint Committee on Reconstruction. He used much of his influence as the patron of fellow townsman Ulysses S. Grant (*q.v.*).

Washburne was largely responsible for Grant's promotion to brigadier general after his Missouri campaigns, to major general after Fort Donelson, and after Chattanooga to the revived rank of lieutenant general. He also saw to the promotion of others from Galena, including John A. Rawlins (*q.v.*). He supported Grant for President in 1868, and Grant returned the favor by appointing Washburne Secretary of State and, after a few days, minister to France. Washburne served through the hazardous period of the French Commune and until 1877, when he returned to Illinois. In 1880, he was an aspirant for the Republican presidential nomination, which brought him into conflict with Grant. In retirement, Washburne was elected president of the Chicago Historical Society. He died in Chicago on October 22, 1887. Hunt, *Israel, Elihu and Cadwallader Washburn.*

Mark A. Plummer

WAUD, Alfred Rudolf, *artist,* was born in London on October 2, 1828. He studied art and worked as a scene painter in theaters before coming to the United States in 1850. By 1860, he was working as an illustrator for the *New York Illustrated News.* In the spring of 1861, the *News* sent him to Washington, and in July he rode into Virginia on the darkroom wagon of Mathew Brady (*q.v.*), to witness the first battle at Bull Run. Waud joined the staff of *Harper's Weekly* late that year. Assigned to cover the Army of the Potomac, he was present at every major battle from the Peninsula campaign to the siege of Petersburg. His drawings, more than 200 of which *Harper's* reproduced during the war, satisfied the American public's demand for realism and drama, and the accuracy of his work and his daring under fire won the admiration of the Union troops whose life he shared.

Unlike Winslow Homer (*q.v.*), who made only a few trips to the front before returning to his New York studio to work up his illustrations for *Harper's,* Waud did all his drawings in the field and inscribed detailed instructions to the engravers in their margins. In his secondary role as a correspondent for *Harper's,* Waud wrote colorful and entertaining accounts of the battles, the life in camp, and the vicissitudes of the "special artist." His strongly pro-Union sentiments are revealed in his descriptions of the Confederate forces as the "horde," "rabble," and "devilish grey coats."

After the war, *Harper's* sent Waud and another artist–correspondent, Theodore Davis (*q.v.*), into the South to record and report on the progress of Reconstruction. He remained with *Harper's* until 1870, then joined the short-lived *Every Saturday,* for which he covered the great Chicago fire in 1871. The next year he was back in the South, making drawings for the two-volume *Picturesque America* (1872–1874), edited by William Cullen Bryant (*q.v.*). In the 1880s, Waud contributed drawings for *Battles and Leaders of the Civil War* and the memoirs of George B. McClellan (*q.v.*). He was touring Southern battlefields to prepare a new series of Civil War drawings when he died in Marietta, Georgia, on April 6, 1891. Ray, *Alfred R. Waud.*

Ben Bassham

WAYNE, James Moore, *Supreme Court justice,* was born in 1790 in Savannah, Georgia. He graduated from the College of New Jersey (later Princeton), read law for a time in New Haven, Connecticut, then returned to Georgia for additional study and was admitted to the bar in 1811. During the War of 1812, he served as captain of a local militia unit. He was elected to the Georgia legislature in 1815, and mayor of Savannah two years later. Becoming a circuit judge in 1822, Wayne gained a measure of popularity in the state, and successfully ran for Congress in 1828. He was a loyal Jacksonian, which won him a Supreme Court appointment in 1835. Unlike other Southerners on the Court, Wayne favored the creative use of national power. He believed in exclusive Federal jurisdiction over interstate commerce, and defended corporations against state laws that impaired contractual obligations. On the slavery question, Wayne could find no justification for Federal intervention, and argued for a broad decision in the *Dred Scott* case that would finally settle the question of slavery in the territories.

The Civil War was perhaps more personally painful to Wayne than to any of his colleagues. His son joined the Confederate Army, but Wayne stayed at his post even though a Confederate court confiscated his Georgia property. His vote was critical in a 5–4 decision upholding the constitutionality of President Abraham Lincoln's (*q.v.*) blockade proclamation in the Prize Cases. He likewise refused to order the release of a soldier who challenged the army's reenlistment policies. Wayne often performed the duties of Chief Justice during Roger Taney's (*q.v.*) increasingly severe and frequent illnesses. He followed the Court's majority through the thicket of Reconstruction cases, but his health prevented him from taking a leading role. He died in Washington, D.C., on July 5, 1867. Lawrence, *James Moore Wayne*; Swisher, *The Taney Period.*

George C. Rable

WEBB, Alexander Stewart, *general*, was born on February 15, 1835, in New York City. He graduated from West Point in 1855, and following field and garrison duty, served as a mathematics professor at West Point until the outbreak of the Civil War. As an artillery lieutenant, he was engaged at Bull Run, and then was appointed to the staff of General William F. Barry (*q.v.*), chief of artillery of the Army of the Potomac. Webb served with distinction during the Peninsula campaign, was reassigned to the chief of staff of the V Corps, and served with this organization during the Maryland campaign. In January 1863, following staff duty at the camp of instruction in Washington, he returned to the staff of the V Corps.

On June 23, 1863, Webb was promoted to brigadier general and assigned to command a brigade in the II Corps. At Gettysburg, his command was severely engaged on July 2, and helped repulse Pickett's charge on July 3. Webb was so conspicuously brave that he was awarded the Medal of Honor in 1891. At Spotsylvania, on May 11, 1864, he was shot in the head, but recovered and returned to duty in January 1865 as chief of staff to General George G. Meade (*q.v.*). He held this important position until the close of the war.

Webb is probably best remembered for his gallant stand at the "angle" at Gettysburg, but some of his most important work was the staff work he performed for the Army of the Potomac in its 1865 campaign. In December 1870 Webb was discharged at his own request, to accept the position of president of the College of the City of New York. He held this post until his retirement in 1902, and died in Riverdale, New York, on February 12, 1911. Coddington, *Gettysburg Campaign*; Pfanz, *Gettysburg: The Second Day.*

D. Scott Hartwig

WEBB, James Watson, *editor, diplomat*, was born on February 2, 1802, in Claverack, New York. In 1819, he was commissioned in the U.S. Army, spent most of his service at Fort Dearborn and Detroit, and in 1827 resigned after a quarrel with his commanding officer. His father-in-law, a prominent New York City merchant, purchased him a share in the *New York Morning Courier*, which Webb joined as editor and owner. His search for political patronage to strengthen the *Courier*'s finances involved him in party politics. He supported Andrew Jackson until the President vetoed the bill to recharter the Bank of the United States. Joining Jackson's opponents, whom he helped to name "Whigs," he became a friend and supporter of William Henry Seward (*q.v.*).

Webb advocated a conservative Whiggery of territorial expansion, government aid to business enterprise, nativism, and hostility to social reform. He also denounced abolitionists and supporters of the Wilmot Proviso for endangering the Union, and advocated colonizing blacks outside the United States. Nevertheless, the controversy over slavery in Kansas, the collapse of the Whig party, the weakness of the Native American (Know-Nothing) party, and his personal ties to Seward caused him to join the Republicans and to campaign against allowing slavery in the territories. In 1860, Webb supported Seward for the Republican presidential nomination, and during the secession crisis supported Seward's efforts to compromise with the South.

After the firing on Fort Sumter, Webb called for massive action against the Confederacy. In 1861, facing serious financial difficulties, he sold the *Courier* to the *New York World*, and with Seward's help was appointed U.S. minister to Brazil. He vigorously protested the supplying of Confederate privateers in Brazilian ports, and promoted better commercial relations between the two nations. Unfortunately, he took no serious interest in the Brazilians, whom he regarded as his inferiors, and tried to bully them into accepting his views. Even less to his credit, Webb used his position to enrich himself, once going so far as to threaten to break diplomatic relations so Brazil would pay a questionable claim, two-thirds of which he received. He left his post in May 1869 and died in New York City on June 7, 1884. Crouthamel, *James Watson Webb*.

George McJimsey

WEBSTER, Edwin Hanson, *congressman*, was born in Harford county, Maryland, on March 31, 1829. He graduated from Dickinson College in 1847, and in 1851 was admitted to the bar. His first effort as a Whig candidate for public office in 1851 failed, but four years later, as an American, he was elected to the Maryland Senate and became president of that body. He served in the U.S. House from 1859 to 1865. In the sectional crisis, Webster supported the Union. He endorsed Governor Thomas Hicks's (*q.v.*) refusal to call the state legislature into special session, and in the House he favored the Crittenden Compromise proposals. Initially a Conditional Unionist who opposed the introduction of the slavery issue, by 1863 he sharply changed his position and joined the ranks of the Unconditional Unionists.

Webster organized the 7th Maryland Volunteers in 1862, and served as its colonel when Congress was not in session, until he resigned his commission in December 1863. Following his reelection for a fourth term, Webster resigned in August 1865 to accept an appointment by President Andrew Johnson (*q.v.*) as collector of the Port of Baltimore, where, much to the chagrin of the Radicals, he shifted Federal patronage in favor of the conservatives. After retiring from office in 1869, he returned to his law practice, until he was again appointed to the collectorship in 1882 by President Chester A. Arthur. He died in Bel Air, Maryland, on April 24, 1893. Clark, *Politics in Maryland During the Civil War*; Wagandt, *Mighty Revolution.*

Richard R. Duncan

WEED, Thurlow, *editor, special diplomatic agent,* was born on November 15, 1797, in Cairo, New York. He began his newspaper career with little formal education, and became publisher of the *Rochester* (New York) *Telegraph* (1825–1826) and of the Albany *Evening Journal* (1830–1863). The *Evening Journal* took a prominent lead in the formation of both the Whig and the Republican parties, and was opposed to both the Jackson administration and nullification. Weed was active in the nomination of William Henry Harrison in 1836 and in 1840, of Henry Clay in 1844, of Winfield Scott (*q.v.*) in 1852, and of John C. Frémont (*q.v.*) in 1856.

With the collapse of the Whig party, Weed supported the Republicans in the election of 1856, and managed William H. Seward's (*q.v.*) unsuccessful bid for the Republican nomination in 1860. He supported Abraham Lincoln's (*q.v.*) election in 1860 and again in 1864. Weed was consulted by Lincoln during the 1860 campaign and afterward, and had considerable influence on appointments. His efforts on behalf of the Union included securing recruits and supplies, and confidential errands for the government at home and diplomatic efforts in Europe. Weed was in Washington when the Union Army moved toward Bull Run in July 1861, and witnessed the rout of Federal forces. In the winter of 1861–1862, Seward sent Weed as a special agent to England to conciliate public opinion. He joined Archbishop John Hughes (*q.v.*) and other agents as a propagandist for the North, to counteract the activities of Southern diplomats in Europe. This was his most important Civil War mission. In France, he joined with American Minister William Dayton (*q.v.*) to conciliate public opinion there following the *Trent* affair. When he left England for the United States, Charles Francis Adams (*q.v.*) spoke well of him.

Upon his return, Weed continued to express his views through the editorial columns of the *Journal* until 1863. Even after leaving the paper, he addressed issues in his letters to the press. His influence declined after the 1864 election, and his support of Andrew Johnson's (*q.v.*) Reconstruction policies diminished his political leadership greatly. By the mid-1860s, Weed had become very wealthy, some of this wealth earned in questionable ways. The largest part of his fortune, which amounted to approximately $1 million at his death, was in his hands at the end of the war. Weed died in New York City on November 22, 1882. Van Deusen, *Thurlow Weed.*

Ronald D. Rietveld

WEITZEL, Godfrey, *general,* was born on November 1, 1835, in Cincinnati, Ohio. He graduated from West Point in 1855, was commissioned in the Corps of Engineers, and served four years in the construction and repair of fortifications guarding the approaches to New Orleans. After this assignment, Weitzel returned to West Point, where he taught engineering for two years.

Weitzel worked as an engineer in the defenses of Washington, D.C., until February 1862, then was sent to New Orleans as the chief engineer under Major General Benjamin F. Butler (*q.v.*). He served as mayor of the city for a brief time after its capture, then was commissioned as brigadier general of Volunteers on August 29, 1862. Later he commanded a division under Nathaniel P. Banks (*q.v.*) in the siege of Port Hudson. Weitzel led the 1st Division in a failed assault on Sabine Pass, Texas, in September 1863, and the following spring returned to the East to become chief engineer of Butler's Army of the James in operations around Petersburg.

On October 1, 1864, Weitzel took command of the XVIII Corps, and was promoted to major general in November as the commander of the all-black XXV Corps. In December, he again served under Butler, this time in a failed attack on Fort Fisher. The mistakes of this battle had no effect on Weitzel, who was given command of all the troops north of the Appomattox River during the final assault on Lee's army.

Weitzel remained in the Volunteer service until March 1866, when he reverted to his Regular rank of captain of engineers. Five months later, he was promoted to major, and held this rank for sixteen years. Weitzel spent the remainder of his career working on navigational projects in the Great Lakes region, and received a promotion to lieutenant colonel in the Regular Army on June 23, 1882. He died in Philadelphia on March 19, 1884. Hewitt, *Port Hudson*; Robertson, *Back Door to Richmond*; Sommers, *Richmond Redeemed.*

Mitchell A. Yockelson

WELD, Theodore Dwight, *abolitionist, propagandist,* was born on November 23, 1803, in Hampton, Connecticut. While a youth, his family moved to New York and settled near Utica. Educated in the local schools, he entered the Oneida Institute to begin studying for the ministry. During these years, he met Charles G. Finney, a noted revivalist, and immersed himself in the cause of temperance.

After 1830, however, Weld discovered his true calling and devoted himself to the antislavery cause. So intense were his convictions that in 1834 he was expelled from the Lane Seminary in Cincinnati for organizing nine days of debates that culminated in the position that slavery ought to be abolished immediately. Weld led almost forty students out of the seminary to serve as agents for the American Anti-Slavery Society in New York and the Midwest. Among Weld's converts were Joshua R. Giddings (*q.v.*) and Edwin M. Stanton (*q.v.*). In the early 1840s, he served as an adviser to the antislavery Whigs in Congress, and encouraged them to break with their party over the slavery issue. Among his numerous tracts was *American Slavery as It Is* (1839), which may have served as the basis for Harriet Beecher Stowe's (*q.v.*), *Uncle Tom's Cabin.*

Although deeply humanitarian and zealous in his pursuit of abolitionism, Weld lacked the flamboyance of others in the movement. Modest to a fault, he eschewed the limelight, preferring to prepare pamphlets rather than present speeches, especially after 1850. Nevertheless, Weld was to Western abolitionism what William Lloyd Garrison (*q.v.*) was to the antislavery movement in New England; he was primarily responsible for galvanizing public opinion and support for abolitionism in the developing regions of the nation. Weld died in Hyde Park, Massachusetts, on February 3, 1895. Abzug, *Passionate Liberator*; Thomas, *Theodore Weld.*

James W. Geary

WELLES, Gideon, *Secretary of the Navy,* was born on July 1, 1802, in Glastonbury, Connecticut. Wealthy and well educated, he planned to study law, but found his profession in September 1825 when he began contributing to the *Hartford Times.* In early 1826, he became its editor. An ardent Jacksonian, Welles served from 1827 to 1835 in the state legislature, where he fought against banks and the imprisonment of debtors, and backed a general incorporation law and the separation of church and state. When Andrew Jackson appointed Welles postmaster of Hartford in 1836, he resigned his editorship, but continued to contribute to newspapers and magazines.

Dismissed by a Whig administration in 1841, Welles was frustrated politically until 1846, just prior to the Mexican War, when James K. Polk made him chief of the Navy Department's Bureau of Provisions and Clothing. Welles remained in that position until 1849, making both useful acquaintances and valuable observations on how the department functioned during a war. After he ran unsuccessfully as Democratic candidate for the U.S. Senate in 1850, Welles's opposition to the Kansas–Nebraska Bill led him to the Republican party, which he helped to found in Connecticut. In 1856, he was its nominee for governor and was on the Republican National Committee.

Welles led his state's delegation at the 1860 Chicago convention that nominated Abraham Lincoln (*q.v.*). President Lincoln appointed Welles Secretary of the Navy, which he rapidly expanded after the Civil War started. Though he depended heavily upon his assistant secretary, Gustavus V. Fox (*q.v.*), who in effect was chief of naval operations, Welles made the important decisions, and the responsibilities, successes, and failures were his. He ordered the acquisition of the bases on the Confederacy's seacoast that made the blockade a crushing reality; the penetration of its rivers that severed and pierced the South; and the fruitless attacks on Charleston, South Carolina. Welles supported the development of new ironclad vessels (particularly John Ericsson's *Monitor*), of heavy naval guns, and of improved steam engines.

Honest, dependable, and methodical, Welles kept waste to a minimum. He was also a loyal and trustworthy political adviser to Lincoln and Andrew Johnson (*q.v.*). A shy, moderate man, he offered his conservative political, social, and economic opinions with unfailing courtesy. He opposed inflation, arbitrary arrests, and suppression of newspapers; accepted emancipation as a military necessity; maintained that the Southern states had never left the Union; and supported Lincoln's and Johnson's lenient Reconstruction proposals. Hostile to the Radical Republicans, he stood by Johnson, and by 1868 had returned to the Democratic party. In 1872, he supported the Liberal Republican movement, and in 1876 vigorously championed Samuel J. Tilden's claims to the presidency in the crisis following that disputed election.

Through his *Diary*, Welles has profoundly influenced Civil War history. He shrewdly judged people, keenly observed their actions, and preserved his sharp, frequently uncharitable, observations. A cautious man, Welles wrote primarily to justify and defend his course against potential attacks, but the result is far more than a self-serving apology. Welles's *Diary* is a vigorous, one-sided history of seven momentous years (1862–1869). It is at times gossipy and moralizing, petty and mean, yet it is also honest and perceptive, grand and sublime. He died in Hartford, Connecticut, on February 11, 1878. Niven, *Gideon Welles*; Welles, *Diary*.

Ari Hoogenboom

WENTWORTH, John, *editor*, was born in Sandwich, New Hampshire, on March 5, 1815. He graduated from Dartmouth in 1836, then moved successively to Michigan and Chicago, where he arrived with only thirty dollars in his pocket. On October 25, 1836, Wentworth ate his first meal at Mrs. Harriet Murphy's boardinghouse, and for the next forty-nine years celebrated the anniversary of his arrival in Chicago by taking dinner with her. Within a month, he was in charge of the editorial portion of the weekly *Chicago Democrat* and was studying law. He attended the law department at Harvard University in 1841, was admitted to the bar that same year, and began his practice in Chicago.

Meanwhile, Wentworth had purchased the *Chicago Democrat*, and in 1840 started the *Daily Democrat*, the leading Northwestern newspaper for years. He was elected to the 28th Congress in 1843 (where he was the youngest member of the House), and was reelected to the 29th, 30th, 31st, and 33rd Congresses. He had an interest in national internal improvements in spite of his party's policy against it. In 1848, the Illinois state legislature instructed the Illinois senators, Stephen A. Douglas (*q.v.*) and James Shields, to vote for the Wilmot Proviso. Only Wentworth and Edward D. Baker (*q.v.*) of the Illinois delegation did so in the House. Northern Illinois was divided on the Proviso, and discontent with the proslavery attitude in the northern districts resulted in Wentworth's reelection to the House; his opposition to the proslavery position of the platform was well known. He opposed the Kansas–Nebraska Bill in 1853–1854, and on May 29, 1856, he allied with other Conscience Democrats and threw in his lot with the new Republican party.

Wentworth was elected mayor of Chicago in 1857 on a Republican Fusion ticket, and announced that he would take no salary for the position. He served for one year and declined another term, but was elected again in 1860. Wentworth's great physical stature—300 pounds and a height of 6 feet, 6 inches—earned him the sobriquet "Long John." He supported Abraham Lincoln's (*q.v.*) candidacy for senator in 1858, and shortly after the election encouraged Illinois Republicans to present Lincoln's name to the Republican National Convention in 1860, first for President and next for Vice President.

Wentworth was elected to the 1861 convention that revised the Illinois state constitution. Meanwhile, he acquired lots and land in Chicago and Cook county, and gained the reputation of holding title to more real estate than any other man in the city of Chicago. By December 1863, Wentworth was listed at a Washington conference as uncommitted to Lincoln's reelection in 1864 and friendly to the candidacy of Salmon P. Chase (*q.v.*). In the 1864 congressional race, Wentworth, on the Union (Republican) ticket, defeated Cyrus H. McCormick, the Democratic candidate and noted inventor and manufacturer of the reaper. He later joined a revolt against Ulysses S. Grant's (*q.v.*) administration, and after serving in the 39th Congress, returned to Chicago to practice law. He died there on October 16, 1888. Fehrenbacher, *Chicago Giant.*

Ronald D. Rietveld

WESSELLS, Henry Walton, *general,* was born on February 20, 1809, at Litchfield, Connecticut. He graduated from West Point in 1833, and fought in the wars against the Indians and Mexico. He was made major of the 6th U.S. Infantry in June 1861, and colonel of the 8th Kansas that September. He was transferred east for the Peninsula campaign, and was promoted on April 25, 1862, to brigadier general of Volunteers. He was wounded at Seven Pines, then posted to Suffolk, Virginia, and later to North Carolina. While commanding the subdistrict of Albemarle, he was compelled to surrender the garrison of Plymouth, North Carolina, on April 20, 1864. Held prisoner for several months, he was among the officers who, the Union charged, had been sent to besieged Charleston to be placed under friendly fire. After exchange, he was assigned on November 11, 1864, to be commissary general of prisoners of war east of the Mississippi. After February 1, 1865, he was transferred to command the draft rendezvous at Hart's Island, New York. Following the war, he continued in the Regular Army, becoming lieutenant colonel of the 18th U.S. Infantry later in 1865. He was on duty against Indians in the West until 1871, when he retired. He died on January 12, 1889, in Dover, Delaware. Hesseltine, *Civil War Prisons.*

Frank L. Byrne

WEST, Joseph Rodman, *general,* was born on September 19, 1822, in New Orleans. In 1824, his family moved to Philadelphia. He attended the University of Pennsylvania (1836–1837), returned to New Orleans in 1841, and remained there for several years. With the outbreak of the Mexican War, he enlisted as a private in the Mounted Volunteers on July 17, 1846, and eight days later was promoted to captain and attached to the Maryland and District of Columbia Volunteers. West moved to California in 1849, where he became owner of the *San Francisco Price Current.*

Early in the Civil War, West joined a California regiment and was commissioned lieutenant colonel on August 5, 1861. On June 1, 1862, he was promoted to colonel and regimental command of the 1st California Volunteers, and to brigadier general on October 25, 1862. His regiment participated in campaigns in New Mexico and Arizona that returned the area to Union control. In early 1863, he led a successful campaign against bands of Apaches, and was placed in command of the District of Arizona. Afterward, West was given command of a division of General Nathaniel P. Banks's (*q.v.*) VII Corps, and participated in the disastrous combined operations of the Red River campaign into Louisiana in early 1864. He continued to participate in Western operations, and was placed in command of cavalry in the Department of the Gulf. He was promoted to major general upon being mustered out of service on January 4, 1866.

Following the war, West participated in Radical Republican politics as a customs official in New Orleans from 1867 to 1871, and as a U.S. senator from Louisiana from 1871 to 1877. He also served on the District of Columbia Commission during Chester Arthur's administration. West died in Washington, D.C., on October 31, 1898. Josephy, *Civil War in the American West*; Starr, *Union Cavalry*, vol. 3.

Carl L. Davis

WHALEY, Kellian Van Rensalear, *congressman,* was born on May 6, 1821, near Utica, New York. While a youth, he moved to Ohio, where he attended public school. In 1842, he settled in Ceredo, Virginia (now West Virginia), where he operated a lumber and timber business. At the outbreak of the Civil War, Whaley was elected as a Unionist Republican to the 37th Congress. He also joined the Union Army, commanding troops at the battle of Guyandotte. Taken prisoner by the Confederates, Whaley escaped and resumed his seat in Congress. He was reelected to the 38th and 39th Congresses as an Unconditional Unionist. A delegate to the 1864 Republican National Convention, he nominated Abraham Lincoln (*q.v.*) to a second term. At Lincoln's death, Whaley served on the national committee appointed to accompany the President's remains to Illinois. Following the war, he was collector of customs at Brazos de Santiago, Texas. Whaley returned to West Virginia and died in Point Pleasant on May 20, 1876. Atkinson, *Prominent Men of West Virginia*; Stutler, *West Virginia in the Civil War.*

Frank R. Levstik

WHEATON, Frank, *general,* was born in Providence, Rhode Island, on May 8, 1833. He left Brown University before graduating, to serve as a civil engineer on the Mexican border survey (the university awarded him a master's degree in 1865). His capable performance and bravery on the survey (1850–1855) were rewarded with a first lieutenancy in the 1st Cavalry in 1855. He next participated in the Cheyenne expedition and the Mormon War, and served as a staff officer with Edwin V. Sumner (*q.v.*), Persifor F. Smith, and William S. Harney.

In 1860, Wheaton left the Indian Territory for recruiting duty in Albany, New York. When the war began, he became captain in the 4th Cavalry, and lieutenant colonel (later colonel) of the 2nd Rhode Island. His able command of his regiment from First Bull Run through Sharpsburg earned him a star on November 29, 1862. Assigned to the 3rd Brigade, 3rd Division, VI Corps (later the 1st Brigade, 2nd Division), he fought well at Chancellorsville, Rappahannock Bridge, and the Wilderness. Often when a VI Corps divisional command fell vacant, Wheaton was chosen to fill it. He led the 3rd Division at Gettysburg, and the 2nd Division at Weldon Railroad and again at Fort Stevens. General David A. Russell's (*q.v.*) death, on September 19, 1864, brought Wheaton permanent command of the 1st Division and distinction at Fisher's Hill, Cedar Creek, Jones's Farm, and Sailor's Creek.

A citizen-soldier in that he was not educated for war, Wheaton possessed a natural aptitude that won him deserved prominence in both the Volunteer and Regular establishments. In a corps renowned for its fighting generals, he stood out as an inspiring, effective combat leader at regimental, brigade, and divisional levels. The best general from Rhode Island and one of the best non–West Point generals, he was, withal, among the North's most distinguished fighting commanders. After the war, Wheaton led the 1st Division, Provisional Corps. As lieutenant colonel, 39th Infantry and 21st Infantry, and colonel, 2nd Infantry, he saw much action in the Indian wars. Promoted to brigadier general in the Regular Army in 1892, he received a second star in 1897, just before retiring. Wheaton died in Washington, D.C., on June 18, 1903. Bartlett, *Memoirs of Rhode Island Officers*; Rhea, *Battle of the Wilderness*.

Richard J. Sommers

WHEELER, Ezra, *congressman*, was born on December 23, 1820, in Chenango county, New York. He graduated from Union College in 1842, and in 1849 he moved to Green Lake county, Wisconsin. A Democrat, he was a member of the state Assembly in 1853, and a judge of the Green Lake County Court from 1854 to 1862, when he was elected to a single term in the 38th Congress. Wheeler continued his law practice in Berlin, Wisconsin, until 1870, when he moved to Pueblo, Colorado, for reasons of health. There he was appointed registrar of the Public Land Office on June 27, 1871. He died in Pueblo on September 19, 1871. *Dictionary of Wisconsin Biography*.

Charles E. Twining

WHEELER, William Almon, *congressman*, was born in Malone, New York, on June 19, 1819. After graduating from Franklin Academy in Malone, he spent two years at the University of Vermont, turned to the law, and was admitted to the bar in 1845. He managed a local bank and, from 1853 to 1866, a railroad company. A staunch Whig, he served with distinction in both houses of the New York legislature. In 1855, Wheeler became a Republican. He was well respected throughout the state and was presiding officer of the state constitutional convention in 1867.

In a period of low public morality, Wheeler was conspicuous as an honest man. Roscoe Conkling (*q.v.*), a leader in the state Republican machine, offered him several opportunities that he declined. In most other ways he was not conspicuous. In the 37th Congress, he regularly supported the Lincoln (*q.v.*) administration, and for the rest of the war he recruited for the Army and generally encouraged support for the Union cause.

Elected to the 41st and the succeeding three Congresses, Wheeler had his greatest influence in committee work. He was well respected by his colleagues, but not known by the public at large. Although he was chairman of the Committee on Pacific Railroads, he was untouched by the scandals that ruined the reputations of so many of his colleagues. He won prominence, however, in settling a disputed election in Louisiana in 1874 with the "Wheeler adjustment." Honesty and party regularity aided in his selection as the vice presidential nominee in 1876, but the major reason for the nomination was that he geographically balanced the ticket with Rutherford B. Hayes (*q.v.*). After his term as Vice President, Wheeler returned to Malone, where he died on June 4, 1887. Fitch, *Encyclopedia of Biography of New York*, vol. 2.

Richard W. Brown, Jr.

WHIPPLE, Amiel Weeks, *general,* was born on October 15, 1816, in Greenwich, Massachusetts. He graduated from West Point in 1841, worked on coastal surveys along the Atlantic and the Gulf of Mexico, assisted in the survey of the boundary between Canada and New England in conjunction with the Webster–Ashburton Treaty, and helped fix the new United States border with Mexico before the Gadsden Purchase of 1853. Promoted to captain in 1855, he worked on lighthouses and on the opening of the Great Lakes to navigation until the outbreak of the Civil War.

Whipple acted as chief topographical engineer for Irvin McDowell (*q.v.*) during First Bull Run, and he remained with McDowell in that capacity afterward. Promoted to major in the engineers in September 1861, he received an appointment as brigadier general of Volunteers on April 16, 1862, commanding first a brigade and later a division within the defenses of Washington. In November 1862 Whipple was given a division in the III Corps, and at Fredericksburg he sent troops into battle for the first time. Of his two small brigades, one approached Marye's Heights late in the battle and suffered relatively light casualties. Whipple made his debut on a battlefield at Chancellorsville, where his division suffered more than a thousand casualties. A sharpshooter shot Whipple through the abdomen as he sat his horse near the front lines. He was evacuated to Washington, where he died of peritonitis on May 7, 1863. Furgurson, *Chancellorsville.*

William Marvel

WHITE, Albert Smith, *congressman,* was born in Blooming Grove, New York, on October 24, 1803. He graduated from Union College in 1822, studied law, and was admitted to the New York bar in 1825, the year that he moved to Indiana. He served as assistant clerk in the Indiana House of Representatives (1830) and as clerk (1831–1835). In 1836, White was elected to the U.S. House of Representatives as a Whig, and in 1839 he was elected to the Senate. Throughout his first period in Congress, he was conscientiously antislavery. Although he declined to run for reelection in 1844, the growing sectionalism kept his attention. He opposed the annexation of Texas for fear of extending slavery. In 1852, while the Senate was debating a bill for apportioning House membership, White gave an impassioned yet scholarly plea for "popular" rather than "party" representation, and advocated Federal power as opposed to states' rights.

In 1860, White was elected to the House of Representatives as a Republican. As chair of a committee to consider compensated emancipation, he recommended that $180 million be appropriated to compensate loyal slave owners, and that $20 million be used to aid in the colonization of freedmen. His plan to compensate loyal slave owners for voluntarily freeing their slaves had Abraham Lincoln's (*q.v.*) support, but not that of his constituents, and he lost his bid for reelection in 1862. In March 1863, on the day he left Congress, White was appointed to the commission to adjust claims of Minnesota and Dakota citizens that resulted from the Sioux raids of 1862. In January 1864, Lincoln appointed him judge of the U.S. District Court for Indiana. White died near Stockwell, Indiana, on September 4, 1864. Woollen, *Biographical and Historical Sketches of Early Indiana.*

Raymond L. Shoemaker

WHITE, Chilton Allen, *congressman,* was born in Georgetown, Ohio, on February 6, 1826. He was educated in the public schools, read law, and taught school. When the Mexican War began, he became the orderly sergeant of Company G, 1st Ohio Volunteers. After a year's service, White returned to Georgetown to finish his law studies, and was admitted to the Ohio bar in 1848. A Democrat, he served for two years as Brown county's prosecuting attorney. In 1859 and 1860, he was a member of the Ohio Senate.

White was elected to the 37th and 38th Congresses. He was critical of Abraham Lincoln's (*q.v.*) war policies, and wary of too much presidential power. He spoke against emancipation, and called for an end of the war. Unlike other Democrats, who during the debates on the national conscription bill focused on the charge that the $300 commutation fee would be unfair to workingmen, White was one of the few members of the opposition party to consistently question the appropriateness of the exemption fee on the basis of principle. He failed to be reelected to the 39th Congress in 1864. In 1873, he was a delegate to the Ohio Constitutional Convention in Georgetown. White died in Georgetown on December 7, 1900. *BDUSC*; Geary, *We Need Men.*

Thomas H. Smith

WHITE, Joseph Worthington, *congressman,* was born on October 2, 1822, in Cambridge, Ohio. He attended the public schools, worked in a dry goods store, then moved to Columbus, where he worked in the county clerk's office. In 1838, he returned to Cambridge and attended Cambridge Academy. The same year, he traveled back to Columbus, and clerked in the U.S. courts until 1842. Returning to Cambridge again, he taught school, studied law, and was admitted to the Ohio bar in 1844. In 1845, White was elected prosecuting attorney for Guernsey county as a Democrat, and won reelection in 1847. For a time he served on the Cambridge city council and was the city's mayor. White attended the 1860 Democratic National Convention in Charleston, South Carolina, and was elected to the 38th Congress in the 1862 Democratic landslide in Ohio. He was defeated for reelection in 1864. In Ohio's 1863 gubernatorial race, White supported Clement L. Vallandigham (*q.v.*), the Democratic nominee. Following the war, he returned to his law practice in Cambridge, where he died on August 6, 1892. Robson, *Biographical Encyclopaedia of Ohio*; Wolfe, *Stories of Guernsey County.*

Thomas H. Smith

WHITEAKER, John, *governor,* was born on May 4, 1820, in Dearborn county, Indiana. After a short residence in Illinois, he moved to Missouri in 1845, and in 1849 joined the California gold rush. In 1851, he returned to Missouri, and a year later moved his family to Oregon. He farmed near Eugene and pursued a political career. A lifelong Democrat, Whiteaker was elected in 1856 as a probate judge and in 1857 as a territorial legislator. In June 1858 he defeated another Democrat to become the first governor of the state.

Relatively obscure at the time of his nomination, Whiteaker received the support of Joe Lane's (*q.v.*) faction of the Democratic party because he was a reliable and ardent proslavery man (he had favored the introduction of slavery into Oregon). As governor, he championed the Breckinridge–Lane ticket. He opposed the doctrine of secession, warned that a war to free slaves might result in the enslavement of whites, and announced that Oregon would not furnish troops for Abraham Lincoln's (*q.v.*) "wicked and unnatural war."

Because the governor rejected the President's call for volunteers, Senator Edward Baker (*q.v.*) received permission to create the 1st Oregon Cavalry. Whiteaker again demonstrated his antiwar sentiments by appointing Benjamin Stark (*q.v.*), who shared his political views, to fill Baker's term after his death at Ball's Bluff. The governor's statements and actions in 1861 angered most Oregonians, and some damned him as a traitor.

Although Whiteaker left office in 1862 under heavy criticism, he quickly rebuilt his political career. He was a delegate to the Democratic National Convention in 1864, and a member of the state legislature. In 1878, he was elected to the U.S. House, and in 1885 he was named collector of internal revenue in Oregon. Voters remembered him not as an antiwar governor but as a frugal executive who asked for the development of local industries and other measures designed to assist frontiersmen. A rural people made "Old Whit" their spokesman. He died in Eugene on October 2, 1902. Edwards, "Department of the Pacific"; Johannsen, *Frontier Politics*.

G. Thomas Edwards

WHITMAN, Walt, *poet*, was born on May 31, 1819, in Huntington, New York. A son of a Quaker carpenter, he attended public schools in Brooklyn, where his family moved in 1823. At thirteen, he began working in a newspaper office. The source of Whitman's poetic genius lay in his struggle to counteract feelings of isolation associated with his complex personality. For years, however, he masked his inner turmoil. In the 1840s, he edited a succession of newspapers in the vicinity of New York City and published conventional poetry and prose. Politically Whitman was a Democrat and, like many New York Democrats, showed a passing interest in Free Soil sentiments in 1848. But he was preoccupied with more transcendent issues, which led to his publication of *Leaves of Grass* in 1855. A celebration of himself and humanity, this collection of poems was a commercial failure.

Whitman wrote in a revolutionary style that was difficult to understand, and his exploration of sexual themes shocked many of his contemporaries. Nevertheless, he resolved henceforth to follow his literary inclinations. During the Civil War, Whitman's humanitarian concerns led him to Washington, D.C. From December 1862 to the end of the war, he nursed wounded soldiers in the capital's hospitals. He worked on his own, and supported himself as a clerk in the Interior Department. In Washington, he identified with Abraham Lincoln (*q.v.*), whom he probably never met. After Lincoln's death, Whitman wrote his finest poem, "When Lilies Last in the Dooryard Bloom'd"—an elegy for the assassinated leader. He remained in Washington until 1873, when a paralytic stroke forced him to give up government employment. He died on March 26, 1892, in Camden, New Jersey. Kaplan, *Walt Whitman*; Miller, *Walt Whitman*.

Stanley Harrold

WHITTIER, John Greenleaf, *poet, abolitionist*, was born on December 17, 1807, in Haverhill, Massachusetts. He lived in near isolation on his father's farm until the age of twenty, when the editors William Lloyd Garrison (*q.v.*) and Abijah W. Thayer, whose newspapers had published his poems, persuaded his father to send him to the Haverhill Academy. Under Garrison's influence, he became an abolitionist. Whittier was a delegate to the Philadelphia convention that formed the American Anti-Slavery Society in December 1833, and signed its Declaration of Sentiments. From 1838 to 1840, he edited the *Pennsylvania Freeman* (successor to Benjamin Lundy's *National Enquirer*), and later aided Gamaliel Bailey in editing the *National Era*. His inclination toward electoral politics early distinguished him from Garrison.

Whittier was elected to the Massachusetts legislature in 1834, and ran unsuccessfully for Congress in 1842 on the Liberty ticket. He urged other antislavery advocates to stand for office. Thus he mobilized Liberty party support for the senatorial candidacy of John P. Hale (*q.v.*) in 1845, and encouraged Charles Sumner (*q.v.*) to run for the Senate in 1851. Whittier thought of himself as a founder of the Republican party. Republican leaders, crediting him with having significant political influence, especially among Quakers, sought his support for their campaigns and programs. Whittier characterized Abraham Lincoln's (*q.v.*) victory in 1860 as "the triumph of our principles—so long delayed," welcomed secession, and opposed compromise efforts during the winter of 1860–1861.

Whittier corresponded with Sumner and Henry Wilson (*q.v.*) throughout the war, urging a forthright emancipation policy. He advocated votes for the freedmen, and supported the impeachment of Andrew Johnson (*q.v.*). His wartime poems, especially "Ein Feste Burg," portrayed the war as a revolutionary experience having strongly religious, even apocalyptic, overtones: "We wait beneath the furnace-blast/The pangs of transformation." During the summer of 1864, he became concerned that John C. Frémont's (*q.v.*) third-party candidacy might lead to Lincoln's defeat. Accordingly, in August, he visited Frémont to urge him to quit the race. Jessie Benton Frémont credited Whittier with being the decisive influence in her husband's decision to withdraw.

Whittier's post–Civil War poetry reached a wide public and earned him a comfortable income. Only Henry Wadsworth Longfellow enjoyed greater popular esteem. Whittier died on September 7, 1892, in Amesbury, Massachusetts. Mordell, *Quaker Militant*; Pollard, *Whittier*; Wagenknecht, *Whittier*.

Merton L. Dillon

WICKLIFFE, Charles Anderson, *congressman*, was born on June 8, 1788, near Springfield, Kentucky. A lawyer, he saw active duty as a staff officer during the War of 1812, and was present at the battle of the Thames. He served three terms in the state legislature, and between 1823 and 1833 served five successive terms in Congress, the first two as a Whig and the final three as a Democrat. In 1836, Wickliffe was elected lieutenant governor on the Whig ticket, and assumed the office of governor (1839–1840) after the death of James Clark. He was Postmaster General (1841–1845), and was President James K. Polk's secret emissary to England and France for negotiations regarding the annexation of Texas (1845).

Following Abraham Lincoln's (*q.v.*) election, Wickliffe participated in a number of pro-Union conferences, but while he advocated peaceful reconciliation, he was also active in the Union State Defense Committee, a secret organization formed to arm Kentucky's pro-Union Home Guards. Running on the Union party ticket, he was elected to the 37th Congress on June 20, 1861. Ironically, his son served as a lieutenant colonel in the Confederate Army. The seventy-three-year-old Kentuckian, with his snow-white hair and "presence of imposing dignity," played a minor role during his final term in Congress. He did not seek renomination and returned to Wickland, his Nelson county estate, when his term ended on March 3, 1863.

A slave owner, Wickliffe expressed a devotion to the Union equaled by his opposition to the Lincoln administration. In June 1863 he was asked by Kentucky's Peace Democrats to run for governor. Wickliffe's party condemned secession, but denounced the Emancipation Proclamation and called for a "just and constitutional" prosecution of the war. Federal military authorities declared that a vote for Wickliffe would be regarded as proof of Confederate sympathy, and openly took steps to ensure his defeat. Wickliffe afterward served as a delegate to the 1864 Democratic National Convention and strongly supported George B. McClellan's (*q.v.*) bid for the presidency. At the close of the war, he resumed the practice of law in Bardstown, Kentucky. He died on October 31, 1869, near Ilchester, Maryland. Harrison, *Kentucky's Governors*; Kleber, *Kentucky Encyclopedia*.

James M. Prichard

WILDER, Abel Carter, *congressman,* was born on March 18, 1828, in Mendon, Massachusetts. While engaged in business in Rochester, New York, he became interested in the Free Soil movement, and in March 1857, moved to the Kansas Territory, where he entered heavily into land speculation at Leavenworth. He campaigned against the Lecompton Constitution, and in May 1859 served as a delegate to the Osawatomie Convention, which organized the Republican party in Kansas. Wilder soon became secretary of the territory's first Republican Central Committee, and ultimately served two terms as its chairman. He also acted as chairman of the Kansas delegation to the 1860 Republican National Convention in Chicago, which nominated Abraham Lincoln (*q.v.*), though Wilder supported William H. Seward (*q.v.*).

In August 1861, Lincoln appointed Wilder a brigade commissary with headquarters at Fort Scott. In November 1862 he was elected to the 38th Congress, and served until 1864, when he failed to gain his party's nomination. Following the war, Wilder returned to Rochester, where he engaged in newspaper publishing. He died in San Francisco on December 22, 1875. Connelly, *Standard History of Kansas*, vol. 3; Plummer, *Frontier Governor.*

Christopher Phillips

WILKINSON, Morton Smith, *senator,* was born on January 22, 1819, in Onondaga county, New York. After studying at a local academy, he read law; moved to Eaton Rapids, Michigan, in 1847; became the first practicing attorney in the Minnesota Territory; and settled eventually in Mankato. He served in the legislature in 1849, helped write the territorial law code in 1851, was active in creating the Minnesota Republican party, ran unsuccessfully for Congress in 1857, and in 1859 was elected U.S. senator. During the secession crisis Wilkinson took an adamant Unionist position, arguing for war if necessary to preserve the Union, then staunchly supported Abraham Lincoln's (*q.v.*) war measures throughout the conflict. He chaired the Committee on Revolutionary Claims and served on the Committee on Indian Affairs, proving to be antagonistic toward the Sioux after their 1862 uprising in Minnesota.

Wilkinson apparently did little to maintain his power base among Minnesota Republicans, for complaints mounted about his laxity in performing constituent services, failure to deliver patronage, and indifferent hospitality toward visitors to Washington. Despite a personal plea from Lincoln to Minnesota Republican legislators on his behalf, Wilkinson was denied reelection in 1865. He was elected to Congress in 1868, then tried unsuccessfully to oust Senator Alexander Ramsey (*q.v.*) in 1869.

At odds with the Minnesota Republican leadership, and uneasy over the Grant administration scandals, Wilkinson supported the insurgent presidential candidacy of Horace Greeley (*q.v.*) in 1872, ran for Congress unsuccessfully as a Democrat, then switched permanently to the Democratic party. He spent his last years practicing law in Mankato, serving as a state legislator from 1874 to 1877, and as Faribault county prosecuting attorney from 1880 to 1884, and running unsuccessfully for Congress in 1888. He died in Wells, Minnesota, on February 4, 1894. Folwell, *History of Minnesota*, vol. 2.

Roger A. Fischer

WILLCOX, Orlando Bolivar, *general*, was born in Detroit, Michigan, on April 16, 1823. He graduated from West Point in 1847, and was assigned to the 4th Artillery and Tilghman's Maryland Battery. After occupation duty in Mexico, he served in Kansas, New Mexico, and Florida. In 1857, he resigned his first lieutenancy to practice law in Detroit, where he commanded a militia company. Commissioned a colonel of the 1st Michigan, he rushed east to help save Washington. By late May 1861, however, Federal forces there were assuming the offensive. On May 24, Willcox's regiment and the 11th New York occupied Alexandria, Virginia, the first Confederate town to fall.

Willcox was captured when he was wounded while leading a brigade at First Bull Run. He and other captive officers were designated to die if the United States executed Confederate naval prisoners as pirates. Neither side fulfilled its threat, and Willcox was exchanged in August 1862. Promoted to brigadier general, he succeeded to the recently vacated command of the 1st Division, IX Corps, and for most of the war served with this corps. He led the division during the Maryland campaign, and the corps at Fredericksburg and during its first two months in Kentucky. After a few months in command of the District of Indiana and Michigan, Willcox led a large new division, called the Left Wing, during the Army of the Ohio's East Tennessee campaign. He served at the battle of

Blue Springs, helped guard the tenuous supply line to Kentucky during the siege of Knoxville, then rejoined the IX Corps and its 2nd Division.

When the IX Corps returned east in April 1864, Willcox took command of its veteran 3rd Division. The consolidation of early September returned him to the 1st Division. He figured prominently in most of Ulysses S. Grant's (*q.v.*) battles from May 6, 1864, to April 2, 1865. Though criticized by the Crater court of inquiry for not pressing the attack, Willcox redeemed himself in his next two battles, Globe Tavern and Poplar Spring Church. Then on March 25, 1865, he contained the Confederates' initial rupture of his line at Fort Stedman until his and other forces could recapture it.

Willcox was one of the few Eastern Theater officers of prominence in early 1861 who made good during the war. Unlike many others who were soon eclipsed, he continually justified his early elevation to high command. He commanded the District of Washington, D.C., after Appomattox, then resigned in January 1866 to resume his law practice. Six months later, he reconsidered and returned to duty as colonel of the 29th Infantry. In 1869, Willcox transferred to the 12th Infantry and spent the next thirteen years garrisoning California and, with only limited success, fighting Apaches. Promoted to brigadier general commanding the Department of the Missouri in 1886, he retired the following year. He subsequently headed the National Soldiers Home (1889–1893). In 1905, he moved to Cobourg, Ontario, Canada, where he died on May 10, 1907. Marvel, *Burnside*; Sommers, *Richmond Redeemed.*

Richard J. Sommers

WILLEY, Waitman Thomas, *senator*, was born near Buffalo Creek, Virginia (now West Virginia), on October 18, 1811. He graduated from Madison College (now Allegheny College), was admitted to the bar in 1833, and opened his law practice at Morgantown. Willey served as clerk of Monongalia county and Circuit Courts of Law and Chancery between 1841 and 1852. Elected to the Virginia Constitutional Convention of 1850–1851, he advocated proportional representation for the western counties on the basis of universal white male suffrage. In 1852, he was the unsuccessful Whig candidate for Congress from his district.

In 1859, Willey received the Whig nomination for lieutenant governor of Virginia, but lost the election. In 1860, as a member of the Constitutional Union party, he was a delegate to the convention that nominated the Bell–Everett ticket. Elected to the Virginia Convention of 1861, he voted against the secession ordinance. Willey played a prominent role in the proceedings of the First and Second Wheeling Conventions (May and June 1861), which led to the creation of the Reorganized Government of Virginia on June 20, 1861. Elected U.S. Senator from Virginia by the Wheeling legislature, he served in that capacity until 1863, when he was elected one of the first U.S. senators from the state of West Virginia. His first term ended in 1865, and he was elected as a Republican for a full term ending on March 4, 1871.

During the war Willey, unlike his more conservative colleague John S. Carlile (*q.v.*), championed the war policies of the Lincoln (*q.v.*) administration, including emancipation. After the West Virginia Constitutional Convention of 1862 submitted a constitution to Congress containing no provision on emancipation, the Republican majority balked. Willey then offered an amendment, which bears his name, calling for gradual emancipation. After the constitution was ratified by the people, West Virginia was admitted to the Union on January 1, 1863. In 1868, Willey voted for President Andrew Johnson's (*q.v.*) conviction on impeachment charges.

In 1870 the Republicans lost control of West Virginia to a coalition of conservative Union and ex-Confederate Democrats. Thus, when Willey's term in the Senate expired in 1871, he returned to the practice of law in Morgantown. He was a delegate to the West Virginia Constitutional Convention of 1872, but played no significant role in its deliberations. Willey remained active in party politics, serving as a delegate-at-large at the Republican National Convention of 1876. He died In Morgantown on May 2, 1900. Ambler, *Waitman Thomas Willey*; Curry, *House Divided*; Moore, *Banner in the Hills.*

Richard Orr Curry

WILLIAMS, Alpheus Starkey, *general*, was born on September 20, 1810, in Deep River, Connecticut. A Yale graduate (class of 1831), he passed the bar and established himself as a lawyer and entrepreneur in Detroit. At various times between 1836 and 1861, he was a bank president, newspaper owner, judge, and city postmaster. Williams supported the Whig party, and became extensively involved in the local militia, serving as lieutenant colonel of the 1st Michigan Volunteers during the Mexican War.

In June 1861, the governor appointed Williams a brigadier general of Michigan Volunteers, in charge of training at Detroit. On August 9, 1861, President Abraham Lincoln (*q.v.*) appointed him brigadier general of U.S. Volunteers, to rank from May 17. From 1861 to 1865, Williams's primary responsibility was that of commander of the 1st Division of whatever corps he was assigned to, but he occasionally filled in as a corps commander. He did so notably at Gettysburg, where he replaced Major General Henry W. Slocum (*q.v.*) of the XII Corps, and was posted in the defense of Culp's Hill, a key point in the Union fishhook-shaped defense. During the Atlanta campaign Williams replaced Major General Joseph Hooker (*q.v.*) of the XX Corps. He served commendably through fighting in the Eastern and Western theaters, including the 1862 Shenandoah Valley campaign, Antietam, Chancellorsville, Chattanooga, the March to the Sea, and the Carolinas.

Williams's long service was marked by competence and loyalty, and was remarkably free of grandstanding or backstabbing. Supporters of the citizen-soldier concept could point to him as a model, to the disappointment of General Emory Upton (*q.v.*) and other Regular Army officers who deplored Volunteers' holding high rank. He consistently performed well, but evidently could not gain a permanent corps command, a posting usually filled by West Pointers. His collected letters to his daughters, published as *From the Cannon's Mouth*, are a valuable source. After the war, Williams participated in politics as a Democrat, serving as U.S. minister to El Salvador from 1866 to 1869, losing the race for governor of Michigan in 1870, and winning two terms to the U.S. House in 1874 and 1876. He died in Washington, D.C., on December 21, 1878. Castel, *Decision in the West*; Coddington, *Gettysburg Campaign.*

Joseph G. Dawson III

WILLIAMS, Thomas, *congressman,* was born in Greensburg, Pennsylvania, on August 28, 1806. He attended Dickinson College, and was admitted to the bar in 1828. Williams entered politics in 1834 by helping to organize a protest meeting against Andrew Jackson's banking policies. That meeting led to the formation of the Whig party, and Williams was included among its influential leaders. Four year later, he successfully ran for the state Senate, and was re-elected in 1840. Depressed by the disarray in the national Whig party, and concerned over an apparent heart problem, Williams decided in 1843 to retire from politics. For the next ten years, he attended to his lucrative law practice in Pittsburgh, turning aside overtures to return to politics. The growing sectional controversy elicited his concern, and he helped to found the Republican party in Pittsburgh.

In 1860, Williams won a seat in the Pennsylvania legislature, and in 1862 he gained his first national office by winning election to Congress. He aligned himself with the more liberal elements of the Republican party, and at the end of the war was among those who advocated a stricter Reconstruction policy. As a member of the House Judiciary Committee, Williams was in the midst of the battle between the Radical Republicans and President Andrew Johnson (*q.v.*). He introduced the Tenure of Office Act into Congress, and when the House impeached Johnson, it appointed Williams to be one of the floor managers in the trial before the Senate. Obviously fatigued and depressed by the trial's outcome, Williams retired from office in 1869, returned to Pittsburgh, and died in Allegheny City, Pennsylvania, on June 16, 1872. Dewitt, *Impeachment and Trial of Andrew Johnson*; Holt, *Forging a Majority*; Konkle, *Life and Speeches of Thomas Williams.*

W. Wayne Smith

WILLIAMS, Thomas, *general,* was born on January 10, 1815, in Albany, New York. He was a private in the Black Hawk War, and graduated from West Point in 1837 as an artillery subaltern. For the next seven years he fought in the Seminole Wars, served on garrison duty in Florida, and was an instructor at the Military Academy. During the Mexican War, Williams served as aide-de-camp to General Winfield Scott (*q.v.*), and was breveted captain and major for gallantry. He spent the next ten years in garrison at several different posts, and participated in another round of fighting against the Seminoles.

When the Civil War began, Williams was at the Artillery School for Practice at Fort Monroe. He was appointed major of the 5th Artillery on May 14, then named brigadier general of Volunteers on September 28. Williams initially acted as inspector general of the Department of Virginia, then returned to the artillery and took part in Ambrose E. Burnside's (*q.v.*) North Carolina expedition. As a result of this expedition, he took command of Fort Hatteras until March 1862, then was assigned to a brigade in Benjamin F. Butler's (*q.v.*) land operations against New Orleans. Once New Orleans was occupied, Williams and his brigade were detailed to the occupation of Baton Rouge. On August 5, 1862, his brigade was caught in an attack on the city by the forces of John C. Breckinridge. Williams and his men were greatly outnumbered, but posted a successful defense of their position. However, Williams was killed that day by a rifle ball in the chest. Hewitt, *Port Hudson*; Marvel, *Burnside*.

Mitchell A. Yockelson

WILMOT, David, *senator,* was born in Bethany, Pennsylvania, on January 20, 1814. In 1834, he was admitted to the Pennsylvania bar, and during the next decade became active in Democratic politics. He was elected as a Democrat to the 29th through the 31st Congresses (1845–1851). Wilmot created a permanent place for himself in U.S. history when he introduced his famous Proviso, which would exclude slavery from any territory taken in the war with Mexico. He tried to assure his slave state colleagues that abolition was far from his motive. Indeed, he wished to open the land for settlement only by whites. Despite Wilmot's reassurances, Southern congressmen objected vehemently to the motion, and although it twice passed in the House, it fell short of a majority in the Senate.

By 1850, Wilmot's Free Soil proclivities had alienated much of his Democratic constituency, and he realized that his chances for reelection to the 32nd Congress were slim. Rather than experience a defeat, he endorsed his law partner, Galusha A. Grow (*q.v.*), for his seat. Wilmot played an instrumental role in the formation of the Republican party in 1854, and in 1857 ran unsuccessfully as a Republican for governor of Pennsylvania. During the secession winter, he represented Pennsylvania at the ill-fated Peace Conference. Wilmot also sought a Senate seat in 1861, but the party machinery behind Simon Cameron (*q.v.*) gave its support to Edgar Cowan (*q.v.*), and Wilmot's bid fell short. When Cameron relinquished his Senate seat for a Cabinet appointment, Wilmot realized his Senate ambition, serving the remaining two years of Cameron's term. He failed to obtain the Republican nomination for a second Senate term, and his public career as an elected official came to an end. Appointed by President Lincoln as a judge on the Court of Claims, Wilmot served there until his death in Towanda, Pennsylvania, on March 16, 1868. Going, *David Wilmot.*

Philip J. Avillo, Jr.

WILSON, Henry, *senator,* was born on February 16, 1812, near Farmington, New Hampshire. His parents christened their son Jeremiah Jones Colbath, but in 1833 he changed his name to Henry Wilson. He then moved to Natick, Massachusetts, and became a successful shoemaker. He obtained a meager education at several New Hampshire academies, but was largely self-taught. In 1840, Wilson was elected as a Whig to the Massachusetts legislature, and served in either the upper or the lower house for eight of the next twelve years. Politics replaced business as his all-consuming career, for it provided him with both an outlet for his ambition and a vehicle for his antislavery convictions. As a Whig legislator, he tried to get his party to take a strongly antislavery stance. Failing in that endeavor, he became a Conscience Whig, and in 1848 helped organize the Free Soil party. After a brief sojourn with the Know-Nothings, Wilson became one of the founders of the Republican party. In 1855, he was elected to the U.S. Senate, a position he held for the next seventeen years.

During the secession crisis, Wilson opposed any compromise over slavery in the territories, and warned Southerners that they risked war by endangering the Union. After Fort Sumter, he returned home to recruit the 22nd Massachusetts, became its colonel, and then resigned his commission to give full attention to his Senate duties. As chairman of the Senate Committee on Military Affairs, Wilson was intimately connected with the important military legislation enacted during the war. Initially, he favored raising Volunteers by state action, and did everything he could to aid state governors in that task. Enlistments fell, however, and by 1862 Wilson obtained congressional approval for the Militia Draft Act. This also proved inadequate, and in 1863 he presented a measure instituting national conscription. He worked incessantly to lessen the draft's impact, by obtaining commutation and substitution provisions and by recommending bounties to encourage volunteering. He also played an important role in obtaining legislation to recruit blacks into the Union Army.

During the first year of the war, Wilson ardently defended the Lincoln (*q.v.*) administration against criticisms about military appointments, suspension of the writ of habeas corpus, military arrests of civilians, and the granting of war contracts. Wilson's eagerness to strike against slavery, however, brought him into conflict with the President. He constantly urged Lincoln to issue an emancipation proclamation, criticized him for not allowing generals in the field to free slaves, and complained of the War Department's initial reluctance to recruit black troops. Wilson sponsored or supported a variety of antislavery measures in Congress, and was especially proud of authoring a bill emancipating slaves in the District of Columbia. Since the Emancipation Proclamation exempted the border states, he sought legislation to free slaves there by providing compensation for their owners. When this attempt failed, he obtained a measure drafting border state slaves into the Army, thereby freeing them and their families. He also sponsored a law equalizing the pay of black and white soldiers.

During the war, Wilson championed the rights of free blacks, sought Federal aid for the education of blacks in the District of Columbia, and worked for the repeal of discriminatory laws there. In 1865, he unsuccessfully sought sweeping legislation that would have forbidden discrimination in public transportation anywhere in the country. Greatly concerned about the future of newly freed slaves in the South, he played a key role in the creation of the Freedmen's Bureau, and then kept a watchful eye on its operations. At the end of the war, Wilson continued his battle to guarantee blacks equality under the law. Despite the passions aroused by the civil conflict, he bore no animosity toward white Southerners, and opposed proposals for confiscating their property or denying them political rights. Rather, he recommended a Reconstruction program based on amnesty for ex-Confederates and suffrage for blacks. In 1872, after playing an important role in the passage of the Congressional Reconstruction program, Wilson was elected Vice President of the United States. He died in Washington, D.C., on November 22, 1875. Abbott, *Cobbler in Congress*; McKay, *Henry Wilson.*

Richard H. Abbott

WILSON, James Falconer, *congressman,* was born in Newark, Ohio, on October 19, 1828. He read law while working as a harness maker, and was admitted to the bar in 1851. In 1853, he moved to Fairfield, Iowa, and set up practice. A temperance advocate, Wilson became active in Republican politics, served in the state legislature from 1857 to 1861, was elected to fill a vacancy in Congress in 1861, and was reelected for three more terms, declining renomination in 1868. Immediately after taking his seat in the House, he offered a resolution to prohibit the Army from returning fugitive slaves to their owners. Chair of the Judiciary Committee by his second term, Wilson moved a resolution calling for Congress to pass an amendment to end slavery. He also promoted greater use of black soldiers, freedom for families of black soldiers, repeal of the Fugitive Slave Law, and black suffrage in the District of Columbia. He also was instrumental in early moves to forbid payment of the Confederate debt.

During Reconstruction, Wilson vigorously opposed Andrew Johnson's (*q.v.*) policies while asserting the prerogatives of Congress. He was a leader in the fight for the Civil Rights Bill of 1866, and sought to ensure Southern loyalty by maintaining a Republican presence in the South via the notes of freedmen and loyal whites. His committee rejected the charges brought against Johnson in the first attempt to remove the President, but Wilson, who had helped draft the Tenure of Office Act, regarded Johnson's violation of the act as sufficient cause for impeachment. He served on the committee to draw up new charges, and was one of the impeachment managers in the Senate trial. Wilson refused appointment as Secretary of State in 1869, but he did accept appointment as a government director of the Union Pacific Railroad. He was involved in the Crédit Mobilier scandal, but denied any wrongdoing. Wilson died in Fairfield, Iowa, on April 22, 1895. Ross, "James F. Wilson," *Annals of Iowa*; Sage, *William Boyd Allison.*

Hubert H. Wubben

WILSON, James Harrison, *general,* was born near Shawneetown, Illinois, on September 2, 1837. He graduated in 1860 from West Point, and entered duty with the topographical engineers. After service with the engineers, Wilson volunteered to join General George B. McClellan's (*q.v.*) staff, seeing such a post as an avenue to promotion. He served through the Maryland campaign and was subsequently assigned to Ulysses S. Grant's (*q.v.*) staff. During the Vicksburg and Chattanooga campaigns, Grant came to value and admire Wilson for his remarkable abilities, despite his opinionated nature and penchant for angering his superiors with blunt observations. In the fall of 1863, Grant rewarded Wilson with promotion to brigadier general of Volunteers. He was subsequently named chief of the Cavalry Bureau in Washington, D.C., where his energy and zeal brought significant improvements in equipment and weapons in the Federal cavalry.

At Grant's personal request, General Philip Sheridan (*q.v.*) selected Wilson as a division commander in the Army of the Potomac Cavalry Corps. Wilson started slowly, but learned quickly and became an aggressive, stubborn fighter. In the fall of 1864, Grant sent him to be chief of cavalry in the Department of Mississippi. Near the close of the fighting, he led the largest cavalry expedition of the war, numbering some 12,000, which resulted in the capture of the industrial center of Selma, Alabama. Perhaps the best evaluation of Wilson's ability as a soldier was Grant's statement to Sherman when he sent Wilson to Mississippi in 1864: "I believe Wilson will add fifty per cent to the effectiveness of your cavalry."

Following the war, Wilson resigned after five years' service in the engineers to work in the railroad industry. He also wrote prolifically on the war, sparing no one from his censorious pen. Wilson returned to the Army as a major general in the Spanish–American War and the Boxer Rebellion. At age eighty, he attempted to serve in World War I. He died on February 23, 1925, in Wilmington, Delaware. Jones, *Yankee Blitzkrieg*; Longacre, *From Union Stars to Top Hat*.

D. Scott Hartwig

WILSON, Robert, *senator,* was born near Staunton, Virginia, in November 1800. He received an elementary education, and worked in the Circuit Court clerk's office in Staunton, which provided valuable experience for his later career. Wilson moved to Howard county, Missouri, in 1820 and served successively as probate judge (1823–1827) and Circuit Court clerk (1828–1840). He studied law, and was admitted to the bar in the late 1830s. He also served as brigadier general of militia during the Mormon War in 1838. Wilson was in the state House from 1845 to 1846, and in the state Senate from 1855 to 1861. A staunch Whig, he was a great admirer of Henry Clay. He declined the gubernatorial nomination of the Constitutional Unionists in 1860, but was elected a delegate to the convention that in 1861 decided against secession. When its president, Sterling Price, defected to the Confederacy, Wilson presided over the subsequent sessions of this body, which sat periodically until 1863.

Following the expulsion of Waldo P. Johnson from the U.S. Senate, Wilson was appointed to the vacancy by acting Governor Willard P. Hall (*q.v.*) on

January 17, 1862, and served until November 13, 1863. He did not seek election to a full term. Wilson was a strong conservative, especially with regard to President Abraham Lincoln's (*q.v.*) proposals for compensated emancipation in the border states in 1862. He was a delegate to the Democratic National Convention in 1864, and supported the presidential nomination of General George B. Mc-Clellan (*q.v.*). Wilson remained active in local Democratic politics following the war, and died in Marshall, Missouri, on May 10, 1870. Parrish, *Turbulent Partnership*; Stewart, *Bench and Bar of Missouri*.

William E. Parrish

WINDOM, William, *congressman*, was born on May 10, 1827, in Belmont county, Ohio. He studied at Martinsburg Academy, read law, was admitted to the bar in 1850, and in 1852 was elected public prosecutor of Knox county, Ohio, as a Whig. Three years later, he moved to Winona, Minnesota, opened a law office, and became active in Republican politics. Windom was elected to Congress in 1858, and was reelected by comfortable margins from 1860 through 1866. His major achievement was the leadership he provided in winning House passage of the 1862 Homestead Act.

As chairman of the House Committee on Indian Affairs, Windom won a reputation for moderation, although he loathed the Sioux for killing more than 500 of his constituents during the 1862 uprising. He served on the House Committee of Thirty-three in early 1861, opposed any extension of slavery into the Western territories, then became a strong supporter of Abraham Lincoln (*q.v.*) and the Union war effort. His loyalty to Lincoln included opposition to the Wade–Davis Manifesto, although after Lincoln's death he sided with the Radicals against Andrew Johnson (*q.v.*) on Reconstruction issues, and voted for Johnson's removal from office.

Windom did not seek reelection in 1868, but after a brief retirement, he was appointed to the Senate to replace Daniel S. Norton in July 1870. He served until 1883, with an eight-month interlude in 1881 as Secretary of the Treasury during President James A. Garfield's (*q.v.*) administration. His Senate career was highlighted by his advocacy of high tariffs and international bimetallism, as well as his chairmanships of the Appropriations Committee (1876–1881) and the Foreign Relations Committee (1881–1883). Windom was retired involuntarily in 1883, moved to New York to practice law, and in 1889 was selected by President Benjamin Harrison to serve a second stint as Treasury Secretary. He died in New York City on January 29, 1891. Folwell, *History of Minnesota*, vols. 2, 3; Salisbury, *William Windom*.

Roger A. Fischer

WINFIELD, Charles Henry, *congressman*, was born on April 22, 1822, in Crawford, New York. He was admitted to the bar in 1846, and established a practice in Goshen, New York. From 1850 to 1856, he served as district attorney of Orange county. Winfield was elected as a Democrat to the House of Representatives in 1862, was reelected in 1864, and became temporary chairman of the New York Democratic convention in 1865. He voted consistently with Democratic party regulars: not opposed in principle to the war itself, but hostile to most of the policies of the Republican administration, especially those related to race. In the 38th Congress, Winfield had been appointed to the Committee on Private Land Claims, but in the 39th Congress he sat on the far more important Ways and Means Committee, the Foreign Affairs Committee, and the Committee on Coinage, Weights, and Measures. Winfield did not run for reelection in 1866. Following expiration of the 39th Congress in 1867, he returned to his Orange county law practice. Winfield died in Walden, New York, on June 10, 1888. Benedict, *Compromise of Principle*.

James C. Mohr

WITTENMYER, Annie Turner, *relief leader,* was born in Sandy Springs, Ohio, on August 26, 1827. In 1847, she married William Wittenmyer, an older, wealthy merchant, and moved to Keokuk, Iowa, in 1852. Her husband died shortly before the Civil War, leaving her a substantial inheritance. Since all but one of her five children had died in infancy, she was free to devote herself to charitable works, many connected with the Methodist Church. With troops gathering at Keokuk, Wittenmyer began to help the sick and became secretary of the local Soldiers' Aid Society. She inspired women in other towns to form similar groups, and her society in Keokuk became a forwarding agent for relief supplies from the whole state. She visited the field to nurse the wounded, and came under fire at Vicksburg and elsewhere.

In September 1862, Wittenmyer became one of several Iowa women designated as a paid "state sanitary agent." Cooperating with the Western Sanitary Commission of St. Louis, she became embroiled in a controversy over whether that group or the U.S. Sanitary Commission should control the Iowa effort; also debated was whether women's work should be merged with (and under) men's. Resigning her position in 1864, Wittenmyer turned to creating special diet kitchens attached to military hospitals. Supported by the U.S. Christian Commission, she pioneered in what finally became an established aspect of military hospitals. Among her later efforts were attempts to aid veterans and soldiers' dependents. In 1889–1890 she was president of the Women's Relief Corps, attached to the leading Union veterans' group. Wittenmyer was also first president of the Woman's Christian Temperance Union. She died in Saratoga, Pennsylvania, on February 2, 1900. Wittenmyer, *Under the Guns*.

Frank L. Byrne

WOOD, Benjamin, *publisher, congressman,* was born on October 13, 1820, in Shelbyville, Kentucky. He finally settled in New York City, where his brother, Fernando Wood (*q.v.*), helped him become editor and publisher of the *New York Daily News*. The newspaper aided Benjamin Wood's political career because it catered to the interests of the city's poorer classes, who in return rewarded him with their votes. Moreover, he gained added political stature among pro-Southern New Yorkers by championing slavery and favoring its extension. During the secession crisis, Wood supported the emerging Confederacy and warned against coercion. By the logic of these commitments, he became a strong Peace Democrat.

Although elected to the 37th and 38th Congresses, Wood took little part in debates and often missed roll calls. Even so, he used this forum, plus his newspaper, to assail the war effort, the administration, the Emancipation Proclamation, War Democrats, and the erosion of states' rights, and to demand an armistice followed by negotiations. On two occasions—when the post office denied his paper mailing privileges, which forced its suspension for over a year, and when Congress investigated his loyalty—Wood's activities appeared treasonous.

Wood perhaps reached the limits of notoriety in 1863, when his attacks on conscription helped to foment the New York draft riots. He continued to press his ideas even when he was defeated for reelection in 1864, and the Confederacy's end was apparent. Despite his conduct during the war, his constituents elected him to the state Senate in 1866, and returned him to the 47th Congress. During all of these political activities, Wood remained the *Daily News*'s publisher until his death in New York City on February 21, 1900. *BDUSC*; Curry, *Blueprint for Modern America.*

Jerome Mushkat

WOOD, Fernando, *congressman*, was born on June 14, 1812, in Philadelphia. Because of his father's business failures, he received little formal education and learned early in life to rely on his native intelligence and charm. These traits aided Wood when he moved to New York City, where he amassed a fortune in the shipping trade. He then invested heavily in real estate, and turned toward a full-time political career.

A Tammany Hall Democrat, Wood served one term in the 27th Congress before being elected mayor of New York City three times during the 1850s. A prototype machine politician, his ambitions alienated Tammany and led to the formation of his own personal machine, Mozart Hall. During this period, Wood expanded his political base by becoming known as one of New York's leading Southern supporters. As secession developed, his sympathies clearly lay with the emerging Confederacy. When war began, patriotic compulsions initially forced him to support coercion.

In 1862, Wood was elected as a Peace Democrat to the 38th Congress. At once, he became a national figure. Along with his brother, Congressman Benjamin Wood (*q.v.*), he defended conservative constitutional principles, sought a negotiated peace, opposed emancipation, and condemned the War Democrats. In late 1864, when the Union's victory seemed inevitable, the pragmatic Wood attempted a prowar shift. His Peace Democratic activities, Tammany's hostility, and Mozart Hall's decline prevented his reelection. Two years later, Wood was elected to the 40th Congress, where he again supported Southern interests, this time through President Andrew Johnson (*q.v.*).

Now at peace with Tammany, Wood was reelected to Congress for the next seven terms. He capped his career in 1877, when the Democrats won control of Congress, by becoming majority floor leader and chairman of the Committee on Ways and Means. Wood died in Hot Springs, Arkansas, on February 14, 1881. Mushkat, *Fernando Wood.*

Jerome Mushkat

WOOD, Thomas John, *general,* was born on September 25, 1823, in Munfordville, Kentucky. He graduated from West Point in 1845, and was commissioned in the topographical engineers. In the Mexican War, he was on the staff of General Zachary Taylor. He later transferred to the cavalry, serving in Kansas and on the Utah expedition. Wood was a mustering officer for Indiana troops when the Civil War began. In October 1861 he was made a brigadier general of Volunteers and assigned to command a brigade in the Army of the Ohio. In the spring of 1862, he led a division at Shiloh and in the advance on Corinth. He fought at Perryville and at Stones River, where he was badly wounded on December 31, 1862. Despite his wound, Wood refused to leave the field until the day's fighting was over.

Wood's most controversial battle was Chickamauga, where, on September 20, 1863, a misunderstanding by the Federal high command resulted in an order for Wood to move to support another division. The movement left a gap in the line at a point where it was soon struck by a massive Confederate attack. The Southerners poured through the gap, and routed half of the Northern army. Technically one cannot fault Wood for obeying an order, but he almost certainly realized that the movement would create a break in the line, and he should have so informed his superiors. Wood led a division of the IV Corps in the fighting around Chattanooga in the advance to relieve Knoxville, and in the Atlanta campaign. At Lovejoy's Station, Georgia, his leg was shattered, but he refused to leave the field. He led his division at Franklin, and at Nashville he commanded the IV Corps. He served a short while in 1865 as the military administrator of Mississippi.

James A. Garfield (*q.v.*), who did not like most West Point graduates, once referred to Wood as a very narrow and impetuous man, possessed of neither prudence nor brains. A more balanced judgment would be that Wood was a reasonably steady and dependable, but not a spectacular, officer. After retiring from active service in 1868, he lived in Dayton, Ohio. He was active in veterans' affairs, and became a member of the board of visitors of the Military Academy. He died in Dayton on February 25, 1906. Castel, *Decision in the West*; Cozzens, *This Terrible Sound.*

Richard M. McMurry

WOODBRIDGE, Frederick Enoch, *congressman,* was born in Vergennes, Vermont, on August 29, 1818. He graduated from the University of Vermont in 1841 and, after studying law in his father's office, was admitted to the bar in 1843. In addition to his law practice, Woodbridge was vice president and manager of the Rutland & Washington Railroad. He served in the state legislature in 1849, 1857, 1858, and 1876, and repeatedly was the town's mayor. He was state auditor (1850–1852) and state's attorney of Addison county (1854–1858). In 1860 and 1861, he was a member of the Vermont Senate, serving as president pro tem in the latter session.

Woodbridge was elected to the U.S. House of Representatives in 1862, and was reelected in 1864 and 1866. In 1867, he served as a member of the House Judiciary Subcommittee investigating Andrew Johnson (*q.v.*). Woodbridge and committee chairman James F. Wilson (*q.v.*) of Iowa dissented from the final report recommending impeachment. Although they censured Johnson's policies, they believed that impeachment was unjustified. However, in 1868, after the removal of Secretary of War Edwin Stanton (*q.v.*), Woodbridge became an important advocate of impeachment. Upon his retirement from Congress, he resumed his law practice in Vergennes, where he died on April 25, 1888. Crockett, *Vermont*, vol. 4.

D. Gregory Sanford

WOODRUFF, George Catlin, *congressman,* was born in Litchfield, Connecticut, on December 1, 1805. He graduated from Yale University in 1825, studied law, and was admitted to the Connecticut bar in 1827. In 1832, he was appointed postmaster of Litchfield, and occupied that post until 1846. He was elected as a Democrat to the Connecticut House of Representatives in 1851, and served one year. In 1861, Woodruff replaced Otis Ferry in the House of Representatives after Ferry accepted a commission in the Army, and later in the same year was elected to Congress. Woodruff sought reelection in 1862, but lost. He returned to his law practice in 1863, and in 1865 again became a member of the Connecticut House. As one of the few Democrats in the legislature that year, he was chosen minority leader. According to the *Hartford Courant,* a Republican newspaper, Woodruff "made hosts of friends among the majority by his gentlemanly bearing and his fairness in debate." He served one other term in the Connecticut House, in 1874. He died in Litchfield on November 21, 1885. Lane, *Political History of Connecticut;* Niven, *Connecticut for the Union.*

Joanna D. Cowden

WOODS, Charles Robert, *general,* was born in Newark, Ohio, on February 19, 1827. He graduated from West Point in 1852, and served on the frontier and in several garrison assignments until the outbreak of the Civil War. In January 1861, as a lieutenant of the 9th U.S. Infantry, Woods commanded a 200-man detail on the *Star of the West,* when that vessel attempted to reach Fort Sumter. The following fall, Woods held temporary command of the 10th U.S. Infantry in western Virginia. He was then made colonel of the 76th Ohio Volunteers, which he led at Fort Donelson and Shiloh.

In the advance on Corinth, Mississippi, Woods commanded a brigade. In late 1862 and in 1863, he led troops at Chickasaw Bluffs, Arkansas Post, and Vicksburg. He was promoted to brigadier general of Volunteers, effective August 4, 1863. Woods won praise for his gallant conduct in the fighting around Chattanooga in November 1863. His brigade was part of the XV Corps in the Atlanta Campaign; Woods was in command of the 1st Division, XV Corps from July 15 to August 15, 1864. In late August, he was given command of the 3rd Division, XVII Corps, which he held for about a month. Woods resumed command of the 1st Division, XV Corps for the March to the Sea. Meanwhile, he had been made brevet major general of Volunteers. Woods was an admirable and competent commander. He remained in the Regular Army after the war, retired in 1874, and lived near Newark, Ohio, until his death there on February 26, 1885. Bearss, *Vicksburg Campaign*; Jones, *"Black Jack": John A. Logan*; Lucas, *Sherman and the Burning of Columbia*.

                                                                    Richard M. McMurry

WOOL, John Ellis, *general,* was born on February 29, 1784, in Newburgh, New York. He suffered reverses as a merchant, studied law briefly, and ran unsuccessfully for public office. He excelled as a militia officer, and in the spring of 1812, obtained a commission as a captain in the 13th Infantry Regiment. He was cited for bravery at the battles of Queenston and Plattsburgh, and was breveted a lieutenant colonel. Wool served for twenty-five years as an inspector general, first in the Northern Division (1816–1821), and later as one of the two Army inspector generals (1821–1841). He was promoted to brigadier general in 1841, and placed in command of the Eastern Department.

When the Mexican War broke out, Wool supervised the muster of twelve Volunteer regiments, then led a division from San Antonio, Texas, into Mexico, where he joined Zachary Taylor's forces at Saltillo. Wool selected the battlefield at Buena Vista, and as field commander repulsed a much larger Mexican army under Santa Anna. He commanded the occupation forces in northeastern Mexico during the last six months of the war, and was breveted a major general. Sent to the Division of the Pacific from 1854 to 1857, Wool grappled with filibusters, vigilantes, and hostile Indians, then resumed command in the East.

At the outbreak of the Civil War, Wool telegraphed state governors from Maine to Illinois to seize Federal arsenals, and expedited troop shipments by sea from New York City to Washington, D.C. He took command of Fortress Monroe in August, and there outfitted navy expeditions bound for the Southern capes, created work programs for black refugees, encouraged prisoner-of-war exchanges, and commanded an amphibious force that captured Norfolk in May 1862. Transferred to the Middle Department (Baltimore), Wool tried to suppress Confederate sympathizers and protect the Baltimore & Ohio Railroad west to Harper's Ferry.

Reassigned in January 1863 to head the Department of New York and New England, Wool strengthened seacoast defenses and stimulated enlistments. In mid-July he battled a mob protesting the draft call in New York City. On August 1, 1863, Wool was retired after fifty-two years of service as an officer. He published articles against George B. McClellan (*q.v.*) in the 1864 election, and two years later was the honorary chairman of the Soldiers and Sailors Convention held in Cleveland. He died in Troy, New York, on November 10, 1869. Harwood P. Hinton, "John Ellis Wool," in Spiller, *Dictionary of American Military Biography*, vol. 3, pp. 1212–1215.

Harwood P. Hinton

WORCESTER, Samuel Thomas, *congressman*, was born in Hollis, New Hampshire, on August 30, 1804. He attended the state's common schools, and in 1830 graduated from Harvard University. After studying law, he was admitted to the bar in 1835. Shortly thereafter, he moved to Norwalk, Ohio, and began to practice law. Becoming involved in local politics, Worcester was elected to the Ohio Senate in 1849 and 1850. He also served as judge of the Court of Common Pleas in 1859 and 1860. Worcester is best known for filling John Sherman's (*q.v.*) unexpired term when the Ohio Senate elected Sherman to the U.S. Senate in 1861. Worcester served in the 37th Congress between July 4, 1861, and March 3, 1863; was a member of the Committee on Agriculture; and actively supported the establishment of the Department of Agriculture. He returned to Norwalk, where he practiced law and helped build several libraries. He died in Nashua, New Hampshire, on December 6, 1882. *BDUSC.*

Thomas H. Smith

WORTHINGTON, Henry Gaither, *congressman*, was born on February 28, 1829, in Cumberland, Maryland. Following a preparatory education, he studied law, and in 1852 settled in Tuolumne county, California. In late 1853, he joined William Walker in an attempt to seize Sonora, Mexico, and may have been with Walker in Nicaragua. Worthington opened a law office in San Francisco in 1861, and that September, he was elected as a Republican to the California Assembly. In 1862, he supported bills to repeal the ban on blacks' testifying against whites in court. In contrast, he supported a $2.50 monthly tax on all Chinese not subject to the foreign miners' tax.

In 1863, Worthington left California for Nevada Territory, and on November 8, 1864, became the first congressman from the new state. He served only from December 21, 1864, to March 3, 1865, but during that time he supported the 13th Amendment. His bill establishing Federal courts for Nevada also protected mining rights. On April 19, Worthington was one of the pallbearers at President Abraham Lincoln's (*q.v.*) funeral.

Later in 1865, Worthington failed to be reelected, and looked for opportunity elsewhere. By February 1867, he was in Nebraska, seeking a Senate seat. In 1868, President Andrew Johnson (*q.v.*) appointed him minister to Uruguay. The next summer, he was the American minister in the Argentine Republic. By late 1870, Worthington was active in the reconstruction of South Carolina, where he picked up the title of "General" from a militia command. From 1875 to 1877, he was collector of the Port of Charleston. He settled in Washington, D.C., and died there on July 29, 1909. *BDUSC.*

Robert J. Chandler

WRIGHT, George, *general,* was born at Norwich, Vermont, on October 21, 1803. He graduated from West Point in 1822, then served in Wisconsin, and in the Seminole and Mexican Wars. In Mexico, he soldiered under Zachary Taylor and Winfield Scott (*q.v.*), participated in most of the significant battles, and at Molino del Rey was wounded while leading a charge. Appointed colonel of the 9th Infantry in 1855, Wright established headquarters at Fort Vancouver. Named brigadier general of Volunteers in September 1861, he held several commands during the Civil War: the Department of Oregon, 1860–1861; the District of Southern California, 1861; the Department of the Pacific, October 20, 1861– July 1, 1864; and the District of California, 1864–1865.

Wright at first expressed displeasure because he had not been promoted while less experienced men received high rank in the burgeoning military establishment. After his promotion and selection as commander of the Department of the Pacific, he accepted his fate as an isolated officer during a momentous war. He was General Edwin Sumner's (*q.v.*) personal choice to replace him in a vast, sensitive department with headquarters in San Francisco. Wright commanded the largest military force ever assembled in the Far West—about 6,000 troops in 1862—most of whom were Volunteers recruited in California, supported by a few units of Regulars. He was to protect the frontier against Indians, to keep a watch on Western secessionists, to safeguard the coastline (especially at San Francisco), and to move troops eastward. General James Carleton led his California Column to secure New Mexico, General Patrick Connor (*q.v.*) marched a force into Utah, and various officers led patrols along the Oregon Trail to shield immigrants from Indian raiders.

Wright granted these and other subordinates considerable independence, and generally handled his duties to the satisfaction of his Eastern superiors and Western supporters. Apparently he was removed from command because the government sought a position for Major General Irvin McDowell (*q.v.*), and because Wright promoted the risky plan of driving the French from Mexico. En route to a new assignment, Wright was drowned on July 30, 1865, when his ship sank off Crescent City, California. Edwards, "Department of the Pacific"; Schlicke, *General George Wright.*

G. Thomas Edwards

WRIGHT, Hendrick Bradley, *congressman,* was born in Plymouth, Pennsylvania, on April 24, 1808. He graduated from Dickinson College in 1829, was admitted to the bar in 1831, and began the practice of law in Wilkes-Barre. He was a delegate to the Democratic National Conventions in 1848, 1852, 1860, 1868, and 1876. In 1860, he campaigned for Stephen A. Douglas (*q.v.*). When

George W. Scranton (*q.v.*), who had been elected to the 37th Congress, died, Wright was elected to fill the vacancy. His earlier experience in Congress was reflected in his appointment to the important Committee on Military Affairs and the active role he played throughout the 37th Congress.

Paramount among Wright's concerns was the restoration of the Union. He clashed openly with Peace Democrat Clement L. Vallandigham (*q.v.*), establishing himself as a leader of the War Democrats. Unlike Vallandigham, who proposed welcoming the seceded South back into the Union unconditionally, Wright declared that he, too, was for peace, but only after the Rebels surrendered. At the same time, he opposed the expansion of the war's goals. Consistent with this position, he endorsed John J. Crittenden's (*q.v.*) resolutions limiting the scope of the war, and on several occasions he opposed confiscation measures before the House. Wright's negrophobia was often at the root of that opposition. He was against the use of black troops for fear that their presence would lower the morale of white soldiers and jeopardize the loyalty of the border states.

At the conclusion of the 37th Congress, Wright withdrew from congressional politics and began focusing his attention on the labor movement, particularly the plight of Pennsylvania's coal miners. With labor support, he was elected to the 45th and 46th Congresses. The Knights of Labor faction within the Pennsylvania Democratic party tried unsuccessfully in 1878 to nominate Wright for governor. At the conclusion of the 46th Congress, Wright retired from public life, after nearly half a century of political activity. He died in Wilkes-Barre on September 2, 1881. Curry, *Blueprint for Modern America*; Shankman, *Pennsylvania Antiwar Movement*.

Philip J. Avillo, Jr.

WRIGHT, Horatio Gouverneur, *general,* was born in Clinton, Connecticut, on March 6, 1820. He graduated from West Point in 1841. As lieutenant and captain of engineers, he taught at West Point (1842–1844), served in Florida (1846–1856), and was Chief Engineer Joseph Totten's assistant in Washington (1856–1861). In April 1861 Wright shared the blame for the Norfolk fiasco, and in July, as chief engineer, 3rd Division, Department of Northeastern Virginia, he experienced the disaster at First Bull Run. Despite inauspicious beginnings (and missing the Mexican War), his high West Point standing and Old Army staff prominence marked him as promising.

Promoted to brigadier general on September 14, 1861, Wright commanded the 3rd Brigade, South Carolina expedition. In South Carolina and Florida, he did not actually lead troops in combat until Secessionville, a Union defeat. Assignments to minor posts and a defeat did not harm him. That August, he became a major general commanding the new Department of the Ohio. This vast territory, full of many targets but few veteran defenders, abounded with raiders, guerrillas, and Copperheads. Wright's main contribution was garrisoning threatened Cincinnati in force. He deserves no credit for clearing Braxton Bragg from Kentucky, and he did not succeed in protecting supply lines once the front returned to Tennessee.

In March 1863, Congress refused Wright confirmation as major general. He briefly held subordinate command in Kentucky, but returned east to command the 1st Division, VI Corps in May 1863. Preferring field service to the West Point superintendency that August, he temporarily led the VI Corps in its great Rappahannock Bridge victory in November. Following John Sedgwick's (*q.v.*) death, on May 9, 1864, Wright was elevated over senior officers to succeed him. With corps command came promotion to major general. His corps served in the Army of the Potomac from Spotsylvania through First Reams' Station. In July, his troops rushed northward just in time to save Washington, but his small army could not secure the Potomac frontier.

Partially to blame for that failure, Wright clearly could not solve the Shenandoah Valley problem. Philip Sheridan (*q.v.*) received that mission, and Wright became merely senior corps commander. He fought well enough, but as temporary army commander at Cedar Creek, he displayed almost disastrous lack of precautions. His final wartime service, though, was outstanding: his attacks were decisive in the great victories at Petersburg (April 2) and Sailor's Creek.

Like most engineers, Wright was thought capable of high command, and neither lack of opportunity nor reverses denied him repeated advancement. His hesitancy, restraint, and indecisiveness made him unfit for independent command. But when responsibility lay elsewhere, and Wright was a prominent subordinate, he could elicit and deliver the power of a division or corps with devastating effect. In his hands, the VI Corps became one of the mightiest striking forces of the Union Army. Following Appomattox, he served in Virginia and as Sheridan's principal subordinate in the Southwest. As a lieutenant colonel and colonel of engineers, he figured prominently in coastal defense, public works, and ordnance. In 1879, Wright became brigadier general and chief of engineers. He retired in 1884, and died in Washington, D.C., on July 2, 1899.
Catton, *Grant Takes Command*; Matter, *If It Takes All Summer*; Rhea, *Battle of the Wilderness*.

Richard J. Sommers

WRIGHT, Joseph Albert, *senator, diplomat*, was born on April 17, 1810, in Washington, Pennsylvania. He moved with his family to Monroe county, Indiana, where he attended Indiana University, graduating in 1825. After studying law, and being admitted to the bar in 1829, he moved to Rockville, where he established a practice. A Democrat, Wright served in the Indiana House of Representatives (1833–1834, 1836–1837) and the Senate (1839–1840). He won election to the U.S. House of Representatives (1843–1845) before becoming Indiana's tenth governor (December 5, 1849–January 12, 1857). An advocate of colonization, temperance, and scientific agriculture, Wright was a popular

Democrat during the 1850s, leading the opposition against Jesse Bright's (*q.v.*) long dominance of state Democratic politics.

After serving as U.S. minister to Prussia (1857–1861), Wright endorsed Abraham Lincoln's (*q.v.*) war policy, advocating the preservation of the Union at all costs. Indiana Governor Oliver H.P. Morton (*q.v.*) appointed Wright to fill the Senate seat vacated by Jesse Bright's expulsion, thereby strengthening Morton's Union party in Indiana; Wright held this position from February 24, 1862, to January 14, 1863. In the fall of 1862, he was one of forty-eight congressmen who petitioned Lincoln to give Lewis Wallace (*q.v.*) of Indiana a field command. Appointed U.S. commissioner to the Hamburg (Germany) Exhibition (1863), Wright later resumed his post as U.S. minister to Prussia (1865–1867). He died in Berlin on May 11, 1867. Shepherd, *Biographical Directory of the Indiana General Assembly*, vol. 1; Stampp, *Indiana Politics During the Civil War*; Walsh, *Centennial History of the Indiana General Assembly*.

David G. Vanderstel

WRIGHT, William, *senator*, was born in Clarksville, New York, on November 13, 1790. He fought in the War of 1812, and by 1815 was associated with Peet, Smith & Company of Bridgeport, Connecticut, manufacturers of harnesses and saddles, in which his father-in-law, William Peet, was a major partner. For several years, Wright managed the company branch in Charleston, South Carolina, and became one of the owners of the firm; Smith & Wright subsequently became one of the largest leather manufacturers in the United States.

Although a nominal Whig, Wright objected to abolitionist influences within the party. He became a Democrat in 1851 because of widespread opposition to the Compromise of 1850 among Northern Whigs. In 1853, he was selected U.S. senator with the support of the Joint Companies, the canal and railroad monopoly that exercised great power in New Jersey politics, particularly in the Democratic party. Wright intrigued unsuccessfully to secure reelection in 1858, after control of the legislature passed to the anti-Democratic Opposition party.

In 1860, Wright was a delegate to the Democratic National Convention at Charleston, and later supported the Breckinridge ticket. The *Newark Journal*, of which he was primary owner, took an extreme pro-Southern stance during the secession crisis, leading to accusations that Wright's politics reflected his large stake in Southern trade. Wright's reentry to the Senate occurred on the heels of a decisive Democratic victory in the 1862 state elections. The death of incumbent U.S. Senator John R. Thomson (*q.v.*) gave the new legislature the opportunity to make a short interim appointment and a selection for a full term. James W. Wall (*q.v.*), the popular Copperhead leader, was forced to accept the two-month term. Both Wall and prominent Republicans asserted privately that Wright won the six-year term through lavish expenditure of money.

Wright was identified with the Peace Democrats because his *Newark Journal* was the most outspokenly antiadministration daily newspaper published in the state. He appears to have had little influence in the Senate. He never spoke, voted only sporadically, and was continually absent during 1866, when he was in declining health. He died in Newark, New Jersey, on November 1, 1866. *BDUSC.*

Daniel W. Crofts

Y

YATES, Richard, *governor,* was born on January 15, 1815, in Warsaw, Kentucky. In 1828, he was sent to Miami University at Oxford, Ohio. In 1831, Yates accompanied his father into Illinois, first to Springfield and then, in 1833, to the tiny Island Grove and Berlin settlements west of Springfield. He was sent to the new Illinois College at Jacksonville, where in 1835 he became its first graduate. Upon graduation, he was accepted as an apprentice into the law offices of John J. Hardin, one of the most influential Whigs in the district. Topping off his apprenticeship with a term at Transylvania University, Yates was admitted to the bar in 1837. Subsequently, he began a successful law practice in Jacksonville.

During the 1840s, Yates was elected three times to the Illinois General Assembly. In 1850, he was elected to a congressional seat once occupied by Abraham Lincoln (*q.v.*). Yates supported Western economic interests and the liberal reform issues of the day. Probably at Lincoln's urging, he ran in 1854, as an anti-Nebraksa candidate for Congress, in a campaign that brought Lincoln out of political "retirement" to support him. He was unsuccessful, but by 1856 was one of the established leaders of the Republican party, and in 1860 he was elected governor.

As governor, Yates favored a war of blood, terror, and Old Testament vengeance. A man of exaggerated sentiment, he stretched toward the melodramatic, the theatrical, the clenched fist. Lincoln was too cautious, too concilatory, too compassionate. The President, whom he had known since his New Salem days, bewildered him. He had difficulty adjusting to Lincoln's new importance and was inclined to regard him as a very ordinary man.

Assessing Ulysses S. Grant's (*q.v.*) talents in much the same way, Yates reluctantly appointed him to his first important military command, but saw no image of Grant's future when he did so. The hard-drinking, rough-and-tumble Yates was antislavery, but unsympathetic toward African Americans, and looked on opposition as disloyalty. He struggled to recruit troops and the materials of war, quarreled with a Democratic constitutional convention, and was briefly famous for proroguing the Democratic state legislature.

Following his governorship, Yates (described as "the Soldiers' Friend") served a term in the Senate, where he loyally followed the Radical program. By this time, much of the fire of his youth had been extinguished by the alcoholism that had plagued him nearly all of his life. His later days were tragic and his senatorial career disgraced. Many called for his resignation, but this he refused. Yates finished his term, obtained a minor government commission, and died in St. Louis on September 23, 1873. Hesseltine, *Lincoln's War Governors*; Yates, *Richard Yates*.

Jack Nortrup

YEAMAN, George Helm, *congressman*, was born on November 1, 1829, in Hardin county, Kentucky. His formal education was limited, but he read law on his own, and gained admission to the bar in 1851. From 1854 to 1858, he was judge of Daviess county while practicing law and editing the weekly *Owensboro Gazette*. A Whig before the Civil War, Yeaman in 1860 supported the Constitutional Union candidacy of John Bell. As one of Kentucky's Unionist coalition in 1861, he opposed the calling of a state convention to consider secession as a possible course of action. The issue was resolved in August 1861 when the Unionists won control of the legislature.

Yeaman gained a seat in the legislature by a close vote. His plans to raise a regiment of Union Volunteer troops were abandoned in October 1862 when he won a special election to fill a place left vacant in the U.S. House of Representatives by the death at Perryville of James S. Jackson (*q.v.*). In August 1863, Yeaman won a full term. In Congress, Yeaman served on the Committee on Military Affairs. By the end of his service he had aligned himself with the conservative Republicans. In December 1862 he had offered a resolution that condemned the Emancipation Proclamation, but the motion was tabled by a decisive vote.

By 1865, Yeaman spoke in support of the 13th Amendment, which, although never ratified by Kentucky, abolished slavery in December of that year. Like other conservative Kentuckians, Yeaman's most significant service was his role in holding the strategically vital Bluegrass State in the Union. Defeated for reelection in August 1865, Yeaman served from late 1865 until 1870 as the American minister to Denmark. After 1870, he practiced law in New York. There he affiliated with the "halfbreed" Republican supporters of James A. Garfield (*q.v.*), lectured on constitutional law at Columbia College, and served as president of the Medico-Legal Society. Yeaman died in Jersey City, New Jersey, on February 23, 1908. Curry, *Blueprint for Modern America.*

Richard G. Stone

YEATMAN, James Erwin, *head of Western Sanitary Commission,* was born near Wartrace, Tennessee, on August 27, 1818. He was educated privately and at the New Haven Commercial School, moved to St. Louis in 1842 to represent his father's interests there, and quickly took a prominent place in the city's business and social circles. A Whig before the Civil War, Yeatman took a strong stand for the Union while trying to play a conciliatory role between the military at St. Louis and the regime of Governor Claiborne Jackson.

Yeatman's great contribution to the war effort was his leadership of the Western Sanitary Commission, established by General John C. Frémont (*q.v.*) in September 1861. Under his leadership, the commission pioneered the concept of railroad hospital cars and had four floating hospitals devised from old steamboats for use on the Mississippi and other Western rivers. It also set up the "flying hospital" to accompany an army on the march. The commission provided extensive services to soldiers on leave, white and black refugees who flocked to St. Louis, and orphans of both races whom its agents sought out. All told, the commission administered some $3.5 million in aid.

Following the war, Yeatman devoted his time to his various business enterprises while continuing to be active in many charitable activities. He died in St. Louis on July 7, 1901. Parrish, *History of Missouri,* vol. 3; Parrish, "Western Sanitary Commission," *Civil War History.*

William E. Parrish

YOUNG, Brigham, *religious leader,* was born in Whitingham, Vermont, on June 1, 1801, and was brought up in western New York. He was baptized into the Church of Jesus Christ of Latter-day Saints in 1832, accepting the leadership of Joseph Smith. Through the agonizing days of Mormon persecutions in Ohio, Illinois, and Nebraska, Young became more and more the spiritual leader of the church, and was elected its president in 1847. Then came the momentous move to Utah, and the building of Salt Lake City and other communities in Zion.

By the time of the Civil War, the Mormons had experienced the Mormon War, and relations with the Union were sometimes strained. The Federal government obviously was concerned with the stand of Utah Territory in the war, because of its vital geographical position astride the mail routes and telegraph lines to California. Despite rumors over the years, there is no evidence that the Mormons were pro-Confederate. They were primarily interested in preserving their new home in Utah Territory, and in promulgating their faith within the Union. Young wanted Utah Territory to become a state, but the Federal appointees as territorial governor during the war proved to be less than successful in this regard.

In response to a call from President Abraham Lincoln (*q.v.*) early in 1862,

Young furnished a company of the Nauvoo Legion, or militia, to protect the trails eastward in what became Wyoming. In the fall of 1862, a force of California Union Volunteers under Colonel Patrick Connor (*q.v.*) arrived from the Pacific Coast, officially to help protect the trails from the Indians, although Connor believed his troops were there to watch the Mormons. Until the end of the war, there was a continual rivalry between Young and Connor. It was principally a confrontation of words in sermons, official reports, and the press. There were no armed clashes, but a variety of vexing incidents did ensue.

Lincoln and the Federal government trod carefully with the citizens of Utah, although Congress in 1862 outlawed polygamy, which angered the Mormons. Brigham Young was an important figure in the Civil War. He skillfully developed a workable relationship with the Union, leading his people eventually into full participation in the United States. He continued to head his church until his death in Salt Lake City on August 29, 1877. Long, *Saints and the Union.*

E. B. Long

Z

ZOOK, Samuel Kosciuszko, *general,* was born on March 27, 1821, in Chester county, Pennsylvania. He served in the Pennsylvania and New York militias, and was named colonel of the 57th New York on October 19, 1861. After service in the Peninsula campaign, he missed Second Bull Run and Sharpsburg. As a brigade commander at Fredericksburg, he was wounded and lost most of his men, yet was praised by Winfield Scott Hancock (*q.v.*) and promoted to brigadier general. Zook distinguished himself at Gettysburg when he took his brigade, as part of John C. Caldwell's (*q.v.*) division, into the thick of the fighting in the Wheat Field. His decision to alter his brigade's movement in order to arrive earlier and more advantageously may have been one of the more critical decisions of the day. Zook was mortally wounded as the heaviest fighting began, and died in a field hospital on the evening of July 2. Pfanz, *Gettysburg: The Second Day*; Tucker, *Hancock the Superb.*

John T. Hubbell

Bibliography

Complete references for the sources mentioned in the text appear below except for the following titles that have been abbreviated: (1) *BDGUS* for Robert Sobel and John Raimo, eds., *Biographical Directory of the Governors of the United States, 1789–1978*; and (2) *BDUSC* for United States Congress, *Biographical Directory of the United States Congress, 1774–1989*. Some titles were modified in the interests of conserving space, for example, Davis, *Bull Run* for William C. Davis, *Battle at Bull Run*; and Hesseltine, *Lincoln's War Governors* for William Best Hesseltine, *Lincoln and the War Governors*.

Abbott, Richard H. *Cobbler in Congress: The Life of Henry Wilson, 1812–1875.* Lexington: University Press of Kentucky, 1972.

Abbott, Richard H. *Ohio's War Governors.* Columbus: Ohio State University Press for the Ohio Historical Society, 1962.

Abzug, Robert H. *Passionate Liberator: Theodore Dwight Weld and the Dilemma of Reform.* New York: Oxford University Press, 1980.

Adams, George Worthington. *Doctors in Blue: The Medical History of the Union Army in the Civil War.* New York: H. Schuman, 1952.

Adams, John R. *Harriet Beecher Stowe.* Updated ed. Boston: Twayne Publishers, 1989.

Aldrich, Lewis Cass, ed. *History of Yates County, New York, with Illustrations and Biographical Sketches of Some of Its Prominent Men and Pioneers.* Syracuse, NY: D. Mason & Co., 1892.

Alexander, De Alva Stanwood. *Political History of the State of New York.* 2 vols. New York: H. Holt & Co., 1906.

Ambler, Charles Henry. *Francis H. Pierpont: Union War Governor and Father of West Virginia.* Chapel Hill: University of North Carolina Press, 1937.

Ambler, Charles Henry. *The Makers of West Virginia and Their Work.* Huntington, WV: Gentry Bros., 1942.

Ambler, Charles Henry. *Waitman Thomas Willey: Orator, Churchman, Humanitarian; Together with a History of Wesley Methodist Church, Morgantown, West Virginia.* Huntington, WV: Standard Printing and Publishing Co., 1954.

Ambler, Charles Henry. *West Virginia: The Mountain State.* 2nd ed. Englewood Cliffs, NJ: Prentice-Hall, 1958.

Ambrose, Stephen E. *Halleck: Lincoln's Chief of Staff.* Baton Rouge: Louisiana State University Press, 1962.

Ambrose, Stephen E. *Upton and the Army.* Baton Rouge: Louisiana State University Press, 1964.

Anderson, David D. *Robert Ingersoll.* New York: Twayne Publishers, 1972.

Anderson, David L. "Between Two Cultures: Frederick F. Low in China." *California History* 49 (Fall 1980): 240–254.

Anderson, David L. *Imperialism and Idealism: American Diplomats in China, 1861–1898.* Bloomington: Indiana University Press, 1985.

Andrews, C. C. *History of the Campaign of Mobile; Including the Co-operative Operations of Gen. Wilson's Cavalry in Alabama.* New York: D. Van Nostrand, 1867.

Angle, Paul M. *One Hundred Years of Law: An Account of the Law Office Which John T. Stuart Founded in Springfield, Illinois, a Century Ago.* Springfield, IL: Brown, Hay, and Stephens, 1928.

Armstong, William H. *Warrior in Two Camps: Ely S. Parker, Union General and Seneca Chief.* Syracuse, NY: Syracuse University Press, 1978.

Athearn, Robert G. *Thomas Francis Meagher: An Irish Revolutionary.* Boulder: University of Colorado Press, 1949.

Atkinson, George W., and Alvaro F. Gibbens. *Prominent Men of West Virginia: Biographical Sketches, the Growth and Advancement of the State, a Compendium of Returns of Every Election, a Record of Every State Officer.* Wheeling, WV: W. L. Gallin, 1890.

Austin, James C. *Petroleum V. Nasby.* New York: Twayne Publishers, 1965.

Bailes, Kendall E. *Rider on the Wind: Jim Lane and Kansas.* Shawnee Mission, KS: Wagon Wheel Press, 1962.

Baker, James H. *Lives of the Governors of Minnesota.* St. Paul: Minnesota Historical Society, 1908.

Baker, Jean H. *Mary Todd Lincoln: A Biography.* New York: W.W. Norton & Co., 1987.

Baker, Jean H. *The Politics of Continuity: Maryland Political Parties from 1858 to 1870.* Baltimore: Johns Hopkins University Press, 1973.

Baker, La Fayette C. *History of the United States Secret Service.* Philadelphia: L. C. Baker, 1867.

Banes, Charles H. *History of the Philadelphia Brigade. Sixty-ninth, Seventy-first, Seventy-second, and One Hundred and Sixth Pennsylvania Volunteers.* Philadelphia: J. B. Lippincott & Co., 1876.

Banner, Lois W. *Elizabeth Cady Stanton: A Radical for Women's Rights.* Boston: Little, Brown, 1980.

[Barnard, F. A.]. *American Biographical History of Eminent and Self-Made Men . . . Michigan Volume.* Cincinnati, OH: Western Biographical Publishing Company, 1878.

Barnard, George N. *Photographic Views of Sherman's Campaign.* With a new preface by Beaumont Newhall. New York: Dover Publications, 1977.

Barnard, Harry. *Rutherford B. Hayes and His America.* Indianapolis, IN: Bobbs-Merrill, 1954.

Barrett, John G. *The Civil War in North Carolina.* Chapel Hill: University of North Carolina Press, 1963.

Barrett, John G. *Sherman's March Through the Carolinas.* Chapel Hill: University of North Carolina Press, 1956.

Bartlett, John Russell. *Memoirs of Rhode Island Officers Who Were Engaged in the Service of Their Country During the Great Rebellion with the South. Illustrated with Thirty-four Portraits.* Providence, RI: S. S. Rider & Brother, 1867.

Basso, Ralph. "Nationalism, Nativism, and the Black Soldier: Daniel Ullman, a Biography of a Man Living in a Period of Transition, 1810–1892." Ph.D. dissertation, St. John's University, 1986.

Bates, Samuel P. *History of Pennsylvania Volunteers, 1861–65.* 2 vols. Harrisburg, PA: B. Singerly, 1869.

Baughman, A. J. *A Centennial Biographical History of Richland County, Ohio.* Chicago: Lewis Publishing Co., 1901.

Baum, Dale. *The Civil War Party System: The Case of Massachusetts, 1848–1876.* Chapel Hill: University of North Carolina Press, 1984.

Baxter, Maurice G. *Orville H. Browning, Lincoln's Friend and Critic.* Bloomington: Indiana University Press, 1957.

Beakes, Samuel W. *Past and Present of Washtenaw County, Michigan, Together with Biographical Sketches of Many of Its Prominent and Leading Citizens and Illustrious Dead.* Chicago: S. J. Clarke Publishing Co., 1906.

Bearss, Edwin C. *The Battle of Jackson, July 10–17, 1863.* Baltimore, MD: Gateway Press, 1981.

Bearss, Edwin C. *The Campaign for Vicksburg.* 3 vols. Dayton, OH: Morningside House Press, 1985–1986.

Bearss, Edwin C. *Forrest at Brice's Cross Roads and in North Mississippi in 1864.* Dayton, OH: Press of Morningside Bookshop, 1979.

Belden, Thomas Graham, and Marva Robins Belden. *So Fell the Angels.* Boston: Little, Brown & Co., 1956.

Belknap, Michal R., ed. *American Political Trials.* Westport, CT: Greenwood Press, 1981.

Belknap, William W. *History of the Fifteenth Regiment, Iowa Veteran Volunteer Infantry, from October, 1861, to August, 1865, When Disbanded at the End of the War.* Keokuk, IA: R. B. Ogden & Son, 1887.

Belmont, August. *A Few Letters and Speeches of the Late Civil War.* New York: Privately published, 1870.

Belz, Herman. *A New Birth of Freedom: The Republican Party and Freedmen's Rights, 1861 to 1866.* Westport, CT: Greenwood Press, 1976.

Belz, Herman. *Reconstructing the Union: Theory and Policy During the Civil War.* Ithaca, NY: Published for the American Historical Association by Cornell University Press, 1969.

Benedict, Michael Les. *A Compromise of Principle: Congressional Republicans and Reconstruction, 1863–1869.* New York: Norton, 1974.

Berryman, John R. *History of the Bench and Bar of Wisconsin*. Chicago: H. C. Cooper, Jr., 1898.

Bicknell, Thomas Williams. *The History of the State of Rhode Island and Providence Plantations*. New York: American Historical Society, 1917.

Bigelow, John. *Retrospections of an Active Life*. 5 vols. New York: Baker and Taylor Co., 1909–1913.

Biographical Album of Prominent Pennsylvanians. 3 vols. Philadelphia: American Biographical Publishing Co., 1888–1890.

Biographical and Reminiscent History of Richland, Clay and Marion Counties, Illinois. Indianapolis, IN: B. F. Bowen, 1909.

The Biographical Encyclopedia of Illinois of the Nineteenth Century. Philadelphia: Galaxy Publishing Co., 1875.

Biographical Encyclopedia of Kentucky of the Dead and Living Men of the Nineteenth Century. Cincinnati, OH: J. M. Armstrong, 1878.

Biographical Encyclopedia of Pennsylvania of the Nineteenth Century. Philadelphia: Galaxy Publishing Company, 1874.

A Biographical History of Eminent and Self-Made Men of Indiana. Cincinnati, OH: Western Biographical Publishing Co., 1880.

Biographical Review: This Volume Contains Biographical Sketches of the Leading Citizens of Broome County, New York. Boston: Biographical Review Publishing Co., 1894.

Biographical Review: This Volume Contains Biographical Sketches of the Leading Citizens of Delaware County, New York. Boston: Biographical Review Publishing Co., 1895.

Biographical Review of Dane County, Wisconsin; Containing Biographical Sketches of Pioneers and Leading Citizens. Chicago: Biographical Review Publishing Co., 1893.

Blackmar, Frank W. *Charles Robinson, the First State Governor of Kansas*. Topeka, KS: Crane and Co., 1901.

Blackwell, Alice Stone. *Lucy Stone: Pioneer of Woman's Rights*. 2nd ed. N.P.: Alice Stone Blackwell Committee, 1930.

Blaine, James Gillespie. *Twenty Years of Congress: From Lincoln to Garfield. With a Review of the Events which Led to the Political Revolution of 1860*. 2 vols. Norwich, CT: Henry Bill Publishing Co., 1884–1886.

Blair, Harry C., and Rebecca Tarshis. *Colonel Edward D. Baker: Lincoln's Constant Ally, Together with Four of His Great Orations*. Portland: Oregon Historical Society, 1960.

Blair, Walter, and Hamlin Hill. *America's Humor: From Poor Richard to Doonesbury*. New York: Oxford University Press, 1978.

Blank, Charles. ''The Waning of Radicalism: Massachusetts Republicans and Reconstruction Issues in the Early 1870's.'' Ph.D. dissertation, Brandeis University, 1972.

Blight, David W. *Frederick Douglass' Civil War: Keeping Faith in Jubilee*. Baton Rouge: Louisiana State University Press, 1989.

Bloss, G.M.D. *Life and Speeches of George H. Pendleton*. Cincinnati, OH: Miami Printing and Publishing Co., 1868.

Blue, Frederick J. *Salmon P. Chase: A Life in Politics*. Kent, OH: Kent State University Press, 1987.

Bogart, Ernest Ludlow, and Charles Manfred Thompson. *The Industrial State, 1870–1893.* Springfield: Illinois Centennial Commission, 1920.

Bogue, Allan G. *The Congressman's Civil War.* Cambridge, UK: Cambridge University Press, 1989.

Bogue, Allan G. *The Earnest Men: Republicans of the Civil War Senate.* Ithaca, NY: Cornell University Press, 1981.

Bogue, Allan G. "William Parker Cutler's Congressional Diary of 1862–63." *Civil War History* 33 (December 1987):315–330.

Boutwell, George S. *Reminiscences of Sixty Years in Public Affairs.* New York: McClure, Phillips & Co., 1902.

Bradford, James C., ed. *Captains of the Old Steam Navy: Makers of the American Naval Tradition, 1840–1880.* Annapolis, MD: Naval Institute Press, 1986.

Bradford, Sarah H. *Harriet Tubman: The Moses of Her People.* New York: For the author by G. R. Lockwood & Son, 1886.

Bradley, Erwin S. *Simon Cameron, Lincoln's Secretary of War: A Political Biography.* Philadelphia: University of Pennsylvania Press, 1966.

Bradley, Erwin S. *The Triumph of Militant Republicanism.* Philadelphia: University of Pennsylvania Press, 1964.

Bradsby, H. C. *History of Bradford County, Pennsylvania; with Biographical Selections.* Chicago: S. B. Nelson, 1891.

Brigham, Johnson. *James Harlan.* Iowa City: State Historical Society of Iowa, 1913.

Brock, Peter. *Pacifism in the United States: From the Colonial Era to the First World War.* Princeton, NJ: Princeton University Press, 1968.

Brockett, L. P., and Mary C. Vaughan. *Woman's Work in the Civil War: A Record of Herosim, Patriotism and Patience.* Philadelphia: Zeigler, McCurdy & Co., 1867.

Brodie, Fawn. *Thaddeus Stevens, Scourge of the South.* New York: W. W. Norton & Co., 1959.

Brooks, Noah. *Washington, D.C., in Lincoln's Time.* Edited by Herbert Mitgang. New York: Century Co., 1895; reprint, Chicago: Quadrangle Books, 1971.

Brown, Charles H. *William Cullen Bryant.* New York: Scribner's, 1971.

Brown, Dee Alexander. *The Bold Cavaliers: Morgan's 2nd Kentucky Cavalry Raiders.* Philadelphia: Lippincott, 1959.

Brown, Dee Alexander. *Grierson's Raid.* Urbana: University of Illinois Press, 1954.

Brown, Francis. *Raymond of the Times.* New York: W.W. Norton Co., 1951.

Brown, Ira V. "William D. Kelley and Radical Reconstruction." *Pennsylvania Magazine of History and Biography* 85 (July 1961):316–329.

Brown, Kent Masterson. *Cushing of Gettysburg: The Story of a Union Artillery Commander.* Lexington: University Press of Kentucky, 1993.

Browning, Orville Hickman. *The Diary of Orville Hickman Browning.* 2 vols. Edited by Theodore Calvin Pease and James G. Randall. Springfield: Illinois State Historical Society, 1925–1933.

Brownlow, W. G. *Sketches of the Rise, Progress, and Decline of Secession; with a Narrative of Personal Adventures Among the Rebels.* Philadelphia: G. W. Childs, 1862.

Bruce, Robert V. *Lincoln and the Tools of War.* Indianapolis, IN: Bobbs-Merrill, 1956.

Brummer, Sidney David. *Political History of New York State During the Period of the Civil War.* New York: Longmans, Green, & Co., 1911.

Buckingham, Samuel G. *The Life of William A. Buckingham, the War Governor of Con-*

necticut, with a Review of His Public Acts, and Especially the Distinguished Services He Rendered His Country During the War of the Rebellion; with Which Is Incorporated, a Condensed Account of the More Important Campaigns of the War, and Information from Private Sources and Family and Official Documents. Springfield, MA: W. F. Adams Co., 1894.

Burton, E. Milby. *The Siege of Charleston, 1861–1865.* Columbia: University of South Carolina Press, 1970.

Burton, Theodore E. *John Sherman.* Boston: Houghton, Mifflin Co., 1906.

Byrne, Frank L. *Prophet of Prohibition: Neal Dow and His Crusade.* Madison: State Historical Society of Wisconsin for the Department of History, University of Wisconsin, 1961; reprint, Gloucester, MA: Peter Smith, 1969.

Calhoun, Charles W. *Gilded Age Cato: The Life of Walter Q. Gresham.* Lexington: University Press of Kentucky, 1988.

Carlson, Oliver. *The Man Who Made News, James Gordon Bennett.* New York: Duell, Sloan and Pearce, 1942.

Carpenter, John A. *Sword and Olive Branch: Oliver Otis Howard.* Pittsburgh, PA: University of Pittsburgh Press, 1964.

Carroll, Charles. *Rhode Island: Three Centuries of Democracy.* 4 vols. New York: Lewis Historical Publishing Co., 1932.

Carse, Robert. *Department of the South: Hilton Head Island in the Civil War.* Columbia, SC: State Printing Co., 1961.

Case, Lynn M., and Warren F. Spencer. *The United States and France: Civil War Diplomacy.* Philadelphia: University of Pennsylvania Press, 1970.

Castel, Albert. *Decision in the West: The Atlanta Campaign of 1864.* Lawrence: University Press of Kansas, 1992.

Castel, Albert. *A Frontier State at War: Kansas, 1861–1865.* Ithaca, NY: Published for the American Historical Association by Cornell University Press, 1958.

Castel, Albert. *General Sterling Price and the Civil War in the West.* Baton Rouge: Louisiana State University Press, 1968.

Castel, Albert. *The Presidency of Andrew Johnson.* Lawrence: Regents Press of Kansas, 1979.

Catton, Bruce. *Glory Road: The Bloody Route from Fredericksburg to Gettysburg.* Vol. 2 in *The Army of the Potomac.* Garden City, NY: Doubleday & Co., 1952.

Catton, Bruce. *Grant Moves South.* Boston: Little, Brown, 1960.

Catton, Bruce. *Grant Takes Command.* Boston: Little, Brown, 1969.

Catton, Bruce. *Mr. Lincoln's Army.* Vol. 1 in *The Army of the Potomac.* Garden City, NY: Doubleday & Co., 1953.

Catton, Bruce. *Never Call Retreat.* Vol. 3 in *The Centennial History of the Civil War.* Garden City, NY: Doubleday & Co., 1965.

Catton, Bruce. *A Stillness at Appomattox.* Vol. 3 in *The Army of the Potomac.* Garden City, NY: Doubleday & Co., 1953.

Catton, Bruce. *Terrible Swift Sword.* Vol. 2 in *The Centennial History of the Civil War.* Garden City, NY: Doubleday & Co., 1963.

Chase, Salmon P. *Inside Lincoln's Cabinet: The Civil War Diaries of Salmon P. Chase.* Edited by David Donald. New York: Longmans, Green & Co., 1954.

Cheek, William, and Aimee Lee Cheek. *John Mercer Langston and the Fight for Black Freedom, 1829–65.* Urbana: University of Illinois Press, 1989.

Chester, Giraud. *Embattled Maiden: The Life of Anna Dickinson.* New York: Putnam, 1951.

Chidsey, Donald Barr. *The Gentleman from New York: A Life of Roscoe Conkling.* New Haven, CT: Yale University Press, 1935.

Cimbala, Paul A. "The 'Talisman Power': Davis Tillson, the Freedmen's Bureau, and Free Labor in Reconstruction Georgia, 1865–1866." *Civil War History* 28 (June 1982):153–171.

Clark, Charles Branch. *Politics in Maryland During the Civil War.* Chestertown, MD: N.p., 1952. Collection of articles that had appeared in *Maryland Historical Magazine* from September 1941 to June 1946.

Clark, Clifford E., Jr. *Henry Ward Beecher: Spokesman for a Victorian America.* Urbana: University of Illinois Press, 1978.

Clark, Dan Elbert. *Samuel Jordan Kirkwood.* Iowa City: State Historical Society of Iowa, 1917.

[Clark, Will Leach, et al.]. *History of the Counties of Woodbury and Plymouth, Iowa; Including an Extended Sketch of Sioux City, Their Early Settlement and Progress to the Present Time: A Description of Their Historic and Interesting Localities; Sketches of the Townships, Cities and Villages; Portraits of Some of the Prominent Men, and Biographies of Many of the Representative Citizens.* Chicago: A. Warner & Co., 1890–1891.

Clayton, W. Woodford. *History of Onondaga County, New York, with Illustrations and Biographical Sketches of Some of Its Prominent Men and Pioneers.* Syracuse, NY: D. Mason & Co., 1878.

Cleaves, Freeman. *Meade of Gettysburg.* Norman: University of Oklahoma Press, 1960.

Coddington, Edwin B. *The Gettysburg Campaign: A Study in Command.* New York: Scribner's, 1968.

Coffin, Howard. *Full Duty: Vermonters in the Civil War.* Woodstock, VT: Countryman Press, 1993.

Cole, Arthur C. *The Era of the Civil War, 1848–1870.* Vol. 3 of *Centennial History of Illinois.* Springfield: Illinois Centennial Commission, 1919.

Cole, Cornelius. *Memoirs of Cornelius Cole.* New York: McLoughlin Brothers, 1908.

Collin, Henry P. *A Twentieth Century History and Biographical Record of Branch County, Michigan.* New York: Lewis Publishing Co., 1906.

Collins, Lewis, and Richard H. Collins. *History of Kentucky: Revised, Enlarged Fourfold and Brought Down to the Year 1874 by His Son Richard H. Collins.* 2 vols. Covington, KY: Collins & Co., 1874.

The Columbian Biographical Dictionary and Portrait Gallery of the Representative Men of the United States: Wisconsin Volume. Chicago: Lewis Publishing Co., 1895.

Combined History of Shelby and Moultrie Counties, Illinois; with Illustrations Descriptive of Their Scenery, and Biographical Sketches of Some of Their Prominent Men and Pioneers. Philadelphia: Brink, McDonough, Co., 1881.

Connelly, William E. *A Standard History of Kansas and Kansans.* 5 vols. Chicago: Lewis Co., 1918.

Conrad, Earl. *Harriet Tubman.* Washington, DC: Associated Publishers, 1943.

Conrad, Henry C. *History of the State of Delaware from the Earliest Settlements to the Year 1907.* 3 vols. Wilmington, DE: H.C. Conrad, 1908.

Cook, Robert. *Baptism of Fire: The Republican Party in Iowa, 1838–1878.* Ames: Iowa State University Press, 1994.

Cooling, Benjamin Franklin. *Forts Henry and Donelson: The Key to the Confederate Heartland.* Knoxville: University of Tennessee Press, 1987.

Cooling, Benjamin Franklin. *Symbol, Sword, and Shield: Defending Washington During the Civil War.* 2nd rev. ed. Shippensburg, PA: White Mane Publishing Co., 1991.

Coons, John W., comp. *Indiana at Shiloh: Report of the Commission.* Indianapolis: Indiana Shiloh National Park Commission, 1904.

Cornish, Dudley Taylor. *The Sable Arm: Negro Troops in the Union Army, 1861–1865.* New York: Longmans, Green & Co., 1956.

Cornish, Dudley Taylor, and Virginia Jeans Laas. *Lincoln's Lee: The Life of Samuel Phillips Lee, United States Navy, 1812–1897.* Lawrence: University Press of Kansas, 1986.

Corwin, Thomas. *Life and Speeches of Thomas Corwin: Orator, Lawyer and Statesman.* Edited by Josiah Morrow. Cincinnati, OH: W.H. Anderson & Co., 1986.

Coryell, Janet L. *Neither Heroine nor Fool: Anna Ella Carroll of Maryland.* Kent, OH: Kent State University Press, 1990.

Coulter, E. Merton. *The Civil War and Readjustment in Kentucky.* Chapel Hill: University of North Carolina Press, 1926.

Coulter, E. Merton. *William G. Brownlow: Fighting Parson of the Southern Highlands.* Knoxville: University of Tennessee Press, 1971.

Cox, Jacob D. *Atlanta.* New York: C. Scribner's Sons, 1882.

Cox, Jacob D. *Military Reminiscences of the Civil War.* 2 vols. New York: C. Scribner's Sons, 1900.

Cox, Lawanda, and John H. Cox. *Politics, Principles, and Prejudice, 1865–1866: Dilemma of Reconstruction America.* New York: Atheneum, 1969.

Cozzens, Peter. *This Terrible Sound: The Battle of Chickamauga.* Urbana: University of Illinois Press, 1992.

Craig, Berry F. "Henry Cornelius Burnett: Champion of Southern Rights." *Register of the Kentucky Historical Society* 77 (October 1979):266–274.

Cramer, C. H. "The Political Metamorphosis of Robert Green Ingersoll." *Journal of the Illinois State Historical Society* 36 (Autumn 1943):271–283.

Crapo, Henry Howland. *The Story of Henry Howland Crapo, 1804–1869, Told by Henry Howland Crapo, [Jr.], in 1933.* Boston: Thomas Todd Co., 1933.

Crawford, Mary Caroline. *Famous Families of Massachusetts.* 2 vols. Boston: Little, Brown & Co., 1930.

Crawford, Samuel W. *The History of Fort Sumpter [sic]: Being an Inside History of the Affairs in South Carolina, and Washington, 1860–1, and the Conditions and Events in the South Which Brought on the Rebellion: The Genesis of the Civil War.* New York: F.P. Harper, 1896.

Cresap, Bernarr. *Appomattox Commander: The Story of General E.O.C. Ord.* South Brunswick, NJ: A. S. Barnes, 1981.

Crockett, Walter Hill. *Vermont: The Green Mountain State.* 4 vols. New York: Century History Co., 1921.

Croffut, W. A., and John M. Morris. *The Military and Civil History of Connecticut During the War of 1861–1865. Comprising a Detailed Account of the Various Regiments and Batteries, Through March, Encampment, Bivouac, and Battle: Also Instances of Distinguished Personal Gallantry, and Biographical Sketches of Many Heroic Soldiers: Together with a Record of the Patriotic Action of*

Citizens at Home, and of the Liberal Support Furnished by the State in Its Executive and Legislative Departments. New York: L. Bill, 1868.

Crouthamel, James L. *James Watson Webb: A Biography.* Middletown, CT: Wesleyan University Press, 1969.

Curl, Donald W. *Murat Halstead and the Cincinnati Commercial.* Boca Raton: University Presses of Florida, 1980.

Current, Richard N. *The Civil War Era, 1848–1873.* Vol. 2 in *The History of Wisconsin.* Madison: State Historical Society of Wisconsin, 1976.

Current, Richard N. *Old Thad Stevens, a Story of Ambition.* Madison: University of Wisconsin Press, 1942.

Curry, Leonard P. *Blueprint for Modern America: Nonmilitary Legislation of the First Civil War Congress.* Nashville, TN: Vanderbilt University Press, 1968.

Curry, Richard Orr. *A House Divided: A Study of Statehood Politics and the Copperhead Movement in West Virginia.* Pittsburgh, PA: University of Pittsburgh Press, 1964.

Dana, Charles A. *Recollections of the Civil War: With the Leaders at Washington and in the Field in the Sixties.* New York: D. Appleton and Co., 1897.

Dana, Richard Henry, Jr. *The Journal of Richard Henry Dana, Jr.* Edited by Robert F. Lucid. Cambridge, MA: Belknap Press of Harvard University Press, 1968.

Davis, Aaron J., ed. *History of Clarion County, Pennsylvania; with Illustrations and Biographical Sketches of Some of Its Prominent Men and Pioneers.* Syracuse, NY: Mason Co., 1887.

Davis, Carl L. *Arming the Union: Small Arms in the Civil War.* Port Washington, NY: Kennikat Press, 1973.

Davis, Stanton Ling. *Pennsylvania Politics, 1860–1863.* Cleveland, OH: Western Reserve University Press, 1935.

Davis, William C. *Battle at Bull Run: A History of the First Major Campaign of the Civil War.* New York: Doubleday, 1977.

Davis, William C. *The Battle of New Market.* Garden City, NY: Doubleday, 1975.

Dawley, Alan. *Class and Community: The Industrial Revolution in Lynn.* Cambridge, MA: Harvard University Press, 1976.

Dawson, Joseph G., III. *Army Generals and Reconstruction: Louisiana, 1862–1877.* Baton Rouge: Louisiana State University Press, 1982.

De Trobriand, Regis. *Four Years with the Army of the Potomac.* Translated by George K. Dauchy. Boston: Ticknor and Co., 1889.

Dell, Christopher. *Lincoln and the War Democrats: The Grand Erosion of Conservative Tradition.* Rutherford, NJ: Fairleigh Dickinson University Press, 1975.

Dewitt, David Miller. *The Impeachment and Trial of Andrew Johnson, Seventeenth President of the United States: A History.* New York: Macmillan Co., 1903.

Dickinson, Anna E. *A Ragged Register (of People, Places and Opinions).* New York: Harper & Brothers, 1879.

Dictionary of Wisconsin Biography. Madison: State Historical Society of Wisconsin, 1960.

Dix, Morgan, comp. *Memoirs of John Adams Dix.* 2 vols. New York: Harper Brothers, 1883.

Dodge, Grenville M. *Personal Recollections of President Abraham Lincoln, General Ulysses S. Grant and General William T. Sherman.* Council Bluffs, IA: Monarch Printing Co., 1914.

Donald, David. *Charles Sumner and the Coming of the Civil War.* New York: Alfred A. Knopf, 1960.

Donald, David. *Charles Sumner and the Rights of Man.* New York: Alfred A. Knopf, 1970.

Dorfman, Joseph. *The Economic Mind in American Civilization.* 5 vols. New York: Viking Press, 1946–1959.

Dorn, Helen P. "Samuel Medary—Journalist and Politician, 1801–1864." *Ohio State Archaeological and Historical Quarterly* 53 (January–March 1944):14–38.

Dorsey, Florence L. *Road to the Sea: The Story of James B. Eads and the Mississippi River.* New York: Rinehart, 1947.

Dow, Neal. *The Reminiscences of Neal Dow: Recollections of Eighty Years.* Portland, ME: Evening Express Publishing Co., 1898.

Dowden, Albert Ricker. "John Gregory Smith." *Vermont History* 32 (April 1964):79–97.

Dowdey, Clifford. *The Seven Days: The Emergence of Lee.* Boston: Little, Brown & Co., 1964.

Doyle, William B., ed. *Centennial History of Summit County, Ohio and Representative Citizens.* Chicago: Biographical Publishing Co., 1908.

Du Pont, Samuel Francis. *Samuel Francis Du Pont: A Selection from His Civil War Letters.* 3 vols. Edited by John D. Hayes. Ithaca, NY: Published for the Eleutherian Mills Historical Library by Cornell University Press, 1969.

Duberman, Martin. *James Russell Lowell.* Boston: Houghton Mifflin Co., 1966.

Duberman, Martin B. *Charles Francis Adams, 1807–1886.* Boston: Houghton Mifflin Co., 1960.

DuBois, Ellen Carol. *Feminism and Suffrage: The Emergence of an Independent Women's Movement in America, 1848–1869.* Ithaca, NY: Cornell University Press, 1978.

Dufour, Charles L. *The Night the War Was Lost.* Garden City, NY: Doubleday, 1960.

Dunbar, Willis F. *Michigan: A History of the Wolverine State.* Grand Rapids, MI: Eerdmans, 1965; revised edition by George S. May. Grand Rapids, MI: Eerdmans, 1980.

Duncan, Bingham. *Whitelaw Reid: Journalist, Politician, Diplomat.* Athens: University of Georgia Press, 1975.

Dunne, Edward F. *Illinois: The Heart of the Nation.* 5 vols. Chicago: Lewis Publishing Co., 1933.

Durant, Samuel W. *History of St. Lawrence County, New York with Illustrations and Biographical Sketches of Some of Its Prominent Men and Pioneers.* Philadelphia: L. H. Everts Co., 1878.

Durden, Robert F. *James Shepherd Pike: Republicanism and the American Negro, 1850–1882.* Durham, NC: Duke University Press, 1957.

Dyer, Brainerd. "Thomas H. Dudley." *Civil War History* 1 (December 1955):401–413.

Dykstra, Robert R. *Bright Radical Star: Black Freedom and White Supremacy on the Hawkeye Frontier.* Cambridge, MA: Harvard University Press, 1993.

Eaton, John, and Ethel Osgood Mason. *Grant, Lincoln, and the Freedmen; Reminiscences of the Civil War with Special Reference to the Work for the Contrabands and Freedmen of the Mississippi Valley.* New York: Longmans, Green, & Co., 1907.

Edwards, G. Thomas. "Benjamin Stark, the U.S. Senate, and the 1862 Membership Issues [Part I]." *Oregon Historical Quarterly* 72 (December 1971):315–338.

Edwards, G. Thomas. "Benjamin Stark, the U.S. Senate, and the 1862 Membership Issues [Part II]." *Oregon Historical Quarterly* 73 (March 1972):31–59.

Edwards, Glenn Thomas. "The Department of the Pacific in the Civil War Years." Ph.D. dissertation, University of Oregon, 1963.

Edwards, G. Thomas, "Holding the Far West for the Union: The Army in 1861." *Civil War History* 14 (December 1968):307–324.

Edwards, William B. *Civil War Guns. The Complete Story of Federal and Confederate Arms: Design, Manufacture, Identification, Procurement, Issue, Employment, Effectiveness, and Postwar Disposal.* Harrisburg, PA: Stackpole Books, 1962.

Egle, William H., ed. *Andrew Gregg Curtin: His Life and Services.* Philadelphia: Avil Printing Co., 1895.

Elliott, Charles Winslow. *Winfield Scott: The Soldier and the Man.* New York: Macmillan Co., 1937.

Elliott, Russell R. *Servant of Power: A Political Biography of Senator William M. Stewart.* Reno: University of Nevada Press, 1983.

Emerson, William A. *Fitchburg, Massachusetts: Past and Present.* Fitchburg, MA: Press of Blanchard & Brown, 1887.

Engle, Stephen D. *Yankee Dutchman: The Life of Franz Sigel.* Fayetteville: University of Arkansas Press, 1993.

Evans, Elwood, comp. *History of the Pacific Northwest: Washington and Oregon; Embracing an Account of the Original Discoveries on the Pacific Coast of North America and a Description of the Conquest, Settlement and Subjugation of the Vast Country Included in the Original Territory of Oregon; also Interesting Biographies of the Earliest Settlers and More Prominent Men and Women of the Pacific Northwest.* 2 vols. Portland, OR: North Pacific History Company, 1889.

Evans, Frank B. *Pennsylvania Politics 1872–1877: A Study in Political Leadership.* Harrisburg: Pennsylvania Historical and Museum Commission, 1966.

Evans, Herndon J. *The Newspaper Press in Kentucky.* Lexington: University Press of Kentucky, 1976.

Evans, Nelson W. *A History of Scioto County, Ohio, Together with a Pioneer Record of Southern Ohio.* Portsmouth, OH: N.W. Evans, 1903.

Fairman, Charles. *Mr. Justice Miller and the Supreme Court, 1862–1890.* Cambridge, MA: Harvard University Press, 1939.

Farish, Thomas Edwin. *History of Arizona.* 8 vols. Phoenix, AZ [San Francisco, CA: Filmer Brothers Electrotype Company], 1915–1918.

Fehrenbacher, Don E. *Chicago Giant: A Biography of "Long John" Wentworth.* Madison, WI: American History Research Center, 1957.

Fehrenbacher, Don E. *Lincoln in Text and Context: Collected Essays.* Stanford, CA: Stanford University Press, 1987.

Fertig, James Walter. *The Secession and Reconstruction of Tennessee.* Chicago: University of Chicago Press, 1898.

Fessenden, Francis. *Life and Public Services of William Pitt Fessenden: United States Senator from Maine 1854–1864, Secretary of the Treasury 1864–1865, United States Senator from Maine 1865–1869.* 2 vols. Boston: Houghton, Mifflin, 1907.

Field, Edward. *State of Rhode Island and Providence Plantations at the End of the Century.* 3 vols. Boston: Mason Publishing Company, 1902.

Fischer, LeRoy H. *Lincoln's Gadfly, Adam Gurowski.* Norman: University of Oklahoma Press, 1964.

Fish, Carl Russell. *The Civil Service and Patronage.* New York: Russell & Russell, 1904.

Fishel, Edwin C. "Pinkerton and McClellan: Who Deceived Whom?" *Civil War History* 34 (June 1988):115–142.

Fisher, Sidney George. *A Philadelphia Perspective: The Diary of Sidney George Fisher Covering the Years 1834–1871.* Edited by Nicholas B. Wainwright. Philadelphia: Historical Society of Pennsylvania, 1967.

Fitch, Charles Elliott. *Encyclopedia of Biography of New York, a Life Record of Men and Women Whose Sterling Character and Energy and Industry Have Made Them Pre-eminent in Their Own and Many Other States.* 3 vols. Boston: American Historical Society, 1916.

Folwell, William Watts. *A History of Minnesota.* 4 vols. Saint Paul: Minnesota Historical Society, 1921–1930.

Foner, Eric. *Free Soil, Free Labor, Free Men: The Ideology of the Republican Party Before the Civil War.* New York: Oxford University Press, 1970.

Forbes, Edwin. *A Civil War Artist at the Front: Edwin Forbes' Life Studies of the Great Army.* Edited by William Forrest Dawson. New York: Oxford University Press, 1957.

Forbes, Edwin. *Thirty Years After: An Artist's Memoir of the Civil War.* Introduction by William J. Cooper. Baton Rouge: Louisiana State University Press, 1993.

Force, M. F. *From Fort Henry to Corinth.* New York: Charles Scribner's Sons, 1881.

Foulke, William Dudley. *Life of Oliver P. Morton, Including His Important Speeches.* 2 vols. Indianapolis, IN: Bowen-Merrill Co., 1898.

Fox, Gustavus Vasa. *Confidential Correspondence of Gustavus Vasa Fox, Assistant Secretary of the Navy, 1861–1865.* 2 vols. Edited by Robert Means Thompson and Richard Wainwright. New York: Printed for the Naval History Society by De Vinne Press, 1918–1920.

Frassanito, William A. *Antietam: The Photographic Legacy of America's Bloodiest Day.* New York: Charles Scribner's Sons, 1978.

Frassanito, William A. *Gettysburg: A Journey in Time.* New York: Charles Scribner's Sons, 1975.

Fredrickson, George M. *The Inner Civil War: Northern Intellectuals and the Crisis of the Union.* New York: Harper & Row, 1965.

Freemon, Frank R. "Lincoln Finds a Surgeon General: William A. Hammond and the Transformation of the Union Army Medical Bureau." *Civil War History* 33 (March 1987):5–21.

Freidel, Frank. *Francis Lieber: Nineteenth-Century Liberal.* Baton Rouge: Louisiana State University Press, 1948.

Friedman, Lawrence J. *Gregarious Saints: Self and Community in American Abolitionism.* Cambridge, UK, and New York: Cambridge University Press, 1981.

Friedman, Leon, and Fred L. Israel, eds. *The Justices of the United States Supreme Court, 1789–1969.* 5 vols. New York: Chelsea House in association with Bowker, 1969–1978.

Frothingham, Paul Revere. *Edward Everett: Orator and Statesman.* Boston: Houghton Mifflin Co., 1925.

Fry, Joseph A. *Henry S. Sanford: Diplomacy and Business in Nineteenth-Century America.* Reno: University of Nevada Press, 1982.

Fuess, Claude M. *Carl Schurz, Reformer, 1829–1906.* Port Washington, NY: Kennikat Press, 1963.

Furgurson, Ernest B. *Chancellorsville 1863: The Souls of the Brave.* New York: Alfred A. Knopf, 1992.

Futhey, J. Smith, and Gilbert Cope. *History of Chester County, Pennsylvania, with Genealogical and Biographical Sketches.* Philadelphia: Louis H. Everts, 1881.

Gallagher, Gary W., ed. *The Second Day at Gettysburg: Essays on Confederate and Union Leadership.* Kent, OH: Kent State University Press, 1993.

Gambee, Budd Leslie, Jr. *Frank Leslie and His Illustrated Newspaper, 1855–1860.* Ann Arbor: Department of Library Science, University of Michigan, 1964.

Gardner, Albert Ten Eyck. *Winslow Homer, American Artist: His World and His Work.* New York: Bramhall House, 1961.

Geary, James W. *We Need Men: The Union Draft in the Civil War.* DeKalb: Northern Illinois University Press, 1991.

George, Mary Karl. *Zachariah Chandler: A Political Biography.* East Lansing: Michigan State University Press, 1969.

Gerteis, Louis S. *From Contraband to Freedman: Federal Policy Toward Southern Blacks, 1861–1865.* Westport, CT: Greenwood Press, 1973.

Gibbon, John. *Personal Recollections of the Civil War.* New York: G. P. Putnam's Sons, 1928.

Gillmore, Quincy A. *Engineer and Artillery Operations Against the Defenses of Charleston Harbor in 1863.* New York: D. Nostrand, 1868.

Glatthaar, Joseph T. *Forged in Battle: The Civil War Alliance of Black Soldiers and White Officers.* New York: Free Press, 1990.

Going, Charles Buxton. *David Wilmot, Free Soiler: A Biography of the Great Advocate of the Wilmot Proviso.* New York: D. Appleton & Co., 1924.

Goodrich, Lloyd. *Winslow Homer's America.* New York: Tudor Publishing Co., 1969.

Goodrich, Thomas. *Bloody Dawn: The Story of the Lawrence Massacre.* Kent, OH: Kent State University Press, 1991.

Gordon, George Henry. *History of the Campaign of the Army of Virginia, Under John Pope . . . from Cedar Mountain to Alexandria, 1862.* Boston: Houghton, Osgood and Co., 1880.

Gosnell, H. Allen. *Guns on the Western Waters: The Story of River Gunboats in the Civil War.* Baton Rouge: Louisiana State University Press, 1949.

Goss, Dwight. *History of Grand Rapids and Its Industries.* Chicago: C. F. Cooper, 1906.

Graham, Howard Jay. *Everyman's Constitution: Historical Essays on the Fourteenth Amendment, the "Conspiracy Theory," and American Constitutionalism.* Madison: State Historical Society of Wisconsin, 1968.

Grant, Ulysses S. *The Papers of Ulysses S. Grant.* 18 vols. Edited by John Y. Simon. Carbondale: Southern Illinois University Press, 1967–1991.

Gravely, William. *Gilbert Haven, Methodist Abolitionist: A Study in Race, Religion, and Reform, 1850–1880.* Edited by the Commission on Archives and History of the United Methodist Church. Nashville, TN: Abingdon Press, 1973.

Gray, Leslie Burns. *The Source and the Vision: Nevada's Role in the Civil War Amendments and the Reconstruction Legislation.* Sparks, NV: Gray Trust, 1990.

Gray, Ralph D., ed. *Gentlemen from Indiana: National Party Candidates, 1836–1940.* Indianapolis: Indiana Historical Bureau, 1977.

Grebner, Constantin. *"We Were the Ninth": A History of the Ninth Regiment, Ohio Volunteer Infantry, April 17, 1861, to June 7, 1864.* Translated and edited by Frederic Trautmann. Kent, OH: Kent State University Press, 1987.

Greenbie, Marjorie Barstow. *My Dear Lady: The Story of Anna Ella Carroll, the "Great Unrecognized Member of Lincoln's Cabinet."* New York: McGraw-Hill, 1940.

Gregory, John G. *History of Milwaukee, Wisconsin.* 4 vols. Chicago: Clarke Publishing Co., 1931.

Gresham, Matilda. *Life of Walter Quinton Gresham, 1832–1895.* 2 vols. Chicago: Rand, McNally & Co., 1919.

Grinnell, Josiah Bushnell. *Men and Events of Forty Years: Autobiographical Reminiscences of an Active Career from 1850 to 1890.* Boston: Lothrop Co., 1891.

Hafendorfer, Kenneth A. *Perryville: Battle for Kentucky.* 2nd ed. Louisville, KY: K. H. Press, 1991.

Hagerman, Edward. *The American Civil War and the Origins of Modern Warfare: Ideas, Organization, and Field Command.* Bloomington: Indiana University Press, 1988.

Hain, H. H. *History of Perry County, Pennsylvania, Including Descriptions of Indians and Pioneer Life from the Time of Earliest Settlement, Sketches of Its Noted Men and Women and Many Professional Men.* Harrisburg, PA: Hain-Moore Co., 1922.

Hallock, William H. *Life of Gerard Hallock: Thirty-three Years Editor of the New York Journal of Commerce. Illustrated in Biography, Professional Writings, Correspondence, Controversies, etc.* New York: Oakley, Mason, 1869.

Halstead, Murat. *Three Against Lincoln: Murat Halstead Reports the Caucuses of 1860.* Edited by William B. Hesseltine. Baton Rouge: Louisiana State University Press, 1960.

Hanchett, William. *Irish: Charles G. Halpine in Civil War America.* Syracuse, NY: Syracuse University Press, 1970.

Hanchett, William. *The Lincoln Murder Conspiracies: Being an Account of the Hatred Felt by Many Americans for President Abraham Lincoln During the Civil War and the First Complete Examination and Refutation of the Many Theories, Hypotheses, and Speculations Put Forward Since 1865 Concerning Those Presumed to Have Aided, Abetted, Controlled, or Directed the Murderous Act of John Wilkes Booth in Ford's Theater the Night of April 14.* Urbana: University of Illinois Press, 1983.

Hancock, Harold Bell. *Delaware During the Civil War.* Wilmington: Historical Society of Delaware, 1961.

Harlow, Ralph V. *Gerrit Smith, Philanthropist and Reformer.* New York: Holt and Co., 1939.

Harper, Ida H. *The Life and Work of Susan B. Anthony.* 3 vols. Indianapolis, IN: Bowen-Merrill Co., 1899–1908.

Harper, Robert S. *Lincoln and the Press.* New York: McGraw-Hill, 1951.

Harrington, Fred H. *Fighting Politician: Major General N.P. Banks.* Philadelphia: University of Pennsylvania Press, 1948.

Harrison, John M. *The Man Who Made Nasby: David Ross Locke.* Chapel Hill: University of North Carolina Press, 1968.

Harrison, Lowell, ed. *Kentucky's Governors, 1792–1985.* Lexington: University Press of Kentucky, 1985.

Hassard, John R. G. *Life of the Most Reverend John Hughes, D.D., First Archbishop of New York with Extracts from His Private Correspondence.* New York: D. Appleton and Co., 1866.

Hassler, Warren W., Jr. *Commanders of the Army of the Potomac.* Baton Rouge: Louisiana State University Press, 1962.

Hassler, Warren W., Jr. *General George B. McClellan: Shield of the Union.* Baton Rouge: Louisiana State University Press, 1957.

Hatch, Louis C., ed. *Maine: A History.* 5 vols. New York: American Historical Society, 1919.

Hawley, Joseph R. *Major General Joseph R. Hawley, Soldier and Editor (1826–1905). Civil War Military Letters with Gen. William T. Sherman's Letter Concerning the Responsibility of the Decision of the March to the Sea.* Edited by Albert D. Putnam. [Hartford?]: Connecticut Civil War Centennial Commission, 1964.

Haynes, Martin A. *A History of the Second Regiment, New Hampshire Volunteer Infantry, in the War of the Rebellion.* Lakeport, NH: N.p., 1896.

Hays, Elinor Rice. *Morning Star: A Biography of Lucy Stone, 1818–1893.* New York: Harcourt, Brace & World, 1961.

Hebert, Walter H. *Fighting Joe Hooker.* Indianapolis, IN: Bobbs-Merrill, 1944.

Hendrick, Jesse Burton. *Lincoln's War Cabinet.* Boston: Little, Brown and Co., 1946.

Hendrickson, James E. *Joe Lane of Oregon: Machine Politics and the Sectional Crisis, 1849–1861.* New Haven, CT: Yale University Press, 1967.

Henig, Gerald S. *Henry Winter Davis: Antebellum and Civil War Congressman from Maryland.* New York: Twayne Publishers, 1974.

Hennessy, John. *Return to Bull Run: The Campaign and Battle of Second Manassas.* New York: Simon and Schuster, 1993.

Herndon, Richard, comp., and Edwin M. Bacon, ed. *Men of Progress: One Thousand Biographical Sketches and Portraits of Leaders in Business and Professional Life in the Commonwealth of Massachusetts.* Boston: New England Magazine, 1896.

Hesseltine, William Best. *Civil War Prisons: A Study in War Psychology.* Columbus: Ohio State University Press, 1930.

Hesseltine, William Best. *Lincoln and the War Governors.* New York: Alfred A. Knopf, 1948.

Hewitt, Lawrence L. *Port Hudson: Confederate Bastion on the Mississippi.* Baton Rouge: Louisiana State University Press, 1987.

Heyman, Max L., Jr. *Prudent Soldier: A Biography of Major General E.R.S. Canby, 1817–1873: His Military Service in the Indian Campaigns, in the Mexican War, in California, New Mexico, Utah, and Oregon; in the Civil War in the Trans-Mississippi West, and as Military Governor in the Post-war South.* Glendale, CA: A. H. Clark Co., 1959.

Hicken, Victor. *Illinois in the Civil War.* 2nd ed. Urbana: University of Illinois Press, 1991.

Hirshson, Stanley P. *Grenville M. Dodge: Soldier, Politician, Railroad Pioneer.* Bloomington: Indiana University Press, 1967.

Historical Collections of the Mahoning Valley: Containing an Account of the Two Pioneer Reunions; Together with a Selection of Interesting Facts, Traditions, Biographical Sketches, Anecdotes, etc., Relating to the Sale and Settlement of the Lands Belonging to the Connecticut Land Company, and History and Reminiscences, Both General and Local. Youngstown, OH: Mahoning Valley Historical Society, 1876.

The History of Fond du Lac County, Wisconsin; Containing . . . War Record, Biographical Sketches . . . History of Wisconsin . . . etc. Chicago: Western Historical Co., 1880.

The History of Iowa County, Wisconsin; Containing an Account of Its Settlement,

Growth, Development and Resources . . . Biographical Sketches. Chicago: Western Historical Co., 1881.

History of Union County, Kentucky. A Complete Account of the Settlement, Organization, and Government of the County, Together with Facts and Figures Concerning Institutions and Resources of the County, and Biographical Sketches of Its Leading Citizens. Evansville, IN: Courier Co., 1886.

History of Wyoming County, New York, with Illustrations and Biographical Sketches of Some of Its Prominent Men and Pioneers. New York: F. W. Beers & Co., 1880.

Hitchcock, Ethan Allen. *Fifty Years in Camp and Field: Diary of Major-General Ethan Allan Hitchcock, U.S.A.* Edited by W. A. Croffut. New York: G. P. Putnam Co., 1909.

Hittell, Theodore H. *History of California.* 4 vols. San Francisco: N. J. Stone, 1897.

Holcombe, John W., and Hubert M. Skinner. *Life and Public Services of Thomas A. Hendricks with Selected Speeches and Writings.* Indianapolis, IN: Carlon and Hollenbeck, 1886.

Hollister, Orland J. *Life of Schuyler Colfax.* New York: Funk & Wagnalls, 1886.

Holt, Michael F. *Forging a Majority: The Formation of the Republican Party in Pittsburgh, 1840–1860.* New Haven, CT: Yale University Press, 1969.

Honeywell, Roy John. *Chaplains of the United States Army.* Washington, DC: Office of the Chief of Chaplains, Department of the Army, 1958.

Hood, James Larry. "For the Union: Kentucky's Unconditional Unionist Congressmen and the Development of the Republican Party in Kentucky, 1863–1865." *Register of the Kentucky Historical Society* 76 (July 1978):197–215.

Hood, James Larry. "The Union and Slavery: Congressman Brutus J. Clay of the Bluegrass." *Register of the Kentucky Historical Society* 75 (July 1977):214–221.

Hoogenboom, Ari. "Gustavus Vasa Fox and the Relief of Fort Sumter." *Civil War History* 9 (December 1963):383–398.

Hooper, Osman Castle. *History of Ohio Journalism, 1793–1933.* Columbus, OH: Spahr & Glenn Co., 1933.

Horan, James D. *Mathew Brady: Historian with a Camera.* New York: Crown Publishers, 1955.

Horan, James D. *The Pinkertons: The Detective Dynasty That Made History.* New York: Crown Publishers, 1968.

Horn, Stanley Fitzgerald. *The Decisive Battle of Nashville.* Baton Rouge: Louisiana State University Press, 1956.

Horner, Harlan Hoyt. *Lincoln and Greeley.* Urbana: University of Illinois Press, 1953.

Horowitz, Robert F. *The Great Impeacher: A Political Biography of James M. Ashley.* New York: Brooklyn College Press; distributed by Columbia University Press, 1979.

Howard, Harry N. *Turkey, the Straits and U.S. Policy.* Baltimore, MD: Johns Hopkins University Press, 1974.

Howard, Robert West. *The Great Iron Trail: The Story of the First Transcontinental Railroad.* New York: Putnam, 1962.

Hudson, Frederic. *Journalism in the United States, from 1690 to 1872.* New York: Harper & Brothers, 1873.

Hughes, Nathaniel Cheairs. *The Battle of Belmont: Grant Strikes South.* Chapel Hill: University of North Carolina Press, 1991.

Humes, Thomas William. *The Loyal Mountaineers of Tennessee.* Knoxville, TN: Ogden Brothers & Co., 1888.

Humphreys, Henry H. *Andrew Atkinson Humphreys: A Biography.* Philadelphia: John C. Winston Co., 1924.

Hungerford, Edward. *Men and Iron: The History of the New York Central.* New York: Thomas Y. Crowell Company, 1938.

Hunt, Gaillard, comp. *Israel, Elihu and Cadwallader Washburn: A Chapter in American Biography.* New York: Macmillan Co., 1925.

Hunt, H. Draper. *Hannibal Hamlin of Maine, Lincoln's First Vice-President.* Syracuse, NY: Syracuse University Press, 1969.

Huston, James A. *The Sinews of War: Army Logistics, 1775–1953.* Washington, DC: Office of the Chief of Military History, United States Army, 1966.

Ilisevich, Robert D. *Galusha A. Grow: The People's Candidate.* Pittsburgh, PA: University of Pittsburgh Press, 1988.

Imholte, John Quinn. *The First Volunteers: History of the First Minnesota Volunteer Regiment, 1861–1865.* Minneapolis, MN: Ross & Haines, 1963.

Irwin, Richard B. *History of the Nineteenth Army Corps.* New York: G. P. Putnam's Sons, 1893.

James, Alfred P. "General James Scott Negley." *Western Pennsylvania Historical Magazine* 14 (April 1931):69–91.

Jellison, Charles A. *Fessenden of Maine: Civil War Senator.* Syracuse, NY: Syracuse University Press, 1962.

Johannsen, Robert W. *Frontier Politics and the Sectional Conflict: The Pacific Northwest on the Eve of the Civil War.* Seattle: University of Washington Press, 1955.

Johannsen, Robert W. *Stephen A. Douglas.* New York: Oxford University Press, 1973.

Johns, Jane Martin. *Personal Recollections of Early Decatur, Abraham Lincoln, Richard J. Oglesby and the Civil War.* Edited by Howard C. Schaub. Decatur, IL: Decatur chapter, Daughters of the American Revolution, 1912.

Johnson, E. Polk. *History of Kentucky and Kentuckians: The Leaders and Representative Men in Commerce, Industry and Modern Activities.* 3 vols. Chicago: Lewis Publishing Co., 1912.

Johnson, Ludwell H. *Red River Campaign: Politics and Cotton in the Civil War.* Baltimore, MD: Johns Hopkins University Press, 1958; reprint, Kent, OH: Kent State University Press, 1993.

Jones, James P. *"Black Jack": John A. Logan and Southern Illinois in the Civil War Era.* Tallahassee: Florida State University Press, 1967.

Jones, James P. "General Jefferson C. Davis, USA, and Sherman's Georgia Campaign." *Georgia Historical Quarterly* 47 (September 1963):231–248.

Jones, James Pickett. *Yankee Blitzkrieg: Wilson's Raid Through Alabama and Georgia.* Athens: University of Georgia Press, 1976.

Jones, Paul. *The Irish Brigade.* Washington, DC: R. B. Luce, 1969.

Jones, Robert H. *The Civil War in the Northwest: Nebraska, Wisconsin, Iowa, Minnesota, and the Dakotas.* Norman: University of Oklahoma Press, 1960.

Jordan, David M. *Roscoe Conkling of New York: Voice in the Senate.* Ithaca, NY: Cornell University Press, 1971.

Jordan, David M. *Winfield Scott Hancock: A Soldier's Life.* Bloomington: Indiana University Press, 1988.

Jordon, John W., et al., eds. *Historic Homes and Institutions and Genealogical and*

Personal Memoirs of the Lehigh Valley, Pennsylvania. 2 vols. New York: Lewis
   Publishing Co., 1905.
Josephy, Alvin M., Jr. *The Civil War in the American West.* New York: Alfred A. Knopf,
   1991.
Kaplan, Justin. *Walt Whitman: A Life.* New York: Simon and Schuster, 1980.
Kaplan, Lawrence S. "The Brahmin as Diplomat in Nineteenth Century America: Ev-
   erett, Bancroft, Motley, Lowell." *Civil War History* 19 (March 1973):5–28.
Katz, Irving. *August Belmont: A Political Biography.* New York: Columbia University
   Press, 1968.
Keasbey, Anthony Q. "John T. Nixon." *Proceedings of the New Jersey Historical So-
   ciety. Second Series* 11 (1890):39–51.
Keasbey, Anthony Q. "Richard S. Field." *Proceedings of the New Jersey Historical
   Society, Second Series* 2 (1872):111–132.
Keller, Allan. *Morgan's Raid.* Indianapolis, IN: Bobbs-Merrill, 1961.
Keller, Morton. *The Art and Politics of Thomas Nast.* New York: Oxford University
   Press, 1968.
Kelley, Darwin N. *Milligan's Fight Against Lincoln.* New York: Exposition Press, 1973.
Kenworthy, Leonard S. *The Tall Sycamore of the Wabash: Daniel Wolsey Voorhees.*
   Boston: B. Humphries, 1936.
Kerr, Andrea Moore. *Lucy Stone: Speaking out for Equality.* New Brunswick, NJ: Rut-
   gers University Press, 1992.
Key, Jack D., and Bonnie Ellen Blustein. *William Alexander Hammond, M.D. (1828–
   1900): The Publications of an American Neurologist.* Rochester, MN: Davies
   Printing Co., 1983.
Kimball, Gayle. *The Religious Ideas of Harriet Beecher Stowe: Her Gospel of Wom-
   anhood.* New York: Mellen Press, 1982.
King, Willard L. *Lincoln's Manager, David Davis.* Cambridge, MA: Harvard University
   Press, 1960.
Kinsley, Philip. *The Chicago Tribune: Its First Hundred Years.* 3 vols. Chicago: Tribune
   Co., 1943–1946.
Kirwan, Albert D. *John J. Crittenden: The Struggle for the Union.* Lexington: University
   Press of Kentucky, 1962.
Kleber, John E., et al., eds. *The Kentucky Encyclopedia.* Lexington: University Press of
   Kentucky, 1992.
Klein, Philip S. *President James Buchanan: A Biography.* University Park: Pennsylvania
   State University Press, 1962.
Klement, Frank L. *The Copperheads in the Middle West.* Chicago: University of Chicago
   Press, 1960.
Klement, Frank L. *Dark Lanterns: Secret Political Societies, Conspiracies, and Treason
   Trials in the Civil War.* Baton Rouge: Louisiana State University Press, 1984.
Klement, Frank L. "Jane Grey Swisshelm and Lincoln: A Feminist Fusses and Frets."
   Abraham Lincoln Quarterly 6 (December 1950):227–238.
Klement, Frank L. *The Limits of Dissent: Clement L. Vallandigham and the Civil War.*
   Lexington: University Press of Kentucky, 1970.
Klotter, James C. *The Breckinridges of Kentucky, 1760–1981.* Lexington: University
   Press of Kentucky, 1986.
Knapp, Charles Merriam. *New Jersey Politics During the Period of the Civil War and
   Reconstruction.* Geneva, NY: W. F. Humphrey, 1924.

Knox, John Jay, et al. *History of Banking in the United States.* New York: B. Rhodes & Co., 1900.

Konkle, Burton Alva. *The Life and Speeches of Thomas Williams.* Philadelphia: Campion & Company, 1905.

Krick, Robert K. *Stonewall Jackson at Cedar Mountain.* Chapel Hill: University of North Carolina Press, 1990.

Krug, Mark M. *Lyman Trumbull: Conservative Radical.* New York: A. S. Barnes, 1965.

Lamers, William M. *The Edge of Glory: A Biography of General William S. Rosecrans, U.S.A..* New York: Harcourt, Brace, 1961.

Lane, J. Robert. *A Political History of Connecticut During the Civil War.* Washington, DC: Catholic University of America Press, 1941.

Lane, Samuel A. *Fifty Years and over of Akron and Summit County.* Akron, OH: Beacon Job Department, 1892.

Lang, William. *History of Seneca County, from the Close of the Revolutionary War to July, 1880: Embracing Many Personal Sketches of Pioneers, Anecdotes, and Faithful Descriptions of Events Pertaining to the Organization of the County and Its Progress.* Springfield, OH: Transcript Printing Co., 1880.

Langston, John Mercer. *From Virginia Plantation to the National Capitol; or, The First and Only Negro Representative in Congress from the Old Dominion.* Hartford, CT: American Publishing Co., 1894.

Lanman, Charles. *Biographical Annals of the Civil Government of the United States During Its First Century.* Washington, DC: James Anglim, 1876.

Lannie, Vincent P. *Public Money and Parochial Education: Bishop Hughes, Governor Seward, and the New York School Controversy.* Cleveland, OH: Press of Case Western Reserve University, 1968.

Lawrence, Alexander A. *James Moore Wayne, Southern Unionist.* Chapel Hill: University of North Carolina Press, 1943.

Leake, Paul. *History of Detroit: Chronicle of Its Progress, Its Industries, Its Institutions, and the People of the Fair City of the Straits.* New York: Lewis Publishing Co., 1912.

Leech, Margaret. *Reveille in Washington, 1860–1865.* New York: Harper & Brothers, 1941.

Levin, David. *History as Romantic Art: Bancroft, Prescott, Motley, and Parkman.* Stanford, CA: Stanford University Press, 1959.

Levin, H., ed. *The Lawyers and Lawmakers of Kentucky.* Chicago: Lewis Publishing Co., 1897.

Lewis, Charles L. *David Glasgow Farragut.* 2 vols. Annapolis, MD: United States Naval Institute, 1941–1943.

Lewis, Lloyd. *Sherman: Fighting Prophet.* New York: Harcourt, Brace and Co., 1932.

Lewis, Martin Deming. *Lumberman from Flint: The Michigan Career of Henry H. Crapo, 1855–1869.* Detroit: Wayne State University Press, 1958.

Liddell Hart, B. H. *Sherman: Soldier, Realist, American.* New York: Praeger, 1958.

Limbaugh, Ronald H. *Rocky Mountain Carpetbaggers: Idaho's Territorial Governors, 1863–1890.* Moscow: University Press of Idaho, 1982.

Lindsey, David. *"Sunset" Cox: Irrepressible Democrat.* Detroit: Wayne State University Press, 1959.

Livermore, Mary Ashton Rice. *The Story of My Life: Or, the Sunshine and Shadow of Seventy Years . . . with Hitherto Unrecorded Incidents and Recollections of Three*

Years' Experience as an Army Nurse in the Great Civil War, and Reminiscences of Twenty-five Years' Experiences on the Lecture Platform . . . to Which Is Added Six of Her Most Popular Lectures. Hartford, CT: A. D. Worthington and Co., 1898.

Long, E. B. *The Saints and the Union: Utah Territory During the Civil War.* Urbana: University of Illinois Press, 1981.

Longacre, Edward G. *The Cavalry at Gettysburg: A Tactical Study of Mounted Operations During the Civil War's Pivotal Campaign, 9 June–14 July 1863.* Rutherford, NJ: Fairleigh Dickinson University Press, 1986.

Longacre, Edward G. *From Union Stars to Top Hat: A Biography of the Extraordinary General James Harrison Wilson.* Harrisburg, PA: Stackpole Books, 1972.

Longacre, Edward G. *The Man Behind the Guns: A Biography of General Henry Jackson Hunt, Chief of Artillery, Army of the Potomac.* South Brunswick, NJ: A.S. Barnes, 1977.

Lord, Francis A. *Lincoln's Railroad Man: Herman Haupt.* Rutherford, NJ: Fairleigh Dickinson University Press, 1969.

Losson, Christopher Thomas. "Jacob Dolson Cox: A Military Biography." Ph.D. dissertation, University of Mississippi, 1993.

Love, William De Loss. *Wisconsin in the War of the Rebellion: A History of All Regiments and Batteries the State Has Sent to the Field, and Deeds of Her Citizens, Governors and Other Military Officers, and State and National Legislators to Suppress the Rebellion.* 2nd ed. Chicago: Church and Goodman, 1866.

Low, Frederick F. *Some Reflections of an Early California Governor Contained in a Short Dictated Memoir by Frederick F. Low, Ninth Governor of California, and Notes from an Interview Between Governor Low and Hubert Howe Bancroft in 1883.* Edited by Robert H. Becker. [Sacramento, CA]: Sacramento Book Collectors Club, 1959.

Lucas, Marion Brunson. *Sherman and the Burning of Columbia.* College Station: Texas A&M University Press, 1976.

Lyford, James O. *Life of Edward H. Rollins: A Political Biography.* Boston: D. Estes & Co., 1906.

Lyman, Theodore. *Meade's Headquarters, 1863–1865. Letters of Colonel Theodore Lyman from the Wilderness to Appomattox.* Edited by George R. Agassiz. Boston: Atlantic Monthly Press, 1922.

McAllister, Robert. *The Civil War Letters of General Robert McAllister.* Edited by James I. Robertson, Jr. New Brunswick, NJ: Published for the New Jersey Civil War Centennial Commission by Rutgers University Press, 1965.

McCabe, James D., Jr. *The Life and Public Services of Horatio Seymour; Together with a Complete and Authentic Life of Francis P. Blair, Jr.* New York: United States Publishing Co., 1868.

McCarter, J. M., and B. F. Jackson. *Historical and Biographical Encyclopaedia of Delaware.* Wilmington, DE: Aldine Publishing and Engraving Co., 1882.

McClintock, John N. *Colony, Province, State, 1623–1888: History of New Hampshire.* Boston: B. B. Russell, 1888.

McClure, A. H. *Old Time Notes of Pennsylvania: A Connected and Chronological Record of the Commercial, Industrial and Educational Advancement of Pennsylvania, and the Inner History of All Political Movements Since the Adoption of the Constitution of 1838.* 2 vols. Philadelphia: John C. Winston Co., 1905.

MacColl, E. Kimbark, and Harry H. Stein. *Merchants, Money and Power: The Portland Establishment, 1843–1913*. Portland, OR: Georgian Press, 1988.

McCulloch, Hugh. *Men and Measures of Half a Century; Sketches and Comments*. New York: C. Scribner's Sons, 1889.

McDonough, James Lee. *Schofield: Union General in the Civil War and Reconstruction*. Tallahassee: Florida State University Press, 1972.

McDonough, James Lee. *Shiloh—In Hell Before Night*. Knoxville: University of Tennessee Press, 1977.

McDonough, James Lee. *Stones River—Bloody Winter in Tennessee*. Knoxville: University of Tennessee Press, 1980.

McFeely, William S. *Frederick Douglass*. New York: W. W. Norton Co., 1991.

McFeely, William S. *Grant: A Biography*. New York: W. W. Norton Co., 1981.

McJimsey, George T. *Genteel Partisan: Manton Marble, 1834–1917*. Ames: Iowa State University Press, 1971.

McKay, Ernest. *Henry Wilson: Practical Radical, a Portrait of a Politician*. Port Washington, NY: Kennikat Press, 1971.

McKee, Irving. *"Ben Hur" Wallace: The Life of General Lew Wallace*. Berkeley: University of California Press, 1947.

McKelvey, Blake. *Rochester: The Flower City, 1855–1890*. Cambridge, MA: Harvard University Press, 1949.

McKitrick, Eric L. *Andrew Johnson and Reconstruction*. Chicago: University of Chicago Press, 1960.

McMullin, Thomas A., and David Walker. *Biographical Directory of American Territorial Governors*. Westport, CT: Meckler, 1984.

McPherson, James M. *Abraham Lincoln and the Second American Revolution*. New York: Oxford University Press, 1991.

McPherson, James M. *The Struggle for Equality: Abolitionists and the Negro in the Civil War and Reconstruction*. Princeton, NJ: Princeton University Press, 1964.

Magdol, Edward. *Owen Lovejoy: Abolitionist in Congress*. New Brunswick, NJ: Rutgers University Press, 1967.

Marshall, Helen E. *Dorothea Dix: Forgotten Samaritan*. Chapel Hill: University of North Carolina Press, 1937.

Marszalek, John F. *Sherman: A Soldier's Passion for Order*. New York: Free Press, 1993.

Marvel, William. *Burnside*. Chapel Hill: University of North Carolina Press, 1991.

Matter, William D. *If It Takes All Summer: The Battle of Spotsylvania*. Chapel Hill: University of North Carolina Press, 1988.

Meade, George Gordon, Jr., ed. *The Life and Letters of George G. Meade, Major-General United States Army*. 2 vols. New York: C. Scribner's Sons, 1913.

Meany, Edmond S. "George E. Cole." *Washington Historical Quarterly* 1 (January 1907):88–89.

Melendy, H. Brett, and Benjamin F. Gilbert. *The Governors of California: Peter H. Burnett to Edmund G. Brown*. Georgetown, CA: Talisman Press, 1965.

Memorial Record of Northeastern Indiana. Chicago: Lewis Publishing Co., 1896.

Meredith, Roy. *Mr. Lincoln's Camera Man: Mathew B. Brady*. 2nd rev. ed. New York: Dover Publications, 1974.

Merriam, George S. *The Life and Times of Samuel Bowles*. 2 vols. New York: Century Co., 1885.

Merrill, Horace Samuel. *Bourbon Democracy of the Middle West, 1865–1896.* Baton Rouge: Louisiana State University Press, 1953.

Merrill, James M. *Du Pont, the Making of an Admiral: A Biography of Samuel Francis Du Pont.* New York: Dodd, Mead, 1986.

Michie, Peter S. *The Life and Letters of General Emory Upton, Colonel of the Fourth Regiment of Artillery, and Brevet Major-General, U.S. Army.* New York: D. Appleton & Co., 1885.

Michigan Biographies, Including Members of Congress, Elective State Officers, Justices of the Supreme Court, Members of the Michigan Legislature, Board of Regents of the University of Michigan, State Board of Agriculture and State Board of Education. 2 vols. Lansing: Michigan Historical Commission, 1924.

Miers, Earl Schenck. *The Web of Victory: Grant at Vicksburg.* New York: Alfred A. Knopf, 1955.

Miller, James E., Jr. *Walt Whitman.* Updated ed. Boston: Twayne Publishers, 1990.

Mitchel, F. A. *Ormsby MacKnight Mitchel: Astronomer and General.* Boston: Houghton Mifflin Co., 1887.

Mitchell, Broadus. *Frederick Law Olmsted, a Critic of the Old South.* Baltimore, MD: Johns Hopkins University Press, 1924.

Mitchell, Donald Grant. *Daniel Tyler: A Memorial Volume Containing His Autobiography and War Record, Some Account of His Later Years, with Various Reminiscences and the Tributes of Friends.* New Haven, CT: Privately printed, 1883.

Mitchell, Stewart. *Horatio Seymour of New York.* Cambridge, MA: Harvard University Press, 1938.

Mohr, James C. *The Radical Republicans and Reform in New York During Reconstruction.* Ithaca, NY: Cornell University Press, 1973.

Monaghan, Jay. *Civil War on the Western Border, 1854–1865.* Boston: Little, Brown & Co., 1955.

Montgomery, Morton L., comp. *Historical and Biographical Annals of Berks County, Pennsylvania; Embracing a Concise History of the County and a Genealogical and Biographical Record of Representative Families.* 2 vols. Chicago: J. H. Beers & Co., 1909.

Moore, George E. *A Banner in the Hills: West Virginia's Statehood.* New York: Appleton-Century-Crofts, 1963.

Moore, Kenneth A. "Frederick Holbrook." *Vermont History* 32 (April 1964):65–78.

Moran, Benjamin. *The Journal of Benjamin Moran, 1857–1865.* 2 vols. Edited by Sarah Agnes Wallace and Frances Elma Gillespie. Chicago: University of Chicago Press, 1948–1949.

Mordell, Albert. *Quaker Militant: John Greenleaf Whittier.* Boston: Houghton Mifflin Co., 1933.

Morgan, H. Wayne. *From Hayes to McKinley: National Party Politics, 1877–1896.* Syracuse, NY: Syracuse University Press, 1969.

Morris, Dan, and Inez Morris. *Who Was Who in American Politics: A Biographical Dictionary of over 4,000 Men and Women Who Contributed to the United States Political Scene from Colonial Days up to and Including the Immediate Past.* New York: Hawthorn Books, 1974.

Morrow, Lynn. "Joseph Washington McClurg: Entrepreneur, Politician, Citizen." *Missouri Historical Review* 78 (January 1984):168–201.

Mott, Frank Luther. *A History of American Magazines, 1741–1930.* 5 vols. Cambridge, MA: Harvard University Press, 1938–1968.

Moulton, Augustus F. *Memorials of Maine: A Life Record of Men and Women of the Past, Whose Sterling Character and Energy and Industry Have Made Them Preeminent in Their Own and Many Other States.* New York: American Historical Society, 1916.

Munroe, James Phinney. *A Life of Francis Amasa Walker.* New York: H. Holt and Company, 1923.

Murdock, Eugene C. *One Million Men: The Civil War Draft in the North.* Madison: State Historical Society of Wisconsin, 1971.

Murdock, Eugene C. *Patriotism Limited, 1862–1865: The Civil War Draft and the Bounty System.* Kent, OH: Kent State University Press, 1967.

Murfin, James W. *The Gleam of Bayonets: The Battle of Antietam and the Maryland Campaign of 1862.* New York: Thomas Yoseloff, 1965.

Musgrove, Richard W. *History of the Town of Bristol, Grafton County, New Hampshire.* Bristol, NH: Printed by R. W. Musgrove, 1904.

Mushkat, Jerome. *Fernando Wood: A Political Biography.* Kent, OH: Kent State University Press, 1990.

Mushkat, Jerome. *The Reconstruction of the New York Democracy, 1861–1874.* Rutherford, NJ: Fairleigh Dickinson University Press, 1981.

Myles, Myrtle Tate. *Nevada's Governors from Territorial Days to the Present, 1861–1971.* [Sparks, NV: Western Printing and Publishing Co., 1972].

Naef, Weston J. *Era of Exploration: The Rise of Landscape Photography in the American West.* Buffalo, NY: Albright–Knox Art Gallery, 1975.

Naisawald, L. Van Loan. *Grape and Canister: The Story of the Field Artillery of the Army of the Potomac, 1861–1865.* New York: Oxford University Press, 1960.

Neely, Mark E., Jr. *The Abraham Lincoln Encyclopedia.* New York: McGraw-Hill, 1982.

Neely, Mark E., Jr., and R. Gerald McMurtry. *The Insanity File: The Case of Mary Todd Lincoln.* Carbondale: Southern Illinois University Press, 1986.

Nesbit, Robert C. *Wisconsin: A History.* Madison: University of Wisconsin Press, 1973.

Neu, Irene D. *Erastus Corning: Merchant and Financier, 1794–1872.* Ithaca, NY: Cornell University Press, 1960.

Nevins, Allan. *The Evening Post: A Century of Journalism.* New York: Boni and Liveright, 1922.

Newell, Graham S. "Erastus Fairbanks." *Vermont History* 32 (April 1964): 59–64.

Newhall, Beaumont, and Nancy Newhall. *T. H. O'Sullivan: Photographer.* Rochester, NY: Eastman House, 1966.

Nichols, Roy Franklin. *The Disruption of American Democracy.* New York: Macmillan Company, 1948.

Nicklason, Fred. "The Civil War Contracts Committee." *Civil War History* 17 (September 1971):232–244.

Niven, John. *Connecticut for the Union: The Role of the State in the Civil War.* New Haven, CT: Yale University Press, 1965.

Niven, John. *Gideon Welles: Lincoln's Secretary of the Navy.* New York: Oxford University Press, 1973.

Nolan, Alan T. *The Iron Brigade: A Military History.* 2nd ed. Madison: State Historical Society of Wisconsin, 1975.

North, James W. *The History of Augusta, Maine.* Somersworth, ME: New England History Press, 1981.

Norton, Frederick Calvin. *The Governors of Connecticut: Biographies of the Chief Executives of the Commonwealth That Gave to the World the First Written Constitution Known to History.* Hartford, CT: Connecticut Magazine, 1905.

Nugent, Walter T. K. *Money and American Society, 1865–1880.* New York: Free Press, 1968.

Nye, Wilbur Sturtevant. *Here Come the Rebels! Maps by the Author.* Baton Rouge: Louisiana State University Press, 1965.

Oates, Stephen B. *To Purge This Land with Blood: A Biography of John Brown.* 2nd ed. Amherst: University of Massachusetts Press, 1984.

Oates, Stephen B. *With Malice Toward None: The Life of Abraham Lincoln.* New York: Harper & Row, 1977.

Oates, Stephen B. *A Woman of Valor: Clara Barton and the Civil War.* New York: Free Press, 1994.

O'Connor, Richard. *Sheridan the Inevitable.* Indianapolis, IN: Bobbs-Merrill Co., 1953.

O'Connor, Richard. *Thomas: Rock of Chickamauga.* New York: Prentice-Hall, 1948.

O'Connor, Thomas H. *Lords of the Loom: The Cotton Whigs and the Coming of the Civil War.* New York: Scribner's, 1968.

Ostrander, Stephen M. *A History of the City of Brooklyn and Kings County.* Brooklyn, NY: Published by subscription, 1894.

Paine, Albert Bigelow. *Thomas Nast, His Period and His Pictures.* New York: Macmillan Co., 1904.

Palmer, John M., ed. *The Bench and Bar of Illinois: Historical and Reminiscent; with Contributions from a Number of the Foremost Members of the Legal Profession in the State.* Chicago: Lewis Publishing Co., 1899.

Park, James. *The Life and Services of Horace Maynard.* Knoxville, TN: N.p., 1903.

Parker, William Belmont. *The Life and Public Service of Justin Smith Morrill.* Boston: Houghton Mifflin Co., 1924.

Parrish, William E. *Missouri Under Radical Rule, 1865–1870.* Columbia: University of Missouri Press, 1965.

Parrish, William E. *Turbulent Partnership: Missouri and the Union, 1861–1865.* Columbia: University of Missouri Press, 1963.

Parrish, William E. "The Western Sanitary Commission." *Civil War History* 36 (March 1990):17–35.

Parrish, William E., et al., eds. *A History of Missouri.* 5 vols. Columbia: University of Missouri Press, 1971–1986.

Parsons, Stanley B. *Populist Context: Rural vs. Urban Power on a Great Plains Frontier.* Westport, CT: Greenwood Press, 1973.

Patrick, Marsena Rudolph. *Inside Lincoln's Army: The Diary of Marsena Rudolph Patrick, Provost Marshal General, Army of the Potomac.* Edited by David S. Sparks. New York: Thomas Yoseloff, 1964.

Patton, James W. *Unionism and Reconstruction in Tennessee, 1860–1869.* Chapel Hill: University of North Carolina Press, 1934.

Pauli, Hertha E. *Her Name Was Sojourner Truth.* New York: Appleton-Century-Crofts, 1962.

Payne, Charles E. *Josiah Bushnell Grinnell.* Iowa City: State Historical Society of Iowa, 1938.

Pearson, Henry Greenleaf. *James S. Wadsworth of Geneseo: Brevet Major-General of United States Volunteers.* New York: C. Scribner's Sons, 1913.

Pearson, Henry Greeleaf. *The Life of John A. Andrew: Governor of Massachusetts, 1861–1865.* 2 vols. Boston: Houghton Mifflin Co., 1904.

Peat, Wilbur D., et al. *Portraits and Painters of the Governors of Indiana, 1800–1978.* Indianapolis: Indiana Historical Society, 1978.

Peck, William F. *History of Rochester and Monroe County, New York; from the Earliest Historic Times to the Beginning of 1907; also Biographical Sketches of Some of the More Prominent Citizens of Rochester and Monroe County.* New York: Pioneer Publishing Company, 1908.

Perrin, W. H., et al. *Kentucky. A History of the State, Embracing a Concise Account of the Origin and Development of the Virginia Colony; Its Expansion Westward and the Settlement of the Frontier Beyond the Alleghenies; the Erection of Kentucky as an Independent State, and Its Subsequent Development.* 8th ed. Louisville, KY: F. A. Battey & Co., 1888.

Perry, Lewis. *Radical Abolitionism: Anarchy and the Government of God in Antislavery Thought.* Ithaca, NY: Cornell University Press, 1973.

Peskin, Allan. *Garfield.* Kent, OH: Kent State University Press, 1978.

Peterson, F. Ross. *Idaho: A Bicentennial History.* New York: W. W. Norton & Co., 1976.

Peterson, Norma L. *Freedom and Franchise: The Political Career of Benjamin Gratz Brown.* Columbia: University of Missouri Press, 1965.

Pfanz, Harry W. *Gettysburg—Culp's Hill and Cemetery Hill.* Chapel Hill: University of North Carolina Press, 1993.

Pfanz, Harry W. *Gettysburg: The Second Day.* Chapel Hill: University of North Carolina Press, 1987.

Phelps, Alonzo. *Contemporary Biography of California's Representative Men, with Contributions from Distinguished Scholars and Scientists.* 2 vols. San Francisco: A. L. Bancroft, 1881–1882.

Phillips, Catherine Coffin. *Cornelius Cole: California Pioneer and United States Senator: A Study in Personality and Achievements Bearing upon the Growth of a Commonwealth.* San Francisco: J. H. Nash, 1929.

Phillips, Christopher. *Damned Yankee: The Life of General Nathaniel Lyon.* Columbia: University of Missouri Press, 1990.

Phisterer, Frederick, comp. *New York in the War of the Rebellion, 1861–1865.* 3rd ed. 6 vols. Albany, NY: J. B. Lyon Co., 1912.

Pinkerton, Allan. *The Spy of the Rebellion: Being a True History of the Spy System of the United States Army During the Late Rebellion, Revealing Many Secrets of the War Hitherto not Made Public Compiled from Official Reports Prepared for President Lincoln, General McClellan and the Provost-Marshal-General.* New York: G. W. Dillingham, 1888.

Plummer, Mark A. *Frontier Governor: Samuel J. Crawford of Kansas.* Lawrence: University Press of Kansas, 1971.

Plummer, Mark A. "Richard J. Oglesby, Lincoln's Rail-Splitter." *Journal of the Illinois State Historical Society* 80 (Spring 1987):2–12.

Plummer, Mark A. *Robert G. Ingersoll: Peoria's Pagan Politician.* Macomb: Western Illinois University Press, 1984.

Pollard, John Albert. *John Greenleaf Whittier: Friend of Man.* Boston: Houghton Mifflin Co., 1949.

Pond, George E. *The Shenandoah Valley in 1864.* New York: C. Scribner's Sons, 1883.

Poore, Benjamin Perley. *Perley's Reminiscences of Sixty Years in the National Metropolis.* 2 vols. Philadelphia: Hubbard Brothers, 1886.

Porte, Joel. *Representative Man: Ralph Waldo Emerson in His Time.* New York: Oxford University Press, 1979.

Porter, George H. *Ohio Politics During the Civil War Period.* New York: Columbia University Press, 1911.

Portrait and Biographical Record of Buchanan and Clinton Counties, Missouri; Containing Biographical Sketches of Prominent and Representative Citizens, Together with Biographies and Portraits of All the Presidents of the United States. Chicago: Chapman Bros., 1893.

Portrait and Biographical Record of Seneca and Schuyler Counties, New York; Containing Portraits and Biographical Sketches of Prominent and Representative Citizens of the Counties, Together with Biographies and Portraits of All the Presidents of the United States. New York: Chapman Publishing Co., 1895.

Portrait and Biographical Record of the Willamette Valley, Oregon; Containing Original Sketches of Many Well Known Citizens of the Past and Present. Chicago: Chapman Publishing Co., 1903.

Potter, David M. *The Impending Crisis, 1848–1861.* Completed and edited by Don E. Fehrenbacher. New York: Harper & Row, 1976.

Powell, William H. *The Fifth Army Corps (Army of the Potomac): A Record of Operations During the Civil War in the United States of America, 1861–1865.* New York: G. P. Putnam's Sons, 1896.

Pratt, Harry E. "The Repudiation of Lincoln's War Policy in the 1862 Stuart–Swett Congressional Campaign." *Journal of the Illinois State Historical Society* 23 (April 1931):129–140.

Prentice, George. *The Life of Gilbert Haven; Bishop of the Methodist Episcopal Church.* New York: Phillips & Hunt, 1883.

Quarles, Benjamin. *The Black Abolitionists.* New York: Oxford University Press, 1969.

Quarles, Benjamin. *Frederick Douglass.* Washington, DC: Associated Publishers, 1948.

Quarles, Benjamin. *The Negro in the Civil War.* Boston: Little, Brown & Co., 1953.

Radcliffe, George L. P. *Governor Thomas H. Hicks of Maryland and the Civil War.* Baltimore, MD: Johns Hopkins University Press, 1901.

Ramage, James A. *Rebel Raider: The Life of General John Hunt Morgan.* Lexington: University Press of Kentucky, 1986.

Rand, John C., ed. *One of a Thousand: A Series of Biographical Sketches of One Thousand Representative Men Resident in the Commonwealth of Massachusetts A.D. 1888–89.* Boston: First National Publishing Company, 1890.

Randall, J. G. *Lincoln the President.* 4 vols. Volume 4 coauthored by Richard N. Current. New York: Dodd, Mead & Co., 1945–1955.

Randall, Ruth Painter. *Mary Lincoln: Biography of a Marriage.* Boston: Little, Brown & Co., 1953.

Rawley, James A. *Edwin D. Morgan, 1811–1833: Merchant in Politics.* New York: Columbia University Press, 1955.

Ray, Frederic E. *Alfred R. Waud: Civil War Artist.* New York: Viking Press, 1974.

Rayback, Joseph G. *Free Soil: The Election of 1848*. Lexington: University Press of Kentucky, 1971.

Reavis, L. U. *St. Louis: The Future Great City of the World*. 3rd ed. St. Louis, MO: Published by order of the St. Louis County Court, 1871.

Reed, Rowena. *Combined Operations in the Civil War*. Annapolis, MD: Naval Institute Press, 1978.

Reid, Whitelaw. *Ohio in the War: Her Statesmen, Her Generals, and Soldiers*. 2 vols. Cincinnati, OH: Moore, Wilstach & Baldwin, 1868.

Reid, Whitelaw. *A Radical View: The "Agate" Dispatches of Whitelaw Reid, 1861–1865*. 2 vols. Edited by James G. Smart. Memphis, TN: Memphis State University Press, 1976.

Reno, Conrad. *Memoirs of the Judiciary and Bar of New England for the Nineteenth Century with a History of the Judicial System of New England*. 2 vols. Boston: Century Memorial Publishing Co., 1900.

Rezneck, Samuel. *Profiles out of the Past of Troy, New York, Since 1789*. Troy, NY: Greater Troy Chamber of Commerce, 1970.

Rhea, Gordon C. *The Battle of the Wilderness, May 5–6, 1864*. Baton Rouge: Louisiana State University Press, 1994.

Rice, Allen Thorndike, ed. *Reminiscences of Abraham Lincoln by Distinguished Men of His Time*. New York: North American Publishing Co., 1885.

Richards, Kent D. *Isaac I. Stevens: Young Man in a Hurry*. 2nd ed. Pullman: Washington State University Press, 1993.

Richardson, Elmo R., and Alan W. Farley. *John Palmer Usher: Lincoln's Secretary of the Interior*. Lawrence: University Press of Kansas, 1960.

Richter, William L. *The Army in Texas During Reconstruction, 1865–1870*. College Station: Texas A&M University Press, 1987.

Riddle, Albert G. *Recollections of War Times: Reminiscences of Men and Events in Washington, 1860–1865*. New York: G. P. Putnam's Sons, 1895.

Riddleberger, Patrick W. *George Washington Julian, Radical Republican: A Study in Nineteenth-Century Politics and Reform*. Indianapolis: Indiana Historical Bureau, 1966.

Ridge, Martin. *Ignatius Donnelly: The Portrait of a Politician*. Chicago: University of Chicago Press, 1962.

Risch, Erna. *Quartermaster Support of the Army: A History of the Corps, 1775–1939*. Washington, DC: Center of Military History, United States Army, 1989.

Robbins, David E. "The Congressional Career of William Ralls Morrison." Ph.D. dissertation, University of Illinois, 1963.

Robertson, William Glenn. *Back Door to Richmond: The Bermuda Hundred Campaign, April–June 1864*. Newark: University of Delaware Press, 1987.

Robson, Charles, ed. *The Biographical Encyclopaedia of Ohio of the Nineteenth Century*. Cincinnati, OH: Galaxy Publishing Co., 1876.

Rolle, Andrew F. *John C. Frémont: Character as Destiny*. Norman: University of Oklahoma Press, 1991.

Rose, Willie Lee. *Rehearsal for Reconstruction: The Port Royal Experiment*. Indianapolis, IN: Bobbs-Merrill, 1964.

Rosebault, Charles J. *When Dana Was the Sun: A Story of Personal Journalism*. New York: R. M. McBride & Co., 1931.

Roseboom, Eugene H. "The Mobbing of the *Crisis*." *Ohio State Archaeological and Historical Quarterly* 59 (April 1950):150–153.

Roske, Ralph J. *His Own Counsel: The Life and Times of Lyman Trumbull*. Reno: University of Nevada Press, 1979.

Ross, Earle D. "James F. Wilson, Legalistic Free Soiler: A Neglected Biography." *Annals of Iowa* 32 (July 1954):365–375.

Ross, Ishbel. *Angel of the Battlefield: The Life of Clara Barton*. New York: Harper & Row, 1956.

Rossbach, Jeffery S. *Ambivalent Conspirators: John Brown, the Secret Six, and a Theory of Slave Violence*. Philadelphia: University of Pennsylvania Press, 1982.

Russell, A. P. *Thomas Corwin: A Sketch*. Cincinnati, OH: R. Clarke & Co., 1881.

Ryland, William James. *Alexander Ramsey: A Study of a Frontier Politician and the Transition of Minnesota from a Territory to a State*. Philadelphia: Harris & Partridge Co., 1941.

Sage, Leland L. *A History of Iowa*. Ames: Iowa State University Press, 1974.

Sage, Leland L. *William Boyd Allison: A Study in Practical Politics*. Iowa City: State Historical Society of Iowa, 1956.

Salisbury, Robert S. *William Windom, Apostle of Positive Government*. Lanham, MD: University Press of America, 1993.

Samuels, Peggy. *The Illustrated Biographical Encyclopedia of Artists of the American West*. Garden City, NY: Doubleday, 1976.

Schafer, Joseph. *Carl Schurz, Militant Liberal*. Evansville, WI: Antes Press, 1930.

Schlicke, Carl P. *General George Wright: Guardian of the Pacific Coast*. Norman: University of Oklahoma Press, 1988.

Scott, Franklin Daniel. "The Political Career of William R. Morrison." *Transactions of the Illinois State Historical Society* 33 (1926):134–171.

Sears, Stephen W. *George B. McClellan: The Young Napoleon*. New York: Ticknor & Fields, 1988.

Sears, Stephen W. *Landscape Turned Red: The Battle of Antietam*. New Haven, CT: Ticknor & Fields, 1983.

Sears, Stephen W. *To the Gates of Richmond: The Peninsula Campaign*. New York: Ticknor & Fields, 1992.

Seaton, Josephine. *William Winston Seaton of the "National Intelligencer." A Biographical Sketch. With Passing Notices of His Associates and Friends*. Boston: J. R. Osgood and Co., 1871.

Sefton, James E. *Andrew Johnson and the Uses of Constitutional Power*. Boston: Little, Brown & Co., 1980.

Seitz, Don C. *Artemus Ward (Charles Farrar Browne): A Biography and Bibliography*. New York: Harper & Brothers, 1919.

Seitz, Don C. *The James Gordon Bennetts, Father and Son, Proprietors of the New York Herald*. Indianapolis, IN: Bobbs-Merrill Co., 1928.

Seward, Frederick William. *Reminiscences of a War-Time Statesman and Diplomat, 1830–1915, by Frederick W. Seward, Assistant Secretary of State During the Administrations of Lincoln, Johnson, and Hayes*. New York: G. P. Putnam's Sons, 1916.

Sewell, Richard H. *John P. Hale and the Politics of Abolition*. Cambridge, MA: Harvard University Press, 1965.

Shankman, Arnold M. *The Pennsylvania Antiwar Movement, 1861–1865.* Rutherford, NJ: Fairleigh Dickinson University Press, 1980.

Shannon, Fred A. *The Organization and Administration of the Union Army.* 2 vols. Cleveland, OH: Arthur H. Clark Co., 1928.

Shapiro, Samuel. *Richard Henry Dana, Jr., 1815–1882.* East Lansing: Michigan State University Press, 1961.

Shaw, Archer H. *The Plain Dealer: One Hundred Years in Cleveland.* New York: Alfred A. Knopf, 1942.

Shaw, Robert Gould. *Blue-eyed Child of Fortune: The Civil War Letters of Colonel Robert Gould Shaw.* Edited by Russell Duncan. Athens: University of Georgia Press, 1992.

Shea, William L., and Earl J. Hess. *Pea Ridge: Civil War Campaign in the West.* Chapel Hill: University of North Carolina Press, 1992.

Sheahan, James W. *The Life of Stephen A. Douglas.* New York: Harper & Brothers, 1860.

Shepherd, Rebecca A., comp. and ed. *A Biographical Directory of the Indiana General Assembly.* 2 vols. Indianapolis: Select Committee on the Centennial History of the Indiana General Assembly, Indiana Historical Bureau, 1980–1984.

Sheridan, Philip Henry. *Personal Memoirs of P.H. Sheridan, General, United States Army.* 2 vols. New York: Charles L. Webster & Co., 1888.

Sherman, John. *John Sherman's Recollections of Forty Years in the House, Senate and Cabinet: An Autobiography.* 2 vols. Chicago: Werner Co., 1895.

Shippee, Lester Burrell. "Jane Grey Swisshelm: Agitator." *Mississippi Valley Historical Review* 7 (December 1930):206–227.

Shuck, Oscar T. *Representative and Leading Men of the Pacific: Being Original Sketches of the Lives and Characters of the Principal Men . . . to Which Are Added Their Speeches, Addresses, Orations, Eulogies, Lectures and Poems. . . .* San Francisco: Bacon and Company, 1870.

Silbey, Joel H. *A Respectable Minority: The Democratic Party in the Civil War Era, 1860–1868.* New York: W. W. Norton & Co., 1977.

Silver, David M. *Lincoln's Supreme Court.* Urbana: University of Illinois Press, 1956.

Smalley, Eugene Virgil. *A History of the Republican Party from Its Organization to the Present Time; to Which Is Added a Political History of Minnesota from a Republican Point of View, and Biographical Sketches of Leading Minnesota Republicans.* St. Paul, MN: E. V. Smalley, 1896.

Smiley, David L. *Lion of White Hall: The Life of Cassius M. Clay.* Madison: University of Wisconsin Press, 1962.

Smith, Charles Perrin. *Charles Perrin Smith: New Jersey Political Reminiscences, 1828–1882.* Edited by Hermann K. Platt. New Brunswick, NJ: Rutgers University Press, 1965.

Smith, Charles W. *Life and Military Services of Brevet Major-General Robert S. Foster.* Indianapolis, IN: E. J. Hecker, 1915.

Smith, Elbert B. *Francis Preston Blair.* New York: Free Press, 1980.

Smith, Henry P. *History of Cortland County with Illustrations and Biographical Sketches of Some of Its Prominent Men and Pioneers.* Syracuse, NY: D. Mason & Co., 1885.

Smith, Henry P., ed. *History of Essex County with Illustrations and Biographical*

Sketches of Some of Its Prominent Men and Pioneers. Syracuse, NY: D. Mason & Co., 1885.

Smith, John E., ed. *Our Country and Its People: A Descriptive and Biographical Record of Madison County, New York.* Boston: Boston History Company, 1899.

Smith, Timothy Lawrence. *Revivalism and Social Reform: American Protestantism on the Eve of the Civil War.* New York: Harper & Row, 1965.

Smith, Walter George. *Life and Letters of Thomas Kilby Smith, Brevet Major-General, United States Volunteers, 1820–1887.* New York: G. P. Putnam's Sons, 1897.

Smith, Willard H. *Schuyler Colfax: The Changing Fortunes of a Political Idol.* Indianapolis: Indiana Historical Bureau, 1952.

Smith, William Benjamin. *James Sidney Rollins: Memoir.* New York: De Vinne Press, 1891.

Smith, William E. *The Francis Preston Blair Family in Politics.* 2 vols. New York: Macmillan Co., 1933.

Sobel, Robert, and John Raimo, eds. *Biographical Directory of the Governors of the United States, 1789–1978.* 4 vols. Westport, CT: Meckler Books, 1978; reprint, Westport, CT: Greenwood Press, 1988.

Sokoloff, Alice Hunt. *Kate Chase for the Defense.* New York: Dodd, Mead, & Co., 1971.

Sommers, Richard J. *Richmond Redeemed: The Siege at Petersburg.* Garden City, NY: Doubleday, 1981.

Speed, Thomas, et al. *Union Regiments of Kentucky.* Published under the auspices of the Union Soldiers and Sailors Monument Association. Louisville, KY: Courier-Journal Job Printing Co., 1897.

Spence, Clark C. *Territorial Politics and Government in Montana, 1864–89.* Urbana: University of Illinois Press, 1975.

Spiller, Roger T., et al., eds. *Dictionary of American Military Biography.* 3 vols. Westport, CT: Greenwood Press, 1984.

Sprague, Homer B. *History of the 13th Infantry Regiment of Connecticut Volunteers During the Great Rebellion.* Hartford, CT: Case, Lockwood & Co., 1867.

St. Hill, Thomas Nast. *Thomas Nast, Cartoons and Illustrations.* New York: Dover Publications, 1974.

Stampp, Kenneth M. *America in 1857: A Nation on the Brink.* New York: Oxford University Press, 1990.

Stampp, Kenneth M. *Indiana Politics During the Civil War.* Indianapolis: Indiana Historical Bureau, 1949.

Stanton, Elizabeth Cady, et al., eds. *History of Women's Suffrage.* 6 vols. New York: Fowler & Wells, 1881–1922.

Stanwood, Edward. *James Gillespie Blaine.* Boston: Houghton Mifflin Co., 1908.

Staples, Thomas S. *Reconstruction in Arkansas, 1862–1874.* New York: Columbia University Press, 1923.

Starling, Edmund Lyne. *History of Henderson County, Kentucky.* Henderson, KY: N.p., 1887.

Starr, Stephen Z. *Colonel Grenfell's Wars: The Life of a Soldier of Fortune.* Baton Rouge: Louisiana State University Press, 1971.

Starr, Stephen Z. *Jennison's Jayhawkers: A Civil War Cavalry Regiment and Its Commander.* Baton Rouge: Louisiana State University Press, 1974.

Starr, Stephen Z. *The Union Cavalry in the Civil War.* 3 vols. Baton Rouge: Louisiana State University Press, 1979–1985.

Steele, Janet E. *The Sun Shines for All: Journalism and Ideology in the Life of Charles A. Dana.* Syracuse, NY: Syracuse University Press, 1993.

Steiner, Bernard C. *Life of Reverdy Johnson.* Baltimore, MD: Norman, Remington Co., 1914.

Stellhorn, Paul A., and Michael J. Birkner, eds. *The Governors of New Jersey, 1664–1974: Biographical Essays.* Trenton: New Jersey Historical Commission, 1982.

Sterling, Dorothy. *Freedom Train: The Story of Harriet Tubman.* Garden City, NY: Doubleday, 1954.

Stewart, A.J.D., ed. *The History of the Bench and Bar of Missouri; with Reminscences of the Prominent Lawyers of the Past, and a Record of the Law's Leaders of the Present.* St. Louis, MO: Legal Publishing Co., 1898.

Stewart, James Brewer. *Joshua R. Giddings and the Tactics of Radical Politics.* Cleveland, OH: Press of Case Western Reserve University, 1970.

Stewart, James Brewer. *Wendell Phillips: Liberty's Hero.* Baton Rouge: Louisiana State University Press, 1986.

Stewart, James Brewer. *William Lloyd Garrison and the Challenge of Emancipation.* Arlington Heights, IL: H. Davidson, 1992.

Stiles, Edward H. *Recollections and Sketches of Notable Lawyers and Public Men of Early Iowa Belonging to the First and Second Generations; with Anecdotes and Incidents Illustrative of the Times.* Des Moines, IA: Homestead Publishers, 1916.

Storke, Elliot G. *History of Cayuga County, New York; with Illustrations and Biographical Sketches of Some of Its Prominent Men and Pioneers.* Syracuse, NY: Mason, 1879.

Strong, George Templeton. *Diary of the Civil War, 1860–1865.* Edited by Allan Nevins. New York: Macmillan Co., 1962.

Stuart, Addison A. *Iowa Colonels and Regiments: Being a History of Iowa Regiments in the War of the Rebellion; and Containing a Description of the Battles in Which They Have Fought.* Des Moines, IA: Mills & Co., 1865.

Sturgis, S. D. *The Other Side, as Viewed by Generals Grant, Sherman, and Other Distinguished Officers, Being a Defence [sic] of His Campaign into N.E. Mississippi in the Year 1864.* Washington, DC: N.p., 1882.

Stutler, Boyd B. *West Virginia in the Civil War.* Charleston, WV: Education Foundation, 1966.

Swanberg, W. A. *First Blood: The Story of Fort Sumter.* New York: Charles Scribner's Sons, 1957.

Swanberg, W. A. *Sickles the Incredible.* New York: Charles Scribner's Sons, 1956.

Swisher, Carl B. *Stephen J. Field: Craftsman of the Law.* Washington, DC: Brookings Institution, 1930.

Swisher, Carl B. *The Taney Period, 1836–64.* Vol. 5 of *The History of the Supreme Court of the United States.* New York: Macmillan, 1971–1984.

Swisshelm, Jane Grey. *Crusader and Feminist: Letters of Jane Grey Swisshelm, 1858–1865.* Edited by Arthur J. Larsen. Saint Paul: Minnesota Historical Society, 1934.

Sword, Wiley, *Embrace an Angry Wind: The Confederacy's Last Hurrah, Spring Hill, Franklin, and Nashville.* New York: HarperCollins Publishers, 1992.

Sword, Wiley, *Shiloh: Bloody April.* Rev. ed. Dayton, OH: Morningside Bookshop Press, 1983.

Taft, Robert. *Artists and Illustrators of the Old West, 1850–1900.* New York: Bonanza Books, 1953.

Taft, Robert. *Photography and the American Scene: A Social History.* New York: Macmillan Co., 1938; reprint, New York: Dover Publications, 1964.

Tapp, Hambleton. *Kentucky: Decades of Discord, 1865–1900.* Frankfort: Kentucky Historical Society, 1977.

Taylor, Charles W. *Biographical Sketches and Review of the Bench and Bar of Indiana; Containing Biographies and Sketches of Eminent Judges and Lawyers of Indiana, Together with a History of the Judiciary of the State and Review of the Bar from the Earliest Times to the Present, with Anecdotes, Reminiscences, etc.* Indianapolis, IN: Bench and Bar Publishing Co., 1895.

Taylor, James E. *With Sheridan up the Shenandoah Valley in 1864: Leaves from a Special Artist's Sketchbook and Diary.* Cleveland, OH: Western Reserve Historical Society, n.d.; reprint, Dayton, OH: Morningside House Press, 1989.

Temple, Wayne C., and Justin G. Turner. "Lincoln's 'Castine': Noah Brooks." *Lincoln Herald* 72–74 (Fall 1970–Winter 1972). Series of articles.

Ten Broek, Jacobus. *Equal Under Law.* New York: Collier Books, 1965.

Tenney, William J. *Military and Naval History of the Rebellion in the United States. With Biographical Sketches of Deceased Officers.* New York: D. Appleton & Co., 1865.

Thomas, Benjamin Platt. *Abraham Lincoln: A Biography.* New York: Alfred A. Knopf, 1952.

Thomas, Benjamin Platt. *Theodore Weld: Crusader for Freedom.* New Brunswick, NJ: Rutgers University Press, 1950.

Thomas, Benjamin P., and Harold M. Hyman. *Stanton: The Life and Times of Lincoln's Secretary of War.* New York: Alfred A. Knopf, 1962.

Thomas, John L. *The Liberator, William Lloyd Garrison: A Biography.* Boston: Little, Brown & Co., 1963.

Thornbrough, Emma Lou. *Indiana in the Civil War Era, 1850–1880.* Vol. 3 in *The History of Indiana.* Indianapolis: Indiana Historical Bureau, 1965.

Tillinghast, P. E., et al., comps. *History of the Twelfth Regiment, Rhode Island Volunteers, in the Civil War, 1862–1863.* Providence, RI: Snow & Farnham, 1904.

Tinkcom, Henry Marlin. *John White Geary: Soldier-Statesman, 1819–1873.* Philadelphia: University of Pennsylvania Press, 1940.

Tredway, G. R. *Democratic Opposition to the Lincoln Administration in Indiana.* Indianapolis: Indiana Historical Bureau, 1973.

Trefousse, Hans L. *Ben Butler: The South Called Him Beast!* New York: Twayne Publishers, 1957.

Trefousse, Hans L. *Benjamin Franklin Wade: Radical Republican from Ohio.* New York: Twayne Publishers, 1963.

Trefousse, Hans L. *Carl Schurz: A Biography.* Knoxville: University of Tennessee Press, 1982.

Trulock, Alice Rains. *In the Hands of Providence: Joshua L. Chamberlain and the American Civil War.* Chapel Hill: University of North Carolina Press, 1992.

Tucker, Glenn. *Hancock the Superb.* Indianapolis, IN: Bobbs-Merrill, 1960.

Turner, George E. *Victory Rode the Rails: The Strategic Place of the Railroads in the Civil War.* Indianapolis, IN: Bobbs-Merrill, 1953.

Turpie, David. *Sketches of My Own Times.* Indianapolis, IN: Bobbs-Merrill Co., 1903.

Tutorow, Norman E. *Leland Stanford: Man of Many Careers.* Menlo Park, CA: Pacific Coast Publishers, 1971.

United States Congress. *Biographical Directory of the United States Congress, 1774–1989*. Bicentennial ed. Washington, DC: Government Printing Office, 1989.

Utley, Henry, and Bryon M. Cutcheon. *Michigan as a Province, Territory, and State: The Twenty-sixth Member of the Federal Union*. 4 vols. New York: Publishing Society of Michigan, 1906.

Utley, Robert M. *Frontier Regulars: The United States Army and the Indian, 1866–1891*. New York: Macmillan, 1974.

Uya, Okon Edet. *From Slavery to Public Service: Robert Smalls, 1839–1915*. New York: Oxford University Press, 1971.

Vallandigham, James L. *A Life of Clement L. Vallandigham*. Baltimore, MD: Turnbull Brothers, 1872.

Van Deusen, Glyndon G. *Thurlow Weed: Wizard of the Lobby*. Boston: Little, Brown & Co., 1947.

Van Deusen, Glyndon G. *William Henry Seward*. New York: Oxford University Press, 1967.

Veatch, William A. *James Clifford Veatch: Scholar, Solicitor, Statesman and Soldier*. Redmond, OR: W. A. Veatch, 1980.

Wagandt, Charles Lewis. *The Mighty Revolution: Negro Emancipation in Maryland, 1862–1864*. Baltimore, MD: Johns Hopkins University Press, 1964.

Wagenknecht, Edward. *John Greenleaf Whittier: A Portrait in Paradox*. New York: Oxford University Press, 1967.

Wainwright, Charles S. *A Diary of Battle: The Personal Journals of Colonel Charles S. Wainwright, 1861–1865*. Edited by Allan Nevins. New York: Harcourt, Brace & World, 1962.

Waite, Otis F.R. *New Hampshire in the Great Rebellion. Containing Histories of the Several New Hampshire Regiments, and Biographical Notices of Many of the Prominent Actors in the Civil War of 1861–65*. Claremont, NH: Tracy, Chase & Co., 1870.

Waldsmith, Thomas. "James F. Gibson: Out of the Shadows." *Stereo World* 2 (January–February 1976):1, 5, 20.

Walker, Francis A. *History of the Second Army Corps in the Army of the Potomac*. New York: C. Scribner's Sons, 1886.

Wallace, Andrew. "General August V. Kautz and the Southwestern Frontier." Ph.D. dissertation, University of Arizona, 1968.

Wallace, Lew. *Lew Wallace: An Autobiography*. 2 vols. New York: Harper and Brothers, 1906.

Wallace, Willard M. *Soul of the Lion: A Biography of General Joshua L. Chamberlain*. New York: T. Nelson, 1960.

Waller, Altina L. *Reverend Beecher and Mrs. Tilton: Sex and Class in Victorian America*. Amherst: University of Massachusetts Press, 1982.

Walsh, Justin E. *The Centennial History of the Indiana General Assembly, 1816–1978*. Indianapolis: Select Committee on the Centennial History of the Indiana General Assembly, Indiana Historical Bureau, 1987.

Walsh, Justin E. *To Print the News and Raise Hell! A Biography of Wilbur F. Storey*. Chapel Hill: University of North Carolina Press, 1968.

Weigley, Russell F. *Quartermaster General of the Union Army: A Biography of M. C. Meigs*. New York: Columbia University Press, 1959.

Weigley, Russell F., et al., eds. *Philadelphia: A 300 Year History.* New York: W. W. Norton, 1982.

Weisner, Stephen G. *Embattled Editor: The Life of Samuel Bowles.* Lanham, MD: University Press of America, 1986.

Welcher, Frank J. *The Union Army, 1861–1865: Organization and Operations.* 2 vols. Bloomington: Indiana University Press, 1989–1993.

Welles, Gideon, *Diary.* 3 vols. Edited by Howard K. Beale. New York: W. W. Norton, 1960.

West, Richard S., Jr. *Lincoln's Scapegoat General: A Life of Benjamin F. Butler, 1818–1893.* Boston: Houghton Mifflin, 1965.

West, Richard S., Jr. *The Second Admiral: A Life of David Dixon Porter, 1813–1891.* New York: Coward-McCann, 1937.

Wheeler, Kenneth W., ed. *For the Union: Ohio Leaders in the Civil War.* Columbus: Ohio State University Press, 1968.

Wheeler, Richard. *Lee's Terrible Swift Sword: From Antietam to Chancellorsville, an Eyewitness History.* New York: HarperCollins, 1992.

[Whitman, Benjamin]. *Nelson's Biographical Dictionary and Historical Reference Book of Erie County, Pennsylvania; Containing a Condensed History of Pennsylvania, of Erie County, and of the Several Cities, Boroughs and Townships in the County, also Portraits and Biographies of the Governors Since 1790, and of Numerous Representative Citizens.* Erie, PA: S. B. Nelson, 1896.

Wightman, Edward King. *From Antietam to Fort Fisher: The Civil War Letters of Edward King Wightman, 1862–1865.* Edited by Edward G. Longacre. Rutherford, NJ: Fairleigh Dickinson University Press, 1985.

Wiley, Samuel T., and W. Scott Garner, eds. *Biographical and Portrait Cyclopaedia of Niagara County, New York.* Philadelphia: Gresham Publishing Co., 1892.

Williams, Charles E. *The Life of Abner Coburn: A Review of the Public and Private Career of the Late ex-Governor of Maine.* Bangor, ME: T. W. Burr, 1885.

Williams, Frederick D. *The Wild Life of the Army: Civil War Letters of James A. Garfield.* East Lansing: Michigan State University Press, 1964.

Williams, Frederick Wells. *Anson Burlingame and the First Chinese Mission to Foreign Powers.* New York: Scribner's, 1912.

Williams, H. Clay, ed. *Biographical Encyclopedia of Vermont of the Nineteenth Century.* Boston: Metropolitan Publishing & Engraving Co., 1885.

Williams, Kenneth P. *Lincoln Finds a General.* 5 vols. New York: Macmillan Co., 1949–1959.

Williams, T. Harry. *Hayes of the Twenty-Third: The Civil War Volunteer Officer.* New York: Alfred A. Knopf, 1965.

Williams, T. Harry. *Lincoln and His Generals.* New York: Alfred A. Knopf, 1952.

Wilmerding, John. *Winslow Homer.* New York: Praeger Publishers, 1972.

Wilson, Dorothy Clarke. *Stranger and Traveler: The Story of Dorothea Dix, American Reformer.* Boston: Little, Brown & Co., 1975.

Wilson, Forrest. *Crusader in Crinoline: The Life of Harriet Beecher Stowe.* Philadelphia: J. B. Lippincott Co., 1941.

Wilson, James Harrison. *The Life of John A. Rawlins: Lawyer, Assistant Adjutant General, Chief of Staff, Major General of Volunteers, and Secretary of War.* New York: Neale Publishing Co., 1916.

Wilson, James Harrison. *Under the Old Flag: Recollections of Military Operations in the War for the Union, the Spanish War, the Boxer Rebellion, etc.* 2 vols. New York: D. Appleton and Co., 1912.

Winters, John D. *The Civil War in Louisiana.* Baton Rouge: Louisiana State University Press, 1963.

Wittenmyer, Annie. *Under the Guns: A Woman's Reminiscences of the Civil War.* Boston: E. B. Stillings & Co., 1895.

Wolfe, William G. *Stories of Guernsey County, Ohio; History of an Average Ohio County.* Cambridge, OH: N.p., 1943.

Woollen, William Wesley. *Biographical and Historical Sketches of Early Indiana.* Indianapolis, IN: Hammond & Co., 1883.

Wooster, Robert. *Nelson A. Miles and the Twilight of the Frontier Army.* Lincoln: University of Nebraska Press, 1993.

Wubben, Hubert H. *Civil War Iowa and the Copperhead Movement.* Ames: Iowa State University Press, 1980.

Wyatt-Brown, Bertram. *Lewis Tappan and the Evangelical War Against Slavery.* Cleveland, OH: Press of Case Western Reserve University, 1969.

Yacovone, Donald. *Samuel Joseph May and the Dilemmas of the Liberal Persuasion, 1797–1871.* Philadelphia: Temple University Press, 1991.

Yates, Richard, and Catharine Yates Pickering. *Richard Yates: Civil War Governor.* Edited by John H. Krenkel. Danville, IL: Interstate Printers & Publishers, 1966.

York, Robert M. *George B. Cheever: Religious and Social Reformer, 1807–1890.* Orono, ME: Printed at the University Press, 1955.

Younger, Edward. *John A. Kasson: Politics and Diplomacy from Lincoln to McKinley.* Iowa City: State Historical Society of Iowa, 1955.

Index

Page numbers in *italics* indicate location of main entries.

About the Editors and Contributors

JAMES W. GEARY is Professor of Libraries and Media Services at Kent State University. The former army paratrooper completed his undergraduate work at the State University of New York at Buffalo and his graduate studies at Kent State University. The author of *We Need Men: The Union Draft in the Civil War*, he is the recipient of the 1992 Ohio Library Foundation Research Award for his study "Post-Centennial Trends in Civil War Monographic Literature, 1966–1990," which appeared in *Collection Management*. He also has published articles in *American Archivist, Historian*, and other scholarly journals.

JOHN T. HUBBELL is Professor of History and Director of the Kent State University Press. Following three years of service in the U.S. Marine Corps, he completed his undergraduate work at Northeastern Oklahoma State College and his graduate studies at the University of Oklahoma and the University of Illinois. The Editor of *Civil War History* since 1965, he is the author of *Battles Lost and Won: Essays From Civil War History*. His articles have appeared in *Georgia Historical Quarterly, Journal of Negro History, Phylon*, and other scholarly journals.

RICHARD H. ABBOTT is Professor of History at Eastern Michigan University.

ALAN C. AIMONE is Chief of Special Collections in the United States Military Academy's Library at West Point.

DAVID L. ANDERSON is Professor of History at the University of Indianapolis.

PHILIP J. AVILLO, JR., is Associate Professor and Chair of the Department of History and Political Science at York College of Pennsylvania.

BEN BASSHAM is Professor of Art History at Kent State University.

DALE BAUM is Associate Professor of History at Texas A&M University.

EDWIN C. BEARSS is Chief Historian, National Park Service, Department of the Interior.

GEORGE M. BLACKBURN is Professor of History at Central Michigan University.

FREDERICK J. BLUE is Professor of History at Youngstown State University.

RICHARD W. BROWN, JR., is Professor of History at Ithaca College.

FRANK L. BYRNE is Professor Emeritus of History at Kent State University.

ALBERT CASTEL is Professor Emeritus of History at Western Michigan University.

ROBERT J. CHANDLER is the Senior Research Historian in the History Department at the Wells Fargo Bank, San Francisco.

BOYD CHILDRESS is Social Sciences Reference Librarian and History Bibliographer at the Auburn University Library.

B. FRANKLIN COOLING is Chief Historian, History Division, U.S. Department of Energy.

DUDLEY T. CORNISH is Professor Emeritus of History at Pittsburg State University.

JOANNA D. COWDEN is Professor of History at California State University, Chico.

WILLIAM COYLE is Professor of English at Florida Atlantic University.

DANIEL W. CROFTS is Professor of History at Trenton State College.

RICHARD ORR CURRY is Professor Emeritus of History at the University of Connecticut.

CARL L. DAVIS is Professor of History at Stephen F. Austin State University.

WILLIAM C. DAVIS is the author of various Civil War studies and resides in Mechanicsburg, Pennsylvania.

JOSEPH G. DAWSON III is Associate Professor of History at Texas A&M University.

DONNA M. DeBLASIO is Research Historian at the Ohio Historical Society.

MERTON L. DILLON is Professor Emeritus of History at The Ohio State University.

BRUCE J. DINGES is Editor of *Journal of Arizona History* and Director of Publications at the Arizona Historical Society.

MARIO R. DiNUNZIO is Professor of History at Providence College.

DAVID DIXON is Associate Professor of History at Slippery Rock University of Pennsylvania.

RICHARD R. DUNCAN is Associate Professor of History at Georgetown University.

ROBERT F. DURDEN is Professor of History at Duke University.

G. THOMAS EDWARDS is Professor of History at Whitman College.

FREDRIC F. ENDRES is Professor of Journalism and Mass Communication at Kent State University.

KATHLEEN L. ENDRES is Associate Professor of Communication at the University of Akron.

NORMAN B. FERRIS is Professor of History at Middle Tennessee State University.

LeROY H. FISCHER is Oppenheim Professor Emeritus of History at Oklahoma State University.

ROGER A. FISCHER is Professor of History at the University of Minnesota, Duluth.

J. K. FOLMAR is Professor of History at California University of Pennsylvania.

JOSEPH A. FRY is Professor of History at the University of Nevada, Las Vegas.

EMILY GEORGE, R.S.M., was Provincial Administrator for the Sisters of Mercy of the Americas, Regional Community of Detroit.

NORMAN A. GRAEBNER is Professor Emeritus of History at the University of Virginia.

ALLEN C. GUELZO is Grace F. Kea Associate Professor of American History at Eastern College.

MARTIN HARDWICK HALL was Professor of History at the University of Texas, Arlington.

WILLIAM HANCHETT is Professor Emeritus of History at San Diego State University.

HAROLD B. HANCOCK was Professor Emeritus of History at Otterbein College.

SAMUEL B. HAND is Professor Emeritus of History at the University of Vermont.

LOWELL H. HARRISON is Professor Emeritus of History at Western Kentucky University.

STANLEY HARROLD is Professor of History at South Carolina State University.

D. SCOTT HARTWIG is the author of various Civil War studies and a Supervisory Park Ranger at the Gettysburg National Military Park.

WARREN W. HASSLER, JR., is Professor Emeritus of History at Pennsylvania State University.

VICTOR HICKEN is Professor Emeritus of History at Western Illinois University.

HARWOOD P. HINTON is Professor Emeritus of History at the University of Arizona and Senior Editor of the *Handbook of Texas* for the Texas Historical Association.

ARI HOOGENBOOM is Professor of History at Brooklyn College of the City University of New York.

ROBERT F. HOROWITZ holds a Ph.D. in history from the City University of New York and is the Campaign Director of the Jewish Federation of Greater Philadelphia.

JAMES J. HUDSON was Professor Emeritus of History and Dean of the Graduate School at the University of Arkansas in Fayetteville.

H. DRAPER HUNT is Professor of History at the University of Southern Maine.

LARRY JOCHIMS is Historian in the Historic Preservation Office, Kansas State Historical Society.

LUDWELL H. JOHNSON is Professor Emeritus of History at the College of William and Mary.

ROBERT H. JONES is Professor Emeritus of History at the University of Akron.

LAWRENCE S. KAPLAN is University Professor Emeritus of History at Kent State University.

FRANK L. KLEMENT was Professor Emeritus of History at Marquette University.

JEFFREY LASH is an Archivist in the Archival Projects Branch, Textual Projects Division, National Archives and Records Administration.

FRANK R. LEVSTIK is the Regional Administrator for Archives and Records at the Kentucky Department for Libraries and Archives.

DAVID LINDSEY was Professor of History at California State University, Los Angeles.

LORI A. LISOWSKI is an Archivist in the Archival Projects Branch, Textual Projects Division, National Archives and Records Administration.

E. B. LONG was Associate Professor of American Studies at the University of Wyoming.

EDWARD G. LONGACRE is Staff Historian, Headquarters, Air Combat Command, Langley Air Force Base, Virginia.

MARION B. LUCAS is Professor of History at Western Kentucky University.

ARCHIE P. McDONALD is Regent's Professor of History at Stephen F. Austin State University.

JAMES LEE McDONOUGH is Professor of History at Auburn University.

GEORGE McJIMSEY is Professor and Chair of the History Department at Iowa State University.

MICHAEL J. McMANUS holds a Ph.D. in history from the University of Wisconsin and is a partner in the firm of McManus, Perkins, and Associates, Ltd., in Madison, Wisconsin.

RICHARD M. McMURRY is the author of various Civil War studies and resides in Decatur, Georgia.

WILLIAM MARVEL is the author of various Civil War studies and resides in South Conway, New Hampshire.

DAVID E. MEERSE holds a Ph.D. in history from the University of Illinois and is the Stated Clerk for the Presbytery of New York City.

JAMES C. MOHR is Professor and Chair of the History Department at the University of Oregon.

JAMES L. MORRISON, JR., is Professor Emeritus of History at York College of Pennsylvania.

JEROME MUSHKAT is Professor of History at the University of Akron.

JACK NORTRUP was Professor of History at Tri-State University.

PETER J. PARISH is Professor Emeritus of American History, and former Director of the Institute of United States Studies, University of London.

WILLIAM E. PARRISH is Professor of History at Mississippi State University.

ALLAN PESKIN is Professor of History at Cleveland State University.

CHRISTOPHER PHILLIPS is Assistant Professor of History at Emporia State University.

MARK A. PLUMMER is Professor of History at Illinois State University.

LAWRENCE N. POWELL is Associate Professor of History at Tulane University.

WALTER L. POWELL is the Historic Preservation Officer for the Borough of Gettysburg.

JAMES M. PRICHARD is the Research Room Supervisor at the Kentucky Department for Libraries and Archives.

BENJAMIN QUARLES is Professor Emeritus of History at Morgan State University.

GEORGE C. RABLE is Professor of History at Anderson University, Indiana.

KENT D. RICHARDS is Professor of History at Central Washington University.

PATRICK W. RIDDLEBERGER is History Professor Emeritus at Southern Illinois University, Edwardsville.

RONALD D. RIETVELD is Professor of History at California State University, Fullerton.

ROGER L. ROSENTRETER is the Editor of *Michigan History Magazine* at the Michigan Bureau of History.

D. GREGORY SANFORD is the State Archivist of Vermont.

THOMAS F. SCHWARTZ is the State Historian at the Illinois Historic Preservation Agency.

JAMES E. SEFTON is Professor of History at California State University, Northridge.

RICHARD H. SEWELL is Professor of History at the University of Wisconsin, Madison.

RAYMOND L. SHOEMAKER is Assistant Executive Director at the Indiana Historical Society.

JOHN Y. SIMON is Professor of History and Executive Director, Ulysses S. Grant Association, at Southern Illinois University, Carbondale.

JAMES G. SMART is Professor of History at Keene State College.

THOMAS H. SMITH is a former Director of the Ohio Historical Society and is a historical consultant in the Dallas–Fort Worth metropolitan area.

W. WAYNE SMITH is Professor of History at Indiana University of Pennsylvania.

RICHARD J. SOMMERS is the Chief Archivist–Historian of the U.S. Army Military History Institute, Carlisle Barracks.

ROGER J. SPILLER is George C. Marshall Professor of Military History at the U.S. Army Command and General Staff College.

STEPHEN Z. STARR was Director of the Cincinnati Historical Society.

LESLIE J. STEGH is Archivist at Deere and Company in Moline, Illinois.

JAMES BREWER STEWART is Professor of History at Macalester College.

WILLIAM N. STILL, JR., is Professor of History at East Carolina University.

RICHARD G. STONE is Professor of History at Western Kentucky University.

ROY P. STONESIFER, JR., is Professor of History at Edinboro University of Pennsylvania.

LORNA LUTES SYLVESTER is Associate Editor of *Indiana Magazine of History*.

WAYNE C. TEMPLE is Chief Deputy Director of the Illinois State Archives and served as editor of *Lincoln Herald* for fifteen years.

HANS L. TREFOUSSE is Distinguished Professor of History at Brooklyn College of the City University of New York.

JOHN B. B. TRUSSELL, JR., a retired U.S. Army colonel and former Chief of the History Division, Pennsylvania Historical and Museum Commission, resides in Mechanicsburg, Pennsylvania.

CHARLES E. TWINING holds a Ph.D. in history from the University of Wisconsin and is a consultant in the Seattle, Washington, area.

DAVID G. VANDERSTEL is Assistant Editor of the *Encyclopedia of Indianapolis* at the POLIS Research Center, Indiana University at Indianapolis.

CAM WALKER is Associate Professor of History at the College of William and Mary.

RUSSELL F. WEIGLEY is Professor of History at Temple University.

FRANK J. WETTA is Dean, School of Arts and Sciences, Daytona Beach Community College.

FREDERICK D. WILLIAMS is Professor Emeritus of History at Michigan State University.

DAVID L. WILSON is Associate Professor of History at Southern Illinois University, Carbondale.

HUBERT H. WUBBEN is Professor Emeritus of History at Oregon State University.

MITCHELL A. YOCKELSON is a Reference Archivist in the Military Reference Branch, National Archives and Records Administration.

ISBN 0-313-20920-0

EAN

9 780313 209208

HARDCOVER BAR CODE